The Writer's Presence
A Pool of Readings

SEVENTH EDITION

EDITED BY

DONALD MCQUADE
University of California, Berkeley

ROBERT ATWAN
Series Editor, The Best American Essays

Emerson College

Bedford/St. Martin's   Boston ♦ New York

For Bedford/St. Martin's

Executive Editor: Leasa Burton
Developmental Editor: Deja Earley
Production Supervisor: Samuel Jones
Marketing Manager: Molly Parke
Project Management: Books By Design, Inc.
Photo Researcher: Julie Tesser
Permissions Manager: Kalina K. Ingham
Senior Art Director: Anna Palchik
Text Design: Tom Carling
Cover Design: Marine Miller
Cover Photo: Person reading a book on the beach © Steven Errico/Corbis
Composition: Carol Keller, Books By Design, Inc.
Printing and Binding: RR Donnelley and Sons

President: Joan E. Feinberg
Editorial Director: Denise B. Wydra
Editor in Chief: Karen S. Henry
Director of Marketing: Karen R. Soeltz
Director of Production: Susan W. Brown
Associate Director, Editorial Production: Elise S. Kaiser
Manager, Publishing Services: Andrea Cava

Library of Congress Control Number: 2011921717

Copyright © 2012, 2009, 2006, 2003 by Bedford/St. Martin's.

Manufactured in the United States of America.

6 5 4
f e

For information, write: Bedford/St. Martin's, 75 Arlington Street, Boston, MA 02116
(617-399-4000)

ISBN: 978-0-312-67262-1

Acknowledgments

Preface for Instructors

At the center of our work on this new edition of *The Writer's Presence* is our commitment to creating an effective tool for teaching critical reading and writing. This commitment is reflected in our efforts to design *The Writer's Presence* to achieve three fundamental instructional objectives: to introduce students to a wide range of prose genres emphasizing a strong authorial presence and voice; to allow writing instructors maximum flexibility in assigning reading materials and writing models; and to support composition teachers and students as effectively as possible with helpful, though unobtrusive, editorial and pedagogical features. We are confident that the readings we have selected, the ways we have chosen to arrange that material, and the instructional resources we have provided both in the book and in the comprehensive instructor's manual as well as online will make this a uniquely useful collection that will satisfy the requirements of most first-year writing programs.

The Writer's Presence combines eminently readable—and teachable—writing with a simple organization and minimal editorial apparatus. Each selection showcases a writer's unique voice and provides students with accessible models they can use to develop their own voices in the writing they produce. Engaging readings arranged alphabetically by author and by four types of writing—personal, expository, and argumentative essays, as well as short fiction—offer instructors the freedom to explore a wide range of pedagogical options, readily adaptable to the specific abilities and needs of particular students.

ESTABLISHED FEATURES OF *THE WRITER'S PRESENCE*

We continue to work diligently to ensure that the book's enduring features are as useful to instructors and as helpful to students as possible. (For information on features new to this edition, see page vi.)

Diverse Selections with a Strong Writer's Presence

Each of the selections in *The Writer's Presence* displays the distinctive signature that characterizes memorable prose: the presence of a lively individual imagination attempting to explore the self, shape information into meaning, or contend with issues. There are 120 essays, including 2 graphic selections and 7 short stories, plus 33 writer's commentaries that offer an array of voices, genres, and styles from different times and cultures. Women writers and writers of color are strongly represented. Ranging widely across subjects, methods of development, and stylistic patterns, the selections also illustrate both the expectations and the uncertainties that surface when a writer attempts to create a memorable presence in prose.

We have built this book—like previous editions—out of first-rate reading and teaching material proven to work in the writing classroom. We continue to feature a large number of authors whose works instructors have repeatedly enjoyed teaching over the years. These classroom favorites include such acclaimed writers as Maya Angelou, James Baldwin, Joan Didion, Annie Dillard, Malcolm Gladwell, Edward Hoagland, Langston Hughes, Jamaica Kincaid, George Orwell, Scott Russell Sanders, Jonathan Swift, Alice Walker, E. B. White, and Virginia Woolf. In fact, as this list of writers clearly indicates, *The Writer's Presence* could also serve as an introduction to the essay as a literary genre and to literary nonfiction in general. For instructors with even more literary ambitions, we have included paired selections so that certain writers can be shown working in two different genres. These writers are Raymond Carver, Sherman Alexie, and Jamaica Kincaid.

Flexible Organization

The organization of *The Writer's Presence* displays a broad range of private, personal, expository, argumentative, and creative writing without imposing an order or specifying an instructional context in which to work with individual selections. In that sense, the contents of *The Writer's Presence* can truly be called "a pool of readings." The nonfiction selections that constitute the first three parts are divided into the three most commonly taught types of nonfiction—personal essays, exposition, and argumentation. That is the extent of the book's overarching structure. Within each part, we present the writers in alphabetical order to make the selections easy to retrieve, assign, analyze, and interpret, regardless of instructional emphasis. To make it even easier to explore different approaches, *The Writer's Presence* includes alternate tables of contents that allow the book to be used as a thematic reader, a short prose reader, or a rhetorical modes reader with an emphasis on contemporary argument, with each selection chosen to play multiple roles.

Helpful and Unobtrusive Apparatus

As in previous editions, we continue to keep instructional apparatus to a minimum, striving for a middle ground between too much and too little. The headnotes in *The Writer's Presence* provide important biographical information and publication lists, along with engaging and useful quotations from the author and, whenever possible, indicate the selection's original source. Many selections provide provocative glimpses of lives and places, and readers naturally want to know when a selection was written and how and where it originally appeared. We don't want readers to infer mistakenly that an excerpt is actually an essay, as this would distort their approach to the selection and may also be unfair to the author. For example, we want readers to know at the outset that Maya Angelou's "What's Your Name, Girl?" is taken from her award-winning autobiography, *I Know Why the Caged Bird Sings*, and was not originally intended to stand alone as an essay.

Our classroom experience suggests that many students can be guided in their assessment or rereading of a selection by carefully constructed follow-up questions. In this edition we have retained "The Reader's Presence," the small collection of questions after each selection. These questions can be used by student readers and writers to enhance their understanding of the selection, or the questions can stimulate productive analysis and group discussion in the classroom.

We have designed "The Reader's Presence" to cover some of the dominant features of the selection and to refer to matters of content, style, and structure. As the title indicates, the questions will often draw attention to the specific ways in which readers are present in a piece of writing—either as an implied reader (the reader imagined by the writer) or as an actual reader. The concept of presence—both the writer's and the reader's—is discussed more fully in the "Introduction for Students."

"Writer at Work" Selections

These thirty-two supplemental readings include excerpts from interviews and essays in which authors discuss their writing processes and their identities as writers or in which a writer's work or composing process is usefully analyzed. We chose each to demonstrate to students that effective writing is thoughtful work done by real people.

Uniquely Extensive Instructor's Manual

Although the amount of instructional apparatus in *The Writer's Presence* is carefully managed, a wealth of specific instructional activities appears in *Resources for Teaching The Writer's Presence*, the most comprehensive instructor's manual available for any composition reader.

The resources in this guide to *The Writer's Presence* include the following four parts in each entry:

- "Approaching the Essay" provides a thorough overview of pedagogically effective ways to work with the essay in the classroom.

- "Additional Activities" offers imaginative classroom material and exercises, connections to other essays in the book, and collaborative projects.

- "Generating Writing" includes a range of writing exercises—from suggestions for informal writing to essay assignments and ideas for research papers.

- "The Reader's Presence" addresses the questions that follow each selection in the text, pointing to illuminating passages in the selection and anticipating possible responses from students.

This comprehensive teaching tool is available in print or as a PDF, which is downloadable at the book's catalog page: **bedfordstmartins.com/writerspresence/catalog**.

FEATURES NEW TO THIS EDITION

For the seventh edition of *The Writer's Presence*, we have strengthened the book's key features: its flexible format and its emphasis on authorial presence. We have also introduced new features that we believe will enhance the book's appeal to teachers and students in and beyond the classroom.

Thirty-Nine New Selections

The compelling new essays include works by such well-known contemporary authors as Charles Bowden, Augusten Burroughs, Michael Chabon, Barbara Ehrenreich, Anne Fadiman, Jonathan Safran Foer, Malcolm Gladwell, Christopher Hitchens, Ha Jin, Michael Lewis, Martha Nussbaum, David Foster Wallace, and Elie Wiesel.

Authors Relatively New to Anthologies

To present the freshest and most compelling nonfiction available, we have chosen to complement the work of established and frequently anthologized authors with that of writers who are now finding their way into major collections: Chris Abani, Joan Acocella, Nicholas Carr, Daniel Gilbert, Cynthia Gorney, Dinaw Mengestu, Barack Obama, Michael J. Sandel, James Shreeve, Manil Suri, and Robert Vivian. Included here, for example, are Dinaw Mengestu's reflections on what it means to be "from" somewhere, Daniel Gilbert's explorations of how our anticipation of happiness is flawed and misleading, and Michael J. Sandel's argument that the potential rise of "designer babies" is ethically complicated.

More Emphasis on Academic Writing

The Internet, Facebook, and text messaging play significant roles in the daily writing lives of many, if not all, of today's students. For this reason, we have been especially attentive to including selections that help students transition from the conventions of their daily correspondence to the expectations and traditions of academic writing. For this seventh edition of *The Writer's Presence*, we present a new feature, "On Writing: Practical Advice from Successful Writers," which introduces students to the pleasures and challenges of writing by invoking the perspectives and wisdom of celebrated professional writers. This feature, located after the introduction for students, collects lively, teachable quotations from such acclaimed writers as E. B. White and Maya Angelou and provides students with the opportunity to learn how accomplished writers conceptualize the compositional task at hand in succinct and engaging terms.

New Sample Student Papers

The Writer's Presence now features highly teachable examples of successful student writing by including two source-driven sample essays. Students can follow other undergraduates as they engage in meaningful terms with the thinking and writing of professional writers, all with an eye on improving their own compositional efforts. For example, student Sabrina Verchot draws imaginatively and convincingly on secondary sources to challenge Camille Paglia's argument in "The Pitfalls of Plastic Surgery."

More Teachable Images and Visual Texts

The Writer's Presence also introduces author photos with each "Writer at Work" selection as well as new, thought-provoking images to complement specific reading and writing assignments. For example, a vintage corset ad accompanies and illuminates Siri Hustvedt's piece, "Eight Days in a Corset"; powerful and stark photos of the U.S.–Mexico border accompany Charles Bowden's essay "Our Wall"; and a photo is included that originally accompanied Christopher Hitchens's essay, "Believe Me, It's Torture."

More Connections Between and Among Selections

In response to suggestions from instructors, we have continued to strengthen the interconnection questions following each reading—questions aimed at helping students recognize and explore the many thematic and stylistic links between and among selections. Each work of fiction is also connected to at least one nonfiction selection on a related theme.

More "Writer at Work" Selections

For the seventh edition we have expanded the acclaimed "Writer at Work" commentaries in which authors discuss their writing habits and identities as writers. This edition features, for example, a commentary by Lars Eighner on the challenges of writing while homeless, and another by Errol Morris on why he believes in truth, along with an original draft of the Declaration of Independence.

ADDITIONAL ELECTRONIC AND PRINT RESOURCES FOR TEACHING AND LEARNING

The Writer's Presence doesn't stop with a book. Online, you'll find both free and affordable premium resources to help students get even more out of the book and your course. You'll also find convenient instructor resources, such as downloadable sample syllabi, classroom activities, and even a nationwide community of teachers. To learn more about or to order any of the products listed here, contact your Bedford/St. Martin's sales representative, e-mail sales support (sales_support@bfwpub.com), or visit the Web site at bedfordstmartins.com.

Companion Web Site for *The Writer's Presence*

bedfordstmartins.com/writerspresence
Free and open resources for *The Writer's Presence* provide students with easy-to-access reference materials, visual tutorials, and support for working with sources.

- Reading comprehension quizzes for every selection in the book

- *AuthorLinks* with reliable online sources for every author in the book

- Five free videos of real writers from *VideoCentral*

- Three free tutorials from *ix visual exercises* by Cheryl E. Ball and Kristin L. Arola

- *Research and Documentation Online* by Diana Hacker

- *Bedford Bibliographer*, a tool for collecting source information and making a bibliography in MLA, APA, and *Chicago* styles

VideoCentral is a growing collection of videos for the writing class that captures real-world, academic, and student writers talking about how and why they write. *VideoCentral* can be packaged with *The Writer's Presence* for free. An activation code is required. To order *VideoCentral* packaged with the print book, use ISBN 1-4576-1015-9 or 978-1-4576-1015-8.

Re:Writing Plus gathers all the Bedford/St. Martin's premium digital content for composition into one online collection. It includes hundreds of model documents, the first ever peer-review game, and *VideoCentral*. *Re:Writing Plus* can be purchased separately or packaged with the print book at a significant discount. An activation code is required. To order *Re:Writing Plus* packaged with the print book, use ISBN 1-4576-1014-0 or 978-1-4576-1014-1.

i·series on CD-ROM

Add more value to your text by choosing one of the following CD-ROMs, free when packaged with *The Writer's Presence*. This popular series presents multimedia tutorials in a flexible format—with activities that can't be done in a book. To learn more about package options or any of the following products, contact your Bedford/St. Martin's sales representative or visit bedfordstmartins.com.

ix visual exercises helps students put into practice key rhetorical and visual concepts. To order *ix visual exercises* packaged with the print book, use ISBN 1-4576-1246-1 or 978-1-4576-1246-6.

i·claim: visualizing argument offers a new way to see argument—with six tutorials, an illustrated glossary, and more than seventy multimedia arguments. To order *i·claim: visualizing argument* packaged with the print book, use ISBN 1-4576-1017-5 or 978-1-4576-1017-2.

i·cite: visualizing sources brings research to life through an animated introduction, four tutorials, and hands-on source practice. To order *i·cite: visualizing sources* packaged with the print book, use ISBN 1-4576-1018-3 or 978-1-4576-1018-9.

Instructor Resources

You have a great deal to accomplish in your course. Bedford/St. Martin's wants to make it easy for you to find the support you need—and to get it quickly.

Resources for Teaching The Writer's Presence is available in a PDF that can be downloaded from bedfordstmartins.com/writerspresence/catalog. In addition to chapter overviews and teaching tips, the instructor's manual includes sample syllabi and suggestions for classroom activities.

TeachingCentral (bedfordstmartins.com/teachingcentral) offers the entire list of Bedford/St. Martin's print and online professional resources in one place. You'll find landmark reference works, sourcebooks on pedagogical issues, award-winning collections, and practical advice for the classroom—all free for instructors.

Bits (bedfordbits.com) collects creative ideas for teaching a range of composition topics in an easily searchable blog. A community of teachers—leading scholars, authors, and editors—discuss revision, research, grammar and style, technology, peer review, and much more. Take, use, adapt, and pass the ideas around. Then, come back to the site to comment or share your own suggestions.

Bedford Coursepacks allow you to easily integrate our most popular content into your own course management system. For details, visit bedfordstmartins.com/coursepacks.

ACKNOWLEDGMENTS

Each revision of *The Writer's Presence* has been developed through frequent correspondence and conversations—on the phone, in person, in letters, and on the Internet—with the many teachers and an appreciable number of students who have worked with *The Writer's Presence* in their writing classes. We continue to learn a great deal from these discussions, and we are grateful to the colleagues and friends who graciously have allowed us into their already crowded lives to seek advice and encouragement. Since its inception, *The Writer's Presence* has been and continues to be a truly collaborative enterprise.

In the same way we originally developed *The Writer's Presence*, this revision has emerged from spirited discussions with instructors. We are grateful to these colleagues across the country who took the time to tell us about what did—and did not—work well when they used the sixth edition: Natalie Bakopoulos, University of Michigan; Quinton Blackwell, Towson University; Jan S. Carpenter, College of Southern Idaho; Gina Crace, Towson University; Rosemary B. Day, Central New Mexico Community College; Lisa del Rosso, New York University; Trevor Dodge, Clackamas Community College; Lisa Dresdner, Norwalk Community College; Laurie Engberg, Portland Community College; Nancy Enright, Seton Hall University; Alex Fitzner, Pellissippi State Community College; Tom Flanigan, Idaho State University; Daniel Glynn, Highland Community College; Joshua Grasso, East Central University; Cortney Green, Central Carolina Technical College; Valerie Grey, Portland Community College; Amy Hobbs Harris, Central State University; Lee Harrison, Houston Community College Southwest; Brenda S. Hines, Highland Community College; Cristopher Hollingsworth, University of South Alabama; Mary Hurst, Cuyahoga Community College; Valerie N. Jensen, Green River Community College; Claire Kageyama, Houston Community College; Linda Legters, Norwalk Community College; Diana Lurz, Rogers State University; Stephen Mathewson, Central New Mexico Community College; Robert A. Mayer, College of Southern Idaho; Melissa McFarland, Central Carolina Technical College; Kevin McKelvey, University of Indianapolis; Lamont Missick, Barry University; Rebecca Napier, Pellissippi State Community College; Keith S. Norris, Pellissippi State Community College; Joey R. Poole, Central Carolina Technical College; Yekaterina Z. Raese, Pellissippi State Community College; David Smith, Milton Academy; Leslie E. St. Martin, College of the Canyons; Diane Tetreault, Bentley University; Brenda Tuberville, Rogers State University; and Raymond Watkins, Central Carolina Technical College.

We would also like to acknowledge those instructors who offered thoughtful responses and imaginative suggestions for improving previous editions: James Adams, Susan J. Allspaw, Lisa Altomari, Linda Baker, Natalie Bakopoulos, Anne Balay, Helen Barnes, Maurice H. Barr, Bette Bauer, Todd W. Bersley, Gerri Black, Scott Brookman, Ann Lightcap Bruno, Larry Brunt, Jennifer Buckley, Irene Burgess, Ruth Elizabeth Burks, Deborah Burnham, Dolores M. Burton, Greg Bryant, Susan Cannata, Jan S. Carpenter, Diane Challis, Jimmy Cheshire, Chet Childress, Louis Cicciarelli, Alice Cleveland, Rosanne Colosi, Michel S. Connell, Kimberly Connor, Chase Crossingham, Ellen Davis, Michael G. Davros, Peggy C. de Broux, Jessica Deforest, Lisa Del Torto, Mary Devaney, Gayatri Devi, Emily Dial-Driver, Debra DiPiazza, Trevor Dodge, Jamye Doerfler, Maria Rowena P. Dolorico, Eileen Donovan-Kranz, Clark Draney, Nina Dulin-Mallory, Susan M. Eisenthal, Alex Fagan, Grace Farrell, Todd Fox, Adria Fulkerson, Joan Gabriele, Christie Anderson Garcia, Deborah Garfinkle, Jane Gatewood, Sharon Gerring, Michael Gorman, Russell Green, Rae Greiner, Brian Hale, Sarah Hanselman, Lee Harrison, Lori Harrison-Kahan, Dave Hendrickson, Curtis W. Herr, Brenda S. Hines, Benjamin Hoffman, Tim Hohmann, Susanna Horng, Jack Jacobs, Goldie Johnson, Nancy B. Johnson, Matthew Kelley, Kate Kessler, Ronald L. King, Laura Kjosen, Elizabeth Klem, Dianne Layden, Mary Ann Lee, Donna Levy, Jennifer Liddell, Anthony W. Lilly II, Genoveva Llosa, Terri Long, Diana Lurz, Harriet Malinowitz, Barbara Mallonee, Denice Martone, Debra Matier, Robert A. Mayer, Laura McBride, Elizabeth McConnell, Michele F. McGinn, Paul Mendonca, Ilene Miele, Andrew Mossin, Cathryn A. Myers, Lolly Ockerstrom, Barbara Ohrstrom, Kathy O'Shaughnessy, Jean Pace, Cheryl Pallant, Sally Parr, Marty Patton, Jesse Peters, Gary D. Pratt, Catherine S. Quick, Colleen Richmond, Larry Rodgers, Robert Rogan, Jan Zlotnick Schmidt, Lissa Schneider, Marilyn S. Scott, Larry Severeid, Joanne Sibicky, Kimberly Skeen, Andrew Sidle, Robert Singleton, Constance Fletcher Smith, Nancy Sorenson, Roger Sorkin, Robert L. Stapleton, J. F. Stenerson, Karen Stewart, Chad R. Stockton, Steven Strang, Pamela Topping, Mary Turnbull, Donna M. Turner, Damon Tutunjian, Sandra Urban, Jennifer Lynne Von Ammon, Michael M. Walker, Kathleen G. White, Mary Robin Whitney, Anthony Wilson, Ed Wiltse, and Sallie Wolf.

We would especially like to acknowledge our colleagues from the Expository Writing Program at New York University who talked with us and shared their ideas as we planned the first edition of this book—Lisa Altomari, Karen Boiko, Darlene Forrest, Alfred Guy, Mary Helen Kolisnyk, Jim Marcall, Denice Martone, and Will McCormack.

We also extend our thanks to the professional staff at Bedford/St. Martin's for their innumerable contributions to this revision. We are grateful for the unfailing support and imaginative and convincing recommendations we received from our previous editors, especially Carolyn Lengel. We are most grateful to Deja Earley, who has managed every aspect of this seventh edition with great insight, excellent judgment, and unfailing dedication. We are also grateful to Regina Tavani for her superb work and resourcefulness bringing together the inevitable and the innumerable loose ends throughout the project's development. Many thanks to Herb Nolan of Books By Design, Inc., for his outstanding work moving this large manuscript through production with such good cheer and exemplary professionalism. Special thanks to Andrea Cava for managing the entire process with impeccable and quiet attentiveness and intelligence.

As ever, Joan Feinberg, the president of Bedford/St. Martin's, offered us spirited encouragement and first-rate and rigorous advice, as well as engaging suggestions for improving the project. When our conversations veered occasionally toward uncertainty, we relied on her steady editorial presence — and that of Editor in Chief Karen Henry — to help us convert pedagogical principle into sound instructional practice.

Sam Ruddick, Ph.D., researched and wrote the headnotes for this edition, in addition to preparing the comprehensive instructor's manual that accompanies this collection, *Resources for Teaching The Writer's Presence*. Dr. Ruddick is a professor of English and composition at the University of Massachusetts Lowell. We are very grateful to Dr. Ruddick for the intelligence, imagination, energy, and wealth of teaching experience he brings to the project. His work is an invaluable pedagogical tool to help instructors teach their students to read and write more effectively. We continue to be grateful to Cassandra Cleghorn of Williams College; Alfred Guy of Yale University; Joanna Imm of the University of Arizona; Jon Roberts of St. Thomas Aquinas College; Shelley Salamensky of the University of California, Los Angeles; Alix Schwartz of the University of California, Berkeley; Kate Silverstein; Darryl Stephens; and MaryJo Thomas; their very helpful suggestions are still amply evident in the instructor's manual. Christine McQuade and Michael Hsu offered invaluable assistance in strengthening the pedagogy of this project. We are especially grateful to Kyle J. Giacomozzi for his assistance through every phase of the project. We extend our thanks as well to Elaine Kosta and Kalina Ingham, who managed the challenging process of securing reprint permissions with great skill and attentiveness. Julie Tesser made the work of art research and permissions gathering seem effortless; she far exceeded our expectations, and we'd like to acknowledge her work with special thanks. Finally, we hope that Gregory and Emily Atwan, along with Susanne, Christine, and Marc McQuade, will once again share our satisfaction in seeing this project in print and our pleasure in continuing our productive collaboration.

Donald McQuade
Robert Atwan
March 2011

Contents

1. PERSONAL WRITING
Exploring Our Own Lives   23

is about much more than being black, and, for that matter, being black is about much more than my skin color."

2. EXPOSITORY WRITING
Shaping Information 281

that landscape in the early morning, with the sun at your back, is to lose the sense of proportion. Your imagination comes to life, and this, you think, is where Creation was begun."

3. ARGUMENTATIVE WRITING
Contending with Issues

631

coercive racist stereotypes at work in the trend among black women to thin their noses and among Asian women to 'Westernize' their eyes?"

Alternate Tables of Contents

Selections Arranged by Theme

EDUCATION

ETHICS AND MORALITY

GENDER ROLES

HISTORY AND BIOGRAPHY

LANGUAGE AND LITERATURE

LAW, POLITICS, AND SOCIETY

THE NATURAL ENVIRONMENT

PHILOSOPHY, SPIRITUALITY, AND RELIGION

POPULAR CULTURE AND MASS MEDIA

PSYCHOLOGY AND HUMAN BEHAVIOR

RACIAL AND ETHNIC IDENTITY

Selections Arranged by Common Rhetorical Modes and Patterns of Development

CONSTRUCTING NARRATIVES

Narratives That Lead to a Sudden Insight or a Decision

WRITING DESCRIPTION: PERSONS, PLACES, THINGS

USING COMPARISONS

DEFINING WORDS AND CONCEPTS

SUPPLYING INSTANCES AND EXAMPLES

CLASSIFYING IDEAS

ANALYZING AND DESCRIBING PROCESSES

ANALYZING AND DESCRIBING IMAGES

ESTABLISHING CAUSES AND EFFECTS

FORMING ANALOGIES

FASHIONING ARGUMENTS: EIGHT METHODS

Arguing from Personal Experience

Arguing from Factual Evidence

Correcting Popular Misconceptions

Countering Other Arguments

Arguing from Personal Authority and Expertise

Short Essay Contents

A Complete Short Essay Reader (6 pages or fewer)

Introduction for Students:
The Writer's Presence

PRESENCE IS A WORD—like *charisma*—that we reserve for people who create powerful and memorable impressions. Many public figures and political leaders are said to "have presence"—Martin Luther King Jr., Eleanor Roosevelt, and John F. Kennedy and his wife Jacqueline Kennedy Onassis are a few superb examples—as well as many athletes, dancers, and musicians. In fact, the quality of presence is found abundantly in the performing arts, where top entertainers and actors self-consciously fashion—through style, costume, and gesture—an instantly recognizable public presence. Clearly, people with presence are able to command our attention. How do they do it?

Presence is far easier to identify than it is to define. We recognize it when we see it, but how do we capture it in words? Virtually everyone would agree, for example, that when LeBron James steps onto a basketball court, he displays an exceptional degree of presence; we acknowledge this regardless of whether we are basketball fans. But what is it about such individuals that commands our attention? How can we begin to understand this elusive characteristic known as presence?

On one level, *presence* simply means "being present." But the word is more complex than that; it suggests much more than the mere fact of being physically present. Most dictionaries define *presence* as an ability to project a sense of self-assurance, poise, ease, or dignity. We thus speak of someone's "stage presence" or "presence of mind." But the word is also used today to suggest an impressive personality, an individual who can make his or her presence felt. As every college student knows, to be present in a classroom is not the same thing as *having a presence* there. We may be present in body but not in spirit. In that sense, presence is also a matter of individual energy and exertion, of putting something of ourselves into whatever we do.

Presence is especially important in writing, which is what this book is about. Just as we notice individual presence in sports or music or conversation, so too we discover it in good writing. If what we read seems dreary, dull, or dead, it's usually because the writer forgot to include an important ingredient: *personal presence*. That doesn't mean that your essays should be written *in* the first-person singular (this book contains many exceptional essays that aren't) but that your essays should be written *by* the first-person singular. Interesting essays are produced by a real and distinct person, not an automaton following a set of mechanical rules and abstract principles.

PRESENCE IN WRITING

How can someone be present in writing? How can you project yourself into an essay so that it seems that you're personally there, even though all your reader sees are words on a piece of paper?

The Writer's Presence shows you how this is done. It shows how a wide variety of talented writers establish a distinct presence in many different kinds of writing and for many different purposes and audiences. Although the book offers numerous examples of methods for establishing presence, several are worth pointing out at the start. Let's examine four of the chief ways an experienced writer can be present in an essay.

1. Through Personal Experience. One of the most straightforward ways for the writer to make his or her presence felt in an essay is to include appropriate personal experiences. Of course, many assignments may call for a personal essay and, in those cases, you will naturally be putting episodes from your own life at the center of your writing. But writers also find ways to build their personal experiences into essays that are informative or argumentative, essays on topics other than themselves. They do this to show their close connection with a subject, to offer testimony, or to establish their personal authority on a subject. Many of the essays in this collection offer clear illustrations of how writers incorporate personal experience into an essay on a specific topic or issue.

Look, for example, at the essay by Amy Cunningham, "Why Women Smile" (page 347). This essay is primarily an explanation of a cultural phenomenon—the way women are socially conditioned to maintain a smiling attitude. However, Cunningham begins the essay not with a general observation but with a personal anecdote: "After smiling brilliantly for nearly four decades, I now find myself trying to quit." Although her essay is not "personal," her opening sentence, besides establishing her own connection with the topic, provides readers with a personal motive for her writing.

One of the first places to look for the writer's presence is in the motive, the purpose, for putting words down on paper or on the computer screen. The extent of your success in making clear your motive for writing will largely depend on your interest both in the subject and in your ideas about the subject. It is extremely difficult for any writer to establish a presence when he or she is either bored with—or simply uninterested in—the subject at hand. But a writer who demonstrates what Virginia Woolf calls a "fierce attachment to an idea" can create a presence that attracts and holds a reader's attention.

2. Through Voice. Another way a writer makes his or her presence felt is through creating a distinctive and an identifiable *voice*. All words are composed of sounds, and language itself is something nearly all of us originally learned through *hearing*. Any piece of writing can be read aloud, though many readers have developed such ingrained habits of silent reading that they no longer *hear* the writing. Good writers, however, want their words to be heard. They want their sentences to have rhythm, cadence, and balance.

Experienced authors revise a great deal of their writing just to make sure the sentences *sound* right. They're writing for the reader's ear as well as the reader's mind.

In many respects, voice is the writer's "signature," what finally distinguishes the work of one writer from another. Consider how quickly we recognize voice. We've *heard* only the opening lines of a comedy routine on television, yet we instantly recognize the speaker. So, too, whenever we read a piece of writing, we ought to think of it as an experience similar to listening to someone speak aloud. Doing so adds drama to writing and reading. Here is what the poet Robert Frost has to say on the subject:

> Everything written is as good as it is dramatic. . . . A dramatic necessity goes deep into the nature of the sentence. Sentences are not different enough to hold the attention unless they are dramatic. No ingenuity of varying structure will do. All that can save them is the speaking tone of voice somehow entangled in the words and fastened to the page for the ear of the imagination. That is all that can save poetry from singing, all that can save prose from itself. (Preface to *A Way Out,* in *Selected Prose of Robert Frost*)

Frost spent a good portion of his celebrated public life encouraging people to cultivate what he called "the hearing imagination."

A more specific dimension of voice is *tone,* which refers not only to the implied relationship of the writer to the reader but also to the manner the writer adopts in addressing the reader. Tone suggests not the writer's attitudes themselves but the way those attitudes are revealed. In either projecting or analyzing tone, writers and readers ought to consider its intensity, the force with which the writer's attitudes are expressed. The strength of the writer's tone depends on such factors as the seriousness of the situation, the nature and extent of the writer's involvement in the situation, and the control the writer exercises over expression. In practical terms, tone is usually a matter of diction and individual word choice.

A writer's voice is usually fairly consistent from essay to essay and can be detected quickly by an experienced reader who pays attention to "the hearing imagination." To be distinctive and effective, a writer's voice need not be strange, artificial, or self-consciously literary. Many essayists develop a casual, familiar, flexible tone of voice that allows them to range easily from the intimate to the intellectual. Sentence rhythm and word choice play a large part in determining a writer's tone of voice. Observe how Raymond Carver begins an essay about his father (page 60):

> My dad's name was Clevie Raymond Carver. His family called him Raymond and friends called him C. R. I was named Raymond Clevie Carver, Jr. I hated the "Junior" part. When I was little my dad called me Frog, which was okay. . . .

Carver's voice here is casual and almost childlike, a quality he is striving for in an essay intended to be candid, intimate, and low key. Throughout the essay, for example, he rarely uses the word *father* but always the more colloquial *dad.* If you read this passage aloud, you will get the feeling that someone is speaking directly to you.

3. Through Point of View. Another sure way for writers to establish presence is through the point of view they adopt toward a subject. In this sense, point of view comprises the "where" of the writer's presence. Sometimes a point of view can be a literal reality, an actual place or situation in which writers physically locate themselves. This occurs most frequently in autobiographical essays in which the writer is present both as the narrator and as a character. For example, in "A Clack of Tiny Sparks: Remembrances of a Gay Boyhood" (page 78), Bernard Cooper is always meticulous about telling us his actual location at any given moment in his writing. The essay begins, "Theresa Sanchez sat behind me in ninth-grade algebra."

Or consider the tremendous importance of point of view—this time in terms of perspective—to another essayist in the volume, Brent Staples, in "Just Walk on By: A Black Man Ponders His Power to Alter Public Space" (page 217). This is how Staples opens his essay:

> My first victim was a woman—white, well dressed, probably in her early twenties. I came upon her late one evening on a deserted street in Hyde Park, a relatively affluent neighborhood in an otherwise mean, impoverished section of Chicago. As I swung onto the avenue behind her, there seemed to be a discreet, uninflammatory distance between us. Not so. She cast back a worried glance. To her, the youngish black man—a broad six feet two inches with a beard and billowing hair, both hands shoved into the pockets of a bulky military jacket—seemed menacingly close. After a few more quick glimpses, she picked up her pace and was soon running in earnest. Within seconds she disappeared into a cross street.

To see why he frightens people, Staples needs to see himself in the stereotypical ways that others see him. Thus, by the middle of this opening paragraph (in the sentence beginning "To her"), he literally switches the point of view from his own perspective to that of the young and terrified white woman, describing his appearance as she would perceive it.

Point of view is not always a matter of a specific location or position. Writers are not always present in their essays as dramatic characters. In many reflective, informative, or argumentative essays, the point of view is determined more by a writer's intellectual attitude or opinions—an angle of vision—than by a precise physical perspective. As an example of how a writer establishes a personal perspective without a dominant first-person narrator, consider the following passage from John Taylor Gatto's "Against School" (page 665), an argumentative essay against America's traditional school system. Although Gatto from time to time introduces his own personal background, he makes his point of view—opposition to modern education—clear to the reader without ever referring directly to himself. Note his comparison between how schools train children and how concerned parents might better handle the job:

> Now for the good news. Once you understand the logic behind modern schooling, its tricks and traps are fairly easy to avoid. School trains children to be employees and

consumers; teach your own to be leaders and adventurers. School trains children to obey reflexively; teach your own to think critically and independently. Well-schooled kids have a low threshold for boredom; help your own to develop an inner life so that they'll never be bored. Urge them to take on the serious material, the *grown-up* material, in history, literature, philosophy, music, art, economics, theology—all the stuff schoolteachers know well enough to avoid. Challenge your kids with plenty of solitude so that they can learn to enjoy their own company, to conduct inner dialogues.

There is no first-person singular here, nor a dramatically rendered self. Yet this passage conveys a distinct point of view.

4. Through Verbal Patterns. A writer can also be present in an essay as a *writer*—that is, as a person consciously crafting and shaping his or her work. This artistic presence is not always obvious. Yet when we begin to detect in our reading certain kinds of repeated elements—a metaphor or an image, a twist on an earlier episode, a conclusion that echoes the opening—we become aware that someone is deliberately shaping experience or ideas in a special manner. We often find this type of presence in imaginative literature—especially in novels and poems—as well as in essays that possess a distinct literary flavor.

To see an example of creating a presence through verbal patterns, look at the opening paragraph of E. B. White's now-classic essay, "Once More to the Lake" (page 260).

One summer, along about 1904, my father rented a camp on a lake in Maine and took us all there for the month of August. We all got ringworm from some kittens and had to rub Pond's Extract on our arms and legs night and morning, and my father rolled over in a canoe with all his clothes on; but outside of that the vacation was a success and from then on none of us ever thought there was any place in the world like that lake in Maine. We returned summer after summer—always on August 1st for one month. I have since become a salt-water man, but sometimes in summer there are days when the restlessness of the tides and the fearful cold of the sea water and the incessant wind that blows across the afternoon and into the evening make me wish for the placidity of a lake in the woods. A few weeks ago this feeling got so strong I bought myself a couple of bass hooks and a spinner and returned to the lake where we used to go, for a week's fishing and to revisit old haunts.

If, in rereading this opening, you circle every use of the word *and*, you will clearly see a pattern of repetition. *And*, of course, is a very unobtrusive word, and you may not notice right away how White keeps it present throughout the passage. This repetition alone may strike you at first as of no special importance, but as you read through the essay and see how much of White's central theme depends on the idea of return and repetition, you will get a better sense of why the little word *and*—a word that subtly reinforces the idea of repetition itself—is so significant.

E. B. White is present in his essay in more obvious ways—he is both telling the story and appearing in it as a character. But he is also present to us as a writer, someone consciously shaping the language and form of his essay. We are dealing here with three levels of presence (which might also be described as three levels of "I"). If this sounds confusing, just think of a movie in which a single person directs, stars, and perhaps plays one or more other roles in the making of the film. It's not that uncommon. If you watch the 2004 film *Million Dollar Baby*, for example, you can observe the multiple presences of Clint Eastwood. Not only is Eastwood visibly present in the film as one of the main characters, but we also can detect his creative and shaping presence as the director and as a producer (roles for which he won two Oscars), and as the composer of the film's score. The audience can directly see him on the screen as an actor; the audience can also infer his presence as a composer, as a producer, and especially as a director—presences that, though less directly observable, are still original and powerful.

THE SELECTIONS IN THIS BOOK

Many selections in this book feature the first-person point of view directly. These selections appear mostly in Part 1, "Personal Writing: Exploring Our Own Lives." In most of these selections, the writer appears as both narrator and main character, and the writer's presence is quite observable.

But private and personal writing provide only a fraction of the different types of nonfiction that appear regularly in books, newspapers, and magazines. Many essays are written on specific topics and deal with specific issues. Most of the essays appearing in America's dominant periodicals, for example, are intended to be either informative or persuasive; the author wants to convey information about a particular subject (a Civil War battle, for example) or wants to express an opinion about a particular issue (such as how to deal with terrorism). Parts 2 and 3, "Expository Writing: Shaping Information" and "Argumentative Writing: Contending with Issues," contain a large number of selections that illustrate writing intended to inform, argue, and persuade.

You'll notice, however, a strong writer's presence in many of the informative and persuasive essays. This is deliberate. To write informatively or persuasively about subjects other than yourself doesn't mean that you have to disappear as a writer. Sometimes you will want to insert your own experiences and testimony into an argumentative essay; at other times you will want to assume a distinct viewpoint concerning a piece of information; and at still other times—though you may not introduce the first-person singular—you will make your presence strongly felt in your tone of voice or simply in the way you arrange your facts and juxtapose details (see the Gatto passage on page 665). At the heart of the word *information* is *form*. Writers don't passively receive facts and information in a totally finished format; they need to shape their information, to give it form. This shaping or patterning is something the writer *contributes*. A large part of the instructional purpose of this collection is to encourage you to pay more attention to the different ways writers are present in their work.

Presence in Fiction

An individual writer's presence and voice are perhaps more easily discerned in nonfiction than in fiction. The reason for this is that a novelist or short story writer invents and gives voices to numerous characters who should not be confused with the author. Sometimes a story is told by an invented character who also should not be closely identified with his or her author. A good example of this technique can be found in John Updike's "A & P" (page 949), in which a story is narrated in the distinctive voice of its main character, Sammy, a teenager who is working at a small suburban supermarket. Although the story is written in the first-person singular—exactly like most personal essays—the character and voice are fictional and do not correspond to any real person. Sammy is not John Updike, nor does he necessarily speak like John Updike would if we met him.

To further complicate matters, this biographical gap between narrator and author remains even when a story that is told in the third person appears to be written in the voice of the author. The third-person narrator is also invented, and the narrative voice and presence may have little to do with the life of the author who created it. So in what ways can the writer's presence be observed in a story if we cannot attach to its teller any biographical connection with its author? In fiction, we often find a writer's presence in a distinctive style of writing; in certain repeated patterns; in the dynamics of structure and plot; and, of course, in the ethical, spiritual, or intellectual values a story may be intended to illustrate. In certain stories, to be sure, a particular character may clearly represent the author's own values, and in those cases we might argue that the writer becomes "present" in that character. As we can see in Part 4, "The Short Story: Seven Modern Classics," an author may refuse to locate his or her moral and psychological values within a particular character but will expect instead that the reader will derive these values from the overall perspective of the story itself. Unlike essayists, short story writers rarely state their ethical or aesthetic values directly and explicitly. As the novelist D. H. Lawrence aptly put it, in fiction we must trust the tale and not the teller.

THE READER'S PRESENCE

Because almost all writing (and *all* published writing) is intended to be read, we can't dismiss the importance of the reader. Just as we find different levels of a writer's presence in a given piece of writing, so too can we detect different ways in which a reader can be present.

An author writes a short essay offering an opinion about gun control. The author herself has been the victim of a shooting, and her piece, though it includes her personal experiences, is largely made up of a concrete plan to eliminate all guns—even hunting rifles—from American life. She would like lawmakers to adopt her plan. Yet, in writing her essay, she imagines that there will be a great deal of resistance to her argument. In other words, she imagines a reader who will most likely disagree with her and who needs to be won over. Let's imagine she gets her essay published in *Newsweek*.

Now imagine three people in a dentist's office who within the same afternoon pick up this issue of *Newsweek* and read the essay. One of them has also been victimized by guns (her son was accidentally wounded by a hunter), and she reads the essay with great sympathy and conviction. She understands perfectly what this woman has gone through and believes in her plan completely. The next reader, a man who has never once in his life committed a crime and has no tolerance for criminals, is outraged by the essay. He was practically brought up in the woods and loves to hunt. He could never adopt a gun control plan that would in effect criminalize hunting. He's ready to fire off a letter attacking this woman's plan. The third reader also enjoys hunting and has always felt that hunting rifles should be exempt from any government regulation of firearms. But he finds the writer's plan convincing and feasible. He spends the rest of the day trying to think of counterarguments.

Obviously, these are only three of many possibilities. But you can see from this example the differences between the reader imagined by the writer and some actual readers. The one person who completely agreed with the writer was not the kind of reader the author had originally imagined or was trying to persuade; she was already persuaded. And though the other two readers were part of her intended audience, one of them could never be persuaded to her point of view, whereas the other one might.

The differences briefly outlined here are distinctions between what can be called *implied readers* and *actual readers*. The implied reader is the reader imagined by the writer for a particular piece of writing. In constructing arguments, for example, it is usually effective to imagine readers we are *trying* to win over to our views. Otherwise, we are simply asking people who already agree with us to agree with us—what's commonly known as "preaching to the converted" or "preaching to the choir."

In informative or critical essays, a writer also needs to be careful about the implied reader. For example, it's always important to ask how much your intended audience may already know about your subject. Here's a practical illustration. If you were asked to write a review of a recent film for your college newspaper, you would assume your readers had not yet seen the film (or else you might annoy them by giving away some surprises). However, if you were asked to write a critical essay about the same movie for a film course, you could assume your readers had seen the film. It's the same movie, and you have the same opinions about it, but your two essays have two different purposes, and in the process of writing them you imagine readers with two different levels of knowledge about the film.

Actual readers, of course, differ from implied readers in that they are real people who read the writing—not readers intended or imagined by the writer. As you read the essays in this collection, you should be aware of at least two readers—(1) the reader you think the writer imagines for the essay and (2) the reader you are in actuality. Sometimes you will seem very close to the kind of reader the writer is imagining. In those cases, you might say that you "identify" with a particular writer, essay, or point of view. At other times, however, you will notice a great distance between the reader the author imagines and you as an actual reader. For example, you may feel excluded by the author on the basis of race, gender, class, or expected knowledge and educational level. Or you may feel you know more than the author does about a particular topic.

To help you get accustomed to your role as a reader, each selection in the book is followed by a set of questions, "The Reader's Presence." These questions are designed to orient you to the various levels of reading suggested by the selection. Some questions will ask you to identify the kind of reader you think the author imagines; other questions will prompt you to think about specific ways you may differ from the author's intended reader; still others will help you to make connections between and among the selections and authors. In general, the questions are intended to make you more deeply aware of your *presence* as a reader.

In this brief introduction, we covered only two types of readers (imagined and actual), but some literary essays, such as Jonathan Swift's "A Modest Proposal" (page 831) and David Foster Wallace's "Consider the Lobster" (page 839), demand more complex consideration. Whenever we think more than these two types of readers need to be identified in an essay, we will introduce this information in the questions.

We hope you will find *The Writer's Presence* a stimulating book to read and think about. To make our presence felt as writers is as much a matter of self-empowerment as it is of faith. It requires the confidence that we can affect others, determine a course of action, or even surprise ourselves by new ideas or by acquiring new powers of articulation.

Part of the enduring pleasure of writing is precisely that element of surprise, of originality—that lifelong pleasure of discovering new resources of language, finding new means of knowing ourselves, and inventing new ways to be present in the world.

ON WRITING:
Practical Advice from

ONE OF THE MOST reassuring discoveries any student of writing can make is that there is no single way to write, no fail-proof formula to produce successful essays. Anyone seriously interested in learning to write can benefit from reading what other writers have to say about the challenges and pleasures of the writing process. The pages that follow provide an opportunity for you to study the writing process from the points of view of experienced writers—from how they search for an idea and then develop it in a first draft to how they revise and then prepare that idea for presentation in a final draft.

Like all writers, published authors invariably speak of the problems and the pleasures of struggling to convey a clear sense of their ideas. They frequently touch on their respect for and anxiety about mastering the skills required to write effective prose. They also describe the distinctive ways in which they compose: how they go about generating ideas for an essay, how they deal with the frustrations of procrastination and the dead ends that disrupt their progress, how they revise, and how they determine when their essays are finished and ready to be read by an audience.

The perspectives these writers present on the composing process are as varied as their backgrounds and interests. Yet the methods they follow when writing can be grouped into three general phases: **getting started, drafting, and revising**. Experienced writers usually start by searching for and then deciding on a subject to write about, developing their ideas about the subject, clarifying their purpose in writing, organizing their thoughts, and considering the audience they want to address. In the drafting phase, they usually carry out their detailed plan in a first draft. In the revising phase, they study what they have written and determine how they can improve it. These designations are not a lock-step series of discrete stages that writers work

GETTING STARTED

IN THE FIRST of the three phases of the writing process, a writer usually chooses a subject to write about if one has not been assigned, discovers a purpose for writing about the subject, generates a thesis or a controlling idea (also called a *governing idea*), and then develops that idea in various preliminary exercises (often involving brainstorming and freewriting) or in an outline or some other form that will serve as the basis for producing a first draft of an essay. This is the most difficult phase of writing for most people. Because they usually face so many challenges and obstacles at this point in the writing process, most writers seem to have more to say about this phase than any other.

10

Successful Writers

through in exactly the same manner each time. They are simply patterns of activities that describe what happens when writers write.

As every writer knows, at least intuitively, writing is not a linear but a recursive process. Writing rarely proceeds neatly from one phase to the next. Rather the phases frequently overlap, making the process often appear messy. Yet, in tracing the movements of a writer's mind at work on an idea, we can discover and describe patterns, but the specific circumstances and the particular moves writers make are never exactly the same every time.

Integral to each phase of the composing process is **reading**. Reading and writing function much like breathing in and breathing out. They are inextricably linked, and each is infused with an intention. Writers read what others have written with a sense of purpose: to gather information, to understand concepts and the details that support them, to evaluate ideas, to engage in critical thinking, to assess explanations and the assumptions that inform arguments, to be entertained, to visit or envision other places and people, to challenge or inspire others, or to expand the limits of what is imagined as possible.

Reading what other writers have to say about writing should assure you that all writers—whether they are professionals, classmates, or you—grapple with many of the same basic issues as well as the same frustrations and pleasures of writing. You may also be pleasantly surprised and pleased to learn that in many instances the observations and solutions of these professional writers are similar to those you may have developed in your own writing. In addition, you may find that these writers will offer new suggestions that can help you improve your writing. Recognizing what is unique and shared about the writing experience will enable you to place yourself in the company of other writers while distinguishing your own voice from theirs.

■ **MARK TWAIN**

"The secret of getting ahead is getting started. The secret of getting started is breaking your complex overwhelming tasks into small manageable tasks, and then starting on the first one."

(Samuel Langhorne Clemens, 1835–1910, American author and humorist)

■ **JACK LONDON**

"You can't wait for inspiration. You have to go after it with a club."

(1876–1916, American author and journalist)

■ **MAYA ANGELOU**

"When I start a project, the first thing I do is write down, in longhand, everything I know about the subject, every thought I've ever had on it."

(b. 1928, American poet and autobiographer. See also page 31.)

■ AKHIL SHARMA

"Writing . . . is very hard and the fact that you will find it very hard does not mean that you are stupid."

(b. 1971, Indian American author)

■ ELIZABETH HARDWICK

"I'm not sure I understand the process of writing. There is, I'm sure, something strange about imaginative concentration. The brain slowly begins to function in a different way, to make mysterious connections. Say, it is Monday, and you write a very bad draft, but if you keep trying, on Friday, words, phrases, appear almost unexpectedly. I don't know why you can't do it on Monday, or why I can't. I'm the same person, no smarter, I have nothing more at hand. . . . It's one of the things writing students don't understand. They write a first draft and are quite disappointed, or often should be disappointed. They don't understand that they have merely begun, and that they may be merely beginning even in the second or third draft."

(1916–2007, American author and literary critic)

DEALING WITH PROCRASTINATION

The tendency to procrastinate remains one of the most common obstacles many writers face when they set out to put pen to paper or fingers on the keyboard. There is no one easy aspect of writing, other than postponing it. Many writers—whether they are professionals or students—share this trait.

■ PAUL RUDNICK

"Writing is 90 percent procrastination: reading magazines, eating cereal out of the box, watching infomercials. It's a matter of doing everything you can to avoid writing, until it is about four in the morning and you reach the point where you have to write."

(b. 1957, American playwright and novelist)

■ DOUGLAS ADAMS

"I love deadlines. I like the whooshing sound they make as they fly by."

(1952–2001, English author and playwright)

■ TAYARI JONES

"[To deal with writer's block] I just keep at it. I think it's a lot like using a pen that isn't working. You can make the scribbling motion and nothing happens, until suddenly it does. Who knows why. But it does. Thank the lord."

(b. 1970, African American novelist)

■ MARGARET ATWOOD

"If I waited for perfection, I would never write a word."

(b. 1939, Canadian author and literary critic)

■ JAMES THURBER

"Don't get it right, just get it written."

(1894–1961, American author and humorist)

■ JOHN STEINBECK

"Write freely and as rapidly as possible and throw the whole thing on paper. Never correct or rewrite until the whole thing is down. Rewriting in process is usually found to be an excuse for not going on."

(1902–1968, American novelist)

■ JOSEPH HELLER

"Every writer I know has trouble writing."

(1923–1999, American satirical novelist)

■ ERNEST HEMINGWAY

"There is no rule on how to write. Sometimes it comes easily and perfectly: sometimes it's like drilling rock and then blasting it out with charges."

(1899–1961, American author and journalist)

■ MARTIN AMIS

"A lot of the time seems to be spent making coffee or trolling around, or throwing darts, or playing pinball, or picking your nose, trimming your fingernails, or staring at the ceiling. . . . Writing is waiting, for me certainly. It wouldn't bother me a bit if I didn't write one word in the morning. I'd just think, you know, not yet."

(b. 1949, English novelist)

■ MAYA ANGELOU

"One of the problems we have as writers is we don't take ourselves seriously while writing; being serious is setting aside a time and saying if it comes, good; if it doesn't come, good, I'll just sit here."

(b. 1928, American poet and autobiographer. See also page 31.)

■ ANNA QUINDLEN

"People have writer's block not because they can't write, but because they despair of writing eloquently."

(b. 1953, American author and columnist)

■ WILLIAM JAMES

"Nothing is so fatiguing as the eternal hanging on of an uncompleted task."

(1842–1910, American psychologist and philosopher)

■ RICHARD FORD

"Writing can be complicated, exhausting, isolating, abstracting, boring, dulling, briefly exhilarating; it can be made to be grueling and demoralizing. And occasionally it can produce rewards. But it's never as hard as, say, piloting an L-1011 into O'Hare on a snowy night in January, or doing brain surgery when you have to stand up for ten hours straight, and once you start you can't just stop. If you're a writer, you can stop anywhere, any time, and no one will care or ever know. Plus, the results might be better if you do."

(b. 1944, American author)

GENERATING IDEAS

Writers rely on a seemingly limitless supply of strategies and tactics to generate a subject for an essay and to start exploring their ideas about these subjects—from deliberate reading and research to discussions with friends as well as random mental associations. For many writers, as Henry Miller (1891–1980, American novelist and painter) observes, "writing, like life itself, is a voyage of discovery."

In order to develop practiced confidence in their ability to choose an engaging subject to focus on in an essay, many writers often identify subjects in the issues and concerns in the world around them. To help keep track of their ideas about a subject, writers often rely on a journal, a daily written record of one's experiences and thoughts on particular subjects. Journal entries are usually more focused and related than those in a diary, which poses no restrictions on subject or focus.

Many writers find that they can discover ideas about a subject by writing down everything they know about it. Often called *freewriting* or *nonstop writing*, this strategy involves pouring out words, thoughts, or feelings, without concern for grammar or punctuation or coherence. Other writers prefer to develop ideas through *brainstorming*. Unlike freewriting, which produces ideas by linking

■ E. L. DOCTOROW

"Writing is an exploration. You start from nothing and learn as you go. . . . Writing is like driving at night in the fog. You can only see as far as your headlights, but you can make the whole trip that way. . . . "

(b. 1931, American novelist)

■ F. SCOTT FITZGERALD

"All good writing is swimming under water and holding your breath."

(1896–1940, American novelist)

ENVISIONING AN AUDIENCE

Imagining an audience looms large in the mind of every writer. Often, the writer's view of the reader helps determine the extent of an essay's success. The writer usually asks: "Who is my reader? What do I need to do to help that person to understand and appreciate what I want to say about my particular subject?" The first question addresses the knowledge, background, and predispositions of the reader toward the subject. The second points to the kinds of information or appeals to which the reader is most likely to respond.

Not all writers concern themselves with the question of audience from the outset of their work. Some writers regard audience as a matter for revision—as an important consideration only after they have articulated their idea and established control of their thinking in writing. Given that student writers prepare papers to satisfy course requirements, they are also of course mindful of their instructor's presence in their audience. Some students are intimidated by this recognition, others imagine themselves writing for a teacher with whom they feel comfortable, still others write with peers and an instructor in mind. But whether they are writing for a teacher, peers, or an audience beyond the classroom, the fact that someone will read their writing imposes a good deal of discipline on most student writers. Thinking about readers helps writers make decisions about appropriate subjects, the kinds of examples to use, the kind and level of diction to use, and the overall organization of the essay—each of which enables them to be clear and compelling in their prose.

■ DON DeLILLO

"I don't have a sense of a so-called ideal reader and certainly not of a readership, that terrific entity. I write for the page."

(b. 1936, American novelist and essayist. See also page 355.)

■ MARIANNE MOORE

"Any writer overwhelmingly honest about pleasing himself is almost sure to please others."

(1887–1972, American poet)

or associating one thought with another, brainstorming records thoughts as they occur, with no regard for their relation to one another. When writers brainstorm, they often leap from one thought to another without stopping to explore the seeming connections between what may be two completely unrelated ideas.

Exercises such as freewriting and brainstorming are excellent confidence builders, especially for relatively inexperienced writers. They can help writers generate a great deal of prose in a very short time. These exercises also enable writers to see quickly what they have to say about a subject—while resisting the urge to edit their work prematurely. Whether you write in a journal or on the back of a napkin, thinking in writing is perhaps the best way to discover the potential of a subject to engage an audience. After all, a practiced writer is usually an effective writer.

■ ERNEST HEMINGWAY

"Work every day. No matter what has happened the day or night before, get up and bite on the nail."

(1899–1961, American novelist and Nobel Laureate)

■ WILLIAM FAULKNER

"Get it down. Take chances. It may be bad, but it's the only way you can do anything really good."

(1897–1962, American novelist and Nobel Laureate)

■ JOAN DIDION

"I write entirely to find out what I'm thinking, what I'm looking at, what I see and what it means. What I want and what I fear."

(b. 1934, American essayist and novelist. See also page 366.)

■ FRANÇOIS MAURIAC

"Each of us is like a desert, and a literary work is like a cry from the desert, or like a pigeon let loose with a message in its claws, or like a bottle thrown into the sea. The point is: to be heard—even if by one single person."

(1885–1970, French author and Nobel Laureate)

■ GABRIEL GARCÍA MÁRQUEZ

"When I'm writing I'm always aware that this friend is going to like this, or that another friend is going to like that paragraph or chapter, always thinking of specific people. In the end all books are written for your friends."

(b. 1928, Colombian novelist and journalist)

■ BARBARA KINGSOLVER

"Close the door. Write with no one looking over your shoulder. Don't try to figure out what other people want to hear from you; figure out what you have to say. It's the one and only thing you have to offer."

(b. 1955, American novelist and essayist)

DRAFTING

WRITERS WORK in a strikingly wide range of different ways to produce a complete first draft. Some write to discover what they want to say. In one sense, these writers need to see what their ideas look like on paper in order to explore, develop, and revise a first draft. Other writers proceed at a much slower pace: they think carefully about what they want to say before they commit themselves to writing. These writers usually regard thinking and writing as separate, sequential intellectual activities. Still other writers create their own distinctive blend of these write/rewrite and think/write styles of drafting.

◼ YAEL HEDAYA

"This is what I always tell my students. Writing is not about leaping forward like an antelope, or some other graceful creature. Writing is about moving like a crab. Sideways."

(b. 1964, Israeli novelist)

◼ ANNIE DILLARD

"When you write, you lay out a line of words. The line of words is a miner's pick, a woodcarver's gouge, a surgeon's probe. You wield it, and it digs a path you follow. Soon you find yourself deep in new territory. Is it a dead end or have you located the real subject? You will know tomorrow, or this time next year."

(b. 1945, American essayist. See also page 371.)

◼ MICHAEL CHABON

"When I finish a first draft, it's always just as much of a mess as it's always been. I still make the same mistakes every time."

(b. 1963, American novelist and essayist. See also page 343.)

◼ MALCOLM GLADWELL

"Good writing does not succeed or fail on the strength of its ability to persuade. It succeeds or fails on the strength of its ability to engage you, to make you think, to give you a glimpse into someone else's head."

(b. 1963, Canadian author. See also page 411.)

◼ JACQUES BARZUN

"Convince yourself that you are working in clay, not marble, on paper, not eternal bronze: Let that first sentence be as stupid as it wishes."

(b. 1907, French-born American historian of ideas and culture)

REVISING

WHEN WRITERS REVISE, they reexamine what they have written with an eye on strengthening their control over their ideas. In some instances, as they revise, they expand or delete, substitute or reorder. In other instances, they revise to clarify or to emphasize—to reinforce or tone down particular points. More generally, they often revise either to simplify what they have written or to add a nuance. Revising provides writers with the opportunity to rethink their drafts, to help them accomplish their intentions more clearly or more fully. Revising also involves such larger concerns as determining whether the draft is logically consistent, whether its thesis or main idea is supported adequately, whether it is organized clearly enough, and whether it satisfies its audience's reasonable expectations or needs—in engaging and accessible terms. Revising enables writers to make sure their essays are as clear, precise, and effective as possible. Revising is crucial to successful writing.

◼ ELIE WIESEL

"Writing is not like painting where you add. It is not what you put on the canvas that the reader sees. Writing is more like a sculpture where you remove, you eliminate in order to make the work visible. Even those pages you remove somehow remain."

(b. 1928, Jewish-American author and Nobel Laureate. See also page 267.)

▓ IAIN BANKS

"Writing is like everything else: the more you do it the better you get. Don't try to perfect as you go along, just get to the end of the damn thing. Accept imperfections. Get it finished and then you can go back. . . ."

(b. 1954, Scottish author)

▓ TOBIAS WOLFF

"For a young writer, the best thing to do is get it out. I certainly have to. I have to write at length before I can write in brief. I have to see what the terrain is before I single out that telling moment, that telling detail and cut away the others. But I have to write the others to get to that one. So you don't want to start off in a stingy way when you write. You want to be extravagant. You know you're going to rewrite anyway, so what the hell? Pump it out, see what comes. And be free in your composition. You can be an editor later. But you don't want to be an editor and a writer at the same time, when you're doing that first draft. I think that's a mistake."

(b. 1945, American author. See also page 276.)

▓ E. M. FORSTER

"How do I know what I think until I see what I say?"

(1879–1970, English novelist and essayist)

▓ LILLIAN HELLMAN

"Nothing you write, if you hope to be any good, will ever come out as you first hoped."

(1905–1984, American playwright)

▓ GEORGE ORWELL

"A scrupulous writer, in every sentence that he writes, will ask himself at least four questions, thus: (1) What am I trying to say? (2) What words will express it? (3) What image or idiom will make it clearer? (4) Is this image fresh enough to have an effect?"

(1903–1950, English novelist and essayist. See also page 180.)

▓ ELMORE LEONARD

"My most important piece of advice to all you would-be writers: when you write, try to leave out all the parts readers skip."

(b. 1925, American novelist and screenwriter)

▓ ROBERT CORMIER

"The beautiful part of writing is that you don't have to get it right the first time, unlike, say, a brain surgeon. You can always do it better, find the exact word, the apt phrase, the leaping simile."

(1925–2000, American author and columnist)

▓ DINAW MENGESTU

"A good writing day is one in which I don't end up flinging myself against a wall or curled up on a couch in a state of nearly blinding frustration. On a good writing day the sentences come out easily, and I know when I'm finished that they are the right ones, whether there are hundreds of them or two."

(b. 1978, African novelist. See also page 170.)

▓ MICHAEL CHABON

"I love cutting. It hurts for a second but it immediately feels great afterward. You feel lighter, relieved of bad dreams and heavy burdens. I can watch two or three hundred pages go down the tubes with the equanimity of a lab assistant gassing a rat."

(b. 1963, American author. See also page 343.)

■ NAOMI SHIHAB NYE

"If a teacher told me to revise, I thought that meant my writing was a broken-down car that needed to go to the repair shop. I felt insulted. I didn't realize the teacher was saying, 'Make it shine. It's worth it.' Now I see revision as a beautiful word of hope. It's a new vision of something. It means you don't have to be perfect the first time. What a relief!"

(b. 1952, Palestinian poet and novelist)

■ CHRIS ABANI

"I cut the parts I love the most."

(b. 1966, Nigerian author and poet. See also page 25.)

■ E. B. WHITE

"The main thing I try to do is write as clearly as I can. Because I have the greatest respect for the reader, and if he's going to the trouble of reading what I've written—I'm a slow reader myself and I guess most people are—why, the least I can do is make it as easy as possible for him to find out what I'm trying to say, trying to get at. I rewrite a good deal to make it clear."

(1899–1985, American essayist. See also page 260.)

■ VLADIMIR NABOKOV

"I have rewritten—often several times—every word I have ever published. My pencils outlast their erasers."

(1899–1977, Russian novelist)

■ ISAAC BASHEVIS SINGER

"The waste basket is the writer's best friend."

(1902–1991, American author and Nobel Laureate)

■ ELMORE LEONARD

"If it sounds like writing, I rewrite it."

(b. 1925, American novelist and screenwriter)

WORKING WITH WORDS

One of the most important principles to learn about writing well is that ideas don't generate writing as much as thinking in writing produces ideas. To write effectively doesn't mean that writers are required to come up with as many new ideas—or words—as possible about a subject but rather that they focus on generating the greatest impact from the ideas that they have already committed to paper. As soon as words appear on a page, it's possible to see whether they express adequately the idea the writer is trying to convey, whether the word choices bring the subject to life or smother it with too many syllables or adjectives. Successful writers realize that there is power and elegance in simple prose and in carefully chosen diction and punctuation. Arranging and rearranging words, deciding whether an exclamation point or a semicolon best supports the writer's purpose—these basic decisions are the means by which the craft of writing is elevated to art.

■ PICO IYER

"Punctuation marks are the road signs placed along the highways of our communication—to control speeds, provide directions, and prevent head-on collisions."

(b. 1957, English essayist and novelist. See also page 693.)

■ STEPHEN KING

"Any word you have to hunt for in a thesaurus is the wrong word. There are no exceptions to this rule."

(b. 1947, American novelist. See also page 451.)

■ ELLEN GOODMAN

"I rewrite a great deal. I'm always fiddling, always changing something. I'll write a few words—then I'll change them. I add. I subtract. I work and fiddle and keep working and fiddling, and I only stop at the deadline."

(b. 1941, American columnist)

■ JOHN MCPHEE

"[T]he aural part of writing is a big, big thing to me. I can't stand a sentence until it sounds right, and I'll go over it again and again. . . . I always read the second draft aloud, as a way of moving forward. . . . I read aloud so I can hear if it's fitting together or not. It's just as much a part of the composition as going out and buying a ream of paper."

(b. 1931, American author of narrative nonfiction)

■ ANNIE DILLARD

"On plenty of days the writer can write three or four pages, and on plenty of other days he concludes he must throw them away."

(b. 1945, American essayist. See also page 371.)

■ SUSAN SONTAG

"I don't write easily or rapidly. My first draft usually has only a few elements worth keeping. I have to find what those are and build from them and throw out what doesn't work, or what simply is not alive."

(1933–2004, American essayist)

■ SCOTT ADAMS

"Creativity is allowing yourself to make mistakes. Art is knowing which ones to keep."

(b. 1957, American creator of the *Dilbert* comic strip and the author of several nonfiction works)

■ BARBARA TUCHMAN

"Nothing is more satisfying than to write a good sentence. It is no fun to write lumpishly, dully, in prose the reader must plod through like wet sand. But it is a pleasure to achieve, if one can, a clear running prose that is simple yet full of surprises. This does not just happen. It requires skill, hard work, a good ear, and continued practice."

(1912–1989, American historian)

■ MARK TWAIN

"I notice that you use plain, simple language, short words and brief sentences. That is the way to write English—it is the modern way and the best way. Stick to it; don't let fluff and flowers and verbosity creep in. When you catch an adjective, kill it. No, I don't mean utterly, but kill most of them—then the rest will be valuable. They weaken when they are close together. They give strength when they are wide apart. An adjective habit, or a wordy, diffuse, flowery habit, once fastened upon a person, is as hard to get rid of as any other vice. . . . Substitute 'damn' every time you're inclined to write 'very'; your editor will delete it and the writing will be just as it should be."

(Samuel Langhorne Clemens, 1835–1910, American author and humorist)

LEWIS THOMAS

"Exclamation points are the most irritating of all. Look! they say, look at what I just said! How amazing is my thought! It is like being forced to watch someone else's small child jumping up and down crazily in the center of the living room shouting to attract attention. If a sentence really has something of importance to say, something quite remarkable, it doesn't need a mark to point it out. And if it is really, after all, a banal sentence needing more zing, the exclamation point simply emphasizes its banality!"

(1913–1993, American physician and essayist)

WENDELL BERRY

"A sentence is both the opportunity and the limit of thought—what we have to think with, and what we have to think in."

(b. 1934, American novelist and essayist)

ROBERT FROST

"All the fun is in how you say a thing."

(1874–1963, American poet)

ON READING

ONE OF THE MOST productive exercises for any writer to practice is to read with a writer's eye. Successful writers read with focused and sustained attention to the choices writers make and to the consequences of those choices—much like how a director views a well-made film, how a musician hears a beautiful piece of music, or how a pastry chef envisions someone savoring a delicious croissant. They take pleasure and satisfaction in practicing their craft, but they also seek to learn from what they create. They notice what works and what doesn't, and they continuously ask themselves why. The same principle applies to writers: successful writers know that careful reading can produce clear and engaging prose.

EUDORA WELTY

"There's still a strange moment with every book when I move from the position of writer to the position of reader and I suddenly see my words with the eyes of the cold public. It gives me a terrible sense of exposure, as if I'd gotten sunburned."

(1909–2001, American novelist)

TONY HILLERMAN

"When I was teaching writing—and I still say it—I taught that the best way to learn to write is by reading. Reading critically, noticing paragraphs that get the job done, how your favorite writers use verbs, all the useful techniques. A scene catches you? Go back and study it. Find out how it works."

(1925–2008, American author of detective novels)

GEORGE BERNARD SHAW

"As soon as I open [a book], I occupy the book, I stomp around in it. I underline passages, scribble in the margins, leave my mark. . . . I like to be able to hear myself responding to a book, answering it, agreeing and disagreeing in a manner I recognize as peculiarly my own."

(1856–1950, Irish playwright)

TESS GALLAGHER

"When you start reading in a certain way, that's already the beginning of your writing. You're learning what you admire and you're learning to love other writers. The love of other writers is an important first step. To be a voracious, loving reader."

(b. 1943, American poet and essayist)

■ DINAW MENGESTU

"Like most writers, I take apart my sentences over and over. A bad or unpolished sentence or phrase can ruin an entire paragraph for me so I try as much as possible to work over each sentence without destroying any of its initial integrity."

(b. 1978, African novelist. See also page 170.)

■ JONATHAN SWIFT

"Proper words in proper places, make the true definition of style."

(1667–1745, Anglo-Irish satirist and essayist. See also page 831.)

■ DONALD HALL

"The paragraph [is] a mini-essay; it is also a maxi-sentence."

(b. 1928, American poet and essayist)

■ B. J. CHUTE

"Grammar is to a writer what anatomy is to a sculptor, or the scales to a musician. You may loathe it, it may bore you, but nothing will replace it, and once mastered it will support you like a rock."

(1913–1987, American novelist)

■ FRANCINE PROSE

"Like most—maybe all—writers, I learned to write by writing and, by example, by reading books."

(b. 1947, American author)

■ EDMUND BURKE

"To read without reflecting is like eating without digesting."

(1729–1797, Anglo-Irish statesman, author, orator, political theorist, and philosopher)

■ MASON COOLEY

"Reading gives us someplace to go when we have to stay where we are."

(1927–2002, American aphorist)

■ STEPHEN KING

"The real importance of reading is that it creates an ease and intimacy with the process of writing; one comes to the country of the writer with one's papers and identification pretty much in order. Constant reading will pull you into a place (a mind-set, if you like the phrase) where you can write eagerly and without self-consciousness. It also offers you a constantly growing knowledge of what has been done and what hasn't, what is trite and what is fresh, what works and what just lies there dying (or dead) on the page. The more you read, the less apt you are to make a fool of yourself with your pen or word processor. . . . '[R]ead a lot, write a lot' is the great commandment."

(b. 1947, American novelist. See also page 451.)

■ JOHN GARDNER

"What this means, in practical terms for the student writer, is that in order to achieve mastery he must read widely and deeply and must write not just carefully but continually, thoughtfully assessing and reassessing what he writes, because practice, for the writer as for the concert pianist, is the heart of the matter."

(1933–1982, American novelist and university professor)

■ NATHANIEL HAWTHORNE

"Easy reading is damned hard writing."

(1804–1864, American novelist. See also page 438.)

■ WILLIAM FAULKNER

"Read, read, read. Read everything—trash, classics, good and bad, and see how they do it. Just like a carpenter who works as an apprentice and studies the master. Read! You'll absorb it. Then write. If it is good, you'll find out. If it's not, throw it out the window."

(1897–1962, American novelist and Nobel Laureate)

■ MONTESQUIEU

"I have never known any distress that an hour's reading did not relieve."

(1689–1755, French social commentator and political thinker)

■ WALTER SAVAGE LANDOR

"What is reading but silent conversation?"

(1775–1864, English writer and poet)

■ CYNTHIA OZICK

"I read in order to write. I read out of obsession with writing. . . . I read in order to find out what I need to know."

(b. 1928, American novelist and essayist)

WRITING IS A SKILL that develops over time and with frequent practice. Writing flourishes when someone has something important to say—and responds to the writer's interest in wanting to have an idea understood by others. Developing the ability to surprise oneself—to be able to express something that one did not previously think one knew or could express —can be an enormously satisfying experience. In this sense, writing offers the opportunity to transform the world already formed by the words of others into a world of possibility—a world that writers create with the words they craft on a blank page.

PERSONAL WRITING

Exploring Our Own Lives

Chris Abani

THE LOTTERY

Nigerian-born author **CHRIS ABANI** (b. 1966) published his first novel, *Masters of the Board*, in 1985 when he was just eighteen years old. It took as its premise a fictional, neo-Nazi takeover of Nigeria. The Nigerian government arrested the eighteen-year-old Abani under suspicion of planning a coup, imprisoning him for six months. He was imprisoned twice more in connection with his writing before moving to the United States in 1999. The recipient of numerous writing awards, including the 2001 PEN USA Freedom-to-Write Award, the 2001 Prince Claus Award, a 2003 Lannan Literary Fellowship, and the 2005 PEN/Hemingway Book Prize, Abani is currently a professor at

> **Chris Abani was imprisoned in connection with his writing a total of three times before leaving Nigeria for London.**

the University of California, Riverside. His recent books include the novels *Graceland* (2005), *Becoming Abigail: A Novella* (2006), and *The Virgin of Flames* (2007), as well as the poetry collections *Hands Washing Water* (2006), *Dog Woman* (2004), and *Daphne's Lot* (2003). His 2001 poetry collection, *Kalakuta Republic*, deals with his and others' experiences as political prisoners at the hands of Nigeria's military regime. The essay included here, "The Lottery," appeared in the *New York Times* in 2004.

EVEN THOUGH it was a wet, rainy afternoon, I was glad my aunt had taken me to the market with her. Even her religious fanaticism, which sometimes prompted her to proselytize, embarrassingly, to complete strangers, wasn't enough to deaden my good mood. The rainy season in Nigeria was my favorite even as a 10-year-old. It had something to do with the light. It was crisp, like a new bank note or a thing washed and starched. And then there was the way everything smelled.

I inhaled deeply. The scent was a balanced mix of wet earth and the dry roughness of rope. There was continuity to that smell, as if it were the essence of the land itself. I closed my eyes for a moment. Other scents in the market broke through the smell of wet earth—the throat-burning sharpness of peppers, dried fish, the animal-funk of goats and chickens.

Suddenly, a lone voice screamed one word over and over: "Thief! Thief! Thief!" It was picked up slowly, as if the drizzle that afternoon had dampened the scent of blood. My aunt froze and faced the sound, nose sniffing the air like a lioness sensing prey. A man's voice, tired and breathless, tried to counter the rising chant with a feeble retort: "It's a lie! It's a lie!"

I drew nearer to my aunt, confused and more than a little afraid, but she shook off my clutching hand. Her head turned like an antenna seeking a signal. The sound of a chase grew closer—desperate, pounding feet and shouts. A man with a wild expression came around a corner and nearly knocked over a stall. Young men were almost on his heels, followed some distance behind by a larger cluster. The man ran past us, and it seemed as if I could see the pores in his skin. As he pushed past, my aunt slapped him across the face. He flinched but didn't stop; he was headed for the courtyard in the middle of the market, where the retired elders sat daily to dispense justice. I imagined the man bursting into the clearing, cries of "Sanctuary, sanctuary!" breaking from his lips. The council of elders was the highest court in my community, besides, of course, the civil system. It arbitrated on everything from murder to marital disputes, and its authority was never questioned. I felt certain the man would be safe there.

This was the mob justice I had read about in the newspaper editorials   5
that my father made my homework. Rife with condemnations of the mob lynchings that were becoming the norm in the 70's, the editorials pointed out that these victims of vigilante justice received no trials and that the crimes they were accused of were never investigated. The editorials went a step further to suggest that most of those killed this way were probably innocent. But in the terror of that moment, editorials were of little use to the man running for his life and would do little to placate the angry horde. My aunt dragged me along behind the crowd that swept past us.

The man stood in the middle of the clearing facing the elders while the crush of people pressed around them. In the center of this sacred space, the sole elder to stand up and call for tolerance was booed and pelted with rotten fruit. He sat down quickly and turned his face away. I was sure that the man was about to be lynched. How could the crowd ignore the elder's intervention? And why didn't the other elders speak out?

The mob was oddly silent; its loud breathing filled the space. The accused man began to beg, but people were too busy picking up stones and tree branches, anything that could be used as a weapon. A young man broke through the crowd carrying an old rubber tire and a metal can. He hung the tire from the accused's neck. This singular action ended the man's pleas for mercy. Resigned, he sobbed softly, mumbling inaudibly, but he didn't move as the young man emptied the contents of the can onto him. The young man smiled and talked as he went about his task: "You see why crime doesn't pay? I am doing this for you, you know. If you burn here, you won't burn in hell. God is reasonable."

Finishing, he held up a box of matches. The crowd roared. The elder who had tried intervening spoke again, but nobody listened. Someone called out, "Bring the children forward so that they can learn." My aunt hustled me to the front. Next to me stood a girl. Her face was impassive; I was ashamed at my fear. I never saw the match fall, but I felt the heat as the man erupted into a sheet of flame, burning like a lighthouse in the drizzly haze. "Watch," my aunt said as I tried to turn away from the writhing figure.

As the man burned, people began to file past him in an orderly manner like the offertory[1] line in the Catholic church I attended. As they walked past, they spat on the incandescent figure. My aunt spat. I looked away, hand held over my nose at the smell of burning flesh, horrified that it reminded me of kebabs. "Spit," she snapped, rapping me on the head with her knuckles. I spat. ●

The Reader's Presence

1. Why do you think Abani titled his essay "The Lottery"? Does anything in the essay refer directly to a lottery? What connection do you think Abani wants his readers to see between the idea of a lottery and the central event of the essay?

2. What is the importance of Abani's fifth paragraph? How does it affect your understanding of the essay? Suppose that paragraph had not been included in the essay—what would you then make of the story? Do you think Abani should have saved this fifth paragraph for last? Why or why not?

3. **CONNECTIONS:** Compare this short essay with Langston Hughes's short selection titled "Salvation" (page 118). What key similarities can you find? In what ways are characters alike? Can you see any similarities in the way each narrative unfolds? If so, describe them.

Sherman Alexie
THE JOY OF READING AND WRITING: SUPERMAN AND ME

SHERMAN ALEXIE (b. 1966) is a Spokane/Coeur d'Alene Indian who grew up on the Spokane Indian Reservation in Wellpinit, Washington. He was born hydrocephalic and underwent a brain operation at the age of six months, which he was not expected to survive. As a youth, Alexie left the reservation for a public high school where he excelled in academics

---

[1] *offertory:* A solemn part of the Catholic Mass in which bread and wine are offered to God. —EDS.

and became a star player on the basketball team. He attended Gonzaga University in Spokane on a scholarship and then transferred to Washington State University, where his experience in a poetry workshop encouraged him to become a writer. Soon after graduation he received the Washington State Arts Commission Poetry Fellowship and a National Endowment for the Arts Poetry Fellowship. His first collection of short stories, *The Lone Ranger and Tonto Fistfight in Heaven* (1993), received a PEN/Hemingway Award for Best First Book of Fiction. He was subsequently named one of Granta's Best of Young American Novelists and published a novel titled *Reservation Blues* (1995), followed the next year by *Indian Killer* (1996). Since 1997 Alexie has written for the screen; his screenplay for the movie *Smoke Signals*, based on his short story "This Is What It Means to Say Phoenix, Arizona" (page 873), received the Christopher Award in 1999. He has published some twenty books of fiction and poetry, including *Ten Little Indians* (2003), short stories; *Dangerous Astronomy* (2005), poetry; *Flight* (2007), a novel; *The Absolutely True Diary of a Part-Time Indian* (2007), his first book aimed at young adults, which won the 2007 National Book Award for Young People's Literature; *Face* (2009), poetry; and, most recently, *War Dances* (2010), which won the PEN/Faulkner Award for Fiction.

> **"I'm a good writer who may be a great writer one day. I'm harder on myself than anybody."**

Alexie has commented on his own work, "I'm a good writer who may be a great writer one day. I'm harder on myself than anybody."

I LEARNED TO READ with a Superman comic book. Simple enough, I suppose. I cannot recall which particular Superman comic book I read, nor can I remember which villain he fought in that issue. I cannot remember the plot, nor the means by which I obtained the comic book. What I can remember is this: I was 3 years old, a Spokane Indian boy living with his family on the Spokane Indian Reservation in eastern Washington state. We were poor by most standards, but one of my parents usually managed to find some minimum-wage job or another, which made us middle-class by reservation standards. I had a brother and three sisters. We lived on a combination of irregular paychecks, hope, fear, and government surplus food.

My father, who is one of the few Indians who went to Catholic school on purpose, was an avid reader of westerns, spy thrillers, murder mysteries, gangster epics, basketball player biographies, and anything else he could find. He bought his books by the pound at Dutch's Pawn Shop, Goodwill, Salvation Army, and Value Village. When he had extra money, he bought new novels at supermarkets, convenience stores, and hospital gift shops. Our house was filled with books. They were stacked in crazy piles in the bathroom, bedrooms, and living room. In a fit of unemployment-inspired creative energy, my father built a set of bookshelves and soon filled them with a random assortment of books about the Kennedy assassination, Watergate, the Vietnam War, and the entire 23-book series of the Apache westerns. My father loved books, and since I loved my father with an aching devotion, I decided to love books as well.

I can remember picking up my father's books before I could read. The words themselves were mostly foreign, but I still remember the exact moment when I first understood, with a sudden clarity, the purpose of a paragraph. I didn't have the vocabulary to say "paragraph," but I realized that a paragraph was a fence that held words. The words inside a paragraph worked together for a common purpose. They had some specific reason for being inside the same fence. This knowledge delighted me. I began to think of everything in terms of paragraphs. Our reservation was a small paragraph within the United States. My family's house was a paragraph, distinct from the other paragraphs of the LeBrets to the north, the Fords to our south, and the Tribal School to the west. Inside our house, each family member existed as a separate paragraph but still had genetics and common experiences to link us. Now, using this logic, I can see my changed family as an essay of seven paragraphs: mother, father, older brother, the deceased sister, my younger twin sisters, and our adopted little brother.

At the same time I was seeing the world in paragraphs, I also picked up that Superman comic book. Each panel, complete with picture, dialogue, and narrative was a three-dimensional paragraph. In one panel, Superman breaks through a door. His suit is red, blue, and yellow. The brown door shatters into many pieces. I look at the narrative above the picture. I cannot read the words, but I assume it tells me that "Superman is breaking down the door." Aloud, I pretend to read the words and say, "Superman is breaking down the door." Words, dialogue, also float out of Superman's mouth. Because he is breaking down the door, I assume he says, "I am breaking down the door." Once again, I pretend to read the words and say aloud, "I am breaking down the door." In this way, I learned to read.

This might be an interesting story all by itself. A little Indian boy teaches himself to read at an early age and advances quickly. He reads "Grapes of Wrath" in kindergarten when other children are struggling through "Dick and Jane." If he'd been anything but an Indian boy living on the reservation, he might have been called a prodigy. But he is an Indian boy living on the reservation and is simply an oddity. He grows into a man who often speaks of his childhood in the third person, as if it will somehow dull the pain and make him sound more modest about his talents.

A smart Indian is a dangerous person, widely feared and ridiculed by Indians and non-Indians alike. I fought with my classmates on a daily basis. They wanted me to stay quiet when the non-Indian teacher asked for answers, for volunteers, for help. We were Indian children who were expected to be stupid. Most lived up to those expectations inside the classroom but subverted them on the outside. They struggled with basic reading in school but could remember how to sing a few dozen powwow songs.

5

They were monosyllabic in front of their non-Indian teachers but could tell complicated stories and jokes at the dinner table. They submissively ducked their heads when confronted by a non-Indian adult but would slug it out with the Indian bully who was 10 years older. As Indian children, we were expected to fail in the non-Indian world. Those who failed were ceremonially accepted by other Indians and appropriately pitied by non-Indians.

I refused to fail. I was smart. I was arrogant. I was lucky. I read books late into the night, until I could barely keep my eyes open. I read books at recess, then during lunch, and in the few minutes left after I had finished my classroom assignments. I read books in the car when my family traveled to powwows or basketball games. In shopping malls, I ran to the bookstores and read bits and pieces of as many books as I could. I read the books my father brought home from the pawnshops and secondhand. I read the books I borrowed from the library. I read the backs of cereal boxes. I read the newspaper. I read the bulletins posted on the walls of the school, the clinic, the tribal offices, the post office. I read junk mail. I read auto-repair manuals. I read magazines. I read anything that had words and paragraphs. I read with equal parts joy and desperation. I loved those books, but I also knew that love had only one purpose. I was trying to save my life.

Despite all the books I read, I am still surprised I became a writer. I was going to be a pediatrician. These days, I write novels, short stories, and poems. I visit schools and teach creative writing to Indian kids. In all my years in the reservation school system, I was never taught how to write poetry, short stories, or novels. I was certainly never taught that Indians wrote poetry, short stories, and novels. Writing was something beyond Indians. I cannot recall a single time that a guest teacher visited the reservation. There must have been visiting teachers. Who were they? Where are they now? Do they exist? I visit the schools as often as possible. The Indian kids crowd the classroom. Many are writing their own poems, short stories, and novels. They have read my books. They have read many other books. They look at me with bright eyes and arrogant wonder. They are trying to save their lives. Then there are the sullen and already defeated Indian kids who sit in the back rows and ignore me with theatrical precision. The pages of their notebooks are empty. They carry neither pencil nor pen. They stare out the window. They refuse and resist. "Books," I say to them. "Books," I say. I throw my weight against their locked doors. The door holds. I am smart. I am arrogant. I am lucky. I am trying to save our lives.

The Reader's Presence

1. What does literacy mean to Alexie? What are his associations with reading? with writing? How does he use his reading and his writing to establish his ties to the community? What aspects of his identity are bound up with reading and writing?

2. How did the young Alexie use popular culture to educate himself? What did comic books teach him? How does Alexie use the figure of Superman, and aspects of action-hero stories more generally, to give structure and coherence to his essay?

3. **CONNECTIONS:** Alexie uses the metaphor of "breaking down the door" to describe the act of learning to read. What are the connotations of this metaphor? How does it compare with Frederick Douglass's account of his acquisition of literacy in "Learning to Read and Write" (page 86) in which he says that he sometimes felt as though "learning to read had been a curse rather than a blessing"? As he encountered arguments for and against slavery in the books he read, Douglass felt that reading deepened his already vivid experience of slavery: "It had given me a view of my wretched condition, without the remedy" (paragraph 6). Is literacy a means to freedom for Alexie as it was, ultimately, for Douglass? If so, freedom from what or freedom to do what?

Maya Angelou

"WHAT'S YOUR NAME, GIRL?"

MAYA ANGELOU (b. 1928) grew up in St. Louis, Missouri, and in Stamps, Arkansas, a victim of poverty, discrimination, and abuse. Angelou confronts the pain and injustice of her childhood in *I Know Why the Caged Bird Sings* (1969), from which the selection "'What's Your Name, Girl?'" is taken. James Baldwin, who suggested she write about her childhood, praised this book as the mark of the "beginning of a new era in the minds and hearts of all black men and women." Angelou, who has received more than a hundred honorary degrees, is currently Reynolds Professor of American Studies at Wake Forest University. In addition to the several volumes of her autobiography, Angelou is the author of articles, short stories, and poetry. Some of her publications include

> **"When I'm writing, everything shuts down."**

Hallelujah! The Welcome Table (2004), a collection of essays, and several books of poetry, including *Amazing Peace: A Christmas Poem* (2005), *Mother: A Cradle to Hold Me* (2006), and *Poetry for Young People: Maya Angelou* (2007). Her recording of her autobiographical work *A Song Flung Up to Heaven* won a Grammy in 2002. Her most recent book is *Letter to My Daughter* (2008), a collection of her thoughts on living well, dedicated to "the daughter she never had but sees all around her."

||||||||||||||||||||||||||||||||||||||||||||||||||||||||||||||||||||||||||||||||||||||||||||||||||||||||||||||||||||||||||||||||||||||||||||||||||||||||||

Angelou describes a typical day in her life as a writer in this way: "When I'm writing, everything shuts down. I get up about five. . . . I get in my car and drive off to a hotel room: I can't write in my house, I take a hotel room and ask them to take everything off the walls so there's me, the Bible, *Roget's Thesaurus*, and some good, dry sherry and I'm at work by 6:30. I write on the bed lying down—one elbow is darker than the other, really black from leaning on it—and I write in longhand on yellow pads. Once into it, all disbelief is suspended, it's beautiful. I hate to go, but I've set for myself 12:30 as the time to leave, because after that it's an indulgence, it becomes stuff I am going to edit out anyway. . . . After dinner I re-read what I have written . . . if April is the cruelest month, then 8:00 at night is the cruellest hour because that's when I start to edit and all that pretty stuff I've written gets axed out. So if I've written ten or twelve pages in six hours, it'll end up as three or four if I'm lucky."

RECENTLY A WHITE WOMAN from Texas, who would quickly describe herself as a liberal, asked me about my hometown. When I told her that in Stamps[1] my grandmother had owned the only Negro general merchandise store since the turn of the century, she exclaimed, "Why, you were a debutante." Ridiculous and even ludicrous. But Negro girls in small Southern towns, whether poverty-stricken or just munching along on a few of life's necessities, were given as extensive and irrelevant preparations for adulthood as rich white girls shown in magazines. Admittedly the training was not the same. While white girls learned to waltz and sit gracefully with a teacup balanced on their knees, we were lagging behind, learning the mid-Victorian values with very little money to indulge them. (Come and see Edna Lomax spending the money she made picking cotton on five balls of ecru tatting thread. Her fingers are bound to snag the work and she'll have to repeat the stitches time and time again. But she knows that when she buys the thread.)

We were required to embroider and I had trunkfuls of colorful dishtowels, pillowcases, runners, and handkerchiefs to my credit. I mastered the art of crocheting and tatting, and there was a lifetime's supply of dainty doilies that would never be used in sacheted dresser drawers. It went without saying that all girls could iron and wash, but the finer touches around the home, like setting a table with real silver, baking roasts, and cooking vegetables without meat, had to be learned elsewhere. Usually at the source of those habits. During my tenth year, a white woman's kitchen became my finishing school.

Mrs. Viola Cullinan was a plump woman who lived in a three-bedroom house somewhere behind the post office. She was singularly unattractive until she smiled, and then the lines around her eyes and mouth which made her look perpetually dirty disappeared, and her face looked like the mask of an impish elf. She usually rested her smile until late afternoon when her women friends dropped in and Miss Glory, the cook, served them cold drinks on the closed-in porch.

[1] *Stamps:* A town in southwestern Arkansas. — EDS.

The exactness of her house was inhuman. This glass went here and only here. That cup had its place and it was an act of impudent rebellion to place it anywhere else. At twelve o'clock the table was set. At 12:15 Mrs. Cullinan sat down to dinner (whether her husband had arrived or not). At 12:16 Miss Glory brought out the food.

It took me a week to learn the difference between a salad plate, a bread   5
plate, and a dessert plate.

Mrs. Cullinan kept up the tradition of her wealthy parents. She was from Virginia. Miss Glory, who was a descendant of slaves that had worked for the Cullinans, told me her history. She had married beneath her (according to Miss Glory). Her husband's family hadn't had their money very long and what they had "didn't 'mount to much."

As ugly as she was, I thought privately, she was lucky to get a husband above or beneath her station. But Miss Glory wouldn't let me say a thing against her mistress. She was very patient with me, however, over the housework. She explained the dishware, silverware, and servants' bells.

The large round bowl in which soup was served wasn't a soup bowl, it was a tureen. There were goblets, sherbet glasses, ice-cream glasses, wine glasses, green glass coffee cups with matching saucers, and water glasses. I had a glass to drink from, and it sat with Miss Glory's on a separate shelf from the others. Soup spoons, gravy boat, butter knives, salad forks, and carving platter were additions to my vocabulary and in fact almost represented a new language. I was fascinated with the novelty, with the fluttering Mrs. Cullinan and her Alice-in-Wonderland house.

Her husband remains, in my memory, undefined. I lumped him with all the other white men that I had ever seen and tried not to see.

On our way home one evening, Miss Glory told me that Mrs. Cullinan   10
couldn't have children. She said that she was too delicate-boned. It was hard to imagine bones at all under those layers of fat. Miss Glory went on to say that the doctor had taken out all her lady organs. I reasoned that a pig's organs included the lungs, heart, and liver, so if Mrs. Cullinan was walking around without these essentials, it explained why she drank alcohol out of unmarked bottles. She was keeping herself embalmed.

When I spoke to Bailey[2] about it, he agreed that I was right, but he also informed me that Mr. Cullinan had two daughters by a colored lady and that I knew them very well. He added that the girls were the spitting image of their father. I was unable to remember what he looked like, although I had just left him a few hours before, but I thought of the Coleman girls. They were very light-skinned and certainly didn't look very much like their mother (no one ever mentioned Mr. Coleman).

My pity for Mrs. Cullinan preceded me the next morning like the Cheshire cat's smile. Those girls, who could have been her daughters, were beautiful. They didn't have to straighten their hair. Even when they were caught in the rain, their braids still hung down straight like tamed snakes.

---

[2] *Bailey:* Angelou's brother. —EDS.

Their mouths were pouty little cupid's bows. Mrs. Cullinan didn't know what she missed. Or maybe she did. Poor Mrs. Cullinan.

For weeks after, I arrived early, left late, and tried very hard to make up for her barrenness. If she had had her own children, she wouldn't have had to ask me to run a thousand errands from her back door to the back door of her friends. Poor old Mrs. Cullinan.

Then one evening Miss Glory told me to serve the ladies on the porch. After I set the tray down and turned toward the kitchen, one of the women asked, "What's your name, girl?" It was the speckled-face one. Mrs. Cullinan said, "She doesn't talk much. Her name's Margaret."

"Is she dumb?"   15

"No. As I understand it, she can talk when she wants to but she's usually quiet as a little mouse. Aren't you, Margaret?"

I smiled at her. Poor thing. No organs and couldn't even pronounce my name correctly.[3]

"She's a sweet little thing, though."

"Well, that may be, but the name's too long. I'd never bother myself. I'd call her Mary if I was you."

I fumed into the kitchen. That horrible woman would never have the   20 chance to call me Mary because if I was starving I'd never work for her. I decided I wouldn't pee on her if her heart was on fire. Giggles drifted in off the porch and into Miss Glory's pots. I wondered what they could be laughing about.

Whitefolks were so strange. Could they be talking about me? Everybody knew that they stuck together better than the Negroes did. It was possible that Mrs. Cullinan had friends in St. Louis who heard about a girl from Stamps being in court and wrote to tell her. Maybe she knew about Mr. Freeman.[4]

My lunch was in my mouth a second time and I went outside and relieved myself on the bed of four-o'clocks. Miss Glory thought I might be coming down with something and told me to go on home, that Momma would give me some herb tea, and she'd explain to her mistress.

I realized how foolish I was being before I reached the pond. Of course Mrs. Cullinan didn't know. Otherwise she wouldn't have given me the two nice dresses that Momma cut down, and she certainly wouldn't have called me a "sweet little thing." My stomach felt fine, and I didn't mention anything to Momma.

That evening I decided to write a poem on being white, fat, old, and without children. It was going to be a tragic ballad. I would have to watch her carefully to capture the essence of her loneliness and pain.

---

[3] *couldn't even pronounce my name correctly:* Angelou's first name is actually Marguerite. —EDS.

[4] *Mr. Freeman:* A friend of Angelou's mother; he was convicted of raping Angelou when she was a child. —EDS.

The very next day, she called me by the wrong name. Miss Glory and I   25
were washing up the lunch dishes when Mrs. Cullinan came to the doorway.
"Mary?"

Miss Glory asked, "Who?"

Mrs. Cullinan, sagging a little, knew and I knew. "I want Mary to go
down to Mrs. Randall's and take her some soup. She's not been feeling well
for a few days."

Miss Glory's face was a wonder to see. "You mean Margaret, ma'am.
Her name's Margaret."

"That's too long. She's Mary from now on. Heat that soup from last night
and put it in the china tureen and, Mary, I want you to carry it carefully."

Every person I knew had a hellish horror of being "called out of his   30
name." It was a dangerous practice to call a Negro anything that could be
loosely construed as insulting because of the centuries of their having been
called niggers, jigs, dinges, blackbirds, crows, boots, and spooks.

Miss Glory had a fleeting second of feeling sorry for me. Then as she
handed me the hot tureen she said, "Don't mind, don't pay that no mind.
Sticks and stones may break your bones, but words . . . You know, I been
working for her for twenty years."

She held the back door open for me. "Twenty years; I wasn't much older
than you. My name used to be Hallelujah. That's what Ma named me, but
my mistress give me 'Glory,' and it stuck. I likes it better too."

I was in the little path that ran behind the houses when Miss Glory
shouted, "It's shorter too."

For a few seconds it was a toss-up over whether I would laugh (imagine
being named Hallelujah) or cry (imagine letting some white woman rename
you for her convenience). My anger saved me from either outburst. I had to
quit the job, but the problem was going to be how to do it. Momma wouldn't
allow me to quit for just any reason.

"She's a peach. That woman is a real peach." Mrs. Randall's maid was   35
talking as she took the soup from me, and I wondered what her name used
to be and what she answered to now.

For a week I looked into Mrs. Cullinan's face as she called me Mary. She
ignored my coming late and leaving early. Miss Glory was a little annoyed
because I had begun to leave egg yolk on the dishes and wasn't putting
much heart in polishing the silver. I hoped that she would complain to our
boss, but she didn't.

Then Bailey solved my dilemma. He had me describe the contents of
the cupboard and the particular plates she liked best. Her favorite piece
was a casserole shaped like a fish and the green glass coffee cups. I kept
his instructions in mind, so on the next day when Miss Glory was hanging
out clothes and I had again been told to serve the old biddies on the porch,
I dropped the empty serving tray. When I heard Mrs. Cullinan scream,
"Mary!" I picked up the casserole and two of the green glass cups in readiness. As she rounded the kitchen door I let them fall on the tiled floor.

I could never absolutely describe to Bailey what happened next, because each time I got to the part where she fell on the floor and screwed up her ugly face to cry, we burst out laughing. She actually wobbled around on the floor and picked up shards of the cups and cried, "Oh, Momma. Oh, dear Gawd. It's Momma's china from Virginia. Oh, Momma, I sorry."

Miss Glory came running in from the yard and the women from the porch crowded around. Miss Glory was almost as broken up as her mistress. "You mean to say she broke our Virginia dishes? What we gone do?"

Mrs. Cullinan cried louder. "That clumsy nigger. Clumsy little black 40 nigger."

Old speckled-face leaned down and asked, "Who did it, Viola? Was it Mary? Who did it?"

Everything was happening so fast I can't remember whether her action preceded her words, but I know that Mrs. Cullinan said, "Her name's Margaret, goddamn it, her name's Margaret!" And she threw a wedge of the broken plate at me. It could have been the hysteria which put her aim off, but the flying crockery caught Miss Glory right over her ear and she started screaming.

I left the front door wide open so all the neighbors could hear.

Mrs. Cullinan was right about one thing. My name wasn't Mary. ▉

The Reader's Presence

1. At the center of this autobiographical episode is the importance of people's names in African American culture. Where does Angelou make this point clear? If she hadn't explained the problem of names directly, how might your interpretation of the episode be different? To what extent do the names of things also play an important role in the essay? What does it mean to be "called out of [one's] name" (paragraph 30)?

2. Consider Marguerite's final act carefully. What turns her sympathetic feelings for Mrs. Cullinan to anger? Why does she respond by deliberately destroying Mrs. Cullinan's china? What else could she have done? Why was that act especially appropriate? What does the china represent? How does Angelou establish our sympathy, or lack thereof, for Marguerite in the final paragraphs?

3. **CONNECTIONS:** Many coming-of-age stories involve an account not only of the child's acquisition of language but also, and perhaps more important, of the importance of social context to communication. Miss Glory's training of Marguerite as a maid involves "additions to [her] vocabulary and in fact almost represented a new language" (paragraph 8). How does her education compare to that of Malcolm X in "My First Conk" (page 153)? What is the relation between language and power in each essay?

James Baldwin

NOTES OF A NATIVE SON

JAMES BALDWIN (1924–1987) grew up in New York City but moved to France in 1948 because he felt personally and artistically stifled as a gay African American man in the United States. His first novels, *Go Tell It on the Mountain* (1956) and *Giovanni's Room* (1956), and his first collection of essays, *Notes of a Native Son* (1955), were published during Baldwin's first stay abroad, where he was able to write critically about race, sexual identity, and social injustice in America. "Once I found myself on the other side of the ocean," he told an interviewer, "I could see where I came from very clearly, and I could see that I carried myself, which is my home, with me. You can never escape that. I am the grandson of a slave, and I am a writer. I must deal with both."

After nearly a decade in France, he returned to New York and became a national figure in the civil rights movement. After Baldwin's death, Henry Louis Gates Jr. eulogized him as the conscience of the nation, for he

> **"I am the grandson of a slave, and I am a writer. I must deal with both."**

"educated an entire generation of Americans about the civil-rights struggle and the sensibility of Afro-Americans as we faced and conquered the final barriers in our long quest for civil rights." Baldwin continues to educate through his essays, collected in *The Price of the Ticket: Collected Nonfiction* (1985).

When asked if he approached the writing of fiction and nonfiction in different ways, Baldwin responded, "Every form is different, no one is easier than another. . . . An essay is not simpler, though it may seem so. An essay is clearly an argument. The writer's point of view in an essay is always absolutely clear. The writer is trying to make the readers see something, trying to convince them of something. In a novel or a play you're trying to show them something. The risks, in any case, are exactly the same."

The title essay of the book *Notes of a Native Son* first appeared in *Harper's* magazine in 1955. In it, Baldwin recounts the death of his father, whose funeral took place on Baldwin's nineteenth birthday—the same day a bloody race riot broke out in Harlem.

ONE

On the twenty-ninth of July, in 1943, my father died. On the same day, a few hours later, his last child was born. Over a month before this, while all our energies were concentrated in waiting for these events, there had been, in Detroit, one of the bloodiest race riots of the century. A few hours after my father's funeral, while he lay in state in the undertaker's chapel, a race riot broke out in Harlem. On the morning of the third of August, we drove my father to the graveyard through a wilderness of smashed plate glass.

The day of my father's funeral had also been my nineteenth birthday. As we drove him to the graveyard, the spoils of injustice, anarchy, discontent, and hatred were all around us. It seemed to me that God himself had devised, to mark my father's end, the most sustained and brutally dissonant of codas. And it seemed to me, too, that the violence which rose all about us as my father left the world had been devised as a corrective for the pride of his eldest son. I had declined to believe in that apocalypse which had been central to my father's vision; very well, life seemed to be saying, here is something that will certainly pass for an apocalypse until the real thing comes along. I had inclined to be contemptuous of my father for the conditions of his life, for the conditions of our lives. When his life had ended I began to wonder about that life and also, in a new way, to be apprehensive about my own.

I had not known my father very well. We had got on badly, partly because we shared, in our different fashions, the vice of stubborn pride. When he was dead I realized that I had hardly ever spoken to him. When he had been dead a long time I began to wish I had. It seems to be typical of life in America, where opportunities, real and fancied, are thicker than anywhere else on the globe, that the second generation has no time to talk to the first. No one, including my father, seems to have known exactly how old he was, but his mother had been born during slavery. He was of the first generation of free men. He, along with thousands of other Negroes, came North after 1919 and I was part of that generation which had never seen the landscape of what Negroes sometimes call the Old Country.

He had been born in New Orleans and had been quite a young man there during the time that Louis Armstrong, a boy, was running errands for the dives and honky-tonks of what was always presented to me as one of the most wicked of cities—to this day, whenever I think of New Orleans, I also helplessly think of Sodom and Gomorrah. My father never mentioned Louis Armstrong, except to forbid us to play his records; but there was a picture of him on our wall for a long time. One of my father's strong-willed female relatives had placed it there and forbade my father to take it down. He never did, but he eventually maneuvered her out of the house and when, some years later, she was in trouble and near death, he refused to do anything to help her.

He was, I think, very handsome. I gather this from photographs and from my own memories of him, dressed in his Sunday best and on his way to preach a sermon somewhere, when I was little. Handsome, proud, and

5

ingrown, "like a toenail," somebody said. But he looked to me, as I grew older, like pictures I had seen of African tribal chieftains: he really should have been naked, with warpaint on and barbaric mementos, standing among spears. He could be chilling in the pulpit and indescribably cruel in his personal life and he was certainly the most bitter man I have ever met; yet it must be said that there was something else in him, buried in him, which lent him his tremendous power and, even, a rather crushing charm. It had something to do with his blackness, I think—he was very black—with his blackness and his beauty, and with the fact that he knew that he was black but did not know that he was beautiful. He claimed to be proud of his blackness but it had also been the cause of much humiliation and it had fixed bleak boundaries to his life. He was not a young man when we were growing up and he had already suffered many kinds of ruin; in his outrageously demanding and protective way he loved his children, who were black like him and menaced, like him; and all these things sometimes showed in his face when he tried, never to my knowledge with any success, to establish contact with any of us. When he took one of his children on his knee to play, the child always became fretful and began to cry; when he tried to help one of us with our homework the absolutely unabating tension which emanated from him caused our minds and our tongues to become paralyzed, so that he, scarcely knowing why, flew into a rage and the child, not knowing why, was punished. If it ever entered his head to bring a surprise home for his children, it was, almost unfailingly, the wrong surprise and even the big watermelons he often brought home on his back in the summertime led to the most appalling scenes. I do not remember, in all those years, that one of his children was ever glad to see him come home. From what I was able to gather of his early life, it seemed that this inability to establish contact with other people had always marked him and had been one of the things which had driven him out of New Orleans. There was something in him, therefore, groping and tentative, which was never expressed and which was buried with him. One saw it most clearly when he was facing new people and hoping to impress them. But he never did, not for long. We went from church to smaller and more improbable church, he found himself in less and less demand as a minister, and by the time he died none of his friends had come to see him for a long time. He had lived and died in an intolerable bitterness of spirit and it frightened me, as we drove him to the graveyard through those unquiet, ruined streets, to see how powerful and overflowing this bitterness could be and to realize that this bitterness now was mine.

When he died I had been away from home for a little over a year. In that year I had had time to become aware of the meaning of all my father's bitter warnings, had discovered the secret of his proudly pursed lips and rigid carriage: I had discovered the weight of white people in the world. I saw that this had been for my ancestors and now would be for me an awful thing to live with and that the bitterness which had helped to kill my father could also kill me.

He had been ill a long time—in the mind, as we now realized, reliving instances of his fantastic intransigence in the new light of his affliction and endeavoring to feel a sorrow for him which never, quite, came true. We had not known that he was being eaten up by paranoia, and the discovery that his cruelty, to our bodies and our minds, had been one of the symptoms of his illness was not, then, enough to enable us to forgive him. The younger children felt, quite simply, relief that he would not be coming home anymore. My mother's observation that it was he, after all, who had kept them alive all these years meant nothing because the problems of keeping children alive are not real for children. The older children felt, with my father gone, that they could invite their friends to the house without fear that their friends would be insulted or, as had sometimes happened with me, being told that their friends were in league with the devil and intended to rob our family of everything we owned. (I didn't fail to wonder, and it made me hate him, what on earth we owned that anybody else would want.)

His illness was beyond all hope of healing before anyone realized that he was ill. He had always been so strange and had lived, like a prophet, in such unimaginably close communion with the Lord that his long silences which were punctuated by moans and hallelujahs and snatches of old songs while he sat at the living-room window never seemed odd to us. It was not until he refused to eat because, he said, his family was trying to poison him that my mother was forced to accept as a fact what had, until then, been only an unwilling suspicion. When he was committed, it was discovered that he had tuberculosis and, as it turned out, the disease of his mind allowed the disease of his body to destroy him. For the doctors could not force him to eat, either, and, though he was fed intravenously, it was clear from the beginning that there was no hope for him.

In my mind's eye I could see him, sitting at the window, locked up in his terrors; hating and fearing every living soul including his children who had betrayed him, too, by reaching toward the world which had despised him. There were nine of us. I began to wonder what it could have felt like for such a man to have had nine children whom he could barely feed. He used to make little jokes about our poverty, which never, of course, seemed very funny to us; they could not have seemed very funny to him, either, or else our all too feeble response to them would never have caused such rages. He spent great energy and achieved, to our chagrin, no small amount of success in keeping us away from the people who surrounded us, people who had all-night rent parties[1] to which we listened when we should have been sleeping, people who cursed and drank and flashed razor blades on Lenox Avenue. He could not understand why, if they had so much energy to spare, they could not use it to make their lives better. He treated almost everybody on our block with a most uncharitable asperity and neither they, nor, of course, their children were slow to reciprocate.

---

1 **rent parties:** Part of a Harlem tradition; musicians were often hired and contributions taken to help pay the rent for needy tenants.—EDS.

The only white people who came to our house were welfare workers   10
and bill collectors. It was almost always my mother who dealt with them,
for my father's temper, which was at the mercy of his pride, was never to be
trusted. It was clear that he felt their very presence in his home to be a violation: this was conveyed by his carriage, almost ludicrously stiff, and by his
voice, harsh and vindictively polite. When I was around nine or ten I wrote
a play which was directed by a young, white schoolteacher, a woman, who
then took an interest in me, and gave me books to read and, in order to corroborate my theatrical bent, decided to take me to see what she somewhat
tactlessly referred to as "real" plays. Theater-going was forbidden in our
house, but, with the really cruel intuitiveness of a child, I suspected that the
color of this woman's skin would carry the day for me. When, at school, she
suggested taking me to the theater, I did not, as I might have done if she had
been a Negro, find a way of discouraging her, but agreed that she should
pick me up at my house one evening. I then, very cleverly, left all the rest to
my mother, who suggested to my father, as I knew she would, that it would
not be very nice to let such a kind woman make the trip for nothing. Also,
since it was a schoolteacher, I imagine that my mother countered the idea of
sin with the idea of "education," which word, even with my father, carried
a kind of bitter weight.

Before the teacher came my father took me aside to ask *why* she was
coming, what *interest* she could possibly have in our house, in a boy like
me. I said I didn't know but I, too, suggested that it had something to do
with education. And I understood that my father was waiting for me to say
something—I didn't quite know what; perhaps that I wanted his protection
against this teacher and her "education." I said none of these things and
the teacher came and we went out. It was clear, during the brief interview
in our living room, that my father was agreeing very much against his will
and that he would have refused permission if he had dared. The fact that
he did not dare caused me to despise him: I had no way of knowing that
he was facing in that living room a wholly unprecedented and frightening
situation.

Later, when my father had been laid off from his job, this woman became
very important to us. She was really a very sweet and generous woman and
went to a great deal of trouble to be of help to us, particularly during one
awful winter. My mother called her by the highest name she knew: she said
she was a "Christian." My father could scarcely disagree but during the
four or five years of our relatively close association he never trusted her and
was always trying to surprise in her open, Midwestern face the genuine,
cunningly hidden, and hideous motivation. In later years, particularly when
it began to be clear that this "education" of mine was going to lead me to
perdition, he became more explicit and warned me that my white friends
in high school were not really my friends and that I would see, when I was
older, how white people would do anything to keep a Negro down. Some of
them could be nice, he admitted, but none of them were to be trusted and
most of them were not even nice. The best thing was to have as little to do

with them as possible. I did not feel this way and I was certain, in my innocence, that I never would.

But the year which preceded my father's death had made a great change in my life. I had been living in New Jersey, working in defense plants, working and living among southerners, white and black. I knew about the south, of course, and about how southerners treated Negroes and how they expected them to behave, but it had never entered my mind that anyone would look at me and expect *me* to behave that way. I learned in New Jersey that to be a Negro meant, precisely, that one was never looked at but was simply at the mercy of the reflexes the color of one's skin caused in other people. I acted in New Jersey as I had always acted, that is as though I thought a great deal of myself—I had to *act* that way—with results that were, simply, unbelievable. I had scarcely arrived before I had earned the enmity, which was extraordinarily ingenious, of all my superiors and nearly all my co-workers. In the beginning, to make matters worse, I simply did not know what was happening. I did not know what I had done, and I shortly began to wonder what *anyone* could possibly do, to bring about such unanimous, active, and unbearably vocal hostility. I knew about Jim Crow but I had never experienced it. I went to the same self-service restaurant three times and stood with all the Princeton boys before the counter, waiting for a hamburger and coffee; it was always an extraordinarily long time before anything was set before me; but it was not until the fourth visit that I learned that, in fact, nothing had ever been set before me: I had simply picked something up. Negroes were not served there, I was told, and they had been waiting for me to realize that I was always the only Negro present. Once I was told this, I determined to go there all the time. But now they were ready for me and, though some dreadful scenes were subsequently enacted in that restaurant, I never ate there again.

It was the same story all over New Jersey, in bars, bowling alleys, diners, places to live. I was always being forced to leave, silently, or with mutual imprecations. I very shortly became notorious and children giggled behind me when I passed and their elders whispered or shouted—they really believed that I was mad. And it did begin to work on my mind, of course; I began to be afraid to go anywhere and to compensate for this I went places to which I really should not have gone and where, God knows, I had no desire to be. My reputation in town naturally enhanced my reputation at work and my working day became one long series of acrobatics designed to keep me out of trouble. I cannot say that these acrobatics succeeded. It began to seem that the machinery of the organization I worked for was turning over, day and night, with but one aim: to eject me. I was fired once, and contrived, with the aid of a friend from New York, to get back on the payroll; was fired again, and bounced back again. It took a while to fire me for the third time, but the third time took. There were no loopholes anywhere. There was not even any way of getting back inside the gates.

That year in New Jersey lives in my mind as though it were the year   15
during which, having an unsuspected predilection for it, I first contracted
some dread, chronic disease, the unfailing symptom of which is a kind of
blind fever, a pounding in the skull and fire in the bowels. Once this disease
is contracted, one can never be really carefree again, for the fever, without
an instant's warning, can recur at any moment. It can wreck more important
things than race relations. There is not a Negro alive who does not have this
rage in his blood—one has the choice, merely, of living with it consciously
or surrendering to it. As for me, this fever has recurred in me, and does, and
will until the day I die.

My last night in New Jersey, a white friend from New York took me to
the nearest big town, Trenton, to go to the movies and have a few drinks. As
it turned out, he also saved me from, at the very least, a violent whipping.
Almost every detail of that night stands out very clearly in my memory. I
even remember the name of the movie we saw because its title impressed
me as being so patly ironical. It was a movie about the German occupation
of France, starring Maureen O'Hara and Charles Laughton and called *This
Land Is Mine*. I remember the name of the diner we walked into when the
movie ended: it was the "American Diner." When we walked in the count-
erman asked what we wanted and I remember answering with the casual
sharpness which had become my habit: "We want a hamburger and a cup of
coffee, what do you think we want?" I do not know why, after a year of such
rebuffs, I so completely failed to anticipate his answer, which was, of course,
"We don't serve Negroes here." This reply failed to discompose me, at least
for the moment. I made some sardonic comment about the name of the diner
and we walked out into the streets.

This was the time of what was called the "brownout," when the lights
in all American cities were very dim. When we reentered the streets something happened to me which had the force of an optical illusion, or a nightmare. The streets were very crowded and I was facing north. People were
moving in every direction but it seemed to me, in that instant, that all of
the people I could see, and many more than that, were moving toward
me, against me, and that everyone was white. I remember how their faces
gleamed. And I felt, like a physical sensation, a *click* at the nape of my neck
as though some interior string connecting my head to my body had been
cut. I began to walk. I heard my friend call after me, but I ignored him.
Heaven only knows what was going on in his mind, but he had the good
sense not to touch me—I don't know what would have happened if he
had—and to keep me in sight. I don't know what was going on in my mind,
either; I certainly had no conscious plan. I wanted to do something to crush
these white faces, which were crushing me. I walked for perhaps a block or
two until I came to an enormous, glittering, and fashionable restaurant in
which I knew not even the intercession of the Virgin would cause me to be
served. I pushed through the doors and took the first vacant seat I saw, at a
table for two, and waited.

I do not know how long I waited and I rather wonder, until today, what I could possibly have looked like. Whatever I looked like, I frightened the waitress who shortly appeared, and the moment she appeared all of my fury flowed toward her. I hated her for her white face, and for her great, astounded, frightened eyes. I felt that if she found a black man so frightening I would make her fright worthwhile.

She did not ask me what I wanted, but repeated, as though she had learned it somewhere, "We don't serve Negroes here." She did not say it with the blunt, derisive hostility to which I had grown so accustomed, but, rather, with a note of apology in her voice, and fear. This made me colder and more murderous than ever. I felt I had to do something with my hands. I wanted her to come close enough for me to get her neck between my hands.

So I pretended not to have understood her, hoping to draw her closer. And   20 she did step a very short step closer, with her pencil poised incongruously over her pad, and repeated the formula: ". . . don't serve Negroes here."

Somehow, with the repetition of that phrase, which was already ringing in my head like a thousand bells of a nightmare, I realized that she would never come any closer and that I would have to strike from a distance. There was nothing on the table but an ordinary watermug half full of water, and I picked this up and hurled it with all my strength at her. She ducked and it missed her and shattered against the mirror behind the bar. And, with that sound, my frozen blood abruptly thawed, I returned from wherever I had been, I *saw*, for the first time, the restaurant, the people with their mouths open, already, as it seemed to me, rising as one man, and I realized what I had done, and where I was, and I was frightened. I rose and began running for the door. A round, potbellied man grabbed me by the nape of the neck just as I reached the doors and began to beat me about the face. I kicked him and got loose and ran into the streets. My friend whispered, "*Run!*" and I ran.

My friend stayed outside the restaurant long enough to misdirect my pursuers and the police, who arrived, he told me, at once. I do not know what I said to him when he came to my room that night. I could not have said much. I felt, in the oddest, most awful way, that I had somehow betrayed him. I lived it over and over and over again, the way one relives an automobile accident after it has happened and one finds oneself alone and safe. I could not get over two facts, both equally difficult for the imagination to grasp, and one was that I could have been murdered. But the other was that I had been ready to commit murder. I saw nothing very clearly but I did see this: that my life, my *real* life, was in danger, and not from anything other people might do but from the hatred I carried in my own heart.

TWO

I had returned home around the second week in June—in great haste because it seemed that my father's death and my mother's confinement were both but a matter of hours. In the case of my mother, it soon became clear that she had simply made a miscalculation. This had always been her tendency and I don't believe that a single one of us arrived in the world, or has since arrived anywhere else, on time. But none of us dawdled so intolerably about the business of being born as did my baby sister. We sometimes amused ourselves, during those endless, stifling weeks, by picturing the baby sitting within in the safe, warm dark, bitterly regretting the necessity of becoming a part of our chaos and stubbornly putting it off as long as possible. I understood her perfectly and congratulated her on showing such good sense so soon. Death, however, sat as purposefully at my father's bedside as life stirred within my mother's womb and it was harder to understand why he so lingered in that long shadow. It seemed that he had bent, and for a long time, too, all of his energies toward dying. Now death was ready for him but my father held back.

All of Harlem, indeed, seemed to be infected by waiting. I had never before known it to be so violently still. Racial tensions throughout this country were exacerbated during the early years of the war, partly because the labor market brought together hundreds of thousands of ill-prepared people and partly because Negro soldiers, regardless of where they were born, received their military training in the south. What happened in defense plants and army camps had repercussions, naturally, in every Negro ghetto. The situation in Harlem had grown bad enough for clergymen, policemen, educators, politicians, and social workers to assert in one breath that there was no "crime wave" and to offer, in the very next breath, suggestions as to how to combat it. These suggestions always seemed to involve playgrounds, despite the fact that racial skirmishes were occurring in the playgrounds, too. Playground or not, crime wave or not, the Harlem police force had been augmented in March, and the unrest grew—perhaps, in fact, partly as a result of the ghetto's instinctive hatred of policemen. Perhaps the most revealing news item, out of the steady parade of reports of muggings, stabbings, shootings, assaults, gang wars, and accusations of police brutality, is the item concerning six Negro girls who set upon a white girl in the subway because, as they all too accurately put it, she was stepping on their toes. Indeed she was, all over the nation.

I had never before been so aware of policemen, on foot, on horseback,　25 on corners, everywhere, always two by two. Nor had I ever been so aware of small knots of people. They were on stoops and on corners and in doorways, and what was striking about them, I think, was that they did not seem to be talking. Never, when I passed these groups, did the usual sound of a curse or a laugh ring out and neither did there seem to be any hum of gossip. There was certainly, on the other hand, occurring between them communication extraordinarily intense. Another thing that was striking was the unexpected diversity of the people who made up these groups. Usually, for example, one would see a group of sharpies standing on the street corner, jiving the passing chicks; or a group of older men, usually, for some reason, in the

vicinity of a barber shop, discussing baseball scores, or the numbers, or making rather chilling observations about women they had known. Women, in a
general way, tended to be seen less often together—unless they were church
women, or very young girls, or prostitutes met together for an unprofessional
instant. But that summer I saw the strangest combinations: large, respectable, churchly matrons standing on the stoops or the corners with their hair
tied up, together with a girl in sleazy satin whose face bore the marks of gin
and the razor, or heavy-set, abrupt, no-nonsense older men, in company
with the most disreputable and fanatical "race" men,[2] or these same "race"
men with the sharpies, or these sharpies with the churchly women. Seventh
Day Adventists and Methodists and Spiritualists seemed to be hobnobbing
with Holyrollers and they were all, alike, entangled with the most flagrant
disbelievers; something heavy in their stance seemed to indicate that they
had all, incredibly, seen a common vision, and on each face there seemed to
be the same strange, bitter shadow.

The churchly women and the matter-of-fact, no-nonsense men had
children in the Army. The sleazy girls they talked to had lovers there, the
sharpies and the "race" men had friends and brothers there. It would have
demanded an unquestioning patriotism, happily as uncommon in this country as it is undesirable, for these people not to have been disturbed by the
bitter letters they received, by the newspaper stories they read, not to have
been enraged by the posters, then to be found all over New York, which
described the Japanese as "yellow-bellied Japs." It was only the "race" men,
to be sure, who spoke ceaselessly of being revenged—how this vengeance
was to be exacted was not clear—for the indignities and dangers suffered
by Negro boys in uniform; but everybody felt a directionless, hopeless bitterness, as well as that panic which can scarcely be suppressed when one
knows that a human being one loves is beyond one's reach, and in danger.
This helplessness and this gnawing uneasiness does something, at length, to
even the toughest mind. Perhaps the best way to sum all this up is to say that
the people I knew felt, mainly, a peculiar kind of relief when they knew that
their boys were being shipped out of the south, to do battle overseas. It was,
perhaps, like feeling that the most dangerous part of a dangerous journey
had been passed and that now, even if death should come, it would come
with honor and without the complicity of their countrymen. Such a death
would be, in short, a fact with which one could hope to live.

It was on the twenty-eighth of July, which I believe was a Wednesday,
that I visited my father for the first time during his illness and for the last time
in his life. The moment I saw him I knew why I had put off this visit so long.
I had told my mother that I did not want to see him because I hated him. But
this was not true. It was only that I *had* hated him and I wanted to hold on
to this hatred. I did not want to look on him as a ruin: it was not a ruin I had

---

2 *"race" men:* Baldwin seems to be thinking of self-appointed spokesmen for racial consciousness and not serious black leaders. —EDS.

hated. I imagine that one of the reasons people cling to their hates so stubbornly is because they sense, once hate is gone, that they will be forced to
deal with pain.

We traveled out to him, his older sister and myself, to what seemed to be
the very end of a very Long Island. It was hot and dusty and we wrangled,
my aunt and I, all the way out, over the fact that I had recently begun to
smoke and, as she said, to give myself airs. But I knew that she wrangled
with me because she could not bear to face the fact of her brother's dying.
Neither could I endure the reality of her despair, her unstated bafflement as
to what had happened to her brother's life, and her own. So we wrangled
and I smoked and from time to time she fell into a heavy reverie. Covertly, I
watched her face, which was the face of an old woman; it had fallen in, the
eyes were sunken and lightless; soon she would be dying, too.

In my childhood—it had not been so long ago—I had thought her beautiful. She had been quick-witted and quick-moving and very generous with
all the children and each of her visits had been an event. At one time one
of my brothers and myself had thought of running away to live with her.
Now she could no longer produce out of her handbag some unexpected and
yet familiar delight. She made me feel pity and revulsion and fear. It was
awful to realize that she no longer caused me to feel affection. The closer
we came to the hospital the more querulous she became and at the same
time, naturally, grew more dependent on me. Between pity and guilt and
fear I began to feel that there was another me trapped in my skull like a
jack-in-the-box who might escape my control at any moment and fill the air
with screaming.

She began to cry the moment we entered the room and she saw him   30
lying there, all shriveled and still, like a little black monkey. The great,
gleaming apparatus which fed him and would have compelled him to be
still even if he had been able to move brought to mind, not beneficence,
but torture; the tubes entering his arm made me think of pictures I had seen
when a child, of Gulliver, tied down by the pygmies on that island. My aunt
wept and wept, there was a whistling sound in my father's throat; nothing
was said; he could not speak. I wanted to take his hand, to say something.
But I do not know what I could have said, even if he could have heard me.
He was not really in that room with us, he had at last really embarked on
his journey; and though my aunt told me that he said he was going to meet
Jesus, I did not hear anything except that whistling in his throat. The doctor
came back and we left, into that unbearable train again, and home. In the
morning came the telegram saying that he was dead. Then the house was
suddenly full of relatives, friends, hysteria, and confusion and I quickly left
my mother and the children to the care of those impressive women, who, in
Negro communities at least, automatically appear at times of bereavement
armed with lotions, proverbs, and patience, and an ability to cook. I went
downtown. By the time I returned, later the same day, my mother had been
carried to the hospital and the baby had been born.

THREE

For my father's funeral I had nothing black to wear and this posed a nagging problem all day long. It was one of those problems, simple, or impossible of solution, to which the mind insanely clings in order to avoid the mind's real trouble. I spent most of that day at the downtown apartment of a girl I knew, celebrating my birthday with whisky and wondering what to wear that night. When planning a birthday celebration one naturally does not expect that it will be up against competition from a funeral and this girl had anticipated taking me out that night, for a big dinner and a night club afterwards. Sometime during the course of that long day we decided that we would go out anyway, when my father's funeral service was over. I imagine I decided it, since, as the funeral hour approached, it became clearer and clearer to me that I would not know what to do with myself when it was over. The girl, stifling her very lively concern as to the possible effects of the whisky on one of my father's chief mourners, concentrated on being conciliatory and practically helpful. She found a black shirt for me somewhere and ironed it and, dressed in the darkest pants and jacket I owned, and slightly drunk, I made my way to my father's funeral.

The chapel was full, but not packed, and very quiet. There were, mainly, my father's relatives, and his children, and here and there I saw faces I had not seen since childhood, the faces of my father's one-time friends. They were very dark and solemn now, seeming somehow to suggest that they had known all along that something like this would happen. Chief among the mourners was my aunt, who had quarreled with my father all his life; by which I do not mean to suggest that her mourning was insincere or that she had not loved him. I suppose that she was one of the few people in the world who had, and their incessant quarreling proved precisely the strength of the tie that bound them. The only other person in the world, as far as I knew, whose relationship to my father rivaled my aunt's in depth was my mother, who was not there.

It seemed to me, of course, that it was a very long funeral. But it was, if anything, a rather shorter funeral than most, nor, since there were no overwhelming, uncontrollable expressions of grief, could it be called—if I dare to use the word—successful. The minister who preached my father's funeral sermon was one of the few my father had still been seeing as he neared his end. He presented to us in his sermon a man whom none of us had ever seen—a man thoughtful, patient, and forbearing, a Christian inspiration to all who knew him, and a model for his children. And no doubt the children, in their disturbed and guilty state, were almost ready to believe this; he had been remote enough to be anything and, anyway, the shock of the incontrovertible, that it was really our father lying up there in that casket, prepared the mind for anything. His sister moaned and this grief-stricken moaning was taken as corroboration. The other faces held a dark, noncommittal thoughtfulness. This was not the man they had known, but they had scarcely expected to be confronted with *him*; this was, in a sense deeper than questions of fact, the man they had not known, and the man they had not known may have been the real one. The real man, whoever he had been, had suffered and now he was dead: this was all that was sure and all that mattered now. Every man in the chapel hoped that when his hour came he, too, would be eulogized, which is to say forgiven, and that all of his lapses, greeds, errors, and strayings from the truth would be invested with coherence and looked upon with charity. This was perhaps the last thing human beings could give each other and it was what they demanded, after all, of the Lord. Only the Lord saw the midnight tears, only He was present when one of His children, moaning and wringing hands, paced up and down the room. When one slapped one's child in anger the recoil in the heart reverberated through heaven and became part of the pain of the universe. And when the children were hungry and sullen and distrustful and one watched them, daily, growing wilder, and further away, and running headlong into danger, it was the Lord who knew what the charged heart endured as the strap was laid to the backside; the Lord alone who knew what one *would* have said if one had had, like the Lord, the gift of the living word. It was the Lord who knew of the impossibility every parent in that room faced: how to prepare the child for the day when the child would be despised and how to *create* in the child—by what means?—a stronger antidote to this poison than one had found for oneself. The avenues, side streets, bars, billiard halls, hospitals, police stations, and even the playgrounds of Harlem—not to mention the houses of correction, the jails, and the morgue—testified to the potency of the poison while remaining silent as to the efficacy of whatever antidote, irresistibly raising the question of whether or not such an antidote existed; raising, which was worse, the question of whether or not an antidote was desirable; perhaps poison should be fought with poison. With these several schisms in the mind and with more terrors in the heart than could be named, it was better not to judge the man who had gone down under an impossible burden. It was better to remember: *Thou knowest this man's fall; but thou knowest not his wrassling.*

While the preacher talked and I watched the children—years of changing their diapers, scrubbing them, slapping them, taking them to school, and scolding them had had the perhaps inevitable result of making me love them, though I am not sure I knew this then—my mind was busily breaking out with a rash of disconnected impressions. Snatches of popular songs, indecent jokes, bits of books I had read, movie sequences, faces, voices, political issues—I thought I was going mad; all these impressions suspended, as it were, in the solution of the faint nausea produced in me by the heat and liquor. For a moment I had the impression that my alcoholic breath, inefficiently disguised with chewing gum, filled the entire chapel. Then someone began singing one of my father's favorite songs and, abruptly, I was with him, sitting on his knee, in the hot, enormous, crowded church which was the first church we attended. It was the Abyssinian Baptist Church on 138th Street. We had not gone there long. With this image, a host of others came. I had forgotten, in the rage of my growing up, how proud my father had been of me when I was little. Apparently, I had had a voice and my father had liked to show me off before the members of the church. I had forgotten what he had looked like when he was pleased but now I remembered that he had always been grinning with pleasure when my solos ended. I even remembered certain expressions on his face when he teased my mother—had he loved her? I would never know. And when had it all begun to change? For now it seemed that he had not always been cruel. I remembered being taken for a haircut and scraping my knee on the footrest of the barber's chair and I remembered my father's face as he soothed my crying and applied the stinging iodine. Then I remembered our fights, fights which had been of the worst possible kind because my technique had been silence.

I remembered the one time in all our life together when we had really   35
spoken to each other.

It was on a Sunday and it must have been shortly before I left home. We were walking, just the two of us, in our usual silence, to or from church. I was in high school and had been doing a lot of writing and I was, at about this time, the editor of the high school magazine. But I had also been a Young Minister and had been preaching from the pulpit. Lately, I had been taking fewer engagements and preached as rarely as possible. It was said in the church, quite truthfully, that I was "cooling off."

My father asked me abruptly, "You'd rather write than preach, wouldn't you?"

I was astonished at his question—because it was a real question. I answered, "Yes."

That was all we said. It was awful to remember that that was all we had *ever* said.

The casket now was opened and the mourners were being led up the   40
aisle to look for the last time on the deceased. The assumption was that the family was too overcome with grief to be allowed to make this journey alone and I watched while my aunt was led to the casket and, muffled in black, and shaking, led back to her seat. I disapproved of forcing the children to look on their dead father, considering that the shock of his death, or, more truthfully, the shock of death as a reality, was already a little more than a child could bear, but my judgment in this matter had been overruled and there they were, bewildered and frightened and very small, being led, one by one, to the casket. But there is also something very gallant about children at such moments. It has something to do with their silence and gravity and with the fact that one cannot help them. Their legs, somehow, seem *exposed*, so that it is at once incredible and terribly clear that their legs are all they have to hold them up.

I had not wanted to go to the casket myself and I certainly had not wished to be led there, but there was no way of avoiding either of these forms. One of the deacons led me up and I looked on my father's face. I cannot say that it looked like him at all. His blackness had been equivocated by powder and there was no suggestion in that casket of what his power had or could have been. He was simply an old man dead, and it was hard to believe that he had ever given anyone either joy or pain. Yet, his life filled that room. Further up the avenue his wife was holding his newborn child. Life and death so close together, and love and hatred, and right and wrong, said something to me which I did not want to hear concerning man, concerning the life of man.

After the funeral, while I was downtown desperately celebrating my birthday, a Negro soldier, in the lobby of the Hotel Braddock, got into a fight with a white policeman over a Negro girl. Negro girls, white policemen, in or out of uniform, and Negro males—in or out of uniform—were part of the furniture of the lobby of the Hotel Braddock and this was certainly not the first time such an incident had occurred. It was destined, however, to receive an unprecedented publicity, for the fight between the policeman and the soldier ended with the shooting of the soldier. Rumor, flowing immediately to the streets outside, stated that the soldier had been shot in the back, an instantaneous and revealing invention, and that the soldier had died protecting a Negro woman. The facts were somewhat different—for example, the soldier had not been shot in the back, and was not dead, and the girl seems to have been as dubious a symbol of womanhood as her white counterpart in Georgia usually is, but no one was interested in the facts. They preferred the invention because this invention expressed and corroborated their hates and fears so perfectly. It is just as well to remember that people are always doing this. Perhaps many of those legends, including Christianity, to which the world clings began their conquest of the world with just some such concerted surrender to distortion. The effect, in Harlem, of this particular legend was like the effect of a lit match in a tin of gasoline. The mob gathered before the doors of the Hotel Braddock simply began to swell and to spread in every direction, and Harlem exploded.

The mob did not cross the ghetto lines. It would have been easy, for example, to have gone over Morningside Park on the west side or to have crossed the Grand Central railroad tracks at 125th Street on the east side, to wreak havoc in white neighborhoods. The mob seems to have been mainly interested in something more potent and real than the white face, that is, in white power, and the principal damage done during the riot of the summer of 1943 was to white business establishments in Harlem. It might have been a far bloodier story, of course, if, at the hour the riot began, these establishments had still been open. From the Hotel Braddock the mob fanned out, east and west along 125th Street, and for the entire length of Lenox, Seventh, and Eighth avenues. Along each of these avenues, and along each major side street—116th, 125th, 135th, and so on—bars, stores, pawnshops, restaurants, even little luncheonettes had been smashed open and entered and looted—looted, it might be added, with more haste than efficiency. The shelves really looked as though a bomb had struck them. Cans of beans and soup and dog food, along with toilet paper, corn flakes, sardines and milk tumbled every which way, and abandoned cash registers and cases of beer leaned crazily out of the splintered windows and were strewn along the avenues. Sheets, blankets, and clothing of every description formed a kind of path, as though people had dropped them while running. I truly had not realized that Harlem *had* so many stores until I saw them all smashed open; the first time the word *wealth* ever entered my mind in relation to Harlem was when I saw it scattered in the streets. But one's first, incongruous impression of plenty was countered immediately by an impression of waste. None of this was doing anybody any good. It would have been better to have left the plate glass as it had been and the goods lying in the stores.

It would have been better, but it would also have been intolerable, for Harlem had needed something to smash. To smash something is the ghetto's chronic need. Most of the time it is the members of the ghetto who smash each other, and themselves. But as long as the ghetto walls are standing there will always come a moment when these outlets do not work. That summer, for example, it was not enough to get into a fight on Lenox Avenue, or curse out one's cronies in the barber shops. If ever, indeed, the violence which fills Harlem's churches, pool halls, and bars erupts outward in a more direct fashion, Harlem and its citizens are likely to vanish in an apocalyptic flood. That this is not likely to happen is due to a great many reasons, most hidden and powerful among them the Negro's real relation to the white American. This relation prohibits, simply, anything as uncomplicated and satisfactory as pure hatred. In order really to hate white people, one has to blot so much out of the mind—and the heart—that this hatred itself becomes an exhausting and self-destructive pose. But this does not mean, on the other hand, that love comes easily: the white world is too powerful, too complacent, too ready with gratuitous humiliation, and, above all, too ignorant and too innocent for that. One is absolutely forced to make perpetual qualifications and one's own reactions are always canceling each other out. It is this, really, which has driven so many people mad, both white and black. One is always in the position of having to decide between amputation and gangrene. Amputation is swift but time may prove that the amputation was not necessary—or one may delay the amputation too long. Gangrene is slow, but it is impossible to be sure that one is reading one's symptoms right. The idea of going through life as a cripple is more than one can bear, and equally unbearable is the risk of swelling up slowly, in agony, with poison. And the trouble, finally, is that the risks are real even if the choices do not exist.

"But as for me and my house," my father had said, "we will serve the   45
Lord." I wondered, as we drove him to his resting place, what this line had meant for him. I had heard him preach it many times. I had preached it once myself, proudly giving it an interpretation different from my father's. Now the whole thing came back to me, as though my father and I were on our way to Sunday school and I were memorizing the golden text: *And if it seem evil unto you to serve the Lord, choose you this day whom you will serve; whether the gods which your fathers served that were on the other side of the flood, or the gods of the Amorites, in whose land ye dwell: but as for me and my house, we will serve the Lord.* I suspected in these familiar lines a

meaning which had never been there for me before. All of my father's texts and songs, which I had decided were meaningless, were arranged before me at his death like empty bottles, waiting to hold the meaning which life would give them for me. This was his legacy: nothing is ever escaped. That bleakly memorable morning I hated the unbelievable streets and the Negroes and whites who had, equally, made them that way. But I knew that it was folly, as my father would have said, this bitterness was folly. It was necessary to hold on to the things that mattered. The dead man mattered, the new life mattered; blackness and whiteness did not matter; to believe that they did was to acquiesce in one's own destruction. Hatred, which could destroy so much, never failed to destroy the man who hated and this was an immutable law.

It began to seem that one would have to hold in the mind forever two ideas which seemed to be in opposition. The first idea was acceptance, the acceptance, totally without rancor, of life as it is, and men as they are: in the light of this idea, it goes without saying that injustice is a commonplace. But this did not mean that one could be complacent, for the second idea was of equal power: that one must never, in one's own life, accept these injustices as commonplace but must fight them with all one's strength. This fight begins, however, in the heart and it now had been laid to my charge to keep my own heart free of hatred and despair. This intimation made my heart heavy and, now that my father was irrecoverable, I wished that he had been beside me so that I could have searched his face for the answers which only the future would give me now. ●

The Reader's Presence

1. Why does Baldwin open with three events: his father's death, his youngest sibling's birth, and the race riots in Detroit and Harlem? How did the death of his father serve to change Baldwin's thinking about how he would deal with racism in his life? How does Baldwin make peace with his father's memory?

2. At the end of the essay, Baldwin remembers a biblical passage his father used to quote. How does Baldwin reinterpret the passage after his father's death? What does it mean in the context of being his father's son? How does it help him make sense of the race riots in Harlem?

3. **CONNECTIONS:**   Examine Baldwin's description of the Harlem race riots in the third section of his essay. How does Baldwin approach the riots as a native of Harlem and as an African American? What explanations does he give for the violence? How does he use the riots to explain the relations between white and black America? Compare Baldwin's discussion of the Harlem race riots to Martin Luther King Jr.'s consideration of nonviolence in "Letter from Birmingham Jail" (page 716) written eight years later. Which author takes a more personal view of race relations at the time? In your opinion, would King concur with Baldwin's assessment of the riots? Do you think after reading Baldwin's essay that Baldwin would agree with King's philosophy? These are long essays and among the most important documents of African American literary history. How would you compare and contrast the racial attitudes of both Baldwin and King as reflected in these two outstanding works?

The Writer at Work

JAMES BALDWIN on Black English

In the following piece, Baldwin takes up a subject that is periodically scrutinized by the American mass media: Is black English a language and, if so, what kind of language is it? Whatever its current status in the eyes of the dominant society, black English is an indisputable fact of everyday life for many Americans. When Baldwin writes that blacks have "endured and transcended" American racism by means of language, he echoes William Faulkner's belief that our compulsion to talk is what will save the human race.

Since Baldwin wrote this piece in 1979, the language he so ardently defends as necessary to African American strength in the face of "brutal necessity" (that is, in defense against racism) has entered the mainstream through the spread of hip-hop culture. What might Baldwin say about white speakers of black English? Are they simply another example of the appropriation of subcultural forms by the dominant culture, a means of containing or defusing resistance? The "rules of the language are dictated by what the language must convey," Baldwin writes. Who is using black English today? For what purposes?

❝ The argument concerning the use, or the status, or the reality, of black English is rooted in American history and has absolutely nothing to do with the question the argument supposes itself to be posing. The argument has nothing to do with language itself but with the *role* of language. Language, incontestably, reveals the speaker. Language, also, far more dubiously, is meant to define the other—and, in this case, the other is refusing to be defined by a language that has never been able to recognize him.

People evolve a language in order to describe and thus control their circumstances, or in order not to be submerged by a reality that they cannot articulate. (And, if they cannot articulate it, they *are* submerged.) A Frenchman living in Paris speaks a subtly and crucially different language from that of the man living in Marseilles; neither sounds very much like a man living in Quebec; and they would all have great difficulty in apprehending what the man from Guadeloupe, or Martinique, is saying, to say nothing of the man from Senegal—although the "common" language of all these areas is French. But each has paid, and is paying, a different price for this "common" language, in which, as it turns out, they are not saying, and cannot be saying, the

same things: They each have very different realities to articulate, or control.

What joins all languages, and all
men, is the necessity to confront life, in
order, not inconceivably, to outwit death:
The price for this is the acceptance, and
achievement, of one's temporal identity.
So that, for example, though it is not
taught in the schools (and this has the
potential of becoming a political issue)
the south of France still clings to its
ancient and musical Provençal, which
resists being described as a "dialect."
And much of the tension in the Basque
countries, and in Wales, is due to the
Basque and Welsh determination not to
allow their languages to be destroyed.
This determination also feeds the flames
in Ireland, for among the many indignities the Irish have been forced to undergo
at English hands is the English contempt
for their language.

It goes without saying, then, that
language is also a political instrument,
means, and proof of power. It is the most
vivid and crucial key to identity: It
reveals the private identity, and connects
one with, or divorces one from, the
larger, public, or communal identity.
There have been, and are, times, and
places, when to speak a certain language
could be dangerous, even fatal. Or, one
may speak the same language, but in
such a way that one's antecedents are
revealed, or (one hopes) hidden. This is
true in France, and is absolutely true in
England: The range (and reign) of accents
on that damp little island make England
coherent for the English and totally
incomprehensible for everyone else.
To open your mouth in England is (if I
may use black English) to "put your
business in the street": You have confessed your parents, your youth, your
school, your salary, your self-esteem,
and, alas, your future.

Now, I do not know what white
Americans would sound like if there
had never been any black people in the
United States, but they would not sound
the way they sound. *Jazz*, for example,
is a very specific sexual term, as in
jazz me, baby, but white people puri-
fied it into the Jazz Age. *Sock it to me*,
which means, roughly, the same thing,
has been adopted by Nathaniel Hawthorne's descendants with no qualms
or hesitations at all, along with *let it
all hang out* and *right on! Beat to his
socks*, which was once the black's most
total and despairing image of poverty,
was transformed into a thing called the
Beat Generation, which phenomenon
was, largely, composed of *uptight*,
middle-class white people, imitating poverty, trying to *get down*, to get *with it*,
doing their *thing*, doing their despairing
best to be *funky*, which we, the blacks,
never dreamed of doing—we *were* funky,
baby, like *funky* was going out of style.

Now, no one can eat his cake and
have it, too, and it is late in the day to
attempt to penalize black people for having created a language that permits the
nation its only glimpse of reality, a language without which the nation would be
even more *whipped* than it is.

I say that the present skirmish is
rooted in American history, and it is.
Black English is the creation of the black
diaspora. Blacks came to the United
States chained to each other, but from
different tribes: Neither could speak the
other's language. If two black people,
at that bitter hour of the world's history,
had been able to speak to each other,
the institution of chattel slavery could
never have lasted as long as it did. Subsequently, the slave was given, under the
eye, and the gun, of his master, Congo
Square, and the Bible—or in other words,
and under these conditions, the slave

began the formation of the black church, and it is within this unprecedented tabernacle that black English began to be formed. This was not, merely, as in the European example, the adoption of a foreign tongue, but an alchemy that transformed ancient elements into a new language: *A language comes into existence by means of brutal necessity, and the rules of the language are dictated by what the language must convey.*

There was a moment, in time, and in this place, when my brother, or my mother, or my father, or my sister, had to convey to me, for example, the danger in which I was standing from the white man standing just behind me, and to convey this with a speed, and in a language, that the white man could not possibly understand, and that, indeed, he cannot understand, until today. He cannot afford to understand it. This understanding would reveal to him too much about himself, and smash that mirror before which he has been frozen for so long.

Now, if this passion, this skill, this (to quote Toni Morrison) "sheer intelligence," this incredible music, the mighty achievement of having brought a people utterly unknown to, or despised by "history"—to have brought this people to their present, troubled, troubling, and unassailable and unanswerable place—if this absolutely unprecedented journey does not indicate that black English is a language, I am curious to know what definition of language is to be trusted.

A people at the center of the Western world, and in the midst of so hostile a population, has not endured and transcended by means of what is patronizingly called a "dialect." We, the blacks, are in trouble, certainly, but we are not doomed, and we are not inarticulate because we are not compelled to defend a morality that we know to be a lie.

The brutal truth is that the bulk of white people in America never had any interest in educating black people, except as this could serve white purposes. It is not the black child's language that is in question, it is not his language that is despised: It is his experience. A child cannot be taught by anyone who despises him, and a child cannot afford to be fooled. A child cannot be taught by anyone whose demand, essentially, is that the child repudiate his experience, and all that gives him sustenance, and enter a limbo in which he will no longer be black, and in which he knows that he can never become white. Black people have lost too many black children that way.

And, after all, finally, in a country with standards so untrustworthy, a country that makes heroes of so many criminal mediocrities, a country unable to face why so many of the nonwhite are in prison, or on the needle, or standing, futureless, in the streets—it may very well be that both the child, and his elder, have concluded that they have nothing whatever to learn from the people of a country that has managed to learn so little.**"**

Augusten Burroughs
ABSOLUTELY FABULOUS

AUGUSTEN BURROUGHS (b. 1965) was born Christopher Robison in Pittsburgh, Pennsylvania. He dropped out of school after the sixth grade and obtained a general equivalency diploma (GED) at age seventeen. At eighteen he changed his name to Augusten Burroughs. He was a successful advertising copywriter in Manhattan for many years before publishing his first novel, *Sellevision*, in 2000. Although *Sellevision* was well received, it was not until the 2002 publication of his childhood memoir, *Running with Scissors*, that Burroughs achieved some measure of celebrity. His subsequent books of nonfiction, including *Dry* (2003), a memoir of his struggle with alcoholism; *Magical Thinking* (2003); and *Possible Side Effects* (2006), have consistently made the best-seller list. His most recent books are *A Wolf at the Table: A Memoir of My Father* (2008) and *You Better Not Cry: Stories for Christmas* (2009). He writes a monthly column for *Details*, and his essays have appeared in publications like the *New York Times*, *House & Garden*, *BlackBook Magazine*, *Attitude*, and *Out*. Much of his writing is characterized by dark humor and a candid approach to uncomfortable topics. In 2005, *Entertainment Weekly* ranked him one of the twenty-five funniest people in America.

> In 2005, *Entertainment Weekly* ranked Augusten Burroughs one of the twenty-five funniest people in America.

I AM A MONTH AWAY from having abs. At the moment I have a flat stomach, etched with shadows that imply musculature — but only when I stand, which I do frequently, at a three-quarter angle in front of mirrors, with my shirt lifted.

Elsewhere in the world bombs explode, villages flood, mothers and children are tortured to death and their bodies abandoned to rot in the sun. But here in the mirror before me remains a resilient layer of blubber over the muscle. Probably five pounds. And they are stubborn, these last five. These inner five. They are like the Secret Service, tightly cloistering the president.

But I *will* reach that prize muscle. If I have to give up every four-carbohydrate almond I currently enjoy (two a day), I will. If I have to choke down my dry salad without the grilled chicken, I will. If I have to throw up after consuming one of my hateful, meager meals, then throw up I will. In fact, I have asked some women I know, "How do you make yourself vomit after eating?"

At first my question is met with looks of horror. Not only have I been politically incorrect, it's as if I have entered their private space—the women's restroom—and am banging on closed stall doors saying "What's going on in there?" The women also feel the question implicates them. *Well, how on earth would I know?* their awkward laughter says.

But a handful of them do know. So an instant later, when we have turned   5
a corner and are walking down a hallway; when we have exited the elevator; when the person who was walking behind us has ducked into a store, these women whisper something like "The trick is to drink a lot of water." Or "You have to eat a lot. You can't just have some little salad and barf it up. Volume—bloating—is the key."

There are many keys, I learn.

But none of them will unlock the contents of my stomach. I was both bemused and appalled a few weeks ago to find myself with most of my hand spidering down my throat, my fingers slick. I was spitting up and gagging into a 200-year-old toilet after breaking my perverse madman's diet by eating one of the bread sticks that arrived, unasked for, with my austere dinner. And no matter how far down my throat I plunged my fingers, I could not vomit. It infuriated me.

I hadn't intended to eat the stick of bread. I only wanted to examine it: a specimen. People actually eat these? Yes, weaker people. The old me would have eaten it, I thought, smug, superior. And instantly, shockingly, the stick was in my mouth and I was chewing with the kind of fierce, male determination that builds bridges and skyscrapers. The bread vanished in an instant and I ran to the bathroom. If I don't get this thing out now, I was thinking, I will never get the abs.

If a doctor had appeared before me, miraculously, and said, "You have cancer," I would have said, "Do I have one more month to live?" Because my only thought would have been *I can get the abs in four weeks.*

Two months before this madness began I was 30 pounds overweight. I   10
found a decade-old photograph of myself and noted with horror that my face had had actual planes back then. Bevels. Angles. I had become used to my doughy, swollen, carbohydrate-infected face. The rest of the 30 pounds had gathered around my middle. I had belly fat, flank fat, and, most appalling of all, back fat.

How long had it been, exactly, since I'd seen the inside of a gym? Since I'd been in handsome shape and had, very nearly—but not as nearly as now—abs? Four years. Had it been that long? Yes. It had.

Seeing my reflection that afternoon, I decided: This is the day. Today. Right now.

At first, I could do exactly four minutes on the elliptical trainer at my gym. And my heart was hysterical inside my chest. It was spasming and screaming "Oh my God, what have you done with the sofa?"

So, like a ruthless executioner atop a Mayan pyramid, I beheaded from my diet anything and everything that made me happy: Lusty brownies, earthy and chocolaty and with the tiniest crackle when you bite into them, shattering the glossy, shellacked surface. Cookies. Candy bars. French fries, bread, butter, meat, cheese, pears. All that was left were a few greens, drizzled with air.

The next day I was able to do four minutes and 20 seconds.   15

Each day, after the elliptical trainer, I would do crunches, gently, the way my chiropractor had taught me. Raise your torso just 10 degrees, Adam's apple pointed at the ceiling. I never counted. I continued until I couldn't.

Weeks passed. Facial bones began to break the surface. I ordered new jeans online, and by the time they were delivered I needed a smaller size. I inspected my stomach constantly. I inhaled to see the convex lines. I exhaled and saw the softness that remained above the muscle and felt my face flush with rage. I knew something was distorted; I sensed that I had lost all perspective. But I did not care. When I looked down? I needed to see only ripples.

Friends gasped when they saw me. "My God, you look wonderful," they'd say, followed by "Are you okay?" I noted the blurry line between beauty and sickness—how beauty came first.

It has been almost two months. When I lift up my shirt I see that the abs are coming. If I continue to starve, if I continue to channel my rage into kinetic energy, the abs will come. The laws of physics promise this. We are, if we do the math right, owed abs, each of us.

And yet? I do not require abs for any rational reason. I'm not single. I'm   20
not 22. I'm not a model. I don't go to the beach. Never will somebody eat whipped cream off my stomach.

But one doesn't chase after abs or thinness or plump lips because one has thought it through. One chases because one needs. The need is vigorous and all-consuming. It is blind and it is mindless, too: Ask "But why?" and the need will reply, "You disgust me."

Funny, but I would never be with somebody who had abs. I like a little extra padding on a person. I like a man with a bit of a belly—a football player's build. On a woman, I like something a little more 19th-century—curves and bulges, voluptuous mounds and promising, elegant hills.

Admitting this lifts the veil, and I get it. It has been almost 10 years since I stopped drinking. The need knows it won't get a martini. So it seduces me through my stomach—"Psst, feeling empty? Abs, dude, abs"—like I'm a dog on a chase, oblivious to the reasonable call of my master and the swiftly approaching car.

And, with the full knowledge that I am again addicted to something and that all addiction is toxic, is circular, erodes and controls, I stop eating for four days, and unleash my resentment on my stomach through crunches, and raise the intensity on the elliptical trainer. And one evening very soon, possibly even tomorrow, there they will be: abs. I will stare at my reflection, at my achieved goal. Abs. I am now that guy with the stomach. I am him.

And I know exactly what I will feel. I will feel: oh.   25

Because in the pursuit of beauty, there is no finish line. Nothing about us will ever be perfect. The need will always, always be there. There will always be just one more thing we could do. Or get. Or lose.

It is a fool's marathon. But I don't care. I will run it anyway. ▣

The Reader's Presence

1. Burroughs writes with intensity about his determination to lose weight and develop abdominal muscle (abs). Yet what is his reason for losing weight and developing his abs? What triggered his determination? Why is he willing to put himself through so much distress to develop these muscles? Do you find his explanations satisfactory? Why or why not?

2. Notice that Burroughs decided not to wait until he had developed abs to write his essay but wrote it prior to achieving his goal. Why do you think he made this compositional decision? What would you have done as a writer? Can you think of any advantages in deciding to write precisely at this stage of his quest? As a reader, would you like to know whether he achieved his goal? Or do you find the conclusion satisfying as is? Explain your reasons for thinking one way or another.

3. **CONNECTIONS:**   Consider "Absolutely Fabulous" in connection with Daniel Akst's "What Meets the Eye" (page 293). In what ways can Akst's explanation of why looks are important shed additional light on Burroughs's motivation to develop abdominal muscle?

Raymond Carver
MY FATHER'S LIFE

Son of a laborer and a homemaker in Clatskanie, Oregon, **RAYMOND CARVER** (1938–1988) resembled the characters in the short stories for which he is widely acclaimed. Once a manual laborer, a gas station attendant, and a janitor himself, Carver acquired his vision of the working class and the desperate lives of ordinary folk through direct experience. The Pacific Northwest of Carver's writing is peopled with types such as "the waitress, the bus driver, the mechanic, the hotel keeper" — people Carver feels are "good people." First published in

Esquire in 1984, "My Father's Life," Carver's account of his father's hardships during the Great Depression, puts a biographical spin on these "good people." Carver's short story collections, *Will You Please Be Quiet, Please?* (1976), *Cathedral* (1984), and *Where I'm Calling From* (1988), were all nominated for the National Book Critics Circle Award. Both *Cathedral* and *Where I'm Calling From* were also nominated for the Pulitzer Prize for fiction in 1985 and 1989, respectively. Carver's poetry is collected in *Where Water Comes Together with Other Water* (1985), recipient of the 1986 Los Angeles Times Book Prize; *Ultramarine* (1986); and *A New Path to the Waterfall* (1989).

> **"Writers don't need tricks or gimmicks."**

In his essay "On Writing," Carver states, "Writers don't need tricks or gimmicks or even necessarily to be the smartest fellows on the block. At the risk of appearing foolish, a writer sometimes needs to be able to just stand and gape at this or that thing—a sunset or an old shoe—in absolute and simple amazement."

For an example of Carver's fiction, see "What We Talk About When We Talk About Love" (page 884).

MY DAD'S NAME was Clevie Raymond Carver. His family called him Raymond and friends called him C. R. I was named Raymond Clevie Carver, Jr. I hated the "Junior" part. When I was little my dad called me Frog, which was okay. But later, like everybody else in the family, he began calling me Junior. He went on calling me this until I was thirteen or fourteen and announced that I wouldn't answer to that name any longer. So he began calling me Doc. From then until his death, on June 17, 1967, he called me Doc, or else Son.

When he died, my mother telephoned my wife with the news. I was away from my family at the time, between lives, trying to enroll in the School of Library Science at the University of Iowa. When my wife answered the phone, my mother blurted out, "Raymond's dead!" For a moment, my wife thought my mother was telling her that I was dead. Then my mother made it clear *which* Raymond she was talking about and my wife said, "Thank God. I thought you meant *my* Raymond."

My dad walked, hitched rides, and rode in empty boxcars when he went from Arkansas to Washington State in 1934, looking for work. I don't know whether he was pursuing a dream when he went out to Washington. I doubt it. I don't think he dreamed much. I believe he was simply looking for steady work at decent pay. Steady work was meaningful work. He picked apples for a time and then landed a construction laborer's job on the Grand Coulee Dam. After he'd put aside a little money, he bought a car and drove back to Arkansas to help his folks, my grandparents, pack up for the move west. He said later that they were about to starve down there, and this wasn't meant as a figure of speech. It was during that short while in Arkansas, in a town called Leola, that my mother met my dad on the sidewalk as he came out of a tavern.

"He was drunk," she said. "I don't know why I let him talk to me. His eyes were glittery. I wish I'd had a crystal ball." They'd met once, a year or so before, at a dance. He'd had girlfriends before her, my mother told me. "Your dad always had a girlfriend, even after we married. He was my first and last. I never had another man. But I didn't miss anything."

They were married by a justice of the peace on the day they left for Washington, this big, tall country girl and a farmhand-turned-construction worker. My mother spent her wedding night with my dad and his folks, all of them camped beside the road in Arkansas.

In Omak, Washington, my dad and mother lived in a little place not much bigger than a cabin. My grandparents lived next door. My dad was still working on the dam, and later, with the huge turbines producing electricity and the water backed up for a hundred miles into Canada, he stood in the crowd and heard Franklin D. Roosevelt when he spoke at the construction site. "He never mentioned those guys who died building that dam," my dad said. Some of his friends had died there, men from Arkansas, Oklahoma, and Missouri.

He then took a job in a sawmill in Clatskanie, Oregon, a little town alongside the Columbia River. I was born there, and my mother has a picture of my dad standing in front of the gate to the mill, proudly holding me up to face the camera. My bonnet is on crooked and about to come untied. His hat is pushed back on his forehead, and he's wearing a big grin. Was he going in to work or just finishing his shift? It doesn't matter. In either case, he had a job and a family. These were his salad days.

In 1941 we moved to Yakima, Washington, where my dad went to work as a saw filer, a skilled trade he'd learned in Clatskanie. When war broke out, he was given a deferment because his work was considered necessary to the war effort. Finished lumber was in demand by the armed services, and he kept his saws so sharp they could shave the hair off your arm.

After my dad had moved us to Yakima, he moved his folks into the same neighborhood. By the mid-1940s the rest of my dad's family—his brother, his sister, and her husband, as well as uncles, cousins, nephews, and most of their extended family and friends—had come out from Arkansas. All because my dad came out first. The men went to work at Boise Cascade, where my dad worked, and the women packed apples in the canneries. And in just a little while, it seemed—according to my mother—everybody was better off than my dad. "Your dad couldn't keep money," my mother said. "Money burned a hole in his pocket. He was always doing for others."

The first house I clearly remember living in, at 1515 South Fifteenth Street, in Yakima, had an outdoor toilet. On Halloween night, or just any night, for the hell of it, neighbor kids, kids in their early teens, would carry our toilet away and leave it next to the road. My dad would have to get somebody to help him bring it home. Or these kids would take the toilet and stand it in somebody else's backyard. Once they actually set it on fire.

5

10

But ours wasn't the only house that had an outdoor toilet. When I was old enough to know what I was doing, I threw rocks at the other toilets when I'd see someone go inside. This was called bombing the toilets. After a while, though, everyone went to indoor plumbing until, suddenly, our toilet was the last outdoor one in the neighborhood. I remember the shame I felt when my third-grade teacher, Mr. Wise, drove me home from school one day. I asked him to stop at the house just before ours, claiming I lived there.

I can recall what happened one night when my dad came home late to find that my mother had locked all the doors on him from the inside. He was drunk, and we could feel the house shudder as he rattled the door. When he'd managed to force open a window, she hit him between the eyes with a colander and knocked him out. We could see him down there on the grass. For years afterward, I used to pick up this colander—it was as heavy as a rolling pin—and imagine what it would feel like to be hit in the head with something like that.

It was during this period that I remember my dad taking me into the bedroom, sitting me down on the bed, and telling me that I might have to go live with my Aunt LaVon for a while. I couldn't understand what I'd done that meant I'd have to go away from home to live. But this, too—whatever prompted it—must have blown over, more or less, anyway, because we stayed together, and I didn't have to go live with her or anyone else.

I remember my mother pouring his whiskey down the sink. Sometimes she'd pour it all out and sometimes, if she was afraid of getting caught, she'd only pour half of it out and then add water to the rest. I tasted some of his whiskey once myself. It was terrible stuff, and I don't see how anybody could drink it.

After a long time without one, we finally got a car, in 1949 or 1950, a 1938 Ford. But it threw a rod the first week we had it, and my dad had to have the motor rebuilt.

"We drove the oldest car in town," my mother said. "We could have had a Cadillac for all he spent on car repairs." One time she found someone else's tube of lipstick on the floorboard, along with a lacy handkerchief. "See this?" she said to me. "Some floozy left this in the car."

Once I saw her take a pan of warm water into the bedroom where my dad was sleeping. She took his hand from under the covers and held it in the water. I stood in the doorway and watched. I wanted to know what was going on. This would make him talk in his sleep, she told me. There were things she needed to know, things she was sure he was keeping from her.

Every year or so, when I was little, we would take the North Coast Limited across the Cascade Range from Yakima to Seattle and stay in the Vance Hotel and eat, I remember, at a place called the Dinner Bell Cafe. Once we went to Ivar's Acres of Clams and drank glasses of warm clam broth.

In 1956, the year I was to graduate from high school, my dad quit his job at the mill in Yakima and took a job in Chester, a little sawmill town in northern California. The reasons given at the time for his taking the job had to do with a higher hourly wage and the vague promise that he might, in a few years' time, succeed to the job of head filer in this new mill. But I think, in the main, that my dad had grown restless and simply wanted to try his luck elsewhere. Things had gotten a little too predictable for him in Yakima. Also, the year before, there had been the deaths, within six months of each other, of both his parents.

But just a few days after graduation, when my mother and I were packed to move to Chester, my dad penciled a letter to say he'd been sick for a while. He didn't want us to worry, he said, but he'd cut himself on a saw. Maybe he'd got a tiny sliver of steel in his blood. Anyway, something had happened and he'd had to miss work, he said. In the same mail was an unsigned postcard from somebody down there telling my mother that my dad was about to die and that he was drinking "raw whiskey."

When we arrived in Chester, my dad was living in a trailer that belonged   20
to the company. I didn't recognize him immediately. I guess for a moment I didn't want to recognize him. He was skinny and pale and looked bewildered. His pants wouldn't stay up. He didn't look like my dad. My mother began to cry. My dad put his arm around her and patted her shoulder vaguely, like he didn't know what this was all about, either. The three of us took up life together in the trailer, and we looked after him as best we could. But my dad was sick, and he couldn't get any better. I worked with him in the mill that summer and part of the fall. We'd get up in the mornings and eat eggs and toast while we listened to the radio, and then go out the door with our lunch pails. We'd pass through the gate together at eight in the morning, and I wouldn't see him again until quitting time. In November I went back to Yakima to be closer to my girlfriend, the girl I'd made up my mind I was going to marry.

He worked at the mill in Chester until the following February, when he collapsed on the job and was taken to the hospital. My mother asked if I would come down there and help. I caught a bus from Yakima to Chester, intending to drive them back to Yakima. But now, in addition to being physically sick, my dad was in the midst of a nervous breakdown, though none of us knew to call it that at the time. During the entire trip back to Yakima, he didn't speak, not even when asked a direct question. ("How do you feel, Raymond?" "You okay, Dad?") He'd communicate, if he communicated at all, by moving his head or by turning his palms up as if to say he didn't know or care. The only time he said anything on the trip, and for nearly a month afterward, was when I was speeding down a gravel road in Oregon and the car muffler came loose. "You were going too fast," he said.

Back in Yakima a doctor saw to it that my dad went to a psychiatrist. My mother and dad had to go on relief, as it was called, and the county paid for the psychiatrist. The psychiatrist asked my dad, "Who is the President?" He'd had a question put to him that he could answer. "Ike," my dad said. Nevertheless, they put him on the fifth floor of Valley Memorial Hospital and began giving him electroshock treatment. I was married by then and about to start my own family. My dad was still locked up when my wife went into this same hospital, just one floor down, to have our first baby. After she had delivered, I went upstairs to give my dad the news. They let me in through a steel door and showed me where I could find him. He was sitting on a couch with a blanket over his lap. *Hey,* I thought. *What in hell is happening to my dad?* I sat down next to him and told him he was a grandfather. He waited a minute and then he said, "I feel like a grandfather." That's all he said. He didn't smile or move. He was in a big room with a lot of other people. Then I hugged him, and he began to cry.

Somehow he got out of there. But now came the years when he couldn't work and just sat around the house trying to figure what next and what he'd done wrong in his life that he'd wound up like this. My mother went from job to crummy job. Much later she referred to that time he was in the hospital, and those years just afterward, as "when Raymond was sick." The word *sick* was never the same for me again.

In 1964, through the help of a friend, he was lucky enough to be hired on at a mill in Klamath, California. He moved down there by himself to see if he could hack it. He lived not far from the mill, in a one-room cabin not much different from the place he and my mother had started out living in when they went west. He scrawled letters to my mother, and if I called she'd read them aloud to me over the phone. In the letters, he said it was touch and go. Every day that he went to work, he felt like it was the most important day of his life. But every day, he told her, made the next day that much easier. He said for her to tell me he said hello. If he couldn't sleep at night, he said, he thought about me and the good times we used to have. Finally, after a couple of months, he regained some of his confidence. He could do the work and didn't think he had to worry that he'd let anybody down ever again. When he was sure, he sent for my mother.

He'd been off from work for six years and had lost everything in that time—home, car, furniture, and appliances, including the big freezer that had been my mother's pride and joy. He'd lost his good name too—Raymond Carver was someone who couldn't pay his bills—and his self-respect was gone. He'd even lost his virility. My mother told my wife, "All during that time Raymond was sick we slept together in the same bed, but we didn't have relations. He wanted to a few times, but nothing happened. I didn't miss it, but I think he wanted to, you know."

During those years I was trying to raise my own family and earn a living. But, from one thing and another, we found ourselves having to move a lot. I couldn't keep track of what was going down in my dad's life. But I did have a chance one Christmas to tell him I wanted to be a writer. I might as well have told him I wanted to become a plastic surgeon. "What are you going to write about?" he wanted to know. Then, as if to help me out, he said, "Write about stuff you know about. Write about some of those fishing trips we took." I said I would, but I knew I wouldn't. "Send me what you write," he said. I said I'd do that, but then I didn't. I wasn't writing anything about fishing, and I didn't think he'd particularly care about, or even necessarily understand, what I was writing in those days. Besides, he wasn't a reader. Not the sort, anyway, I imagined I was writing for.

Guilt?

Then he died. I was a long way off, in Iowa City, with things still to say to him. I didn't have the chance to tell him goodbye, or that I thought he was doing great at his new job. That I was proud of him for making a comeback.

My mother said he came in from work that night and ate a big supper. Then he sat at the table by himself and finished what was left of a bottle of whiskey, a bottle she found hidden in the bottom of the garbage under some coffee grounds a day or so later. Then he got up and went to bed, where my mother joined him a little later. But in the night she had to get up and make a bed for herself on the couch. "He was snoring so loud I couldn't sleep," she said. The next morning when she looked in on him, he was on his back with his mouth open, his cheeks caved in. *Graylooking*, she said. She knew he was dead—she didn't need a doctor to tell her that. But she called one anyway, and then she called my wife.

Among the pictures my mother kept of my dad and herself during those early days in Washington was a photograph of him standing in front of a car, holding a beer and a stringer of fish. In the photograph he is wearing his hat back on his forehead and has this awkward grin on his face. I asked her for it and she gave it to me, along with some others. I put it up on my wall, and each time we moved, I took the picture along and put it up on another wall. I looked at it carefully from time to time, trying to figure out some things about my dad, and maybe myself in the process. But I couldn't. My dad just kept moving further and further away from me and back into time. Finally, in the course of another move, I lost the photograph. It was then that I tried to recall it, and at the same time make an attempt to say something about my dad, and how I thought that in some important ways we might be alike. I wrote the poem when I was living in an apartment house in an urban area south of San Francisco, at a time when I found myself, like my dad, having trouble with alcohol. The poem was a way of trying to connect up with him.

how to connect a poem

PHOTOGRAPH OF MY FATHER IN HIS TWENTY-SECOND YEAR

October. Here in this dank, unfamiliar kitchen
I study my father's embarrassed young man's face.
Sheepish grin, he holds in one hand a string
of spiny yellow perch, in the other
a bottle of Carlsberg beer.

In jeans and flannel shirt, he leans
against the front fender of a 1934 Ford.
He would like to pose brave and hearty for his posterity,
wear his old hat cocked over his ear.
All his life my father wanted to be bold.

But the eyes give him away, and the hands
that limply offer the string of dead perch
and the bottle of beer. Father, I love you,
yet how can I say thank you, I who can't hold my liquor either
and don't even know the places to fish.

The poem is true in its particulars, except that my dad died in June and   30
not October, as the first word of the poem says. I wanted a word with more
than one syllable to it to make it linger a little. But more than that, I wanted
a month appropriate to what I felt at the time I wrote the poem—a month
of short days and failing light, smoke in the air, things perishing. June was
summer nights and days, graduations, my wedding anniversary, the birthday of one of my children. June wasn't a month your father died in.

After the service at the funeral home, after we had moved outside, a
woman I didn't know came over to me and said, "He's happier where he
is now." I stared at this woman until she moved away. I still remember the
little knob of a hat she was wearing. Then one of my dad's cousins—I didn't
know the man's name—reached out and took my hand. "We all miss him,"
he said, and I knew he wasn't saying it just to be polite.

I began to weep for the first time since receiving the news. I hadn't been
able to before. I hadn't had the time, for one thing. Now, suddenly, I couldn't
stop. I held my wife and wept while she said and did what she could do to
comfort me there in the middle of that summer afternoon.

I listened to people say consoling things to my mother, and I was glad
that my dad's family had turned up, had come to where he was. I thought I'd
remember everything that was said and done that day and maybe find a way
to tell it sometime. But I didn't. I forgot it all, or nearly. What I do remember
is that I heard our name used a lot that afternoon, my dad's name and mine.
But I knew they were talking about my dad. *Raymond*, these people kept
saying in their beautiful voices out of my childhood. *Raymond*. ■

The Reader's Presence

1. You may have noticed that Carver begins and ends his essay with a reference to his
and his father's name. Of what importance is this information at the opening? What
do we learn about his relationship with his father through their names? How do
names matter in the final paragraph?

2. Reread the essay with particular attention to the conversations between father and
son. How many reported conversations can you find? What do the conversations
sound like? Can you find any pattern to them? If so, describe that pattern. To what
extent do these conversations help you understand Carver's relationship with his
father?

3. **CONNECTIONS:**   Carver includes one of his own poems in his essay (paragraph 29),
as does Alice Walker in "Beauty: When the Other Dancer Is the Self" (page 244).
How do these writers explore the margins between poetry and prose? What do you
think a poem communicates that a passage of prose may not?

Judith Ortiz Cofer

SILENT DANCING

Born in Puerto Rico in 1952, **JUDITH ORTIZ COFER** moved to New Jersey in 1955. Her poetry has appeared in numerous literary magazines, and several collections of her poems have been published. Her first novel, *The Line of the Sun* (1989), was nominated for the Pulitzer Prize. "Silent Dancing" is from Cofer's 1990 essay collection, *Silent Dancing: A Partial Remembrance of a Puerto Rican Childhood*, which won a PEN/Martha Albrand special citation for nonfiction. Among her notable books are *The Latin Deli: Prose and Poetry* (1993), *An Island Like You: Stories of the Barrio* (1995), *Woman in Front of the Sun* (2000), *The Meaning of Consuelo* (2003), and *Call Me Maria* (2004). Her third volume of poetry, *A Love Story Beginning in Spanish*, was published in 2005.

> **"The 'infinite variety' and power of language interest me."**

Reflecting on her life as a writer, Cofer has said, "The 'infinite variety' and power of language interest me. I never cease to experiment with it. As a native Puerto Rican, my first language was Spanish. It was a challenge, not only to learn English, but to master it enough to teach it and—the ultimate goal—to write poetry in it." Cofer is professor of English and creative writing at the University of Georgia.

WE HAVE A HOME MOVIE of this party. Several times my mother and I have watched it together, and I have asked questions about the silent revelers coming in and out of focus. It is grainy and of short duration, but it's a great visual aid to my memory of life at that time. And it is in color—the only complete scene in color I can recall from those years.

We lived in Puerto Rico until my brother was born in 1954. Soon after, because of economic pressures on our growing family, my father joined the United States Navy. He was assigned to duty on a ship in Brooklyn Yard—a place of cement and steel that was to be his home base in the States until his retirement more than twenty years later. He left the Island first, alone, going to New York City and tracking down his uncle who lived with his family across the Hudson River in Paterson, New Jersey. There my father found a tiny apartment in a huge tenement that had once housed Jewish families but was just being taken over and transformed by Puerto Ricans, overflowing from New York City. In 1955 he sent for us. My mother was only twenty years old, I was not quite three, and my brother was a toddler when we arrived at *El Building*, as the place had been christened by its newest residents.

My memories of life in Paterson during those first few years are all in shades of gray. Maybe I was too young to absorb vivid colors and details, or to discriminate between the slate blue of the winter sky and the darker hues of the snow-bearing clouds, but that single color washes over the whole period. The building we lived in was gray, as were the streets, filled with slush the first few months of my life there. The coat my father had bought for me was similar in color and too big; it sat heavily on my thin frame.

I do remember the way the heater pipes banged and rattled, startling all of us out of sleep until we got so used to the sound that we automatically shut it out or raised our voices above the racket. The hiss from the valve punctuated my sleep (which has always been fitful) like a nonhuman presence in the room—a dragon sleeping at the entrance of my childhood. But the pipes were also a connection to all the other lives being lived around us. Having come from a house designed for a single family back in Puerto Rico—my mother's extended-family home—it was curious to know that strangers lived under our floor and above our heads, and that the heater pipe went through everyone's apartments. (My first spanking in Paterson came as a result of playing tunes on the pipes in my room to see if there would be an answer.) My mother was as new to this concept of beehive life as I was, but she had been given strict orders by my father to keep the doors locked, the noise down, ourselves to ourselves.

It seems that Father had learned some painful lessons about prejudice 5 while searching for an apartment in Paterson. Not until years later did I hear how much resistance he had encountered with landlords who were panicking at the influx of Latinos into a neighborhood that had been Jewish for a couple of generations. It made no difference that it was the American phenomenon of ethnic turnover which was changing the urban core of Paterson, and that the human flood could not be held back with an accusing finger.

"You Cuban?" one man had asked my father, pointing at his name tag on the Navy uniform—even though my father had the fair skin and light-brown hair of his northern Spanish background, and the name Ortiz is as common in Puerto Rico as Johnson is in the United States.

"No," my father had answered, looking past the finger into his adversary's angry eyes. "I'm Puerto Rican."

"Same shit." And the door closed.

My father could have passed as European, but we couldn't. My brother and I both have our mother's black hair and olive skin, and so we lived in El Building and visited our great-uncle and his fair children on the next block. It was their private joke that they were the German branch of the family. Not many years later that area too would be mainly Puerto Rican. It was as if the heart of the city map were being gradually colored brown—café con leche[1] brown. Our color.

*The movie opens with a sweep of the living room. It is "typical" immi-   10
grant Puerto Rican decor for the time: The sofa and chairs are square and
hard-looking, upholstered in bright colors (blue and yellow in this instance),
and covered with the transparent plastic that furniture salesmen then were
so adept at convincing women to buy. The linoleum on the floor is light blue;
if it had been subjected to spike heels (as it was in most places), there were
dime-sized indentations all over it that cannot be seen in this movie. The
room is full of people dressed up: dark suits for the men, red dresses for the
women. When I have asked my mother why most of the women are in red
that night, she has shrugged, "I don't remember. Just a coincidence." She
doesn't have my obsession for assigning symbolism to everything.*

*The three women in red sitting on the couch are my mother, my
eighteen-year-old cousin, and her brother's girlfriend. The novia is just up
from the Island, which is apparent in her body language. She sits up formally,
her dress pulled over her knees. She is a pretty girl, but her posture makes
her look insecure, lost in her full-skirted dress, which she has carefully tucked
around her to make room for my gorgeous cousin, her future sister-in-law. My
cousin has grown up in Paterson and is in her last year of high school. She
doesn't have a trace of what Puerto Ricans call la mancha (literally, the stain:
the mark of the new immigrant—something about the posture, the voice, or
the humble demeanor that makes it obvious to everyone the person has just
arrived on the mainland). My cousin is wearing a tight, sequined, cocktail
dress. Her brown hair has been lightened with peroxide around the bangs,
and she is holding a cigarette expertly between her fingers, bringing it up to
her mouth in a sensuous arc of her arm as she talks animatedly. My mother,
who has come up to sit between the two women, both only a few years younger
than herself, is somewhere between the poles they represent in our culture.*

It became my father's obsession to get out of the barrio, and thus we
were never permitted to form bonds with the place or with the people who
lived there. Yet El Building was a comfort to my mother, who never got over
yearning for *la isla*. She felt surrounded by her language: The walls were
thin, and voices speaking and arguing in Spanish could be heard all day.
Salsas blasted out of radios, turned on early in the morning and left on for
company. Women seemed to cook rice and beans perpetually—the strong
aroma of boiling red kidney beans permeated the hallways.

Though Father preferred that we do our grocery shopping at the supermarket when he came home on weekend leaves, my mother insisted that she
could cook only with products whose labels she could read. Consequently,

---

[1] **café con leche:** Coffee with cream. In Puerto Rico it is sometimes prepared with boiled milk.—COFER'S NOTE.

during the week I accompanied her and my little brother to *La Bodega*—a hole-in-the-wall grocery store across the street from El Building. There we squeezed down three narrow aisles jammed with various products. Goya's and Libby's—those were the trademarks that were trusted by her *mamá*, so my mother bought many cans of Goya beans, soups, and condiments, as well as little cans of Libby's fruit juices for us. And she also bought Colgate toothpaste and Palmolive soap. (The final *e* is pronounced in both these products in Spanish, so for many years I believed that they were manufactured on the Island. I remember my surprise at first hearing a commercial on television in which Colgate rhymed with "ate.") We always lingered at La Bodega, for it was there that Mother breathed best, taking in the familiar aromas of the foods she knew from Mamá's kitchen. It was also there that she got to speak to the other women of El Building without violating outright Father's dictates against fraternizing with our neighbors.

Yet Father did his best to make our "assimilation" painless. I can still see him carrying a real Christmas tree up several flights of stairs to our apartment, leaving a trail of aromatic pine. He carried it formally, as if it were a flag in a parade. We were the only ones in El Building that I knew of who got presents on both Christmas day and *dia de Reyes*, the day when the Three Kings brought gifts to Christ and to Hispanic children.

Our supreme luxury in El Building was having our own television set. It 15 must have been a result of Father's guilty feelings over the isolation he had imposed on us, but we were among the first in the barrio to have one. My brother quickly became an avid watcher of Captain Kangaroo and Jungle Jim, while I loved all the series showing families. By the time I started first grade, I could have drawn a map of Middle America as exemplified by the lives of characters in *"Father Knows Best," "The Donna Reed Show," "Leave It to Beaver," "My Three Sons,"* and (my favorite) *"Bachelor Father,"* where John Forsythe treated his adopted teenage daughter like a princess because he was rich and had a Chinese houseboy to do everything for him. In truth, compared to our neighbors in El Building, *we* were rich. My father's Navy check provided us with financial security and a standard of life that the factory workers envied. The only thing his money could not buy us was a place to live away from the barrio—his greatest wish, Mother's greatest fear.

In the home movie the men are shown next, sitting around a card table set up in one corner of the living room, playing dominoes. The clack of the ivory pieces was a familiar sound. I heard it in many houses on the Island and in many apartments in Paterson. In "Leave It to Beaver," the Cleavers played bridge in every other episode; in my childhood, the men started every social occasion with a hotly debated round of dominoes. The women would sit around and watch, but they never participated in the games.

Here and there you can see a small child. Children were always brought to parties and, whenever they got sleepy, were put to bed in the host's bedroom. Babysitting was a concept unrecognized by the Puerto Rican women

||||||||||||||||||||||||||||||||||||||||||||||||||||||||||||||||||||||||||||||||||||||||||||||||||||||||||||||||||||||||||||||||||||||||||||||||||||||||||||||||||||||||

I knew: A responsible mother did not leave her children with any stranger. And in a culture where children are not considered intrusive, there was no need to leave the children at home. We went where our mother went.

Of my preschool years I have only impressions: the sharp bite of the wind in December as we walked with our parents toward the brightly lit stores downtown; how I felt like a stuffed doll in my heavy coat, boots, and mittens; how good it was to walk into the five-and-dime and sit at the counter drinking hot chocolate. On Saturdays our whole family would walk downtown to shop at the big department stores on Broadway. Mother bought all our clothes at Penney's and Sears, and she liked to buy her dresses at the women's specialty shops like Lerner's and Diana's. At some point we'd go into Woolworth's and sit at the soda fountain to eat.

We never ran into other Latinos at these stores or when eating out, and it became clear to me only years later that the women from El Building shopped mainly in other places—stores owned by other Puerto Ricans or by Jewish merchants who had philosophically accepted our presence in the city and decided to make us their good customers, if not real neighbors and friends. These establishments were located not downtown but in the blocks around our street, and they were referred to generically as *La Tienda, El Bazar, La Bodega, La Botánica.* Everyone knew what was meant. These were the stores where your face did not turn a clerk to stone, where your money was as green as anyone else's.

One New Year's Eve we were dressed up like child models in the Sears   20
catalogue: my brother in a miniature man's suit and bow tie, and I in black patent-leather shoes and a frilly dress with several layers of crinoline underneath. My mother wore a bright red dress that night, I remember, and spike heels; her long black hair hung to her waist. Father, who usually wore his Navy uniform during his short visits home, had put on a dark civilian suit for the occasion: We had been invited to his uncle's house for a big celebration. Everyone was excited because my mother's brother Hernan—a bachelor who could indulge himself with luxuries—had bought a home movie camera, which he would be trying out that night.

Even the home movie cannot fill in the sensory details such a gathering left imprinted in a child's brain. The thick sweetness of women's perfumes mixing with the ever-present smells of food cooking in the kitchen: meat and plantain *pasteles,* as well as the ubiquitous rice dish made special with pigeon peas—*gandules*—and seasoned with precious *sofrito*[2] sent up from the Island by somebody's mother or smuggled in by a recent traveler. *Sofrito* was one of the items that women hoarded, since it was hardly ever in stock at La Bodega. It was the flavor of Puerto Rico.

---

[2] ***sofrito:*** A cooked condiment. A sauce composed of a mixture of fatback, ham, tomatoes, and many island spices and herbs. It is added to many Puerto Rican dishes for a distinctive flavor.—COFER'S NOTE.

The men drank Palo Viejo rum, and some of the younger ones got weepy. The first time I saw a grown man cry was at a New Year's Eve party: He had been reminded of his mother by the smells in the kitchen. But what I remember most were the boiled *pasteles*—plantain or yucca rectangles stuffed with corned beef or other meats, olives, and many other savory ingredients, all wrapped in banana leaves. Everybody had to fish one out with a fork. There was always a "trick" pastel—one without stuffing—and whoever got that one was the "New Year's Fool."

There was also the music. Long-playing albums were treated like precious china in these homes. Mexican recordings were popular, but the songs that brought tears to my mother's eyes were sung by the melancholy Daniel Santos, whose life as a drug addict was the stuff of legend. Felipe Rodríguez was a particular favorite of couples, since he sang about faithless women and brokenhearted men. There is a snatch of one lyric that has stuck in my mind like a needle on a worn groove: *De piedra ha de ser mi cama, de piedra la cabezera . . . la mujer que a mi me quiera . . . ha de quererme de veras. Ay, Ay, Ay, corazón, porque no amas.*[3] . . . I must have heard it a thousand times since the idea of a bed made of stone, and its connection to love, first troubled me with its disturbing images.

The five-minute home movie ends with people dancing in a circle—the creative filmmaker must have set it up so that all of them could file past him. It is both comical and sad to watch silent dancing. Since there is no justification for the absurd movements that music provides for some of us, people appear frantic, their faces embarrassingly intense. It's as if you were watching sex. Yet for years I've had dreams in the form of this home movie. In a recurring scene, familiar faces push themselves forward into my mind's eyes, plastering their features into distorted close-ups. And I'm asking them: "Who is *she*? Who is the old woman I don't recognize? Is she an aunt? Somebody's wife? Tell me who she is."

"See the beauty mark on her cheek as big as a hill on the lunar landscape of her face—well, that runs in the family. The women on your father's side of the family wrinkle early; it's the price they pay for that fair skin. The young girl with the green stain on her wedding dress is *La Novia*—just up from the Island. See, she lowers her eyes when she approaches the camera, as she's supposed to. Decent girls never look at you directly in the face. *Humilde*, humble, a girl should express humility in all her actions. She will make a good wife for your cousin. He should consider himself lucky to have met her only weeks after she arrived here. If he marries her quickly, she will make him a good Puerto Rican–style wife; but if he waits too long, she will be corrupted by the city—just like your cousin there."

"She means me. I do what I want. This is not some primitive island I live on. Do they expect me to wear a black mantilla on my head and go to mass every day?

---

[3] ***De piedra ha de ser . . . amas:*** Lyrics from a popular romantic ballad (called a *bolero* in Puerto Rico). Freely translated: "My bed will be made of stone, of stone also my headrest (or pillow), the woman who (dares to) love me, will have to love me for real. Ay, Ay, Ay, my heart, why can't you (let me) love. . . ."—COFER'S NOTE.

Not me. I'm an American woman, and I will do as I please. I can type faster than anyone in my senior class at Central High, and I'm going to be a secretary to a lawyer when I graduate. I can pass for an American girl anywhere—I've tried it. At least for Italian, anyway—I never speak Spanish in public. I hate these parties, but I wanted the dress. I look better than any of these *humildes* here. My life is going to be different. I have an American boyfriend. He is older and has a car. My parents don't know it, but I sneak out of the house late at night sometimes to be with him. If I marry him, even my name will be American. I hate rice and beans—that's what makes these women fat."

"Your *prima*[4] is pregnant by that man she's been sneaking around with. Would I lie to you? I'm your *Tía Política*,[5] your great-uncle's common-law wife—the one he abandoned on the Island to go marry your cousin's mother. *I* was not invited to this party, of course, but I came anyway. I came to tell you that story about your cousin that you've always wanted to hear. Do you remember the comment your mother made to a neighbor that has always haunted you? The only thing you heard was your cousin's name, and then you saw your mother pick up your doll from the couch and say: 'It was as big as this doll when they flushed it down the toilet.' This image has bothered you for years, hasn't it? You had nightmares about babies being flushed down the toilet, and you wondered why anyone would do such a horrible thing. You didn't dare ask your mother about it. She would only tell you that you had not heard her right, and yell at you for listening to adult conversations. But later, when you were old enough to know about abortions, you suspected.

"I am here to tell you that you were right. Your cousin was growing an *Americanito* in her belly when this movie was made. Soon after she put something long and pointy into her pretty self, thinking maybe she could get rid of the problem before breakfast and still make it to her first class at the high school. Well, *Niña*,[6] her screams could be heard downtown. Your aunt, her mamá, who had been a midwife on the Island, managed to pull the little thing out. Yes, they probably flushed it down the toilet. What else could they do with it—give it a Christian burial in a little white casket with blue bows and ribbons? Nobody wanted that baby—least of all the father, a teacher at her school with a house in West Paterson that he was filling with real children, and a wife who was a natural blonde.

"Girl, the scandal sent your uncle back to the bottle. And guess where your cousin ended up? Irony of ironies. She was sent to a village in Puerto Rico to live with a relative on her mother's side: a place so far away from civilization that you have to ride a mule to reach it. A real change in scenery. She found a man there—women like that cannot live without male company—but believe me, the men in Puerto Rico know how to put a saddle on a woman like her. *La Gringa*,[7] they call her. Ha, ha, ha. *La Gringa* is what she always wanted to be. . . ."

---

[4] ***prima:*** Female cousin.—COFER'S NOTE.
[5] ***Tía Política:*** Aunt by marriage.—COFER'S NOTE.
[6] ***Niña:*** Girl.—COFER'S NOTE.
[7] ***La Gringa:*** Derogatory epithet used here to ridicule a Puerto Rican girl who wants to look like a blonde North American.—COFER'S NOTE.

The old woman's mouth becomes a cavernous black hole I fall into. And as I fall, I can feel the reverberations of her laughter. I hear the echoes of her last mocking words: *La Gringa, La Gringa!* And the conga line keeps moving silently past me. There is no music in my dream for the dancers.

When Odysseus visits Hades to see the spirit of his mother, he makes an   25 offering of sacrificial blood, but since all the souls crave an audience with the living, he has to listen to many of them before he can ask questions. I, too, have to hear the dead and the forgotten speak in my dream. Those who are still part of my life remain silent, going around and around in their dance. The others keep pressing their faces forward to say things about the past.

My father's uncle is last in line. He is dying of alcoholism, shrunken and shriveled like a monkey, his face a mass of wrinkles and broken arteries. As he comes closer I realize that in his features I can see my whole family. If you were to stretch that rubbery flesh, you could find my father's face, and deep within *that* face—my own. I don't want to look into those eyes ringed in purple. In a few years he will retreat into silence, and take a long, long time to die. *Move back, Tío,* I tell him. *I don't want to hear what you have to say. Give the dancers room to move. Soon it will be midnight. Who is the New Year's Fool this time?* ●

The Reader's Presence

1. In "Silent Dancing," Cofer explores the personal, familial, and communal transformations that resulted from moving in the 1950s to Paterson, New Jersey—to "a huge tenement that had once housed Jewish families" (paragraph 2) and to a new community that emerged from the sprawling barrio that Puerto Ricans "overflowing from New York City" (paragraph 2) called home. Reread the essay carefully, and summarize the transformations that occurred in the life of the narrator, her family, and their larger Puerto Rican community.

2. Cofer uses an account of a home movie to create a structure for her essay. What are the specific advantages and disadvantages of this strategy? How, for example, does the home movie serve as "a great visual aid" (paragraph 1) to recounting life in the barrio of Paterson, New Jersey? What effect does the fact that the home movie is in color have on what Cofer notices? on how she writes?

3. Because Cofer's essay is built around the occasion of watching a home movie, the narrator assumes the position of an observer of the scenes and people Cofer describes. What specific strategies as a writer does Cofer use to establish a presence for herself in this narrative and descriptive account of growing up?

4. **CONNECTIONS:**   In his attempt to aid the family's "assimilation" into American culture, Cofer's father forbids his wife and children from making friends in "El Building." Cofer and her mother were expected "to keep the doors locked, the noise down, ourselves to ourselves" (paragraph 3). As a result, Cofer at times feels alienated from her own relatives. How does her situation compare to that of the narrator of Maxine Hong Kingston's "No Name Woman" (page 458)?

The Writer at Work

JUDITH ORTIZ COFER on Memory and Personal Essays

SILENT DANCING: *A Partial Remembrance of a Puerto Rican Childhood*

JUDITH ORTIZ COFER

In setting out to write essays recounting her family history, Judith Ortiz Cofer found in Virginia Woolf a brilliant mentor and guide who taught her how to release the creative power of memory. In the following preface to *Silent Dancing: A Partial Remembrance of a Puerto Rican Childhood*, Cofer pays tribute to Woolf, who "understood that the very act of reclaiming her memories could provide a writer with confidence in the power of art to discover meaning and truth in ordinary events." How do Cofer's remarks in the preface (which she called "Journey to a Summer's Afternoon"), along with Woolf's "The Death of the Moth" (page 625), help illuminate the artistry of Cofer's own essay, "Silent Dancing"?

The author at the age of two, from the cover of *Silent Dancing: A Partial Remembrance of a Puerto Rican Childhood*, by Judith Ortiz Cofer. Published in 1990 by Arte Publico Press (Houston, Texas).

❝ As one gets older, childhood years are often conveniently consolidated into one perfect summer's afternoon. The events can be projected on a light blue screen; the hurtful parts can be edited out, and the moments of joy brought in sharp focus to the foreground. It is our show. But with all that on the cutting room floor, what remains to tell?

Virginia Woolf, whose vision guided my efforts as I tried to recall the faces and words of the people who are a part of my "summer's afternoon," wrote of the problem of writing truth from memory. In "A Sketch of the Past" she says, "But if I turn to my mother, how difficult it is to single her out as she really was; to imagine what she was thinking, to put a single sentence into her mouth." She accepts the fact that in writing about one's life, one often has to rely on that combination of memory, imagination, and strong emotion that may result in "poetic truth." In preparing to write her memoirs Woolf said, "I dream, I make up pictures of a summer's afternoon."

In one of her essays from her memoir *Moments of Being*, Woolf recalls the figure of her beautiful and beloved mother who died while the author was still a child, leaving her a few precious "moments of being" from which the mature woman must piece together a childhood. And she does so not to showcase her life, extraordinary as it was, but rather out of a need most of us feel at some point to study ourselves and our lives in retrospect; to understand what people and events formed us (and, yes, what and who hurt us, too).

From "A Sketch of the Past": "Many bright colors; many distinct sounds; some human beings, caricatures; several violent moments of being, always including a circle of the scene they cut out: and all surrounded by a vast space—that is a rough visual description of childhood. This is how I shape it; and how I see myself as a child. . . ."

　　This passage illustrates the approach that I was seeking in writing about my family. I wanted the essays to be, not just family history, but also creative explorations of known territory. I wanted to trace back through scenes based on my "moments of being" the origins of my creative imagination. As a writer, I am, like most artists, interested in the genesis of ideas: How does a poem begin? Can the process be triggered at will? What compels some of us to examine and re-examine our lives in poems, stories, novels, memoirs?

　　Much of my writing begins as a meditation on past events. But memory for me is the "jumping off" point; I am not, in my poetry and my fiction writing, a slave to memory. I like to believe that the poem or story contains the "truth" of art rather than the factual, historical truth that the journalist, sociologist, scientist—most of the rest of the world—must adhere to. Art gives me that freedom. But in writing these "essays" (the Spanish word for essay, *ensayo*, suits my meaning here better—it can mean "a rehearsal," an exercise or practice), I faced the possibility that the past is mainly a creation of the imagination also, although there are facts one can research and confirm. The biographer's time-honored task can be employed on one's own life too. There are birth, marriage, and death certificates on file, there are letters and family photographs in someone's desk or attic; and there are the relatives who have assigned themselves the role of genealogist or family bard, recounting at the least instigation the entire history of your clan. One can go

to these sources and come up with a *Life* in several volumes that will make your mother proud and give you the satisfaction of having "preserved" something. I am not interested in merely "canning" memories, however, and Woolf gave me the focus that I needed to justify this work. Its intention is not to chronicle my life—which in my case is still very much "in-progress," nor are there any extraordinary accomplishments to showcase; neither is it meant to be a record of public events and personal histories (in fact, since most of the characters in these essays are based on actual, living persons and real places, whenever I felt that it was necessary to protect their identities, I changed names, locations, etc.). Then, what is the purpose of calling this collection nonfiction or a memoir? Why not just call it fiction? Once again I must turn to my literary mentor for this project, Virginia Woolf, for an answer: like her, I wanted to try to connect myself to the threads of lives that have touched mine and at some point converged into the tapestry that is my memory of childhood. Virginia Woolf understood that the very act of reclaiming her memories could provide a writer with confidence in the power of art to discover meaning and truth in ordinary events. She was a time-traveler who saw the past as a real place one could return to by following the tracks left by strong emotions: "I feel that strong emotion must leave its trace; and it is only a question of discovering how we can get ourselves attached to it, so that we shall be able to live our lives through from the start."[1]

　　It was this winding path of memory, marked by strong emotions, that I followed in my *ensayos* of a life. **"**

[1]All quotes by Virginia Woolf are from *Moments of Being* (Harcourt Brace Jovanovich, Inc.).—COFER'S NOTE.

Bernard Cooper

A CLACK OF TINY SPARKS: REMEMBRANCES OF A GAY BOYHOOD

Born (1951), raised, and still residing in Los Angeles, **BERNARD COOPER** received his BFA and MFA from the California Institute of the Arts. He has taught at the Otis/Parsons Institute of Art and Design and Southern California Institute of Architecture, Los Angeles, and at the UCLA writing program; he is now an art critic for *Los Angeles Magazine*. His two collections of personal essays, *Maps to Any-where* (1990) and *Truth Serum* (1996), cover a wide range of topics from the aging of his father, to his gay awakening, to the future of American life and culture. A collection of short stories, *Guess Again*, was published in 2000

> **"The world only seems real and vivid and meaningful to me in the smaller details."**

and his latest memoir, *The Bill from My Father*, in 2006. Cooper contributes to various periodicals such as *Harper's*, where "A Clack of Tiny Sparks: Remembrances of a Gay Boyhood" first appeared in January 1991.

Commenting on his 1993 novel, *A Year of Rhymes*, Cooper notes, "One of the reasons why there is so much detail in my work is that I'm a person that essentially shies away from abstractions, from Large Issues and Big Ideas. The world only seems real and vivid and meaningful to me in the smaller details, what's heard and felt and smelled and tasted."

THERESA SANCHEZ sat behind me in ninth-grade algebra. When Mr. Hubbley faced the blackboard, I'd turn around to see what she was reading; each week a new book was wedged inside her copy of *Today's Equations*. The deception worked; from Mr. Hubbley's point of view, Theresa was engrossed in the value of X, but I knew otherwise. One week she perused *The Wisdom of the Orient*, and I could tell from Theresa's contemplative expression that the book contained exotic thoughts, guidelines handed down from high. Another week it was a paperback novel whose title, *Let Me Live My Life*, appeared in bold print atop every page, and whose cover, a gauzy photograph of a woman biting a strand of pearls, head thrown back in an attitude of ecstasy, confirmed my suspicion that Theresa Sanchez was mature beyond her years. She was the tallest girl in school. Her bouffant hairdo, streaked with blond, was higher than the flaccid bouffants of other girls. Her smooth skin, plucked eyebrows, and painted fingernails suggested hours of pampering, a worldly and sensual vanity that placed her within the domain of adults. Smiling dimly, steeped in daydreams, Theresa moved through the crowded halls with a languid, self-satisfied indifference to those around her. "You are merely children," her posture seemed to say. "I can't be bothered." The week Theresa hid *101 Ways to Cook Hamburger* behind her algebra book, I could stand it no longer and, after the bell rang, ventured a question.

"Because I'm having a dinner party," said Theresa. "Just a couple of intimate friends."

No fourteen-year-old I knew had ever given a dinner party, let alone used the word "intimate" in conversation. "Don't you have a mother?" I asked.

Theresa sighed a weary sigh, suffered my strange inquiry. "Don't be so naïve," she said. "Everyone has a mother." She waved her hand to indicate the brick school buildings outside the window. "A higher education should have taught you that." Theresa draped an angora sweater over her shoulders, scooped her books from the graffiti-covered desk, and just as she was about to walk away, she turned and asked me, "Are you a fag?"

There wasn't the slightest hint of rancor or condescension in her voice. The tone was direct, casual. Still I was stunned, giving a sidelong glance to make sure no one had heard. "No," I said. Blurted really, with too much defensiveness, too much transparent fear in my response. Octaves lower than usual, I tried a "Why?"

Theresa shrugged. "Oh, I don't know. I have lots of friends who are fags. You remind me of them." Seeing me bristle, Theresa added, "It was just a guess." I watched her erect, angora back as she sauntered out the classroom door.

She had made an incisive and timely guess. Only days before, I'd invited Grady Rogers to my house after school to go swimming. The instant Grady shot from the pool, shaking water from his orange hair, freckled shoulders shining, my attraction to members of my own sex became a matter I could no longer suppress or rationalize. Sturdy and boisterous and gap-toothed, Grady was an inveterate backslapper, a formidable arm wrestler, a wizard at basketball. Grady was a boy at home in his body.

My body was a marvel I hadn't gotten used to; my arms and legs would sometimes act of their own accord, knocking over a glass at dinner or flinching at an oncoming pitch. I was never singled out as a sissy, but I could have been just as easily as Bobby Keagan, a gentle, intelligent, and introverted boy reviled by my classmates. And although I had always been aware of a tacit rapport with Bobby, a suspicion that I might find with him a rich friendship, I stayed away. Instead, I emulated Grady in the belief that being seen with him, being like him, would somehow vanquish my self-doubt, would make me normal by association.

Apart from his athletic prowess, Grady had been gifted with all the trappings of what I imagined to be a charmed life: a fastidious, aproned mother who radiated calm, maternal concern; a ruddy, stoic father with a knack for home repairs. Even the Rogerses' small suburban house in Hollywood, with its spindly Colonial furniture and chintz curtains, was a testament to normalcy.

Grady and his family bore little resemblance to my clan of Eastern Euro- 10 pean Jews, a dark and vociferous people who ate with abandon—matzo and halvah and gefilte fish; foods the goyim couldn't pronounce—who cajoled one another during endless games of canasta, making the simplest remark about the weather into a lengthy philosophical discourse on the sun and the seasons and the passage of time. My mother was a chain-smoker, a dervish in a frowsy housedress. She showed her love in the most peculiar and obsessive ways, like spending hours extracting every seed from a watermelon before she served it in perfectly bite-sized, geometric pieces. Preoccupied and perpetually frantic, my mother succumbed to bouts of absentmindedness so profound she'd forget what she was saying midsentence, smile and blush and walk away. A divorce attorney, my father wore roomy, iridescent suits, and the intricacies, the deceits inherent in his profession, had the effect of making him forever tense and vigilant. He was "all wound up," as my mother put it. But when he relaxed, his laughter was explosive, his disposition prankish: "Walk this way," a waitress would say, leading us to our table, and my father would mimic the way she walked, arms akimbo, hips liquid, while my mother and I were wracked with laughter. Buoyant or brooding, my parents' moods were unpredictable, and in a household fraught with extravagant emotion it was odd and awful to keep my longing secret.

One day I made the mistake of asking my mother what a "fag" was. I knew exactly what Theresa had meant but hoped against hope it was not what I thought; maybe "fag" was some French word, a harmless term like "naïve." My mother turned from the stove, flew at me, and grabbed me by the shoulders. "Did someone call you that?" she cried.

"Not me," I said. "Bobby Keagan."

"Oh," she said, loosening her grip. She was visibly relieved. And didn't answer. The answer was unthinkable.

For weeks after, I shook with the reverberations from that afternoon in the kitchen with my mother, pained by the memory of her shocked expression and, most of all, her silence. My longing was wrong in the eyes of my mother, whose hazel eyes were the eyes of the world, and if that longing continued unchecked, the unwieldy shape of my fate would be cast, and I'd be subjected to a lifetime of scorn.

During the remainder of the semester, I became the scientist of my own 15 desire, plotting ways to change my yearning for boys into a yearning for girls. I had enough evidence to believe that any habit, regardless of how compulsive, how deeply ingrained, could be broken once and for all: The plastic cigarette my mother purchased at the Thrifty pharmacy—one end was red to approximate an ember, the other tan like a filtered tip—was designed to wean her from the real thing. To change a behavior required self-analysis, cold resolve, and the substitution of one thing for another: plastic, say, for tobacco. Could I also find a substitute for Grady? What I needed to do, I figured, was kiss a girl and learn to like it.

This conclusion was affirmed one Sunday morning when my father, seeing me wrinkle my nose at the pink slabs of lox he layered on a bagel, tried to convince me of its salty appeal. "You should try some," he said. "You don't know what you're missing."

"It's loaded with protein," added my mother, slapping a platter of sliced onions onto the dinette table. She hovered above us, cinching her housedress, eyes wet from onion fumes, the mock cigarette dangling from her lips.

My father sat there chomping with gusto, emitting a couple of hearty grunts to dramatize his satisfaction. And still I was not convinced. After a loud and labored swallow, he told me I may not be fond of lox today, but sooner or later I'd learn to like it. One's tastes, he assured me, are destined to change.

"Live," shouted my mother over the rumble of the Mixmaster. "Expand your horizons. Try new things." And the room grew fragrant with the batter of a spice cake.

The opportunity to put their advice into practice, and try out my plan to   20
adapt to girls, came the following week when Debbie Coburn, a member of Mr. Hubbley's algebra class, invited me to a party. She cornered me in the hall, furtive as a spy, telling me her parents would be gone for the evening and slipping into my palm a wrinkled sheet of notebook paper. On it were her address and telephone number, the lavender ink in a tidy cursive. "Wear cologne," she advised, wary eyes darting back and forth. "It's a make-out party. Anything can happen."

The Santa Ana wind blew relentlessly the night of Debbie's party, careening down the slopes of the Hollywood hills, shaking the road signs and stoplights in its path. As I walked down Beachwood Avenue, trees thrashed, surrendered their leaves, and carob pods bombarded the pavement. The sky was a deep but luminous blue, the air hot, abrasive, electric. I had to squint in order to check the number of the Coburns' apartment, a three-story building with glitter embedded in its stucco walls. Above the honeycombed balconies was a sign that read BEACHWOOD TERRACE in lavender script resembling Debbie's.

From down the hall, I could hear the plaintive strains of Little Anthony's "I Think I'm Going Out of My Head." Debbie answered the door bedecked in an Empire dress, the bodice blue and orange polka dots, the rest a sheath of black and white stripes. "Op art," proclaimed Debbie. She turned in a circle, then proudly announced that she'd rolled her hair in orange juice cans. She patted the huge unmoving curls and dragged me inside. Reflections from the swimming pool in the courtyard, its surface ruffled by wind, shuddered over the ceiling and walls. A dozen of my classmates were seated on the sofa or huddled together in corners, their whispers full of excited imminence, their bodies barely discernible in the dim light. Drapes flanking the sliding glass doors bowed out with every gust of wind, and it seemed that the room might lurch from its foundations and sail with its cargo of silhouettes into the hot October night.

Grady was the last to arrive. He tossed a six-pack of beer into Debbie's arms, barreled toward me, and slapped my back. His hair was slicked back with Vitalis, lacquered furrows left by the comb. The wind hadn't shifted a single hair. "Ya ready?" he asked, flashing the gap between his front teeth and leering into the darkened room. "You bet," I lied.

Once the beers had been passed around, Debbie provoked everyone's attention by flicking on the overhead light. "Okay," she called. "Find a partner." This was the blunt command of a hostess determined to have her guests aroused in an orderly fashion. Everyone blinked, shuffled about, and grabbed a member of the opposite sex. Sheila Garabedian landed beside me—entirely at random, though I wanted to believe she was driven by passion—her timid smile giving way to plain fear as the light went out. Nothing for a moment but the heave of the wind and the distant banter of dogs. I caught a whiff of Sheila's perfume, tangy and sweet as Hawaiian Punch. I probed her face with my own, grazing the small scallop of an ear, a velvety temple, and though Sheila's trembling made me want to stop, I persisted with my mission until I found her lips, tightly sealed as a private letter. I held my mouth over hers and gathered her shoulders closer, resigned to the possibility that, no matter how long we stood there, Sheila would be too scared to kiss me back. Still, she exhaled through her nose, and I listened to the squeak of every breath as though it were a sigh of inordinate pleasure. Diving within myself, I monitored my heartbeat and respiration, trying to will stimulation into being, and all the while an image intruded, an image of Grady erupting from our pool, rivulets of water sliding down his chest. "Change," shouted Debbie, switching on the light. Sheila thanked me, pulled away, and continued her routine of gracious terror with every boy throughout the evening. It didn't matter whom I held—Margaret Sims, Betty Vernon, Elizabeth Lee—my experiment was a failure; I continued to picture Grady's wet chest, and Debbie would bellow "change" with such fervor, it could have been my own voice, my own incessant reprimand.

Our hostess commandeered the light switch for nearly half an hour. 25 Whenever the light came on, I watched Grady pivot his head toward the newest prospect, his eyebrows arched in expectation, his neck blooming with hickeys, his hair, at last, in disarray. All that shuffling across the carpet charged everyone's arms and lips with static, and eventually, between low moans and soft osculations, I could hear the clack of tiny sparks and see them flare here and there in the dark like meager, short-lived stars.

I saw Theresa, sultry and aloof as ever, read three more books—*North American Reptiles, Bonjour Tristesse*, and *MGM: A Pictorial History*—before she vanished early in December. Rumors of her fate abounded. Debbie Coburn swore that Theresa had been "knocked up" by an older man, a traffic cop, she thought, or a grocer. Nearly quivering with relish, Debbie told me and Grady about the home for unwed mothers in the San Fernando

Valley, a compound teeming with pregnant girls who had nothing to do but touch their stomachs and contemplate their mistake. Even Bobby Keagan, who took Theresa's place behind me in algebra, had a theory regarding her disappearance colored by his own wish for escape; he imagined that Theresa, disillusioned with society, booked passage to a tropical island, there to live out the rest of her days without restrictions or ridicule. "No wonder she flunked out of school," I overheard Mr. Hubbley tell a fellow teacher one afternoon. "Her head was always in a book."

Along with Theresa went my secret, or at least the dread that she might divulge it, and I felt, for a while, exempt from suspicion. I was, however, to run across Theresa one last time. It happened during a period of torrential rain that, according to reports on the six o'clock news, washed houses from the hillsides and flooded the downtown streets. The halls of Joseph Le Conte Junior High were festooned with Christmas decorations: crepe-paper garlands, wreaths studded with plastic berries, and one requisite Star of David twirling above the attendance desk. In Arts and Crafts, our teacher, Gerald (he was the only teacher who allowed us—*required* us—to call him by his first name), handed out blocks of balsa wood and instructed us to carve them into bugs. We would paint eyes and antennae with tempera and hang them on a Christmas tree he'd made the previous night. "Voilà," he crooned, unveiling his creation from a burlap sack. Before us sat a tortured scrub, a wardrobe-worth of wire hangers that were bent like branches and soldered together. Gerald credited his inspiration to a Charles Addams cartoon he's seen in which Morticia, grimly preparing for the holidays, hangs vampire bats on a withered pine. "All that red and green," said Gerald. "So predictable. *So boring.*"

As I chiseled a beetle and listened to rain pummel the earth, Gerald handed me an envelope and asked me to take it to Mr. Kendrick, the drama teacher. I would have thought nothing of his request if I hadn't seen Theresa on my way down the hall. She was cleaning out her locker, blithely dropping the sum of its contents—pens and textbooks and mimeographs—into a trash can. "Have a nice life," she sang as I passed. I mustered the courage to ask her what had happened. We stood alone in the silent hall, the reflections of wreaths and garlands submerged in brown linoleum.

"I transferred to another school. They don't have grades or bells, and you get to study whatever you want." Theresa was quick to sense my incredulity. "Honest," she said. "The school is progressive." She gazed into a glass cabinet that held the trophies of track meets and intramural spelling bees. "God," she sighed, "this place is so . . . barbaric." I was still trying to decide whether or not to believe her story when she asked me where I was headed. "Dear," she said, her exclamation pooling in the silence, "that's no ordinary note, if you catch my drift." The envelope was blank and white; I looked up at Theresa, baffled. "Don't be so naïve," she muttered, tossing an empty bottle of nail polish into the trash can. It struck bottom with a resolute thud. "Well," she said, closing her locker and breathing deeply, "bon voyage." Theresa swept through the double doors and in seconds her figure was obscured by rain.

As I walked toward Mr. Kendrick's room, I could feel Theresa's insinu- 30
ation burrow in. I stood for a moment and watched Mr. Kendrick through
the pane in the door. He paced intently in front of the class, handsome in his
shirt and tie, reading from a thick book. Chalked on the blackboard behind
him was THE ODYSSEY BY HOMER. I have no recollection of how Mr. Kendrick
reacted to the note, whether he accepted it with pleasure or embarrassment,
slipped it into his desk drawer or the pocket of his shirt. I have scavenged
that day in retrospect, trying to see Mr. Kendrick's expression, wondering if
he acknowledged me in any way as his liaison. All I recall is the sight of his
mime through a pane of glass, a lone man mouthing an epic, his gestures
ardent in empty air.

Had I delivered a declaration of love? I was haunted by the need to
know. In fantasy, a kettle shot steam, the glue released its grip, and I read
the letter with impunity. But how would such a letter begin? Did the common
endearments apply? This was a message between two men, a message for
which I had no precedent, and when I tried to envision the contents, apart
from a hasty, impassioned scrawl, my imagination faltered.

Once or twice I witnessed Gerald and Mr. Kendrick walk together into
the faculty lounge or say hello at the water fountain, but there was nothing especially clandestine or flirtatious in their manner. Besides, no matter
how acute my scrutiny, I wasn't sure, short of a kiss, exactly what to look
for—what semaphore of gesture, what encoded word. I suspected there
were signs, covert signs that would give them away, just as I'd unwittingly
given myself away to Theresa.

In the school library, a *Webster's* unabridged dictionary lay on a wooden
podium, and I padded toward it with apprehension; along with clues to the
bond between my teachers, I risked discovering information that might
incriminate me as well. I had decided to consult the dictionary during lunch
period, when most of the students would be on the playground. I clutched
my notebook, moving in such a way as to appear both studious and nonchalant, actually believing that, unless I took precautions, someone would see
me and guess what I was up to. The closer I came to the podium, the more
obvious, I thought, was my endeavor; I felt like the model of The Visible
Man in our science class, my heart's undulations, my overwrought nerves
legible through transparent skin. A couple of kids riffled through the card
catalogue. The librarian, a skinny woman whose perpetual whisper and
rubber-soled shoes caused her to drift through the room like a phantom,
didn't seem to register my presence. Though I'd looked up dozens of words
before, the pages felt strange beneath my fingers. *Homer* was the first word
I saw. *Hominid. Homogenize.* I feigned interest and skirted other words
before I found the word I was after. Under the heading HO·MO·SEX·U·AL
was the terse definition: *adj. Pertaining to, characteristic of, or exhibiting
homosexuality.—n. A homosexual person.* I read the definition again and
again, hoping the words would yield more than they could. I shut the dictionary, swallowed hard, and, none the wiser, hurried away.

As for Gerald and Mr. Kendrick, I never discovered evidence to prove or dispute Theresa's claim. By the following summer, however, I had overheard from my peers a confounding amount about homosexuals: They wore green on Thursday, couldn't whistle, hypnotized boys with a piercing glance. To this lore, Grady added a surefire test to ferret them out.

"A test?" I said.

"You ask a guy to look at his fingernails, and if he looks at them like this" — Grady closed his fingers into a fist and examined his nails with manly detachment — "then he's okay. But if he does this" — he held out his hands at arm's length, splayed his fingers, and coyly cocked his head — "you'd better watch out." Once he'd completed his demonstration, Grady peeled off his shirt and plunged into our pool. I dove in after. It was early June, the sky immense, glassy, placid. My father was cooking spareribs on the barbecue, an artist with a basting brush. His apron bore the caricature of a frazzled French chef. Mother curled on a chaise lounge, plumes of smoke wafting from her nostrils. In a stupor of contentment she took another drag, closed her eyes, and arched her face toward the sun.

Grady dog-paddled through the deep end, spouting a fountain of chlo-rinated water. Despite shame and confusion, my longing for him hadn't diminished; it continued to thrive without air and light, like a luminous fish in the dregs of the sea. In the name of play, I swam up behind him, encircled his shoulders, astonished by his taut flesh. The two of us flailed, pretended to drown. Beneath the heavy press of water, Grady's orange hair wavered, a flame that couldn't be doused.

I've lived with a man for seven years. Some nights, when I'm half-asleep and the room is suffused with blue light, I reach out to touch the expanse of his back, and it seems as if my fingers sink into his skin, and I feel the plea-sure a diver feels the instant he enters a body of water.

I have few regrets. But one is that I hadn't said to Theresa, "Of course I'm a fag." Maybe I'd have met her friends. Or become friends with her. Imagine the meals we might have concocted: hamburger Stroganoff, Swedish meat-balls in a sweet translucent sauce, steaming slabs of Salisbury steak. ●

The Reader's Presence

1. Cooper's first stirrings of attraction for his friend Grady occur in a swimming pool. What importance does swimming play in Cooper's essay? How does it provide him with a cluster of images for sexual experience?

2. Why does Cooper attend the "make-out party"? What does he hope will happen? Why do you think he ends his description of the party with the observation of the "clack of tiny sparks"? Why do you think he used that image for his title?

3. **CONNECTIONS:** In paragraph 15, Cooper writes that he became "the scientist of [his] own desire," as he tried to understand — and to resist — his "yearning for

||||||||||||||||||||||||||||||||||||||||||||||||||||||||||||||||||||||||||||||||||||||||||||||||||||||||||||||||||||||||||||||||||||||

boys." In what ways does Cooper's experience resemble Andrew Sullivan's in "The M-Word: Why It Matters to Me" (page 223). What differences do you find in the author's process of self-discovery? Children often turn to dictionaries to solve mysteries they are too shy to ask people about. How does Cooper's discovery of the definition of "homosexual" compare to Frederick Douglass's attempt to discover the meaning of "abolition" in the following essay, "Learning to Read and Write"?

Frederick Douglass
LEARNING TO READ AND WRITE

Born into slavery, **FREDERICK DOUGLASS** (1817?–1895) was taken from his mother as an infant and denied any knowledge of his father's identity. He escaped to the north at the age of twenty-one and created a new identity for himself as a free man. He educated himself and went on to become one of the most eloquent orators and persuasive writers of the nineteenth century. He was a national leader in the abolition movement and, among other activities, founded and edited the *North Star* and *Douglass' Monthly*. His public service included appointments as U.S. marshal and consul general to the Republic of Haiti. His

> Born into slavery, Frederick Douglass was taken from his mother as an infant and denied any knowledge of his father's identity.

most lasting literary accomplishment was his memoirs, which he revised several times before they were published as *The Life and Times of Frederick Douglass* (1881 and 1892). "Learning to Read and Write" is taken from these memoirs.

Douglass overcame his initial reluctance to write his memoirs because, as he put it, "not only is slavery on trial, but unfortunately, the enslaved people are also on trial. It is alleged that they are, naturally, inferior; that they are so low in the scale of humanity, and so utterly stupid, that they are unconscious of their wrongs, and do not apprehend their rights." Therefore, wishing to put his talents to work "to the benefit of my afflicted people," Douglass agreed to write the story of his life.

I LIVED IN MASTER HUGH'S FAMILY about seven years. During this time, I succeeded in learning to read and write. In accomplishing this, I was compelled to resort to various stratagems. I had no regular teacher. My mistress, who had kindly commenced to instruct me, had, in compliance with the advice and direction of her husband, not only ceased to instruct, but had set her face against my being instructed by anyone else. It is due, however, to my mistress to say of her, that she did not adopt this course of treatment immediately. She at first lacked the depravity indispensable to shutting me up in mental darkness. It was at least necessary for her to have some training in the exercise of irresponsible power, to make her equal to the task of treating me as though I were a brute.

My mistress was, as I have said, a kind and tender-hearted woman; and in the simplicity of her soul she commenced, when I first went to live with her, to treat me as she supposed one human being ought to treat another. In entering upon the duties of a slaveholder, she did not seem to perceive that I sustained to her the relation of a mere chattel, and that for her to treat me as a human being was not only wrong, but dangerously so. Slavery proved as injurious to her as it did to me. When I went there, she was a pious, warm, and tender-hearted woman. There was no sorrow or suffering for which she had not a tear. She had bread for the hungry, clothes for the naked, and comfort for every mourner that came within her reach. Slavery soon proved its ability to divest her of these heavenly qualities. Under its influence, the tender heart became stone, and the lamb-like disposition gave way to one of tiger-like fierceness. The first step in her downward course was in her ceasing to instruct me. She now commenced to practice her husband's precepts. She finally became even more violent in her opposition than her husband himself. She was not satisfied with simply doing as well as he had commanded; she seemed anxious to do better. Nothing seemed to make her more angry than to see me with a newspaper. She seemed to think that here lay the danger. I have had her rush at me with a face made all up of fury, and snatch from me a newspaper, in a manner that fully revealed her apprehension. She was an apt woman; and a little experience soon demonstrated, to her satisfaction, that education and slavery were incompatible with each other.

From this time I was most narrowly watched. If I was in a separate room any considerable length of time, I was sure to be suspected of having a book, and was at once called to give an account of myself. All this, however, was too late. The first step had been taken. Mistress, in teaching me the alphabet, had given me the *inch*, and no precaution could prevent me from taking the *ell*.

The plan which I adopted, and the one by which I was most successful, was that of making friends of all the little white boys whom I met in the street. As many of these as I could, I converted into teachers. With their kindly aid, obtained at different times and in different places, I finally succeeded in learning to read. When I was sent to errands, I always took my book with me, and by doing one part of my errand quickly, I found time to get a lesson before my return. I used also to carry bread with me, enough of which was always in the house, and to which I was always welcome; for I was much better off in this regard than many of the poor white children in our neighborhood. This bread I used to bestow upon the hungry little urchins, who, in return, would give me that more valuable bread of knowledge. I am strongly tempted to give the names of two or three of those little boys, as a testimonial of the gratitude and affection I bear them; but prudence forbids — not that it would injure me, but it might embarrass them; for it is almost an unpardonable offense to teach slaves to read in this Christian country. It is enough to say of the dear little fellows, that they lived on Philpot Street, very near Durgin and Bailey's ship-yard. I used to talk this matter of slavery over with them. I would sometimes say to them, I wished I could be as free as they would be when they got to be men. "You will be free as soon as you are twenty-one, *but I am a slave for life!* Have not I as good a right to be free as you have?" These words used to trouble them; they would express for me the liveliest sympathy, and console me with the hope that something would occur by which I might be free.

I was now about twelve years old, and the thought of being *a slave for*   5
life began to bear heavily upon my heart. Just about this time, I got hold of a book entitled *The Columbian Orator.* Every opportunity I got, I used to read this book. Among much of other interesting matter, I found in it a dialogue between a master and his slave. The slave was represented as having run away from his master three times. The dialogue represented the conversation which took place between them, when the slave was retaken the third time. In this dialogue, the whole argument in behalf of slavery was brought forward by the master, all of which was disposed of by the slave. The slave was made to say some very smart as well as impressive things in reply to his master — things which had the desired though unexpected effect; for the conversation resulted in the voluntary emancipation of the slave on the part of the master.

In the same book, I met with one of Sheridan's[1] mighty speeches on and in behalf of Catholic emancipation. These were choice documents to me. I read them over and over again with unabated interest. They gave tongue to interesting thoughts of my own soul, which had frequently flashed through my mind, and died away for want of utterance. The moral which I gained from the dialogue was the power of truth over the conscience of even a slaveholder. What I got from Sheridan was a bold denunciation of slavery, and a powerful vindication of human rights. The reading of these documents enabled me to utter my thoughts, and to meet the arguments brought forward to sustain slavery; but while they relieved me of one difficulty, they brought on another even more painful than the one of which I was relieved. The more I read, the more I was led to abhor and detest my enslavers. I could regard them in no other light than a band of successful robbers, who had left their homes, and gone to Africa, and stolen us from our homes, and in a strange land reduced us to slavery. I loathed them as being the meanest

---

[1] **Sheridan's:** Richard Brinsley Butler Sheridan (1751–1816), Irish dramatist and orator. — EDS.

$100 REWARD.

Ran away from my farm, near Buena Vista P. O., Prince George's County, Maryland, on the first day of April, 1855, my servant MATHEW TURNER.

He is about five feet six or eight inches high; weighs from one hundred and sixty to one hundred and eighty pounds; he is very black, and has a remarkably thick upper lip and neck; looks as if his eyes are half closed; walks slow, and talks and laughs loud.

I will give One Hundred Dollars reward to whoever will secure him in jail, so that I get him again, no matter where taken.

MARCUS DU VAL.

BUENA VISTA P O., MD.,
MAY 10, 1855.

1855 advertisement to capture a runaway slave.

as well as the most wicked of men. As I read and contemplated the subject, behold! that very discontentment which Master Hugh had predicted would follow my learning to read had already come, to torment and sting my soul to unutterable anguish. As I writhed under it, I would at times feel that learning to read had been a curse rather than a blessing. It had given me a view of my wretched condition, without the remedy. It opened my eyes to the horrible pit, but to no ladder upon which to get out. In moments of agony, I envied my fellow-slaves for their stupidity. I have often wished myself a beast. I preferred the condition of the meanest reptile to my own. Anything, no matter what, to get rid of thinking! It was this everlasting thinking of my condition that tormented me. There was no getting rid of it. It was pressed upon me by every object within sight or hearing, animate or inanimate. The silver trump of freedom had roused my soul to eternal wakefulness. Freedom now appeared, to disappear no more forever. It was heard in every sound, and seen in every thing. It was ever present to torment me with a sense of my wretched condition. I saw nothing without seeing it, I heard nothing without hearing it, and felt nothing without feeling it. It looked from every star, it smiled in every calm, breathed in every wind, and moved in every storm.

I often found myself regretting my own existence, and wishing myself dead; and but for the hope of being free, I have no doubt but that I should have killed myself, or done something for which I should have been killed. While in this state of mind, I was eager to hear anyone speak of slavery. I was a ready listener. Every little while, I could hear something about the abolitionists. It was some time before I found what the word meant. It was always used in such connections as to make it an interesting word to me. If a slave ran away and succeeded in getting clear, or if a slave killed his master, set fire to a barn, or did anything very wrong in the mind of a slaveholder, it was spoken of as the fruit of *abolition*. Hearing the word in this connection very often, I set about learning what it meant. The dictionary afforded me little or no help. I found it was "the act of abolishing"; but then I did not know what was to be abolished. Here I was perplexed. I did not dare to ask anyone about its meaning, for I was satisfied that it was something they wanted me to know very little about. After a patient waiting, I got one of our city papers, containing an account of the number of petitions from the North, praying for the abolition of slavery in the District of Columbia, and of the slave trade between the States. From this time I understood the words *abolition* and *abolitionist*, and always drew near when that word was spoken, expecting to hear something of importance to myself and fellow-slaves. The light broke in upon me by degrees. I went one day down on the wharf of Mr. Waters; and seeing two Irishmen unloading a scow of stone, I went, unasked, and helped them. When we had finished, one of them came to me and asked me if I were

1860 advertisement to capture a runaway slave.

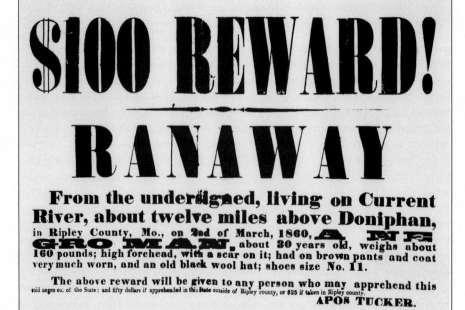

a slave. I told him I was. He asked, "Are ye a slave for life?" I told him that I was. The good Irishman seemed to be deeply affected by the statement. He said to the other that it was a pity so fine a little fellow as myself should be a slave for life. He said it was a shame to hold me. They both advised me to run away to the North; that I should find friends there, and that I should be free. I pretended not to be interested in what they said, and treated them as if I did not understand them; for I feared they might be treacherous. White men have been known to encourage slaves to escape, and then, to get the reward, catch them and return them to their masters. I was afraid that these seemingly good men might use me so; but I nevertheless remembered their advice, and from that time I resolved to run away. I looked forward to a time at which it would be safe for me to escape. I was too young to think of doing so immediately; besides, I wished to learn how to write, as I might have occasion to write my own pass. I consoled myself with the hope that I should one day find a good chance. Meanwhile, I would learn to write.

The idea as to how I might learn to write was suggested to me by being in Durgin and Bailey's ship-yard, and frequently seeing the ship carpenters, after hewing, and getting a piece of timber ready for use, write on the timber the name of that part of the ship for which it was intended. When a piece of timber was intended for the larboard side, it would be marked thus—"L." When a piece was for the starboard side, it would be marked thus—"S." A piece for the larboard side forward, would be marked thus—"L.F." When a piece was for starboard side forward, it would be marked thus—"S.F." For larboard aft, it would be marked thus—"L.A." For starboard aft, it would be marked thus—"S.A." I soon learned the names of these letters, and for what they were intended when placed upon a piece of timber in the shipyard. I immediately commenced copying them, and in a short time was able to make the four letters named. After that, when I met with any boy who I knew could write, I would tell him I could write as well as he. The next word would be, "I don't believe you. Let me see you try it." I would then make the letters which I had been so fortunate as to learn, and ask him to beat that. In this way I got a good many lessons in writing, which it is quite possible I should never have gotten in any other way. During this time, my copy-book was the board fence, brick wall, and pavement; my pen and ink was a lump of chalk. With these, I learned mainly how to write. I then commenced and continued copying the Italics in *Webster's Spelling Book*, until I could make them all without looking in the book. By this time, my little Master Thomas had gone to school, and learned how to write, and had written over a number of copy-books. These had been brought home, and shown to some of our near neighbors, and then laid aside. My mistress used to go to class meeting at the Wilk Street meeting-house every Monday afternoon, and leave me to take care of the house. When left thus, I used to spend the time in writing in the spaces left in Master Thomas's copy-book, copying what he had written. I continued to do this until I could write a hand very similar to that of Master Thomas. Thus, after a long, tedious effort for years, I finally succeeded in learning how to write.

||||||||||||||||||||||||||||||||||||||||||||||||||||||||||||||||||||||||||||||||||||||||||||||||||||||||||||||||||||||||||||||||||||||||||||||||||||||||||

The Reader's Presence

1. What sort of audience does Douglass anticipate for his reminiscence? How much does he assume his readers know about the conditions of slavery?

2. What books seem to matter most to Douglass? Why? What are his motives for wanting to read and write? For Douglass, what is the relationship between literacy and freedom? How does he move from curiosity to anguish to "eternal wakefulness" in paragraph 6? What is the relationship between learning to read and learning to write?

3. **CONNECTIONS:**   Read Azar Nafisi's excerpt from "Reading *Lolita* in Tehran" (page 511) and consider Nafisi's students' challenges in obtaining an education. What obstacles do the girls overcome to join Nafisi's class? How do the difficulties Douglass faced in getting an education compare with those of Nafisi's students?

Anne Fadiman

UNDER WATER

ANNE FADIMAN (b. 1953) is an American author and teacher. Her first book, *The Spirit Catches You and You Fall Down*, an account of an epileptic Hmong child and her family living in Merced, California, won the National Book Critics' Circle Award in 1997. She was the editor of the prestigious American literary quarterly, *The American Scholar*, for seven years, and her essays have appeared in *Harper's*, the *New Yorker*, and the *New York Times*, among many other publications. She has won national magazine awards for both reporting and essays. Her other books include *Ex Libris: Confessions of a Common Reader* (1998) and *At Large and At Small: Familiar Essays* (2007), an essay collection from which this selection is taken.

> "Books wrote our life story."

In *Ex Libris*, Anne Fadiman reflected on the role of books in her life by saying that "books wrote our life story, and as they accumulated on our shelves (and on our windowsills, and underneath our sofa, and on top of our refrigerator), they became chapters in it themselves."

I WAS AN IMPATIENT CHILD who disliked obstructions: traffic jams, clogged bathtub drains, catsup bottles you had to bang. I liked to drop twigs into the stream that ran through our backyard and watch them float downstream, coaxed around rocks and branches by the distant pull of the ocean. If they hit a snag, I freed them.

When I was eighteen, rushing through life as fast as I could, I was a student on a month-long wilderness program in western Wyoming. On the third day of the course we went canoeing on the Green River, a tributary of the Colorado that begins in the glaciers of the Wind River range and flows south across the sagebrush plains. Swollen by warm-weather runoff from an unusually deep snowpack, the Green was higher and swifter that month—June of 1972—than it had been in forty years. A river at flood stage can have strange currents. There is not enough room in the channel for the water to move downstream in an orderly fashion, so it collides with itself and forms whirlpools and boils and souseholes.[1] Our instructors decided to stick to their itinerary nevertheless, but they put in at a relatively easy section of the Green, one that the flood had merely upgraded, in the international system of whitewater classification, from Class I to Class II. There are six levels of difficulty, and Class II was not an unreasonable challenge for novice paddlers.

The Green River did not seem dangerous to me. It seemed magnificently unobstructed. Impediments to progress—the rocks and stranded trees that under normal conditions would protrude above the surface—were mostly submerged. The river carried our aluminum canoe high and lightly, like a child on a pair of broad shoulders. We could rest our paddles on the gunwales and let the water do our work. The sun was bright and hot. Every few minutes I dipped my bandanna in the river, draped it over my head, and let an ounce or two of melted glacier run down my neck.

I was in the bow of the third canoe. We rounded a bend and saw, fifty feet ahead, a standing wave in the wake of a large black boulder. The students in the lead canoe were attempting to avoid the boulder by backferrying, slipping crabwise across the current by angling their boat diagonally and stroking backward. Done right, backferrying allows paddlers to hover midstream and carefully plan their course instead of surrendering to the water's impetuous pace. But if they lean upstream—a natural inclination, as few people choose to lean toward the difficulties that lie ahead—the current can overflow the lowered gunwale and flip the boat. And that is what happened to the lead canoe.

I wasn't worried when I saw it go over. Knowing that we might capsize in the fast water, our instructors had arranged to have our gear trucked to our next campsite. The packs were safe. The water was little more than

5

---

[1] *boils and souseholes:* Terms from whitewater canoeing or rafting. Boils are small spots of agitated or swirling water; souseholes are formed by water flowing over submerged objects, usually rocks. —EDS.

waist-deep, and the paddlers were both wearing life jackets. They would be fine. One was already scrambling onto the right-hand bank.

But where was the second paddler? Gary, a local boy from Rawlins a year or two younger than I, seemed to be hung up on something. He was standing at a strange angle in the middle of the river, just downstream from the boulder. Gary was the only student on the course who had not brought sneakers, and one of his mountaineering boots had become wedged between two rocks. The instructors would come around the bend in a moment and pluck him out, like a twig from a snag.

But they didn't come. The second canoe pulled over to the bank and ours followed. Thirty seconds passed, maybe a minute. Then we saw the standing wave bend Gary's body forward at the waist, push his face underwater, stretch his arms in front of him, and slip his orange life jacket off his shoulders. The life jacket lingered for a moment at his wrists before it floated downstream, its long white straps twisting in the current. His shirtless torso was pale and undulating, and it changed shape as hills and valleys of water flowed over him, altering the curve of the liquid lens through which we watched him. I thought: *He looks like the flayed skin of St. Bartholomew in the Sistine Chapel.*[2] As soon as I had the thought, I knew that it was dishonorable. To think about anything outside the moment, outside Gary, was a crime of inattention. I swallowed a small, sour piece of self-knowledge: I was the sort of person who, instead of weeping or shouting or praying during a crisis, thought about something from a textbook (H. W. Janson's *History of Art,* page 360).

Once the flayed man had come, I could not stop the stream of images: Gary looked like a piece of seaweed. Gary looked like a waving handkerchief, Gary looked like a hula dancer. Each simile was a way to avoid thinking about what Gary *was,* a drowning boy. To remember these things is dishonorable, too, for I have long since forgotten Gary's last name and the color of his hair and the sound of his voice.

I do not remember a single word that anyone said. Somehow we got into one of the canoes, all five of us, and tried to ferry the twenty feet or so to the middle of the river. The current was so strong, and we were so incompetent, that we never even got close. Then we tried it on foot, linking arms to form a chain. The water was so cold that it stung. And it was noisy, not the roar and crash of whitewater but a groan, a terrible bass grumble, from the stones that were rolling and leaping down the riverbed. When we got close to Gary, we couldn't see him. All we could see was the reflection of the sky. A couple of times, groping blindly, one of us touched him, but he was as slippery as soap. Then our knees buckled and our elbows unlocked, and we rolled downstream, like the stones. The river's rocky load, moving invisibly beneath its smooth surface, pounded and scraped us. Eventually the current heaved us, blue-lipped and panting, onto the bank. In that other world

---

[2] ***Sistine Chapel:*** The famed ceiling of the Sistine Chapel in Rome, one of the artistic wonders of the world, was painted by Michelangelo between 1508 and 1512. The figure of St. Bartholomew appears in one of the ceiling's many panels. —EDS.

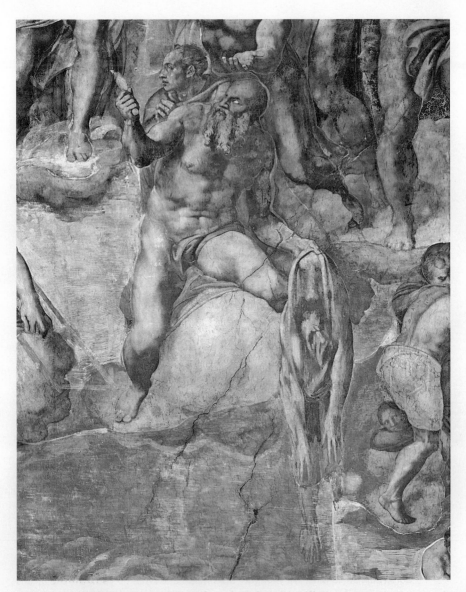

Detail from Michelangelo's famed "Sistine Chapel" showing the figure of St. Bartholomew.

above the water, the only sounds were the buzzing of bees and flies. Our wet sneakers kicked up red dust. The air smelled of sage and rabbitbrush and sunbaked earth.

We tried again and again, back and forth between the worlds. Wet, dry, cold, hot, turbulent, still.

At first I assumed that we would save him. He would lie on the bank and the sun would warm him while we administered mouth-to-mouth

10

resuscitation. If we couldn't get him out, we would hold him upright in the river; maybe he could still breathe. But the Green River was flowing at nearly three thousand cubic feet—about ninety tons—per second. At that rate, water can wrap a canoe around a boulder like tinfoil. Water can uproot a tree. Water can squeeze the air out of a boy's lungs, undo knots, drag off a life jacket, lever a boot so tightly into the riverbed that even if we had had ropes—the ropes that were in the packs that were in the trucks—we never could have budged him.

We kept going in, not because we had any hope of saving Gary after the first ten minutes but because we needed to save face. It would have been humiliating if the instructors had come around the bend and found us sitting in the sagebrush, a docile row of five with no hypothermia and no skinned knees. Eventually, they did come. The boats had been delayed because one of them had nearly capsized, and the instructors had made the students stop and practice backferrying until they learned not to lean upstream. Even though Gary had already drowned, the instructors did all the same things we had done, more competently but no more effectively, because they, too, would have been humiliated if they hadn't skinned their knees. Men in wetsuits, belayed with ropes, pried the body out the next morning.

Twenty-seven years have passed. My life seems too fast now, so obstructions bother me less than they once did. I am no longer in a hurry to see what is around the next bend. I find myself wanting to backferry, to hover midstream, suspended. If I could do that, I might avoid many things: harsh words, foolish decisions, moments of inattention, regrets that wash over me, like water. ▨

The Reader's Presence

1. Read Anne Fadiman's opening paragraph very carefully. What is its relevance to the rest of her short personal essay? What images in the paragraph will be repeated later? What would you consider the key word of the paragraph? In what ways does that word inform the entire essay?

2. At the moment of crisis, the author says she pictured a figure that appears in Michelangelo's famous ceiling painting in the Sistine Chapel in Rome (paragraph 7). Why does Fadiman consider her thought "dishonorable"? What do you think she means by a "crime of inattention"? How do these self-criticisms reappear in the essay's final paragraph?

3. **CONNECTIONS:** Compare and contrast "Under Water" with Chris Abani's "The Lottery" (page 25). Both essays depict a young person witnessing the death of someone, yet in very different circumstances. What similarities in narration do you see between the two selections? In your opinion, how differently do the authors respond to the tragic event they witnessed?

Henry Louis Gates Jr.

IN THE KITCHEN

The critic, educator, writer, and activist **HENRY LOUIS GATES JR.** (b. 1950) is perhaps the most recent in a long line of African American intellectuals who are also public figures. In 1979 he became the first African American to earn a PhD from Cambridge University in its eight-hundred-year history. He has been the recipient of countless honors, including a Carnegie Foundation Fellowship, a Mellon Fellowship, a MacArthur "genius" grant for his work in literary theory, and the 1998 National Medal for the Humanities. Gates is the Alphonse Fletcher University Professor and the director of the W. E. B. Du Bois Institute for African and African American Research at Harvard University. He has been at the forefront of the movement to expand the literary canon that is studied in American schools to include the works of non-European authors. He is also known for his work as a "literary archaeologist," uncovering literally thousands of previously unknown stories, poems, and reviews written by African American authors between 1829 and 1940 and making those texts available to modern readers. He is co-editor with Kwame Anthony Appiah of *Encarta Africana*, an encyclopedia of the African diaspora published on CD-ROM, and in print as *Africana: The Encyclopedia of the African and African American Experience* (1999); the expanded five-volume edition was published in 2005. Gates has written and produced a number of documentaries aired on public television, including *African American Lives* in 2006, and *Oprah's Roots: An African American Lives Special* in 2007, which further examined the genealogical and genetic heritage of African Americans. His latest documentary work is the four-hour sequel to *African American Lives*, which aired on PBS in February 2008.

> "I'm trying to recollect a lost era . . . a whole world that simply no longer exists."

Among Gates's more recent books are *America Behind the Color Line: Dialogues with African Americans* (2004), *The Annotated UNCLE TOM'S CABIN* (2006), and *Finding Oprah's Roots: Finding Your Own* (2007), a companion book to the PBS documentary. His most recent book, *Tradition and the Black Atlantic: Critical Theory and the African Diaspora*, was published in 2010. He also edited *In Search of Our Roots: How 19 Extraordinary African Americans Reclaimed Their Past* (2009).

|||||||||||||||||||||||||||||||||||||||||||||||||||||||||||||||||||||||||||||||||||||||||||||||||||||||||||||||||||||||||||||||||||||||||||||||||||||||||||||||||||||||||

"In the Kitchen" is taken from Gates's 1995 book *Colored People*, a memoir of his early life as part of the middle-class "colored" community of Piedmont, West Virginia. About *Colored People*, Gates says, "I'm trying to recollect a lost era, what I can call a *sepia time*, a whole world that simply no longer exists.

WE ALWAYS HAD A GAS STOVE in the kitchen, though electric cooking became fashionable in Piedmont, like using Crest toothpaste rather than Colgate, or watching Huntley and Brinkley rather than Walter Cronkite. But for us it was gas, Colgate, and good ole Walter Cronkite, come what may. We used gas partly out of loyalty to Big Mom, Mama's mama, because she was mostly blind and still loved to cook, and she could feel her way better with gas than with electric.

But the most important thing about our gas-equipped kitchen was that Mama used to do hair there. She had a "hot comb"—a fine-tooth iron instrument with a long wooden handle—and a pair of iron curlers that opened and closed like scissors: Mama would put them into the gas fire until they glowed. You could smell those prongs heating up.

I liked what that smell meant for the shape of my day. There was an intimate warmth in the women's tones as they talked with my mama while she did their hair. I knew what the women had been through to get their hair ready to be "done," because I would watch Mama do it herself. How that scorched kink could be transformed through grease and fire into a magnificent head of wavy hair was a miracle to me. Still is.

Mama would wash her hair over the sink, a towel wrapped round her shoulders, wearing just her half-slip and her white bra. (We had no shower until we moved down Rat Tail Road into Doc Wolverton's house, in 1954.) After she had dried it, she would grease her scalp thoroughly with blue Bergamot hair grease, which came in a short, fat jar with a picture of a beautiful colored lady on it. It's important to grease your scalp real good, my mama would explain, to keep from burning yourself.

Of course, her hair would return to its natural kink almost as soon as   5
the hot water and shampoo hit it. To me, it was another miracle how hair so "straight" would so quickly become kinky again once it even approached some water.

My mama had only a "few" clients whose heads she "did"—and did, I think, because she enjoyed it, rather than for the few dollars it brought in. They would sit on one of our red plastic kitchen chairs, the kind with the shiny metal legs, and brace themselves for the process. Mama would stroke that red-hot iron, which by this time had been in the gas fire for a half hour or more, slowly but firmly through their hair, from scalp to strand's end. It made a scorching, crinkly sound, the hot iron did, as it burned its way through the damp kink, leaving in its wake the straightest of hair strands, each of them standing up long and tall but drooping at the end, like the top of a heavy

Odetta Holmes Felious Gorden.

willow tree. Slowly, steadily, with deftness and grace, Mama's hands would transform a round mound of Odetta kink[1] into a darkened swamp of everglades. The Bergamot made the hair shiny; the heat of the hot iron gave it a brownish-red cast. Once all the hair was as straight as God allows kink to get, Mama would take the well-heated curling iron and twirl the straightened strands into more or less loosely wrapped curls. She claimed that she owed her strength and skill as a hairdresser to her wrists, and her little finger would poke out the way it did when she sipped tea. Mama was a southpaw, who wrote upside down and backwards to produce the cleanest, roundest letters you've ever seen.

The "kitchen" she would all but remove from sight with a pair of shears bought for this purpose. Now, the *kitchen* was the room in which we were sitting, the room where Mama did hair and washed clothes, and where each of us bathed in a galvanized tub. But the word has another meaning, and the "kitchen" I'm speaking of now is the very kinky bit of hair at the back of the head, where our neck meets the shirt collar. If there ever was one part of our African past that resisted assimilation, it was the kitchen. No matter how hot the iron, no matter how powerful the chemical, no matter how stringent the mashed-potatoes-and-lye formula of a man's "process," neither God nor woman nor Sammy Davis, Jr., could straighten the kitchen. The kitchen was permanent, irredeemable, invincible kink. Unassimilably African. No matter what you did, no matter how hard you tried, nothing could dekink a person's kitchen. So you trimmed it off as best you could.

---

[1] ***Odetta kink:*** A reference to Odetta Holmes Felious Gorden, a popular African American folk singer of the 1960s who helped popularize the hairstyle known as the "afro." —EDS.

When hair had begun to "turn," as they'd say, or return to its natural kinky glory, it was the kitchen that turned first. When the kitchen started creeping up the back of the neck, it was time to get your hair done again. The kitchen around the back, and nappy edges at the temples.

Sometimes, after dark, Mr. Charlie Carroll would come to have his hair done. Mr. Charlie Carroll was very light-complected and had a ruddy nose, the kind of nose that made me think of Edmund Gwenn playing Kris Kringle in *Miracle on 34th Street*. At the beginning, they did it after Rocky and I had gone to sleep. It was only later that we found out he had come to our house so Mama could iron his hair — not with a comb and curling iron but with our very own Proctor-Silex steam iron. For some reason, Mr. Charlie would conceal his Frederick Douglass mane[2] under a big white Stetson hat, which I never saw him take off. Except when he came to our house, late at night, to have his hair pressed.

(Later, Daddy would tell us about Mr. Charlie's most prized piece of   10 knowledge, which the man would confide only after his hair had been pressed, as a token of intimacy. "Not many people know this," he'd say in a tone of circumspection, "but George Washington was Abraham Lincoln's daddy." Nodding solemnly, he'd add the clincher: "A white man told me." Though he was in dead earnest, this became a humorous refrain around the house — "a white man told me" — used to punctuate especially preposterous assertions.)

My mother furtively examined my daughters' kitchens whenever we went home for a visit in the early eighties. It became a game between us.

Frederick Douglass.

---

2 ***Frederick Douglass mane:*** Frederick Douglass (1817?–1895), an escaped slave who became a prominent African American writer, abolitionist, and orator (see page 86). — Eds.

I had told her not to do it, because I didn't like the politics it suggested of "good" and "bad" hair. "Good" hair was straight. "Bad" hair was kinky. Even in the late sixties, at the height of Black Power, most people could not bring themselves to say "bad" for "good" and "good" for "bad." They still said that hair like white hair was "good," even if they encapsulated it in a disclaimer like "what we used to call 'good.'"

Maggie would be seated in her high chair, throwing food this way and that, and Mama would be cooing about how cute it all was, remembering how I used to do the same thing, and wondering whether Maggie's flinging her food with her left hand meant that she was going to be a southpaw too. When my daughter was just about covered with Franco-American Spaghet-tiOs, Mama would seize the opportunity and wipe her clean, dipping her head, tilted to one side, down under the back of Maggie's neck. Sometimes, if she could get away with it, she'd even rub a curl between her fingers, just to make sure that her bifocals had not deceived her. Then she'd sigh with satisfaction and relief, thankful that her prayers had been answered. No kink . . . yet. "Mama!" I'd shout, pretending to be angry. (Every once in a while, if no one was looking, I'd peek too.)

I say "yet" because most black babies are born with soft, silken hair. Then, sooner or later, it begins to "turn," as inevitably as do the seasons or the leaves turn on a tree. And if it's meant to turn, it *turns*, no matter how hard you try to stop it. People once thought baby oil would stop it. They were wrong.

Everybody I knew as a child wanted to have good hair. You could be as ugly as homemade sin dipped in misery and still be thought attractive if you had good hair. Jesus Moss was what the girls at Camp Lee, Virginia, had called Daddy's hair during World War II. I know he played that thick head of hair for all it was worth, too. Still would, if he could.

My own hair was "not a bad grade," as barbers would tell me when they cut my head for the first time. It's like a doctor reporting the overall results of the first full physical that he had given you. "You're in good shape" or "Blood pressure's kind of high; better cut down on salt." 15

I spent much of my childhood and adolescence messing with my hair. I definitely wanted straight hair. Like Pop's.

When I was about three, I tried to stick a wad of Bazooka bubble gum to that straight hair of his. I suppose what fixed that memory for me is the spank-ing I got for doing so: he turned me upside down, holding me by the feet, the better to paddle my behind. Little *nigger*, he shouted, walloping away. I started to laugh about it two days later, when my behind stopped hurting.

When black people say "straight," of course, they don't usually mean "straight" literally, like, say, the hair of Peggy Lipton (the white girl on *The Mod Squad*) or Mary of Peter, Paul and Mary fame; black people call that "stringy" hair. No, "straight" just means not kinky, no matter what con-tours the curl might take. Because Daddy had straight hair, I would have done *anything* to have straight hair—and I used to try everything to make it straight, short of getting a process, which only riffraff were dumb enough to do.

Of the wide variety of techniques and methods I came to master in the great and challenging follicle prestidigitation, almost all had two things in common: a heavy, oil-based grease and evenly applied pressure. It's no accident that many of the biggest black companies in the fifties and sixties made hair products. Indeed, we do have a vast array of hair grease. And I have tried it all, in search of that certain silky touch, one that leaves neither the hand nor the pillow sullied by grease.

I always wondered what Frederick Douglass put on *his* hair, or Phillis   20
Wheatley.[3] Or why Wheatley has that rag on her head in the little engraving in the frontispiece of her book. One thing is for sure: you can bet that when Wheatley went to England to see the Countess of Huntington, she did not stop by the Queen's Coiffeur on the way. So many black people still get their hair straightened that it's a wonder we don't have a national holiday for Madame C. J. Walker, who invented the process for straightening kinky hair, rather than for Dr. King. Jheri-curled or "relaxed" — it's still fried hair.

I used all the greases, from sea-blue Bergamot, to creamy vanilla Duke (in its orange-and-white jar), to the godfather of grease, the formidable Murray's. Now, Murray's was some *serious* grease. Whereas Bergamot was like oily Jell-O and Duke was viscous and sickly sweet, Murray's was light brown and *hard*. Hard as lard and twice as greasy, Daddy used to say whenever the subject of Murray's came up. Murray's came in an orange can with a screw-on top. It was so hard that some people would put a match to the can, just to soften it and make it more manageable. In the late sixties, when Afros came into style, I'd use Afro-Sheen. From Murray's to Duke to Afro-Sheen: that was my progression in black consciousness.

We started putting hot towels or washrags over our greased-down Murray's-coated heads, in order to melt the wax into the scalp and follicles. Unfortunately, the wax had a curious habit of running down your neck, ears, and forehead. Not to mention your pillowcase.

Another problem was that if you put two palmfuls of Murray's on your head, your hair turned white. Duke did the same thing. It was a challenge: if you got rid of the white stuff, you had a magnificent head of wavy hair. Murray's turned kink into waves. Lots of waves. Frozen waves. A hurricane couldn't have blown those waves around.

That was the beauty of it. Murray's was so hard that it froze your hair into the wavy style you brushed it into. It looked really good if you wore a part. A lot of guys had parts *cut* into their hair by a barber, with clippers or a straight-edge razor. Especially if you had kinky hair — in which case you'd generally wear a short razor cut, or what we called a Quo Vadis.

Being obsessed with our hair, we tried to be as innovative as possible.   25
Everyone knew about using a stocking cap, because your father or your

---

[3] *Phillis Wheatley* (1753?–1784): An African-born slave who became America's first major black poet. — EDS.

uncle or the older guys wore them whenever something really big was about to happen, secular or sacred, a funeral or a dance, a wedding or a trip in which you confronted official white people, or when you were trying to look really sharp. When it was time to be clean, you wore a stocking cap. If the event was really a big one, you made a new cap for the occasion.

A stocking cap was made by asking your mother for one of her hose, cutting it with a pair of scissors about six inches or so from the open end, where the elastic goes to the top of the thigh. Then you'd knot the cut end, and behold—a conical-shaped hat or cap, with an elastic band that you pulled down low on your forehead and down around your neck in the back. A good stocking cap, to work well, had to fit tight and snug, like a press. And it had to fit that tightly because it *was* a press: it pressed your hair with the force of the hose's elastic. If you greased your hair down real good and left the stocking cap on long enough—*voilà*: you got a head of pressed-against-the-scalp waves. If you used Murray's, and if you wore a stocking cap to sleep, you got a *whole lot* of waves. (You also got a ring around your forehead when you woke up, but eventually that disappeared.)

And then you could enjoy your concrete 'do. Swore we were bad, too, with all that grease and those flat heads. My brother and I would brush it out a bit in the morning so it would look—ahem—"natural."

Grown men still wear stocking caps, especially older men, who generally keep their caps in their top drawer, along with their cuff links and their see-through silk socks, their Maverick tie, their silk handkerchief, and whatever else they prize most.

A Murrayed-down stocking cap was the respectable version of the process, which, by contrast, was most definitely not a cool thing to have, at least if you weren't an entertainer by trade.

Zeke and Keith and Poochie and a few other stars of the basketball team 30 all used to get a process once or twice a year. It was expensive, and to get one you had to go to Pittsburgh or D.C. or Uniontown, someplace where there were enough colored people to support a business. They'd disappear, then reappear a day or two later, strutting like peacocks, their hair burned slightly red from the chemical lye base. They'd also wear "rags" or cloths or handkerchiefs around it when they slept or played basketball. Do-rags, they were called. But the result was *straight* hair with a hint of wave. No curl. Do-it-yourselfers took their chances at home with a concoction of mashed potatoes and lye.

The most famous process, outside of what Malcolm X describes in his *Autobiography* and maybe that of Sammy Davis, Jr., was Nat King Cole's. Nat King Cole had patent-leather hair.

"That man's got the finest process money can buy." That's what Daddy said the night Cole's TV show aired on NBC, November 5, 1956. I remember the date because everyone came to our house to watch it and to celebrate one of Daddy's buddies' birthdays. Yeah, Uncle Joe chimed in, they can do shit to his hair that the average Negro can't even *think* about—secret shit.

Nat King Cole.

Nat King Cole was *clean.* I've had an ongoing argument with a Nigerian friend about Nat King Cole for twenty years now. Not whether or not he could sing; any fool knows that he could sing. But whether or not he was a handkerchief-head for wearing that patent-leather process.

Sammy Davis's process I detested. It didn't look good on him. Worse still, he liked to have a fried strand dangling down the middle of his forehead, shaking it out from the crown when he sang. But Nat King Cole's hair was a thing unto itself, a beautifully sculpted work of art that he and he alone should have had the right to wear.

The only difference between a process and a stocking cap, really, was   35
taste; yet Nat King Cole—unlike, say, Michael Jackson—looked *good* in his process. His head looked like Rudolph Valentino's in the twenties, and some say it was Valentino that the process imitated. But Nat King Cole wore a process because it suited his face, his demeanor, his name, his style. He was as clean as he wanted to be.

I had forgotten all about Nat King Cole and that patent-leather look until the day in 1971 when I was sitting in an Arab restaurant on the island of Zanzibar, surrounded by men in fezzes and white caftans, trying to learn how to eat curried goat and rice with the fingers of my right hand, feeling two million miles from home, when all of a sudden the old transistor radio sitting on top of a china cupboard stopped blaring out its Swahili music to play "Fly Me to the Moon" by Nat King Cole. The restaurant's din was not affected at all, not even by half a decibel. But in my mind's eye, I saw it: the King's sleek black magnificent tiara. I managed, barely, to blink back the tears. ●

The Reader's Presence

1. At what point in the essay do you, as a reader, begin to become aware of the social or political significance of the hair-straightening process? At what point in his own development does Gates begin to ascribe a political significance to hair? How would you describe his attitude toward the "kitchen"? toward the "process"? toward the prominent black Americans whom he names in the essay?

2. How would you characterize the author's voice in this essay? Which words and phrases hark back to the language of his home and family? How does Gates integrate these words and phrases into the text? What difference, if any, does it make to you as a reader when he puts certain words, such as *kitchen* or *good*, in quotation marks, as opposed to the passages in which phrases (such as "ugly as homemade sin dipped in misery" [paragraph 14]) are not set off in the text in this way?

3. **CONNECTIONS:** Gates makes explicit reference to Malcolm X's description of his own first home hair-straightening process (paragraph 31). Reread that description in "My First Conk" (page 153). How do the two descriptions compare in terms of detail and tone? Are both essays staging an argument? If so, what are their main assertions, and what do they use as evidence? Might Gates's essay be read as a response to Malcolm X's admission of shame? If so, what sort of response is it?

The Writer at Work

HENRY LOUIS GATES JR. on the Writer's Voice

Skilled at critical and academic writing, Henry Louis Gates Jr. hoped to find ways to tell stories about his growing up in a small West Virginia community. In writing his memoir, *Colored People*, Gates found the voice he wanted. The following comments appeared in a 1995 collection, *Swing Low: Black Men Writing*, edited by Rebecca Carroll.

❝ My father told stories all the time when I was growing up. My mother used to call them "lies." I didn't know that "lies" was the name for stories in the black vernacular, I just thought it was her own word that she had made up. I was inspired by those "lies," though, and knew that I wanted to tell some too one day.

When I was ten or twelve, I had a baseball column in the local newspaper. I was the scorekeeper for the minor-league games in my town—I would compile all of the facts, and then the editor and I would put together a narrative. I did that every week during the summer. The best part was seeing my name in print. After that, I was hooked—hooked to seeing my name in black and white on paper.

At fourteen or fifteen, I read James Baldwin's work and became fascinated with the idea of writing. When I started reading about black people through the writings of black people, suddenly I was seized by the desire to write. I was in awe of how writers were able to take words and create an illusion of the world that people could step into—a world where people opened doors and shut doors, fell in love and out of love, where people lived and died. I wanted to be able to create those worlds too. I knew I had a voice even before I knew what a "writer's voice" meant. I didn't know what it was, but I could hear it, and I knew when my rhythm was on—it was almost as if I could hear myself write. I thought I had a unique take on the world and trusted my sensibility. It struck me that perhaps it would be a good thing to share it with other people. . . .

I don't think that the prime reason for writing is to save the world, or to save black people. I do it because it makes me feel good. I want to record my vision and to entertain people. When I was writing reviews, although it was an intriguing way to discuss literature, I would have a lot of black people say to me, "I'm having a hard time understanding you, brother." I've always had two conflicting voices within me, one that wants to be outrageous and on the edge, always breaking new ground, and another that wants to

be loved by the community for that outrageousness. It is very difficult to expect that people will let you have it both ways like that. Those who really care about a community are the ones who push the boundaries and create new definitions, but generally they get killed for doing that, which is what I mean when I refer to myself as a griot in the black community—the one who makes the wake-up call, who loves his people enough to truly examine the status quo.

The wonderful thing about *Colored People* is that everybody gets it and can appreciate it because it is a universal story. It is my segue from nonfiction to fiction. I wrote it to preserve a world that has passed away, and to reveal some secrets—not for the shock value, but because I want to re-create a voice that black people use when there are no white people around. Oftentimes in black literature, black authors get all lockjawed in their writing because they are doing it for a white audience, and not for themselves. You don't hear the voice of black people when it's just us in the kitchen, talking out the door and down the road, and that is the voice that I am trying to capture in *Colored People*. Integration may have cost us that voice. We cannot take it for granted and must preserve it whenever possible. I don't know what kind of positive language and linguistic rituals are being passed down in the fragmented, dispossessed black underclass. I think it's very different from when and where I was raised, when there was a stronger sense of community, and that language was everywhere I turned.**𝟿𝟿**

Michihiko Hachiya

FROM *HIROSHIMA DIARY*

On August 6, 1945, the United States dropped an atomic bomb on the Japanese city of Hiroshima and introduced a new, devastating weapon into modern war. Two days later, the U.S. military dropped another bomb, on Nagasaki, forcing the Japanese government into an unconditional surrender. For years, the Japanese survivors of the blasts suffered from unhealing burns, radiation poisoning, cancers, and a score of other illnesses. At first, the Japanese had no idea what had hit them, though rumors of a new secret weapon circulated rapidly. Most Americans today know of the bombing mainly through repeated images of the mushroom cloud itself; rarely do they see photographs or footage of the destruction and casualties. One of the most vivid accounts of the bombing and its immediate aftermath can be found in a diary kept by a Hiroshima physician, **MICHIHIKO HACHIYA** (1903–1980), who, though severely injured himself, miraculously found the time to record both his professional observations of a medical nightmare and his human impressions of an utterly destroyed community. Published on the tenth anniversary of the bombing of Hiroshima, *Hiroshima Diary* (1955) gained widespread attention. The diary runs only for some two months, from the moment of the blast on the sunny morning of August 6 to the end of September, when the American occupation was well under way.

> At first, the Japanese had no idea what had hit them, though rumors of a new secret weapon circulated rapidly.

 WHAT HAD HAPPENED?

August 6, 1945

Badly injured from the blast, Dr. Hachiya managed to make his way to the hospital where he served as director and which, fortunately, was quite near his house. He spent several days in bed and did not begin writing his diary until August 8. As we can see from the following passage, however, the events were still fresh in his mind.

The hour was early; the morning still, warm, and beautiful. Shimmering leaves, reflecting sunlight from a cloudless sky, made a pleasant contrast with shadows in my garden as I gazed absently through wide-flung doors opening to the south.

Clad in drawers and undershirt, I was sprawled on the living room floor exhausted because I had just spent a sleepless night on duty as an air warden in my hospital.

Suddenly, a strong flash of light startled me — and then another. So well does one recall little things that I remember vividly how a stone lantern in the garden became brilliantly lit and I debated whether this light was caused by a magnesium flare or sparks from a passing trolley.

Garden shadows disappeared. The view where a moment before all had been so bright and sunny was now dark and hazy. Through swirling dust I could barely discern a wooden column that had supported one corner of my house. It was leaning crazily and the roof sagged dangerously.

Moving instinctively, I tried to escape, but rubble and fallen timbers   5
barred the way. By picking my way cautiously I managed to reach the *rōka*[1] and stepped down into my garden. A profound weakness overcame me, so I stopped to regain my strength. To my surprise I discovered that I was completely naked. How odd! Where were my drawers and undershirt?

What had happened?

All over the right side of my body I was cut and bleeding. A large splinter was protruding from a mangled wound in my thigh, and something warm trickled into my mouth. My cheek was torn, I discovered as I felt it gingerly, with the lower lip laid wide open. Embedded in my neck was a sizable fragment of glass which I matter-of-factly dislodged, and with the detachment of one stunned and shocked I studied it and my blood-stained hand.

Where was my wife?

Suddenly thoroughly alarmed, I began to yell for her: "Yaeko-san! Yaeko-san! Where are you?"

Blood began to spurt. Had my carotid artery been cut? Would I bleed to   10
death? Frightened and irrational, I called out again: "It's a five-hundred-ton bomb! Yaeko-san, where are you? A five-hundred-ton bomb has fallen!"

Yaeko-san, pale and frightened, her clothes torn and blood-stained, emerged from the ruins of our house holding her elbow. Seeing her, I was reassured. My own panic assuaged, I tried to reassure her.

"We'll be all right," I exclaimed. "Only let's get out of here as fast as we can."

She nodded, and I motioned for her to follow me.

The shortest path to the street lay through the house next door so through the house we went — running, stumbling, falling, and then running again until in headlong flight we tripped over something and fell sprawling into the street. Getting to my feet, I discovered that I had tripped over a man's head.

"Excuse me! Excuse me, please!" I cried hysterically.   15

---

[1] *rōka:* A narrow outside hall. — EDS.

There was no answer. The man was dead. The head had belonged to a young officer whose body was crushed beneath a massive gate.

We stood in the street, uncertain and afraid, until a house across from us began to sway and then with a rending motion fell almost at our feet. Our own house began to sway, and in a minute it, too, collapsed in a cloud of dust. Other buildings caved in or toppled. Fires sprang up and whipped by a vicious wind began to spread.

It finally dawned on us that we could not stay there in the street, so we turned our steps towards the hospital. Our home was gone; we were wounded and needed treatment; and after all, it was my duty to be with my staff. This latter was an irrational thought—what good could I be to anyone, hurt as I was.

We started out, but after twenty or thirty steps I had to stop. My breath became short, my heart pounded, and my legs gave way under me. An over-powering thirst seized me and I begged Yaeko-san to find me some water. But there was no water to be found. After a little my strength somewhat returned and we were able to go on.

I was still naked, and although I did not feel the least bit of shame, I was   20 disturbed to realize that modesty had deserted me. On rounding a corner we came upon a soldier standing idly in the street. He had a towel draped across his shoulder, and I asked if he would give it to me to cover my naked-ness. The soldier surrendered the towel quite willingly but said not a word. A little later I lost the towel, and Yaeko-san took off her apron and tied it around my loins.

Our progress towards the hospital was interminably slow, until finally, my legs, stiff from drying blood, refused to carry me farther. The strength, even the will, to go on deserted me, so I told my wife, who was almost as badly hurt as I, to go on alone. This she objected to, but there was no choice. She had to go ahead and try to find someone to come back for me.

Yaeko-san looked into my face for a moment, and then, without say-ing a word, turned away and began running towards the hospital. Once, she looked back and waved and in a moment she was swallowed up in the gloom. It was quite dark now, and with my wife gone, a feeling of dreadful loneliness overcame me.

I must have gone out of my head lying there in the road because the next thing I recall was discovering that the clot on my thigh had been dislodged and blood was again spurting from the wound. I pressed my hand to the bleeding area and after a while the bleeding stopped and I felt better.

Could I go on?

I tried. It was all a nightmare—my wounds, the darkness, the road ahead.   25 My movements were ever so slow; only my mind was running at top speed.

In time I came to an open space where the houses had been removed to make a fire lane. Through the dim light I could make out ahead of me the hazy outlines of the Communications Bureau's big concrete building, and beyond it the hospital. My spirits rose because I knew that now someone would find me; and if I should die, at least my body would be found.

I paused to rest. Gradually things around me came into focus. There were the shadowy forms of people, some of whom looked like walking ghosts. Others moved as though in pain, like scarecrows, their arms held out from their bodies with forearms and hands dangling. These people puzzled me until I suddenly realized that they had been burned and were holding their arms out to prevent the painful friction of raw surfaces rubbing together. A naked woman carrying a naked baby came into view. I averted my gaze. Perhaps they had been in the bath. But then I saw a naked man, and it occurred to me that, like myself, some strange thing had deprived them of their clothes. An old woman lay near me with an expression of suffering on her face; but she made no sound. Indeed, one thing was common to everyone I saw — complete silence. . . .

PIKADON

August 9, 1945

As the wounded poured into Dr. Hachiya's hospital, the physicians tried to make sense of the symptoms and injuries, which did not resemble those of ordinary bombings. Because many of the patients with horrible symptoms showed no obvious signs of injuries, Dr. Hachiya could only speculate about what might have occurred. He had no idea as yet what type of weapon had been used against them.

Today, Dr. Hanaoka's[2] report on the patients was more detailed. One observation particularly impressed me. Regardless of the type of injury, nearly everybody had the same symptoms. All had a poor appetite, the majority had nausea and gaseous indigestion, and over half had vomiting.

Not a few had shown improvement since yesterday. Diarrhea, though, continued to be a problem and actually appeared to be increasing. Distinctly alarming was the appearance of blood in the stools of patients who earlier had only diarrhea. The isolation of these people was becoming increasingly difficult.

One seriously ill man complained of a sore mouth yesterday, and today,   30 numerous small hemorrhages began to appear in his mouth and under his skin. His case was the more puzzling because he came to the hospital complaining of weakness and nausea and did not appear to have been injured at all.

This morning, other patients were beginning to show small subcutaneous hemorrhages, and not a few were coughing and vomiting blood in addition to passing it in their stools. One poor woman was bleeding from her privates. Among these patients there was not one with symptoms typical of anything we knew, unless you could excuse those who developed signs of severe brain disease before they died.

2 *Dr. Hanaoka:* Head of internal medicine. —EDS.

Dr. Hanaoka believed the patients could be divided into three groups:

1. Those with nausea, vomiting, and diarrhea who were improving.

2. Those with nausea, vomiting, and diarrhea who were remaining stationary.

3. Those with nausea, vomiting, and diarrhea who were developing hemorrhage under the skin or elsewhere.

Had these patients been burned or otherwise injured, we might have tried to stretch the logic of cause and effect and assume that their bizarre symptoms were related to injury, but so many patients appeared to have received no injury whatsoever that we were obliged to postulate an insult heretofore unknown.

The only other possible cause for the weird symptoms observed was a sudden change in atmospheric pressure. I had read somewhere about bleeding that follows ascent to high altitudes and about bleeding in deep

People walking through the ruins of Hiroshima in the weeks following the atomic bomb blast. Photo by Bernard Hoffman.

sea divers who ascend too rapidly from the depths. Having never seen such injury I could not give much credence to my thoughts.

Still, it was impossible to dismiss the thought that atmospheric pressure   35
had had something to do with the symptoms of our patients. During my student days at Okayama University, I had seen experiments conducted in a pressure chamber. Sudden, temporary deafness was one symptom everyone complained of if pressure in the chamber was abruptly altered.

Now, I could state positively that I heard nothing like an explosion when we were bombed the other morning, nor did I remember any sound during my walk to the hospital as houses collapsed around me. It was as though I walked through a gloomy, silent motion picture. Others whom I questioned had had the same experience.

Those who experienced the bombing from the outskirts of the city characterized it by the word: *pikadon*.[3]

How then could one account for my failure and the failure of others to hear an explosion except on the premise that a sudden change in atmospheric pressure had rendered those nearby temporarily deaf: Could the bleeding we were beginning to observe be explained on the same basis?

Since all books and journals had been destroyed, there was no way to corroborate my theories except by further appeal to the patients. To that end Dr. Katsube[4] was asked to discover what else he could when he made ward rounds.

It was pleasing to note my scientific curiosity was reviving, and I lost no   40
opportunity to question everyone who visited me about the bombing of Hiroshima. Their answers were vague and ambiguous, and on one point only were they in agreement: a new weapon had been used. *What* the new weapon was became a burning question. Not only had our books been destroyed, but our newspapers, telephones, and radios as well. . . . 🔳

The Reader's Presence

1. In many ways it is fortunate that one of the diaries kept immediately after the atomic blast was written by a medical doctor. Why? How does it contribute to the diary's historical value? Could this be a disadvantage? Would you have preferred to read a patient's diary instead? Why or why not?

2. Hachiya's first entry, on August 6, was written a few days after the events it depicts. What indications do you receive from the writing that the entry was predated? Can you detect any differences from the second entry (August 9), which was apparently composed on the stated day?

---

[3] *pikadon: Pika* means a glitter, sparkle, or bright flash of light, like a flash of lightning. *Don* means a boom! or loud sound. Together, the words came to mean to the people of Hiroshima an explosion characterized by a flash and a boom. Hence: "flash-boom!" Those who remember the flash only speak of the "*pika*"; those who were far enough from the hypocenter to experience both speak of the "*pikadon*." —EDS.

[4] *Dr. Katsube:* Chief of surgery. —EDS.

3. **CONNECTIONS:**   Hachiya's confusion reveals itself in his writing in many ways: short paragraphs, multiple questions, and unconfirmed guesses. Throughout, his matter-of-fact language belies his panic. How does Hachiya's characterization of the bombing of Hiroshima compare with Don DeLillo's account of the attack on the World Trade Center (page 355)? Is a survivor's account of a disaster necessarily more vivid than that of someone who witnesses it from a distance?

Edward Hoagland
On Stuttering

EDWARD HOAGLAND (b. 1932) is an essayist, a nature writer, and a novelist. Before his graduation from Harvard University, his first novel, *Cat Man* (1956), was accepted for publication and won the Houghton Mifflin Literary Fellowship Award. He has received several other honors, including a Guggenheim Fellowship, an O. Henry Award, an award from the American Academy of Arts and Letters, and a Lannan Foundation Award. Having taught at Bennington College in Vermont for almost twenty years, Hoagland retired in 2005. Hoagland's essays cover a wide range of top-ics, such as personal experiences, wild animals,

> "Most of us live like stand-up comedians on a vaudeville stage."

travels to other countries, and ecological crises. Among his many highly regarded books are *Walking the Dead Diamond River* (1973), *African Calliope* (1979), *Balancing Acts* (1992), *Tigers & Ice* (1999), and *Hoagland on Nature* (2004). His latest book, *Early in the Season: A British Columbia Journal*, was published in 2009.

In his memoir, *Compass Points* (2001), Hoagland writes: "Most of us live like stand-up comedians on a vaudeville stage—the way an essayist does—by our humble wits, messing up, swallowing an aspirin, knowing Hollywood won't call, thinking no one we love will die today, just another day of sunshine and rain."

STUTTERING is like trying to run with loops of rope around your feet. And yet you feel that you do want to run because you may get more words out that way before you trip: an impulse you resist so other people won't tell you to "calm down" and "relax." Because they themselves may stammer a little bit when jittery or embarrassed, it's hard for a real stutterer like me to convince a new acquaintance that we aren't perpetually in such a nervous state and that it's quite normal for us to be at the mercy of strangers. Strangers are usually civilized, once the rough and sometimes inadvertently hurtful process of recognizing what is wrong with us is over (that we're not laughing, hiccuping, coughing, or whatever) and in a way we plumb them for traces of schadenfreude. A stutterer knows who the good guys are in any crowded room, as well as the location of each mocking gleam, and even the St. Francis type, who will wait until he thinks nobody is looking to wipe a fleck of spittle off his face.

I've stuttered for more than sixty years, and the mysteries of the encumbrance still catch me up: being reminded every morning that it's engrained in my fiber, although I had forgotten in my dreams. Life can become a matter of measuring the importance of anything you have to say. Is it better to remain a pleasant cipher who ventures nothing in particular but chuckles immoderately at everyone else's conversation, or instead to subject your several companions to the ordeal of watching you struggle to expel opinions that are either blurred and vitiated, or made to sound too emphatic, by all the huffing and puffing, the facial contortions, tongue biting, blushing, and suffering? "Write it down," people often said to me in school; indeed I sold my first novel before I left college.

Self-confidence can reduce a stutter's dimensions (in that sense you do "outgrow" it), as will affection (received or felt), anger, sexual arousal, and various other hormonal or pheromonal states you may dip into in the shorter term. Yet it still lurks underfoot, like a trapdoor. I was determined not to be impeded and managed to serve a regular stint in the Army by telling the draft-board psychiatrist that I wanted to and was only stammering from "nervousness" with him. Later I also contrived to become a college professor, thanks to the patience of my early students. Nevertheless, through childhood and adolescence, when I was almost mute in public, I could talk without much difficulty to one or two close friends, and then to the particular girl I was necking with. In that case, an overlapping trust was then the lubricant, but if it began to evaporate as our hopes for permanence didn't pan out, I'd start regretfully, apologetically but willy-nilly, to stutter with her again. Adrenaline, when I got mad, operated in a similar fashion, though only momentarily. That is, if somebody made fun of me or treated me cavalierly and a certain threshold was crossed, a spurt of chemistry would suddenly free my mouth and—like Popeye grabbing a can of spinach—I could answer him. Poor Billy Budd[1] didn't learn this technique (and his example

---

[1] **Poor Billy Budd:** A reference to the main character in Herman Melville's novella, *Billy Budd* (published 1924). Billy Budd's speech impediment plays a pivotal role in the plot, leading to his hanging.—EDS.

frightened me because of its larger implications). Yet many stutterers develop a snappish temperament, and from not just sheer frustration but the fact that being more than ready to "lose one's temper" (as Billy wasn't) actually helps. As in jujitsu, you can trap an opponent by employing his strength and cruelty against him; and bad guys aren't generally smart enough to know that if they wait me out, I'll bog down helplessly all over again.

Overall, however, stuttering is not so predictable. Whether rested or exhausted, fibbing or speaking the Simon-pure truth, and when in the company of chums or people whom I don't respect, I can be fluent or tied in knots. I learned young to be an attentive listener, both because my empathy for others' worries was honed by my handicap and because it was in my best interest that they talk a lot. And yet a core in you will hemorrhage if you become a mere assenter. How many opinions can you keep to yourself before you choke on them (and turn into a stick of furniture for everybody else)? So, instead, you measure what's worth specifying. If you agree with two-thirds of what's being suggested, is it worth the labor of breathlessly elaborating upon the one-third where you differ? There were plenty of times when a subject might come up that I knew more about than the rest of the group, and it used to gall me if I had held my peace till maybe closeted afterward with a close friend. A stymieing bashfulness can also slide a stutterer into slack language because accurate words are so much harder to say than bland ones. You're tempted to be content with an approximation of what you mean in order to escape the scourge of being exact. A sort of football game is going on in your head—the tacklers live there too—and the very effort of pausing to figure out the right way to describe something will alert them to how to pull you down. Being glib and sloppy generates less blockage.

But it's important not to err in the opposite direction, on the side of tendentiousness, and insist on equal time only because you are a pain in the neck with a problem. You can stutter till your tongue bleeds and your chest is sore from heaving, but so what, if you haven't anything to say that's worth the humiliation? Better to function as a kind of tuning fork, vibrating to other people's anguish or apprehensiveness, as well as your own. A handicap can be cleansing. My scariest moments as a stutterer have been (1) when my daughter was learning to talk and briefly got the impression that she was supposed to do the same; (2) once when I was in the woods and a man shot in my direction and I had to make myself heard loud and fast; and (3) when anticipating weddings where I would need either to propose a toast or say "I do." Otherwise my impediment ceased to be a serious blight about the time I lost my virginity: just a sort of cleft to step around—a squint and gasp of hesitation that indicated to people I might want to be friends with or interview that I wasn't perfect either and perhaps they could trust me.

At worst, during my teens, when I was stuttering on vowels as well as consonants and spitting a few words out could seem interminable, I tried some therapies. But "Slow Speech" was as slow as the trouble itself; and repeatedly writing the first letter of the word that I was stuttering on with my finger in my pocket looked peculiar enough to attract almost as much attention. It did gradually lighten with my maturity and fatherhood, professional recognition, and the other milestones that traditionally help. Nothing "slew" it, though, until at nearly 60 I went semiblind for a couple of years, and this emergency eclipsed—completely trumped—the lesser difficulty. I felt I simply had to talk or die, and so I talked. Couldn't do it gratuitously or lots, but I talked enough to survive. The stutter somehow didn't hold water and ebbed away, until surgery restored my vision and then it returned, like other normalcies.

Such variations can make a stutter seem like a sort of ancillary eccentricity, or a personal Godzilla. But the ball carrier in your head is going to have his good days too—when he can swivel past the tacklers, improvising a broken-field dash so that they are out of position—or even capture their attention with an idea so intriguing that they stop and listen. Not for long, however: The message underlying a stutter is rather like mortality, after all. Real reprieves and fluency are not for you and me. We blunder along, stammering—then not so much—through minor scrapes and scares, but not unscathed. We're not Demosthenes, of course. And poor Demosthenes, if you look him up, ended about as sadly as Billy Budd. People tend to.

The Reader's Presence

1. Why does Hoagland compare his stutter to a football game (paragraph 4)? Explore the metaphor fully. For example, what position does Hoagland play? Who are the tacklers who are trying to pull him down? How many touchdowns does he score in his life, according to his essay? What strategies does he develop to avoid anticipated blockers? Would you say he's winning or losing? Why?

2. In what specific ways do Hoagland's sentences and paragraphs begin and end as you might have anticipated? Can you detect written signs of his stutter? What kinds of verbal hesitations and restatements happen when someone stutters? Where—and with what effects—are there similar hesitations and restatements in Hoagland's essay? Imagine Hoagland speaking this essay. At which points do you think that he would hesitate? Rewrite a paragraph to include the imagined stuttering and compare it to the original paragraph. What changes in meaning occur in the rewritten version?

3. **CONNECTIONS:**   Read David Sedaris's "Me Talk Pretty One Day" (page 212) and compare his and Hoagland's approaches to handling difficulties with speech. What strategies do they use to deal with being less than fluent? To what extent do their limitations affect their feelings about themselves? about the world around them? Who deals more effectively with not being able to communicate easily? Why?

The Writer at Work

EDWARD HOAGLAND on What an Essay Is

Known as one of America's finest essayists, Edward Hoagland began his career writing fiction. In this passage from his Introduction to *The Best American Essays 1999*, Hoagland describes how he thinks essays work and the idiosyncratic ways essayists—like himself—approach the act of writing them. Essays, he reminds us, are different from articles and documents: They don't necessarily offer objective information and they don't require their writers to be authorities about anything other than their own experiences. All good essays, he suggests, encapsulate their writer's presence. In these literary beliefs he is a direct descendent of Montaigne (1533–1592), whom many consider the inventor of the modern essay. Montaigne, too, was skeptical of authority and wrote essays that appear to follow the drifts of an interior dialogue carried on with himself. After reading Hoagland's brief but thoughtful passage, consider how it comments on his essay on stuttering.

❝Essays are how we speak to one another in print—caroming thoughts not merely in order to convey a certain packet of information, but with a special edge or bounce of personal character in a kind of public letter. You multiply yourself as a writer, gaining height as though jumping on a trampoline, if you can catch the gist of what other people have also been feeling and clarify it for them. Classic essay subjects, like the flux of friendship, "On Greed," "On Religion," "On Vanity," or solitude, lying, self-sacrifice, can be major-league yet not require Bertrand Russell to handle them. A layman who has diligently looked into something, walking in the mosses of regret after the death of a parent, for instance, may acquire an intangible authority, even without being memorably angry or funny or possessing a beguiling equanimity. *He* cares; therefore, if he has tinkered enough with his words, we do too.

An essay is not a scientific document. It can be serendipitous or domestic, satire or testimony, tongue-in-cheek or a wail of grief. Mulched perhaps in its own contradictions, it promises no sure objectivity, just the condiment of opinion on a base of observation, and sometimes such leaps of illogic or superlogic that they may work a bit like magic realism in a novel: namely, to simulate the mind's own processes in a murky and incongruous world. More than being instructive, as a magazine article is, an essay has a slant, a seasoned personality behind it that ought to weather well. Even if we think the author is telling us the earth is flat, we might want to listen to him elaborate upon the fringes of his premise because the bristle of his narrative and what he's seen intrigues us. He has a cutting edge, yet balance too. A given body of information is going to be eclipsed, but what lives in art is spirit, not factuality, and we respond to Montaigne's human touch despite four centuries of technological and social change.❞

Langston Hughes

SALVATION

One of the leading figures of the Harlem Renaissance, **LANGSTON HUGHES** (1902–1967) was a prolific writer. He started his career as a poet, but he also wrote fiction, autobiography, biography, history, and plays, and he worked at various times as a journalist. One of his most famous poems, "The Negro Speaks of Rivers," was written while he was in high school. Although Langston Hughes traveled widely, most of his writings are concerned with the lives of urban working-class African Americans.

Hughes used the rhythms of blues and jazz to bring to his writing a distinctive expression of black culture and experience. His work continues to be popular today, especially collections of short stories such as *The Ways of White Folks* (1934), volumes of poetry such as *Montage of a Dream Deferred* (1951), and his series of vignettes on the character Jesse B. Simple, collected and published from 1950 to 1965. Hughes published two volumes of autobiography; "Salvation" is taken from the first of these, *The Big Sea* (1940).

> "I only knew the people I had grown up with, and they weren't the people whose shoes were always shined, who had been to Harvard, or who had heard of Bach. But they seemed to me good people too."

Throughout his work, Hughes refused to idealize his subject. "Certainly," he said, "I personally knew very few people anywhere who were wholly beautiful and wholly good. Besides I felt that the masses of our people had as much in their lives to put into books as did those more fortunate ones who had been born with some means and the ability to work up to a master's degree at a Northern college." Expressing the writer's truism on writing about what one knows best, he continued, "Anyway, I didn't know the upper-class Negroes well enough to write much about them. I only knew the people I had grown up with, and they weren't the people whose shoes were always shined, who had been to Harvard, or who had heard of Bach. But they seemed to me good people too."

I WAS SAVED FROM SIN when I was going on thirteen. But not really saved. It happened like this. There was a big revival at my Auntie Reed's church. Every night for weeks there had been much preaching, singing, praying, and shouting, and some very hardened sinners had been brought to Christ, and the membership of the church had grown by leaps and bounds. Then just before the revival ended, they held a special meeting for children, "to bring the young lambs to the fold." My aunt spoke of it for days ahead. That night I was escorted to the front row and placed on the mourners' bench with all the other young sinners, who had not yet been brought to Jesus.

My aunt told me that when you were saved you saw a light, and something happened to you inside! And Jesus came into your life! And God was with you from then on! She said you could see and hear and feel Jesus in your soul. I believed her. I had heard a great many old people say the same thing and it seemed to me they ought to know. So I sat there calmly in the hot, crowded church, waiting for Jesus to come to me.

The preacher preached a wonderful rhythmical sermon, all moans and shouts and lonely cries and dire pictures of hell, and then he sang a song about the ninety and nine safe in the fold, but one little lamb was left out in the cold. Then he said: "Won't you come? Won't you come to Jesus? Young lambs, won't you come?" And he held out his arms to all us young sinners there on the mourners' bench. And the little girls cried. And some of them jumped up and went to Jesus right away. But most of us just sat there.

A great many old people came and knelt around us and prayed, old women with jet-black faces and braided hair, old men with work-gnarled hands. And the church sang a song about the lower lights are burning, some poor sinners to be saved. And the whole building rocked with prayer and song.

Still I kept waiting to *see* Jesus.   5

Finally all the young people had gone to the altar and were saved, but one boy and me. He was a rounder's son named Westley. Westley and I were surrounded by sisters and deacons praying. It was very hot in the church, and getting late now. Finally Westley said to me in a whisper: "God damn! I'm tired o' sitting here. Let's get up and be saved." So he got up and was saved.

Then I was left all alone on the mourners' bench. My aunt came and knelt at my knees and cried, while prayers and song swirled all around me in the little church. The whole congregation prayed for me alone, in a mighty wail of moans and voices. And I kept waiting serenely for Jesus, waiting, waiting—but he didn't come. I wanted to see him, but nothing happened to me. Nothing! I wanted something to happen to me, but nothing happened.

I heard the songs and the minister saying: "Why don't you come? My dear child, why don't you come to Jesus? Jesus is waiting for you. He wants you. Why don't you come? Sister Reed, what is this child's name?"

"Langston," my aunt sobbed.

"Langston, why don't you come? Why don't you come and be saved?   10
Oh, Lamb of God! Why don't you come?"

Now it was really getting late. I began to be ashamed of myself, holding everything up so long. I began to wonder what God thought about Westley, who certainly hadn't seen Jesus either, but who was now sitting proudly on the platform, swinging his knickerbockered legs and grinning down at me, surrounded by deacons and old women on their knees praying. God had not struck Westley dead for taking his name in vain or for lying in the temple. So I decided that maybe to save further trouble, I'd better lie, too, and say that Jesus had come, and get up and be saved.

So I got up.

Suddenly the whole room broke into a sea of shouting, as they saw me rise. Waves of rejoicing swept the place. Women leaped in the air. My aunt threw her arms around me. The minister took me by the hand and led me to the platform.

When things quieted down, in a hushed silence, punctuated by a few ecstatic "Amens," all the new young lambs were blessed in the name of God. Then joyous singing filled the room.

That night, for the first time in my life but one—for I was a big boy   15 twelve years old—I cried. I cried, in bed alone, and couldn't stop. I buried my head under the quilts, but my aunt heard me. She woke up and told my uncle I was crying because the Holy Ghost had come into my life, and because I had seen Jesus. But I was really crying because I couldn't bear to tell her that I had lied, that I had deceived everybody in the church, that I hadn't seen Jesus, and that now I didn't believe there was a Jesus anymore, since he didn't come to help me. ◼

The Reader's Presence

1. Pay close attention to Hughes's two opening sentences. How would you describe their tone? How do they suggest the underlying pattern of the essay? How do they introduce the idea of deception right from the start? Who is being deceived in the essay? Is it the congregation? God? Hughes's aunt? the reader?

2. Hughes's essay is full of hyperbole, much of it expressing the heightened emotion of religious conversion. What is the purpose of the exclamation points Hughes uses in paragraph 2? Who is speaking these sentences? Where are other examples of overstatement? How does Hughes incorporate lyrics from songs into his prose (see especially paragraph 3)? Why not simply quote from the songs directly? How do these stylistic decisions affect your sense of the scene? Do you feel aligned with Hughes? Why or why not?

3. **CONNECTIONS:** How does Hughes use the character of Westley? Is he essential to the narrative? If so, why? How does his role compare to secondary characters in other essays—for example, Theresa in Bernard Cooper's "A Clack of Tiny Sparks" (page 78) or Shorty in Malcolm X's "My First Conk" (page 153)?

The Writer at Work

LANGSTON HUGHES on *How to Be a Bad Writer (in Ten Easy Lessons)*

Established authors are frequently asked for tips on writing. Here Langston Hughes reverses the practice and offers young writers some memorable advice on how to write poorly. "How to Be a Bad Writer" first appeared in the *Harlem Quarterly* (Spring 1950). Some of Hughes's suggestions no longer seem applicable today, thanks in part to his own literary efforts. But which lessons do you think are still worth paying attention to?

❝1. Use all the clichés possible, such as "He had a gleam in his eye," or "Her teeth were white as pearls."

2. If you are a Negro, try very hard to write with an eye dead on the white market—use modern stereotypes of older stereotypes—big burly Negroes, criminals, low-lifers, and prostitutes.

3. Put in a lot of profanity and as many pages as possible of near-pornography and you will be so modern you pre-date Pompei in your lonely crusade toward the best-seller lists. By all means be misunderstood, unappreciated, and ahead of your time in print and out, then you can be felt-sorry-for by your own self, if not the public.

4. Never characterize characters. Just name them and then let them go for themselves. Let all of them talk the same way. If the reader hasn't imagination enough to make something out of cardboard cut-outs, shame on him!

5. Write about China, Greece, Tibet, or the Argentine pampas—anyplace you've never seen and know nothing about. Never write about anything you know, your home town, or your home folks, or yourself.

6. Have nothing to say, but use a great many words, particularly high-sounding words, to say it.

7. If a playwright, put into your script a lot of hand-waving and spirituals, preferably the ones everybody has heard a thousand times from Marion Anderson to the Golden Gates.

8. If a poet, rhyme June with moon as often and in as many ways as possible. Also use *thee*'s and *thou*'s and *'tis* and *o'er*, and invert your sentences all the time. Never say, "The sun rose, bright and shining." But, rather, "Bright and shining rose the sun."

9. Pay no attention to spelling or grammar or the neatness of the

manuscript. And in writing letters, never sign your name so anyone can read it. A rapid scrawl will better indicate how important and how busy you are.

10. Drink as much liquor as possible and always write under the influence of alcohol. When you can't afford alcohol yourself, or even if you can, drink on your friends, fans, and the general public.

If you are white, there are many more things I can advise in order to be a bad writer, but since this piece is for colored writers, there are some things I know a Negro just will not do, not even for writing's sake, so there is no use mentioning them. **"**

Ha Jin

ARRIVAL

HA JIN (b. 1956) is an award-winning Chinese American author. Born Jin Xuefei, in the Liaoning province of northern China, he grew up in rural China and joined the People's Liberation Army of China at age fourteen, serving for several years along what was then the Sino-Soviet border. He left the army at nineteen and began his studies at Heilongjiang University in Harbin, China, when he was twenty-one. He received a bachelor's degree in English from Heilongjiang in 1981 and a master's degree in American literature at Shandong University in 1984. In 1985, he left China to work toward a PhD in English at Brandeis University in Massachusetts. Although his original intention had been to return to China to teach and write, he

> Ha Jin grew up in rural China and joined the People's Liberation Army of China at age fourteen.

decided to remain in the United States after the Tiananmen Square massacre in 1989. He took the pen name "Ha Jin" when he decided to write exclusively in English, and has published more than a dozen books under that name since 1990, including critically acclaimed novels as well as collections of poetry and short stories. He had only been writing in English for a dozen years when his novel *Waiting* won the National Book Award in 1999. He has also received the PEN/ Faulkner Award, the Flannery O'Connor Award for short fiction, the PEN/Hemingway Award, and the Asian American Literary Award. His most recent books include *A Good Fall* (2009), a short story collection; *A Free Life: A Novel* (2007); and *The Writer as Migrant* (2008), a book of nonfiction on writing in the migrant tradition.

Explaining how the Tiananmen Square massacre changed him, Ha Jin said, "I served in the Chinese army, and the army was called the People's Army, so we were from the people and supposed to serve the people and protect the people. I was shocked that the field armies would go into the city and really suppress civilians. Then my son arrived. That was a turning point. It was clear that he would be an American."

IN COLLEGE, English meant humiliation to me. When I was assigned to major in the language in 1977 at Heilongjiang University,[1] I knew only dozens of English words and was put in the lowest class, where I stayed four years. We were the first group of undergraduates admitted through the entrance exams after the Cultural Revolution,[2] after colleges had been closed for a decade. There was no hope for a late starter like me to catch up with the students in the faster English classes, so I kind of gave up and avoided working hard on my English. But in 1980, writers such as Hemingway, Faulkner, Bellow and Malamud suddenly became immensely popular in China after American literature had mostly been banned for three decades. I was fascinated by their fiction: Their literary subject matter was not confined to politics and social movements, as it was in China, and the techniques they used—such as stream of consciousness and multiple narrative points of view—were unheard of to me. I made up my mind to study American literature after college. For that, I would have to pass an advanced English test, so I began applying myself.

In 1982, I got into the graduate program in American literature at Shandong University,[3] but I was not a good student—at least, my professor didn't like me, probably because I married in my first year there when I was supposed to concentrate on my studies. There were only three graduate students in my year, and we had American professors teaching us most of the time. Back then, no doctoral degree in our field was offered in China, so the only way to continue my graduate work was to go abroad. Beatrice Spade, my American literature professor, encouraged me to apply to some U.S. universities, and in the winter of 1984, I started sending out applications.

The next spring, Brandeis University,[4] which I knew nothing about and which had been recommended to me by Professor Spade, notified me of my

---

[1] *Heilongjiang University:* Located in Harbin, China, the university today numbers 34,000 students. —EDS.

[2] *Cultural Revolution:* A massive political reform movement launched by Mao Zedong in 1965 mainly to suppress counterrevolutionary activities. —EDS.

[3] *Shandong University:* With some 54,000 students on a sprawling campus in Jinan, the university is one of the largest and most prestigious in China. —EDS.

[4] *Brandeis University:* A noted university in Waltham, Massachusetts, just outside Boston. —EDS.

admission and offered me a scholarship, but I wasn't very excited. I was 28, and unable to imagine living outside of China.

Since childhood, I had lived a peripatetic life, most of the time separated from my parents, so I was quite independent. But the United States was so far away and so enigmatic that ever since I had started the application, I had been possessed by a relentless emotion, as if I was about to fall ill. The previous October, Professor Spade had introduced me to a group of top American scholars in a delegation that visited our university. They were staying at a hotel in Jinan City, and I spoke with Professor Alan Trachtenberg, the head of American studies at Yale, for a preliminary interview. I was a bundle of nerves, and when he asked if I had questions for him, I blurted out, "I don't know if I can survive in America." The question, more existential than literal, must have been tormenting me for months and just gushed out. Professor Trachtenberg's eyes flashed behind his glasses—he was surprised, but there was no way for me to clarify, to say that physically I could survive for sure, but that I was more concerned about my quest for a meaningful existence, which I had no idea how to accomplish in the United States.

So, I blew my opportunity with Yale. I had my scholarship from Brandeis, though, and now I had to get permission from my university to go abroad. That meant I would have a J-1 visa that required its holder to return after graduation. To me, this was no problem, as I viewed my studies in America as no more than a sojourn. Besides, the authorities, to prevent me from defecting, would not allow my wife and child to go with me, so I would have to return anyway, the sooner, the better. 5

A schoolmate, Yafei, and I were allowed to leave together. He was going to MIT to study linguistics. After mid-August, we went to Beijing to go through a few days of "the training," which was more like a formality consisting of speeches given by officials and brief introductions to the United States.

One of the officials, a squat, smiling man, told us to be careful about sexual contact with foreigners and not to catch VD, but he also said, "It's understandable if you have a fling with someone when you are there, because we are not puritans."

Everything went smoothly in Beijing, except that three days before our scheduled departure, we were informed that the plane tickets were no longer available, though our school had paid for them long before. Apparently, our tickets had been given to "more important people." Desperate, Yafei contacted a distant relative who had some pull with the airport. To get the tickets, we would have to give the man some brand-name cigarettes. His wife was fond of 555's, and we decided to offer him two cartons. I didn't smoke and had no idea where to buy foreign cigarettes, which regular stores didn't carry. Yafei, always resourceful, got them without difficulty, and we split the cost, each paying 30 yuan,[5] almost half our monthly salary. We took a bus to the man's home to hand him the bribe. He met us in the doorway

---

[5] **yuan:** Basis of Chinese currency; in 2011, a yuan was worth approximately 15 cents.—EDS.

of his apartment and gave us the plane tickets after taking the cigarettes. Though he didn't let us in, through a narrow pane of glass on a door I caught a glimpse of his wife lying in bed smoking. On our way back to our dorm, Yafei said that the woman's father was a high-ranking official. Years later, whenever I thought of going back to China, the image of the young woman with a haggard face and bedraggled hair smoking expensive cigarettes would come to mind and make me wince.

Yafei and I boarded a plane without anyone seeing us off. I had never flown before, so the shifting and tilting cityscape of Beijing viewed from the air was exhilarating. However, the Boeing had a peculiar smell that nauseated us. It was a typical American odor, sharp and artificial, like a combination of chemicals and perfumes. Even lunch, Parmesan chicken and salad, tasted strange and gave off the same awful smell. I would find it everywhere in America, even on vegetables and fruits in supermarkets, but in a week or so I would get used to it, unable to detect it anymore.

Professor Peter Swiggart, a middle-aged man with chestnut hair and a   10
roundish, good-natured face, was assigned by the international program at Brandeis to be my host, so he agreed to pick me up at Logan International Airport.

The moment I sat in the passenger seat of his car, he told me to "buckle up." I had no clue what he was talking about. He pulled his seat belt; still, I didn't know how to use mine, never having seen one in a car before. I thought to myself, *This is like a ride on a plane.* That was the only connection I could make with the seat belt. Professor Swiggart helped me push the buckle into the slot.

My graduate dormitory at Brandeis was a three-story building by the Charles River. I had two roommates. Benny was from Israel, and Hosan from South Korea. Hosan, a broad-framed man with a square face, was a second-year graduate student in the chemistry department, which had a number of Chinese students, so he spread the word among them about my arrival, probably because I was an oddity studying literature instead of science.

The next afternoon, I strolled along the Charles. The sky was clear and high, much higher than the sky in China, thanks to the absence of smog. A pudgy angler was fishing with a tallboy of beer in his hand. Behind us, Canada geese strutted and mallards waddled. A young mother and her toddler boy were tossing potato chips at the waterfowl. Soon the man caught a bass, about a foot and a half long, wriggling like crazy. He unhooked the fish, observed it for a few seconds. "Dammit, it's you again," he said, and, to my amazement, dropped it back into the water.

"You don't keep your fish?" I asked him.

"Nope."   15

"You can't eat it?" I was still baffled.

"I'm fishin' jus' for fun."

It occurred to me that people here had a different view of nature. That night, I wrote in my first letter to my best friend: "By comparison, our old land must be overused and exhausted. Nature is extraordinarily generous to America."

My roommate Benny was a first-year graduate student in Judaic studies. He was a skinny man and had a German girlfriend, Bettina, who had just arrived as a special student, doing graduate work at Brandeis for one year. At first, I thought that they both spoke English fluently, but I soon discovered that their vocabulary wasn't that rich and that they might not know more English than I did. Yet compared with theirs, my spoken English was quite shabby, partly because I had learned it mainly from books. For example, several times I introduced myself as "a freshman," assuming that the word referred to a first-year grad student as well. I couldn't understand the news on TV at all, and it took me two months to be able to follow TV shows. Some Chinese students in our dorm loved watching American wrestling, believing that the stunts, the moves, the pain were all real.

Below us, on the first floor, lived a young Indian couple, both graduate   20
students. The wife, Aparna, was tall and vivacious, specializing in social policy and management. One evening, as we were having tea in their living room, she asked me, "Why didn't you bring your wife and child with you?"

"They were not allowed to come with me," I said.

"Who didn't allow them?"

"The government."

"Why not sue your government?"

Stumped, I didn't know how to answer. But the question has stayed with   25
me since. It shook me, as I realized that democracy fundamentally meant the equality between the individual and the country. Such a thought was something few Chinese would dare to entertain.

When I left home, it was understood between my wife, Lisha, and me that I would live abroad for four years without coming back to visit her, because I was unlikely to be able to afford the airfare. Our 2-year-old son had been staying with her parents, and, right before my departure, Lisha and I went to see him; he was too young to worry about my imminent absence from his life. Even when I said goodbye, he hardly paid me any mind. After my arrival in Boston, I noticed that some Chinese graduate students had their spouses with them, so I began to figure out how to bring Lisha over. I spoke to a woman at the graduate school admissions at Brandeis, saying: "I want my wife to join me here. I miss her terribly." She didn't respond, her face wooden and her eyes dropped, as if I had asked for something beyond reason. The prolonged silence made clear that no assistance would come from her office.

Gradually, I found out that everyone who came here was entitled to have a visa for his or her spouse, but there was another difficulty, namely money. The U.S. Embassy in Beijing would demand that my wife show that I had at least $4,000 in my bank account. To earn that amount, I began working on and off campus. I started in the periodical section of the main library and learned to operate the copiers and the microfilm and microfiche machines. My fellow graduate student Dan Morris used to be a custodian at Waltham

Hospital, but now he was too busy with his studies to keep all the hours, so he split the job with me. We each worked 20 hours a week in the medical building, vacuuming floors, cleaning toilets, washing glass doors, picking up trash from the offices and keeping the parking lot clean. We wore beepers at work so that the doctors and nurses could page us if they needed help. The job was undemanding, but I often got confused. For instance, a patient once told me to keep an eye on his "burgundy station wagon" because its lock was broken. I had no idea what kind of car a station wagon was and had to ask several people about that. A physician who spoke English with a Greek accent often wiggled his forefinger to summon me over when he wanted me to change a light bulb or clean away a patch of vomit on his office floor. I hated that gesture, which at first seemed to mean that he could pull me around with just one finger. But gradually I became accustomed to it as I saw that many others used it without any condescension. Despite some twinge of discomfort, I liked the job, mainly because I could rest my mind while I worked. I had to be very careful about my time and energy. At the outset of the semester, the director of graduate studies had told me that the English department had admitted Asian PhD candidates before, but none of them had survived the intensity of the graduate work, so I had to prove that I could manage it.

For new arrivals in America, there was always the sinister attraction of money. Suddenly one could make $4 or $5 an hour, which was equal to a whole week's wages back home. If you were not careful, you could fall into the money-grubbing trap. Some Chinese students didn't continue with their graduate work because they couldn't stop making money. One fellow from Shanghai started working part time in a museum on campus but soon stopped showing up in his lab in the physics department, dropped out of graduate school within a semester, and began taking courses to learn how to sell real estate. Another in American studies, who loved teaching as a profession, could no longer write his dissertation after taking a clerical job in a bank—sometimes he put in more than 60 hours a week, the overtime even harder to resist.

One evening, as I was cleaning the front entrance of the medical building, a slender Hispanic woman carrying a baby stopped to watch me work. She was under 30, with honey-colored hair, and might have been a single mother. A moment later, she stepped closer and handed her pacifier-sucking baby to me, saying, "You like kids?" Her round eyes were glowing while a hesitant smile cracked her face.

I was perplexed but managed to say, "Sorry, I am busy now." I kept spraying Windex on the glass door. After scraping the glass clean, I observed my face in the mirror inside the men's room. I looked a bit melancholy and frazzled. But how on earth, I wondered, had that woman sensed my yearning for family? 30

My coursework and two part-time jobs kept me so busy that I rarely ate dinner. I would cook twice a week—a potful of rice or spaghetti mixed with vegetables and chicken generally lasted me a few days. Back home, I wouldn't eat chicken or beef, because, unlike pork, they had tasted strange to me. But now I just ate whatever I could get. Fortunately, in America, food was very affordable. But my eating habit soon gave me a stomachache. I went to the infirmary, and the doctor said I had developed a digestive disorder and must eat regularly, three meals a day. That was out of the question, thanks to my hectic schedule. But my stomach problem made Lisha eager to join me here.

Despite my effort to earn money for her visa, she was not sure if she would be able to come. With the help of a doctor's letter about my illness, she had obtained a three-month leave from the school where she taught, but the Chinese authorities wouldn't let her bring our child. She was having difficulty getting a passport even for herself. For two months, she went to various offices every day to ask for permission to visit me. Sometimes she swept floors and wiped desks in those places just to earn the officials' mercy so they might issue her the papers.

During my absence, she had been raising our child alone on her teacher's salary. I missed him and often looked at the photos she mailed me. I could not afford to call home, since it cost more than $3 a minute. Worse, very few families in China had a phone back then, and if I was going to call, Lisha would have to go to an office to wait for the call. When she spoke, there would be people around, listening. Once in a while, she would send me the imprints of our child's hands and feet to give me a better sense of how much he had grown. In the Boston area, I had encountered young couples from China who had their children with them, and I could see that eventually I might be able to bring my son over, too, but the first step was to get his mother out.

However, even after Lisha got her passport, she began having second thoughts about leaving our son behind and coming alone. In her letters, she even bragged teasingly about how orderly her life had become without me around and said that, as we had planned, she could manage without seeing me for four years. I assured her that our family would be reunited in time, but she should come over first. She was worried about her lack of English, as well, and I told her that she could easily learn it once she was here. I also wrote her about American amenities: She could take a hot shower at home every day; she could do laundry in a washer and dryer, no need to hand-launder anything; and she needn't burn honeycomb briquettes to cook, as electric and gas stoves were commonplace in America. What's more, the air here was so fresh and clean that your collar didn't get black even after you wore a white shirt for days, and that you needn't wipe your shoes.

After a few more exchanges of letters, she finally decided to come once 35 I had earned the $4,000.

At the end of the semester, I completed my four courses with decent grades, which convinced the department of my ability. Then, one evening, my friend Jia-yang, a first-year graduate student in the biology department, came by to ask if he could borrow $1,000 from me, saying that his wife was going to apply for a visa, and he needed enough money in his bank account. I was stupefied, as it had never crossed my mind that I could have borrowed cash from friends, perhaps because it was such a big sum. I lent Jia-yang the money, and he promised to lend me some when Lisha began her application. And, two months later, he did. Now Lisha and I wouldn't have to wait for long to be together again, for me to show her my new American life. ▪

The Reader's Presence

1. Before coming to the United States to study, Jin worried whether he could survive in America. "Arrival" is an account of his survival. What did Jin worry about mostly? For example, what do you think he means when he writes "that physically I could survive for sure, but . . . I was more concerned about my quest for a meaningful existence, which I had no idea how to accomplish in the United States" (paragraph 4)? Based on Jin's essay, do you think Jin achieves "a meaningful existence" in America? Why or why not?

2. At one point in his essay, Jin suggests that he never forgot an image associated with the bribe he was forced to make to obtain his plane ticket: "Years later, whenever I thought of going back to China, the image of the young woman with a haggard face and bedraggled hair smoking expensive cigarettes would come to mind and make me wince" (paragraph 8). Why do you think that image affected Jin so powerfully? How is it associated with his native country?

3. **CONNECTIONS:** Compare Jin's "Arrival" with Dinaw Mengestu's "Home at Last" (page 170). What immigrant experiences do you find similar in each selection? Of what importance, for example, is the role of family for each writer?

Jamaica Kincaid

THE ESTRANGEMENT

Born in Antigua in 1949, JAMAICA KINCAID moved to the United States at seventeen to work as an au pair in New York. Although she is known primarily for her fiction, Kincaid is by no means a stranger to nonfiction: she began her writing career as a journalist, penning articles for the *Village Voice* and *Ingenue* magazines. In 1976, she became a staff writer for the *New Yorker*, a position she kept for nine years. Her first book of fiction, a collection of unified short stories centering on

> Born in Antigua in 1949, Jamaica Kincaid moved to the United States at seventeen to work as an au pair in New York.

the coming of age of a Caribbean girl and titled *At the Bottom of the River* (1983), won the Morton Darwen Zabel Award of the American Academy of Arts and Letters and was nominated for the PEN/Faulkner Award. Her first novel, *Annie John* (1985), was a finalist for the

||||||||||||||||||||||||||||||||||||||||||||||||||||||||||||||||||||||||||||||||||||||||||||||||||||||||||||||||||||||||||||||||||||||||||||||||||||||||||||||||||||||||||||||

1985 international Ritz Paris Hemingway Award. Her 1996 book, *The Autobiography of My Mother*, was a finalist for the PEN/Faulkner Award. Her most recent book, *Among Flowers: A Walk in the Himalaya*, was published in 2005. She teaches literature and creative writing at Claremont McKenna College, in Claremont, California.

THREE YEARS before my mother died, I decided not to speak to her again. And why? During a conversation over the telephone, she had once again let me know that my accomplishments — becoming a responsible and independent woman — did not amount to very much, that the life I lived was nothing more than a silly show, that she truly wished me dead. I didn't disagree. I didn't tell her that it would be just about the best thing in the world not to hear this from her.

And so, after that conversation, I never spoke to her, said a word to her of any kind, and then she died and her death was a shock to me, not because I would miss her presence and long for it, but because I could not believe that such a presence could ever be stilled.

For many years and many a time, her children, of which I was the only female, wondered what would happen to her, as we wondered what would happen to us; because she seemed to us not a mother at all but a God, not a Goddess but a God.

How to explain in this brief space what I mean? When we were children and in need of a mother's love and care, there was no better mother to provide such an ideal entity. When we were adolescents, and embracing with adolescent certainty our various incarnations, she could see through the thinness of our efforts, she could see through the emptiness of our aspirations; when we fell apart, there she was, bringing us dinner in jail or in a hospital ward, cold compresses for our temples, or just standing above us as we lay flat on our backs in bed. That sort of mother is God.

Her death was a shock, not because I would miss her, but because I   5
could not believe such a presence could be stilled.

I am the oldest, by 9, 11, and 13 years, of four children. My three brothers and I share only our mother; they have the same father, I have a different one. I knew their father very well, better than they did, but I did not know my own. (When I was seven months in her womb, my mother quarreled with the man with whom she had conceived me and then ran away with the money he had been saving up to establish a little business for himself. He never forgave her.) I didn't mind not knowing my real father, because in the place I am from, Antigua, when people love you, your blood relationship to them is not necessarily the most important component. My mother's husband, the father of my brothers, loved me, and his love took on the shape of a father's love: he told me about himself when he was a boy and the things he loved to do and the ways in which his life changed for better and worse, giving me some idea about how he came to be himself, my father, the father of my brothers, the person married to my mother.

She was a very nice person, apparently; that is what everybody said about her at her funeral. There were descriptions of her good and selfless deeds, kindnesses, generosity, testaments of her love expressed in humor. We, her children, looked at one another in wonder then, for such a person as described was not at all known to us. The person we knew, our Mother, said horrible things to us more often than not.

The youngest of my three brothers died of AIDS when he was 33 years of age. In the years he spent actively dying, our mother tended to him with the greatest tenderness that was absent all the time before he was dying. Before he got sick, before he became afflicted with that disease, his mother, my mother too, quarreled with him and disparaged him. This was enabled by the fact that he did not know how to go off somewhere and make a home of any kind for himself. Yes, he had been unable to move out into the world, away from this woman, his mother, and become the sole possessor of his own destiny, with all the loss and gain that this implies.

The two remaining brothers and I buried her right next to him, and we were not sure we should have done that: for we didn't know even now, if he wanted to spend eternity lying beside her, since we were sure we would rather be dead than spend eternity lying next to her.

Is this clear? It is to me right now as I write it: I would rather be dead   10
than spend eternity with our mother! And do I really mean that when I say it? Yes, I really mean just that: after being my mother's daughter, I would rather be dead than spend eternity with her.

By the time my mother died, I was not only one of her four children, I had become the mother of two children: a girl and then a boy. This was bliss, my two children in love with me, and I with them. Nothing has gone wrong, as far as I can see, but tears have been shed over my not being com-pletely enthusiastic about going to a final basketball game in a snowstorm, or saying something I should have kept in my mind's mouth. A particularly unforgivable act in my children's eyes is a book's dedication I made to them; it read: "With blind, instinctive, and confused love to Annie and Harold, who from time to time are furiously certain that the only thing standing between them and a perfect union with their mother is the garden, and from time to time, they are correct."[1]

I wrote this with a feeling of overbrimming love for them, my children. I was not thinking of my own mother directly, not thinking of her at all con-sciously at that exact time, but then again, I am always thinking of my mother; I believe every action of a certain kind that I make is completely influenced by her, completely infused with her realness, her existence in my life.

I am now middle-aged (59 years of age); I not only hope to live for a very long time after this, I will be angry in eternity if this turns out not to be the case. And so in eternity will my children want to be with me? And in eternity will I, their mother, want to be with them?

In regard to my children, eternity is right now, and I always want to be with them. In regard to my mother, my progenitor, eternity is beyond now,

[1] Kincaid is a dedicated gardener and has written several books on gardening. —EDS.

and is that not forever? I will not speak to her again in person, of that I am certain, but I am not sure that I will never speak to her again. For in eternity is she in me, and are even my children speaking to her? I do not know, I do not know. ▨

The Reader's Presence

1. Note how frequently Kincaid uses repetition in her brief essay—for example, the repetition of the word "eternity" toward the end of the selection. How does her use of repetition throughout the essay affect your response? Select a paragraph to read aloud. How would you describe Kincaid's tone of voice? For example, how would you interpret her tone of voice in her final sentence, which is also deliberately repetitive?

2. When Kincaid writes that she "would rather be dead than spend eternity with our mother" (paragraph 10), what do you think she means? In what way is that remark puzzling? How do you interpret it?

3. **CONNECTIONS:**   Kincaid wrote this essay for a magazine in 2009; compare it with her miniature, one-paragraph short story "Girl" (page 894), published in 1978. Based on this essay, do you think the story is autobiographical? In what ways does the story inform the essay?

Geeta Kothari

IF YOU ARE WHAT YOU EAT, THEN WHAT AM I?

Writer and educator **GEETA KOTHARI** (b. 1962) was born in New York City of Indian parents whose "back home" was New Delhi, India. Kothari is the fiction editor of the literary journal the *Kenyon Review* and teaches at the University of Pittsburgh. She is a two-time recipient of the fellowship in literature from the Pennsylvania Council on the Arts and the editor of an anthology, *Did My Mama Like to Dance? and Other Stories about Mothers and Daughters* (1994). Her fiction and nonfiction

> Geeta Kothari is a two-time recipient of the fellowship in literature from the Pennsylvania Council on the Arts.

work has appeared in a number of journals, including the *Massachusetts Review* and *Fourth Genre*. Her essay "If You Are What You Eat, Then What Am I?" was first published in the *Kenyon Review* in 1999 and was selected for the *Best American Essays 2000*.

Kothari clearly understands the relationship among culture, family, and food and "the tacit codes of the people you live with," as the Michael Ignatieff quotation that opens the essay underscores.

> *To belong is to understand the tacit codes of the people you live with.*
> —*MICHAEL IGNATIEFF, Blood and Belonging*

I

THE FIRST TIME my mother and I open a can of tuna, I am nine years old. We stand in the doorway of the kitchen, in semi-darkness, the can tilted toward daylight. I want to eat what the kids at school eat: bologna, hot dogs, salami—foods my parents find repugnant because they contain pork and meat by-products, crushed bone and hair glued together by chemicals and fat. Although she has never been able to tolerate the smell of fish, my mother buys the tuna, hoping to satisfy my longing for American food.

Indians, of course, do not eat such things.

The tuna smells fishy, which surprises me because I can't remember anyone's tuna sandwich actually smelling like fish. And the tuna in those sandwiches doesn't look like this, pink and shiny, like an internal organ. In fact, this looks similar to the bad foods my mother doesn't want me to eat. She is silent, holding her face away from the can while peering into it like a half-blind bird.

"What's wrong with it?" I ask.

She has no idea. My mother does not know that the tuna everyone else's   5
mothers made for them was tuna *salad*.

"Do you think it's botulism?"

I have never seen botulism, but I have read about it, just as I have read about but never eaten steak and kidney pie.

There is so much my parents don't know. They are not like other parents, and they disappoint me and my sister. They are supposed to help us negotiate the world outside, teach us the signs, the clues to proper behavior: what to eat and how to eat it.

We have expectations, and my parents fail to meet them, especially my mother, who works full time. I don't understand what it means, to have a mother who works outside and inside the home; I notice only the ways in which she disappoints me. She doesn't show up for school plays. She doesn't make chocolate-frosted cupcakes for my class. At night, if I want her attention, I have to sit in the kitchen and talk to her while she cooks the evening meal, attentive to every third or fourth word I say.

We throw the tuna away. This time my mother is disappointed. I go   10
to school with tuna eaters. I see their sandwiches, yet cannot explain the

discrepancy between them and the stinking, oily fish in my mother's hand. We do not understand so many things, my mother and I.

II

On weekends, we eat fried chicken from Woolworth's on the back steps of my father's first-floor office in Murray Hill. The back steps face a small patch of garden—hedges, a couple of skinny trees, and gravel instead of grass. We can see the back windows of the apartment my parents and I lived in until my sister was born. There, the doorman watched my mother, several months pregnant and wearing a sari, slip on the ice in front of the building.

My sister and I pretend we are in the country, where our American friends all have houses. We eat glazed doughnuts, also from Woolworth's, and french fries with catsup.

III

My mother takes a catering class and learns that Miracle Whip and mustard are healthier than mayonnaise. She learns to make egg salad with chopped celery, deviled eggs with paprika, a cream cheese spread with bits of fresh ginger and watercress, chicken liver pâté, and little brown and white checkerboard sandwiches that we have only once. She makes chicken *à la king* in puff pastry shells and eggplant parmesan. She acquires smooth wooden paddles, whose purpose is never clear, two different egg slicers, several wooden spoons, icing tubes, cookie cutters, and an electric mixer.

IV

I learn to make tuna salad by watching a friend. My sister never acquires a taste for it. Instead, she craves:

    bologna
    hot dogs
    bacon
    sausages

and a range of unidentifiable meat products forbidden by my parents. Their restrictions are not about sacred cows, as everyone around us assumes; in a pinch, we are allowed hamburgers, though lamb burgers are preferable. A "pinch" means choosing not to draw attention to ourselves as outsiders, impolite visitors who won't eat what the host serves. But bologna is still taboo.

V

Things my sister refuses to eat: butter, veal, anything with *jeera*.[1] The babysit- 15
ter tries to feed her butter sandwiches, threatens her with them, makes her
cry in fear and disgust. My mother does not disappoint her; she does not
believe in forcing us to eat, in using food as a weapon. In addition to pbj, my
sister likes pasta and marinara sauce, bologna and Wonder bread (when she
can get it), and fried egg sandwiches with turkey, cheese, and horseradish.
Her tastes, once established, are predictable.

VI

When we visit our relatives in India, food prepared outside the house is
carefully monitored. In the hot, sticky monsoons in New Delhi and Bombay,
we cannot eat ice cream, salad, cold food, or any fruit that can't be peeled.
Definitely no meat. People die from amoebic dysentery, unexplained fevers,
strange boils on their bodies. We drink boiled water only, no ice. No sweets
except for jalebi, thin fried twists of dough in dripping hot sugar syrup. If
we're caught outside with nothing to drink, Fanta, Limca, Thums Up (after
Coca-Cola is thrown out by Mr. Gandhi) will do. Hot tea sweetened with
sugar, served with thick creamy buffalo milk, is preferable. It should be
boiled, to kill the germs on the cup.

My mother talks about "back home" as a safe place, a silk cocoon frozen
in time where we are sheltered by family and friends. Back home, my sister
and I do not argue about food with my parents. Home is where they know all
the rules. We trust them to guide us safely through the maze of city streets
for which they have no map, and we trust them to feed and take care of us,
the way parents should.

Finally, though, one of us will get sick, hungry for the food we see our
cousins and friends eating, too thirsty to ask for a straw, too polite to insist
on properly boiled water.

At my uncle's diner in New Delhi, someone hands me a plate of aloo
tikki, fried potato patties filled with mashed channa dal[2] and served with
a sweet and sour chutney. The channa, mixed with hot chilies and spices,
burned my tongue and throat. I reach for my Fanta, discard the paper straw,
and gulp the sweet orange soda down, huge draughts that sting rather than
soothe.

When I throw up later that day (or is it the next morning, when a stom- 20
achache wakes me up from deep sleep?), I cry over the frustration of being
singled out, not from the pain my mother assumes I'm feeling as she holds

---

[1] *jeera:* Cumin.—EDS.
[2] *channa dal:* A dish made of the split kernel of beans in the chickpea family.—EDS.

my hair back from my face. The taste of orange lingers in my mouth, and I remember my lips touching the cold glass of the Fanta bottle.

At that moment, more than anything, I want to be like my cousins.

VII

In New York, at the first Indian restaurant in our neighborhood, my father orders with confidence, and my sister and I play with the silverware until the steaming plates of lamb biryani[3] arrive.

What is Indian food? my friends ask, their noses crinkling up.

Later, this restaurant is run out of business by the new Indo-Pak-Bangladeshi combinations up and down the street, which serve similar food. They use plastic cutlery and Styrofoam cups. They do not distinguish between North and South Indian cooking, or between Indian, Pakistani, and Bangladeshi cooking, and their customers do not care. The food is fast, cheap, and tasty. Dosa, a rice flour crepe stuffed with masala[4] potato, appears on the same trays as chicken makhani.[5]

Now my friends want to know, Do you eat curry at home?   25

One time, my mother makes lamb vindaloo[6] for guests. Like dosa, this is a South Indian dish, one that my Punjabi mother has to learn from a cookbook. For us, she cooks everyday food—yellow dal, rice, chapati, bhaji. Lentils, rice, bread, and vegetables. She has never referred to anything on our table as "curry" or "curried," but I know she has made chicken curry for guests. Vindaloo, she explains, is a curry too. I understand, then, that curry is a dish created for guests, outsiders, a food for people who eat in restaurants.

VIII

I have inherited brown eyes, black hair, a long nose with a crooked bridge, and soft teeth with thin enamel. I am in my twenties, moving to a city far from my parents, before it occurs to me that jeera, the spice my sister avoids, must have an English name. I have to learn that haldi = turmeric, methi = fenugreek. What to make with fenugreek, I do not know. My grandmother used to make methi roti[7] for our breakfast, corn bread with fresh fenugreek leaves served with a lump of homemade butter. No one makes it now that she's gone, though once in a while my mother will get a craving for it and produce a facsimile ("The corn meal here is wrong") that only highlights what she's really missing: the smells and tastes of her mother's house.

---

3 *lamb biryani:* A dish made of lamb, spices, basmati rice, and yogurt. —EDS.
4 *masala:* A blend of spices common to Indian food, often includes cinnamon, cardamom, cumin, caraway, and many others. —EDS.
5 *chicken makhani:* A dish combining chicken with a butter-based tomato sauce. —EDS.
6 *lamb vindaloo:* A spicy marinated lamb dish. —EDS.
7 *roti:* A round puffy flatbread. —EDS.

I will never make my grandmother's methi roti or even my mother's unsatisfactory imitation of it. I attempt chapati:[8] it takes six hours, three phone calls home, and leaves me with an aching back. I have to write translations down: jeera = cumin. My memory is unreliable. But I have always known garam = hot.

IX

My mother learns how to make brownies and apple pie. My father makes only Indian food, except for loaves of heavy, sweet, brown bread that I eat with thin slices of American cheese and lettuce. The recipe is a secret, passed on to him by a woman at work. Years later, when he finally gives it to me, when I ask for it, I end up with three bricks of gluten that even the birds and my husband won't eat.

X

My parents send me to boarding school, outside of London. They imag-   30
ine that I will overcome my shyness and find a place for myself in this all-girls' school. They have never lived in England, but as former subjects of the British Empire, they find London familiar, comfortable in a way New York—my mother's home for over twenty years by now—is not. Americans still don't know what to call us; their Indians live on reservations, not in Manhattan. Because they understand the English, my parents believe the English understand us.

I poke at my first school lunch—thin, overworked pastry in a puddle of lumpy gravy. The lumps are chewy mushrooms, maybe, or overcooked shrimp.

"What is this?" I don't want to ask, but I can't go on eating without knowing.

"Steak and kidney pie."

The girl next to me, red-haired, freckled, watches me take a bite from my plate. She has been put in charge of me, the new girl, and I follow her around all day, a foreigner at the mercy of a reluctant and angry tour guide. She is not used to explaining what is perfectly and utterly natural.

"What, you've never had steak and kidney pie? Bloody hell."   35

My classmates scoff, then marvel, then laugh at my ignorance. After a year, I understand what is on my plate: sausage rolls, blood pudding, Spam, roast beef in a thin, greasy gravy, all the bacon and sausage I could possibly want. My parents do not expect me to starve.

The girls at school expect conformity; it has been bred into them, through years of uniforms and strict rules about proper behavior. I am thirteen and

---

8 ***chapati:*** A type of roti, or flatbread. —EDS.

contrary, even as I yearn for acceptance. I declare myself a vegetarian and doom myself to a diet of cauliflower cheese and baked beans on toast. The administration does not question my decision; they assume it's for vague, undefined religious reasons, although my father, the doctor, tells them it's for my health. My reasons, from this distance of many years, remain murky to me.

Perhaps I am my parents' daughter after all.

XI

When she is three, sitting on my cousin's lap in Bombay, my sister reaches for his plate and puts a chili in her mouth. She wants to be like the grown-ups who dip green chilies in coarse salt and eat them like any other vegetable. She howls inconsolable animal pain for what must be hours. She doesn't have the vocabulary for the oily heat that stings her mouth and tongue, burns a trail through her small tender body. Only hot, sticky tears on my father's shoulder.

As an adult, she eats red chili paste, mango pickle, kimchee,[9] foods that   40 make my eyes water and my stomach gurgle. My tastes are milder. I order raita[10] at Indian restaurants and ask for food that won't sear the roof of my mouth and scar the insides of my cheeks. The waiters nod, and their eyes shift—a slight once-over that indicates they don't believe me. I am Indian, aren't I? My father seems to agree with them. He tells me I'm asking for the impossible, as if he believes the recipes are immutable, written in stone during the passage from India to America.

XII

I look around my boyfriend's freezer one day and find meat: pork chops, ground beef, chicken pieces, Italian sausage. Ham in the refrigerator, next to the homemade Bolognese sauce. Tupperware filled with chili made from ground beef and pork.

He smells different from me. Foreign. Strange.

I marry him anyway.

He has inherited blue eyes that turn gray in bad weather, light brown hair, a sharp pointy nose, and excellent teeth. He learns to make chili with ground turkey and tofu, tomato sauce with red wine and portobello mushrooms, roast chicken with rosemary and slivers of garlic under the skin.

He eats steak when we are in separate cities, roast beef at his mother's   45 house, hamburgers at work. Sometimes I smell them on his skin. I hope

---

9 *kimchee:* A spicy Korean dish made of fermented cabbage and other vegetables. —EDS.
10 *raita:* A yogurt-based condiment, often including cilantro, mint, and cucumber. —EDS.

he doesn't notice me turning my face, a cheek instead of my lips, my nose wrinkled at the unfamiliar, musky smell.

XIII

And then I realize I don't want to be a person who can find Indian food only in restaurants. One day, my parents will be gone, and I will long for the foods of my childhood, the way they long for theirs. I prepare for this day the way people on TV prepare for the end of the world. They gather canned goods they will never eat while I stockpile recipes I cannot replicate. I am frantic, disorganized, grabbing what I can, filing scribbled notes haphazardly. I regret the tastes I've forgotten, the meals I have inhaled without a thought. I worry that I've come to this realization too late.

XIV

Who told my mother about Brie? One day we were eating Velveeta, the next day Brie, Gouda, Camembert, Port Salut, Havarti with caraway, Danish fontina, string cheese made with sheep's milk. Who opened the door to these foreigners that sit on the refrigerator shelf next to last night's dal?

Back home, there is one cheese only, which comes in a tin, looks like Bakelite, and tastes best when melted.

And how do we go from Chef Boyardee to fresh pasta and homemade sauce, made with Redpack tomatoes, crushed garlic, and dried oregano? Macaroni and cheese, made with fresh cheddar and whole milk, sprinkled with bread crumbs and paprika. Fresh eggplant and ricotta ravioli, packed with marinara sauce and fresh mozzarella.

My mother will never cook beef or pork in her kitchen, and the foods she 50 knew in her childhood are unavailable. Because the only alternative to the supermarket, with its TV dinners and canned foods, is the gourmet Italian deli across the street, by default our meals become socially acceptable.

XV

If I really want to make myself sick, I worry that my husband will one day leave me for a meat-eater, for someone familiar who doesn't sniff him suspiciously for signs of alimentary infidelity.

XVI

Indians eat lentils. I understand this as absolute, a decree from an unidentifiable authority that watches and judges me.

So what does it mean that I cannot replicate my mother's dal? She and my father show me repeatedly, in their kitchen, in my kitchen. They coach me over the phone, buy me the best cookbooks, and finally write down their secrets. Things I'm supposed to know but don't. Recipes that should be, by now, engraved on my heart.

Living far from the comfort of people who require no explanation for what I do and who I am, I crave the foods we have shared. My mother convinces me that moong is the easiest dal to prepare, and yet it fails me every time: bland, watery, a sickly greenish-yellow mush. These imperfect imitations remind me only of what I'm missing.

But I have never been fond of moong dal.[11] At my mother's table it is   55
the last thing I reach for. Now I worry that this antipathy toward dal signals something deeper, that somehow I am not my parents' daughter, not Indian, and because I cannot bear the touch and smell of raw meat, though I can eat it cooked (charred, dry, and overdone), I am not American either.

I worry about a lifetime purgatory in Indian restaurants where I will complain that all the food looks and tastes the same because they've used the same masala.

XVII

About the tuna and her attempts to feed us, my mother laughs. She says, "You were never fussy. You ate everything I made and never complained."

My mother is at the stove, wearing only her blouse and petticoat, her sari carefully folded and hung in the closet. She does not believe a girl's place is in the kitchen, but she expects me to know that too much hing can ruin a meal, to know without being told, without having to ask or write it down. Hing = asafoetida.

She remembers the catering class. "Oh, that class. You know, I had to give it up when we got to lobster. I just couldn't stand the way it looked."

She says this apologetically, as if she has deprived us, as if she suspects   60
that having a mother who could feed us lobster would have changed the course of our lives.

Intellectually, she understands that only certain people regularly eat lobster, people with money or those who live in Maine, or both. In her catering class there were people without jobs for whom preparing lobster was a part of their professional training as caterers. Like us, they wouldn't be eating lobster at home. For my mother, however, lobster was just another American food, like tuna—different, strange, not natural yet somehow essential to belonging.

I learned how to prepare and eat lobster from the same girl who taught me tuna salad. I ate bacon at her house, too. And one day this girl, with her houses in the country and Martha's Vineyard, asked me how my uncle was going to pick me up from the airport in Bombay. In 1973, she was surprised to

---

11 **moong dal:** A dish made of split green lentils. —EDS.

hear that he used a car, not an elephant. At home, my parents and I laughed, and though I never knew for sure if she was making fun of me, I still wanted her friendship.

My parents were afraid my sister and I would learn to despise the foods they loved, replace them with bologna and bacon and lose our taste for masala. For my mother, giving up her disgust of lobster, with its hard exterior and foreign smell, would mean renouncing some essential difference. It would mean becoming, decidedly, definitely, American—unafraid of meat in all its forms, able to consume large quantities of protein at any given meal. My willingness to toss a living being into boiling water and then get past its ugly appearance to the rich meat inside must mean to my mother that I am, somehow, someone she is not.

But I haven't eaten lobster in years. In my kitchen cupboards, there is a thirteen-pound bag of basmati rice, jars of lime pickle, mango pickle, and ghee,[12] cans of tuna and anchovies, canned soups, coconut milk, and tomatoes, rice noodles, several kinds of pasta, dried mushrooms, and unlabeled bottles of spices: haldi, jeera, hing. When my husband tries to help me cook, he cannot identify all the spices. He gets confused when I forget their English names and remarks that my expectations of him are unreasonable.

I am my parents' daughter. Like them, I expect knowledge to pass from 65 me to my husband without one word of explanation or translation. I want him to know what I know, see what I see, without having to tell him exactly what it is. I want to believe the recipes never change. ●

The Reader's Presence

1. Kothari worries in the essay whether she is "[her] parents' daughter" (paragraph 38). Why is this of concern? How is that concern related to the title of her essay? At the end of the essay, she says definitively: "I am my parents' daughter" (paragraph 65). How has she reached that conclusion in the process of writing the essay?

2. Consider the ways food relates to cultural identity. How does Kothari characterize American foods? In what ways does she enjoy them? In what ways does she find them distasteful? For example, how is her husband—who is never named—described in terms of his favorite foods? In what ways do husband and wife differ from each other? How does Kothari suggest that their culinary differences could affect their relationship?

3. **CONNECTIONS:** Read Kothari's essay in conjunction with Amy Tan's "Mother Tongue" (page 232). Though one writes about food and the other about language, discuss how each writer deals with the conflict between a family's ethnic values and its assimilation into American culture. You also might consider ethnic cuisine in contrast to American fast food as described by Eric Schlosser in "Why McDonald's Fries Taste So Good" (page 558). Do you think fast-food chains help undermine cultural heritage as it is expressed in various ethnic cuisines, such as Kothari's Indian recipes? Why or why not?

12 *ghee:* Clarified butter. —EDS.

Nancy Mairs
ON BEING A CRIPPLE

NANCY MAIRS (b. 1943) has contributed poetry, short stories, articles, and essays to numerous journals. "On Being a Cripple" comes from *Plaintext*, a collection of essays published in 1986. Her books include *Remembering the Bone House: An Erotics of Place and Space* (1989); *Carnal Acts* (1990); *Ordinary Time: Cycles in Marriage, Faith, and Renewal* (1993); *Waist-High in the World: A Life Among the Nondisabled* (1997); *A Troubled Guest: Life and Death Stories* (2001); and her most recent, *A Dynamic God: Living an Unconventional Catholic Faith* (2007). From 1983 to 1985 Mairs served as assistant director of the Southwest Institute for Research on Women, and she has also taught at the University of Arizona and at UCLA.

> **"I want a prose that is allusive and translucent."**

In *Voice Lessons: On Becoming a (Woman) Writer* (1994), she writes, "I want a prose that is allusive and translucent, that eases you into me and embraces you, not one that baffles you or bounces you around so that you can't even tell where I am. And so I have chosen to work, very, very carefully, with the language we share, faults and all, choosing each word for its capacity, its ambiguity, the space it provides for me to live my life within it, relating rather than opposing each word to the next, each sentence to the next, 'starting on all sides at once . . . twenty times, thirty times, over': the stuttering adventure of the essay."

To escape is nothing. Not to escape is nothing.
—*Louise Bogan*

THE OTHER DAY I was thinking of writing an essay on being a cripple. I was thinking hard in one of the stalls of the women's room in my office building, as I was shoving my shirt into my jeans and tugging up my zipper. Preoccupied, I flushed, picked up my book bag, took my cane down from the hook, and unlatched the door. So many movements unbalanced me, and as I pulled the door open I fell over backward, landing fully clothed on the toilet seat with my legs splayed in front of me: the old beetle-on-its-back routine. Saturday afternoon, the building deserted, I was free to laugh aloud as I wriggled back to my feet, my voice bouncing off the yellowish tiles from all directions. Had anyone been there with me, I'd have been still and faint and hot with chagrin. I decided that it was high time to write the essay.

First, the matter of semantics. I am a cripple. I choose this word to name me. I choose from among several possibilities, the most common of which are "handicapped" and "disabled." I made the choice a number of years ago, without thinking, unaware of my motives for doing so. Even now, I'm not sure what those motives are, but I recognize that they are complex and not entirely flattering. People—crippled or not—wince at the word "cripple," as they do not at "handicapped" or "disabled." Perhaps I want them to wince. I want them to see me as a tough customer, one to whom the fates/ gods/viruses have not been kind, but who can face the brutal truth of her existence squarely. As a cripple, I swagger.

But, to be fair to myself, a certain amount of honesty underlies my choice. "Cripple" seems to me a clean word, straightforward and precise. It has an honorable history, having made its first appearance in the Lindisfarne Gospel in the tenth century. As a lover of words, I like the accuracy with which it describes my condition: I have lost the full use of my limbs. "Disabled," by contrast, suggests any incapacity, physical or mental. And I certainly don't like "handicapped," which implies that I have deliberately been put at a disadvantage, by whom I can't imagine (my God is not a Handicapper General), in order to equalize chances in the great race of life. These words seem to me to be moving away from my condition, to be widening the gap between word and reality. Most remote is the recently coined euphemism "differently abled," which partakes of the same semantic hopefulness that transformed countries from "undeveloped" to "underdeveloped," then to "less developed," and finally to "developing" nations. People have continued to starve in those countries during the shift. Some realities do not obey the dictates of language.

Mine is one of them. Whatever you call me, I remain crippled. But I don't care what you call me, so long as it isn't "differently abled," which strikes me as pure verbal garbage designed, by its ability to describe anyone, to describe no one. I subscribe to George Orwell's thesis that "the slovenliness of our language makes it easier for us to have foolish thoughts."[1] And I refuse to participate in the degeneration of the language to the extent that I deny that I have lost anything in the course of this calamitous disease; I refuse to pretend that the only differences between you and me are the various ordinary ones that distinguish any one person from another. But call me "disabled" or "handicapped" if you like. I have long since grown accustomed to them; and if they are vague, at least they hint at the truth. Moreover, I use them myself. Society is no readier to accept crippledness than to accept death, war, sex, sweat, or wrinkles. I would never refer to another person as a cripple. It is the word I use to name only myself.

I haven't always been crippled, a fact for which I am soundly grateful. 5 To be whole of limb is, I know from experience, infinitely more pleasant and useful than to be crippled; and if that knowledge leaves me open to bitterness at my loss, the physical soundness I once enjoyed (though I did

---

[1] *Orwell:* From his essay "Politics and the English Language" (page 527). —EDS.

not enjoy it half enough) is well worth the occasional stab of regret. Though never any good at sports, I was a normally active child and young adult. I climbed trees, played hopscotch, jumped rope, skated, swam, rode my bicycle, sailed. I despised team sports, spending some of the wretchedest afternoons of my life, sweaty and humiliated, behind a field-hockey stick and under a basketball hoop. I tramped alone for miles along the bridle paths that webbed the woods behind the house I grew up in. I swayed through countless dim hours in the arms of one man or another under the scattered shot of light from mirrored balls, and gyrated through countless more as Tab Hunter and Johnny Mathis gave way to the Rolling Stones, Creedence Clearwater Revival, Cream. I walked down the aisle. I pushed baby carriages, changed tires in the rain, marched for peace.

When I was twenty-eight I started to trip and drop things. What at first seemed my natural clumsiness soon became too pronounced to shrug off. I consulted a neurologist, who told me that I had a brain tumor. A battery of tests, increasingly disagreeable, revealed no tumor. About a year and a half later I developed a blurred spot in one eye. I had, at last, the episodes "disseminated in space and time" requisite for a diagnosis: multiple sclerosis. I have never been sorry for the doctor's initial misdiagnosis, however. For almost a week, until the negative results of the tests were in, I thought that I was going to die right away. Every day for the past nearly ten years, then, has been a kind of gift. I accept all gifts.

Multiple sclerosis is a chronic degenerative disease of the central nervous system, in which the myelin that sheathes the nerves is somehow eaten away and scar tissue forms in its place, interrupting the nerves' signals. During its course, which is unpredictable and uncontrollable, one may lose vision, hearing, speech, the ability to walk, control of bladder and/or bowels, strength in any or all extremities, sensitivity to touch, vibration, and/or pain, potency, coordination of movements—the list of possibilities is lengthy and, yes, horrifying. One may also lose one's sense of humor. That's the easiest to lose and the hardest to survive without.

In the past ten years, I have sustained some of these losses. Characteristic of MS are sudden attacks, called exacerbations, followed by remissions, and these I have not had. Instead, my disease has been slowly progressive. My left leg is now so weak that I walk with the aid of a brace and a cane; and for distances I use an Amigo, a variation on the electric wheelchair that looks rather like an electrified kiddie car. I no longer have much use of my left hand. Now my right side is weakening as well. I still have the blurred spot in my right eye. Overall, though, I've been lucky so far. My world has, of necessity, been circumscribed by my losses, but the terrain left me has been ample enough for me to continue many of the activities that absorb me: writing, teaching, raising children and cats and plants and snakes, reading, speaking publicly about MS and depression, even playing bridge with people patient and honorable enough to let me scatter cards every which way without sneaking a peek.

Lest I begin to sound like Pollyanna, however, let me say that I don't like having MS. I hate it. My life holds realities—harsh ones, some of them—that no right-minded human being ought to accept without grumbling. One of them is fatigue. I know of no one with MS who does not complain of bone-weariness; in a disease that presents an astonishing variety of symptoms, fatigue seems to be a common factor. I wake up in the morning feeling the way most people do at the end of a bad day, and I take it from there. As a result, I spend a lot of time *in extremis* and, impatient with limitation, I tend to ignore my fatigue until my body breaks down in some way and forces rest. Then I miss picnics, dinner parties, poetry readings, the brief visits of old friends from out of town. The offspring of a puritanical tradition of exceptional venerability, I cannot view these lapses without shame. My life often seems a series of small failures to do as I ought.

I lead, on the whole, an ordinary life, probably rather like the one I would have led had I not had MS. I am lucky that my predilections were already solitary, sedentary, and bookish—unlike the world-famous French cellist I have read about, or the young woman I talked with one long afternoon who wanted only to be a jockey. I had just begun graduate school when I found out something was wrong with me, and I have remained, interminably, a graduate student. Perhaps I would not have if I'd thought I had the stamina to return to a full-time job as a technical editor; but I've enjoyed my studies.

In addition to studying, I teach writing courses. I also teach medical students how to give neurological examinations. I pick up freelance editing jobs here and there. I have raised a foster son and sent him into the world, where he has made me two grandbabies, and I am still escorting my daughter and son through adolescence. I go to Mass every Saturday. I am a superb, if messy, cook. I am also an enthusiastic laundress, capable of sorting a hamper full of clothes into five subtly differentiated piles, but a terrible housekeeper. I can do italic writing and, in an emergency, bathe an oil-soaked cat. I play a fiendish game of Scrabble. When I have the time and the money, I'd like to sit on my front steps with my husband, drinking Amaretto and smoking a cigar, as we imagine our counterparts in Leningrad and make sure that the sun gets down once more behind the sharp childish scrawl of the Tucson Mountains.

This lively plenty has its bleak complement, of course, in all the things I can no longer do. I will never run again, except in dreams, and one day I may have to write that I will never walk again. I like to go camping, but I can't follow George and the children along the trails that wander out of a campsite through the desert or into the mountains. In fact, even on the level I've learned never to check the weather or try to hold a coherent conversation: I need all my attention for my wayward feet. Of late, I have begun to catch myself wondering how people can propel themselves without canes. With only one usable hand, I have to select my clothing with care not so much for style as for ease of ingress and egress, and even so, dressing can be laborious.

10

I can no longer do fine stitchery, pick up babies, play the piano, braid my hair. I am immobilized by acute attacks of depression, which may or may not be physiologically related to MS but are certainly its logical concomitant.

These two elements, the plenty and the privation, are never pure, nor are the delight and wretchedness that accompany them. Almost every pickle that I get into as a result of my weakness and clumsiness—and I get into plenty—is funny as well as maddening and sometimes painful. I recall one May afternoon when a friend and I were going out for a drink after finishing up at school. As we were climbing into opposite sides of my car, chatting, I tripped and fell, flat and hard, onto the asphalt parking lot, my abrupt departure interrupting him in mid-sentence. "Where'd you go?" he called as he came around the back of the car to find me hauling myself up by the door frame. "Are you all right?" Yes, I told him, I was fine, just a bit rattly, and we drove off to find a shady patio and some beer. When I got home an hour or so later, my daughter greeted me with "What have you done to yourself?" I looked down. One elbow of my white turtleneck with the green froggies, one knee of my white trousers, one white kneesock were blood-soaked. We peeled off the clothes and inspected the damage, which was nasty enough but not alarming. That part wasn't funny: The abrasions took a long time to heal, and one got a little infected. Even so, when I think of my friend talking earnestly, suddenly, to the hot thin air while I dropped from his view as though through a trap door, I find the image as silly as something from a Marx Brothers movie.

I may find it easier than other cripples to amuse myself because I live propped by the acceptance and the assistance and, sometimes, the amusement of those around me. Grocery clerks tear my checks out of my checkbook for me, and sales clerks find chairs to put into dressing rooms when I want to try on clothes. The people I work with make sure I teach at times when I am least likely to be fatigued, in places I can get to, with the materials I need. My students, with one anonymous exception (in an end-of-the-semester evaluation), have been unperturbed by my disability. Some even like it. One was immensely cheered by the information that I paint my own fingernails; she decided, she told me, that if I could go to such trouble over fine details, she could keep on writing essays. I suppose I became some sort of bright-fingered muse. She wrote good essays, too.

The most important struts in the framework of my existence, of course,   15
are my husband and children. Dismayingly few marriages survive the MS test, and why should they? Most twenty-two- and nineteen-year-olds, like George and me, can vow in clear conscience, after a childhood of chicken pox and summer colds, to keep one another in sickness and in health so long as they both shall live. Not many are equipped for catastrophe: the dismay, the depression, the extra work, the boredom that a degenerative disease can insinuate into a relationship. And our society, with its emphasis on fun and its association of fun with physical performance, offers little encouragement for a whole spouse to stay with a crippled partner. Children experience similar stresses when faced with a crippled parent, and they are more

helpless, since parents and children can't usually get divorced. They hate, of course, to be different from their peers, and the child whose mother is tacking down the aisle of a school auditorium packed with proud parents like a Cape Cod dinghy in a stiff breeze jolly well stands out in a crowd. Deprived of legal divorce, the child can at least deny the mother's disability, even her existence, forgetting to tell her about recitals and PTA meetings, refusing to accompany her to stores or church or the movies, never inviting friends to the house. Many do.

But I've been limping along for ten years now, and so far George and the children are still at my left elbow, holding tight. Anne and Matthew vacuum floors and dust furniture and haul trash and rake up dog droppings and button my cuffs and bake lasagna and Toll House cookies with just enough grumbling so I know that they don't have brain fever. And far from hiding me, they're forever dragging me by racks of fancy clothes or through teeming school corridors, or welcoming gaggles of friends while I'm wandering through the house in Anne's filmy pink babydoll pajamas. George generally calls before he brings someone home, but he does just as many dumb thankless chores as the children. And they all yell at me, laugh at some of my jokes, write me funny letters when we're apart—in short, treat me as an ordinary human being for whom they have some use. I think they like me. Unless they're faking. . . .

Faking. There's the rub. Tugging at the fringes of my consciousness always is the terror that people are kind to me only because I'm a cripple. My mother almost shattered me once, with that instinct mothers have—blind, I think, in this case, but unerring nonetheless—for striking blows along the fault-lines of their children's hearts, by telling me, in an attack on my selfishness, "We all have to make allowances for you, of course, because of the way you are." From the distance of a couple of years, I have to admit that I haven't any idea just what she meant, and I'm not sure that she knew either. She was awfully angry. But at the time, as the words thudded home, I felt my worst fear, suddenly realized. I could bear being called selfish: I am. But I couldn't bear the corroboration that those around me were doing in fact what I'd always suspected them of doing, professing fondness while silently putting up with me because of the way I am. A cripple. I've been a little cracked ever since.

Along with this fear that people are secretly accepting shoddy goods comes a relentless pressure to please—to prove myself worth the burdens I impose, I guess, or to build a substantial account of good will against which I may write drafts in times of need. Part of the pressure arises from social expectations. In our society, anyone who deviates from the norm had better find some way to compensate. Like fat people, who are expected to be jolly, cripples must bear their lot meekly and cheerfully. A grumpy cripple isn't playing by the rules. And much of the pressure is self-generated. Early on I vowed that, if I had to have MS, by God I was going to do it well. This is a class act, ladies and gentlemen. No tears, no recriminations, no faint-heartedness.

One way and another, then, I wind up feeling like Tiny Tim,[2] peering over the edge of the table at the Christmas goose, waving my crutch, piping down God's blessing on us all. Only sometimes I don't want to play Tiny Tim; I'd rather be Caliban,[3] a most scurvy monster. Fortunately, at home no one much cares whether I'm a good cripple or a bad cripple as long as I make vichyssoise with fair regularity. One evening several years ago, Anne was reading at the dining-room table while I cooked dinner. As I opened a can of tomatoes, the can slipped in my left hand and juice spattered me and the counter with bloody spots. Fatigued and infuriated, I bellowed, "I'm so sick of being crippled!" Anne glanced at me over the top of her book. "There now," she said, "do you feel better?" "Yes," I said, "yes, I do." She went back to her reading. I felt better. That's about all the attention my scurviness ever gets.

Because I hate being crippled, I sometimes hate myself for being a crip-   20
ple. Over the years I have come to expect—even accept—attacks of violent self-loathing. Luckily, in general our society no longer connects deformity and disease directly with evil (though a charismatic once told me that I have MS because a devil is in me) and so I'm allowed to move largely at will, even among small children. But I'm not sure that this revision of attitude has been particularly helpful. Physical imperfection, even freed of moral disapprobation, still defies and violates the ideal, especially for women, whose confinement in their bodies as objects of desire is far from over. Each age, of course, has its ideal, and I doubt that ours is any better or worse than any other. Today's ideal woman, who lives on the glossy pages of dozens of magazines, seems to be between the ages of eighteen and twenty-five; her hair has body, her teeth flash white, her breath smells minty, her underarms are dry; she has a career but is still a fabulous cook, especially of meals that take less than twenty minutes to prepare; she does not ordinarily appear to have a husband or children; she is trim and deeply tanned; she jogs, swims, plays tennis, rides a bicycle, sails, but does not bowl; she travels widely, even to out-of-the-way places like Finland and Samoa, always in the company of the ideal man, who possesses a nearly identical set of characteristics. There are a few exceptions. Though usually white and often blonde, she may be black, Hispanic, Asian, or Native American, so long as she is unusually sleek. She may be old, provided she is selling a laxative or is Lauren Bacall. If she is selling a detergent, she may be married and have a flock of strikingly messy children. But she is never a cripple.

Like many women I know, I have always had an uneasy relationship with my body. I was not a popular child, largely, I think now, because I was peculiar: intelligent, intense, moody, shy, given to unexpected actions and inexplicable notions and emotions. But as I entered adolescence, I believed myself unpopular because I was homely; my breasts too flat, my mouth too wide, my hips too narrow, my clothing never quite right in fit or style. I was not, in fact, particularly ugly, old photographs inform me, though I was well off the ideal; but I carried this sense of self-alienation with me into adulthood,

2 **Tiny Tim:** Crippled boy in Charles Dickens's *A Christmas Carol.*—EDS.
3 **Caliban:** A character in William Shakespeare's play *The Tempest.*—EDS.

where it regenerated in response to the depredations of MS. Even with my brace I walk with a limp so pronounced that, seeing myself on the video-tape of a television program on the disabled, I couldn't believe that anything but an inchworm could make progress humping along like that. My shoulders droop and my pelvis thrusts forward as I try to balance myself upright, throwing my frame into a bony S. As a result of contractures, one shoulder is higher than the other and I carry one arm bent in front of me, the fingers curled into a claw. My left arm and leg have wasted into pipe-stems, and I try always to keep them covered. When I think about how my body must look to others, especially to men, to whom I have been trained to display myself, I feel ludicrous, even loathsome.

At my age, however, I don't spend much time thinking about my appearance. The burning egocentricity of adolescence, which assures one that all the world is looking all the time, has passed, thank God, and I'm generally too caught up in what I'm doing to step back, as I used to, and watch myself as though upon a stage. I'm also too old to believe in the accuracy of self-image. I know that I'm not a hideous crone, that in fact, when I'm rested, well dressed, and well made up, I look fine. The self-loathing I feel is neither physically nor intellectually substantial. What I hate is not me but a disease.

I am not a disease.

And a disease is not—at least not singlehandedly—going to determine who I am, though at first it seemed to be going to. Adjusting to a chronic incurable illness, I have moved through a process similar to that outlined by Elisabeth Kübler-Ross in *On Death and Dying*. The major difference—and it is far more significant than most people recognize—is that I can't be sure of the outcome, as the terminally ill cancer patient can. Research studies indicate that, with proper medical care, I may achieve a "normal" life span. And in our society, with its vision of death as the ultimate evil, worse even than decrepitude, the response to such news is, "Oh well, at least you're not going to *die*." Are there worse things than dying? I think that there may be.

I think of two women I know, both with MS, both enough older than I to have served me as models. One took to her bed several years ago and has been there ever since. Although she can sit in a high-backed wheel-chair, because she is incontinent she refuses to go out at all, even though incontinence pants, which are readily available at any pharmacy, could protect her from embarrassment. Instead, she stays at home and insists that her husband, a small quiet man, a retired civil servant, stay there with her except for a quick weekly foray to the supermarket. The other woman, whose illness was diagnosed when she was eighteen, a nursing student engaged to a young doctor, finished her training, married her doctor, accompanied him to Germany when he was in the service, bore three sons and a daughter, now grown and gone. When she can, she travels with her husband; she plays bridge, embroiders, swims regularly; she works, like me, as a symptomatic-patient instructor of medical students in neurology. Guess which woman I hope to be.

At the beginning, I thought about having MS almost incessantly. And because of the unpredictable course of the disease, my thoughts were always terrified. Each night I'd get into bed wondering whether I'd get out again the next morning, whether I'd be able to see, to speak, to hold a pen between my fingers. Knowing that the day might come when I'd be physically incapable of killing myself, I thought perhaps I ought to do so right away, while I still had the strength. Gradually I came to understand that the Nancy who might one day lie inert under a bedsheet, arms and legs paralyzed, unable to feed or bathe herself, unable to reach out for a gun, a bottle of pills, was not the Nancy I was at present, and that I could not presume to make decisions for that future Nancy, who might well not want in the least to die. Now the only provision I've made for the future Nancy is that when the time comes—and it is likely to come in the form of pneumonia, friend to the weak and the old—I am not to be treated with machines and medications. If she is unable to communicate by then, I hope she will be satisfied with these terms.

Thinking all the time about having MS grew tiresome and intrusive, especially in the large and tragic mode in which I was accustomed to considering my plight. Months and even years went by without catastrophe (at least without one related to MS), and really I was awfully busy, what with George and children and snakes and students and poems, and I hadn't the time, let alone the inclination, to devote myself to being a disease. Too, the richer my life became, the funnier it seemed, as though there were some connection between largesse and laughter, and so my tragic stance began to waver until, even with the aid of a brace and a cane, I couldn't hold it for very long at a time.

After several years I was satisfied with my adjustment. I had suffered my grief and fury and terror, I thought, but now I was at ease with my lot. Then one summer day I set out with George and the children across the desert for a vacation in California. Part way to Yuma I became aware that my right leg felt funny. "I think I've had an exacerbation," I told George. "What shall we do?" he asked. "I think we'd better get the hell to California," I said, "because I don't know whether I'll ever make it again." So we went on to San Diego and then to Orange, up the Pacific Coast Highway to Santa Cruz, across to Yosemite, down to Sequoia and Joshua Tree, and so back over the desert to home. It was a fine two-week trip, filled with friends and fair weather, and I wouldn't have missed it for the world, though I did in fact make it back to California two years later. Nor would there have been any point in missing it, since in MS, once the symptoms have appeared, the neurological damage has been done, and there's no way to predict or prevent that damage.

The incident spoiled my self-satisfaction, however. It renewed my grief and fury and terror, and I learned that one never finishes adjusting to MS. I don't know now why I thought one would. One does not, after all, finish adjusting to life, and MS is simply a fact of my life—not my favorite fact, of course—but as ordinary as my nose and my tropical fish and my yellow Mazda station wagon. It may at any time get worse, but no amount of worry or anticipation can prepare me for a new loss. My life is a lesson in losses. I learn one at a time.

And I had best be patient in the learning, since I'll have to do it like it or not. As any rock fan knows, you can't always get what you want. Particularly when you have MS. You can't, for example, get cured. In recent years researchers and the organizations that fund research have started to pay MS some attention even though it isn't fatal; perhaps they have begun to see that life is something other than a quantitative phenomenon, that one may be very much alive for a very long time in a life that isn't worth living. The researchers have made some progress toward understanding the mechanism of the disease: It may well be an autoimmune reaction triggered by a slow-acting virus. But they are nowhere near its prevention, control, or cure. And most of us want to be cured. Some, unable to accept incurability, grasp at one treatment after another, no matter how bizarre: megavitamin therapy, gluten-free diet, injections of cobra venom, hypothermal suits, lymphocytopharesis, hyperbaric chambers. Many treatments are probably harmless enough, but none are curative.

The absence of a cure often makes MS patients bitter toward their doctors. Doctors are, after all, the priests of modern society, the new shamans, whose business is to heal, and many an MS patient roves from one to another, searching for the "good" doctor who will make him well. Doctors too think of themselves as healers, and for this reason many have trouble dealing with MS patients, whose disease in its intransigence defeats their aims and mocks their skills. Too few doctors, it is true, treat their patients as whole human beings, but the reverse is also true. I have always tried to be gentle with my doctors, who often have more at stake in terms of ego than I do. I may be frustrated, maddened, depressed by the incurability of my disease, but I am not diminished by it, and they are. When I push myself up from my seat in the waiting room and stumble toward them, I incarnate the limitation of their powers. The least I can do is refuse to press on their tenderest spots.

This gentleness is part of the reason that I'm not sorry to be a cripple. I didn't have it before. Perhaps I'd have developed it anyway—how could I know such a thing?—and I wish I had more of it, but I'm glad of what I have. It has opened and enriched my life enormously, this sense that my frailty and need must be mirrored in others, that in searching for and shaping a stable core in a life wrenched by change and loss, change and loss, I must recognize the same process, under individual conditions, in the lives around me. I do not deprecate such knowledge, however I've come by it.

All the same, if a cure were found, would I take it? In a minute. I may be a cripple, but I'm only occasionally a loony and never a saint. Anyway, in my brand of theology God doesn't give bonus points for a limp. I'd take a cure; I just don't need one. A friend who also has MS startled me once by asking, "Do you ever say to yourself, 'Why me, Lord?'" "No, Michael, I don't," I told him, "because whenever I try, the only response I can think of is 'Why not?'" If I could make a cosmic deal, who would I put in my place? What in my life would I give up in exchange for sound limbs and a thrilling rush of energy? No one. Nothing. I might as well do the job myself. Now that I'm getting the hang of it. ⬤

The Reader's Presence

1. Mairs's approach to her multiple sclerosis may come across as ironic, jaunty, or tough. Near the beginning of the essay she assumes that her reader is fundamentally alienated from her: "I refuse to pretend that the only differences between you and me are the various ordinary ones that distinguish any one person from another" (paragraph 4). What are those differences? How does the essay attempt to move the reader away from awkwardness or suspicion or hostility? Does it succeed? Why or why not?

2. What does the epigraph from Louise Bogan mean to you? What might it signify in relation to Mairs's essay? What is "escape," in Mairs's context? What meanings might the word *nothing* have?

3. **CONNECTIONS:** "Lest I begin to sound like Pollyanna, however, let me say that I don't like having MS. I hate it" (paragraph 9). Discuss Mairs's admission of hatred for the disease—and for herself (paragraph 20)—in relation to Alice Walker's "abuse" of her injured eye (paragraph 30) in "Beauty: When the Other Dancer Is the Self" (page 244). What is the role of self-loathing in personal growth?

The Writer at Work

NANCY MAIRS on Finding a Voice

In writing workshops and lectures, the essayist Nancy Mairs is often asked what appears to be a simple question: How did you find your voice as a writer? Yet is the question truly a simple one? In the following passage from her book "on becoming a (woman) writer," *Voice Lessons*, Mairs closely examines the question and suggests a way it might be answered. You might want to compare her concern about finding a voice to that of Henry Louis Gates Jr. in "The Writer at Work" on page 105.

❝ The question I am most often asked when I speak to students and others interested in writing is, How did you find your voice? I have some trouble with this locution because "find" always suggests to me the discovery, generally fortuitous, of some lack or loss. I have found an occasional four-leaf clover. I have found a mate. I have, more than once, found my way home. But is a voice susceptible of the same sort of revelation or retrieval? Hasn't mine simply always been there, from my earliest lallation to the "I love you" I called after my husband on his way to school several hours ago?

But of course, I remind myself, the question doesn't concern *my* voice at all but the voice of another woman (also named Nancy Mairs, confusingly enough) whose "utterances" are, except for the occasional public reading, literally inaudible: not, strictly speaking, a voice at all, but a fabrication, a device. And when I look again at the dictionary, I see that "find" can indeed also mean "devise." The voice in question, like the woman called into being to explain its existence, is an invention.

But of whom? For simplicity's sake, we assume that the voice in a work is that of the writer (in the case of nonfiction) or one invented by her (in the case of fiction). This assumption describes the relationship between writer (the woman in front of a luminous screen) and persona (whoever you hear speaking to you right now) adequately for most readers. And maybe for most writers, too. Until

that earnest student in the second row waves a gnawed pencil over her head and asks, timidly as a rule because hers is the first question, "How did you find your voice?"

As though "you" were a coherent entity already existing at some original point, who had only to open her mouth and agitate her vocal chords—or, to be precise, pick up her fingers and diddle the keys—to call the world she had in mind into being. Not just a writer, an Author. But I've examined this process over and over in myself, and the direction of this authorial plot simply doesn't ring true. In the beginning, remember, was the *Word*. Not me. And the question, properly phrased, should probably be asked of my voice: How did you find (devise, invent, contrive) your Nancy?**"**

Malcolm X
MY FIRST CONK

MALCOLM X (1925–1965) is regarded as one of the most influential figures in the struggle for racial equality. Born Malcolm Little in Omaha, Nebraska, his family was frequently the target of racist violence: white supremacists burned their home, and his father, a Baptist minister, was horribly murdered. After his father's death, Malcolm's mother was hospitalized for mental illness, and Malcolm and his seven brothers and sisters were placed in foster homes. Although a gifted student, Malcolm was discouraged by a racist teacher and quit high school. He lived for a while in Lansing, Michigan, and later moved to Boston, where he engaged in various illegal activities, became addicted to narcotics, and was imprisoned for robbery. While in jail Malcolm made extensive use of the prison library and studied philosophy, politics, and the teachings of the Black Muslims' Nation of Islam. After his release from prison, Malcolm worked with Elijah Muhammad, founder and leader of the Nation of Islam, and changed his name to Malcolm X. He became known as an outspoken and articulate minister, championing racial separatism, faith in Allah, and rejection of white society, and he quickly rose to a position of prominence within the organization. While on a pilgrimage to Mecca in 1964, Malcolm X became an orthodox Muslim, adopted the name El-Hajj Malik El-Shabazz, and formed his own religious organization. Hostilities grew between his followers and the Black Muslims, and in 1965 Malcolm X was assassinated in a Harlem ballroom. *The Autobiography of Malcolm X* (1965), from which "My First Conk" is taken, was written with Alex Haley and was published posthumously.

> **While in jail Malcolm made extensive use of the prison library and studied philosophy, politics, and the teachings of the Black Muslims' Nation of Islam.**

Malcolm Little left Lansing, Michigan, and moved into his older sister Ella's house in the Roxbury section of Boston in 1948. In his Autobiography, *Malcolm X describes how he eventually transformed himself from a country bumpkin into a sharp-dressed young cat. Another of those "cats" was a fellow called Shorty who worked in a neighborhood poolroom. A "dark, stubby, conk-headed fellow," Shorty took a liking to the twenty-three-year-old Malcolm and oversaw his urban makeover, a big part of which was to get his hair straightened, or "conked." The term probably derives from* congolene, *a gel-like substance that could be made at home with eggs, potatoes, and corrosive lye. It was then applied like shampoo, with often painful results.*

SHORTY SOON DECIDED that my hair was finally long enough to be conked. He had promised to school me in how to beat the barbershops' three- and four-dollar price by making up congolene, and then conking ourselves.

I took the little list of ingredients he had printed out for me, and went to a grocery store, where I got a can of Red Devil lye, two eggs, and two medium-sized white potatoes. Then at a drugstore near the poolroom, I asked for a large jar of vaseline, a large bar of soap, a large-toothed comb and a fine-toothed comb, one of those rubber hoses with a metal spray-head, a rubber apron, and a pair of gloves.

"Going to lay on that first conk?" the drugstore man asked me. I proudly told him, grinning, "Right!"

Shorty paid six dollars a week for a room in his cousin's shabby apartment. His cousin wasn't at home. "It's like the pad's mine, he spends so much time with his woman," Shorty said. "Now, you watch me—"

He peeled the potatoes and thin-sliced them into a quart-sized Mason   5
fruit jar, then started stirring them with a wooden spoon as he gradually
poured in a little over half the can of lye. "Never use a metal spoon; the lye
will turn it black," he told me.

A jelly-like, starchy-looking glop resulted from the lye and potatoes, and
Shorty broke in the two eggs, stirring real fast—his own conk and dark
face bent down close. The congolene turned pale-yellowish. "Feel the jar,"
Shorty said. I cupped my hand against the outside, and snatched it away.
"Damn right, it's hot, that's the lye," he said. "So you know it's going to
burn when I comb it in—it burns *bad*. But the longer you can stand it, the
straighter the hair."

He made me sit down, and he tied the string of a new rubber apron
tightly around my neck, and combed up my bush of hair. Then, from the
big vaseline jar, he took a handful and massaged it hard all through my hair
and into the scalp. He also thickly vaselined my neck, ears and forehead.
"When I get to washing out your head, be sure to tell me anywhere you feel
any little stinging," Shorty warned me, washing his hands, then pulling on
the rubber gloves, and tying on his own rubber apron. "You always got to
remember that any congolene left in burns a sore into your head."

*"Conking" was popular from the 1920s into the 1960s. This 1962 barbershop photo
shows a man enduring the painful process of having his hair straightened.*

The congolene just felt warm when Shorty started combing it in. But then my head caught fire.

I gritted my teeth and tried to pull the sides of the kitchen table together. The comb felt as if it was raking my skin off.

My eyes watered, my nose was running. I couldn't stand it any longer; I bolted to the washbasin. I was cursing Shorty with every name I could think of when he got the spray going and started soap-lathering my head.

He lathered and spray-rinsed, lathered and spray-rinsed, maybe ten or twelve times, each time gradually closing the hot-water faucet, until the rinse was cold, and that helped some.

"You feel any stinging spots?"

"No," I managed to say. My knees were trembling.

"Sit back down, then. I think we got it all out okay."

The flame came back as Shorty, with a thick towel, started drying my head, rubbing hard. *"Easy, man, easy!"* I kept shouting.

"The first time's always worst. You get used to it better before long. You took it real good, homeboy. You got a good conk."

When Shorty let me stand up and see in the mirror, my hair hung down in limp, damp strings. My scalp still flamed, but not as badly; I could bear it. He draped the towel around my shoulders, over my rubber apron, and began again vaselining my hair.

I could feel him combing, straight back, first the big comb, then the fine-tooth one.

Then, he was using a razor, very delicately, on the back of my neck. Then, finally, shaping the sideburns.

My first view in the mirror blotted out the hurting. I'd seen some pretty conks, but when it's the first time, on your *own* head, the transformation, after the lifetime of kinks, is staggering.

The mirror reflected Shorty behind me. We both were grinning and sweating. And on top of my head was this thick, smooth sheen of shining red hair—real red—as straight as any white man's.

How ridiculous I was! Stupid enough to stand there simply lost in admiration of my hair now looking "white," reflected in the mirror in Shorty's room. I vowed that I'd never again be without a conk, and I never was for many years.

This was my first really big step toward self-degradation: when I endured all of that pain, literally burning my flesh to have it look like a white man's hair. I had joined that multitude of Negro men and women in America who are brainwashed into believing that the black people are "inferior"—and white people "superior"—that they will even violate and mutilate their God-created bodies to try to look "pretty" by white standards.

Look around today, in every small town and big city, from two-bit catfish and soda-pop joints into the "integrated" lobby of the Waldorf-Astoria, and you'll see conks on black men. And you'll see black women wearing these green and pink and purple and red and platinum-blond wigs. They're all more ridiculous than a slapstick comedy. It makes you wonder if the Negro has completely lost his sense of identity, lost touch with himself.

You'll see the conk worn by many, many so-called "upper class" Negroes, and, as much as I hate to say it about them, on all too many Negro entertainers. One of the reasons that I've especially admired some of them, like Lionel Hampton and Sidney Poitier,[1] among others, is that they have kept their natural hair and fought to the top. I admire any Negro man who has never had himself conked, or who has had the sense to get rid of it—as I finally did.

I don't know which kind of self-defacing conk is the greater shame—the one you'll see on the heads of the black so-called "middle class" and "upper class," who ought to know better, or the one you'll see on the heads of the poorest, most downtrodden, ignorant black men. I mean the legal-minimum-wage ghetto-dwelling kind of Negro, as I was when I got my first one. It's generally among these poor fools that you'll see a black kerchief over the man's head, like Aunt Jemima; he's trying to make his conk last longer, between trips to the barbershop. Only for special occasions is this kerchief-protected conk exposed—to show off how "sharp" and "hip" its owner is. The ironic thing is that I have never heard any woman, white or black, express any admiration for a conk. Of course, any white woman with a black man isn't thinking about his hair. But I don't see how on earth a black woman with any race pride could walk down the street with any black man wearing a conk—the emblem of his shame that he is black.

To my own shame, when I say all of this I'm talking first of all about myself—because you can't show me any Negro who ever conked more faithfully than I did. I'm speaking from personal experience when I say of any black man who conks today, or any white-wigged black woman, that if they gave the brains in their heads just half as much attention as they do their hair, they would be a thousand times better off. ●

The Reader's Presence

1. Observe the way Malcolm X narrates the recollections of his first "conk." The reader doesn't learn about how he felt later on in life about the conk until the process is over and he calls it his "first really big step toward self-degradation" (paragraph 23). If he had shared that information from the start, how would that have affected your response? To what extent were you surprised by his reaction to the experience?

2. The writer, of course, was a courageous African American leader who was assassinated in 1965, when he was only forty years old. How does this knowledge affect your reading of this account of his early years? How does Malcolm himself indicate the difference in time between the events he is relating and the time at which he is writing?

---

[1] ***Lionel Hampton and Sidney Poitier:*** Hampton (1908–2002) was a prominent jazz bandleader and an outstanding musician; Poitier (b. 1927) has long been one of the most famous film stars and the first black person to receive an Oscar for Best Actor.—EDS.

3. **CONNECTIONS:**   Read "My First Conk" in connection with Henry Louis Gates Jr.'s "In the Kitchen" (page 97) and Daniel Akst's "What Meets the Eye" (page 293). In what ways does Gates's account of hair styling depart from that described in Malcolm X's memoir? Consider "My First Conk" in relation to the standards of good looks Akst examines in his essay and discuss the older Malcolm's feelings of "self-degradation" in terms of Akst's analysis.

David Mamet

THE RAKE: A FEW SCENES FROM MY CHILDHOOD

DAVID MAMET (b. 1947) is a playwright, screenwriter, and director whose work is appreciated for the attention he pays to language as it is spoken by ordinary people in the contemporary world. His 1984 Pulitzer Prize–winning play, *Glengarry Glen Ross*, explores the psychology of ambition, competition, failure, and despair among a group of Chicago real estate agents who are driven to sell worthless property to unsuspecting customers.

Mamet has said that "playwriting is simply showing how words influence actions and vice versa. All my plays attempt to bring out the poetry in the plain, everyday language people use. That's the only way to put art back in the theater." Mamet's sensitivity to working-class language and experience is due in part to his own work experience in factories, at a real estate agency, and as a window washer, office cleaner, and taxi driver. Mamet has taught

> "Playwriting is simply showing how words influence action and vice versa."

theater at several leading universities and published a number of books about theater and film, including *True and False: Heresy and Common Sense for the Actor* (1997), *Three Uses of the Knife: On the Nature and Purpose of Drama* (1998), and *Bambi vs. Godzilla: On the Nature, Purpose, and Practice of the Movie Business*. Mamet's plays include the often revived *American Buffalo* (1977) and *Speed-the-Plow* (1988), and, more recently, *Ricky Jay: On the Stem* (2002), *Dr. Faustus* (2004), *Romance* (2005), and *November*, his take on politics that opened in New York City in 2008. He has written and directed several films, including Oscar-nominated movies, *The Verdict* (1982) and *Wag the Dog* (1997), *State and Main* (2000), and *Heist* (2001). He was also the producer and writer of the television series, *The Unit* (2006–2007). His latest book, *Theatre*, was published in 2010. "The Rake: A Few Scenes from My Childhood" appeared in *Harper's* in 1992.

THERE WAS THE INCIDENT of the rake and there was the incident of the school play, and it seems to me that they both took place at the round kitchen table.

The table was not in the kitchen proper but in an area called "the nook," which held its claim to that small measure of charm by dint of a waist-high wall separating it from an adjacent area known as the living room.

All family meals were eaten in the nook. There was a dining room to the right, but, as in most rooms of that name at the time and in those surroundings, it was never used.

The round table was of wrought iron and topped with glass; it was noteworthy for that glass, for it was more than once and rather more than several times, I am inclined to think, that my stepfather would grow so angry as to bring some object down on the glass top, shattering it, thus giving us to know how we had forced him out of control.

And it seems that most times when he would shatter the table, as often   5
as that might have been, he would cut some portion of himself on the glass, or that he or his wife, our mother, would cut their hands on picking up the glass afterward, and that we children were to understand, and did understand, that these wounds were our fault.

So the table was associated in our minds with the notion of blood.

The house was in a brand-new housing development in the southern suburbs. The new community was built upon, and now bordered, the remains of what had once been a cornfield. When our new family moved in, there were but a few homes in the development completed, and a few more under construction. Most streets were mud, and boasted a house here or there, and many empty lots marked out by white stakes.

The house we lived in was the development's Model Home. The first time we had seen it, it had signs plastered on the front and throughout the interior telling of the various conveniences it contained. And it had a lawn, and was one of the only homes in the new community that did.

My stepfather was fond of the lawn, and he detailed me and my sister to care for it, and one fall afternoon we found ourselves assigned to rake the leaves.

Why this chore should have been so hated I cannot say, except that we   10
children, and I especially, felt ourselves less than full members of this new, cobbled-together family, and disliked being assigned to the beautification of a home that we found unbeautiful in all respects, and for which we had neither natural affection nor a sense of proprietary interest.

We went to the new high school. We walked the mile down the open two-lane road on one side of which was the just-begun suburban community and on the other side of which was the cornfield.

The school was as new as the community, and still under construction for the first three years of its occupancy. One of its innovations was the notion that honesty would be engendered by the absence of security, and so the lockers were designed and built both without locks and without the possibility of attaching locks. And there was the corresponding rash of thievery and many lectures about the same from the school administration, but it was difficult to point with pride to any scholastic or community tradition supporting the suggestion that we, the students, pull together in this new, utopian way. We were, in school, in an uncompleted building in the midst of a mud field in the midst of a cornfield. Our various sports teams were called The Spartans; and I played on those teams, which were of a wretchedness consistent with their novelty.

Meanwhile my sister interested herself in the drama society. The year after I had left the school she obtained the lead in the school play. It called for acting and singing, both of which she had talent for, and it looked to be a signal triumph for her in her otherwise unremarkable and unenjoyed school career.

On the night of the play's opening, she sat down to dinner with our mother and our stepfather. It may be that they ate a trifle early to allow her to get to the school to enjoy the excitement of opening night. But however it was, my sister had no appetite, and she nibbled a bit at her food, and then she got up from the table to carry her plate back to scrape it in the sink, when my mother suggested that she sit down, as she had not finished her food. My sister said she really had no appetite, but my mother insisted that, as the meal had been prepared, it would be good form to sit and eat it.

My sister sat down with the plate and pecked at her food and she tried   15
to eat a bit, and told my mother that, no, really, she possessed no appetite whatever, and that was due, no doubt, not to the food, but to her nervousness and excitement at the prospect of opening night.

My mother, again, said that, as the food had been cooked, it had to be eaten, and my sister tried and said that she could not; at which my mother nodded. She then got up from the table and went to the telephone and looked the number up and called the school and got the drama teacher and identified herself and told him that her daughter wouldn't be coming to school that night, that, no, she was not ill, but that she would not be coming in. Yes, yes, she said, she knew her daughter had the lead in the play, and, yes, she was aware that many children and teachers had worked hard for it, et cetera, and so my sister did not play the lead in her school play. But I was long gone, out of the house by that time, and well out of it. I heard that story, and others like it, at the distance of twenty-five years.

In the model house our rooms were separated from their room, the master bedroom, by a bathroom and a study. On some weekends I would go alone to visit my father in the city and my sister would stay and sometimes grow frightened or lonely in her part of the house. And once, in the period when my grandfather, then in his sixties, was living with us, she became alarmed at a noise she had heard in the night; or perhaps she just became lonely, and she went out of her room and down the hall, calling for my mother, or my stepfather, or my grandfather, but the house was dark, and no one answered.

And, as she went farther down the hall, toward the living room, she heard voices, and she turned the corner, and saw a light coming from under the closed door in the master bedroom, and heard my stepfather crying, and the sound of my mother weeping. So my sister went up to the door, and she heard my stepfather talking to my grandfather and saying, "Jack. Say the words. Just say the words . . ." And my grandfather in his Eastern European accent, saying with obvious pain and difficulty, "No. No. I can't. Why are you making me do this? Why?" And the sound of my mother crying convulsively.

My sister opened the door, and she saw my grandfather sitting on the bed, and my stepfather standing by the closet and gesturing. On the floor of the closet she saw my mother, curled in a fetal position, moaning and crying and hugging herself. My stepfather was saying, "Say the words. Just say the words." And my grandfather was breathing fast and repeating, "I can't. She knows how I feel about her. I can't." And my stepfather said, "Say the words, Jack. Please. Just say you love her." At which my mother would moan louder. And my grandfather said, "I can't."

My sister pushed the door open farther and said—I don't know what she   20 said, but she asked, I'm sure, for some reassurance, or some explanation, and my stepfather turned around and saw her and picked up a hairbrush from a dresser that he passed as he walked toward her, and he hit her in the face and slammed the door on her. And she continued to hear "Jack, say the words."

She told me that on weekends when I was gone my stepfather ended every Sunday evening by hitting or beating her for some reason or other. He would come home from depositing his own kids back at their mother's house after their weekend visitation, and would settle down tired and angry, and, as a regular matter on those evenings, would find out some intolerable behavior on my sister's part and slap or hit or beat her.

Years later, at my mother's funeral, my sister spoke to our aunt, my mother's sister, who gave a footnote to this behavior. She said when they were young, my mother and my aunt, they and their parents lived in a small flat on the West Side. My grandfather was a salesman on the road from dawn on Monday until Friday night. Their family had a fiction, and that fiction, that article of faith, was that my mother was a naughty child. And each Friday, when he came home, his first question as he climbed the stairs was, "What has she done this week . . . ?" At which my grandmother would tell him the terrible things that my mother had done, after which she, my mother, was beaten.

This was general knowledge in my family. The footnote concerned my grandfather's behavior later in the night. My aunt had a room of her own, and it adjoined her parents' room. And she related that each Friday, when the house had gone to bed, she, through the thin wall, heard my grandfather pleading for sex. "Cookie, please." And my grandmother responding, "No, Jack." "Cookie, please." "No, Jack." "Cookie, please."

And once, my grandfather came home and asked, "What has she done this week?" and I do not know, but I imagine that the response was not completed, and perhaps hardly begun; in any case, he reached and grabbed my mother by the back of the neck and hurled her down the stairs.

And once, in our house in the suburbs there had been an outburst by   25 my stepfather directed at my sister. And she had, somehow, prevailed. It was, I think, that he had the facts of the case wrong, and had accused her of the commission of something for which she had demonstrably had no opportunity, and she pointed this out to him with what I can imagine, given the circumstances, was an understandable, and, given my prejudice, a commendable degree of freedom. Thinking the incident closed she went back to her room to study, and, a few moments later, saw him throw open her door, bat the book out of her hands, and pick her up and throw her against the far wall, where she struck the back of her neck on the shelf.

She was told, the next morning, that her pain, real or pretended, held no weight, and that she would have to go to school. She protested that she could not walk, or, if at all, only with the greatest of difficulty and in great pain; but she was dressed and did walk to school, where she fainted, and was brought home. For years she suffered various headaches; an X-ray taken twenty years later for an unrelated problem revealed that when he threw her against the shelf he had cracked her vertebrae.

When we left the house we left in good spirits. When we went out to dinner, it was an adventure, which was strange to me, looking back, because many of these dinners ended with my sister or myself being banished, sullen or in tears, from the restaurant, and told to wait in the car, as we were in disgrace.

These were the excursions that had ended, due to her or my intolerable arrogance, as it was explained to us.

The happy trips were celebrated and capped with a joke. Here is the joke: My stepfather, my mother, my sister, and I would exit the restaurant, my stepfather and mother would walk to the car, telling us that they would pick us up. We children would stand by the restaurant entrance. They would drive up in the car, open the passenger door, and wait until my sister and I had started to get in. They would then drive away.

They would drive ten or fifteen feet, and open the door again, and we   30 would walk up again, and they would drive away again. They sometimes would drive around the block. But they would always come back, and by that time the four of us would be laughing in camaraderie and appreciation of what, I believe, was our only family joke.

We were raking the lawn, my sister and I. I was raking, and she was stuffing the leaves into a bag. I loathed the job, and my muscles and my mind rebelled, and I was viciously angry, and my sister said something, and I turned and threw the rake at her and hit her in the face.

The rake was split bamboo and metal, and a piece of metal caught her lip and cut her badly.

We were both terrified, and I was sick with guilt, and we ran into the house, my sister holding her hand to her mouth, and her mouth and her hand and the front of her dress covered in blood.

We ran into the kitchen where my mother was cooking dinner, and my mother asked what happened.

Neither of us, myself out of guilt, of course, and my sister out of a desire to avert the terrible punishment she knew I would receive, neither of us would say what occurred.

My mother pressed us, and neither of us would answer. She said that until one or the other answered, we would not go to the hospital; and so the family sat down to dinner where my sister clutched a napkin to her face and the blood soaked the napkin and ran down onto her food, which she had to eat; and I also ate my food and we cleared the table and went to the hospital.

I remember the walks home from school in the frigid winter, along the cornfield that was, for all its proximity to the city, part of the prairie. The winters were viciously cold. From the remove of years, I can see how the area might and may have been beautiful. One could have walked in the stubble of the cornfields, or hunted birds, or enjoyed any of a number of pleasures naturally occurring. ◼

The Reader's Presence

1. Interwoven throughout Mamet's essay are descriptions of suburban developments and model homes; he even uses the word *utopian* (paragraph 12). What is Mamet's attitude toward these ideals? What is his tone in discussing them? Mamet says that he and his sister hated doing yardwork, in part because they "had neither natural affection nor a sense of proprietary interest" (paragraph 10) toward their house. What does this mean?

2. Near the end of the essay, Mamet recalls a "joke" that his family shared. How does he present the joke to the reader? Do you think Mamet wants the reader to think the joke is funny? Why or why not? Would the joke seem different if Mamet had told it at the beginning of the essay? How does he connect this joke back to the story about the rake?

3. **CONNECTIONS:**   Mamet says that "the table was associated in our minds with the notion of blood" (paragraph 6). Do you think the rake also has symbolic value? If so, what does it represent? How does Mamet's use of symbolic objects compare to George Orwell's treatment of the gun and the elephant in "Shooting an Elephant" (page 180)? How does Mamet's account of his relationship with his sister compare to Alice Walker's account of her brothers' role in the "accident" in which she lost the sight in her eye in "Beauty: When the Other Dancer Is the Self" (page 244)?

Adam Mayblum
THE PRICE WE PAY

ADAM MAYBLUM, the thirty-five-year-old managing director of the May Davis Group private investment firm, was in his office on the eighty-seventh floor of the North Tower of the World Trade Center when one of the hijacked planes struck on September 11, 2001. He escaped just before the tower's collapse. The following day, at his home in New Rochelle, New York, Mayblum composed a terse, harrowing e-mail describing his experience and sent the 2,100-word piece out to friends and family. This e-mail quickly circulated throughout the world, bringing Mayblum more than 1,000 responses from strangers offering thanks, sympathy, and prayers. One woman wrote, "The fact that you survived . . . helped to lift the terrible weight from my heart." Mayblum, who disclaims the label of "hero" by pointing out that firefighters and police officers were the ones who rushed in to save lives, attributes the enormous outpouring of support to the fact that his e-mail "helped a lot of people understand what was going on inside the building at the same time they had seen what was going on outside." Mayblum's e-mail was first published as an essay in *DoubleTake Magazine*, and was selected for *The Best American Essays 2002*.

> **Adam Mayblum was in his office on the eighty-seventh floor of the North Tower of the World Trade Center when one of the hijacked planes struck on September 11, 2001.**

MY NAME IS ADAM MAYBLUM. I am alive today. I am committing this to "paper" so I never forget. SO WE NEVER FORGET. I am sure that this is one of thousands of stories that will emerge over the next several days and weeks.

I arrived as usual a little before 8 a.m. My office was on the eighty-seventh floor of 1 World Trade Center, aka: Tower 1, aka: the North Tower. Most of my associates were in by 8:30 a.m. We were standing around, joking around, eating breakfast, checking e-mails, and getting set for the day when the first plane hit just a few stories above us. I must stress that we did not know that it was a plane. The building lurched violently and shook as if it were an earthquake. People screamed. I watched out my window as the building seemed to move ten to twenty feet in each direction. It rumbled and shook long enough for me to get my wits about myself and grab a coworker and seek shelter under a doorway. Light fixtures and parts of the ceiling collapsed. The kitchen was destroyed. We were certain that it was a bomb. We looked out the windows. Reams of paper were flying everywhere, like a ticker tape parade. I looked down at the street. I could see people in Battery Park City looking up. Smoke started billowing in through the holes in the ceiling. I believe that there were thirteen of us.

We did not panic. I can only assume that we thought that the worst was over. The building was standing and we were shaken but alive. We checked the halls. The smoke was thick and white and did not smell like I imagined smoke should smell. Not like your BBQ or your fireplace or even a bonfire. The phones were working. My wife had taken our nine-month-old for his checkup. I called my nanny at home and told her to page my wife, tell her that a bomb went off, I was O.K., and on my way out, I grabbed my laptop. Took off my T-shirt and ripped it into three pieces. Soaked it in water. Gave two pieces to my friends. Tied my piece around my face to act as an air filter. And we all started moving to the staircase. One of my dearest friends said that he was staying until the police or firemen came to get him. In the halls there were tiny fires and sparks. The ceiling had collapsed in the men's bathroom. It was gone along with anyone who may have been in there. We did not go in to look. We missed the staircase on the first run and had to double back. Once in the staircase we picked up fire extinguishers just in case. On the eighty-fifth floor a brave associate of mine and I headed back up to our office to drag out my partner who stayed behind. There was no air, just white smoke. We made the rounds through the office calling his name. No response. He must have succumbed to the smoke. We left defeated in our efforts and made our way back to the stairwell. We proceeded to the seventy-eighth floor where we had to change over to a different stairwell. Seventy-eight is the main junction to switch to the upper floors. I expected to see more people. There were some fifty to sixty more. Not enough. Wires and fires all over the place. Smoke too. A brave man was fighting a fire with the emergency hose. I stopped with friends to make sure that everyone from our office was accounted for. We ushered them and confused people into the stairwell. In retrospect, I recall seeing Harry, my head trader, doing the same several yards behind me. I am only thirty-five. I have known him for over fourteen years. I headed into the stairwell with two friends.

We were moving down very orderly in Stairwell A. Very slowly. No panic. At least not overt panic. My legs could not stop shaking. My heart was pounding. Some nervous jokes and laughter. I made a crack about ruining a brand new pair of Merrells. Even still, they were right, my feet felt great. We all laughed. We checked our cell phones. Surprisingly, there was a very good signal, but the Sprint network was jammed. I heard that the BlackBerry two-way e-mail devices worked perfectly. On the phones, one out of twenty dial attempts got through. I knew I could not reach my wife so I called my parents. I told them what happened and that we were all O.K.

and on the way down. Soon, my sister-in-law reached me. I told her we were fine and moving down. I believe that was about the sixty-fifth floor. We were bored and nervous. I called my friend Angel in San Francisco. I knew he would be watching. He was amazed I was on the phone. He told me to get out, that there was another plane on its way. I did not know what he was talking about. By now the second plane had struck Tower 2. We were so deep into the middle of our building that we did not hear or feel anything. We had no idea what was really going on. We kept making way for wounded to go down ahead of us. Not many of them, just a few. No one seemed seriously wounded. Just some cuts and scrapes. Everyone cooperated. Everyone was a hero yesterday. No questions asked. I had coworkers in another office on the seventy-seventh floor. I tried dozens of times to get them on their cell phones or office lines. It was futile. Later I found that they were alive. One of the many miracles on a day of tragedy.

On the fifty-third floor we came across a very heavyset man sitting on   5
the stairs. I asked if he needed help or was he just resting. He needed help. I knew I would have trouble carrying him because I have a very bad back. But my friend and I offered anyway. We told him he could lean on us. He hesitated, I don't know why. I said do you want to come or do you want us to send help for you. He chose for help. I told him he was on the fifty-third floor in Stairwell A and that's what I would tell the rescue workers. He said O.K. and we left.

On the forty-fourth floor my phone rang again. It was my parents. They were hysterical. I said relax, I'm fine. My father said get out, there is a third plane coming. I still did not understand. I was kind of angry. What did my parents think? Like I needed some other reason to get going? I couldn't move the thousand people in front of me any faster. I know they love me, but no one inside understood what the situation really was. My parents did. Starting around this floor the firemen, policemen, WTC K-9 units without the dogs, anyone with a badge, started coming up as we were heading down. I stopped a lot of them and told them about the man on Fifty-three and my friend on Eighty-seven. I later felt terrible about this. They headed up to find those people and met death instead.

On the thirty-third floor I spoke with a man who somehow knew most of the details. He said two small planes hit the building. Now we all started talking about which terrorist group it was. Was it an internal organization or an external one? The overwhelming but uninformed opinion was Islamic fanatics. Regardless, we now knew that it was not a bomb and there were potentially more planes coming. We understood.

On the third floor the lights went out and we heard and felt this rumbling coming towards us from above. I thought the staircase was collapsing upon itself. It was 10 a.m. now and that was Tower 2 collapsing next door. We did not know that. Someone had a flashlight. We passed it forward and left the stairwell and headed down a dark and cramped corridor to an exit. We could not see at all. I recommended that everyone place a hand on the shoulder of the person in front of them and call out if they hit an obstacle so others

The rubble shortly after the collapse of the first World Trade Center tower in New York City, September 11, 2001. This was the tower from which Adam Mayblum made his escape.

would know to avoid it. They did. It worked perfectly. We reached another stairwell and saw a female officer emerge soaking wet and covered in soot. She said we could not go that way, it was blocked. Go up to Four and use the other exit. Just as we started up she said it was O.K. to go down instead. There was water everywhere. I called out for hands on shoulders again and she said that was a great idea. She stayed behind instructing people to do that. I do not know what happened to her.

We emerged into an enormous room. It was light but filled with smoke. I commented to a friend that it must be under construction. Then we realized where we were. It was the second floor. The one that overlooks the lobby. We were ushered out into the courtyard, the one where the fountain used to be. My first thought was of a TV movie I saw once about nuclear winter and fallout. I could not understand where all of the debris came from. There was at least five inches of this gray pasty dusty drywall soot on the ground as well as a thickness of it in the air. Twisted steel and wires. I heard there were bodies and body parts as well, but I did not look. It was bad enough. We hid under the remaining overhangs and moved out to the street. We were told to keep walking towards Houston Street. The odd thing is that there were very few rescue workers around. Less than five. They all must have been trapped under the debris when Tower 2 fell. We did not know that and could not understand where all of that debris came from. It was just my friend Kern and I now. We were hugging but sad. We felt certain that most of our friends ahead of us died and we knew no one behind us.

We came upon a post office several blocks away. We stopped and looked   10
up. Our building, exactly where our office is (was), was engulfed in flame and smoke. A postal worker said that Tower 2 had fallen down. I looked again and sure enough it was gone. My heart was racing. We kept trying to call our families. I could not get in touch with my wife. Finally I got through to my parents. Relieved is not the word to explain their feelings. They got through to my wife, thank G–d, and let her know I was alive. We sat down. A girl on a bike offered us some water. Just as she took the cap off her bottle we heard a rumble. We looked up and our building, Tower 1, collapsed. I did not note the time, but I am told it was 10:30 a.m. We had been out less than fifteen minutes.

We were mourning our lost friends, particularly the one who stayed in the office, as we were now sure that he had perished. We started walking towards Union Square. I was going to Beth Israel Medical Center to be looked at. We stopped to hear the president speaking on the radio. My phone rang. It was my wife. I think I fell to my knees crying when I heard her voice. Then she told me the most incredible thing. My partner who had stayed behind called her. He was alive and well. I guess we just lost him in the commotion. We started jumping and hugging and shouting. I told my wife that my brother had arranged for a hotel in midtown. He can be very resourceful in that way. I told her I would call her from there. My brother and I managed to get a gypsy cab to take us home to Westchester instead. I cried on my son and held my wife until I fell asleep. As it turns out, my partner, the one who I thought had stayed behind, was behind us with Harry Ramos, our head trader. This is now secondhand information. They came upon Victor, the heavyset man on the fifty-third floor. They helped him. He could barely move. My partner bravely/stupidly tested the elevator on the fifty-second floor. He rode it down to the sky lobby on Forty-four. The doors opened, it was fine. He rode it back up and got Harry and Victor. I don't yet know if anyone else joined them. Once on Forty-four they made their way back into the stairwell. Someplace around the thirty-ninth to thirty-sixth floors they felt the same rumble I felt on the third floor. It was 10 a.m. and Tower 2 was coming down. They had about thirty minutes to get out. Victor said he could no longer move. They offered to have him lean on them. He said he couldn't do it. My partner hollered at him to sit on his butt and scooch down the steps. He said he was not capable of doing it. Harry told my partner to go ahead of them. Harry once had a heart attack and was worried about this man's heart. It was his nature to be this way. He was/is one of the kindest people I know. He would not leave a man behind. My partner went ahead and made it out. He said he was out maybe ten minutes before the building came down. This means that Harry had maybe twenty-five minutes to move Victor thirty-six floors. I guess they moved one floor every 1.5 minutes. Just a guess. This means Harry was around the twentieth floor when the building collapsed. As of now twelve of thirteen people are accounted for. As of 6 p.m. yesterday his wife had not heard from him. I fear that Harry is lost. However, a short while ago I heard that he may be alive. Apparently there is a Web site with survivor names on it and his appears there. Unfortunately, Ramos is not an uncommon name in New York. Pray for him and all those like him.

With regards to the firemen heading upstairs, I realize that they were going up anyway. But it hurts to know that I may have made them move quicker to find my friend. Rationally, I know this is not true and that I am not the responsible one. The responsible ones are in hiding somewhere on this planet and damn them for making me feel like this. But they should know that they failed in terrorizing us. We were calm. Those men and women that went up were heroes in the face of it all. They must have known what was going on and they did their jobs. Ordinary people were heroes, too. Today the images that people around the world equate with power and democracy are gone, but "America" is not an image, it is a concept. That concept is only strengthened by our pulling together as a team. If you want to kill us, leave us alone because we will try to do it by ourselves. If you want to make us stronger, attack and we unite. This is the ultimate failure of terrorism against the United States and the ultimate price we pay to be free, to decide where we want to work, what we want to eat, and when and where we want to go on vacation. The very moment the first plane was hijacked, democracy won. ■

The Reader's Presence

1. Whom does Mayblum talk to as he moves down the stairs? What subject(s) do they discuss? Whom did you talk to following the attacks on the World Trade Center? To what extent do these conversations confirm Mayblum's claim that "If you want to make us stronger, attack and we unite" (paragraph 12)?

2. As Mayblum mentions the floors he passes in his descent, how does the countdown affect his overall story? Point to specific parts of his story that are more hurried than other parts. What about the moments in which he pauses? How do these moments affect your reading?

3. **CONNECTIONS:** Compare Mayblum's account with Don DeLillo's essay on the terrorist attack on the World Trade Center ("In the Ruins of the Future," page 355) and with Michihiko Hachiya's account of the bombing of Hiroshima (page 107). How does each writer position himself in relation to the catastrophic experience related in each essay? Which account do you find most moving? most effective? Why?

Dinaw Mengestu

HOME AT LAST

Ethiopian-born author **DINAW MENGESTU** (b. 1978) immigrated to the United States with his parents when he was just two years old. He received a BA in English from George-town University and an MFA in fiction writing from Columbia University. His debut novel, *The Beautiful Things That Heaven Bears* (2007) was a New York Times Notable Book and was named one of the ten best novels of 2007 by Amazon.com. He has also written extensively for magazines, such as *Harper's* and *Rolling Stone*, on global issues, including the situation in Darfur. His second novel, *How to Read the Air*, was published in 2010. Mengestu has said

> **Dinaw Mengestu's novel is about "what it's like when you are not particularly attached to either of [the] two communities" you belong to.**

that the novel, the story of an Ethiopian American, is "less about trying to figure out how you occupy these two cultural or racial boundaries and more about what it's like when you are not particularly attached to either of [the] two communities." A similar sentiment marks the following essay, "Home at Last," originally published in the Winter 2008 issue of *Open City*.

AT TWENTY-ONE I moved to Brooklyn hoping that it would be the last move I would ever make — that it would, with the gradual accumulation of time, memory, and possessions, become that place I instinctively reverted back to when asked, "So, where are you from?" I was born in Ethiopia like my parents and their parents before them, but it would be a lie to say I was *from* Ethiopia, having left the country when I was only two years old following a military coup and civil war, losing in the process the language and any direct memory of the family and culture I had been born into. I simply am Ethiopian, without the necessary "from" that serves as the final assurance of our identity and origin.

Since leaving Addis Ababa in 1980, I've lived in Peoria, Illinois; in a sub-urb of Chicago; and then finally, before moving to Brooklyn, in Washington, D.C., the de facto[1] capital of the Ethiopian immigrant. Others, I know, have moved much more often and across much greater distances. I've only known a few people, however, that have grown up with the oddly permanent feeling

---

[1] **de facto:** A Latin term often used in the law; it means "in practice" or "for all intents and purposes." — EDS.

of having lost and abandoned a home that you never, in fact, really knew, a feeling that has nothing to do with apartments, houses, or miles, but rather the sense that no matter how far you travel, or how long you stay still, there is no place that you can always return to, no place where you fully belong. My parents, for all that they had given up by leaving Ethiopia, at least had the certainty that they had come from some place. They knew the country's language and culture, had met outside of coffee shops along Addis's main boulevard in the early days of their relationship, and as a result, regardless of how mangled by violence Ethiopia later became, it was irrevocably and ultimately theirs. Growing up, one of my father's favorite sayings was, "Remember, you are Ethiopian," even though, of course, there was nothing for me to remember apart from the bits of nostalgia and culture my parents had imparted. What remained had less to do with the idea that I was from Ethiopia and more to do with the fact that I was not from America.

I can't say when exactly I first became aware of that feeling—that I was always going to and never from—but surely I must have felt it during those first years in Peoria, with my parents, sister, and me always sitting on the edge of whatever context we were now supposed to be a part of, whether it was the all-white Southern Baptist Church we went to every weekend, or the nearly all-white Catholic schools my sister and I attended first in Peoria and then again in Chicago at my parents' insistence. By that point my father, haunted by the death of his brother during the revolution and the ensuing loss of the country he had always assumed he would live and die in, had taken to long evening walks that he eventually let me accompany him on. Back then he had a habit of sometimes whispering his brother's name as he walked ("Shibrew," he would mutter) or whistling the tunes of Amharic[2] songs that I had never known. He always walked with both hands firmly clasped behind his back, as if his grief, transformed into something real and physical, could be grasped and secured in the palms of his hands. That was where I first learned what it meant to lose and be alone. The lesson would be reinforced over the years whenever I caught sight of my mother sitting by herself on a Sunday afternoon, staring silently out of our living room's picture window, recalling, perhaps, her father who had died after she left, or her mother, four sisters, and one brother in Ethiopia—or else recalling nothing at all because there was no one to visit her, no one to call or see. We had been stripped bare here in America, our lives confined to small towns and urban suburbs. We had sacrificed precisely those things that can never be compensated for or repaid—parents, siblings, culture, a memory to a place that dates back more than half a generation. It's easy to see now how even as a family we were isolated from one another—my parents tied and lost to their past; my sister and I irrevocably assimilated. For years we were strangers even among ourselves.

By the time I arrived in Brooklyn I had little interest in where I actually landed. I had just graduated college and had had enough of the fights and

---

2 **Amharic:** Language spoken in North Central Ethiopia. —EDS.

arguments about not being "black" enough, as well as the earlier fights in high school hallways and street corners that were fought for simply being black. Now it was enough, I wanted to believe, to simply be, to say I was in Brooklyn and Brooklyn was home. It wasn't until after I had signed the lease on my apartment that I even learned the name of the neighborhood I had moved into: Kensington, a distinctly regal name at a price that I could afford; it was perfect, in other words, for an eager and poor writer with inflated ambitions and no sense of where he belonged.

After less than a month of living in Kensington I had covered almost   5
all of the neighborhood's streets, deliberately committing their layouts and routines to memory in a first attempt at assimilation. There was an obvious and deliberate echo to my walks, a self-conscious reenactment of my father's routine that I adopted to stave off some of my own emptiness. It wasn't just that I didn't have any deep personal relationships here, it was that I had chosen this city as the place to redefine, to ground, to secure my place in the world. If I could bind myself to Kensington physically, if I could memorize and mentally reproduce in accurate detail the various shades of the houses on a particular block, then I could stake my own claim to it, and in doing so, no one could tell me who I was or that I didn't belong.

On my early-morning walks to the F train I passed in succession a Latin American restaurant and grocery store, a Chinese fish market, a Halal butcher shop, followed by a series of Pakistani and Bangladeshi takeout restaurants. This cluster of restaurants on the corner of Church and McDonald, I later learned, sold five-dollar plates of lamb and chicken biryani in portions large enough to hold me over for a day, and in more financially desperate times, two days. Similarly, I learned that the butcher and fish shop delivery trucks arrived on most days just as I was making my way to the train. If I had time, I found it hard not to stand and stare at the refrigerated trucks with their calf and sheep carcasses dangling from hooks, or at the tanks of newly arrived bass and catfish flapping around in a shallow pool of water just deep enough to keep them alive.

It didn't take long for me to develop a fierce loyalty to Kensington, to think of the neighborhood and my place in it as emblematic of a grander immigrant narrative. In response to that loyalty, I promised to host a "Kensington night" for the handful of new friends that I eventually made in the city, an evening that would have been comprised of five-dollar lamb biryani followed by two-dollar Budweisers at Denny's, the neighborhood's only full-fledged bar—a defunct Irish pub complete with terribly dim lighting and wooden booths. I never hosted a Kensington night, however, no doubt in part because I had established my own private relationship to the neighborhood, one that could never be shared with others in a single evening of cheap South Asian food and beer. I knew the hours of the call of the muezzin that rang from the mosque a block away from my apartment. I heard it in my bedroom every morning, afternoon, and evening, and if I was writing when it called out, I learned that it was better to simply stop and admire it. My landlord's father, an old gray-haired Chinese immigrant who spoke

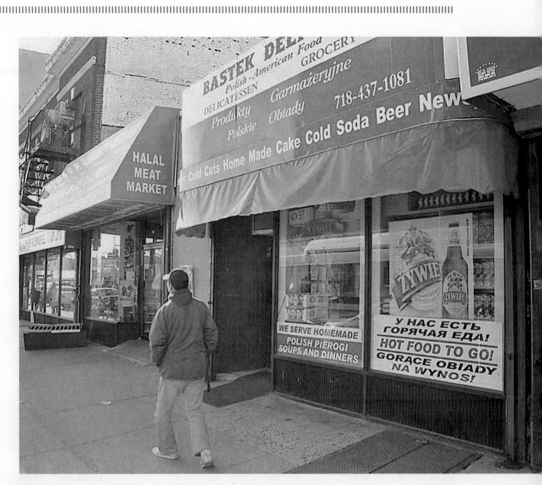

Ethnic diversity in Brooklyn's Kensington neighborhood.

no English, gradually smiled at me as I came and went, just as I learned to say hello, as politely as possible, in Mandarin every time I saw him. The men behind the counters of the Bangladeshi takeout places now knew me by sight. A few, on occasion, slipped an extra dollop of vegetables or rice into my to-go container, perhaps because they worried that I wasn't eating enough. One in particular, who was roughly my age, spoke little English, and smiled wholeheartedly whenever I came in, gave me presweetened tea and free bread, a gesture that I took to be an acknowledgment that, at least for him, I had earned my own, albeit marginal, place here.

And so instead of sitting with friends in a brightly lit fluorescent restaurant with cafeteria-style service, I found myself night after night quietly walking around the neighborhood in between sporadic fits of writing. Kensington was no more beautiful by night than by day, and perhaps this very absence of grandeur allowed me to feel more at ease wandering its streets at night. The haphazard gathering of immigrants in Kensington had turned it

Ethnic restaurant in Brooklyn's Kensington neighborhood.

into a place that even someone like me, haunted and conscious of race and identity at every turn, could slip and blend into.

Inevitably on my way home I returned to the corner of Church and McDonald with its glut of identical restaurants. On warm nights, I had found it was the perfect spot to stand and admire not only what Kensington had become with the most recent wave of migration, but what any close-knit community—whether its people came here one hundred years ago from Europe or a decade ago from Africa, Asia, or the Caribbean—has provided throughout Brooklyn's history: a second home. There, on that corner, made up of five competing South Asian restaurants of roughly equal quality, dozens of Pakistani and Bangladeshi men gathered one night after another to drink chai out of paper cups. The men stood there talking for hours, huddled in factions built in part, I imagine, around restaurant loyalties. Some nights I sat in one of the restaurants and watched from a corner table with a book in hand as an artificial prop. A few of the men always stared, curious no doubt as to what I was doing there. Even though I lived in Kensington, when it came to evening gatherings like this, I was the foreigner and tourist. On other nights I ordered my own cup of tea and stood a few feet away on the edge of the sidewalk, near the subway entrance or at the bus stop, and silently stared. I had seen communal scenes like this before, especially while living in Washington, D.C., where there always seemed to be a cluster of Ethiopians, my age or older, gathered together outside coffee shops and bars all over the city, talking in Amharic with an ease and fluency that I admired and envied. They told jokes that didn't require explanation and debated arguments that were decades in the making. All of this was coupled with the familiarity and comfort of speaking in our native tongue. At any given moment, they could have told you without hesitancy where they were from. And so I had watched, hardly understanding a word, hoping somehow that the simple act of association and observation was enough to draw me into the fold.

Here, then, was a similar scene, this one played out on a Brooklyn cor- 10 ner with a culture and history different from the one I had been born into, but familiar to me nonetheless. The men on that corner in Kensington, just like the people I had known throughout my life, were immigrants in the most complete sense of the word—their loyalties still firmly attached to the countries they had left one, five, or twenty years earlier. If there was one thing I admired most about them, it was that they had succeeded, at least partly, in re-creating in Brooklyn some of what they had lost when they left their countries of origin. Unlike the solitary and private walks my father and I took, each of us buried deep in thoughts that had nowhere to go, this nightly gathering of Pakistani and Bangladeshi men was a makeshift reen-actment of home. Farther down the road from where they stood were the few remaining remnants of the neighborhood's older Jewish community—one synagogue, a kosher deli—proof, if one was ever needed, that Brooklyn is always reinventing itself, that there is room here for us all.

While the men stood outside on the corner, their numbers gradually increasing until they spilled out into the street as they talked loudly among themselves, I once again played my own familiar role of quiet, jealous observer and secret admirer. I have no idea what those men talked about, if they discussed politics, sex, or petty complaints about work. It never mattered anyway. The substance of the conversations belonged to them, and I couldn't have cared less. What I had wanted and found in them, what I admired and adored about Kensington, was the assertion that we can rebuild and remake ourselves and our communities over and over again, in no small part because there have always been corners in Brooklyn to do so on. I stood on that corner night after night for the most obvious of reasons—to be reminded of a way of life that persists regardless of context; to feel, however foolishly, that I too was attached to something. ◼

The Reader's Presence

1. Why does Mengestu consciously try to make the Kensington section of Brooklyn home? What had been previously missing in his life? Why can't he acknowledge that he is *from* Ethiopia? Do you think he succeeds in making Kensington home? How do you interpret his final paragraph?

2. What is Mengestu's reason for not hosting the "Kensington night" he had planned (paragraph 7)? Why do you think—though he says he made new friends in the city—that no friends appear in the essay? Note how often through the course of the essay he is either alone or at the edge of a group of people whose language he doesn't understand. How do you interpret this?

3. **CONNECTIONS:**   Compare Mengestu's essay to Geeta Kothari's "If You Are What You Eat, Then What Am I?" (page 132). How does each essay illuminate ethnic identity in America? What differences and similarities can you find between each author's presentation of separation and assimilation?

Manuel Muñoz

LEAVE YOUR NAME AT THE BORDER

MANUEL MUÑOZ (b. 1972) is a California native who received a BA from Harvard University and an MFA in creative writing from Cornell University. He has published two award-winning collections of short fiction, *Zigzagger* (2003) and *The Faith Healer of Olive Avenue* (2007), and his work has been published widely in mainstream publications, such
as the *New York Times*, as well as in some
of the most prestigious literary magazines
in the country, including *Glimmer Train* and
Boston Review. He received a Whiting Award
and a PEN/O'Henry Award in 2009. His first

> **Manuel Muñoz has said that California's Central Valley and his hometown, Dinuba, "remain the foundation of [his] fiction."**

novel, *What You See in the Dark*, was published in 2011. Although he currently teaches in the Creative Writing Program at the University of Arizona, Tucson, he has said that California's Central Valley and his hometown, Dinuba, "remain the foundation of [his] fiction."

AT THE FRESNO AIRPORT, as I made my way to the gate, I heard a name over the intercom. The way the name was pronounced by the gate agent made me want to see what she looked like. That is, I wanted to see whether she was Mexican. Around Fresno, identity politics rarely deepen into exacting terms, so to say "Mexican" means, essentially, "not white." The slivered self-identifications Chicano, Hispanic, Mexican-American and Latino are not part of everyday life in the Valley. You're either Mexican or you're not. If someone wants to know if you were born in Mexico, they'll ask. Then you're From Over There—*de allá*. And leave it at that.

The gate agent, it turned out, was Mexican. Well-coiffed, in her 30s, she wore foundation that was several shades lighter than the rest of her skin. It was the kind of makeup job I've learned to silently identify at the mall when I'm with my mother, who will say nothing about it until we're back in the car. Then she'll stretch her neck like an ostrich and point to the darkness of her own skin, wondering aloud why women try to camouflage who they are.

I watched the Mexican gate agent busy herself at the counter, profes-sional and studied. Once again, she picked up the microphone and, with authority, announced the name of the missing customer: "Eugenio Reyes, please come to the front desk."

You can probably guess how she said it. Her Anglicized pronunciation wouldn't be unusual in a place like California's Central Valley. I didn't have a Mexican name there either: I was an instruction guide.

When people ask me where I'm from, I say Fresno because I don't expect them to know little Dinuba. Fresno is a booming city of nearly 500,000 these days, with a diversity—white, Mexican, African-American, Armenian, Hmong and Middle Eastern people are all well represented—that shouldn't surprise anyone. It's in the small towns like Dinuba that surround Fresno that the awareness of cultural difference is stripped down to the interactions between the only two groups that tend to live there: whites and Mexicans. When you hear a Mexican name spoken in these towns, regardless of the speaker's background, it's no wonder that there's an "English way of pronouncing it." 5

I was born in 1972, part of a generation that learned both English and Spanish. Many of my cousins and siblings are bilingual, serving as translators for those in the family whose English is barely functional. Others have no way of following the Spanish banter at family gatherings. You can tell who falls into which group: Estella, Eric, Delia, Dubina, Melanie.

It's intriguing to watch "American" names begin to dominate among my nieces and nephews and second cousins, as well as with the children of my hometown friends. I am not surprised to meet 5-year-old Brandon or Kaitlyn. Hardly anyone questions the incongruity of matching these names with last names like Trujillo or Zepeda. The English-only way of life partly explains the quiet erasure of cultural difference that assimilation has attempted to accomplish. A name like Kaitlyn Zepeda doesn't completely obscure her ethnicity, but the half-step of her name, as a gesture, is almost understandable.

Spanish was and still is viewed with suspicion: always the language of the vilified illegal immigrant, it segregated schoolchildren into English-only and bilingual programs; it defined you, above all else, as part of a lower class. Learning English, though, brought its own complications with identity. It was simultaneously the language of the white population and a path toward the richer, expansive identity of "American." But it took getting out of the Valley for me to understand that "white" and "American" were two very different things.

Something as simple as saying our names "in English" was our unwittingly complicit gesture of trying to blend in. Pronouncing Mexican names correctly was never encouraged. Names like Daniel, Olivia and Marco slipped right into the mutability of the English language.

I remember a school ceremony at which the mathematics teacher, a white man, announced the names of Mexican students correctly and caused some confusion, if not embarrassment. Years later we recognized that he spoke in deference to our Spanish-speaking parents in the audience, caring teacher that he was. 10

These were difficult names for a non-Spanish speaker: Araceli, Nadira, Luis (a beautiful name when you glide the *u* and the *i* as you're supposed to). We had been accustomed to having our birth names altered for convenience. Concepción was Connie. Ramón was Raymond. My cousin Esperanza was Hope—but her name was pronounced "Hopie" because any Spanish speaker would automatically pronounce the *e* at the end.

Ours, then, were names that stood as barriers to a complete embrace of an American identity, simply because their pronunciations required a slip into Spanish, the otherness that assimilation was supposed to erase. What to do with names like Amado, Lucio or Élida? There are no English "equivalents," no answer when white teachers asked, "What does your name mean?" when what they really wanted to know was "What's the English one?" So what you heard was a name butchered beyond recognition, a pronunciation that pointed the finger at the Spanish language as the source of clunky sound and ugly rhythm.

My stepfather, from Ojos de Agua, Mexico, jokes when I ask him about the names of Mexicans born here. He deliberately stumbles over pronunciations, imitating our elders who have difficulty with Bradley and Madelyn. "Ashley Sánchez. ¿Tú crees?"[1] He wonders aloud what has happened to the "nombres del rancho"—traditional Mexican names that are hardly given anymore to children born in the States: Heraclio, Madaleno, Otilia, Dominga.

My stepfather's experience with the Anglicization of his name—Antonio to Tony—ties into something bigger than learning English. For him, the erasure of his name was about deference and subservience. Becoming Tony gave him a measure of access as he struggled to learn English and get more fieldwork.

This isn't to say that my stepfather welcomed the change, only that he   15
could not put up much resistance. Not changing put him at risk of being passed over for work. English was a world of power and decisions, of smooth, uninterrupted negotiation. There was no time to search for the right word while a shop clerk waited for him to come up with the English name of the correct part needed out in the field. Clear communication meant you could go unsupervised, or that you were even able to read instructions directly off a piece of paper. Every gesture made toward convincing an employer that English was on its way to being mastered had the potential to make a season of fieldwork profitable.

It's curious that many of us growing up in Dinuba adhered to the same rules. Although as children of farm workers we worked in the fields at an early age, we'd also had the opportunity to stay in one town long enough to finish school. Most of us had learned English early and splintered off into a dual existence of English at school, Spanish at home. But instead of recognizing the need for fluency in both languages, we turned it into a peculiar kind of battle. English was for public display. Spanish was for privacy—and privacy quickly turned to shame.

---

1 *¿Tú crees?:* Can you believe it? —EDS.

The corrosive effect of assimilation is the displacement of one culture over another, the inability to sustain more than one way of being. It isn't a code word for racial and ethnic acculturation only. It applies to needing and wanting to belong, of seeing from the outside and wondering how to get in and then, once inside, realizing there are always those still on the fringe.

When I went to college on the East Coast, I was confronted for the first time by people who said my name correctly without prompting; if they stumbled, there was a quick apology and an honest plea to help with the pronunciation. But introducing myself was painful: already shy, I avoided meeting people because I didn't want to say my name, felt burdened by my own history. I knew that my small-town upbringing and its limitations on Spanish would not have been tolerated by any of the students of color who had grown up in large cities, in places where the sheer force of their native languages made them dominant in their neighborhoods.

It didn't take long for me to assert the power of code-switching in public, the transferring of words from one language to another, regardless of who might be listening. I was learning that the English language composed new meanings when its constrictions were ignored, crossed over or crossed out. Language is all about manipulation, or not listening to the rules.

When I come back to Dinuba, I have a hard time hearing my name   20 said incorrectly, but I have an even harder time beginning a conversation with others about why the pronunciation of our names matters. Leaving a small town requires an embrace of a larger point of view, but a town like Dinuba remains forever embedded in an either/or way of life. My step-father still answers to Tony and, as the United States-born children grow older, their Anglicized names begin to signify who does and who does not "belong"—who was born here and who is *de allá*.

My name is Manuel. To this day, most people cannot say it correctly, the way it was intended to be said. But I can live with that because I love the alliteration of my full name. It wasn't the name my mother, Esmeralda, was going to give me. At the last minute, my father named me after an uncle I would never meet. My name was to have been Ricardo. Growing up in Dinuba, I'm certain I would have become Ricky or even Richard, and the journey toward the discovery of the English language's extraordinary power in even the most ordinary of circumstances would probably have gone unlearned.

I count on a collective sense of cultural loss to once again swing the names back to our native language. The Mexican gate agent announced Eugenio Reyes, but I never got a chance to see who appeared. I pictured an older man, cowboy hat in hand, but I made the assumption on his name alone, the clash of privileges I imagined between someone *de allá* and a Mexican woman with a good job in the United States. Would she speak to him in Spanish? Or would she raise her voice to him as if he were hard of hearing?

But who was I to imagine this man being from anywhere, based on his name alone? At a place of arrivals and departures, it sank into me that the currency of our names is a stroke of luck: because mine was not an easy name, it forced me to consider how language would rule me if I allowed it. Yet I discovered that only by leaving. My stepfather must live in the Valley, a place that does not allow that choice, every day. And Eugenio Reyes—I do not know if he was coming or going. ●

The Reader's Presence

1. Consider the way Muñoz structures his essay. What is his purpose in starting with a name heard over the intercom at the Fresno Airport? What does that incident trigger? In what ways does ending his essay with further reflections on that same moment reinforce his perspective about identity? In what ways does his final paragraph complicate that perspective?

2. As a reader, would you know how to pronounce the author's name correctly? Any of the other Mexican names he mentions? Why do you think Muñoz offers no guide to pronunciation that would help English-speaking readers say the names as the author thinks they should be said? What does he feel is lost when the Mexican names are Anglicized?

3. **CONNECTIONS:** Compare "Leave Your Name at the Border" to Dinaw Mengestu's "Home at Last" (page 170). What identity issues do both writers contend with? You might also compare Muñoz's essay with Richard Rodriguez's longer essay on the Spanish language, "Aria: A Memoir of a Bilingual Childhood" (page 187). What differences in attitude do you find between Muñoz and Rodriguez?

George Orwell
SHOOTING AN ELEPHANT

GEORGE ORWELL (1903–1950) was born Eric Arthur Blair in Bengal, India, the son of a colonial administrator. He was sent to England for his education and attended Eton on a scholarship, but rather than go on to university in 1922 he returned to the East and served with the Indian Imperial Police in Burma. Orwell hated his work and the colonial system; published posthumously, the essay "Shooting an Elephant" was based on his experience in Burma and is found in *Shooting an Elephant and Other Essays* (1950). In 1927, Orwell returned to England and began a career as a professional writer. He served briefly in the Spanish Civil War until he was wounded and then settled in Hertfordshire. Best remembered for his novels *Animal Farm* (1945) and *Nineteen Eighty-Four* (1949), Orwell also wrote articles, essays, and reviews, usually with a political point in mind. In 1969, Irving Howe honored Orwell as "the best English essayist since Hazlitt, perhaps since Dr. Johnson. He was the greatest moral force in English letters during the last several decades: craggy, fiercely polemical, sometimes mistaken, but an utterly free man."

> **"Good prose is like a windowpane."**

In his 1946 essay "Why I Write," Orwell said that from a very early age "I knew that when I grew up I should be a writer." At first he saw writing as a remedy for loneliness, but as he grew up his reasons for writing expanded: "Looking back through my work, I see it is invariably when I lacked a *political* purpose that I wrote lifeless books." In his mature work, he relied on simple, clear prose to express his political and social convictions: "Good prose," he once wrote, "is like a windowpane."

IN MOULMEIN, in Lower Burma, I was hated by large numbers of people — the only time in my life that I have been important enough for this to happen to me. I was subdivisional police officer of the town, and in an aimless, petty kind of way anti-European feeling was very bitter. No one had the guts to raise a riot, but if a European woman went through the bazaars alone somebody would probably spit betel juice over her dress. As a police officer I was an obvious target and was baited whenever it seemed safe to do so. When a nimble Burman tripped me up on the football field and the referee (another Burman) looked the other way, the crowd yelled with hideous laughter. This happened more than once. In the end the sneering yellow faces of young men that met me everywhere, the insults hooted after me when I was at a safe distance, got badly on my nerves. The young Buddhist priests were the worst of all. There were several thousands of them in the town and none of them seemed to have anything to do except stand on street corners and jeer at Europeans.

All this was perplexing and upsetting. For at that time I had already made up my mind that imperialism was an evil thing and the sooner I chucked up my job and got out of it the better. Theoretically — and secretly, of course — I was all for the Burmese and all against the oppressors, the British. As for the job I was doing, I hated it more bitterly than I can perhaps make clear. In a job like that you see the dirty work of Empire at close quarters. The wretched prisoners huddling in the stinking cages of the lockups, the grey, cowed faces of the long-term convicts, the scarred buttocks of the men who had been flogged with bamboos — all these oppressed me with an intolerable sense of guilt. But I could get nothing into perspective. I was young and ill-educated and I had had to think out my problems in the utter silence that is imposed on every Englishman in the East. I did not even know that the British Empire is dying, still less did I know that it is a great deal better than the younger empires that are going to supplant it. All I knew was that I was stuck between my hatred of the empire I served and my rage against the evil-spirited little beasts who tried to make my job impossible. With one part of my mind I thought of the British Raj[1] as an unbreakable tyranny, as something clamped down, *in saecula saeculorum*,[2] upon the will of prostrate peoples; with another part I thought that the greatest joy in the world would be to drive a bayonet into a Buddhist priest's guts. Feelings like these are the normal by-products of imperialism; ask any Anglo-Indian official, if you can catch him off duty.

One day something happened which in a roundabout way was enlightening. It was a tiny incident in itself, but it gave me a better glimpse than I had had before of the real nature of imperialism—the real motives for which despotic governments act. Early one morning the subinspector at a police station the other end of town rang me up on the phone and said that an elephant was ravaging the bazaar. Would I please come and do something about it? I did not know what I could do, but I wanted to see what was happening and I got on to a pony and started out. I took my rifle, an old .44 Winchester and much too small to kill an elephant, but I thought the noise might be useful *in terrorem*.[3] Various Burmans stopped me on the way and told me about the elephant's doings. It was not, of course, a wild elephant, but a tame one which had gone "must."[4] It had been chained up, as tame elephants always are when their attack of "must" is due, but on the previous night it had broken its chain and escaped. Its mahout,[5] the only person who could manage it when it was in that state, had set out in pursuit, but had taken the wrong direction and was now twelve hours' journey away, and in the morning the elephant had suddenly reappeared in the town. The Burmese population had no weapons and were quite helpless against it. It had already destroyed somebody's bamboo hut, killed a cow, and raided some fruit stalls and devoured the stock; also it had met the municipal rubbish van and, when the driver jumped out and took to his heels, had turned the van over and inflicted violence upon it.

The Burmese subinspector and some Indian constables were waiting for me in the quarter where the elephant had been seen. It was a very poor quarter, a labyrinth of squalid bamboo huts, thatched with palmleaf, winding all over a steep hillside. I remember that it was a cloudy, stuffy morning at the beginning of the rains. We began questioning the people as to where the elephant had gone and, as usual, failed to get any definite information. That is invariably the case in the East; a story always sounds clear enough

---

1 *Raj:* The British administration.—EDS.
2 *in saecula saeculorum:* Forever and ever (Latin).—EDS.
3 *in terrorem:* As a warning (Latin).—EDS.
4 *"must":* Sexual arousal.—EDS.
5 *mahout:* Keeper (Hindi).—EDS.

at a distance, but the nearer you get to the scene of events the vaguer it becomes. Some of the people said that the elephant had gone in one direction, some said that he had gone in another, some professed not even to have heard of any elephant. I had almost made up my mind that the whole story was a pack of lies, when we heard yells a little distance away. There was a loud, scandalized cry of "Go away, child! Go away this instant!" and an old woman with a switch in her hand came round the corner of a hut, violently shooing away a crowd of naked children. Some more women followed, clicking their tongues and exclaiming; evidently there was something that the children ought not to have seen. I rounded the hut and saw a man's dead body sprawling in the mud. He was an Indian, a black Dravidian[6] coolie, almost naked, and he could not have been dead many minutes. The people said that the elephant had come suddenly upon him round the corner of the hut, caught him with its trunk, put its foot on his back, and ground him into the earth. This was the rainy season and the ground was soft, and his face had scored a trench a foot deep and a couple of yards long. He was lying on his belly with arms crucified and head sharply twisted to one side. His face was coated with mud, the eyes wide open, the teeth bared and grinning with an expression of unendurable agony. (Never tell me, by the way, that the dead look peaceful. Most of the corpses I have seen looked devilish.) The friction of the great beast's foot had stripped the skin from his back as neatly as one skins a rabbit. As soon as I saw the dead man I sent an orderly to a friend's house nearby to borrow an elephant rifle. I had already sent back the pony, not wanting it to go mad with fright and throw me if it smelled the elephant.

The orderly came back in a few minutes with a rifle and five cartridges,   5 and meanwhile some Burmans had arrived and told us that the elephant was in the paddy fields below, only a few hundred yards away. As I started forward practically the whole population of the quarter flocked out of the houses and followed me. They had seen the rifle and were all shouting excitedly that I was going to shoot the elephant. They had not shown much interest in the elephant when he was merely ravaging their homes, but it was different now that he was going to be shot. It was a bit of fun to them, as it would be to an English crowd; besides, they wanted the meat. It made me vaguely uneasy. I had no intention of shooting the elephant—I had merely sent for the rifle to defend myself if necessary—and it is always unnerving to have a crowd following you. I marched down the hill, looking and feeling a fool, with the rifle over my shoulder and an ever-growing army of people jostling at my heels. At the bottom, when you got away from the huts, there was a metalled road and beyond that a miry waste of paddy fields a thousand yards across, not yet ploughed but soggy from the first rains and dotted with coarse grass. The elephant was standing eight yards from the road, his left side towards us. He took not the slightest notice of the crowd's approach. He was tearing up bunches of grass, beating them against his knees to clean them and stuffing them into his mouth.

6 **Dravidian:** A populous Indian group.—EDS.

I had halted on the road. As soon as I saw the elephant I knew with perfect certainty that I ought not to shoot him. It is a serious matter to shoot a working elephant—it is comparable to destroying a huge and costly piece of machinery—and obviously one ought not to do it if it can possibly be avoided. And at that distance, peacefully eating, the elephant looked no more dangerous than a cow. I thought then and I think now that his attack of "must" was already passing off; in which case he would merely wander harmlessly about until the mahout came back and caught him. Moreover, I did not in the least want to shoot him. I decided that I would watch him for a little while to make sure that he did not turn savage again, and then go home.

But at that moment, I glanced round at the crowd that had followed me. It was an immense crowd, two thousand at the least and growing every minute. It blocked the road for a long distance on either side. I looked at the sea of yellow faces above the garish clothes—faces all happy and excited over this bit of fun, all certain that the elephant was going to be shot. They were watching me as they would watch a conjuror about to perform a trick. They did not like me, but with the magical rifle in my hands I was momentarily worth watching. And suddenly I realized that I should have to shoot the elephant after all: The people expected it of me and I had got to do it; I could feel their two thousand wills pressing me forward, irresistibly. And it was at this moment, as I stood there with the rifle in my hands, that I first grasped the hollowness, the futility of the white man's dominion in the East. Here was I, the white man with his gun, standing in front of the unarmed native crowd—seemingly the leading actor of the piece; but in reality I was only an absurd puppet pushed to and fro by the will of those yellow faces behind. I perceived in this moment that when the white man turns tyrant it is his own freedom that he destroys. He becomes a sort of hollow, posing dummy, the conventionalized figure of a sahib. For it is the condition of his rule that he shall spend his life in trying to impress the "natives," and so in every crisis he has got to do what the "natives" expect of him. He wears a mask, and his face grows to fit it. I had got to shoot the elephant. I had committed myself to doing it when I sent for the rifle. A sahib has got to act like a sahib; he has got to appear resolute, to know his own mind and do definite things. To come all that way, rifle in hand, with two thousand people marching at my heels, and then to trail feebly away, having done nothing—no, that was impossible. The crowd would laugh at me. And my whole life, every white man's life in the East, was one long struggle not to be laughed at.

But I did not want to shoot the elephant. I watched him beating his bunch of grass against his knees, with that preoccupied grandmotherly air that elephants have. It seemed to me that it would be murder to shoot him. At that age I was not squeamish about killing animals, but I had never shot an elephant and never wanted to. (Somehow it always seems worse to kill a *large* animal.) Besides, there was the beast's owner to be considered. Alive, the elephant was worth at least a hundred pounds; dead, he would only be worth the value of his tusks, five pounds, possibly. But I had got to act quickly. I turned to some experienced-looking Burmans who had been there when we arrived, and asked them how the elephant had been behaving. They all said the same thing: He took no notice of you if you left him alone, but he might charge if you went too close to him.

It was perfectly clear to me what I ought to do. I ought to walk up to within, say, twenty-five yards of the elephant and test his behavior. If he charged, I could shoot; if he took no notice of me, it would be safe to leave him until the mahout came back. But also I knew that I was going to do no such thing. I was a poor shot with a rifle and the ground was soft mud into which one would sink at every step. If the elephant charged and I missed him, I should have about as much chance as a toad under a steamroller. But even then I was not thinking particularly of my own skin, only of the watchful yellow faces behind. For at that moment, with the crowd watching me, I was not afraid in the ordinary sense, as I would have been if I had been alone. A white man mustn't be frightened in front of "natives"; and so, in general, he isn't frightened. The sole thought in my mind was that if anything went wrong those two thousand Burmans would see me pursued, caught, trampled on, and reduced to a grinning corpse like that Indian up the hill. And if that happened it was quite probable that some of them would laugh. That would never do. There was only one alternative. I shoved the cartridges into the magazine and lay down on the road to get a better aim.

The crowd grew very still, and a deep, low, happy sigh, as of people who 10 see the theatre curtain go up at last, breathed from innumerable throats. They were going to have their bit of fun after all. The rifle was a beautiful German thing with cross-hair sights. I did not then know that in shooting an elephant one would shoot to cut an imaginary bar running from ear-hole to ear-hole. I ought, therefore, as the elephant was sideways on, to have aimed straight at his ear-hole; actually I aimed several inches in front of this, thinking the brain would be further forward.

When I pulled the trigger I did not hear the bang or feel the kick—one never does when a shot goes home—but I heard the devilish roar of glee that went up from the crowd. In that instant, in too short a time, one would have thought, even for the bullet to get there, a mysterious, terrible change had come over the elephant. He neither stirred nor fell, but every line of his body had altered. He looked suddenly stricken, shrunken, immensely old, as though the frightful impact of the bullet had paralyzed him without knocking him down. At last, after what seemed a long time—it might have been five seconds, I dare say—he sagged flabbily to his knees. His mouth slobbered. An enormous senility seemed to have settled upon him. One could have imagined him thousands of years old. I fired again into the same spot. At the second shot he did not collapse but climbed with desperate slowness to his feet and stood weakly upright, with legs sagging and head drooping. I fired a third time. That was the shot that did it for him. You could see the agony of it jolt his whole body and knock the last remnant of strength from his legs. But in falling he seemed for a moment to rise, for as his hind legs collapsed beneath him he seemed to tower upward like a huge rock toppling, his trunk reaching skywards like a tree. He trumpeted, for the first and only time. And then down he came, his belly towards me, with a crash that seemed to shake the ground even where I lay.

I got up. The Burmans were already racing past me across the mud. It was obvious that the elephant would never rise again, but he was not dead. He was breathing very rhythmically with long rattling gasps, his great mound of a side painfully rising and falling. His mouth was wide open. I could see far down into caverns of pale pink throat. I waited a long time for him to die, but his breathing did not weaken. Finally, I fired my two remaining shots into the spot where I thought his heart must be. The thick blood welled out of him like red velvet, but still he did not die. His body did not even jerk when the shots hit him, the tortured breathing continued without a pause. He was dying, very slowly and in great agony, but in some world remote from me where not even a bullet could damage him further. I felt I had got to put an end to that dreadful noise. It seemed dreadful to see the great beast lying there, powerless to move and yet powerless to die, and not even to be able to finish him. I sent back for my small rifle and poured shot after shot into his heart, and down his throat. They seemed to make no impression. The tortured gasps continued as steadily as the ticking of a clock.

In the end I could not stand it any longer and went away. I heard later that it took him half an hour to die. Burmans were bringing dahs[7] and baskets even before I left, and I was told they had stripped his body almost to the bones by the afternoon.

Afterwards, of course, there were endless discussions about the shooting of the elephant. The owner was furious, but he was only an Indian and could do nothing. Besides, legally I had done the right thing, for a mad elephant has to be killed, like a mad dog, if its owner fails to control it. Among the Europeans opinion was divided. The older men said I was right, the younger men said it was a damn shame to shoot an elephant for killing a coolie, because the elephant was worth more than any damn Coringhee coolie. And afterwards I was very glad that the coolie had been killed; it put me legally in the right and it gave me sufficient pretext for shooting the elephant. I often wondered whether any of the others grasped that I had done it solely to avoid looking a fool. ■

The Reader's Presence

1. At the end of paragraph 2, Orwell gives the perfect expression of ambivalence, the simultaneous holding of two opposed feelings or opinions: "With one part of my mind . . . with another part . . ." How would you describe Orwell's dilemma? How would you react in such a situation? Is Orwell recommending that readers see his behavior as a model of what to do in such a conflict? To what extent is Orwell responsible for the situation in which he finds himself? What does he mean when he says that his conflicted feelings "are the normal by-products of imperialism"?

7 **dahs:** Large knives. —EDS.

2. Some literary critics doubt that Orwell really did shoot an elephant in Burma. No external historical documentation has ever been found to corroborate Orwell's account. Yet what *internal* elements in the essay—what details or features—suggest that the episode is fact and not fiction? In other words, what makes this piece seem to be an essay and not a short story?

3. **CONNECTIONS:**   Orwell's essay describes a state of extreme personal self-consciousness, even vigilance, in a situation in which one's behavior feels somehow "scripted" by society. Orwell writes, "In reality I was only an absurd puppet pushed to and fro by the will of those yellow faces behind" (paragraph 7). How does Orwell's essay compare with Brent Staples's essay "Just Walk on By: A Black Man Ponders His Power to Alter Public Space" (page 217)? Compare especially Orwell's use of the word *fool* in his last paragraph and Staples's use of the same word in the second paragraph of the alternate version of his essay. Do you believe both authors?

Richard Rodriguez

ARIA: A MEMOIR OF A BILINGUAL CHILDHOOD

RICHARD RODRIGUEZ (b. 1944) has contributed articles to many magazines and newspapers, including *Harper's*, *American Scholar*, the *Los Angeles Times*, and the *New York Times*. He is an editor at *Pacific News Services* and a regular essayist on the *News Hour with Jim Lehrer*, for which he received the 1997 George Foster Peabody Award. His most sensational literary accomplishment, however, is his intellectual autobiography, *Hunger of Memory: The Education of Richard Rodriguez* (1982). In it, Rodriguez outlines his positions on issues such as bilingualism, affirmative action, and assimilation, and he concludes that current policies in these areas are misguided and serve only to reinforce current social inequalities. Other books include *Days of Obligation: An Argument with My Mexican Father* (1992) and *Brown: The Last Discovery of America* (2002).

> **"I have come to think of myself as engaged in writing graffiti."**

||||||||||||||||||||||||||||||||||||||||||||||||||||||||||||||||||||||||||||||||||||||||||||||||||||||||||||||||||||||||||||||||||||||||||||||||||

About the experience of writing his autobiography, Rodriguez comments, "By finding public words to describe one's feelings, one can describe oneself to oneself. . . . I have come to think of myself as engaged in writing graffiti."

The following essay originally appeared in the *American Scholar* (winter 1980/81) and later served as the opening chapter in Rodriguez's autobiography *Hunger of Memory*.

I REMEMBER, to start with, that day in Sacramento, in a California now nearly thirty years past, when I first entered a classroom—able to understand about fifty stray English words. The third of four children, I had been preceded by my older brother and sister to a neighborhood Roman Catholic school. But neither of them had revealed very much about their classroom experiences. They left each morning and returned each afternoon, always together, speaking Spanish as they climbed the five steps to the porch. And their mysterious books, wrapped in brown shopping-bag paper, remained on the table next to the door, closed firmly behind them.

An accident of geography sent me to a school where all my classmates were white and many were the children of doctors and lawyers and business executives. On that first day of school, my classmates must certainly have been uneasy to find themselves apart from their families, in the first institution of their lives. But I was astonished. I was fated to be the "problem student" in class.

The nun said, in a friendly but oddly impersonal voice: "Boys and girls, this is Richard Rodriguez." (I heard her sound it out: *Rich-heard Road-ree-guess.*) It was the first time I had heard anyone say my name in English. "Richard," the nun repeated more slowly, writing my name down in her book. Quickly I turned to see my mother's face dissolve in a watery blur behind the pebbled-glass door.

Now, many years later, I hear of something called "bilingual education"—a scheme proposed in the late 1960s by Hispanic-American social activists, later endorsed by a congressional vote. It is a program that seeks to permit non-English-speaking children (many from lower class homes) to use their "family language" as the language of school. Such, at least, is the aim its supporters announce. I hear them, and am forced to say no: It is not possible for a child, any child, ever to use his family's language in school. Not to understand this is to misunderstand the public uses of schooling and to trivialize the nature of intimate life.

Memory teaches me what I know of these matters. The boy reminds the adult. I was a bilingual child, but of a certain kind: "socially disadvantaged," the son of working-class parents, both Mexican immigrants. 5

In the early years of my boyhood, my parents coped very well in America. My father had steady work. My mother managed at home. They were nobody's victims. When we moved to a house many blocks from the Mexican-American section of town, they were not intimidated by those two or three neighbors who initially tried to make us unwelcome. ("Keep your brats away from my sidewalk!") But despite all they achieved, or perhaps because they had so much to achieve, they lacked any deep feeling of ease, of belonging in public. They regarded the people at work or in crowds as being very distant from us. Those were the others, *los gringos*. That term was interchangeable in their speech with another, even more telling: *los americanos*.

I grew up in a house where the only regular guests were my relations. On a certain day, enormous families of relatives would visit us, and there would be so many people that the noise and the bodies would spill out to the backyard and onto the front porch. Then for weeks no one would come. (If the doorbell rang, it was usually a salesman.) Our house stood apart—gaudy yellow in a row of white bungalows. We were the people with the noisy dog, the people who raised chickens. We were the foreigners on the block. A few neighbors would smile and wave at us. We waved back. But until I was seven years old, I did not know the name of the old couple living next door or the names of the kids living across the street.

In public, my father and mother spoke a hesitant, accented, and not always grammatical English. And then they would have to strain, their bodies tense, to catch the sense of what was rapidly said by *los gringos*. At home, they returned to Spanish. The language of their Mexican past sounded in counterpoint to the English spoken in public. The words would come quickly, with ease. Conveyed through those sounds was the pleasing, soothing, consoling reminder that one was at home.

During those years when I was first learning to speak, my mother and father addressed me only in Spanish; in Spanish I learned to reply. By contrast, English (*inglés*) was the language I came to associate with gringos, rarely heard in the house. I learned my first words of English overhearing my parents speaking to strangers. At six years of age, I knew just enough words for my mother to trust me on errands to stores one block away—but no more.

I was then a listening child, careful to hear the very different sounds   10
of Spanish and English. Wide-eyed with hearing, I'd listen to sounds more than to words. First, there were English (gringo) sounds. So many words still were unknown to me that when the butcher or the lady at the drugstore said something, exotic polysyllabic sounds would bloom in the midst of their sentences. Often the speech of people in public seemed to me very loud, booming with confidence. The man behind the counter would literally ask, "What can I do for you?" But by being so firm and clear, the sound of his voice said that he was a gringo; he belonged in public society. There were also the high, nasal notes of middle-class American speech—which I rarely am conscious of hearing today because I hear them so often, but could not stop hearing when I was a boy. Crowds at Safeway or at bus stops were noisy with the birdlike sounds of *los gringos*. I'd move away from them all—all the chirping chatter above me.

My own sounds I was unable to hear, but I knew that I spoke English poorly. My words could not extend to form complete thoughts. And the words I did speak I didn't know well enough to make distinct sounds. (Listeners would usually lower their heads to hear better what I was trying to say.) But it was one thing for *me* to speak English with difficulty; it was more troubling to hear my parents speaking in public: their high-whining vowels and guttural consonants; their sentences that got stuck with "eh" and "ah" sounds; the confused syntax; the hesitant rhythm of sounds so different from the way gringos spoke. I'd notice, moreover, that my parents' voices were softer than those of gringos we would meet.

I am tempted to say now that none of this mattered. (In adulthood I am embarrassed by childhood fears.) And, in a way, it didn't matter very much that my parents could not speak English with ease. Their linguistic difficulties had no serious consequences. My mother and father made themselves understood at the county hospital clinic and at government offices. And yet, in another way, it mattered very much. It was unsettling to hear my parents struggle with English. Hearing them, I'd grow nervous, and my clutching trust in their protection and power would be weakened.

There were many times like the night at a brightly lit gasoline station (a blaring white memory) when I stood uneasily hearing my father talk to a teenage attendant. I do not recall what they were saying, but I cannot forget the sounds my father made as he spoke. At one point his words slid together to form one long word—sounds as confused as the threads of blue and green oil in the puddle next to my shoes. His voice rushed through what he had left to say. Toward the end, he reached falsetto notes, appealing to his listener's understanding. I looked away at the lights of passing automobiles. I tried not to hear any more. But I heard only too well the attendant's reply, his calm, easy tones. Shortly afterward, headed for home, I shivered when my father put his hand on my shoulder. The very first chance that I got, I evaded his grasp and ran on ahead into the dark, skipping with feigned boyish exuberance.

But then there was Spanish: *español*, the language rarely heard away from the house; *español*, the language which seemed to me therefore a private language, my family's language. To hear its sounds was to feel myself specially recognized as one of the family, apart from *los otros*. A simple remark, an inconsequential comment could convey that assurance. My parents would say something to me and I would feel embraced by the sounds of their words. Those sounds said: *I am speaking with ease in Spanish. I am addressing you in words I never use with los gringos. I recognize you as someone special, close, like no one outside. You belong with us. In the family. Ricardo.*

At the age of six, well past the time when most middle-class children no longer notice the difference between sounds uttered at home and words spoken in public, I had a different experience. I lived in a world compounded of sounds. I was a child longer than most. I lived in a magical world, surrounded by sounds both pleasing and fearful. I shared with my family a language enchantingly private—different from that used in the city around us. 15

Just opening or closing the screen door behind me was an important experience. I'd rarely leave home all alone or without feeling reluctance. Walking down the sidewalk, under the canopy of tall trees, I'd warily notice the (suddenly) silent neighborhood kids who stood warily watching me. Nervously, I'd arrive at the grocery store to hear there the sounds of the gringo, reminding me that in this so-big world I was a foreigner. But if leaving home was never routine, neither was coming back. Walking toward our house, climbing the steps from the sidewalk, in summer when the front door was open, I'd hear voices beyond the screen door talking in Spanish. For a second or two I'd stay, linger there listening. Smiling, I'd hear my mother call out, saying in Spanish, "Is that you, Richard?" Those were her words, but all the while her sounds would assure me: *You are home now. Come closer inside. With us. "Sí,"* I'd reply.

Once more inside the house, I would resume my place in the family. The sounds would grow harder to hear. Once more at home, I would grow less conscious of them. It required, however, no more than the blurt of the doorbell to alert me all over again to listen to sounds. The house would turn instantly quiet while my mother went to the door. I'd hear her hard English sounds. I'd wait to hear her voice turn to soft-sounding Spanish, which assured me, as surely as did the clicking tongue of the lock on the door, that the stranger was gone.

Plainly it is not healthy to hear such sounds so often. It is not healthy to distinguish public from private sounds so easily. I remained cloistered by sounds, timid and shy in public, too dependent on the voices at home. And yet I was a very happy child when I was at home. I remember many nights when my father would come back from work, and I'd hear him call out to my mother in Spanish, sounding relieved. In Spanish, his voice would sound the light and free notes that he never could manage in English. Some nights I'd jump up just hearing his voice. My brother and I would come running into the room where he was with our mother. Our laughing (so deep was the pleasure!) became screaming. Like others who feel the pain of public alienation, we transformed the knowledge of our public separateness into a consoling reminder of our intimacy. Excited, our voices joined in a celebration of sounds. *We are speaking now the way we never speak out in public—we are together*, the sounds told me. Some nights no one seemed willing to loosen the hold that sounds had on us. At dinner we invented new words that sounded Spanish, but made sense only to us. We pieced together new words by taking, say, an English verb and giving it Spanish endings. My mother's instructions at bedtime would be lacquered with mock-urgent tones. Or a word like *sí*, sounded in several notes, would convey added measures of feeling. Tongues lingered around the edges of words, especially fat vowels. And we happily sounded that military drum roll, the twirling roar of the Spanish *r*. Family language, my family's sounds: the voices of my parents and sisters and brother. Their voices insisting: *You belong here. We are family members. Related. Special to one another. Listen!* Voices singing and sighing, rising and straining, then surging, teeming with pleasure which burst syllables into fragments of laughter. At times it seemed there was steady quiet only when, from another room, the rustling whispers of my parents faded and I edged closer to sleep.

Supporters of bilingual education imply today that students like me miss a great deal by not being taught in their family's language. What they seem not to recognize is that, as a socially disadvantaged child, I regarded Spanish as a private language. It was a ghetto language that deepened and strengthened my feeling of public separateness. What I needed to learn in school was that I had the right, and the obligation, to speak the public language. The odd truth is that my first-grade classmates could have become bilingual, in the conventional sense of the word, more easily than I. Had they been taught early (as upper middle-class children often are taught) a "second language" like Spanish or French, they could have regarded it simply as another public language. In my case, such bilingualism could not have been so quickly achieved. What I did not believe was that I could speak a single public language.

Without question, it would have pleased me to have heard my teach-   20 ers address me in Spanish when I entered the classroom. I would have felt much less afraid. I would have imagined that my instructors were somehow "related" to me; I would indeed have heard their Spanish as my family's language. I would have trusted them and responded with ease. But I would have delayed—postponed for how long?—having to learn the language of public society. I would have evaded—and for how long?—learning the great lesson of school: that I had a public identity.

Fortunately, my teachers were unsentimental about their responsibility. What they understood was that I needed to speak public English. So their voices would search me out, asking me questions. Each time I heard them I'd look up in surprise to see a nun's face frowning at me. I'd mumble, not really meaning to answer. The nun would persist. "Richard, stand up. Don't look at the floor. Speak up. Speak to the entire class, not just to me!" But I couldn't believe English could be my language to use. (In part, I did not want to believe it.) I continued to mumble. I resisted the teacher's demands. (Did I somehow suspect that once I learned this public language my family life would be changed?) Silent, waiting for the bell to sound, I remained dazed, diffident, afraid.

Because I wrongly imagined that English was intrinsically a public language and Spanish was intrinsically private, I easily noted the difference between classroom language and the language of home. At school, words were directed to a general audience of listeners. ("Boys and girls . . .") Words were meaningfully ordered. And the point was not self-expression alone, but to make oneself understood by many others. The teacher quizzed: "Boys and girls, why do we use that word in this sentence? Could we think of a better word to use there? Would the sentence change its meaning if the words were differently arranged? Isn't there a better way of saying much the same thing?" (I couldn't say. I wouldn't try to say.)

Three months passed. Five. A half year. Unsmiling, ever watchful, my teachers noted my silence. They began to connect my behavior with the slow progress my brother and sisters were making. Until, one Saturday morning, three nuns arrived at the house to talk to our parents. Stiffly they sat on the blue living-room sofa. From the doorway of another room, spying on the visitors, I noted the incongruity, the clash of two worlds, the faces and voices of school intruding upon the familiar setting of home. I overheard one voice gently wondering, "Do your children speak only Spanish at home, Mrs. Rodriguez?" While another voice added, "That Richard especially seems so timid and shy."

That Rich-heard!

With great tact, the visitors continued, "Is it possible for you and your   25 husband to encourage your children to practice their English when they are home?" Of course my parents complied. What would they not do for their children's well-being? And how could they question the Church's authority which those women represented? In an instant they agreed to give up the language (the sounds) which had revealed and accentuated our family's closeness. The moment after the visitors left, the change was observed. "*Ahora,* speak to us only *en inglés,*" my father and mother told us.

At first, it seemed a kind of game. After dinner each night, the family gathered together to practice "our" English. It was still then *inglés,* a language foreign to us, so we felt drawn to it as strangers. Laughing, we would try to define words we could not pronounce. We played with strange English sounds, often over-anglicizing our pronunciations. And we filled the smiling gaps of our sentences with familiar Spanish sounds. But that was cheating, somebody shouted, and everyone laughed.

In school, meanwhile, like my brother and sisters, I was required to attend a daily tutoring session. I needed a full year of this special work. I also needed my teachers to keep my attention from straying in class by calling out, "*Rich-heard!*"—their English voices slowly loosening the ties to my other name, with its three notes, *Ri-car-do.* Most of all, I needed to hear my mother and father speak to me in a moment of seriousness in "broken"—suddenly heartbreaking—English. This scene was inevitable. One Saturday morning I entered the kitchen where my parents were talking, but I did not realize that they were talking in Spanish until, the moment they saw me, their voices changed and they began speaking English. The gringo sounds they uttered startled me. Pushed me away. In that moment of trivial misunderstanding and profound insight, I felt my throat twisted by unsounded grief. I simply turned and left the room. But I had no place to escape to where I could grieve in Spanish. My brother and sisters were speaking English in another part of the house.

Again and again in the days following, as I grew increasingly angry, I was obliged to hear my mother and father encouraging me: "Speak to us *en inglés.*" Only then did I determine to learn classroom English. Thus, sometime afterward it happened: one day in school, I raised my hand to volunteer an answer to a question. I spoke out in a loud voice and I did not think it remarkable when the entire class understood. That day I moved very far from being the disadvantaged child I had been only days earlier. Taken hold at last was the belief, the calming assurance, that I *belonged* in public.

Shortly after, I stopped hearing the high, troubling sounds of *los gringos*. A more and more confident speaker of English, I didn't listen to how strangers sounded when they talked to me. With so many English-speaking people around me, I no longer heard American accents. Conversations quickened. Listening to persons whose voices sounded eccentrically pitched, I might note their sounds for a few seconds, but then I'd concentrate on what they were saying. Now when I heard someone's tone of voice—angry or questioning or sarcastic or happy or sad—I didn't distinguish it from the words it expressed. Sound and word were thus tightly wedded. At the end of each day I was often bemused, and always relieved, to realize how "soundless," though crowded with words, my day in public had been. An eight-year-old boy, I finally came to accept what had been technically true since my birth: I was an American citizen.

But diminished by then was the special feeling of closeness at home. 30
Gone was the desperate, urgent, intense feeling of being at home among those with whom I felt intimate. Our family remained a loving family, but one greatly changed. We were no longer so close, no longer bound tightly together by the knowledge of our separateness from *los gringos*. Neither my older brother nor my sisters rushed home after school any more. Nor did I. When I arrived home, often there would be neighborhood kids in the house. Or the house would be empty of sounds.

Following the dramatic Americanization of their children, even my parents grew more publicly confident—especially my mother. First she learned the names of all the people on the block. Then she decided we needed to have a telephone in our house. My father, for his part, continued to use the word *gringo*, but it was no longer charged with bitterness or distrust. Stripped of any emotional content, the word simply became a name for those Americans not of Hispanic descent. Hearing him, sometimes, I wasn't sure if he was pronouncing the Spanish word *gringo*, or saying gringo in English.

There was a new silence at home. As we children learned more and more English, we shared fewer and fewer words with our parents. Sentences needed to be spoken slowly when one of us addressed our mother or father. Often the parent wouldn't understand. The child would need to repeat himself. Still the parent misunderstood. The young voice, frustrated, would end up saying, "Never mind"—the subject was closed. Dinners would be noisy with the clinking of knives and forks against dishes. My mother would smile softly between her remarks; my father, at the other end of the table, would chew and chew his food while he stared over the heads of his children.

My mother! My father! After English became my primary language, I no longer knew what words to use in addressing my parents. The old Spanish words (those tender accents of sound) I had earlier used—*mamá* and *papá*—I couldn't use any more. They would have been all-too-painful reminders of how much had changed in my life. On the other hand, the words I heard neighborhood kids call their parents seemed equally unsatisfactory. "Mother" and "father," "ma," "papa," "pa," "dad," "pop" (how I hated the all-American sound of that last word)—all these I felt were unsuitable terms of address for *my* parents. As a result, I never used them at home. Whenever I'd speak to my parents, I would try to get their attention by looking at them. In public conversations, I'd refer to them as my "parents" or my "mother" and "father."

My mother and father, for their part, responded differently, as their children spoke to them less. My mother grew restless, seemed troubled and anxious at the scarceness of words exchanged in the house. She would question me about my day when I came home from school. She smiled at my small talk. She pried at the edges of my sentences to get me to say something more. ("What . . . ?") She'd join conversations she overheard, but her intrusions often stopped her children's talking. By contrast, my father seemed to grow reconciled to the new quiet. Though his English somewhat improved, he tended more and more to retire into silence. At dinner he spoke very little. One night his children and even his wife helplessly giggled at his garbled English pronunciation of the Catholic "Grace Before Meals." Thereafter he made his wife recite the prayer at the start of each meal, even on formal occasions when there were guests in the house.

Hers became the public voice of the family. On official business it was 35 she, not my father, who would usually talk to strangers on the phone or in stores. We children grew so accustomed to his silence that years later we would routinely refer to his "shyness." (My mother often tried to explain: Both of his parents died when he was eight. He was raised by an uncle who treated him as little more than a menial servant. He was never encouraged to speak. He grew up alone—a man of few words.) But I realized my father was not shy whenever I'd watch him speaking Spanish with relatives. Using Spanish, he was quickly effusive. Especially when talking with other men, his voice would spark, flicker, flare alive with varied sounds. In Spanish he expressed ideas and feelings he rarely revealed when speaking English. With firm Spanish sounds he conveyed a confidence and authority that English would never allow him.

The silence at home, however, was not simply the result of fewer words passing between parents and children. More profound for me was the silence created by my inattention to sounds. At about the time I no longer bothered to listen with care to the sounds of English in public, I grew careless about listening to the sounds made by the family when they spoke. Most of the time I would hear someone speaking at home and didn't distinguish his sounds from the words people uttered in public. I didn't even pay much attention to my parents' accented and ungrammatical speech—at least not at home. Only when I was with them in public would I become alert to their accents. But even then their sounds caused me less and less concern. For I was growing increasingly confident of my own public identity.

I would have been happier about my public success had I not recalled, sometimes, what it had been like earlier, when my family conveyed its intimacy through a set of conveniently private sounds. Sometimes in public, hearing a stranger, I'd hark back to my lost past. A Mexican farm worker approached me one day downtown. He wanted directions to some place. "*Hijito . . . ,*" he said. And his voice stirred old longings. Another time I was standing beside my mother in the visiting room of a Carmelite convent, before the dense screen which rendered the nuns shadowy figures. I heard several of them speaking Spanish in their busy, singsong, overlapping voices, assuring my mother that, yes, yes, we were remembered, all our family was remembered, in their prayers. Those voices echoed faraway family sounds. Another day a dark-faced old woman touched my shoulder lightly to steady herself as she boarded a bus. She murmured something to me I couldn't quite comprehend. Her Spanish voice came near, like the face of a never-before-seen relative in the instant before I was kissed. That voice, like so many of the Spanish voices I'd hear in public, recalled the golden age of my childhood.

Bilingual educators say today that children lose a degree of "individuality" by becoming assimilated into public society. (Bilingual schooling is a program popularized in the seventies, that decade when middle-class "ethnics" began to resist the process of assimilation—the "American melting pot.") But the bilingualists oversimplify when they scorn the value and necessity of assimilation. They do not seem to realize that a person is individualized in two ways. So they do not realize that, while one suffers a diminished sense of *private* individuality by being assimilated into public society, such assimilation makes possible the achievement of *public* individuality.

Simplistically again, the bilingualists insist that a student should be reminded of his difference from others in mass society, of his "heritage." But they equate mere separateness with individuality. The fact is that only in private—with intimates—is separateness from the crowd a prerequisite for individuality; an intimate "tells" me that I am unique, unlike all others, apart from the crowd. In public, by contrast, full individuality is achieved, paradoxically, by those who are able to consider themselves members of the crowd. Thus it happened for me. Only when I was able to think of myself as an American, no longer an alien in gringo society, could I seek the rights and opportunities necessary for full public individuality. The social and political advantages I enjoy as a man began on the day I came to believe that my name is indeed *Rich-heard Road-ree-guess*. It is true that my public society today is often impersonal; in fact, my public society is usually mass society. But despite the anonymity of the crowd, and despite the fact that the individuality I achieve in public is often tenuous—because it depends on my being one in a crowd—I celebrate the day I acquired my new name. Those middle-class ethnics who scorn assimilation seem to me filled with decadent self-pity, obsessed by the burden of public life. Dangerously, they romanticize public separateness and trivialize the dilemma of those who are truly socially disadvantaged.

If I rehearse here the changes in my private life after my Americaniza- 40
tion, it is finally to emphasize a public gain. The loss implies the gain. The
house I returned to each afternoon was quiet. Intimate sounds no longer
greeted me at the door. Inside there were other noises. The telephone rang.
Neighborhood kids ran past the door of the bedroom where I was reading my
schoolbooks—covered with brown shopping-bag paper. Once I learned the
public language, it would never again be easy for me to hear intimate family
voices. More and more of my day was spent hearing words, not sounds. But
that may only be a way of saying that on the day I raised my hand in class
and spoke loudly to an entire roomful of faces, my childhood started to end.

I grew up the victim of a disconcerting confusion. As I became fluent
in English, I could no longer speak Spanish with confidence. I continued
to understand spoken Spanish, and in high school I learned how to read
and write Spanish. But for many years I could not pronounce it. A powerful
guilt blocked my spoken words; an essential glue was missing whenever I
would try to connect words to form sentences. I would be unable to break
a barrier of sound, to speak freely. I would speak, or try to speak, Spanish,
and I would manage to utter halting, hiccuping sounds which betrayed my
unease. (Even today I speak Spanish very slowly, at best.)

When relatives and Spanish-speaking friends of my parents came to the
house, my brother and sisters would usually manage to say a few words
before being excused. I never managed so gracefully. Each time I'd hear
myself addressed in Spanish, I couldn't respond with any success. I'd know
the words I wanted to say, but I couldn't say them. I would try to speak, but
everything I said seemed to me horribly anglicized. My mouth wouldn't form
the sounds right. My jaw would tremble. After a phrase or two, I'd stutter,
cough up a warm, silvery sound, and stop.

My listeners were surprised to hear me. They'd lower their heads to
grasp better what I was trying to say. They would repeat their questions
in gentle, affectionate voices. But then I would answer in English. No, no,
they would say, we want you to speak to us in Spanish (*"en español"*). But
I couldn't do it. Then they would call me *Pocho*. Sometimes playfully, teasing, using the tender diminutive—*mi pochito*. Sometimes not so playfully
but mockingly, *pocho*. (A Spanish dictionary defines that word as an adjective meaning "colorless" or "bland." But I heard it as a noun, naming the
Mexican-American who, in becoming an American, forgets his native society.) "*¡Pocho!*" my mother's best friend muttered, shaking her head. And my
mother laughed, somewhere behind me. She said that her children didn't
want to practice "our Spanish" after they started going to school. My mother's smiling voice made me suspect that the lady who faced me was not really
angry at me. But searching her face, I couldn't find the hint of a smile.

Embarrassed, my parents would often need to explain their children's
inability to speak fluent Spanish during those years. My mother encountered
the wrath of her brother, her only brother, when he came up from Mexico
one summer with his family and saw his nieces and nephews for the very

first time. After listening to me, he looked away and said what a disgrace it was that my siblings and I couldn't speak Spanish, *"su propria idioma."* He made that remark to my mother, but I noticed that he stared at my father.

One other visitor from those years I clearly remember: a long-time friend of my father from San Francisco who came to stay with us for several days in late August. He took great interest in me after he realized that I couldn't answer his questions in Spanish. He would grab me, as I started to leave the kitchen. He would ask me something. Usually he wouldn't bother to wait for my mumbled response. Knowingly, he'd murmur, *"¿Ay pocho, pocho, donde vas?"* And he would press his thumbs into the upper part of my arms, making me squirm with pain. Dumbly I'd stand there, waiting for his wife to notice us and call him off with a benign smile. I'd giggle, hoping to deflate the tension between us, pretending that I hadn't seen the glittering scorn in his glance. 45

I recount such incidents only because they suggest the fierce power that Spanish had over many people I met at home, how strongly Spanish was associated with closeness. Most of those people who called me a *pocho* could have spoken English to me, but many wouldn't. They seemed to think that Spanish was the only language we could use among ourselves, that Spanish alone permitted our association. (Such persons are always vulnerable to the ghetto merchant and the politician who have learned the value of speaking their clients' "family language" so as to gain immediate trust.) For my part, I felt that by learning English I had somehow committed a sin of betrayal. But betrayal against whom? Not exactly against the visitors to the house. Rather, I felt I had betrayed my immediate family. I knew that my parents had encouraged me to learn English. I knew that I had turned to English with angry reluctance. But once I spoke English with ease, I came to feel guilty. I sensed that I had broken the spell of intimacy which had once held the family so close together. It was this original sin against my family that I recalled whenever anyone addressed me in Spanish and I responded, confounded.

Yet even during those years of guilt, I was coming to grasp certain consoling truths about language and intimacy—truths that I learned gradually. Once, I remember playing with a friend in the backyard when my grandmother appeared at the window. Her face was stern with suspicion when she saw the boy (the *gringo* boy) I was with. She called out to me in Spanish, sounding the whistle of her ancient breath. My companion looked up and watched her intently as she lowered the window and moved (still visible) behind the light curtain, watching us both. He wanted to know what she had said. I started to tell him, to translate her Spanish words into English. The problem was, however, that though I knew how to translate exactly what she had told me, I realized that any translation would distort the deepest meaning of her message: it had been directed only to me. This message of intimacy could never be translated because it did not lie in the actual words she had used but passed through them. So any translation would have seemed wrong; the words would have been stripped of an essential meaning. Finally I decided not to tell my friend anything—just that I didn't hear all she had said.

This insight was unfolded in time. As I made more and more friends outside my house, I began to recognize intimate messages spoken in English in a close friend's confidential tone or secretive whisper. Even more remarkable were those instances when, apparently for no special reason, I'd become conscious of the fact that my companion was speaking *only to me*. I'd marvel then, just hearing his voice. It was a stunning event to be able to break through the barrier of public silence, to be able to hear the voice of the other, to realize that it was directed just to me. After such moments of intimacy outside the house, I began to trust what I heard intimately conveyed through my family's English. Voices at home at last punctured sad confusion. I'd hear myself addressed as an intimate—in English. Such moments were never as raucous with sound as in past times, when we had used our "private" Spanish. (Our English-sounding house was never to be as noisy as our Spanish-sounding house had been.) Intimate moments were usually moments of soft sound. My mother would be ironing in the dining room while I did my homework nearby. She would look over at me, smile, and her voice sounded to tell me that I was her son. *Richard.*

Intimacy thus continued at home; intimacy was not stilled by English. Though there were fewer occasions for it—a change in my life that I would never forget—there were also times when I sensed the deep truth about language and intimacy: *Intimacy is not created by a particular language; it is created by intimates.* Thus the great change in my life was not linguistic but social. If, after becoming a successful student, I no longer heard intimate voices as often as I had earlier, it was not because I spoke English instead of Spanish. It was because I spoke public language for most of my day. I moved easily at last, a citizen in a crowded city of words.

As a man I spend most of my day in public, in a world largely devoid of 50 speech sounds. So I am quickly attracted by the glamorous quality of certain alien voices. I still am gripped with excitement when someone passes me on the street, speaking in Spanish. I have not moved beyond the range of the nostalgic pull of those sounds. And there is something very compelling about the sounds of lower-class blacks. Of all the accented versions of English that I hear in public, I hear theirs most intently. The Japanese tourist stops me downtown to ask me a question and I inch my way past his accent to concentrate on what he is saying. The eastern European immigrant in the neighborhood delicatessen speaks to me and, again, I do not pay much attention to his sounds, nor to the Texas accent of one of my neighbors or the Chicago accent of the woman who lives in the apartment below me. But when the ghetto black teenagers get on the city bus, I hear them. Their sounds in my society are the sounds of the outsider. Their voices annoy me for being so loud—so self-sufficient and unconcerned by my presence, but for the same reason they are glamorous: a romantic gesture against public acceptance. And as I listen to their shouted laughter, I realize my own quietness. I feel envious of them—envious of their brazen intimacy.

I warn myself away from such envy, however. Overhearing those teenagers, I think of the black political activists who lately have argued in favor of using black English in public schools—an argument that varies only slightly from that of foreign-language bilingualists. I have heard "radical" linguists make the point that black English is a complex and intricate version of English. And I do not doubt it. But neither do I think that black English should be a language of public instruction. What makes it inappropriate in classrooms is not something in the language itself but, rather, what lower-class speakers make of it. Just as Spanish would have been a dangerous language for me to have used at the start of my education, so black English would be a dangerous language to use in the schooling of teenagers for whom it reinforces feelings of public separateness.

This seems to me an obvious point to make, and yet it must be said. In recent years there have been many attempts to make the language of the alien a public language. "Bilingual education, two ways to understand . . ." television and radio commercials glibly announce. Proponents of bilingual education are careful to say that above all they want every student to acquire a good education. Their argument goes something like this: Children permitted to use their family language will not be so alienated and will be better able to match the progress of English-speaking students in the crucial first months of schooling. Increasingly confident of their ability, such children will be more inclined to apply themselves to their studies in the future. But then the bilingualists also claim another very different goal. They say that children who use their family language in school will retain a sense of their ethnic heritage and their family ties. Thus the supporters of bilingual education want it both ways. They propose bilingual schooling as a way of helping students acquire the classroom skills crucial for public success. But they likewise insist that bilingual instruction will give students a sense of their identity apart from the English-speaking public.

Behind this scheme gleams a bright promise for the alien child: One can become a public person while still remaining a private person. Who would not want to believe such an appealing idea? Who can be surprised that the scheme has the support of so many middle-class ethnic Americans? If the barrio or ghetto child can retain his separateness even while being publicly educated, then it is almost possible to believe that no private cost need be paid for public success. This is the consolation offered by any of the number of current bilingual programs. Consider, for example, the bilingual voter's ballot. In some American cities one can cast a ballot printed in several languages. Such a document implies that it is possible for one to exercise that most public of rights—the right to vote—while still keeping oneself apart, unassimilated in public life.

It is not enough to say that such schemes are foolish and certainly doomed. Middle-class supporters of public bilingualism toy with the confusion of those Americans who cannot speak standard English as well as they do. Moreover, bilingual enthusiasts sin against intimacy. A Hispanic-American tells me, "I will never give up my family language," and he clutches a group of words as though they were the source of his family ties. He credits to language what he should credit to family members. This is a convenient mistake, for as long as he holds on to certain familiar words, he can ignore how much else has actually changed in his life.

It has happened before. In earlier decades, persons ambitious for social mobility, and newly successful, similarly seized upon certain "family words." Workingmen attempting to gain political power, for example, took to calling one another "brother." The word as they used it, however, could never resemble the word (the sound) "brother" exchanged by two people in intimate greeting. The context of its public delivery made it at best a metaphor; with repetition it was only a vague echo of the intimate sound. Context forced the change. Context could not be overruled. Context will always protect the realm of the intimate from public misuse. Today middle-class white Americans continue to prove the importance of context as they try to ignore it. They seize upon idioms of the black ghetto, but their attempt to appropriate such expressions invariably changes the meaning. As it becomes a public expression, the ghetto idiom loses its sound, its message of public separateness and strident intimacy. With public repetition it becomes a series of words, increasingly lifeless.

The mystery of intimate utterance remains. The communication of intimacy passes through the word and enlivens its sound, but it cannot be held by the word. It cannot be retained or ever quoted because it is too fluid. It depends not on words but on persons.

My grandmother! She stood among my other relations mocking me when I no longer spoke Spanish. *Pocho*, she said. But then it made no difference. She'd laugh, and our relationship continued because language was never its source. She was a woman in her eighties during the first decade of my life — a mysterious woman to me, my only living grandparent, a woman of Mexico in a long black dress that reached down to her shoes. She was the one relative of mine who spoke no word of English. She had no interest in gringo society and remained completely aloof from the public. She was protected by her daughters, protected even by me when we went to Safeway together and I needed to act as her translator. An eccentric woman. Hard. Soft.

When my family visited my aunt's house in San Francisco, my grandmother would search for me among my many cousins. When she found me, she'd chase them away. Pinching her granddaughters, she would warn them away from me. Then she'd take me to her room, where she had prepared for my coming. There would be a chair next to the bed, a dusty jellied candy nearby, and a copy of *Life en Español* for me to examine. "There," she'd say. And I'd sit content, a boy of eight. *Pocho*, her favorite. I'd sift through the pictures of earthquake-destroyed Latin-American cities and blonde-wigged Mexican movie stars. And all the while I'd listen to the sound of my grandmother's voice. She'd pace around the room, telling me stories of her life. Her past. They were stories so familiar that I couldn't remember when I'd heard them for the first time. I'd look up sometimes to listen. Other times she'd look over at me, but she never expected a response. Sometimes I'd smile or nod. (I understood exactly what she was saying.) But it never seemed to matter to her one way or the other. It was enough that I was there. The words she spoke were almost irrelevant to that fact. We were content. And the great mystery remained: intimate utterance.

I learn nothing about language and intimacy listening to those social activists who propose using one's family language in public life. I learn much more simply by listening to songs on a radio, or hearing a great voice at the opera, or overhearing the woman downstairs at an open window singing to herself. Singers celebrate the human voice. Their lyrics are words, but, animated by voice, those words are subsumed into sounds. (This suggests a central truth about language: All words are capable of becoming sounds as we fill them with the "music" of our life.) With excitement I hear the words yielding their enormous power to sound, even though their meaning is never totally obliterated. In most songs, the drama or tension results from the way that the singer moves between words (sense) and notes (song). At one moment the song simply "says" something; at another moment the voice stretches out the words and moves to the realm of pure sound. Most songs are about love: lost love, celebrations of loving, pleas. By simply being occasions when sounds soar through words, however, songs put me in mind of the most intimate moments of life.

Finally, among all types of music, I find songs created by lyric poets most 60 compelling. On no other public occasion is sound so important for me. Written poems on a page seem at first glance a mere collection of words. And yet, without musical accompaniment, the poet leads me to hear the sounds of the words that I read. As song, a poem moves between the levels of sound and sense, never limited to one realm or the other. As a public artifact, the poem can never offer truly intimate sound, but it helps me to recall the intimate times of my life. As I read in my room, I grow deeply conscious of being alone, sounding my voice in search of another. The poem serves, then, as a memory device; it forces remembrance. And it refreshes; it reminds me of the possibility of escaping public words, the possibility that awaits me in intimate meetings.

The child reminds the adult: To seek intimate sounds is to seek the company of intimates. I do not expect to hear those sounds in public. I would dishonor those I have loved, and those I love now, to claim anything else. I would dishonor our intimacy by holding on to a particular language and calling it my family language. Intimacy cannot be trapped within words; it passes through words. It passes. Intimates leave the room. Doors close. Faces move away from the window. Time passes, and voices recede into the dark. Death finally quiets the voice. There is no way to deny it, no way to stand in the crowd claiming to utter one's family language.

The last time I saw my grandmother I was nine years old. I can tell you some of the things she said to me as I stood by her bed, but I cannot quote the message of intimacy she conveyed with her voice. She laughed, holding my hand. Her voice illumined disjointed memories as it passed them again. She remembered her husband—his green eyes, his magic name of Narcissio, his early death. She remembered the farm in Mexico, the eucalyptus trees nearby (their scent, she remembered, like incense). She remembered the family cow, the bell around its neck heard miles away. A dog. She remembered working as a seamstress, how she'd leave her daughters and son for long hours to go into Guadalajara to work. And how my mother would come running toward her in the sun—in her bright yellow dress—on her return. "MMMAAAAMMMMÁÁÁÁ," the old lady mimicked her daughter (my mother) to her daughter's son. She laughed. There was the snap of a cough. An aunt came into the room and told me it was time I should leave. "You can see her tomorrow," she promised. So I kissed my grandmother's cracked face. And the last thing I saw was her thin, oddly youthful thigh, as my aunt rearranged the sheet on the bed.

At the funeral parlor a few days after, I remember kneeling with my relatives during the rosary. Among their voices I traced, then lost, the sounds of individual aunts in the surge of the common prayer. And I heard at that moment what since I have heard very often—the sound the women in my family make when they are praying in sadness. When I went up to look at my grandmother, I saw her through the haze of a veil draped over the open lid of the casket. Her face looked calm—but distant and unyielding to love. It was not the face I remembered seeing most often. It was the face she made in public when the clerk at Safeway asked her some question and I would need to respond. It was her public face that the mortician had designed with his dubious art. ●

The Reader's Presence

1. The writer blames the intrusion of English into his family's private language, Spanish, for a breakdown of communication, and even of caring. How does the Spanish language appear in the essay? What associations does it have for the author? Why does Rodriguez end the essay with the scene of his dying grandmother followed by a glimpse of her corpse?

2. Rodriguez's rhetorical style alternates between persuasive argument and personal drama. Find examples of each. Do these divergent tactics undercut or reinforce each other? Why? What is the purpose of the exclamation points at the beginning of paragraph 33?

3. **CONNECTIONS:** Rodriguez opposes proposals to teach bilingual children in their native languages, wishing to keep native language "private" and fearing that teaching bilingual children in their native languages will further contribute to the marginalization of minorities. Read Walter Benn Michaels's essay, "The Trouble with Diversity" (page 744). Based on your analysis and understanding of Michaels's argument, how do you think Michaels would react to Rodriguez's proposition about bilingual education? Which writer do you find more persuasive, and why?

The Writer at Work

RICHARD RODRIGUEZ on a Writer's Identity

How important is cultural or ethnic identity to a writer? Some writers clearly draw creative strength from their allegiances and affiliations, whereas others prefer to remain independent of groups, even those they are undeniably part of. In the following passage from a 1997 interview published in *The Sun* magazine, Scott London asks Richard Rodriguez some tough questions about Rodriguez's various "identities." Could you have anticipated Rodriguez's responses based on his essay, "Aria: A Memoir of a Bilingual Childhood"?

❝ London: Many people feel that the call for diversity and multiculturalism is one reason the American educational system is collapsing.

Rodriguez: It's no surprise that at the same time that American universities have engaged in a serious commitment to diversity, they have been thought-prisons. We are not talking about diversity in any real way. We are talking about brown, black, and white versions of the same political ideology. It is very curious that the United States and Canada both assume that diversity means only race and ethnicity. They never assume it might mean more Nazis, or more Southern Baptists. That's diversity, too, you know.

London: What do *you* mean by diversity?

Rodriguez: For me, diversity is not a value. Diversity is what you find in Northern Ireland. Diversity is Beirut. Diversity is brother killing brother. Where diversity is *shared*—where I share with you my difference—that can be valuable. But the simple fact that we are unlike each other is a terrifying notion. I have often found

myself in foreign settings where I became suddenly aware that I was not like the people around me. That, to me, is not a pleasant discovery.

London: You've said that it's tough in America to lead an intellectual life outside the universities. Yet you made a very conscious decision to leave academia.

Rodriguez: My decision was sparked by affirmative action. There was a point in my life when affirmative action would have meant something to me—when my family was working-class, and we were struggling. But very early in life I became part of the majority culture and now don't think of myself as a minority. Yet the university said I was one. Anybody who has met a real minority—in the economic sense, not the numerical sense—would understand how ridiculous it is to describe a young man who is already at the university, already well into his studies in Italian and English Renaissance literature, as a minority. Affirmative action ignores our society's real minorities—members of the disadvantaged classes, no matter what their race. We have this ludicrous, bureaucratic sense that certain racial groups, regardless of class, are minorities. So what happens is those "minorities" at the very top of the ladder get chosen for everything.

London: Is that what happened to you?

Rodriguez: Well, when it came time for me to look for jobs, the jobs came looking for me. I had teaching offers from the best universities in the country. I was about to accept one from Yale when the whole thing collapsed on me.

London: What do you mean?

Rodriguez: I had all this anxiety about what it meant to be a minority. My professors—these same men who taught me the intricacies of language—just shied away from the issue. They didn't want to talk about it, other than to suggest I could be a "role model" to other Hispanics—when I went back to my barrio, I suppose. I came from a white, middle-class neighborhood. Was I expected to go back there and teach the woman next door about Renaissance sonnets? The embarrassing truth of the matter was that I was being chosen because Yale University had some peculiar idea about what my skin color or ethnicity signified. Who knows what Yale thought it was getting when it hired Richard Rodriguez? The people who offered me the job thought there was nothing wrong with that. I thought there was something very wrong. I still do. I think race-based affirmative action is crude and absolutely mistaken.

London: I noticed that some university students put up a poster outside the lecture hall where you spoke the other night. It said, "Richard Rodriguez is a disgrace to the Chicano community."

Rodriguez: I sort of like that. I don't think writers should be convenient examples. I don't think we should make people feel settled. I don't try to be a gadfly, but I do think that real ideas are troublesome. There should be something about my work that leaves the reader unsettled. I intend that. The notion of the writer as a kind of sociological sample of a community is ludicrous. Even worse is the notion that writers should provide an example of how to live. Virginia Woolf ended her life by putting a rock in her sweater one day and walking into a lake. She is not a model for how I want to live my life. On the other hand, the bravery of her syntax, of her sentences, written during her deepest depression, is a kind of example for me. But I do not want to become Virginia Woolf. That is not why I read her.

London: What's wrong with being a role model?

Rodriguez: The popular idea of a role model implies that an adult's influence on a child is primarily occupational, that all a black child needs is to see a black doctor, and then this child will think, "Oh, I can become a doctor, too." I have a good black friend who is a doctor, but he didn't become a doctor because he saw other black men who were doctors. He became a doctor because his mother cleaned office buildings at night, and because she loved her children. She grew bowlegged from cleaning office buildings at night, and in the process she taught him something about courage and bravery and dedication to others. I became a writer not because my father was one—my father made false teeth for a living. I became a writer because the Irish nuns who educated me taught me something about bravery with their willingness to give so much to me.

London: There used to be a category for writers and thinkers and intellectuals—"the intelligentsia." But not anymore.

Rodriguez: No, I think the universities have co-opted the intellectual, by and large. But there is an emerging intellectual set coming out of Washington think tanks now. There are people who are leaving the universities and working for the government or in think tanks, simply looking for freedom. The university has become so stultified since the sixties. There is so much you can't do at the university. You can't say this, you can't do that, you can't think this, and so forth. In many ways, I'm free to range as widely as I do intellectually precisely because I'm not at a university. The tiresome Chicanos would be after me all the time. You know: "We saw your piece yesterday, and we didn't like what you said," or, "You didn't sound happy enough," or, "You didn't sound proud enough."

London: You've drawn similar responses from the gay community, I understand.

Rodriguez: Yes, I've recently gotten in trouble with certain gay activists because I'm not gay enough! I am a morose homosexual. I'm melancholy. *Gay* is the last adjective I would use to describe myself. The idea of being gay, like a little sparkler, never occurs to me. So if you ask me if I'm gay, I say no.

After the second chapter of *Days of Obligation*, which is about the death of a friend of mine from AIDS, was published in *Harper's*, I got this rather angry letter from a gay-and-lesbian group that was organizing a protest against the magazine. It was the same old problem: political groups have almost no sense of irony. For them, language has to say exactly what it means. "Why aren't you proud of being gay?" they wanted to know. "Why are you so dark? Why are you so morbid? Why are you so sad? Don't you realize, we're all OK? Let's celebrate that fact." But that is not what writers do. We don't celebrate being "OK." If you want to be OK, take an aspirin.

London: Do you consider yourself more Mexican, or more American?

Rodriguez: In some ways I consider myself more Chinese, because I live in San Francisco, which is becoming a predominantly Asian city. I avoid falling into the black-and-white dialectic in which most of America still seems trapped. I have always recognized that, as an American, I am in relationships with other parts of the world; that I have to measure myself against the Pacific, against Asia. Having to think of myself in relationship to that horizon has liberated me from the black-and-white checkerboard.**"**

Marjane Satrapi

My Speech at West Point

Writer-illustrator and graphic novelist **MARJANE SATRAPI** (b. 1969) was born in Iran and, after a sojourn in Europe and a return to Tehran, now lives and works in France. Her graphic memoir, *Persepolis: The Story of a Childhood* (2003), recounts in comic-book form growing up in Iran from ages six to fourteen, years that saw the overthrow of the Shah, the triumph of the Islamic Revolution, and the devastating effects of war with Iraq. The book was an immediate hit in France, selling more than 150,000 copies, and has been translated into numerous languages. In the United States, *Persepolis* was named a *New York Times* Notable Book and one of *Time* magazine's "Best Comix of the Year." Satrapi co-directed the feature film, *Persepolis*, which won numerous awards including an Oscar nomination for Best Animated Feature Film of 2007. *Persepolis 2: The Story of a Return* (2004) picks up her story with Satrapi's departure for Austria when she was fourteen and continues through her college years back in Tehran. Satrapi's most recent graphic memoirs are *Embroideries* (2005) and *Chicken with Plums* (2006). She has also written several children's books, and her commentary and comics appear in newspapers and magazines around the world, including the *New York Times* and the *New Yorker*.

> **"I figured out a long time ago that, whatever I think I know, I don't know anything. Once I realized that, I really started learning."**

Satrapi was invited to West Point to speak in 2005. After her visit, her book *Persepolis* was put on the required reading list at the academy. "My Speech at West Point" appeared on the Op-Ed page of the *New York Times* on May 29, 2005.

In an interview with *Believer* magazine, Satrapi talked about what she learned not only at West Point but also through traveling and listening to people from so many disparate cultures: "I figured out a long time ago that, whatever I think I know, I don't know anything. Once I realized that, I really started learning. That's a great strength: I know that I don't know. There are some people in Iran who are fundamentalist and others who are not. I have very good Israeli friends. And I have very good American friends. We come from different cultures but share points of view. It's humanism, which we're steadily losing. That's what the comics are about in a way, trying to stop that loss."

When I was invited to speak at West Point, this is how I thought it would be: I'll go to West Point...

The major will show me around without saying a word...

Then, he will shout at me...

YOU DON'T SMOKE HERE

Then, I'll eat with 4,000 cadets in the mess hall...

The meal won't be tasty... PIZZA... half pepperoni

half cheese

After lunch, I will speak in front of 600 people...

I AM AGAINST THE WAR IN IRAQ.

They will all shout at me again...

I will have to continue my speech...

Democracy is not a present you give to people by bombing them.

Their general will order them to hang me...

I will DIE...

BUT...

Here we are!

The major shows me around...

Here they play football. You should come and watch a game sometime!

great...

Can I smoke?

Of course!

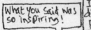

I eat with 4,000 cadets in the mess hall...

The half-pepperoni, half-cheese pizza is worse than what I thought

After my speech, the cadets come to talk to me...

What you said was so inspiring!

It's great to discover another point of view!

They are lovely and intelligent and much more open-minded than I am!

I go back to Manhattan...

I know that I don't know anything

That makes my life even more complicated...

HUDSON RIVER

Later, in my hotel room...

Seven American soldiers and 10 Iraqis died today in Baghdad

There's still things I know that I know: I'm against the war and democracy is not a present you give to people by bombing them

The Reader's Presence

1. How would you describe Satrapi's expectations of West Point as opposed to what she actually experienced on her visit? What do her expectations imply about her view of the military academy? Where may she have received these views? In what ways do they complicate her experience? What elements of Satrapi's narrative do you find humorous? Why?

2. Satrapi's personal narrative is not just told but drawn in black and white. How would you describe her artistic style? What sort of imagery does it resemble? Do you think that the way she depicts herself in the art reinforces the way she describes herself in words? Why or why not? Explain how you see the interrelation of words and images in this graphic essay.

3. **CONNECTIONS:**   Consider Satrapi's graphic essay in connection with other short personal narratives that dramatize a complicated personal experience, such as Jerald Walker's "Scattered Inconveniences" (page 251) or Brent Staples's "Just Walk on By: A Black Man Ponders His Power to Alter Public Space" (page 217). How do these narratives convey complicated moments and emotions and introduce competing perspectives? Of the three selections, choose the one you believe achieves the most satisfying resolution and explain the reasons for your choice.

The Graphic Memoirist at Work

MARJANE SATRAPI on the Language of Words and Images

In an interview with the literary journal *Fourth Genre*, Marjane Satrapi spoke about the unique interaction of words and images in her graphic memoirs and comics in general. The interview was conducted in November 2006 by the journal's interview editor, Robert Root, and it was published in Fall 2007.

❝ *Root:* I'm interested in the use of illustration in the service of autobiography or memoir or other kinds of nonfiction and how that affects the "nonfictionness" of it, the truth of it. People keep referring to your books and to Art Spiegelman's *Maus* and to Alison Bechdel's *Fun Home* as "graphic novels," but it seems to me that a more accurate term would be "graphic memoirs," since they are all autobiographical on some level.

Satrapi: Yes, they *are* autobiographical, but at the same time they search for truth. . . . If you're looking for truth you have to ask it from the Fox News and the *New York Times*. As soon as you write your story, it is a story; this is not a documentary. Of course you have to make fiction, you have to cheat, you have to make some angle around there, because the story has to turn, so that is the reconstruction of what we do. For instance, I don't know, when I write something about people and I'm mean to them, of course I would not use the real names and the real figures, even not the real story. I will create this new personage around myself. Of course, they will always be related to my experiences — what I have seen and what I have heard, or whatever — but any writer will do that, even in science fiction you do that. So the use of the drawing for me is that first of all, I am a very lousy writer. I have tried actually, you know, at one time to write. If I had to write this short article or something, here I am good. But for a novel, just forget about it. I lose all my sense of humor, I lose completely all my decency, and I become completely lousy and pathetic. If I say to myself, "Now you are a serious girl and now you are going to make some serious work," there's nothing worse than wanting to make a serious work for me. So drawing gives me the possibility of this sense of saying what I want to say.

Also, there are many things that you can say through images that you cannot say with the writing. The comics is the only media in the whole world that you can use the image plus the writing plus the imagination and plus be active while reading it. When you watch a picture, a movie, you are passive. Everything is coming to you. When you are reading comics, between one frame to the other what is happening, you have to imagine it yourself. So you are active; you have to take part actually when you read the story. It is the only medium that uses the images in this way. So, for me, comics has only convenience. . . .

Root: You've mentioned before the two languages that you work with, the language of words and the language of image, and how they come together. I wish you would elaborate a little more on that. You've said that you don't write the story and then find images to illustrate the text, that they go together and bounce off of one another. How does that work?

Satrapi: I have a small page on which I know more or less what I want to write in my story. When I start, I have these small little sketches with small drawings of people, and I have short, short dialogues going together, and once in a while I write the dialogue, and once in a while I go the other way. It's like a baby growing up. You don't have first the nose come up and then one eye and then one hand or one leg — all of it grows at the same time. Another thing also: when I work, you know, I am completely in a trance. I'm so concentrated on the work that I don't look at myself working. And I work alone on my books. So since I don't watch myself, it's very difficult for me to know what I'm doing, since I don't see what I'm doing. **"**

David Sedaris

ME TALK PRETTY ONE DAY

DAVID SEDARIS (b. 1956) was born in Johnson City, New York, and raised in Raleigh, North Carolina. He is a dramatist whose plays, written in collaboration with his sister, Amy (one of which won an Obie Award), have been produced at La Mama and Lincoln Center. Sedaris launched his career as a wry, neurotically self-disparaging humorist on National Public Radio's *Morning Edition*, when he read aloud from "The Santaland Diaries," an autobiographical piece about working as a Christmas elf at Macy's. He has since published a number of best-selling collections, including *Barrel Fever* (1994), *Naked* (1997), *Holidays on Ice* (1997), *Me Talk Pretty One Day* (2000), *Dress Your Family in Corduroy and Denim* (2004), and *When You Are Engulfed in Flames* (2008). His newest book, a collection of fables titled *Squirrel Seeks Chipmunk: A Modest Bestiary* (with illustrations by Ian Falconer), was published in 2010 and immediately hit the *New York Times* Best-Seller List for fiction. His

> **"It doesn't really matter what your life was like, you can write about anything."**

essays appear regularly in the *New Yorker* and *Esquire*. In 2001, Sedaris was named Humorist of the Year by *Time* magazine and received the Thurber Prize for American Humor. *New York Magazine* had dubbed Sedaris "the most brilliantly witty New Yorker since Dorothy Parker." He currently divides his time between France and New York City.

Sedaris, who for two years taught writing at the Art Institute of Chicago, laments that the students in his writing classes "were ashamed of their middle-class background . . . they felt like unless they grew up in poverty, they had nothing to write about." Sedaris feels that "it doesn't really matter what your life was like, you can write about anything. It's just the writing of it that is the challenge."

AT THE AGE OF FORTY-ONE, I am returning to school and have to think of myself as what my French textbook calls "a true debutant." After paying my tuition, I was issued a student ID, which allows me a discounted entry fee at movie theaters, puppet shows, and Festyland, a far-flung amusement park that advertises with billboards picturing a cartoon stegosaurus sitting in a canoe and eating what appears to be a ham sandwich.

I've moved to Paris with hopes of learning the language. My school is an easy ten-minute walk from my apartment, and on the first day of class I arrived early, watching as the returning students greeted one another in the school lobby. Vacations were recounted, and questions were raised concerning mutual friends with names like Kang and Vlatnya. Regardless of their nationalities, everyone spoke in what sounded to me like excellent French. Some accents were better than others, but the students exhibited an ease and confidence I found intimidating. As an added discomfort, they were all young, attractive, and well dressed, causing me to feel not unlike Pa Kettle trapped backstage after a fashion show.

The first day of class was nerve-racking because I knew I'd be expected to perform. That's the way they do it here—it's everybody into the language pool, sink or swim. The teacher marched in, deeply tanned from a recent vacation, and proceeded to rattle off a series of administrative announcements. I've spent quite a few summers in Normandy, and I took a monthlong French class before leaving New York. I'm not completely in the dark, yet I understood only half of what this woman was saying.

"If you have not *meimslsxp* or *lgpdmurct* by this time, then you should not be in this room. Has everyone *apzkiubjxow*? Everyone? Good, we shall begin." She spread out her lesson plan and sighed, saying, "All right, then, who knows the alphabet?"

It was startling because (a) I hadn't been asked that question in a while and (b) I realized, while laughing, that I myself did *not* know the alphabet. They're the same letters, but in France they're pronounced differently. I knew the shape of the alphabet but had no idea what it actually sounded like.

"Ahh." The teacher went to the board and sketched the letter *a*. "Do we have anyone in the room whose first name commences with an *ahh*?"

Two Polish Annas raised their hands, and the teacher instructed them to present themselves by stating their names, nationalities, occupations, and a brief list of things they liked and disliked in this world. The first Anna hailed from an industrial town outside of Warsaw and had front teeth the size of tombstones. She worked as a seamstress, enjoyed quiet times with friends, and hated the mosquito.

"Oh, really," the teacher said. "How very interesting. I thought that everyone loved the mosquito, but here, in front of all the world, you claim to detest him. How is it that we've been blessed with someone as unique and original as you? Tell us, please."

The seamstress did not understand what was being said but knew that this was an occasion for shame. Her rabbity mouth huffed for breath, and she stared down at her lap as though the appropriate comeback were stitched somewhere alongside the zipper of her slacks.

The second Anna learned from the first and claimed to love sunshine and detest lies. It sounded like a translation of one of those Playmate of the Month data sheets, the answers always written in the same loopy handwriting: "Turn-ons: Mom's famous five-alarm chili! Turnoffs: insecurity and guys who come on too strong!!!!"

The two Polish Annas surely had clear notions of what they loved and hated, but like the rest of us, they were limited in terms of vocabulary, and this made them appear less than sophisticated. The teacher forged on, and we learned that Carlos, the Argentine bandonion player, loved wine, music, and, in his words, "making sex with the womens of the world." Next came a beautiful young Yugoslav who identified herself as an optimist, saying that she loved everything that life had to offer.

The teacher licked her lips, revealing a hint of the saucebox we would later come to know. She crouched low for her attack, placed her hands on the young woman's desk, and leaned close, saying, "Oh yeah? And do you love your little war?"

While the optimist struggled to defend herself, I scrambled to think of an answer to what had obviously become a trick question. How often is one asked what he loves in this world? More to the point, how often is one asked and then publicly ridiculed for his answer? I recalled my mother, flushed with wine, pounding the tabletop late one night, saying, "Love? I love a good steak cooked rare. I love my cat, and I love . . ." My sisters and I leaned forward, waiting to hear our names. "Tums," our mother said. "I love Tums."

The teacher killed some time accusing the Yugoslavian girl of masterminding a program of genocide, and I jotted frantic notes in the margins of my pad. While I can honestly say that I love leafing through medical textbooks devoted to severe dermatological conditions, the hobby is beyond the reach of my French vocabulary, and acting it out would only have invited controversy.

When called upon, I delivered an effortless list of things that I detest: blood sausage, intestinal pâtés, brain pudding. I'd learned these words the hard way. Having given it some thought, I then declared my love for IBM typewriters, the French word for *bruise*, and my electric floor waxer. It was a short list, but still I managed to mispronounce *IBM* and assign the wrong gender to both the floor waxer and the typewriter. The teacher's reaction led me to believe that these mistakes were capital crimes in the country of France.

"Were you always this *palicmkrexis*?" she asked. "Even a *fiuscrzsa ticiwelmun* knows that a typewriter is feminine."

I absorbed as much of her abuse as I could understand, thinking—but not saying—that I find it ridiculous to assign a gender to an inanimate object incapable of disrobing and making an occasional fool of itself. Why refer to Lady Crack Pipe or Good Sir Dishrag when these things could never live up to all that their sex implied?

The teacher proceeded to belittle everyone from German Eva, who hated laziness, to Japanese Yukari, who loved paintbrushes and soap. Italian, Thai, Dutch, Korean, and Chinese—we all left class foolishly believing that the worst was over. She'd shaken us up a little, but surely that was just an act designed to weed out the deadweight. We didn't know it then, but the coming months would teach us what it was like to spend time in the presence

15

of a wild animal, something completely unpredictable. Her temperament was not based on a series of good and bad days but, rather, good and bad moments. We soon learned to dodge chalk and protect our heads and stomachs whenever she approached us with a question. She hadn't yet punched anyone, but it seemed wise to protect ourselves against the inevitable.

Though we were forbidden to speak anything but French, the teacher would occasionally use us to practice any of her five fluent languages.

"I hate you," she said to me one afternoon. Her English was flawless. "I really, really hate you." Call me sensitive, but I couldn't help but take it personally.   20

After being singled out as a lazy *kfdtinvfm*, I took to spending four hours a night on my homework, putting in even more time whenever we were assigned an essay. I suppose I could have gotten by with less, but I was determined to create some sort of identity for myself: David the hard worker, David the cut-up. We'd have one of those "complete this sentence" exercises, and I'd fool with the thing for hours, invariably settling on something like "A quick run around the lake? I'd love to! Just give me a moment while I strap on my wooden leg." The teacher, through word and action, conveyed the message that if this was my idea of an identity, she wanted nothing to do with it.

My fear and discomfort crept beyond the borders of the classroom and accompanied me out onto the wide boulevards. Stopping for a coffee, asking directions, depositing money in my bank account: these things were out of the question, as they involved having to speak. Before beginning school, there'd been no shutting me up, but now I was convinced that everything I said was wrong. When the phone rang, I ignored it. If someone asked me a question, I pretended to be deaf. I knew my fear was getting the best of me when I started wondering why they don't sell cuts of meat in vending machines.

My only comfort was the knowledge that I was not alone. Huddled in the hallways and making the most of our pathetic French, my fellow students and I engaged in the sort of conversation commonly overheard in refugee camps.

"Sometime me cry alone at night."

"That be common for I, also, but be more strong, you. Much work and someday you talk pretty. People start love you soon. Maybe tomorrow, okay."   25

Unlike the French class I had taken in New York, here there was no sense of competition. When the teacher poked a shy Korean in the eyelid with a freshly sharpened pencil, we took no comfort in the fact that, unlike Hyeyoon Cho, we all knew the irregular past tense of the verb *to defeat*. In all fairness, the teacher hadn't meant to stab the girl, but neither did she spend much time apologizing, saying only, "Well, you should have been *vkkdyo* more *kdeynfulh*."

Over time it became impossible to believe that any of us would ever improve. Fall arrived and it rained every day, meaning we would now be scolded for the water dripping from our coats and umbrellas. It was mid-October when the teacher singled me out, saying, "Every day spent with you is like having a cesarean section." And it struck me that, for the first time since arriving in France, I could understand every word that someone was saying.

Understanding doesn't mean that you can suddenly speak the language. Far from it. It's a small step, nothing more, yet its rewards are intoxicating and deceptive. The teacher continued her diatribe and I settled back, bathing in the subtle beauty of each new curse and insult.

"You exhaust me with your foolishness and reward my efforts with nothing but pain, do you understand me?"

The world opened up, and it was with great joy that I responded, "I know the thing that you speak exact now. Talk me more, you, plus, please, plus." ■

The Reader's Presence

1. How did Sedaris take his experience—auditing a beginner's language class—and turn it into a humorous essay? What were the funniest parts of the essay? An interviewer once wrote that Sedaris's signature is "deadpan" humor. What is deadpan humor? Identify—and characterize the effectiveness of—examples of it in "Me Talk Pretty One Day."

2. Which English words would you substitute for the nonsense words that represent Sedaris's difficulties understanding his teacher's French? Have a classmate tell you what he or she thinks such words as *meimslsxp* (paragraph 4), *palicmkrexis* (paragraph 16), or *kdeynfulh* (paragraph 26) might mean. Did he or she pick the same or similar words to the ones you picked? Point to the clues Sedaris includes in the essay to hint at what such words mean. How would you rewrite the passage with different clues to indicate a different possible meaning for the nonsense words?

3. **CONNECTIONS:** How surprised were you by the last line in the essay? To what extent did you expect that Sedaris would speak fluently because he understood his teacher's French perfectly? Look at some other unexpected last lines in essays that you've read in this collection, such as Bernard Cooper's "A Clack of Tiny Sparks" (page 78) or Jamaica Kincaid's "The Estrangement" (page 129) or any two other last lines you found surprising, and identify how each author goes about setting up the surprise. When you look back, at what point in each essay might you have expected the unexpected? Be as specific as possible in your response.

Brent Staples

JUST WALK ON BY: A BLACK MAN PONDERS HIS POWER TO ALTER PUBLIC SPACE

As he describes in *Parallel Time: Growing Up in Black and White* (1994), **BRENT STAPLES** (b. 1951) escaped a childhood of urban poverty through success in school and his determination to be a writer. Although Staples earned a PhD in psychology from the University of Chicago in 1982, his love of journalism led him to leave the field of psychology and start a career that has taken him to the *New York Times*, where he has served on the editorial board since 1990. Staples contributes to several national magazines, including *Harper's*, the *New York Times Magazine*, and *Ms.*, in which "Just Walk on By" appeared in 1986.

Staples's 1994 memoir, *Parallel Time*, received the Anisfield Wolff Book Award, previously won by such writers as James Baldwin,

> **"I traveled to distant neighborhoods, sat on their curbs, and sketched what I saw in words."**

Ralph Ellison, and Zora Neale Hurston. In it he remembers how in Chicago he prepared for his writing career by keeping a journal. "I wrote on buses, on the Jackson Park el—though only at the stops to keep the writing legible. I traveled to distant neighborhoods, sat on their curbs, and sketched what I saw in words. Thursdays meant free admission at the Art Institute. All day I attributed motives to people in paintings, especially people in Rembrandts. At closing time I went to a nightclub in The Loop and spied on patrons, copied their conversations and speculated about their lives. The journal was more than 'a record of my inner transactions.' It was a collection of stolen souls from which I would one day construct a book."

MY FIRST VICTIM was a woman—white, well dressed, probably in her early twenties. I came upon her late one evening on a deserted street in Hyde Park, a relatively affluent neighborhood in an otherwise mean, impoverished section of Chicago. As I swung onto the avenue behind her, there seemed to be a discreet, uninflammatory distance between us. Not so. She cast back a worried glance. To her, the youngish black man—a broad six feet two inches with a beard and billowing hair, both hands shoved into the pockets of a bulky military jacket—seemed menacingly close. After a few more quick glimpses, she picked up her pace and was soon running in earnest. Within seconds she disappeared into a cross street.

That was more than a decade ago. I was twenty-two years old, a graduate student newly arrived at the University of Chicago. It was in the echo of that terrified woman's footfalls that I first began to know the unwieldy inheritance I'd come into—the ability to alter public space in ugly ways. It was clear that she thought herself the quarry of a mugger, a rapist, or worse. Suffering a bout of insomnia, however, I was stalking sleep, not defenseless wayfarers. As a softy who is scarcely able to take a knife to a raw chicken—let alone hold it to a person's throat—I was surprised, embarrassed, and dismayed all at once. Her flight made me feel like an accomplice in tyranny. It also made it clear that I was indistinguishable from the muggers who occasionally seeped into the area from the surrounding ghetto. That first encounter, and those that followed, signified that a vast, unnerving gulf lay between nighttime pedestrians—particularly women—and me. And I soon gathered that being perceived as dangerous is a hazard in itself. I only needed to turn a corner into a dicey situation, or crowd some frightened, armed person in a foyer somewhere, or make an errant move after being pulled over by a policeman. Where fear and weapons meet—and they often do in urban America—there is always the possibility of death.

In that first year, my first away from my hometown, I was to become thoroughly familiar with the language of fear. At dark, shadowy intersections in Chicago, I could cross in front of a car stopped at a traffic light and elicit the *thunk, thunk, thunk, thunk* of the driver—black, white, male, or female—hammering down the door locks. On less traveled streets after dark, I grew accustomed to but never comfortable with people who crossed to the other side of the street rather than pass me. Then there were the standard unpleasantries with police, doormen, bouncers, cabdrivers, and others whose business is to screen out troublesome individuals *before* there is any nastiness.

I moved to New York nearly two years ago and I have remained an avid night walker. In central Manhattan, the near-constant crowd cover minimizes tense one-on-one street encounters. Elsewhere—visiting friends in Soho,[1] where sidewalks are narrow and tightly spaced buildings shut out the sky—things can get very taut indeed.

Black men have a firm place in New York mugging literature. Norman Podhoretz[2] in his famed (or infamous) 1963 essay, "My Negro Problem—And Ours," recalls growing up in terror of black males; they "were tougher than we were, more ruthless," he writes—and as an adult on the Upper West Side of Manhattan, he continues, he cannot constrain his nervousness when he meets black men on certain streets. Similarly, a decade later, the essayist and novelist Edward Hoagland extols a New York where once "Negro bitterness bore down mainly on other Negroes." Where some

5

---

1 **Soho:** A district of lower Manhattan known for its art galleries.—EDS.
2 **Podhoretz:** A well-known literary critic and editor of *Commentary* magazine.—EDS.

see mere panhandlers, Hoagland sees "a mugger who is clearly screwing up his nerve to do more than just *ask* for money." But Hoagland has "the New Yorker's quick-hunch posture for broken-field maneuvering," and the bad guy swerves away.

I often witness that "hunch posture," from women after dark on the warrenlike streets of Brooklyn where I live. They seem to set their faces on neutral and, with their purse straps strung across their chests bandolier style, they forge ahead as though bracing themselves against being tackled. I understand, of course, that the danger they perceive is not a hallucination. Women are particularly vulnerable to street violence, and young black males are drastically overrepresented among the perpetrators of that violence. Yet these truths are no solace against the kind of alienation that comes of being ever the suspect, against being set apart, a fearsome entity with whom pedestrians avoid making eye contact.

It is not altogether clear to me how I reached the ripe old age of twenty-two without being conscious of the lethality nighttime pedestrians attributed to me. Perhaps it was because in Chester, Pennsylvania, the small, angry industrial town where I came of age in the 1960s, I was scarcely noticeable against a backdrop of gang warfare, street knifings, and murders. I grew up one of the good boys, had perhaps a half-dozen fistfights. In retrospect, my shyness of combat has clear sources.

Many things go into the making of a young thug. One of those things is the consummation of the male romance with the power to intimidate. An infant discovers that random flailings send the baby bottle flying out of the crib and crashing to the floor. Delighted, the joyful babe repeats those motions again and again, seeking to duplicate the feat. Just so, I recall the points at which some of my boyhood friends were finally seduced by the perception of themselves as tough guys. When a mark cowered and surrendered his money without resistance, myth and reality merged—and paid off. It is, after all, only manly to embrace the power to frighten and intimidate. We, as men, are not supposed to give an inch of our lane on the highway; we are to seize the fighter's edge in work and in play and even in love; we are to be valiant in the face of hostile forces.

Unfortunately, poor and powerless young men seem to take all this nonsense literally. As a boy, I saw countless tough guys locked away; I have since buried several, too. They were babies, really—a teenage cousin, a brother of twenty-two, a childhood friend in his midtwenties—all gone down in episodes of bravado played out in the streets. I came to doubt the virtues of intimidation early on. I chose, perhaps even unconsciously, to remain a shadow—timid, but a survivor.

The fearsomeness mistakenly attributed to me in public places often has 10
a perilous flavor. The most frightening of these confusions occurred in the late 1970s and early 1980s when I worked as a journalist in Chicago. One day, rushing into the office of a magazine I was writing for with a deadline story in hand, I was mistaken for a burglar. The office manager called

security and, with an ad hoc posse, pursued me through the labyrinthine halls, nearly to my editor's door. I had no way of proving who I was. I could only move briskly toward the company of someone who knew me.

Another time I was on assignment for a local paper and killing time before an interview. I entered a jewelry store on the city's affluent Near North Side. The proprietor excused herself and returned with an enormous red Doberman pinscher straining at the end of a leash. She stood, the dog extended toward me, silent to my questions, her eyes bulging nearly out of her head. I took a cursory look around, nodded, and bade her good night. Relatively speaking, however, I never fared as badly as another black male journalist. He went to nearby Waukegan, Illinois, a couple of summers ago to work on a story about a murderer who was born there. Mistaking the reporter for the killer, police hauled him from his car at gunpoint and but for his press credentials would probably have tried to book him. Such episodes are not uncommon. Black men trade tales like this all the time.

In "My Negro Problem—And Ours," Podhoretz writes that the hatred he feels for blacks makes itself known to him through a variety of avenues—one being his discomfort with that "special brand of paranoid touchiness" to which he says blacks are prone. No doubt he is speaking here of black men. In time, I learned to smother the rage I felt at so often being taken for a criminal. Not to do so would surely have led to madness—via that special "paranoid touchiness" that so annoyed Podhoretz at the time he wrote the essay.

I began to take precautions to make myself less threatening. I move about with care, particularly late in the evening. I give a wide berth to nervous people on subway platforms during the wee hours, particularly when I have exchanged business clothes for jeans. If I happen to be entering a building behind some people who appear skittish, I may walk by, letting them clear the lobby before I return, so as not to seem to be following them. I have been calm and extremely congenial on those rare occasions when I've been pulled over by the police.

And on late-evening constitutionals along streets less traveled by, I employ what has proved to be an excellent tension-reducing measure: I whistle melodies from Beethoven and Vivaldi and the more popular classical composers. Even steely New Yorkers hunching toward nighttime destinations seem to relax, and occasionally they even join in the tune. Virtually everybody seems to sense that a mugger wouldn't be warbling bright, sunny selections from Vivaldi's *Four Seasons*. It is my equivalent of the cowbell that hikers wear when they know they are in bear country. ●

The Reader's Presence

1. Why does Staples use the word *victim* in his opening sentence? In what sense is the white woman a "victim"? How is Staples using the term? As readers, how might we interpret the opening sentence upon first reading? How does the meaning of the term change in rereading?

2. In rereading the essay, pay close attention to the way Staples handles points of view. When does he shift viewpoints or perspectives? What is his purpose in doing so? What are some of the connections Staples makes in this essay between the point of view one chooses and one's identity?

3. **CONNECTIONS:**   How does Staples behave on the street? How does he deal with the woman's anxiety? How has he "altered" his own public behavior? In what ways is his behavior on the street similar to his "behavior" as a writer? Compare this version of the essay to the alternate version that follows. What are the changes and how do those changes influence the essay's effect on the reader? How do you compare Staples's strategies—in both versions—to those of Malcolm X in "My First Conk" (page 153)?

The Writer at Work

Another Version of *Just Walk on By*

When he published his memoir, *Parallel Time*, in 1994, Brent Staples decided to incorporate his earlier essay into the book. He also decided to revise it substantially. As you compare the two versions, note the passages Staples retained and those he chose not to carry forward into book form. Do you agree with his changes? Why in general do you think he made them? If you had been his editor, what revision strategy would you have suggested?

❝ At night, I walked to the lakefront whenever the weather permitted. I was headed home from the lake when I took my first victim. It was late fall, and the wind was cutting. I was wearing my navy pea jacket, the collar turned up, my hands snug in the pockets. Dead leaves scuttled in shoals along the streets. I turned out of Blackstone Avenue and headed west on 57th Street, and there she was, a few yards ahead of me, dressed in business clothes and carrying a briefcase. She looked back at me once, then again, and picked up her pace. She looked back

again and started to run. I stopped where I was and looked up at the surrounding windows. What did this look like to people peeking out through their blinds? I was out walking. But what if someone had thought they'd seen something they hadn't and called the police. I held back the urge to run. Instead, I walked south to The Midway, plunged into its darkness, and remained on The Midway until I reached the foot of my street.

I'd been a fool. I'd been walking the streets grinning good evening at people who were frightened to death of me. I did violence to them by just being. How had I missed this? I kept walking at night, but from then on I paid attention.

I became expert in the language of fear. Couples locked arms or reached for each other's hand when they saw me. Some crossed to the other side of the street. People who were carrying on conversations went mute and stared straight ahead, as though avoiding my eyes would save them. This reminded me of an old wives' tale: that rabid dogs didn't bite if you avoided their eyes. The determination to avoid my eyes made me invisible to classmates and professors whom I passed on the street.

It occurred to me for the first time that I was big. I was 6 feet 1½ inches tall, and my long hair made me look bigger. I weighed only 170 pounds. But the navy pea jacket that Brian had given me was broad at the shoulders, high at the collar, making me look bigger and more fearsome than I was.

I tried to be innocuous but didn't know how. The more I thought about how I moved, the less my body belonged to me; I became a false character riding along inside it. I began to avoid people. I turned out of my way into side streets to spare them the sense that they were being stalked. I let them clear the lobbies of buildings before I entered, so they wouldn't feel trapped. Out of nervousness I began to whistle and discovered I was good at it. My whistle was pure and sweet—and also in tune. On the street at night I whistled popular tunes from the Beatles and Vivaldi's *Four Seasons*. The tension drained from people's bodies when they heard me. A few even smiled as they passed me in the dark.

Then I changed. I don't know why, but I remember when. I was walking west on 57th Street, after dark, coming home from the lake. The man and the woman walking toward me were laughing and talking but clammed up when they saw me. The man touched the woman's elbow, guiding her toward the curb. Normally I'd have given way and begun to whistle, but not this time. This time I veered toward them and aimed myself so that they'd have to part to avoid walking into me. The man stiffened, threw back his head and assumed the stare: eyes dead ahead, mouth open. His face took on a bluish hue under the sodium vapor streetlamps. I suppressed the urge to scream into his face. Instead I glided between them, my shoulder nearly brushing his. A few steps beyond them I stopped and howled with laughter. I called this game Scatter the Pigeons.

Fifty-seventh Street was too well lit for the game to be much fun; people didn't feel quite vulnerable enough. Along The Midway were heart-stopping strips of dark sidewalk, but these were so frightening that few people traveled them. The stretch of Blackstone between 57th and 55th provided better hunting. The block was long and lined with young trees that blocked out the streetlight and obscured the heads of people coming toward you.

One night I stooped beneath the branches and came up on the other side, just as a couple was stepping from their car into their town house. The woman pulled her purse close with one hand and reached for her husband with the other. The two of them stood frozen as I bore down on them. I felt a surge of power: these people were mine; I could do with them as I wished. If I'd been younger, with less to lose, I'd have robbed them, and it would have been easy. All I'd have to do was stand silently before them until they surrendered their money. I thundered, "Good evening!" into their bleached-out faces and cruised away laughing.

I held a special contempt for people who cowered in their cars as they waited for the light to change at 57th and Woodlawn. The intersection was always deserted at night, except for a car or two

> stuck at the red. *Thunk! Thunk! Thunk!* they hammered down the door locks when I came into view. Once I had hustled across the street, head down, trying to seem harmless. Now I turned brazenly into the headlights and laughed. Once across, I paced the sidewalk, glaring until the light changed. They'd made me terrifying. Now I'd show them how terrifying I could be. **"**

Andrew Sullivan

THE M-WORD: WHY IT MATTERS TO ME

ANDREW SULLIVAN (b. 1963) was born in southern England, and grew up near his birthplace. He attended Oxford University, where he studied modern history and modern languages. In 1984, he won a Harkness Fellowship to the John F. Kennedy School of Government at Harvard University, and graduated with a master's degree in Public Administration in 1986. Upon graduation, he began PhD work at Harvard in political science, and from 1991 to 1996 he was acting editor of the *New Republic*.

Openly gay, Sullivan has been an outspoken advocate of gay issues. His 1993 *New Republic* essay, "The Politics of Homosexuality," remains one of the most influential articles of the decade on the subject of gay rights; his controversial essay, "Why Men Are Different," put him on the cover of *Time* magazine. Sullivan has worked as a contributing writer and columnist for the *New York Times Magazine*, a regular contributor to the *New York Times Book Review*, and a weekly columnist

> Sullivan took up blogging in 2000 and writes daily on his blog, *The Daily Dish*, on the *Atlantic Online*.

for the *Sunday Times of London*. He writes often for *Time* magazine, in which his essay, "The M-Word: Why It Matters to Me," appeared in 2004. Sullivan's books include *Virtually Normal: An Argument About Homosexuality* (1995), *Love Undetectable: Notes on Friendship, Sex, and Survival* (1998), and, most recently, *The Conservative Soul: Fundamentalism, Freedom, and the Future of the Right* (2006). Sullivan took up blogging in 2000 and writes daily on his blog, *The Daily Dish*, on the *Atlantic Online*.

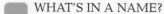

WHAT'S IN A NAME?

Perhaps the best answer is a memory.

As a child, I had no idea what homosexuality was. I grew up in a traditional home—Catholic, conservative, middle class. Life was relatively simple: education, work, family. I was brought up to aim high in life, even though my parents hadn't gone to college. But one thing was instilled in me. What matters is not how far you go in life, how much money you make, how big a name you make for yourself. What really matters is family, and the love you have for one another. The most important day of your life was not graduation from college or your first day at work or a raise or even your first house. The most important day of your life was when you got married. It was on that day that all your friends and all your family got together to celebrate the most important thing in life: your happiness, your ability to make a new home, to form a new but connected family, to find love that puts everything else into perspective.

But as I grew older, I found that this was somehow not available to me. I didn't feel the things for girls that my peers did. All the emotions and social rituals and bonding of teenage heterosexual life eluded me. I didn't know why. No one explained it. My emotional bonds to other boys were one-sided; each time I felt myself falling in love, they sensed it, pushed it away. I didn't and couldn't blame them. I got along fine with my buds in a nonemotional context; but something was awry, something not right. I came to know almost instinctively that I would never be a part of my family the way my siblings one day might be. The love I had inside me was unmentionable, anathema—even, in the words of the Church I attended every Sunday, evil. I remember writing in my teenage journal one day: "I'm a professional human being. But what do I do in my private life?"

So, like many gay men of my generation, I retreated. I never discussed   5
my real life. I couldn't date girls and so immersed myself in schoolwork, in the debate team, school plays, anything to give me an excuse not to confront reality. When I looked toward the years ahead, I couldn't see a future. There was just a void. Was I going to be alone my whole life? Would I ever have a "most important day" in my life? It seemed impossible, a negation, an undoing. To be a full part of my family I had to somehow not be me. So like many gay teens, I withdrew, became neurotic, depressed, at times close to suicidal. I shut myself in my room with my books, night after night, while my peers developed the skills needed to form real relationships, and loves. In wounded pride, I even voiced a rejection of family and marriage. It was the only way I could explain my isolation.

It took years for me to realize that I was gay, years later to tell others, and more time yet to form any kind of stable emotional bond with another man. Because my sexuality had emerged in solitude—and without any link to the idea of an actual relationship—it was hard later to reconnect sex to love and self-esteem. It still is. But I persevered, each relationship slowly growing longer than the last, learning in my twenties and thirties what my straight friends found out in their teens. But even then, my parents and friends never asked the question they would have asked automatically if I were straight: So when are you going to get married? When is your relationship going to be public? When will we be able to celebrate it and affirm it and support it? In fact, no one—no one—has yet asked me that question.

When people talk about "gay marriage," they miss the point. This isn't about gay marriage. It's about marriage. It's about family. It's about love. It isn't about religion. It's about civil marriage licenses—available to atheists as well as believers. These family values are not options for a happy and stable life. They are necessities. Putting gay relationships in some other category—civil unions, domestic partnerships, civil partnerships, whatever—may alleviate real human needs, but, by their very euphemism, by their very separateness, they actually build a wall between gay people and their own families. They put back the barrier many of us have spent a lifetime trying to erase.

It's too late for me to undo my own past. But I want above everything else to remember a young kid out there who may even be reading this now. I want to let him know that he doesn't have to choose between himself and his family any more. I want him to know that his love has dignity, that he does indeed have a future as a full and equal part of the human race. Only marriage will do that. Only marriage can bring him home. ●

The Reader's Presence

1. Why do you think Sullivan uses the term *M-Word* in his title? Would you know before reading the essay what it stands for? Why not simply use the full word? In what way does using only the letter to stand for the word affect the way you consider that word?

2. In paragraph 7, Sullivan refers to a "euphemism." What is a euphemism and what examples does he give? In what way do euphemisms "build a wall between gay people and their own families"? Given his argument, do you think Sullivan would consider the term *same-sex marriage* (which he doesn't use) a euphemism? Why or why not?

3. **CONNECTIONS:** Compare Sullivan's essay to Calvin Trillin's "A Traditional Family" (page 581). Which essayist in your opinion is more committed to traditional family values? What evidence can you supply to support your opinion?

The Writer at Work

ANDREW SULLIVAN on Essays and Blogs

"The word *blog*," Sullivan writes in "Why I Blog," an essay that appeared in *The Atlantic* in November 2008, "is a conflation of two words: *Web* and *log*. It contains in its four letters a concise and accurate self-description: it is a log of thoughts and writing posted publicly on the World Wide Web. In the monosyllable vernacular of the Internet, *Web log* soon became the word *blog*."

In the essay, Sullivan both examines the immediate origins of blogs and links the relatively recent online genre to the traditional essay, which developed centuries ago as a way of expressing one's ideas more informally than the intellectual conventions of the time required. The writer credited with establishing the popularity of an informal style in prose discourse is the French author, Michel Eyquem de Montaigne (1533–1592), who usually is referred to simply as Montaigne. After retiring from public life, Montaigne began developing a personal, quirky, candid, and digressive manner of composition, paying more attention to the *processes* of his thinking than perhaps any writer before him. He decided to give his unusual productions a name—*essais*, a word that in French means trials or attempts, thus characterizing their tentative and informal nature. The *Essais* appeared in print in France between 1580 and 1588 and ever since have exerted an enormous influence on writers and thinkers. That influence can be felt on practically every page of this anthology.

❝. . . Perhaps the quintessential blogger *avant la letter*[1] was Montaigne. His essays were published in three major editions, each one longer and more complex than the previous. A passionate skeptic, Montaigne amended, added to, and amplified the essays for each edition, making them three-dimensional through time. In the best modern translations, each essay is annotated, sentence by sentence, paragraph by paragraph, by small letters (A, B, and C) for each major edition, helping the reader see how each rewrite added to or subverted, emphasized or ironized, the version before. Montaigne was living his skepticism,

daring to show how a writer evolves, changes his mind, learns new things, shifts perspectives, grows older—and that this, far from being something that needs to be hidden behind a veneer of unchanging authority, can become a virtue, a new way of looking at the pretensions of authorship and text and truth. Montaigne, for good measure, also peppered his essays with myriads of what bloggers would call external links. His own thoughts are strewn with and complicated by the aphorisms and anecdotes of others. Scholars of the sources note that many of these "money quotes" were deliberately taken out of context, adding layers of irony to writing that was already saturated in empirical doubt.

To blog is therefore to let go of your writing in a way, to hold it at arm's length,

[1] *avant la lettre:* French, meaning before the term existed; in this case, Montaigne was a blogger before the word *blog* existed.—EDS.

open it to scrutiny, allow it to float in the ether for a while, and to let others, as Montaigne did, pivot you toward relative truth. A blogger will notice this almost immediately upon starting. Some e-mailers, unsurprisingly, know more about a subject than the blogger does. They will send links, stories, and facts, challenging the blogger's view of the world, sometimes outright refuting it, but more frequently adding context and nuance and complexity to an idea. The role of a blogger is not to defend against this but to embrace it. He is similar in this way to the host of a dinner party. He can provoke discussion or take a position, even passionately, but he also must create an atmosphere in which others want to participate.

That atmosphere will inevitably be formed by the blogger's personality. The blogosphere may, in fact, be the least veiled of any forum in which a writer dares to express himself. Even the most careful and self-aware blogger will reveal more about himself than he wants to in a few unguarded sentences and publish them before he has the sense to hit Delete. The wise panic that can paralyze a writer—the fear that he will be exposed, undone, humiliated—is not available to a blogger. You can't have blogger's block. You have to express yourself now, while your emotions roil, while your temper flares, while your humor lasts. You can try to hide yourself from real scrutiny, and the exposure it demands, but it's hard. And that's what makes blogging as a form stand out: it is rich in personality. The faux intimacy of the Web experience, the closeness of the e-mail and the instant message, seeps through. You feel as if you know bloggers as they go through their lives, experience the same things you are experiencing, and share the moment. When readers of my blog bump into me in person, they invariably address me as Andrew. Print readers don't do that. It's Mr. Sullivan to them. **"**

Manil Suri

KEYS TO THE KINGDOM

Born and raised in Bombay (now Mumbai), India, **MANIL SURI** (b. 1959) came to the United States as a student when he was twenty and obtained his PhD in applied mathematics from Carnegie Mellon University in 1983. He began working as a professor in the Department of Mathematics and Statistics at the University of Maryland Baltimore County (UMBC) and reports happily that it is "the only job [he's] ever had." His first novel, *The Death of Vishnu* (2001), has been translated into twenty-two languages. Suri was named a *Time* magazine

"Person to Watch" in 2000 and received a Guggenheim Fellowship for fiction in 2004. His second novel, *The Age of Shiva* (2008), is now available in paperback from W.W. Norton. Suri has written extensively on India and has said: "With this book [*The Age of Shiva*], I immersed myself in modern India. I understood what enormous challenges have been met since independence, and what a tremendous bond I have with the country of my birth. It is a source of joy to me that my book is being released in India's anniversary year of six decades of independence." His August 2007 essay, "What Unites India?" was published in the sixtieth independence-day anniversary issue of *India Today* and deals with topics in modern India. In addition to his work as an essayist and fiction writer, Suri still works in the field of numerical analysis and is interested in finding ways to bring mathematics to the public at large. He has said: "I'd like to help push mathematics into the cultural arena. Perhaps even put a mathematician on Oprah."

> **Manil Suri was named a *Time* magazine "Person to Watch" in 2000.**

WHEN I WAS GROWING UP in what was then Bombay, my mother promised to take me to Disneyland. Snow White and Mickey Mouse live there, she'd say, running her fingertips over the pictures in my storybooks, and that's where we'll meet them one day. When I got too old to believe this, she tantalized me with stories of the rides instead. Toy trains and swirling teacups, boats weaving through magic kingdoms, cable cars swinging through the air. They were so different from the boring local rides that hadn't changed since she was a girl: the merry-go-round, the giant wheel, the elephant or camel that plodded around at every fair.

Like other middle-class families in Bombay at the time, we rarely had the money to go anywhere on vacation, much less to travel to the United States. But America was always present—in the Paramount movies at the New Empire and the MGM movies at the Metro; in the "Archie" comics and the Hardy Boys novels for rent at the book lender's; and, once, in a jar of Tang that a wealthy relative presented to me. It was not until 1979, when I was 20, that I finally came to the United States as a student; five years later, after I had started teaching at the University of Maryland Baltimore County, my mother arrived in Baltimore for a summer visit. Disneyland was still at the top of her list. She had known, she insisted, from the day she first heard about the place, in 1955—even before I was born, when she was still working at the welfare ministry in Delhi—that she would one day accompany me there. "Besides, what else is there to see in America?" she said.

I was not as enthusiastic. I felt no nostalgia for Mickey Mouse. (Who was Minnie, anyway, Mickey's sister, or his wife?) I had no desire to be churned around in a rotating teacup or to be photographed with Snow White. Five years in America had trained me to peel back every image and look for the

*The "Mad Tea Party" ride at Disneyland in Anaheim, California, that Manil Suri
visited with his mother.*

commercial motive beneath it. Disneyland would no longer be "the experience of a lifetime" that the tour ads in the *Times of India* had promised. I was
too eager to assimilate, to be hip, to leave my naïvete behind.

We arrived at Disneyland on a June morning in 1984. There were banners at the entrance, proclaiming 1984 the year of Donald Duck's 50th birthday. My mother wanted to buy a pass for three days, but when I balked
at the price she reluctantly allowed herself to be negotiated down to two.
There were 52 attractions listed in the guide. We would have to hit 26 that
day, she said.

Once inside, we saw people photographing a cartoon character wad-   5
dling down Main Street—a duck that I did not recognize. My mother told
me that we would take pictures with Mickey later, if there was time. Right
now, the Disneyland Railroad train was about to leave, and she hustled me

onboard. "It's my second childhood," she said, "and I want to have more fun this time." I remembered her telling me how, as a child, she had fallen to the ground in a faint every time she felt neglected.

The first ride my mother decided we would go on was a river safari of some kind. My mind reeled as the guide announced we were on the Irrawaddy, then the Congo, then the Amazon, but my mother didn't care. She was too busy being regaled by the mechanical elephants, taking pictures of the giant hippo maws that our boat was tripping open alongside. Her excitement only grew with each subsequent attraction—the singing flowers, the talking animals, the dancing cartoon characters, all of which began to blur together in my mind. I noticed I had started picking up on the behavior of the parents around me—holding my mother's hand so that she wouldn't get lost, steering her away from the expensive souvenirs, shepherding her from ride to ride. She allowed herself to be led, without protest.

My mother loved everything. And she carefully checked off each ride in her guide with a ballpoint pen when it was over. She was especially captivated by the Enchanted Tiki Room, not because of the animated tropical birds but because it was presented by Dole Pineapple. What a startling country, she said, where even the fruits had brand names! For several weeks afterward, whenever we went to a grocery store, she headed for the produce section to see if the pineapples they stocked were Dole.

We went to a Chinese restaurant that evening. My mother kept leafing through the menu, unable to decide. "You order," she said, as if still hung over from her role as a child. "For me, anything is fine." When the rice and the chicken and the pork came out, my mother looked disappointedly at the plates. "The fish on the menu sounded so good—how come you didn't order it?"

As we walked through the entrance on the second morning, I was in a funk, anticipating another day of endless lines. It had taken an hour to get there in the Los Angeles traffic, and my mother had been plotting our itinerary the whole way. Twenty-six rides remained to be endured, including the teacups waiting to subject me to their nausea-inducing spin.

On Main Street, Goofy was holding court. Children were running toward   10
him, tugging their parents along, then being held up by their fathers to hug his neck. Goofy wagged his head and flopped his ears, and the kids in the crowd began to laugh. Even the adults were smiling—it was a Disney poster come to life.

"Quick, the camera," my mother said. She went over and hugged Goofy.

Through the lens, I saw a giant dog with a woman two-thirds his size. Her eyes were in the dog's shadow, and in her hand she clutched her guide. She didn't look like a girl, not quite—her smile was too wistful for a child. I gazed at the longing on her face even after the shutter had clicked, as if absorbing it for the first time. It struck me that we no longer had years left to spend in each other's company—only eight weeks remained of her visit, I realized.

Suddenly, the park came alive around me. Every zone scintillating with excitement, every nook throbbing with possibility—I started seeing Disneyland through my mother's eyes. Rides whooshed, a train tooted in the distance, people waved from cable cars gliding through the sky. The squeals of children, so grating just a moment ago, began to sound agreeable, endearing.

We managed to hit all the remaining 26 rides that day. I barreled us through, invigorated by my mother's eagerness—even the dreaded teacups failed to derail me. We had just enough time at the end to squeeze in an extra go-round on the floating safari. The plunge from Burma into the Congo was still geographically disorienting, but I laughed at the elephant antics along with everyone else this time.

After that, for the rest of my mother's visit, I went to every movie and   15
attraction she wanted to see, cheerfully, unflinchingly. I took her to Niagara Falls and New York City and Atlantic City, made sure to order fish at restaurants, even drove several times to Arlington for the salt-crusted Cambodian-style shrimp that she fell in love with. As her departure date grew closer, our activity got more frenetic—like in one of those movies about terminal illness, where the parents try to pack in every experience to enrich the last days of their child. For the first time, at the airport, it was my turn to be left behind.

It wasn't quite as tragic as that—some years later, my mother was back for her second visit. We even got to look together through the Disneyland photos in my album one day. "Thanks for introducing us," she said, when she came to her picture with Goofy. "Thanks for taking me."

Later on during that second trip, I reluctantly accompanied her to see the Broadway production of "Cats." My mother had heard about the musical for years in India, and it was now on the top of her list. She emerged from the theater exultant. "Truly, the experience of a lifetime," she declared. ●

The Reader's Presence

1. Why did Suri eventually lose interest in visiting Disneyland? How did his stay in the United States as a student and then as a teacher affect his interest? How do you explain the change that comes over him on the second day of visiting Disneyland with his mother after his initial lack of enthusiasm for the park?

2. What is your response to Suri's conclusion? Do you think he might have more effectively ended his essay at the conclusion of paragraph 15 ("For the first time, at the airport, it was my turn to be left behind")? Why do you think he added the next two paragraphs? What do they contribute to the essay? How would you have ended the essay?

3. **CONNECTIONS:** How does Suri's essay compare to another essay about a visit to a famous tourist site, Nathaniel Hawthorne's "My Visit to Niagara" (page 438)? Compare the initial responses each writer has toward the site and the changes they undergo. You might also compare Suri's essay to Ha Jin's "Arrival" (page 122) in terms of the way each immigrant writer forms a relationship with America.

Amy Tan
MOTHER TONGUE

AMY TAN (b. 1952) was born in California several years after her parents immigrated to the United States from China. She started writing as a child and won a writing contest at age eight. As an adult, Tan made her living as a freelance business writer for many years. In 1989 she published a best-selling novel, *The Joy Luck Club*, followed by the novel *The Kitchen God's Wife* (1991); the children's books *The Moon Lady* (1992) and *Sagwa, The Chinese Siamese Cat* (1994); and the novels *The Hundred Secret Senses* (1995) and *The Boneset-ter's Daughter* (2001). Her latest books are *The Opposite of Fate* (2003), a collection of autobiographical essays, and *Saving Fish from Drowning* (2005), a novel. "Mother Tongue" originally appeared in the *Threepenny Review* in 1990.

> **"I had a very unliterary background, but I had a determination to write for myself."**

Commenting on the art of writing, Tan has said, "I had a very unliterary background, but I had a determination to write for myself." She believes that the goal of every serious writer of literature is "to try to find your voice and your art, because it comes from your own experiences, your own pain."

I AM NOT A SCHOLAR of English or literature. I cannot give you much more than personal opinions on the English language and its variations in this country or others.

I am a writer. And by that definition, I am someone who has always loved language. I am fascinated by language in daily life. I spend a great deal of my time thinking about the power of language—the way it can evoke an emotion, a visual image, a complex idea, or a simple truth. Language is the tool of my trade. And I use them all—all the Englishes I grew up with.

Recently, I was made keenly aware of the different Englishes I do use. I was giving a talk to a large group of people, the same talk I had already given to half a dozen other groups. The nature of the talk was about my writing, my life, and my book, *The Joy Luck Club*. The talk was going along well enough, until I remembered one major difference that made the whole talk sound wrong. My mother was in the room. And it was perhaps the first time she had heard me give a lengthy speech, using the kind of English I have never used with her. I was saying things like "The intersection of memory upon imagination" and "There is an aspect of my fiction that relates to thus-and-thus"—a speech filled with carefully wrought grammatical phrases, burdened, it suddenly seemed to me, with nominalized forms, past perfect tenses, conditional phrases, all the forms of standard English that I had learned in school and through books, the forms of English I did not use at home with my mother.

Just last week, I was walking down the street with my mother, and I again found myself conscious of the English I was using, the English I do use with her. We were talking about the price of new and used furniture and I heard myself saying this: "Not waste money that way." My husband was with us as well, and he didn't notice any switch in my English. And then I realized why. It's because over the twenty years we've been together I've often used that same kind of English with him, and sometimes he even uses it with me. It has become our language of intimacy, a different sort of English that relates to family talk, the language I grew up with.

So you'll have some idea of what this family talk I heard sounds like, I'll   5
quote what my mother said during a recent conversation which I videotaped and then transcribed. During this conversation, my mother was talking about a political gangster in Shanghai who had the same last name as her family's, Du, and how the gangster in his early years wanted to be adopted by her family, which was rich by comparison. Later, the gangster became more powerful, far richer than my mother's family, and one day showed up at my mother's wedding to pay his respects. Here's what she said in part:

"Du Yusong having business like fruit stand. Like off the street kind. He is Du like Du Zong—but not Tsung-ming Island people. The local people call putong, the river east side, he belong to that side local people. That man want to ask Du Zong father take him in like become own family. Du Zong father wasn't look down on him, but didn't take seriously, until that man big like become a mafia. Now important person, very hard to inviting him. Chinese way, came only to show respect, don't stay for dinner. Respect for making big celebration, he shows up. Mean gives lots of respect. Chinese custom. Chinese social life that way. If too important won't have to stay too long. He come to my wedding. I didn't see, I heard it. I gone to boy's side, they have YMCA dinner. Chinese age I was nineteen."

You should know that my mother's expressive command of English belies how much she actually understands. She reads the *Forbes* report, listens to *Wall Street Week*, converses daily with her stockbroker, reads all of Shirley MacLaine's books with ease—all kinds of things I can't begin to understand. Yet some of my friends tell me they understand 50 percent of what my mother says. Some say they understand 80 to 90 percent. Some say they understand none of it, as if she were speaking pure Chinese. But to me, my mother's English is perfectly clear, perfectly natural. It's my mother

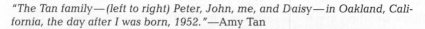

tongue. Her language, as I hear it, is vivid, direct, full of observation and imagery. That was the language that helped shape the way I saw things, expressed things, made sense of the world.

Lately, I've been giving more thought to the kind of English my mother speaks. Like others, I have described it to people as "broken" or "fractured" English. But I wince when I say that. It has always bothered me that I can think of no way to describe it other than "broken," as if it were damaged and needed to be fixed, as if it lacked a certain wholeness and soundness. I've heard other terms used, "limited English," for example. But they seem just as bad, as if everything is limited, including people's perceptions of the limited English speaker.

I know this for a fact, because when I was growing up, my mother's "limited" English limited *my* perception of her. I was ashamed of her English. I believed that her English reflected the quality of what she had to say. That is, because she expressed them imperfectly her thoughts were imperfect. And I had plenty of empirical evidence to support me: the fact that people in department stores, at banks, and at restaurants did not take her seriously, did not give her good service, pretended not to understand her, or even acted as if they did not hear her.

My mother has long realized the limitations of her English as well. When   10
I was fifteen, she used to have me call people on the phone to pretend I was

"The Tan family—(left to right) Peter, John, me, and Daisy—in Oakland, California, the day after I was born, 1952."—Amy Tan

she. In this guise, I was forced to ask for information or even to complain and yell at people who had been rude to her. One time it was a call to her stockbroker in New York. She had cashed out her small portfolio and it just so happened we were going to go to New York the next week, our very first trip outside California. I had to get on the phone and say in an adolescent voice that was not very convincing, "This is Mrs. Tan."

And my mother was standing in the back whispering loudly, "Why he don't send me check, already two weeks late. So mad he lie to me, losing me money."

And then I said in perfect English, "Yes, I'm getting rather concerned. You had agreed to send the check two weeks ago, but it hasn't arrived."

Then she began to talk more loudly. "What he want, I come to New York tell him front of his boss, you cheating me?" And I was trying to calm her down, make her be quiet, while telling the stockbroker, "I can't tolerate any more excuses. If I don't receive the check immediately, I am going to have to speak to your manager when I'm in New York next week." And sure enough, the following week there we were in front of this astonished stockbroker, and I was sitting there red-faced and quiet, and my mother, the real Mrs. Tan, was shouting at his boss in her impeccable broken English.

We used a similar routine just five days ago, for a situation that was far less humorous. My mother had gone to the hospital for an appointment, to find out about a benign brain tumor a CAT scan had revealed a month ago. She said she had spoken very good English, her best English, no mistakes. Still, she said, the hospital did not apologize when they said they had lost the CAT scan and she had come for nothing. She said they did not seem to have any sympathy when she told them she was anxious to know the exact diagnosis, since her husband and son had both died of brain tumors. She said they would not give her any more information until the next time and she would have to make another appointment for that. So she said she would not leave until the doctor called her daughter. She wouldn't budge. And when the doctor finally called her daughter, me, who spoke in perfect English—lo and behold—we had assurances the CAT scan would be found, promises that a conference call on Monday would be held, and apologies for any suffering my mother had gone through for a most regrettable mistake.

I think my mother's English almost had an effect on limiting my possibilities in life as well. Sociologists and linguists probably will tell you that a person's developing language skills are more influenced by peers. But I do think that the language spoken in the family, especially in immigrant families which are more insular, plays a large role in shaping the language of the child. And I believe that it affected my results on achievement tests, IQ tests, and the SAT. While my English skills were never judged as poor, compared to math, English could not be considered my strong suit. In grade school I did moderately well, getting perhaps B's, sometimes B-pluses, in English and scoring perhaps in the sixtieth or seventieth percentile on achievement tests. But those scores were not good enough to override the opinion that my true abilities lay in math and science, because in those areas I achieved A's and scored in the ninetieth percentile or higher.

This was understandable. Math is precise; there is only one correct answer. Whereas, for me at least, the answers on English tests were always a judgment call, a matter of opinion and personal experience. Those tests were constructed around items like fill-in-the-blank sentence completion, such as "Even though Tom was _____, Mary thought he was _____." And the correct answer always seemed to be the most bland combinations of thoughts, for example, "Even though Tom was shy, Mary thought he was charming," with the grammatical structure "even though" limiting the correct answer to some sort of semantic opposites, so you wouldn't get answers like, "Even though Tom was foolish, Mary thought he was ridiculous." Well, according to my mother, there were very few limitations as to what Tom could have been and what Mary might have thought of him. So I never did well on tests like that.

The same was true with word analogies, pairs of words in which you were supposed to find some sort of logical, semantic relationship—for example, "*Sunset* is to *nightfall* as _____ is to _____." And here you would be presented with a list of four possible pairs, one of which showed the same kind of relationship: *red* is to *stoplight, bus* is to *arrival, chills* is to *fever, yawn* is to *boring.* Well, I could never think that way. I knew what the tests were asking, but I could not block out of my mind the images already created by the first pair, "*sunset* is to *nightfall*"—and I would see a burst of colors against a darkening sky, the moon rising, the lowering of a curtain of stars. And all the other pairs of words—*red, bus, stoplight, boring*—just threw up a mass of confusing images, making it impossible for me to sort out something as logical as saying: "A sunset precedes nightfall" is the same as "a chill precedes a fever." The only way I would have gotten that answer right would have been to imagine an associative situation, for example, my being disobedient and staying out past sunset, catching a chill at night, which turns into feverish pneumonia as punishment, which indeed did happen to me.

I have been thinking about all this lately, about my mother's English, about achievement tests. Because lately I've been asked, as a writer, why there are not more Asian Americans represented in American literature. Why are there few Asian Americans enrolled in creative writing programs? Why do so many Chinese students go into engineering? Well, these are broad sociological questions I can't begin to answer. But I have noticed in surveys—in fact, just last week—that Asian students, as a whole, always do significantly better on math achievement tests than in English. And this makes me think that there are other Asian-American students whose English spoken in the home might also be described as "broken" or "limited." And perhaps they also have teachers who are steering them away from writing and into math and science, which is what happened to me.

Fortunately, I happen to be rebellious in nature and enjoy the challenge of disproving assumptions made about me. I became an English major my first year in college, after being enrolled as pre-med. I started writing nonfiction as a freelancer the week after I was told by my former boss that writing was my worst skill and I should hone my talents toward account management.

But it wasn't until 1985 that I finally began to write fiction. And at first   20 I wrote using what I thought to be wittily crafted sentences, sentences that would finally prove I had mastery over the English language. Here's an example from the first draft of a story that later made its way into *The Joy Luck Club*, but without this line: "That was my mental quandary in its nascent state." A terrible line, which I can barely pronounce.

Fortunately, for reasons I won't get into today, I later decided I should envision a reader for the stories I would write. And the reader I decided upon was my mother, because these were stories about mothers. So with this reader in mind—and in fact she did read my early drafts—I began to write stories using all the Englishes I grew up with: the English I spoke to my mother, which for lack of a better term might be described as "simple"; the English she used with me, which for lack of a better term might be described as "broken"; my translation of her Chinese, which could certainly be described as "watered down"; and what I imagined to be her translation of her Chinese if she could speak in perfect English, her internal language, and for that I sought to preserve the essence, but neither an English nor a Chinese structure. I wanted to capture what language ability tests can never reveal: her intent, her passion, her imagery, the rhythms of her speech, and the nature of her thoughts.

Apart from what any critic had to say about my writing, I knew I had succeeded where it counted when my mother finished reading my book and gave me her verdict: "So easy to read."

The Reader's Presence

1. In paragraph 2, Tan mentions "all the Englishes" she grew up with. What were those "Englishes"? What is odd about the term? How does the oddity of the word reinforce the point of her essay?

2. In paragraph 20, Tan gives an example of a sentence that she once thought showed her "mastery" of English. What does she now find wrong with that sentence? What do you think of it? What would her mother have thought of it? What sort of reader does that sentence anticipate?

3. **CONNECTIONS:**   What exactly is Tan's "mother tongue"? What does the phrase usually mean? Would you call her mother's English "broken English"? What does that phrase imply? Why does Tan write with her mother in mind as her ideal reader? How does Tan's determination to keep her mother linked to her writing compare with Richard Rodriguez's profound sense of having irrecoverably lost a connection with his parents in "Aria: A Memoir of a Bilingual Childhood" (page 187)? Does Rodriguez's distinction between private and public languages hold true for Tan?

Robert Vivian

TOWN

ROBERT VIVIAN (b. 1967) is an essayist, a poet, and a playwright. He grew up in the Dundee neighborhood of Omaha and holds the PhD in English from the University of Nebraska–Lincoln. More than twenty of his plays have been produced, and several have been published, with monologues appearing in *Best Men and Women's Stage Monologues* anthologies in 1995, 1996, 1997, and 1998. His work in drama and other genres has also appeared in prestigious mainstream and literary magazines, including *Harper's*, *Alaska Quarterly Review*, *Creative Nonfiction*, and *Glimmertrain*. His essay collection, *Cold Snap as Yearning* (2002), won the Society of Midland Authors Award for Nonfiction and the Nebraska Book Award for Nonfiction in 2002. The first install-ment of a trilogy in progress (*The Tall Grass Trilogy*), his first novel, *The Mover of Bones*, was published by the University of Nebraska Press in 2006. The second installment, *Lamb Bright Saviors* (2010), moved *Publishers Weekly* to dub Robert Vivian a "latter-day Faulkner." Despite his success as a novelist, Vivian remains committed to working in other genres. An assistant professor of English at Alma College in Michigan, he has said that he wants to "keep growing and changing," and that teaching allows him to do that.

> **Robert Vivian has said that he wants to "keep growing and changing," and that teaching allows him to do that.**

FOR SEVERAL YEARS NOW I've wondered in a slow-burning ache if I'll ever be able to chronicle what it's like to live in a small town in the middle of Michigan that's struggling to hang on, if I can somehow take the trains passing through night after night, offering up their long, drawn-out wails, and make of them, or of the water tower standing above abandoned oil fields or the rickety porches on the south side of town, a kind of sense, if only to myself, in order to say this is what it's like here, without sanctimony or censure or the least trace of sentimentality.

It's very important, perhaps even critical, to say something about a town like Alma,[1] to arrive at some understanding of it, even if it's partial and imperfect, to tug on the sleeve of the cosmos and inquire after this particular

[1] **Alma:** A town in Central Michigan with a population of approximately 10,000 and the home of Alma College. —EDS.

238

tiny corner of its staggering debris field and set forth an accurate portrait about the place where I have lived for almost eight years now. How I came to be here isn't that important, only the fact that enough time has passed for the spirit of this place to gradually fill me up so that I must appear like someone afflicted with bouts of inexplicable sighing, sudden bursts of exhalation that suggest resignation or ennui but which are just a way to maintain stability in the midst of the town's continuous outpouring of moon vibes.

Alma's downtown storefront windows are unlike any other windows in the world. It seems that you can't really look through them. When you try to, they instead appear to frame your entire existence in some as yet unnamed and ghostly dimension no one has ever defined. There's no way to escape the gravity of the reflections in these windows, no way to elude what they have in store for you, how they seem to do the work of X-rays connecting the living and the dead in a continuum that goes on forever. Maybe this borders on the preposterous, teeters at the edge of good taste. But stand a few minutes in front of Stacey's Men's Shop or the Cobbler Shop and look for yourself with a continued stare, at this same glass plunging down into fathomless depths, see around your reflection the aura of a gray sky pressing down and passing cars whose brake lights offer only a fleeting reprieve.

Litter and blowing trash flock like torn paper birds in startling, catastrophic numbers in the fallow fields behind Wal-Mart, punctuated here and there by itinerant trash bags that manage to play their ragged arpeggios if you're close enough to hear them. This is a distinctly forlorn and landlocked type of music usually reserved for wandering mystics, the kind of music that draws its inspiration from the spectral wastes of a man-made void. But above the fields and their legions of piping trash you can still watch the pastel bands of the sun going down over a distant tree line as radiant as anywhere else in the world and know that God and beauty are as mysteriously and abundantly here as they are in the fading twilight of a Tuscan vineyard or a wine glass filled with chardonnay glowing on a sunlit table.

At the Big Boy diner north of town, the forty-foot monstrous man-doll out front lofts a burger the circumference of a tractor tire, his garish expression so demonic and naïve you can see it for miles around, illuminated by a searchlight driving its wedging V deep into the night. To sit in a booth at Big Boy in the middle of winter is to come in contact with something so overwhelmingly sad and American as to be indistinguishable from facing your own mortality in the form of a trip to the salad bar arranged on a melting bank of ice. The ketchup-stained menus are bendable placards from the rough proximity of exile, where the missing children are.

A few years ago I sat in a booth at this Big Boy and watched the traffic going by on Highway 46, the headlights of the cars and trucks on that two-lane highway so hypnotic it took me several minutes to remember where I was. The red upholstery of the booth was like gruesome ribbons of congealed blood somehow turned into cushions. I looked around at my fellow diners.

The Big Boy statue at the original Bob's Big Boy restaurant in Toluca Lake, California. The restaurant has since become a national franchise.

We had all come here for whatever reason to eat and stare out these same windows, a little lost and dreamy above our croutons and chocolate milk shakes and banana splits. Did any of us have the slightest idea what being in this Big Boy meant? Was heartbreak ever more subtle? These aren't quaint or harmless questions. They're among the most important ever uttered. Not because I'm the one asking them, but because they're waiting for each one of us to somehow come to terms with them wherever we happen to be.

The radiant, startling truth is that a small town like Alma burns eternity into your soul and it won't let up, not for love, not for time, not for walking the dog at midnight. Alma makes smoking tinder of my own waking thoughts and visions. I eat a cheeseburger at the Main Cafe and can hear it crying at a frequency beyond any known decibel; I watch the blinking salt trucks in winter spray their minerals over a blanket of snow and feel the fine gray fanning-out of an odd reassurance; I smell the effluvium from the CAFO[2] eight miles west of town, hauling aloft its invisible clouds of apocalypse in early August, and touch the weathered hands of the farmer's wife counting out change under an awning buffeted by a gust of wind at the farmer's market that displays all the homegrown fruits and vegetables I could ever want to eat, and I know that this town has done a number on me in ways no map has ever charted. Little by little I'm pulling into middle age here, which I don't rightly know is a good thing or a bad thing, only that it is. I find myself unaccountably and inexorably drawn to billboards advertising 1-800 numbers for pregnant teenage girls and hotlines for bad credit and giant pictures of mud-covered ATVs, tooling around on my bike on hot summer days through the trailer parks out of sheer wanton curiosity and even esteem, loving the lonely dirt roads just outside of town for the dust they inevitably raise, loving the calls of cicadas and the birds sounding from hidden grooves in the fields.

I like going to the Shell gas station to buy wine and gasoline, to pay for a Beaujolais at a place with deer jerky for sale on the counter in old pickle jars and handwritten signs asking for donations for children sick from leukemia, to look out the wide, plate glass windows in late July and see fields of sunflowers raising their delicate throats to the sun only to droop back down once the day is done. I like driving by the legion of deer that come out to feed at twilight next to one of the busiest streets leading into town, traffic and these graceful ungulates living peacefully side by side within feet of each other as if some agreement has been struck between them and underwritten in paradise. Such strange incongruities have cast a lasting spell on me. I could live here for the rest of my life or leave tomorrow, staying or going not all that important somehow despite the incessant tug-of-war between the two that has stretched me out in a gradual crucifixion, the yin and yang of loving and hating a certain place, the need to go and the need to stay. "Contradictions feed us," Czeslaw Milosz[3] said, and in this he was prophetic. My family hasn't come to visit me and I'm secretly glad of this, for I don't think I could handle the subtle but relentless psychic pressure of trying to explain the unexplainable, to tell them how I've come to live here or what it might mean, which is no one's fault, not even the town's.

For whatever reason and whatever cause, I'm not the kind of person who chooses where to go, only submits to the place where he is bidden. I've wondered at this many times, how I end up in the places I do. The destinations occur less out of volition than some other appeasing fate that bends me to its will: places like Samsun, Turkey, and Miami, Oklahoma; Wroclaw, Poland, and Lincoln, Nebraska. I've been called to live in this town for however long and let its river of dreams run through me in order to offer a report of what it's like, even if no one cares to read about or listen to it.

---

[2] **CAFO:** The initials stand for Concentrated Animal Feeding Operation, controversial facilities subject to regulation by the Environmental Protection Agency. — EDS.

[3] **Czeslaw Milosz** (1911–2004): Nobel Prize–winning Polish poet who defected from the Soviet Union in 1951 and eventually became a U.S. citizen and a professor at the University of California, Berkeley. — EDS.

Somehow I've always known this and guarded it like a secret that isn't   10
mine to understand. I'm not supposed to fall in love with the beautiful dark-
haired girl behind the dry cleaning counter, but I need to be in quiet awe
of her and carry this awe forward like the lit end of a Lucky Strike. I'm supposed to notice and say how I can already see the middle-aged woman she
will become, the incipient lines around her eyes like the faintest crinkles of
wrapping paper, just the gentlest forecast of a sorrow years from happening.
I'm grateful for her beauty and the flashing tiny doors of her perfect teeth,
the wrinkling sound of my newly pressed clothes in the see-through plastic,
the fact that she knows what I smell like and the fact that this will never be
mentioned between us.

Intimacy is such a hushed and heartbreaking thing that I think it happens between strangers every bit as much as it does between lifelong lovers,
sometimes even more so. One day I was running in the woods down by the
polluted Pine River when I saw two men in camouflage outfits. One of the
men was kneeling down in front of the other engaged in telltale bobbing as
I ran on by as fast and loudly as I could, to the sudden startled yelp of the
standing man, who had his hands on the shoulders of his ten-minute lover. I
had accidentally interrupted an act that was strictly between them and their
own relentless fantasies—and eternity was burning each one of us up even
then, sparing no corner or aspect of our souls as the beautiful but sick river
flowed past, down by banks littered with debris.

I never saw the men again, nor ever wanted to, but I can still hear the
standing one yelp and gasp, can see the flashing whites of his eyes and the
astonishment that signaled his instant understanding of the reckoning that
had suddenly found him on the trail and was just as suddenly gone, the
stranger who now held his secret though he had no way of knowing that
I didn't or couldn't judge him for it. How fast can desire or lust turn into
something else, into terror and remorse? Running by, I saw in a revelation
as big as my life the standing man pulling up his pants like he was hauling
in empty fishing nets, gathering into his hands a sorrowful impotence that
lapped the town and his secret life of coming to these woods, of getting in his
car or truck dressed in hunting gear in order to achieve the release no other
corner of his life offered.

I didn't feel scandalized, didn't feel anger or outrage, just sorrow and
continuing wonder that these things happen in a town like Alma and happen everywhere, that the men's camouflage outfits disguised nothing, only
revealed a deeper truth. In fact I was almost grateful to see them, almost
glad that I could run on by within feet of their undeniable postures, that the
trail I was on gave me room to get around them and room to keep on going
into trees filled with shaking wires of lemon light and toward the teeming,
hoarse-throated chorus of frogs that call out every March back near the cemetery in a low-lying bog.

This town has given me so much, but taken away almost as much. It has
claimed my youth, my wild freedom, my ability to move about unencumbered

and unattached throughout all of sprawling Middle America. Some of what it has given me defies the confines of category—fish heads nailed to garage walls and cars and trucks parked on front lawns, tornado sirens sounding the first weekend of every month in spring and summer and the hoods of SUVs strapped down with dead deer. I've seen monster trucks driving by with Confederate flags frosted into their rear windows, I've seen the geese come and go, honking their messages to the sky—have seen how the seasons change the town into something holy and almost everlasting, how the quiet reverence of the first snow blesses the houses and the lawns and the city park where teenagers go to try out new tricks on their skateboards. I've stood over the sluice gates of the river and watched the sun go down in a mist of rainbows, have walked home drunk more nights than I can count from one of the town's two bars, which smell of dog hair and smoke—have pledged my fidelities to the town and revoked all citizenship elsewhere, pondered its formidable black-eyed ugliness and astonishing beauty with those same passing trains calling almost every night for all these years.

Someday I'll say good-bye to this town or it will say good-bye to me: we   15
will come to a mutual understanding that need not be discussed. Alma will add me to the greater universal fire, or I'll take these same burns to another place in the configuration of our enigma. I'll walk down some other sidewalk in some other town or city, waiting for my life to catch up with me even as the new town does its slow, steady termite work of beetling through the webby darkness of my flesh. Any place is good enough to die in and good enough to leave. Any place has the power to shake and remake a person into something he could never know before. When I leave I'll keep walking and I won't turn around, because I know that wherever I go the way is always forward toward a place that is no place at all but a state of being filled with gratitude in the inescapable and headlong leaning of home. ◼

The Reader's Presence

1. In many ways, Vivian's essay is a tribute to the small midwestern town he has lived in for eight years. But as keen as the author seems about the town, how does he also complicate matters by making the reader believe he would find—and actually in the future might find—other places equally fascinating? Why do you think that is, based on what he finds so appealing about Alma?

2. How would you describe the poetic quality of Vivian's prose? Select a few sentences in the essay and discuss their poetic characteristics. How do imagery and surprising observations contribute to the quality of Vivian's prose?

3. **CONNECTIONS:** Compare "Town" to Dinaw Mengestu's tribute to his Brooklyn neighborhood in "Home at Last" (page 170). Which author, in your opinion, seems more closely attached to the place he has chosen to live? Imagine Mengestu in Alma, Michigan, and Vivian in the Kensington section of Brooklyn—do you think each writer's essay would essentially remain the same even though the hometown had changed? Explain your answer.

Alice Walker

BEAUTY: WHEN THE OTHER DANCER IS THE SELF

ALICE WALKER (b. 1944) was awarded the Pulitzer Prize and the American Book Award for her second novel, *The Color Purple* (1982), which was made into a popular film. This novel helped establish Walker's reputation as one of America's most important contemporary writers. In both her fiction and nonfiction, she shares her compassion for the black women of America whose lives have long been largely excluded from or distorted in literary representation. Walker is also the author of other novels, short stories, several volumes of poetry, a children's biography of Langston Hughes, essays, and criticism. Her books of poetry and prose include *The Temple of My Familiar* (1989), *Possessing the Secret of Joy: A Novel* (1992), *By the Light of My Father's Smile* (1998), *The Way Forward Is with a Broken Heart* (2000), *Absolute Trust in the Goodness of the Earth* (2003), and *Now Is the Time to Open Your Heart* (2004). Her most recent work includes a collection of essays and ruminations, *We Are the Ones We Have Been Waiting For* (2006), an illustrated poem for children, *Why War Is Never a Good Idea* (2007), *Hard Times Require Furious Dancing: New Poems* (2010), and *Overcoming Speechlessness: A Poet Encounters the Horror in Rwanda, Eastern Congo, and Palestine/Israel* (2010). "Beauty: When the Other Dancer Is the Self" comes from her 1983 collection, *In Search of Our Mothers' Gardens*.

> "You have to go to the bottom of the well with creativity. You have to give it everything you've got, but at the same time you have to leave that last drop for the creative spirit or for the earth itself."

When asked by an interviewer about her writing habits, Walker replied, "I think it was Hemingway who said that each day that you write, you don't try to write to the absolute end of what you feel and think. You leave a little, you know, so that the next day you have something else to go on. And I would take it a little further—the thing is being able to create out of fullness, and that in order to create out of fullness, you have to let it well up. . . . In creation you must always leave something. You have to go to the bottom of the well with creativity. You have to give it everything you've got, but at the same time you have to leave that last drop for the creative spirit or for the earth itself."

IT IS A BRIGHT SUMMER DAY in 1947. My father, a fat, funny man with beautiful eyes and a subversive wit, is trying to decide which of his eight children he will take with him to the county fair. My mother, of course, will not go. She is knocked out from getting most of us ready: I hold my neck stiff against the pressure of her knuckles as she hastily completes the braiding and the beribboning of my hair.

My father is the driver for the rich old white lady up the road. Her name is Miss Mey. She owns all the land for miles around, as well as the house in which we live. All I remember about her is that she once offered to pay my mother thirty-five cents for cleaning her house, raking up piles of her magnolia leaves, and washing her family's clothes, and that my mother—she of no money, eight children, and a chronic earache—refused it. But I do not think of this in 1947. I am two-and-a-half years old. I want to go everywhere my daddy goes. I am excited at the prospect of riding in a car. Someone has told me fairs are fun. That there is room in the car for only three of us doesn't faze me at all. Whirling happily in my starchy frock, showing off my biscuit-polished patent-leather shoes and lavender socks, tossing my head in a way that makes my ribbons bounce, I stand, hands on hips, before my father. "Take me, Daddy," I say with assurance; "I'm the prettiest!"

Later, it does not surprise me to find myself in Miss Mey's shiny black car, sharing the back seat with the other lucky ones. Does not surprise me that I thoroughly enjoy the fair. At home that night I tell the unlucky ones all I can remember about the merry-go-round, the man who eats live chickens, and the teddy bears, until they say: that's enough, baby Alice. Shut up now, and go to sleep.

It is Easter Sunday, 1950. I am dressed in a green, flocked, scalloped-hem dress (handmade by my adoring sister, Ruth) that has its own smooth satin petticoat and tiny hot-pink roses tucked into each scallop. My shoes, new T-strap patent leather, again highly biscuit-polished. I am six years old and have learned one of the longest Easter speeches to be heard that day, totally unlike the speech I said when I was two: "Easter lilies / pure and white / blossom in / the morning light." When I rise to give my speech I do so on a great wave of love and pride and expectation. People in the church stop rustling their new crinolines. They seem to hold their breath. I can tell they admire my dress, but it is my spirit, bordering on sassiness (womanishness), they secretly applaud.

"That girl's a little *mess*," they whisper to each other, pleased.   5

Naturally I say my speech without stammer or pause, unlike those who stutter, stammer, or, worst of all, forget. This is before the word "beautiful" exists in people's vocabulary, but "Oh, isn't she the *cutest* thing!" frequently floats my way. "And got so much sense!" they gratefully add . . . for which thoughtful addition I thank them to this day.

It was great fun being cute. But then, one day, it ended.

I am eight years old and a tomboy. I have a cowboy hat, cowboy boots, checkered shirt and pants, all red. My playmates are my brothers, two and four years older than I. Their colors are black and green, the only difference in the way we are dressed. On Saturday nights we all go to the picture show, even my mother; Westerns are her favorite kind of movie. Back home, "on the ranch," we pretend we are Tom Mix, Hopalong Cassidy, Lash LaRue (we've even named one of our dogs Lash LaRue); we chase each other for hours rustling cattle, being outlaws, delivering damsels from distress. Then my parents decide to buy my brothers guns. These are not "real" guns. They shoot BBs, copper pellets my brothers say will kill birds. Because I am a girl, I do not get a gun. Instantly I am relegated to the position of Indian. Now there appears a great distance between us. They shoot and shoot at everything with their new guns. I try to keep up with my bow and arrows.

One day while I am standing on top of our makeshift "garage"—pieces of tin nailed across some poles—holding my bow and arrow and looking out toward the fields, I feel an incredible blow in my right eye. I look down just in time to see my brother lower his gun.

Both brothers rush to my side. My eye stings, and I cover it with my   10
hand. "If you tell," they say, "we will get a whipping. You don't want that to happen, do you?" I do not. "Here is a piece of wire," says the older brother, picking it up from the roof; "say you stepped on one end of it and the other flew up and hit you." The pain is beginning to start. "Yes," I say. "Yes, I will say that is what happened." If I do not say this is what happened, I know my brothers will find ways to make me wish I had. But now I will say anything that gets me to my mother.

Confronted by our parents we stick to the lie agreed upon. They place me on a bench on the porch and I close my left eye while they examine the right. There is a tree growing from underneath the porch that climbs past the railing to the roof. It is the last thing my right eye sees. I watch as its trunk, its branches, and then its leaves are blotted out by the rising blood.

I am in shock. First there is intense fever, which my father tries to break using lily leaves bound around my head. Then there are chills: my mother tries to get me to eat soup. Eventually, I do not know how, my parents learn what has happened. A week after the "accident" they take me to see a doctor. "Why did you wait so long to come?" he asks, looking into my eye and shaking his head. "Eyes are sympathetic," he says. "If one is blind, the other will likely become blind too."

This comment of the doctor's terrifies me. But it is really how I look that bothers me most. Where the BB pellet struck there is a glob of whitish scar tissue, a hideous cataract, on my eye. Now when I stare at people—a favorite pastime, up to now—they will stare back. Not at the "cute" little girl, but at her scar. For six years I do not stare at anyone, because I do not raise my head.

Years later, in the throes of a mid-life crisis, I ask my mother and sister whether I changed after the "accident." "No," they say, puzzled. "What do you mean?"

What do I mean?   15

I am eight, and, for the first time, doing poorly in school, where I have been something of a whiz since I was four. We have just moved to the place where the "accident" occurred. We do not know any of the people around us because this is a different county. The only time I see the friends I knew is when we go back to our old church. The new school is the former state penitentiary. It is a large stone building, cold and drafty, crammed to overflowing with boisterous, ill-disciplined children. On the third floor there is a huge circular imprint of some partition that has been torn out.

"What used to be here?" I ask a sullen girl next to me on our way past it to lunch.

"The electric chair," says she.

At night I have nightmares about the electric chair, and about all the people reputedly "fried" in it. I am afraid of the school, where all the students seem to be budding criminals.

"What's the matter with your eye?" they ask, critically.   20

When I don't answer (I cannot decide whether it was an "accident" or not), they shove me, insist on a fight.

My brother, the one who created the story about the wire, comes to my rescue. But then brags so much about "protecting" me, I become sick.

After months of torture at the school, my parents decide to send me back to our old community, to my old school. I live with my grandparents and the teacher they board. But there is no room for Phoebe, my cat. By the time my grandparents decide there *is* room, and I ask for my cat, she cannot be found. Miss Yarborough, the boarding teacher, takes me under her wing, and begins to teach me to play the piano. But soon she marries an African—a "prince," she says—and is whisked away to his continent.

At my old school there is at least one teacher who loves me. She is the teacher who "knew me before I was born" and bought my first baby clothes. It is she who makes life bearable. It is her presence that finally helps me turn on the one child at the school who continually calls me "one-eyed bitch." One day I simply grab him by his coat and beat him until I am satisfied. It is my teacher who tells me my mother is ill.

My mother is lying in bed in the middle of the day, something I have   25
never seen. She is in too much pain to speak. She has an abscess in her ear. I stand looking down on her, knowing that if she dies, I cannot live. She is being treated with warm oils and hot bricks held against her cheek. Finally a doctor comes. But I must go back to my grandparents' house. The weeks pass but I am hardly aware of it. All I know is that my mother might die, my father is not so jolly, my brothers still have their guns, and I am the one sent away from home.

"You did not change," they say.

Did I imagine the anguish of never looking up?

I am twelve. When relatives come to visit I hide in my room. My cousin Brenda, just my age, whose father works in the post office and whose mother is a nurse, comes to find me. "Hello," she says. And then she asks, looking at my recent school picture, which I did not want taken, and on which the "glob," as I think of it, is clearly visible, "You still can't see out of that eye?"

"No," I say, and flop back on the bed over my book.

That night, as I do almost every night, I abuse my eye. I rant and rave at   30
it, in front of the mirror. I plead with it to clear up before morning. I tell it I hate and despise it. I do not pray for sight. I pray for beauty.

"You did not change," they say.

I am fourteen and baby-sitting for my brother Bill, who lives in Boston. He is my favorite brother and there is a strong bond between us. Understanding my feelings of shame and ugliness he and his wife take me to a local hospital, where the "glob" is removed by a doctor named O. Henry. There is still a small bluish crater where the scar tissue was, but the ugly white stuff is gone. Almost immediately I become a different person from the girl who does not raise her head. Or so I think. Now that I've raised my head I win the boyfriend of my dreams. Now that I've raised my head I have plenty of friends. Now that I've raised my head classwork comes from my lips as faultlessly as Easter speeches did, and I leave high school as valedictorian, most popular student, and *queen*, hardly believing my luck. Ironically, the girl who was voted most beautiful in our class (and was) was later shot twice through the chest by a male companion, using a "real" gun, while she was pregnant. But that's another story in itself. Or is it?

"You did not change," they say.

It is now thirty years since the "accident." A beautiful journalist comes to visit and to interview me. She is going to write a cover story for her magazine that focuses on my latest book. "Decide how you want to look on the cover," she says. "Glamorous, or whatever."

Never mind "glamorous," it is the "whatever" that I hear. Suddenly all I   35
can think of is whether I will get enough sleep the night before the photography session: If I don't, my eye will be tired and wander, as blind eyes will.

At night in bed with my lover I think up reasons why I should not appear on the cover of a magazine. "My meanest critics will say I've sold out," I say. "My family will now realize I write scandalous books."

"But what's the real reason you don't want to do this?" he asks.

"Because in all probability," I say in a rush, "my eye won't be straight."

"It will be straight enough," he says. Then, "Besides, I thought you'd made your peace with that."

And I suddenly remember that I have.   40

I remember:

I am talking to my brother Jimmy, asking if he remembers anything unusual about the day I was shot. He does not know I consider that day the last time my father, with his sweet home remedy of cool lily leaves, chose me, and that I suffered and raged inside because of this. "Well," he says, "all I remember is standing by the side of the highway with Daddy, trying to flag down a car. A white man stopped, but when Daddy said he needed somebody to take his little girl to the doctor, he drove off."

I remember:

I am in the desert for the first time. I fall totally in love with it. I am so overwhelmed by its beauty, I confront for the first time, consciously, the meaning of the doctor's words years ago: "Eyes are sympathetic. If one is blind, the other will likely become blind too." I realize I have dashed about the world madly, looking at this, looking at that, storing up images against the fading of the light. *But I might have missed seeing the desert!* The shock of that possibility—and gratitude for over twenty-five years of sight—sends me literally to my knees. Poem after poem comes—which is perhaps how poets pray.

ON SIGHT

I am so thankful I have seen
The Desert
And the creatures in the desert
And the desert Itself.

The desert has its own moon
Which I have seen
With my own eye.
There is no flag on it.

Trees of the desert have arms
All of which are always up
That is because the moon is up
The sun is up
Also the sky
The Stars
Clouds
None with flags.

If there were flags, I doubt
the trees would point.
Would you?

But mostly, I remember this:

45

I am twenty-seven, and my baby daughter is almost three. Since her birth I have worried about her discovery that her mother's eyes are different from other people's. Will she be embarrassed? I think. What will she say? Every day she watches a television program called *Big Blue Marble*. It begins with a picture of the earth as it appears from the moon. It is bluish, a little battered-looking, but full of light, with whitish clouds swirling around it. Every time I see it I weep with love, as if it is a picture of Grandma's house. One day when I am putting Rebecca down for her nap, she suddenly focuses on my eye. Something inside me cringes, gets ready to try to protect myself. All children are cruel about physical differences, I know from experience, and that they don't always mean to be is another matter. I assume Rebecca will be the same.

But no-o-o-o. She studies my face intently as we stand, her inside and me outside her crib. She even holds my face maternally between her dimpled little hands. Then, looking every bit as serious and lawyerlike as her father, she says, as if it may just possibly have slipped my attention: "Mommy, there's a *world* in your eye." (As in, "Don't be alarmed, or do anything crazy.") And then, gently, but with great interest: "Mommy, where did you *get* that world in your eye?"

For the most part, the pain left then. (So what, if my brothers grew up to buy even more powerful pellet guns for their sons and to carry real guns themselves. So what, if a young "Morehouse[1] man" once nearly fell off the steps of Trevor Arnett Library because he thought my eyes were blue.) Crying and laughing I ran to the bathroom, while Rebecca mumbled and sang herself to sleep. Yes indeed, I realized, looking into the mirror. There *was* a world in my eye. And I saw that it was possible to love it: that in fact, for all it had taught me of shame and anger and inner vision, I *did* love it. Even to see it drifting out of orbit in boredom, or rolling up out of fatigue, not to mention floating back at attention in excitement (bearing witness, a friend has called it), deeply suitable to my personality, and even characteristic of me.

That night I dream I am dancing to Stevie Wonder's song "Always" (the name of the song is really "As," but I hear it as "Always"). As I dance, whirling and joyous, happier than I've ever been in my life, another bright-faced dancer joins me. We dance and kiss each other and hold each other through the night. The other dancer has obviously come through all right, as I have done. She is beautiful, whole, and free. And she is also me. ●

The Reader's Presence

1. In her opening paragraph, Walker refers to her father's "beautiful eyes." How does that phrase take on more significance in rereading? Can you find other words, phrases, or images that do the same? For example, why might Walker have mentioned the pain of having her hair combed?

2. Note that Walker uses the present tense throughout the essay. Why might this be unusual, given her subject? What effect does it have for both writer and reader? Try rewriting the opening paragraph in the past tense. What difference do you think it makes?

3. **CONNECTIONS:**   What is the meaning of Walker's occasional italicized comments? What do they have in common? Whose comments are they? To whom do they seem addressed? What time frame do they seem to be in? What purpose do you think they serve? How do they compare to those of Judith Ortiz Cofer in "Silent Dancing" (page 68)?

---

[1] *Morehouse:* Morehouse College, a black men's college in Atlanta, Georgia. —EDS.

Jerald Walker

SCATTERED INCONVENIENCES

JERALD WALKER (b. 1964) was born and raised on Chicago's South Side. He attended the Iowa Writers' Workshop and later earned a PhD in interdisciplinary studies from the University of Iowa. The winner of a James A. Michener Fellowship, he has published works in numerous periodicals such as the *Iowa Review*, the *Chronicle of Higher Education*, *Mother Jones*, *Harvard Review*, and *Creative Nonfiction*, and his essays have been selected for both *The Best American Essays* and *The Best African American Essays*. He is an associate professor in the Department of Writing, Literature, and Publishing at Emerson College in Boston. His memoir, *Street Shadows: A Memoir of Race, Rebellion, and Redemption* (2010) received the 2011 L. L. Winship/PEN New England Award. "Scattered Inconveniences" appeared in the *North American Review* in 2006.

> Jerald Walker was born and raised on Chicago's South Side.

HE BARRELED up on our left, momentarily matched our speed, then surged forward and waved a cowboy hat out the window, a bull rider in a brown Chevy. Somehow I knew he would swerve into our lane and slow down, and as he did the sound of his horn came to us over the rumble of our truck's engine. We were in a seventeen-foot Ryder that held everything we owned, junk, pretty much, with ten feet to spare. Those were, we believed, the final days of poverty. After not being able to find a teaching job for three years since completing her doctorate in art history, my wife had landed a rare tenure-track position at a state college in New England, twelve hundred miles east of Iowa City where we'd spent ten years living with tornadoes, academics, and hippies. I was going to be a stay-at-home dad, watching our fifteen-month-old during the day and writing at night. It was the perfect scenario, one we'd dreamt of for so long. All I had to do now was prevent the man in the Chevy from killing us.

I gripped the steering wheel tighter, checked the rearview mirrors in case a sudden maneuver was necessary. There were no vehicles within twenty yards, besides our reckless escort, just ten feet away.

"This guy's drunk or something," Brenda said.

I shook my head. "I *told you* we shouldn't drive in the middle of the night."

"It's only eight."   5

I checked the clock on the dashboard. "8:10."

"Well, you could just *slow down*," she said, "and let him go."

"Or," I responded, "I could crush him."

"And injure your son in the process?"

I glanced to my right. Adrian slept between us in his child seat, oblivious   10
that we were being menaced by a fool, and that his daddy, in certain situations, particularly those that involved motor vehicles and testosterone, was
a fool, too. I tugged at his harness, and confirmed that it was secure, then
gunned the engine and lurched the truck forward. Brenda punched my arm. I
lifted my foot off the accelerator and watched the speedometer topple from 70
to 55, where I leveled off. For a few seconds there was a gentlemanly distance
between us and the Chevy, and then it slowed, too, until it was again ten feet
from our bumper. This time I held my ground. I could feel Brenda tensing. I
lowered my window and gave him the finger, Adrian stirring as wind tore into
the cab. Brenda called me an ass, though not audibly. We'd been together long
enough that the actual use of words, at times like those, was unnecessary.

The Chevy suddenly braked and I had to as well to avoid a collision.
My heart was racing now. I tried hard to believe that we weren't dealing
with something more ominous than a souse. We were in Indiana, a state I
vaguely remembered hearing was a breeding ground for racists; perhaps
the random sight of a black family had proved too irresistible, a cat straying
into an angry dog's view.

But I had heard similar things about Iowa, only later to experience no
problems. "No problems" is not to say "nothing," though, for there were
what a black intellectual referred to as "scattered inconveniences"—women
crossing the street or removing their purses from grocery carts at my approach,
security guards following me in department stores. Once, while I was working out in the university's gym, two young men, looking my way and laughing, began mimicking the walk of a gorilla. Silly, all of it, confirmation that
the bigotry my parents faced no longer exists, that its sledgehammer impact
has been reduced, for the most part, to pebbles pitched from a naughty child's
hand. I tell myself to find victory in encounters such as these. And I usually
do. But sometimes I can't because of one simple truth: I am a racist.

Like a recovering alcoholic, I recognize that to define myself by my disease is in some way to help guard against relapse, that there is daily salvation in this constant reminder of who and what I am. My quest to be rid of all
traces of this scourge has not been easy, though I have made good progress,
considering I was born during the sixties in a segregated Chicago. The communities I grew up in were dangerous and poor, and it was the common
opinion of nearly everyone I knew that, when all was said and done, whites
were to blame. Whites discriminated against us. Whites denied us decent
housing. Whites caused us to have high unemployment and failed schools.
Crack had come from whites, and so too had AIDS. Whites, in some vague
and yet indisputable way, made the winos drink and gangbangers kill. I

came to believe, at a very early age, that in order to succeed I would have to beat the system through the mastery of some criminal enterprise, or join it in the form of a Sambo, a sell-out, an Oreo, an Uncle Tom. In other words, I'd have to be my brother Clyde.

Clyde, who said things like, "Whites aren't an obstacle to success," and "Only *you* can stop *you*."

We didn't like Clyde.   15

We watched him with disgust as he became a teenager and continued to speak without slang or profanity. He wore straight-legs and loafers instead of bellbottoms and four-inch stacks, his only concession to soulful style an afro, which *could* have been bigger. He held a job during high school and still earned straight A's. After graduation he studied computers when his friends aspired to be postal clerks or pimps.

Our father threw him out. He was twenty-one. My twin brother and I, at fourteen, just on the threshold of a decade of lawlessness, had come home one night drunk. Clyde beat us sober with a pool stick. Outside of a few times at church, it was many years before we saw him socially again. I didn't know where he spent his exile. I was not surprised, though, when he resurfaced in the eighties in a Ford AeroStar with a Ronald Reagan sticker on his bumper. He'd rejected liberal black ideology his whole life, and so his emergence as a staunch conservative made perfect sense, as much sense as me, twenty years later, being tempted to crush a white man on I-80.

The Chevy switched lanes again, this time to the right. The driver was shouting at us through his opened window. I ignored him. He blew his horn.

Brenda asked, "What do you think he wants?"

"Our lives," I said.   20

He blew his horn again.

"I'm going to open my window and see what he wants."

"Do *not* do that!"

She opened her window. I couldn't make out what he was saying, and Brenda was practically hanging out the window to hear him. I leaned towards them while trying to keep the truck steady. Brenda suddenly whirled to face me. Her eyes were wide. "Stop the truck!" she demanded.

"Why?"   25

"The back door is open! The washer's about to fall out!"

We were towing our car behind us; the perilousness of the situation was instantly clear.

I put on my right signal and began to work my way to the shoulder. The man tooted his horn and gave me a thumbs-up, then rode off into the night. Adrian was crying and I wondered for how long. His pacifier had fallen. Brenda rooted it from his seat and slipped it between his lips. He puffed on it fiendishly, like it was long-denied nicotine.

We'd come to a stop. Our hazards were flashing. Cars and trucks rocked us gently as they hurled themselves east, towards the Promised Land. Before I opened my door, Brenda and I exchanged a quick glance. I did not have to actually say I was sorry. She did not have to actually say she forgave me. ◼

The Reader's Presence

1. Why does Walker title his essay "Scattered Inconveniences"? Where in the essay do we find the phrase used? Who said it and in what context does it appear? What meaning does it take on with respect to racism? Do you think the incident Walker describes is an example of a scattered inconvenience in the same sense that the phrase appears in the essay? Why or why not?

2. In paragraph 12, Walker admits to being "a racist." In what sense is he one? Is his racism shown in the essay? If so, how? If not, why does he introduce the subject? Consider Walker's brother Clyde, who plays a fairly large part in this brief essay. What does Clyde's presence have to do with Walker's main point in the essay?

3. **CONNECTIONS:**   Consider Walker's essay along with Brent Staples's "Just Walk on By: A Black Man Ponders His Power to Alter Public Space" (page 217). How would you differentiate the racial factors in each essay? How does Staples's essay conform to Walker's advice on how to tell a good story?

The Writer at Work

JERALD WALKER on Telling a Good Story

As a creative writing instructor, Jerald Walker wants his students to concentrate more on story *telling* and less on the lesson or point they want to make. Nevertheless, invited by the editors to discuss his own essay and what it means to him as a reader (and not as a writer), Walker discovers that it contains a moral or point he did not set out to make. His brief explanation makes us aware that writing to a large extent is an act of discovery. But that discovery could only happen in the process of constructing the story.

❝One thing I constantly urge my creative writing students to do is to lay off the metaphors. Go easy on morals, lessons, and "points"—it's the reader's job to worry about those. Your job is simply to try to tell a good story. That was what I tried to do in "Scattered Inconveniences." However, much to my delight (I was tempted to say "surprise," but I've come to expect surprises in the act of writing, so now I'm merely delighted when they occur), I later discovered it to be highly metaphorical. As a *reader* of this essay, I could make a case that the man in the Chevy represents the sin of American racism—slavery, discrimination, and other forms of bigotry that may at any moment barrel forth to make terribly disruptive appearances in our lives. When it cannot appear itself, which these days is more often the case than not, for an exceedingly long and reckless life has left it frail and feeble, it sends an able representative, known as paranoia. I have experienced a great deal of paranoia in the black community. On Chicago's South Side, where I was raised, there always seemed to be the suspicion, if not the outright prediction, that the blatant racism practiced in previous generations would make a triumphant comeback—indeed, in the minds of some people it never left. The paranoia created by racism, it seems to me, is often worse than racism itself, in the way that not knowing something is often worse than knowing. The phrase, "*Please*, Doc, just give it to me straight!" comes to mind.

But as my wife, son, and I traveled in our truck through Indiana, I could not have it given to me straight. I did not know the intentions of the man in the Chevy. And so, regrettably, I assumed the worst. Here my actions were metaphorical, too, for what better way to express how so many racial conflicts could be averted if we simply learned to give each other the benefit of the doubt. For me, that is sometimes easier said than done, but it is what I—what we all—must constantly aspire to if complete racial reconciliation will ever be achieved. Which leads me to another metaphor, as embodied in Adrian, my toddler, sleeping so peacefully until I lost my cool; he is, of course, the future. As a result of fear and mistrust, the future is placed in jeopardy. Perhaps that is ultimately the lesson of "Scattered Inconveniences"; maybe that is its moral or "point." I will leave that for each reader to decide, because, as the *writer*, I did not set out with any of these in mind. I was simply trying to tell a good story. **"**

The Student at Work

LAUREN CARTER / Isn't Watermelon Delicious?

Lauren Carter (b. 1978) graduated in 2005 from Bridgewater State University in Massachusetts with a degree in English. While at Bridgewater, Carter served as editor in chief of the literary magazine *The Bridge*, where her essay, "Isn't Watermelon Delicious?" first appeared. After graduating, she began to write for a newspaper full time and currently works as a freelance writer for several publications. Her topics include music and race, and she encourages fellow student writers not to "look at writing as drudgery [but to] view it as an opportunity to express yourself."

Carter wrote the following essay as a response to an assignment in an undergraduate African American literature course taught at Bridgewater State University by Jerald Walker, the author of the preceding selection. Professor Walker, who now teaches at Emerson College, generously supplied us with the actual assignment.

Assignment: Malon Riggs's documentary *Black Is . . . Black Ain't . . .* ends with the following quotation: "If you have received no clear cut impression of what The Negro in America is like, then you are in the same place with me. There is no The Negro here" (Zora Neale Hurston). Hurston's point, it seems to me, is that Negroes (or coloreds or blacks or Afro-Americans or African Americans) come in such varieties that they are impossible to define as a homogeneous group. Much of this variety can be said to be the result of blues/jazz idiom, how blacks are constantly improvising new identities in an effort to adapt to changing conditions and needs. Likewise, African American fiction writers are constantly improvising on the theme of "blackness" in order to produce works that attempt to offer at least partial definitions of what it means to be African American. In your essay, work your way through the literature read in this class and discuss how each author adds to our understanding of what it means to be black.

As you read Carter's response to the assignment, observe how she blends her personal experiences of being a young black woman with a number of relevant literary works she read for Professor Walker's course. Her essay is prompted by a friend's comment about behavior corresponding to race. Where else does Carter encounter this idea? What questions does she raise about how people understand race?

❝ It was just another Thursday night at Axis. White lights were flashing, music was pumping, and I was mildly buzzed. My best friend Stacey and I were making our way around the edges of the crowded dance floor, looking for a table where we could plop down and briefly escape the frenzy of the hot, crowded club. Then my favorite song came on. I don't remember what song it was; it was a long time ago and I usually had a new favorite song every other week. But at the time, the song that started playing was my favorite one, and I was ecstatic. As soon as I heard the bass line I guzzled what was left of my drink, broke out into some kind of overenthusiastic dance move, and shouted "Let's go!"

Stacey looked over at me and laughed.

"God, Lauren," she said, "sometimes you're so white, and sometimes you're soooo black."

It was an interesting idea. That I could be one or the other, at different times. I wondered when I was which one. So I asked her.

She started to answer, but the music was too loud, and I couldn't really make out what she was saying. I leaned in closer and asked her to repeat what she said, but she waved the idea away, saying we should go dance.

Yes, we should dance, I thought. My favorite song was on and we were attempting to have a conversation meant for a quiet café, not a loud, crowded club.

We never did have that conversation, and I never did get the answer I was looking for. What, exactly, I did that was so white. And what, exactly, I did that was so black. But the idea stuck with me. That a behavior related to a skin tone. That my behavior related to two different ones.

It wasn't a totally new idea. My black cousin Shea had told me for years that I acted "so white." I thought I was just acting like me, but apparently, with my Bart Simpson t-shirt, my "proper" speech, and my affinity for Vanilla Ice, I was masquerading as a white girl in a black girl's body. I didn't know those characteristics belonged exclusively to white people. I thought they belonged to

people who liked the occasional Simpsons t-shirt, spoke the way they had
learned to speak, and enjoyed listening
to extremely cheesy, albeit catchy, quasi-
rap music.

Or at least that's how I feel now.
But then, I felt inferior—way behind
in the race for true blackness. I would
never catch up to her. I'd never know all
the latest black sayings, never listen to
all the latest black music, never wear all
the latest black clothing. I'd never be as
black as she was. Or so I thought.

But that's before I met the Ex-
Colored Man.[1] In his autobiography,
he switched from white to black and
back again, though his skin color never
changed. When he discovered his blackness as a child, he still looked like a
white person. But internally, he realized
there was black blood running through
his veins, or rather blue blood with
black ancestry in it, and he withdrew.
He wasn't what he thought he'd been.
He couldn't stop thinking about his new
blackness. Really, though, nothing had
changed. Externally, at least.

So it kind of surprised me when, at
the end of his story, he chose to become
white again. This, after feeling morti-
fied and ashamed that in a country like
America, with all its talk of democracy
and freedom, the black race could be
persecuted so harshly. While I could
attempt to analyze and judge his decision to forsake his blackness in order
to better his condition, decide whether
he had succumbed to the race game
or merely decided to stop playing, the
validity of his decision isn't as important
as the fact that it could be made. That
he could become white again, simply by

---

[1] *Ex-Colored Man:* Referenced in Works Cited
(page 259). —EDS.

deciding to be. It was a miraculous transformation. Which got me to thinking,
if you can miraculously transform from
black to white, or vice versa, then how
real is either category?

My sister transforms all the time,
depending on who's looking at her. She's
black in terms of ancestry. Partially, anyway. Our mother's Italian, her father's
black. And though her hair came out
extremely nappy, her skin is light. Whiter
than some "white" people's skin, in fact.
Now that she chemically straightens her
hair, most people don't know she's black
unless she tells them. She can pass. Not
among black people, of course, myself
included. We can all see it in her features.
But to the untrained eye, amongst the
world at large, she can generally be perceived as white. So which is she? Is she
what her ancestry dictates, or what other
people's perception decides?

It's a ridiculous question, I know.
But only as ridiculous as the fallacy it's
based on. When you lump a group of
people together based solely on the color
of their skin, of course ridiculous questions like these come up. It'd be the same
if you lumped them together based on
eye color, height, or any other arbitrary
characteristic over which they have no
control.

Funny, that we would choose to separate and define people based on factors
beyond their control. Well, maybe not
funny. But certainly ingenious. And an
excellent way to subordinate one group
in order to elevate another. Because isn't
it true that all of these external factors,
in actuality, say nothing about a person's
character, that the only real measure
of a person is in their actions, not any
physical characteristic? Isn't it true that
anyone who has survived and succeeded
in any facet of life did so almost exclusively because of their intellect, their

intelligence, their will to persevere, not because of the pigment in their skin or the fullness of their features?

When Frederick Douglass found ways to teach himself to read, it wasn't because of his melanin content. It was because of his desire to learn, his ingenuity, his intelligence.

After six months of torture by his brutal master Covey, Douglass made the bold and beautiful statement: "You have seen how a man was made a slave; now you shall see how a slave was made a man."

And when he did make that journey from slavery to manhood, it wasn't because of the coil of his hair, it was because of the color of his character. When Gabriel Prosser[2] decided to lead a revolt in pursuit of freedom, it wasn't because of the size of his muscles, it was because of the size of his spirit. When blacks survived slavery, it wasn't because of the width of their noses or how many calluses they did or didn't have on their hands. It was because of the survival strategies they'd developed over time, none of which had anything to do with appearance.

The folktales and spirituals that emerged out of that era weren't developed because of the shape of someone's kneecaps; they were developed because of a will to overcome seemingly insurmountable obstacles. And when Bigger Thomas, the main character in Richard Wright's famous novel, *Native Son*, became the agent of his own demise, it wasn't, contrary to his own beliefs, because of the darkness of his skin; it was

because of the darkness of his mind, and all of the things he believed he would never, and so never did, achieve.

Maybe life would be simpler if skin color really was an indicator of character, external factors determined internal worth, and similar complexions could unite us all. Then all the dark-skinned peoples of America could heed Marcus Garvey's[3] message and return home to Africa. We could take a giant plane to Uganda, and when it landed we could step down off it with open arms and scream, "Hello black people, I'm finally home!!" But in reality, that probably wouldn't work. Those Ugandans would only point out what I've come to realize over the past semester: that the significance of skin color is that it is the color of one's skin, and not much more. That it does not necessarily imply a common set of values, a standard behavior, a singular way of life.

And why should it? Aren't there a number of ways that human beings can define themselves as individuals? What about gender? Profession? Religious beliefs? Hobbies? Personality? Sexual orientation? Values? What about your attitude towards yourself, towards others, towards life? Isn't it true that race is just one ingredient in a large and complicated recipe? Why must it be the main ingredient and define all the other areas of life? I know that my life is about much more than being black, and, for that matter, being black is about much more than my skin color.

Which leads to the question: What is my blackness about? When am I really

---

[2]*Gabriel Prosser* (1776–1800): A blacksmith who was executed for planning a slave rebellion near Richmond, Virginia, in 1800. —EDS.

[3]*Marcus Garvey* (1887–1940): A Jamaican journalist known for his Black Nationalism movement. —EDS.

black? When I start celebrating Kwan-zaa? When I fill my wardrobe with Roc-A-Wear and Phat Farm? When I stop playing Elton John? Is that what blackness is? A holiday? A piece of clothing? A song?

Funny, I never thought of being black that way. I never considered that a Dashiki would give me blackness, and I never thought that a lack of one would take it away. I always thought of black as a state of mind; a way of looking at the world. Perseverance in the face of any and all obstacles. Winning when everyone says you're bound to lose. I never looked at the color of my skin as evidence of a drum, or a slice of water-melon. I never thought I had to do, have, or say anything at all to be black. I just thought I was.

I never told her so, but when Shea said I was acting "so white," she was wrong. Whites don't have a monopoly on listening to Vanilla Ice, and even if they could have one, I doubt they'd want it. I was acting like me. I don't need to walk the streets with a sandwich board proclaiming what I am. I don't need to act out my blackness, just like I don't need to act out my eye color; it's simply an intrinsic part of who I am.

True, the color of my skin implies an ancestry that the color of my eyes does not, and I'm aware of that ancestry; I draw from it daily. But I don't need to wear Lugz and use slang to prove it. Maya Angelou wrote "I am the dream and the hope of the slave," and I haven't forgotten about those hopes and dreams. I understand the debt that I owe to my ancestors, and I pay it back every day, in my own way, that has nothing to do with what jeans I wear, and has everything to do with how I live my life. The size of

my nose is not my inheritance. The will to survive is.

Stacey's statement in that night-club was probably my first—or at least my most memorable—experience with double consciousness as civil rights activist W. E. B. DuBois described it, of being conscious not only of how you see yourself, but how others see you; I'd never thought of myself solely in terms of white and black, but I realized the extent to which other people could. For a long time after that night I wondered where the line between black and white was, and in what moments I crossed it. I don't wonder about that line anymore. Black-ness no longer boils down to a t-shirt, or a desire to dance. It's just not that simple. Blackness is the legacy left by the people that came before me, and it's the legacy I'll leave behind me when I'm gone.**"**

WORKS CITED

Angelou, Maya. "Still I Rise." *The Complete Collected Poems of Maya Angelou.* New York: Random House, 1994.

Bontemps, Arna. *Black Thunder.* Boston: Beacon Press, 1992.

Douglass, Frederick. *Narrative of the Life of Frederick Douglass, an American Slave.* New York: Barnes & Noble Classics, 2003.

DuBois, W. E. B. *The Souls of Black Folk.* Boston: Bedford/St. Martin's, 1997.

Johnson, James Weldon. *The Autobiography of an Ex-Colored Man.* New York: Vintage Books, 1989.

Wright, Richard. *Native Son.* New York: Perennial, 2003.

E. B. White

ONCE MORE TO THE LAKE

ELWYN BROOKS WHITE (1899–1985) started contributing to the *New Yorker* soon after the magazine began publication in 1925, and in the "Talk of the Town" and other columns helped establish the magazine's reputation for precise and brilliant prose. Collections of his contributions can be found in *Every Day Is Saturday* (1934), *Quo Vadimus?* (1939), and *The Wild Flag* (1946). He also wrote essays for *Harper's* on a regular basis; these essays include "Once More to the Lake" and are collected in *One Man's Meat* (1941). In his comments on this work, the critic Jonathan Yardley observed that White is "one of the few writers of this or any century who has succeeded in transforming the ephemera of journalism into something that demands to be called literature."

> **"I have always felt that the first duty of a writer was to ascend—to make flights, carrying others along if he could manage it."**

Capable of brilliant satire, White could also be sad and serious, as in his compilation of forty years of writing, *Essays* (1977). Among his numerous awards and honors, White received the American Academy of Arts and Letters Gold Medal (1960), a Presidential Medal of Freedom (1963), and a National Medal for Literature (1971). He made a lasting contribution to children's literature with *Stuart Little* (1945), *Charlotte's Web* (1952), and *The Trumpet of the Swan* (1970).

White has written, "I have always felt that the first duty of a writer was to ascend—to make flights, carrying others along if he could manage it." According to White, the writer needs not only courage but also hope and faith to accomplish this goal: "Writing itself is an act of faith, nothing else. And it must be the writer, above all others, who keeps it alive—choked with laughter, or with pain."

ONE SUMMER, along about 1904, my father rented a camp on a lake in Maine and took us all there for the month of August. We all got ringworm from some kittens and had to rub Pond's Extract on our arms and legs night and morning, and my father rolled over in a canoe with all his clothes on; but outside of that the vacation was a success and from then on none of us ever thought there was any place in the world like that lake in Maine. We returned summer after summer—always on August 1st for one month. I have since become a salt-water man, but sometimes in summer there are days when the restlessness of the tides and the fearful cold of the sea water and the incessant wind that blows across the afternoon and into the evening make me wish for the placidity of a lake in the woods. A few weeks ago this feeling got so strong I bought myself a couple of bass hooks and a spinner and returned to the lake where we used to go, for a week's fishing and to revisit old haunts.

I took along my son, who had never had any fresh water up his nose and who had seen lily pads only from train windows. On the journey over to the lake I began to wonder what it would be like. I wondered how time would have marred this unique, this holy spot—the coves and streams, the hills that the sun set behind, the camps and the paths behind the camps. I was sure that the tarred road would have found it out and I wondered in what other ways it would be desolated. It is strange how much you can remember about places like that once you allow your mind to return into the grooves that lead back. You remember one thing, and that suddenly reminds you of another thing. I guess I remembered clearest of all the early mornings, when the lake was cool and motionless, remembered how the bedroom smelled of the lumber it was made of and the wet woods whose scent entered through the screen. The partitions in the camp were thin and did not extend clear to the top of the rooms, and as I was always the first up I would dress softly so as not to wake the others, and sneak out into the sweet outdoors and start out in the canoe, keeping close along the shore in the long shadows of the pines. I remembered being very careful never to rub my paddle against the gunwale for fear of disturbing the stillness of the cathedral.

The lake had never been what you would call a wild lake. There were cottages sprinkled about the shores, and it was in farming country although the shores of the lake were quite heavily wooded. Some of the cottages were owned by nearby farmers, and you would live at the shore and eat your meals at the farmhouse. That's what our family did. But although it wasn't wild, it was a fairly large and undisturbed lake and there were places in it which, to a child at least, seemed infinitely remote and primeval.

I was right about the tar: It led to within half a mile of the shore. But when I got back there, with my boy, and we settled into a camp near a farmhouse and into the kind of summertime I had known, I could tell that it was going to be pretty much the same as it had been before—I knew it, lying in bed the first morning, smelling the bedroom, and hearing the boy sneak quietly out and go off along the shore in a boat. I began to sustain the illusion that he was I, and therefore, by simple transposition, that I was my father. This sensation persisted, kept cropping up all the time we were there. It was not an entirely new feeling, but in this setting it grew much stronger. I seemed to be living a dual existence. I would be in the middle of some simple act, I would be picking up a bait box or laying down a table fork, or I would be saying something, and suddenly it would be not I but my father who was saying the words or making the gesture. It gave me a creepy sensation.

We went fishing the first morning. I felt the same damp moss covering   5
the worms in the bait can, and saw the dragonfly alight on the tip of my rod as it hovered a few inches from the surface of the water. It was the arrival of this fly that convinced me beyond any doubt that everything was as it always had been, that the years were a mirage and there had been no years. The small waves were the same, chucking the rowboat under the chin as we fished at anchor, and the boat was the same boat, the same color green and the ribs broken in the same places, and under the floor-boards the same fresh-water leavings and debris—the dead hellgrammite, the wisps of moss, the rusty discarded fishhook, the dried blood from yesterday's catch. We stared silently at the tips of our rods, at the dragonflies that came and went. I lowered the tip of mine into the water, tentatively, pensively dislodging the fly, which darted two feet away, poised, darted two feet back, and came to rest again a little farther up the rod. There had been no years between the ducking of this dragonfly and the other one—the one that was part of memory. I looked at the boy, who was silently watching his fly, and it was my hands that held his rod, my eyes watching. I felt dizzy and didn't know which rod I was at the end of.

We caught two bass, hauling them in briskly as though they were mackerel, pulling them over the side of the boat in a businesslike manner without any landing net, and stunning them with a blow on the back of the head. When we got back for a swim before lunch, the lake was exactly where we had left it, the same number of inches from the dock, and there was only the merest suggestion of a breeze. This seemed an utterly enchanted sea, this lake you could leave to its own devices for a few hours and come back to, and find that it had not stirred, this constant and trustworthy body of water. In the shallows, the dark, watersoaked sticks and twigs, smooth and old, were undulating in clusters on the bottom against the clean ribbed sand, and the track of the mussel was plain. A school of minnows swam by, each minnow with its small individual shadow, doubling the attendance, so clear and sharp in the sunlight. Some of the other campers were in swimming, along the shore, one of them with a cake of soap, and the water felt thin and clear and unsubstantial. Over the years there had been this person with the cake of soap, this cultist, and here he was. There had been no years.

Up to the farmhouse to dinner through the teeming, dusty field, the road under our sneakers was only a two-track road. The middle track was missing, the one with the marks of the hooves and splotches of dried, flaky manure. There had always been three tracks to choose from in choosing which track to walk in; now the choice was narrowed down to two. For a moment I missed terribly the middle alternative. But the way led past the tennis court, and something about the way it lay there in the sun reassured me; the tape had loosened along the backline, the alleys were green with plantains and other weeds, and the net (installed in June and removed in September) sagged in the dry noon, and the whole place steamed with mid-day heat and hunger and emptiness. There was a choice of pie for dessert, and one was blueberry and one was apple, and the waitresses were the same country girls, there having been no passage of time, only the illusion of it as in a dropped curtain—the waitresses were still fifteen; their hair had been washed, that was the only difference—they had been to the movies and seen the pretty girls with the clean hair.

Summertime, oh summertime, pattern of life indelible, the fade-proof lake, the woods unshatterable, the pasture with the sweetfern and the juniper forever and ever, summer without end; this was the background, and the life along the shore was the design, the cottages with their innocent and tranquil design, their tiny docks with the flagpole and the American flag floating against the white clouds in the blue sky, the little paths over the roots of the trees leading from camp to camp and the paths leading back to the outhouses and the can of lime for sprinkling, and at the souvenir counters at the store the miniature birch-bark canoes and the post cards that showed things looking a little better than they looked. This was the American family at play, escaping the city heat, wondering whether the newcomers in the camp at the head of the cove were "common" or "nice," wondering whether it was true that the people who drove up for Sunday dinner at the farmhouse were turned away because there wasn't enough chicken.

It seemed to me, as I kept remembering all this, that those times and those summers had been infinitely precious and worth saving. There had been jollity and peace and goodness. The arriving (at the beginning of August) had been so big a business in itself, at the railway station the farm wagon drawn up, the first smell of the pine-laden air, the first glimpse of the smiling farmer, and the great importance of the trunks and your father's enormous authority in such matters, and the feel of the wagon under you for the long ten-mile haul, and at the top of the last long hill catching the first view of the lake after eleven months of not seeing this cherished body of water. The shouts and cries of the other campers when they saw you, and the trunks to be unpacked, to give up their rich burden. (Arriving was less exciting nowadays, when you sneaked up in your car and parked it under a tree near the camp and took out the bags and in five minutes it was all over, no fuss, no loud wonderful fuss about trunks).

Peace and goodness and jollity. The only thing that was wrong now, really, was the sound of the place, an unfamiliar nervous sound of the outboard motors. This was the note that jarred, the one thing that would sometimes break the illusion and set the years moving. In those other summertimes all motors were inboard; and when they were at a little distance, the noise they made was a sedative, an ingredient of summer sleep. They were one-cylinder and two-cylinder engines, and some were make-and-break and some were jump-spark, but they all made a sleepy sound across the lake. The one-lungers throbbed and fluttered, and the twin-cylinder ones purred and purred, and that was a quiet sound too. But now the campers all had outboards. In the daytime, in the hot mornings, these motors made a petulant, irritable sound; at night, in the still evening when the afterglow lit the water, they whined about one's ears like mosquitoes. My boy loved our rented outboard, and his great desire was to achieve singlehanded mastery over it, and authority, and he soon learned the trick of choking it a little (but not too much), and the adjustment of the needle valve. Watching him I would remember the things you could do with the old one-cylinder engines with the heavy flywheel, how you could have it eating out of your hand if you got really close to it spiritually. Motor boats in those days didn't have clutches, and you would make a landing by shutting off the motor at the proper time and coasting in with a dead rudder. But there was a way of reversing them, if you learned the trick, by cutting the switch and putting it on again exactly on the final dying revolution of the flywheel, so that it would kick back against compression and begin reversing. Approaching a dock in a strong following breeze, it was difficult to slow up sufficiently by the ordinary coasting method, and if a boy felt he had complete mastery over his motor, he was tempted to keep it running beyond its time and then reverse it a few feet from the dock. It took a cool nerve, because if you threw the switch a twentieth of a second too soon you could catch the flywheel when it still had speed enough to go up past center, and the boat would leap ahead, charging bull-fashion at the dock.

We had a good week at the camp. The bass were biting well and the sun shone endlessly, day after day. We would be tired at night and lie down in the accumulated heat of the little bedrooms after the long hot day and the breeze would stir almost imperceptibly outside and the smell of the swamp drift in through the rusty screens. Sleep would come easily and in the morning the red squirrel would be on the roof, tapping out his gay routine. I kept remembering everything, lying in bed in the mornings—the small steamboat that had a long rounded stern like the lip of a Ubangi, and how quietly she ran on the moonlight sails, when the older boys played their mandolins and the girls sang and we ate doughnuts dipped in sugar, and how sweet the music was on the water in the shining night, and what it had felt like to think about girls then. After breakfast we would go up to the store and the things were in the same place—the minnows in a bottle, the plugs and spinners disarranged and pawed over by the youngsters from the boys' camp, the Fig Newtons and the Beeman's gum. Outside, the road was tarred and cars stood in front of the store. Inside, all was just as it had always been, except there was more Coca-Cola and not so much Moxie and root beer and birch beer and sarsaparilla. We would walk out with a bottle of pop apiece and sometimes the pop would backfire up our noses and hurt. We explored the streams, quietly, where the turtles slid off the sunny logs and dug their way into the soft bottom; and we lay on the town wharf and fed worms to the tame bass. Everywhere we went I had trouble making out which was I, the one walking at my side, the one walking in my pants.

One afternoon while we were there at that lake a thunderstorm came up. It was like the revival of an old melodrama that I had seen long ago with childish awe. The second-act climax of the drama of the electrical disturbance over a lake in America had not changed in any important respect. This was the big scene, still the big scene. The whole thing was so familiar, the first feeling of oppression and heat and a general air around camp of not wanting to go very far away. In midafternoon (it was all the same) a curious darkening of the sky, and a lull in everything that had made life tick; and then the way the boats suddenly swung the other way at their moorings with the coming of a breeze out of the new quarter, and the premonitory rumble. Then the kettle drum, then the snare, then the bass drum and cymbals, then crackling light against the dark, and the gods grinning and licking their chops in the hills. Afterward the calm, the rain steadily rustling in the calm lake, the return of light and hope and spirits, and the campers running out in joy and relief to go swimming in the rain, their bright cries perpetuating the deathless joke about how they were getting simply drenched, and the children screaming with delight at the new sensation of bathing in the rain, and the joke about getting drenched linking the generations in a strong indestructible chain. And the comedian who waded in carrying an umbrella.

When the others went swimming my son said he was going in too. He pulled his dripping trunks from the line where they had hung all through the shower, and wrung them out. Languidly, and with no thought of going in, I watched him, his hard little body, skinny and bare, saw him wince slightly as he pulled up around his vitals the small, soggy, icy garment. As he buckled the swollen belt suddenly my groin felt the chill of death. ■

The Reader's Presence

1. In paragraph 2, White begins to reflect on the way his memory works. How does he follow the process of remembering throughout the essay? Are his memories of the lake safely stored in the past? If not, why not?

2. Go through the essay and identify words and images having to do with the sensory details of seeing, hearing, touching, and so on. How do these details contribute to the overall effect of the essay? How do they anticipate White's final paragraph?

3. **CONNECTIONS:** In paragraph 4, White refers to a "creepy sensation." What is the basis of that sensation? Why is it "creepy"? What is the "dual existence" White feels he is living? How does the essay build the story of White's relationships with both his father and his son? Compare this account of intergenerational intimacy to Raymond Carver's essay "My Father's Life" (page 60).

The Writer at Work

E. B. WHITE on the Essayist

For several generations, E. B. White has remained America's best-known essayist, his works widely available and widely anthologized. Yet in the foreword to his 1977 collected essays, when he addresses the role of the essayist, he sounds wholly modest not only about his career but about his chosen genre: In the world of literature, he writes, the essayist is a "second-class citizen."

Why do you think White thinks of himself that way, and how might that self-deprecation be reconciled with the claims of his final two paragraphs? Do you think White's description of himself as an essayist matches the actual essayist we encounter in "Once More to the Lake"? Also, do you think White's persistent use of the male pronoun is merely for grammatical convenience (the essay was written in 1977) or reflects a gender bias on his part?

❝ The essayist is a self-liberated man, sustained by the childish belief that everything he thinks about, everything that happens to him, is of general interest. He is a fellow who thoroughly enjoys his work, just as people who take bird walks enjoy theirs. Each new excursion of the essayist, each new "attempt," differs from the last and takes him into new country. This delights him. Only a person who is congenitally self-centered has the effrontery and the stamina to write essays.

There are as many kinds of essays as there are human attitudes or poses, as many essay flavors as there are Howard Johnson ice creams. The essayist arises in the morning and, if he has work to do, selects his garb from an unusually extensive wardrobe: he can pull on any sort of shirt, be any sort of person, according to his mood or his subject matter—philosopher, scold, jester, raconteur, confidant, pundit, devil's advocate, enthusiast. I like the essay, have always liked it, and even as a child was at work, attempting to inflict my young thoughts and experiences on others by putting them on paper. I early broke into print in the pages of *St. Nicholas*.[1] I tend still to fall back on the essay form (or lack of form) when an idea strikes me, but I am not fooled about the place of the essay in twentieth century American letters—it stands a short distance down the line. The essayist, unlike the novelist, the poet, and the playwright, must be content in his self-imposed role of second-class citizen. A writer who has his sights trained on the Nobel Prize or other

[1] *St. Nicholas:* A prominent magazine for children, founded in 1873.—EDS.

earthly triumphs had best write a novel, a poem, or a play, and leave the essayist to ramble about, content with living a free life and enjoying the satisfactions of a somewhat undisciplined existence. (Dr. Johnson[2] called the essay "an irregular, undigested piece"; this happy practitioner has no wish to quarrel with the good doctor's characterization.)

There is one thing the essayist cannot do, though—he cannot indulge himself in deceit or in concealment, for he will be found out in no time. Desmond MacCarthy, in his introductory remarks to the 1928 E. P. Dutton & Company edition of Montaigne, observes that Montaigne "had the gift of natural candor. . . ." It is the basic ingredient. And even the essayist's escape from discipline is only a partial escape: the essay, although a relaxed form, imposes its own disciplines,

raises its own problems, and these disciplines and problems soon become apparent and (we all hope) act as a deterrent to anyone wielding a pen merely because he entertains random thoughts or is in a happy or wandering mood.

I think some people find the essay the last resort of the egoist, a much too self-conscious and self-serving form for their tastes; they feel that it is presumptuous of a writer to assume that his little excursions or his small observations will interest the reader. There is some justice in their complaint. I have always been aware that I am by nature self-absorbed and egoistical; to write of myself to the extent I have done indicates a too great attention to my own life, not enough to the lives of others. I have worn many shirts, and not all of them have been a good fit. But when I am discouraged or downcast I need only fling open the door of my closet, and there, hidden behind everything else, hangs the mantle of Michel de Montaigne, smelling slightly of camphor. **"**

[2] ***Dr. Johnson*** (1709–1784): One of the most important and influential essayists and critics of the 18th century. —EDS.

Elie Wiesel

EIGHT SIMPLE, SHORT WORDS

ELIE WIESEL (b. 1928) is a Romanian-born Jewish American writer, teacher, and human-rights activist. Born in Sighet, Transylvania (a historical region of Romania), he was fifteen years old when he was sent with his family to the Nazi concentration camp at Auschwitz. His older sisters survived the experience. His mother and younger sister did not. Elie and his father

II

were transferred to another camp, Buchenwald, where his father died shortly before the camp was liberated in April 1945. After the war, Wiesel studied in Paris, became a journalist, and decided to write a book about his experiences in the death camps. The result was his internationally acclaimed memoir, *Night* (*La Nuit*), originally published in French in 1958 and since translated into more than thirty languages. Wiesel immigrated to the United States in 1955 and became an American citizen. Appointed chairman of the President's Commission on the Holocaust in 1978 by President Jimmy Carter, Wiesel went on to found the United States Holocaust Memorial Council in 1980. He has published more than fifty books of fiction and nonfiction and has received numerous awards for his literary and human rights activities, including the Presidential Medal of Freedom, the U.S. Congressional Gold Medal, the National Humanities Medal, the Medal of Liberty, and the rank of Grand-Croix in the French Legion of Honor. In 1986, Wiesel won the Nobel Prize for Peace. Soon after, with his wife Marion, he established The Elie Wiesel Foundation for Humanity, dedicated to fighting intolerance, indifference, and injustice. Since 1976, he has been the Andrew W. Mellon Professor in the Humanities at Boston University, where he also holds the title of University Professor.

> **Elie Wiesel established The Elie Wiesel Foundation for humanity, dedicated to fighting intolerance, indifference, and injustice.**

In May 1944, the police began rounding up Jews in Wiesel's hometown of Sighet, in what is now Romania, for transport in overcrowded cattle cars to the concentration camps at Auschwitz Birkenau. As the harrowing episode begins, the train has pulled out of the station at Sighet on what would be a four-day journey to the notorious camp.

LYING DOWN was not an option, nor could we all sit down. We decided to take turns sitting. There was little air. The lucky ones found themselves near a window; they could watch the blooming countryside flit by.

After two days of travel, thirst became intolerable, as did the heat.

Freed of normal constraints, some of the young let go of their inhibitions and, under cover of darkness, caressed one another, without any thought of others, alone in the world. The others pretended not to notice.

There was still some food left. But we never ate enough to satisfy our hunger. Our principle was to economize, to save for tomorrow. Tomorrow could be worse yet.

The train stopped in Kaschau, a small town on the Czechoslovakian border. We realized then that we were not staying in Hungary. Our eyes opened. Too late.

The door of the car slid aside. A German officer stepped in accompanied by a Hungarian lieutenant, acting as his interpreter.

5

"From this moment on, you are under the authority of the German Army. Anyone who still owns gold, silver, or watches must hand them over now. Anyone who will be found to have kept any of these will be shot on the spot. Secondly, anyone who is ill should report to the hospital car. That's all."

The Hungarian lieutenant went around with a basket and retrieved the last possessions from those who chose not to go on tasting the bitterness of fear.

"There are eighty of you in the car," the German officer added. "If anyone goes missing, you will all be shot, like dogs."

The two disappeared. The doors clanked shut. We had fallen into the   10
trap, up to our necks. The doors were nailed, the way back irrevocably cut off. The world had become a hermetically sealed cattle car.

There was a woman among us, a certain Mrs. Schächter. She was in her fifties and her ten-year-old son was with her, crouched in a corner. Her husband and two older sons had been deported with the first transport, by mistake. The separation had totally shattered her.

I knew her well. A quiet, tense woman with piercing eyes, she had been a frequent guest in our house. Her husband was a pious man who spent most of his days and nights in the house of study. It was she who supported the family.

Mrs. Schächter had lost her mind. On the first day of the journey, she had already begun to moan. She kept asking why she had been separated from her family. Later, her sobs and screams became hysterical.

On the third night, as we were sleeping, some of us sitting, huddled against each other, some of us standing, a piercing cry broke the silence:

"Fire! I see a fire! I see a fire!"   15

There was a moment of panic. Who had screamed? It was Mrs. Schächter. Standing in the middle of the car, in the faint light filtering through the windows, she looked like a withered tree in a field of wheat. She was howling, pointing through the window:

"Look! Look at this fire! This terrible fire! Have mercy on me!"

Some pressed against the bars to see. There was nothing. Only the darkness of night.

It took us a long time to recover from this harsh awakening. We were still trembling, and with every screech of the wheels, we felt the abyss opening beneath us. Unable to still our anguish, we tried to reassure each other:

"She is mad, poor woman . . ."   20

Someone had placed a damp rag on her forehead. But she nevertheless continued to scream:

"Fire! I see a fire!"

Her little boy was crying, clinging to her skirt, trying to hold her hand:

"It's nothing, Mother! There's nothing there . . . Please sit down . . ." He pained me even more than did his mother's cries.

Some of the women tried to calm her: 25

"You'll see, you'll find your husband and sons again . . . In a few days . . ."

She continued to scream and sob fitfully.

"Jews, listen to me," she cried. "I see a fire! I see flames, huge flames!"

It was as though she were possessed by some evil spirit.

We tried to reason with her, more to calm ourselves, to catch our breath,   30
than to soothe her:

"She is hallucinating because she is thirsty, poor woman . . . That's why she speaks of flames devouring her . . ."

But it was all in vain. Our terror could no longer be contained. Our nerves had reached a breaking point. Our very skin was aching. It was as though madness had infected all of us. We gave up. A few young men forced her to sit down, then bound and gagged her.

Silence fell again. The small boy sat next to his mother, crying. I started to breathe normally again as I listened to the rhythmic pounding of the wheels on the tracks as the train raced through the night. We could begin to doze again, to rest, to dream . . .

And so an hour or two passed. Another scream jolted us. The woman had broken free of her bonds and was shouting louder than before:

"Look at the fire! Look at the flames! Flames everywhere . . ."   35

Once again, the young men bound and gagged her. When they actually struck her, people shouted their approval:

"Keep her quiet! Make that madwoman shut up. She's not the only one here . . ."

She received several blows to the head, blows that could have been lethal. Her son was clinging desperately to her, not uttering a word. He was no longer crying.

The night seemed endless. By daybreak, Mrs. Schächter had settled down. Crouching in her corner, her blank gaze fixed on some faraway place, she no longer saw us.

She remained like that all day, mute, absent, alone in the midst of us.   40
Toward evening she began to shout again:

"The fire, over there!"

She was pointing somewhere in the distance, always the same place. No one felt like beating her anymore. The heat, the thirst, the stench, the lack of air, were suffocating us. Yet all that was nothing compared to her screams, which tore us apart. A few more days and all of us would have started to scream.

But we were pulling into a station. Someone near a window read to us:

"Auschwitz."

Nobody had ever heard that name.   45

The train did not move again. The afternoon went by slowly. Then the doors of the wagon slid open. Two men were given permission to fetch water.

When they came back, they told us that they had learned, in exchange for a gold watch, that this was the final destination. We were to leave the train here. There was a labor camp on the site. The conditions were good. Families would not be separated. Only the young would work in the factories. The old and the sick would find work in the fields.

Confidence soared. Suddenly we felt free of the previous nights' terror. We gave thanks to God.

Mrs. Schächter remained huddled in her corner, mute, untouched by the optimism around her. Her little one was stroking her hand.

Dusk began to fill the wagon. We ate what was left of our food. At ten   50 o'clock in the evening, we were all trying to find a position for a quick nap and soon we were dozing. Suddenly:

"Look at the fire! Look at the flames! Over there!"

With a start, we awoke and rushed to the window yet again. We had believed her, if only for an instant. But there was nothing outside but dark-ness. We returned to our places, shame in our souls but fear gnawing at us nevertheless. As she went on howling, she was struck again. Only with great difficulty did we succeed in quieting her down.

The man in charge of our wagon called out to a German officer stroll-ing down the platform, asking him to have the sick woman moved to a hospital car.

"Patience," the German replied, "patience. She'll be taken there soon."

Around eleven o'clock, the train began to move again. We pressed   55 against the windows. The convoy was rolling slowly. A quarter of an hour later, it began to slow down even more. Through the windows, we saw barbed wire; we understood that this was the camp.

We had forgotten Mrs. Schächter's existence. Suddenly there was a ter-rible scream:

"Jews, look! Look at the fire! Look at the flames!"

And as the train stopped, this time we saw flames rising from a tall chim-ney into a black sky.

Mrs. Schächter had fallen silent on her own. Mute again, indifferent, absent, she had returned to her corner.

We stared at the flames in the darkness. A wretched stench floated in   60 the air. Abruptly, our doors opened. Strange-looking creatures, dressed in striped jackets and black pants, jumped into the wagon. Holding flashlights and sticks, they began to strike at us left and right, shouting:

"Everybody out! Leave everything inside. Hurry up!"

We jumped out. I glanced at Mrs. Schächter. Her little boy was still hold-ing her hand.

In front of us, those flames. In the air, the smell of burning flesh. It must have been around midnight. We had arrived. In Birkenau.

The fifteen-year-old Elie would never see his mother and seven-year-old sis-ter, Tzipora, again. His father was ordered to the crematorium after many months of forced labor. The camp was liberated on April 11, 1945.

The beloved objects that we had carried with us from place to place were now left behind in the wagon and, with them, finally, our illusions.

Every few yards, there stood an SS man, his machine gun trained on us.   65
Hand in hand we followed the throng.

An SS came toward us wielding a club. He commanded:

"Men to the left! Women to the right!"

Eight words spoken quietly, indifferently, without emotion. Eight simple, short words. Yet that was the moment when I left my mother. There was
no time to think, and I already felt my father's hand press against mine: we
were alone. In a fraction of a second I could see my mother, my sisters, move
to the right. Tzipora was holding Mother's hand. I saw them walking farther
and farther away; Mother was stroking my sister's blond hair, as if to protect
her. And I walked on with my father, with the men. I didn't know that this
was the moment in time and the place where I was leaving my mother and
Tzipora forever. I kept walking, my father holding my hand.

Behind me, an old man fell to the ground. Nearby, an SS man replaced
his revolver in its holster.

My hand tightened its grip on my father. All I could think of was not to   70
lose him. Not to remain alone.

The SS officers gave the order.

"Form ranks of fives!"

There was a tumult. It was imperative to stay together.

"Hey, kid, how old are you?"

The man interrogating me was an inmate. I could not see his face, but   75
his voice was weary and warm.

"Fifteen."

"No. You're eighteen."

"But I'm not," I said. "I'm fifteen."

"Fool. Listen to what *I* say."

Then he asked my father, who answered: 80

"I'm fifty."

"No." The man now sounded angry. "Not fifty. You're forty. Do you hear?
Eighteen and forty."

He disappeared into the darkness. Another inmate appeared, unleash-
ing a stream of invectives:

"Sons of bitches, why have you come here? Tell me, why?"

Someone dared to reply: 85

"What do you think? That we came here of our own free will? That we
asked to come here?"

The other seemed ready to kill him:

"Shut up, you moron, or I'll tear you to pieces! You should have hanged
yourselves rather than come here. Didn't you know what was in store for you
here in Auschwitz? You didn't know? In 1944?"

True. We didn't know. Nobody had told us. He couldn't believe his ears.
His tone became even harsher:

"Over there. Do you see the chimney over there? Do you see it? And   90
the flames, do you see them?" (Yes, we saw the flames.) "Over there, that's
where they will take you. Over there will be your grave. You still don't

understand? You sons of bitches. Don't you understand anything? You will be burned! Burned to a cinder! Turned into ashes!"

His anger changed into fury. We stood stunned, petrified. Could this be just a nightmare? An unimaginable nightmare?

I heard whispers around me:

"We must do something. We can't let them kill us like that, like cattle in the slaughterhouse. We must revolt."

There were, among us, a few tough young men. They actually had knives and were urging us to attack the armed guards. One of them was muttering:

"Let the world learn about the existence of Auschwitz. Let everybody   95
find out about it while they still have a chance to escape . . ."

But the older men begged their sons not to be foolish:

"We mustn't give up hope, even now as the sword hangs over our heads. So taught our sages . . ."

The wind of revolt died down. We continued to walk until we came to a crossroads. Standing in the middle of it was, though I didn't know it then, Dr. Mengele,[1] the notorious Dr. Mengele. He looked like the typical SS officer: a cruel, though not unintelligent, face, complete with monocle. He was holding a conductor's baton and was surrounded by officers. The baton was moving constantly, sometimes to the right, sometimes to the left.

In no time, I stood before him.

"Your age?" he asked, perhaps trying to sound paternal.   100

"I'm eighteen." My voice was trembling.

"In good health?"

"Yes."

"Your profession?"

Tell him that I was a student?   105

"Farmer," I heard myself saying.

This conversation lasted no more than a few seconds. It seemed like an eternity.

The baton pointed to the left. I took half a step forward. I first wanted to see where they would send my father. Were he to have gone to the right, I would have run after him.

The baton, once more, moved to the left. A weight lifted from my heart.

We did not know, as yet, which was the better side, right or left, which   110
road led to prison and which to the crematoria. Still, I was happy, I was near my father. Our procession continued slowly to move forward.

Another inmate came over to us:

"Satisfied?"

"Yes," someone answered.

"Poor devils, you are heading for the crematorium."

---

[1] **Dr. Mengele** (1911–1979): The infamous concentration camp physician who inspected prisoners to select those fit for labor and those who would be exterminated. He was also responsible for performing medical experiments on prisoners.—EDS.

Buchenwald, 1945. Wiesel is on the second row from the bottom, seventh from the left.

He seemed to be telling the truth. Not far from us, flames, huge flames, 115
were rising from a ditch. Something was being burned there. A truck drew
close and unloaded its hold: small children. Babies! Yes, I did see this, with
my own eyes . . . children thrown into the flames. (Is it any wonder that ever
since then, sleep tends to elude me?)

So that was where we were going. A little farther on, there was another,
larger pit for adults.

I pinched myself: Was I still alive? Was I awake? How was it possible
that men, women, and children were being burned and that the world kept
silent? No. All this could not be real. A nightmare perhaps . . . Soon I would
wake up with a start, my heart pounding, and find that I was back in the
room of my childhood, with my books . . .

My father's voice tore me from my daydreams:

"What a shame, a shame that you did not go with your mother . . . I saw many children your age go with their mothers . . ."

His voice was terribly sad. I understood that he did not wish to see what 120 they would do to me. He did not wish to see his only son go up in flames.

My forehead was covered with cold sweat. Still, I told him that I could not believe that human beings were being burned in our times; the world would never tolerate such crimes . . .

"The world? The world is not interested in us. Today, everything is possible, even the crematoria . . ." His voice broke.

"Father," I said. "If that is true, then I don't want to wait. I'll run into the electrified barbed wire. That would be easier than a slow death in the flames."

He didn't answer. He was weeping. His body was shaking. Everybody around us was weeping. Someone began to recite Kaddish, the prayer for the dead. I don't know whether, during the history of the Jewish people, men have ever before recited Kaddish for themselves.

"*Yisgadal, veyiskadash, shmey raba* . . . May His name be celebrated 125 and sanctified . . ." whispered my father.

For the first time, I felt anger rising within me. Why should I sanctify His name? The Almighty, the eternal and terrible Master of the Universe, chose to be silent. What was there to thank Him for?

We continued our march. We were coming closer and closer to the pit, from which an infernal heat was rising. Twenty more steps. If I was going to kill myself, this was the time. Our column had only some fifteen steps to go. I bit my lips so that my father would not hear my teeth chattering. Ten more steps. Eight. Seven. We were walking slowly, as one follows a hearse, our own funeral procession. Only four more steps. Three. There it was now, very close to us, the pit and its flames. I gathered all that remained of my strength in order to break rank and throw myself onto the barbed wire. Deep down, I was saying good-bye to my father, to the whole universe, and, against my will, I found myself whispering the words: "*Yisgadal, veyiskadash, shmey raba* . . ." May His name be celebrated and sanctified . . ." My heart was about to burst. There I was face-to-face with the Angel of Death[2] . . .

No. Two steps from the pit, we were ordered to turn left and herded into barracks.

I squeezed my father's hand. He said:

Do you remember Mrs. Schächter, in the train?   130

Never shall I forget that night, the first night in camp, that turned my life into one long night seven times sealed.

Never shall I forget that smoke.

Never shall I forget the small faces of the children whose bodies I saw transformed into smoke under a silent sky.

Never shall I forget those flames that consumed my faith forever.

---

[2] **Angel of Death:** A name by which Dr. Mengele was known. It isn't clear, however, if Wiesel wants to make this connection. —EDS.

|||||||||||||||||||||||||||||||||||||||||||||||||||||||||||||||||||||||||||||||||||||||||||||||||||||||||||||||||||||||||||||||||||||

Never shall I forget the nocturnal silence that deprived me for all eter- 135
nity of the desire to live.

Never shall I forget those moments that murdered my God and my soul
and turned my dreams to ashes.

Never shall I forget those things, even were I condemned to live as long
as God Himself.

Never. ■

The Reader's Presence

1. Why do you think the inmates abuse the newly arrived prisoners? How would you
   describe their tone? Why do they order father and son to lie about their ages? Why
   do they lead the father and son to believe they are headed for the crematorium?

2. Besides offering a historical account of how Jews were herded into concentration
   camps, Wiesel also describes his harrowing religious experience. What impact did
   this experience have on his religious beliefs? What is Wiesel's purpose in the almost
   prayer-like litany that appears at the conclusion of the selection?

3. **CONNECTIONS:**   How do people respond in writing when they have encountered
   horrific events? Compare Wiesel's recollection of his childhood internment at Auschwitz to Adam Mayblum's account of escaping the Twin Towers on 9/11. Wiesel,
   of course, wrote his memoir of his nightmarish experiences in 1958 (originally in
   French), more than a decade after the events occurred. Mayblum wrote his account
   immediately after the event. How do the time frames account for the different ways
   in which each author makes his presence felt in his writing?

Tobias Wolff

PROSPECTING

TOBIAS WOLFF (b. 1945) is an American author, famous for his memoirs and widely
considered to be one of the best short story writers working in American fiction today. His
short story collections include *In the Garden of the North American Martyrs* (1981); *Back in
the World* (1985); *The Night in Question* (1997); and *Our Story Begins: New and Selected
Stories* (2008), which won the Story Prize that year. In addition to his stories and memoirs,

Wolff has also published several novels and novellas, most recently *Old School* (2003). He has received multiple writing awards, including the PEN/Malamud Award and the Rea Award (both for excellence in the short story), the Los Angeles Times Book Prize, and the PEN/Faulkner Award for his novel *The Barracks Thief*, in 1985. He has also been the editor of *Best American Short Stories*, *The Vintage Book of Contemporary American Short Stories*, and *A Doctor's Visit: The Short Stories of Anton Chekhov*, and his work regularly appears in the *New Yorker*, the *Atlantic*, and *Harper's*. But he remains best known for *This Boy's Life* (1989), a memoir of his adolescence in Seattle and the North Cascade Mountains of Washington State, from which the following selection is an excerpt. The book was adapted into a successful film, starring, among others, Leonardo DiCaprio and Robert De Niro in 1993.

> Tobias Wolff is widely considered to be one of the best short story writers working in American fiction today.

Wolff has said that he admires Russian playwright and short story writer Anton Chekhov (1860–1904), for "his humanity, and at the same time his pitilessness."

OUR CAR BOILED OVER AGAIN just after my mother and I crossed the Continental Divide. While we were waiting for it to cool we heard, from somewhere above us, the bawling of an airhorn. The sound got louder and then a big truck came around the corner and shot past us into the next curve, its trailer shimmying wildly. We started after it. "Oh, Toby," my mother said, "he's lost his brakes."

The sound of the horn grew distant, then faded in the wind that sighed in the trees all around us.

By the time we got there, quite a few people were standing along the cliff where the truck went over. It had smashed through the guardrails and fallen hundreds of feet through empty space to the river below, where it lay on its back among the boulders. It looked pitifully small. A stream of thick black smoke rose from the cab, feathering out in the wind. My mother asked whether anyone had gone to report the accident. Someone had. We stood with the others at the cliff's edge. Nobody spoke. My mother put her arm around my shoulder.

For the rest of the day she kept looking over at me, touching me, brushing back my hair. I saw that the time was right to make a play for souvenirs. I knew she had no money for them, and I had tried not to ask, but now that her guard was down I couldn't help myself. When we pulled out of Grand Junction[1] I owned a beaded Indian belt, beaded moccasins, and a bronze horse with a removable, tooled-leather saddle.

---

[1] *Grand Junction:* City in western Colorado that is nearly a mile high. —EDS.

It was 1955 and we were driving from Florida to Utah, to get away from   5
a man my mother was afraid of and to get rich on uranium.[2] We were going
to change our luck.

We'd left Sarasota in the dead of summer, right after my tenth birthday,
and headed West under low flickering skies that turned black and exploded
and cleared just long enough to leave the air gauzy with steam. We drove
through Georgia, Alabama, Tennessee, Kentucky, stopping to cool the
engine in towns where people moved with arthritic slowness and spoke in
thick, strangled tongues. Idlers with rotten teeth surrounded the car to press
peanuts on the pretty Yankee lady and her little boy, arguing among themselves about shortcuts. Women looked up from their flower beds as we drove
past, or watched us from their porches, sometimes impassively, sometimes
giving us a nod and a flutter of their fans.

Every couple of hours the Nash Rambler[3] boiled over. My mother kept
digging into her little grubstake[4] but no mechanic could fix it. All we could
do was wait for it to cool, then drive on until it boiled over again. (My mother
came to hate this machine so much that not long after we got to Utah she
gave it away to a woman she met in a cafeteria.) At night we slept in boggy
rooms where headlight beams crawled up and down the walls and mosquitoes sang in our ears, incessant as the tires whining on the highway outside.
But none of this bothered me. I was caught up in my mother's freedom, her
delight in her freedom, her dream of transformation.

Everything was going to change when we got out West. My mother had
been a girl in Beverly Hills, and the life we saw ahead of us was conjured
from her memories of California in the days before the Crash.[5] Her father,
Daddy as she called him, had been a navy officer and a paper millionaire.
They'd lived in a big house with a turret. Just before Daddy lost all his
money and all his shanty-Irish relatives' money and got himself transferred
overseas, my mother was one of four girls chosen to ride on the Beverly
Hills float in the Tournament of Roses.[6] The float's theme was "The End of
the Rainbow" and it won that year's prize by acclamation. She met Jackie
Coogan. She had her picture taken with Harold Lloyd and Marion Davies,[7]
whose movie *The Sailor Man* was filmed on Daddy's ship. When Daddy was
at sea she and her mother lived a dream life in which, for days at a time, they
played the part of sisters.

---

[2] **uranium:** After World War II, uranium was sought for nuclear weapons and by the mid-fifties
many people hoped to strike it rich by prospecting for the ore with the help of Geiger counters.
Colorado, Utah, and Wyoming were considered good sources of uranium. — EDS.

[3] **Nash Rambler:** One of the nation's earliest compact cars, the inexpensive Ramblers were
manufactured between 1950 and 1955. They are now a collector's item. — EDS.

[4] **grubstake:** The funds supplied to a mining prospector for start-up ventures, with promise of
a stake in the profits. — EDS.

[5] **the Crash:** The stock market crash of 1929 that triggered the Great Depression. — EDS.

[6] **Tournament of Roses:** The famous parade held on January 1 in Pasadena, California, since
1890. The parade features flowered floats and marching bands and is followed by the Rose Bowl
college football game. — EDS.

[7] **Jackie Coogan, Harold Lloyd, Marion Davies:** Famous motion picture stars of the nineteen
twenties and thirties. — EDS.

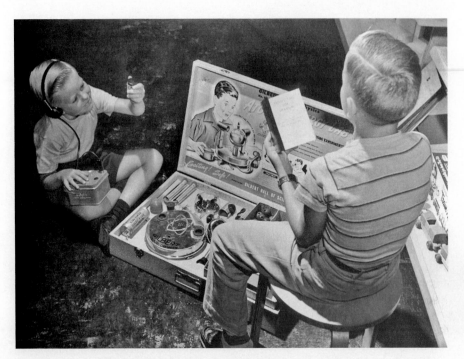

1950. Toy Exhibition. Two boys try out a U-239 Geiger counter, and a government manual on how to prospect for uranium. © Topham/The Image Works.

And the *cars* my mother told me about as we waited for the Rambler to cool—I should have seen the cars! Daddy drove a Franklin touring car. She'd been courted by a boy who had his own Chrysler convertible with a musical horn. And of course there was the Hernandez family, neighbors who'd moved up from Mexico after finding oil under their cactus ranch. The family was large. When they were expected to appear somewhere together they drove singly in a caravan of identical Pierce-Arrows.

Something like that was supposed to happen to us. People in Utah were   10
getting up poor in the morning and going to bed rich at night. You didn't need to be a mining engineer or a mineralogist. All you needed was a Geiger counter. We were on our way to the uranium fields, where my mother would get a job and keep her eyes open. Once she learned the ropes she'd start prospecting for a claim of her own.

And when she found it she planned to do some serious compensating: for the years of hard work, first as a soda jerk and then as a novice secretary, that had gotten her no farther than flat broke and sometimes not that far. For the breakup of our family five years earlier. For the misery of her long affair with a violent man. She was going to make up for lost time, and I was going to help her.

We got to Utah the day after the truck went down. We were too late—months too late. Moab and the other mining towns had been overrun.

All the motels were full. The locals had rented out their bedrooms and living rooms and garages and were now offering trailer space in their front yards for a hundred dollars a week, which was what my mother could make in a month if she had a job. But there were no jobs, and people were getting ornery. There's been murders. Prostitutes walked the streets in broad daylight, drunk and bellicose. Geiger counters cost a fortune. Everyone told us to keep going.

My mother thought things over. Finally she bought a poor man's Geiger counter, a black light that was supposed to make uranium trace glow, and we started for Salt Lake City. She figured there must be ore somewhere around there. The fact that nobody else had found any meant that we would have the place pretty much to ourselves. To tide us over she planned to take a job with the Kennecott Mining Company, whose personnel officer had responded to a letter of inquiry she'd sent from Florida some time back. He had warned her against coming, said there was no work in Salt Lake and that his own company was about to go out on strike. But his letter was so friendly! My mother just knew she'd get a job out of him. It was as good as guaranteed.

So we drove on through the desert. As we drove, we sang—Irish ballads, folk songs, big-band blues. I was hooked on "Mood Indigo."[8] Again and again I world-wearily crooned "You ain't been blue, no, no, no" while my mother eyed the temperature gauge and babied the engine. Then my throat dried up and left me croaking. I was too excited anyway. Our trail was ending. Burma Shave ads[9] and bullet-riddled mileage signs ticked past. As the numbers on those signs grew smaller we began calling them out at the top of our lungs. ◼

The Reader's Presence

1. What is the effect of opening with a big truck losing its brakes and falling hundreds of feet off a cliff? How does the scene establish a mood for the selection? How does it affect your sense of what's to come in the story?

2. What sense do you get of Toby's mother? What sort of personality does she seem to have? What details does Wolff offer that help us understand her attitudes and motivations? How does her response to the rejection letter from a company in Salt Lake City in paragraph 13 characterize her attitude?

3. **CONNECTIONS:** Compare "Prospecting" with Manil Suri's "Keys to the Kingdom" (page 227). How do both selections characterize mothers? In what ways do the mothers, though of entirely different backgrounds, seem alike? You might compare both of these accounts of mothers to that of Jamaica Kincaid in "The Estrangement" (page 129), which offers a different perspective on ways of writing about family.

---

8 *"Mood Indigo":* A popular song, first recorded in 1930.—EDS.
9 *Burma Shave ads:* Humorous small signs running in a sequence on highway billboards to promote a popular shaving cream.—EDS.

EXPOSITORY WRITING

Shaping Information

Joan Acocella

A FEW TOO MANY

JOAN ACOCELLA (b. 1945), also known as Joan Ross Acocella, is a dance critic for the *New Yorker* and the author of *Mark Morris* (1993), the first serious examination of the renowned choreographer of the same name. She has also written books on literature, *Willa Cather and the Politics of Criticism* (2000), and psychology, *Creating Hysteria: Women and Multiple Personality Disorder* (1999). Her latest book, *Twenty-Eight Artists and Two Saints* (2007), is a collection of essays on various dancers; artists; authors; choreographers; and, as the title indicates, saints, namely Mary Magdalene and Joan of Arc. Acocella received a Guggenheim Fellowship in 1993, and her work has been anthologized in *Best American Essays*. Regarding her work as a dance and book critic, she has said, "I try to describe with love what I love." Like many of her essays, this selection was originally published in the *New Yorker*.

> Regarding her work as a dance and book critic, Joan Acocella has said, "I try to describe with love what I love."

OF THE MISERIES regularly inflicted on humankind, some are so minor and yet, while they last, so painful that one wonders how, after all this time, a remedy cannot have been found. If scientists do not have a cure for cancer, that makes sense. But the common cold, the menstrual cramp? The hangover is another condition of this kind. It is a preventable malady: don't drink. Nevertheless, people throughout time have found what seemed to them good reason for recourse to alcohol. One attraction is alcohol's power to disinhibit—to allow us, at last, to tell off our neighbor or make an improper suggestion to his wife. Alcohol may also persuade us that we have found the truth about life, a comforting experience rarely available in the sober hour. Through the lens of alcohol, the world seems nicer. ("I drink to make other people interesting," the theatre critic George Jean Nathan used to say.) For all these reasons, drinking cheers people up. See Proverbs 31:6–7: "Give . . . wine unto those that be of heavy hearts. Let him drink, and forget his poverty, and remember his misery no more." It works, but then, in the morning, a new misery presents itself.

A hangover peaks when alcohol that has been poured into the body is finally eliminated from it—that is, when the blood-alcohol level returns to zero. The toxin is now gone, but the damage it has done is not. By fairly common consent, a hangover will involve some combination of headache, upset stomach, thirst, food aversion, nausea, diarrhea, tremulousness, fatigue, and a general feeling of wretchedness. Scientists haven't yet found all the reasons for this network of woes, but they have proposed various causes. One is withdrawal, which would bring on the tremors and also sweating. A second factor may be dehydration. Alcohol interferes with the secretion of the hormone that inhibits urination. Hence the heavy traffic to the rest rooms at bars and parties. The resulting dehydration seems to trigger the thirst and lethargy. While that is going on, the alcohol may also be inducing hypoglycemia (low blood sugar), which converts into light-headedness and muscle weakness, the feeling that one's bones have turned to jello. Meanwhile, the body, to break down the alcohol, is releasing chemicals that may be more toxic than alcohol itself; these would result in nausea and other symptoms. Finally, the alcohol has produced inflammation, which in turn causes the white blood cells to flood the bloodstream with molecules called cytokines. Apparently, cytokines are the source of the aches and pains and lethargy that, when our bodies are attacked by a flu virus—and likewise, perhaps, by alcohol—encourage us to stay in bed rather than go to work, thereby freeing up the body's energy for use by the white cells in combatting the invader. In a series of experiments, mice that were given a cytokine inducer underwent dramatic changes. Adult males wouldn't socialize with young males new to their cage. Mothers displayed "impaired nest-building." Many people will know how these mice felt.

But hangover symptoms are not just physical; they are cognitive as well. People with hangovers show delayed reaction times and difficulties with attention, concentration, and visual-spatial perception. A group of airplane pilots given simulated flight tests after a night's drinking put in substandard performances. Similarly, automobile drivers, the morning after, get low marks on simulated road tests. Needless to say, this is a hazard, and not just for those at the wheel. There are laws against drunk driving, but not against driving with a hangover.

Hangovers also have an emotional component. Kingsley Amis, who was, in his own words, one of the foremost drunks of his time, and who wrote three books on drinking, described this phenomenon as "the metaphysical hangover": "When that ineffable compound of depression, sadness (these two are not the same), anxiety, self-hatred, sense of failure and fear for the future begins to steal over you, start telling yourself that what you have is a hangover. . . . You have not suffered a minor brain lesion, you are not all that bad at your job, your family and friends are not leagued in a conspiracy of barely maintained silence about what a shit you are, you have not come at last to see life as it really is." Some people are unable to convince themselves of this. Amis described the opening of Kafka's *Metamorphosis*, with the hero discovering that he has been changed into a bug, as the best literary representation of a hangover.

The severity of a hangover depends, of course, on how much you drank 5
the night before, but that is not the only determinant. What, besides alcohol,

did you consume at that party? If you took other drugs as well, your hangover may be worse. And what kind of alcohol did you drink? In general, darker drinks, such as red wine and whiskey, have higher levels of congeners—impurities produced by the fermentation process, or added to enhance flavor—than do light-colored drinks such as white wine, gin, and vodka. The greater the congener content, the uglier the morning. Then there are your own characteristics—for example, your drinking pattern. Unjustly, habitually heavy drinkers seem to have milder hangovers. Your sex is also important. A woman who matches drinks with a man is going to get drunk faster than he, partly because she has less body water than he does, and less of the enzyme alcohol dehydrogenase, which breaks down alcohol. Apparently, your genes also have a vote, as does your gene pool. Almost forty percent of East Asians have a variant, less efficient form of aldehyde dehydrogenase, another enzyme necessary for alcohol processing. Therefore, they start showing signs of trouble after just a few sips—they flush dramatically—and they get drunk fast. This is an inconvenience for some Japanese and Korean businessmen. They feel that they should drink with their Western colleagues. Then they crash to the floor and have to make awkward phone calls in the morning.

Hangovers are probably as old as alcohol use, which dates back to the Stone Age. Some anthropologists have proposed that alcohol production may have predated agriculture; in any case, it no doubt stimulated that development, because in many parts of the world the cereal harvest was largely given over to beer-making. Other prehistorians have speculated that alcohol intoxication may have been one of the baffling phenomena, like storms, dreams, and death, that propelled early societies toward organized religion. The ancient Egyptians, who, we are told, made seventeen varieties of beer, believed that their god Osiris invented this agreeable beverage. They buried their dead with supplies of beer for use in the afterlife.

Alcohol was also one of our ancestors' foremost medicines. Berton Roueché, in a 1960 article on alcohol for the *New Yorker*, quoted a prominent fifteenth-century German physician, Hieronymus Brunschwig, on the range of physical ills curable by brandy: head sores, pallor, baldness, deafness, lethargy, toothache, mouth cankers, bad breath, swollen breasts, short-windedness, indigestion, flatulence, jaundice, dropsy, gout, bladder infections, kidney stones, fever, dog bites, and infestation with lice or fleas. Additionally, in many times and places, alcohol was one of the few safe things to drink. Water contamination is a very old problem.

Some words for hangover, like ours, refer prosaically to the cause: the Egyptians say they are "still drunk," the Japanese "two days drunk," the Chinese "drunk overnight." The Swedes get "smacked from behind." But it is in languages that describe the effects rather than the cause that we begin to see real poetic power. Salvadorans wake up "made of rubber," the French with a "wooden mouth" or a "hair ache." The Germans and the Dutch say they have a "tomcat," presumably wailing. The Poles, reportedly, experience a "howling of kittens." My favorites are the Danes, who get "carpenters in the forehead." In keeping with the saying about the Eskimos' nine words for snow, the Ukrainians have several words for hangover. And, in keeping with the Jews-don't-drink rule, Hebrew didn't even have one word until recently. Then the experts at the Academy of the Hebrew Language, in Tel Aviv, decided that such a term was needed, so they made one up: *hamarmoret*, derived from the word for fermentation. (*Hamarmoret* echoes a usage of Jeremiah's, in Lamentations 1:20, which the King James Bible translates as "My bowels are troubled.") There is a biochemical basis for Jewish abstinence. Many Jews—fifty percent, in one estimate—carry a variant gene for alcohol dehydrogenase. Therefore, they, like the East Asians, have a low tolerance for alcohol.

As for hangover remedies, they are legion. There are certain unifying themes, however. When you ask people, worldwide, how to deal with a hangover, their first answer is usually the hair of the dog. The old faithful in this category is the Bloody Mary, but books on curing hangovers—I have read three, and that does not exhaust the list—describe more elaborate potions, often said to have been invented in places like Cap d'Antibes by bartenders with names like Jean-Marc. An English manual, Andrew Irving's *How to Cure a Hangover* (2004), devotes almost a hundred pages to hair-of-the-dog recipes, including the Suffering Bastard (gin, brandy, lime juice, bitters, and ginger ale); the Corpse Reviver (Pernod, champagne, and lemon juice); and the Thomas Abercrombie (two Alka-Seltzers dropped into a double shot of tequila). Kingsley Amis suggests taking Underberg bitters, a highly alcoholic digestive: "The resulting mild convulsions and cries of shock are well worth witnessing. But thereafter a comforting glow supervenes." Many people, however, simply drink some more of what they had the night before. My Ukrainian informant described his morning-after protocol for a vodka hangover as follows: "two shots of vodka, then a cigarette, then another shot of vodka." A Japanese source suggested wearing a sake-soaked surgical mask.

Application of the hair of the dog may sound like nothing more than a 10 way of getting yourself drunk enough so that you don't notice you have a hangover, but, according to Wayne Jones, of the Swedish National Laboratory of Forensic Medicine, the biochemistry is probably more complicated than that. Jones's theory is that the liver, in processing alcohol, first addresses itself to ethanol, which is the alcohol proper, and then moves on to methanol, a secondary ingredient of many wines and spirits. Because methanol breaks down into formic acid, which is highly toxic, it is during this second stage that the hangover is most crushing. If at that point you pour in more alcohol, the body will switch back to ethanol processing. This will not eliminate the hangover—the methanol (indeed, more of it now) is still waiting for you round the bend—but it delays the worst symptoms. It may also mitigate them somewhat. On the other hand, you are drunk again, which may create difficulty about going to work.

As for the non-alcoholic means of combatting hangover, these fall into three categories: before or while drinking, before bed, and the next morning. Many people advise you to eat a heavy meal with lots of protein and fats, before or while drinking. If you can't do that, at least drink a glass of milk. In Africa, the same purpose is served by eating peanut butter. The other most frequent before-and-during recommendation is water, lots of it. Proponents of this strategy tell you to ask for a glass of water with every drink you order, and then make yourself chug-a-lug the water before addressing the drink.

A recently favored antidote, both in Asia and in the West, is sports drinks, taken either the morning after or, more commonly, at the party itself. A fast-moving bar drink these days is Red Bull, an energy drink, mixed with vodka or with the herbal liqueur Jägermeister. (The latter cocktail is a Jäg-bomb.) Some people say that the Red Bull holds the hangover at bay, but apparently its primary effect is to blunt the depressive force of alcohol—no surprise, since an eight-ounce serving of Red Bull contains more caffeine than two cans of Coke. According to fans, you can rock all night. According to Maria Lucia Souza-Formigoni, a psychobiology researcher at the Federal University of São Paolo, that's true, and dangerous. After a few drinks with Red Bull, you're drunk but you don't know it, and therefore you may engage in high-risk behaviors—driving, going home with a questionable companion—rather than passing out quietly in your chair. Red Bull's manufacturers have criticized the methodology of Souza-Formigoni's study and have pointed out that they never condoned mixing their product with alcohol.

When you get home, is there anything you can do before going to bed? Those still able to consider such a question are advised, again, to consume buckets of water, and also to take some Vitamin C. Koreans drink a bowl of water with honey, presumably to head off the hypoglycemia. Among the young, one damage-control measure is the ancient Roman method, induced vomiting. Nic van Oudtshoorn's *The Hangover Handbook* (1997) thoughtfully provides a recipe for an emetic: mix mustard powder with water. If you have "bed spins," sleep with one foot on the floor.

Now to the sorrows of the morning. The list-topping recommendation, apart from another go at the water cure, is the greasy-meal cure. (An American philosophy professor: "Have breakfast at Denny's." An English teenager: "Eat two McDonald's hamburgers. They have a secret ingredient for hangovers.") Spicy foods, especially Mexican, are popular, along with eggs, as in the Denny's breakfast. Another egg-based cure is the prairie oyster, which involves vinegar, Worcestershire sauce, and a raw egg yolk to be consumed whole. Sugar, some say, should be reapplied. A reporter at the *Times*: "Drink a six-pack of Coke." Others suggest fruit juice. In Scotland, there is a soft drink called Irn-Bru, described to me by a local as tasting like melted plastic. Irn-Bru is advertised to the Scots as "Your Other National Drink." Also widely employed are milk-based drinks. Teenagers recommend milkshakes and smoothies. My contact in Calcutta said buttermilk. "You can also pour it over your head," he added. "Very soothing."

Elsewhere on the international front, many people in Asia and the Near   15
East take strong tea. The Italians and the French prefer strong coffee. (Italian
informant: add lemon. French informant: add salt. Alcohol researchers: stay
away from coffee—it's a diuretic and will make you more dehydrated.) Germans eat pickled herring; the Japanese turn to pickled plums; the Vietnamese drink a wax-gourd juice. Moroccans say to chew cumin seeds; Andeans,
coca leaves. Russians swear by pickle brine. An ex-Soviet ballet dancer told
me, "Pickle juice or a shot of vodka or pickle juice with a shot of vodka."

Many folk cures for hangovers are soups: *menudo* in Mexico, *mondongo*
in Puerto Rico, *iskembe çorbasi* in Turkey, *patsa* in Greece, *khashi* in Georgia. The fact that all of the above involve tripe may mean something. Hun-
garians favor a concoction of cabbage and smoked meats, sometimes forth-
rightly called "hangover soup." The Russians' morning-after soup, *solyanka*,
is, of course, made with pickle juice. The Japanese have traditionally relied
on miso soup, though a while ago there was a fashion for a vegetable soup
invented and marketed by one Kazu Tateishi, who claimed that it cured cancer as well as hangovers.

I read this list of food cures to Manuela Neuman, a Canadian researcher
on alcohol-induced liver damage, and she laughed at only one, the six-pack
of Coke. Many of the cures probably work, she said, on the same distraction
principle as the hair of the dog: "Take the spicy foods, for example. They
divert the body's attention away from coping with the alcohol to coping with
the spices, which are also a toxin. So you have new problems—with your
stomach, with your esophagus, with your respiration—rather than the problem with the headache, or that you are going to the washroom every five
minutes." The high-fat and high-protein meals operate in the same way,
she said. The body turns to the food and forgets about the alcohol for the
time being, thus delaying the hangover and possibly alleviating it. As for
the differences among the many food recommendations, Neuman said that
any country's hangover cure, like the rest of its cultural practices, is an adaptation to the environment. Chilies are readily available in Mexico, peanut
butter in Africa. People use what they have. Neuman also pointed out that
local cures will reflect the properties of local brews. If Russians favor pickle
juice, they are probably right to, because their drink is vodka: "Vodka is a
very pure alcohol. It doesn't have the congeners that you find, for example,
in whiskey in North America. The congeners are also toxic, independent of
alcohol, and will have their own effects. With vodka you are just going to
have pure-alcohol effects, and one of the most important of those is dehydration. The Russians drink a lot of water with their vodka, and that combats the
dehydration. The pickle brine will have the same effect. It's salty, so they'll
drink more water, and that's what they need."

Many hangover cures—soups, the greasy breakfast—are comfort foods,
and that, apart from any sworn-by ingredients, may be their chief therapeu-
tic property, but some other remedies sound as though they were devised by
the witches in *Macbeth*. Kingsley Amis recommended a mixture of Bovril

and vodka. There is also a burnt-toast cure. Such items suggest that what some hungover people are seeking is not so much relief as atonement. The same can be said of certain non-food recommendations, such as exercise. One source says that you should do a forty-minute workout, another that you should run six miles—activities that may have little attraction for the hung over. Additional procedures said to be effective are an intravenous saline drip and kidney dialysis, which, apart from their lack of appeal, are not readily available.

There are other noningested remedies. Amazon will sell you a refrigeratable eye mask, an aromatherapy inhaler, and a vinyl statue of St. Vivian, said to be the patron saint of the hung over. She comes with a stand and a special prayer.

The most widely used over-the-counter remedy is no doubt aspirin. Advil, or ibuprofen, and Alka-Seltzer—there is a special formula for hangovers, Alka-Seltzer Wake-Up Call—are probably close runners-up. (Tylenol, or acetaminophen, should not be used, because alcohol increases its toxicity to the liver.) Also commonly recommended are Vitamin C and B-complex vitamins. But those are almost home remedies. In recent years, pharmaceutical companies have come up with more specialized formulas: Chaser, NoHang, BoozEase, PartySmart, Sob'r-K HangoverStopper, Hangover Prevention Formula, and so on. In some of these, such as Sob'r-K and Chaser, the primary ingredient is carbon, which, according to the manufacturers, soaks up toxins. Others are herbal compounds, featuring such ingredients as ginseng, milk thistle, borage, and extracts of prickly pear, artichoke, and guava leaf. These and other OTC[1] remedies aim to boost biochemicals that help the body deal with toxins. A few remedies have scientific backing. Manuela Neuman, in lab tests, found that milk-thistle extract, which is an ingredient in NoHang and Hangover Helper, does protect cells from damage by alcohol. A research team headed by Jeffrey Wiese, of Tulane University, tested prickly-pear extract, the key ingredient in Hangover Prevention Formula, on human subjects and found significant improvement with the nausea, dry mouth, and food aversion but not with other, more common symptoms, such as headache. 20

Five years ago, there was a flurry in the press over a new OTC remedy called RU-21 (i.e., Are you twenty-one?). According to the reports, this wonder drug was the product of twenty-five years of painstaking research by the Russian Academy of Sciences, which developed it for KGB agents[2] who wanted to stay sober while getting their contacts drunk and prying information out of them. During the Cold War, we were told, the formula was a state secret, but in 1999 it was declassified. Now it was ours! "HERE'S ONE COMMUNIST PLOT AMERICANS CAN REALLY GET BEHIND," the headline in the *Washington Post* said. "BOTTOMS UP TO OUR BUDDIES IN RUSSIA," the *Cleveland Plain Dealer* said. The literature on RU-21 was mysterious, however.

---

[1] **OTC:** Over the counter.—EDS.

[2] **KGB:** State security police of the former Soviet Union, responsible for external espionage, internal counterintelligence, and internal "crimes against the state."—EDS.

If the formula was developed to keep your head clear, how come so many reports said that it didn't suppress the effects of alcohol? Clearly, it couldn't work both ways. When I put this question to Emil Chiaberi, a co-founder of RU-21's manufacturer, Spirit Sciences, in California, he answered, "No, no, no. It is true that succinic acid" —a key ingredient of RU-21— "was tested at the Russia Academy of Sciences, including secret laboratories that worked for the KGB. But it didn't do what they wanted. It didn't keep people sober, and so it never made it with the KGB men. Actually, it does improve your condition a little. In Russia, I've seen people falling under the table plenty of times—they drink differently over there—and if they took a few of these pills they were able to get up and walk around, and maybe have a couple more drinks. But no, what those scientists discovered, really by accident, was a way to prevent hangover." (Like many other OTC remedies, RU-21 is best taken before or while drinking, not the next morning.) Asians love the product, Chiaberi says. "It flies off the shelves there." In the United States, it is big with the Hollywood set: "For every film festival—Sundance, the Toronto Film Festival—we get calls asking us to send them RU-21 for parties. So it has that glamour thing."

Most cures for hangover—indeed most statements about hangover— have not been tested. Jeffrey Wiese and his colleagues, in a 2000 article in *Annals of Internal Medicine*, reported that in the preceding thirty-five years more than forty-seven hundred articles on alcohol intoxication had been published, but that only a hundred and eight of these dealt with hangover. There may be more information on hangover cures in college newspapers— a rich source—than in the scientific literature. And the research that has been published is often weak. A team of scientists attempting to review the literature on hangover cures were able to assemble only fifteen articles, and then they had to throw out all but eight on methodological grounds. There have been more studies in recent years, but historically this is not a subject that has captured scientists' hearts.

Which is curious, because anyone who discovered a widely effective hangover cure would make a great deal of money. Doing the research is hard, though. Lab tests with cell samples are relatively simple to conduct, as are tests with animals, some of which have been done. In one experiment, with a number of rats suffering from artificially induced hangovers, ninety percent of the animals died, but in a group that was first given Vitamins B and C, together with cysteine, an amino acid contained in some OTC remedies, there were no deaths. (Somehow this is not reassuring.) The acid test, however, is in clinical trials, with human beings, and these are complicated. Basically, what you have to do is give a group of people a lot to drink, apply the remedy in question, and then, the next morning, score them on a number of measures in comparison with people who consumed the same amount of alcohol without the remedy. But there are many factors that you have to control for: the sex of the subjects; their general health; their family history; their past experience with alcohol; the type of alcohol you give them; the amount of food and water they consume before, during, and after; and the circumstances under which they drink, among other variables. (Wiese and his colleagues, in their prickly-pear experiment, provided music so that the subjects could dance, as at a party.) Ideally, there should also be a large sample—many subjects.

All that costs money, and researchers do not pay out of pocket. They depend on funding institutions—typically, universities, government agencies, and foundations. With all those bodies, a grant has to be OK'd by an ethics committee, and such committees' ethics may stop short of getting people drunk. For one thing, they are afraid that the subjects will hurt themselves. (All the studies I read specified that the subjects were sent home by taxi or limousine after their contribution to science.) Furthermore, many people believe that alcohol abusers *should* suffer the next morning—that this is a useful deterrent. Robert Lindsey, the president of the National Council on Alcoholism and Drug Dependence, told me that he wasn't sure about that. His objection to hangover-cure research was simply that it was a misuse of resources: "Fifteen million people in this country are alcohol-dependent. That's a staggering number! They need help: not with hangovers but with the cause of hangovers—alcohol addiction." Robert Swift, an alcohol researcher who teaches at Brown University, counters that if scientists, through research, could provide the public with better information on the cognitive impairments involved in hangover, we might be able to prevent accidents. He compares the situation to the campaigns against distributing condoms, on the ground that this would increase promiscuity. In fact, the research has shown that free condoms did not have that effect. What they did was cut down on unwanted pregnancies and sexually transmitted disease.

Manufacturers of OTC remedies are sensitive to the argument that they are enablers, and their literature often warns against heavy drinking. The message may be unashamedly mixed, however. The makers of NoHang, on their Web page, say what your mother would: "It is recommended that you drink moderately and responsibly." At the same time, they tell you that with NoHang "you can drink the night away." They list the different packages in which their product can be bought: the Bender (twelve tablets), the Party Animal (twenty-four), the It's Noon Somewhere (forty-eight). Among the testimonials they publish is one by "Chad S.," from Chicago: "After getting torn up all day on Saturday, I woke up Sunday morning completely hangover-free. I must have had like twenty drinks." Researchers address the moral issue less hypocritically. Wiese and his colleagues describe the damage done by hangovers—according to their figures, the cost to the U.S. economy, in absenteeism and poor job performance, is a hundred and forty-eight billion dollars a year (other estimates are far lower, but still substantial)—and they mention the tests with the airplane pilots, guaranteed to scare anyone. They also say that there is no experimental evidence indicating that hangover relief encourages further drinking. (Nor, they might have added, have there been any firm findings on this matter.) Manuela Neuman, more philosophically, says that some people, now and then, are going to drink too much, no

25

matter what you tell them, and that we should try to relieve the suffering caused thereby. Such reasoning seems to have cut no ice with funding institutions. Of the meagre research I have read in support of various cures, all was paid for, at least in part, by pharmaceutical companies.

A truly successful hangover cure is probably going to be slow in coming. In the meantime, however, it is not easy to sympathize with the alcohol disciplinarians, so numerous, for example, in the United States. They seem to lack a sense of humor and, above all, the tragic sense of life. They appear not to know that many people have a lot that they'd like to forget. In the words of the English aphorist William Bolitho, "The shortest way out of Manchester is . . . a bottle of Gordon's gin," and if that relief is temporary the reformers would be hard put to offer a more lasting solution. Also questionable is the moral emphasis of the temperance folk, their belief that drinking is a lapse, a sin, as if getting to work on time, or living a hundred years, were the crown of life. They forget alcohol's relationship to camaraderie, sharing, toasts. Those, too, are moral matters. Even hangovers are related to social comforts. Alcohol investigators describe the bad things that people do on the morning after. According to Genevieve Ames and her research team at the Prevention Research Center, in Berkeley, hungover assembly-line workers are more likely to be criticized by their supervisors, to have disagreements with their co-workers, and to feel lousy. Apart from telling us what we already know, such findings are incomplete, because they do not talk about the jokes around the water cooler—the fellowship, the badge of honor. Yes, there are safer ways of gaining honor, but how available are they to most people?

Outside the United States, there is less finger-wagging. British writers, if they recommend a cure, will occasionally say that it makes you feel good enough to go out and have another drink. They are also more likely to tell you about the health benefits of moderate drinking—how it lowers one's risk of heart disease, Alzheimer's, and so on. English fiction tends to portray drinking as a matter of getting through the day, often quite acceptably. In P. G. Wodehouse's Jeeves and Wooster series, a hangover is the occasion of a happy event, Bertie's hiring of Jeeves. Bertie, after "a late evening," is lying on the couch in agony when Jeeves rings his doorbell. "'I was sent by the agency, sir,' he said. 'I was given to understand that you required a valet.'" Bertie says he would have preferred a mortician. Jeeves takes one look at Bertie, brushes past him, and vanishes into the kitchen, from which he emerges a moment later with a glass on a tray. It contains a prairie oyster. Bertie continues, "I would have clutched at anything that looked like a lifeline that morning. I swallowed the stuff. For a moment I felt as if somebody . . . was strolling down my throat with a lighted torch, and then everything seemed suddenly to get all right. The sun shone in through the window; birds twittered in the tree-tops; and, generally speaking, hope dawned once more. 'You're engaged,' I said." Here the hangover is a comedy, or at least a fact of life. So it has been, probably, since the Stone Age, and so it is likely to be for a while yet. ◾

The Reader's Presence

1. What do you think Acocella's purpose was in writing this essay? What role do the anecdotes and scientific studies that she cites play in supporting her purpose? What personal opinions, if any, does Acocella reveal about alcohol consumption? Of those, which are stated explicitly and which are implied?

2. Identify a passage in which Acocella writes about a specific facet of alcohol consumption through multiple lenses: scientific, cultural, historical, anecdotal, and so on. What effect(s) does this approach have on your understanding of the subject? To what extent does each of the various sources Acocella cites seem relevant to her overarching purpose in writing this essay? Which did you find most compelling? Explain why.

3. **CONNECTIONS:**   Compare the moral implications raised in this essay with those in David Foster Wallace's "Consider the Lobster" (page 839). How would you describe the tone each writer uses when discussing the moral questions surrounding each of their topics? How does this tone affect your reading of each essay? How would your reading differ if the authors' tones were reversed—that is, if Wallace wrote about lobsters with the tone with which Acocella wrote about hangovers—and vice versa?

Daniel Akst

WHAT MEETS THE EYE

New York–born writer **DANIEL AKST** (b. 1956) divides his time between fiction and nonfiction, journalism and commentary. He has written two novels, *St. Burl's Obituary* (1996), a PEN/Faulkner Award finalist, and *The Webster Chronicle* (2001). His nonfiction account of financial fraud in southern California, *Wonder Boy*, was listed in *Business Week*'s best books of 1990. Akst began his career in journalism while still attending college at the University of Pennsylvania and continued as a reporter while at New York University, where he took graduate courses in economics and finance. Akst has been a regular columnist for the

> Daniel Akst's latest book examines what he calls "the central problem of our time: how to save ourselves from what we want."

Los Angeles Times and the Sunday business section of the New York Times, writing, as he describes it, "about the intersection of money and culture." He is a regular contributor to the Wall Street Journal and his articles have appeared in numerous publications, including Salon, the Christian Science Monitor, Forbes, Fortune, Money, Newsday, Slate, and Smithsonian. His commentaries have been aired on NPR's Marketplace, and Nightly Business Report for PBS. He is a contributing editor to the Wilson Quarterly, in which this essay, "What Meets the Eye," first appeared in 2005. His latest book, We Have Met the Enemy: Self-Control in an Age of Excess (2011), is a "wide-ranging examination of the central problem of our time: how to save ourselves from what we want."

EVERYONE KNOWS looks shouldn't matter. Beauty, after all, is only skin deep, and no right-thinking person would admit to taking much account of how someone looks outside the realm of courtship, that romantic free-trade zone traditionally exempted from the usual tariffs of rationality. Even in that tender kingdom, where love at first sight is still readily indulged, it would be impolitic, if not immature, to admit giving too much weight to a factor as shallow as looks. Yet perhaps it's time to say what we all secretly know, which is that looks do matter, maybe even more than most of us think.

We infer a great deal from people's looks — not just when it comes to mating (where looks matter profoundly), but in almost every other aspect of life as well, including careers and social status. It may not be true that blondes have more fun, but it's highly likely that attractive people do, and they start early. Mothers pay more attention to good-looking babies, for example, but, by the same token, babies pay more attention to prettier adults who wander into their fields of vision. Attractive people are paid more on the job, marry more desirable spouses, and are likelier to get help from others when in evident need. Nor is this all sheer, baseless prejudice. Human beings appear to be hard-wired to respond to how people and objects look, an adaptation without which the species might not have made it this far. The unpleasant truth is that, far from being only skin deep, our looks reflect all kinds of truths about difference and desire — truths we are, in all likelihood, biologically programmed to detect.

Sensitivity to the signals of human appearances would naturally lead to successful reproductive decisions, and several factors suggest that this sensitivity may be bred in the bone. Beauty may even be addictive. Researchers at London's University College have found that human beauty stimulates a section of the brain called the ventral striatum, the same region activated in drug and gambling addicts when they're about to indulge their habit. Photos of faces rated unattractive had no effect on the volunteers to whom they were shown, but the ventral striatum did show activity if the picture was of an attractive person, especially one looking straight at the viewer. And the responses occurred even when the viewer and the subject of the photo were of the same sex. Good-looking people just do something to us, whether we like it or not.

People's looks speak to us, sometimes in a whisper and sometimes in a shout, of health, reproductive fitness, agreeableness, social standing, and intelligence. Although looks in mating still matter much more to men than to women, the importance of appearance appears to be rising on both sides of the gender divide. In a fascinating cross-generational study of mating preferences, every 10 years different groups of men and women were asked to rank 18 characteristics they might want enhanced in a mate. The importance of good looks rose "dramatically" for both men and women from 1939 to 1989, the period of the study, according to David M. Buss, an evolutionary psychologist at the University of Texas. On a scale of 1 to 3, the importance men gave to good looks rose from 1.50 to 2.11. But for women, the importance of good looks in men rose from 0.94 to 1.67. In other words, women in 1989 considered a man's looks even more important than men considered women's looks 50 years earlier. Since the 1930s, Buss writes, "physical appearance has gone up in importance for men and women about equally, corresponding with the rise in television, fashion magazines, advertising, and other media depictions of attractive models."

In all likelihood this trend will continue, driven by social and technological changes that are unlikely to be reversed anytime soon—changes such as the new ubiquity of media images, the growing financial independence of women, and the worldwide weakening of the institution of marriage. For better or worse, we live now in an age of appearances. It looks like looks are here to stay.

5

The paradox, in such an age, is that the more important appearances become, the worse most of us seem to look—and not just by comparison with the godlike images alternately taunting and bewitching us from every billboard and TV screen. While popular culture is obsessed with fashion and style, and our prevailing psychological infirmity is said to be narcissism, fully two-thirds of American adults have abandoned conventional ideas of attractiveness by becoming overweight. Nearly half of this group is downright obese. Given their obsession with dieting—a $40 billion-plus industry in the United States—it's not news to these people that they're sending an unhelpful message with their inflated bodies, but it's worth noting here nonetheless.

Social scientists have established what most of us already know in this regard, which is that heavy people are perceived less favorably in a variety of ways. Across cultures—even in places such as Fiji, where fat is the norm—people express a preference for others who are neither too slim nor too heavy. In studies by University of Texas psychologist Devendra Singh, people guessed that the heaviest figures in photos were eight to 10 years older than the slimmer ones, even though the faces were identical. (As the nation's bill for hair dye and facelifts attests, looking older is rarely desirable, unless you happen to be an underage drinker.)

America's weight problem is one dimension of what seems to be a broader-based national flight from presentability, a flight that manifests itself unmistakably in the relentless casualness of our attire. Contrary to the desperate contentions of some men's clothiers, for example, the suit is really dying. Walk around midtown Manhattan, and these garments are striking by their absence. Consumer spending reflects this. In 2004, according to NPD Group, a marketing information firm, sales of "active sportswear," a category that includes such apparel as warm-up suits, were $39 billion, nearly double what was spent on business suits and other tailored clothing. The irony is that the more athletic gear we wear, from plum-colored velour track suits to high-tech sneakers, the less athletic we become.

The overall change in our attire did not happen overnight. America's clothes, like America itself, have been getting more casual for decades, in a trend that predates even Nehru jackets and the "full Cleveland" look of a pastel leisure suit with white shoes and belt, but the phenomenon reaches something like an apotheosis in the vogue for low-riding pajama bottoms and flip-flops outside the home. Visit any shopping mall in summer—or many deep-Sunbelt malls year round—and you'll find people of all sizes, ages, and weights clomping through the climate-controlled spaces in tank tops, T-shirts, and running shorts. Tops—and nowadays often bottoms— emblazoned with the names of companies, schools, and places make many of these shoppers look like walking billboards. Bulbous athletic shoes, typi- cally immaculate on adults who go everywhere by car, are the functional equivalent of SUVs for the feet. Anne Hollander, an observant student of clothing whose books include *Sex and Suits* (1994), has complained that we've settled on "a sandbox aesthetic" of sloppy comfort, the new classics— sweats, sneakers, and jeans—persist year after year, transcending fashion altogether.

We've come to this pass despite our seeming obsession with how we   10
look. Consider these 2004 numbers from the American Society of Plastic Surgeons: 9.2 million cosmetic surgeries (up 24 percent from 2000) at a cost of $8.4 billion, and that doesn't count 7.5 million "minimally invasive" pro- cedures, such as skin peels and Botox injections (collectively up 36 percent). Cosmetic dentistry is also booming, as is weight-loss surgery. Although most of this spending is by women, men are focusing more and more on their appearance as well, which is obvious if you look at the evolution of men's magazines over the years. Further reflecting our concern with both looks and rapid self-transformation is a somewhat grisly new genre of reality TV: the extreme makeover show, which plays on the audience's presumed desire to somehow look a whole lot better fast.

But appearances in this case *are* deceiving. The evidence suggests that a great many of us do not care nearly enough about how we look, and that even those who care very much indeed still end up looking terrible. In understanding why, it's worth remembering that people look the way they do for two basic reasons—on purpose and by accident—and both can be as revealing as a neon tube top.

Let's start with the purposeful. Extremes in casual clothing have several important functions. A big one nowadays is camouflage. Tent-like T-shirts and sweatsuits cover a lot of sins, and the change in our bodies over time is borne out by the sizes stores find themselves selling. In 1985, for example, the top-selling women's size was eight. Today, when, as a result of size infla-tion, an eight (and every other size) is larger than it used to be, NPD Group reports that the top-selling women's size is 14. Camouflage may also account for the popularity of black, which is widely perceived as slimming as well as cool.

That brings us to another motive for dressing down—way down—which is status. Dressing to manifest disregard for society—think of the loose, baggy hipsters in American high schools—broadcasts self-determination by flaunting the needlessness of having to impress anybody else. We all like to pretend we're immune to "what people think," but reaching for sta-tus on this basis is itself a particularly perverse—and egregious—form of status seeking. For grownups, it's also a way of pretending to be young, or at least youthful, since people know instinctively that looking young often means looking good. Among the truly young, dressing down is a way to avoid any embarrassing lapses in self-defining rebelliousness. And for the young and fit, sexy casual clothing can honestly signal a desire for short-term rather than long-term relationships. Indeed, researchers have shown that men respond more readily to sexy clothing when seeking a short-term relationship, perhaps because more modest attire is a more effective signal of sexual fidelity, a top priority for men in the marriage market, regardless of nation or tribe.

Purposeful slovenliness can have its reasons, then, but what about care-lessness? One possible justification is that, for many people, paying attention to their own looks is just too expensive. Clothes are cheap, thanks to imports, but looking good can be costly for humans, just as it is for other species. A signal such as beauty, after all, is valuable in reproductive terms only if it has credibility, and it's been suggested that such signals are credible indicators of fitness precisely because in evolutionary terms they're so expensive. The peacock's gaudy tail, for example, attracts mates in part because it signals that the strutting bird is robust enough not only to sustain his fancy plumage but to fend off predators it also attracts. Modern humans who want to strut their evolutionary stuff have to worry about their tails too. They have to work them off. Since most of us are no longer paid to perform physical labor, get-ting exercise requires valuable time and energy, to say nothing of a costly gym membership. And then there is the opportunity cost—the pleasure lost by forgoing fried chicken and Devil Dogs. Eating junk food, especially fast food, is probably also cheaper, in terms of time, than preparing a low-calorie vegetarian feast at home.

These costs apparently strike many Americans as too high, which may   15
be why we as a culture have engaged in a kind of aesthetic outsourcing, transferring the job of looking good—of providing the desired supply of physical beauty—to the specialists known as "celebrities," who can afford

to devote much more time and energy to the task. Offloading the chore of looking great into a small, gifted corps of professionals saves the rest of us a lot of trouble and expense, even if it has opened a yawning aesthetic gulf between the average person (who is fat) and the average model or movie star (who is lean and toned within an inch of his or her life).

Although the popularity of Botox and other such innovations suggests that many people do want to look better, it seems fair to conclude that they are not willing to pay any significant price to do so, since the great majority do not in fact have cosmetic surgery, exercise regularly, or maintain anything like their ideal body weight. Like so much in our society, physical attractiveness is produced by those with the greatest comparative advantage, and consumed vicariously by the rest of us—purchased, in a sense, ready made.

Whether our appearance is purposeful or accidental, the outcome is the same, which is that a great many of us look awful most of the time, and as a consequence of actions or inactions that are at least substantially the result of free will.

Men dressed like boys? Flip-flops at the office? Health care workers who never get near an operating room but nevertheless dress in shapeless green scrubs? These sartorial statements are not just casual. They're also of a piece with the general disrepute into which looking good seems to have fallen. On its face, so to speak, beauty presents some serious ideological problems in the modern world. If beauty were a brand, any focus group that we convened would describe it as shallow and fleeting or perhaps as a kind of eye candy that is at once delicious and bad for you. As a society, we consume an awful lot of it, and we feel darn guilty about it.

Why should this be so? For one thing, beauty strikes most of us as a natural endowment, and as a people we dislike endowments. We tax inheritances, after all, on the premise that they are unearned by their recipients and might produce something like a hereditary aristocracy, not unlike the one produced by the competition to mate with beauty. Money plays a role in that competition; there's no denying that looks and income are traditionally awfully comfortable with each other, and today affluent Americans are the ones least likely to be overweight. By almost any standard, then, looks are a seemingly unfair way of distinguishing oneself, discriminating as they do on the basis of age and generally running afoul of what the late political scientist Alan Wildavsky called "the rise of radical egalitarianism," which was at the very least suspicious of distinction and advantage, especially a distinction as capricious and as powerful as appearance.

Appearance can be a source of inequality, and achieving some kind of   20 egalitarianism in this arena is a longstanding and probably laudable American concern. The Puritans eschewed fancy garb, after all, and Thoreau warned us to beware of enterprises that require new clothes. Nowadays, at a time of increased income inequality, our clothes paradoxically confer less distinction than ever. Gender distinctions in clothing, for instance, have been blurred in favor of much greater sartorial androgyny, to the extent that nobody would any longer ask who wears the pants in any particular household (because the correct answer would be, "everybody"). The same goes for age distinctions (short pants long ago lost their role as uniform of the young), class distinctions (the rich wear jeans too), and even distinctions between occasions such as school and play, work and leisure, or public and private. Who among us hasn't noticed sneakers, for example, at a wedding, in a courtroom, or at a concert, where you spot them sometimes even on the stage?

The problem is that, if anything, looks matter even more than we think, not just because we're all hopelessly superficial, but because looks have always told us a great deal of what we want to know. Looks matter for good reason, in other words, and delegating favorable appearances to an affluent elite for reasons of cost or convenience is a mistake, both for the individuals who make it and for the rest of us as well. The slovenliness of our attire is one of the things that impoverish the public sphere, and the stunning rise in our weight (in just 25 years) is one of the things that impoverish our health. Besides, it's not as if we're evolving anytime soon into a species that's immune to appearances. Looks seem to matter to all cultures, not just our image-besotted one, suggesting that efforts to stamp out looksism (which have yet to result in hiring quotas on behalf of the homely) are bucking millions of years of evolutionary development.

The degree of cross-cultural consistency in this whole area is surprising. Contrary to the notion that beauty is in the eye of the beholder, or at the very least in the eye of the culture, studies across nations and tribal societies have found that people almost everywhere have similar ideas about what's attractive, especially as regards the face (tastes in bodies seem to vary a bit more, perhaps allowing for differing local evolutionary ecologies). Men everywhere, even those few still beyond the reach of Hollywood and Madison Avenue, are more concerned about women's looks than women are about men's, and their general preference for women who look young and healthy is probably the result of evolutionary adaptation.

The evidence for this comes from the field of evolutionary psychology. Whatever one's view of this burgeoning branch of science, one thing it has produced (besides controversy) is an avalanche of disconcerting research about how we look. Psychologists Michael R. Cunningham, of the University of Louisville, and Stephen R. Shamblen cite evidence that babies as young as two or three months old look longer at more attractive faces. New mothers of less attractive offspring, meanwhile, have been found to pay more attention to other people (say, hospital room visitors) than do new mothers of better-looking babies. This may have some basis in biological necessity, if you bear in mind that the evolutionary environment, free as it was of antibiotics and pediatricians, might have made it worthwhile indeed for mothers to invest themselves most in the offspring likeliest to survive and thrive.

The environment today, of course, is very different, but it may only amplify the seeming ruthlessness of the feelings and judgments we make. "In one study," reports David M. Buss, the evolutionary psychologist who reported on the multi-generational study of mating preferences, "after groups of men looked at photographs of either highly attractive women or women of average attractiveness, they were asked to evaluate their commitment to their current romantic partner. Disturbingly, the men who had viewed pictures of attractive women thereafter judged their actual partners to be less attractive than the men who had viewed analogous pictures of women who were average in attractiveness. Perhaps more important, the men who had viewed attractive women thereafter rated themselves as less committed, less satisfied, less serious, and less close to their actual partners." In another study, men who viewed attractive nude centerfolds promptly rated themselves as less attracted to their own partners.

Even if a man doesn't personally care much what a woman looks like, 25 he knows that others do. Research suggests that being with an attractive woman raises a man's status significantly, while dating a physically unattractive woman moderately lowers a man's status. (The effect for women is quite different; dating an attractive man raises a woman's status only somewhat, while dating an unattractive man lowers her status only nominally.) And status matters. In the well-known "Whitehall studies" of British civil servants after World War II, for example, occupational grade was strongly correlated with longevity. The higher the bureaucrat's ranking, the longer the life. And it turns out that Academy Award–winning actors and actresses outlive other movie performers by about four years, at least according to a study published in the *Annals of Internal Medicine* in 2001. "The results," write authors Donald A. Redelmeier and Sheldon M. Singh, "suggest that success confers a survival advantage." So if an attractive mate raises a man's status, is it really such a wonder that men covet trophy wives?

In fact, people's idea of what's attractive, influenced by the body types that are associated with status in a given time and place (which suggests that culture plays at least some role in ideas of attractiveness). As any museumgoer can tell you, the big variation in male preferences across time and place is in plumpness, and Buss contends that this is a status issue: In places where food is plentiful, such as the United States, high-status people distinguish themselves by being thin.

There are reasons besides sex and status to worry about how we look. For example, economists David S. Hamermesh, of the University of Texas, and Jeff E. Biddle, of Michigan State University, have produced a study suggesting that better-looking people make more money. "Holding constant demographic and labor-market characteristics," they wrote in a well-known 1993 paper, "plain people earn less than people of average looks, who earn less than the good-looking. The penalty for plainness is five to 10 percent, slightly larger than the premium for beauty." A 1998 study of attorneys (by the same duo) found that some lawyers also benefit by looking better. Yet another study found that better-looking college instructors—especially men—receive higher ratings from their students.

Hamermesh and some Chinese researchers also looked into whether primping pays, based on a survey of Shanghai residents. They found that beauty raises women's earnings (and, to a lesser extent, men's), but that spending on clothing and cosmetics helps only a little. Several studies have even found associations between appearance preferences and economic cycles. Psychologists Terry F. Pettijohn II, of Ohio State University, and Abraham Tesser, of the University of Georgia, for example, obtained a list of the Hollywood actresses with top box-office appeal in each year from 1932 to 1995. The researchers scanned the actresses' photos into a computer, did various measurements, and determined that, lo and behold, the ones who were most popular during social and economic good times had more "neoteny"—more childlike features, including bigger eyes, smaller chins, and rounder cheeks. During economic downturns, stronger and more rectangular female faces—in other words, faces that were more mature—were preferred.

It's not clear whether this is the case for political candidates as well, but looks matter in this arena too. In a study that appeared recently [2005] in *Science*, psychologist Alexander Todorov and colleagues at Princeton University showed photographs of political candidates to more than 800 students, who were asked to say who had won and why based solely on looks. The students chose correctly an amazing 69 percent of the time, consistently picking candidates they judged to look the most competent, meaning those who looked more mature. The losers were more likely to have babyfaces, meaning some combination of a round face, big eyes, small nose, high forehead, and small chin. Those candidates apparently have a hard time winning elections.

To scientists, a convenient marker for physical attractiveness in people 30 is symmetry, as measured by taking calipers to body parts [such] as wrists, elbows, and feet to see how closely the pairs match. The findings of this research can be startling. As summarized by biologist Randy Thornhill and psychologist Steven W. Gangestad, both of the University of New Mexico, "In both sexes, relatively low asymmetry seems to be associated with increased genetic, physical, and mental health, including cognitive skill and IQ. Also, symmetric men appear to be more muscular and vigorous, have a lower basal metabolic rate, and may be larger in body size than asymmetric men. . . . Symmetry is a major component of developmental health and overall condition and appears to be heritable." The researchers add that more symmetrical men have handsomer faces, more sex partners, and their first sexual experience at an earlier age, and they get to sex more quickly with a new romantic partner. "Moreover," they tell us, "men's symmetry predicts a relatively high frequency of their sexual partners' copulatory orgasms."

Those orgasms are sperm retaining, suggesting that symmetric men may have a greater chance of getting a woman pregnant. It doesn't hurt that the handsomest men may have the best sperm, at least according to a study at Spain's University of Valencia, which found that men with the healthiest, fastest sperm were those whose faces were rated most attractive by women. There's evidence that women care more about men's looks for short-term relationships than for marriage, and that as women get closer to the most fertile point of the menstrual cycle, their preference for "symmetrical" men grows stronger, according to Thornhill and Gangestad. Ovulating women prefer more rugged, masculinized faces, whereas the rest of the time they prefer less masculinized or even slightly feminized faces. Perhaps predictably, more-symmetrical men are likelier to be unfaithful and tend to invest less in a relationship.

Asymmetric people may have some idea that they're behind the eight ball here. William Brown and his then-colleague at Dalhousie University in Halifax, Nova Scotia, looked at 50 people in heterosexual relationships, measuring such features as hands, ears, and feet, and then asked about jealousy. The researchers found a strong correlation between asymmetry and romantic jealousy, suggesting that asymmetrical lovers may suspect they're somehow less desirable. Brown's explanation: "If jealousy is a strategy to retain your mate, then the individual more likely to be philandered on is more likely to be jealous."

In general, how we look communicates something about how healthy we are, how fertile, and probably how useful in the evolutionary environment. This may be why, across a range of cultures, women prefer tall, broad-shouldered men who seem like good reproductive specimens, in addition to offering the possibility of physical protection. Men, meanwhile, like pretty women who appear young. Women's looks seem to vary depending on where they happen to be in the monthly fertility cycle. The University of Liverpool biologist John Manning measured women's ears and fingers and had the timing of their ovulation confirmed by pelvic exams. He found a 30 percent decline in asymmetries in the 24 hours before ovulation—perhaps more perceptible to our sexual antennae than to the conscious mind. In general, symmetrical women have more sex partners, suggesting that greater symmetry makes women more attractive to men.

To evolutionary biologists, it makes sense that men should care more about the way women look than vice versa, because youth and fitness matter so much more in female fertility. And while male preferences do vary with time and place there's also some remarkable underlying consistency. Devendra Singh, for instance, found that the waist-to-hip ratio was the most important factor in women's attractiveness to men in 18 cultures he studied. Regardless of whether lean or voluptuous women happen to be in fashion, the favored shape involves a waist/hip ratio of about 0.7. "Audrey Hepburn and Marilyn Monroe represented two very different images of beauty to filmgoers in the 1950s," writes Nancy Etcoff, who is a psychologist at Massachusetts General Hospital. "Yet the 36-24-34 Marilyn and the 31.5-22-31 Audrey both had versions of the hourglass shape and waist-to-hip ratios of 0.7." Even Twiggy, in her 92-pound heyday, had a waist/hip ratio of 0.73.

Despite wildly divergent public images, actresses Audrey Hepburn, in black, and Marilyn Monroe shared one thing: a waist/hip ratio of 0.7.

Is it cause for despair that looks are so important? The bloom of youth 35 is fleeting, after all, and the bad news that our appearance will inevitably broadcast about us cannot be kept under wraps forever. Besides, who could live up to the impossible standards propagated by our powerful aesthetic-industrial complex? It's possible that the images of models and actresses and even TV newscasters, most of them preternaturally youthful and all selected for physical fitness, have driven most Americans to quit the game, insisting that they still care about how they look even as they retire from the playing field to console themselves with knife and fork.

If the pressure of all these images has caused us to opt out of caring about how we look, that's a shame, because we're slaves of neither genes nor fashion in this matter. By losing weight and exercising, simply by making ourselves healthier, we can change the underlying data our looks report. The advantages are almost too obvious to mention, including lower medical costs, greater confidence, and a better quality of life in virtually every way.

There's no need to look like Brad Pitt or Jennifer Lopez, and no reason for women to pursue Olive Oyl[1] thinness (a body type men do not especially prefer). Researchers, in fact, have found that people of both sexes tend to prefer averageness in members of the opposite sex: The greater the number of faces poured (by computer) into a composite, the higher it's scored in attractiveness by viewers. That's in part because "bad" features tend to be averaged out. But the implication is clear: You don't need to look like a movie star to benefit from a favorable appearance, unless, of course, you're planning a career in movies.

To a bizarre extent, looking good in America has become the province of an appearance aristocracy—an elect we revere for their seemingly unattainable endowment of good looks. Physical attractiveness has become too much associated with affluence and privilege for a country as democratically inclined as ours. We can be proud at least that these lucky lookers no longer have to be white or even young. Etcoff notes that, in tracking cosmetic surgery since the 1950s, the American Academy of Facial Plastic and Reconstructive Surgery reports a change in styles toward wider, fuller-tipped noses and narrower eyelids, while makeup styles have tended toward fuller lips and less pale skin shades. She attributes these changes to the recalibration of beauty norms as the result of the presence of more Asian, African, and Hispanic features in society.

But what's needed is a much more radical democratization of physical beauty, a democratization we can achieve not by changing the definition of beauty but by changing ourselves. Looking nice is something we need to take back from the elites and make once again a broadly shared, everyday attribute, as it once was when people were much less likely to be fat and much more likely to dress decently in public. Good looks are not just an endowment, and the un-American attitude that looks are immune to self-improvement only breeds the kind of fatalism that is blessedly out of character in America.

As a first step, maybe we can stop pretending that our appearance   40 doesn't—or shouldn't—matter. A little more looksism, if it gets people to shape up, would probably save some lives, to say nothing of some marriages. Let's face it. To a greater extent than most of us are comfortable with, looks tell us something, and right now what they say about our health, our discipline, and our mutual regard isn't pretty. ■

---

1 *Olive Oyl:* A cartoon character created in 1919 by Elzie Crisler Segar for his comic strip "Thimble Theater," which later was renamed "Popeye," to recognize the popularity of the sailor character featured in the comic strip.—EDS.

The Reader's Presence

1. If, as Akst notes, humans are "hard-wired to respond to how people and objects look" (paragraph 2), why has society developed attitudes that consider beauty as "only skin deep" (paragraph 1)? How does the author explain this apparent inconsistency? Discuss why you agree or disagree with his explanation.

2. Note that Akst's essay on a common subject—the significance of good looks—relies on a number of scientific and professional studies. Make a list of the various disciplines that help provide Akst with evidence and support. For example, how does research in evolutionary biology contribute? How does economics contribute? What reports, if any, did you find either surprising or obvious, and why?

3. **CONNECTIONS:**   Read Akst's essay in conjunction with Camille Paglia's "The Pitfalls of Plastic Surgery" (page 774). Explain how Paglia's responses to the subject of looks and beauty conform to Akst's. How does Paglia offer alternative insights into the topic? For example, how are Paglia's norms about beauty different from those Akst cites in his essay? Which author do you agree with on the significance of good looks, and why?

Akhil Reed Amar

SECOND THOUGHTS: WHAT THE RIGHT TO BEAR ARMS REALLY MEANS

Constitutional law scholar **AKHIL REED AMAR** (b. 1958) is the Sterling Professor of Law and Political Science at Yale University. He teaches constitutional law at both Yale College, from which he graduated in 1980, and Yale Law School, where he received his law degree in 1984. Before joining the Yale faculty in 1985, Amar served as law clerk to Stephen Breyer, who is now a Supreme Court Justice. He co-edited, with other noted experts, a leading constitutional law casebook, *Process of Constitutional Decisionmaking: Cases and Materials* (2002), and has authored many

> "As I see it, text without context is empty. . . . The right to 'bear arms' could mean no more than an entitlement to possess the stuffed forelimbs of grizzlies and Kodiaks."

law review articles and scholarly books, including *The Constitution and Criminal Procedure: First Principles* (1997); *For the People: What the Constitution Really Says About Your Rights* (1998), co-written with Alan Hirsch; *The Bill of Rights: Creation and Reconstruction* (1998); and his most recent book, *America's Constitution: A Biography* (2005). Amar's articles on constitutional issues have been published in the *New York Times*, the *Washington Post*, the *Los Angeles Times*, the *American Lawyer*, *Slate*, and the *New Republic*, where his essay "Second Thoughts: What the Right to Bear Arms Really Means" appeared in 1999. In another essay, titled "Rethinking Originalism" (2005), Amar jokes about the importance of context in analyzing the Second Amendment: "As I see it, text without context is empty. Constitutional interpretation heedless of enactment history becomes a pun-game: The right to 'bear arms' could mean no more than an entitlement to possess the stuffed forelimbs of grizzlies and Kodiaks."

> **The Second Amendment to the U.S. Constitution**
> "Amendment 2: A well regulated Militia, being necessary to the security of a free State, the right of the people to keep and bear Arms, shall not be infringed."

SO WHAT *does* the Second Amendment mean? A lot, says the National Rifle Association. Not much, say gun-control groups. Until recently, it didn't much matter who was right—on all but the mildest of measures, the NRA had the votes (and the cash), and that was that. Then came Littleton. Now proposals for serious federal gun controls are in the air. Thus far, the House and Senate have failed to agree on any specific gun measures, and whatever Congress ultimately decides in conference promises to be modest at best, targeting only gun shows and youngsters. But prominent politicians and civic leaders are now arguing for far more sweeping restrictions on guns, including mandatory licensing schemes and strict limits on the number of weapons that may be purchased in a single transaction. Would such measures violate the Constitution? Is the NRA right after all? No, but neither are its leading critics. Properly construed, the Second Amendment means quite a lot, but not what the NRA thinks.

Begin with the words of the amendment itself: "A well regulated militia being necessary to the security of a free state, the right of the people to keep and bear arms shall not be infringed." This curious syntax has perplexed most modern readers. How do the two main clauses with different subject-nouns fit together? Do these words guarantee a right of militias, as the second clause seems to say? In one corner, gun controllers embrace a narrow, statist reading, insisting that the amendment merely confers a right on state governments to establish professional state militias like the National Guard or local SWAT teams. No ordinary citizen is covered by the amendment in this view. In the other corner, gun owners and their supporters read the amendment in a broad, libertarian way, arguing that it protects a right of every individual to have guns for self-protection, for hunting, and even for sport. Virtually nothing having to do with personal weaponry is outside the amendment in this view. Both readings are wrong.

The statist reading sidesteps the obvious fact that the amendment's actual command language—"shall not be infringed"—appears in its second clause, which speaks of "the people" and not "the states." A quick look at the Tenth Amendment—which draws a sharp distinction between "the states" and "the people"—makes clear that these two phrases are not identical and that the Founders knew how to say "states" when they meant states. What's more, the eighteenth-century "militia" referred to by the first clause was not remotely like today's National Guard. It encompassed virtually all voters—somewhat like today's Swiss militia—rather than a small group of paid, semiprofessional volunteers.

But the libertarian reading must contend with textual embarrassments of its own. The amendment speaks of a right of "the people" collectively rather than a right of "persons" individually. And it uses a distinctly military phrase: "bear arms." A deer hunter or target shooter carries a gun but does not, strictly speaking, bear arms. The military connotation was even more obvious in an earlier draft of the amendment, which contained additional language that "no one religiously scrupulous of bearing arms shall be compelled to render military service in person." Even in the final version, note how the military phrase "bear arms" is sandwiched between a clause that talks about the "militia" and a clause (the Third Amendment) that regulates the quartering of "soldiers" in times of "war" and "peace." Likewise, state constitutions in place in 1789 consistently used the phrase "bear arms" in military contexts and no other.

By now it should be evident that we need to understand how all the words of the amendment fit together, and how they, in turn, mesh with other words in the Constitution. The amendment's syntax seems odd only because modern readers persistently misread the words "militia" and "people," imposing twentieth-century assumptions on an eighteenth-century text. The key subject-nouns were simply different ways of saying the same thing: at the Founding, the militia was the people and the people were the militia. Indeed, the earlier draft of the amendment linked the two clauses with linchpin language speaking of "a well regulated militia, composed of the body of the people." The linchpin was later pulled out as clumsy and redundant. A modern translation of the amendment might thus be: "An armed and militarily trained citizenry being conducive to freedom, the right of the electorate to organize itself militarily shall not be infringed."

Call this the communitarian reading as opposed to the statist and libertarian readings that dominate modern discourse. Statists anachronistically read the "militia" to mean the government (the paid professional officialdom) rather than the people (the ordinary citizenry). Equally anachronistically, libertarians read "the people" to mean atomized private persons, each hunting in his own private Idaho, rather than the citizenry acting collectively.

5

But, when the Constitution speaks of "the people" rather than "persons," the collective connotation is primary. "We the People" in the preamble do ordain and establish the Constitution as public citizens meeting together in conventions and acting in concert, not as private individuals pursuing our respective hobbies. The only other reference to "the people" in the Philadelphia Constitution of 1787 appears a sentence away from the preamble, and here, too, the meaning is public and political, not private and individualistic. Every two years, "the people"—that is, the voters—elect the House. To see the key distinction another way, recall that women in 1787 had the rights of "persons" (such as freedom to worship and protections of privacy in their homes) but did not directly participate in the acts of "the people"—they did not vote in constitutional conventions or for Congress, nor were they part of the militia/people at the heart of the Second Amendment.

The rest of the Bill of Rights confirms this communitarian reading. The core of the First Amendment's assembly clause, which textually abuts the Second Amendment, is the right of "the people"—in essence, voters—to "assemble" in constitutional conventions and other political conclaves. So, too, the core rights retained and reserved to "the people" in the Ninth and Tenth Amendments were rights of the people collectively to govern themselves democratically. The Fourth Amendment is trickier: "The right of the people to be secure in their persons, houses, papers, and effects against unreasonable searches and seizures, shall not be violated." Here, the collective "people" wording is paired with more individualistic language of "persons." And these words obviously focus on the private domain, protecting individuals in their private homes more than in the public square. Why, then, did the Fourth Amendment use the words "the people" at all? Probably to highlight the role that jurors—acting collectively and representing the electorate—would play in deciding which searches were reasonable and how much to punish government officials who searched and seized improperly. An early draft of James Madison's amendment protecting jury rights helps make this linkage obvious and also resonates with the language of the Second Amendment: "[T]he trial by jury, as one of the best securities to the rights of the people, ought to remain inviolate." Note the obvious echoes here—"security" (Second Amendment), "secure" (Fourth Amendment), and "securities" (draft amendment); "shall not be infringed," "shall not be violated," and "ought to remain inviolate"; and, of course, "the right of the people" in all three places.

If we want an image of the people's militia at the Founding, we should think first of the militia's cousin, the jury. Like the militia, the jury was a local body countering imperial power—summoned by the government but standing outside it, representing the people, collectively. Like jury service, militia participation was both a right and a duty of qualified voters who were regularly summoned to discharge their public obligations. Like the jury, the militia was composed of amateurs arrayed against, and designed to check, permanent and professional government officials (judges and prosecutors, in the case of the jury; a standing army in the case of the militia). Like the jury, the militia embodied collective political action rather than private pursuits.

Founding history confirms this. The Framers envisioned Minutemen bearing guns, not Daniel Boone gunning bears. When we turn to state constitutions, we consistently find arms-bearing and militia clauses intertwined with rules governing standing armies, troop-quartering, martial law, and civilian supremacy. Libertarians cannot explain this clear pattern that has everything to do with the military and nothing to do with hunting. Conversely, statists make a hash of all these state constitutional provisions using language very similar to the Second Amendment to affirm rights *against* state governments.

Keeping the jury-militia analogy in mind, we can see the kernel of truth   10
in these competing accounts and also what's missing from each. Statists are right to see the amendment as localist and to note that law and government help bring the militia together. So, too, with the jury. Twelve private citizens who simply get together on their own to announce the guilt of a fellow citizen are not a lawful jury but a lynch mob. Similarly, private citizens who choose to own guns today are not a well-regulated militia of the people; they are gun clubs. But what the statist reading misses is that, when the law summons the citizenry together, these citizens act as the people *outside* of government, rather than as a professional and permanent government bureaucracy. A lynch mob is not a jury, but neither is the Occupational Safety and Health Administration. Likewise, the NRA and other gun clubs are not the militia, but neither is the National Guard. Libertarians rightly recoil at the authoritarianism of their opponents in the debate but wrongly privatize what is an inherently collective and political right. It is as if Ross Perot[1] insisted that the First Amendment guaranteed him the right to conduct his own poll and, on the basis of this private poll, to proclaim himself president.

But to see all this is to see what makes the Second Amendment so slippery today: the legal and social structure on which the amendment is built no longer exists. The Founders' juries—grand, petit, and civil—are still around today, but the Founders' militia is not. America is not Switzerland. Voters no longer muster for militia practice in the town square.

Of course, we are free today to read the Second Amendment more broadly if we choose. Thoughtful legal scholars of all stripes—from Sanford Levinson on the left to Eugene Volokh on the right—have reminded us that other amendments have been read generously; why not the Second? But, given that a broad reading is a policy choice rather than a clear constitutional command, it must be functionally justified. And the mere fact that, say, the First Amendment has been read expansively is not an automatic argument for equal treatment for the Second. For example, violent felons, even while in prison and especially after their release, obviously have a First Amendment right to print their opinions in newspapers. Yet such felons have never had a Second Amendment right to own guns. Even the NRA accepts

---

1 **Ross Perot** (b. 1930): An American businessman from Texas, who founded Electronic Data Systems (EDS) in 1962. He sold EDS to General Motors in 1984, and founded Perot Systems in 1988. One of the wealthiest Americans, Perot is most widely known as a candidate for president of the United States in 1992 and 1996.—EDS.

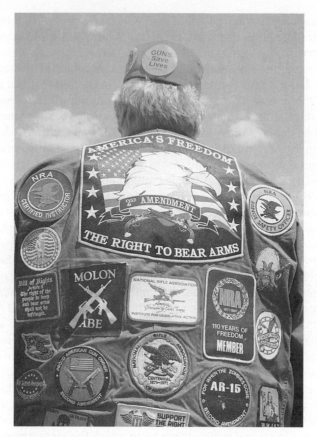

*Second Amendment activists gathered at the foot of
the Washington Monument in the nation's capital on
April 19, 2010.*

this double standard. But what underlies it? The obvious functional idea that
sticks and stones and guns in the hands of dangerous felons can indeed hurt
others in ways that their words cannot.

Especially today's guns. At the Founding, single-fire muskets had certain attractive and democratic properties. A person had to get close to you
to kill you, and, in getting close, he typically rendered himself vulnerable
to counterattack. It took time to reload, and so one person could not kill
dozens in a few seconds. One person, one gun, one shot was not as perfect
a system of majority rule as one person, one vote, but the side with the most
men often won; and, as lawyer Brent McIntosh emphasizes in a forthcoming
2000[2] essay in the *Alabama Law Review*, there was a rough proportionality
of capacity to kill and be killed. Virtually all male citizens were trained in

[2] Brent J. McIntosh, "The Revolutionary Second Amendment," 51 (2000): 673. http://www.saf
.org/LawReviews/McIntosh1.htm. — EDS.

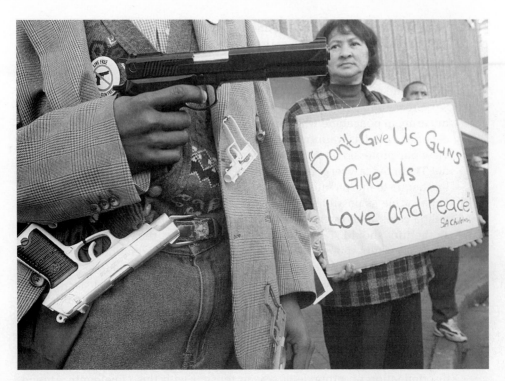

Adorned with toy guns, anti-gun lobbyists protest against the easy availability of firearms on the streets of Cape Town, July 18, 2002, as part of a United Nations campaign aimed at stemming the proliferation of small arms worldwide.

the use of weapons and had them handy. What's more, madmen were constrained by the strong social network of the well-regulated militia. Today, technological and social limits have been loosened, perhaps rendering madmen more dangerous.

So, if we seek broad readings of the amendment faithful to the core values of the Founding, here are a few that the NRA hasn't proposed but that are at least as plausible as their preferred broad readings:

Take the "mil" out of the militia. In highly sophisticated scholarship transcending the typical statist-versus-libertarian debate, Indiana law professor David Williams has emphasized how the militia bound citizens together in a common venture. It played an important social function in the community and embodied a democratic culture in which rich and poor citizens from all walks of life came together as equals—as with the jury. Without some forms of democratic glue, our culture risks flying apart, especially in today's world of increasing demographic diversity and specialization of labor. Thus, a broad modern reading of the amendment would call for compulsory or quasi-compulsory national service, with both military and nonmilitary alternatives,

15

like Volunteers in Service to America or the Civilian Conservation Corps. (Recall that an early version of the amendment provided for compulsory military service with an opt-out for conscientious objectors.) Instead of bowling alone, Americans would band together, building a more solid base of social capital and civic virtue.

Create an Army that truly looks like America. At the Founding, a standing army in peacetime was viewed with dread and seen as the Other — mercenaries, convicts, vagrants, aliens — rather than ordinary citizens. Today, we view our professional Armed Forces with pride. These forces represent Us, not Them. As lawyer-journalist Alan Hirsch has noted, the Founders' militia has begun to morph into today's Army. If so, women and gays should play as equal a role as possible in today's institutions of collective self-defense. The militia celebrated by the Second Amendment should reflect the people, just as the jury should. To put the point another way, the Second Amendment says that voters should bear arms and that arms-bearers should vote. Since the Nineteenth Amendment has made women equal voters, the Second Amendment demands that they be given equal status in arms. (Allowing women to buy guns at the local Wal-Mart might make them equal in communitarian arms-bearing — it fails to include them on equal terms in modern America's militia-substitute.)

And what's true for women may also be true for gay men: the Armed Forces' discrimination on grounds of sexual orientation is, formally at least, discrimination on grounds of sex, in tension with this Nineteenth Amendment ideal. (If Leslie has sex with John, it is a form of sex discrimination to treat Leslie one way if she is a woman and a different way if he is a man.) Formal sex discriminations can be justified in some cases, but they should be closely interrogated. For example, separate bathrooms for men and women are, formally, a kind of sex discrimination, but this arrangement is widely seen as justified by legitimate privacy concerns. So, too, certain sex-based exclusions in military policy might be justifiable, where these exclusions reflect real physical differences relevant to modern warfare. But, where exclusions of women and gays are justified merely by the need to maintain "morale" and "unit cohesion," we should be wary: similar arguments were once used to maintain racial discrimination in our Armed Forces.

Rethink presidential power to use military force unilaterally. At the Founding, standing armies were feared as engines of executive despotism and military adventurism. If the president could simply command hired guns who would mindlessly obey, he would have less need to persuade his fellow citizens before pursuing risky policies. Thus, the Founders' reliance on a militia effectively decentralized and democratized decisions about whether and how to go to war. In a brilliant article in the May 1991 *University of Pennsylvania Law Review*, Harvard's Elaine Scarry argues that our modern military system has betrayed the values and vision of the Second Amendment. Today's Minuteman missiles, she suggests, are far less democratic than the Founders' Minuteman muskets.

These, then, are a few broad readings that in various ways try to stay true to the vision of the Founders' Second Amendment while also making modern sense. None of these readings is compelled, and all of them would require much more elaboration before they should be accepted.

But is there nothing to be said for the strong libertarian view? In fact,   20
there is a great deal to be said on behalf of an individual right to keep a gun in one's home for self-defense, as even Harvard Law School's Laurence Tribe—no pawn of the NRA—has publicly acknowledged of late. But the best constitutional arguments for this view come not from the Founding but from the Reconstruction some fourscore years later.

Even with regard to the Founding, it's simplistic to deny any link between collective self-protection and individual self-defense. Lawyer and legal scholar Don Kates reminds us that, somewhat like standing armies, roving bands of thugs and pirates posed a threat to law-abiding citizens, and a trusty musket in every home was indeed part of a system of community policing against predators. (Note that the amendment encompasses the right to "keep" as well as "bear" arms.) But this was not the main image of the Second Amendment at the Founding. Rather, the amendment was about Lexington and Concord and Bunker Hill. When arms were outlawed, only the king's men would have arms.

The amendments forged in the afterglow of the Revolution reflected obvious anxiety about a standing army controlled by the new imperial government and affection for the good old militia. But things looked different to Americans after a bloody Civil War. Massachusetts militiamen had once died for liberty at Bunker Hill, but more recently Mississippi militiamen had killed for slavery at Vicksburg. The imperial Redcoats at the Founding were villains, but the boys in blue who had won under Grant and Sherman were heroes—at least in the eyes of Reconstruction Republicans. And, when this generation took its turn rewriting the Constitution, it significantly recast the right to weapons. Textually, the Fourteenth Amendment proclaimed the need to protect fundamental "privileges" and "immunities" of citizens. The amendment explicitly limited state governments, but its authors made clear that no government, state or federal, had the right to violate fundamental rights of citizens. Although the Supreme Court ignored this language for almost a century, there are recent signs that suggest the justices may be willing to give this clause a second look.

And, if they do, gun groups would have reason to cheer. As scholars such as Stephen Halbrook, Michael Kent Curtis, Robert Cottrol, and Ray Diamond have documented in great detail, the framers of the Fourteenth Amendment strongly believed in an individual right to own and keep guns in one's home for self-protection. Most obviously, blacks and Unionists down South could not always count on the local police to keep white night-riders at bay. When guns were outlawed, only Klansmen would have guns. Thus, the Reconstruction Congress made quite clear that a right to keep a gun at home for self-protection was indeed a constitutional right—a true "privilege" or "immunity" of citizens.

That's the good news for the NRA—with the even better news that, if the Court took this Reconstruction vision seriously, state and local governments would be limited along with federal officials. But the bad news, at least for the most ardent gun lovers, is that whatever Fourteenth Amendment right exists is a limited one. Virtually no one today is seriously arguing to take away all guns from homes. (And actually trying to do so would be a nightmare for anyone who cares about liberty and privacy, given that guns are stashed everywhere and may well outnumber people in America.) Instead, most proposals seek to regulate rather than prohibit—limiting the amount and type of ammunition, restricting the number of guns one can buy in a given week, and so on. Requiring registration of guns and even licenses with practical and book tests, on the model of licensing drivers, sends some gun lovers up the wall—the first step toward confiscation, they predict in dire tones. But this is hard to take seriously. The authors of the Second Amendment, after all, were perfectly comfortable knowing that the government would know who had guns—every voter—and also were perfectly comfortable requiring those who owned guns to be properly trained and monitored in their use. Realistic gun control today may not be exactly what the Framers had in mind when they said that the armed citizenry should be "well regulated." But—at least in a world that is so distant from the Founders—it's close enough. ▪

The Reader's Presence

1. In paragraph 2, Amar summarizes the "statist" and the "libertarian" readings of the Second Amendment to the U.S. Constitution. Summarize the particular points of reasoning that inform each interpretation. What specific terms does Amar use to characterize each? Amar ends the second paragraph by asserting: "Both readings are wrong." Summarize the main points he offers for his alternative reading of the Second Amendment, and then discuss the extent to which you find his analysis reasonable and convincing. How does Amar's own interpretation take into account "the kernel of truth [he sees] in these competing accounts and also what's missing from each" (paragraph 10)? Summarize—and then characterize—the relevance of his jury-militia analogy to his interpretation of the Second Amendment.

2. What do you notice about the syntax and tone in the opening paragraph of Amar's essay? What would you identify as the pivotal sentence in this paragraph? What changes in syntax and tone do you notice after this point? With what effect(s)? In the second sentence of his first paragraph Amar sets up a contrast between those who think that the Second Amendment means "A lot," and those who think that it means "Not much." What moves does Amar make in this paragraph in order to stake out a position between these two extremes? With what effect(s)? How might the structure of this opening paragraph be said to represent the structure for the rest of Amar's analysis of the different interpretations of the Second Amendment? Please be as specific as possible.

3. **CONNECTIONS:**   After you have settled into an understanding of Amar's interpretation of the Second Amendment—and especially his analysis of its phrasing—read
Stephen Jay Gould's essay "Sex, Drugs, Disasters, and the Extinction of Dinosaurs" (page 430). Which essay do you think is more successful in making observations—and drawing reasonable inferences—about what Gould calls the failure
"to separate fascinating claims" (paragraph 2) from the methods used to establish
facts? Point to specific examples to support your responses. Explain why you think
one writer is more successful in unpacking the distinctions others use to construct
their analyses and arguments, what Gould calls "testable proposals" (paragraph 4),
"intriguing ideas" (paragraph 5), and "useless speculation" (paragraph 5). Do you
find Amar's or Gould's analysis more engaging and reasonable? Explain why.

Dave Barry

BEAUTY AND THE BEAST

DAVE BARRY (b. 1947) is an American author known primarily for his nationally syndicated humor column. In addition to his column for the *Miami Herald*, where he worked from
1983 through 2005, he has published dozens of books of fiction and nonfiction, including
Dave Barry Turns 40 (1990), *Dave Barry's Complete Guide to Guys* (1995), *Dave Barry in
Cyberspace* (1996), *"The Greatest Inven-
tion in the History of Mankind Is Beer"
and Other Manly Insights from Dave Barry*
(2001), *Dave Barry's History of the Millennium (So Far)* (2007), and *I'll Mature When
I'm Dead* (2010). With Ridley Pearson, he is
also the co-author of the successful *Peter and
the Starcatchers* series, a series of novels for
children based on J. M. Barrie's *Peter Pan*. The

> "As an English major, I had
> experience writing long
> authoritative-sounding essays
> without any knowledge of
> my topic, which is . . . the
> essence of journalism."

winner of a Pulitzer Prize for commentary in 1988, Dave Barry has been widely praised for his
use of humor in journalism. Of his writing career, Barry has said that he was attracted to the
newspaper business because he was an English major: "This meant I had experience writing
long, authoritative-sounding essays without any knowledge of my topic, which is of course the
essence of journalism."

IF YOU'RE A MAN, at some point a woman will ask you how she looks.

"How do I look?" she'll ask.

You must be careful how you answer this question. The best technique is to form an honest yet sensitive opinion, then collapse on the floor with some kind of fatal seizure. Trust me, this is the easiest way out. Because you will never come up with the right answer.

The problem is that women generally do not think of their looks in the same way that men do. Most men form an opinion of how they look in the seventh grade, and they stick to it for the rest of their lives. Some men form the opinion that they are irresistible stud muffins, and they do not change this opinion even when their faces sag and their noses bloat to the size of eggplants and their eyebrows grow together to form what appears to be a giant forehead-dwelling tropical caterpillar.

Most men, I believe, think of themselves as average-looking. Men will   5 think this even if their faces cause heart failure in cattle at a range of 300 yards. Being average does not bother them; average is fine, for men. This is why men never ask anybody how they look. Their primary form of beauty care is to shave themselves, which is essentially the same form of beauty care that they give to their lawns. If, at the end of his four-minute daily beauty regimen, a man has managed to wipe most of the shaving cream out of his hair and is not bleeding too badly, he feels that he has done all he can, so he stops thinking about his appearance and devotes his mind to more critical issues, such as the Super Bowl.

Women do not look at themselves this way. If I had to express, in three words, what I believe most women think about their appearance, those words would be: "not good enough." No matter how attractive a woman may appear to be to others, when she looks at herself in the mirror, she thinks: woof. She thinks that at any moment a municipal animal-control officer is going to throw a net over her and haul her off to the shelter.

Why do women have such low self-esteem? There are many complex psychological and societal reasons, by which I mean Barbie. Girls grow up playing with a doll proportioned such that, if it were human, it would be seven feet tall and weigh 81 pounds, of which 53 pounds would be bosoms. This is a difficult appearance standard to live up to, especially when you contrast it with the standard set for little boys by their dolls . . . excuse me, by their action figures. Most of the action figures that my son played with when he was little were hideous-looking. For example, he was very fond of an action figure (part of the He-Man series) called "Buzz-Off," who was part human, part flying insect. Buzz-Off was not a looker. But he was extremely self-confident. You could not imagine Buzz-Off saying to the other action figures: "Do you think these wings make my hips look big?"

But women grow up thinking they need to look like Barbie, which for most women is impossible, although there is a multibillion-dollar beauty industry devoted to convincing women that they must try. I once saw an Oprah show wherein supermodel Cindy Crawford dispensed makeup tips to the studio audience. Cindy had all these middle-aged women applying beauty products to their faces; she stressed how important it was to apply them in a certain way, using the tips of their fingers. All the women dutifully did this, even though it was obvious to any sane observer that, no matter how carefully they applied these products, they would never look remotely like Cindy Crawford, who is some kind of genetic mutation.

I'm not saying that men are superior. I'm just saying that you're not going to get a group of middle-aged men to sit in a room and apply cosmetics to themselves under the instruction of Brad Pitt, in hopes of looking more like him. Men would realize that this task was pointless and demeaning. They would find some way to bolster their self-esteem that did not require looking like Brad Pitt. They would say to Brad: "Oh YEAH? Well what do you know about LAWN CARE, pretty boy?"

Of course many women will argue that the reason they become obsessed   10 with trying to look like Cindy Crawford is that men, being as shallow as a drop of spit, WANT women to look that way. To which I have two responses:

1. Hey, just because WE'RE idiots, that does not mean YOU have to be; and

2. Men don't even notice 97 percent of the beauty efforts you make anyway. Take fingernails. The average woman spends 5,000 hours per year worrying about her fingernails; I have never once, in more than 40 years of listening to men talk about women, heard a man say, "She has a nice set of fingernails!" Many men would not notice if a woman had upward of four hands.

Anyway, to get back to my original point: If you're a man, and a woman asks you how she looks, you're in big trouble. Obviously, you can't say she looks bad. But you also can't say that she looks great, because she'll think you're lying, because she has spent countless hours, with the help of the multibillion-dollar beauty industry, obsessing about the differences between herself and Cindy Crawford. Also, she suspects that you're not qualified to judge anybody's appearance. This is because you have shaving cream in your hair. ●

The Reader's Presence

1. Barry makes a number of broad claims in this essay. How does he support—or fail to support—each of these claims? How specific or general is he in the explanations he offers? How does his approach affect your willingness to accept his explanations?

2. Comment on the role humor plays in Barry's essay. How would you read and understand the essay differently if Barry had simply explained each of his points in a straightforward manner? With which, if any, of Barry's more exaggerated or improbable statements did you find yourself agreeing? Explain why.

3. **CONNECTIONS:**   In both this essay and Barbara Ehrenreich's "Will Women Still Need Men?" (page 650), the authors use humorous generalizations to explain the points they are making. Find examples of this approach in both essays. Consider, specifically, how each writer justifies the generalizations that he or she makes. Are the two authors essentially using the same technique, or do their approaches differ? Explain.

Michael Bérubé

ANALYZE, DON'T SUMMARIZE

MICHAEL BÉRUBÉ, born in New York City in 1961, is the Paterno Family Professor in Literature at Pennsylvania State University, where he teaches literature and cultural studies or, as he calls it, "dangeral studies" for the controversy such studies engender. "I would be selling students short if my classes did not reflect some of my beliefs about literary theory, or feminism, or postmodernism, or multiculturalism, since I have spent my entire adult life studying such things," he told a reporter in 2006. Known for sparring with conservative critics of academia, Bérubé has become a noted advocate of "liberal" liberal education, a defender of the humanities, and "the professor the right loves to hate." His books include *Marginal Forces/Cultural Centers: Tolson, Pynchon, and the Politics of the Canon* (1992); *Public Access: Literary Theory and American Cultural Politics* (1994); and *The Employment of English: Theory, Jobs, and the Future of Literary Studies* (1998). His 1996 book dealing with his son born with Down syndrome, *Life as We Know It: A Father, a Family, and an Exceptional Child* (1996), was a *New York Times* Notable Book of the Year. His most recent works are *What's Liberal About the Liberal Arts? Classroom Politics and "Bias" in Higher Education* (2006), *Rhetorical Occasions: Essays on Humans and the Humanities* (2006), and *The Left at War (Cultural Front)* (2009). He has written articles for many publications, including *Harper's*, the *New Yorker*, *Dissent*, the *New York Times Magazine*, the *Village Voice*, the *Washington Post*, and the *Nation*, as well as numerous scholarly journals such as the *Chronicle of Higher Education*, where his essay, "Analyze, Don't Summarize," appeared in 2004.

> Michael Bérubé has become a noted advocate of "liberal" liberal education, a defender of the humanities, and "the professor the right loves to hate."

THE FIRST TIME a student asked me about my "grading system," I was nonplused—and a bit intimidated. It was an innocent question, but I heard it as a challenge: I was a 25-year-old graduate student teaching my first section in an English-literature class at the University of Virginia, and I really didn't know *what* my grading system was. Nor did I feel comfortable saying, "Well, it's like Justice Stewart's definition of pornography, really—I simply know an A paper when I see one."

I fumbled my way through a reply, but I was unsettled enough by the exchange to seek the advice of the professor in charge of the course (and roughly a dozen teaching assistants). He went on a sublime rant that I've never forgotten, though I'm sure I've embellished it over the years. "These students come in here," he fumed, "with the idea that *you* have to explain yourself. 'You gave me a B-plus,' they say. 'What did you take points off for?' I tell them, 'Your paper was not born with an A. Your paper was born with a "nothing," and I made up my mind about it as I read it. That's what the marginalia are—they're the record of my responses to your arguments.'"

Today I've incorporated versions of that rant into my own teaching handouts: I try to explain the differences among superior, mediocre, and failing papers, and I tell students that my skills as a reader have been honed by my many experiences with professional editors, who attend carefully to paragraph transitions, dangling modifiers, and inaccurate citations. But I've never been able to give my students a visceral idea of what goes through my head as I read their work—until now.

Like many sports fans, I've grown a bit tired of ESPN's 25th-anniversary hyper-self-awareness of itself as a sports medium. While it's great to see the network poke fun at its early years, when its anchors wore dorky sport coats and weren't always sure when they were on the air, it's really quite tedious to be reminded of how sports-television hype helped hype TV sports.

The show *Around the Horn* has come to epitomize the general decline to me. Another half-hour program with which it's paired, *Pardon the Interruption*, gives us two volatile, opinionated sportscasters disagreeing with each other in rapid-fire fashion, with but a handful of seconds devoted to each topic. *Around the Horn* takes that format and makes a game show of it, offering us sportswriters competing for whose commentary will "win" by the end of the show.

I still play an organized sport—ice hockey—and as an amateur (and aged) player, I have to say that sports talk shows like this make me wonder whether some people don't see sports as simply an opportunity for endless metacommentary . . . and, of course, as gainful employment for an entire entourage of chattering parasites. In all that noise, I think, where are the games themselves?

Imagine my surprise, then, when I watched *Around the Horn* one afternoon and realized that here, at last, was my grading system in practice.

The idea behind *Around the Horn* is simple. There are a host and four contestants, each of whom speaks briefly on a series of up-to-the-moment sports topics. Points are awarded for smart—or merely plausible—remarks, and points are deducted for obviously foolish or factually inaccurate ones. There's a mute button involved, too, and players get eliminated as the show progresses (but those aspects of the game, so far as I can tell, have no counterpart in the world of paper-grading). And—of course, for this is the point of all such sports metacommentary—the viewers at home get to disagree with and complain about the commentary, as well as the officiating.

My standard undergraduate survey-course guides for paper-writing tell students things like this: "Assume a hypothetical readership composed of people who have already read the book. That means you shouldn't say, 'In class, we discussed the importance of the clam chowder in Chapter Five.' But more important, it means *you don't have to summarize the novel.* We're your readers, and we've read the book. However, we haven't read it in quite the way *you're* reading it. We haven't focused on the same scenes and passages you're bringing to our attention, and we haven't yet seen how your argument might make sense of the book for us."

But not all of my students see the point. Every semester I'm approached   10 by some who don't quite understand why they're being asked to make an *argument* out of literary criticism. Why shouldn't they simply record their impressions of the works before them? When I tell them that an observation is not a thesis, and that their thesis isn't sufficiently specific or useful if they can't imagine anyone plausibly disagreeing with it, they ask me why they can't simply explain *what happens in the novel.*

But in what world, exactly, would such an enterprise count as analysis? Not in any world I know—not even in the ephemeral pop-culture world of sports metacommentary. Can you imagine someone showing up on *Around the Horn* and saying to host Tony Reali, "Well, Tony, let me point out that last night, the Red Sox swept the Tigers and crept to within three games of the Yankees."

"And?"

"And nothing. I'm just pointing out that the Sox won, 3–1, on a four-hitter by Schilling, while the Yanks blew another late-inning lead."

No one does that, because no one in the sports world confuses summaries with analyses.

I also tell students that an essay of 2,000 words doesn't give them all that   15 much space to get going.

"You've only got a few pages to make that argument of yours. You don't need a grand introductory paragraph that begins, 'Mark Twain is one of Earth's greatest writers.' It's far better to start by giving us some idea of what you'll be arguing and why. If you like, you can even begin by pointing us to a particularly important passage that will serve as the springboard for your larger discussion: 'Not long after the second scaffold scene in *The Scarlet Letter,* when Arthur Dimmesdale joins hands with Hester Prynne and her daughter Pearl, Nathaniel Hawthorne asks us to reconsider the meaning of the scarlet A on Hester's breast.'"

On *Around the Horn,* commentators have to make their points in 15 seconds, which, as people who know me can testify, just happens to be roughly the amount of time it takes me to utter 2,000 words. So here, too, the analogy holds up.

Seriously, the sports-talk analogy is useful simply as a handy way of distinguishing between summary and analysis—and, more important, as an illustration of what happens in my grading process when a student paper cites textual evidence so compelling and unusual that it makes me go back and reread the passage in question (good!), suggests that a novel's conclusion fails to resolve the questions and tensions raised by the rest of the narrative (interesting!—possibly good, depending on the novel we're talking about), or makes claims that are directly contradicted by the literary text itself (bad! the mute button for you!).

So in a sense, I do "take off" points as I go—but then I add them back on as well, sentence by sentence, paragraph by paragraph, as I weigh the claims my students advance and the means by which they advance them.

The rules for literary analysis are the same rules in play for any kind of   20
analysis: mastery of the material. Cogency of supporting evidence. Ability to imagine and rebut salient counterarguments. Extra points for wit and style, points off for mind-numbing clichés, and permanent suspension for borrowing someone else's argument without proper attribution.

And yet, every year, I'm left with a handful of students who tell me that if *that's* what I want, I should simply assign topics to each student. "Not a chance," I reply. "Most of the mental labor of your paper takes place when you try to figure out just what you want to argue and why." As books like Thomas McLaughlin's *Street Smarts and Critical Theory* and Gerald Graff's *Clueless in Academe* have argued (with wit and style), students seem to understand this principle perfectly well when it comes to music, sports, and popular culture. It's our job to show them how it might apply to the study of literature.

My students, too, are often suspicious of what they regard as an idiosyncratic and a subjective enterprise that varies from English professor to English professor. But I can tell them there's really nothing mysterious about its mechanics. In fact, if they want to watch it in action, they can tune in to ESPN any weekday afternoon, 5 p.m. Eastern. ●

The Reader's Presence

1. Bérubé creates an analogy between grading student essays and watching sports commentary on ESPN. Outline the points of similarity between an instructor's responding to student writing and a television commentator's comments about sports. Which aspects of this analogy do you find most—and least—convincing? What aspects of this analogy, if any, has Bérubé omitted? Summarize the distinctions Bérubé draws between "analysis" and "summary." What is the significance of Bérubé's point that "an observation is not a thesis" (paragraph 10)?

2. In paragraph 21, Bérubé notes, "As books like Thomas McLaughlin's *Street Smarts and Critical Theory* and Gerald Graff's *Clueless in Academe* have argued (with wit and style), students seem to understand this principle perfectly well when it comes to music, sports, and popular culture." Explain the extent to which you agree—or

disagree—with Bérubé's assertion here. What evidence can you point to in support of—or to argue against—the spirit and substance of Bérubé's claim?

3. As you reread Bérubé's essay, what are the specific words and phrases that you think most accurately and effectively characterize his tone toward grading student essays? Toward television commentators on sports? What do you notice about Bérubé's choice of adjectives and verbs? What are his attitudes toward what he calls "marginalia" (paragraph 2)? What do you understand him to mean when he talks about "sports as simply an opportunity for endless metacommentary" (paragraph 6)? Comment on the effectiveness of Bérubé's use of "entourage" in the phrase "an entire entourage of chattering parasites" (paragraph 6). Examine carefully Bérubé's "rules for literary analysis" in paragraph 20. Apply these criteria to the strengths and weaknesses of his essay. Which of these rules does his essay most—and least—effectively illustrate? Please be as specific as possible in your response.

4. **CONNECTIONS:** In his essay "Politics and the English Language" (page 527), George Orwell observes: "Modern English, especially written English, is full of bad habits which spread by imitation and which can be avoided if one is willing to take the necessary trouble" (paragraph 2). Orwell proceeds to list—and then to illustrate and analyze—six rules for writing good prose. Compare and contrast Orwell's and Bérubé's rules of writing. Based on these rules, which writer practices his craft more effectively? Explain why, and support your response with detailed analyses of each writer's prose.

Charles Bowden

OUR WALL

CHARLES BOWDEN (b. 1945) is probably best known for writing about the Mexican-American border. A contributing editor for *GQ* and *Mother Jones*, he has also contributed to national publications such as *Harper's*, the *New York Times Book Review*, and *Esquire*. He is the author of many books of nonfiction, including (to name just a few) *Murder City: Ciudad Juarez and the Global Economy's New Killing Fields* (2010), *Dreamland: The Way Out of Juarez* (2010), *Some of the Dead Are Still Breathing* (2009), *A Shadow in the City: Confessions of an Undercover Drug Warrior* (2005), and *Down by the River: Drugs, Money,*

Murder, and Family (2004). He was a Lannan Writing Residency Fellow in Marfa, Texas, in 2001, and his 2006 collaboration with photographer Michael Berman, *Inferno*, received the Border Regional Library Association's Southwest Book Award. A strong advocate for immigration reform and a sharp critic of U.S. border policy, Bowden has called NAFTA "a machine producing poor people" and likened U.S. foreign policy (regarding Mexico) to "making war on the poor."

> **Advocating immigration reform and criticizing U.S. border policy, Bowden has likened American foreign policy toward Mexico to "making war on the poor."**

IN THE SPRING OF 1929, a man named Patrick Murphy left a bar in Bisbee, Arizona, to bomb the Mexican border town of Naco, a bunny hop of about ten miles (16 kilometers). He stuffed dynamite, scrap iron, nails, and bolts into suitcases and dropped the weapons off the side of his crop duster as part of a deal with Mexican rebels battling for control of Naco, Sonora. When his flight ended, it turned out he'd hit the wrong Naco, managing to destroy property mainly on the U.S. side, including a garage and a local mining company. Some say he was drunk, some say he was sober, but everyone agrees he was one of the first people to bomb the United States from the air.

Borders everywhere attract violence, violence prompts fences, and eventually fences can mutate into walls. Then everyone pays attention because a wall turns a legal distinction into a visual slap in the face. We seem to love walls, but are embarrassed by them because they say something unpleasant about the neighbors—and us. They flow from two sources: fear and the desire for control. Just as our houses have doors and locks, so do borders call forth garrisons, customs officials, and, now and then, big walls. They give us divided feelings because we do not like to admit we need them.

Now as the United States debates fortifying its border with Mexico, walls have a new vogue. At various spots along the dusty, 1,952-mile (3,141 kilometers) boundary, fences, walls, and vehicle barriers have been constructed since the 1990s to slow the surge in illegal immigration. In San Diego, nine miles (14 kilometers) of a double-layered fence have been erected. In Arizona, the state most overrun with illegal crossings, 65 miles (105 kilometers) of barriers have been constructed already. Depending on the direction of the ongoing immigration debate, there may soon be hundreds more miles of walls.

The 800 or so residents of Naco, Arizona, where Patrick Murphy is part of the local lore, have been living in the shadow of a 14-foot-high (four meters) steel wall for the past decade. National Guard units are helping to extend the 4.6-mile (7.4 kilometers) barrier 25 miles (40 kilometers) deeper into the desert. The Border Patrol station is the biggest building in the tiny

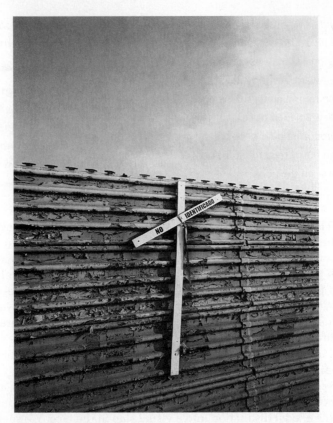

Memorial at a border wall in Tijuana, Mexico.

town; the copper roof glistens under the blistering sun. In 2005, a pioneering bit of guerrilla theater took place here when the Minutemen, a citizen group devoted to securing the border, staked out 20 miles (32 kilometers) of the line and patrolled it. Today about 8,000 people live in Naco, Sonora, on the Mexican side of the metal wall that slashes the two communities.

Only a dirt parking lot separates the Gay 90s bar from the Naco wall.   5
Inside, the patrons are largely bilingual and have family ties on both sides of the line. Janet Warner, one of the bartenders, has lived here for years and is one of those fortunate souls who has found her place in the sun. But thanks to the racks of stadium lights along the wall, she has lost her nights, and laments the erasure of the brilliant stars that once hung over her life. She notes that sometimes Mexicans jump the new steel wall, come in for a beer, then jump back into Mexico. The bar began in the late 1920s as a casino and with the end of Prohibition added alcohol. The gambling continued until 1961, when a new county sheriff decided to clean up things. On the back wall are photographs of Ronald and Nancy Reagan when they'd stop by on their way to a nearby Mexican ranch.

The bar is one of only a handful of businesses left. The commercial street leading to the border is lined with defunct establishments, all dead because the U.S. government sealed the entry to Mexico after 9/11 and rerouted it to the east. Leonel Urcadez, 54, a handsome man who has owned the bar for decades, has mixed feelings about the wall. "You get used to it," he says. "When they first built it, it was not a bad idea—cars were crossing illegally from Mexico and the Border Patrol would chase them. But it's so ugly."

The two Nacos came into being in 1897 around a border crossing that connected copper mines in both nations. By 1901 a railroad linked the mines. A big miners' strike in 1906, one cherished by Mexicans as foreshadowing the revolution in 1910, saw troops from both nations facing each other down at the line. The town of Naco on the Mexican side changed hands many times during the actual revolution—at first the prize was revenue from the customs house. Later, when Arizona voted itself dry in 1915, the income came from the saloons. Almost every old house in Naco, Arizona, has holes from the gun battles. The Naco Hotel, with its three-foot (one meter) mud walls, advertised its bulletproof rooms.

Border Field State Park, California. This stretch of upended railway track that looks like a work of contemporary art marks the western extent of the U.S.-Mexico border.

The boundary between Mexico and the United States has always been zealously insisted upon by both countries. But initially Mexicans moved north at will. The U.S. patrols of the border that began in 1904 were mainly to keep out illegal Asian immigrants. Almost 900,000 Mexicans legally entered the United States to flee the violence of the revolution. Low population in both nations and the need for labor in the American Southwest made this migration a nonevent for decades. The flow of illegal immigrants exploded after the passage of the North American Free Trade Agreement in the early 1990s, a pact that was supposed to end illegal immigration but wound up dislocating millions of Mexican peasant farmers and many small-industrial workers.

The result: Naco was overrun by immigrants on their way north. At night, dozens, sometimes hundreds, of immigrants would crowd into motel rooms and storage rental sheds along the highway. The local desert was stomped into a powder of dust. Naco residents found their homes broken into by desperate migrants. Then came the wall in 1996, and the flow of people spread into the high desert outside the town.

The Border Patrol credits the wall, along with better surveillance tech- 10
nology, with cutting the number of illegal immigrants captured near Naco's 33-mile (53 kilometers) border by half in the past year. Before this new heightening of enforcement, the number caught each week, hiding in arroyos thick with mesquite and yucca, often exceeded the town's population. At the moment, the area is relatively quiet as "coyotes," or people smugglers, pause to feel out the new reality, and the National Guard has been sent in to assist the Border Patrol. At the nearby abandoned U.S. Army camp, the roofs are collapsing and the adobe bricks dribble mud onto the floor. Scattered about are Mexican water bottles—illegals still hole up here after climbing the wall.

Residents register a hodgepodge of feelings about the wall. Even those who have let passing illegal immigrants use their phones or given them a ride say the exodus has to stop. And even those sick of finding trash in their yards understand why the immigrants keep coming.

"Sometimes I feel sorry for the Mexicans," says Bryan Tomlinson, 45, a custodial engineer for the Bisbee school district. His brother Don chimes in, "But the wall's a good thing."

A border wall seems to violate a deep sense of identity most Americans cherish. We see ourselves as a nation of immigrants with our own goddess, the Statue of Liberty, a symbol so potent that dissident Chinese students fabricated a version of it in 1989 in Tiananmen Square as the visual representation of their yearning for freedom.

Walls are curious statements of human needs. Sometimes they are built to keep restive populations from fleeing. The Berlin Wall was designed to keep citizens from escaping from communist East Germany. But most walls are for keeping people out. They all work for a while, until human appetites or sheer numbers overwhelm them. The Great Wall of China, built mostly after the mid-14th century, kept northern tribes at bay until the Manchu conquered China in the 17th century. Hadrian's Wall, standing about 15 feet (5 meters) high, 9 feet (3 meters) wide, and 73 miles (117 kilometers) long, kept the crazed tribes of what is now Scotland from running amok in Roman Britain—from A.D. 122 until it was overrun in 367. Then you have the Maginot Line, a series of connected forts built by France after World War I to keep the German army from invading. It was a success, except for one flaw: The troops of the Third Reich simply went around its northwestern end and invaded France through the Netherlands and Belgium. Now tourists visit its labyrinth of tunnels and underground barracks.

In 1859 a rancher named Thomas Austin released 24 rabbits in Australia   15 because, he noted, "the introduction of a few rabbits could do little harm and might provide a touch of home, in addition to a spot of hunting." By that simple act, he launched one of the most extensive barriers ever erected by human beings: the rabbit fences of Australia, which eventually reached 2,023 miles (3,256 kilometers). Within 35 years, the rabbits had overrun the continent, a place lacking sufficient and dedicated rabbit predators. For a century and a half, the Australian government has tried various solutions: imported fleas, poisons, trappers. Nothing has dented the new immigrants. The fences themselves failed almost instantly—rabbits expanded faster than the barriers could be built, careless people left gates open, holes appeared, and, of course, the rabbits simply dug under them.

In Naco all the walls of the world are present in one compact bundle. You have Hadrian's Wall or the Great Wall of China because the barrier is intended to keep people out. You have the Maginot Line because a 15-minute walk takes you to the end of the existing steel wall. You have the rabbit fences of Australia because people still come north illegally, as do the drugs.

Perhaps the closest thing to the wall going up on the U.S.-Mexico border is the separation wall being built by Israel in the West Bank. Like the new American wall, it is designed to control the movement of people, but it faces the problem of all walls—rockets can go over it, tunnels can go under it. It offends people, it comforts people, it fails to deliver security. And it keeps expanding.

Rodolfo Santos Esquer puts out *El Mirador*, a weekly newspaper in Naco, Sonora, and he finds the wall hateful. He stands in his cramped office—a space he shares with a small shop peddling underwear—and says, "It looks like the Berlin Wall. It is horrible. It is ugly. You feel more racism now. It is a racist wall. If people get close to the wall, the Border Patrol calls the Mexican police, and they go and question people."

And then he lightens up because he is a sunny man, and he says it actually hasn't changed his life or the lives of most people in town. Except that the coyotes[1] now drive to the end of the wall before crossing. And as the

---

[1] *coyotes:* Smugglers paid to take people illegally across the U.S-Mexico border.—EDS.

wall grows in length, the coyotes raise their rates. Santos figures half the town is living off migrants going north—either feeding them and housing them or guiding them into the U.S. Passage to Phoenix, about 200 miles (320 kilometers) away, is now $1,500 and rising. He notes that after the wall went up in 1996, the migration mushroomed. He wonders if there is a connection, if the wall magically beckons migrants. Besides, he says, people just climb over it with ropes.

Santos fires up his computer and shows an image he snapped in the 20 cemetery of a nearby town. There, there, he points as he enlarges a section of the photo. Slowly a skull-shaped blur floats into view against the black of the night—a ghost, he believes. The border is haunted by ghosts—the hundreds who die each year from heat and cold, the ones killed in car wrecks as the packed vans of migrants flee the Border Patrol, and the increasing violence erupting between smugglers and the agents of Homeland Security. Whenever heat is applied to one part of the border, the migration simply moves to another part. The walls in southern California drove immigrants into the Arizona desert and, in some cases, to their deaths. We think of walls as statements of foreign policy, and we forget the intricate lives of the people we wall in and out.

Emanuel Castillo Erúnez, 23, takes crime and car wreck photos for *El Mirador*. He went north illegally when he was 17, walked a few days, then was picked up and returned to Mexico. He sits on a bench in the plaza, shielded by a New York Yankees cap, and sums up the local feeling about the wall simply: "Some are fine with it, some are not." He thinks of going north again, but then he thinks of getting caught again. And so he waits.

There is a small-town languor about Naco, Sonora, and the wall becomes unnoticeable in this calm. The Minutemen and National Guard terrify people. At the Hospedaje Santa María, four people wait for a chance to go over the wall and illegally enter the wealth of the United States. It is a run-down, two-story building, one of many boarding houses for migrants in Naco. Salvador Rivera, a solid man in his early 30s, has been here about a year. He worked in Washington State, but, when his mother fell ill, he returned home to Nayarit, Mexico, and is now having trouble getting past the increased security. He left behind an American girlfriend he can no longer reach.

"For so many years, we Mexicans have gone to the U.S. to work. I don't understand why they put up a wall to turn us away. It's not like we're robbing anybody over there, and they don't pay us very much."

But talk of the wall almost has to be prompted. Except for those engaged in smuggling drugs or people, border crossers in Naco, Sonora, continue to enter through the main gate, as they always have. They visit relatives on the other side, as they always have. What has changed is this physical statement, a big wall lined with bright lights, that says, yes, we are two nations.

Jesús Gastelum Ramírez lives next door to the wall, makes neon signs, 25 and looks like Willie Nelson. He watches people climb the wall and he understands a reality forgotten by most U.S. lawmakers—that simply to go through the wire instantly raises a person's income tenfold. Gastelum knows many of his neighbors smuggle people, and he understands.

Until recently, a volleyball team from the Mexican Naco and a team from the U.S. Naco used to meet once a year at the point where the wall ends on the west side of town, put up a net on the line, bring kegs of beer, and play a volleyball game. People from both Nacos would stream out to the site and watch. And then the wall would no longer exist for a spell. But it always confronts the eye.

Dan Duley, 50, operates heavy equipment and is a native of the Naco area. He was living in Germany after serving in the Air Force when the Berlin Wall came down, and he thought that was a fine thing. But here he figures something has to be done. "We need help," he says. "We're being invaded. They've taken away our jobs, our security. I'm just a blue-collar man living in a small town. And I just wish the government cared about a man who was blue."

But then, as in many conversations on the border, the rhetoric calms down. Duley, along with many other Naco residents, believes the real solution has to be economic, that jobs must be created in Mexico. There is an iron law on this border: The closer one gets to the line, the more rational the talk becomes because everyone has personal ties to people on the other side. Everyone realizes the wall is a police solution to an economic problem. The Mexicans will go over it, under it, or try to tear holes in it. Or, as is often the case, enter legally with temporary visiting papers and then melt into American communities. Of the millions of illegal immigrants living in the United States, few would have come if there wasn't a job waiting for them.

Over in Naco, Sonora, the final night of a fiesta is in full roar. Men drinking beer move by on horseback, groups of girls in high heels prance past. Nearby, folks play bingo, and in the band shell a group does a sound check for the big dance. Looming over the whole party is a giant statue of Father Hidalgo with his bald head and wild eyes. He launched the Mexican Wars of Independence in 1810. Two blocks away, the steel wall glows under a battery of lights.

In the Gay 90s bar in Naco, Arizona, a *quinceañera*, the 15th-birthday   30 celebration that introduces a young girl to the world, is firing up. There are 200 people in the saloon's back room, half from Mexico and half from the U.S. The boys wear rented tuxedo vests, the girls are dressed like goddesses. One man walks in with a baby in a black polka-dot dress with pink trim.

The birthday girl, Alyssa, stands with her family for an official portrait.

Walls come and go, but *quinceañeras* are forever, I say to the man with the baby. He nods his head and smiles.

The steel barrier is maybe a hundred feet (30 meters) away. Outside in the darkness, Mexicans are moving north, and Border Patrol agents are hunting them down. Tomorrow, work will continue on the construction of the wall as it slowly creeps east and west from the town. Tourists already come to look at it.

I have no doubt someday archaeologists will do excavations here and write learned treatises about the Great Wall of the United States. Perhaps one of them will be the descendant of a Mexican stealing north at this moment in the midnight hour.

The Reader's Presence

1. From his first paragraph to his last, Bowden refers to the two towns of Naco, one in the United States and the other directly across the border in Mexico. What is the significance of these two towns? How do they play a key role in the way Bowden structures and develops his essay?

2. Bowden's essay is about barriers currently being built on the Mexican-American border. What, then, is his purpose in mentioning various walls and fences in world history, as he does in paragraphs 14–15? What is the relevance of the walls and fences to his main topic?

3. **CONNECTIONS:** Compare "Our Wall" to the following selection, David Brooks's "People Like Us." Who do the words *Our* and *Us* stand for in each essay? Do you think David Brooks's perspective on human behavior applies to the people Bowden speaks with in both Naco, Arizona, and Naco, Mexico? Why or why not?

David Brooks
PEOPLE LIKE US

DAVID BROOKS (b. 1961) was born in Toronto and grew up in New York City and in a suburb of Philadelphia. A journalist, columnist, and self-described "comic sociologist," Brooks has authored two books of cultural commentary, *Bobos in Paradise: The New Upper Class and How They Got There* (2001) and *On Paradise Drive: How We Live Now (and Always Have) in the Future Tense* (2004), and he edited the anthology *Backward and Upward: The New Conservative Writing* (1995). After graduating from the University of Chicago, Brooks worked as a reporter for the *Wall Street Journal*. Since that time, he has served as a senior editor at the *Weekly Standard* and as a contributing editor at the *Atlantic* and *Newsweek*, where the managing editor praised his "dead-on eye for the foibles of the Beltway—and his strong sense of how what happens in the capital's conservative circles affects the rest of the country." Brooks presents commentary on *National Public Radio* and on *The Newshour with Jim Lehrer*. In 2003 he joined the *New York Times* as an op-ed columnist.

> **In a PBS interview in 2000, David Brooks argued that people tend to gravitate to like-minded, like-cultured people— a "congealing pot" of people just like themselves.**

In a PBS interview in 2000, Brooks argued that people tend to gravitate to like-minded, like-cultured people—a "congealing pot" of people just like themselves: "Now if you look at the *New York Times* wedding page, it's this great clash of résumés. . . . Harvard marries Yale. Princeton marries Stanford. Magna cum laude marries magna cum laude. You never get a magna cum laude marrying a summa cum laude because the tensions would be too great in that wedding." "People Like Us" first appeared in the *Atlantic* in 2003. Brooks's latest book is *The Social Animal: The Hidden Sources of Love, Character, and Achievement* (2011).

MAYBE IT'S TIME to admit the obvious. We don't really care about diversity all that much in America, even though we talk about it a great deal. Maybe somewhere in this country there is a truly diverse neighborhood in which a black Pentecostal minister lives next to a white anti-globalization activist, who lives next to an Asian short-order cook, who lives next to a professional golfer, who lives next to a postmodern-literature professor and a cardiovascular surgeon. But I have never been to or heard of that neighborhood. Instead, what I have seen all around the country is people making strenuous efforts to group themselves with people who are basically like themselves.

Human beings are capable of drawing amazingly subtle social distinctions and then shaping their lives around them. In the Washington, D.C., area Democratic lawyers tend to live in suburban Maryland, and Republican lawyers tend to live in suburban Virginia. If you asked a Democratic lawyer to move from her $750,000 house in Bethesda, Maryland, to a $750,000 house in Great Falls, Virginia, she'd look at you as if you had just asked her to buy a pickup truck with a gun rack and to shove chewing tobacco in her kid's mouth. In Manhattan the owner of a $3 million SoHo loft would feel out of place moving into a $3 million Fifth Avenue apartment. A West Hollywood interior decorator would feel dislocated if you asked him to move to Orange County. In Georgia a barista from Athens would probably not fit in serving coffee in Americus.

It is a common complaint that every place is starting to look the same. But in the information age, the late writer James Chapin once told me, every place becomes more like itself. People are less often tied down to factories and mills, and they can search for places to live on the basis of cultural affinity. Once they find a town in which people share their values, they flock there, and reinforce whatever was distinctive about the town in the first place. Once Boulder, Colorado, became known as congenial to politically progressive mountain bikers, half the politically progressive mountain bikers in the country (it seems) moved there; they made the place so culturally pure that it has become practically a parody of itself.

But people love it. Make no mistake—we are increasing our happiness by segmenting off so rigorously. We are finding places where we are comfortable and where we feel we can flourish. But the choices we make toward that end lead to the very opposite of diversity. The United States might be a diverse nation when considered as a whole, but block by block and institution by institution it is a relatively homogeneous nation.

When we use the word "diversity" today we usually mean racial integration. But even here our good intentions seem to have run into the brick wall of human nature. Over the past generation reformers have tried heroically, and in many cases successfully, to end housing discrimination. But recent patterns aren't encouraging: according to an analysis of the 2000 census data, the 1990s saw only a slight increase in the racial integration of neighborhoods in the United States. The number of middle-class and upper-middle-class African-American families is rising, but for whatever reasons—racism, psychological comfort—these families tend to congregate in predominantly black neighborhoods.

In fact, evidence suggests that some neighborhoods become more segregated over time. New suburbs in Arizona and Nevada, for example, start out reasonably well integrated. These neighborhoods don't yet have reputations, so people choose their houses for other, mostly economic reasons. But as neighborhoods age, they develop personalities (that's where the Asians live, and that's where the Hispanics live), and segmentation occurs. It could be that in a few years the new suburbs in the Southwest will be nearly as segregated as the established ones in the Northeast and the Midwest.

Even though race and ethnicity run deep in American society, we should in theory be able to find areas that are at least culturally diverse. But here, too, people show few signs of being truly interested in building diverse communities. If you run a retail company and you're thinking of opening new stores, you can choose among dozens of consulting firms that are quite effective at locating your potential customers. They can do this because people with similar tastes and preferences tend to congregate by ZIP code.

The most famous of these precision marketing firms is Claritas, which breaks down the U.S. population into sixty-two psycho-demographic clusters, based on such factors as how much money people make, what they like to read and watch, and what products they have bought in the past.

Berkeley, New Jersey, 2003. As David Brooks writes, "what I have seen all around the country is people making strenuous efforts to group themselves with people who are basically like themselves."

For example, the "suburban sprawl" cluster is composed of young families making about $41,000 a year and living in fast-growing places such as Burnsville, Minnesota, and Bensalem, Pennsylvania. These people are almost twice as likely as other Americans to have three-way calling. They are two and a half times as likely to buy Light n' Lively Kid Yogurt. Members of the "towns & gowns" cluster are recent college graduates in places such as Berkeley, California, and Gainesville, Florida. They are big consumers of DoveBars and *Saturday Night Live*. They tend to drive small foreign cars and to read *Rolling Stone* and *Scientific American*.

Looking through the market research, one can sometimes be amazed by how efficiently people cluster—and by how predictable we all are. If you wanted to sell imported wine, obviously you would have to find places where rich people live. But did you know that the sixteen counties with the greatest proportion of imported-wine drinkers are all in the same three metropolitan areas (New York, San Francisco, and Washington, D.C.)? If you tried to open a motor-home dealership in Montgomery County, Pennsylvania, you'd probably go broke, because people in this ring of the Philadelphia suburbs think RVs are kind of uncool. But if you traveled just a short way north, to Monroe County, Pennsylvania, you would find yourself in the fifth motor-home-friendliest county in America.

Geography is not the only way we find ourselves divided from people   10
unlike us. Some of us watch Fox News, while others listen to NPR. Some like David Letterman, and others—typically in less urban neighborhoods—like Jay Leno. Some go to charismatic churches; some go to mainstream churches. Americans tend more and more often to marry people with education levels similar to their own, and to befriend people with backgrounds similar to their own.

My favorite illustration of this latter pattern comes from the first, non-controversial chapter of *The Bell Curve*. Think of your twelve closest friends, Richard J. Herrnstein and Charles Murray write. If you had chosen them randomly from the American population, the odds that half of your twelve closest friends would be college graduates would be six in a thousand. The odds that half of the twelve would have advanced degrees would be less than one in a million. Have any of your twelve closest friends graduated from Harvard, Stanford, Yale, Princeton, Caltech, MIT, Duke, Dartmouth, Cornell, Columbia, Chicago, or Brown? If you chose your friends randomly from the American population, the odds against your having four or more friends from those schools would be more than a billion to one.

Many of us live in absurdly unlikely groupings, because we have organized our lives that way.

It's striking that the institutions that talk the most about diversity often practice it the least. For example, no group of people sings the diversity anthem more frequently and fervently than administrators at just such elite universities. But elite universities are amazingly undiverse in their values, politics, and mores. Professors in particular are drawn from a rather narrow segment of the population. If faculties reflected the general population, 32 percent of professors would be registered Democrats and 31 percent would be registered Republicans. Forty percent would be evangelical Christians. But a recent study of several universities by the conservative Center for the Study of Popular Culture and the American Enterprise Institute found that roughly 90 percent of those professors in the arts and sciences who had registered with a political party had registered Democratic. Fifty-seven professors at Brown were found on the voter-registration rolls. Of those, fifty-four were Democrats. Of the forty-two professors in the English, history, sociology, and political-science departments, all were Democrats. The results at Harvard, Penn State, Maryland, and the University of California at Santa Barbara were similar to the results at Brown.

What we are looking at here is human nature. People want to be around others who are roughly like themselves. That's called community. It probably would be psychologically difficult for most Brown professors to share an office with someone who was pro-life, a member of the National Rifle Association, or an evangelical Christian. It's likely that hiring committees would subtly—even unconsciously—screen out any such people they encountered. Republicans and evangelical Christians have sensed that they are not welcome at places like Brown, so they don't even consider working there. In fact, any registered Republican who contemplates a career in academia these days is both a hero and a fool. So, in a semi–self-selective pattern, brainy people with generally liberal social mores flow to academia, and brainy people with generally conservative mores flow elsewhere.

The dream of diversity is like the dream of equality. Both are based on ideals we celebrate even as we undermine them daily. (How many times have you seen someone renounce a high-paying job or pull his child from an elite college on the grounds that these things are bad for equality?) On the one hand, the situation is appalling. It is appalling that Americans know so little about one another. It is appalling that many of us are so narrow-minded that we can't tolerate a few people with ideas significantly different from our own. It's appalling that evangelical Christians are practically absent from entire professions, such as academia, the media, and filmmaking. It's appalling that people should be content to cut themselves off from everyone unlike themselves.

The segmentation of society means that often we don't even have arguments across the political divide. Within their little validating communities, liberals and conservatives circulate half-truths about the supposed awfulness of the other side. These distortions are believed because it feels good to believe them.

On the other hand, there are limits to how diverse any community can or should be. I've come to think that it is not useful to try to hammer diversity into every neighborhood and institution in the United States. Sure, Augusta National should probably admit women, and university sociology departments should probably hire a conservative or two. It would be nice if all neighborhoods had a good mixture of ethnicities. But human nature being what it is, most places and institutions are going to remain culturally homogeneous.

It's probably better to think about diverse lives, not diverse institutions. Human beings, if they are to live well, will have to move through a series of institutions and environments, which may be individually homogeneous but, taken together, will offer diverse experiences. It might also be a good idea to make national service a rite of passage for young people in this country: it would take them out of their narrow neighborhood segment and thrust them in with people unlike themselves. Finally, it's probably important for adults to get out of their own familiar circles. If you live in a coastal, socially liberal neighborhood, maybe you should take out a subscription to *The Door*, the evangelical humor magazine; or maybe you should visit Branson, Missouri. Maybe you should stop in at a megachurch. Sure, it would be superficial familiarity, but it beats the iron curtains that now separate the nation's various cultural zones.

Look around at your daily life. Are you really in touch with the broad diversity of American life? Do you care? ●

The Reader's Presence

1. Brooks begins his argument by "admit[ting] the obvious": Americans don't care about diversity, they just like to talk as if they do. What was your initial reaction to Brooks's so-called admission? What is the effect of admitting something that many of his readers will instinctually reject? How is your opinion affected by his evidence? How well has he supported this assertion by the end of the essay?

2. Brooks claims that it is human nature for people to group together with those who have similar ideals and backgrounds. What might be the advantages of such grouping? What might be lost if Americans were truly integrated? What is lost by segregating by religion, politics, race, class, profession, and sexuality?

3. **CONNECTIONS:** Compare Brooks's observations about how we prefer to be around "people who are basically like themselves" (paragraph 1) to E. B. White's classic essay "Once More to the Lake" (page 260). In what ways can Brooks's point play a factor in evaluating White's essay, which was written decades earlier? In what ways does White's lake community support Brooks's perspective on diversity? For a more direct comparison of ideas, compare Brooks's essay with Walter Benn Michaels's "The Trouble with Diversity" (page 744). After reading each selection closely, list the points Brooks and Michaels agree on and those they don't. What major differences do you see between the conclusions each writer reaches?

Stephen L. Carter

THE INSUFFICIENCY OF HONESTY

Law professor and writer **STEPHEN L. CARTER** (b. 1954) is an insightful and incisive critic of contemporary cultural politics. His first book, *Reflections of an Affirmative Action
Baby* (1992), criticizes affirmative action policies that reinforce racial stereotypes rather than
break down structures of discrimination. Carter's critique emerges from his own experience as
an African American student at Stanford University and at Yale University Law School. After
graduating from Yale, Carter served as a law clerk for Supreme Court justice Thurgood Marshall
and eventually joined the faculty at Yale as
professor of law, where he has served since
1991 as the William Cromwell Professor of
Law. Carter has published widely on legal and
social topics, including his books *The Culture
of Disbelief: How American Law and Politics
Trivialize Religious Devotion* (1993), *The
Confirmation Mess: Cleaning Up the Federal Appointments Process* (1994), *Civility: Manners,
Morals, and the Etiquette of Democracy* (1998), *The Dissent of the Governed: A Meditation on
Law, Religion, and Loyalty* (1998), and *God's Name in Vain: The Right and Wrongs of Religion
in Politics* (2000).

> **"There's no piece of writing that
> can't be improved by spending
> more time on it. The discipline
> is to make yourself stop."**

Carter is also a prolific writer of novels; his most recent novels include *New England
White* (2007), *Palace Council* (2008), and *Jericho's Fall* (2009). Carter's best-selling novel *The
Emperor of Ocean Park* (2002) took him four years to complete. Carter says, "One of the best
pieces of advice about writing I ever received was from a professor at law school who said to
me, 'Stephen, there's no piece of writing that can't be improved by spending more time on it.
The discipline is to make yourself stop.'"

"The Insufficiency of Honesty" first appeared in *Integrity* in 1996.

A COUPLE OF YEARS AGO I began a university commencement address
by telling the audience that I was going to talk about integrity. The crowd
broke into applause. Applause! Just because they had heard the word "integrity": that's how starved for it they were. They had no idea how I was using the
word, or what I was going to say about integrity, or, indeed, whether I was for
it or against it. But they knew they liked the idea of talking about it.

Very well, let us consider this word "integrity." Integrity is like the
weather: everybody talks about it but nobody knows what to do about it.

Integrity is that stuff that we always want more of. Some say that we need to return to the good old days when we had a lot more of it. Others say that we as a nation have never really had enough of it. Hardly anybody stops to explain exactly what we mean by it, or how we know it is a good thing, or why everybody needs to have the same amount of it. Indeed, the only trouble with integrity is that everybody who uses the word seems to mean something slightly different.

For instance, when I refer to integrity, do I mean simply "honesty"? The answer is no; although honesty is a virtue of importance, it is a different virtue from integrity. Let us, for simplicity, think of honesty as not lying; and let us further accept Sissela Bok's[1] definition of a lie: "any intentionally deceptive message which is *stated*." Plainly, one cannot have integrity without being honest (although, as we shall see, the matter gets complicated), but one can certainly be honest and yet have little integrity.

When I refer to integrity, I have something very specific in mind. Integrity, as I will use the term, requires three steps: discerning what is right and what is wrong; acting on what you have discerned, even at personal cost; and saying openly that you are acting on your understanding of right and wrong. The first criterion captures the idea that integrity requires a degree of moral reflectiveness. The second brings in the ideal of a person of integrity as steadfast, a quality that includes keeping one's commitments. The third reminds us that a person of integrity can be trusted.

The first point to understand about the difference between honesty and integrity is that a person may be entirely honest without ever engaging in the hard work of discernment that integrity requires; she may tell us quite truthfully what she believes without ever taking the time to figure out whether what she believes is good and right and true. The problem may be as simple as someone's foolishly saying something that hurts a friend's feelings; a few moments of thought would have revealed the likelihood of the hurt and the lack of necessity for the comment. Or the problem may be more complex, as when a man who was raised from birth in a society that preaches racism states his belief in one race's inferiority as a fact, without ever really considering that perhaps this deeply held view is wrong. Certainly the racist is being honest—he is telling us what he actually thinks—but his honesty does not add up to integrity.

5

TELLING EVERYTHING YOU KNOW

A wonderful epigram sometimes attributed to the filmmaker Sam Goldwyn goes like this: "The most important thing in acting is honesty; once you learn

---

1 **Sissela Bok** (b. 1934): A Swedish-born scholar, philosopher, ethicist, and the author of many books, including *Lying: Moral Choice in Public and Private Life* (1978). She is the wife of Derek Bok, an interim president (2006–2007) of Harvard University.—EDS.

to fake that, you're in." The point is that honesty can be something one *seems* to have. Without integrity, what passes for honesty often is nothing of the kind; it is fake honesty—or it is honest but irrelevant and perhaps even immoral.

Consider an example. A man who has been married for fifty years confesses to his wife on his deathbed that he was unfaithful thirty-five years earlier. The dishonesty was killing his spirit, he says. Now he has cleared his conscience and is able to die in peace.

The husband has been honest—sort of. He has certainly unburdened himself. And he has probably made his wife (soon to be his widow) quite miserable in the process, because even if she forgives him, she will not be able to remember him with quite the vivid image of love and loyalty that she had hoped for. Arranging his own emotional affairs to ease his transition to death, he has shifted to his wife the burden of confusion and pain, perhaps for the rest of her life. Moreover, he has attempted his honesty at the one time in his life when it carries no risk; acting in accordance with what you think is right and risking no loss in the process is a rather thin and unadmirable form of honesty.

Besides, even though the husband has been honest in a sense, he has now twice been unfaithful to his wife: once thirty-five years ago, when he had his affair, and again when, nearing death, he decided that his own peace of mind was more important than hers. In trying to be honest he has violated his marriage vow by acting toward his wife not with love but with naked and perhaps even cruel self-interest.

As my mother used to say, you don't have to tell people everything you   10
know. Lying and nondisclosure, as the law often recognizes, are not the same thing. Sometimes it is actually illegal to tell what you know, as, for example, in the disclosure of certain financial information by market insiders. Or it may be unethical, as when a lawyer reveals a confidence entrusted to her by a client. It may be simple bad manners, as in the case of a gratuitous comment to a colleague on his or her attire. And it may be subject to religious punishment, as when a Roman Catholic priest breaks the seal of the confessional—an offense that carries automatic excommunication.

In all the cases just mentioned, the problem with telling everything you know is that somebody else is harmed. Harm may not be the intention, but it is certainly the effect. Honesty is most laudable when we risk harm to ourselves; it becomes a good deal less so if we instead risk harm to others when there is no gain to anyone other than ourselves. Integrity may counsel keeping our secrets in order to spare the feelings of others. Sometimes, as in the example of the wayward husband, the reason we want to tell what we know is precisely to shift our pain onto somebody else—a course of action dictated less by integrity than by self-interest. Fortunately, integrity and self-interest often coincide, as when a politician of integrity is rewarded with our votes. But often they do not, and it is at those moments that our integrity is truly tested.

ERROR

Another reason that honesty alone is no substitute for integrity is that if forth-rightness is not preceded by discernment, it may result in the expression of an incorrect moral judgment. In other words, I may be honest about what I believe, but if I have never tested my beliefs, I may be wrong. And here I mean "wrong" in a particular sense: the proposition in question is wrong if I would change my mind about it after hard moral reflection.

Consider this example. Having been taught all his life that women are not as smart as men, a manager gives the women on his staff less-challeng-ing assignments than he gives the men. He does this, he believes, for their own benefit: he does not want them to fail, and he believes that they will if he gives them tougher assignments. Moreover, when one of the women on his staff does poor work, he does not berate her as harshly as he would a man, because he expects nothing more. And he claims to be acting with integrity because he is acting according to his own deepest beliefs.

The manager fails the most basic test of integrity. The question is not whether his actions are consistent with what he most deeply believes but whether he has done the hard work of discerning whether what he most deeply believes is right. The manager has not taken this harder step.

Moreover, even within the universe that the manager has constructed   15 for himself, he is not acting with integrity. Although he is obviously wrong to think that the women on his staff are not as good as the men, even were he right, that would not justify applying different standards to their work. By so doing he betrays both his obligation to the institution that employs him and his duty as a manager to evaluate his employees.

The problem that the manager faces is an enormous one in our practical politics, where having the dialogue that makes democracy work can seem impossible because of our tendency to cling to our views even when we have not examined them. As Jean Bethke Elshtain[2] has said, borrowing from John Courtney Murray,[3] our politics are so fractured and contentious that we often cannot reach *disagreement*. Our refusal to look closely at our own most cherished principles is surely a large part of the reason. Socrates thought the unexamined life not worth living. But the unhappy truth is that few of us actually have the time for constant reflection on our views — on public or private morality. Examine them we must, however, or we will never know whether we might be wrong.

None of this should be taken to mean that integrity as I have described it presupposes a single correct truth. If, for example, your integrity-guided

---

[2] *Jean Bethke Elshtain* (b. 1941): A feminist political philosopher and professor of social and political ethics at the University of Chicago Divinity School. She serves on the Board of Advisors of the Bible Literacy Project, publishers of the curriculum "The Bible and Its Influence" for public high school literature courses. — EDS.

[3] *John Courtney Murray, SJ* (1904–1967): A Jesuit priest, theologian, and widely respected in-tellectual who was especially known for his efforts to reconcile Catholicism and religious pluralism, religious freedom, and American politics. — EDS.

search tells you that affirmative action is wrong, and my integrity-guided search tells me that affirmative action is right, we need not conclude that one of us lacks integrity. As it happens, I believe—both as a Christian and as a secular citizen who struggles toward moral understanding—that we *can* find true and sound answers to our moral questions. But I do not pretend to have found very many of them, nor is an exposition of them my purpose here.

It is the case not that there aren't any right answers but that, given human fallibility, we need to be careful in assuming that we have found them. However, today's political talk about how it is wrong for the government to impose one person's morality on somebody else is just mindless chatter. *Every* law imposes one person's morality on somebody else, because law has only two functions: to tell people to do what they would rather not or to forbid them to do what they would.

And if the surveys can be believed, there is far more moral agreement in America than we sometimes allow ourselves to think. One of the reasons that character education for young people makes so much sense to so many people is precisely that there seems to be a core set of moral understandings—we might call them the American Core—that most of us accept. Some of the virtues in this American Core are, one hopes, relatively noncontroversial. About 500 American communities have signed on to Michael Josephson's[4] program to emphasize the "six pillars" of good character: trustworthiness, respect, responsibility, caring, fairness, and citizenship. These virtues might lead to a similarly noncontroversial set of political values: having an honest regard for ourselves and others, protecting freedom of thought and religious belief, and refusing to steal or murder.

HONESTY AND COMPETING RESPONSIBILITIES

A further problem with too great an exaltation of honesty is that it may 20 allow us to escape responsibilities that morality bids us bear. If honesty is substituted for integrity, one might think that if I say I am not planning to fulfill a duty, I need not fulfill it. But it would be a peculiar morality indeed that granted us the right to avoid our moral responsibilities simply by stating our intention to ignore them. Integrity does not permit such an easy escape.

Consider an example. Before engaging in sex with a woman, her lover tells her that if she gets pregnant, it is her problem, not his. She says that she understands. In due course she does wind up pregnant. If we believe, as I hope we do, that the man would ordinarily have a moral responsibility toward both the child he will have helped to bring into the world and the child's mother, then his honest statement of what he intends does not spare him that responsibility.

---

4 ***Michael Josephson*** (b. 1942): A prominent ethicist as well as founder and president of Josephson Institute and its CHARACTER COUNTS! Project.—EDS.

This vision of responsibility assumes that not all moral obligations stem from consent or from a stated intention. The linking of obligations to promises is a rather modern and perhaps uniquely Western way of looking at life, and perhaps a luxury that the well-to-do can afford. As Fred and Shulamit Korn (a philosopher and an anthropologist) have pointed out, "If one looks at ethnographic accounts of other societies, one finds that, while obligations everywhere play a crucial role in social life, promising is not preeminent among the sources of obligation and is not even mentioned by most anthropologists." The Korns have made a study of Tonga, where promises are virtually unknown but the social order is remarkably stable. If life without any promises seems extreme, we Americans sometimes go too far the other way, parsing not only our contracts but even our marriage vows in order to discover the absolute minimum obligation that we have to others as a result of our promises.

That some societies in the world have worked out evidently functional structures of obligation without the need for promise or consent does not tell us what *we* should do. But it serves as a reminder of the basic proposition that our existence in civil society creates a set of mutual responsibilities that philosophers used to capture in the fiction of the social contract. Nowadays, here in America, people seem to spend their time thinking of even cleverer ways to avoid their obligations, instead of doing what integrity commands and fulfilling them. And all too often honesty is their excuse. ◼

The Reader's Presence

1. If Carter intends his essay to be a discussion of honesty, why does he begin with a consideration of the concept of integrity? How are the terms related? In what important ways are they different? What does integrity involve that honesty doesn't?

2. Notice that in this essay Carter never once offers a dictionary definition of the words *honesty* and *integrity*. Look up each term in a standard dictionary. As a reader, do you think such definitions would have made Carter's distinctions clearer? Why or why not? Why do you think Carter chose not to define the words according to their common dictionary meanings? How does he define them? How are his considerations of honesty and integrity related to his conclusion?

3. **CONNECTIONS:** In "Why Women Smile" (page 347), Amy Cunningham argues that women often "smile in lieu of showing what's really on [their] minds" (paragraph 3). Would Carter classify this kind of smiling as insufficiently honest? Why or why not? Cunningham notes that she is "trying to quit" smiling (paragraph 1); would not smiling show greater integrity, as Carter explains it?

Michael Chabon

FAKING IT

MICHAEL CHABON (b. 1963) is a Pulitzer Prize–winning author. His first novel, *The Mysteries of Pittsburgh* (1988), was widely praised by critics. *Wonder Boys*, his 1995 best-selling novel, was made into a successful film starring Michael Douglas and Tobey Maguire. *The Amazing Adventures of Kavalier & Clay* (2000) won the 2001 Pulitzer Prize for fiction and was nominated for the National Book Critics' Circle Award in 2000. A Washington, D.C. native, Chabon has also published collections of short stories, many of which first appeared in the *New Yorker*. His novel, *The Yiddish Policemen's Union*, set in an alternate

> *Wonder Boys*, Michael Chabon's 1995 best-selling novel, was made into a successful film starring Michael Douglas and Tobey Maguire.

reality, won the 2008 Hugo Award for Best Novel. His essay collections, *Manhood for Amateurs: The Pleasures and Regrets of a Husband, Father, and Son* (2009) and *Maps and Legends* (2008), have also received critical acclaim. This essay, "Faking It," was taken from *Manhood for Amateurs*.

AT ONE TIME there was a pair of hooks on the back of the bathroom door from which one could hang a couple of towels, but people used the towels as vines, webbing, and rope for games of Tarzan, Spider-Man, and Look! I'm a Dead Guy That Hung Themself, and now, to serve four children, there remained one wall-mounted towel rack with only two bars. This situation encouraged the general tendency among the children to leave their soggy bath towels in Noguchi-like[1] arrangements on the floor. The parents allocated resources for a pilot program of nag-based maintenance, targeted yelling, and regular exercises in stumbling over damp bath towels in dark bedrooms, but when emotional funding at last ran out, it became apparent that someone would have to put up a second towel rack. Responsibility for this task logically fell to the person who knew, kind of, how to use an electric drill.

You should have seen me. I had my cordless Makita in its blue high-impact plastic case. I had a ratcheting screwdriver, a nice Sears Craftsman

---

1 **Isamu Noguchi** (1904–1988): Japanese American artist, landscape architect, and sculptor. —EDS.

hammer, a mechanical pencil with a good eraser, and (that most beautifully named of all tools) a spirit level. I sat down on the tile floor of the bathroom with the new chrome towel rack from Restoration Hardware and its gnomic instruction sheet, and I ran the fingers of one hand across the designated stretch of beadboard while sagely stroking my whiskers with the fingers of the other. I strongly suspect that I may well have looked as if I knew what I was doing.

I managed to sustain the appearance of competence over nearly the entire course of the next three hours, except for the painful minute that followed my dropping one of the metal towel bars onto my right thumb, behind whose nail, like a ghost on an old television screen, a grayish-blue blotch immediately made manifest. But from the moment I began to trace with my pencil the prospective outline of one of the faceplates against the beadboard until the moment when, holding my breath, I insinuated two ominously heavy towels into the works of the now-mounted towel rack, I was expecting, at every instant, disaster: molly bolts sliding with a creak of splintering wood from their holes, nickel-plated towel bars clanging against the floor.

I knew how to use my tools, more or less. I understood the rudimentary physics of tension and load that were supposed to hold the rack together and keep it fixed to the wall. And yet on both the deepest and the most practical levels, I had no reason to believe, no evidence from prior experience of myself, physics, or life itself, that I knew how or would be able to pull off the job. In fact, I had encountered a certain amount of tragedy in my dealings with molly bolts over the years.

"You're going to put that up?" my wife had asked me when I brought the   5
rack home from the store. She didn't sound dubious so much as surprised, as if I were also proposing to weave a new set of bath towels from cotton I had grown and harvested myself.

"Duh," I said coolly. "No biggie."

This is an essential element of the business of being a man: to flood everyone around you in a great radiant arc of bullshit, one whose source and object of greatest intensity is yourself. To behave as if you have everything firmly under control even when you have just sailed your boat over the falls. "To keep your head," wrote Rudyard Kipling in his classic poem "If," which articulated the code of high-Victorian masculinity in whose fragmentary shadow American men still come of age, "when all about you are losing theirs"; but in reality, the trick of being a man is to give the appearance of keeping your head when, deep inside, the truest part of you is crying out, *Oh, shit!*

Perhaps in the end there is little difference between keeping one's head and appearing to do so; perhaps the effort required to feign unconcern and control over a situation itself imparts a measure of control. If so, then the essence of traditional male virtue lies in imposture, in an ongoing act of dissimulation—fronting—which hardly conforms to the classic Kipling model of square-dealing candor.

I have no doubt that the male impulse to downplay his own lack of fitness for a job, to refuse to acknowledge his inadequacy, insufficiency, or lack of preparation, has been and continues to be responsible for a large share of the world's woes, in the form of the accidents, errors, and calamities that result from specific or overarching acts of faking it, a grim encyclopedia of which the G. W. Bush administration readily affords. There is also the more subtle damage that is done repeatedly to boys who grow up learning from their fathers and the men around them the tragic lesson that failure is not a human constant but a kind of aberration of gender, a flaw in a man, to be concealed.

Men's refusal to stop and ask for directions, a foundational cliché of women's criticism, analysis, and stand-up mockery of male behavior, is a perfect example of this tendency to put up a front, in that it views as aberrant a condition—being lost—that is ineluctable, a given of human existence. We are born lost and spend vast stretches of our lives on wrong turns and backtracking. In this respect, male fronting resembles a number of other behaviors typically ascribed to men and masculinity, in that it proceeds by denying essential human conditions or responses—say public displays of mutual affection, grief, or triumph—marking them as feminine, infantile, socially unacceptable.

I learned to pretend that I know what I am doing from my own father, an extremely intelligent and well-informed man whose intermittent bouts with mistakenness and inaccuracy visibly cost him bitter pain and embarrassment, and shocked the hell out of me when I was a child. By fiat and consensus, fathers are always right, so that when facts or events inevitably conspire to prove them wrong, they and their sons alike totter on the brink of an abyss. I have never forgotten the day—I can't have been older than five—when I watched in silent horror as my father, imperturbable and confident and disdaining the instruction sheet, assembled an entire barbecue grill with its key pieces upside down and backward. I remember my mounting anxiety about whether I should point out his mistake to him, and most clearly of all I remember the sharp and mocking look my mother gave him when at last I betrayed him.

When I became a father, I made a promise to myself not to pretend to knowledge I did not possess, not to claim authority I plainly lacked, not to hide my doubts and uncertainties, my setbacks and regrets, from my children. And so I have tried to share them over the years as I have been fired from screenwriting jobs or proved wrong or led to look a fool. I have made a point (until the recent advent of GPS) to stop and ask for directions. But sometimes I waver in my resolve. My sense of myself as a father, my sense of fathers, is so deeply caught up with some kind of primal longing (which I think we all share) for inerrancy, for the word of God, for a rock and a redeemer, a mighty hand and an outstretched arm, for the needle that always always finds true north in a storm.

And maybe that longing in one's wife and children runs beyond the understanding of even the most painfully self-conscious of fathers. One recent winter my family and I found ourselves stuck in Jackson Hole, Wyoming, in the middle of a snowstorm. All flights out were canceled. There was a flight home from Idaho Falls, a drive of two hours through a high mountain pass, or three hours by an easier route that skirted the mountains. Either way, there would be snow, ice, unknown chances. If we wanted, we could wait for an airline-chartered bus that might eventually depart for Idaho Falls, getting us home to Oakland no one could say when. Or we could sit tight, wait it out, and hope to get home sometime tomorrow or the next day.

I didn't give it a moment's thought. We had rented a big strong four-by-four. It had the tires and the muscle for the roads up there. I liked the way I felt behind its wheel, competent and unperturbed by weather. The fact that I had not driven in a blizzard in twenty years barely entered the conscious register of my thoughts.

"Let's drive," I told my wife. "I'll go the long way around."   15

She looked at me with a strange expression, then said okay; later, after we had made it safely and without incident up and down through ice and rain and snowfall that was at times blinding, my wife told me that she initially thought I was dangerously insane when I proposed driving to Idaho Falls through a blizzard. But then she had heard something in my voice that reassured her; she'd seen something in my eyes. I looked as if I knew what I was doing. And though I gripped the wheel with bloodless hands and prayed wildly to the gods of the interstate trucker whom I carefully tailed all the way to Idaho, in the backseat the kids calmly watched their iPod videos, and my wife studied the map and gossiped with me, and none of them knew or suspected for a moment—for I never betrayed, by word or deed, my secret—that I was in way over my head. I was the father and the husband; they were safe with me. We made it to the airport right on time to catch the next flight home.

"I knew you could do it," my wife said, and I thought about saying, "Well, that makes one of us." But I held my tongue and nodded with a Kiplingesque modesty, because the truth was that in the absence of any evidence or experience or reason to think so, I had known that I could do it, too. I had no choice, do you see, but to know that.

By the way, the towels are still hanging from the rack in the bathroom. And I fully expect, at any moment, in the dead of night, to hear a telltale clatter on the tiles. ◼

The Reader's Presence

1. Chabon observes, "I have no doubt that the male impulse to downplay his own lack of fitness for a job, to refuse to acknowledge his inadequacy, insufficiency, or lack of preparation, has been and continues to be responsible for a large share of the world's woes" (paragraph 9). Given the overall context of this expository essay, to which of the "world's woes" might Chabon be referring? Comment on the effectiveness of each of the examples Chabon cites throughout the essay to support this explanation. Which examples do you find most engaging and memorable? Explain why.

2. Compare the story Chabon tells about installing a bathroom towel bar with the one he tells about driving through a blizzard. In what specific ways do these stories relate to each other? What point(s) does each illustrate? Why do you think they appear where they do in the essay?

3. **CONNECTIONS:** Compare the generalizations Chabon makes about men in this essay to the ones Dave Barry makes in "Beauty and the Beast" (page 315). In what specific ways are these generalizations similar and in what ways are they different? Compare, too, the ways in which both writers draw on personal experience to support their claims. How would you characterize the tone of voice of each writer? How does this tone affect your reading of each essay?

Amy Cunningham
WHY WOMEN SMILE

AMY CUNNINGHAM (b. 1955) has been writing on psychological issues and modern life for magazines such as *Redbook*, *Glamour*, and the *Washington Post Magazine* since she graduated from the University of Virginia in 1977 with a BA in English. Cunningham says that the essay reprinted here grew out of her own experience as an "easy to get along with

person" who was raised by southerners in the suburbs of Chicago. She also recalls that when writing it, "I was unhappy with myself for taking too long, for not being efficient the way I thought a professional writer should be — but the work paid off and now I think it is one of the best essays I've written." "Why Women Smile" originally appeared in *Lear's* in 1993.

> "Good writing has less to do with talent and more to do with the discipline of staying seated . . . in front of the computer and getting the work done."

Looking back on her writing career, Cunningham notes, "When I was younger I thought if you had talent you would make it as a writer. I'm surprised to realize now that good writing has less to do with talent and more to do with the discipline of staying seated in the chair, by yourself, in front of the computer and getting the work done."

AFTER SMILING BRILLIANTLY for nearly four decades, I now find myself trying to quit. Or, at the very least, seeking to lower the wattage a bit.

Not everyone I know is keen on this. My smile has gleamed like a cheap plastic night-light so long and so reliably that certain friends and relatives worry that my mood will darken the moment my smile dims. "Gee," one says, "I associate you with your smile. It's the essence of you. I should think you'd want to smile more!" But the people who love me best agree that my smile — which springs forth no matter where I am or how I feel — hasn't been serving me well. Said my husband recently, "Your smiling face and unthreatening demeanor make people like you in a fuzzy way, but that doesn't seem to be what you're after these days."

Smiles are not the small and innocuous things they appear to be: Too many of us smile in lieu of showing what's really on our minds. Indeed, the success of the women's movement might be measured by the sincerity — and lack of it — in our smiles. Despite all the work we American women have done to get and maintain full legal control of our bodies, not to mention our destinies, we still don't seem to be fully in charge of a couple of small muscle groups in our faces.

We smile so often and so promiscuously — when we're angry, when we're tense, when we're with children, when we're being photographed, when we're interviewing for a job, when we're meeting candidates to employ — that the Smiling Woman has become a peculiarly American archetype. This isn't entirely a bad thing, of course. A smile lightens the load, diffuses unpleasantness, redistributes nervous tension. Women doctors smile more than their male counterparts, studies show, and are better liked by their patients.

Oscar Wilde's[1] old saw that "a woman's face is her work of fiction" is   5
often quoted to remind us that what's on the surface may have little connection to what we're feeling. What is it in our culture that keeps our smiles on automatic pilot? The behavior seems to be an equal blend of nature and nurture. Research has demonstrated that since females often mature earlier than males and are less irritable, girls smile more than boys from the very beginning. But by adolescence, the differences in the smiling rates of boys and girls are so robust that it's clear the culture has done more than its share of the dirty work. Just think of the mothers who painstakingly embroidered the words ENTER SMILING on little samplers, and then hung their handiwork on doors by golden chains. Translation: "Your real emotions aren't welcome here."

Clearly, our instincts are another factor. Our smiles have their roots in the greetings of monkeys, who pull their lips up and back to show their fear of attack, as well as their reluctance to vie for a position of dominance. And like the opossum caught in the light by the clattering garbage cans, we, too, flash toothy grimaces when we make major mistakes. By declaring ourselves nonthreatening, our smiles provide an extremely versatile means of protection.

---

[1] *Oscar Wilde* (1854–1900): An Irish writer, poet, aesthete, and popular playwright in the early 1890s remembered for his epigrams and his early death. — EDS.

Our earliest baby smiles are involuntary reflexes having only the vaguest connection to contentment or comfort. In short, we're genetically wired to pull on our parents' heartstrings. As Desmond Morris[2] explains in *Babywatching*, this is our way of attaching ourselves to our caretakers, as truly as baby chimps clench their mothers' fur. Even as babies we're capable of projecting onto others (in this case, our parents) the feelings we know we need to get back in return.

Bona fide social smiles occur at two-and-a-half to three months of age, usually a few weeks after we first start gazing with intense interest into the faces of our parents. By the time we are six months old, we are smiling and laughing regularly in reaction to tickling, feedings, blown raspberries, hugs, and peekaboo games. Even babies who are born blind intuitively know how to react to pleasurable changes with a smile, though their first smiles start later than those of sighted children.

Psychologists and psychiatrists have noted that babies also smile and laugh with relief when they realize that something they thought might be dangerous is not dangerous after all. Kids begin to invite their parents to indulge them with "scary" approach-avoidance games; they love to be chased or tossed up into the air. (It's interesting to note that as adults, we go through the same gosh-that's-shocking-and-dangerous-but-it's-okay-to-laugh-and-smile cycles when we listen to raunchy stand-up comics.)

From the wilds of New Guinea to the sidewalks of New York, smiles are   10
associated with joy, relief, and amusement. But smiles are by no means limited to the expression of positive emotions: People of many different cultures smile when they are frightened, embarrassed, angry, or miserable. In Japan, for instance, a smile is often used to hide pain or sorrow.

Psychologist Paul Ekman, the head of the University of California's Human Interaction Lab in San Francisco, has identified 18 distinct types of smiles, including those that show misery, compliance, fear, and contempt. The smile of true merriment, which Dr. Ekman calls the Duchenne Smile, after the nineteenth-century French doctor who first studied it, is characterized by heightened circulation, a feeling of exhilaration, and the employment of two major facial muscles: the zygomaticus major of the lower face, and the orbicularis oculi, which crinkles the skin around the eyes. But since the average American woman's smile often has less to do with her actual state of happiness than it does with the social pressure to smile no matter what, her baseline social smile isn't apt to be a felt expression that engages the eyes like this. Ekman insists that if people learned to read smiles, they could see the sadness, misery, or pain lurking there, plain as day.

Evidently, a woman's happy, willing deference is something the world wants visibly demonstrated. Woe to the waitress, the personal assistant or receptionist, the flight attendant, or any other woman in the line of public

---

2 ***Desmond Morris*** (b. 1928): Distinguished zoologist and author of the best-selling *The Naked Ape* (1967) and *Babywatching* (1992).—EDS.

These photos from Paul Ekman's study show the difference between the social smile (left) and the true enjoyment smile (right).

service whose smile is not offered up to the boss or client as proof that there are no storm clouds—no kids to support, no sleep that's been missed—rolling into the sunny workplace landscape. Women are expected to smile no matter where they line up on the social, cultural, or economic ladder: College professors are criticized for not smiling, political spouses are pilloried for being too serious, and women's roles in films have historically been smiling ones. It's little wonder that men on the street still call out, "Hey, baby, smile! Life's not *that* bad, is it?" to women passing by, lost in thought.

A friend remembers being pulled aside by a teacher after class and asked, "What is wrong, dear? You sat there for the whole hour looking so sad!" "All I could figure," my friend says now, "is that I wasn't smiling. And the fact that *she* felt sorry for me for looking normal made me feel horrible."

Ironically, the social laws that govern our smiles have completely reversed themselves over the last two thousand years. Women weren't always expected to seem animated and responsive; in fact, immoderate laughter was once considered one of the more conspicuous vices a woman could have, and mirth was downright sinful. Women were kept apart, in some cultures even veiled, so that they couldn't perpetuate Eve's seductive, evil work. The only smile deemed appropriate on a privileged woman's face was the serene, inward smile of the Virgin Mary at Christ's birth, and even that expression was best directed exclusively at young children. Cackling laughter and wicked glee were the kinds of sounds heard only in hell.

What we know of women's facial expressions in other centuries comes   15
mostly from religious writings, codes of etiquette, and portrait paintings. In fifteenth century Italy, it was customary for artists to paint lovely, blank-faced

women in profile. A viewer could stare endlessly at such a woman, but she could not gaze back. By the Renaissance, male artists were taking some pleasure in depicting women with a semblance of complexity, Leonardo da Vinci's *Mona Lisa*,[3] with her veiled enigmatic smile, being the most famous example.

The Golden Age of the Dutch Republic[4] marks a fascinating period for studying women's facial expressions. While we might expect the drunken young whores of Amsterdam to smile devilishly (unbridled sexuality and lasciviousness were *supposed* to addle the brain), it's the faces of the Dutch women from fine families that surprise us. Considered socially more free, these women demonstrate a fuller range of facial expressions than their European sisters. Frans Hals's[5] 1622 portrait of Stephanus Geraerdt and

3 **Mona Lisa** (above): Widely recognized as one of the most important works of art in history, this sixteenth-century portrait painted in oil by Leonardo di ser Piero da Vinci (1452–1519) is on display at the Musée du Louvre in Paris as "Portrait of Lisa Gherardini, wife of Francesco del Giocondo." —EDS.

4 **Golden Age of the Dutch Republic:** A period in Dutch history, ranging across the seventeenth century, in which Dutch achievements in trade, science, art, and military were highly acclaimed. —EDS.

5 **Frans Hals** (c. 1582/83–1666): One of the most celebrated painters during the Dutch Golden Age. —EDS.

Isabella Coymans, a married couple, is remarkable not just for the full, friendly smiles on each face but for the frank and mutual pleasure the couple take in each other.

In the 1800s, sprightly, pretty women began appearing in advertisements for everything from beverages to those newfangled Kodak Land cameras.[6] Women's faces were no longer impassive, and their willingness to bestow status, to offer, proffer, and yield, was most definitely promoted by their smiling images. The culture appeared to have turned the smile, originally a bond shared between intimates, into a socially required display that sold capitalist ideology as well as kitchen appliances. And female viewers soon began to emulate these highly idealized pictures. Many longed to be more like her, that perpetually smiling female. She seemed so beautiful. So content. So whole.

By the middle of the nineteenth century, the bulk of America's smile burden was falling primarily to women and African-American slaves, providing a very portable means of protection, a way of saying, "I'm harmless. I won't assert myself here." It reassured those in power to see signs of gratitude and contentment in the faces of subordinates. As long ago as 1963, adman David Ogilvy declared the image of a woman smiling approvingly at a product clichéd, but we've yet to get the message. Cheerful Americans still appear in ads today, smiling somewhat less disingenuously than they smiled during the middle of the century, but smiling broadly nonetheless.

Other countries have been somewhat reluctant to import our "Don't worry, be happy" American smiles. When McDonald's opened in Moscow not long ago [1990] and when EuroDisney debuted in France last year [1992], the Americans involved in both business ventures complained that they couldn't get the natives they'd employed to smile worth a damn.

Europeans visiting the United States for the first time are often surprised   20 at just how often Americans smile. But when you look at our history, the relentless good humor (or, at any rate, the pretense of it) falls into perspective. The American wilderness was developed on the assumption that this country had a shortage of people in relation to its possibilities. In countries with a more rigid class structure or caste system, fewer people are as captivated by the idea of quickly winning friends and influencing people. Here in the States, however, every stranger is a potential associate. Our smiles bring new people on board. The American smile is a democratic version of a curtsy or doffed hat, since, in this land of free equals, we're not especially formal about the ways we greet social superiors.

The civil rights movement never addressed the smile burden by name, but activists worked on their own to set new facial norms. African-American

---

6 ***Kodak Land camera:*** An instant camera, invented by American scientist Edwin Land and first sold in 1948. —EDS.

males stopped smiling on the streets in the 1960s, happily aware of the unsettling effect this action had on the white population. The image of the simpleminded, smiling, white-toothed black was rejected as blatantly racist, and it gradually retreated into the distance. However, like the women of Sparta and the wives of samurai, who were expected to look happy upon learning their sons or husbands had died in battle, contemporary American women have yet to unilaterally declare their faces their own property.

For instance, imagine a woman at a morning business meeting being asked if she could make a spontaneous and concise summation of a complicated project she's been struggling to get under control for months. She might draw the end of her mouth back and clench her teeth—Eek!—in a protective response, a polite, restrained expression of her surprise, not unlike the expression of a conscientious young schoolgirl being told to get out paper and pencil for a pop quiz. At the same time, the woman might be feeling resentful of the supervisor who sprang the request, but she fears taking that person on. So she holds back a comment. The whole performance resolves in a weird grin collapsing into a nervous smile that conveys discomfort and unpreparedness. A pointed remark by way of explanation or self-defense might've worked better for her—but her mouth was otherwise engaged.

We'd do well to realize just how much our smiles misrepresent us, and swear off for good the self-deprecating grins and ritual displays of deference. Real smiles have beneficial physiological effects, according to Paul Ekman. False ones do nothing for us at all.

"Smiles are as important as sound bites on television," insists producer and media coach Heidi Berenson, who has worked with many of Washington's most famous faces. "And women have always been better at understanding this than men. But the smile I'm talking about is not a cutesy smile. It's an authoritative smile. A genuine smile. Properly timed, it's tremendously powerful."

To limit a woman to one expression is like editing down an orchestra to one instrument. And the search for more authentic means of expression isn't easy in a culture in which women are still expected to be magnanimous smilers, helpmates in crisis, and curators of everybody else's morale. But change is already floating in the high winds. We see a boon in assertive female comedians who are proving that women can *dish out* smiles, not just wear them. Actress Demi Moore has stated that she doesn't like to take smiling roles. Nike is running ads that show unsmiling women athletes sweating, reaching, pushing themselves. These women aren't overly concerned with issues of rapport; they're not being "nice" girls—they're working out.

If a woman's smile were truly her own, to be smiled or not, according to how the *woman* felt, rather than according to what someone else needed, she would smile more spontaneously, without ulterior, hidden motives. As

Rainer Maria Rilke[7] wrote in *The Journal of My Other Self*, "Her smile was not meant to be seen by anyone and served its whole purpose in being smiled."

That smile is my long-term aim. In the meantime, I hope to stabilize on the smile continuum somewhere between the eliciting grin of Farrah Fawcett[8] and the haughty smirk of Jeane Kirkpatrick.[9] ▮

The Reader's Presence

1. Cunningham presents an informative précis of the causes and effects of smiling in Western culture. Consider the points of view from which she addresses this subject. Summarize and evaluate her treatment of smiling from psychological, physiological, sociological, and historical points of view. Which do you find most incisive? Why? What other points of view does she introduce into her discussion of smiling? What effects do they create? What does she identify as the benefits (and the disadvantages) of smiling?

2. At what point in this essay does Cunningham address the issue of gender? Characterize the language she uses to introduce this issue. She distinguishes between the different patterns—and the consequences—experienced by men and women who smile. Summarize these differences and assess the nature and the extent of the evidence she provides for each of her points. What more general distinctions does she make about various kinds of smiles? What are their different purposes and degrees of intensity? What information does she provide about smiling as an issue of nationality and race? What is the overall purpose of this essay? Where—and how—does Cunningham create and sustain a sense of her own presence in this essay? What does she set as her personal goal in relation to smiling?

3. **CONNECTIONS:** Cunningham presents an explanation of the causes of an activity that few of her readers think of in both scientific and historical terms. Compare her use of science and history to that of Stephen Jay Gould in "Sex, Drugs, Disasters, and the Extinction of Dinosaurs" (page 430). How does each writer establish her or his authority in these fields? What is each writer's argument? To what extent does each argument depend on factual evidence?

---

[7] ***Rainer Maria Rilke*** (1875–1926): Austrian poet, art critic, and author of *Letters to a Young Poet* (1929) and *The Journal of My Other Self* (1930).—EDS.

[8] ***Farrah Fawcett*** (1947–2009): American actress who became an international celebrity after appearing in the television series *Charlie's Angels* in 1976.—EDS.

[9] ***Jeane Kirkpatrick*** (1926–2006): An American ambassador to the United Nations during the administration of President Ronald Reagan.—EDS.

Don DeLillo

IN THE RUINS OF THE FUTURE: REFLECTIONS ON TERROR, LOSS, AND TIME IN THE SHADOW OF SEPTEMBER

DON DELILLO was born in the Bronx, New York, in 1936, the son of Italian immigrants, and grew up in an Italian American neighborhood. He attended Cardinal Hayes High School and then majored in communication arts at Fordham University, graduating with a BA in 1958. During the 1960s, he worked as a copywriter for the renowned ad agency Ogilvy and Mather. He did not start writing his first novel, *Americana*, until about 1967. But after it appeared in print in 1971, he continued to write prolifically, publishing five novels in only seven years: *End Zone* (1972), *Great Jones Street* (1973), *Ratner's Star* (1976), *Players* (1977), and *Running Dog* (1978). Although popular with reviewers and a small but fanatical readership, DeLillo had difficulty reaching a wide audience until the publication of *White Noise* (1985), which won the National Book Award, and *Mao II* (1991), which won the PEN/Faulkner Award. DeLillo's work surveys recent history and portrays American culture since the 1950s, dealing with such themes as paranoia, terrorist violence, and consumerism. His novels include *Libra* (1988), *Underworld* (1997), *The Body Artist* (2001), *Cosmopolis* (2003), and *Falling Man* (2007), which traces the changes in people's perception of the world and themselves after 9/11. His essay "In the Ruins of the Future," which first appeared in *Harper's* in December 2001, was written just weeks after the September 11 attack and appears to be the seed from which his later novel *Falling Man* emerged. His most recent book, *Point Omega*, was published in 2010.

> "Language lives in everything it touches and can be an agent of redemption, the thing that delivers us, paradoxically, from history's flat, thin, tight, and relentless designs."

DeLillo's work reflects a fascination with language—its power to free the writer and to shape narrative and history. "Language lives in everything it touches and can be an agent of redemption, the thing that delivers us, paradoxically, from history's flat, thin, tight, and relentless designs, its arrangement of stark pages, and that allows us to find an unconstraining otherness, a free veer from time and place and fate."

I.

IN THE PAST DECADE the surge of capital markets has dominated discourse and shaped global consciousness. Multinational corporations have come to seem more vital and influential than governments. The dramatic climb of the Dow and the speed of the Internet summoned us all to live permanently in the future, in the utopian glow of cyber-capital, because there is no memory there and this is where markets are uncontrolled and investment potential has no limit.

All this changed on September 11. Today, again, the world narrative belongs to terrorists. But the primary target of the men who attacked the Pentagon and the World Trade Center was not the global economy. It is America that drew their fury. It is the high gloss of our modernity. It is the thrust of our technology. It is our perceived godlessness. It is the blunt force of our foreign policy. It is the power of American culture to penetrate every wall, home, life, and mind.

Terror's response is a narrative that has been developing over years, only now becoming inescapable. It is *our* lives and minds that are occupied now. This catastrophic event changes the way we think and act, moment to moment, week to week, for unknown weeks and months to come, and steely years. Our world, parts of our world, have crumbled into theirs, which means we are living in a place of danger and rage.

The protesters in Genoa, Prague, Seattle, and other cities want to decelerate the global momentum that seemed to be driving unmindfully toward a landscape of consumer-robots and social instability, with the chance of self-determination probably diminishing for most people in most countries. Whatever acts of violence marked the protests, most of the men and women involved tend to be a moderating influence, trying to slow things down, even things out, hold off the white-hot future.

The terrorists of September 11 want to bring back the past.   5

II

Our tradition of free expression and our justice system's provisions for the rights of the accused can only seem an offense to men bent on suicidal terror.

We are rich, privileged, and strong, but they are willing to die. This is the edge they have, the fire of aggrieved belief. We live in a wide world, routinely filled with exchange of every sort, an open circuit of work, talk, family, and expressible feeling. The terrorist, planted in a Florida town, pushing his supermarket cart, nodding to his neighbor, lives in a far narrower format. This is his edge, his strength. Plots reduce the world. He builds a plot around his anger and our indifference. He lives a certain kind of apartness, hard and tight. This is not the self-watcher, the soft white dangling boy who shoots someone to keep from disappearing into himself. The terrorist shares a secret and a self. At a certain point he and his brothers may begin to feel less motivated by politics and personal hatred than by brotherhood itself. They share the codes and protocols of their mission here and something deeper as well, a vision of judgment and devastation.

Does the sight of a woman pushing a stroller soften the man to her humanity and vulnerability, and her child's as well, and all the people he is here to kill?

This is his edge, that he does not see her. Years here, waiting, taking flying lessons, making the routine gestures of community and home, the credit card, the bank account, the post-office box. All tactical, linked, layered. He knows who we are and what we mean in the world—an idea, a righteous fever in the brain. But there is no defenseless human at the end of his gaze.

The sense of disarticulation we hear in the term "Us and Them" has never been so striking, at either end.   10

We can tell ourselves that whatever we've done to inspire bitterness, distrust, and rancor, it was not so damnable as to bring this day down on our heads. But there is no logic in apocalypse. They have gone beyond the bounds of passionate payback. This is heaven and hell, a sense of armed martyrdom as the surpassing drama of human experience.

He pledges his submission to God and meditates on the blood to come.

III

The [George W.] Bush Administration was feeling a nostalgia for the Cold War. This is over now. Many things are over. The narrative ends in the rubble, and it is left to us to create the counter-narrative.

There are a hundred thousand stories crisscrossing New York, Washington, and the world. Where we were, whom we know, what we've seen or heard. There are the doctors' appointments that saved lives, the cell phones that were used to report the hijackings. Stories generating others and people running north out of the rumbling smoke and ash. Men running in suits and ties, women who'd lost their shoes, cops running from the skydive of all that towering steel.

People running for their lives are part of the story that is left to us.   15

There are stories of heroism and encounters with dread. There are stories that carry around their edges the luminous ring of coincidence, fate, or premonition. They take us beyond the hard numbers of dead and missing and give us a glimpse of elevated being. For a hundred who are arbitrarily dead, we need to find one person saved by a flash of forewarning. There are configurations that chill and awe us both. Two women on two planes, best of friends, who die together and apart, Tower 1 and Tower 2. What desolate epic tragedy might bear the weight of such juxtaposition? But we can also ask what symmetry, bleak and touching both, takes one friend, spares the other's grief?

The brother of one of the women worked in one of the towers. He managed to escape.

In Union Square Park, about two miles north of the attack site, the improvised memorials are another part of our response. The flags, flower beds, and votive candles, the lamppost hung with paper airplanes, the passages from the Koran and the Bible, the letters and poems, the cardboard John Wayne, the children's drawings of the Twin Towers, the hand-painted signs for Free Hugs, Free Back Rubs, the graffiti of love and peace on the tall equestrian statue.

There are many photographs of missing persons, some accompanied by hopeful lists of identifying features. (Man with panther tattoo, upper right arm.) There is the saxophonist, playing softly. There is the sculptured flag of rippling copper and aluminum, six feet long, with two young people still attending to the finer details of the piece.

Then there are the visitors to the park. The artifacts on display represent   20 the confluence of a number of cultural tides, patriotic and multidevotional and retro hippie. The visitors move quietly in the floating aromas of candlewax, roses, and bus fumes. There are many people this mild evening, and in their voices, manner, clothing, and in the color of their skin they recapitulate the mix we see in the photocopied faces of the lost.

For the next fifty years, people who were not in the area when the attacks occurred will claim to have been there. In time, some of them will believe it. Others will claim to have lost friends or relatives, although they did not.

This is also the counter-narrative, a shadow history of false memories and imagined loss.

The Internet is a counter-narrative, shaped in part by rumor, fantasy, and mystical reverberation.

The cell phones, the lost shoes, the handkerchiefs mashed in the faces of running men and women. The box cutters and credit cards. The paper that came streaming out of the towers and drifted across the river to Brooklyn back yards: status reports, résumés, insurance forms. Sheets of paper driven into concrete, according to witnesses. Paper slicing into truck tires, fixed there.

These are among the small objects and more marginal stories in the   25 sifted ruins of the day. We need them, even the common tools of the terrorists, to set against the massive spectacle that continues to seem unmanageable, too powerful a thing to set into our frame of practiced response.

IV

Ash was spattering the windows. Karen was half dressed, grabbing the kids and trying to put on some clothes and talking with her husband and scooping things to take out to the corridor, and they looked at her, twin girls, as if she had fourteen heads.

September 11, 2001: moments after the second tower in the World Trade Center had collapsed.

They stayed in the corridor for a while, thinking there might be secondary explosions. They waited, and began to feel safer, and went back to the apartment.

At the next impact, Marc knew in the sheerest second before the shock wave broadsided their building that it was a second plane, impossible, striking the second tower. Their building was two blocks away, and he'd thought the first crash was an accident.

They went back to the hallway, where others began to gather, fifteen or twenty people.

Karen ran back for a cell phone, a cordless phone, a charger, water, sweaters, snacks for the kids, and then made a quick dash to the bedroom for her wedding ring.

From the window she saw people running in the street, others locked shoulder to shoulder, immobilized, with debris coming down on them. People were trampled, struck by falling objects, and there was ash and paper everywhere, paper whipping through the air, no sign of light or sky.

Cell phones were down. They talked on the cordless, receiving information measured out in eyedrops. They were convinced that the situation outside was far more grave than it was here.

Smoke began to enter the corridor.

Then the first tower fell. She thought it was a bomb. When she talked to someone on the phone and found out what had happened, she felt a surreal relief. Bombs and missiles were not falling everywhere in the city. It was not all-out war, at least not yet.

Marc was in the apartment getting chairs for the older people, for the woman who'd had hip surgery. When he heard the first low drumming rumble, he stood in a strange dead calm and said, "Something is happening." It sounded exactly like what it was, a tall tower collapsing.   35

The windows were surfaced with ash now. Blacked out completely, and he wondered what was out there. What remained to be seen and did he want to see it?

They all moved into the stairwell, behind a fire door, but smoke kept coming in. It was gritty ash, and they were eating it.

He ran back inside, grabbing towels off the racks and washcloths out of drawers and drenching them in the sink, and filling his bicycle water bottles, and grabbing the kids' underwear.

He thought the crush of buildings was the thing to fear most. This is what would kill them.

Karen was on the phone, talking to a friend in the district attorney's office, about half a mile to the north. She was pleading for help. She begged, pleaded, and hung up. For the next hour a detective kept calling with advice and encouragement.   40

Marc came back out to the corridor. I think we *might* die, he told himself, hedging his sense of what would happen next.

The detective told Karen to stay where they were.

When the second tower fell, my heart fell with it. I called Marc, who is my nephew, on his cordless. I couldn't stop thinking of the size of the towers and the meager distance between those buildings and his. He answered, we talked. I have no memory of the conversation except for his final remark, slightly urgent, concerning someone on the other line, who might be sending help.

Smoke was seeping out of the elevator shaft now. Karen was saying goodbye to her father in Oregon. Not hello-goodbye. But goodbye-I-think-we-are-going-to-die. She thought smoke would be the thing that did it.

People sat on chairs along the walls. They chatted about practical matters. They sang songs with the kids. The kids in the group were cooperative because the adults were damn scared.   45

There was an improvised rescue in progress. Karen's friend and a colleague made their way down from Centre Street, turning up with two policemen they'd enlisted en route. They had dust masks and a destination, and they searched every floor for others who might be stranded in the building.

They came out into a world of ash and near night. There was no one else to be seen now on the street. Gray ash covering the cars and pavement, ash falling in large flakes, paper still drifting down, discarded shoes, strollers, briefcases. The members of the group were masked and toweled, children in adults' arms, moving east and then north on Nassau Street, trying not to look around, only what's immediate, one step and then another, all closely focused, a pregnant woman, a newborn, a dog.

They were covered in ash when they reached shelter at Pace University, where there was food and water, and kind and able staff members, and a gas-leak scare, and more running people.

Workers began pouring water on the group. *Stay wet, stay wet.* This was the theme of the first half hour.

Later a line began to form along the food counter.   50

Someone said, "I don't want cheese on that."

Someone said, "I like it better not so cooked."

Not so incongruous really, just people alive and hungry, beginning to be themselves again.

V

Technology is our fate, our truth. It is what we mean when we call ourselves the only superpower on the planet. The materials and methods we devise make it possible for us to claim our future. We don't have to depend on God or the prophets or other astonishments. We are the astonishment. The miracle is what we ourselves produce, the systems and networks that change the way we live and think.

But whatever great skeins of technology lie ahead, ever more complex,   55
connective, precise, micro-fractional, the future has yielded, for now, to medieval expedience, to the old slow furies of cutthroat religion.

Kill the enemy and pluck out his heart.

If others in less scientifically advanced cultures were able to share, wanted to share, some of the blessings of our technology, without a threat to their faith or traditions, would they need to rely on a God in whose name they kill the innocent? Would they need to invent a God who rewards violence against the innocent with a promise of "infinite paradise," in the words of a handwritten letter found in the luggage of one of the hijackers?

For all those who may want what we've got, there are all those who do not. These are the men who have fashioned a morality of destruction. They want what they used to have before the waves of Western influence. They surely see themselves as the elect of God whether or not they follow the central precepts of Islam. It is the presumptive right of those who choose violence and death to speak directly to God. They will kill and then die. Or they will die first, in the cockpit, in clean shoes, according to instructions in the letter.

Six days after the attacks, the territory below Canal Street is hedged with barricades. There are few civilians in the street. Police at some checkpoints, troops in camouflage gear at others, wearing gas masks, and a pair of state troopers in conversation, and ten burly men striding east in hard hats, work pants, and NYPD jackets. A shop owner tries to talk a cop into letting him enter his place of business. He is a small elderly man with a Jewish accent, but there is no relief today. Garbage bags are everywhere in high broad stacks. The area is bedraggled and third-worldish, with an air of permanent emergency, everything surfaced in ash.

It is possible to pass through some checkpoints, detour around others.   60
At Chambers Street I look south through the links of the National Rent-A-Fence barrier. There stands the smoky remnant of filigree that marks the last tall thing, the last sign in the mire of wreckage that there were towers here that dominated the skyline for over a quarter of a century.

Ten days later and a lot closer, I stand at another barrier with a group of people, looking directly into the strands of openwork façade. It is almost too close. It is almost Roman, I-beams for stonework, but not nearly so salvageable. Many here describe the scene to others on cell phones.

"Oh my god I'm standing here," says the man next to me.

The World Trade towers were not only an emblem of advanced technology but a justification, in a sense, for technology's irresistible will to realize in solid form whatever becomes theoretically allowable. Once defined, every limit must be reached. The tactful sheathing of the towers was intended to reduce the direct threat of such straight-edge enormity, a giantism that eased over the years into something a little more familiar and comfortable, even dependable in a way.

Now a small group of men have literally altered our skyline. We have fallen back in time and space. It is their technology that marks our moments, the small lethal devices, the remote-control detonators they fashion out of radios, or the larger technology they borrow from us, passenger jets that become manned missiles.

Maybe this is a grim subtext of their enterprise. They see something   65
innately destructive in the nature of technology. It brings death to their customs and beliefs. Use it as what it is, a thing that kills.

VI

Nearly eleven years ago, during the engagement in the Persian Gulf, people had trouble separating the war from coverage of the war. After the first euphoric days, coverage became limited. The rush of watching all that eerie green night-vision footage, shot from fighter jets in combat, had been so intense that it became hard to honor the fact that the war was still going on, untelevised. A layer of consciousness had been stripped away. People shuffled around, muttering. They were lonely for their war.

The events of September 11 were covered unstintingly. There was no confusion of roles on TV. The raw event was one thing, the coverage another. The event dominated the medium. It was bright and totalizing, and some of us said it was unreal. When we say a thing is unreal, we mean it is too real, a phenomenon so unaccountable and yet so bound to the power of objective fact that we can't tilt it to the slant of our perceptions. First the planes struck the towers. After a time it became possible for us to absorb this, barely. But when the towers fell. When the rolling smoke began moving downward, floor to floor. This was so vast and terrible that it was outside imagining even as it happened. We could not catch up to it. But it was real, punishingly so, an expression of the physics of structural limits and a void in one's soul, and there was the huge antenna falling out of the sky, straight down, blunt end first, like an arrow moving backward in time.

The event itself has no purchase on the mercies of analogy or simile. We have to take the shock and horror as it is. But living language is not diminished. The writer wants to understand what this day has done to us. Is it too soon? We seem pressed for time, all of us. Time is scarcer now. There is a sense of compression, plans made hurriedly, time forced and distorted. But language is inseparable from the world that provokes it. The writer begins in the towers, trying to imagine the moment, desperately. Before politics, before history and religion, there is the primal terror. People falling from the towers hand in hand. This is part of the counter-narrative, hands and spirits joining, human beauty in the crush of meshed steel.

In its desertion of every basis for comparison, the event asserts its singularity. There is something empty in the sky. The writer tries to give memory, tenderness, and meaning to all that howling space.

VII

We like to think America invented the future. We are comfortable with the   70
future, intimate with it. But there are disturbances now, in large and small ways, a chain of reconsiderations. Where we live, how we travel, what we think about when we look at our children. For many people, the event has changed the grain of the most routine moment.

We may find that the ruin of the towers is implicit in other things. The new PalmPilot at fingertip's reach, the stretch limousine parked outside the hotel, the midtown skyscraper under construction, carrying the name of a major investment bank — all haunted in a way by what has happened, less assured in their authority, in the prerogatives they offer.

There is fear of other kinds of terrorism, the prospect that biological and chemical weapons will contaminate the air we breathe and the water we drink. There wasn't much concern about this after earlier terrorist acts. This time we are trying to name the future, not in our normally hopeful way but guided by dread.

What has already happened is sufficient to affect the air around us, psychologically. We are all breathing the fumes of lower Manhattan, where traces of the dead are everywhere, in the soft breeze off the river, on rooftops and windows, in our hair and on our clothes.

Think of a future in which the components of a microchip are the size of atoms. The devices that pace our lives will operate from the smart quantum spaces of pure information. Now think of people in countless thousands massing in anger and vowing revenge. Enlarged photos of martyrs and holy men dangle from balconies, and the largest images are those of a terrorist leader.

Two forces in the world, past and future. With the end of Communism, the ideas and principles of modern democracy were seen clearly to prevail, whatever the inequalities of the system itself. This is still the case. But now there is a global theocratic state, unboundaried and floating and so obsolete it must depend on suicidal fervor to gain its aims.

Ideas evolve and de-evolve, and history is turned on end.

VIII

On Friday of the first week a long series of vehicles moves slowly west on Canal Street. Dump trucks, flatbeds, sanitation sweepers. There are giant earthmovers making a tremendous revving sound. A scant number of pedestrians, some in dust masks, others just standing, watching, the indigenous people, clinging to walls and doorways, unaccustomed to traffic that doesn't bring buyers and sellers, goods and cash. The fire rescue car and state police cruiser, the staccato sirens of a line of police vans. Cops stand at the saw-horse barriers, trying to clear the way. Ambulances, cherry pickers, a fleet of Con Ed trucks, all this clamor moving south a few blocks ahead, into the cloud of sand and ash.

One month earlier I'd taken the same walk, early evening, among crowds of people, the panethnic swarm of shoppers, merchants, residents and passersby, with a few tourists as well, and the man at the curbstone doing acupoint massage, and the dreadlocked kid riding his bike on the sidewalk. This was the spirit of Canal Street, the old jostle and stir unchanged for many decades and bearing no sign of SoHo just above, with its restaurants and artists' lofts, or TriBeCa below, rich in architectural textures. Here were hardware bargains, car stereos, foam rubber and industrial plastics, the tattoo parlor and the pizza parlor.

Then I saw the woman on the prayer rug. I'd just turned the corner, heading south to meet some friends, and there she was, young and slender, in a silk headscarf. It was time for sunset prayer, and she was kneeling, upper body pitched toward the edge of the rug. She was partly concealed by a couple of vendors' carts, and no one seemed much to notice her. I think there was another woman seated on a folding chair near the curbstone. The figure on the rug faced east, which meant most immediately a storefront just a foot and a half from her tipped head but more distantly and pertinently toward Mecca, of course, the holiest city of Islam.

Some prayer rugs include a *mihrab* in their design, an arched element   80 representing the prayer niche in a mosque that indicates the direction of Mecca. The only locational guide the young women needed was the Manhattan grid.

I looked at her in prayer and it was clearer to me than ever, the daily sweeping taken-for-granted greatness of New York. The city will accommodate every language, ritual, belief, and opinion. In the rolls of the dead of September 11, all these vital differences were surrendered to the impact and flash. The bodies themselves are missing in large numbers. For the survivors, more grief. But the dead are their own nation and race, one identity, young or old, devout or unbelieving—a union of souls. During the *hadj*, the annual pilgrimage to Mecca, the faithful must eliminate every sign of status, income, and nationality, the men wearing identical strips of seamless white cloth, the women with covered heads, all recalling in prayer their fellowship with the dead.

Allahu akbar. God is great. ◼

The Reader's Presence

1. From the title's linking of the past and the future to statements such as "history is turned on end" (paragraph 76), DeLillo's essay is absorbed with time. Trace the way time is used in the piece. How does the writer make schematic use of past and future to evoke the warring forces of the world? How does he vary tenses and points of view to report the events of September 11 and their aftermath? Why is time central to DeLillo's understanding of these events?

2. For the most part, DeLillo's discussion of the terrorists themselves is unspecific with respect to nationality, religion, or political affiliation. He first mentions Islam several pages into the essay, in section V. How does DeLillo build the reader's sense of "the enemy"? How is Islam woven through the essay? Why might DeLillo resist giving too narrow an articulation of "us" and "them"?

3. **CONNECTIONS:** Compare DeLillo's account of the very recent past to Barbara Tuchman's history of the distant past in "'This Is the End of the World': The Black Death" (page 584). Which sections of DeLillo's essay read like a historian's account and which read more like the primary accounts of the plague's disastrous effects? Compare section IV to Michihiko Hachiya's journal of the days immediately following the bombing of Hiroshima in "From *Hiroshima Diary*" (page 107). Why do you think DeLillo varies his style so dramatically from section to section? What are the advantages and disadvantages of writing about an event whose meaning is still being discovered?

Joan Didion

ON MORALITY

The author of novels, short stories, screenplays, and essays, **JOAN DIDION** (b. 1934) began her career in 1956 as a staff writer at *Vogue* magazine in New York. In 1963, she published her first novel, *Run River*, and the following year returned to her native California. Didion's essays have appeared in periodicals ranging from *Mademoiselle* to the *National Review*. Her essay "On Morality" can be found in her collection of essays, *Slouching Towards Bethlehem* (1968). Didion's other nonfiction publications include *The White Album* (1979), *Salvador* (1983), *Miami* (1987), *After Henry* (1992), *Political Fictions* (2001), *Fixed Ideas: America since 9.11* (2003), and *Where I Was From* (2003). Her essays, written between 1968 and 2003, are collected in *We Tell Ourselves Stories in Order to Live* (2006). *The Year of Magical Thinking* (2005), Didion's account of grief and survival after the loss of her husband of forty years, John Gregory Dunne, and the near-fatal illness of their only child, won the 2005 National Book Award for Nonfiction; Didion adapted her tragic memoir into a play, which opened on Broadway in 2007, starring Vanessa Redgrave and directed by David Hare.

> "I write entirely to find out what's on my mind, what I'm thinking, what I'm looking at, what I'm seeing and what it means, what I want and what I'm afraid of."

Didion has defined a writer as "a person whose most absorbed and passionate hours are spent arranging words on pieces of paper. I write entirely to find out what's on my mind, what I'm thinking, what I'm looking at, what I'm seeing and what it means, what I want and what I'm afraid of." She has also said that "all writing is an attempt to find out what matters, to find the pattern in disorder, to find the grammar in the shimmer. Actually I don't know whether you find the grammar in the shimmer or you impose a grammar on the shimmer, but I am quite specific about the grammar—I mean it literally. The scene that you see in your mind finds its own structure; the structure dictates the arrangement of the words. . . . All the writer has to do really is to find the words." However, she warns, "You have to be alone to do this."

AS IT HAPPENS I am in Death Valley, in a room at the Enterprise Motel and Trailer Park, and it is July, and it is hot. In fact it is 119°. I cannot seem to make the air conditioner work, but there is a small refrigerator, and I can wrap ice cubes in a towel and hold them against the small of my back. With the help of the ice cubes I have been trying to think, because *The American Scholar* asked me to, in some abstract way about "morality," a word I distrust more every day, but my mind veers inflexibly toward the particular.

Here are some particulars. At midnight last night, on the road in from Las Vegas to Death Valley Junction, a car hit a shoulder and turned over. The driver, very young and apparently drunk, was killed instantly. His girl was found alive but bleeding internally, deep in shock. I talked this afternoon to the nurse who had driven the girl to the nearest doctor, 185 miles across the floor of the Valley and three ranges of lethal mountain road. The nurse explained that her husband, a talc miner, had stayed on the highway with the boy's body until the coroner could get over the mountains from Bishop, at dawn today. "You can't just leave a body on the highway," she said. "It's immoral."

It was one instance in which I did not distrust the word, because she meant something quite specific. She meant that if a body is left alone for even a few minutes on the desert, the coyotes close in and eat the flesh. Whether or not a corpse is torn apart by coyotes may seem only a sentimental consideration, but of course it is more: one of the promises we make to one another is that we will try to retrieve our casualties, try not to abandon our dead to the coyotes. If we have been taught to keep our promises—if, in the simplest terms, our upbringing is good enough—we stay with the body, or have bad dreams.

I am talking, of course, about the kind of social code that is sometimes called, usually pejoratively, "wagon-train morality." In fact that is precisely what it is. For better or worse, we are what we learned as children: my own childhood was illuminated by graphic litanies of the grief awaiting those who failed in their loyalties to each other. The Donner-Reed Party,[1] starving in the Sierra snows, all the ephemera of civilizations gone save that one vestigial taboo, the provision that no one should eat his own blood kin. The Jayhawkers,[2] who quarreled and separated not far from where I am tonight. Some of them died in the Funerals and some of them died down near Badwater[3] and most of the rest of them died in the Panamints.[4] A woman who got through gave the Valley its name. Some might say that the Jayhawkers were killed by the desert summer, and the Donner Party by the mountain winter, by circumstances beyond control; we were taught instead that they

[1] **Donner-Reed Party:** A group of pioneers who set out for California in a wagon train. Delayed by a series of accidents, they spent the winter of 1846–1847 snowbound in the Sierra Nevada mountains. To survive, some resorted to cannibalism, eating those who had died of sickness or starvation.—EDS.

[2] **Jayhawkers:** A group of 36 single men who left Illinois in April 1849 to cross the plains in search of gold in California. After getting lost in what is now known as Death Valley and struggling with hunger and thirst, 33 arrived at the San Francisquito Ranch north of Los Angeles in February 1850.—EDS.

[3] **Badwater:** An unincorporated community in Badwater Basin, Death Valley, California, the point of lowest elevation in the United States.—EDS.

[4] **Panamints:** A short, rugged, mountain range on the northern edge of the Mojave Desert, in Death Valley National Park, Inyo County, California.—EDS.

had somewhere abdicated their responsibilities, somehow breached their primary loyalties, or they would not have found themselves helpless in the mountain winter or the desert summer, would not have given way to acrimony, would not have deserted one another, would not have *failed*. In brief, we heard such stories as cautionary tales, and they still suggest the only kind of "morality" that seems to me to have any but the most potentially mendacious meaning.

You are quite possibly impatient with me by now; I am talking, you want to say, about a "morality" so primitive that it scarcely deserves the name, a code that has as its point only survival, not the attainment of the ideal good. Exactly. Particularly out here tonight, in this country so ominous and terrible that to live in it is to live with antimatter, it is difficult to believe that "the good" is a knowable quantity. Let me tell you what it is like out here tonight. Stories travel at night on the desert. Someone gets in his pickup and drives a couple of hundred miles for a beer, and he carries news of what is happening, back wherever he came from. Then he drives another hundred miles for another beer, and passes along stories from the last place as well as from the one before; it is a network kept alive by people whose instincts tell them that if they do not keep moving at night on the desert they will lose all reason. Here is a story that is going around the desert tonight: over across the Nevada line, sheriff's deputies are diving in some underground pools, trying to retrieve a couple of bodies known to be in the hole. The widow of one of the drowned boys is over there; she is eighteen, and pregnant, and is said not to leave the hole. The divers go down and come up, and she just stands there and stares into the water. They have been diving for ten days but have found no bottom to the caves, no bodies and no trace of them, only the black 90° water going down and down and down, and a single translucent fish, not classified. The story tonight is that one of the divers has been hauled up incoherent, out of his head, shouting—until they got him out of there so that the widow could not hear—about water that got hotter instead of cooler as he went down, about light flickering through the water, about magma, about underground nuclear testing.

That is the tone stories take out here, and there are quite a few of them tonight. And it is more than the stories alone. Across the road at the Faith Community Church a couple of dozen old people, come here to live in trailers and die in the sun, are holding a prayer sing. I cannot hear them and do not want to. What I can hear are occasional coyotes and a constant chorus of "Baby the Rain Must Fall" from the jukebox in the Snake Room next door, and if I were also to hear those dying voices, those Midwestern voices drawn to this lunar country for some unimaginable atavistic rites, *rock of ages cleft for me*, I think I would lose my own reason. Every now and then I imagine I hear a rattlesnake, but my husband says that it is a faucet, a paper rustling, the wind. Then he stands by a window, and plays a flashlight over the dry wash outside.

5

What does it mean? It means nothing manageable. There is some sinister hysteria in the air out here tonight, some hint of the monstrous perversion to which any human idea can come. "I followed my own conscience." "I did what I thought was right." How many madmen have said it and meant it? How many murderers? Klaus Fuchs[5] said it, and the men who committed the Mountain Meadows Massacre[6] said it, and Alfred Rosenberg[7] said it. And, as we are rotely and rather presumptuously reminded by those who would say it now, Jesus said it. Maybe we have all said it, and maybe we have been wrong. Except on that most primitive level—our loyalties to those we love—what could be more arrogant than to claim the primacy of personal conscience? ("Tell me," a rabbi asked Daniel Bell when he said, as a child, that he did not believe in God. "Do you think God cares?") At least some of the time, the world appears to me as a painting by Hieronymous Bosch;[8] were I to follow my conscience then, it would lead me out onto the desert with Marion Faye, out to where he stood in *The Deer Park* looking east to Los Alamos and praying, as if for rain, that it would happen: "*. . . let it come and clear the rot and the stench and the stink, let it come for all of everywhere, just so it comes and the world stands clear in the white dead dawn.*"

Of course you will say that I do not have the right, even if I had the power, to inflict that unreasonable conscience upon you; nor do I want you to inflict your conscience, however reasonable, however enlightened, upon me. ("We must be aware of the dangers which lie in our most generous wishes," Lionel Trilling[9] once wrote. "Some paradox of our nature leads us, when once we have made our fellow men the objects of our enlightened interest, to go on to make them the objects of our pity, then of our wisdom, ultimately of our coercion.") That the ethic of conscience is intrinsically insidious seems scarcely a revelatory point, but it is one raised with increasing infrequency; even those who do raise it tend to segue with troubling readiness into the quite contradictory position that the ethic of conscience is dangerous when it is "wrong," and admirable when it is "right."

You see I want to be quite obstinate about insisting that we have no way of knowing—beyond that fundamental loyalty to the social code—what is "right" and what is "wrong," what is "good" and what "evil." I dwell so upon this because the most disturbing aspect of "morality" seems to me to be the frequency with which the word now appears; in the press, on television, in the most perfunctory kinds of conversation. Questions of straightforward

---

5 ***Klaus Fuchs*** (1911–1988): A German physicist and spy convicted in 1950 of providing research on the atomic bomb to the Soviet Union during and shortly after World War II.—EDS.

6 ***Mountain Meadows Massacre:*** The murder of 120 emigrants from Arkansas who were passing through southern Utah in September 1857 to California.—EDS.

7 ***Alfred Rosenberg*** (1893–1946): An early and intellectually influential member of the Nazi Party.—EDS.

8 ***Hieronymous Bosch*** (c. 1450–1516): A Dutch painter renowned for using fantastic imagery to illustrate moral and religious concepts and narratives.—EDS.

9 ***Lionel Trilling*** (1905–1975): An American literary critic, author, and educator.—EDS.

power (or survival) politics, questions of quite indifferent public policy, questions of almost anything: they are all assigned these factitious moral burdens. There is something facile going on, some self-indulgence at work. Of course we would all like to "believe" in something, like to assuage our private guilts in public causes, like to lose our tiresome selves; like, perhaps, to transform the white flag of defeat at home into the brave white banner of battle away from home. And of course it is all right to do that; that is how, immemorially, things have gotten done. But I think it is all right only so long as we do not delude ourselves about what we are doing, and why. It is all right only so long as we remember that all the *ad hoc* committees, all the picket lines, all the brave signatures in *The New York Times*, all the tools of agitprop straight across the spectrum, do not confer upon anyone any *ipso facto* virtue. It is all right only so long as we recognize that the end may or may not be expedient, may or may not be a good idea, but in any case has nothing to do with "morality." Because when we start deceiving ourselves into thinking not that we want something or need something, not that it is a pragmatic necessity for us to have it, but that it is a *moral imperative* that we have it, then is when we join the fashionable madmen, and then is when the thin whine of hysteria is heard in the land, and then is when we are in bad trouble. And I suspect we are already there. ●

The Reader's Presence

1. The simple, direct, and hard-edged prose of Didion's essay demonstrates her remarkable ability to discover in her own experience concrete parallels to an abstract issue: the state of American values. In the opening paragraph, Didion states that *morality* is "a word I distrust." How does she illustrate this statement? What abstract point does she make with the examples she introduces? What does Didion say the consequence would be if we were to abandon a dead body? Does she mean this consequence to be taken literally or figuratively or both? Point to specific passages to support your response. What does Didion mean by the phrase "wagon-train morality" (paragraph 4)?

2. Create a point-by-point summary of Didion's thoughts on morality. What percentage of the summary is specific and concrete? What percentage is abstract? Using the examples in this essay, show how Didion demonstrates what she calls the tendency of her mind to veer "inflexibly toward the particular" (paragraph 1). When does Didion's essay return to considering morality in abstract terms? Why do you think Didion allows the essay to return to an abstract consideration of morality? With what effect(s)?

3. **CONNECTIONS:**   Didion's essay focuses on moral issues and values in contemporary American life. How would you distinguish between "morality" and "ethics"? As soon as you think you have a clear distinction in mind, read Stephen L. Carter's essay "The Insufficiency of Honesty" (page 337). In what specific ways are the distinctions Carter draws between "honesty" and "integrity" similar to—and different from—the distinctions you have drawn between "morality" and "ethics"? Which distinction do you find most clear and convincing? Explain why, and point to specific passages in each essay to support your response.

Annie Dillard
THE DEATH OF A MOTH

ANNIE DILLARD (b. 1945) was awarded the Pulitzer Prize for general nonfiction in 1974 for *Pilgrim at Tinker Creek*, which she describes (borrowing from Henry David Thoreau) as "a meteorological journal of the mind." She graduated from Hollins College in 1967; Tinker Creek is nearby. She has also published poetry in *Tickets for a Prayer Wheel* (1975) and *Mornings Like This: Found Poems* (1995), literary theory in *Living by Fiction* (1982), essays in *Teaching a Stone to Talk: Expeditions and Encounters* (1982) and *For the Time Being* (1999), and an autobiography in *An American Childhood* (1987). Dillard's first novel was *The Living* (1992), and her most recent is *The Maytrees* (2007); the *Annie Dillard Reader* was published in 1994. She was contributing editor to *Harper's* magazine for almost a decade, and she taught creative writing at Wesleyan University where she is now professor emeritus. "The Death of a Moth" first appeared in *Harper's* magazine in May, 1976.

> **"A sentence is a machine; it has a job to do. An extra word is like a sock in a machine."**

In her 1997 essay "Advice to Young Writers," Dillard argues, "Don't use any extra words. A sentence is a machine; it has a job to do. An extra word in a sentence is like a sock in a machine."

I LIVE ALONE WITH CATS who sleep on my legs. There is a yellow one, and a black one whose name is Small. In the morning I joke to the black one, Do you remember last night? Do you remember? I throw them both out before breakfast, so I can eat.

There is a spider, too, in the bathroom, of uncertain lineage, bulbous at the abdomen and drab, whose six-inch mess of web works, works somehow, works miraculously, to keep her alive and me amazed. The web is in the corner behind the toilet, connecting tile wall to tile wall. The house is new, the bathroom immaculate, save for the spider, her web, and the sixteen or so corpses she's tossed to the floor.

The corpses appear to be mostly sow bugs, those little armadillo creatures who live to travel flat out in houses, and die round. In addition to sow-bug husks, hollow and sipped empty of color, there are what seem to be two or three wingless moth bodies, one new flake of earwig, and three spider carcasses crinkled and clenched.

I wonder on what fool's errand an earwig, or a moth, or a sow bug, would visit that clean corner of the house behind the toilet; I have not noticed any blind parades of sow bugs blundering into corners. Yet they do hazard there, at a rate of more than one a week, and the spider thrives. Yesterday she was working on the earwig, mouth on gut; today he's on the floor. It must take a certain genius to throw things away from there, to find a straight line through that sticky tangle to the floor.

Today the earwig shines darkly, and gleams, what there is of him: a dor-   5
sal curve of thorax and abdomen, and a smooth pair of pincers by which I knew his name. Next week, if the other bodies are any indication, he'll be shrunk and gray, webbed to the floor with dust. The sow bugs beside him are curled and empty, fragile, a breath away from brittle fluff. The spiders lie on their sides, translucent and ragged, their legs drying in knots. The moths stagger against each other, headless, in a confusion of arcing strips of chi-tin like peeling varnish, like a jumble of buttresses for cathedral vaults, like nothing resembling moths, so that I would hesitate to call them moths, except that I have had some experience with the figure Moth reduced to a nub.

Two summers ago I was camped alone in the Blue Ridge Mountains of Virginia. I had hauled myself and gear up there to read, among other things, *The Day on Fire*, by James Ullman, a novel about Rimbaud that had made me want to be a writer when I was sixteen; I was hoping it would do it again. So I read every day sitting under a tree by my tent, while warblers sang in the leaves overhead and bristle worms trailed their inches over the twiggy dirt at my feet; and I read every night by candlelight, while barred owls called in the forest and pale moths seeking mates massed round my head in the clearing, where my light made a ring.

Moths kept flying into the candle. They would hiss and recoil, reeling upside down in the shadows among my cooking pans. Or they would singe their wings and fall, and their hot wings, as if melted, would stick to the first thing they touched—a pan, a lid, a spoon—so that the snagged moths could struggle only in tiny arcs, unable to flutter free. These I could release by a quick flip with a stick; in the morning I would find my cooking stuff deco-rated with torn flecks of moth wings, ghostly triangles of shiny dust here and there on the aluminum. So I read, and boiled water, and replenished candles, and read on.

One night a moth flew into the candle, was caught, burnt dry, and held. I must have been staring at the candle, or maybe I looked up when a shadow crossed my page; at any rate, I saw it all. A golden female moth, a biggish one with a two-inch wingspread, flapped into the fire, dropped abdomen into the wet wax, stuck, flamed, and frazzled in a second. Her moving wings ignited like tissue paper, like angels' wings, enlarging the circle of light in the clearing and creating out of the darkness the sudden blue sleeves of my sweater, the green leaves of jewelweed by my side, the ragged red trunk of a pine; at once the light contracted again and the moth's wings vanished in a fine, foul smoke. At the same time, her six legs clawed, curled, blackened, and ceased, disappearing utterly. And her head jerked in spasms, making a spattering noise; her antennae crisped and burnt away and her heaving mouthparts cracked like pistol fire. When it was all over, her head was, so far as I could determine, gone, gone the long way of her wings and legs. Her head was a hole lost to time. All that was left was the glowing horn shell of her abdomen and thorax—a fraying, partially collapsed gold tube jammed upright in the candle's round pool.

And then this moth-essence, this spectacular skeleton, began to act as a wick. She kept burning. The wax rose in the moth's body from her soaking abdomen to her thorax to the shattered hole where her head should have been, and widened into flame, a saffron-yellow flame that robed her to the ground like an immolating[1] monk. That candle had two wicks, two winding flames of identical light, side by side. The moth's head was fire. She burned for two hours, until I blew her out.

She burned for two hours without changing, without swaying or kneel-   10 ing—only glowing within, like a building fire glimpsed through silhouetted walls, like a hollow saint, like a flame-faced virgin gone to God, while I read by her light, kindled, while Rimbaud in Paris burnt out his brain in a thousand poems, while night pooled wetly at my feet.

So. That is why I think those hollow shreds on the bathroom floor are moths. I believe I know what moths look like, in any state.

I have three candles here on the table which I disentangle from the plants and light when visitors come. The cats avoid them, although Small's tail caught fire once; I rubbed it out before she noticed. I don't mind living alone. I like eating alone and reading. I don't mind sleeping alone. The only time I mind being alone is when something is funny; then, when I am laughing at something funny, I wish someone were around. Sometimes I think it is pretty funny that I sleep alone. ◼

The Reader's Presence

1. What types of images does Dillard use throughout the essay and especially when describing the moth that flew into her candle (paragraphs 8–10)? What responses do these images evoke? Why do you think Dillard chose them?

2. Why do you think Dillard ends her essay the way she does? How do the final two paragraphs affect the meaning of the rest of the essay? How would your reading of the work differ if the essay ended two paragraphs earlier?

3. **CONNECTIONS:** Compare Dillard's essay to Virginia Woolf's "The Death of the Moth" (page 625). How would you describe the writer's tone in each essay? In what specific way(s) are they similar and in what ways are they different? Given that Dillard assumes much of her audience would be familiar with Woolf's essay, how does Dillard craft her essay to resonate with Woolf's?

---

1 *immolating:* In this context, setting oneself on fire (as an act of protest).—EDS.

The Writer at Work

ANNIE DILLARD on the Writing Life

One of the nation's outstanding nonfiction writers—who prefers to think of herself as an "all-purpose writer" rather than an essayist—Annie Dillard is also a professor emeritus of creative writing at Wesleyan University. Dillard once said that a commitment to writing is "like living any dedicated life." How is this idea reflected in the following excerpt from her book *The Writing Life* (1989)? What does Dillard believe drives the creative artist and writer? Does her tough-minded advice apply only to artistic expression? In what other areas of human activity or expression might it also apply?

❝ Push it. Examine all things intensely and relentlessly. Probe and search each object in a piece of art. Do not leave it, do not course over it, as if it were understood, but instead follow it down until you see it in the mystery of its own specificity and strength. Giacometti's[1] drawings and paintings show his bewilderment and persistence. If he had not acknowledged his bewilderment, he would not have persisted. A twentieth-century master of drawing, Rico Lebrun, taught that "the draftsman must aggress; only by persistent assault will the live image capitulate and give up its secret to an unrelenting line." Who but an artist fierce to know—not fierce to seem to know—would suppose that a live image possessed a secret? The artist is willing to give all his or her strength and life to probing with blunt instruments those same secrets no one can describe in any way but with those instruments' faint tracks.

[1] *Alberto Giacometti* (1901–1966): A renowned Swiss sculptor, painter, draftsman, and printmaker. —EDS.

Admire the world for never ending on you—as you would admire an opponent, without taking your eyes from him, or walking away.

One of the few things I know about writing is this: spend it all, shoot it, play it, lose it, all, right away, every time. Do not hoard what seems good for a later place in the book, or for another book; give it, give it all, give it now. The impulse to save something good for a better place later is the signal to spend it now. Something more will arise for later, something better. These things fill from behind, from beneath, like well water. Similarly, the impulse to keep to yourself what you have learned is not only shameful, it is destructive. Anything you do not give freely and abundantly becomes lost to you. You open your safe and find ashes.

After Michelangelo died, someone found in his studio a piece of paper on which he had written a note to his apprentice, in the handwriting of his old age: 'Draw, Antonio, draw, Antonio, draw and do not waste time.' ❞

Brian Doyle

THE GREATEST NATURE ESSAY EVER

Journalist, essayist, and editor **BRIAN DOYLE** (b. 1956) was born in New York, educated "fitfully" at the University of Notre Dame, and now lives and works in Portland, Oregon, where he is editor of *Portland Magazine* at the University of Portland. Doyle is noted for writing books with spiritual and religious themes, including *Two Voices: A Father and Son Discuss Family and Faith* (1998), co-written with his father, Jim Doyle; *Credo: Essays on Grace, Altar Boys, Bees, Kneeling, Saints, the Mass, Priests, Strong Women, Epiphanies, a Wake, and the Haunting Thin Energetic Dusty Figure of Jesus the Christ* (1999); *Saints Passionate & Peculiar: Brief Exuberant Essays for Teens* (2002); *Leaping: Revelations & Epiphanies* (2003); *Spirited Men: Story, Soul, & Substance* (2004); *The Wet Engine: Exploring the Mad Wild Miracle of the Heart* (2005); *The Grail: A Year Ambling and Shambling through an Oregon Vineyard in Pursuit of the Best Pinot Noir Wine in the Whole Wild World* (2006); *Epiphanies & Elegies: Very Short Stories* (2007); and *Thirsty for the Joy: Australian and American Voices* (2007). He also edited the anthology *God Is Love: Essays from PORTLAND MAGAZINE* (2003). He is a columnist for *The Age* news-

> Brian Doyle says that as a writer, he doesn't feel "a responsibility to edify," adding that such writing tends "toward sermon and homily and lecture," a tendency he calls "boring."

paper in Melbourne, Australia, and the recipient of the *American Scholar*'s Best Essay Award in 2000, for an essay on Plutarch. Doyle's essays and poems have appeared in numerous magazines, journals, and newspapers, including the *Atlantic Monthly, Harper's, Commonweal, American Scholar, Georgia Review*, the *Times of London*, the *Sydney Morning Herald*, the *Kansas City Star*, the *San Francisco Chronicle, Newsday*, and *Orion*, where this essay, "The Greatest Nature Essay *Ever*," originally appeared in 2008.

One thing Doyle cautions against, in this essay and elsewhere, is writing that sermonizes. In an interview on quotidiana.org, he said that, as a writer, he doesn't "have a responsibility to edify," adding that such writing tends "toward sermon and homily and lecture," a tendency he calls "boring."

||||||||||||||||||||||||||||||||||||||||||||||||||||||||||||||||||||||||||||||||||||||||||||||||||||||||||||||||||||||||||||||||||||||||||

■ . . . WOULD BEGIN with an image so startling and lovely and wondrous that you would stop riffling through the rest of the mail, take your jacket off, sit down at the table, adjust your spectacles, tell the dog to lie *down*, tell the kids to make their *own* sandwiches for heavenssake, that's why god gave you *hands*, and read straight through the piece, marveling that you had indeed seen or smelled or heard *exactly* that, but never quite articulated it that way, or seen or heard it articulated that way, and you think, *man, this is why I read nature essays, to be startled and moved like that, wow.*

The next two paragraphs would smoothly and gently move you into a story, seemingly a small story, a light tale, easily accessed, something personal but not self-indulgent or self-absorbed on the writer's part, just sort of a cheerful nutty everyday story maybe starring an elk or a mink or a child, but then there would suddenly be a sharp sentence where the dagger enters your heart and the essay spins on a dime like a skater, and you are plunged into waaay deeper water, you didn't see it coming at all, and you actually shiver, your whole body shimmers, and much later, maybe when you are in bed with someone you love and you are trying to evade his or her icy feet, you think, *my god, stories do have roaring power, stories are the most crucial and necessary food, how come we never hardly say that out loud?*

The next three paragraphs then walk inexorably toward a line of explosive Conclusions on the horizon like inky alps. Probably the sentences get shorter, more staccato. Terser. Blunter. Shards of sentences. But there's no opinion or commentary, just one line fitting into another, each one making plain inarguable sense, a goat or even a senator could easily understand the sentences and their implications, and there's no shouting, no persuasion, no eloquent pirouetting, no pronouncements and accusations, no sermons or homilies, just calm clean clear statements one after another, fitting together like people holding hands.

Then an odd paragraph, this is a most unusual and peculiar essay, for right here where you would normally expect those alpine Conclusions, some Advice, some Stern Instructions & Directions, there's only the quiet murmur of the writer tiptoeing back to the story he or she was telling you in the second and third paragraphs. The story slips back into view gently, a little shy, holding its hat, nothing melodramatic, in fact it offers a few gnomic questions without answers, and then it gently slides away off the page and off the stage, it almost evanesces or dissolves, and it's only later after you have read the essay three times with mounting amazement that you see quite how the writer managed the stagecraft there, but that's the stuff of another essay for another time.

And finally the last paragraph. It turns out that the perfect nature essay 5 is quite short, it's a lean taut thing, an arrow and not a cannon, and here at the end there's a flash of humor, and a hint or tone or subtext of sadness, a touch of rue, you can't quite put your finger on it but it's there, a dark thread in the fabric, and there's also a shot of espresso hope, hope against all odds and sense, but rivetingly there's no call to arms, no clarion brassy trumpet blast, no website to which you are directed, no hint that you, yes you, should be ashamed of how much water you use or the car you drive or the fact that you just turned the thermostat up to seventy, or that you actually have not voted in the past two elections despite what you told the kids and the goat. Nor is there a rimshot ending, a bang, a last twist of the dagger. Oddly, sweetly, the essay just ends with a feeling eerily like a warm hand brushed against your cheek, and you sit there, near tears, smiling, and then you stand up. Changed. ●

The Reader's Presence

1. What responses does Doyle elicit from his readers by beginning his essay with an ellipsis? by presenting his opening paragraph as a single sentence? What other stylistic devices does Doyle use—and with what effect(s)? For example, Doyle suggests that the greatest essay ever "would begin with an image so startling and lovely and wondrous that you would stop riffling through the rest of the mail." Point to specific examples of Doyle's use of figurative language in this sentence and throughout his essay.

2. What in your judgment are the most important features of "the greatest nature essay *ever*"? To what extent does Doyle's own essay satisfy the criteria he articulates for such an essay? Please be as specific as possible in your response. Which of these criteria do you find most engaging as a reader? Explain why.

3. **CONNECTIONS:** After you have created a list of the criteria that Doyle identifies as the distinguishing features of the "greatest nature essay *ever*," apply these criteria to one of the following essays: E. B. White, "Once More to the Lake" (page 260); Annie Dillard, "The Death of a Moth" (page 371); Virginia Woolf, "The Death of the Moth" (page 625); Nathaniel Hawthorne, "My Visit to Niagara" (page 438).

Lars Eighner
ON DUMPSTER DIVING

LARS EIGHNER (b. 1948) was born in Texas and attended the University of Texas at Austin. An essayist and a fiction writer, he contributes regularly to the *Threepenny Review*, *Advocate Men*, the *Guide*, and *Inches*. He has published several collections of short stories, essays, and gay erotica. His most recent publications include a camp novel, *Pawn to Queen Four* (1995); a collection of essays, *Gay Cosmos* (1995); an erotic short story collection,

|||||||||||||||||||||||||||||||||||||||||||||||||||||||||||||||||||||||||||||||||||||||||||||||||||||||||||||||||||||||||||||||||||||||||||||||||||||

Whispered in the Dark (1995); and *WANK: The Tapes* (1998). Eighner writes a blog on his Web site, larseighner.com.

Eighner became homeless in 1988, after he lost his job as a mental-hospital attendant. "On Dumpster Diving" is Eighner's prize-winning essay based on this experience, later reprinted as part of his full-length book about homelessness, *Travels with Lizbeth: Three Years on the Road and on the Streets* (1993). Eighner and Lizbeth, Eighner's dog, became homeless again in 1996. Friends organized a fund under the auspices of the *Texas Observer* and obtained an apartment for Eighner and Lizbeth in Austin. Lizbeth has since passed away.

> **"A writer needs talent, luck, and persistence. You can make do with two out of three, and the more you have of one, the less you need of the others."**

On what is required to find success as a writer, Eighner has said, "I was not making enough money to support myself as a housed person, but I was writing well before I became homeless. . . . A writer needs talent, luck, and persistence. You can make do with two out of three, and the more you have of one, the less you need of the others."

LONG BEFORE I began Dumpster diving I was impressed with Dumpsters, enough so that I wrote the Merriam-Webster research service to discover what I could about the word "Dumpster." I learned from them that "Dumpster" is a proprietary word belonging to the Dempster Dumpster company.

Since then I have dutifully capitalized the word although it was lowercased in almost all of the citations Merriam-Webster photocopied for me. Dempster's word is too apt. I have never heard these things called anything but Dumpsters. I do not know anyone who knows the generic name for these objects. From time to time, however, I hear a wino or hobo give some corrupted credit to the original and call them Dipsy Dumpsters.

I began Dumpster diving about a year before I became homeless.

I prefer the term "scavenging" and use the word "scrounging" when I mean to be obscure. I have heard people, evidently meaning to be polite, using the word "foraging," but I prefer to reserve that word for gathering nuts and berries and such which I do also according to the season and the opportunity. "Dumpster diving" seems to me to be a little too cute and, in my case, inaccurate because I lack the athletic ability to lower myself into the Dumpsters as the true divers do, much to their increased profit.

I like the frankness of the word "scavenging," which I can hardly think of without picturing a big black snail on an aquarium wall. I live from the refuse of others. I am a scavenger. I think it a sound and honorable niche, although if I could I would naturally prefer to live the comfortable consumer life, perhaps—and only perhaps—as a slightly less wasteful consumer owing to what I have learned as a scavenger.

5

While my dog Lizbeth and I were still living in the house on Avenue B in Austin, as my savings ran out, I put almost all my sporadic income into rent. The necessities of daily life I began to extract from Dumpsters. Yes, we ate from Dumpsters. Except for jeans, all my clothes came from Dumpsters. Boom boxes, candles, bedding, toilet paper, medicine, books, a typewriter, a virgin male love doll, change sometimes amounting to many dollars: I acquired many things from the Dumpsters.

I have learned much as a scavenger. I mean to put some of what I have learned down here, beginning with the practical art of Dumpster diving and proceeding to the abstract.

What is safe to eat?

After all, the finding of objects is becoming something of an urban art. Even respectable employed people will sometimes find something tempting sticking out of a Dumpster or standing beside one. Quite a number of people, not all of them of the bohemian type, are willing to brag that they found this or that piece in the trash. But eating from Dumpsters is the thing that separates the dilettanti from the professionals.

Eating safely from the Dumpsters involves three principles: using the   10 senses and common sense to evaluate the condition of the found materials, knowing the Dumpsters of a given area and checking them regularly, and seeking always to answer the question "Why was this discarded?"

Perhaps everyone who has a kitchen and a regular supply of groceries has, at one time or another, made a sandwich and eaten half of it before discovering mold on the bread or got a mouthful of milk before realizing the milk had turned. Nothing of the sort is likely to happen to a Dumpster diver because he is constantly reminded that most food is discarded for a reason. Yet a lot of perfectly good food can be found in Dumpsters.

Canned goods, for example, turn up fairly often in the Dumpsters I frequent. All except the most phobic people would be willing to eat from a can even if it came from a Dumpster. Canned goods are among the safest of foods to be found in Dumpsters, but are not utterly foolproof.

Although very rare with modern canning methods, botulism is a possibility. Most other forms of food poisoning seldom do lasting harm to a healthy person. But botulism is almost certainly fatal and often the first symptom is death. Except for carbonated beverages, all canned goods should contain a slight vacuum and suck air when first punctured. Bulging, rusty, dented cans and cans that spew when punctured should be avoided, especially when the contents are not very acidic or syrupy.

Heat can break down the botulin, but this requires much more cooking than most people do to canned goods. To the extent that botulism occurs at all, of course, it can occur in cans on pantry shelves as well as in cans from Dumpsters. Need I say that home-canned goods found in Dumpsters are simply too risky to be recommended.

From time to time one of my companions, aware of the source of my   15 provisions, will ask, "Do you think these crackers are really safe to eat?" For some reason it is most often the crackers they ask about.

This question always makes me angry. Of course I would not offer my companion anything I had doubts about. But more than that I wonder why he cannot evaluate the condition of the crackers for himself. I have no special knowledge and I have been wrong before. Since he knows where the food comes from, it seems to me he ought to assume some of the responsibility for deciding what he will put in his mouth.

For myself I have few qualms about dry foods such as crackers, cookies, cereal, chips, and pasta if they are free of visible contaminants and still dry and crisp. Most often such things are found in the original packaging, which is not so much a positive sign as it is the absence of a negative one.

Raw fruits and vegetables with intact skins seem perfectly safe to me, excluding of course the obviously rotten. Many are discarded for minor imperfections which can be pared away. Leafy vegetables, grapes, cauliflower, broccoli, and similar things may be contaminated by liquids and may be impractical to wash.

Candy, especially hard candy, is usually safe if it has not drawn ants. Chocolate is often discarded only because it has become discolored as the cocoa butter de-emulsified. Candying after all is one method of food preservation because pathogens do not like very sugary substances.

All of these foods might be found in any Dumpster and can be evaluated 20 with some confidence largely on the basis of appearance. Beyond these are foods which cannot be correctly evaluated without additional information.

I began scavenging by pulling pizzas out of the Dumpster behind a pizza delivery shop. In general prepared food requires caution, but in this case I knew when the shop closed and went to the Dumpster as soon as the last of the help left.

Such shops often get prank orders, called "bogus." Because help seldom stays long at these places pizzas are often made with the wrong topping, refused on delivery for being cold, or baked incorrectly. The products to be discarded are boxed up because inventory is kept by counting boxes: A boxed pizza can be written off; an unboxed pizza does not exist.

I never placed a bogus order to increase the supply of pizzas and I believe no one else was scavenging in this Dumpster. But the people in the shop became suspicious and began to retain their garbage in the shop overnight.

While it lasted I had a steady supply of fresh, sometimes warm pizza. Because I knew the Dumpster I knew the source of the pizza, and because I visited the Dumpster regularly I knew what was fresh and what was yesterday's.

The area I frequent is inhabited by many affluent college students. I 25 am not here by chance; the Dumpsters in this area are very rich. Students throw out many good things, including food. In particular they tend to throw everything out when they move at the end of a semester, before and after breaks, and around midterm when many of them despair of college. So I find it advantageous to keep an eye on the academic calendar.

The students throw food away around the breaks because they do not know whether it has spoiled or will spoil before they return. A typical discard is a half jar of peanut butter. In fact nonorganic peanut butter does not require refrigeration and is unlikely to spoil in any reasonable time. The student does not know that, and since it is Daddy's money, the student decides not to take a chance.

Opened containers require caution and some attention to the question "Why was this discarded?" But in the case of discards from student apartments, the answer may be that the item was discarded through carelessness, ignorance, or wastefulness. This can sometimes be deduced when the item is found with many others, including some that are obviously perfectly good.

Some students, and others, approach defrosting a freezer by chucking out the whole lot. Not only do the circumstances of such a find tell the story, but also the mass of frozen goods stays cold for a long time and items may be found still frozen or freshly thawed.

Yogurt, cheese, and sour cream are items that are often thrown out while they are still good. Occasionally I find a cheese with a spot of mold, which of course I just pare off, and because it is obvious why such a cheese was discarded, I treat it with less suspicion than an apparently perfect cheese found in similar circumstances. Yogurt is often discarded, still sealed, only because the expiration date on the carton had passed. This is one of my favorite finds because yogurt will keep for several days, even in warm weather.

Students throw out canned goods and staples at the end of semesters and when they give up college at midterm. Drugs, pornography, spirits, and the like are often discarded when parents are expected—Dad's day, for example. And spirits also turn up after big party weekends, presumably discarded by the newly reformed. Wine and spirits, of course, keep perfectly well even once opened.

My test for carbonated soft drinks is whether they still fizz vigorously. Many juices or other beverages are too acid or too syrupy to cause much concern provided they are not visibly contaminated. Liquids, however, require some care.

One hot day I found a large jug of Pat O'Brien's Hurricane mix. The jug had been opened, but it was still ice cold. I drank three large glasses before it became apparent to me that someone had added the rum to the mix, and not a little rum. I never tasted the rum and by the time I began to feel the effects I had already ingested a very large quantity of the beverage. Some divers would have considered this a boon, but being suddenly and thoroughly intoxicated in a public place in the early afternoon is not my idea of a good time.

I have heard of people maliciously contaminating discarded food and even handouts, but mostly I have heard of this from people with vivid imaginations who have had no experience with the Dumpsters themselves. Just before the pizza shop stopped discarding its garbage at night, jalapeños began showing up on most of the discarded pizzas. If indeed this was meant to discourage me it was a wasted effort because I am a native Texan.

For myself, I avoid game, poultry, pork, and egg-based foods whether I find them raw or cooked. I seldom have the means to cook what I find, but when I do I avail myself of plentiful supplies of beef which is often in very

30

good condition. I suppose fish becomes disagreeable before it becomes dangerous. The dog is happy to have any such thing that is past its prime and, in fact, does not recognize fish as food until it is quite strong.

Home leftovers, as opposed to surpluses from restaurants, are very often   35
bad. Evidently, especially among students, there is a common type of personality that carefully wraps up even the smallest leftover and shoves it into the back of the refrigerator for six months or so before discarding it. Characteristic of this type are the reused jars and margarine tubs which house the remains.

I avoid ethnic foods I am unfamiliar with. If I do not know what it is supposed to look like when it is good, I cannot be certain I will be able to tell if it is bad.

No matter how careful I am I still get dysentery at least once a month, oftener in warm weather. I do not want to paint too romantic a picture. Dumpster diving has serious drawbacks as a way of life.

I learned to scavenge gradually, on my own. Since then I have initiated several companions into the trade. I have learned that there is a predictable series of stages a person goes through in learning to scavenge.

At first the new scavenger is filled with disgust and self-loathing. He is ashamed of being seen and may lurk around, trying to duck behind things, or he may try to dive at night.

(In fact, most people instinctively look away from a scavenger. By skulk-   40
ing around, the novice calls attention to himself and arouses suspicion. Diving at night is ineffective and needlessly messy.)

Every grain of rice seems to be a maggot. Everything seems to stink. He can wipe the egg yolk off the found can, but he cannot erase the stigma of eating garbage out of his mind.

That stage passes with experience. The scavenger finds a pair of running shoes that fit and look and smell brand new. He finds a pocket calculator in perfect working order. He finds pristine ice cream, still frozen, more than he can eat or keep. He begins to understand: People do throw away perfectly good stuff, a lot of perfectly good stuff.

At this stage, Dumpster shyness begins to dissipate. The diver, after all, has the last laugh. He is finding all manner of good things which are his for the taking. Those who disparage his profession are the fools, not he.

He may begin to hang onto some perfectly good things for which he has neither a use nor a market. Then he begins to take note of the things which are not perfectly good but are nearly so. He mates a Walkman with broken earphones and one that is missing a battery cover. He picks up things which he can repair.

At this stage he may become lost and never recover. Dumpsters are full   45
of things of some potential value to someone and also of things which never have much intrinsic value but are interesting. All the Dumpster divers I have known come to the point of trying to acquire everything they touch. Why not take it, they reason, since it is all free.

This is, of course, hopeless. Most divers come to realize that they must restrict themselves to items of relatively immediate utility. But in some cases the diver simply cannot control himself. I have met several of these pack-rat types. Their ideas of the values of various pieces of junk verge on the psychotic. Every bit of glass may be a diamond, they think, and all that glistens, gold.

I tend to gain weight when I am scavenging. Partly this is because I always find far more pizza and doughnuts than water-packed tuna, non-fat yogurt, and fresh vegetables. Also I have not developed much faith in the reliability of Dumpsters as a food source, although it has been proven to me many times. I tend to eat as if I have no idea where my next meal is coming from. But mostly I just hate to see food go to waste and so I eat much more than I should. Something like this drives the obsession to collect junk.

As for collecting objects, I usually restrict myself to collecting one kind of small object at a time, such as pocket calculators, sunglasses, or campaign buttons. To live on the street I must anticipate my needs to a certain extent: I must pick up and save warm bedding I find in August because it will not be found in Dumpsters in November. But even if I had a home with extensive storage space I could not save everything that might be valuable in some contingency.

I have proprietary feelings about my Dumpsters. As I have suggested, it is no accident that I scavenge from Dumpsters where good finds are common. But my limited experience with Dumpsters in other areas suggests to me that it is the population of competitors rather than the affluence of the dumpers that most affects the feasibility of survival by scavenging. The large number of competitors is what puts me off the idea of trying to scavenge in places like Los Angeles.

Curiously, I do not mind my direct competition, other scavengers, so much as I hate the can scroungers.   50

People scrounge cans because they have to have a little cash. I have tried scrounging cans with an able-bodied companion. Afoot a can scrounger simply cannot make more than a few dollars a day. One can extract the necessities of life from the Dumpsters directly with far less effort than would be required to accumulate the equivalent value in cans.

Can scroungers, then, are people who *must* have small amounts of cash. These are drug addicts and winos, mostly the latter because the amounts of cash are so small.

Spirits and drugs do, like all other commodities, turn up in Dumpsters and the scavenger will from time to time have a half bottle of a rather good wine with his dinner. But the wino cannot survive on these occasional finds; he must have his daily dose to stave off the DTs. All the cans he can carry will buy about three bottles of Wild Irish Rose.

I do not begrudge them the cans, but can scroungers tend to tear up the Dumpsters, mixing the contents and littering the area. They become so specialized that they can see only cans. They earn my contempt by passing up change, canned goods, and readily hockable items.

There are precious few courtesies among scavengers. But it is a common   55
practice to set aside surplus items: pairs of shoes, clothing, canned goods,
and such. A true scavenger hates to see good stuff go to waste and what he
cannot use he leaves in good condition in plain sight.

Can scroungers lay waste to everything in their path and will stir one of
a pair of good shoes to the bottom of a Dumpster, to be lost or ruined in the
muck. Can scroungers will even go through individual garbage cans, something I have never seen a scavenger do.

Individual garbage cans are set out on the public easement only on garbage days. On other days going through them requires trespassing close to
a dwelling. Going through individual garbage cans without scattering litter
is almost impossible. Litter is likely to reduce the public's tolerance of scavenging. Individual garbage cans are simply not as productive as Dumpsters;
people in houses and duplexes do not move as often and for some reason
do not tend to discard as much useful material. Moreover, the time required
to go through one garbage can that serves one household is not much less
than the time required to go through a Dumpster that contains the refuse of
twenty apartments.

But my strongest reservation about going through individual garbage
cans is that this seems to me a very personal kind of invasion to which I
would object if I were a householder. Although many things in Dumpsters
are obviously meant never to come to light, a Dumpster is somehow less
personal.

I avoid trying to draw conclusions about the people who dump in the
Dumpsters I frequent. I think it would be unethical to do so, although I know
many people will find the idea of scavenger ethics too funny for words.

Dumpsters contain bank statements, bills, correspondence, and other   60
documents, just as anyone might expect. But there are also less obvious
sources of information. Pill bottles, for example. The labels on pill bottles
contain the name of the patient, the name of the doctor, and the name of the
drug. AIDS drugs and antipsychotic medicines, to name but two groups, are
specific and are seldom prescribed for any other disorders. The plastic compacts for birth control pills usually have complete label information.

Despite all of this sensitive information, I have had only one apartment
resident object to my going through the Dumpster. In that case it turned
out the resident was a university athlete who was taking bets and who was
afraid I would turn up his wager slips.

Occasionally a find tells a story. I once found a small paper bag containing some unused condoms, several partial tubes of flavored sexual lubricant,
a partially used compact of birth control pills, and the torn pieces of a picture
of a young man. Clearly she was through with him and planning to give up
sex altogether.

Dumpster things are often sad—abandoned teddy bears, shredded
wedding books, despaired-of sales kits. I find many pets lying in state in
Dumpsters. Although I hope to get off the streets so that Lizbeth can have

a long and comfortable old age, I know this hope is not very realistic. So I suppose when her time comes she too will go into a Dumpster. I will have no better place for her. And after all, for most of her life her livelihood has come from the Dumpster. When she finds something I think is safe that has been spilled from the Dumpster I let her have it. She already knows the route around the best Dumpsters. I like to think that if she survives me she will have a chance of evading the dog catcher and of finding her sustenance on the route.

Silly vanities also come to rest in the Dumpsters. I am a rather accomplished needleworker. I get a lot of materials from the Dumpsters. Evidently sorority girls, hoping to impress someone, perhaps themselves, with their mastery of a womanly art, buy a lot of embroider-by-number kits, work a few stitches horribly, and eventually discard the whole mess. I pull out their stitches, turn the canvas over, and work an original design. Do not think I refrain from chuckling as I make original gifts from these kits.

I find diaries and journals. I have often thought of compiling a book of literary found objects. And perhaps I will one day. But what I find is hopelessly commonplace and bad without being, even unconsciously, camp. College students also discard their papers. I am horrified to discover the kind of paper which now merits an A in an undergraduate course. I am grateful, however, for the number of good books and magazines the students throw out.   65

In the area I know best I have never discovered vermin in the Dumpsters, but there are two kinds of kitty surprise. One is alley cats which I meet as they leap, claws first, out of Dumpsters. This is especially thrilling when I have Lizbeth in tow. The other kind of kitty surprise is a plastic garbage bag filled with some ponderous, amorphous mass. This always proves to be used cat litter.

City bees harvest doughnut glaze and this makes the Dumpster at the doughnut shop more interesting. My faith in the instinctive wisdom of animals is always shaken whenever I see Lizbeth attempt to catch a bee in her mouth, which she does whenever bees are present. Evidently some birds find Dumpsters profitable, for birdie surprise is almost as common as kitty surprise of the first kind. In hunting season all kinds of small game turn up in Dumpsters, some of it, sadly, not entirely dead. Curiously, summer and winter, maggots are uncommon.

The worst of the living and near-living hazards of the Dumpsters are the fire ants. The food that they claim is not much of a loss, but they are vicious and aggressive. It is very easy to brush against some surface of the Dumpster and pick up half a dozen or more fire ants, usually in some sensitive area such as the underarm. One advantage of bringing Lizbeth along as I make Dumpster rounds is that, for obvious reasons, she is very alert to ground-based fire ants. When Lizbeth recognizes the signs of fire ant infestation around our feet she does the Dance of the Zillion Fire Ants. I have learned not to ignore this warning from Lizbeth, whether I perceive the tiny ants or not, but to remove ourselves at Lizbeth's first pas de bourrée.[1] All the more so because the ants are the worst in the months I wear flip-flops, if I have them.

(Perhaps someone will misunderstand the above. Lizbeth does the Dance of the Zillion Fire Ants when she recognizes more fire ants than she cares to eat, not when she is being bitten. Since I have learned to react promptly, she does not get bitten at all. It is the isolated patrol of fire ants that falls in Lizbeth's range that deserves pity. Lizbeth finds them quite tasty.)

By far the best way to go through a Dumpster is to lower yourself into it. Most of the good stuff tends to settle at the bottom because it is usually weightier than the rubbish. My more athletic companions have often demonstrated to me that they can extract much good material from a Dumpster I have already been over.

To those psychologically or physically unprepared to enter a Dumpster, I recommend a stout stick, preferably with some barb or hook at one end. The hook can be used to grab plastic garbage bags. When I find canned goods or other objects loose at the bottom of a Dumpster I usually can roll them into a small bag that I can then hoist up. Much Dumpster diving is a matter of experience for which nothing will do except practice.

Dumpster diving is outdoor work, often surprisingly pleasant. It is not entirely predictable; things of interest turn up every day and some days there are finds of great value. I am always very pleased when I can turn up exactly the thing I most wanted to find. Yet in spite of the element of change, scavenging more than most other pursuits tends to yield returns in some proportion to the effort and intelligence brought to bear. It is very sweet to turn up a few dollars in change from a Dumpster that has just been gone over by a wino.

The land is now covered with cities. The cities are full of Dumpsters. I think of scavenging as a modern form of self-reliance. In any event, after ten years of government service, where everything is geared to the lowest common denominator, I find work that rewards initiative and effort refreshing. Certainly I would be happy to have a sinecure again, but I am not heartbroken not to have one anymore.

I find from the experience of scavenging two rather deep lessons. The first is to take what I can use and let the rest go by. I have come to think that there is no value in the abstract. A thing I cannot use or make useful, perhaps by trading, has no value however fine or rare it may be. I mean useful in a broad sense — so, for example, some art I would think useful and valuable, but other art might be otherwise for me.

I was shocked to realize that some things are not worth acquiring, but now I think it is so. Some material things are white elephants that eat up the possessor's substance.

The second lesson is of the transience of material being. This has not quite converted me to a dualist, but it has made some headway in that

---

[1] **pas de bourrée:** A transitional ballet step. — EDS.

direction. I do not suppose that ideas are immortal, but certainly mental things are longer-lived than other material things.

Once I was the sort of person who invests material objects with sentimental value. Now I no longer have those things, but I have the sentiments yet.

Many times in my travels I have lost everything but the clothes I was wearing and Lizbeth. The things I find in Dumpsters, the love letters and ragdolls of so many lives, remind me of this lesson. Now I hardly pick up a thing without envisioning the time I will cast it away. This I think is a healthy state of mind. Almost everything I have now has already been cast out at least once, proving that what I own is valueless to someone.

Anyway, I find my desire to grab for the gaudy bauble has been largely sated. I think this is an attitude I share with the very wealthy—we both know there is plenty more where what we have came from. Between us are the rat-race millions who have confounded their selves with the objects they grasp and who nightly scavenge the cable channels looking for they know not what.

I am sorry for them. ● 80

The Reader's Presence

1. At the center of "On Dumpster Diving" is Eighner's effort to bring out from the shadows of contemporary American life the lore and practices of scavenging, what he calls "a modern form of self-reliance." His essay also provides a compelling account of his self-education as he took to the streets for "the necessities of daily life" (paragraph 6). Outline the stages in this process, and summarize the ethical and moral issues and the questions of decorum that Eighner confronted along the way. Show how this process reflects the structure of his essay, "beginning with the practical art of Dumpster diving and proceeding to the abstract" (paragraph 7).

2. One of the most remarkable aspects of Eighner's essay is the tone (the attitude) he expresses toward his subject. Select a paragraph from the essay. Read it aloud. How would you characterize the sound of his voice? Does he sound, for example, tough-minded? polite? strident? experienced? cynical? something else? Consider, for example, paragraph 34, where he notes: "For myself, I avoid game, poultry, pork, and egg-based foods whether I find them raw or cooked." Where have you heard talk like this before? Do you notice any changes as the essay develops, or does Eighner maintain the same tone in discussing his subject? What responses does he elicit from his readers when he speaks of scavenging as a "profession" and a "trade"?

3. Consider Eighner's relationship with his readers. Does he consider himself fundamentally different from or similar to his audience? In what specific ways? Consider, for example, the nature of the information Eighner provides in the essay. Does he expect his readers to be familiar with the information? How does he characterize his own knowledgeability about this often-noticed but rarely discussed activity in urban America? Comment on his use of irony in presenting information about Dumpster diving and in anticipating his readers' responses to the circumstances within which he does the work of his trade.

4. **CONNECTIONS:**   Compare Eighner's description of Dumpster diving to one of the most famous essays in the English language, Jonathan Swift's "A Modest Proposal" (page 831). Both essays deal with economics and the effects of poverty. In what ways does each author use humor and satire? How does each author introduce us to the grim realities of poverty? What role does food play in each essay? You might also compare Eighner's essay to Peter Singer's "The Singer Solution to World Poverty" (page 814). Discuss how applicable you find Singer's "solution" to Eighner's problems.

The Writer at Work

LARS EIGHNER on the Challenges of Writing While Homeless

Lars Eighner and Lizbeth.

In the summer of 1989, Lars Eighner, without a job and with no place to live, began writing about his experiences as a homeless person trying to survive in the college town of Austin, Texas. When one of his essays, "On Dumpster Diving," was published in the prestigious literary journal, the *Threepenny Review* (Fall 1991), it became immediately clear that he had contributed one of the best and most authentic accounts of life on the American streets. The essay, now a modern classic and reprinted widely, was collected in *Travels with Lizbeth: Three Years on the Road and on the Streets* in 1993. For that volume, Eighner included an introduction (excerpted here) in which he discussed the challenges that confront a homeless writer.

❝When I began this account I was living under a shower curtain in a stand of bamboo in a public park. I did not undertake to write about homelessness, but wrote what I knew, as an artist paints a still life, not because he is especially fond of fruit, but because the subject is readily at hand.

In the summer of 1989, when I was in the bamboo, I supposed interest in homelessness had peaked in the presidential election of the previous year. Moreover, I thought my experiences with homelessness were atypical.

I still think my experiences were atypical, but I have come to disbelieve in typical homelessness. I had some advantages and some disadvantages and I chose the course that seemed mostly likely to provide the survival of myself and my dog Lizbeth on the most comfortable terms of which our situation would admit.

I did not often associate with other homeless people. I avoided the homeless shelters and hobo jungles. I did not attempt to survive on the streets of a very large city, but made my way for the most part in a liberal and affluent area of an overgrown college town. Although I often despaired of improving my material situation, I seldom lacked for a feeling of self-worth or a sense of mission. On the other hand, I spent most of my time in Texas, where a general contempt for the poor is reflected in a useless, vestigial social welfare system. I handicapped myself by adopting from the first a policy of not stealing and not begging on the streets. And, of course, I would not be parted from Lizbeth. I do not pretend to speak for the homeless. I think no one could speak for all the various people who have in common the condition of being homeless. I do not know many of the homeless, but of the condition of being homeless I know something, and that is part of what I have written about.

In truth, becoming homeless was a long process that I can date only arbitrarily. I had been without a reliable income for about a year before I left the shack I had been living in. For about five months after I left the shack I traveled and imposed on friends and strangers, so that I spent only part of the time on the streets. Moreover, throughout that first period I believed I had one prospect or another of improving my situation and I did not regard myself as truly homeless.

When I had the opportunity to get off the street for a week or a month or even for only a night, I did so; my object was not to explore homelessness but to get off the street. I have recounted these events in the ordinary narrative manner, but have only summarized the events of my longer stopovers. Eventually I became homeless enough to suit anyone's definition. In spite of the challenges that homelessness presented, the chief characteristic of my experience of homelessness was tedium. The days and nights that Lizbeth and I were literally without a roof over our heads, although by far the majority of the more than two years encompassed here, are represented by relatively few examples. One of those days was so much like each of the others that to call any of them typical would be an understatement. Our immediate needs I met with more or less trouble, but once that was done I could do no more. Day after day I could aspire, within reason, to nothing more than survival. Although the planets wandered among the stars and the moon waxed and waned, the identical naked barrenness of existence was exposed to me, day in and day out. I do not think I could write a narrative that would quite capture the unrelenting ennui of homelessness, but if I were to write it, no one could bear to read it. I spare myself as much as the reader in not attempting to recall so many empty hours. Every life has trivial occurrences, pointless episodes, and unresolved mysteries, but a homeless life has these and virtually nothing else. I have found it best in some parts to abandon a strictly chronological account and to treat in essay form experiences that relate to a single subject although they occurred in disparate times and places. **🙰**

Joseph Epstein

THE PERPETUAL ADOLESCENT

A self-described "stickler for language," **JOSEPH EPSTEIN** (b. 1937) has authored many books of literary criticism, social commentary, personal essays, and fiction. His essays and articles are found in numerous publications, including *Commentary*, the *New Yorker*, *Harper's*, the *New Republic*, and the *New York Review of Books*. He was a lecturer in English and writing at Northwestern University from 1974 to 2002 and an editor of the Phi Beta Kappa magazine *American Scholar* for more than two decades. In his "Life and Letters" column in that magazine, Epstein declared his principles regarding the use and abuse of language: "Take out all language that is pretentious and imprecise, under-educated and over-intellectualized. Question all language that says more than it means, that leaves the ground but doesn't really fly. Question authority only after you have first seriously consulted it; it isn't always as stupid as it looks. Never forget that today's hot new phrase becomes tomorrow's cold dead cliché." Now retired from teaching, Epstein has continued to write prodigiously; his books of essays and stories include *Narcissus Leaves the Pool* (1999), *Snobbery* (2002), *Envy* (2003), *Fabulous Small Jews* (2003), *Friendship: An Exposé* (2006), *In a Cardboard Belt! Essays Personal, Literary, and Savage* (2007), *Fred Astaire* (2008), and *The Love Song of A. Jerome Minkoff and Other Stories* (2010).

> **"Question authority only after you have first seriously consulted it; it isn't always as stupid as it looks."**

In a 2003 interview, Epstein described writing about people who are "caught in a cultural switch. That is to say they grew up with one set of values and now there is another. . . . I like to think of myself as a kind of chronicler of people caught in the switch." In his essay "The Perpetual Adolescent," Epstein comments on such a "cultural switch" in the United States since World War II. The essay is taken from the March 15, 2003, issue of the *Weekly Standard*, to which Epstein is a regular contributor.

WHENEVER ANYONE under the age of 50 sees old newsreel film of Joe DiMaggio's 56-game hitting streak of 1941, he is almost certain to be brought up by the fact that nearly everyone in the male-dominated crowds—in New York, Boston, Chicago, Detroit, Cleveland—seems to be wearing a suit and a fedora or other serious adult hat. The people in those earlier baseball crowds, though watching a boyish game, nonetheless had a radically differ-ent conception of themselves than most Americans do now. A major depres-sion was ending, a world war was on. Even though they were watching an entertainment that took most of them back to their boyhoods, they thought of themselves as adults, no longer kids, but grown-ups, adults, men.

How different from today, when a good part of the crowd at any ball-game, no matter what the age, is wearing jeans and team caps and T-shirts; and let us not neglect those (one hopes) benign maniacs who paint their faces in home-team colors or spell out, on their bare chests, the letters of the names of star players: S-O-S-A.

Part of the explanation for the suits at the ballpark in DiMaggio's day is that in the 1940s and even '50s there weren't a lot of sport, or leisure, or casual clothes around. Unless one lived at what H. L. Mencken[1] called "the country-club stage of culture"—unless, that is, one golfed, played tennis, or sailed—one was likely to own only the clothes one worked in or better. Far from casual Fridays, in those years there weren't even casual Sundays. Wearing one's "Sunday best," a cliché of the time, meant wearing the good clothes one reserved for church.

Dressing down may first have set in on the West Coast, where a certain informality was thought to be a new way of life. In the 1960s, in universities casual dress became absolutely *de rigueur* among younger faculty, who, in their ardor to destroy any evidence of their being implicated in evil hierar-chy, wished not merely to seem in no wise different from their students but, more important, to seem always young; and the quickest path to youthful-ness was teaching in jeans, T-shirts, and the rest of it.

This informality has now been institutionalized. Few are the restaurants that could any longer hope to stay in business if they required men to wear a jacket and tie. Today one sees men wearing baseball caps—some worn backwards—while eating indoors in quite good restaurants. In an episode of *The Sopranos*, Tony Soprano, the mafia don, representing life of a differ-ent day, finds this so outrages his sense of decorum that, in a restaurant he frequents, he asks a man, in a quiet but entirely menacing way, to remove his goddamn hat.

Life in that different day was felt to observe the human equivalent of the Aristotelian unities: to have, like a good drama, a beginning, middle, and end. Each part, it was understood, had its own advantages and detrac-tions, but the middle—adulthood—was the lengthiest and most earnest part, where everything serious happened and much was at stake. To violate the boundaries of any of the three divisions of life was to go against what was natural and thereby to appear unseemly, to put one's world somehow out of joint, to be, let us face it, a touch, and perhaps more than a touch, grotesque.

5

---

[1] *H(enry) L(ouis) "H. L." Mencken* (1880–1956): An influential journalist, essayist, magazine editor, satirist, and critic of American life and culture.—EDS.

Today, of course, all this has been shattered. The ideal almost everywhere is to seem young for as long as possible. The health clubs and endemic
workout clothes, the enormous increase in cosmetic surgery (for women and
men), the special youth-oriented television programming and moviemak-
ing, all these are merely the more obvious signs of the triumph of youth culture. When I say youth culture, I do not mean merely that the young today
are transcendent, the group most admired among the various age groups in
American society, but that youth is no longer viewed as a transitory state,
through which one passes on the way from childhood to adulthood, but an
aspiration, a vaunted condition in which, if one can only arrange it, to settle
in perpetuity.

This phenomenon is not something that happened just last night; it
has been underway for decades. Nor is it something that can be changed
even by an event as cataclysmic as that of September 11, which at first was
thought to be so sobering as to tear away all shreds of American innocence.
As a generalization, it allows for a wide variety of exceptions. There still
are adults in America; if names are wanted, I would set out those of Alan
Greenspan, Jeane Kirkpatrick, Robert Rubin, Warren Buffett, Sol Linowitz,[2]
and many more. But such men and women, actual grown-ups, now begin
to appear a bit anomalous; they no longer seem representative of the larger
culture.

The shift into youth culture began in earnest, I suspect, during the 10
or so years following 1951, the year of the publication of *Catcher in the
Rye.* Salinger's novel exalts the purity of youth and locates the enemy—a
clear case of Us versus Them—in those who committed the sin of having
grown older, which includes Holden Caulfield's pain-in-the-neck parents,
his brother (the sellout screenwriter), and just about everyone else who has
passed beyond adolescence and had the rather poor taste to remain alive.

The case for the exaltation of the young is made in Wordsworth's "Inti-   10
mation of Immortality," with its idea that human beings are born with great
wisdom from which life in society weans them slowly but inexorably. Plato
promulgated this same idea long before: For him we all had wisdom in the
womb, but it was torn from us at the exact point that we came into the world.
Rousseau gave it a French twist, arguing that human beings are splendid
all-around specimens—noble savages, really—with life out in society turning us mean and loutish, which is another way of saying that the older we
are, the worse we get. We are talking about Romanticism here, friend, which
never favors the mature, let alone the aged.

The triumph of youth culture has conquered perhaps nowhere more
completely than in the United States. The John F. Kennedy administration,

---

2 *Alan Greenspan . . . Sol Linowitz:* Greenspan: five-term chairman of the Federal Reserve
System; Kirkpatrick: former Reagan cabinet member and United Nations representative; Rubin:
Secretary of the Treasury under President Clinton; Buffett: world-famous multi-billionaire; Linowitz
(d. 2005): cofounder and chairman of Xerox, who also served in the Johnson and Carter administra-
tions.—EDS.

with its emphasis on youthfulness, beginning with its young president—the first president routinely not to wear a serious hat—gave it its first public prominence. Soon after the assassination of Kennedy, the Free Speech Movement, which spearheaded the student revolution, positively enshrined the young. Like Yeats's Byzantium, the '60s utopia posited by the student radicals was "no country for old men"[3] or women. One of the many tenets in its credo—soon to become a cliché, but no less significant for that—was that no one over 30 was to be trusted. (If you were part of that movement and 21 years old in 1965, you are 60 today. Good morning, Sunshine.)

Music was a key element in the advance of youth culture. The dividing moment here is the advent of Elvis. On one side were those who thought Elvis an amusing and largely freakish phenomenon—a bit of a joke—and on the other, those who took him dead seriously as a figure of youthful rebellion, the musical equivalent of James Dean in the movie *Rebel Without a Cause* [1955], another early winning entry in the glorification-of-youth sweepstakes then forming. Rock 'n' roll presented a vinyl curtain, with those committed to retaining their youth on one side, those wanting to claim adulthood on the other. The Beatles, despite the very real charms of their non-druggie music, solidified things. So much of hard rock 'n' roll came down to nothing more than a way of saying bugger off to adult culture.

Reinforcement for these notions—they were not yet so coherent as to qualify as ideas—was to be found in the movies. Movies for some years now have been made not only increasingly for the young but by the young. I once worked on a movie script with a producer who one day announced to me that it was his birthday. When I wished him happy returns of the day, he replied that it wasn't so happy for him; he was turning 41, an uncomfortably old age in Hollywood for someone who hadn't many big success-scalps on his belt.

Robert Redford, though now in his mid-sixties, remains essentially a guy in jeans, a handsome graduate student with wrinkles. Paul Newman, now in his late seventies, seems uncomfortable in a suit. Hugh Grant, the English actor, may be said to be professionally boyish, and in a recent role, in the movie *About a Boy*, is described in the *New York Times* as a character who "surrounds himself with gadgets, videos, CDs, and other toys" and who "is doing everything in his power to avoid growing up." The actor Jim Carrey, who is 42, not long ago said of the movie *The Majestic*, in which he stars, "It's about manhood. It's about adulthood," as if italicizing the rarity of such movies. He then went on to speak about himself in standard self-absorbed adolescent fashion: "You've got that hole you're left with by whatever your parents couldn't give you." Poor baby.

Jim Carrey's roles in movies resemble nothing so much as comic-book   15 characters come to life. And why, just now, does so much of contemporary

---

3 ***"no country for old men":*** One of the most famous poems by Irish poet William Butler Yeats, "Sailing to Byzantium," begins: "That is no country for old men."—EDS.

entertainment come in the form of animation or comic-book cartooning? Such television shows as *The Simpsons* and *King of the Hill*, the occasional back page in the *New York Times Book Review* or the *New Yorker* and the comic-book novel, all seem to feel that the animated cartoon and comic-book formats are very much of the moment. They are of course right, at least if you think of your audience as adolescent, or, more precisely, as being unwilling quite to detach themselves from their adolescence.

Recent history has seemed to be on the side of keeping people from growing up by supplying only a paucity of stern tests of the kind out of which adulthood is usually formed. We shall never have another presidential candidate tested by the Depression or by his experience in World War II. These were events that proved crucibles for the formation of adult character, not to say manliness. Henceforth all future presidential—and congressional—candidates will come with a shortage of what used to pass for significant experience. Crises for future politicians will doubtless be about having to rethink their lives when they didn't get into Brown or found themselves unequipped emotionally for Stanford Business School.

Corporate talent these days feels no weightier. Pictures of heads of corporations in polo shirts with designer logos in the business section of the *New York Times*, fresh from yet another ephemeral merger, or acquiring an enormous raise after their company has recorded another losing year, do not inspire confidence. "The trouble with Enron," said an employee of the company in the aftermath of that corporation's appalling debacle, "is that there weren't any grown-ups."

The increasing affluence the United States enjoyed after World War II, extending into the current day, also contributed heavily to forming the character I've come to think of as the perpetual American adolescent. Earlier, with less money around, people were forced to get serious, to grow up—and fast. How quickly the Depression generation was required to mature! How many stories one used to hear about older brothers going to work at 18 or earlier, so that a younger brother might be allowed to go to college, or simply to help keep the family afloat! With lots of money around, certain kinds of pressure were removed. More and more people nowadays are working, as earlier generations were not, with a strong safety net of money under them. All options opened, they now swim in what Kierkegaard[4] called "a sea of possibilities," and one of these possibilities in America is to refuse to grow up for a longer period than has been permitted any other people in history.

All this is reinforced by the play of market forces, which strongly encourage the mythical dream of perpetual youthfulness. The promise behind 95 percent of all advertising is that of recaptured youth, whose deeper promise is lots more sex yet to go. The ads for the $5,000 wristwatch, the $80,000 car, the khakis, the vodka, the pharmaceuticals to regrow hair and recapture

---

4 ***Søren Kierkegaard*** (1813–1855): Danish philosopher. —EDS.

ardor, all whisper display me, drive me, wear me, drink me, swallow me, and you stop the clock—youth, Baby, is yours.

The whole sweep of advertising, which is to say of market, culture [20] since soon after World War II has been continuously to lower the criteria of youthfulness while extending the possibility for seeming youthful to older and older people. To make the very young seem older—all those 10- and 12-year-old Britney Spears and Jennifer Lopez imitators, who already know more about brand-name logos than I do about English literature—is another part of the job. It's not a conspiracy, mind you, not six or eight international ad agencies meeting in secret to call the shots, but the dynamics of marketing itself, finding a way to make it more profitable all around by convincing the young that they can seem older and the old that they can seem a lot younger. Never before has it been more difficult to obey the injunction to act one's age.

Two of the great television sitcom successes of recent years, *Seinfeld* and *Friends*, though each is different in its comic tone, are united by the theme of the permanent adolescent loose in the big city. One takes the characters in *Seinfeld* to be in their middle to late thirties, those in *Friends* in their late twenties to early thirties. Charming though they may be, both sets of characters are oddly stunted. They aren't quite anywhere and don't seem to be headed anywhere, either. Time is suspended for them. Aimless and shameless, they are in the grip of the everyday *Sturm und Drang*[5] of adolescent self-absorption. Outside their rather temporary-looking apartments, they scarcely exist. Personal relations provide the full drama of their lives. Growth and development aren't part of the deal. They are still, somehow, in spirit, locked in a high school of the mind, eating dry cereal, watching a vast quantity of television, hoping to make ecstatic sexual scores. Apart from the high sheen of the writing and the comic skill of the casts, I wonder if what really attracts people to these shows—*Friends*[6] still, *Seinfeld* in its reruns—isn't the underlying identification with the characters because of the audience's own longing for a perpetual adolescence, cut loose, free of responsibility, without the real pressures that life, that messy business, always exerts.

Time for the perpetual adolescents is curiously static. They are in no great hurry: to succeed, to get work, to lay down achievements. Perhaps this is partly because longevity has increased in recent decades—if one doesn't make it to 90 nowadays, one feels slightly cheated—but more likely it is that time doesn't seem to the perpetual adolescent the excruciatingly finite matter, the precious commodity, it indubitably is. For the perpetual adolescent, time is almost endlessly expandable. Why not go to law school in one's late

---

[5] ***Sturm und Drang:*** German for "storm and stress." The phrase refers to a literary movement in the late eighteenth century that emphasized the emotional conflicts of unconventional youth.—EDS.

[6] Both *Friends* and *Seinfeld* are now in reruns.—EDS.

thirties, or take the premed requirements in one's early forties, or wait even later than that to have children? Time enough to toss away one's 20s, maybe even one's 30s; 40 is soon enough to get serious about life; maybe 50, when you think about it, is the best time really to get going in earnest.

The old hunger for life, the eagerness to get into the fray, has been replaced by an odd patience that often looks more like passivity. In the 1950s, people commonly married in their twenties, which may or may not have been a good thing, but marriage did prove a forcing house into adulthood, for men and women, especially where children issued from the marriage, which they usually did fairly quickly. I had two sons by the time I was 26, which, among other things, made it impossible, either physically or spiritually, for me to join the general youth movement of the 1960s, even though I still qualified by age. It also required me to find a vocation. By 30, one was supposed to be settled in life: wife, children, house, job— "the full catastrophe," as Zorba the Greek[7] liked to say. But it was also a useful catastrophe. Today most people feel that they can wait to get serious about life. Until then one is feeling one's way, still deciding, shopping around, contributing to the formation of a new psychological type: the passive-nonaggressive.

Not everywhere is nonaggression the psychological mode of choice. One hears about the young men and women working the 14-hour days at low six-figure jobs in front-line law firms; others sacrificing to get into MBA programs, for the single purpose of an early financial score. But even here one senses an adolescent spirit to the proceedings. The old model for ambition was solid hard work that paid off over time. One began at a low wage, worked one's way up through genuine accomplishment, grew wealthier as one grew older, and, with luck, retired with a sense of financial security and pleasure in one's achievement. But the new American ambition model features the kid multimillionaire—the young man or woman who breaks the bank not long out of college. An element of adolescent impatience enters in here—I want it, *now!*—and also an element of continued youthfulness.

The model of the type may be the professional athlete. "The growth   25 of professional basketball over the past twenty-odd years, from a relatively minor spectator sport to a mass-cultural phenomenon," notes Rebecca Mead, in the *New Yorker*, "is an example of the way in which all of American culture is increasingly geared to the tastes of teenage boys." Mead writes this in an article about Shaquille O'Neal,[8] the 32-year-old center for the Los Angeles Lakers, who earns, with endorsements, 30-odd million dollars a year and lives the life of the most privileged possible junior high school boy: enjoying food fights, go-carts, motorcycles, the run of high rides at amusement parks. It may be a wonderful, but it's also a strange life.

---

[7] ***Zorba the Greek:*** Nikos Kazantzakis's *Zorba the Greek* was published in the United States in 1953 and became a major film in 1964.—EDS.

[8] ***Shaquille O'Neal*** (b. 1972): Formerly a center for the Boston Celtics.—EDS.

And yet what is so wrong about any of this? If one wants to dress like a kid, spin around the office on a scooter, not make up one's mind about what work one wants to do until one is 40, be noncommittal in one's relationships—what, really, are the consequences? I happen to think that the consequences are genuine, and fairly serious.

"Obviously it is normal to think of oneself as younger than one is," W. H. Auden, a younger son, told Robert Craft,[9] "but fatal to want to be younger." I'm not sure about fatal, but it is at a minimum degrading for a culture at large to want to be younger. The tone of national life is lowered, made less rich. The first thing lowered is expectations, intellectual and otherwise. To begin with education, one wonders if the dumbing down of culture one used to hear so much about and which continues isn't connected to the rise of the perpetual adolescent.

Consider contemporary journalism, which tends to play everything to lower and lower common denominators. Why does the *New York Times*, with its pretensions to being our national newspaper, choose to put on its front pages stories about Gennifer Flowers's career as a chanteuse in New Orleans, the firing of NFL coaches, the retirement of Yves Saint Laurent, the canceling of the singer Mariah Carey's recording contract? Slow-news days is a charitable guess; a lowered standard of the significant is a more realistic one. Since the advent of its new publisher, a man of the baby boomer generation, an aura of juvenilia clings to the paper. Frank Rich and Maureen Dowd, two of the paper's most-read columnists, seem not so much the type of the bright college student but of the sassy high-school student—the clever, provocative editor of the school paper out to shock the principal—even though both are in their early 50s.

Television comes closer and closer to being a wholly adolescent form of communication. Clicking the remote from major network news shows, one slides smoothly from superficiality to triviality. When Tom Brokaw announces that some subject will be covered "in depth," what he really means is that roughly 90 seconds, perhaps two minutes, will be devoted to it. It's scarcely original to note that much of contemporary journalism, print and electronic, is pitched to the short attention span, the soundbite, photo-op, quickie take, the deep distaste for complexity—in short, so much is pitched to the adolescent temperament.

Political correctness and so many of the political fashions of our day—from academic feminism to cultural studies to queer theory—could only be perpetrated on adolescent minds: minds, that is, that are trained to search out one thing and one thing only: Is my teacher, or this politician, or that public spokesman, saying something that is likely to be offensive to me or members of any other victim group? Only an adolescent would find it worthwhile to devote his or her attention chiefly to the hunting of offenses, the possibility of slights, real and imagined.

---

9 ***Robert Lawson Craft*** (b. 1923): An American conductor and writer.—EDS.

Self-esteem, of which one currently hears so much, is at bottom another essentially adolescent notion. The great psychological sin of our day is to violate the self-esteem of adolescents of all ages. One might have thought that such self-esteem as any of us is likely to command would be in place by the age of 18. (And what is the point of having all that much self-esteem anyhow, since its logical culminating point can only be smug complacence?) Even in nursing homes, apparently, patients must be guarded against a feeling of their lowered consequence in the world. Self-esteem has become a womb to tomb matter, so that, in contemporary America, the inner and the outer child can finally be made one in the form of the perpetual adolescent.

The coarsening of American culture seems part of the adolescent phenomenon. Television commercials have gotten grosser and grosser. The level of profanity on prime-time television shows has risen greatly over the years. Flicks known to their audiences as "gross-out movies," featuring the slimy and hideous, are part of the regular film menu. Florence King, writing about this phenomenon in her column in the *National Review*, noted: "Since arrested development is as American as apple pie, it is easy to identify the subconscious motivation of the adult male Ughs who produce all these revolting movies and commercials." What makes these things possible is what is known as "niche programming," or the aiming of entertainment at quite specific segments of the audience—African Americans, or teenagers, or the educated classes, or the beer brutes. But increasingly, apparently, we are all being forced into that largest of niches, the American adolescent mentality.

Consider now what must be taken as the most consequential adolescent act in American history during the past half century: the Bill Clinton–Monica Lewinsky relationship. I hesitate to call it an affair, because an affair implies a certain adult style: the good hotel room, the bottle of excellent wine, the peignoir, the Sulka pajamas. With Bill and Monica, you had instead the pizza, the canoodling under the desk, the cigar business, even the whole thing going without consummation. No matter what one's politics, one has to admit that our great national scandal was pure high school.

In a 1959 review of Iona and Peter Opie's *The Lore and Language of School Children*, the poet Philip Larkin[10] revealed first sensing a sharp waning of his interest in Christianity when he read the Bible verse that promises one will return to one's childish state upon entry into Heaven. Larkin wanted nothing more to do with being a child or with the company of children. He looked forward to "money, keys, wallets, letters, books, long-playing records, drinks, the opposite sex, and other solaces of adulthood."

I wanted these things, too, and as soon as possible. From roughly the   35
age of 14, I wanted to stay out all night, to dress like Fred Astaire, to drink and smoke cigarettes with the elegance of William Powell, to have the company of serious women like Susan Hayward and Ingrid Bergman.[11] As I grew

---

10 *Philip Larkin* (1922–1985): A British poet who was known for his witty formal verse.—EDS.
11 *Susan Hayward and Ingrid Bergman:* Glamorous film stars of the 1940s and 1950s.—EDS.

older, I sadly began to realize it wasn't going to happen, at least not in the way I had hoped. What happened instead was the triumph of youth culture, with its adoration of youth, in and for itself, and as a time in one's life of purity and goodness always in danger of being despoiled by the corruption of growing older, which is also to say, of "growing up."

At a certain point in American life, the young ceased to be viewed as a transient class and youth as a phase of life through which everyone soon passed. Instead, youthfulness was vaunted and carried a special moral status. Adolescence triumphed, becoming a permanent condition. As one grew older, one was presented with two choices, to seem an old fogey for attempting to live according to one's own standard of adulthood, or to go with the flow and adapt some variant of pulling one's long gray hair back into a ponytail, struggling into the spandex shorts, working on those abs, and ending one's days among the Rip Van With-Its. Not, I think, a handsome set of alternatives.

The greatest sins, Santayana[12] thought, are those that set out to strangle human nature. This is of course what is being done in cultivating perpetual adolescence, while putting off maturity for as long as possible. Maturity provides a more articulated sense of the ebb and flow, the ups and downs, of life, a more subtly reticulated graph of human possibility. Above all, it values a clear and fit conception of reality. Maturity is ever cognizant that the clock is running, life is finite, and among the greatest mistakes is to believe otherwise. Maturity doesn't exclude playfulness or high humor. Far from it. The mature understand that the bitterest joke of all is that the quickest way to grow old lies in the hopeless attempt to stay forever young. ●

The Reader's Presence

1. What does Epstein believe caused the shift toward adolescent culture? When did it happen? What are some of the earliest examples he cites of youth culture triumphing over maturity? Do you agree that most Americans behave in an "adolescent" way? Why or why not?

2. What areas of life does Epstein believe have been negatively affected by our immaturity? What are the consequences of youth culture's triumph over adulthood? What does Epstein's interpretation suggest about what he values?

3. **CONNECTIONS:** Read John Taylor Gatto's "Against School" (page 665). What does Gatto suggest are the benefits of treating adults like children? Who benefits? How does Gatto's argument about Americans' immaturity differ from Epstein's?

---

12 **Santayana:** Spanish-born George Santayana (1863–1952) was an influential American philosopher. —EDS.

James Fallows

THROWING LIKE A GIRL

Journalist **JAMES FALLOWS** (b. 1949) has written extensively on government, war and defense, and the economy. He graduated with a BA degree in American history and literature from Harvard University, and received an MA degree in economics from Oxford University. Before becoming national correspondent for the *Atlantic Monthly*, a position he has held for more than twenty-five years, Fallows was an editor at the *Washington Monthly* and *U.S. News & World Report*. Fallows writes on a variety of national and international issues. His latest book, *Postcards from Tomorrow Square: Reports from China* (2009), is a collection of essays on contemporary China, all of which were originally published in the *Atlantic Monthly*. His article, "The Fifty-First State," which first appeared in the *Atlantic Monthly*, won the National Magazine Award in 2003. His books include *National Defense* (1981), which won the National Book Award; *Looking at the Sun: The Rise of the New East Asian Economic and Political System* (1995); *Breaking the News: How the Media Undermine American Democracy* (1996); and *Free Flight: From Airline Hell to a New Age of Travel* (2001). His essay, "Throwing Like a Girl," first appeared in the *Atlantic Monthly* in August 1996.

MOST PEOPLE remember the 1994 baseball season for the way it ended—with a strike rather than a World Series. I keep thinking about the way it began. On opening day, April 4, Bill Clinton went to Cleveland and, like many Presidents before him, threw out a ceremonial first pitch. That same day Hillary Rodham Clinton went to Chicago and, like no First Lady before her, also threw out a first ball, at a Cubs game in Wrigley Field.

The next day photos of the Clintons in action appeared in newspapers around the country. Many papers, including the *New York Times* and the *Washington Post*, chose the same two photos to run. The one of Bill Clinton showed him wearing an Indians cap and warm-up jacket. The President, throwing lefty, had turned his shoulders sideways to the plate in preparation for delivery. He was bringing the ball forward from behind his head in a clean-looking throwing action as the photo was snapped. Hillary Clinton was pictured wearing a dark jacket, a scarf, and an oversized Cubs hat. In preparation for her throw she was standing directly facing the plate. A right-hander, she had the elbow of her throwing arm pointed out in front of her. Her forearm was tilted back, toward her shoulder. The ball rested on her upturned palm. As the picture was taken, she was in the middle of an action that can only be described as throwing like a girl.

The phrase "throwing like a girl" has become an embattled and offensive one. Feminists smart at its implication that to do something "like a girl" is to do it the wrong way. Recently, on the heels of the O. J. Simpson case, a book appeared in which the phrase was used to help explain why male athletes, especially football players, were involved in so many assaults against women. Having been trained (like most American boys) to dread the accusation of doing anything "like a girl," athletes were said to grow into the assumption that women were valueless, and natural prey.

I grant the justice of such complaints. I am attuned to the hurt caused by similar broad-brush stereotypes when they apply to groups I belong to—"dancing like a white man," for instance, or "speaking foreign languages like an American," or "thinking like a Washingtonian."

Still, whatever we want to call it, the difference between the two Clintons in what they were doing that day is real, and it is instantly recognizable. And since seeing those photos I have been wondering, Why, exactly, do so many women throw "like a girl"? If the motion were easy to change, presumably a woman as motivated and self-possessed as Hillary Clinton would have changed it. (According to her press secretary, Lisa Caputo, Mrs. Clinton spent the weekend before opening day tossing a ball in the Rose Garden with her husband, for practice.) Presumably, too, the answer to the question cannot be anything quite as simple as, because they *are* girls.

A surprising number of people think that there is a structural difference between male and female arms or shoulders—in the famous "rotator cuff," perhaps—that dictates different throwing motions. "It's in the shoulder joint," a well-educated woman told me recently. "They're hinged differently." Someday researchers may find evidence to support a biological theory of throwing actions. For now, what you'll hear if you ask an orthopedist, an anatomist, or (especially) the coach of a women's softball team is that there is no structural reason why men and women should throw in different ways. This point will be obvious to any male who grew up around girls who liked to play baseball and became good at it. It should be obvious on a larger scale this summer, in broadcasts of the Olympic Games. This year [1996], for the first time, women's fast-pitch softball teams will compete in the Olympics. Although the pitchers in these games will deliver the ball underhand, viewers will see female shortstops, center fielders, catchers, and so on pegging the ball to one another at speeds few male viewers could match.

Even women's tennis is a constant if indirect reminder that men's and women's shoulders are "hinged" the same way. The serving motion in tennis is like a throw—but more difficult, because it must be coordinated with the toss of the tennis ball. The men in professional tennis serve harder than the women, because they are bigger and stronger. But women pros serve harder than most male amateurs have ever done, and the service motion for good players is the same for men and women alike. There is no expectation in college or pro tennis that because of their anatomy female players must "serve like a girl." "I know many women who can throw a lot harder and better than the normal male," says Linda Wells, the coach of the highly

5

successful women's softball team at Arizona State University. "It's not gender that makes the difference in how they throw."

So what is it, then? Since Hillary Clinton's ceremonial visit to Wrigley Field, I have asked men and women how they learned to throw, or didn't. Why did I care? My impetus was the knowledge that eventually my sons would be grown and gone. If my wife, in all other ways a talented athlete, could learn how to throw, I would still have someone to play catch with. My research left some women, including my wife, thinking that I am some kind of obsessed lout, but it has led me to the solution to the mystery. First let's be clear about what there is to be explained.

At a superficial level it's easy to tick off the traits of an awkward-looking throw. The fundamental mistake is the one Mrs. Clinton appeared to be making in the photo: trying to throw a ball with your body facing the target, rather than rotating your shoulders and hips ninety degrees away from the target and then swinging them around in order to accelerate the ball. A throw looks bad if your elbow is lower than your shoulder as your arm comes forward (unless you're throwing sidearm). A throw looks really bad if, as the ball leaves your hand, your wrist is "inside your elbow" — that is, your elbow joint is bent in such a way that your forearm angles back toward your body and your wrist is closer to your head than your elbow is. Slow-motion film of big-league pitchers shows that when they release the ball, the throwing arm is fully extended and straight from shoulder to wrist. The combination of these three elements — head-on stance, dropped elbow, and wrist inside the elbow — mechanically dictates a pushing rather than a hurling motion, creating the familiar pattern of "throwing like a girl."

It is surprisingly hard to find in the literature of baseball a deeper expla-   10
nation of the mechanics of good and bad throws. Tom Seaver's pitching for the Mets and the White Sox got him into the Hall of Fame, but his book *The Art of Pitching* is full of bromides that hardly clarify the process of throwing, even if they might mean something to accomplished pitchers. His chapter "The Absolutes of Pitching Mechanics," for instance, lays out these four unhelpful principles: "Keep the Front Leg Flexible!" "Rub Up the Baseball." "Hide the Baseball!" "Get it Out, Get it Up!" (The fourth refers to the need to get the ball out of the glove and into the throwing hand in a quick motion.)

A variety of other instructional documents, from *Little League's Official How-to-Play Baseball Book* to *Softball for Girls & Women*, mainly reveal the difficulty of finding words to describe a simple motor activity that everyone can recognize. The challenge, I suppose, is like that of writing a manual on how to ride a bike, or how to kiss. Indeed, the most useful description I've found of the mechanics of throwing comes from a man whose specialty is another sport: Vic Braden made his name as a tennis coach, but he has attempted to analyze the physics of a wide variety of sports so that they all will be easier to teach.

Braden says that an effective throw involves connecting a series of links in a "kinetic chain." The kinetic chain, which is Braden's tool for analyzing most sporting activity, operates on a principle like that of crack-the-whip. Momentum builds up in one part of the body. When that part is suddenly stopped, as the end of the "whip" is stopped in crack-the-whip, the momentum is transferred to and concentrated in the next link in the chain. A good throw uses six links of chain, Braden says. The first two links involve the lower body, from feet to waist. The first motion of a throw (after the body has been rotated away from the target) is to rotate the legs and hips back in the direction of the throw, building up momentum as large muscles move body mass. Then those links stop—a pitcher stops turning his hips once they face the plate—and the momentum is transferred to the next link. This is the torso, from waist to shoulders, and since its mass is less than that of the legs, momentum makes it rotate faster than the hips and legs did. The torso stops when it is facing the plate, and the momentum is transferred to the next link—the upper arm. As the upper arm comes past the head, it stops moving forward, and the momentum goes into the final links—the forearm and wrist, which snap forward at tremendous speed.

This may sound arcane and jerkily mechanical, but it makes perfect sense when one sees Braden's slow-mo movies of pitchers in action. And it explains why people do, or don't, learn how to throw. The implication of Braden's analysis is that throwing is a perfectly natural action (millions and millions of people can do it) but not at all innate. A successful throw involves an intricate series of actions coordinated among muscle groups, as each link of the chain is timed to interact with the next. Like bike riding or skating, it can be learned by anyone—male or female. No one starts out knowing how to ride a bike or throw a ball. Everyone has to learn.

Readers who are happy with their throwing skills can prove this to themselves in about two seconds. If you are right-handed, pick up a ball with your left hand and throw it. Unless you are ambidextrous or have some other odd advantage, you will throw it "like a girl." The problem is not that your left shoulder is hinged strangely or that you don't know what a good throw looks like. It is that you have not spent time training your leg, hip, shoulder, and arm muscles on that side to work together as required for a throw. The actor John Goodman, who played football seriously and baseball casually when he was in high school, is right-handed. When cast in the 1992 movie *The Babe*, he had to learn to bat and throw left-handed, for realism in the role of Babe Ruth. For weeks before the filming began, he would arrive an hour early at the set of his TV show, *Roseanne*, so that he could practice throwing a tennis ball against a wall left-handed. "I made damn sure no one could see me," Goodman told me recently. "I'm hard enough on myself without the derisive laughter of my so-called friends." When *The Babe* was released, Goodman told a newspaper interviewer, "I'll never say something like 'He throws like a girl' again. It's not easy to learn how to throw."

What Goodman discovered is what most men have forgotten: that if they know how to throw now, it is because they spent time learning at some point long ago. (Goodman says that he can remember learning to ride a bicycle but not learning to throw with his right hand.) This brings us back to the roots of the "throwing like a girl" phenomenon. The crucial factor is not that males and females are put together differently but that they typically spend their early years in different ways. Little boys often learn how to throw without noticing that they are learning. Little girls are more rarely in environments that encourage them to learn in the same way. A boy who wonders why a girl throws the way she does is like a Frenchman who wonders why so many Americans speak French "with an accent."

"For young boys it is culturally acceptable and politically correct to develop these skills," says Linda Wells, of the Arizona State softball team. "They are mentored and networked. Usually girls are not coached at all, or are coached by Mom—or if it's by Dad, he may not be much of an athlete. Girls are often stuck with the bottom of the male talent pool as examples. I would argue that rather than learning to 'throw like a girl,' they learn to throw like poor male athletes. I say that a bad throw is 'throwing like an old man.' This is not gender, it's acculturation."

Almost any motor skill, from doing handstands to dribbling a basketball, is easier to learn if you start young, which is why John Goodman did not realize that learning to throw is difficult until he attempted it as an adult. Many girls reach adulthood having missed the chance to learn to throw when that would have been easiest to do. And as adults they have neither John Goodman's incentive to teach their muscles a new set of skills nor his confidence that the feat is possible. Five years ago, Joseph Russo, long a baseball coach at St. John's University, gave athletic-talent tests to actresses who were trying out for roles in *A League of Their Own*, a movie about women's baseball. Most of them were "well coordinated in general, like for dancing," he says. But those who had not happened to play baseball or softball when they were young had a problem: "It sounds silly to say it, but they kept throwing like girls." (The best ball-field talents, by the way, were Madonna, Demi Moore, and the rock singer Joan Jett, who according to Russo "can really hit it hard." Careful viewers of *A League of Their Own* will note that only in a fleeting instant in one scene is the star, Geena Davis, shown actually throwing a ball.)

I'm not sure that I buy Linda Wells's theory that most boys are "mentored" or "networked" into developing ball skills. Those who make the baseball team, maybe. But for a far larger number the decisive ingredient seems to be the hundreds of idle hours spent throwing balls, sticks, rocks, and so on in the playground or the back yard. Children on the playground, I think, demonstrate the moment when the kinetic chain begins to work. It is when a little boy tries to throw a rock farther than his friend can or to throw a stick over a telephone wire thirty feet up. A toddler's first, instinctive throw is a push from the shoulder, showing the essential traits of "throwing like a girl." But when a child is really trying to put some oomph into the throw, his

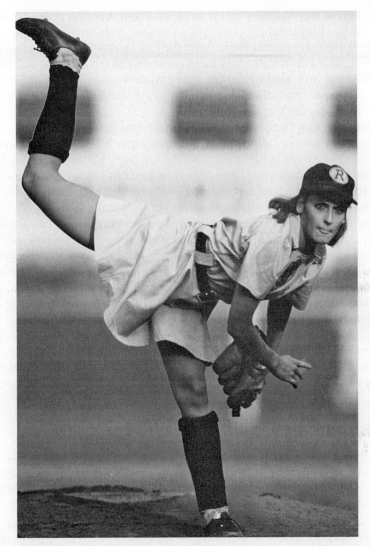

Lori Petty, who plays pitcher Kit Keller (#23) in the 1992 film
A League of Their Own.

natural instinct is to wind up his body and let fly with the links of the chain.
Little girls who do the same thing—compete with each other in distance
throwing—learn the same way, but whereas many boys do this, few girls do.
Tammy Richards, a woman who was raised on a farm in central California,
says that she learned to throw by trying to heave dried cow chips farther
than her brother could. It may have helped that her father, Bob Richards,
was a former Olympic competitor in the decathlon (and two-time Olympic
champion in the pole vault) and that he taught all his sons and daughters to
throw not only the ball but also the discus, the shotput, and the javelin.

Is there a way to make up for lost time if you failed to invest those long hours on the playground years ago? Of course. Adults may not be able to learn to speak unaccented French, but they can learn to ride a bike, or skate, or throw. All that is required for developing any of these motor skills is time for practice—and spending that time requires overcoming the sense of embarrassment and futility that adults often have when attempting something new. Here are two tips that may help.

One is a surprisingly valuable drill suggested by the Little League's   20
How-to-Play handbook. Play catch with a partner who is ten or fifteen feet away—but do so while squatting with the knee of your throwing side touching the ground. When you start out this low, you have to keep the throw high to get the ball to your partner without bouncing it. This encourages a throw with the elbow held well above the shoulder, where it belongs.

The other is to play catch with a person who can throw like an athlete but is using his or her off hand. The typical adult woman hates to play catch with the typical adult man. She is well aware that she's not looking graceful and reacts murderously to the condescending tone in his voice ("That's more like it, honey!"). Forcing a right-handed man to throw left-handed is the great equalizer. He suddenly concentrates his attention on what it takes to get hips, shoulder, and elbow working together. He is suddenly aware of the strength of character needed to ignore the snickers of onlookers while learning new motor skills. He can no longer be condescending. He may even be nervous, wondering what he'll do if his partner makes the breakthrough first and he's the one still throwing like a girl.

The Reader's Presence

1. Fallows acknowledges the objections of feminists to the phrase "throwing like a girl" (paragraph 4). What other activities are linked to one gender or the other? Which gender gathers more negative associations? Why might feminists challenge the phrase? In your opinion, does Fallows satisfactorily answer such objections?

2. As a reporter, Fallows has covered many serious issues. Where does his use of language indicate that this essay is a lighter piece? Where does Fallows use an exaggerated or self-mocking tone? How does his use of humor affect the reader's reception of his message?

3. **CONNECTIONS:** Reread Fallows's essay, focusing on his descriptions of physical movement, especially in paragraphs 9 through 14. Is it possible to understand his idea of the "kinetic chain" (paragraph 12) only by reading a description of it, or must the reader also enact it with his or her body? Compare Fallows's anatomically detailed account to Annie Dillard's "The Death of a Moth" (page 371). How does each writer integrate such "close focus" description into his or her larger overarching point? Do these passages slow the pace of the essays? If they do, to what extent? If they don't, explain why they don't.

Daniel Gilbert

NEXT TO NOTHING

A Professor of Psychology at Harvard University, **DANIEL GILBERT** (b. 1957) is well known for his research in social psychology. The author of the international bestseller, *Stumbling on Happiness* (2006), from which the selection below is taken, Gilbert is particularly interested in the subject of affective forecasting—the human tendency to predict the emotions we will feel in the future—and cognitive bias: the systematic errors in our thinking that cause us to predict incorrectly. With long time collaborator Timothy Wilson (University of Virginia), Daniel Gilbert coined the phrase "psychological immune system" to describe the system of coping mechanisms (rationalization, self-affirmation, and self-deception, to name but a few) that people use to deal with negative emotions. Gilbert has won numerous honors and awards for his research, including a Guggenheim Fellowship and the American Psychological Association's Distinguished Scientific Award for an Early Career Contribution to Psychology. His book, *Stumbling on Happiness*, won the 2007 Royal Society Prize for Science Books and has been translated into over two-dozen languages.

> Daniel Gilbert coined the phrase "psychological immune system" to describe the system of coping mechanisms (rationalization, self-affirmation, and self-deception, to name but a few) that people use to deal with negative emotions.

IF YOU HAVE no special talents or intriguing deformities but are still harboring a secret desire to get into *Guinness World Records*, here's something you might try: March into your boss's office on Monday morning and say, "I've been with the company for some time, I believe my work has been excellent, and I'd like a fifteen percent pay cut . . . though I could settle for ten if that's all the firm can manage right now." The Guinness folks will be taking careful notes because in the long and often contentious history of labor relations, it is unlikely that anyone has ever before demanded a pay cut. Indeed, people *hate* pay cuts, but research suggests that the reason they hate pay cuts has very little to do with the *pay* part and everything to do with the *cut* part. For instance, when people are asked whether they would prefer to have a job at which they earned $30,000 the first year, $40,000 the second year, and $50,000 the third year, or a job at which they earned $60,000 then

$50,000 then $40,000, they generally prefer the job with the increasing wages, despite the fact that they would earn less money over the course of the three years. This is quite curious. Why would people be willing to reduce their total income in order to avoid experiencing a cut in pay?

COMPARING WITH THE PAST

If you've ever fallen asleep one night with the television blaring and been awakened another night by a single footstep, then you already know the answer. The human brain is not particularly sensitive to the absolute magnitude of stimulation, but it is extraordinarily sensitive to differences and changes—that is, to the *relative* magnitude of stimulation. For example, if I blindfolded you and asked you to hold a wooden block in your hand, would you be able to tell if I then placed a pack of gum on top of it? The right answer is "It depends," and what it depends on is the weight of the block. If the block weighed only an ounce, then you'd immediately notice the 500 percent increase in weight when I added a five-ounce pack of gum. But if the block weighed ten pounds, then you'd never notice the .03 percent increase in weight. There is no answer to the question "Can people detect five ounces?" because brains do not detect ounces, they detect changes in ounces and differences in ounces, and the same is true for just about every physical property of an object. Our sensitivity to relative rather than absolute magnitudes is not limited to physical properties such as weight, brightness, or volume. It extends to subjective properties, such as value, goodness, and worth, as well.[1] For instance, most of us would be willing to drive across town to save $50 on the purchase of a $100 radio but not on the purchase of a $100,000 automobile because $50 seems like a fortune when we're buying radios ("Wow, Target has the same radio for half off!") but a pittance when we're buying cars ("Like I'm going to schlep across the city just to get this car for one twentieth of a percent less?")[2]

Economists shake their heads at this kind of behavior and will correctly tell you that your bank account contains absolute dollars and not "percentages off." If it is worth driving across town to save $50, then it doesn't matter which item you're saving it on because when you spend these dollars on gas and groceries, the dollars won't know where they came from.[3] But these economic arguments fall on deaf ears because human beings don't think

[1] D. Kahneman and A. Tversky, "Prospect Theory: An Analysis of Decision Under Risk," *Econometrica* 47 (1979): 263–91.

[2] J. W. Pratt, D. A. Wise, and R. Zeckhauser, "Price Differences in Almost Competitive Markets," *Quarterly Journal of Economics* 93 (1979): 189–211; A. Tversky and D. Kahneman, "The Framing of Decisions and the Psychology of Choice," *Science* 211 (1981): 453–58; R. H. Thaler, "Toward a Positive Theory of Consumer Choice," *Journal of Economic Behavior and Organization* I (1980): 39–60.

[3] R. H. Thaler, "Mental Accounting Matters," *Journal of Behavioral Decision Making* 12 (1999): 183–206.

in absolute dollars. They think in relative dollars, and fifty is or isn't a lot of dollars depending on what it is relative to (which is why people who don't worry about whether their mutual fund manager is keeping 0.5 or 0.6 percent of their investment will nonetheless spend hours scouring the Sunday paper for a coupon that gives them 40 percent off a tube of toothpaste). Marketers, politicians, and other agents of influence know about our obsession with relative magnitudes and routinely turn it to their own advantage. For instance, one ancient ploy involves asking someone to pay an unrealistically large cost ("Would you come to our Save the Bears meeting next Friday and then join us Saturday for a protest march at the zoo?") before asking them to pay a smaller cost ("Okay then, could you at least contribute five dollars to our organization?"). Studies show that people are much more likely to agree to pay the small cost after having first contemplated the large one, in part because doing so makes the small cost seem so . . . er, bearable.[4]

Because the subjective value of a commodity is relative, it shifts and changes depending on what we compare the commodity to. For instance, every morning on my walk to work I stop at my neighborhood Starbucks and hand $1.89 to the barista, who then hands me twenty ounces of better-than-average coffee. I have no idea what it costs Starbucks to make this coffee, and I have no idea why they have chosen to charge me this particular amount, but I do know that if I stopped in one morning and found that the price had suddenly jumped to $2.89, I would immediately do one of two things: I would compare the new price to the price I used to pay, conclude that coffee at Starbucks had gotten too damned expensive, and invest in one of those vacuum-sealed travel mugs and start brewing my coffee at home; or I would compare the new price to the price of other things I could buy with the same amount of cash (e.g., two felt-tip markers, a thirty-two-inch branch of artificial bamboo, or 1/100th of the twenty-CD boxed set *The Complete Miles Davis at Montreux*) and conclude that the coffee at Starbucks was a bargain. In theory I could make either of these comparisons, so which one would I actually make?

We both know the answer to that: I'd make the easy one. When I encounter a $2.89 cup of coffee, it's all too easy for me to recall what I paid for coffee the day before and not so easy for me to imagine all the other things I might buy with my money.[5] Because it is so much easier for me to *remember the past* than to *generate new possibilities*, I will tend to compare the present with the past even when I *ought* to be comparing it with the possible. And that is indeed what I *ought* to be doing because it really doesn't *matter*

[margin: 5]

---

[4] R. B. Cialdini et al., "Reciprocal Concessions Procedure for Inducing Compliance: The Door-in-the-Face Technique," *Journal of Personality and Social Psychology* 31 (1975): 206–15. There is some controversy about whether this effect is, in fact, a result of the contrast between the large and small requests. See J. P. Dillard, "The Current Status of Research on Sequential-Request Compliance Techniques," *Personality and Social Psychology Bulletin* 17 (1991): 283–88.

[5] D. Kahneman and D. T. Miller, "Norm Theory: Comparing Reality to Its Alternatives," *Psychological Review* 93 (1986): 136–53.

what coffee cost the day before, the week before, or at any time during the Hoover administration. Right now I have absolute dollars to spend and the only question I need to answer is how to spend them in order to maximize my satisfaction. If an international bean embargo suddenly caused the price of coffee to skyrocket to $10,000 per cup, then the only question I would need to ask myself is: "What else can I do with ten thousand dollars, and will it bring me more or less satisfaction than a cup of coffee?" If the answer is "more," then I should walk away. If the answer is "less," then I should get a cup of coffee. And an accountant with a whip.

The fact that it is so much easier to remember the past than to generate the possible causes us to make plenty of weird decisions. For instance, people are more likely to purchase a vacation package that has been marked down from $600 to $500 than an identical package that costs $400 but that was on sale the previous day for $300.[6] Because it is easier to compare a vacation package's price with its former price than with the price of other things one might buy, we end up preferring bad deals that have become decent deals to great deals that were once amazing deals. The same tendency leads us to treat commodities that have a "memorable past" differently from those that don't. For example, imagine that you have a $20 bill and a $20 concert ticket in your wallet, but when you arrive at the concert you realize that you've lost the ticket en route. Would you buy a new one? Most people say no.[7] Now imagine that instead of a $20 bill and a $20 ticket, you have two $20 bills in your wallet, and when you arrive at the concert you realize that you've lost one of the bills en route. Would you buy a concert ticket? Most people say yes. It doesn't take a logician to see that the two examples are identical in all the ways that matter: In both cases you've lost a piece of paper that was valued at $20 (a ticket or a bill), and in both cases you must now decide whether to spend the money that remains in your wallet on a concert. Nonetheless, our stubborn insistence on comparing the present to the past leads us to reason differently about these functionally equivalent cases. When we lose a $20 bill and then contemplate buying a concert ticket for the first time, the concert has no past, and hence we correctly compare the cost of seeing the concert with other possibilities ("Should I spend twenty dollars to see the concert, or should I buy some new sharkskin mittens?"). But when we lose a ticket we've previously purchased and contemplate "replacing it," the concert has a past, and hence we compare the current cost of seeing the concert ($40) with its previous cost ($20) and feel disinclined to see a performance whose price has suddenly doubled. ●

---

6 O. E. Tykocinski and T. S. Pittman, "The Consequences of Doing Nothing: Inaction Inertia as Avoidance of Anticipated Counterfactual Regret," *Journal of Personality and Social Psychology* 75 (1998): 607–16; and O. E. Tykocinski, T. S. Pittman, and E. E. Tuttle, "Inaction Inertia: Forgoing Future Benefits as a Result of an Initial Failure to Act," *Journal of Personality and Social Psychology* 68 (1995): 793–803.

7 D. Kahneman and A. Tversky, "Choices, Values, and Frames," *American Psychologist* 39 (1984): 341–50.

The Reader's Presence

1. What is the point of Gilbert's first example of an employee asking for a pay cut? What is the pay cut in question? Do you think the example that people would prefer to take less overall by opting for an increase in pay instead of a decrease—despite the difference in total amount—makes sense? Why or why not? What other factors might come into play?

2. Why does Gilbert introduce the example of vacation packages (paragraph 6)? What psychological principle does the example illustrate? Put the principle into your own words to show why people "are more likely to purchase a vacation package that has been marked down from $600 to $500 than an identical package that costs $400 but that was on sale the previous day for $300." What appears irrational about the decision from an economic point of view? In your opinion, is it irrational from a psychological point of view? Explain why or why not.

3. **CONNECTIONS:** Daniel Gilbert is a trained psychologist who is examining economic behavior. Compare "Next to Nothing" with the selection by two economists, Steven D. Levitt and Stephen J. Dubner, who examine psychological behavior in "What Should You Worry About?" (page 475). In what ways do the disciplines of the authors help them understand what appears to be irrational human behavior?

Malcolm Gladwell

SMALL CHANGE: WHY THE REVOLUTION WILL NOT BE TWEETED

MALCOLM GLADWELL (b. 1963) is a best-selling author and staff writer for the *New Yorker*. Son of a British father and a Jamaican mother, Gladwell was born in England and moved to the United States as a child. He began his journalism career at the *American Spectator*, a conservative monthly magazine. He started writing for the *Washington Post* in 1987, serving as a science writer before becoming the paper's New York City bureau chief. He left the *Post* in 1996 to write for the *New Yorker*. Gladwell is known for his best-

> "Ideas and products and messages and behaviors spread just like viruses do."

selling books *The Tipping Point: How Little Things Can Make a Big Difference* (2000), *Blink: The Power of Thinking Without Thinking* (2005), and *Outliers: The Story of Success* (2008). His most recent book, *What the Dog Saw: And Other Adventures* (2009), is a collection of shorter works originally published in the *New Yorker.* "Small Change: Why the Revolution Will Not Be Tweeted" first appeared in the October 4, 2010 issue of the *New Yorker.*

Gladwell's writing tends to be concerned with illuminating the patterns behind everyday life and identifying the origins of major events and the trends in minor ones. According to Gladwell, "Ideas and products and messages and behaviors spread just like viruses do." He was named one of *Time* magazine's 100 Most Influential People in 2005.

AT FOUR-THIRTY in the afternoon on Monday, February 1, 1960, four college students sat down at the lunch counter at the Woolworth's in downtown Greensboro, North Carolina. They were freshmen at North Carolina A. & T., a black college a mile or so away.

"I'd like a cup of coffee, please," one of the four, Ezell Blair, said to the waitress.

"We don't serve Negroes here," she replied.

The Woolworth's lunch counter was a long L-shaped bar that could seat sixty-six people, with a standup snack bar at one end. The seats were for whites. The snack bar was for blacks. Another employee, a black woman who worked at the steam table, approached the students and tried to warn them away. "You're acting stupid, ignorant!" she said. They didn't move. Around five-thirty, the front doors to the store were locked. The four still didn't move. Finally, they left by a side door. Outside, a small crowd had gathered, including a photographer from the Greensboro *Record.* "I'll be back tomorrow with A. & T. College," one of the students said.

By next morning, the protest had grown to twenty-seven men and four   5 women, most from the same dormitory as the original four. The men were dressed in suits and ties. The students had brought their schoolwork, and studied as they sat at the counter. On Wednesday, students from Greensboro's "Negro" secondary school, Dudley High, joined in, and the number of protesters swelled to eighty. By Thursday, the protesters numbered three hundred, including three white women, from the Greensboro campus of the University of North Carolina. By Saturday, the sit-in had reached six hundred. People spilled out onto the street. White teenagers waved Confederate flags. Someone threw a firecracker. At noon, the A. & T. football team arrived. "Here comes the wrecking crew," one of the white students shouted.

By the following Monday, sit-ins had spread to Winston-Salem, twenty-five miles away, and Durham, fifty miles away. The day after that, students at Fayetteville State Teachers College and at Johnson C. Smith College, in Charlotte, joined in, followed on Wednesday by students at St. Augustine's College and Shaw University, in Raleigh. On Thursday and Friday, the protest crossed state lines, surfacing in Hampton and Portsmouth, Virginia, in

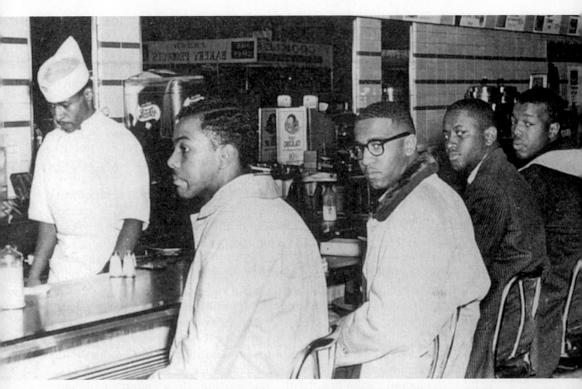

The four college students at the lunch counter at Woolworth's in downtown Greensboro, North Carolina, February 2, 1960.

Rock Hill, South Carolina, and in Chattanooga, Tennessee. By the end of the month, there were sit-ins throughout the South, as far west as Texas. "I asked every student I met what the first day of the sitdowns had been like on his campus," the political theorist Michael Walzer wrote in *Dissent*. "The answer was always the same: 'It was like a fever. Everyone wanted to go.'" Some seventy thousand students eventually took part. Thousands were arrested and untold thousands more radicalized. These events in the early sixties became a civil-rights war that engulfed the South for the rest of the decade—and it happened without e-mail, texting, Facebook, or Twitter.

The world, we are told, is in the midst of a revolution. The new tools of social media have reinvented social activism. With Facebook and Twitter and the like, the traditional relationship between political authority and popular will has been upended, making it easier for the powerless to collaborate, coordinate, and give voice to their concerns. When ten thousand protesters took to the streets in Moldova in the spring of 2009 to protest against their country's Communist government, the action was dubbed the Twitter Revolution, because of the means by which the demonstrators had been brought together. A few months after that, when student protests rocked Tehran, the

State Department took the unusual step of asking Twitter to suspend scheduled maintenance of its Web site, because the Administration didn't want such a critical organizing tool out of service at the height of the demonstrations. "Without Twitter the people of Iran would not have felt empowered and confident to stand up for freedom and democracy," Mark Pfeifle, a former national-security adviser, later wrote, calling for Twitter to be nominated for the Nobel Peace Prize. Where activists were once defined by their causes, they are now defined by their tools. Facebook warriors go online to push for change. "You are the best hope for us all," James K. Glassman, a former senior State Department official, told a crowd of cyber activists at a recent conference sponsored by Facebook, A. T. & T., Howcast, MTV, and Google. Sites like Facebook, Glassman said, "give the U.S. a significant competitive advantage over terrorists. Some time ago, I said that Al Qaeda was 'eating our lunch on the Internet.' That is no longer the case. Al Qaeda is stuck in Web 1.0. The Internet is now about interactivity and conversation."

These are strong, and puzzling, claims. Why does it matter who is eating whose lunch on the Internet? Are people who log on to their Facebook page really the best hope for us all? As for Moldova's so-called Twitter Revolution, Evgeny Morozov, a scholar at Stanford who has been the most persistent of digital evangelism's critics, points out that Twitter had scant internal significance in Moldova, a country where very few Twitter accounts exist. Nor does it seem to have been a revolution, not least because the protests—as Anne Applebaum suggested in the *Washington Post*—may well have been a bit of stagecraft cooked up by the government. (In a country paranoid about Romanian revanchism,[1] the protesters flew a Romanian flag over the Parliament building.) In the Iranian case, meanwhile, the people tweeting about the demonstrations were almost all in the West. "It is time to get Twitter's role in the events in Iran right," Golnaz Esfandiari wrote, this past summer, in *Foreign Policy*. "Simply put: There was no Twitter Revolution inside Iran." The cadre of prominent bloggers, like Andrew Sullivan, who championed the role of social media in Iran, Esfandiari continued, misunderstood the situation. "Western journalists who couldn't reach—or didn't bother reaching?—people on the ground in Iran simply scrolled through the English-language tweets post with tag #iranelection," she wrote. "Through it all, no one seemed to wonder why people trying to coordinate protests in Iran would be writing in any language other than Farsi."

Some of this grandiosity is to be expected. Innovators tend to be solipsists. They often want to cram every stray fact and experience into their new model. As the historian Robert Darnton has written, "The marvels of communication technology in the present have produced a false consciousness about the past—even a sense that communication has no history, or had nothing of importance to consider before the days of television and the Internet." But there is something else at work here, in the outsized enthusiasm

---

[1] **revanchism** (from the French: *revanche*, "revenge"): A term used to describe a political policy of a nation or an ethnic group, intended to regain lost territory or standing.—EDS.

for social media. Fifty years after one of the most extraordinary episodes of social upheaval in American history, we seem to have forgotten what activism is.

Greensboro in the early nineteen-sixties was the kind of place where   10 racial insubordination was routinely met with violence. The four students who first sat down at the lunch counter were terrified. "I suppose if anyone had come up behind me and yelled 'Boo,' I think I would have fallen off my seat," one of them said later. On the first day, the store manager notified the police chief, who immediately sent two officers to the store. On the third day, a gang of white toughs showed up at the lunch counter and stood ostentatiously behind the protesters, ominously muttering epithets such as "burr-head nigger." A local Ku Klux Klan leader made an appearance. On Saturday, as tensions grew, someone called in a bomb threat, and the entire store had to be evacuated.

The dangers were even clearer in the Mississippi Freedom Summer Project of 1964, another of the sentinel campaigns of the civil-rights movement. The Student Nonviolent Coordinating Committee recruited hundreds of Northern, largely white unpaid volunteers to run Freedom Schools, register black voters, and raise civil-rights awareness in the Deep South. "No one should go *anywhere* alone, but certainly not in an automobile and certainly not at night," they were instructed. Within days of arriving in Mississippi, three volunteers—Michael Schwerner, James Chaney, and Andrew Goodman—were kidnapped and killed, and, during the rest of the summer, thirty-seven black churches were set on fire and dozens of safe houses were bombed; volunteers were beaten, shot at, arrested, and trailed by pickup trucks full of armed men. A quarter of those in the program dropped out. Activism that challenges the status quo—that attacks deeply rooted problems—is not for the faint of heart.

What makes people capable of this kind of activism? The Stanford sociologist Doug McAdam compared the Freedom Summer dropouts with the participants who stayed, and discovered that the key difference wasn't, as might be expected, ideological fervor. "*All* of the applicants—participants and withdrawals alike—emerge as highly committed, articulate supporters of the goals and values of the summer program," he concluded. What mattered more was an applicant's degree of personal connection to the civil-rights movement. All the volunteers were required to provide a list of personal contacts—the people they wanted kept apprised of their activities—and participants were far more likely than dropouts to have close friends who were also going to Mississippi. High-risk activism, McAdam concluded, is a "strong-tie" phenomenon.

This pattern shows up again and again. One study of the Red Brigades, the Italian terrorist group of the nineteen-seventies, found that seventy percent of recruits had at least one good friend already in the organization. The same is true of the men who joined the mujahideen in Afghanistan. Even revolutionary actions that look spontaneous, like the demonstrations in East

Germany that led to the fall of the Berlin Wall, are, at core, strong-tie phenomena. The opposition movement in East Germany consisted of several hundred groups, each with roughly a dozen members. Each group was in limited contact with the others: at the time, only thirteen percent of East Germans even had a phone. All they knew was that on Monday nights, outside St. Nicholas Church in downtown Leipzig, people gathered to voice their anger at the state. And the primary determinant of who showed up was "critical friends"—the more friends you had who were critical of the regime the more likely you were to join the protest.

So one crucial fact about the four freshmen at the Greensboro lunch counter—David Richmond, Franklin McCain, Ezell Blair, and Joseph McNeil—was their relationship with one another. McNeil was a roommate of Blair's in A. & T.'s Scott Hall dormitory. Richmond roomed with McCain one floor up, and Blair, Richmond, and McCain had all gone to Dudley High School. The four would smuggle beer into the dorm and talk late into the night in Blair and McNeil's room. They would all have remembered the murder of Emmett Till in 1955, the Montgomery bus boycott that same year, and the showdown in Little Rock in 1957. It was McNeil who brought up the idea of a sit-in at Woolworth's. They'd discussed it for nearly a month. Then McNeil came into the dorm room and asked the others if they were ready. There was a pause, and McCain said, in a way that works only with people who talk late into the night with one another, "Are you guys chicken or not?" Ezell Blair worked up the courage the next day to ask for a cup of coffee because he was flanked by his roommate and two good friends from high school.

The kind of activism associated with social media isn't like this at all. The 15 platforms of social media are built around weak ties. Twitter is a way of following (or being followed by) people you may never have met. Facebook is a tool for efficiently managing your acquaintances, for keeping up with the people you would not otherwise be able to stay in touch with. That's why you can have a thousand "friends" on Facebook, as you never could in real life.

This is in many ways a wonderful thing. There is strength in weak ties, as the sociologist Mark Granovetter has observed. Our acquaintances—not our friends—are our greatest source of new ideas and information. The Internet lets us exploit the power of these kinds of distant connections with marvellous efficiency. It's terrific at the diffusion of innovation, interdisciplinary collaboration, seamlessly matching up buyers and sellers, and the logistical functions of the dating world. But weak ties seldom lead to high-risk activism.

In a new book called *The Dragonfly Effect: Quick, Effective, and Powerful Ways to Use Social Media to Drive Social Change*, the business consultant Andy Smith and the Stanford Business School professor Jennifer Aaker tell the story of Sameer Bhatia, a young Silicon Valley entrepreneur who came down with acute myelogenous leukemia. It's a perfect illustration of social media's strengths. Bhatia needed a bone-marrow transplant, but he could not find a match among his relatives and friends. The odds were best with a donor of his ethnicity, and there were few South Asians in the national bone-marrow database. So Bhatia's business partner sent out an e-mail explaining Bhatia's plight to more than four hundred of their acquaintances, who forwarded the e-mail to their personal contacts; Facebook pages and YouTube videos were devoted to the Help Sameer campaign. Eventually, nearly twenty-five thousand new people were registered in the bone-marrow database, and Bhatia found a match.

But how did the campaign get so many people to sign up? By not asking too much of them. That's the only way you can get someone you don't really know to do something on your behalf. You can get thousands of people to sign up for a donor registry, because doing so is pretty easy. You have to send in a cheek swab and—in the highly unlikely event that your bone marrow is a good match for someone in need—spend a few hours at the hospital. Donating bone marrow isn't a trivial matter. But it doesn't involve financial or personal risk; it doesn't mean spending a summer being chased by armed men in pickup trucks. It doesn't require that you confront socially entrenched norms and practices. In fact, it's the kind of commitment that will bring only social acknowledgment and praise.

The evangelists of social media don't understand this distinction; they seem to believe that a Facebook friend is the same as a real friend and that signing up for a donor registry in Silicon Valley today is activism in the same sense as sitting at a segregated lunch counter in Greensboro in 1960. "Social networks are particularly effective at increasing motivation," Aaker and Smith write. But that's not true. Social networks are effective at increasing *participation*—by lessening the level of motivation that participation requires. The Facebook page of the Save Darfur Coalition has 1,282,339 members, who have donated an average of nine cents apiece. The next biggest Darfur charity on Facebook has 22,073 members, who have donated an average of thirty-five cents. Help Save Darfur has 2,797 members, who have given, on average, fifteen cents. A spokesperson for the Save Darfur Coalition told *Newsweek*, "We wouldn't necessarily gauge someone's value to the advocacy movement based on what they've given. This is a powerful mechanism to engage this critical population. They inform their community, attend events, volunteer. It's not something you can measure by looking at a ledger." In other words, Facebook activism succeeds not by motivating people to make a real sacrifice but by motivating them to do the things that people do when they are not motivated enough to make a real sacrifice. We are a long way from the lunch counters of Greensboro.

The students who joined the sit-ins across the South during the winter   20
of 1960 described the movement as a "fever." But the civil-rights movement was more like a military campaign than like a contagion. In the late nineteen-fifties, there had been sixteen sit-ins in various cities throughout the South, fifteen of which were formally organized by civil-rights organizations like the NAACP and CORE. Possible locations for activism were scouted. Plans were drawn up. Movement activists held training sessions

and retreats for would-be protesters, The Greensboro Four were a product of this groundwork: all were members of the NAACP Youth Council. They had close ties with the head of the local NAACP chapter. They had been briefed on the earlier wave of sit-ins in Durham, and had been part of a series of movement meetings in activist churches. When the sit-in movement spread from Greensboro throughout the South, it did not spread indiscriminately. It spread to those cities which had preexisting "movement centers" — a core of dedicated and trained activists ready to turn the "fever" into action.

The civil-rights movement was high-risk activism. It was also, crucially, strategic activism: a challenge to the establishment mounted with precision

Dignity keeps pace with bigotry: a young African-American man walks next to a Caucasian young man during a lunch counter sit-down demonstration.

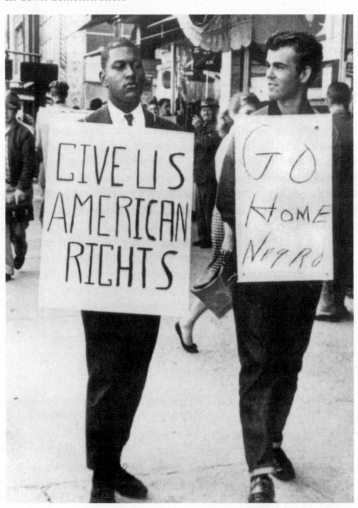

and discipline. The NAACP was a centralized organization, run from New York according to highly formalized operating procedures. At the Southern Christian Leadership Conference, Martin Luther King, Jr., was the unquestioned authority. At the center of the movement was the black church, which had, as Aldon D. Morris points out in his superb 1984 study, "The Origins of the Civil Rights Movement," a carefully demarcated division of labor, with various standing committees and disciplined groups. "Each group was task-oriented and coordinated its activities through authority structures," Morris writes. "Individuals were held accountable for their assigned duties, and important conflicts were resolved by the minister, who usually exercised ultimate authority over the congregation."

This is the second crucial distinction between traditional activism and its online variant: social media are not about this kind of hierarchical organization. Facebook and the like are tools for building *networks*, which are the opposite, in structure and character, of hierarchies. Unlike hierarchies, with their rules and procedures, networks aren't controlled by a single central authority. Decisions are made through consensus, and the ties that bind people to the group are loose.

This structure makes networks enormously resilient and adaptable in low-risk situations. Wikipedia is a perfect example. It doesn't have an editor, sitting in New York, who directs and corrects each entry. The effort of putting together each entry is self-organized. If every entry in Wikipedia were to be erased tomorrow, the content would swiftly be restored, because that's what happens when a network of thousands spontaneously devote their time to a task.

There are many things, though, that networks don't do well. Car companies sensibly use a network to organize their hundreds of suppliers, but not to design their cars. No one believes that the articulation of a coherent design philosophy is best handled by a sprawling, leaderless organizational system. Because networks don't have a centralized leadership structure and clear lines of authority, they have real difficulty reaching consensus and setting goals. They can't think strategically; they are chronically prone to conflict and error. How do you make difficult choices about tactics or strategy or philosophical direction when everyone has an equal say?

The Palestine Liberation Organization originated as a network, and the international-relations scholars Mette Eilstrup-Sangiovanni and Calvert Jones argue in a recent essay in *International Security* that this is why it ran into such trouble as it grew: "Structural features typical of networks—the absence of central authority, the unchecked autonomy of rival groups, and the inability to arbitrate quarrels through formal mechanisms—made the P.L.O. excessively vulnerable to outside manipulation and internal strife."

In Germany in the nineteen-seventies, they go on, "the far more unified and successful left-wing terrorists tended to organize hierarchically, with professional management and clear divisions of labor. They were concentrated geographically in universities, where they could establish central leadership, trust, and camaraderie through regular, face-to-face meetings."

They seldom betrayed their comrades in arms during police interrogations. Their counterparts on the right were organized as decentralized networks, and had no such discipline. These groups were regularly infiltrated, and members, once arrested, easily gave up their comrades. Similarly, Al Qaeda was most dangerous when it was a unified hierarchy. Now that it has dissipated into a network, it has proved far less effective.

The drawbacks of networks scarcely matter if the network isn't interested in systemic change—if it just wants to frighten or humiliate or make a splash—or if it doesn't need to think strategically. But if you're taking on a powerful and organized establishment you have to be a hierarchy. The Montgomery bus boycott required the participation of tens of thousands of people who depended on public transit to get to and from work each day. It lasted a *year*. In order to persuade those people to stay true to the cause, the boycott's organizers tasked each local black church with maintaining morale, and put together a free alternative private carpool service, with forty-eight dispatchers and forty-two pickup stations. Even the White Citizens Council, King later said, conceded that the carpool system moved with "military precision." By the time King came to Birmingham, for the climactic showdown with Police Commissioner Eugene (Bull) Connor, he had a budget of a million dollars, and a hundred full-time staff members on the ground, divided into operational units. The operation itself was divided into steadily escalating phases, mapped out in advance. Support was maintained through consecutive mass meetings rotating from church to church around the city.

Boycotts and sit-ins and nonviolent confrontations—which were the weapons of choice for the civil-rights movement—are high-risk strategies. They leave little room for conflict and error. The moment even one protester deviates from the script and responds to provocation, the moral legitimacy of the entire protest is compromised. Enthusiasts for social media would no doubt have us believe that King's task in Birmingham would have been made infinitely easier had he been able to communicate with his followers through Facebook, and contented himself with tweets from a Birmingham jail. But networks are messy: think of the ceaseless pattern of correction and revision, amendment and debate, that characterizes Wikipedia. If Martin Luther King, Jr., had tried to do a wiki-boycott in Montgomery, he would have been steamrollered by the white power structure. And of what use would a digital communication tool be in a town where ninety-eight percent of the black community could be reached every Sunday morning at church? The things that King needed in Birmingham—discipline and strategy—were things that online social media cannot provide.

The bible of the social-media movement is Clay Shirky's *Here Comes Everybody*. Shirky, who teaches at New York University, sets out to demonstrate the organizing power of the Internet, and he begins with the story of Evan, who worked on Wall Street, and his friend Ivanna, after she left her smart phone, an expensive Sidekick, on the back seat of a New York City taxicab. The telephone company transferred the data on Ivanna's lost phone to a new phone, whereupon she and Evan discovered that the Sidekick was now in the hands of a teenager from Queens, who was using it to take photographs of herself and her friends.

When Evan e-mailed the teenager, Sasha, asking for the phone back,   30 she replied that his "white ass" didn't deserve to have it back. Miffed, he set up a Web page with her picture and a description of what had happened. He forwarded the link to his friends, and they forwarded it to their friends. Someone found the MySpace page of Sasha's boyfriend, and a link to it found its way onto the site. Someone found her address online and took a video of her home while driving by; Evan posted the video on the site. The story was picked up by the news filter Digg. Evan was now up to ten e-mails a minute. He created a bulletin board for his readers to share their stories, but it crashed under the weight of responses. Evan and Ivanna went to the police, but the police filed the report under "lost," rather than "stolen," which essentially closed the case. "By this point millions of readers were watching," Shirky writes, "and dozens of mainstream news outlets had covered the story." Bowing to the pressure, the NYPD reclassified the item as "stolen." Sasha was arrested, and Evan got his friend's Sidekick back.

Shirky's argument is that this is the kind of thing that could never have happened in the pre-Internet age—and he's right. Evan could never have tracked down Sasha. The story of the Sidekick would never have been publicized. An army of people could never have been assembled to wage this fight. The police wouldn't have bowed to the pressure of a lone person who had misplaced something as trivial as a cell phone. The story, to Shirky, illustrates "the ease and speed with which a group can be mobilized for the right kind of cause" in the Internet age.

Shirky considers this model of activism an upgrade. But it is simply a form of organizing which favors the weak-tie connections that give us access to information over the strong-tie connections that help us persevere in the face of danger. It shifts our energies from organizations that promote strategic and disciplined activity and toward those which promote resilience and adaptability. It makes it easier for activists to express themselves, and harder for that expression to have any impact. The instruments of social media are well suited to making the existing social order more efficient. They are not a natural enemy of the status quo. If you are of the opinion that all the world needs is a little buffing around the edges, this should not trouble you. But if you think that there are still lunch counters out there that need integrating it ought to give you pause.

Shirky ends the story of the lost Sidekick by asking, portentously, "What happens next?"—no doubt imagining future waves of digital protesters. But he has already answered the question. What happens next is more of the same. A networked, weak-tie world is good at things like helping Wall Streeters get phones back from teenage girls. *Viva la revolución.* ∎

The Reader's Presence

1. Reread the first six paragraphs of Gladwell's essay. What do they lead you to believe will be the focus of his essay? Point to specific words and phrases to support your response. How does the scene that Gladwell describes relate to the point he is making in this essay? What are the effects of Gladwell's decision not to mention anything about social media until the end of this opening section?

2. Point to specific ways in which Gladwell recounts the events of the Greensboro lunch counter sit-in differently from the way he relates the story of the New Yorker who lost her Sidekick. What compositional strategies does Gladwell use to make the effects of reading about these two events seem so different?

3. **CONNECTIONS:**   Compare Gladwell's essay with Nicholas Carr's "Is Google Making Us Stupid?" (page 633). How does each author use historical facts to support the points he is making? In what specific ways are the authors' uses of historical facts similar? How are they different? In what ways do their claims support each other? In what ways are they at odds?

Cynthia Gorney
THE URGE TO MERGE

CYNTHIA GORNEY (b. 1954) is an American journalist. A member of the faculty of the Berkeley Graduate School of Journalism since 1999, she was a reporter for the *Washington Post* from 1975 through 1991 and the paper's South American bureau chief from 1980 through 1982. She has also written for the *New Yorker*, *National Geographic*, *Harper's*, *Sports Illustrated*, the *New York Times Magazine*, *Runner's World*, *O: The Oprah Magazine*, and the *American Journalism Review*, among other magazines. She is currently a contributing writer for the *New York Times Magazine* and *National Geographic*. She has received an American Society of Newspaper Editors feature writing award, and her book, *Articles of Faith: A Frontline History of the Abortion Wars* (1998), was nominated for the *Los Angeles Times* Book Prize.

HERE IS the Caldecott Tunnel Problem. If there's another person with you right now, you may end up raising your voices as you consider it. I'm just warning, is all. The last time I brought up the Caldecott Tunnel Problem among friends, two people who had been a happy couple for a long time started arguing, and then they looked at each other as if something new and disturbing were presenting itself, and when I got up to go, one of them was pounding the table and yelling at her beloved, "But that is *so wrong!*"

Anyway, the problem. Near where I live, which happens to be Northern California but that's not relevant, there's a three-bore tunnel that runs east-west under some steep hills that separate the suburbs (east) from Oakland and Berkeley and eventually San Francisco (west). If you're driving east-west around here, you use the Caldecott Tunnel; you could go winding over the hills and bypass the problem altogether, but it would take forever and you don't want to. The freeway leading to the Caldecott is called Highway 24, and on the suburban side of the tunnel it courses like a river beneath open sloping grassland, all golden and Tuscan right now in summer.

So here you are, let us say, heading west toward the Caldecott at the end of a July afternoon. The geography, what with the hills rising on either side, pretty much requires you to focus on the thing that is about to happen in front of you—you can see it coming, and sometimes from quite a distance, depending on how bad the backup is. The trick about the Caldecott is that although each bore is two lanes wide, the middle bore switches direction, by means of signage and mechanically raised cone separators, contingent on the flow of the main morning and evening commute. So if you're driving out of the suburbs toward Oakland at the end of the day, the cars coming the opposite way take that middle bore, which means your side of 24 is being coned off into the one remaining bore on the right—a four-lane to a two-lane funnel.

This is the point at which the North American driving populace, as you know, cleaves into two camps.

Two-thirds of us, according to calculations I have made while brooding inordinately about this inside my Subaru, are lineuppers, slowing rapidly from 70 to 30 or 20 or whatever and taking our places—courteously and patiently, as our mothers taught us to do, respecting the broad tenets of social justice and the primacy of fairness to all persons on the road, regardless of income or ethnicity or car model or perceived level of personal importance—where was I? Oh. Sorry. Taking our places at the end of the line, I was saying, the long two-lane line that has formed to the right, creeping toward the mouth of our tunnel bore. There is still some empty lane space beside us on the left, true, where the cones are gradually closing those left lanes down. But people are *already lined up*. If we passed them on the left to get in, farther ahead, we would be cutting the line.

One-third of us, on the other hand, zoom on by. For purposes of this problem, I shall call these sidezoomers. (When I raised the Caldecott Tunnel Problem with my father, who is 83, he startled me by suggesting a longer label that included more bad words than I believe I have ever heard him use

5

TO KNOW THE PROBLEM
YOU MUST LIVE THE PROBLEM...
EXIBIT A - Anatomy of the issue at hand. Knowledge is power
and knowing, is half the battle...

Long suffering
lineuppers in
through-lane.

Sidezoomer
hustling for
maximum
advantage

Ersatz exit-laner
finally making
intentions known

Sidezoomer
engaging in
instant butt-in.

Blissful
non-bottlenecked
other way drivers

Genuine
exit-laner
blamelessly
proceeding

Hostile lineupper
holding two-inch
space between
cars to block
sidezoomer.

This illustration originally accompanied Gorney's essay in
The New York Times Magazine *for August 3, 2008.*

at one time.) Sidezoomers have a variety of strategies, each exaggerated by
the configuration of the Caldecott but replicated in bottlenecks across the
land: there are the ones who zoom by a few dozen cars, angling in when
they see a plausible opening; and there are the ones who zoom all the way
up, to the very top of the cone-off funnel, at which point they thrust their
aggressive little self-entitled fenders toward the lineup and nudge themselves in. And there are those who opt for frontage-road sidezooming, which
requires maneuvering into the far-right highway lane in order to get off at a
certain pretunnel exit that dumps cars onto a surface street alongside Highway 24. They zip along that street and get back on 24 at the next entrance,

slipping in ahead of the bumper-to-bumper lineup they just bypassed. So now they're cutting the line, too, but from the right.

And that very last exit lane before the tunnel, also on the right? You can't get back onto the highway once you've exited there, but if you're a sidezoomer you can slide into the empty exit-only lane, still on the highway but pretending you're leaving, and then you drive and drive right past all the lineuppers until whoops, now at the last minute you've changed your mind and you're not exiting at all; you're sneaking back into the line.

Not in front of me, though.

Until recently, I had the idea that I was somewhat overwrought about this. I supposed there were not all that many drivers gritting their teeth behind their steering wheels, practicing what Jerry Seinfeld once called the stare-ahead, while declining to let the sidezoomers in and musing at the same time that this is the *problem* with modern American capitalism, really, this anti-aristocratic all-men-are-created-equal narrative we pretend to cherish while simultaneously celebrating the individual's right to do what-ever advances his own interests without technically breaking the law, Gordon Gekko[1] triumphant over César Chávez,[2] and that is an *exit-only* lane, you rodent, so no, you are *not* cutting in front of me unless you look as if you might have a gun in your car, in which case, O.K., but you're still a rodent.

I was mistaken, as it turns out. There are a lot of people who feel this   10 way.

I know this because a while ago I began asking around—politely, I mean, trying to avoid words like "bullying" and "lowlife," making inquiries as to who lines up at bottlenecks and who sidezooms. The truth is, I had come to be a tiny bit rattled by uncertainty. I kept studying that empty lane space on either side of our lineup. Something about the physics was not working out. I bought a textbook called *Traffic Flow Fundamentals*, hoping for instructions as to the technically correct way to enter a lane-drop funnel, but the explanations looked like this:

When $k = k_j$, $\mu = 0$ (vehicles bumper to bumper but no movement):

$$0 = \alpha_0 \ln \left(\frac{c_2}{k_j} \right)$$

So I started consulting professionals on my own: traffic engineers, the highway police, queuing theorists. The learning curve, it must be said, was robust. I hadn't known queuing had theories. But of course it does, mathe-maticians and business-operations people have to work them out, the heart-attack patient gets in ahead of the sprained ankle and nobody has a prob-lem with that, and anybody who has been to Europe intuitively understands what one engineer meant when in midsentence he said to me, "perfect England," meaning culturally mandated compulsive queuing, and, "perfect

---

1 **Gordon Gekko:** The main antagonist of the film *Wall Street* (1987) and the antihero of the 2010 film *Wall Street: Money Never Sleeps.*—EDS.

2 **César Chávez** (1927–1993): American farm worker, labor leader, and civil rights activ-ist.—EDS.

Italy," meaning culturally mandated compulsive nonqueuing. I learned about the father of modern queuing theory, an early 1900s Dane whose specific who-goes-first challenge was the new Copenhagen telephone system, which required callers, disembodied but queued nonetheless, to be moved along in a way both maximally efficient and acceptable to all. I learned some of the ways a crush of traffic is and is not like a crush of opera fans outside Lincoln Center—the speed factor, the isolating qualities of an auto's steel bubble, the coarsening effect of no-eye-contact anonymity. I learned that Officer Sam Morgan, of the California Highway Patrol, occasionally uses the term "cranial-rectal inversion" when referring to drivers of especially poor judgment, which was one of the most satisfactory things I learned all summer, come to think of it. I asked each professional the same questions:

1. If you were inside your personal vehicle, approaching a bottleneck that offered you the options of lineup or sidezoom, which option would you select?

2. For practical purposes—maximum vehicle flow, minimal hang-up — who's right?

A University of Washington engineer named Bill Beaty, who was one of the first traffic scholars I located, has come up with his own bottleneck-behavior labels: Cheaters and Vigilantes. He disapproves of both. When I acknowledged belonging to the choleric wing of the vigilante order, he was unyielding but sympathetic. "That's just human," he said. Beaty is a proponent of the third-way prescription, which I'll get to in a minute; he's an electrical engineer, not formally trained in traffic flow but so interested in it that for a decade he has kept up a link-filled Web page, http://amasci.com/amateur/traffic/links.html, connecting to scores of diagrams and scholarly papers and discussion groups, a whole subuniverse of people preoccupied with the physics and psychology of traffic. (You can click from Beaty's page to a comic Italian animated traffic short, a German traffic-flow simulator that twitches and rotates and a live-cam shot of one nasty section of Seattle's I-5.)

It wasn't until I'd spent weeks wandering this subuniverse that Tom   15
Vanderbilt and I stumbled upon each other, like tourists buried in the same obscure travel guide, and started comparing notes. Vanderbilt is a journalist in Brooklyn who got worked up over an East Coast version of the Caldecott Tunnel Problem a few years ago, after negotiating a freeway bottleneck one day in what he described to me as a "very 'Sopranos'" stretch of urban New Jersey. A lineupper by disposition, Vanderbilt unaccountably switched modes, joined the sidezoomers and cut in late. Then he worried and ruminated about what he had done. The book he ended up writing just came out: *Traffic: Why We Drive the Way We Do (and What It Says About Us)*.

Vanderbilt's book is terrific. He writes about the traffic law Julius Caesar imposed to manage chariot jams. He deconstructs "injunctive norms" (what the law tells us to do) versus "descriptive norms" (what the behavior of those around us tells us to do). He has a chapter called "Why Ants Don't Get Into Traffic Jams (and Humans Do)," which was particularly interesting to read; it seems there's an ant species, the New World army ant, that organizes its perfectly flowing commute processions along principles similar to those Beaty and my traffic experts invoked as they explained why the Caldecott backup is not *entirely*, and I say this with some reluctance, the sidezoomers' fault.

The experts drew schematics in my notebook for me. They asked me to envision rice pouring smoothly through a kitchen funnel. They pointed out, as a Virginia Tech computer-science professor named Chris Barrett put it, that "if you move over too soon, you have this big empty piece of real estate, which could absorb that many more cars." And I would say, yes, but they still all have to squish into the same two-lane tunnel, right? And the experts would say yes, but what really botches the flow is the stop-and-go part—which is accentuated both by the guy hanging around up there trying to last-minute jam his way in *and* by the hostile party in the Subaru who won't let him, thus prompting him to try again in front of the next car, whose driver brakes while deciding whether to go into high-, medium- or low-level snit, and so on. Nearly every time I asked one of the traffic people to assume the role of the great vehicle arranger in the sky, remote-controlling each of us bottleneck drivers as if we were so many video-game characters, the reply went as follows:

First, everybody remains unruffled, without abrupt changes of lane or speed, as the lane-drop comes into view. Everybody takes three deep, cleansing breaths—all right, the experts didn't say that but they meant to—and considers both the imminent needs of everybody else and the system as a smoothly functioning whole.

Then everybody begins to slow, not too much, all in concert. All cars remain in their lanes, using all the real estate. (On the question of frontage roads and exit-only lanes, the experts waffled; those are arguably part of the real estate, they agreed, but they are meant for a different purpose, and this scenario relies upon everybody buying into the same rules. So no frontage-roading or fake-exit-laning, unless there's a sign specifically instructing otherwise.) People in the narrowing left lanes refrain from shooting ahead, while people in the right through lanes—this is hard to swallow, for those of us inclined toward vigilantism, but crucial—leave big spaces in front of their cars for the merging that is about to commence. We resist the freeze-out-the-sidezoomer urge. We prepare to invite them in.

Finally, at clearly marked or somehow mutually agreed upon places, everybody starts conducting beautiful "zipper merges." That's the technical term—one-two, one-two or one-two-three, one-two-three—as indicated by the roadway configuration. The process has now worked at its ideal efficiency/equitability ratio: if all have behaved correctly, the tunnel passage has been both benign and, relatively speaking, quick. Personal sacrifice has been called for, to be sure. The former sidezoomers have sacrificed the

20

pleasure of high-speed bypass, also known as I Beat Out the Stupid Sheep Just Now, Ha Ha (less truculent rendition: I Want to Get Home More Than I Care About Strangers Whose Faces I Can't Even See). The former lineuppers have sacrificed the pleasure of self-congratulatory umbrage, also known as Hmph, Good Thing Society Has People Like Me. Together we have all ascended to the traffic decorum of the army ants, who as Vanderbilt observes are among the earth's most accomplished commuters, managing to get from one place to another in large groups without cutting each other off, deciding their time is more valuable than everybody else's, or—apparently this is the fast-lane domination method for certain traveling land crickets—eating anybody who gets in the way.

One afternoon a few weeks ago, Sam Morgan took me out to the Caldecott in his California Highway Patrol black-and-white, a big sedan that Morgan pulled to the shoulder so we could watch the lineupper-sidezoomer minuet from a neutral vantage point. I figured it would take a seriously dumb person to do something offensive with Morgan sitting right there, but lo, here came the exit-only-lane zoomers, gunning it past the lineup and then cutting in. Red Dodge pickup. Black Camaro. Blue Prius—great, Mr. Environmentally Superior, *you* have the personal-sacrifice thing down big time—white Toyota. Morgan watched them, alert but calm. "No violation here," he said.

Morgan resembles John Wayne, except African-American and in a CHP uniform. Every time I tried to prod him into moral pronouncements about fairness, he assumed a serene Buddha face and reminded me that his job was to enforce the law. It is legal to use the exit-only lane for sidezooming—in California, at least—as long as you do your cut-in before the lane line turns solid (meaning no more lane-changing permitted) near the end. It is legal to frontage-road sidezoom, as long as you observe the stop sign along the way. It is legal to be a full-on lineupper vigilante, for that matter, since you are "established" and therefore have priority in your lane, as long as your refusal to let a sidezoomer in doesn't rise to the level of unlawfully unsafe driving. "It's not a matter of fairness or unfairness," Morgan said. "It's a matter of there's no violation, no one is being injured. Ergo, chill out. Enjoy life. You're spending too much energy pounding the dashboard."

Morgan gave me the Buddha look, crinkled the corners of his eyes in amusement and drove us to the operations building above the Caldecott. In civilian life he said, he's primarily a lineupper, just because he knows this will occasion the least vitriol. As a rule, he lets all sidezoomers in. "When I'm plainclothes, people cut me off all the time," he said. "My thought is, If you knew who I am, you probably wouldn't do that."

Well, exactly. No disrespect toward Morgan, but if you've spent your working life being a big-shouldered guy in a patrol car, you have maybe transcended the tendency many of us have toward driving around in a state of constant micronegotiation with the world, which is so unfathomable in most respects, so beyond our field of vision and our ability to do anything about it, although not by God along the asphalt beneath our wheels. The first time I deliberately made special invite room for a sidezoomer this summer—a lane-drop bottleneck en route to Lake Tahoe, me dubiously opening the extra-long space in front of my car—I swear I could see the zoomer beside me start to accelerate, hesitate and then with me murmuring, *Come on pal, we can do this together*, finally shrug his SUV into the merge. Neither of us had to brake. I'll be honest, though: I missed my minuscule occasion of power, and I'm guessing he did, too, both of us having recently paid $4.69 per gallon even assuming he uses regular. "In the overall scheme of things, it's a very short amount of time," Morgan remarked as we got out of the black-and-white, and I followed him up some stairs to the monitor room, where two operations workers were gazing at multiple screen images of the Caldecott.

We all stood there, watching sidezoomers cut in one after another at the top of the line. One worker, Anthony Padilla, said, "That's what I do."   25

The other worker, Tim Miller, swung his head around fast. "*I* get in *line*," he said.

I asked Padilla to elaborate—to present his case to Miller and me, as if he were chatting with us right after we'd all made it through the tunnel. "Um, I'm an aggressive driver," Padilla said. "I would say. . . ." He stopped and smiled. He didn't look even a little bit apologetic. He looked, in fact, like a fisherman holding up a big shining catch. "I would say, 'Well, the lane was open—and I took it.'"

Padilla and Miller studied each other. Then Miller turned to Morgan, who was contemplating them both impassively, his hands folded before him. "But I don't have to let him in, do I?" Miller asked.

"Nope," Morgan said. "You don't." ●

The Reader's Presence

1. Gorney draws on a variety of sources in her essay—from her own personal observations to quotations from computer-science professors. What is the effect of drawing on multiple sources in order to explain the points she is making? How does this decision affect the persuasiveness of her argument? How would you read the essay differently if she relied only on one source?

2. How would you describe the tone of voice Gorney uses in her essay? Given the topic, comment on the effects of Gorney's use of this stylistic choice. Point to specific words and phrases to support each point you make. Comment on Gorney's use of sentence and paragraph structure. In what specific ways does the structure of her sentences and paragraphs reflect the point she is trying to make about merging in traffic?

3. **CONNECTIONS:**   Compare Gorney's essay with Joan Acocella's "A Few Too Many" (page 283). Both present in-depth examinations of common experiences. Identify—and comment on the effectiveness of—the specific ways in which each author explores her topic. In what ways does each writer treat her subject differently? How would you describe the style of humor each author uses? What are the effects of each?

Stephen Jay Gould

SEX, DRUGS, DISASTERS, AND THE EXTINCTION OF DINOSAURS

STEPHEN JAY GOULD (1941–2002) was professor of geology and zoology at Harvard University and curator of invertebrate paleontology at Harvard's Museum of Comparative Zoology. He published widely on evolution and other topics and earned a reputation for making technical subjects readily comprehensible to lay readers without trivializing the material. His *The Panda's Thumb* (1980) won the American Book Award, and *The Mismeasure of Man* (1981) won the National Book Critics Circle Award. Gould published more than one hundred articles in scientific journals, and he contributed to national magazines as well. "Sex, Drugs, Disasters, and the Extinction of Dinosaurs" appeared in *Discover* magazine in 1984. More recently, Gould wrote *Questioning the Millennium: A Rationalist's Guide to a Precisely Arbitrary Countdown* (1997), *Leonardo's Mountain of Clams and the Diet of Worms: Essays on Natural History* (1998), *Rocks of Ages: Science & Religion in the Fullness of Life* (1999), *The Lying Stones of Marrakesh* (2001), and *The Structure of Evolutionary Theory* (2001). Among many other honors

> "I don't think the concepts of science are intrinsically more difficult than the professional notions in any other field."

and awards, he was a fellow of the National Science Foundation and the MacArthur Foundation. In 1999 Gould became president of the American Association for the Advancement of Science. John Updike comments that "Gould, in his scrupulous explication of [other scientists'] carefully wrought half-truths, abolishes the unnecessary distinction between the humanities and science, and honors the latter as a branch of humanistic thought, fallible and poetic."

When asked if he found it difficult to write about complex scientific concepts in language that is accessible to general readers, Gould replied, "I don't see why it should be that difficult. . . . Every field has its jargon. I think scientists hide behind theirs perhaps more than people in other professions do—it's part of our mythology—but I don't think the concepts of science are intrinsically more difficult than the professional notions in any other field."

SCIENCE, in its most fundamental definition, is a fruitful mode of inquiry, not a list of enticing conclusions. The conclusions are the consequence, not the essence.

My greatest unhappiness with most popular presentations of science concerns their failure to separate fascinating claims from the methods that scientists use to establish the facts of nature. Journalists, and the public, thrive on controversial and stunning statements. But science is, basically, a way of knowing—in P. B. Medawar's[1] apt words, "the art of the soluble." If the growing corps of popular science writers would focus on *how* scientists develop and defend those fascinating claims, they would make their greatest possible contribution to public understanding.

Consider three ideas, proposed in perfect seriousness to explain that greatest of all titillating puzzles—the extinction of dinosaurs. Since these three notions invoke the primally fascinating themes of our culture—sex, drugs, and violence—they surely reside in the category of fascinating claims. I want to show why two of them rank as silly speculation, while the other represents science at its grandest and most useful.

Science works with the testable proposals. If, after much compilation and scrutiny of data, new information continues to affirm a hypothesis, we may accept it provisionally and gain confidence as further evidence mounts. We can never be completely sure that a hypothesis is right, though we may be able to show with confidence that it is wrong. The best scientific hypotheses are also generous and expansive: They suggest extensions and implications that enlighten related, and even far distant, subjects. Simply consider how the idea of evolution has influenced virtually every intellectual field.

Useless speculation, on the other hand, is restrictive. It generates no   5
testable hypothesis, and offers no way to obtain potentially refuting evidence. Please note that I am not speaking of truth or falsity. The speculation may well be true; still, if it provides, in principle, no material for affirmation or rejection, we can make nothing of it. It must simply stand forever as an intriguing idea. Useless speculation turns in on itself and leads nowhere; good science, containing both seeds for its potential refutation and implications for more and different testable knowledge, reaches out. But, enough preaching. Let's move on to dinosaurs, and the three proposals for their extinction.

1. **Sex:** Testes function only in a narrow range of temperature (those of mammals hang externally in a scrotal sac because internal body temperatures are too high for their proper function). A worldwide rise in temperature at the close of the Cretaceous period caused the testes of dinosaurs to stop functioning and led to their extinction by sterilization of males.

---

[1] *Sir Peter Brian Medawar* (1915–1987): A Brazilian-born British scientist renowned for his research on how the immune system rejects or accepts tissue transplants. Co-winner of the 1960 Nobel Prize in medicine.—EDS.

2. **Drugs:** Angiosperms (flowering plants) first evolved toward the end of the dinosaurs' reign. Many of these plants contain psychoactive agents, avoided by mammals today as a result of their bitter taste. Dinosaurs had neither means to taste the bitterness nor livers effective enough to detoxify the substances. They died of massive overdoses.

3. **Disasters:** A large comet or asteroid struck the earth some 65 million years ago, lofting a cloud of dust into the sky and blocking sunlight, thereby suppressing photosynthesis and so drastically lowering world temperatures that dinosaurs and hosts of other creatures became extinct.

Before analyzing these three tantalizing statements, we must establish a basic ground rule often violated in proposals for the dinosaurs' demise. *There is no separate problem of the extinction of dinosaurs.* Too often we divorce specific events from their wider contexts and systems of cause and effect. The fundamental fact of dinosaur extinction is its synchrony with the demise of so many other groups across a wide range of habitats, from terrestrial to marine.

The history of life has been punctuated by brief episodes of mass extinction. A recent analysis by University of Chicago paleontologists Jack Sepkoski and Dave Raup, based on the best and most exhaustive tabulation of data ever assembled, shows clearly that five episodes of mass dying stand well above the "background" extinctions of normal times (when we consider all mass extinctions, large and small, they seem to fall in a regular 26-million-year cycle). The Cretaceous debacle, occurring 65 million years ago and separating the Mesozoic and Cenozoic eras of our geological time scale, ranks prominently among the five. Nearly all the marine plankton (single-celled floating creatures) died with geological suddenness; among marine invertebrates, nearly 15 percent of all families perished, including many previously dominant groups, especially the ammonites (relatives of squids in coiled shells). On land, the dinosaurs disappeared after more than 100 million years of unchallenged domination.

In this context, speculations limited to dinosaurs alone ignore the larger phenomenon. We need a coordinated explanation for a system of events that includes the extinction of dinosaurs as one component. Thus it makes little sense, though it may fuel our desire to view mammals as inevitable inheritors of the earth, to guess that dinosaurs died because small mammals ate their eggs (a perennial favorite among untestable speculations). It seems most unlikely that some disaster peculiar to dinosaurs befell these massive beasts—and that the debacle happened to strike just when one of history's five great dyings had enveloped the earth for completely different reasons.

The testicular theory, an old favorite from the 1940s, had its root in an interesting and thoroughly respectable study of temperature tolerances in the American alligator, published in the staid *Bulletin of the American Museum of Natural History* in 1946 by three experts on living and fossil reptiles—E. H. Colbert, my own first teacher in paleontology; R. B. Cowles; and C. M. Bogert.

The first sentence of their summary reveals a purpose beyond alliga- 10 tors: "This report describes an attempt to infer the reactions of extinct rep- tiles, especially the dinosaurs, to high temperatures as based upon reactions observed in the modern alligator." They studied, by rectal thermometry, the body temperatures of alligators under changing conditions of heating and cooling. (Well, let's face it, you wouldn't want to try sticking a thermometer under a 'gator's tongue.) The predictions under test go way back to an old theory first stated by Galileo in the 1630s—the unequal scaling of surfaces and volumes. As an animal, or an object, grows (provided its shape doesn't change), surface areas must increase more slowly than volumes—since sur- faces get larger as length squared, while volumes increase much more rap- idly, as length cubed. Therefore, small animals have high ratios of surface to volume, while large animals cover themselves with relatively little surface.

Among cold-blooded animals lacking any physiological mechanism for keeping their temperatures constant, small creatures have a hell of a time keeping warm—because they lose so much heat through their relatively large surfaces. On the other hand, large animals, with their relatively small surfaces, may lose heat so slowly that, once warm, they may maintain effec- tively constant temperatures against ordinary fluctuations of climate. (In fact, the resolution of the "hot-blooded dinosaur" controversy that burned so brightly a few years back may simply be that, while large dinosaurs pos- sessed no physiological mechanism for constant temperature, and were not therefore warm-blooded in the technical sense, their large size and rela- tively small surface area kept them warm.)

Colbert, Cowles, and Bogert compared the warming rates of small and large alligators. As predicted, the small fellows heated up (and cooled down) more quickly. When exposed to a warm sun, a tiny 50-gram (1.76-ounce) alligator heated up one degree Celsius every minute and a half, while a large alligator, 260 times bigger at 13,000 grams (28.7 pounds), took seven and a half minutes to gain a degree. Extrapolating up to an adult 10-ton dinosaur, they concluded that a one-degree rise in body temperature would take eighty-six hours. If large animals absorb heat so slowly (through their relatively small surfaces), they will also be unable to shed any excess heat gained when temperatures rise above a favorable level.

The authors then guessed that large dinosaurs lived at or near their optimum temperatures; Cowles suggested that a rise in global tempera- tures just before the Cretaceous extinction caused the dinosaurs to heat up beyond their optimal tolerance—and, being so large, they couldn't shed the unwanted heat. (In a most unusual statement within a scientific paper, Col- bert and Bogert then explicitly disavowed this speculative extension of their empirical work on alligators.) Cowles conceded that this excess heat prob- ably wasn't enough to kill or even to enervate the great beasts, but since tes- tes often function only within a narrow range of temperature, he proposed that this global rise might have sterilized all the males, causing extinction by natural contraception.

The overdose theory has recently been supported by UCLA psychiatrist Ronald K. Siegel. Siegel has gathered, he claims, more than 2,000 records of animals who, when given access, administer various drugs to themselves — from a mere swig of alcohol to massive doses of the big H. Elephants will swill the equivalent of twenty beers at a time, but do not like alcohol in concentrations greater than 7 percent. In a silly bit of anthropocentric speculation, Siegel states that "elephants drink, perhaps, to forget . . . the anxiety produced by shrinking rangeland and the competition for food."

Since fertile imaginations can apply almost any hot idea to the extinc- 15 tion of dinosaurs, Siegel found a way. Flowering plants did not evolve until late in the dinosaurs' reign. These plants also produced an array of aromatic, amino-acid-based alkaloids — the major group of psychoactive agents. Most mammals are "smart" enough to avoid these potential poisons. The alkaloids simply don't taste good (they are bitter); in any case, we mammals have livers happily supplied with the capacity to detoxify them. But, Siegel speculates, perhaps dinosaurs could neither taste the bitterness nor detoxify the substances once ingested. He recently told members of the American Psychological Association: "I'm not suggesting that all dinosaurs OD'd on plant drugs, but it certainly was a factor." He also argued that death by overdose may help explain why so many dinosaur fossils are found in contorted positions. (Do not go gentle into that good night.)[2]

Extraterrestrial catastrophes have long pedigrees in the popular literature of extinction, but the subject exploded again in 1979, after a long lull, when the father-son, physicist-geologist team of Luis and Walter Alvarez proposed that an asteroid, some 10 km in diameter, struck the earth 65 million years ago (comets, rather than asteroids, have since gained favor. Good science is self-corrective).

The force of such a collision would be immense, greater by far than the megatonnage of all the world's nuclear weapons. In trying to reconstruct a scenario that would explain the simultaneous dying of dinosaurs on land and so many creatures in the sea, the Alvarezes proposed that a gigantic dust cloud, generated by particles blown aloft in the impact, would so darken the earth that photosynthesis would cease and temperatures drop precipitously. (Rage, rage against the dying of the light.)[3] The single-celled photosynthetic oceanic plankton, with life cycles measured in weeks, would perish outright, but land plants might survive through the dormancy of their seeds (land plants were not much affected by the Cretaceous extinction, and any adequate theory must account for the curious pattern of differential survival). Dinosaurs would die by starvation and freezing; small, warm-blooded mammals, with more modest requirements for food and better regulation of

---

2 ***Do not go gentle into that good night.":*** A poem composed in 1951 by the Welsh poet Dylan Thomas (1914–1953) and considered to be among his finest works. — EDS.

3 ***"Rage, rage against the dying of the light.":*** The final line of the poem "Do Not Go Gentle into That Good Night" by Dylan Thomas. — EDS.

body temperature, would squeak through. "Let the bastards freeze in the dark," as bumper stickers of our chauvinistic neighbors in sunbelt states proclaimed several years ago during the Northeast's winter oil crisis.

All three theories, testicular malfunction, psychoactive overdosing, and asteroidal zapping, grab our attention mightily. As pure phenomenology, they rank about equally high on any hit parade of primal fascination. Yet one represents expansive science, the others restrictive and untestable specula-tion. The proper criterion lies in evidence and methodology; we must probe behind the superficial fascination of particular claims.

How could we possibly decide whether the hypothesis of testicular fry-ing is right or wrong? We would have to know things that the fossil record cannot provide. What temperatures were optimal for dinosaurs? Could they avoid the absorption of excess heat by staying in the shade, or in caves? At what temperatures did their testicles cease to function? Were late Cretaceous climates ever warm enough to drive the internal temperatures of dinosaurs close to this ceiling? Testicles simply don't fossilize, and how could we infer their temperature tolerances even if they did? In short, Cowles's hypoth-esis is only an intriguing speculation leading nowhere. The most damning statement against it appeared right in the conclusion of Colbert, Cowles, and Bogert's paper, when they admitted: "It is difficult to advance any defi-nite arguments against the hypothesis." My statement may seem paradoxi-cal—isn't a hypothesis really good if you can't devise any arguments against it? Quite the contrary. It is simply untestable and unusable.

Siegel's overdosing has even less going for it. At least Cowles extrapo-lated his conclusion from some good data on alligators. And he didn't com-pletely violate the primary guideline of siting dinosaur extinction in the context of a general mass dying—for rise in temperature could be the root cause of a general catastrophe, zapping dinosaurs by testicular malfunc-tion and different groups for other reasons. But Siegel's speculation cannot touch the extinction of ammonites or oceanic plankton (diatoms make their own food with good sweet sunlight; they don't OD on the chemicals of ter-restrial plants). It is simply a gratuitous, attention-grabbing guess. It cannot be tested, for how can we know what dinosaurs tasted and what their livers could do? Livers don't fossilize any better than testicles.

The hypothesis doesn't even make any sense in its own context. Angio-sperms were in full flower ten million years before dinosaurs went the way of all flesh. Why did it take so long? As for the pains of a chemical death recorded in contortions of fossils, I regret to say (or rather I'm pleased to note for the dinosaurs' sake) that Siegel's knowledge of geology must be a bit deficient: muscles contract after death and geological strata rise and fall with motions of the earth's crust after burial—more than enough reason to distort a fossil's pristine appearance.

The impact story, on the other hand, has a sound basis in evidence. It can be tested, extended, refined, and, if wrong, disproved. The Alvarezes did not just construct an arresting guess for public consumption. They proposed their hypothesis after laborious geochemical studies with Frank Asaro and

20

Helen Michael had revealed a massive increase of iridium in rocks deposited right at the time of extinction. Iridium, a rare metal of the platinum group, is virtually absent from indigenous rocks of the earth's crust; most of our iridium arrives on extraterrestrial objects that strike the earth.

The Alvarez hypothesis bore immediate fruit. Based originally on evidence from two European localities, it led geochemists throughout the world to examine other sediments of the same age. They found abnormally high amounts of iridium everywhere—from continental rocks of the western United States to deep sea cores from the South Atlantic.

Cowles proposed his testicular hypothesis in the mid-1940s. Where has it gone since then? Absolutely nowhere, because scientists can do nothing with it. The hypothesis must stand as a curious appendage to a solid study of alligators. Siegel's overdose scenario will also win a few press notices and fade into oblivion. The Alvarezes' asteroid falls into a different category altogether, and much of the popular commentary has missed this essential distinction by focusing on the impact and its attendant results, and forgetting what really matters to a scientist—the iridium. If you talk just about asteroids, dust, and darkness, you tell stories no better and no more entertaining than fried testicles or terminal trips. It is the iridium—the source of testable evidence—that counts and forges the crucial distinction between speculation and science.

The proof, to twist a phrase, lies in the doing. Cowles's hypothesis has   25
generated nothing in thirty-five years. Since its proposal in 1979, the Alvarez hypothesis has spawned hundreds of studies, a major conference, and attendant publications. Geologists are fired up. They are looking for iridium at all other extinction boundaries. Every week exposes a new wrinkle in the scientific press. Further evidence that the Cretaceous iridium represents extraterrestrial impact and not indigenous volcanism continues to accumulate. As I revise this essay in November 1984 (this paragraph will be out of date when the book is published),[4] new data include chemical "signatures" of other isotopes indicating unearthly provenance, glass spherules of a size and sort produced by impact and not by volcanic eruptions, and high-pressure varieties of silica formed (so far as we know) only under the tremendous shock of impact.

My point is simply this: Whatever the eventual outcome (I suspect it will be positive), the Alvarez hypothesis is exciting, fruitful science because it generates tests, provides us with things to do, and expands outward. We are having fun, battling back and forth, moving toward a resolution, and extending the hypothesis beyond its original scope.

As just one example of the unexpected, distant cross-fertilization that good science engenders, the Alvarez hypothesis made a major contribution to a theme that has riveted public attention in the past few months—so-called nuclear winter. In a speech delivered in April 1982, Luis Alvarez

---

4 *The Flamingo's Smile* (1985), in which Gould included this essay.—EDS.

calculated the energy that a ten-kilometer asteroid would release on impact. He compared such an explosion with a full nuclear exchange and implied that all-out atomic war might unleash similar consequences.

This theme of impact leading to massive dust clouds and falling temperatures formed an important input to the decision of Carl Sagan[5] and a group of colleagues to model the climatic consequences of nuclear holocaust. Full nuclear exchange would probably generate the same kind of dust cloud and darkening that may have wiped out the dinosaurs. Temperatures would drop precipitously and agriculture might become impossible. Avoidance of nuclear war is fundamentally an ethical and political imperative, but we must know the factual consequences to make firm judgments. I am heartened by a final link across disciplines and deep concerns—another criterion, by the way, of science at its best.[6] A recognition of the very phenomenon that made our evolution possible by exterminating the previously dominant dinosaurs and clearing a way for the evolution of large mammals, including us, might actually help to save us from joining those magnificent beasts in contorted poses among the strata of the earth. ●

The Reader's Presence

1. Although the title of Gould's essay focuses on the extinction of dinosaurs, his overriding interest is in demonstrating the way science works, and his purpose is to make that process fully accessible and understandable to the general public. Where does he lay out this central claim, and how does he demonstrate, clarify, and complicate it as his essay proceeds?

2. Reread Gould's essay with special attention to his use of tone, diction, syntax, and metaphor. How does he use these compositional strategies to make information accessible to his readers? Point to passages where Gould uses the diction and syntax of a serious scientist. When—and with what effects—does his prose sound more colloquial? Does his tone remain consistent throughout the essay? If not, when and how does it change? With what effects?

3. **CONNECTIONS:** What distinctions does Gould draw among "testable proposals" (paragraph 4), "intriguing ideas" (paragraph 5), and "useless speculation" (paragraph 5)? What features of each does he identify? How does Gould encourage critical thinking in his reader? Compare Gould's compositional tactics to those of Malcolm Gladwell in "Small Change: Why the Revolution Will Not Be Tweeted" (page 411). Where does each writer use wit and humor to "translate" for the reader facts that might otherwise seem arcane?

---

[5] ***Carl Sagan*** (1934–1996): An American astronomer and astrochemist who did much to make the study of astronomy, astrophysics, and other natural sciences accessible to wide audiences. He also promoted the Search for Extra-Terrestrial Intelligence (SETI).—EDS.

[6] This quirky connection so tickles my fancy that I break my own strict rule about eliminating redundancies from [this essay]. . . .—AUTHOR'S NOTE.

Nathaniel Hawthorne
MY VISIT TO NIAGARA

Born in Salem, Massachusetts, **NATHANIEL HAWTHORNE** (1804–1864) is best known as the author of *The Scarlet Letter* (1850), but he was also a prolific short story and nonfiction writer. He worked briefly as the editor of the *American Magazine of Useful and Entertaining Knowledge*, but he spent much of his professional life (prior to the publication of *The Scarlet Letter*) working in government, first at the Customs House in Boston and later as the surveyor for the District of Salem and Beverly, Massachusetts. He was closely associated with other American writers of the period, including Henry Wadsworth Longfellow, Oliver Wendell Holmes, Herman Melville, Ralph Waldo Emerson, and Henry David Thoreau. Much of his fiction is set in New England and deals with themes of guilt and sin. Hawthorne was particularly troubled by the idea of ancestral sin: His ancestors were directly involved in the Salem witch trials. His great-great grandfather, John Hathorne, was one of the judges who oversaw the infamous trials, in which

> Nathaniel Hawthorne's great-great grandfather, John Hathorne, was one of the judges who oversaw the Salem witch trials, and it has been suggested that Hawthorne added the "w" to his last name to distance himself from his ancestors.

many innocent men and women were sentenced to death. It has even been suggested that Hawthorne added the "w" to the spelling of his last name to distance himself from his ancestors. "My Visit to Niagara," first published anonymously, by the author of "The Gray Champion," in the *New England Magazine*, February, 1835, stands apart from much of Hawthorne's work in its comparatively light nature. He never included it in any of his later collections.

NEVER DID A PILGRIM approach Niagara with deeper enthusiasm, than mine. I had lingered away from it, and wandered to other scenes, because my treasury of anticipated enjoyments, comprising all the wonders of the world, had nothing else so magnificent, and I was loth to exchange the pleasures of hope for those of memory so soon. At length, the day came. The stage-coach, with a Frenchman and myself on the back seat, had already left Lewiston, and in less than an hour would set us down in Manchester. I began to listen for the roar of the cataract,[1] and trembled with a sensation like

---

1 *cataract:* A large waterfall. — EDS.

438

dread, as the moment drew nigh, when its voice of ages must roll, for the first time, on my ear. The French gentleman stretched himself from the window, and expressed loud admiration, while, by a sudden impulse, I threw myself back and closed my eyes. When the scene shut in, I was glad to think, that for me the whole burst of Niagara was yet in futurity. We rolled on, and entered the village of Manchester, bordering on the falls.

I am quite ashamed of myself here. Not that I ran, like a madman, to the falls, and plunged into the thickest of the spray—never stopping to breathe, till breathing was impossible; not that I committed this, or any other suitable extravagance. On the contrary, I alighted with perfect decency and composure, gave my cloak to the black waiter, pointed out my baggage, and inquired, not the nearest way to the cataract, but about the dinner-hour. The interval was spent in arranging my dress. Within the last fifteen minutes, my mind had grown strangely benumbed, and my spirits apathetic, with a slight depression, not decided enough to be termed sadness. My enthusiasm was in a deathlike slumber. Without aspiring to immortality, as he did, I could have imitated that English traveller, who turned back from the point where he first heard the thunder of Niagara, after crossing the ocean to behold it. Many a western trader, by-the-by, has performed a similar act of heroism with more heroic simplicity, deeming it no such wonderful feat to dine at the hotel and resume his route to Buffalo or Lewiston, while the cataract was roaring unseen.

Such has often been my apathy, when objects, long sought, and earnestly desired, were placed within my reach. After dinner—at which, an unwonted and perverse epicurism detained me longer than usual—I lighted a cigar and paced the piazza, minutely attentive to the aspect and business of a very ordinary village. Finally, with reluctant step, and the feeling of an intruder, I walked towards Goat Island. At the toll-house, there were further excuses for delaying the inevitable moment. My signature was required in a huge leger, containing similar records innumerable, many of which I read. The skin of a great sturgeon, and other fishes, beasts, and reptiles; a collection of minerals, such as lie in heaps near the falls; some Indian moccasins, and other trifles, made of deer-skin and embroidered with beads; several newspapers from Montreal, New-York, and Boston; all attracted me in turn. Out of a number of twisted sticks, the manufacture of a Tuscarora Indian, I selected one of curled maple, curiously convoluted, and adorned with the carved images of a snake and a fish. Using this as my pilgrim's staff, I crossed the bridge. Above and below me were the rapids, a river of impetuous snow, with here and there a dark rock amid its whiteness, resisting all the physical fury, as any cold spirit did the moral influences of the scene. On reaching Goat Island, which separates the two great segments of the falls, I chose the right-hand path, and followed it to the edge of the American cascade. There, while the falling sheet was yet invisible, I saw the vapor that never vanishes, and the Eternal Rainbow of Niagara.

It was an afternoon of glorious sunshine, without a cloud, save those of the cataracts. I gained an insulated rock, and beheld a broad sheet of brilliant and unbroken foam, not shooting in a curved line from the top of the precipice, but falling headlong down from height to depth. A narrow stream diverged from the main branch, and hurried over the crag by a channel of its own, leaving a little pine-clad island and a streak of precipice, between itself and the larger sheet. Below arose the mist, on which was painted a dazzling sunbow, with two concentric shadows—one, almost as perfect as the original brightness; and the other, drawn faintly round the broken edge of the cloud.

Still, I had not half seen Niagara. Following the verge of the island, the   5
path led me to the Horse-shoe, where the real, broad St. Lawrence, rushing along on a level with its banks, pours its whole breadth over a concave line of precipice, and thence pursues its course between lofty crags towards Ontario. A sort of bridge, two or three feet wide, stretches out along the edge of the descending sheet, and hangs upon the rising mist, as if that were the foundation of the frail structure. Here I stationed myself, in the blast of wind, which the rushing river bore along with it. The bridge was tremulous beneath me, and marked the tremor of the solid earth. I looked along the whitening rapids, and endeavored to distinguish a mass of water far above the falls, to follow it to their verge, and go down with it, in fancy, to the abyss of clouds and storm. Casting my eyes across the river, and every side, I took in the whole scene at a glance, and tried to comprehend it in one vast idea. After an hour thus spent, I left the bridge, and, by a staircase, winding almost interminably round a post, descended to the base of the precipice. From that point, my path lay over slippery stones, and among great fragments of the cliff, to the edge of the cataract, where the wind at once enveloped me in spray, and perhaps dashed the rainbow round me. Were my long desires fulfilled? And had I seen Niagara?

Oh, that I had never heard of Niagara till I beheld it. Blessed were the wanderers of old, who heard its deep roar sounding through the woods, as the summons to an unknown wonder, and approached its awful brink, in all the freshness of native feeling. Had its own mysterious voice been the first to warn me of its existence, then, indeed, I might have knelt down and worshipped. But I had come thither haunted with a vision of foam and fury, and dizzy cliffs, and an ocean tumbling down out of the sky—a scene, in short, which Nature had too much good taste and calm simplicity to realize. My mind had struggled to adapt these false conceptions to the reality, and finding the effort vain, a wretched sense of disappointment weighed me down. I climbed the precipice, and threw myself on the earth—feeling that I was unworthy to look at the Great Falls, and careless about beholding them again.

All that night, as there has been and will be, for ages past and to come, a rushing sound was heard, as if a great tempest were sweeping through the air. It mingled with my dreams, and made them full of storm and whirlwind. Whenever I awoke, and heard this dread sound in the air, and the windows rattling as with a mighty blast, I could not rest again, till, looking forth, I saw how bright the stars were, and that every leaf in the garden was motionless. Never was a summer-night more calm to the eye, nor a gale of autumn louder to the ear. The rushing sound proceeds from the rapids, and the rattling of the

Alvan Fisher, The Great Horseshoe Falls, Niagara. *This 1820 painting is held at the National Museum of American Art, Smithsonian Institution.*

casements is but an effect of the vibration of the whole house, shaken by the jar of the cataract. The noise of the rapids draws the attention from the true voice of Niagara, which is a dull, muffled thunder, resounding between the cliffs. I spent a wakeful hour at midnight, in distinguishing its reverberations, and rejoiced to find that my former awe and enthusiasm were reviving.

Gradually, and after much contemplation, I came to know, by my own feelings, that Niagara is indeed a wonder of the world, and not the less wonderful, because time and thought must be employed in comprehending it. Casting aside all pre-conceived notions, and preparation to be dire-struck or delighted, the beholder must stand beside it in the simplicity of his heart, suffering the mighty scene to work its own impression. Night after night, I dreamed of it, and was gladdened every morning by the consciousness of a growing capacity to enjoy it. Yet I will not pretend to the all-absorbing enthusiasm of some more fortunate spectators, nor deny, that very trifling causes would draw my eyes and thoughts from the cataract.

The last day that I was to spend at Niagara, before my departure for the far west, I sat upon the Table Rock. This celebrated station did not now, as of old, project fifty feet beyond the line of the precipice, but was shattered by the fall of an immense fragment, which lay distant on the shore below. Still, on the utmost verge of the rock, with my feet hanging over it, I felt as if suspended in the open air. Never before had my mind been in such perfect unison with the scene. There were intervals, when I was conscious of nothing but the great river, rolling calmly into the abyss, rather descending than precipitating itself, and acquiring tenfold majesty from its unhurried motion. It came like the march of Destiny. It was not taken by surprise, but seemed to have anticipated, in all its course through the broad lakes, that it must pour their collected waters down this height. The perfect foam of the river, after its descent, and the ever-varying shapes of mist, rising up, to become clouds in the sky, would be the very picture of confusion, were it merely transient, like the rage of a tempest. But when the beholder has stood awhile and perceives no lull in the storm, and considers that the vapor and the foam are as everlasting as the rocks which produce them, all this turmoil assumes a sort of calmness. It soothes, while it awes the mind.

Leaning over the cliff, I saw the guide conducting two adventurers   10 behind the falls. It was pleasant, from that high seat in the sunshine, to observe them struggling against the eternal storm of the lower regions, with heads bent down, now faltering, now pressing forward, and finally swallowed up in their victory. After their disappearance, a blast rushed out with an old hat, which it had swept from one of their heads. The rock, to which they were directing their unseen course, is marked, at a fearful distance on the exterior of the sheet, by a jet of foam. The attempt to reach it, appears both poetical and perilous, to a looker-on, but may be accomplished without much more difficulty or hazard, than in stemming a violent northeaster. In a few moments, forth came the children of the mist. Dripping and breathless, they crept along the base of the cliff, ascended to the guide's cottage, and received, I presume, a certificate of their achievement, with three verses of sublime poetry on the back.

My contemplations were often interrupted by strangers who came down from Forsyth's to take their first view of the falls. A short, ruddy, middle-aged gentleman, fresh from old England, peeped over the rock, and evinced his approbation by a broad grin. His spouse, a very robust lady, afforded a sweet example of maternal solicitude, being so intent on the safety of her little boy that she did not even glance at Niagara. As for the child, he gave himself wholly to the enjoyment of a stick of candy. Another traveller, a native American, and no rare character among us, produced a volume of Captain Hall's tour, and labored earnestly to adjust Niagara to the captain's description, departing, at last, without one new idea or sensation of his own. The next comer was provided, not with a printed book, but with a blank sheet of foolscap, from top to bottom of which, by means of an ever-pointed pencil, the cataract was made to thunder. In a little talk, which we had together, he awarded his approbation to the general view, but censured the position of Goat Island, observing that it should have been thrown farther to the right, so as to widen the American falls, and contract those of the Horse-shoe. Next appeared two traders of Michigan, who declared, that, upon the whole, the sight was worth looking at; there certainly was an immense water-power here; but that, after all, they would go twice as far to see the noble stone-works of Lockport,

*An 1834 advertisement for tours of Niagara Falls led
by Samuel Hooker, a prominent tour guide in his day.*

where the Grand Canal is locked down a descent of sixty feet. They were succeeded by a young fellow, in a home-spun cotton dress, with a staff in his hand, and a pack over his shoulders. He advanced close to the edge of the rock, where his attention, at first wavering among the different components of the scene, finally became fixed in the angle of the Horse-shoe falls, which is, indeed, the central point of interest. His whole soul seemed to go forth and be transported thither, till the staff slipped from his relaxed grasp, and falling down—down—down—struck upon the fragment of the Table Rock.

In this manner, I spent some hours, watching the varied impression, made by the cataract, on those who disturbed me, and returning to unwearied contemplation, when left alone. At length, my time came to depart.

There is a grassy footpath, through the woods, along the summit of the bank, to a point whence a causeway, hewn in the side of the precipice, goes winding down to the ferry, about half a mile below the Table Rock. The sun was near setting, when I emerged from the shadow of the trees, and began the descent. The indirectness of my downward road continually changed the point of view, and shewed me, in rich and repeated succession—now, the whitening rapids and the majestic leap of the main river, which appeared more deeply massive as the light departed, now, the lovelier picture, yet still sublime, of Goat Island, with its rocks and grove, and the lesser falls, tumbling over the right bank of the St. Lawrence, like a tributary stream, now, the long vista of the river, as it eddied and whirled between the cliffs, to pass through Ontario towards the sea, and everywhere to be wondered at, for this one unrivalled scene. The golden sunshine tinged the sheet of the American cascade, and painted on its heaving spray the broken semicircle of a rainbow, Heaven's own beauty crowning earth's sublimity. My steps were slow, and I paused long at every turn of the descent, as one lingers and pauses, who discerns a brighter and brightening excellence in what he must soon behold no more. The solitude of the old wilderness now reigned over the whole vicinity of the falls. My enjoyment became the more rapturous, because no poet shared it—nor wretch, devoid of poetry, profaned it: but the spot, so famous through the world, was all my own! ▪

The Reader's Presence

1. In addition to providing a fascinating description of seeing Niagara Falls for the first time, Hawthorne's essay constitutes a primer on the principle of encountering the natural world directly rather than through what Hawthorne calls "pre-conceived notions" (paragraph 8) and the perspectives of others. What other principles about how we ought to see the natural world can you infer from reading Hawthorne's essay?

2. Summarize the different reactions Hawthorne has to anticipating—and then seeing—Niagara Falls. Which does he seem more interested in exploring with his readers? Point to specific passages to support your response. Hawthorne seems quite conscious of his readers—especially when he says "I am quite ashamed of myself here" (paragraph 2). After seeing Niagara Falls for the first time, he says "a wretched sense of disappointment weighed me down" (paragraph 6). What, more specifically, evokes this sense of being "ashamed" in anticipation of seeing Niagara Falls and then being overcome by a "wretched sense of disappointment"? How and when—and with what effect(s)—does Hawthorne's attitude toward himself change?

3. **CONNECTIONS:**   Much of Hawthorne's essay is written in the form of first-person narration and description. Yet, Hawthorne also manages to convey a great deal of information about seeing Niagara Falls for the first time. Compare and contrast Hawthorne's use of personal narration and description with the ways these rhetorical modes function in Walker Percy's essay "The Loss of the Creature" (page 539). What percentage of Percy's essay is devoted to personal narration and to generalizations about seeing a "wonder of the world" for the first time? Which essay do you find more informative *and* more memorable? Explain why.

Siri Hustvedt

EIGHT DAYS IN A CORSET

Writer, essayist, and poet **SIRI HUSTVEDT** (b. 1955) was born and raised in Northfield, Minnesota, where she attended St. Olaf's College before earning her PhD in English literature from Columbia University in New York City. She lives in Brooklyn, New York, with her husband, writer Paul Auster, and their daughter.

Hustvedt has authored numerous books of fiction and nonfiction, including five novels: *The Blindfold* (1992), *The Enchantment of Lily Dahl* (1996), *What I Loved* (2003), *The Sorrows of an American* (2008), and her most recent, *The Shaking Woman or a History of My Nerves* (2010). Her first book of essays, *Yonder*, was published in 1998, followed by *Mysteries of the Rectangle* (2005), a collection of personal essays on the paintings that "tell us something about what it means to be human." Her essay, "Eight Days in a Corset," is taken from *A Plea for Eros* (2006), a collection of personal and critical essays about writing and writers. Her work has appeared in a number of anthologies, journals, and magazines, including the *Paris Review Anthology* and *Best American Short Stories*, *Fiction* magazine, the *Observer*, and *Modern Painters*. A self-described "migraineur," she contributes to the *New York Times* blog, "Migraine: Perspectives on a Headache."

> **"Writing isn't a job so much as a compulsion."**

In an interview with Powell's Books "Ink Q & A," Hustvedt was asked the inevitable question: Why do you write? "Writing isn't a job so much as a compulsion. I've been writing since I was very young because, for some strange reason, I must write, and also because when I write I feel more alive and closer to the world than when I'm not writing."

LAST SUMMER, I worked as an extra in the film version of Henry James's novel *Washington Square*. I am not an actress. Agnieszka Holland, the director, is a friend of my husband's and mine, and the person she was really interested in was our daughter, Sophie, who was cast as one of Mrs. Almond's children. Under a blasting June sun, Sophie and I arrived in Baltimore for a fitting. Sophie was dressed first, and she looked as pretty as a young heroine in any book. One of the two wardrobe women handed me a corset, a hoopskirt, and a petticoat, which I put on, and then she tightened my stays. They searched for a dress long enough to fit me, and I climbed into it in front of a long, wide mirror in the changing room.

Within a few minutes, I felt faint. I began to suffer from the feeling I always have when I am faint—acute embarrassment. This time there was the added burden of fear: that I would crash to the floor in front of my eight-year-old daughter: I began to sway, dropped, but did not black out. I wish I could say that they cried, "Loosen her stays!" hurried out for smelling salts, and waved my ashen face with a fan. But they didn't. They kindly brought me water and grapes as I recovered. I joked about filling the role too well, about becoming in a matter of minutes the classic image of a swooning nineteenth-century lady, and yet I don't believe it was the corset. I had almost fainted in front of a mirror once before—in a yoga class. That time I was wearing dance tights and a sweatshirt. My teacher was correcting my posture, and without warning I collapsed and found myself breathing deeply with my head between my knees.

Mirrors are where I check myself—for parsley stuck in my teeth, for blemishes and dirty hair—where I ponder which shoes go with which dress. But every once in a while, they become something more than that—the site of a body I know will eventually give up the ghost. As in fairy tales and folklore, the mirror displays for an instant my ghost double, and I don't like seeing her. It is a moment when I am a stranger to myself. But a foreign reflection in a mirror is not always a shock. There is something appealing about transformations, and clothes are the fastest route to leaping out of your own life and into someone else's. The whalebone corset I wore for eight days catapulted me into another time and another aesthetic, and I liked it.

The corset is a vilified article of clothing. It was and is blamed for a host of feminine miseries, both physical and spiritual, for ruining women's bodies and for closing their minds. It is interesting to note, however, that while women wore them, it was male doctors who led the campaign against the corset. Most women were for it. In the twentieth century, feminists joined physicians and attacked the garment as crippling. No doubt there were women who, in the heat of summer or in front of a parlor fire in winter, lost consciousness in corsets too tightly laced for their own good. But wearing mine day in and day out, I fell prey to its charms. Wearing a corset is a little like finding oneself in a permanent embrace, a hug around the middle that goes on and on. This is pleasant and vaguely erotic—a squeeze that lasts.

But the feeling of a corset is only part of its effect. Like all clothing, 5
more than anything else, it is an idea. In this case it promotes an idea of a woman's body as radically different from a man's. In the summer of 1986, I traveled in Asia with my three sisters and we visited both a Buddhist monastery and a Buddhist nunnery in the mountains of Taiwan. Those monks and nuns looked *exactly* alike—small, trim, hairless bodies with shaved heads. The monks had orange robes, the nuns white. Had they all stripped naked and stood together, the difference between them would have been ridiculously small, would have been no more nor less than what the difference truly is—genital variation and a few secondary sexual characteristics in the chest and hips. The truth about clothes, hairdos, and makeup had never hit

As this 1885 advertisement for Madame Dean's Spinal Supporting Corset illustrates, advertising has always drawn heavily on traditional religious images and forms of discourse.

me so hard. The cultural trappings of sex are overwhelming. We make them and live them and are them.

The corset takes the difference between men and women and runs wild with it. The inward slope of a woman's waist becomes extreme, and the tension of lacing the waist pushes the breasts upward. Suddenly, I had new breasts. I did not know how much my body had changed until I saw a photograph of myself in costume and marveled at this addition to my anatomy.

The corset leaves most of the breasts free and does not cover the genitals. By lodging itself securely between upper and lower body parts, its effect is to articulate them more sharply and define them as separate erotic zones. The corset helped to create a notion of femininity, and the lines it produced have gone in and out of fashion ever since. If I had never seen a corset before or had never imagined myself in one, it probably wouldn't have had much power; but I grew up on nineteenth-century novels and studied the illustrations of Dickens and Thackeray very closely. Snug in my corset, with a body I had never seen before, I became an illustration to myself of a world I had only read about.

The corset did not live alone, however: In the 1860s, the time during which James set his novel, it was joined by other garments essential to the American bourgeois woman: the hoopskirt and the petticoat padded at the hips. The padding exaggerates the tiny waist created by the corset, and the hoop turns a woman into a kind of walking bell. The hoop's threat is real. You sit, and if you are not careful, it flies up over your head. No one can scrub floors in a hoop. If you're wearing one, it's a sign that during the day you are *never* on your knees. It is possible to arrange flowers in a hoop, lift a teacup, read a book, and point out tasks to your servants. The hoop was a sign of class; its restriction meant luxury. Like the Chinese aristocrat with fingernails a yard long, it tells a story: "I do not work for money." And I did notice among some of the extras a touch of envy among those who were cast as maids in sad, gray dresses for those of us who swished along in our private balloons. Our movements might have been hampered, but we took up a lot of space, and that space, I realized, was a matter of pride.

And then, alas, they did my hair. I liked the corset. I was amused by my petticoats and laughed at the hoop, except when I had to back slowly into a bathroom stall wearing the crazy thing. (Women of the period did not back into stalls. Their underwear was open, and they could pee standing up. Yes, like a man.) The hairdo was another matter. I am six feet tall. I was forty-one years old. When they had finished with me, I looked like a giraffe in ringlets. The only people in the world who come by ringlets naturally are babies. During that period every woman who could afford to be curled was—young, old, and in between. It was baby fashion, and to my mind it made every woman over twenty look ridiculous. Like the hourglass figure, the longing for infancy through garments or hairdos comes and goes. The short shifts of the sixties were a movement back to childhood, as were the big eyes and ringlets of the same period. Only a few years ago I read about the fashion among teenagers and young club-goers to drape pacifiers around their necks after they had squeezed themselves into baby clothes. Female Peter Pans.

In other words, the idea is what matters. Clothes give us insight into culture and its wishes, and into individuals and their desires. More than who you are, clothes articulate what you want to be. Ringlets were hard for me, because I like to think of myself as a grown-up, because I strive for a certain dignity in my apparel, but that dignity is no more than a message I want to communicate, and who knows if it is successful? I love clothes and have often pined for them—the beautiful dress or coat in the window. My desire is for a transformation I imagine will take place, a kind of enchantment of my own body.

Children are closer to fantastic transformations than adults, closer to the   10 spell of costume and the change that comes from illusion, but we all are prone to it, and hiding behind the silk nightgown or the stockings or the pin-striped suit is a story we have heard and repeated to ourselves. These stories are often clichés, worn narratives we hold close to our hearts. I am chang-ing into the silk nightgown, have brushed my hair and pinched my cheeks. I walk into the bedroom and there he is—the hero, Clark Gable or William Powell, depending on my mood. He turns, gasps, "You look . . ." Fill in the blank. Whatever the words are, it is never: "You look like yourself."

Any meaningful piece of clothing is a part of a broader cultural story. Years ago I went to a Halloween party as a man. In a borrowed suit, my face wiped clean of all makeup, and my hair hidden under a hat, I looked at myself in the mirror and was unprepared for the change. Women flirt with men's clothing all the time, but when you go all the way, the result is striking. I felt manly. My stride lengthened. My manner changed. It was easy to play at being a man, as easy as playing at being a woman. The suit unleashed a fantasy of maleness I heartily enjoyed. Another time, I was walking down a dark street in New York on my way to a large party. I was in my early twenties then and experimented occasionally with wild attire. In a red jumpsuit and heels, which added several inches to my already tower-ing frame, I passed a man who began spewing insults at me. I kept walking. It took several seconds for me to digest what was happening. The man had mistaken me for a transvestite. The experience, both comic and sad, gave me a sudden insight into the venom that appearances can produce, not to speak of the often hazy line between femininity and its parodic double.

Every once in a while, a piece of clothing jumps out of one culture and into another. I spent three months in Thailand in 1975 as a student, and I vividly remember seeing a gang of motorcycle toughs roaring through the streets of Chiang Mai in the rain, wearing shower caps. Several of those caps were decorated with flowers and other beacons of feminine adornment. I was amazed, but nobody else was. My cultural associations didn't apply. The shower cap had been born again somewhere else with a totally different signification.

While it is true that certain individuals are fixed on an idea that rigidly determines them—whether it be "I do not care about clothes at all" or "I am a sex goddess"—most of us have or have had over time many different dreams. I own a black dress that reminds me of Audrey Hepburn. I do not suffer from the delusion that I look like Audrey Hepburn in that dress, but her exquisite form wrapped in Givenchy has bewitched it nevertheless, and her magic is part of my pleasure in wearing it. Movies and books are strong drugs to clothes lovers. Katharine Hepburn striding along in trousers, Lana

Turner in a towel, Claudette Colbert in a man's pajama top, Marilyn Monroe in anything. Tolstoy lavished his attention on the details of women's clothes and bodies, on Natasha at her first ball and Ellen's white shoulders above her low-cut gown. Jane Eyre's plain dress is a tonic against the frippery of the silly females who visit Rochester. And all these images are taken from moments in larger stories that captivate us, stories about people who are living out their lives and their romantic entanglements, both comic and tragic.

My daughter dresses up. She is a rich woman, then a poor one, starving in the streets. She is an old peasant woman selling apples. She is on the phone saying, "Let's have lunch," in an English accent. She sashays down the stairs snapping her gum and practicing her Brooklyn voice. She is wearing my shoes and singing "Adelaide's Lament." She is always somebody else. My husband says I have two personas at least, the stooped four-eyed scholar and the elegant lady. One lives at home. The other goes out. Thinking collapses my body, and I forget what I look like anyway. In a good dress, I stand up straight and never slump. I live up to the dress I know I am wearing even though I do not see myself wearing it. Others see me more often than I see myself. My family knows what I look like better than I do. I offer the mirror a placid face like an inanimate statue, and from time to time the frozen image may frighten me. But I also laugh a lot and smile. I wrinkle my face in concern, and I wave my hands when I talk, and this I never see.

In the end, wearing clothes is an act of the imagination, an invention of   15
self, a fiction. Several years ago, I was sitting in the Carlyle Hotel with my husband having a drink. I was wearing a beautiful dress. I remember that he looked across the table at me with pleasure and said, "When you were a little girl growing up in the sticks of Minnesota, did you ever imagine you would be sitting in this elegant hotel wearing that extraordinary dress?"

And I said, "Yes." Because of course, I did. ●

The Reader's Presence

1. Hustvedt builds her essay on her experience working as an extra—and wearing a corset for eight days—during the filming of Henry James's *Washington Square*. In paragraph 15, she observes: "In the end, wearing clothes is an act of the imagination, an invention of self, a fiction." Throughout her essay, Hustvedt unfolds examples of the "transformations" that wearing different kinds of clothing afford her—and women more generally. Create a list of these transformations. Which do you find Hustvedt to have unpacked most engagingly? Explain why.

2. Summarize—and comment on—the literal and figurative importance of the mirror in Hustvedt's essay. What does Hustvedt mean when she talks about her "ghost double" (paragraph 3)? Summarize—and then comment on—Hustvedt's attitudes toward the corset. In what specific ways does Hustvedt illustrate and validate her assertion that the corset is responsible for "ruining women's bodies and for closing their minds" (paragraph 4)? In what specific ways—and why—does she fall "prey to its charms" (paragraph 4)? In addition to femininity and sexuality, what larger issues does Hustvedt address in her essay? How successfully?

3. In paragraph 10, she observes: "Children are closer to fantastic transformations than adults, closer to the spell of costume and the change that comes from illusion, but we are all prone to it . . . a story we have heard and repeated to ourselves. These stories are often clichés, worn narratives we hold close to our hearts." How does Hustvedt use specific word choices (especially verbs and adjectives) and phrasing to resist the lure of clichés in telling her story? Comment on the effectiveness of her use of simile and metaphor.

4. **CONNECTIONS:**   In paragraph 11, Hustvedt observes: "Any meaningful piece of clothing is part of a broader cultural story." She proceeds to recount the story of dressing as a man for a Halloween party and the effects of doing so both on her and on those who saw her. She concludes that the experience of dressing in a red jumpsuit and being mistaken for a transvestite is "both comic and sad, [and] gave me sudden insight into the venom that appearances can produce" (paragraph 11). Compare and contrast Hustvedt's conclusion about the relationship between clothing and social expectations, and clothing and gender with that of Dave Barry in "Beauty and the Beast" (page 315). Which writer makes the more engaging and convincing case about the relationship between looks (and especially clothing) and social expectations and gender identity? Explain why.

Stephen King

EVERYTHING YOU NEED TO KNOW ABOUT WRITING SUCCESSFULLY — IN TEN MINUTES

STEPHEN KING was born in 1947 in Portland, Maine. He began writing stories early in his life, but it was his discovery of a box of horror and science fiction novels in the attic of his aunt's house that made him decide to pursue a career as a writer. He published his first short stories in pulp horror magazines while in high school. After graduating from the University of Maine at Orono in 1970, King, while working at a low-paying job in a laundry, began writing his first novel, *Carrie*

> **Stephen King's discovery of horror and science fiction novels in his aunt's attic prompted him to pursue a writing career.**

(1974). *Carrie* was followed by some forty more novels, including a series written under the pen name Richard Bachman, as well as numerous novellas, short story collections, and screenplays. His critically acclaimed work of nonfiction, *On Writing* (2000), the source of the following essay, was completed while he was recovering painfully from a much-publicized accident.

Stephen King has commented that, as a creative writer, he always hopes for "that element of inspiration which lifts you past the point where the characters are just you, where you do achieve something transcendental and the people are really people in the story."

 I. THE FIRST INTRODUCTION

THAT'S RIGHT. I know it sounds like an ad for some sleazy writers' school, but I really am going to tell you everything you need to pursue a successful and financially rewarding career writing fiction, and I really am going to do it in ten minutes, which is exactly how long it took me to learn. It will actually take you twenty minutes or so to read this article, however, because I have to tell you a story, and then I have to write a second introduction. But these, I argue, should not count in the ten minutes.

II. THE STORY, OR, HOW STEPHEN KING LEARNED TO WRITE

When I was a sophomore in high school, I did a sophomoric thing which got me in a pot of fairly hot water, as sophomoric didoes often do. I wrote and published a small satiric newspaper called *The Village Vomit*. In this little paper I lampooned a number of teachers at Lisbon (Maine) High School, where I was under instruction. These were not very gentle lampoons; they ranged from the scatological to the downright cruel.

Eventually, a copy of this paper found its way into the hands of a faculty member, and since I had been unwise enough to put my name on it (a fault, some critics would argue, of which I have still not been entirely cured). I was brought into the office. The sophisticated satirist had by that time reverted to what he really was: a fourteen-year-old kid who was shaking in his boots and wondering if he was going to get a suspension . . . what we called a "three-day vacation" in those dim days of 1964.

I wasn't suspended. I was forced to make a number of apologies—they were warranted, but they tasted like dog-dirt in my mouth—and spent a week in detention hall. And the guidance counselor arranged what he no doubt thought of as a more constructive channel for my talents. This was a job—contingent upon the editor's approval—writing sports for the Lisbon Enterprise, a twelve-page weekly of the sort with which any small-town resident will be familiar. This editor was the man who taught me everything

I know about writing in ten minutes. His name was John Gould—not the famed New England humorist or the novelist who wrote *The Greenleaf Fires*, but a relative of both, I believe.

He told me he needed a sports writer, and we could "try each other out," if I wanted.   5

I told him I knew more about advanced algebra than I did sports.

Gould nodded and said, "You'll learn."

I said I would at least try to learn. Gould gave me a huge roll of yellow paper and promised me a wage of 1/2 [cts.] per word. The first two pieces I wrote had to do with a high school basketball game in which a member of my school team broke the Lisbon High scoring record. One of these pieces was a straight piece of reportage. The second was a feature article.

I brought them to Gould the day after the game, so he'd have them for the paper, which came out Fridays. He read the straight piece, made two minor corrections, and spiked it. Then he started in on the feature piece with a large black pen and taught me all I ever needed to know about my craft. I wish I still had the piece,—it deserves to be framed, editorial corrections and all—but I can remember pretty well how it went and how it looked when he had finished with it. Here's an example:

> → *thrash out*
> *the owd*
> *vig positive*
> *or over exaggerated*
> *description*
>
> Last night, in the ~~well-loved~~ gymnasium of Lisbon High School, partisans and Jay Hills fans alike were stunned by an athletic performance unequalled in school history: Bob Ransom, ~~known as Bullet Bob for both his size and accuracy~~, scored thirty-seven points. Yes, you heard me right. ~~Plus~~ he did it with grace, and speed . . . and with an odd courtesy as well, committing only two personal fouls in his ~~knight-like~~ quest for a record which has eluded Lisbon ~~thincladℓ~~ players since ~~the years of Korea~~ 1953 . . .
>
> *fluff*
> *Be efficient.*
> *Be "economical."*

When Gould finished marking up my copy in the manner I have indi-   10
cated above, he looked up and must have seen something on my face. I think he must have thought it was horror, but it was not: It was revelation.

"I only took out the bad parts, you know," he said. "Most of it's pretty good."

"I know," I said, meaning both things; yes, most of it was good, and yes, he had only taken out the bad parts. "I won't do it again."

"If that's true," he said, "you'll never have to work again. You can do this for a living."

Then he threw back his head and laughed.

And he was right: I am doing this for a living, and as long as I can keep   15
on, I don't expect ever to have to work again.

III. THE SECOND INTRODUCTION

All of what follows has been said before. If you are interested enough in writing to be a purchaser of this magazine [*Writer*], you will have either heard or read all (or almost all) of it before. Thousands of writing courses are taught across the United States each year; seminars are convened; guest lecturers talk, then answer questions, and it all boils down to what follows.

I am going to tell you these things again because often people will only listen—really listen—to someone who makes a lot of money doing the thing he's talking about. This is sad but true. And I told you the story above not to make myself sound like a character out of a Horatio Alger novel but to make a point: I saw, I listened, and I learned. Until that day in John Gould's little office, I had been writing first drafts of stories that might run 2,500 words. The second drafts were apt to run 3,300 words. Following that day, my 2,500-word first drafts became 2,200-word second drafts. And two years after that, I sold the first one.

So here it is, with all the bark stripped off. It'll take ten minutes to read, and you can apply it right away . . . if you listen.

IV. EVERYTHING YOU NEED TO KNOW ABOUT WRITING SUCCESSFULLY

1. Be talented

This, of course, is the killer. What is talent? I can hear someone shouting, and here we are, ready to get into a discussion right up there with "What is the meaning of life?" for weighty pronouncements and total uselessness. For the purposes of the beginning writer, talent may as well be defined as eventual success—publication and money. If you wrote something for which someone sent you a check, if you cashed the check and it didn't bounce, and if you then paid the light bill with the money, I consider you talented.

Now some of you are really hollering. Some of you are calling me one 20 crass money-fixated creep. Nonsense. Worse than nonsense, off the subject. We're not talking about good or bad here. I'm interested in telling you how to get your stuff published, not in critical judgments of who's good or bad. As a rule, the critical judgments come after the check's been spent, any-way. I have my own opinions, but most times I keep them to myself. People who are published steadily and are paid for what they are writing may be either saints or trollops, but they are clearly reaching a great many some-ones who want what they have. Ergo, they are communicating. Ergo, they are talented. The biggest part of writing successfully is being talented, and in the context of marketing, the only bad writer is one who doesn't get paid. If you're not talented, you won't succeed. And if you're not succeeding, you should know when to quit.

When is that? I don't know. It's different for each writer. Not after six rejection slips, certainly, nor after sixty. But after six hundred? Maybe. After six thousand? My friend, after six thousand pinks, it's time you tried painting or computer programming.

Further, almost every aspiring writer knows when he is getting warmer—you start getting little jotted notes on your rejection slips, or personal letters . . . maybe a commiserating phone call. It's lonely out there in the cold, but there are encouraging voices . . . unless there is nothing in your words that warrants encouragement. I think you owe it to yourself to skip as much of the self-illusion as possible. If your eyes are open, you'll know which way to go . . . or when to turn back.

2. Be neat

Type. Double-space. Use a nice heavy white paper. If you've marked your manuscript a lot, do another draft.

3. Be self-critical

If you haven't marked up your manuscript a lot, you did a lazy job. Only God gets things right the first time. Don't be a slob.

4. Remove every extraneous word

You want to get up on a soapbox and preach? Fine. Get one, and try your local park. You want to write for money? Get to the point. And if you remove the excess garbage and discover you can't find the point, tear up what you wrote and start all over again . . . or try something new.

5. Never look at a reference book while doing a first draft

You want to write a story? Fine. Put away your dictionary, your encyclopedias, your *World Almanac*, and your thesaurus. Better yet, throw your thesaurus into the wastebasket. The only things creepier than a thesaurus are those little paperbacks college students too lazy to read the assigned novels buy around exam time. Any word you have to hunt for in a thesaurus is the wrong word. There are no exceptions to this rule. You think you might have misspelled a word? O.K., so here is your choice: Either look it up in the dictionary, thereby making sure you have it right—and breaking your train of thought and the writer's trance in the bargain—or just spell it phonetically and correct it later. Why not? Did you think it was going to go somewhere? And if you need to know the largest city in Brazil and you find you don't have it in your head, why not write in Miami, or Cleveland? You can check it . . . but later. When you sit down to write, write. Don't do anything else except go to the bathroom, and only do that if it absolutely cannot be put off.

25

6. Know the markets

Only a dimwit would send a story about giant vampire bats surrounding a high school to *McCall's*. Only a dimwit would send a tender story about a mother and daughter making up their differences on Christmas Eve to *Playboy* . . . but people do it all the time. I'm not exaggerating; I have seen such stories in the slush piles of the actual magazines. If you write a good story, why send it out in an ignorant fashion? Would you send your kid out in a snowstorm dressed in Bermuda shorts and a tank top? If you like science fiction, read science fiction novels and magazines. If you want to write mysteries, read the magazines. And so on. It isn't just a matter of knowing what's right for the present story; you can begin to catch on, after a while, to overall rhythms, editorial likes and dislikes, a magazine's slant. Sometimes your reading can influence the next story, and create a sale.

7. Write to entertain

Does this mean you can't write "serious fiction"? It does not. Somewhere along the line pernicious critics have invested the American reading and writing public with the idea that entertaining fiction and serious ideas do not overlap. This would have surprised Charles Dickens, not to mention Jane Austen, John Steinbeck, William Faulkner, Bernard Malamud, and hundreds of others. But your serious ideas must always serve your story, not the other way around. I repeat: If you want to preach, get a soapbox.

8. Ask yourself frequently, "Am I having fun?"

The answer needn't always be yes. But if it's always no, it's time for a new project or a new career.

9. How to evaluate criticism

Show your piece to a number of people—ten, let us say. Listen carefully to   30
what they tell you. Smile and nod a lot. Then review what was said very carefully. If your critics are all telling you the same thing about some facet of your story—a plot twist that doesn't work, a character who rings false, stilted narrative, or half a dozen other possibles—change it. It doesn't matter if you really like that twist or that character; if a lot of people are telling you something is wrong with your piece, it is. If seven or eight of them are hitting on that same thing, I'd still suggest changing it. But if everyone—or even most everyone—is criticizing something different, you can safely disregard what all of them say.

10. Observe all rules for proper submission

Return postage, self-addressed envelope, etc.

11. An agent? Forget it. For now.

Agents get 10 percent to 15 percent of monies earned by their clients. Fifteen percent of nothing is nothing. Agents also have to pay the rent. Beginning writers do not contribute to that or any other necessity of life. Flog your stories around yourself. If you've done a novel, send around query letters to publishers, one by one, and follow up with sample chapters and/or the complete manuscript. And remember Stephen King's First Rule of Writers and Agent, learned by bitter personal experience: You don't need one until you're making enough for someone to steal . . . and if you're making that much, you'll be able to take your pick of good agents.

12. If it's bad, kill it

When it comes to people, mercy killing is against the law. When it comes to fiction, it is the law.

That's everything you need to know. And if you listened, you can write everything and anything you want. Now I believe I will wish you a pleasant day and sign off.

My ten minutes are up.   ●   35

The Reader's Presence

1. Why does King include sections I through III, even though they are not part of the "ten minutes"? What does the first introduction actually introduce? the second? How effectively does section II work with section IV? For example, how many rules did King learn when John Gould edited his story? Which rules does he break in his own essay? Why do you think he breaks them?

2. King is best known for writing horror novels, stories that scare people. What fears does he play on throughout this essay? How does he go about setting up suspenseful situations? What does he do to frighten people in this essay? If the rules are monsters, which ones do you think are the most frightening? Why?

3. By King's definition, a talented author is one who has been paid for his or her writing. Pick an author in this collection whom you consider talented and evaluate him or her according to King's rules. How successful should this writer be according to King? What other rules of success does the writer's essay suggest should be added to King's list?

4. **CONNECTIONS:**   King's essay represents an approach to an ongoing debate between money and art. Signalled by terms like *practicality* and *popularity*, the money side holds that you should write to make money. Signalled by phrases like "art for art's sake" or "selling out," the art side holds that you should write to please yourself. George Orwell in "George Orwell on the Four Reasons for Writing" (page 538) represents another approach to this debate when he lists "four great motives for writing" (paragraph 1). Read Orwell's essay and determine how well each of the motives would lead to the kind of successful writing that King imagines. For example, how well—or how poorly—does Orwell's desire to "share an experience which one feels is valuable" (paragraph 3) lead to King's "eventual success—publication and money" (paragraph 19)?

Maxine Hong Kingston
NO NAME WOMAN

MAXINE HONG KINGSTON (b. 1940) won the National Book Critics Circle Award for nonfiction with her first book, *The Woman Warrior: Memoirs of a Girlhood among Ghosts* (1976). "No Name Woman" is the opening chapter of this book, which *Time* magazine named one of the top ten nonfiction works of the 1970s. Her other works include *China Men* (1980), which won the American Book Award; *Tripmaster Monkey: His Fake Book* (1988), a picaresque novel; and *To Be the Poet* (2002), a collection of her lectures and verse. A manuscript entitled *The Fourth Book of Peace* was destroyed, along with her home and all of her possessions, in a 1991 Oakland–Berkeley fire, but Kingston started over and published *The Fifth Book of Peace* in 2003. Kingston's writing often blurs the distinction between fiction and nonfiction. She edited *Veterans of War, Veterans of Peace* (2006), a collection of writing by survivors of war compiled from her healing workshops. Her narratives blend autobiography, history, myth, and legend, drawing on the stories she remembers from her childhood in the Chinese American community of Stockton,

> **"My life as a writer had been a long struggle with pronouns."**

California. Kingston's essays, stories, and poems also appear in numerous magazines, and she received the 1997 National Medal for the Humanities. In 2004, she retired as a senior lecturer for creative writing at the University of California, Berkeley. Her most recent book, *I Love a Broad Margin to My Life* (2011), is a reflection on aging.

Kingston has said that before writing *The Woman Warrior*, "My life as a writer had been a long struggle with pronouns. For 30 years I wrote in the first-person singular. At a certain point I was thinking that I was self-centered and egotistical, solipsistic, and not very developed as a human being, nor as an artist, because I could only see from this one point of view." She began to write in the third person because "I thought I had to overcome this self-centeredness." As she wrote her third novel, Kingston experienced the disappearance of her authorial voice. "I feel that this is an artistic as well as psychological improvement on my part. Because I am now a much less selfish person."

"YOU MUST NOT TELL ANYONE," my mother said, "what I am about to tell you. In China your father had a sister who killed herself. She jumped into the family well. We say that your father has all brothers because it is as if she had never been born.

"In 1924 just a few days after our village celebrated seventeen hurry-up weddings — to make sure that every young man who went 'out on the road' would responsibly come home —your father and his brothers and your grandfather and his brothers and your aunt's new husband sailed for America, the Gold Mountain. It was your grandfather's last trip. Those lucky enough to get contracts waved good-bye from the decks. They fed and guarded the stowaways and helped them off in Cuba, New York, Bali, Hawaii. 'We'll meet in California next year,' they said. All of them sent money home.

"I remember looking at your aunt one day when she and I were dressing; I had not noticed before that she had such a protruding melon of a stomach. But I did not think, 'She's pregnant,' until she began to look like other pregnant women, her shirt pulling and the white tops of her black pants showing. She could not have been pregnant, you see, because her husband had been gone for years. No one said anything. We did not discuss it. In early summer she was ready to have the child, long after the time when it could have been possible.

"The village had also been counting. On the night the baby was to be born the villagers raided our house. Some were crying. Like a great saw, teeth strung with lights, files of people walked zigzag across our land, tearing the rice. Their lanterns doubled in the disturbed black water, which drained away through the broken bunds.[1] As the villagers closed in, we could see that some of them, probably men and women we knew well, wore white masks. The people with long hair hung it over their faces. Women with short hair made it stand up on end. Some had tied white bands around their foreheads, arms, and legs.

"At first they threw mud and rocks at the house. Then they threw eggs   5
and began slaughtering our stock. We could hear the animals scream their deaths—the roosters, the pigs, a last great roar from the ox. Familiar wild heads flared in our night windows; the villagers encircled us. Some of the faces stopped to peer at us, their eyes rushing like searchlights. The hands flattened against the panes, framed heads, and left red prints.

"The villagers broke in the front and the back doors at the same time, even though we had not locked the doors against them. Their knives dripped with the blood of our animals. They smeared blood on the doors and walls. One woman swung a chicken, whose throat she had slit, splattering blood in red arcs about her. We stood together in the middle of our house, in the family hall with the pictures and tables of the ancestors around us, and looked straight ahead.

"At that time the house had only two wings. When the men came back we would build two more to enclose our courtyard and a third one to begin a second courtyard. The villagers pushed through both wings, even your grandparents' rooms, to find your aunt's, which was also mine until the men returned. From this room a new wing for one of the younger families would grow. They ripped up her clothes and shoes and broke her combs, grinding

---

1 **bunds:** An embankment around rice fields to help prevent flooding. — EDS.

them underfoot. They tore her work from the loom. They scattered the cooking fire and rolled the new weaving in it. We could hear them in the kitchen breaking our bowls and banging the pots. They overturned the great waist-high earthenware jugs; duck eggs, pickled fruits, vegetables burst out and mixed in acrid torrents. The old woman from the next field swept a broom through the air and loosed the spirits-of-the-broom over our heads. 'Pig.' 'Ghost.' 'Pig,' they sobbed and scolded while they ruined our house.

"When they left, they took sugar and oranges to bless themselves. They cut pieces from the dead animals. Some of them took bowls that were not broken and clothes that were not torn. Afterward we swept up the rice and sewed it back up into sacks. But the smells from the spilled preserves lasted. Your aunt gave birth in the pigsty that night. The next morning when I went up for the water, I found her and the baby plugging up the family well.

"Don't let your father know that I told you. He denies her. Now that you have started to menstruate, what happened to her could happen to you. Don't humiliate us. You wouldn't like to be forgotten as if you had never been born. The villagers are watchful."

Whenever she had to warn us about life, my mother told stories that ran   10
like this one, a story to grow up on. She tested our strength to establish realities. Those in the emigrant generations who could not reassert brute survival died young and far from home. Those of us in the first American generations have had to figure out how the invisible world the emigrants built around our childhoods fit in solid America.

The emigrants confused the gods by diverting their curses, misleading them with crooked streets and false names. They must try to confuse their offspring as well, who, I suppose, threaten them in similar ways—always trying to get things straight, always trying to name the unspeakable. The Chinese I know hide their names; sojourners take new names when their lives change and guard their real names with silence.

Chinese-Americans, when you try to understand what things in you are Chinese, how do you separate what is peculiar to childhood, to poverty, insanities, one family, your mother who marked your growing with stories, from what is Chinese? What is Chinese tradition and what is the movies?

If I want to learn what clothes my aunt wore, whether flashy or ordinary, I would have to begin, "Remember Father's drowned-in-the-well sister?" I cannot ask that. My mother has told me once and for all the useful parts. She will add nothing unless powered by Necessity, a riverbank that guides her life. She plants vegetable gardens rather than lawns; she carries the odd-shaped tomatoes home from the fields and eats food left for the gods.

Whenever we did frivolous things, we used up energy; we flew high kites. We children came up off the ground over the melting cones our parents brought home from work and the American movie on New Year's Day—*Oh, You Beautiful Doll* with Betty Grable one year, and *She Wore a Yellow Ribbon* with John Wayne another year. After the one carnival ride each, we paid in guilt; our tired father counted his change on the dark walk home.

Adultery is extravagance. Could people who hatch their own chicks and   15
eat the embryos and the heads for delicacies and boil the feet in vinegar for
party food, leaving only the gravel, eating even the gizzard lining—could
such people engender a prodigal aunt? To be a woman, to have a daughter in
starvation time was a waste enough. My aunt could not have been the lone
romantic who gave up everything for sex. Women in the old China did not
choose. Some man had commanded her to lie with him and be his secret evil.
I wonder whether he masked himself when he joined the raid on her family.

Perhaps she encountered him in the fields or on the mountain where
the daughters-in-law collected fuel. Or perhaps he first noticed her in the
marketplace. He was not a stranger because the village housed no strangers. She had to have dealings with him other than sex. Perhaps he worked
an adjoining field, or he sold her the cloth for the dress she sewed and wore.
His demand must have surprised, then terrified her. She obeyed him; she
always did as she was told.

When the family found a young man in the next village to be her husband, she stood tractably beside the best rooster, his proxy, and promised
before they met that she would be his forever. She was lucky that he was her
age and she would be the first wife, an advantage secure now. The night she
first saw him, he had sex with her. Then he left for America. She had almost
forgotten what he looked like. When she tried to envision him, she only saw
the black and white face in the group photograph the men had had taken
before leaving.

The other man was not, after all, much different from her husband. They
both gave orders: she followed. "If you tell your family, I'll beat you. I'll kill
you. Be here again next week." No one talked sex, ever. And she might have
separated the rapes from the rest of living if only she did not have to buy her
oil from him or gather wood in the same forest. I want her fear to have lasted
just as long as rape lasted so that the fear could have been contained. No
drawn-out fear. But women at sex hazarded birth and hence lifetimes. The
fear did not stop but permeated everywhere. She told the man, "I think I'm
pregnant." He organized the raid against her.

On nights when my mother and father talked about their life back home,
sometimes they mentioned an "outcast table" whose business they still
seemed to be settling, their voices tight. In a commensal tradition, where food
is precious, the powerful older people made wrongdoers eat alone. Instead
of letting them start separate new lives like the Japanese, who could become
samurais and geishas, the Chinese family, faces averted but eyes glowering
sideways, hung on to the offenders and fed them leftovers. My aunt must
have lived in the same house as my parents and eaten at an outcast table.
My mother spoke about the raid as if she had seen it, when she and my
aunt, a daughter-in-law to a different household, should not have been living together at all. Daughters-in-law lived with their husbands' parents, not
their own; a synonym for marriage in Chinese is "taking a daughter-in-law."
Her husband's parents could have sold her, mortgaged her, stoned her. But

they had sent her back to her own mother and father, a mysterious act hinting at disgraces not told me. Perhaps they had thrown her out to deflect the avengers.

She was the only daughter; her four brothers went with her father, husband, and uncles "out on the road" and for some years became western men. When the goods were divided among the family, three of the brothers took land, and the youngest, my father, chose an education. After my grandparents gave their daughter away to her husband's family, they had dispensed all the adventure and all the property. They expected her alone to keep the traditional ways, which her brothers, now among the barbarians, could fumble without detection. The heavy, deep-rooted women were to maintain the past against the flood, safe for returning. But the rare urge west had fixed upon our family, and so my aunt crossed boundaries not delineated in space.
20

The work of preservation demands that the feelings playing about in one's guts not be turned into action. Just watch their passing like cherry blossoms. But perhaps my aunt, my forerunner, caught in a slow life, let dreams grow and fade and after some months or years went toward what persisted. Fear at the enormities of the forbidden kept her desires delicate, wire and bone. She looked at a man because she liked the way the hair was tucked behind his ears, or she liked the question-mark line of a long torso curving at the shoulder and straight at the hip. For warm eyes or a soft voice or a slow walk—that's all—a few hairs, a line, a brightness, a sound, a pace, she gave up family. She offered us up for a charm that vanished with tiredness, a pigtail that didn't toss when the wind died. Why, the wrong lighting could erase the dearest thing about him.

It could very well have been, however, that my aunt did not take subtle enjoyment of her friend, but, a wild woman, kept rollicking company. Imagining her free with sex doesn't fit, though. I don't know any women like that, or men either. Unless I see her life branching into mine, she gives me no ancestral help.

To sustain her being in love, she often worked at herself in the mirror, guessing at the colors and shapes that would interest him, changing them frequently in order to hit on the right combination. She wanted to look back.

On a farm near the sea, a woman who tended her appearance reaped a reputation for eccentricity. All the married women blunt-cut their hair in flaps about their ears or pulled it back in tight buns. No nonsense. Neither style blew easily into heart-catching tangles. And at their weddings they displayed themselves in their long hair for the last time. "It brushed the back of my knees," my mother tells me. "It was braided, and even so, it brushed the backs of my knees."

At the mirror my aunt combed individuality into her bob. A bun could have been contrived to escape into black streamers blowing in the wind or in quiet wisps about her face, but only the older women in our picture album wear buns. She brushed her hair back from her forehead, tucking the flaps behind her ears. She looped a piece of thread, knotted into a circle between her index fingers and thumbs, and ran the double strand across her forehead.
25

When she closed her fingers as if she were making a pair of shadow geese bite, the string twisted together catching the little hairs. Then she pulled the thread away from her skin, ripping the hairs out neatly, her eyes watering from the needles of pain. Opening her fingers, she cleaned the thread, then rolled it along her hairline and the tops of the eyebrows. My mother did the same to me and my sisters and herself. I used to believe that the expression "caught by the short hairs" meant a captive held with a depilatory string. It especially hurt at the temples, but my mother said we were lucky we didn't have to have our feet bound when we were seven. Sisters used to sit on their beds and cry together, she said, as their mothers or their slave removed the bandages for a few minutes each night and let the blood gush back into their veins. I hope that the man my aunt loved appreciated a smooth brow, that he wasn't just a tits-and-ass man.

Once my aunt found a freckle on her chin, at a spot that the almanac said predestined her for unhappiness. She dug it out with a hot needle and washed the wound with peroxide.

More attention to her looks than these pullings of hairs and pickings at spots would have caused gossip among the villagers. They owned work clothes and good clothes, and they wore good clothes for feasting the new seasons. But since a woman combing her hair hexes beginnings, my aunt rarely found an occasion to look her best. Women looked like great sea snails—the corded wood, babies, and laundry they carried were the whorls on their backs. The Chinese did not admire a bent back; goddesses and warriors stood straight. Still there must have been a marvelous freeing of beauty when a worker laid down her burden and stretched and arched.

Such commonplace loveliness, however, was not enough for my aunt. She dreamed of a lover for the fifteen days of New Year's, the time for families to exchange visits, money, and food. She plied her secret comb. And sure enough she cursed the year, the family, the village, and herself.

Even as her hair lured her imminent lover, many other men looked at her. Uncles, cousins, nephews, brothers would have looked, too, had they been home between journeys. Perhaps they had already been restraining their curiosity, and they left, fearful that their glances, like a field of nesting birds, might be startled and caught. Poverty hurt, and that was their first reason for leaving. But another, final reason for leaving the crowded house was the never-said.

She may have been unusually beloved, the precious only daughter, spoiled and mirror-gazing because of the affection the family lavished on her. When her husband left, they welcomed the chance to take her back from the in-laws; she could live like the little daughter for just a while longer. There are stories that my grandfather was different from other people, "crazy ever since the little Jap bayoneted him in the head." He used to put his naked penis on the dinner table, laughing. And one day he brought home a baby girl, wrapped up inside his brown western-style greatcoat. He had traded one of his sons, probably my father, the youngest, for her. My grandmother made him trade back. When he finally got a daughter of his

30

own, he doted on her. They must have all loved her, except perhaps my father, the only brother who never went back to China, having once been traded for a girl.

Brothers and sisters, newly men and women, had to efface their sexual color and present plain miens. Disturbing hair and eyes, a smile like no other, threatened the ideal of five generations living under one roof. To focus blurs, people shouted face to face and yelled from room to room. The immigrants I know have loud voices, unmodulated to American tones even after years away from the village where they called their friendships out across the fields. I have not been able to stop my mother's screams in public libraries or over telephones. Walking erect (knees straight, toes pointed forward, not pigeon-toed, which is Chinese-feminine) and speaking in an inaudible voice, I have tried to turn myself American-feminine. Chinese communication was loud, public. Only sick people had to whisper. But at the dinner table, where the family members came nearest one another, no one could talk, not the outcasts nor any eaters. Every word that falls from the mouth is a coin lost. Silently they gave and accepted food with both hands. A preoccupied child who took his bowl with one hand got a sideways glare. A complete moment of total attention is due everyone alike. Children and lovers have no singularity here, but my aunt used a secret voice, a separate attentiveness.

She kept the man's name to herself throughout her labor and dying; she did not accuse him that he be punished with her. To save her inseminator's name she gave silent birth.

He may have been somebody in her own household, but intercourse with a man outside the family would have been no less abhorrent. All the village were kinsmen, and the titles shouted in loud country voices never let kinship be forgotten. Any man within visiting distance would have been neutralized as a lover— "brother," "younger brother," "older brother" —115 relationship titles. Parents researched birth charts probably not so much to assure good fortune as to circumvent incest in a population that has but one hundred surnames. Everybody has eight million relatives. How useless then sexual mannerisms, how dangerous.

As if it came from an atavism deeper than fear, I used to add "brother" silently to boys' names. It hexed the boys, who would or would not ask me to dance, and made them less scary and as familiar and deserving of benevolence as girls.

But, of course, I hexed myself also—no dates. I should have stood up, 35 both arms waving, and shouted out across libraries, "Hey, you! Love me back." I had no idea, though, how to make attraction selective, how to control its direction and magnitude. If I made myself American-pretty so that the five or six Chinese boys in the class fell in love with me, everyone else—the Caucasian, Negro, and Japanese boys—would too. Sisterliness, dignified and honorable, made much more sense.

Attraction eludes control so stubbornly that whole societies designed to organize relationships among people cannot keep order, not even when they bind people to one another from childhood and raise them together.

Among the very poor and the wealthy, brothers married their adopted sisters, like doves. Our family allowed some romance, paying adult brides' prices and providing dowries so that their sons and daughters could marry strangers. Marriage promises to turn strangers into friendly relatives—a nation of siblings.

In the village structure, spirits shimmered among the live creatures, balanced and held in equilibrium by time and land. But one human being flaring up into violence could open up a black hole, a maelstrom that pulled in the sky. The frightened villagers, who depended on one another to maintain the real, went to my aunt to show her a personal, physical representation of the break she made in the "roundness." Misallying couples snapped off the future, which was to be embodied in true offspring. The villagers punished her for acting as if she could have a private life, secret and apart from them.

If my aunt had betrayed the family at a time of large grain yields and peace, when many boys were born, and wings were being built on many houses, perhaps she might have escaped such severe punishment. But the men—hungry, greedy, tired of planting in dry soil, cuckolded—had been forced to leave the village in order to send food-money home. There were ghost plagues, bandit plagues, wars with the Japanese, floods. My Chinese brother and sister had died of an unknown sickness. Adultery, perhaps only a mistake during good times, became a crime when the village needed food.

The round moon cakes and round doorways, the round tables of graduated size that fit one roundness inside another, round windows and rice bowls—these talismans had lost their power to warn this family of the law: A family must be whole, faithfully keeping the descent line by having sons to feed the old and the dead who in turn look after the family. The villagers came to show my aunt and lover-in-hiding a broken house. The villagers were speeding up the circling of events because she was too shortsighted to see that her infidelity had already harmed the village, that waves of consequences would return unpredictably, sometimes in disguise, as now, to hurt her. This roundness had to be made coin-sized so that she would see its circumference: Punish her at the birth of her baby. Awaken her to the inexorable. People who refused fatalism because they could invent small resources insisted on culpability. Deny accidents and wrest fault from the stars.

After the villagers left, their lanterns now scattering in various directions   40
toward home, the family broke their silence and cursed her. "Aiaa, we're going to die. Death is coming. Death is coming. Look what you've done. You've killed us. Ghost! Dead Ghost! Ghost! You've never been born." She ran out into the fields, far enough from the house so that she could no longer hear their voices, and pressed herself against the earth, her own land no more. When she felt the birth coming, she thought that she had been hurt. Her body seized together. "They've hurt me too much," she thought. "This is gall, and it will kill me." With forehead and knees against the earth, her body convulsed and then relaxed. She turned on her back, lay on the ground. The black well of sky and stars went out and out forever; her body and her complexity seemed to disappear. She was one of the stars, a bright

dot in blackness, without home, without a companion, in eternal cold and silence. An agoraphobia rose in her, speeding higher and higher, bigger and bigger; she would not be able to contain it; there would be no end to fear.

Flayed, unprotected against space, she felt pain return, focusing her body. This pain chilled her—a cold, steady kind of surface pain. Inside, spasmodically, the other pain, the pain of the child, heated her. For hours she lay on the ground, alternately body and space. Sometimes a vision of normal comfort obliterated reality: She saw the family in the evening gambling at the dinner table, the young people massaging their elders' backs. She saw them congratulating one another, high joy on the mornings the rice shoots came up. When these pictures burst, the stars drew yet further apart. Black space opened.

She got to her feet to fight better and remembered that old-fashioned women gave birth in their pigsties to fool the jealous, pain-dealing gods, who do not snatch piglets. Before the next spasms could stop her, she ran to the pigsty, each step a rushing out into emptiness. She climbed over the fence and knelt in the dirt. It was good to have a fence enclosing her, a tribal person alone.

Laboring, this woman who had carried her child as a foreign growth that sickened her every day, expelled it at last. She reached down to touch the hot, wet, moving mass, surely smaller than anything human, and could feel that it was human after all—fingers, toes, nails, nose. She pulled it up on to her belly, and it lay curled there, butt in the air, feet precisely tucked one under the other. She opened her loose shirt and buttoned the child inside. After resting, it squirmed and thrashed and she pushed it up to her breast. It turned its head this way and that until it found her nipple. There, it made little snuffling noises. She clenched her teeth at its preciousness, lovely as a young calf, a piglet, a little dog.

She may have gone to the pigsty as a last act of responsibility: She would protect this child as she had protected its father. It would look after her soul, leaving supplies on her grave. But how would this tiny child without family find her grave when there would be no marker for her anywhere, neither in the earth nor the family hall? No one would give her a family hall name. She had taken the child with her into the wastes. At its birth the two of them had felt the same raw pain of separation, a wound that only the family pressing tight could close. A child with no descent line would not soften her life but only trail after her, ghostlike, begging her to give it purpose. At dawn the villagers on their way to the fields would stand around the fence and look.

Full of milk, the little ghost slept. When it awoke, she hardened her breasts against the milk that crying loosens. Toward morning she picked up the baby and walked to the well.   45

Carrying the baby to the well shows loving. Otherwise abandon it. Turn its face into the mud. Mothers who love their children take them along. It was probably a girl; there is some hope of forgiveness for boys.

"Don't tell anyone you had an aunt. Your father does not want to hear her name. She has never been born." I have believed that sex was unspeakable and words so strong and fathers so frail that "aunt" would do my father mysterious harm. I have thought that my family, having settled among immigrants who had also been their neighbors in the ancestral land, needed to clean their name, and a wrong word would incite the kinspeople even here. But there is more to this silence: They want me to participate in her punishment. And I have.

In the twenty years since I heard this story I have not asked for details nor said my aunt's name; I do not know it. People who comfort the dead can also chase after them to hurt them further—a reverse ancestor worship. The real punishment was not the raid swiftly inflicted by the villagers, but the family's deliberately forgetting her. Her betrayal so maddened them, they saw to it that she would suffer forever, even after death. Always hungry, always needing, she would have to beg food from other ghosts, snatch and steal it from those whose living descendants give them gifts. She would have to fight the ghosts massed at crossroads for the buns a few thoughtful citizens leave to decoy her away from village and home so that the ancestral spirits could feast unharassed. At peace, they could act like gods, not ghosts, their descent lines providing them with paper suits and dresses, spirit money, paper houses, paper automobiles, chicken, meat, and rice into eternity—essences delivered up in smoke and flames, steam and incense rising from each rice bowl. In an attempt to make the Chinese care for people outside the family, Chairman Mao[2] encourages us now to give our paper replicas to the spirits of outstanding soldiers and workers, no matter whose ancestors they may be. My aunt remains forever hungry. Goods are not distributed evenly among the dead.

My aunt haunts me—her ghost drawn to me because now, after fifty years of neglect, I alone devote pages of paper to her, though not origamied into houses and clothes. I do not think she always means me well. I am telling on her, and she was a spite suicide, drowning herself in the drinking water. The Chinese are always very frightened of the drowned one, whose weeping ghost, wet hair hanging and skin bloated, waits silently by the water to pull down a substitute. ●

The Reader's Presence

1. Kingston's account of her aunt's life and death is a remarkable blend of fact and speculation. Consider the overall structure of "No Name Woman." How many versions of the aunt's story do we hear? Where, for example, does the mother's story end? Where does the narrator's begin? Which version do you find more compelling? Why? What does the narrator mean when she says that her mother's stories "tested our strength to establish realities" (paragraph 10)?

2. The narrator's version of her aunt's story is replete with such words and phrases as *perhaps* and *It could very well have been*. The narrator seems far more speculative about her aunt's life than her mother is. At what point does the narrator raise doubts

---

[2] **Chairman Mao** (1893–1976): Political theorist, guerilla warfare strategist, poet, and leader of the Chinese Revolution, Mao Zedong helped found the People's Republic of China in 1949, and ruled the nation until his death in 1976. — EDS.

about the veracity of her mother's version of the aunt's story? What purpose does the mother espouse in telling the aunt's story? Is it meant primarily to express family lore? to issue a warning? Point to specific passages to verify your response. What is the proposed moral of the story? Is that moral the same for the mother as for the narrator? Explain.

3. **CONNECTIONS:**   What line does Kingston draw between the two cultures represented in the story: between the mother, a superstitious, cautious Chinese woman, and the narrator, an American-born child trying to "straighten out" her mother's confusing story? How does the narrator resolve the issue by thinking of herself as neither Chinese nor American, but as Chinese American? How does she imagine her relationship to her distant aunt? Compare Kingston's depiction of relationships across generations and cultures to those in N. Scott Momaday's "The Way to Rainy Mountain" (page 504) and to those in Richard Rodriguez's "Aria: A Memoir of a Bilingual Childhood" (page 187). How does language feature in each writer's family? How do problems of comprehension become occasions for creative play in each essay?

The Writer at Work

MAXINE HONG KINGSTON on Writing for Oneself

In the fire that raged through the Oakland, California, hills in 1991, Maxine Hong Kingston lost, along with her entire house, all her copies of a work in progress. In the following interview conducted by Diane Simmons at Kingston's new home in 1997, the writer discusses how the fire and the loss of her work have transformed her attitude toward her own writing. Confronted with a similar loss (whether the work was on paper or hard drive), most authors would try to recapture as best they could what they had originally written. Why do you think Kingston wants to avoid that sort of recovery? The following exchange is from the opening of that long interview, which appeared in a literary periodical, the *Crab Orchard Review* (Spring/Summer 1998). Simmons is the author of *Maxine Hong Kingston* (New York: Twayne Publishers, 1999).

I began by asking Ms. Kingston to talk about the book that was lost, and where she was going with her recent work.

Kingston: In the book that I lost in the fire, I was working on an idea of finding the book of peace again. There was a myth that there were three lost books of peace and so I was going to find the book of peace for our time. I imagine that it has to do with how to wage peace on earth and that there would be tactics on how to wage peace and how to stop war. I see that the books of war are popular; they are taught in the military academies; they're translated into all different languages. They [are used to] help corporate executives succeed in business. And people don't even think about the books of peace; people don't even know about them. I'm the only one that knows about it.

And so I was writing this and that was what was burned in the fire. What I'm working on now I'm calling *The Fifth Book of Peace*. I'm not recalling and remembering what I had written. To me it's the pleasure of writing to be constantly discovering, going into the new. To recall word by word what I had written before sounds like torture and agony for me. I know I can do it, I'm sure I can do it if I want to. One of my former students volunteered to hypnotize me so I could recall, but that seemed so wrong to me.

Simmons: How much was lost?

Kingston: About 200 written, rewritten pages, so it was very good. But I had wanted to rewrite it again and I think to recall word by word would freeze me into a version and I didn't want to do that.

Simmons: Is the book you are working on now the same project, the same version?

Kingston: Yes, but it is not the same words. It's not the same story. It's the same idea that I want to work on peace. At one point I called it the global novel. But since then I've been thinking of it as a book of peace. And the one big difference is the Book of Peace was a work of fiction. I was imagining fictional characters. But after the fire I wanted to use writing for my personal self. I wanted to write directly what I was thinking and feeling, not imagining fictional other people. I wanted to write myself. I wanted to write in the way I wrote when I was a child which is to say my deepest feelings and thoughts as they could come out in a personal way and not for public consumption. It's not even for other people

to read but for myself, to express myself, and it doesn't matter whether this would be published. I don't even want to think about publication or readers, but this is for my own expression of my own suffering or agony.

Simmons: You've said that that's how you wrote in the beginning.

Kingston: I always begin like that. I always have to begin like that. Getting back to the roots of language in myself. It's almost like diary writing which is not for others.

Simmons: You don't mean that you don't want other people to read it necessarily.

Kingston: That's not a consideration. I don't want to think about any of that. I think of this as going back to a primitive state of what writing is for me, which is that I am finding my own voice again.

Simmons: Was it lost?

Kingston: Well, I started not to think about it anymore. After a while I had such an effective public voice, from childhood to now, I had found it and I had created it.

Simmons: Where do we see that public voice?

Kingston: The public voice is the voice that's in all my books.

Simmons: Even *Woman Warrior*?

Kingston: Yes. All my works. That is a public voice. What I mean by the private, personal voice is what I write when I'm trying to figure out things, what I write that's just for me. I get to be the reader and nobody else gets to read this. For years now I have not written in that way. I usually don't write diaries as an adult and so after the fire I needed to get to that again. I had forgotten about it.

Simmons: You are going back to before *Woman Warrior*, to before being a writer.

Kingston: Yes. Before being a writer who publishes.

Simmons: Why do you think the fire caused you to turn away from fiction?

Kingston: At the same time my father died; he died a few weeks before the fire. At that time I felt I'd lost a lot. So I wanted to say what I felt about all that, about all my losses. And I don't see that as writing for publication. I see that as writing for myself, to put into words my losses. And so I started there, and wrote and wrote and wrote. But as I was writing, it became some of the things I was thinking in the book that burned; those would come into the writing, and then of course I go back to that very *id*[1] basic place. I'm old enough and civilized enough now so that the sentences and the words that come out are very elegant, very good, very crafted. I don't return to a place that's not crafted anymore. So all this stuff that I wrote down is going to be part of *The Fifth Book of Peace.*

[1] *id:* Latin for *it;* in Freudian psychoanalysis it stands for primitive impulses that derive from the unconscious part of the human psyche.

Dan Koeppel

HOW TO FALL 35,000 FEET — AND SURVIVE

DAN KOEPPEL (b. 1962) is a well-known outdoors and nature writer. He has written for the *New York Times Magazine, Outside, Popular Mechanics,* and many mountain biking magazines, and was inducted into the Mountain Bike Hall of Fame in 2003 for his writings on the subject. He was the editor of *Mountain Bike* magazine until 1996 and is a former commentator for Public Radio International's *Marketplace.* His books include *To See Every Bird on Earth: A Father, a Son, and a Lifelong Obsession* (2005) and *Banana: The Fate of the Fruit That Changed the World* (2007). Suspected of being a spy, Koeppel was imprisoned briefly in Africa while researching *Banana,* which deals with the surprisingly complex social, economic, and political history of the popular fruit.

> Suspected of being a spy, Dan Koeppel was imprisoned briefly in Africa while researching his book *Banana,* which deals with the surprisingly complex social, economic, and political history of the popular fruit.

6:59:00 AM—35,000 FEET

YOU HAVE A LATE NIGHT and an early flight. Not long after takeoff, you drift to sleep. Suddenly, you're wide awake. There's cold air rushing everywhere, and sound. Intense, horrible sound. *Where am I?*, you think. *Where's the plane?*

You're 6 miles up. You're alone. You're falling.

Things are bad. But now's the time to focus on the good news. (Yes, it goes beyond surviving the destruction of your aircraft.) Although gravity is against you, another force is working in your favor: time. Believe it or not, you're better off up here than if you'd slipped from the balcony of your high-rise hotel room after one too many drinks last night.

Or at least you will be. Oxygen is scarce at these heights. By now, hypoxia is starting to set in. You'll be unconscious soon, and you'll cannonball at least a mile before waking up again. When that happens, remember what you are about to read. The ground, after all, is your next destination.

Granted, the odds of surviving a 6-mile plummet are extraordinarily slim, but at this point you've got nothing to lose by understanding your situation. There are two ways to fall out of a plane. The first is to free-fall, or drop from the sky with absolutely no protection or means of slowing your descent. The second is to become a wreckage rider, a term coined by Massachusetts-based amateur historian Jim Hamilton, who developed the Free Fall Research Page—an online database of nearly every imaginable human plummet. That classification means you have the advantage of being attached to a chunk of the plane. In 1972, Serbian flight attendant Vesna Vulovic was traveling in a DC-9 over Czechoslovakia when it blew up. She fell 33,000 feet, wedged between her seat, a catering trolley, a section of aircraft and the body of another crew member, landing on—then sliding down—a snowy incline before coming to a stop, severely injured but alive.

Surviving a plunge surrounded by a semiprotective cocoon of debris is more common than surviving a pure free-fall, according to Hamilton's statistics; 31 such confirmed or "plausible" incidents have occurred since the 1940s. Free-fallers constitute a much more exclusive club, with just 13 confirmed or plausible incidents, including perennial Ripley's Believe It or Not superstar Alan Magee—blown from his B-17 on a 1943 mission over France. The New Jersey airman, more recently the subject of a *MythBusters* episode, fell 20,000 feet and crashed into a train station; he was subsequently captured by German troops, who were astonished at his survival.

Whether you're attached to crumpled fuselage or just plain falling, the concept you'll be most interested in is *terminal velocity*. As gravity pulls you toward earth, you go faster. But like any moving object, you create drag—more as your speed increases. When downward force equals upward resistance, acceleration stops. You max out.

Depending on your size and weight, and factors such as air density, your speed at that moment will be about 120 mph—and you'll get there after a

5

surprisingly brief bit of falling: just 1,500 feet, about the same height as Chicago's Sears (now Willis) Tower. Equal speed means you hit the ground with equal force. The difference is the clock. Body meets Windy City sidewalk in 12 seconds. From an airplane's cruising altitude, you'll have almost enough time to read this entire article.

7:00:20 AM—22,000 FEET

By now you've descended into breathable air. You sputter into consciousness. At this altitude, you've got roughly 2 minutes until impact. Your plan is simple. You will enter a Zen state and decide to live. You will understand, as Hamilton notes, "that it isn't the fall that kills you—it's the landing."

Keeping your wits about you, you take aim.   10

But at what? Magee's landing on the stone floor of that French train station was softened by the skylight he crashed through a moment earlier. Glass hurts, but it gives. So does grass. Haystacks and bushes have cushioned surprised-to-be-alive free-fallers. Trees aren't bad, though they tend to skewer. Snow? Absolutely. Swamps? With their mucky, plant-covered surface, even more awesome. Hamilton documents one case of a sky diver who, upon total parachute failure, was saved by bouncing off high-tension wires. Contrary to popular belief, water is an awful choice. Like concrete, liquid doesn't compress. Hitting the ocean is essentially the same as colliding with a sidewalk, Hamilton explains, except that pavement (perhaps unfortunately) won't "open up and swallow your shattered body."

With a target in mind, the next consideration is body position. To slow your descent, emulate a sky diver. Spread your arms and legs, present your chest to the ground, and arch your back and head upward. This adds friction and helps you maneuver. But don't relax. This is not your landing pose.

The question of how to achieve ground contact remains, regrettably, given your predicament, a subject of debate. A 1942 study in the journal *War Medicine* noted "distribution and compensation of pressure play large parts in the defeat of injury." Recommendation: wide-body impact. But a 1963 report by the Federal Aviation Agency argued that shifting into the classic sky diver's landing stance—feet together, heels up, flexed knees and hips—best increases survivability. The same study noted that training in wrestling and acrobatics would help people survive falls. Martial arts were deemed especially useful for hard-surface impacts: "A 'black belt' expert can reportedly crack solid wood with a single blow," the authors wrote, speculating that such skills might be transferable.

The ultimate learn-by-doing experience might be a lesson from Japanese parachutist Yasuhiro Kubo, who holds the world record in the activity's banzai category. The sky diver tosses his chute from the plane and then jumps out after it, waiting as long as possible to retrieve it, put it on and pull the ripcord. In 2000, Kubo—starting from 9,842 feet—fell for 50 seconds before recovering his gear. A safer way to practice your technique would be at one of the wind-tunnel simulators found at about a dozen U.S. theme parks and malls. But neither will help with the toughest part: sticking the landing. For that you might consider—though it's not exactly advisable—a leap off the world's highest bridge, France's Millau Viaduct; its platform towers 891 feet over mostly spongy farmland.

Water landings—if you must—require quick decision-making. Studies of bridge-jump survivors indicate that a feet-first, knife-like entry (aka "the pencil") best optimizes your odds of resurfacing. The famed cliff divers of Acapulco, however, tend to assume a head-down position, with the fingers of each hand locked together, arms outstretched, protecting the head. Whichever you choose, first assume the free-fall position for as long as you can. Then, if a feet-first entry is inevitable, the most important piece of advice, for reasons both unmentionable and easily understood, is to *clench your butt.*

No matter the surface, definitely don't land on your head. In a 1977 "Study of Impact Tolerance Through Free-Fall Investigations," researchers at the Highway Safety Research Institute found that the major cause of death in falls—they examined drops from buildings, bridges and the occasional elevator shaft (oops!)—was cranial contact. If you have to arrive top-down, sacrifice your good looks and land on your face, rather than the back or top of your head. You might also consider flying with a pair of goggles in your pocket, Hamilton says, since you're likely to get watery eyes—impairing accuracy—on the way down.

7:02:19 AM—1,000 FEET

Given your starting altitude, you'll be just about ready to hit the ground as you reach this section of instruction (based on the average adult reading speed of 250 words per minute). The basics have been covered, so feel free to concentrate on the task at hand. But if you're so inclined, here's some supplemental information—though be warned that none of it will help you much at this point.

Statistically speaking, it's best to be a flight crew member, a child, or traveling in a military aircraft. Over the past four decades, there have been at least a dozen commercial airline crashes with just one survivor. Of those documented, four of the survivors were crew, like the flight attendant Vulovic, and seven were passengers under the age of 18. That includes Mohammed el-Fateh Osman, a 2-year-old wreckage rider who lived through the crash of a Boeing jet in Sudan in 2003, and, more recently, 14-year-old Bahia Bakari, the sole survivor of last June's Yemenia Airways plunge off the Comoros Islands.

Crew survival may be related to better restraint systems, but there's no consensus on why children seem to pull through falls more often. The Federal Aviation Agency study notes that kids, especially those under the age of 4, have more flexible skeletons, more relaxed muscle tonus, and a higher proportion of subcutaneous fat, which helps protect internal organs. Smaller people—whose heads are lower than the seat backs in front of them—are better shielded from debris in a plane that's coming apart. Lower body weight reduces terminal velocity, plus reduced surface area decreases the chance of impalement upon landing.

7:02:25 AM—0 FEET

The ground. Like a Shaolin master, you are at peace and prepared. *Impact.* 20
You're alive. What next? If you're lucky, you might find that your injuries are minor, stand up and smoke a celebratory cigarette, as British tail gunner Nicholas Alkemade did in 1944 after landing in snowy bushes following an 18,000-foot plummet. (If you're a smoker, you're *super extra lucky*, since you've technically gotten to indulge during the course of an airliner trip.) More likely, you'll have tough work ahead.

Follow the example of Juliane Koepcke. On Christmas Eve 1971, the Lockheed Electra she was traveling in exploded over the Amazon. The next morning, the 17-year-old German awoke on the jungle floor, strapped into her seat, surrounded by fallen holiday gifts. Injured and alone, she pushed the death of her mother, who'd been seated next to her on the plane, out of her mind. Instead, she remembered advice from her father, a biologist: To find civilization when lost in the jungle, follow water. Koepcke waded from tiny streams to larger ones. She passed crocodiles and poked the mud in front of her with a stick to scare away stingrays. She had lost one shoe in the fall and was wearing a ripped miniskirt. Her only food was a bag of candy, and she had nothing but dark, dirty water to drink. She ignored her broken collarbone and her wounds, infested with maggots.

On the tenth day, she rested on the bank of the Shebonya River. When she stood up again, she saw a canoe tethered to the shoreline. It took her hours to climb the embankment to a hut, where, the next day, a group of lumberjacks found her. The incident was seen as a miracle in Peru, and free-fall statistics seem to support those arguing for divine intervention: According to the Geneva-based Aircraft Crashes Record Office, 118,934 people have died in 15,463 plane crashes between 1940 and 2008. Even when you add failed-chute sky divers, Hamilton's tally of confirmed or plausible lived-to-tell-about-it incidents is only 157, with 42 occurring at heights over 10,000 feet.

But Koepcke never saw survival as a matter of fate. She can still recall the first moments of her fall from the plane, as she spun through the air in her seat. That wasn't under her control, but what happened when she regained consciousness was. "I had been able to make the correct decision—to leave the scene of the crash," she says now. And because of experience at her parents' biological research station, she says, "I did not feel fear. I knew how to move in the forest and the river, in which I had to swim with dangerous animals like caimans and piranhas."

Or, by now, you're wide awake, and the aircraft's wheels have touched safely down on the tarmac. You understand the odds of any kind of accident on a commercial flight are slimmer than slim and that you will likely never have to use this information. But as a courtesy to the next passenger, consider leaving your copy of this guide in the seat-back pocket. ◼

The Reader's Presence

1. What do you think the overall purpose is for Koeppel in writing this essay? With this goal in mind, comment on his decision to address the reader directly. How would you characterize Koeppel's tone of voice in the essay?

2. What do you notice about Koeppel's use of historical facts and research? How does he transition from the description of a real-time free fall, on the one hand, to the historical anecdotes, on the other? What effect(s) does weaving together these two narratives have on the sense of elapsed time in the essay?

3. **CONNECTIONS:**   Consider the "advice" given in this essay to that given in Joan Acocella's "A Few Too Many" (page 283). Compare and contrast the writer's tone of voice in each essay. In what specific ways do the essays diverge in terms of style? Consider diction, sentence structure, and overarching purpose as you develop your response. In what ways — and with what effects — does each writer draw on research or scientific evidence and for what purpose?

Steven D. Levitt and Stephen J. Dubner

WHAT SHOULD YOU WORRY ABOUT?

STEVEN D. LEVITT (b. 1967) and **STEPHEN J. DUBNER** (b. 1963) teamed up to write the enormously popular and influential book *Freakonomics: A Rogue Economist Explores the Hidden Side of Everything* (2006), which was on the *New York Times* best-seller list for over two years, selling more than 3 million copies worldwide. The team followed up their success in 2009 with *SuperFreakonomics: Global Cooling, Patriotic Prostitutes, and Why Suicide Bombers Should Buy Life Insurance*, which debuted at number two on the *New York Times* best-seller list.

Levitt graduated from Harvard University and received his PhD from the Massachusetts Institute of Technology. He has been a professor of economics at the University of Chicago since 1997 and is the director of the Becker Center on Chicago Price Theory, a research center administered by the Graduate School of Business at the University of Chicago that emphasizes the role of markets and incentives in understanding economics and human behavior—fundamental elements of the new study of "freakonomics." An award-winning economist, Levitt was named one of *Time* magazine's "100 People Who Shape Our World" and, in 2004, received the John Bates Clark Medal, which recognizes the most influential economist in America under the age of forty. In 2009, he co-founded—with a group of leading economists, including John List and Andrew Rosenfield—a business and philanthropy consulting firm called The Greatest Good.

> In 2004, Steven Levitt won the John Bates Clark Medal, which recognizes the most influential economist in America under the age of forty.

Author and journalist Stephen J. Dubner received his MFA from Columbia University in New York City. In addition to co-writing *Freakonomics*, he is the author of two books of nonfiction/memoir, *Turbulent Souls: A Catholic Son's Return to His Jewish Family* (1998) and *Confessions of a Hero-Worshipper* (2003); and a book for young children, *The Boy with Two Belly Buttons* (2007). His work appears frequently in the *New Yorker* and in the *New York Times*, and it has been anthologized in *Best American Sports Writing* and *Best American Crime Writing*, among other collections. Both writers contribute to the *New York Times* blog, "Freakonomics."

HUMANS ARE GOOD at many things—typing, inventing stuff—but we're bad at assessing risk. Day after day, we get bent out of shape over things we shouldn't worry about so much, like airplane crashes and lightning strikes, instead of things we should, like heart disease and the flu.

So how can we find out what's truly dangerous? Economics. Upon hearing the word, most people think of incomprehensible charts and jargon and promptly change the subject. However, we can use the field's powerful ideas and tools, along with huge piles of data, to understand topics that aren't typically associated with economics. Topics like shark attacks.

Think back to the summer of 2001, or what the U.S. media dubbed the "Summer of the Shark." The prime example was the story of Jessie Arbogast, an 8-year-old who was playing in the warm, shallow Pensacola, Florida, waves when a bull shark ripped off his right arm and a big chunk of his thigh.

The media was full of such chilling tales. Here's the lead paragraph from one article published that summer:

"Sharks come silently, without warning. There are three ways they strike: the hit-and-run, the bump-and-bite, and the sneak attack. The hit-   5 and-run is the most common. The shark may see the sole of a swimmer's foot, think it's a fish, and take a bite before realizing this isn't its usual prey."

A reasonable person might never go near the ocean again. But how many shark attacks do you think actually happened that year?

Take a guess—and then cut that figure in half, and now cut it in half a few more times. During all of 2001, there were 68 shark attacks worldwide, of which just four were fatal.

Not only were the numbers lower than the media hysteria implied, but they were not much higher than those of previous years or of the years that followed. Between 1995 and 2005, there were on average 60.3 shark attacks worldwide each year, with a high of 79 and a low of 46. There were on average 5.9 fatalities per year, with a high of 11 and a low of three. In other words, the headlines during the summer of 2001 might just as easily have read "Shark Attacks About Average This Year."

Elephants, meanwhile, kill at least 200 people a year. Why aren't we petrified of them? Probably because their victims tend to live far from the world's media centers. It may also have to do with our perceptions gleaned from the movies. Friendly elephants are a staple of children's films like *Babar* and *Dumbo*; sharks are typecast as villains.

There are any number of topics about which our fears run far out of proportion to reality. For instance, whom are you more afraid of: strangers or people you know?   10

While "strangers" is the obvious answer, it's probably wrong. Three out of four murder victims knew their assailants; about seven of 10 rape victims knew theirs. While the public is justifiably horrified when a stranger snatches a child off the street, the data show that such kidnappings are extremely rare.

As for the crime of identity theft, most of us fear nameless, faceless perpetrators—say, a far-off ring of teenage hackers. We try to thwart them by endlessly changing our PINs (and forgetting them). But it turns out that nearly half of identity-theft victims are ripped off by someone they know. And fully 90 percent of thefts happen offline, not on the Internet.

Fear sometimes distorts our thinking to the point where we become convinced that certain threats are so enormous as to be unstoppable. Every generation has at least one such problem—the plague, polio. Today, it's global warming.

The average global ground temperature over the past 100 years has risen 1.3 degrees Fahrenheit, or 0.74 degrees Celsius. But even the most brilliant climate scientists are unable to predict exactly what will happen to the Earth as a result of those atmospheric changes and when anything will happen.

We humans tend to respond to uncertainty with more emotion—fear,   15
blame, paralysis—than advisable. Uncertainty also has a nasty way of making us conjure the very worst possibilities. With global warming, these are downright biblical: hellish temperatures, rising oceans, a planet in chaos.

But instead of panicking and collectively wringing our hands, it might help us to look at other "unsolvable" problems humanity has had to deal with.

Like, well, horse manure. As urban populations exploded in the 19th century, horses were put to work in countless ways, from pulling streetcars and coaches to powering manufacturing equipment. Our cities became filled with horses—for example, in 1900, New York City was home to some 200,000 of them, or one for every 17 people.

Unfortunately, they produced a slew of what economists refer to as "negative externalities." These included noise, gridlock, high insurance costs, and far too many human traffic fatalities.

The worst problem was the manure. The average horse produces about 24 pounds of it a day. In New York, that added up to nearly 5 million pounds. A day. It lined the streets like banks of snow and was piled as high as 60 feet in vacant lots. It stank to the heavens. And it was a fertile breeding ground for flies that spread deadly disease.

City planners everywhere were confounded. It seemed as if cities could not survive without the horse—but they couldn't survive with it, either.   20

And then the problem vanished. The horse was kicked to the curb by the electric streetcar and the automobile.

Virtually every unsolvable problem we've faced in the past has turned out to be quite solvable, and the script has nearly always been the same: A band of clever, motivated people—scientists usually—find an answer. With polio, it was the creation of a vaccine. If the best minds in the world focus their attention on global warming, hopefully we can handle that, too.

Yes, it is an incredibly large and challenging problem. But, as history has shown us again and again, human ingenuity is bound to be even larger.

The Reader's Presence

1. The authors argue that knowledge of economics can help us better assess risk. Why do you think they chose shark attacks as their lead example? In what way does economics help us understand that being attacked by a shark is less of a risk than most people realize? Are you persuaded by their example? Why or why not?

2. What does our fear of global warming have to do with "horse manure" (paragraph 17)? In what ways do both examples support the view that economics can solve what appear to be insurmountable problems? What do the authors propose people do to solve the problems associated with global warming?

3. **CONNECTIONS:** The next selection, by Michael Lewis, "The Mansion: A Subprime Parable" also deals with a current economic problem. Read Lewis's essay in the context of Levitt and Dubner's "What Should You Worry About?" In what ways does Lewis's essay deal with our assessment of risk? How would you apply Levitt and Dubner's economic approach to danger to the conditions Lewis writes about?

Michael Lewis

THE MANSION: A SUBPRIME PARABLE

MICHAEL LEWIS (b. 1960) is an American author. Although he is probably best known for penning *The Blind Side: Evolution of a Game* (2006), the book that later became the basis for the 2009 film, *The Blind Side*, Michael Lewis began as a financial writer. Originally from New Orleans, Lewis earned a bachelor's degree in art history from Princeton University, but his desire to make money on Wall Street eventually prompted him to enroll in the London School of Economics to pursue a master's degree in economics. He went to work for an investment bank, Salomon Brothers, during the late 1980s but was soon disillusioned by the dishonesty he perceived in the way Wall Street seemed to toy with other people's money. He wrote his first book, *Liar's Poker*

> **Working for Salomon Brothers during the late 1980s, Lewis became disillusioned by the dishonest ways Wall Street played with other people's money.**

(1989), based on his experiences, and has since written many best-selling books on subjects ranging from money to sports. Some titles include *Moneyball: The Art of Winning an Unfair Game* (2003), *The New New Thing: A Silicon Valley Story* (1999), and, most recently, *The Big Short: Inside the Doomsday Machine* (2010). He has written for *Slate*, the *New York Times Magazine*, and many other high-profile periodicals, including Condé Nast's *Portfolio*. He joined *Vanity Fair* as a contributing editor in 2009.

I WAS LOOKING to return to New Orleans, where I'd grown up, to write a book. The move would uproot my wife and three children from California, and I felt a little bad about that. They needed a place to live, but places to live in New Orleans are hard to find. Ever since Hurricane Katrina, the real estate market there has been in turmoil. Owners want to sell, buyers want to rent, and the result is a forest of for sale signs and an army of workers commuting from great distances.

At the bottom of every real estate ad I saw was the name of the same agent. One woman ruled the market, it seemed, and her name was Eleanor Farnsworth. I called her and threw myself on her mercy. She thought my problem over and then said, "I only know of one place that would work for you." She'd suggested it to Brad Pitt and Angelina Jolie, she said, before selling them their more modest place in the French Quarter.

That shouldn't have been a selling point; it should have been a warning. I should have asked the price. Instead, I asked the address.

As soon as I saw it, I knew it—the mansion. The most conspicuously grand house in New Orleans. As a child, I'd ridden my bike past it 2,000 times and always felt a tiny bit unnerved. It wasn't just a mansion; it seemed like the biggest mansion on the street with all the mansions, St. Charles Avenue, an object of fascination for the tourists on the clanging streetcars. But it was hard to imagine a human being standing beside it, much less living inside it, and as far as I could tell, none ever did. There was never any sign of life around it; it was just this awesome, silent pile of pale stone. The Frick Museum,[1] but closed.

5

Inside, it was even more awesome than outside. It was as if the architect had set out to show just how much space he could persuade a rich man to waste. The entryway was a kind of ballroom, which gave way to a curved staircase, a replica of one in the Palace of Versailles.[2] The living room wasn't a kind of ballroom; it was a ballroom, with $80,000 worth of gold on the ceiling. The bedrooms were the size of giant living rooms. The changing rooms and closets and bathrooms were the size of bedrooms. There were two of everything that the rest of the world has one of: two dining rooms, two full kitchens, two half kitchens. Ten bathrooms and seven bedrooms.

I didn't ask the price—I was renting—so I didn't know that the last time it changed hands it had sold for close to $7 million, and was now valued at $10 million. I imagined how it would feel to live in such a place. What it wouldn't feel like, clearly, was anything close to being in the other houses in which I'd lived.

Upper middle class: That's how I've always thought of myself. Upper middle class is the class into which I was born, the class to which I was always told I belonged, and the class with which, until this moment, I'd never had a problem. Upper middle class is a sneaky designation, however. It's a way of saying "I'm well-off" without having to say "I'm rich," even if, by most standards, you are. Upper-middle-classness has allowed me to feel like I'm not only competing in the same financial league as most Americans—I'm winning! Playing in the middle class, I have enjoyed huge success.

In this house, I now glimpsed the problem with upper-middle-classness: It isn't really a class. It's a space between classes. The space may once have been bridgeable, but lately it's become a chasm. Middle-class people fantasize about travel upgrades; upper-class people can't imagine life without a jet. Middle-class people help their children with their homework so they'll have a chance of getting into Princeton; upper-class people buy Princeton a new building. Middle-class people have homes; upper-class people have monuments. A man struggling to hold on to the illusion that he is upper middle class has become like a character in a cartoon earthquake: He looks down

---

1 **Frick Museum:** New York City art museum that was once the home of the multimillionaire Henry Clay Frick. — EDS.
2 **Palace of Versailles:** The luxurious palace of Louis XIV. — EDS.

Since the 1980s Americans have desired to live in supersized, newly constructed houses that opponents began calling McMansions as a way of criticizing their mass-produced quality (like fast food) and lack of architectural integrity.

and sees his feet being dragged ever farther apart by a quickly widening fissure. His legs stretch, then splay, and finally he plunges into the abyss.

This house, and everything it represents, stands on the more appealing side of the chasm. "It's perfect," I said.

Every few days, I googled the house and stared at it. Then a funny thing　10 happened: It began to shrink. Sure it's big, I told myself, but houses come bigger. The White House, for instance. I told my wife and children only that I'd found a house with a swimming pool and enough bathrooms for everyone to have his or her own. Which is to say, they really had no idea what they were getting into. How could they? It didn't occur to them that not only would they have their own bathrooms, they'd need to decide before dinner which of the two dining rooms to eat in — and afterward, which of the three dishwashers to not put their dishes in. To believe it, and to grasp its full upper-class implications, they'd need to see it.

On the day we move in, we're all stuffed together, Beverly Hillbillies-style, in a rented, dirty, gold Hyundai Sonata. For fun, as I drive up and down St. Charles Avenue, I ask them to guess which of these improbably large houses is ours.

"That one?"

"No."

"That one!"

The exercise turns giddy. Each house is bigger than the last. The girls   15
squeal in the backseat and press their noses against the windows, while
their mother, in the front, does her best to remain calm. We pass in front of
the mansion and they look right past it. The thing takes up an entire city
block, and somehow they can't see it. It's too implausible. It's not a home.
It's a mint.

We circle around the block and approach from the rear, the Sonata rolling up the long driveway and coming to a stop beneath the grand stone
porte cochere. "This is our new house?" asks Quinn, age eight.

"This is our new house," I say.

She begins to hyperventilate.

"Omigodomigodomigod!"

My small children plunge from the rental car into the driveway. They   20
leap up and down as if they've just won an N.B.A. championship. By the time
we get inside, they're gasping. They sprint off to inspect their new home.

"There's another floor!"

"Daddy! There's an elevator!"

My children love me. They have a house with an elevator.

In all the public finger-pointing about the American real estate bust, surprisingly little attention has been paid to its origin. There's obviously a long
list of people and ideas that can share in the blame: ratings agencies, mortgage brokers, big Wall Street firms, small Wall Street firms, Angelo Mozilo,[3]
Alan Greenspan.[4] Every few weeks, the *New York Times* runs a piece exposing some new way in which a big Wall Street firm has exploited some poor or
middle-class family. The rich people on Wall Street blame their bosses. The
brokers at Merrill Lynch blame Stan O'Neal,[5] the traders at Bear Stearns blame
Jimmy Cayne.[6] Everyone blames Countrywide. But all of this misses the point:
However terrible the sins of the financial markets, they're merely a reflection
of a cultural predisposition. To blame the people who lend the money for the
real estate boom is like blaming the crack dealers for creating addicts.

Americans feel a deep urge to live in houses that are bigger than they   25
can afford. This desire cuts so cleanly through the population that it touches
just about everyone. It's the acceptable lust.

Consider, for example, the Garcias. On May 30, the *New York Times* ran
a story about a couple, Lilia and Jesus Garcia, who were behind on their
mortgage payments and in danger of losing their homes. The Garcias had
a perfectly nice house near Stockton, California, that they bought in 2003
for 160 grand. Given their joint income of $65,000, they could afford to bor-
row about $160,000 against a home. But then, in 2006, they stumbled upon

---

[3] **Angelo Mozilo** (b. 1938): Was founder, chairman, and CEO of Countrywide Financial, one of
the nation's largest mortgage loan companies. — EDS.

[4] **Alan Greenspan** (b. 1926): A noted economist, was Chairman of the Federal Reserve from
1987 to 2006. — EDS.

[5] **Stan O'Neal** (b. 1951): Was the CEO of Merrill Lynch from 2003 to 2008. — EDS.

[6] **Jimmy Cayne** (b. 1934): Was the CEO of Bear Stearns from 1993 to 2008. — EDS.

their dream house. The new property was in Linden, California, and, judging from its picture, had distinctly mansionlike qualities. Its price, $535,000, was a stretch.

Then, of course, the market turned. The Garcias failed to make their mortgage payments and couldn't sell their original house. They owed the bank about $700,000 and were facing eviction. The mistake supposedly illustrated by the Garcias' predicament was that they held on to their former home in Stockton as an investment. The moral: Americans are in their current bind because so many of them saw houses as moneymaking opportunities.

But the real moral is that when a middle-class couple buys a house they can't afford, defaults on their mortgage, and then sits down to explain it to a reporter from the *New York Times*, they can be confident that he will overlook the reason for their financial distress: the peculiar willingness of Americans to risk it all for a house above their station. People who buy something they cannot afford usually hear a little voice warning them away or prodding them to feel guilty. But when the item in question is a house, all the signals in American life conspire to drown out the little voice. The tax code tells people like the Garcias that while their interest payments are now gargantuan relative to their income, they're deductible. Their friends tell them how impressed they are—and they mean it. Their family tells them that while theirs is indeed a big house, they have worked hard, and Americans who work hard deserve to own a dream house. Their kids love them for it.

Across America, some version of this drama has become a social norm. As of this spring, one in 11 mortgages was either past due—like Ed McMahon's[7] $4.8 million jumbo loan on his property—or in foreclosure, like Evander Holyfield's[8] $10 million Georgia estate. It's no good pretending that Americans didn't know they couldn't afford such properties, or that they were seduced into believing they could afford them by mendacious mortgage brokers or Wall Street traders. If they hadn't lusted after the bigger house, they never would have met the mortgage brokers in the first place. The money-lending business didn't create the American desire for unaffordable housing. It simply facilitated it.

It's this desire we must understand. More than any other possession, houses are what people use to say, "Look how well I'm doing!" Given the financial anxieties and indignities suffered by the American middle class, it's hardly surprising that a lower-middle-class child who grows up in a small house feels a burning need to acquire a bigger one. The wonder is how an upper-middle-class child who grew up in a big and perfectly enviable house is inexorably drawn to a mansion.

30

When you move into a house you cannot afford, the first thing you notice is everything that you suddenly need—things that, before you arrived, you

---

[7] **Ed McMahon** (1923–2009): American TV personality, most famous for his role on *The Tonight Show*. — EDS.

[8] **Evander Holyfield** (b. 1962): A four-time heavyweight boxing champion. — EDS.

didn't even want. The dressing room was a microcosm of our mansion's ability to instruct. It wasn't a closet, but a room as big as the master bedroom we'd left behind in California. Even after my wife had stored her countless pairs of shoes, there was more than enough space for all of my stuff. Three weeks later, I noticed a door near the master-bedroom suite that I hadn't seen before; it was like a magical door that someone had carved into the wall while I slept. What could it be? I opened it to find . . . another huge dressing room! Inside, I could have fit every stitch of clothing I owned, three times over. It seemed weird to just leave it empty, but I didn't have anything left to put in it, so I closed the door and pretended the room wasn't there. But the thought occurred: Maybe I need more clothes.

The pool was another example. Because we moved in during the winter, we didn't pay that much attention to it at first. Had we bothered to dip our fingers in, we'd have discovered that it was not merely heated but was saltwater. It was a full six weeks before we really even noticed the pool house. Full bathroom, full kitchen, shiny new Viking range, and a fridge stuffed with 24 bottles of champagne. For a few weeks I felt that all of this was excessive. Then one day I became aware of the inconvenience of having to walk, dripping wet, from the pool back into the main house. This is what you need a pool house for—so you can make the transition from water to dry land without the trouble of walking the whole 15 yards back into the house and climbing a long flight of stairs to the giant dressing room. From that moment on, it seemed to me terribly inconvenient to not have a pool house. How on earth did people with pools, but no special house adjacent to them, cope?

The problems posed by the mansion were different from the problems posed by most other houses. How to locate loved ones, for instance. There's been no room inside any home I'd ever lived in from which, if I yelled at the top of my lungs, I couldn't be heard in every other room. The mansion required a new approach to human communications. Standing inside the mansion and screaming at the top of your lungs, you knew for certain that your voice wasn't reaching at least half the house. If you wanted to find someone, you could run around the house, but that took ages and presupposed that the other person was not similarly wandering in the void. A trek up the Himalayan staircases quickly became the subject of an elaborate cost-benefit analysis. How badly do I really want to find my six-year-old daughter? How much does my one-year-old son's diaper really need to be changed? After a while, it seemed only natural to my wife to begin with the assumption that her husband could not be found. Even when she knew for a fact that I was somewhere in the house, she'd begin her search with a phone call. She'd call my cell when I was two flights up and she'd call my cell when I was a room away. One afternoon she called my cell 20 minutes after I had come home with our three children and had gone looking for her to take them off my hands.

"Where are you?" she asked.

"I'm in the house taking care of the kids," I said, a little indignantly.   35
"Well, you can't be watching them very closely," she said, "because I'm in the house taking care of the kids."

Even though you couldn't find anybody, all sorts of people could find you. People stumbled into other people's spaces and terrified them. The house was so vast that the sound waves that normally precede the arrival of a living creature got lost. And so while there was, in theory, a great deal of privacy, there was, in practice, none. The mansion came with a gardener, a pool man, a caretaker, and a housekeeper. Any one of these people might turn up anyplace, anytime. The housekeeper, a sweet woman, came twice a week. She developed a habit of turning up over my right shoulder without warning and, as I stared helplessly at my computer screen, booming, "How's that book of yours coming along??!!!"

"Ah!" I'd yell, and leap out of my chair.

"Always writing, writing, writing!" she'd say with a laugh. (Writing in the mansion never ceased to be inherently comical.)

Money was another problem. It was suddenly going out faster than it   40
was coming in. When I'd finally gotten around to asking the real estate agent what the mansion cost to rent, she'd said — in the most offhand tone, as if it were the least important thing about the house — "I'll have to see, but I think it's around 13." Thirteen. The extra digits are just assumed. One reason is that no one can bring themselves to actually utter the sentence: "Your rent will be $13,000 a month."

Thirteen thousand dollars a month is not the rent I was raised to pay. When I let it slip to my mother what I'd be paying, she just said, "Oh, Michael," in exactly the same tone she'd have used if I'd informed her that I'd just run over the neighbor with a truck or been diagnosed with pancreatic cancer. Thirteen thousand dollars a month might be a record rent in New Orleans, but it was really just the ante.

We'd been there only three weeks when the first bills arrived. Utilities were $2,700. That turned out not to include water, which was another $1,000. Think of it: $1,000 a month for water you don't drink. (The drinking water came in truckloads from a spring-water company.) How did we use so much water? you might reasonably ask. The answer is, we didn't. The mansion did. The pool, the fountains, the sprinklers that came on in the wee hours to keep the great lawn lush and green — all were suddenly necessary. So, it turned out, was cable, at $800 a month. Who was I to argue? I wasn't even entirely sure how many televisions we had. Nine, at least. I thought I'd found the last of them when, two months after we'd arrived, I opened a cabinet and found another.

Walking into the mansion after school one day, my younger daughter, Dixie, asked, "Daddy, what's a Daddy Warbucks?" She'd caught a ride with a new friend's babysitter, who didn't know where we lived. Instead of giving the babysitter directions, the friend's mother had just said, "They live in the Daddy Warbucks house."

The first request for money came exactly 11 days after we arrived. A former schoolmate was calling on behalf of our high school; its fundraising department had somehow learned that I'd not only moved back to town but had moved into the mansion. My old school friend had a number in mind, somewhere between $25,000 and $100,000. Two days later, we had another old friend to dinner and—in hopes that she'd spread the word—I spoke of my amazement that anyone thought we could fork over 100 grand on a whim. "It's funny you should say that," she said. She'd just spoken with the director of a New Orleans museum, who had also heard we'd moved into the mansion. "He's trying to figure out the best way to approach you," she said.

We'd become an engineering problem.   45

Late one night the doorbell rings. There on our great stone porch is a man, obviously down on his luck, doing his best to appear subservient.

"I was just wondering if you have anything," he asks.

"Have anything?" I ask back.

"Some work that might be done, you know."

It's a feudal exchange right out of the 11th century. Vassal calling on lord   50 with the mutual understanding that lord owes vassal employment. The only thing missing is the offer of a freshly slaughtered rabbit.

A couple of months into our stay, we all sit in the formal dining room, under the gilded ceiling and the crystal chandelier, eating packaged tortellini off paper plates. We are Cuban peasants in late 1959 who have just moved into a Havana mansion on the heels of the rich owner, who has fled in terror from the revolution. Dixie, then five, blurts out, "I hate it when people say, 'Oh, I love your house,' because then I have to say, 'It's not my house.'" To which Quinn adds, "Yeah, I hate it when people say, 'You must be rich.'"

This was new. My children had taken to their new splendor like ducks to water. They'd see the St. Charles streetcar rolling past, and the tourists gawking and pointing at their new house, and their first reaction was not to cringe but to perform. They'd throw on their most princesslike dresses and run out front and dance around the malfunctioning marble fountain, pissing water in all the wrong directions, and wave to the commoners. One morning, as Quinn descended the staircases, overdressed for school, she announced, "I need to look good. I'm the girl who lives in the mansion."

But after a few months, the charm of pretending to be something they know they are not is wearing off.

There's a moment in the life of every American child when it dawns on him or her that the divvying up of material spoils is neither arbitrary nor a matter of personal choice, that money is a tool used by grownups to order and rank themselves, and that the easiest way to establish those rankings is through their houses. At first, everyone's house appears more or less the same; at any rate, you don't spend much time dwelling on the differences. But then, one day, someone's house is either so much humbler or so much grander than anything you've ever seen that you realize: A house is not just a house. It's one of the tools people use to rank me.

Children are basically communists. Seeing other children's material   55
prosperity, they follow their first instinct, which isn't to understand it or stew
about it. It's to ask for some of it—to get invited to the mansion. As far as I
knew, my children had never given much thought to what their house said
about them and their place in the world. They'd been friends with rich kids
and poor kids, without dwelling on the differences. That had just changed.

I resist the urge to explain how their misery might be good training for
grown-up American life; how we are, quite obviously, a nation of financial
imposters, poised to seize the first opportunity to live in houses we cannot
afford; and how, if they want to fit in, they'll need to learn to handle the
stress. They will have to learn these important lessons for themselves.

Instead, I turn my attention to survival. The mansion was not satisfied
with making us uneasy. It wanted us out. It preferred us to leave quietly,
without a fuss. But if we didn't, it was prepared to get violent.

The first inkling of this came one lazy Sunday afternoon. I was father-
ing my one-year-old son by teaching him how best to watch an NBA
game—which is to say, in high-def with surround sound. Our bliss was disrupted by the cry of a small child. It was muted, as if someone were calling out from inside the walls. It was from inside the walls. Our girls, with
their 10-year-old cousin, were trapped inside the elevator, which had mysteriously jolted to a stop. I tried to yank the metal gate off its hinges to get
into the shaft, but failed. It wouldn't have mattered anyway, as they were
between floors. For a good 20 minutes, I grunted and groaned and sweated
and pretended that this wasn't anything I couldn't handle. Then I called the
caretaker, who gave me the number of the man who had made the elevator
work in the first place. By some miracle, he was around and willing to drive
the 20 miles from his home to ours on a Sunday. Two hours later, the girls,
sobbing melodramatically, were sprung. The elevator man turned to me and
said, "I'm surprised you let them in there."

"Why?"

"She didn't tell you about the cat?"   60

No one told me about the cat that had been riding up in the elevator
with its billionaire owner. As they ascended, the cat had jumped out of the
owner's arms and stuck its head out of the metal gate. Its head had been
chopped off.

I shut down the elevator.

A few days later the phone rang. "We want to let you know that we
received a message from the equipment-supervision device on your control
panel," said the voice on the other end of the line. The what on the what?
The mansion, I learned, was equipped with tiny cameras that enabled it, in
effect, to watch its inhabitants. One of these, apparently, had malfunctioned.
I went into the basement, found the video-control panel, and yanked out as
many plugs as I could find.

The next afternoon, the house felt chilly. I hunted down the many ther-
mostats and turned them back up, from the 68 degrees to which they'd
somehow plummeted, to 72. The house ignored the request; no matter what

I did, it remained at exactly 68 degrees. My skin became the world's most sensitive thermometer, an expert on the state of being 69 degrees, because the moment the house would reach that temperature, all hell would break loose—one, then another, and then a third of the massive air-conditioning units that sat outside would begin to purr. Every now and again, I'd feel a brief tingle of warmth, a premonition of climate change, but that moment was always followed by the roar of engines and a correction.

The day after I tried to change the mansion's temperature, early in the   65
morning, the alarm went off. Then the phone rang: It was the alarm company, wanting to know our password. I gave it to them.

"I'm sorry, we don't have that as a password," said the lady on the other end of the phone, and then, as I begged and pleaded ("No, please, no! Let me try again!"), she quickly hung up.

Moments later, two squad cars with lights flashing sped into our driveway. Four police officers leapt out and banged on the front door. The mansion had phoned the cops at exactly the moment I appeared most shockingly arrestable: wearing only underpants and a T-shirt, hair sticking up in six different directions, and without a trace of evidence that I belonged there. I grabbed Dixie ("Daddy, I don't want to go! What if they arrest me too?") and pulled her close to me, as a kind of human shield.

"Sir, we're responding to an alarm signal."

"It was obviously a mistake. Sorry to trouble you."

Silence.   70

"We're just renting the place."

The police drove away, more slowly than they'd arrived. But obviously they weren't the problem. The house had a mind of its own, like one of those old horses you find at dude ranches. You begin with the assumption that you are in control of the beast. Then you try to guide it as much as two feet off the assigned path, and it resists and takes control of the steering. You are left feeling ashamed of whatever cowboy pretense you had to begin with.

I investigated the history of our property. It was built in 1912 by an entrepreneur named E. V. Benjamin, whose son, raised in the mansion, became eccentric enough for a small group of interested residents of New Orleans to create a gathering called the Benjamin Club, whose sole purpose was to swap stories about him. The house then moved into the hands of another very rich man, J. Edgar Monroe, who had made the bulk of his fortune from taking over the Canal Bank. When the bank was closed by the federal government during the Great Depression, he had himself appointed the bank's liquidator, repaid its shareholders, and then bought up a huge chunk of the leftover shares for pennies.

Monroe went on to buy not only this house but also Rosecliffe, the Newport mansion used in the filming of *The Great Gatsby*. He was famous for telling anyone who would listen how much money he had given away to charity. After he donated a music building to Loyola University New Orleans, he insisted that the school mount a plaque on one of its walls with an inscription he wrote:

J. Edgar Monroe has donated to construction of this building $1,000,000.00   75
(one million) in cash. my secretary has strongly urged me to make a plaque
of this donation so that the students of the music school and the public will
know of this gift. father carter, president of loyola university, acknowledged
receipt of four $250,000.00 checks, or $1,000,000.00. mr. monroe has given
over one hundred million dollars ($100,000,000.00) to organized charity of
which the largest share was given to loyola university.

When Monroe's wife, Louise, died in 1989, the old man wrote her obituary. It opened with a paragraph or two about the deceased, but then quickly
moved on to detail her husband's incredible generosity. "Mr. Monroe is still
living and is 92 years of age," he wrote. "He has been very generous and has
given over one hundred million dollars to organized charity . . ." and so on.
He too died in the house a few years later.

Until the mid-1990s, the house had been owned by men who could comfortably afford it. They didn't need the house to prove how rich they were;
everyone knew how rich they were. The moment the house became troubled
was the moment someone who couldn't afford it moved in—a man who was
using it to slake his own thirst for status. He was a lawyer.

Lawyers are upper middle class. But this lawyer grabbed the saddle
horn of magnificence and hung on for dear life—until the day in 2004 when
he was bucked off. There in the dust he lay, exposed—in the *New Orleans
Times-Picayune*—for defrauding his law partners. His firm defended big
companies from class-action suits. To make the kind of money he needed to
live in this house, the poor guy had resorted to allegedly cutting secret deals
with plaintiffs' lawyers. He reportedly gave up his law license to avoid being
formally charged.

The mansion made him do it: That's what I thought when I heard the
story. As sordid as his behavior was, I'm incapable of feeling toward him
anything but sympathy. He wanted this mansion, he bought this mansion,
and then he discovered that the mansion owned him.

The next owner was a woman. She'd grown up middle class in New   80
Orleans, and in her youth had driven past the mansion and fantasized about
owning it. Then she'd married an oil-and-gas billionaire who gave her the
house as a surprise for her birthday.

The billionaire's wife proceeded to spare no expense in redoing it exactly
as she wanted. She spent $250,000 on gold to touch up the gilt fringe of the
moldings and the ceiling medallions. I spoke with the interior decorator she
hired. It was this man who grasped the inappropriateness of a mere lawyer
owning this house. "They tried to shrink it," he said to me one day. "They
painted the walls taupe; they had canopies over the beds to make a room
within the room. They tried to make it homey." The billionaire's wife succeeded in undoing that. The taupe returned to white, the canopies fell, and
the gilding on the ceiling soon gleamed like new. Several million dollars
later, she had the mansion looking as she wanted it to look, which was more
or less like Versailles. Luckily for her, birthday presents are not community
property, because by the time she was finished touching up the house, her

husband was divesting himself of her. No matter what the settlement came to, the property belonged to her outright. But she was not happy.

And neither was her mansion. When we moved in, she'd been trying to sell it for the $10 million or so she had put into it. Characteristically, the house was refusing to give her the money back. It resented people trying to sell it, just as it was beginning to resent people who can't afford it.

Now it was expressing that resentment. It committed an act which, for a New Orleans house in summer, is tantamount to eviction. All by itself, with the temperature outside rising into the low 90s, it shut down its air-conditioning. I do not mean that any of its 11 air-conditioning units broke. A broken unit can be repaired. The repairmen came and went, shaking their heads. There was nothing they could see that was wrong with even one of the mansion's massive air compressors. The problem was deep inside the walls, perhaps in the wiring. The ballroom, interestingly, was still 68 degrees, but the bedrooms were now 83. The house not only had microclimates, but also a unifying theme. The grand public spaces continued to be pleasant and comfortable, as if the mansion, in chasing us out, had no interest in sullying its public reputation. Only its putatively private spaces—bedrooms, bathrooms—were uninhabitable. Amazingly, it could be 83 degrees and humid in one room and 68 and dry in another—on the same floor. For the first time inside a house, it occurred to me that it might rain.

And so we fled, back to where we'd come from: the upper middle class. Obviously this presents new problems. Even as my children grew weary of pretending they were richer than they are, they became accustomed to living as the rich do. On the way back to California, my wife drove Quinn, who'd just turned nine, across the Southwest and then up the coast. They came to Hearst Castle and stopped to take the guided tour. A few minutes into it, as they stood in one of William Randolph Hearst's many bedrooms, the guide asked if anyone had a question. My child raised her hand. The guide smiled indulgently and called on her.

"Why," Quinn asked, "is it so small?" ●   85

The Reader's Presence

1. In his title, Lewis refers to his essay as a "parable." What does a parable mean to you? What connotations does the word have? How does the notion of a parable inform the essay?

2. How does Lewis explain our attraction to big homes? What role does social class play in this attraction? What is the relation between this attraction and the current real estate crisis? In Lewis's opinion, what is responsible for that crisis? Do you agree with him? Explain why or why not.

3. **CONNECTIONS:** Contrast the social world depicted in Lewis's essay with that shown in N. Scott Momaday's "The Way to Rainy Mountain" (page 504). What do you see as the essential differences between both worlds? What different roots are behind each one?

Abraham Lincoln

GETTYSBURG ADDRESS

ABRAHAM LINCOLN (1809–1865), the sixteenth president of the United States, led the country through a bloody civil war in which one side "would *make* war rather than let the nation survive; and the other would *accept* war rather than let it perish." During his presidency, Lincoln, who is still widely admired as both a political figure and a writer, wrote notable documents such as the Emancipation Proclamation and several poignant and moving speeches, including the Gettysburg Address.

Four months after the Battle of Gettysburg, Lincoln joined in a dedication of a national cemetery on the battlefield. The "Gettysburg Address," delivered on November 19, 1863, would become one of the most famous—and shortest—speeches given by a U.S. president. The text that follows has been widely accepted as the "final" version of the "Gettysburg Address." It comes from the "Bliss copy" of the speech—the fifth and final version of the text that Lincoln copied out by hand, probably sometime in early 1864.

> **"A house divided against itself cannot stand."**

FOUR SCORE and seven years ago our fathers brought forth on this continent, a new nation, conceived in Liberty, and dedicated to the proposition that all men are created equal.

Now we are engaged in a great civil war, testing whether that nation, or any nation so conceived and so dedicated, can long endure. We are met on a great battle-field of that war. We have come to dedicate a portion of that field, as a final resting place for those who here gave their lives that that nation might live. It is altogether fitting and proper that we should do this.

But, in a larger sense, we can not dedicate—we can not consecrate—we can not hallow—this ground. The brave men, living and dead, who struggled here, have consecrated it, far above our poor power to add or detract. The world will little note, nor long remember what we say here, but it can never forget what they did here. It is for us the living, rather, to be dedicated here to the unfinished work which they who fought here have thus far so nobly advanced. It is rather for us to be here dedicated to the great task remaining before us—that from these honored dead we take increased devotion to that cause for which they gave the last full measure of devotion—that we here highly resolve that these dead shall not have died in vain—that this nation, under God, shall have a new birth of freedom—and that government of the people, by the people, for the people, shall not perish from the earth.

The Reader's Presence

1. What historical event does Lincoln refer to at the beginning and end of the "Gettysburg Address"? Why do you think he chose to place this information in a position of such prominence? Why is this event relevant to the dedication of a cemetery?

2. Consider Lincoln's strategy of repetition. What phrases and sentence structures does he repeat? What is the effect of the repetition? Read the speech aloud. Do you find the repetition more or less effective when the words are spoken? Why?

3. **CONNECTIONS:** Compare and contrast Lincoln's "Gettysburg Address" to Thomas Jefferson's draft of "The Declaration of Independence" (page 695). Focus on their respective uses of such rhetorical devices as repetition, parallel structure, alliteration, and antithesis (a figure of speech in which an opposition or a contrast of ideas is expressed by parallelism of words that are the opposites of, or strongly contrasted with, each other). Which writer uses these rhetorical devices more successfully? Support your response by pointing to specific examples of each rhetorical device.

The Writer at Work

ABRAHAM LINCOLN's Hay Draft of the "Gettysburg Address"

Abraham Lincoln, 1850 and 1860.

Two of the five surviving versions of the "Gettysburg Address" in Lincoln's own handwriting were written down just before or just after he gave the speech on November 19, 1863. Scholars disagree about whether one of these two drafts—known as the "Nicolay Draft" and the "Hay Draft"—might have been the pages Lincoln read from on the field at Gettysburg; both drafts differ somewhat from contemporary accounts of the speech that the president delivered that day. Both also differ from the final "Bliss copy" that has become the standard version of the "Gettysburg Address" (see previous page).

The images on the following pages show the pages of the Hay Draft of the "Gettysburg Address," the second version that Lincoln wrote. Note the additions and changes Lincoln has made to this draft of his speech. Compare this version, written very close to the time of the speech's delivery, with the final version made several months later. As the fame of the "Gettysburg Address" continued to grow, Lincoln kept revising the words for an increasingly wide audience that had not been present to hear him speak. What do Lincoln's continuing revisions suggest about his hopes for this text? Which version do you find more compelling?

Four score and seven years ago our fathers brought forth, upon this continent, a new nation, conceived in Liberty, and dedicated to the proposition that all men are created equal.

Now we are engaged in a great Civil war, testing whether that nation, or any nation, so conceived, and so dedicated, can long endure. We are met here on a great battle-field of that war. We ~~are~~ have ~~come~~ ~~to~~ to dedicate a portion of it as ~~the~~ a final resting place for those who here gave their lives that that nation might live. It is altogether fitting and proper that we should do this.

But in a larger sense we can not dedicate— we can not consecrate— we can not hallow this ground. The brave men, living and dead, who struggled here, have consecrated it far above our poor power to add or detract. The world will little note, nor long remember, what we say here, but can never forget what they did here. It is for us, the living, rather to be dedicated here to the unfinished work which they have, thus far, so nobly carried on. It is rather

for us to be here dedicated to the great
task remaining before us— that from these
honored dead we take increased devotion
to the cause for which they here gave
the last full measure of devotion— that
we here highly resolve that these dead
shall not have died in vain; that this
nation shall have a new birth of freedom;
and that this government of the people, by
the people, for the people, shall not perish
from the earth.

There are five known manuscript versions of Lincoln's "Gettysburg Address." This manuscript, known as the Hay Draft, features Lincoln's handwritten corrections. It was discovered in 1906, during a search for the "original manuscript" of the Address among the papers of John Hay, Lincoln's personal secretary.

James McBride

HIP-HOP PLANET

Writer, journalist, and musician **JAMES McBRIDE** (b. 1957) grew up in Harlem in New York City, the son of a black father and a white, Jewish mother, and the eighth of twelve siblings. The title of his best-selling memoir, *The Color of Water: A Black Man's Tribute to His White Mother* (1996), refers to the answer his mother gave him when he asked about the color of God's skin. McBride's first novel, *Miracle of St. Anna* (2002) has been made into a film by Spike Lee. His second novel, *Song Yet Sung* (2008), set in pre–Civil War Maryland, is the story of a slave girl who can see the future. McBride began his dual career as journalist and musician early, studying composition at the Oberlin Conservatory of Music in Ohio and receiving his master's in journalism from Columbia University in New York at age 22. He has been a staff writer for the *Washington Post*, *People* magazine, and the *Boston Globe*, and he has written articles for the *New York Times*, *Essence*, *Rolling Stone*, and *National Geographic*, where his essay "Hip-Hop Planet" appeared in April 2007. McBride is a composer, lyricist, producer, and performer, playing tenor saxophone. He has written for such music luminaries as Anita Baker, Grover Washington Jr., and Gary Burton, and he has recorded and performed with numerous jazz and pop artists. His collaboration with Ed Shockly on the musical *Bobos* won the Stephen Sondheim Award and the Richard Rodgers Foundation Horizon Award. He holds several honorary doctorates and was appointed a Distinguished Writer in Residence at New York University in 2005. He is married with three children and lives in Pennsylvania and New York.

> **"The nice thing about rap music, . . . good rap that's straight ahead and deals with truth really gets to the point and takes you places, just like a good book will. . . . It's all storytelling."**

McBride often talks about writing in the context of music, likening writing fiction to playing jazz and, in an interview with Powell's Books, rap music to storytelling: "The nice thing about rap music, and I know people give rap a bad rap, good rap that's straight ahead and deals with truth really gets to the point and takes you places, just like a good book will. And it's all valid. It's no more or less valid than Def Leppard or Henri Salvador, the French singer. It's all storytelling."

THIS IS MY NIGHTMARE: My daughter comes home with a guy and says, "Dad, we're getting married." And he's a rapper, with a mouthful of gold teeth, a do-rag on his head, muscles popping out of his arms, and a thug attitude. And then the nightmare gets deeper, because before you know it, I'm hearing the pitter-patter of little feet, their offspring, cascading through my living room, cascading through my life, drowning me with the sound of my own hypocrisy, because when I was young, I was a knucklehead, too, hearing my own music, my own sounds. And so I curse the day I saw his face, which is a reflection of my own, and I rue the day I heard his name, because I realize to my horror that rap—music seemingly without melody, sensibility, instruments, verse, or harmony, music with no beginning, end, or middle, music that doesn't even seem to be music—rules the world. It is no longer my world. It is his world. And I live in it. I live on a hip-hop planet.

HIGH-STEPPING

I remember when I first heard rap. I was standing in the kitchen at a party in Harlem. It was 1980. A friend of mine named Bill had just gone on the blink. He slapped a guy, a total stranger, in the face right in front of me. I can't remember why. Bill was a fellow student. He was short-circuiting. Problem was, the guy he slapped was a big guy, dude wearing a do-rag who'd crashed the party with three friends, and, judging by the fury on their faces, there would be no Martin Luther King moments in our immediate future.

There were no white people in the room, though I confess I wished there had been, if only to hide the paleness of my own frightened face. We were black and Latino students about to graduate from Columbia University's journalism school, having learned the whos, whats, wheres, and whys of American reporting. But the real storytellers of the American experience came from the world of the guy that Bill had just slapped. They lived less than a mile from us in the South Bronx. They had no journalism degrees. No money. No credibility. What they did have, however, was talent.

Earlier that night, somebody tossed a record on the turntable, which sent my fellow students stumbling onto the dance floor, howling with delight, and made me, a jazz lover, cringe. It sounded like a broken record. It was a version of an old hit record called "Good Times," the same four bars looped over and over. And on top of this loop, a kid spouted a rhyme about how he was the best disc jockey in the world. It was called "Rapper's Delight." I thought it was the most ridiculous thing I'd ever heard. More ridiculous than Bill slapping that stranger.

Bill survived that evening, but in many ways, I did not. For the next 26 years, I high-stepped past that music the way you step over a crack in the sidewalk. I heard it pounding out of cars and alleyways from Paris to Abidjan, yet I never listened. It came rumbling out of boomboxes from Johannesburg to Osaka, yet I pretended not to hear. I must have strolled past the corner of St. James Place and Fulton Street in my native Brooklyn where a fat kid

5

named Christopher Wallace, aka Biggie Smalls, stood amusing friends with rhyme, a hundred times, yet I barely noticed. I high-stepped away from that music for 26 years because it was everything I thought it was, and more than I ever dreamed it would be, but mostly, because it held everything I wanted to leave behind.

In doing so, I missed the most important cultural event of my lifetime.

Not since the advent of swing jazz in the 1930s has an American music exploded across the world with such overwhelming force. Not since the Beatles invaded America and Elvis packed up his blue suede shoes has a music crashed against the world with such outrage. This defiant culture of song, graffiti, and dance, collectively known as hip-hop, has ripped popular music from its moorings in every society it has permeated. In Brazil, rap rivals samba in popularity. In China, teens spray-paint graffiti on the Great Wall. In France it has been blamed, unfairly, for the worst civil unrest that country has seen in decades.

Its structure is unique, complex, and at times bewildering. Whatever music it eats becomes part of its vocabulary, and as the commercial world falls into place behind it to gobble up the powerful slop in its wake, it metamorphoses into the Next Big Thing. It is a music that defies definition, yet defines our collective societies in immeasurable ways. To many of my generation, despite all attempts to exploit it, belittle it, numb it, classify it, and analyze it, hip-hop remains an enigma, a clarion call, a cry of "I am" from the youth of the world. We'd be wise, I suppose, to start paying attention.

BURNING MAN

Imagine a burning man. He is on fire. He runs into the room. You put out the flames. Then another burning man arrives. You put him out and go about your business. Then two, three, four, five, ten appear. You extinguish them all, send them to the hospital. Then imagine no one bothers to examine why the men caught fire in the first place. That is the story of hip-hop.

It is a music dipped in the boiling cauldron of race and class, and for   10 that reason it is clouded with mystics, snake oil salesmen, two-bit scholars, race-baiters, and sneaker salesmen, all professing to know the facts, to be "real," when the reality of race is like shifting sand, dependent on time, place, circumstance, and who's telling the history. Here's the real story: In the mid-1970s, New York City was nearly broke. The public school system cut funding for the arts drastically. Gone were the days when you could wander into the band room, rent a clarinet for a minimal fee, and march it home to squeal on it and drive your parents nuts.

The kids of the South Bronx and Harlem came up with something else. In the summer of 1973, at 1595 East 174th Street in the Bronx River Houses, a black teenager named Afrika Bambaataa stuck a speaker in his mother's first-floor living room window, ran a wire to the turntable in his bedroom, and set the housing project of 3,000 people alight with party music. At the same time, a Jamaican teenager named Kool DJ Herc was starting up the scene in the East Bronx, while a technical whiz named Grandmaster Flash was rising to prominence a couple of miles south. The Bronx became a music magnet for Puerto Ricans, Jamaicans, Dominicans, and black Americans from the surrounding areas. Fab 5 Freddy, Kurtis Blow, and Melle Mel were only a few of the pioneers. Grand Wizard Theodore, Kool DJ AJ, the Cold Crush Brothers, Spoony Gee, and the Rock Steady Crew of B-boys showed up to "battle"—dance, trade quips and rhymes, check out each other's records and equipment—not knowing as they strolled through the doors of the community center near Bambaataa's mother's apartment that they were writing musical history. Among them was an MC named Lovebug Starski, who was said to utter the phrase "hip-hop" between breaks to keep time.

This is how it worked: One guy, the DJ, played records on two turntables. One guy—or girl—served as master of ceremonies, or MC. The DJs learned to move the record back and forth under the needle to create a "scratch," or to drop the needle on the record when the beat was the hottest, playing "the break" over and over to keep the folks dancing. The MCs "rapped" over the music to keep the party going. One MC sought to outchat the other. Dance styles were created—"locking" and "popping" and "breaking." Graffiti artists spread the word of the "I" because the music was all about identity: I am the best. I spread the most love in the Bronx, in Harlem, in Queens. The focus initially was not on the MCs, but on the dancers, or B-boys. Commercial radio ignored it. DJs sold mix tapes out of the back of station wagons. "Rapper's Delight" by the Sugarhill Gang—the song I first heard at that face-slapping party in Harlem—broke the music onto radio in 1979.

That is the short history.

The long history is that spoken-word music made its way here on slave ships from West Africa centuries ago: Ethnomusicologists trace hip-hop's roots to the dance, drum, and song of West African griots, or storytellers, its pairing of word and music the manifestation of the painful journey of slaves who survived the middle passage. The ring shouts, field hollers, and spirituals[1] of early slaves drew on common elements of African music, such as call and response and improvisation. "Speech-song has been part of black culture for a long, long time," says Samuel A. Floyd, director of the Center for Black Music Research at Columbia College in Chicago. The "dozens," "toasts," and "signifying" of black Americans—verbal dueling, rhyming, self-deprecating tales, and stories of blacks outsmarting whites—were defensive, empowering strategies.

You can point to jazz musicians such as Oscar Brown, Jr., Edgar "Eddie" Jefferson, and Louis Armstrong, and blues greats such as John Lee Hooker, and easily find the foreshadowing of rap music in the verbal play of their work. Black performers such as poet Nikki Giovanni and Gil Scott-Heron, a pianist 15

---

[1] *ring shouts, field hollers, and spirituals:* Various types of music and circle dances that drew from African sources but were adapted by slave communities as they developed new forms of expression in the pre–Civil War American South. — EDS.

and vocalist who put spoken political lyrics to music (most famously in "The Revolution Will Not Be Televised"), elevated spoken word to a new level.

But the artist whose work arguably laid the groundwork for rap as we know it was Amiri Baraka, a beat poet out of Allen Ginsberg's Greenwich Village scene. In the 1950s and '60s, Baraka performed with shrieks, howls, cries, stomps, verse floating ahead of or behind the rhythm, sometimes in staccato syncopation. It was performance art, delivered in a dashiki and Afro, in step with the anger of a bold and sometimes frightening nationalistic black movement, and it inspired what might be considered the first rap group, the Last Poets.

I was 13 when I first heard the Last Poets in 1970. They scared me. To black America, they were like the relatives you hoped wouldn't show up at your barbecue because the boss was there—the old Aunt Clementine who would arrive, get drunk, and pull out her dentures. My parents refused to allow us to play their music in our house—so my siblings waited until my parents went to work and played it anyway. They were the first musical group I heard to use the N-word on a record, with songs like "N------ Are Scared of Revolution." In a world where blacks were evolving from "Negroes" to "blacks," and the assassinations of civil rights leaders Malcolm X and Martin Luther King, Jr., still reverberated in the air like a shotgun blast, the Last Poets embodied black power. Their records consisted of percussion and spoken-word rhyme. They were wildly popular in my neighborhood. Their debut recording sold 400,000 records in three months, says Last Poet member Umar Bin Hassan. "No videos, no radio play, strictly word of mouth." The group's demise coincided with hip-hop's birth in the 1970s.

It's unlikely that the Last Poets ever dreamed the revolution they sang of would take the form it has. "We were about the movement," Abiodun Oyewoke, a founder of the group, says. "A lot of today's rappers have talent. But a lot of them are driving the car in the wrong direction."

THE CROSSOVER

Highways wrap around the city of Dayton, Ohio, like a ribbon bowtied on a box of chocolates from the local Esther Price candy factory. They have six ladies at the plant who do just that: Tie ribbons around boxes all day. Henry Rosenkranz can tell you about it. "I love candy," says Henry, a slim white teenager in glasses and a hairnet, as he strolls the factory, bucket in hand. His full-time after-school job is mopping the floors.

Henry is a model American teenager—and the prototypical consumer at which the hip-hop industry is squarely aimed, which has his parents sitting up in their seats. The music that was once the purview of black America has gone white and gone commercial all at once. A sea of white faces now rises up to greet rap groups as they perform, many of them teenagers like Henry, a NASCAR fanatic and self-described redneck. "I live in Old North Dayton," he says. "It's a white, redneck area. But hip-hop is so prominent with country

20

people . . . if you put them behind a curtain and hear them talk, you won't know if they're black or white. There's a guy I work with, when Kanye West sings about a gold digger, he can relate because he's paying alimony and child support."

Obviously, it's not just working-class whites, but also affluent, suburban kids who identify with this music with African-American roots. A white 16-year-old hollering rap lyrics at the top of his lungs from the driver's seat of his dad's late-model Lexus may not have the same rationale to howl at the moon as a working-class kid whose parents can't pay for college, yet his own anguish is as real to him as it gets. What attracts white kids to this music is the same thing that prompted outraged congressmen to decry jazz during the 1920s and Tipper Gore[2] to campaign decades later against violent and sexually explicit lyrics: life on the other side of the tracks; its "cool" or illicit factor, which black Americans, like it or not, are always perceived to possess.

Hip-hop has continually changed form, evolving from party music to social commentary with the 1982 release of Grandmaster Flash and the Furious Five's "The Message." Today, alternative hip-hop artists continue to produce socially conscious songs, but most commercial rappers spout violent lyrics that debase women and gays. Beginning with the so-called gangsta rap of the '90s, popularized by the still unsolved murders of rappers Biggie Smalls and Tupac Shakur, the genre has become dominated by rappers who brag about their lives of crime. 50 Cent, the hip-hop star of the moment, trumpets his sexual exploits and boasts that he has been shot nine times.

"People call hip-hop the MTV music now," scoffs Chuck D., of Public Enemy, known for its overtly political rap. "It's Big Brother controlling you. To slip something in there that's indigenous to the roots, that pays homage to the music that came before us, it's the Mount Everest of battles."

Most rap songs unabashedly function as walking advertisements for luxury cars, designer clothes, and liquor. Agenda Inc., a "pop culture brand strategy agency" listed Mercedes-Benz as the number one brand mentioned in *Billboard*'s top 20 singles in 2005. Hip-hop sells so much Hennessy cognac, listed at number six, that the French makers, deader than yesterday's beer a decade ago, are now rolling in suds. The company even sponsored a contest to win a visit to its plant in France with a famous rapper.

In many ways, the music represents an old dream. It's the pot of gold to   25 millions of kids like Henry, who quietly agonizes over how his father slaves 14 hours a day at two tool-and-die machine jobs to make ends meet. Like teenagers across the world, he fantasizes about working in the hip-hop business and making millions himself.

"My parents hate hip-hop," Henry says, motoring his 1994 Dodge Shadow through traffic on the way home from work on a hot October afternoon. "But I can listen to Snoop Dogg and hear him call women whores, and

---

2 ***Tipper Gore:*** Mary Elizabeth ("Tipper") Gore is the ex-wife of former U.S. vice president Al Gore. In 1985, she founded an organization that advocated putting warning labels on albums with explicit lyrics. — EDS.

I know he has a wife and children at home. It's just a fantasy. Everyone has the urge deep down to be a bad guy or a bad girl. Everyone likes to talk the talk, but not everyone will walk the walk."

FULL CIRCLE

You breathe in and breathe out a few times and you are there. Eight hours and a wake-up shake on the flight from New York, and you are on the tarmac in Dakar, Senegal. Welcome to Africa. The assignment: Find the roots of hip-hop. The music goes full circle. The music comes home to Africa. That whole bit. Instead it was the old reporter's joke: You go out to cover a story and the story covers you. The stench of poverty in my nostrils was so strong it pulled me to earth like a hundred-pound ring in my nose. Dakar's Sandaga market is full of "local color"—unless you live there. It was packed and filthy, stalls full of new merchandise surrounded by shattered pieces of life everywhere, broken pipes, bicycle handlebars, fruit flies, soda bottles, beggars, dogs, cell phones. A teenager beggar, his body malformed by polio, crawled by on hands and feet, like a spider. He said, "Hey brother, help me." When I looked into his eyes, they were a bottomless ocean.

The Hotel Teranga is a fortress, packed behind a concrete wall where beggars gather at the front gate. The French tourists march past them, the women in high heels and stonewashed jeans. They sidle through downtown Dakar like royalty, haggling in the market, swimming in the hotel pool with their children, a scene that resembles Birmingham, Alabama, in the 1950s—the blacks serving, the whites partying. Five hundred yards away, Africans eat off the sidewalk and sell peanuts for a pittance. There is a restlessness, a deep sense of something gone wrong in the air.

The French can't smell it, even though they've had a mouthful back home. A good amount of the torching of Paris suburbs in October 2005 was courtesy of the children of immigrants from former French African colonies, exhausted from being bottled up in housing projects for generations with no job prospects. They telegraphed the punch in their music—France is the second largest hip-hop market in the world—but the message was ignored. Around the globe, rap music has become a universal expression of outrage, its macho pose borrowed from commercial hip-hop in the U.S.

In Dakar, where every kid is a microphone and turntable away from 30 squalor, and American rapper Tupac Shakur's picture hangs in market stalls of folks who don't understand English, rap is king. There are hundreds of rap groups in Senegal today. French television crews troop in and out of Dakar's nightclubs filming the kora harp lute[3] and *tama*[4] talking drum with

---

3 **kora harp lute:** In West Africa, a popular 21-string instrument played with both hands and used by storytellers and bards. — EDS.

4 **tama:** A flexible West African drum, known as a "talking drum," popular in Senegal; it is placed under the shoulder and can be manipulated to produce a wide range of tones and sounds. — EDS.

regularity. But beneath the drumming and the dance lessons and the jingling sound of tourist change, there is a quiet rage, a desperate fury among the Senegalese, some of whom seem to bear an intense dislike of their former colonial rulers.

"We know all about French history," says Abdou Ba, a Senegalese producer and musician. "We know about their kings, their castles, their art, their music. We know everything about them. But they don't know much about us."

Assane N'Diaye, 19, loves hip-hop music. Before he left his Senegalese village to work as a DJ in Dakar, he was a fisherman, just like his father, like his father's father before him. Tall, lean, with a muscular build and a handsome chocolate face, Assane became a popular DJ, but the equipment he used was borrowed, and when his friend took it back, success eluded him. He has returned home to Toubab Dialaw, about 25 miles south of Dakar, a village marked by a huge boulder, perhaps 40 feet high, facing the Atlantic Ocean.

About a century and a half ago, a local ruler led a group of people fleeing slave traders to this place. He was told by a white trader to come here, to Toubab Dialaw. When he arrived, the slavers followed. A battle ensued. The ruler fought bravely but was killed. The villagers buried him by the sea and marked his grave with a small stone, and over the years it is said to have sprouted like a tree planted by God. It became a huge, arching boulder that stares out to sea, protecting the village behind it. When the fishermen went deep out to sea, the boulder was like a lighthouse that marked the way home. The Great Rock of Toubab Dialaw is said to hold a magic spirit, a spirit that Assane N'Diaye believes in.

In the shadow of the Great Rock, Assane has built a small restaurant, Chez Las, decorated with hundreds of seashells. It is where he lives his hip-hop dream. At night, he and his brother and cousin stand by the Great Rock and face the sea. They meditate. They pray. Then they write rap lyrics that are worlds away from the bling-bling culture of today's commercial hip-hoppers. They write about their lives as village fishermen, the scarcity of catch forcing them to fish in deeper and deeper waters, the hardship of fishing for 8, 10, 14 days at a time in an open pirogue in rainy season, the high fee they pay to rent the boat, and the paltry price their catches fetch on the market. They write about the humiliation of poverty, watching their town sprout up around them with rich Dakarians and richer French. And they write about the relatives who leave in the morning and never return, surrendered to the sea, sharks, and God.

The dream, of course, is to make a record. They have their own demo, their own logo, and their own name, Salam T. D. (for Toubab Dialaw). But rap music represents a deeper dream: a better life. "We want money to help our parents," Assane says over dinner. "We watch our mothers boil water to cook and have nothing to put in the pot."

He fingers his food lightly. "Rap doesn't belong to American culture," he says. "It belongs here. It has always existed here, because of our pain and our hardships and our suffering."

35

On this cool evening in a restaurant above their village, these young men, clad in baseball caps and T-shirts, appear no different from their African-American counterparts, with one exception. After a dinner of chicken and rice, Assane says something in Wolof[5] to the others. Silently and without ceremony, they take every bit of the leftover dinner—the half-eaten bread, rice, pieces of chicken, the chicken bones—and dump them into a plastic bag to give to the children in the village. They silently rise from the table and proceed outside. The last I see of them, their regal figures are outlined in the dim light of the doorway, heading out to the darkened village, holding on to that bag as though it held money.

THE CITY OF GODS

Some call the Bronx River Houses the City of Gods, though if God has been by lately, he must've slipped out for a chicken sandwich. The 10 drab, red-brick buildings spread out across 14 acres, coming into view as you drive east across the East 174th Street Bridge. The Bronx is the hallowed holy ground of hip-hop, the place where it all began. Visitors take tours through this neighborhood now, care of a handful of fortyish "old-timers," who point out the high and low spots of hip-hop's birthplace.

It is a telling metaphor for the state of America's racial landscape that you need a permit to hold a party in the same parks and playgrounds that produced the music that changed the world. The rap artists come and go, but the conditions that produced them linger. Forty percent of New York City's black males are jobless. One in three black males born in 2001 will end up in prison. The life expectancy of black men in the U.S. ranks below that of men in Sri Lanka and Colombia. It took a massive hurricane in New Orleans for the United States to wake up to its racial realities.

That is why, after 26 years, I have come to embrace this music I tried so   40 hard to ignore. Hip-hop culture is not mine. Yet I own it. Much of it I hate. Yet I love it, the good of it. To confess a love for a music that, at least in part, embraces violence is no easy matter, but then again our national anthem talks about bombs bursting in air, and I love that song, too. At its best, hip-hop lays bare the empty moral cupboard that is our generation's legacy. This music that once made visible the inner culture of America's greatest social problem, its legacy of slavery, has taken the dream deferred to a global scale. Today, 2 percent of the Earth's adult population owns more than 50 percent of its household wealth, and indigenous cultures are swallowed with the rapidity of a teenager gobbling a bag of potato chips. The music is calling. Over the years, the instruments change, but the message is the same. The drums are pounding out a warning. They are telling us something. Our children can hear it.

The question is: Can we? ■

---

5 ***Wolof:*** The most widely used language in Senegal; "banana" is a Wolof word. — EDS.

The Reader's Presence

1. "Hip-Hop Planet" features a popular topic covered by an experienced journalist. What characteristics of the selection seem to belong to the personal essay? What characteristics seem to belong to a journalistic article? How are these two components of the selection brought together? Would you prefer if the selection used only a single method—for example, interviews and information told in the third person without a personal response? Explain why or why not.

2. Discuss McBride's attitude toward hip-hop. Why did he dislike it at first? What did he come to admire about it? What does McBride still not like about the music? What does he think about today's commercial rap artists? In what ways do they differ from the groups McBride enjoys most? How would you describe the differences? Do those differences matter to you?

3. **CONNECTIONS:** Compare McBride's evaluation of hip-hop culture to Joseph Epstein's analysis of "The Perpetual Adolescent" (page 390). After considering both selections carefully, make a list of all the points on which you think McBride and Epstein would agree. Then make a list of what you think their disagreements might be. Which account of adolescence do you find more engaging and convincing? Use your lists to explain why.

N. Scott Momaday
THE WAY TO RAINY MOUNTAIN

N. SCOTT MOMADAY (b. 1934) was born on a Kiowa Indian reservation in Oklahoma and grew up surrounded by the cultural traditions of his people. He has taught at the University of California, Berkeley; Stanford University; Columbia University; Princeton University; and the University of Arizona. His first novel, *House Made of Dawn* (1968), won a Pulitzer Prize. The author of poetry and autobiography, Momaday has edited a collection of Kiowa oral literature. His books include *Ancestral Voice: Conversations with N. Scott Momaday* (1989), *The Ancient Child* (1989), *In the Presence of the Sun: Stories and Poems* (1991), *Circle of Wonder: A Native American Christmas Story* (1994), *The Man Made of Words: Essays, Stories, Passages* (1997), and *In the Bear's House* (1999). "The Way to Rainy Mountain" appears as the introduction to the book of that name, published in 1969. Among his more recent books is a collection of Momaday's plays, *Three Plays: The Indolent Boy, Children of the Sun, and the Moon in Two Windows* (2007) and *Four Arrows and Magpie* (2006), a book for young children, which Momaday also illustrated. In 2007, Momaday was awarded the National Medal of Arts, "for his writings and his work that celebrate and preserve Native American art and oral tradition."

> **"I listen to what I write. I work with it until it is what I want it to be in my hearing."**

Momaday thinks of himself as a story-teller. When asked to compare his written voice with his speaking voice, he replied, "My physical voice is something that bears on my writing in an important way. I listen to what I write. I work with it until it is what I want it to be in my hearing. I think that the voice of my writing is very much like the voice of my speaking. And I think in both cases it's distinctive. At least, I mean for it to be. I think that most good writers have individual voices, and that the best writers are those whose voices are most distinctive—most recognizably individual."

A SINGLE KNOLL rises out of the plain in Oklahoma, north and west of the Wichita Range. For my people, the Kiowas, it is an old landmark, and they gave it the name Rainy Mountain. The hardest winter in the world is there. Winter brings blizzards, hot tornadic winds arise in the spring, and in summer the prairie is an anvil's edge. The grass turns brittle and brown, and it cracks beneath your feet. There are green belts along the rivers and creeks, linear groves of hickory and pecan, willow and witch hazel. At a distance in July or August, the steaming foliage seems almost to writhe in fire. Great green and yellow grasshoppers are everywhere in the tall grass, popping up like corn to sting the flesh, and tortoises crawl about on the red earth, going nowhere in plenty of time. Loneliness is an aspect of the land. All things in the plain are isolate; there is no confusion of objects in the eye, but *one* hill or *one* tree or *one* man. To look upon that landscape in the early morning, with the sun at your back, is to lose the sense of proportion. Your imagination comes to life, and this, you think, is where Creation was begun.

I returned to Rainy Mountain in July. My grandmother had died in the spring, and I wanted to be at her grave. She had lived to be very old and at last infirm. Her only living daughter was with her when she died, and I was told that in death her face was that of a child.

I like to think of her as a child. When she was born, the Kiowas were living the last great moment of their history. For more than a hundred years they had controlled the open range from the Smoky Hill River to the Red, from the headwaters of the Canadian to the fork of the Arkansas and Cimarron. In alliance with the Comanches, they had ruled the whole of the southern Plains. War was their sacred business, and they were among the finest horsemen the world has ever known. But warfare for the Kiowas was pre-eminently a matter of disposition rather than of survival, and they never

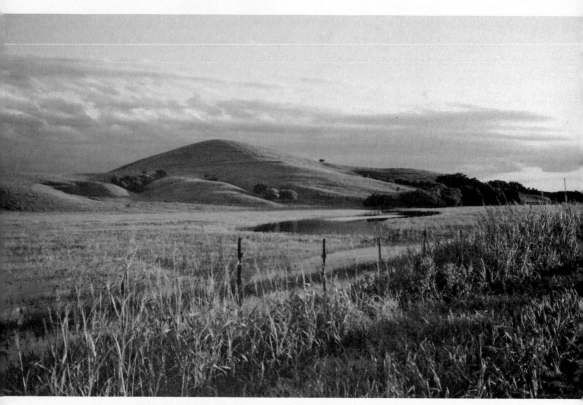

Rainy Mountain, Kiowa Holy Place, Oklahoma.

understood the grim, unrelenting advance of the U.S. Cavalry. When at last, divided and ill-provisioned, they were driven onto the Staked Plains in the cold rains of autumn, they fell into panic. In Palo Duro Canyon they abandoned their crucial stores to pillage and had nothing then but their lives. In order to save themselves, they surrendered to the soldiers of Fort Sill and were imprisoned in the old stone corral that now stands as a military museum. My grandmother was spared the humiliation of those high gray walls by eight or ten years, but she must have known from birth the affliction of defeat, the dark brooding of old warriors.

Her name was Aho, and she belonged to the last culture to evolve in North America. Her forebears came down from the high country in western Montana nearly three centuries ago. They were a mountain people, a mysterious tribe of hunters whose language has never been positively classified in any major group. In the late seventeenth century they began a long migration to the south and east. It was a journey toward the dawn, and it led to a golden age. Along the way the Kiowas were befriended by the Crows, who gave them the culture and religion of the Plains. They acquired horses, and their ancient nomadic spirit was suddenly free of the ground. They acquired Tai-me, the sacred Sun Dance doll, from that moment the object and symbol of their worship, and so shared in the divinity of the sun. Not least, they acquired the sense of destiny, therefore courage and pride. When they entered upon the southern Plains they had been transformed. No longer were they slaves to the simple necessity of survival; they were a lordly and dangerous society of fighters and thieves, hunters and priests of the sun. According to their origin myth, they entered the world through a hollow log. From one point of view, their migration was the fruit of an old prophecy, for indeed they emerged from a sunless world.

Although my grandmother lived out her long life in the shadow of Rainy   5
Mountain, the immense landscape of the continental interior lay like memory in her blood. She could tell of the Crows, whom she had never seen, and of the Black Hills, where she had never been. I wanted to see in reality what she had seen more perfectly in the mind's eye, and traveled fifteen hundred miles to begin my pilgrimage.

Yellowstone, it seemed to me, was the top of the world, a region of deep lakes and dark timber, canyons and waterfalls. But, beautiful as it is, one might have the sense of confinement there. The skyline in all directions is close at hand, the high wall of the woods and deep cleavages of shade. There is a perfect freedom in the mountains, but it belongs to the eagle and the elk, the badger and the bear. The Kiowas reckoned their stature by the distance they could see, and they were bent and blind in the wilderness.

Descending eastward, the highland meadows are a stairway to the plain. In July the inland slope of the Rockies is luxuriant with flax and buckwheat, stonecrop and larkspur. The earth unfolds and the limit of the land recedes. Clusters of trees, and animals grazing far in the distance, cause the vision to reach away and wonder to build upon the mind. The sun follows a longer course in the day, and the sky is immense beyond all comparison. The great billowing clouds that sail upon it are shadows that move upon the grain like water, dividing light. Farther down, in the land of the Crows and Blackfeet, the plain is yellow. Sweet clover takes hold of the hills and bends upon itself to cover and seal the soil. There the Kiowas paused on their way; they had come to the place where they must change their lives. The sun is at home on the plains. Precisely there does it have the certain character of a god. When the Kiowas came to the land of the Crows, they could see the dark lees of the hills at dawn across the Bighorn River, the profusion of light on the grain shelves, the oldest deity ranging after the solstices. Not yet would they veer southward to the caldron of the land that lay below; they must wean their blood from the northern winter and hold the mountains a while longer in their view. They bore Tai-me in procession to the east.

A dark mist lay over the Black Hills, and the land was like iron. At the top of the ridge I caught sight of Devil's Tower upthrust against the gray sky as if in the birth of time the core of the earth had broken through its crust and the motion of the world was begun. There are things in nature that engender an awful quiet in the heart of man; Devil's Tower is one of them. Two centuries ago, because they could not do otherwise, the Kiowas made a legend at the base of the rock. My grandmother said:

Eight children were there at play, seven sisters and their brother. Suddenly the boy was struck dumb; he trembled and began to run upon his hands and feet. His fingers became claws, and his body was covered with fur. Directly there was a bear where the boy had been. The sisters were terrified; they ran, and the bear ran after them. They came to the stump of a great tree, and the tree spoke to them. It bade them climb upon it, and as they did so it began to rise into the air. The bear came to kill them, but they were just beyond its reach. It reared against the tree and scored the bark all around with its claws. The seven sisters were borne into the sky, and they became the stars of the Big Dipper.

From that moment, and so long as the legend lives, the Kiowas have kinsmen in the night sky. Whatever they were in the mountains, they could be no more. However tenuous their well-being, however much they had suffered and would suffer again, they had found a way out of the wilderness.

My grandmother had a reverence for the sun, a holy regard that now is all but gone out of mankind. There was a wariness in her, and an ancient awe. She was a Christian in her later years, but she had come a long way about, and she never forgot her birthright. As a child she had been to the Sun Dances; she had taken part in those annual rites, and by them she had learned the restoration of her people in the presence of Tai-me. She was about seven when the last Kiowa Sun Dance was held in 1887 in the Washita River above Rainy Mountain Creek. The buffalo were gone. In order to consummate the ancient sacrifice—to impale the head of a buffalo bull upon the medicine tree—a delegation of old men journeyed into Texas, there to beg and barter for an animal from the Goodnight herd. She was ten when the Kiowas came together for the last time as a living Sun Dance culture. They could find no buffalo; they had to hang an old hide from the sacred tree. Before the dance could begin, a company of soldiers rode out from Fort Sill under orders to disperse the tribe. Forbidden without cause the essential act of their faith, having seen the wild herds slaughtered and left to rot upon the ground, the Kiowas backed away forever from the medicine tree. That was July 20, 1890, at the great bend of the Washita. My grandmother was there. Without bitterness, and for as long as she lived, she bore a vision of deicide.

Now that I can have her only in memory, I see my grandmother in the 10 several postures that were peculiar to her: standing at the wood stove on a winter morning and turning meat in a great iron skillet; sitting at the south window, bent above her beadwork, and afterwards, when her vision failed, looking down for a long time into the fold of her hands; going out upon a cane, very slowly as she did when the weight of age came upon her; praying. I remember her most often at prayer. She made long, rambling prayers out of suffering and hope, having seen many things. I was never sure that I had the right to hear, so exclusive were they of all mere custom and company. The last time I saw her she prayed standing by the side of her bed at night, naked to the waist, the light of a kerosene lamp moving upon her dark skin. Her long, black hair, always drawn and braided in the day, lay upon her shoulders and against her breasts like a shawl. I do not speak Kiowa, and I never understood her prayers, but there was something inherently sad in the sound, some merest hesitation upon the syllables of sorrow. She began in a high and descending pitch, exhausting her breath to silence; then again and again—and always the same intensity of effort, of something that is, and is not, like urgency in the human voice. Transported so in the dancing light among the shadows of her room, she seemed beyond the reach of time. But that was illusion; I think I knew then that I should not see her again.

Houses are like sentinels in the plain, old keepers of the weather watch. There, in a very little while, wood takes on the appearance of great age. All colors wear soon away in the wind and rain, and then the wood is burned gray and the grain appears and the nails turn red with rust. The window-panes are black and opaque; you imagine there is nothing within, and indeed there are many ghosts, bones given up to the land. They stand here and there against the sky, and you approach them for a longer time than you expect. They belong in the distance; it is their domain.

Once there was a lot of sound in my grandmother's house, a lot of coming and going, feasting and talk. The summers there were full of excitement and reunion. The Kiowas are a summer people; they abide the cold and keep to themselves, but when the season turns and the land becomes warm and vital they cannot hold still; an old love of going returns upon them. The aged visitors who came to my grandmother's house when I was a child were made of lean and leather, and they bore themselves upright. They wore great black hats and bright ample shirts that shook in the wind. They rubbed fat upon their hair and wound their braids with strips of colored cloth. Some of them painted their faces and carried the scars of old and cherished enmities. They were an old council of warlords, come to remind and be reminded of who they were. Their wives and daughters served them well. The women might indulge themselves; gossip was at once the mark and compensation of their servitude. They made loud and elaborate talk among themselves, full of jest and gesture, fright and false alarm. They went abroad in fringed and flowered shawls, bright beadwork and German silver. They were at home in the kitchen, and they prepared meals that were banquets.

There were frequent prayer meetings, and great nocturnal feasts. When I was a child I played with my cousins outside, where the lamplight fell upon the ground and the singing of the old people rose up around us and carried away into the darkness. There were a lot of good things to eat, a lot of laughter and surprise. And afterwards, when the quiet returned, I lay down with my grandmother and could hear the frogs away by the river and feel the motion of the air.

Now there is a funereal silence in the rooms, the endless wake of some final word. The walls have closed in upon my grandmother's house. When I returned to it in mourning, I saw for the first time in my life how small it was. It was late at night, and there was a white moon, nearly full. I sat for a long time on the stone steps by the kitchen door. From there I could see out across the land; I could see the long row of trees by the creek, the low light upon the rolling plains, and the stars of the big dipper. Once I looked at the moon and caught sight of a strange thing. A cricket had perched upon the hand-rail, only a few inches away from me. My line of vision was such that the creature filled the moon like a fossil. It had gone there, I thought, to live and die, for there, of all places, was its small definition made whole and eternal. A warm wind rose up and purled like the longing within me.

The next morning I awoke at dawn and went out on the dirt road to   15
Rainy Mountain. It was already hot, and the grasshoppers began to fill the air. Still, it was early in the morning, and the birds sang out of the shadows. The long yellow grass on the mountain shone in the bright light, and a scissortail hied above the land. There, where it ought to be, at the end of a long and legendary way, was my grandmother's grave. Here and there on the dark stones were ancestral names. Looking back once, I saw the mountain and came away. ▨

The Reader's Presence

1. Momaday tells several stories in this selection, including the history of the Kiowa people, the story of his grandmother's life and death, the story of his homecoming, and the legend of Devil's Tower. How does each story overlap and intertwine with the others? What forces compel the telling or creation of each story? What needs do the stories satisfy? Look, for example, at the legend related in paragraph 8. The Kiowas made this legend "because they could not do otherwise." Why could they have not done otherwise? How does this embedded legend enhance and complicate the other stories Momaday tells here?

2. From the beginning of this essay, Momaday sets his remarks very firmly in space and then in time. Discuss the importance of physical space in this essay. Why does Momaday take the journey to Rainy Mountain—a fifteen-hundred-mile "pilgrimage" (paragraph 5)? Why does he say that his grandmother's vision of this landscape is more nearly perfect than his, even though she has never actually seen the landscape he travels? Consider the many remarks about perspective, and change of perspective, that Momaday includes, as well as his remarks on proportion. What significance does he attach to these remarks? More generally, consider the temporal journeys that run parallel to the spatial journeys: the Kiowas' "journey toward the dawn [that] led to a golden age" (paragraph 4) and Momaday's own journeys that he relates in the essay. How would you characterize the sense of space and time and the relation between the two that are conveyed in this essay?

3. **CONNECTIONS:**   In the interview quoted in the introductory note to this selection, Momaday talks about capturing his speaking voice in his writing. What are some of the phrases and passages that make you hear his distinctive voice as you read? Point to—and analyze—specific words and phrases to discuss how Momaday creates the effect he is aiming for. Compare Momaday's voice to Calvin Trillin's in "A Traditional Family" (page 581). What common techniques do these writers use to make their prose appealing to the reader's ear?

Azar Nafisi

FROM READING LOLITA IN TEHRAN

AZAR NAFISI (b. 1950) was raised in Tehran, Iran, and educated in England and the United States. Having returned to Iran in the 1970s to teach English literature, she experienced firsthand the revolution and its aftermath, when strict Islamic religious codes were imposed; the harshest restrictions were placed on women. Nafisi has said that "before the revolution I had an image of myself as a woman, as a writer, as an academician, as a person with a set of values." Afterward, even the smallest public gestures were forbidden, from kissing her husband in public to shaking hands with a colleague. Fearing she would "become someone who was a stranger to herself," Nafisi resigned her university position in 1995 and for two years took a group of her best students "underground" for weekly discussions of Western authors, including Vladimir Nabokov, the author of *Lolita* and the subject of Nafisi's scholarly work.

> **"I think if a civilization or a culture does not take its own works of literature seriously it goes downhill. You need imagination in order to imagine a future that doesn't exist."**

"Unfortunately you have to be deprived of something in order to understand its worth," Nafisi told an interviewer. "I think if a civilization or a culture does not take its own works of literature seriously it goes downhill. You need imagination in order to imagine a future that doesn't exist."

Nafisi left Iran with her family in 1997. She is currently a Visiting Fellow at the Foreign Policy Institute of the Johns Hopkins University School of Advanced International Studies and the director of the Dialogue Project, an education and policy initiative for the development of democracy and human rights in the Muslim world. This essay, adapted from Nafisi's memoir *Reading Lolita in Tehran* (2003), first appeared in the *Chronicle of Higher Education*. She has since published a second memoir, *Things I've Been Silent About: Memories of a Prodigal Daughter* (2008), which focuses on her family.

IN THE FALL OF 1995, after resigning from my last academic post, I decided to indulge myself and fulfill a dream. I chose seven of my best and most committed students and invited them to come to my home every Thursday morning to discuss literature. They were all women—to teach a mixed class in the privacy of my home was too risky, even if we were discussing harmless works of fiction.

For nearly two years, almost every Thursday morning, rain or shine, they came to my house, and almost every time, I could not get over the shock of seeing them shed their mandatory veils and robes and burst into color. When my students came into that room, they took off more than their scarves and robes. Gradually, each one gained an outline and a shape, becoming her own inimitable self. Our world in that living room with its window framing my beloved Elburz Mountains became our sanctuary, our self-contained universe, mocking the reality of black-scarved, timid faces in the city that sprawled below.

The theme of the class was the relationship between fiction and reality. We would read Persian classical literature, such as the tales of our own lady of fiction, Scheherazade, from *A Thousand and One Nights*, along with Western classics — *Pride and Prejudice, Madame Bovary, Daisy Miller, The Dean's December*, and *Lolita*, the work of fiction that perhaps most resonated with our lives in the Islamic Republic of Iran. For the first time in many years, I felt a sense of anticipation that was not marred by tension: I would not need to go through the tortuous rituals that had marked my days when I taught at the university — rituals governing what I was forced to wear, how I was expected to act, the gestures I had to remember to control.

Life in the Islamic Republic was as capricious as the month of April, when short periods of sunshine would suddenly give way to showers and storms. It was unpredictable: The regime would go through cycles of some tolerance, followed by a crackdown. Now, in the mid-1990s, after a period of relative calm and so-called liberalization, we had again entered a time of hardships. Universities had once more become the targets of attack by the cultural purists, who were busy imposing stricter sets of laws, going so far as to segregate men and women in classes and punishing disobedient professors.

The University of Allameh Tabatabai, where I had been teaching since   5
1987, had been singled out as the most liberal university in Iran. It was rumored that someone in the Ministry of Higher Education had asked, rhetorically, if the faculty at Allameh thought they lived in Switzerland. Switzerland had somehow become a byword for Western laxity. Any program or action that was deemed un-Islamic was reproached with a mocking reminder that Iran was by no means Switzerland.

The pressure was hardest on the students. I felt helpless as I listened to their endless tales of woe. Female students were being penalized for running up the stairs when they were late for classes, for laughing in the hallways, for talking to members of the opposite sex. One day Sanaz had barged into class near the end of the session, crying. In between bursts of tears, she explained that she was late because the female guards at the door, finding a blush in her bag, had tried to send her home with a reprimand.

Why did I stop teaching so suddenly? I had asked myself this question many times. Was it the declining quality of the university? The ever-increasing indifference among the remaining faculty members and students? The daily struggle against arbitrary rules and restrictions?

I often went over in my mind the reaction of the university officials to my letter of resignation. They had harassed and limited me in all manner of ways, monitoring my visitors, controlling my actions, refusing my long-overdue tenure; and when I resigned, they infuriated me by suddenly commiserating and by refusing to accept my resignation. The students had threatened to boycott classes, and it was of some satisfaction to me to find out later that despite threats of reprisals, they in fact did boycott my replacement. Everyone thought I would break down and eventually return. It took two more years before they finally accepted my resignation.

Teaching in the Islamic Republic, like any other vocation, was subservient to politics and subject to arbitrary rules. Always, the joy of teaching was marred by diversions and considerations forced on us by the regime—how well could one teach when the main concern of university officials was not the quality of one's work but the color of one's lips, the subversive potential of a single strand of hair? Could one really concentrate on one's job when what preoccupied the faculty was how to excise the word "wine" from a Hemingway story, when they decided not to teach Brontë because she appeared to condone adultery?

In selecting students for study in my home, I did not take into consideration their ideological or religious backgrounds. Later, I would count it as the class's great achievement that such a mixed group, with different and at times conflicting backgrounds, personal as well as religious and social, remained so loyal to its goals and ideals. One reason for my choice of these particular girls was the peculiar mixture of fragility and courage I sensed in them. They were what you would call loners, who did not belong to any particular group or sect. I admired their ability to survive not despite but in some ways because of their solitary lives.

One of the first books we read was Nabokov's *Invitation to a Beheading*. Nabokov creates for us in this novel not the actual physical pain and torture of a totalitarian regime but the nightmarish quality of living in an atmosphere of perpetual dread. Cincinnatus C. is frail, he is passive, he is a hero without knowing or acknowledging it: He fights with his instincts, and his acts of writing are his means of escape. He is a hero because he refuses to become like all the rest.

We formed a special bond with Nabokov despite the difficulty of his prose. This went deeper than our identification with his themes. His novels are shaped around invisible trapdoors, sudden gaps that constantly pull the carpet from under the reader's feet. They are filled with mistrust of what we call everyday reality, an acute sense of that reality's fickleness and frailty. There was something, both in his fiction and in his life, that we instinctively related to and grasped, the possibility of a boundless freedom when all options are taken away.

Nabokov used the term "fragile unreality" to explain his own state of exile; it also describes our existence in the Islamic Republic of Iran. We lived in a culture that denied any merit to literary works, considering them important only when they were handmaidens to something seemingly more urgent—namely, ideology. This was a country where all gestures, even the most private, were interpreted in political terms. The colors of my head scarf or my father's tie were symbols of Western decadence and imperialist tendencies. Not wearing a beard, shaking hands with members of the opposite sex, clapping or whistling in public meetings, were likewise considered Western and therefore decadent, part of the plot by imperialists to bring down our culture.

Our class was shaped within this context. There, in that living room, we rediscovered that we were also living, breathing human beings; and no matter how repressive the state became, no matter how intimidated and frightened we were, like Lolita we tried to escape and to create our own little pockets of freedom. And, like Lolita, we took every opportunity to flaunt our insubordination: by showing a little hair from under our scarves, insinuating a little color into the drab uniformity of our appearances, growing our nails, falling in love, and listening to forbidden music.

How can I create this other world outside the room? I have no choice   15
but to appeal to your imagination. Let's imagine one of the girls, say Sanaz, leaving my house, and let us follow her from there to her final destination. She says her goodbyes and puts on her black robe and scarf over her orange shirt and jeans, coiling her scarf around her neck to cover her huge gold earrings. She directs wayward strands of hair under the scarf, puts her notes into her large bag, straps it on over her shoulder, and walks out into the hall. She pauses for a moment on top of the stairs to put on thin, lacy, black gloves to hide her nail polish.

We follow Sanaz down the stairs, out the door, and into the street. You might notice that her gait and her gestures have changed. It is in her best interest not to be seen, not to be heard or noticed. She doesn't walk upright, but bends her head toward the ground and doesn't look at passers-by. She walks quickly and with a sense of determination. The streets of Tehran and other Iranian cities are patrolled by militia, who ride in white Toyota patrols—four gun-carrying men and women, sometimes followed by a minibus. They are called the Blood of God. They patrol the streets to make sure that women like Sanaz wear their veils properly, do not wear makeup, do not walk in public with men who are not their fathers, brothers, or husbands. If she gets on a bus, the seating is segregated. She must enter through the rear door and sit in the back seats, allocated to women.

You might well ask, What is Sanaz thinking as she walks the streets of Tehran? How much does this experience affect her? Most probably, she tries to distance her mind as much as possible from her surroundings. Perhaps she is thinking of her distant boyfriend and the time when she will meet him in Turkey. Does she compare her own situation with her mother's when she was the same age? Is she angry that women of her mother's generation could walk the streets freely, enjoy the company of the opposite sex, join the police force, become pilots, live under laws that were among the most progressive in the world regarding women? Does she feel humiliated by the new laws, by the fact that after the revolution, the age of marriage was lowered from eighteen to nine, that stoning became once more the punishment for adultery and prostitution?

In the course of nearly two decades, the streets have been turned into a war zone, where young women who disobey the rules are hurled into patrol cars, taken to jail, flogged, fined, forced to wash the toilets and humiliated—and, as soon as they leave, they go back and do the same thing. Is she aware, Sanaz, of her own power? Does she realize how dangerous she can be when her every stray gesture is a disturbance to public safety? Does she think how vulnerable are the Revolutionary Guards, who for over eighteen years have patrolled the streets of Tehran and have had to endure young women like herself, and those of other generations, walking, talking, showing a strand of hair just to remind them that they have not converted?

These girls had both a real history and a fabricated one. Although they came from very different backgrounds, the regime that ruled them had tried to make their personal identities and histories irrelevant. They were never free of the regime's definition of them as Muslim women.

Take the youngest in our class, Yassi. There she is, in a photograph I   20
have of the students, with a wistful look on her face. She is bending her head to one side, unsure of what expression to choose. She is wearing a thin white-and-gray scarf, loosely tied at the throat—a perfunctory homage to her family's strict religious background. Yassi was a freshman who audited my graduate courses in my last year of teaching. She felt intimidated by the older students, who, she thought, by virtue of their seniority, were blessed not only with greater knowledge and a better command of English but also with more wisdom. Although she understood the most difficult texts better than many of the graduate students, and although she read the texts more dutifully and with more pleasure than most, she felt secure only in her terrible sense of insecurity.

About a month after I had decided privately to leave Allameh Tabatabai, Yassi and I were standing in front of the green gate at the entrance of the university. What I remember most distinctly about the university now is that green gate. I owe my memory of that gate to Yassi: She mentioned it in one of her poems. The poem is called "How Small Are the Things That I Like." In it, she describes her favorite objects—an orange backpack, a colorful coat, a bicycle just like her cousin's—and she also describes how much she likes to enter the university through the green gate. The gate appears in this poem, and in some of her other writings, as a magical entrance into the forbidden world of all the ordinary things she had been denied in life.

Yet that green gate was closed to her, and to all my girls. Next to the gate there was a small opening with a curtain hanging from it. Through this opening all the female students went into a small, dark room to be inspected. Yassi would describe later what was done to her in this room: "I would first be checked to see if I have the right clothes: the color of my coat, the length of my uniform, the thickness of my scarf, the form of my shoes, the objects in my bag, the visible traces of even the mildest makeup, the size of my rings and their level of attractiveness, all would be checked before I could enter the campus of the university, the same university in which men also study. And to them the main door, with its immense portals and emblems and flags, is generously open."

In the sunny intimacy of our encounter that day, I asked Yassi to have an ice cream with me. We went to a small shop, where, sitting opposite each other with two tall *cafés glacés* between us, our mood changed. We became, if not somber, quite serious. Yassi came from an enlightened religious family that had been badly hurt by the revolution. They felt the Islamic Republic was a betrayal of Islam rather than its assertion. At the start of the revolution, Yassi's mother and older aunt joined a progressive Muslim women's group that, when the new government started to crack down on its former supporters, was forced to go underground. Yassi's mother and aunt went into hiding for a long time. This aunt had four daughters, all older than Yassi, all of whom in one way or another supported an opposition group that was popular with young religious Iranians. They were all but one arrested, tortured, and jailed. When they were released, every one of them married within a year. They married almost haphazardly, as if to negate their former rebellious selves. Yassi felt that they had survived the jail but could not escape the bonds of traditional marriage.

To me, Yassi was the real rebel. She did not join any political group or organization. As a teenager she had defied family traditions and, in the face of strong opposition, had taken up music. Listening to any form of nonreligious music, even on the radio, was forbidden in her family, but Yassi forced her will. Her rebellion did not stop there: She did not marry the right suitor at the right time and instead insisted on leaving her hometown, Shiraz, to go to college in Tehran. Now she lived partly with her older sister and husband and partly in the home of an uncle with fanatical religious leanings. The university, with its low academic standards, its shabby morality, and its ideological limitations, had been a disappointment to her.

What could she do? She did not believe in politics and did not want to 25 marry, but she was curious about love. That day, she explained why all the normal acts of life had become small acts of rebellion and political insubordination to her and to other young people like her. All her life she was shielded. She was never let out of sight; she never had a private corner in which to think, to feel, to dream, to write. She was not allowed to meet any young men on her own. Her family not only instructed her on how to behave around men, but seemed to think they could tell her how she should feel about them as well. What seems natural to someone like you, she said, is so strange and unfamiliar to me.

Again she repeated that she would never get married. She said that for her a man always existed in books, that she would spend the rest of her life with Mr. Darcy[1]—even in the books, there were few men for her. What was wrong with that? She wanted to go to America, like her uncles, like me. Her mother and her aunts had not been allowed to go, but her uncles were given the chance. Could she ever overcome all the obstacles and go to America? Should she go to America? She wanted me to advise her; they all wanted that. But what could I offer her, she who wanted so much more from life than she had been given?

There was nothing in reality that I could give her, so I told her instead about Nabokov's "other world." I asked her if she had noticed how in most of Nabokov's novels, there was always the shadow of another world, one that was attainable only through fiction. It is this world that prevents his heroes and heroines from utter despair, that becomes their refuge in a life that is consistently brutal.

Take *Lolita*. This was the story of a twelve-year-old girl who had nowhere to go. Humbert had tried to turn her into his fantasy, into his dead love, and he had destroyed her. The desperate truth of Lolita's story is not the rape of a twelve-year-old by a dirty old man but the confiscation of one individual's life by another. We don't know what Lolita would have become if Humbert had not engulfed her. Yet the novel, the finished work, is hopeful, beautiful even, a defense not just of beauty but of life, ordinary everyday life, all the normal pleasures that Lolita, like Yassi, was deprived of.

Warming up and suddenly inspired, I added that, in fact, Nabokov had taken revenge against our own solipsizers; he had taken revenge on the Ayatollah Khomeini and those like him. They had tried to shape others according to their own dreams and desires, but Nabokov, through his portrayal of Humbert, had exposed all solipsists who take over other people's lives. She, Yassi, had much potential; she could be whatever she wanted to be—a good wife or a teacher and poet. What mattered was for her to know what she wanted.

I want to emphasize that we were not Lolita, the Ayatollah was not Humbert, and this republic was not what Humbert called his princedom by the sea. *Lolita* was not a critique of the Islamic Republic, but it went against the grain of all totalitarian perspectives.   30

At some point, the truth of Iran's past became as immaterial to those who had appropriated it as the truth of Lolita's is to Humbert. It became immaterial in the same way that Lolita's truth, her desires and life, must lose color before Humbert's one obsession, his desire to turn a twelve-year-old unruly child into his mistress.

This is how I read *Lolita*. Again and again as we discussed *Lolita* in that class, our discussions were colored by my students' hidden personal sorrows

---

1 **Mr. Darcy:** The leading male character in Jane Austen's classic novel *Pride and Prejudice* (1813). — EDS.

and joys. Like tear stains on a letter, these forays into the hidden and the personal shaded all our discussions of Nabokov.

Humbert never possesses his victim; she always eludes him, just as objects of fantasy are always simultaneously within reach and inaccessible. No matter how they may be broken, the victims will not be forced into submission.

This was on my mind one Thursday evening after class, as I was looking at the diaries my girls had left behind, with their new essays and poems. At the start of our class, I had asked them to describe their image of themselves. They were not ready then to face that question, but every once in a while I returned to it and asked them again. Now, as I sat curled up on the love seat, I looked at dozens of pages of their recent responses.

I have one of these responses in front of me. It belongs to Sanaz, who   35 handed it in shortly after a recent experience in jail, on trumped-up morality charges. It is a simple drawing in black and white, of a naked girl, the white of her body caught in a black bubble. She is crouched in an almost fetal position, hugging one bent knee. Her other leg is stretched out behind her. Her long, straight hair follows the same curved line as the contour of her back, but her face is hidden. The bubble is lifted in the air by a giant bird with long black talons. What interests me is a small detail: the girl's hand reaches out of the bubble and holds on to the talon. Her subservient nakedness is dependent on that talon, and she reaches out to it.

The drawing immediately brought to my mind Nabokov's statement in his famous afterword to *Lolita*, about how the "first little throb of Lolita" went through him in 1939 or early 1940, when he was ill with a severe attack of intercostal neuralgia. He recalls that "the initial shiver of inspiration was somehow prompted by a newspaper story about an ape in the Jardin des Plantes, who, after months of coaxing by a scientist, produced the first drawing ever charcoaled by an animal: this sketch showed the bars of the poor creature's cage."

The two images, one from the novel and the other from reality, reveal a terrible truth. Its terribleness goes beyond the fact that in each case an act of violence has been committed. It goes beyond the bars, revealing the victim's proximity and intimacy with its jailer. Our focus in each is on the delicate spot where the prisoner touches the bar, on the invisible contact between flesh and cold metal.

Most of the other students expressed themselves in words. Manna saw herself as fog, moving over concrete objects, taking on their form but never becoming concrete herself. Yassi described herself as a figment. Nassrin, in one response, gave me the *Oxford English Dictionary*'s definition of the word "paradox." Implicit in almost all of their descriptions was the way they saw themselves in the context of an outside reality that prevented them from defining themselves clearly and separately.

Manna had once written about a pair of pink socks for which she was reprimanded by the Muslim Students' Association. When she complained to a favorite professor, he started teasing her about how she had already ensnared and trapped her man, Nima, and did not need the pink socks to entrap him further.

These students, like the rest of their generation, were different from my   40 generation in one fundamental aspect. My generation complained of a loss, the void in our lives that was created when our past was stolen from us, making us exiles in our own country. Yet we had a past to compare with the present; we had memories and images of what had been taken away. But my girls spoke constantly of stolen kisses, films they had never seen, and the wind they had never felt on their skin. This generation had no past. Their memory was of a half-articulated desire, something they never had. It was this lack, their sense of longing for the ordinary, taken-for-granted aspects of life, that gave their words a certain luminous quality akin to poetry.

I had asked my students if they remembered the dance scene in *Invitation to a Beheading*: The jailer invites Cincinnatus to a dance. They begin a waltz and move out into the hall. In a corner they run into a guard: "They described a circle near him and glided back into the cell, and now Cincinnatus regretted that the swoon's friendly embrace had been so brief." This movement in circles is the main movement of the novel. As long as he accepts the sham world the jailers impose upon him, Cincinnatus will remain their prisoner and will move within the circles of their creation. The worst crime committed by totalitarian mind-sets is that they force their citizens, including their victims, to become complicit in their crimes. Dancing with your jailer, participating in your own execution, that is an act of utmost brutality. My students witnessed it in show trials on television and enacted it every time they went out into the streets dressed as they were told to dress. They had not become part of the crowd who watched the executions, but they did not have the power to protest them, either.

The only way to leave the circle, to stop dancing with the jailer, is to find a way to preserve one's individuality, that unique quality which evades description but differentiates one human being from the other. That is why, in their world, rituals—empty rituals—become so central.

There was not much difference between our jailers and Cincinnatus's executioners. They invaded all private spaces and tried to shape every gesture, to force us to become one of them, and that in itself is another form of execution.

In the end, when Cincinnatus is led to the scaffold, and as he lays his head on the block, in preparation for his execution, he repeats the magic mantra: "by myself." This constant reminder of his uniqueness, and his attempts to write, to articulate and create a language different from the one imposed upon him by his jailers, saves him at the last moment, when he takes his head in his hands and walks away toward voices that beckon him from that other world, while the scaffold and all the sham world around him, along with his executioner, disintegrate. ▪

The Reader's Presence

1. What does literature represent to Nafisi's students? How do the young women's experiences in Iran shape their interpretations and understandings of Nabokov?

2. Why is Cincinnatus's execution a metaphor Nafisi's students can relate to? What is the meaning of Cincinnatus's mantra "by myself" (paragraph 44)? How does Cincinnatus "save" himself in the end? Is this ending hopeful for Nafisi's students? Why or why not?

3. **CONNECTIONS:** The strict moral regulations imposed by the Islamic regime are, Nafisi suggests, motivated by fear. When picturing her student Sanaz on the street, Nafisi asks, "Does she realize how dangerous she can be when her every stray gesture is a disturbance to public safety?" (paragraph 18). How is the education of women a potential threat to public safety in Iran? Read Sherman Alexie's "The Joy of Reading and Writing: Superman and Me" (page 27). How does Alexie characterize his education as subversive? Who is threatened by his learning?

Danielle Ofri
SAT

DANIELLE OFRI (b. 1965) demonstrates that it is possible to be a productive writer while pursuing a busy life or career. The possessor of both an MD and a PhD, she is an attending physician at Bellevue Hospital and assistant professor of medicine at New York University School of Medicine. She is also editor-in-chief and co-founder of the *Bellevue Literary Review* and the associate chief editor of the award-winning medical textbook *The Bellevue Guide to Outpatient Medicine*. Her essays have appeared in the *New York Times*, the *Los Angeles Times*, *Best American Essays*, *Best American Science Writing*, the *New England Journal of Medicine*, the *Missouri Review*, *Tikkun*, the *Journal of the American Medical Association*, and the *Lancet*. Her Web site, danielleofri.com, explores the relationship between literature and medicine. A frequent guest on National Public Radio, Ofri lives in New York City with her husband and three children.

Her first collection, *Singular Intimacies: Becoming a Doctor at Bellevue* (2003), was described by physician/author Perri Klass as "a beautiful book about souls and bodies, sadness and healing at a legendary hospital." Ofri co-edited with her colleagues *The Best of the Bellevue Literary Review* (2008), a collection of writings from that journal. Her essay, "SAT," is taken from her 2005 book, *Incidental Findings: Lessons from My Patients in the Art of Medicine*. A *New York Times* profile reports, "To Dr. Ofri every patient's history is a mystery story, a narrative that unfolds full of surprises, exposing the vulnerability at the human core." Her most recent book, *Medicine in Translation: Journeys with My Patients*, was published in 2010.

> **Danielle Ofri demonstrates that it is possible to be a productive writer while pursuing a busy career. In addition to professionally editing and writing, she is an attending physician at Bellevue Hospital and assistant professor of medicine at New York University School of Medicine.**

"NEMESIO RIOS?" I called out to the crowded waiting room of our medical clinic. I'd just finished a long stint attending on the wards and I was glad to be back to the relatively sane life of the clinic. "Nemesio Rios?" I called out again.

"Yuh," came a grunt, as a teenaged boy in baggy jeans with a ski hat pulled low over his brow hoisted himself up. He sauntered into my office and slumped into the plastic chair next to my desk.

"What brings you to the clinic today?"

He shrugged. "Feel all right, but they told me to come today," he said, slouching lower into the chair, his oversize sweatshirt reaching nearly to his knees. The chart said he'd been in the ER two weeks ago for a cough.

"How about a regular checkup?" He shrugged again. His eyes were   5
deep brown, tucked deep beneath his brow.

Past medical history? None. Past surgical history? None. Meds? None. Allergies? None. Family history? None.

"Where were you born?" I asked, wanting to know his nationality.

"Here."

"Here in New York?"

"Yeah, in this hospital."   10

"A Bellevue baby!" I said with a grin, noticing that his medical record number had only six digits (current numbers had nine digits). "A genuine Bellevue baby."

There was a small smile, but I could see him working hard to suppress it. "My mom's from Mexico."

"Have you ever been there?" I asked, curious.

"You sound like my mom." He rolled his eyes. "She's always trying to get me to go. She's over there right now visiting her sisters."

"You don't want to go visit?"   15

"Mexico? Just a bunch of corrupt politicians." Nemesio shifted his unlaced sneakers back and forth on the linoleum floor, causing a dull screech each time.

I asked about his family. In a distracted voice, as though he'd been through this a million times before, he told me that he was the youngest of eight, but now that his sister got married, it was only he and his mother left in the house. I asked about his father.

"He lives in Brooklyn." Nemesio poked his hand in and out of the pocket of his sweatshirt. "He's all right, I guess, but he drinks a lot," he said, his voice trailing off. "Doesn't do anything stupid, but he drinks."

"Are you in school now?"

"Me?" he said, his voice perking up for the first time from his baseline   20
mumble. "I'm twenty. I'm done! Graduated last year."

"What are you doing now?"

"Working in a kitchen. It's all right, I guess."

"Any thoughts about college?"

"You sound like my cousin in Connecticut. He's in some college there and he's always bugging me about going to college. But I'm lazy. No one to kick my lazy butt."

"What do you want to do when you grow up?"   25

"What I *really* want to do? I want to play basketball." He gave a small laugh. "But they don't take five-foot-seven guys in the NBA."

"Anything else besides basketball?"

He thought for a minute. "Comics. I like to draw comics. I guess I could be an artist that draws comics." His eye caught the tiny Monet poster I'd taped above the examining table. "That's pretty cool, that painting."

"There are a lot of great art schools here in New York." My comment floated off into empty space. We were silent for a few minutes. I made a few notes in the chart.

"That stuff about peer pressure is a bunch of crap," he said abruptly,   30
forcefully, sitting up in his chair, speaking directly toward the poster in front of him.

I leaned closer toward Nemesio, trying to figure out what this sudden outburst was related to. But he continued, staring straight forward, lecturing at the empty room, as if I weren't there.

"Anyone who tells you they do something because of peer pressure is full of crap." He was even more animated now, even angry. "People always asking me to do stuff, but I can make my own mind up." His hands came out of his sweatshirt pocket and began gesticulating in the air. "My brother and his friends, they're always drinking beer. But I don't like the taste of it. I don't believe in peer pressure."

Speech ended, Nemesio settled back into his chair, resumed his slouched posture, and repositioned his hands into his pockets. Then he glanced up at the ceiling and added quietly, almost wistfully, "But if beer tasted like apple juice, I might be drinking it every day."

He was quiet for a few minutes. One hand slid out of his pocket and started fiddling with the zipper on his sweatshirt.

Without warning he swiveled in his chair to face me directly, his whole   35
body leaning into my desk. "You ever face peer pressure, Doc?"

His eyes were right on mine, and I was caught off guard by this sudden shift in his voice and body language. I felt unexpectedly on the spot. Who does he see? I wondered. Do I represent the older generation or the medical profession or women or non-Hispanic whites? Or all of the above?

Nemesio refused to let my gaze wander off his. He demanded an answer to his question, and our doctor–patient encounter had obviously taken an abrupt turn. I could tell that a lot was riding on my answer, though I wasn't sure what exactly was at stake. Did he need me to provide a reassuring societal answer about how bad drugs are? Or did he need me to identify with him, to say that I've been where he's been, even if that was not exactly the truth?

"Yes," I said, after debating in my head for a moment, trying to think of something sufficiently potent to satisfy the question but not so sordid as to embarrass myself. "I have."

He stared at me, waiting for me to continue. His eyes looked younger and younger.

"In my first year of college," I said. "In the very first week. Everyone was   40
sitting in the stairwell and they were passing a joint around. Everyone took a drag. When it came to me I hesitated. I wasn't really interested in smoking, but everyone else was doing it."

"So what did you do?"

"I didn't want anyone to think I was a little kid, so I took a drag too."

"Did you like it?"

"No, I just hacked and coughed. I didn't even *want* the stupid joint to begin with, and I couldn't believe I was doing it just because everyone else was."

"That peer pressure is crap." Nemesio stated it as a fact and then sank   45
back into his seat.

"You're right. It is. It took me a little while to figure that out."

He pushed the ski hat back from his brow a few inches. "In my high school there was this teacher that was always on my case. She was always bugging me to study and take the tests. What a pain in the butt she was." He pulled the hat all the way off. "But now there's no one around to kick my lazy butt. I could get to college easy, but I'm just lazy."

My mind wandered back to a crisp autumn day in my second month of medical school. Still overwhelmed by the pentose-phosphate shunt and other minutiae of biochemistry, our Clinical Correlation group—led by two fourth-year students—promised us first-year students a taste of clinical medicine.

The CC student leaders had obtained permission for a tour of the New York City medical examiner's office. All suspicious death—murders, suicides, and the like—were investigated here.

The autumn sun dazzled against the bright turquoise bricks of the ME   50
building, which stood out in sharp contrast to the gray concrete buildings
lining First Avenue. We congregated on the steps, endeavoring to look
nonchalant.

The security guard checked our ID cards as well as our letter of entry.
We followed him through the metal detector, down the whitewashed concrete hallway, into the unpainted service elevator with a hand-pulled metal
grate.

We stared at our sneakers as the elevator lurched downward. It creaked
past several floors and landed with a jolt. Out we spilled, gingerly, onto the
raw concrete floor. Our first stop was the morgue. The cavernous walk-in
refrigerator was icy and silent. There was a Freon smell, the kind I recalled
from the frozen food departments in grocery stores. As a child, when I went
shopping with my mother I used to lean into the bins of ice cream and frozen
waffles and inhale that curiously appealing, vaguely sweet, chemical fra-
grance. But here the odor was intensified—magnified by the rigid chill and
bleak soundlessness of the room.

Nine naked corpses lay on shelves, their wizened bodies covered with
skin that glowed a ghastly green from the low-wattage fluorescent lights.
These were the unclaimed bodies, mostly elderly men found on the streets.
The ones that were never identified, never claimed by relatives. The ones
that were sent next door to the medical school. These were the subjects of
our first-year anatomy course.

From there we were herded into the autopsy room. Loosely swinging
doors delivered us into a shock of cacophonous noise and harsh bright lights.
We stumbled into each other, a discombobulated mass at the entranceway,
blinking to adjust from the stark silence of the morgue. The autopsy room was
long and rectangular. The high ceilings and brisk yellow walls lent an odd air
of cheeriness. Seven metal tables lay parallel in the center. Six of them were
surrounded by groups of pathology residents performing autopsies. The residents wore long rubber gloves and industrial-strength aprons. The sound of
their voices and their clanking instruments echoed in the room.

The only body I had ever opened was my cadaver in anatomy lab, which   55
was preserved in formaldehyde and completely dried out. I'd never actually seen blood. In the autopsy room there was blood everywhere. Residents
were handling organs—weighing hearts, measuring kidneys, taking samples from livers—then replacing them in the open corpses. Their aprons
were spotted with scarlet streaks. Blood streamed down the troughs that
surrounded each table.

It was disgusting, but I wasn't nauseated. These bodies didn't look like
people anymore. It was more like a cattle slaughterhouse: cows and pigs
lined up to be transformed into sterile packages of cellophane-wrapped
chopped meat. The slaughterhouse that compelled you to vow lifetime veg-
etarianism, a resolve that lasted only until the next barbecue with succu-
lent, browned burgers that looked nothing like the disemboweled carcasses
you'd seen earlier.

Then I spied the last table, the only one without a sea of activity around it. Lying on the metal table was a young boy who didn't look older than twelve. He was wearing new Nikes and one leg of his jeans was rolled up to the knee. His bright red basketball jersey was pushed up, revealing a smooth brown chest. He looked as if he were sleeping.

I tiptoed closer. Could he really be dead? There was not a mark on his body. Every part was in its place. His clothes were crisp and clean. There was no blood, no dirt, no sign of struggle. He wasn't anything like the gutted carcasses on the other tables. His expression was serene, his face without blemish. His skin was plump. He was just a beautiful boy sleeping.

I wanted to rouse him, to tell him to get out of this house of death, quick, before the rubber-aproned doctors got to him. There is still time, I wanted to say. Get out while you can!

I leaned over his slender, exposed, adolescent chest. I peered closer.   60
There, just over his left nipple, was a barely perceptible hole. Smaller than the tip of my little finger. A tiny bullet hole.

I stared at that hole. That ignominious hole. That hole that stole this boy's life. I wanted to rewind the tape, to give him a chance to dodge six inches to the right. That's all he'd need—just six inches. Who would balk over six inches?

Somebody pulled on my arm. Time to go.

For months after my visit to the medical examiner's office, I had nightmares. But they weren't about bloody autopsies or refrigerated corpses. I dreamt only about the boy, that beautiful, untouched, intact boy. The one who'd had the misfortune to fall asleep in the autopsy room.

At night, he would creep into my bed. On the street, I could feel his breath on the back of my neck. In the library, while I battled the Krebs cycle and the branches of the trigeminal nerve, he would slip silently into the pages of my book. His body was so perfect, so untouched.

Except for that barely perceptible hole.   65

Now I looked at Nemesio Rios sitting before me; his beautiful body adrift in the uncertainty of adolescence, made all the rockier by the unfair burdens of urban poverty. Research has shown that health status and life expectancy are directly correlated with socioeconomic status and earning power. Whether this is related to having health insurance, or simply to having more knowledge to make healthier lifestyle choices, there is no doubt that being poor is bad for your health.

As I scribbled in his chart, an odd thought dawned on me: the best thing that I, as a physician, could recommend for Nemesio's long-term health would be to take the SAT and get into college. Too bad I couldn't just write a prescription for that.

"Have you taken the SAT yet?" I asked Nemesio.

"Nah. I can't stand U.S. history. What's the point of knowing U.S. history?"

I twisted my stethoscope around my finger. "Ever hear of McCarthy?"   70
He shrugged. "Yeah, maybe."

"McCarthy tried to intimidate people to turn in their friends and coworkers. Anyone who might believe differently from him. I'd hate to see that part of U.S. history repeated."

He nodded slowly. "Yeah, I guess. I wouldn't want nobody to tell me what to think. That peer pressure is crap."

"Besides," I added, "there's no U.S. history on the SAT."

Nemesio turned toward me, his eyes opened wide. "Yeah? No U.S. history?" His cheeks were practically glowing. 75

"No history. Just math and English."

"Wow," he said. "No U.S. history. That's pretty cool." His tone of voice changed abruptly as his gaze plummeted to the floor. "But damn, I can't remember those fractions and stuff."

"Sure you can," I said. "It's all the same from high school. If you review it, it'll all come back to you."

In medical school, I had taught an SAT prep course on the weekends to help pay my living expenses. For kids in more affluent neighborhoods, these courses were standard. But it didn't seem fair, because for Nemesio, his health depended on it.

"Listen," I said. "I'll make you a deal. You go out and buy one of those 80 SAT review books and bring it to our next appointment. I bet we can brush you up on those fractions."

He shifted in his seat and I could just detect a hint of a swagger in his torso. "Okay, Doc. I'll take you on."

Nemesio stood up to go and then turned quickly back to me. "College ain't so bad, but what I really want is to play basketball."

Now it was my turn to nod. "There's nothing like a good ballgame. I played point guard in college."

"You? You even shorter than me."

"That's why I had to find another career." 85

He grinned. "You and me both." Nemesio put his ski hat on and pulled it carefully down over his forehead. Then he slouched out the door.

Nemesio and I met three times over the next two months. While my stethoscope and blood pressure cuff sat idle, we reviewed algebra, analogies, geometry, and reading comprehension. With only a little prodding, Nemesio was able to recall what he had learned in high school. And he thought it was "really cool" when I showed him the tricks and shortcuts that I recalled from the SAT prep course.

I lost touch with Nemesio after that. Many days I thought about him, wondering how things turned out. If this were a movie, he'd score a perfect 1600 and be off to Princeton on full scholarship. But Harlem isn't Hollywood, and the challenges in real life are infinitely more complex. I don't know if Nemesio ever got into college — any college — or if he even took the SAT exam. But he did learn a bit more about fractions, and I learned a bit more about the meaning of preventative medicine. At the end of each visit, I would face the clinic billing sheet. The top fifty diagnoses were listed — the most common and important medical issues, according to Medicaid, that faced our patients. I scrutinized them each time, because I was required to check one off, to check off Nemesio Rios's most salient medical diagnosis and treatment, to identify the most pressing issues for his health, to categorize the medical interventions deemed necessary for this patient's well-being, otherwise the clinic wouldn't get reimbursed.

SAT prep was not among them. ■

The Reader's Presence

1. Ofri uses dialogue extensively throughout the essay. What are the effects of this choice? How would the essay be different if she had not used her patient's own words?

2. Why does Ofri juxtapose the material about Nemesio Rios with the material about her experiences in the morgue? Is the fact that Ofri does not reveal the outcome of Nemesio's story disturbing? Does this uncertainty make the essay more or less believable? Why?

3. **CONNECTIONS:** Ofri argues that continuing his education is the best step her patient can take to safeguard his health. Do you agree? Read John Taylor Gatto's "Against School" (page 665). Does Gatto's argument apply to a case like that of Ofri's young patient? Why or why not?

George Orwell
POLITICS AND THE ENGLISH LANGUAGE

During his lifetime, **GEORGE ORWELL** was well known for the political positions he laid out in his essays. The events that inspired Orwell to write his essays have long since passed, but his writing continues to be read and enjoyed. Orwell demonstrates that political writing need not be narrowly topical—it can speak to enduring issues and concerns. He suggested as much in 1946 when he wrote, "What I have most wanted to do throughout the past ten years is to make political writing into an art. My starting point is always a feeling of

> "My starting point is always a feeling of partisanship, a feeling of injustice."

partisanship, a feeling of injustice. . . . But I could not do the work of writing a book, or even a long magazine article, if it were not also an aesthetic experience." "Politics and the English Language" appears in *Shooting an Elephant and Other Essays* (1950).

For more information about Orwell, see page 180.

MOST PEOPLE who bother with the matter at all would admit that the English language is in a bad way, but it is generally assumed that we cannot by conscious action do anything about it. Our civilization is decadent and our language—so that argument runs—must inevitably share in the general collapse. It follows that any struggle against the abuse of language is a sentimental archaism, like preferring candles to electric light or hansom cabs to airplanes. Underneath this lies the half-conscious belief that language is a natural growth and not an instrument which we shape for our own purposes.

Now, it is clear that the decline of a language must ultimately have political and economic causes: It is not due simply to the bad influence of this or that individual writer. But an effect can become a cause, reinforcing the original cause and producing the same effect in an intensified form, and so on indefinitely. A man may take to drink because he feels himself to be a failure, and then fail all the more completely because he drinks. It is rather the same thing that is happening to the English language. It becomes ugly and inaccurate because our thoughts are foolish, but the slovenliness of our language makes it easier for us to have foolish thoughts. The point is that the process is reversible. Modern English, especially written English, is full of bad habits which spread by imitation and which can be avoided if one is willing to take the necessary trouble. If one gets rid of these habits one can think more clearly, and to think clearly is a necessary first step towards political regeneration: so that the fight against bad English is not frivolous and is not the exclusive concern of professional writers. I will come back to this presently, and I hope that by that time the meaning of what I have said here will have become clearer. Meanwhile, here are five specimens of the English language as it is now habitually written.

These five passages have not been picked out because they are especially bad—I could have quoted far worse if I had chosen—but because they illustrate various of the mental vices from which we now suffer. They are a little below the average, but are fairly representative samples. I number them so that I can refer back to them when necessary:

> (1) I am not, indeed, sure whether it is true to say that the Milton who once seemed not unlike a seventeenth-century Shelley had not become, out of an experience ever more bitter in each year, more alien [sic] to the founder of that Jesuit sect which nothing could induce him to tolerate.
>
> Professor Harold Laski (*Essay in Freedom of Expression*).

> (2) Above all, we cannot play ducks and drakes with a native battery of idioms which prescribes such egregious collections of vocals as the Basic *put up with* for *tolerate* or *put at a loss* for *bewilder.*
>
> Professor Lancelot Hogben (*Interglossa*).

(3) On the one side we have the free personality: By definition it is not neurotic, for it has neither conflict nor dream. Its desires, such as they are, are transparent, for they are just what institutional approval keeps in the forefront of consciousness; another institutional pattern would alter their number and intensity; there is little in them that is natural, irreducible, or culturally dangerous. But *on the other side*, the social bond itself is nothing but the mutual reflection of these self-secure integrities. Recall the definition of love. Is not this the very picture of a small academic? Where is there a place in this hall of mirrors for either personality or fraternity?

Essay on psychology in *Politics* (New York).

(4) All the "best people" from the gentlemen's clubs, and all the frantic fascist captains, united in common hatred of Socialism and bestial horror of the rising tide of the mass revolutionary movement, have turned to acts of provocation, to foul incendiarism, to medieval legends of poisoned wells, to legalize their own destruction of proletarian organizations, and rouse the agitated petty-bourgeoisie to chauvinistic fervor on behalf of the fight against the revolutionary way out of the crisis.

Communist pamphlet.

(5) If a new spirit *is* to be infused into this old country, there is one thorny and contentious reform which must be tackled, and that is the humanization and galvanization of the B.B.C. Timidity here will bespeak cancer and atrophy of the soul. The heart of Britain may be sound and of strong beat, for instance, but the British lion's roar at present is like that of Bottom in Shakespeare's *Midsummer Night's Dream*—as gentle as any sucking dove. A virile new Britain cannot continue indefinitely to be traduced in the eyes or rather ears, of the world by the effete languors of Langham Place, brazenly masquerading as "standard English." When the *Voice of Britain* is heard at nine o'clock, better far and infinitely less ludicrous to hear aitches honestly dropped than the present priggish, inflated, inhibited, school-ma'amish arch braying of blameless bashful mewing maidens!

Letter in *Tribune*.

Each of these passages has faults of its own, but, quite apart from avoidable ugliness, two qualities are common to all of them. The first is staleness of imagery: The other is lack of precision. The writer either has a meaning and cannot express it, or he inadvertently says something else, or he is almost indifferent as to whether his words mean anything or not. This mixture of vagueness and sheer incompetence is the most marked characteristic of modern English prose, and especially of any kind of political writing. As soon as certain topics are raised, the concrete melts into the abstract and no one seems able to think of turns of speech that are not hackneyed: Prose consists less and less of *words* chosen for the sake of their meaning, and more and more of *phrases* tacked together like the sections of a prefabricated hen-house. I list below, with notes and examples, various of the tricks by means of which the work of prose-construction is habitually dodged:

Dying Metaphors. A newly invented metaphor assists thought by evoking a visual image, while on the other hand a metaphor which is technically "dead" (e.g., *iron resolution*) has in effect reverted to being an ordinary word and can generally be used without loss of vividness. But in between

5

these two classes there is a huge dump of worn-out metaphors which have lost all evocative power and are merely used because they save people the trouble of inventing phrases for themselves. Examples are: *Ring the changes on, take up the cudgels for, toe the line, ride roughshod over, stand shoulder to shoulder with, play into the hands of, no axe to grind, grist to the mill, fishing in troubled waters, rift within the lute, on the order of the day, Achilles' heel, swan song, hotbed.* Many of these are used without knowledge of their meaning (what is a "rift," for instance?), and incompatible metaphors are frequently mixed, a sure sign that the writer is not interested in what he is saying. Some metaphors now current have been twisted out of their original meaning without those who use them even being aware of the fact. For example, *toe the line* is sometimes written *tow the line.* Another example is *the hammer and the anvil,* now always used with the implication that the anvil gets the worst of it. In real life it is always the anvil that breaks the hammer, never the other way about: A writer who stopped to think what he was saying would be aware of this, and would avoid perverting the original phrase.

Operators or Verbal False Limbs. These save the trouble of picking out appropriate verbs and nouns, and at the same time pad each sentence with extra syllables which give it an appearance of symmetry. Characteristic phrases are *render inoperative, militate against, make contact with, be subjected to, give rise to, give grounds for, have the effect of, play a leading part (role) in, make itself felt, take effect, exhibit a tendency to, serve the purpose of, etc., etc.* The keynote is the elimination of simple verbs. Instead of being a single word, such as *break, stop, spoil, mend, kill,* a verb becomes a *phrase,* made up of a noun or adjective tacked on to some general-purpose verb such as *prove, serve, form, play, render.* In addition, the passive voice is wherever possible used in preference to the active, and noun constructions are used instead of gerunds (*by examination of* instead of *by examining*). The range of verbs is further cut down by means of the *-ize* and *de-* formation, and the banal statements are given an appearance of profundity by means of the *not un-* formation. Simple conjunctions and prepositions are replaced by such phrases as *with respect to, having regard to, the fact that, by dint of, in view of, in the interests of, on the hypothesis that;* and the ends of sentences are saved from anticlimax by such resounding commonplaces as *greatly to be desired, cannot be left out of account, a development to be expected in the near future, deserving of serious consideration, brought to a satisfactory conclusion,* and so on and so forth.

Pretentious Diction. Words like *phenomenon, element, individual* (as noun), *objective, categorical, effective, virtual, basic, primary, promote, constitute, exhibit, exploit, utilize, eliminate, liquidate,* are used to dress up simple statements and give an air of scientific impartiality to biased judgments. Adjectives like *epoch-making, epic, historic, unforgettable, triumphant, age-old, inevitable, inexorable, veritable,* are used to dignify the sordid processes of international politics, while writing that aims at glorifying war usually takes on an archaic color, its characteristic words being: *realm, throne, chariot, mailed fist, trident, sword, shield, buckler, banner, jackboot, clarion.* Foreign words and expressions such as *cul de sac, ancien régime, deus ex machina, mutatis mutandis, status quo, gleichschaltung, weltanschauung,* are used to give an air of culture and elegance. Except for the useful abbreviations *i.e., e.g.,* and *etc.,* there is no real need for any of the hundreds of foreign phrases now current in English. Bad writers, and especially scientific, political, and sociological writers, are nearly always haunted by the notion that Latin or Greek words are grander than Saxon ones, and unnecessary words like *expedite, ameliorate, predict, extraneous, deracinated, clandestine, subaqueous,* and hundreds of others constantly gain ground from their Anglo-Saxon opposite numbers.[1] The jargon peculiar to Marxist writing (*hyena, hangman, cannibal, petty bourgeois, these gentry, lackey, flunkey, mad dog, White Guard, etc.*) consists largely of words and phrases translated from Russian, German, or French; but the normal way of coining a new word is to use a Latin or Greek root with the appropriate affix and, where necessary, the *-ize* formation. It is often easier to make up words of this kind (*deregionalize, impermissible, extramarital, nonfragmentary,* and so forth) than to think up the English words that will cover one's meaning. The result, in general, is an increase in slovenliness and vagueness.

Meaningless Words. In certain kinds of writing, particularly in art criticism and literary criticism, it is normal to come across long passages which are almost completely lacking in meaning.[2] Words like *romantic, plastic, values, human, dead, sentimental, natural, vitality,* as used in art criticism, are strictly meaningless, in the sense that they not only do not point to any discoverable object, but are hardly ever expected to do so by the reader. When one critic writes, "The outstanding feature of Mr. X's work is its living quality," while another writes, "The immediately striking thing about Mr. X's work is its peculiar deadness," the reader accepts this as a simple difference of opinion. If words like *black* and *white* were involved, instead of the jargon words *dead* and *living,* he would see at once that language was being used in an improper way. Many political words are similarly abused. The word *Fascism* has now no meaning except in so far as it signifies "something not desirable." The words *democracy, socialism, freedom, patriotic, realistic, justice,* have each of them several different meanings which cannot be reconciled with one another. In the case of a word like *democracy,* not

---

1 An interesting illustration of this is the way in which the English flower names which were in use till very recently are being ousted by Greek ones, *snapdragon* becoming *antirrhinum, forget-me-not* becoming *myosotis,* etc. It is hard to see any practical reason for this change of fashion: It is probably due to an instinctive turning away from the more homely word and a vague feeling that the Greek word is scientific. — AUTHOR'S NOTE.

2 Example: "Comfort's catholicity of perception and image, strangely Whitmanesque in range, almost the exact opposite in aesthetic compulsion, continues to evoke that trembling atmospheric accumulative hinting at a cruel, an inexorably serene timelessness. . . . Wrey Gardiner scores by aiming at simple bull's-eyes with precision. Only they are not so simple, and through this contented sadness runs more than the surface bitter-sweet of resignation." (*Poetry Quarterly*). — AUTHOR'S NOTE.

only is there no agreed definition, but the attempt to make one is resisted from all sides. It is almost universally felt that when we call a country democratic we are praising it: Consequently the defenders of every kind of regime claim that it is a democracy, and fear that they might have to stop using the word if it were tied down to any one meaning. Words of this kind are often used in a consciously dishonest way. That is, the person who uses them has his own private definition, but allows his hearer to think he means something quite different. Statements like *Marshal Pétain*[3] *was a true patriot, The Soviet Press is the freest in the world, The Catholic Church is opposed to persecution*, are almost always made with intent to deceive. Other words used in variable meanings, in most cases more or less dishonestly, are: *class, totalitarian, science, progressive, reactionary, bourgeois, equality*.

Now that I have made this catalogue of swindles and perversions, let me give another example of the kind of writing that they lead to. This time it must of its nature be an imaginary one. I am going to translate a passage of good English into modern English of the worst sort. Here is a well-known verse from *Ecclesiastes*:

> I returned and saw under the sun, that the race is not to the swift, nor the battle to the strong, neither yet bread to the wise, nor yet riches to men of understanding, nor yet favor to men of skill; but time and chance happeneth to them all.

Here it is in modern English:

> Objective consideration of contemporary phenomena compels the conclusion that success or failure in competitive activities exhibits no tendency to be commensurate with innate capacity, but that a considerable element of the unpredictable must invariably be taken into account.

This is a parody, but not a very gross one. Exhibit (3), above, for instance, contains several patches of the same kind of English. It will be seen that I have not made a full translation. The beginning and ending of the sentence follow the original meaning fairly closely, but in the middle the concrete illustrations — race, battle, bread — dissolve into the vague phrase "success or failure in competitive activities." This had to be so, because no modern writer of the kind I am discussing — no one capable of using phrases like "objective consideration of contemporary phenomena" — would ever tabulate his thoughts in that precise and detailed way. The whole tendency of modern prose is away from concreteness. Now analyze these two sentences a little more closely. The first contains forty-nine words but only sixty syllables, and all its words are those of everyday life. The second contains thirty-eight words of ninety syllables: Eighteen of its words are from Latin roots,

10

---

3 **Pétain:** Henri Philippe Pétain was a World War I French military hero who served as chief of state in France from 1940 to 1945, after France surrendered to Germany. A controversial figure, Pétain was regarded by some to be a patriot who had sacrificed himself for his country, while others considered him to be a traitor. He was sentenced to life imprisonment in 1945, the year before Orwell wrote his essay. — EDS.

and one from Greek. The first sentence contains six vivid images, and only one phrase ("time and chance") that could be called vague. The second contains not a single fresh, arresting phrase, and in spite of its ninety syllables it gives only a shortened version of the meaning contained in the first. Yet without a doubt it is the second kind of sentence that is gaining ground in modern English. I do not want to exaggerate. This kind of writing is not yet universal, and outcrops of simplicity will occur here and there in the worst-written page. Still, if you or I were told to write a few lines on the uncertainty of human fortunes, we should probably come much nearer to my imaginary sentences than to the one from *Ecclesiastes*.

As I have tried to show, modern writing at its worst does not consist in picking out words for the sake of their meaning and inventing images in order to make the meaning clearer. It consists in gumming together long strips of words which have already been set in order by someone else, and making the results presentable by sheer humbug. The attraction of this way of writing is that it is easy. It is easier—even quicker once you have the habit—to say *In my opinion it is a not unjustifiable assumption that* than to say *I think*. If you use ready-made phrases, you not only don't have to hunt about for words; you also don't have to bother with the rhythms of your sentences, since these phrases are generally so arranged as to be more or less euphonious. When you are composing in a hurry—when you are dictating to a stenographer, for instance, or making a public speech—it is natural to fall into a pretentious, Latinized style. Tags like *a consideration which we should do well to bear in mind* or *a conclusion to which all of us would readily assent* will save many a sentence from coming down with a bump. By using stale metaphors, similes, and idioms, you save much mental effort, at the cost of leaving your meaning vague, not only for your reader but for yourself. This is the significance of mixed metaphors. The sole aim of a metaphor is to call up a visual image. When these images clash—as in *The Fascist octopus has sung its swan song, the jackboot is thrown into the melting pot*—it can be taken as certain that the writer is not seeing a mental image of the objects he is naming; in other words he is not really thinking. Look again at the examples I gave at the beginning of this essay. Professor Laski (1) uses five negatives in fifty-three words. One of these is superfluous, making nonsense of the whole passage, and in addition there is the slip—*alien* for akin—making further nonsense, and several avoidable pieces of clumsiness which increase the general vagueness. Professor Hogben (2) plays ducks and drakes with a battery which is able to write prescriptions, and, while disapproving of the everyday phrase *put up with*, is unwilling to look *egregious* up in the dictionary and see what it means; (3), if one takes an uncharitable attitude towards it, is simply meaningless: Probably one could work out its intended meaning by reading the whole of the article in which it occurs. In (4), the writer knows more or less what he wants to say, but an accumulation of stale phrases chokes him like tea leaves blocking a sink. In (5), words and meaning have almost parted company. People who write in this manner usually have a general emotional meaning—they dislike one thing and want to express solidarity with another—but they are not interested in the detail of what they are saying. A scrupulous writer, in every sentence that he writes, will ask himself at least four questions, thus: What am I trying to say? What words will express it? What image or idiom will make it clearer? Is this image fresh enough to have an effect? And he will probably ask himself two more: Could I put it more shortly? Have I said anything that is avoidably ugly? But you are not obliged to go to all this trouble. You can shirk it by simply throwing your mind open and letting the ready-made phrases come crowding in. They will construct your sentences for you—even think your thoughts for you, to a certain extent—and at need they will perform the important service of partially concealing your meaning even from yourself. It is at this point that the special connection between politics and the debasement of language becomes clear.

In our time it is broadly true that political writing is bad writing. Where it is not true, it will generally be found that the writer is some kind of rebel, expressing his private opinions and not a "party line." Orthodoxy, of whatever color, seems to demand a lifeless, imitative style. The political dialects to be found in pamphlets, leading articles, manifestos, White Papers, and the speeches of under-secretaries do, of course, vary from party to party, but they are all alike in that one almost never finds in them a fresh, vivid, homemade turn of speech. When one watches some tired hack on the platform mechanically repeating the familiar phrases—*bestial atrocities*, *iron heel*, *bloodstained tyranny*, *free peoples of the world*, *stand shoulder to shoulder*—one often has a curious feeling that one is not watching a live human being but some kind of dummy: a feeling which suddenly becomes stronger at moments when the light catches the speaker's spectacles and turns them into blank discs which seem to have no eyes behind them. And this is not altogether fanciful. A speaker who uses that kind of phraseology has gone some distance towards turning himself into a machine. The appropriate noises are coming out of his larynx, but his brain is not involved as it would be if he were choosing his words for himself. If the speech he is making is one that he is accustomed to make over and over again, he may be almost unconscious of what he is saying, as one is when one utters the responses in church. And this reduced state of consciousness, if not indispensable, is at any rate favorable to political conformity.

In our time, political speech and writing are largely the defense of the indefensible. Things like the continuance of British rule in India, the Russian purges and deportations, the dropping of the atom bombs on Japan, can indeed be defended, but only by arguments which are too brutal for most people to face, and which do not square with the professed aims of political parties. Thus political language has to consist largely of euphemism, question-begging, and sheer cloudy vagueness. Defenseless villages are bombarded from the air, the inhabitants driven out into the countryside, the cattle machine-gunned, the huts set on fire with incendiary bullets: This is called *pacification*. Millions of peasants are robbed of their farms and sent trudging along the roads with no more than they can carry: This is called *transfer of population* or *rectification of frontiers*. People are imprisoned for years without trial, or shot in the back of the neck or sent to die of scurvy in Arctic lumber camps:[4] This is called *elimination of unreliable elements*. Such phraseology is needed if one wants to name things without calling up mental pictures of them. Consider for instance some comfortable English professor defending Russian totalitarianism. He cannot say outright, "I believe in killing off your opponents when you get good results by doing so." Probably, therefore, he will say something like this:

"While freely conceding that the Soviet régime exhibits certain features which the humanitarian may be inclined to deplore, we must, I think, agree that a certain curtailment of the right to political opposition is an unavoidable concomitant of transitional periods, and that the rigors which the Russian people have been called upon to undergo have been amply justified in the sphere of concrete achievement."

The inflated style is itself a kind of euphemism. A mass of Latin words   15
falls upon the facts like soft snow, blurring the outlines and covering up all the details. The great enemy of clear language is insincerity. When there is a gap between one's real and one's declared aims, one turns as it were instinctively to long words and exhausted idioms, like a cuttlefish squirting out ink. In our age there is no such thing as "keeping out of politics." All issues are political issues, and politics itself is a mass of lies, evasions, folly, hatred, and schizophrenia. When the general atmosphere is bad, language must suffer. I should expect to find — this is a guess which I have not sufficient knowledge to verify — that the German, Russian, and Italian languages have all deteriorated in the last ten or fifteen years, as a result of dictatorship.

But if thought corrupts language, language can also corrupt thought. A bad usage can spread by tradition and imitation, even among people who should and do know better. The debased language that I have been discussing is in some ways very convenient. Phrases like *a not unjustifiable assumption, leaves much to be desired, would serve no good purpose, a consideration which we should do well to bear in mind*, are a continuous temptation, a packet of aspirins always at one's elbow. Look back through this essay, and for certain you will find that I have again and again committed the very faults I am protesting against. By this morning's post I have received a pamphlet dealing with conditions in Germany. The author tells me that he "felt impelled" to write it. I open it at random, and here is almost the first sentence that I see: "(The Allies) have an opportunity not only of achieving a radical transformation of Germany's social and political structure in such a way as to avoid a nationalistic reaction in Germany itself, but at the same time of laying the foundations of a co-operative and unified Europe." You

---

4 **People . . . camps:** Though Orwell is decrying all totalitarian abuse of language, his examples are mainly pointed at the Soviet purges under Joseph Stalin. — EDS.

see, he "feels impelled" to write—feels, presumably, that he has something new to say—and yet his words, like cavalry horses answering the bugle, group themselves automatically into the familiar dreary pattern. The invasion of one's mind by ready-made phrases (*lay the foundations*, *achieve a radical transformation*) can only be prevented if one is constantly on guard against them, and every such phrase anaesthetizes a portion of one's brain.

I said earlier that the decadence of our language is probably curable. Those who deny this would argue, if they produced an argument at all, that language merely reflects existing social conditions, and that we cannot influence its development by any direct tinkering with words and constructions. So far as the general tone or spirit of a language goes, this may be true, but it is not true in detail. Silly words and expressions have often disappeared, not through any evolutionary process but owing to the conscious action of a minority. Two recent examples were *explore every avenue* and *leave no stone unturned*, which were killed by the jeers of a few journalists. There is a long list of flyblown metaphors which could similarly be got rid of if enough people would interest themselves in the jobs; and it should also be possible to laugh the *not un-* formation out of existence,[5] to reduce the amount of Latin and Greek in the average sentence, to drive out foreign phrases and strayed scientific words, and, in general, to make pretentiousness unfashionable. But all these are minor points. The defense of the English language implies more than this, and perhaps it is best to start by saying what it does *not* imply.

To begin with it has nothing to do with archaism, with the salvaging of obsolete words and turns of speech, or with the setting up of a "standard English" which must never be departed from. On the contrary, it is especially concerned with the scrapping of every word or idiom which has outworn its usefulness. It has nothing to do with correct grammar and syntax, which are of no importance so long as one makes one's meaning clear, or with the avoidance of Americanisms, or with having what is called a "good prose style." On the other hand it is not concerned with fake simplicity and the attempt to make written English colloquial. Nor does it even imply in every case preferring the Saxon word to the Latin one, though it does imply using the fewest and shortest words that will cover one's meaning. What is above all needed is to let the meaning choose the word, and not the other way about. In prose, the worst thing one can do with words is to surrender to them. When you think of a concrete object, you think wordlessly, and then, if you want to describe the thing you have been visualizing you probably hunt about till you find the exact words that seem to fit. When you think of something abstract you are more inclined to use words from the start, and unless you make a conscious effort to prevent it, the existing dialect will come rushing in and do the job for you, at the expense of blurring or even changing

---

5 One can cure oneself of the *not un-* formation by memorizing this sentence: *A not unblack dog was chasing a not unsmall rabbit across a not ungreen field.* — AUTHOR'S NOTE.

your meaning. Probably it is better to put off using words as long as possible and get one's meaning as clear as one can through pictures or sensations. Afterwards one can choose—not simply *accept*—the phrases that will best cover the meaning, and then switch round and decide what impression one's words are likely to make on another person. This last effort of the mind cuts out all stale or mixed images, all prefabricated phrases, needless repetitions, and humbug and vagueness generally. But one can often be in doubt about the effect of a word or a phrase, and one needs rules that one can rely on when instinct fails. I think the following rules will cover most cases:

(i) Never use a metaphor, simile, or other figure of speech which you are used to seeing in print.

(ii) Never use a long word where a short one will do.

(iii) If it is possible to cut a word out, always cut it out.

(iv) Never use the passive where you can use the active.

(v) Never use a foreign phrase, a scientific word, or a jargon word if you can think of an everyday English equivalent.

(vi) Break any of these rules sooner than say anything outright barbarous.

These rules sound elementary, and so they are, but they demand a deep change in attitude in anyone who has grown used to writing in the style now fashionable. One could keep all of them and still write bad English, but one could not write the kind of stuff that I quoted in those five specimens at the beginning of this article.

I have not here been considering the literary use of language, but merely language as an instrument for expressing and not for concealing or preventing thought. Stuart Chase and others have come near to claiming that all abstract words are meaningless, and have used this as a pretext for advocating a kind of political quietism. Since you don't know what Fascism is, how can you struggle against Fascism? One need not swallow such absurdities as these, but one ought to recognize that the present political chaos is connected with the decay of language, and the one can probably bring about some improvement by starting at the verbal end. If you simplify your English, you are freed from the worst follies of orthodoxy. You cannot speak any of the necessary dialects, and when you make a stupid remark its stupidity will be obvious, even to yourself. Political language—and with variations this is true of all political parties, from Conservatives to Anarchists—is designed to make lies sound truthful and murder respectable, and to give an appearance of solidity to pure wind. One cannot change this all in a moment, but one can at least change one's own habits, and from time to time one can even, if one jeers loudly enough, send some worn-out and useless phrase—some *jackboot, Achilles' heel, hotbed, melting pot, acid test, veritable inferno,* or other lump of verbal refuse—into the dustbin where it belongs. ■

The Reader's Presence

1. What characteristics of Orwell's own writing demonstrate his six rules for writing good prose (paragraph 18)? (See page 537.) Can you identify five examples in which Orwell practices what he preaches? Can you identify any moments when he seems to slip?

2. Note that Orwell does not provide *positive* examples of political expression. Why do you think this is so? Is Orwell implying that all political language—regardless of party or position—is corrupt? From this essay, can you infer Orwell's political philosophy? Explain your answer.

3. **CONNECTIONS:** Look carefully at Orwell's five examples of bad prose. Would you have identified this writing as "bad" if you had come across it in your college reading? Compare Orwell's list of rules for writing (paragraph 18), and the ideas expressed in paragraph 16, to Langston Hughes's "How to Be a Bad Writer (in Ten Easy Lessons)" (page 121). How does each writer use humor to persuade the reader of the serious effects of writing badly? What does each writer seem to think is at stake in how one writes?

The Writer at Work

GEORGE ORWELL on the Four Reasons for Writing

As the preceding essay shows, George Orwell spent much time considering the art of writing. He believed it was of the utmost political importance to write clearly and accurately. In the following passage from another essay, "Why I Write," Orwell considers a more fundamental aspect of writing: the reasons behind why people write at all. You may observe that he doesn't list the reason most college students write—to respond to an assignment. Why do you think he omitted assigned writing? Can you think of other motives he doesn't take into account?

❝ Putting aside the need to earn a living, I think there are four great motives for writing, at any rate for writing prose. They exist in different degrees in every writer, and in any one writer the proportions will vary from time to time, according to the atmosphere in which he is living. They are:

1. Sheer egoism. Desire to seem clever, to be talked about, to be remembered after death, to get your own back on grown-ups who snubbed you in childhood, etc., etc. It is humbug to pretend that this is not a motive, and a strong one. Writers share this characteristic with scientists, artists, politicians, lawyers,

soldiers, successful businessmen—in short, with the whole top crust of humanity. The great mass of human beings are not acutely selfish. After the age of thirty they abandon individual ambition—in many cases, indeed, they almost abandon the sense of being individuals at all—and live chiefly for others, or are simply smothered under drudgery. But there is also the minority of gifted, willful people who are determined to live their own lives to the end, and writers belong in this class. Serious writers, I should say, are on the whole more vain and self-centered than journalists, though less interested in money.

2. Aesthetic enthusiasm. Perception of beauty in the external world, or, on the other hand, in words and their right arrangement. Pleasure in the impact of one sound on another, in the firmness of good prose or the rhythm of a good story. Desire to share an experience which one feels is valuable and ought not to be missed. The aesthetic motive is very feeble in a lot of writers, but even a pamphleteer or a writer of textbooks will have pet words and phrases which appeal to him for non-utilitarian reasons; or he may feel strongly about typography, width of margins, etc. Above the level of a railway guide, no book is quite free from aesthetic considerations.

3. Historical impulse. Desire to see things as they are, to find out true facts and store them up for the use of posterity.

4. Political purpose—using the word "political" in the widest possible sense. Desire to push the world in a certain direction, to alter other people's idea of the kind of society that they should strive after. Once again, no book is genuinely free from political bias. The opinion that art should have nothing to do with politics is itself a political attitude. **"**

Walker Percy

THE LOSS OF THE CREATURE

WALKER PERCY (1916–1990) received his MD in 1941 and began a career teaching and practicing medicine shortly thereafter. As a resident physician, he contracted tuberculosis, and the disease changed the course of his life. During his recovery, he read extensively in literature, philosophy, and theology, and this reading program became the basis for a new career as a writer. His first novel, *The Moviegoer* (1961), won a National Book Award. He wrote a number of other novels, including *The Thanatos Syndrome* (1987), as well as works of nonfiction such as *Lost in the Cosmos: The Last Self-Help Book* (1983) and *The Message in the Bottle: How Queer Man Is, How Queer Language Is, and What One Has to Do with the Other* (1975), from which this essay, "The Loss of the Creature," is taken.

Percy believed in the ability of writing "to affirm people, to affirm the reader." In an age dominated by scientific ways of thinking, Percy once said, people are left asking questions science can't answer. "But the role of a novelist, or an artist, for that matter, is to tell the truth, to convey a kind of knowledge which cannot be conveyed by science, or psychology, or newspapers."

> **"The role of a novelist, or an artist, for that matter, is to tell the truth, to convey a kind of knowledge which cannot be conveyed by science, or psychology, or newspapers."**

EVERY EXPLORER names his island Formosa, beautiful. To him it is beautiful because, being first, he has access to it and can see it for what it is. But to no one else is it ever as beautiful—except the rare man who manages to recover it, who knows that it has to be recovered.

García López de Cárdenas discovered the Grand Canyon and was amazed at the sight. It can be imagined: One crosses miles of desert, breaks through the mesquite, and there it is at one's feet. Later the government set the place aside as a national park, hoping to pass along to millions the experience of Cárdenas. Does not one see the same sight from the Bright Angel Lodge that Cárdenas saw?

The assumption is that the Grand Canyon is a remarkably interesting and beautiful place and that if it had a certain value P for Cárdenas, the same value P may be transmitted to any number of sightseers—just as Banting's discovery of insulin can be transmitted to any number of diabetics. A counterinfluence is at work, however, and it would be nearer the truth to say that if the place is seen by a million sightseers, a single sightseer does not receive value P but a millionth part of value P.

It is assumed that since the Grand Canyon has the fixed interest value P, tours can be organized for any number of people. A man in Boston decides to spend his vacation at the Grand Canyon. He visits his travel bureau, looks at the folder, signs up for a two-week tour. He and his family take the tour, see the Grand Canyon, and return to Boston. May we say that this man has seen the Grand Canyon? Possibly he has. But it is more likely that what he has done is the one sure way not to see the canyon.

Why is it almost impossible to gaze directly at the Grand Canyon under these circumstances and see it for what it is—as one picks up a strange object from one's back yard and gazes directly at it? It is almost impossible because the Grand Canyon, the thing as it is, has been appropriated by the symbolic

5

complex which has already been formed in the sightseer's mind. Seeing the canyon under approved circumstances is seeing the symbolic complex head on. The thing is no longer the thing as it confronted the Spaniard; it is rather that which has already been formulated—by picture postcard, geography book, tourist folders, and the words *Grand Canyon*. As a result of this preformulation, the source of the sightseer's pleasure undergoes a shift. Where the wonder and delight of the Spaniard arose from his penetration of the thing itself, from a progressive discovery of depths, patterns, colors, shadows, etc., now the sightseer measures his satisfaction *by the degree to which the Canyon conforms to the preformed complex*. If it does so, if it looks just like the postcard, he is pleased; he might even say, "Why it is every bit as beautiful as a picture postcard!" He feels he has not been cheated. But if it does not conform, if the colors are somber, he will not be able to see it directly; he will only be conscious of the disparity between what it is and what it is supposed to be. He will say later that he was unlucky in not being there at the right time. The highest point, the term of the sightseer's satisfaction, is not the sovereign discovery of the thing before him; it is rather the measuring up of the thing to the criterion of the preformed symbolic complex.

Seeing the canyon is made even more difficult by what the sightseer does when the moment arrives, when sovereign knower confronts the thing to be known. Instead of looking at it, he photographs it. There is no confrontation

Tourists, 1989, a painting by Woody Gwyn. From the private collection of Steven Ratner.

at all. At the end of forty years of preformulation and with the Grand Canyon yawning at his feet, what does he do? He waives his right of seeing and knowing and records symbols for the next forty years. For him there is no present; there is only the past of what has been formulated and seen and the future of what has been formulated and not seen. The present is surrendered to the past and the future.

The sightseer may be aware that something is wrong. He may simply be bored; or he may be conscious of the difficulty: that the great thing yawning at his feet somehow eludes him. The harder he looks at it, the less he can see. It eludes everybody. The tourist cannot see it; the bellboy at the Bright Angel Lodge cannot see it: for him it is only one side of the space he lives in, like one wall of a room; to the ranger it is a tissue of everyday signs relevant to his own prospects—the blue haze down there means that he will probably get rained on during the donkey ride.

How can the sightseer recover the Grand Canyon? He can recover it in any number of ways, all sharing in common the stratagem of avoiding the approved confrontation of the tour and the Park Service.

It may be recovered by leaving the beaten track. The tourist leaves the tour, camps in the back country. He arises before dawn and approaches the South Rim through a wild terrain where there are no trails and no railed-in lookout points. In other words, he sees the canyon by avoiding all the facilities for seeing the canyon. If the benevolent Park Service hears about this fellow and thinks he has a good idea and places the following notice in the Bright Angel Lodge: *Consult ranger for information on getting off the beaten track*—the end result will only be the closing of another access to the canyon.

It may be recovered by a dialectical movement which brings one back   10
to the beaten track but at a level above it. For example, after a lifetime of avoiding the beaten track and guided tours, a man may deliberately seek out the most beaten track of all, the most commonplace tour imaginable: he may visit the canyon by a Greyhound tour in the company of a party from Terre Haute—just as a man who has lived in New York all his life may visit the Statue of Liberty. (Such dialectical savorings of the familiar as the familiar are, of course, a favorite stratagem of *The New Yorker* magazine.) The thing is recovered from familiarity by means of an exercise in familiarity. Our complex friend stands behind his fellow tourists at the Bright Angel Lodge and sees the canyon through them and their predicament, their picture taking and busy disregard. In a sense, he exploits his fellow tourists; he stands on their shoulders to see the canyon.

Such a man is far more advanced in the dialectic than the sightseer who is trying to get off the beaten track—getting up at dawn and approaching the canyon through the mesquite. This stratagem is, in fact, for our complex man the weariest, most beaten track of all.

It may be recovered as a consequence of a breakdown of the symbolic machinery by which the experts present the experience to the consumer. A family visits the canyon in the usual way. But shortly after their arrival, the park is closed by an outbreak of typhus in the south. They have the canyon to themselves. What do they mean when they tell the home folks of their good luck: "We had the whole place to ourselves"? How does one see the thing better when the others are absent? Is looking like sucking: the more lookers, the less there is to see? They could hardly answer, but by saying this they testify to a state of affairs which is considerably more complex than the simple statement of the schoolbook about the Spaniard and the millions who followed him. It is a state in which there is a complex distribution of sovereignty, of zoning.

It may be recovered in a time of national disaster. The Bright Angel Lodge is converted into a rest home, a function that has nothing to do with the canyon a few yards away. A wounded man is brought in. He regains consciousness; there outside his window is the canyon.

The most extreme case of access by privilege conferred by disaster is the Huxleyan[1] novel of the adventures of the surviving remnant after the great wars of the twentieth century. An expedition from Australia lands in Southern California and heads east. They stumble across the Bright Angel Lodge, now fallen into ruins. The trails are grown over, the guard rails fallen away, the dime telescope at Battleship Point rusted. But there is the canyon, exposed at last. Exposed by what? By the decay of those facilities which were designed to help the sightseer.

This dialectic of sightseeing cannot be taken into account by planners, for the object of the dialectic is nothing other than the subversion of the efforts of the planners.   15

The dialectic is not known to objective theorists, psychologists, and the like. Yet it is quite well known in the fantasy-consciousness of the popular arts. The devices by which the museum exhibit, the Grand Canyon, the ordinary thing, is recovered have long since been stumbled upon. A movie shows a man visiting the Grand Canyon. But the moviemaker knows something the planner does not know. He knows that one cannot take the sight frontally. The canyon must be approached by the stratagems we have mentioned: the Inside Track, the Familiar Revisited, the Accidental Encounter. Who is the stranger at the Bright Angel Lodge? Is he the ordinary tourist from Terre Haute that he makes himself out to be? He is not. He has another objective in mind, to revenge his wronged brother, counterespionage, etc. By virtue of the fact that he has other fish to fry, he may take a stroll along the rim after supper and then we can see the canyon through him. The movie accomplishes its purpose by concealing it. Overtly the characters (the American family marooned by typhus) and we the onlookers experience pity for the sufferers, and the family experience anxiety for themselves; covertly and in truth they are the happiest of people and we are happy through them, for we have the canyon to ourselves. The movie cashes in on the recovery of sovereignty through disaster. Not only is the canyon now accessible to the remnant; the members of the remnant are now accessible to each other;

---

1 **Huxleyan:** A reference to the English novelist Aldous Huxley (1894–1963), best known for his anti-utopian novel, *Brave New World* (1932). — EDS.

a whole new ensemble of relations becomes possible—friendship, love, hatred, clandestine sexual adventures. In a movie when a man sits next to a woman on a bus, it is necessary either that the bus break down or that the woman lose her memory. (The question occurs to one: Do you imagine there are sightseers who see sights just as they are supposed to? a family who live in Terre Haute, who decide to take the canyon tour, who go there, see it, enjoy it immensely, and go home content? a family who are entirely innocent of all the barriers, zones, losses of sovereignty I have been talking about? Wouldn't most people be sorry if Battleship Point fell into the canyon, carrying all one's fellow passengers to their death, leaving one alone on the South Rim? I cannot answer this. Perhaps there are such people. Certainly a great many American families would swear they had no such problems, that they came, saw, and went away happy. Yet it is just these families who would be happiest if they had gotten the Inside Track and been among the surviving remnant.)

It is now apparent that as between the many measures which may be taken to overcome the opacity, the boredom, of the direct confrontation of the thing or creature in its citadel of symbolic investiture, some are less authentic than others. That is to say, some stratagems obviously serve other purposes than that of providing access to being—for example, various unconscious motivations which it is not necessary to go into here.

Let us take an example in which the recovery of being is ambiguous, where it may under the same circumstances contain both authentic and unauthentic components. An American couple, we will say, drives down into Mexico. They see the usual sights and have a fair time of it. Yet they are never without the sense of missing something. Although Taxco and Cuernavaca are interesting and picturesque as advertised, they fall short of "it." What do the couple have in mind by "it"? What do they really hope for? What sort of experience could they have in Mexico so that upon their return, they would feel that "it" had happened? We have a clue: Their hope has something to do with their own role as tourists in a foreign country and the way in which they conceive this role. It has something to do with other American tourists. Certainly they feel that they are very far from "it" when, after traveling five thousand miles, they arrive at the plaza in Guanajuato only to find themselves surrounded by a dozen other couples from the Midwest.

Already we may distinguish authentic and unauthentic elements. First, we see the problem the couple faces and we understand their efforts to surmount it. The problem is to find an "unspoiled" place. "Unspoiled" does not mean only that a place is left physically intact; it means also that it is not encrusted by renown and by the familiar (as is Taxco), that it has not been discovered by others. We understand that the couple really want to get at the place and enjoy it. Yet at the same time we wonder if there is not something wrong in their dislike of their compatriots. Does access to the place require the exclusion of others?

Let us see what happens. 20

The couple decide to drive from Guanajuato to Mexico City. On the way they get lost. After hours on a rocky mountain road, they find themselves in a tiny valley not even marked on the map. There they discover an Indian village. Some sort of religious festival is going on. It is apparently a corn dance in supplication of the rain god.

The couple know at once that this is "it." They are entranced. They spend several days in the village, observing the Indians and being themselves observed with friendly curiosity.

Now may we not say that the sightseers have at last come face to face with an authentic sight, a sight which is charming, quaint, picturesque, unspoiled, and that they see the sight and come away rewarded? Possibly this may occur. Yet it is more likely that what happens is a far cry indeed from an immediate encounter with being, that the experience, while masquerading as such, is in truth a rather desperate impersonation. I use the word *desperate* advisedly to signify an actual loss of hope.

The clue to the spuriousness of their enjoyment of the village and the festival is a certain restiveness in the sightseers themselves. It is given expression by their repeated exclamations that "this is too good to be true," and by their anxiety that it may not prove to be so perfect, and finally by their downright relief at leaving the valley and having the experience in the bag, so to speak—that is, safely embalmed in memory and movie film.

What is the source of their anxiety during the visit? Does it not mean that the couple are looking at the place with a certain standard of performance in mind? Are they like Fabre,[2] who gazed at the world about him with wonder, letting it be what it is; or are they not like the overanxious mother who sees her child as one performing, now doing badly, now doing well? The village is their child and their love for it is an anxious love because they are afraid that at any moment it might fail them.

We have another clue in their subsequent remark to an ethnologist friend. "How we wished you had been there with us! What a perfect goldmine of folkways! Every minute we would say to each other, if only you were here! You must return with us." This surely testifies to a generosity of spirit, a willingness to share their experience with others, not at all like their feelings toward their fellow Iowans on the plaza at Guanajuato!

I am afraid this is not the case at all. It is true that they longed for their ethnologist friend, but it was for an entirely different reason. They wanted him, not to share their experience, but to certify their experience as genuine.

"This is it" and "Now we are really living" do not necessarily refer to the sovereign encounter of the person with the sight that enlivens the mind and gladdens the heart. It means that now at last we are having the acceptable experience. The present experience is always measured by a prototype, the "it" of their dreams. "Now I am really living" means that now I am filling

25

---

2 **Jean-Henri Fabre** (1823–1913): French scientist who wrote numerous books on insects, including *The Life of the Fly* and *The Life of the Spider*, based on careful observation. — EDS.

the role of sightseer and the sight is living up to the prototype of sights. This quaint and picturesque village is measured by a Platonic ideal of the Quaint and the Picturesque.

Hence their anxiety during the encounter. For at any minute something could go wrong. A fellow Iowan might emerge from a 'dobe hut; the chief might show them his Sears catalogue. (If the failures are "wrong" enough, as these are, they might still be turned to account as rueful conversation pieces: "There we were expecting the chief to bring us a churinga[3] and he shows up with a Sears catalogue!") They have snatched victory from disaster, but their experience always runs the danger of failure.

They need the ethnologist to certify their experience as genuine. This is borne out by their behavior when the three of them return for the next corn dance. During the dance, the couple do not watch the goings-on; instead they watch the ethnologist! Their highest hope is that their friend should find the dance interesting. And if he should show signs of true absorption, an interest in the goings-on so powerful that he becomes oblivious of his friends—then their cup is full. "Didn't we tell you?" they say at last. What they want from him is not ethnological explanations; all they want is his approval.

What has taken place is a radical loss of sovereignty over that which is as much theirs as it is the ethnologist's. The fault does not lie with the ethnologist. He has no wish to stake a claim to the village; in fact, he desires the opposite: he will bore his friends to death by telling them about the village and the meaning of the folkways. A degree of sovereignty has been surrendered by the couple. It is the nature of the loss, moreover, that they are not aware of the loss, beyond a certain uneasiness. (Even if they read this and admitted it, it would be very difficult for them to bridge the gap in their confrontation of the world. Their consciousness of the corn dance cannot escape their consciousness of their consciousness, so that with the onset of the first direct enjoyment, their higher consciousness pounces and certifies: "Now you are doing it! Now you are really living!" and, in certifying the experience, sets it at nought.)

Their basic placement in the world is such that they recognize a priority of title of the expert over his particular department of being. The whole horizon of being is staked out by "them," the experts. The highest satisfaction of the sightseer (not merely the tourist but any layman seer of sights) is that his sight should be certified as genuine. The worst of this impoverishment is that there is no sense of impoverishment. The surrender of title is so complete that it never even occurs to one to reassert title. A poor man may envy the rich man, but the sightseer does not envy the expert. When a caste system becomes absolute, envy disappears. Yet the caste of layman-expert is not the fault of the expert. It is due altogether to the eager surrender of sovereignty by the layman so that he may take up the role not of the person but of the consumer.

---

[3] *churinga:* Ancient sacred stones and wooden boards. — EDS.

I do not refer only to the special relation of layman to theorist. I refer to the general situation in which sovereignty is surrendered to a class of privileged knowers, whether these be theorists or artists. A reader may surrender sovereignty over that which has been written about, just as a consumer may surrender sovereignty over a thing which has been theorized about. The consumer is content to receive an experience just as it has been presented to him by theorists and planners. The reader may also be content to judge life by whether it has or has not been formulated by those who know and write about life. A young man goes to France. He too has a fair time of it, sees the sights, enjoys the food. On his last day, in fact as he sits in a restaurant in Le Havre waiting for his boat, something happens. A group of French students in the restaurant get into an impassioned argument over a recent play. A riot takes place. Madame la concierge joins in, swinging her mop at the rioters. Our young American is transported. This is "it." And he had almost left France without seeing "it"!

But the young man's delight is ambiguous. On the one hand, it is a pleasure for him to encounter the same Gallic temperament he had heard about from Puccini[4] and Rolland.[5] But on the other hand, the source of his pleasure testifies to a certain alienation. For the young man is actually barred from a direct encounter with anything French excepting only that which has been set forth, authenticated by Puccini and Rolland—those who know. If he had encountered the restaurant scene without reading Hemingway, without knowing that the performance was so typically, charmingly French, he would not have been delighted. He would only have been anxious at seeing things get so out of hand. The source of his delight is the sanction of those who know.

This loss of sovereignty is not a marginal process, as might appear from my example of estranged sightseers. It is a generalized surrender of the horizon to those experts within whose competence a particular segment of the horizon is thought to lie. Kwakiutls are surrendered to Franz Boas;[6] decaying Southern mansions are surrendered to Faulkner and Tennessee Williams. So that, although it is by no means the intention of the expert to expropriate sovereignty—in fact he would not even know what sovereignty meant in this context—the danger of theory and consumption is a seduction and deprivation of the consumer.

In the New Mexican desert, natives occasionally come across strange-looking artifacts which have fallen from the skies and which are stenciled: *Return to U.S. Experimental Project, Alamogordo. Reward.* The finder returns the object and is rewarded. He knows nothing of the nature of the object he has found and does not care to know. The sole role of the native, the highest role he can play, is that of finder and returner of the mysterious equipment.

35

---

4 **Giacomo Puccini** (1858–1924): Italian composer of such well-known operas as *La Bohéme* (1896) and *Madame Butterfly* (1904). — EDS.

5 **Romain Rolland** (1866–1944): Nobel Prize–winning French novelist and dramatist. — EDS.

6 **Franz Boas** (1858–1942): Influential German-born American anthropologist who specialized in the languages and cultures of Native Americans; in 1886, he began studying the Kwakiutl tribe of British Columbia. — EDS.

The same is true of the layman's relation to *natural* objects in a modern technical society. No matter what the object or event is, whether it is a star, a swallow, a Kwakiutl, a "psychological phenomenon," the layman who confronts it does not confront it as a sovereign person, as Crusoe[7] confronts a seashell he finds on the beach. The highest role he can conceive himself as playing is to be able to recognize the title of the object, to return it to the appropriate expert and have it certified as a genuine find. He does not even permit himself to see the thing—as Gerard Hopkins[8] could see a rock or a cloud or a field. If anyone asks him why he doesn't look, he may reply that he didn't take that subject in college (or he hasn't read Faulkner).

This loss of sovereignty extends even to oneself. There is the neurotic who asks nothing more of his doctor than that his symptom should prove interesting. When all else fails, the poor fellow has nothing to offer but his own neurosis. But even this is sufficient if only the doctor will show interest when he says, "Last night I had a curious sort of dream; perhaps it will be significant to one who knows about such things. It seems I was standing in a sort of alley—" (I have nothing else to offer you but my own unhappiness. Please say that it, at least, measures up, that it is a proper sort of unhappiness.)

2

A young Falkland Islander walking along a beach and spying a dead dogfish and going to work on it with his jackknife has, in a fashion wholly unprovided in modern educational theory, a great advantage over the Scarsdale high-school pupil who finds the dogfish on his laboratory desk. Similarly the citizen of Huxley's *Brave New World* who stumbles across a volume of Shakespeare in some vine-grown ruins and squats on a potsherd to read it is in a fairer way of getting at a sonnet than the Harvard sophomore taking English Poetry II.

The educator whose business it is to teach students biology or poetry is   40 unaware of a whole ensemble of relations which exist between the student and the dogfish and between the student and the Shakespeare sonnet. To put it bluntly: A student who has the desire to get at a dogfish or a Shakespeare sonnet may have the greatest difficulty in salvaging the creature itself from the educational package in which it is presented. The great difficulty is that he is not aware that there is a difficulty; surely, he thinks, in such a fine classroom, with such a fine textbook, the sonnet must come across! What's wrong with me?

The sonnet and the dogfish are obscured by two different processes. The sonnet is obscured by the symbolic package which is formulated not by the

---

7 ***Robinson Crusoe:*** Title character in Daniel Defoe's novel (1719), a fictional account of a castaway who spends 28 years on a remote tropical island before being rescued. — EDS.

8 ***Gerard Manley Hopkins*** (1844–1889): English poet admired for his observations of nature and his innovative use of rhythm and metrics. — EDS.

sonnet itself but by the *media* through which the sonnet is transmitted, the media which the educators believe for some reason to be transparent. The new textbook, the type, the smell of the page, the classroom, the aluminum windows and the winter sky, the personality of Miss Hawkins—these media which are supposed to transmit the sonnet may only succeed in transmitting themselves. It is only the hardiest and cleverest of students who can salvage the sonnet from this many-tissued package. It is only the rarest student who knows that the sonnet must be salvaged from the package. (The educator is well aware that something is wrong, that there is a fatal gap between the student's learning and the student's life: The student reads the poem, appears to understand it, and gives all the answers. But what does he recall if he should happen to read a Shakespeare sonnet twenty years later? Does he recall the poem or does he recall the smell of the page and the smell of Miss Hawkins?)

One might object, pointing out that Huxley's citizen reading his sonnet in the ruins and the Falkland Islander looking at his dogfish on the beach also receive them in a certain package. Yes, but the difference lies in the fundamental placement of the student in the world, a placement which makes it possible to extract the thing from the package. The pupil at Scarsdale High sees himself placed as a consumer receiving an experience-package; but the Falkland Islander exploring his dogfish is a person exercising the sovereign right of a person in his lordship and mastery of creation. He too could use an instructor and a book and a technique, but he would use them as his subordinates, just as he uses his jackknife. The biology student does not use his scalpel as an instrument; he uses it as a magic wand! Since it is a "scientific instrument," it should do "scientific things."

The dogfish is concealed in the same symbolic package as the sonnet. But the dogfish suffers an additional loss. As a consequence of this double deprivation, the Sarah Lawrence student who scores A in zoology is apt to know very little about a dogfish. She is twice removed from the dogfish, once by the symbolic complex by which the dogfish is concealed, once again by the spoliation of the dogfish by theory which renders it invisible. Through no fault of zoology instructors, it is nevertheless a fact that the zoology laboratory at Sarah Lawrence College is one of the few places in the world where it is all but impossible to see a dogfish.

The dogfish, the tree, the seashell, the American Negro, the dream, are rendered invisible by a shift of reality from concrete thing to theory which Whitehead[9] has called the fallacy of misplaced concreteness. It is the mistaking of an idea, a principle, an abstraction, for the real. As a consequence of the shift, the "specimen" is seen as less real than the theory of the specimen. As Kierkegaard[10] said, once a person is seen as a specimen of a race or a

---

[9] ***Alfred North Whitehead*** (1861–1947): Prominent British philosopher and mathematician. — EDS.

[10] ***Søren Aabye Kierkegaard*** (1813–1855): Danish philosopher and theologian. — EDS.

species, at that very moment he ceases to be an individual. Then there are no more individuals but only specimens.

To illustrate: A student enters a laboratory which, in the pragmatic view, 45 offers the student the optimum conditions under which an educational experience may be had. In the existential view, however—that view of the student in which he is regarded not as a receptacle of experience but as a knowing being whose peculiar property it is to see himself as being in a certain situation—the modern laboratory could not have been more effectively designed to conceal the dogfish forever.

The student comes to his desk. On it, neatly arranged by his instructor, he finds his laboratory manual, a dissecting board, instruments, and a mimeographed list:

Exercise 22

Materials: 1 dissecting board
1 scalpel
1 forceps
1 probe
1 bottle india ink and syringe
1 specimen of *Squalus acanthias*

The clue to the situation in which the student finds himself is to be found in the last item: 1 specimen of *Squalus acanthias*.

The phrase *specimen of* expresses in the most succinct way imaginable the radical character of the loss of being which has occurred under his very nose. To refer to the dogfish, the unique concrete existent before him, as a "specimen of *Squalus acanthias*" reveals by its grammar the spoliation of the dogfish by the theoretical method. This phrase, *specimen of*, example of, instance of, indicates the ontological status of the individual creature in the eyes of the theorist. The dogfish itself is seen as a rather shabby expression of an ideal reality, the species *Squalus acanthias*. The result is the radical devaluation of the individual dogfish. (The *reductio ad absurdum*[11] of Whitehead's shift is Toynbee's[12] employment of it in his historical method. If a gram of NaCl is referred to by the chemist as a "sample of" NaCl, one may think of it as such and not much is missed by the oversight of the act of being of this particular pinch of salt, but when the Jews and the Jewish religion are understood as—in Toynbee's favorite phrase—a "classical example of" such and such a kind of *Voelkerwanderung*,[13] we begin to suspect that something is being left out.)

If we look into the ways in which the student can recover the dogfish (or the sonnet), we will see that they have in common the stratagem of avoiding

11 **reductio ad absurdum:** "A reduction to absurdity" (Latin); the argumentative method by which one shows that a statement carried to its logical conclusion leads to an absurdity. — EDS.

12 **Arnold Toynbee** (1889–1975): British historian who believed that civilizations were formed from responses to adversity. — EDS.

13 **Voelkerwanderung:** Barbarian invasion (German). — EDS.

the educator's direct presentation of the object as a lesson to be learned and restoring access to sonnet and dogfish as beings to be known, reasserting the sovereignty of knower over known.

In truth, the biography of scientists and poets is usually the story of the discovery of the indirect approach, the circumvention of the educator's presentation—the young man who was sent to the *Technikum*[14] and on his way fell into the habit of loitering in book stores and reading poetry; or the young man dutifully attending law school who on the way became curious about the comings and goings of ants. One remembers the scene in *The Heart Is a Lonely Hunter*[15] where the girl hides in the bushes to hear the Capehart in the big house play Beethoven. Perhaps she was the lucky one after all. Think of the unhappy souls inside, who see the record, worry about scratches, and most of all worry about whether they are *getting it*, whether they are bona fide music lovers. What is the best way to hear Beethoven: sitting in a proper silence around the Capehart or eavesdropping from an azalea bush?

However it may come about, we notice two traits of the second situation: (1) an openness of the thing before one—instead of being an exercise to be learned according to an approved mode, it is a garden of delights which beckons to one; (2) a sovereignty of the knower—instead of being a consumer of a prepared experience, I am a sovereign wayfarer, a wanderer in the neighborhood of being who stumbles into the garden.

One can think of two sorts of circumstances through which the thing may be restored to the person. (There is always, of course, the direct recovery: A student may simply be strong enough, brave enough, clever enough to take the dogfish and the sonnet by storm, to wrest control of it from the educators and the educational package.) First by ordeal: The Bomb falls; when the young man recovers consciousness in the shambles of the biology laboratory, there not ten inches from his nose lies the dogfish. Now all at once he can see it, directly and without let,[16] just as the exile or the prisoner or the sick man sees the sparrow at his window in all its inexhaustibility; just as the commuter who has had a heart attack sees his own hand for the first time. In these cases, the simulacrum of everydayness and of consumption has been destroyed by disaster; in the case of the bomb, literally destroyed. Secondly, by apprenticeship to a great man: One day a great biologist walks into the laboratory; he stops in front of our student's desk; he leans over, picks up the dogfish, and, ignoring instruments and procedure, probes with a broken fingernail into the little carcass. "Now here is a curious business," he says, ignoring also the proper jargon of the specialty. "Look here how this little duct reverses its direction and drops into the pelvis. Now if you would look into a coelacanth, you would see that it—" And all at once the student can see. The technician and the sophomore who loves his textbook are

---

14 **Technikum:** Technical school (German). — EDS.
15 **The Heart Is a Lonely Hunter:** A 1940 novel by Carson McCullers (1917–1967). — EDS.
16 **let:** Hindrance; here used in its older sense: The dogfish is seen "without hindrance." Related to the tennis call "let ball," meaning the net interfered with (hindered) the ball. — EDS.

always offended by the genuine research man because the latter is usually a little vague and always humble before the thing; he doesn't have much use for the equipment or the jargon. Whereas the technician is never vague and never humble before the thing; he holds the thing disposed of by the principle, the formula, the textbook outline; and he thinks a great deal of equipment and jargon.

But since neither of these methods of recovering the dogfish is pedagogically feasible—perhaps the great man even less so than the Bomb—I wish to propose the following educational technique which should prove equally effective for Harvard and Shreveport High School. I propose that English poetry and biology should be taught as usual, but that at irregular intervals, poetry students should find dogfishes on their desks and biology students should find Shakespeare sonnets on their dissecting boards. I am serious in declaring that a Sarah Lawrence English major who began poking about in a dogfish with a bobby pin would learn more in thirty minutes than a biology major in a whole semester; and that the latter upon reading on her dissecting board

> That time of year Thou may'st in me behold
> When yellow leaves, or none, or few, do hang
> Upon those boughs which shake against the cold—
> Bare ruin'd choirs where late the sweet birds sang.[17]

might catch fire at the beauty of it.

The situation of the tourist at the Grand Canyon and the biology student are special cases of a predicament in which everyone finds himself in a modern technical society—a society, that is, in which there is a division between expert and layman, planner and consumer, in which experts and planners take special measures to teach and edify the consumer. The measures taken are measures appropriate to the consumer: The expert and the planner *know* and *plan*, but the consumer *needs* and *experiences*.

There is a double deprivation. First, the thing is lost through its packaging. The very means by which the thing is presented for consumption, the very techniques by which the thing is made available as an item of need-satisfaction, these very means operate to remove the thing from the sovereignty of the knower. A loss of title occurs. The measures which the museum curator takes to present the thing to the public are self-liquidating. The upshot of the curator's efforts are not that everyone can see the exhibit but that no one can see it. The curator protests: Why are they so indifferent? Why do they even deface the exhibits? Don't they know it is theirs? But it is not theirs. It is his, the curator's. By the most exclusive sort of zoning, the museum exhibit, the park oak tree, is part of an ensemble, a package, which is almost impenetrable to them. The archaeologist who puts his find in a museum so that everyone can see it accomplishes the reverse of his

55

---

17 The opening lines of William Shakespeare's sonnet 73. — EDS.

expectations. The result of his action is that no one can see it now but the archaeologist. He would have done better to keep it in his pocket and show it now and then to strangers.

The tourist who carves his initials in a public place, which is theoretically "his" in the first place, has good reasons for doing so, reasons which the exhibitor and planner know nothing about. He does so because in his role of consumer of an experience (a "recreational experience" to satisfy a "recreational need") he knows that he is disinherited. He is deprived of his title over being. He knows very well that he is in a very special sort of zone in which his only rights are the rights of a consumer. He moves like a ghost through schoolroom, city streets, trains, parks, movies. He carves his initials as a last desperate measure to escape his ghostly role of consumer. He is saying in effect: I am not a ghost after all; I am a sovereign person. And he establishes title the only way remaining to him, by staking his claim over one square inch of wood or stone.

Does this mean that we should get rid of museums? No, but it means that the sightseer should be prepared to enter into a struggle to recover a sight from a museum.

The second loss is the spoliation of the thing, the tree, the rock, the swallow, by the layman's misunderstanding of scientific theory. He believes that the thing is *disposed of* by theory, that it stands in the Platonic relation of being a *specimen of* such and such an underlying principle. In the transmission of scientific theory from theorist to layman, the expectation of the theorist is reversed. Instead of the marvels of the universe being made available to the public, the universe is disposed of by theory. The loss of sovereignty takes this form: As a result of the science of botany, trees are not made available to every man. On the contrary. The tree loses its proper density and mystery as a concrete existent and, as merely another *specimen of* a species, becomes itself nugatory.

Does this mean that there is no use taking biology at Harvard and Shreveport High? No, but it means that the student should know what a fight he has on his hands to rescue the specimen from the educational package. The educator is only partly to blame. For there is nothing the educator can do to provide for this need of the student. Everything the educator does only succeeds in becoming, for the student, part of the educational package. The highest role of the educator is the maieutic role of Socrates: to help the student come to himself not as a consumer of experience but as a sovereign individual.

The thing is twice lost to the consumer. First, sovereignty is lost: It is   60 theirs, not his. Second, it is radically devalued by theory. This is a loss which has been brought about by science but through no fault of the scientist and through no fault of scientific theory. The loss has come about as a consequence of the seduction of the layman by science. The layman will be seduced as long as he regards beings as consumer items to be experienced rather than prizes to be won, and as long as he waives his sovereign rights as a person and accepts his role of consumer as the highest estate to which the layman can aspire.

As Mounier[18] said, the person is not something one can study and provide for; he is something one struggles for. But unless he also struggles for himself, unless he knows that there is a struggle, he is going to be just what the planners think he is. ■

The Reader's Presence

1. Percy's essay is about the difficulties of seeing the world around us. At the beginning of paragraph 5, Percy asks: "Why is it almost impossible to gaze directly at the Grand Canyon under these circumstances and see it for what it is. . . ? . . . [B]ecause the Grand Canyon . . . has been appropriated by the symbolic complex which has already been formed in the sightseer's mind." What does he mean when he talks about "these circumstances" and "the symbolic complex"? In the next sentence, Percy mentions seeing the Grand Canyon "under approved circumstances." What does he mean here, and how does he extend his point beyond seeing to learning as well?

2. What would you identify as Percy's overall purpose in writing this essay? Where does he announce his purpose? With what terms? Consider Percy's diction. From what sources does he derive his vocabulary? What, for example, do such words as *authenticity*, *appropriation*, *expropriate*, and *sovereignty* have in common? What point of view does he express about each of these words and, more generally, about seeing the world directly? How would you characterize Percy's tone of voice in this essay? Is it, for example, pessimistic or optimistic? What attitude does he finally express about the individual's ability to discover or to recover the world or to do both? Where is this theme of discovery and recovery first introduced in the essay? How is it developed?

3. Outline the structure of Percy's essay. In what specific ways does the structure of the first part of the essay reappear in the second part? What is the general subject of the second part, and how does Percy connect it to the subject of the first part? Percy builds his case for experiencing the world firsthand by exploring a series of examples. Work through several of these examples, and show how they not only support the points he makes but eventually take on a life of their own.

4. **CONNECTIONS:** In his essay "My Visit to Niagara" (page 438), Nathaniel Hawthorne anticipates—by more than one hundred years—Percy's fascination with how people anticipate visiting a place that they already have been encouraged to see through what Hawthorne calls "pre-conceived notions." In what specific ways does reading Hawthorne's essay anticipate the questions and concerns articulated by Percy? Point to specific passages to support your response. In what ways are their perspectives on seeing Niagara Falls and the Grand Canyon different? Which essay do you find more engaging and memorable? Please explain why.

---

[18] *Emmanuel Mounier* (1905–1950): A French philosopher. — EDS.

Katha Pollitt

WHY BOYS DON'T PLAY WITH DOLLS

KATHA POLLITT was born in 1949 in New York City and is considered one of the leading poets of her generation. Her 1982 collection of poetry, *Antarctic Traveller*, won a National Book Critics Circle Award. Her poetry has received many other honors and has appeared in the *Atlantic* and the *New Yorker*. Pollitt also writes essays, and she has gained a reputation for incisive analysis and persuasive argument. She contributes reviews, essays, and social commentary to numerous national publications, many of which are collected in *Reasonable Creatures: Essays on Women and Feminism* (1994). Her collections of essays, *Subject to Debate: Sense and Dissents on Women, Politics, and Culture* (2001) and *Virginity or Death! And Other Social and Political Issues of Our Time* (2006), draw on her twice-monthly column in the *Nation*, where she has been a writer, an associate editor, and a columnist for more than twenty-seven years. Her latest collection of personal essays is *Learning to Drive: And Other Life Stories* (2008). "Why Boys Don't Play with Dolls" appeared in the *New York Times Magazine* in 1995.

Pollitt thinks of writing poems and political essays as two distinct endeavors. "What I want in a poem—one that I read or one that I write—is not an argument, it's not a statement, it has to do with language. . . . There isn't that much political poetry that I find I even want to read once, and almost none that I would want to read again."

IT'S TWENTY-EIGHT YEARS since the founding of NOW,[1] and boys still like trucks and girls still like dolls. Increasingly, we are told that the source of these robust preferences must lie outside society—in prenatal hormonal influences, brain chemistry, genes—and that feminism has reached its natural limits. What else could possibly explain the love of preschool girls for party dresses or the desire of toddler boys to own more guns than Mark from Michigan?[2]

True, recent studies claim to show small cognitive differences between the sexes: he gets around by orienting himself in space, she does it by remembering landmarks. Time will tell if any deserve the hoopla with which each is invariably greeted, over the protests of the researchers themselves. But even if the results hold up (and the history of such research is not encouraging),

---

1 **NOW:** The National Organization for Women was founded in 1966. — EDS.
2 **Mark from Michigan:** Mark Koernke, a former right-wing talk-show host who supports the militia movement's resistance to federal government. — EDS.

we don't need studies of sex-differentiated brain activity in reading, say, to understand why boys and girls still seem so unalike.

The feminist movement has done much for some women, and something for every woman, but it has hardly turned America into a playground free of sex roles. It hasn't even got women to stop dieting or men to stop interrupting them.

Instead of looking at kids to "prove" that differences in behavior by sex are innate, we can look at the ways we raise kids as an index to how unfinished the feminist revolution really is, and how tentatively it is embraced even by adults who fully expect their daughters to enter previously male-dominated professions and their sons to change diapers.

I'm at a children's birthday party. "I'm sorry," one mom silently mouths   5
to the mother of the birthday girl, who has just torn open her present—Tropical Splash Barbie. Now, you can love Barbie or you can hate Barbie, and there are feminists in both camps. But *apologize* for Barbie? Inflict Barbie, against your own convictions, on the child of a friend you know will be none too pleased?

Every mother in that room had spent years becoming a person who had to be taken seriously, not least by herself. Even the most attractive, I'm willing to bet, had suffered over her body's failure to fit the impossible American ideal. Given all that, it seems crazy to transmit Barbie to the next generation. Yet to reject her is to say that what Barbie represents—being sexy, thin, stylish—is unimportant, which is obviously not true, and children know it's not true.

Women's looks matter terribly in this society, and so Barbie, however ambivalently, must be passed along. After all, there are worse toys. The Cut and Style Barbie styling head, for example, a grotesque object intended to encourage "hair play." The grown-ups who give that probably apologize, too.

How happy would most parents be to have a child who flouted sex conventions? I know a lot of women, feminists, who complain in a comical, eyeball-rolling way about their sons' passion for sports: the ruined weekends, obnoxious coaches, macho values. But they would not think of discouraging their sons from participating in this activity they find so foolish. Or do they? Their husbands are sports fans, too, and they like their husbands a lot.

Could it be that even sports-resistant moms see athletics as part of manliness? That if their sons wanted to spend the weekend writing up their diaries, or reading, or baking, they'd find it disturbing? Too antisocial? Too lonely? Too gay?

Theories of innate differences in behavior are appealing. They let parents off the hook—no small recommendation in a culture that holds moms, and sometimes even dads, responsible for their children's every misstep on the road to bliss and success.   10

They allow grown-ups to take the path of least resistance to the dominant culture, which always requires less psychic effort, even if it means more actual work: just ask the working mother who comes home exhausted and nonetheless finds it easier to pick up her son's socks than make him do it himself. They let families buy for their children, without *too* much guilt, the unbelievably sexist junk that the kids, who have been watching commercials since birth, understandably crave.

But the thing that theories do most of all is tell adults that the *adult* world—in which moms and dads still play by many of the old rules even as they question and fidget and chafe against them—is the way it's supposed to be. A girl with a doll and a boy with a truck "explain" why men are from Mars and women are from Venus, why wives do housework and husbands just don't understand.

The paradox is that the world of rigid and hierarchical sex roles evoked by determinist theories is already passing away. Three-year-olds may indeed insist that doctors are male and nurses female, even if their own mother is a physician. Six-year-olds know better. These days, something like half of all medical students are female, and male applications to nursing school are inching upward. When tomorrow's three-year-olds play doctor, who's to say how they'll assign the roles?

With sex roles, as in every area of life, people aspire to what is possible, and conform to what is necessary. But these are not fixed, especially today. Biological determinism may reassure some adults about their present, but it is feminism, the ideology of flexible and converging sex roles, that fits our children's future. And the kids, somehow, know this.

That's why, if you look carefully, you'll find that for every kid who fits 15 a stereotype, there's another who's breaking one down. Sometimes it's the same kid—the boy who skateboards *and* takes cooking in his afterschool program; the girl who collects stuffed animals *and* A-pluses in science.

Feminists are often accused of imposing their "agenda" on children. Isn't that what adults always do, consciously and unconsciously? Kids aren't born religious, or polite, or kind, or able to remember where they put their sneakers. Inculcating these behaviors, and the values behind them, is a tremendous amount of work, involving many adults. We don't have a choice, really, about *whether* we should give our children messages about what it means to be male and female—they're bombarded with them from morning till night.

The question, as always, is what do we want those messages to be? ■

The Reader's Presence

1. Pollitt notes in her opening paragraph that "it's twenty-eight years since the founding of NOW, and boys still like trucks and girls still like dolls." What does Pollitt identify as the competing theories to explain these differences between boys and girls? Which theory does Pollitt prefer, and how does she express her support of it?

2. As you reread the essay, consider carefully the role of the media in upholding the status quo with regard to differentiated roles for girls and boys. As you develop a

response to this question, examine carefully both the media directed principally to children and the media targeted at adults. In the latter category, for instance, Pollitt refers to the media version of scientific research studies into gender differences (paragraph 2) and alludes to popular books that discuss the differences between men and women, such as *Men Are from Mars, Women Are from Venus*, and *You Just Don't Understand* (paragraph 12). Drawing on Pollitt's essay and on your own experience, identify—and discuss—the specific social responsibilities you would like to see America's mass media take more seriously.

3. **CONNECTIONS:** How would you characterize Pollitt's stance toward today's parents? What are some of the reasons she gives to explain parents' choices and actions? Consider Pollitt's argument in the light of Bernard Cooper's essay "A Clack of Tiny Sparks: Remembrances of a Gay Boyhood" (page 78). How does Cooper's account of his parents' attitudes compare with Pollitt's portrait of parents? What general points about childrearing can you draw from the contrasts and commonalities between the essays? How does parenting figure in the transmission of beliefs and practices in America, according to these authors?

Eric Schlosser
WHY MCDONALD'S FRIES TASTE SO GOOD

Investigative reporter and author **ERIC SCHLOSSER** was born in New York City in 1960. A correspondent for the *Atlantic*, and contributor to *Rolling Stone* and the *New Yorker*, he has won numerous journalistic honors and awards. His two-part *Atlantic Monthly* series, "Reefer Madness" and "Marijuana and the Law," won the National Magazine Award in 1994 and became the basis for his best-selling collection of essays, *Reefer Madness: Sex, Drugs, and Cheap Labor in the American Black Market* (2003), an exposé of America's underground economy. *Fast Food Nation: The Dark Side of the All-American Meal* (2001), Schlosser's controversial and influential first book, prompted a reexamination of practices in the meat-processing industry. A best-seller,

> *Fast Food Nation: The Dark Side of the All-American Meal* (2001), Eric Schlosser's first book, prompted a reexamination of practices in the meat-processing industry.

the book was adapted and released as a motion picture in 2006, followed by a companion book for young people, *Chew on This: Everything You Don't Want to Know About Fast Food* (2006).

Of writing *Fast Food Nation*, Schlosser said, "I care about the literary aspects of the book. I tried to make it as clear as possible, and make it an interesting thing to read, but I sacrificed some of that, ultimately, in order to get this out to people and let them know what's going on."

THE FRENCH FRY was "almost sacrosanct for me," Ray Kroc, one of the founders of McDonald's, wrote in his autobiography, "its preparation a ritual to be followed religiously." During the chain's early years french fries were made from scratch every day. Russet Burbank potatoes were peeled, cut into shoestrings, and fried in McDonald's kitchens. As the chain expanded nationwide, in the mid-1960s, it sought to cut labor costs, reduce the number of suppliers, and ensure that its fries tasted the same at every restaurant. McDonald's began switching to frozen french fries in 1966—and few customers noticed the difference. Nevertheless, the change had a profound effect on the nation's agriculture and diet. A familiar food had been transformed into a highly processed industrial commodity. McDonald's fries now come from huge manufacturing plants that can peel, slice, cook, and freeze two million pounds of potatoes a day. The rapid expansion of McDonald's and the popularity of its low-cost, mass-produced fries changed the way Americans eat. In 1960 Americans consumed an average of about eighty-one pounds of fresh potatoes and four pounds of frozen french fries. In 2000 they consumed an average of about fifty pounds of fresh potatoes and thirty pounds of frozen fries. Today McDonald's is the largest buyer of potatoes in the United States.

The taste of McDonald's french fries played a crucial role in the chain's success—fries are much more profitable than hamburgers—and was long praised by customers, competitors, and even food critics. James Beard loved McDonald's fries. Their distinctive taste does not stem from the kind of potatoes that McDonald's buys, the technology that processes them, or the restaurant equipment that fries them: other chains use Russet Burbanks, buy their french fries from the same large processing companies, and have similar fryers in their restaurant kitchens. The taste of a french fry is largely determined by the cooking oil. For decades McDonald's cooked its french fries in a mixture of about 7 percent cottonseed oil and 93 percent beef tallow. The mixture gave the fries their unique flavor—and more saturated beef fat per ounce than a McDonald's hamburger.

In 1990, amid a barrage of criticism over the amount of cholesterol in its fries, McDonald's switched to pure vegetable oil. This presented the company with a challenge: how to make fries that subtly taste like beef without cooking them in beef tallow. A look at the ingredients in McDonald's french fries suggests how the problem was solved. Toward the end of the list is a seemingly innocuous yet oddly mysterious phrase: "natural flavor." That ingredient helps to explain not only why the fries taste so good but also why most fast food—indeed, most of the food Americans eat today—tastes the way it does.

Open your refrigerator, your freezer, your kitchen cupboards, and look at the labels on your food. You'll find "natural flavor" or "artificial flavor" in just about every list of ingredients. The similarities between these two broad categories are far more significant than the differences. Both are man-made additives that give most processed food most of its taste. People usually buy a food item the first time because of its packaging or appearance. Taste usually determines whether they buy it again. About 90 percent of the money that Americans now spend on food goes to buy processed food. The

Advertising poster for the 2004 award-winning documentary by Morgan Spurlock that examined the consequences of surviving for one month entirely on meals from McDonald's.

canning, freezing, and dehydrating techniques used in processing destroy most of food's flavor—and so a vast industry has arisen in the United States to make processed food palatable. Without this flavor industry today's fast food would not exist. The names of the leading American fast-food chains and their best-selling menu items have become embedded in our popular culture and famous worldwide. But few people can name the companies that manufacture fast food's taste.

The flavor industry is highly secretive. Its leading companies will not   5 divulge the precise formulas of flavor compounds or the identities of clients. The secrecy is deemed essential for protecting the reputations of beloved brands. The fast-food chains, understandably, would like the public to believe that the flavors of the food they sell somehow originate in their restaurant kitchens, not in distant factories run by other firms. A McDonald's french fry is one of countless foods whose flavor is just a component in a complex manufacturing process. The look and the taste of what we eat now are frequently deceiving—by design.

THE FLAVOR CORRIDOR

The New Jersey Turnpike runs through the heart of the flavor industry, an industrial corridor dotted with refineries and chemical plants. International Flavors & Fragrances (IFF), the world's largest flavor company, has a manufacturing facility off Exit 8A in Dayton, New Jersey; Givaudan, the world's second-largest flavor company, has a plant in East Hanover. Haarmann & Reimer, the largest German flavor company, has a plant in Teterboro, as does Takasago, the largest Japanese flavor company. Flavor Dynamics has a plant in South Plainfield; Frutarom is in North Bergen; Elan Chemical is in Newark. Dozens of companies manufacture flavors in the corridor between Teaneck and South Brunswick. Altogether the area produces about two-thirds of the flavor additives sold in the United States.

The IFF plant in Dayton is a huge pale-blue building with a modern office complex attached to the front. It sits in an industrial park, not far from a BASF plastics factory, a Jolly French Toast factory, and a plant that manufactures Liz Claiborne cosmetics. Dozens of tractor-trailers were parked at the IFF loading dock the afternoon I visited, and a thin cloud of steam floated from a roof vent. Before entering the plant, I signed a nondisclosure form, promising not to reveal the brand names of foods that contain IFF flavors. The place reminded me of Willy Wonka's chocolate factory. Wonderful smells drifted through the hallways, men and women in neat white lab coats cheerfully went about their work, and hundreds of little glass bottles sat on laboratory tables and shelves. The bottles contained powerful but fragile flavor chemicals, shielded from light by brown glass and round white caps shut tight. The long chemical names on the little white labels were as mystifying to me as medieval Latin. These odd-sounding things would be mixed and poured and turned into new substances, like magic potions.

I was not invited into the manufacturing areas of the IFF plant, where, it was thought, I might discover trade secrets. Instead I toured various laboratories and pilot kitchens, where the flavors of well-established brands are tested or adjusted, and where whole new flavors are created. IFF's snack-and-savory lab is responsible for the flavors of potato chips, corn chips, breads, crackers, breakfast cereals, and pet food. The confectionary lab devises flavors for ice cream, cookies, candies, toothpastes, mouthwashes, and antacids. Everywhere I looked, I saw famous, widely advertised products sitting on laboratory desks and tables. The beverage lab was full of brightly colored liquids in clear bottles. It comes up with flavors for popular soft drinks, sports drinks, bottled teas, and wine coolers, for all-natural juice drinks, organic soy drinks, beers, and malt liquors. In one pilot kitchen I saw a dapper food technologist, a middle-aged man with an elegant tie beneath his crisp lab coat, carefully preparing a batch of cookies with white frosting and pink-and-white sprinkles. In another pilot kitchen I saw a pizza oven, a grill, a milk-shake machine, and a french fryer identical to those I'd seen at innumerable fast-food restaurants.

In addition to being the world's largest flavor company, IFF manufactures the smells of six of the ten best-selling fine perfumes in the United States, including Estée Lauder's Beautiful, Clinique's Happy, Lancôme's Trésor, and Calvin Klein's Eternity. It also makes the smells of household products such as deodorant, dishwashing detergent, bath soap, shampoo, furniture polish, and floor wax. All these aromas are made through essentially the same process: the manipulation of volatile chemicals. The basic science behind the scent of your shaving cream is the same as that governing the flavor of your TV dinner.

"NATURAL" AND "ARTIFICIAL"

Scientists now believe that human beings acquired the sense of taste as a   10
way to avoid being poisoned. Edible plants generally taste sweet, harmful ones bitter. The taste buds on our tongues can detect the presence of half a dozen or so basic tastes, including sweet, sour, bitter, salty, astringent, and umami, a taste discovered by Japanese researchers—a rich and full sense of deliciousness triggered by amino acids in foods such as meat, shellfish, mushrooms, potatoes, and seaweed. Taste buds offer a limited means of detection, however, compared with the human olfactory system, which can perceive thousands of different chemical aromas. Indeed, "flavor" is primarily the smell of gases being released by the chemicals you've just put in your mouth. The aroma of a food can be responsible for as much as 90 percent of its taste.

The act of drinking, sucking, or chewing a substance releases its volatile gases. They flow out of your mouth and up your nostrils, or up the passageway in the back of your mouth, to a thin layer of nerve cells called the olfactory epithelium, located at the base of your nose, right between your eyes. Your brain combines the complex smell signals from your olfactory epithelium with the simple taste signals from your tongue, assigns a flavor to what's in your mouth, and decides if it's something you want to eat.

A person's food preferences, like his or her personality, are formed during the first few years of life, through a process of socialization. Babies innately prefer sweet tastes and reject bitter ones; toddlers can learn to enjoy hot and spicy food, bland health food, or fast food, depending on what the people around them eat. The human sense of smell is still not fully understood. It is greatly affected by psychological factors and expectations. The mind focuses intently on some of the aromas that surround us and filters out the overwhelming majority. People can grow accustomed to bad smells or good smells; they stop noticing what once seemed overpowering. Aroma and memory are somehow inextricably linked. A smell can suddenly evoke a long-forgotten moment. The flavors of childhood foods seem to leave an indelible mark, and adults often return to them, without always knowing why. These "comfort foods" become a source of pleasure and reassurance—a fact that fast-food chains use to their advantage. Childhood memories of Happy Meals, which come with french fries, can translate into frequent adult visits to McDonald's. On average, Americans now eat about four servings of french fries every week.

The human craving for flavor has been a largely unacknowledged and unexamined force in history. For millennia royal empires have been built, unexplored lands traversed, and great religions and philosophies forever changed by the spice trade. In 1492 Christopher Columbus set sail to find seasoning. Today the influence of flavor in the world marketplace is no less decisive. The rise and fall of corporate empires—of soft-drink companies, snack-food companies, and fast-food chains—is often determined by how their products taste.

The flavor industry emerged in the mid-nineteenth century, as processed foods began to be manufactured on a large scale. Recognizing the need for flavor additives, early food processors turned to perfume companies that had long experience working with essential oils and volatile aromas. The great perfume houses of England, France, and the Netherlands produced many of the first flavor compounds. In the early part of the twentieth century Germany took the technological lead in flavor production, owing to its powerful chemical industry. Legend has it that a German scientist discovered methyl anthranilate, one of the first artificial flavors, by accident while mixing chemicals in his laboratory. Suddenly the lab was filled with the sweet smell of grapes. Methyl anthranilate later became the chief flavor compound in grape Kool-Aid. After World War II much of the perfume industry shifted from Europe to the United States, settling in New York City near the garment district and the fashion houses. The flavor industry came with it, later moving to New Jersey for greater plant capacity. Man-made flavor additives were used mostly in baked goods, candies, and sodas until the 1950s, when sales of processed food began to soar. The invention of gas chromatographs and mass spectrometers—machines capable of detecting volatile gases at low levels—vastly increased the number of flavors that could be synthesized. By the mid-1960s flavor companies were churning out compounds to supply the taste of Pop Tarts, Bac-Os, Tab, Tang, Filet-O-Fish sandwiches, and literally thousands of other new foods.

The American flavor industry now has annual revenues of about $1.4 billion. Approximately 10,000 new processed-food products are introduced every year in the United States. Almost all of them require flavor additives. And about nine out of ten of these products fail. The latest flavor innovations and corporate realignments are heralded in publications such as *Chemical Market Reporter*, *Food Chemical News*, *Food Engineering*, and *Food Product Design*. The progress of IFF has mirrored that of the flavor industry as a whole. IFF was formed in 1958, through the merger of two small companies. Its annual revenues have grown almost fifteenfold since the early 1970s, and it currently has manufacturing facilities in twenty countries. 15

Today's sophisticated spectrometers, gas chromatographs, and head-space-vapor analyzers provide a detailed map of a food's flavor components, detecting chemical aromas present in amounts as low as one part per billion. The human nose, however, is even more sensitive. A nose can detect aromas present in quantities of a few parts per trillion—an amount equivalent to about 0.000000000003 percent. Complex aromas, such as those of coffee and roasted meat, are composed of volatile gases from nearly a thousand different chemicals. The smell of a strawberry arises from the interaction of about 350 chemicals that are present in minute amounts. The quality that people seek most of all in a food—flavor—is usually present in a quantity too infinitesimal to be measured in traditional culinary terms such as ounces or teaspoons. The chemical that provides the dominant flavor of bell pepper can be tasted in amounts as low as 0.02 parts per billion; one drop is sufficient to add flavor to five average-size swimming pools. The flavor additive usually comes next to last in a processed food's list of ingredients and often costs less than its packaging. Soft drinks contain a larger proportion of flavor additives than most products. The flavor in a twelve-ounce can of Coke costs about half a cent.

The color additives in processed foods are usually present in even smaller amounts than the flavor compounds. Many of New Jersey's flavor companies also manufacture these color additives, which are used to make processed foods look fresh and appealing. Food coloring serves many of the same decorative purposes as lipstick, eye shadow, mascara—and is often made from the same pigments. Titanium dioxide, for example, has proved to be an especially versatile mineral. It gives many processed candies, frostings, and icings their bright white color; it is a common ingredient in women's cosmetics; and it is the pigment used in many white oil paints and house paints. At Burger King, Wendy's, and McDonald's coloring agents have been added to many of the soft drinks, salad dressings, cookies, condiments, chicken dishes, and sandwich buns.

Studies have found that the color of a food can greatly affect how its taste is perceived. Brightly colored foods frequently seem to taste better than bland-looking foods, even when the flavor compounds are identical. Foods that somehow look off-color often seem to have off tastes. For thousands of years human beings have relied on visual cues to help determine what is edible. The color of fruit suggests whether it is ripe, the color of meat whether it is rancid. Flavor researchers sometimes use colored lights to modify the influence of visual cues during taste tests. During one experiment in the early 1970s people were served an oddly tinted meal of steak and french fries that appeared normal beneath colored lights. Everyone thought the meal tasted fine until the lighting was changed. Once it became apparent that the steak was actually blue and the fries were green, some people became ill.

The federal Food and Drug Administration does not require companies to disclose the ingredients of their color or flavor additives so long as all the chemicals in them are considered by the agency to be GRAS ("generally recognized as safe"). This enables companies to maintain the secrecy of their formulas. It also hides the fact that flavor compounds often contain more ingredients than the foods to which they give taste. The phrase "artificial strawberry flavor" gives little hint of the chemical wizardry and manufacturing skill that can make a highly processed food taste like strawberries.

A typical artificial strawberry flavor, like the kind found in a Burger King   20
strawberry milk shake, contains the following ingredients: amyl acetate, amyl butyrate, amyl valerate, anethol, anisyl formate, benzyl acetate, benzyl isobutyrate, butyric acid, cinnamyl isobutyrate, cinnamyl valerate, cognac essential oil, diacetyl, dipropyl ketone, ethyl acetate, ethyl amyl ketone, ethyl butyrate, ethyl cinnamate, ethyl heptanoate, ethyl heptylate, ethyl lactate, ethyl methylphenylglycidate, ethyl nitrate, ethyl propionate, ethyl valerate, heliotropin, hydroxyphenyl-2-butanone (10 percent solution in alcohol), α-ionone, isobutyl anthranilate, isobutyl butyrate, lemon essential oil, maltol, 4-methylacetophenone, methyl anthranilate, methyl benzoate, methyl cinnamate, methyl heptine carbonate, methyl naphthyl ketone, methyl salicylate, mint essential oil, neroli essential oil, nerolin, neryl isobutyrate, orris butter, phenethyl alcohol, rose, rum ether, y-undecalactone, vanillin, and solvent.

Although flavors usually arise from a mixture of many different volatile chemicals, often a single compound supplies the dominant aroma. Smelled alone, that chemical provides an unmistakable sense of the food. Ethyl-2-methyl butyrate, for example, smells just like an apple. Many of today's highly processed foods offer a blank palette: whatever chemicals are added to them will give them specific tastes. Adding methyl-2-pyridyl ketone makes something taste like popcorn. Adding ethyl-3-hydroxy butanoate makes it taste like marshmallow. The possibilities are now almost limitless. Without affecting appearance or nutritional value, processed foods could be made with aroma chemicals such as hexanal (the smell of freshly cut grass) or 3-methyl butanoic acid (the smell of body odor).

The 1960s were the heyday of artificial flavors in the United States. The synthetic versions of flavor compounds were not subtle, but they did not have to be, given the nature of most processed food. For the past twenty years food processors have tried hard to use only "natural flavors" in their products. According to the FDA, these must be derived entirely from natural sources—from herbs, spices, fruits, vegetables, beef, chicken, yeast, bark, roots, and so forth. Consumers prefer to see natural flavors on a label, out of a belief that they are more healthful. Distinctions between artificial and natural flavors can be arbitrary and somewhat absurd, based more on how the flavor has been made than on what it actually contains.

"A natural flavor," says Terry Acree, a professor of food science at Cornell University, "is a flavor that's been derived with an out-of-date technology." Natural flavors and artificial flavors sometimes contain exactly the same chemicals, produced through different methods. Amyl acetate, for example, provides the dominant note of banana flavor. When it is distilled from bananas with a solvent, amyl acetate is a natural flavor. When it is produced by mixing vinegar with amyl alcohol and adding sulfuric acid as a catalyst, amyl acetate is an artificial flavor. Either way it smells and tastes the same. "Natural flavor" is now listed among the ingredients of everything from Health Valley Blueberry Granola Bars to Taco Bell Hot Taco Sauce.

A natural flavor is not necessarily more healthful or purer than an artificial one. When almond flavor—benzaldehyde—is derived from natural sources, such as peach and apricot pits, it contains traces of hydrogen cyanide, a deadly poison. Benzaldehyde derived by mixing oil of clove and amyl acetate does not contain any cyanide. Nevertheless, it is legally considered an artificial flavor and sells at a much lower price. Natural and artificial flavors are now manufactured at the same chemical plants, places that few people would associate with Mother Nature.

A TRAINED NOSE AND A POETIC SENSIBILITY

The small and elite group of scientists who create most of the flavor in most 25 of the food now consumed in the United States are called "flavorists." They draw on a number of disciplines in their work: biology, psychology, physiology, and organic chemistry. A flavorist is a chemist with a trained nose and a poetic sensibility. Flavors are created by blending scores of different chemicals in tiny amounts—a process governed by scientific principles but demanding a fair amount of art. In an age when delicate aromas and microwave ovens do not easily co-exist, the job of the flavorist is to conjure illusions about processed food and, in the words of one flavor company's literature, to ensure "consumer likeability." The flavorists with whom I spoke were discreet, in keeping with the dictates of their trade. They were also charming, cosmopolitan, and ironic. They not only enjoyed fine wine but could identify the chemicals that give each grape its unique aroma. One flavorist compared his work to composing music. A well-made flavor compound will have a "top note" that is often followed by a "dry-down" and a "leveling-off," with different chemicals responsible for each stage. The taste of a food can be radically altered by minute changes in the flavoring combination. "A little odor goes a long way," one flavorist told me.

In order to give a processed food a taste that consumers will find appealing, a flavorist must always consider the food's "mouthfeel"—the unique combination of textures and chemical interactions that affect how the flavor is perceived. Mouthfeel can be adjusted through the use of various fats, gums, starches, emulsifiers, and stabilizers. The aroma chemicals in a food can be precisely analyzed, but the elements that make up mouthfeel are much harder to measure. How does one quantify a pretzel's hardness, a french fry's crispness? Food technologists are now conducting basic research in rheology, the branch of physics that examines the flow and deformation of materials. A number of companies sell sophisticated devices that attempt to measure mouthfeel. The TA.XT2i Texture Analyzer, produced by the Texture Technologies Corporation, of Scarsdale, New York, performs calculations based on data derived from as many as 250 separate probes. It is essentially a mechanical mouth. It gauges the most-important rheological properties of a food—bounce, creep, breaking point, density, crunchiness, chewiness, gumminess, lumpiness, rubberiness, springiness, slipperiness, smoothness, softness, wetness, juiciness, spreadability, springback, and tackiness.

Some of the most important advances in flavor manufacturing are now occurring in the field of biotechnology. Complex flavors are being made using enzyme reactions, fermentation, and fungal and tissue cultures. All the flavors created by these methods—including the ones being synthesized by fungi—are considered natural flavors by the FDA. The new enzyme-based processes are responsible for extremely true-to-life dairy flavors. One company now offers not just butter flavor but also fresh creamy butter, cheesy butter, milky butter, savory melted butter, and super-concentrated butter flavor, in liquid or powder form. The development of new fermentation techniques, along with new techniques for heating mixtures of sugar and amino acids, have led to the creation of much more realistic meat flavors.

The McDonald's Corporation most likely drew on these advances when it eliminated beef tallow from its french fries. The company will not reveal the exact origin of the natural flavor added to its fries. In response to inquiries from *Vegetarian Journal*, however, McDonald's did acknowledge that its fries derive some of their characteristic flavor from "an animal source." Beef is the probable source, although other meats cannot be ruled out. In France, for example, fries are sometimes cooked in duck fat or horse tallow.

Other popular fast foods derive their flavor from unexpected ingredients. McDonald's Chicken McNuggets contain beef extracts, as does Wendy's Grilled Chicken Sandwich. Burger King's BK Broiler Chicken Breast Patty contains "natural smoke flavor." A firm called Red Arrow Products specializes in smoke flavor, which is added to barbecue sauces, snack foods, and processed meats. Red Arrow manufactures natural smoke flavor by charring sawdust and capturing the aroma chemicals released into the air. The smoke is captured in water and then bottled, so that other companies can sell food that seems to have been cooked over a fire.

The Vegetarian Legal Action Network recently petitioned the FDA to   30
issue new labeling requirements for foods that contain natural flavors. The
group wants food processors to list the basic origins of their flavors on their
labels. At the moment vegetarians often have no way of knowing whether
a flavor additive contains beef, pork, poultry, or shellfish. One of the most
widely used color additives—whose presence is often hidden by the phrase
"color added"—violates a number of religious dietary restrictions, may
cause allergic reactions in susceptible people, and comes from an unusual
source. Cochineal extract (also known as carmine or carminic acid) is made
from the desiccated bodies of female *Dactylopius coccus Costa*, a small insect
harvested mainly in Peru and the Canary Islands. The bug feeds on red cactus berries, and color from the berries accumulates in the females and their
unhatched larvae. The insects are collected, dried, and ground into a pigment. It takes about 70,000 of them to produce a pound of carmine, which is
used to make processed foods look pink, red, or purple. Dannon strawberry
yogurt gets its color from carmine, and so do many frozen fruit bars, candies,
and fruit fillings, and Ocean Spray pink-grapefruit juice drink.

In a meeting room at IFF, Brian Grainger let me sample some of the
company's flavors. It was an unusual taste test—there was no food to taste.
Grainger is a senior flavorist at IFF, a soft-spoken chemist with graying hair,
an English accent, and a fondness for understatement. He could easily be
mistaken for a British diplomat or the owner of a West End brasserie with
two Michelin stars. Like many in the flavor industry, he has an Old World,
old-fashioned sensibility. When I suggested that IFF's policy of secrecy and
discretion was out of step with our mass-marketing, brand-conscious, self-
promoting age, and that the company should put its own logo on the countless products that bear its flavors, instead of allowing other companies to
enjoy the consumer loyalty and affection inspired by those flavors, Grainger
politely disagreed, assuring me that such a thing would never be done. In
the absence of public credit or acclaim, the small and secretive fraternity of
flavor chemists praise one another's work. By analyzing the flavor formula
of a product, Grainger can often tell which of his counterparts at a rival firm
devised it. Whenever he walks down a supermarket aisle, he takes a quiet
pleasure in seeing the well-known foods that contain his flavors.

Grainger had brought a dozen small glass bottles from the lab. After he
opened each bottle, I dipped a fragrance-testing filter into it—a long white
strip of paper designed to absorb aroma chemicals without producing off
notes. Before placing each strip of paper in front of my nose, I closed my
eyes. Then I inhaled deeply, and one food after another was conjured from
the glass bottles. I smelled fresh cherries, black olives, sautéed onions, and
shrimp. Grainger's most remarkable creation took me by surprise. After closing my eyes, I suddenly smelled a grilled hamburger. The aroma was
uncanny, almost miraculous—as if someone in the room were flipping burgers on a hot grill. But when I opened my eyes, I saw just a narrow strip of
white paper and a flavorist with a grin. ▪

The Reader's Presence

1. What do McDonald's french fries have to do with Schlosser's primary aim in this selection? Why does he feature them in the title and use them in the opening to the essay? Why, in your opinion, didn't he use a different example?

2. Describe Schlosser's attitude toward "natural" and "artificial" flavoring (paragraph 4). Does he think one is superior to the other? Why or why not? How critical does he appear toward food additives in general? Do you read his essay as a condemnation of fast food? How does his account of his laboratory visit color your response? Overall, were his laboratory experiences positive or negative? Explain what in his account makes you feel one way or the other.

3. **CONNECTIONS:** Compare and contrast Schlosser's investigative techniques with those of James Fallows in "Throwing Like a Girl" (page 400) or Amy Cunningham in "Why Women Smile" (page 347). How does each writer establish a question to investigate, provoke your interest in the issue, gather information, and conduct the investigation? How important are sources and interviews? What information about sources and interviews is omitted from the essays?

James Shreeve

THE GREATEST JOURNEY

JAMES SHREEVE is the author of several books, including *Nature: The Other Earthlings* (1991), *The Neandertal Enigma: Solving the Mystery of Modern Human Origins* (1995), and *The Genome War: How Craig Venter Tried to Capture the Code of Life and Save the World* (2004). With Donald C. Johanson, he is also the co-author of *Lucy's Child: The Discovery of a Human Ancestor* (1989). His science writing has appeared in the *Atlantic Monthly*, *Discover*, *National Geographic*, *Science*, and *Smithsonian*, and he has been a fellow of the Alfred P. Sloan Foundation as well as the Alicia Patterson Foundation.

EVERYBODY LOVES a good story, and when it's finished, this will be the greatest one ever told. It begins in Africa with a group of hunter-gatherers, perhaps just a few hundred strong. It ends some 200,000 years later with their six and a half billion descendants spread across the Earth, living in peace or at war, believing in a thousand different deities or none at all, their faces aglow in the light of campfires and computer screens.

In between is a sprawling saga of survival, movement, isolation, and conquest, most of it unfolding in the silence of prehistory. Who were those first modern people in Africa? What compelled a band of their descendants to leave their home continent as little as 50,000 years ago and expand into Eurasia? What routes did they take? Did they interbreed with earlier members of the human family along the way? When and how did humans first reach the Americas?

In sum: Where do we all come from? How did we get to where we are today? For decades the only clues were the sparsely scattered bones and artifacts our ancestors left behind on their journeys. In the past 20 years, however, scientists have found a record of ancient human migrations in the DNA of living people. "Every drop of human blood contains a history book written in the language of our genes," says population geneticist Spencer Wells, a *National Geographic* explorer-in-residence.

The human genetic code, or genome, is 99.9 percent identical throughout the world. What's left is the DNA responsible for our individual differences—in eye color or disease risk, for example—as well as some that serves no apparent function at all. Once in an evolutionary blue moon, a random, harmless mutation can occur in one of these functionless stretches, which is then passed down to all of that person's descendants. Generations later, finding that same mutation, or marker, in two people's DNA indicates that they share the same ancestor. By comparing markers in many different populations, scientists can trace their ancestral connections.

In most of the genome, these minute changes are obscured by the genetic reshuffling that takes place each time a mother and father's DNA combine to make a child. Luckily a couple of regions preserve the telltale variations. One, called mitochondrial DNA (mtDNA), is passed down intact from mother to child. Similarly, most of the Y chromosome, which determines maleness, travels intact from father to son.

The accumulated mutations in your mtDNA and (for males) your Y chromosome are only two threads in a vast tapestry of people who have contributed to your genome. But by comparing the mtDNA and Y chromosomes of people from various populations, geneticists can get a rough idea of where and when those groups parted ways in the great migrations around the planet.

In the mid-1980s the late Allan Wilson and colleagues at the University of California, Berkeley, used mtDNA to pinpoint humanity's ancestral home. They compared mtDNA from women around the world and found that women of African descent showed twice as much diversity as their sisters. Since the telltale mutations seem to occur at a steady rate, modern humans must have lived in Africa twice as long as anywhere else. Scientists now calculate that all living humans are related to a single woman who lived roughly 150,000 years ago in Africa, a "mitochondrial Eve." She was not the

Human Migration

⊞ Fossil or artifact site   40,000 years ago Migration date   ➤ Generalized route

SOURCES: SUSAN ANTÓN, NEW YORK UNIVERSITY; ALISON BROOKS, GEORGE WASHINGTON UNIVERSITY; PETER FORSTER, UNIVERSITY OF CAMBRIDGE; JAMES F. O'CONNELL, UNIVERSITY OF UTAH; STEPHEN OPPENHEIMER, OXFORD UNIVERSITY; SPENCER WELLS, NATIONAL GEOGRAPHIC SOCIETY; OFER BAR-YOSEF, HARVARD UNIVERSITY
NGM MAPS

① African Cradle
Most paleoanthropologists and geneticists agree that modern humans arose some 200,000 years ago in Africa. The earliest modern human fossils were found in Omo Kibish, Ethiopia. Sites in Israel hold the earliest evidence of modern humans outside Africa, but that group went no farther, dying out about 90,000 years ago.

② Out of Africa
Genetic data show that a small group of modern humans left Africa for good 70,000 to 50,000 years ago and eventually replaced all earlier types of humans, such as Neandertals. All non-Africans are the descendants of these travelers, who may have migrated around the top of the Red Sea or across its narrow southern opening.

③ The First Australians
Discoveries at two ancient sites—artifacts from Malakunanja and fossils from Lake Mungo—indicate that modern humans followed a coastal route along southern Asia and reached Australia nearly 50,000 years ago. Their descendants, Australian Aborigines, remained genetically isolated on that island continent until recently.

④ Early Europeans
Paleoanthropologists long thought that the peopling of Europe followed a route from North Africa through the Levant. But genetic data show that the DNA of today's western Eurasians resembles that of people in India. It's possible that an inland migration from Asia seeded Europe between 40,000 and 30,000 years ago.

⑤ Populating Asia
Around 40,000 years ago, humans pushed into Central Asia and arrived on the grassy steppes north of the Himalaya. At the same time, they traveled through Southeast Asia and China, eventually reaching Japan and Siberia. Genetic clues indicate that humans in northern Asia eventually migrated to the Americas.

⑥ Into the New World
Exactly when the first people arrived in the Americas is still hotly debated. Genetic evidence suggests it was between 20,000 and 15,000 years ago, when sea levels were low and land connected Siberia to Alaska. Ice sheets would have covered the interior of North America, forcing the new arrivals to travel down the west coast.

Human Migration Map. *Based on the "Human Migration" map from pages 64–65 of the March 2006 issue of* National Geographic, *with permission of National Geographic Maps.*

only woman alive at the time, but if geneticists are right, all of humanity is linked to Eve through an unbroken chain of mothers.

Mitochondrial Eve was soon joined by "Y chromosome Adam," an analogous father of us all, also from Africa. Increasingly refined DNA studies have confirmed this opening chapter of our story over and over: All the variously shaped and shaded people of Earth trace their ancestry to African hunter-gatherers.

Looking more closely at DNA markers in Africa, scientists may have found traces of those founders. Ancestral DNA markers turn up most often among the San people of southern Africa and the Biaka Pygmies of central Africa, as well as in some East African tribes. The San and two of the East African tribes also speak languages that feature a repertoire of unique sounds, including clicks. Perhaps these far-flung people pay witness to an expansion of our earliest ancestors within Africa, like the fading ripples from a pebble dropped in a pond.

What seems virtually certain now is that at a remarkably recent date— probably between 50,000 and 70,000 years ago—one small wavelet from Africa lapped up onto the shores of western Asia. All non-Africans share markers carried by those first emigrants, who may have numbered just a thousand people.

Some archaeologists think the migration out of Africa marked a revolution in behavior that also included more sophisticated tools, wider social networks, and the first art and body ornaments. Perhaps some kind of neurological mutation had led to spoken language and made our ancestors fully modern, setting a small band of them on course to colonize the world. But other scientists see finely wrought tools and other traces of modern behavior scattered around Africa long before those first steps outside the continent. "It's not a 'revolution' if it took 200,000 years," says Alison Brooks of George Washington University.

Whatever tools and cognitive skills the emigrants packed with them, two paths lay open into Asia. One led up the Nile Valley, across the Sinai Peninsula, and north into the Levant. But another also beckoned. Seventy thousand years ago the Earth was entering the last ice age, and sea levels were sinking as water was locked up in glaciers. At its narrowest, the mouth of the Red Sea between the Horn of Africa and Arabia would have been only a few miles wide. Using primitive watercraft, modern humans could have crossed over while barely getting their feet wet.

Once in Asia, genetic evidence suggests, the population split. One group stalled temporarily in the Middle East, while the other followed the coast around the Arabian Peninsula, India, and beyond. Each generation may have pushed just a couple of miles farther.

"The movement was probably imperceptible," says Spencer Wells, who heads the National Geographic Society's Genographic Project, a global effort to refine the picture of early migrations. "It was less of a journey and probably more like walking a little farther down the beach to get away from the crowd."

Over the millennia, a few steps a year and a few hops by boat added   15
up. The wanderers had reached southeastern Australia by 45,000 years ago,
when a man was buried at a site called Lake Mungo. Artifact-bearing soil
layers beneath the burial could be as old as 50,000 years—the earliest evidence of modern humans far from Africa.

No physical trace of these people has been found along the 8,000 miles
from Africa to Australia—all may have vanished as the sea rose after the Ice
Age. But a genetic trace endures. A few indigenous groups on the Andaman
Islands near Myanmar, in Malaysia, and in Papua New Guinea—as well as
almost all Australian Aborigines—carry signs of an ancient mitochondrial
lineage, a trail of genetic bread crumbs dropped by the early migrants.

People in the rest of Asia and Europe share different but equally ancient
mtDNA and Y-chromosome lineages, marking them as descendants of the
other, stalled branch of the African exodus. At first, rough terrain and the Ice
Age climate blocked further progress. Europe, moreover, was a stronghold
of the Neandertals, descendants of a much earlier migration of pre-modern
humans out of Africa.

Finally, perhaps 40,000 years ago, modern humans advanced into the
Neandertals' territory. Overlapping layers of Neandertal and early modern
human artifacts at a cave in France suggest that the two kinds of humans
could have met.

How these two peoples—the destined parvenu and the doomed caretaker of a continent—would have interacted is a potent mystery. Did they
eye each other with wonder or in fear? Did they fight, socialize, or dismiss
each other as alien beings?

All we know is that as modern humans and distinctly more sophisti-   20
cated toolmaking spread into Europe, the once ubiquitous Neandertals were
squeezed into ever shrinking pockets of habitation that eventually petered
out completely. On current evidence, the two groups interbred rarely, if at
all. Neither mtDNA from Neandertal fossils nor modern human DNA bears
any trace of an ancient mingling of the bloodlines.

About the same time as modern humans pushed into Europe, some of the
same group that had paused in the Middle East spread east into Central Asia.
Following herds of game, skirting mountain ranges and deserts, they reached
southern Siberia as early as 40,000 years ago. As populations diverged and
became isolated, their genetic lineages likewise branched and rebranched.
But the isolation was rarely if ever complete. "People have always met other
people, found them attractive, and had children," says molecular anthropologist Theodore Schurr of the University of Pennsylvania.

Schurr's specialty is the peopling of the Americas—one of the last and
most contentious chapters in the human story. The subject seems to attract
fantastic theories (Native Americans are the descendants of the ancient Isra-
elites or the lost civilization of Atlantis) as well as ones tinged with a political
agenda. The "Caucasoid" features of a 9,500-year-old skull from Washington State called Kennewick Man, for instance, have been hailed as proof
that the first Americans came from northern Europe.

In fact most scientists agree that today's Native Americans descend from ancient Asians who crossed from Siberia to Alaska in the last ice age, when low sea level would have exposed a land bridge between the continents. But there's plenty of debate about when they came and where they originated in Asia.

For decades the first Americans were thought to have arrived around 13,000 years ago as the Ice Age eased, opening a path through the ice covering Canada. But a few archaeologists claimed to have evidence for an earlier arrival, and two early sites withstood repeated criticism: the Meadowcroft Shelter in Pennsylvania, now believed to be about 16,000 years old, and Monte Verde in southern Chile, more than 14,000 years old.

The DNA of living Native Americans can help settle some of the disputes. Most carry markers that link them unequivocally to Asia. The same markers cluster in people who today inhabit the Altay region of southern Siberia, suggesting it was the starting point for a journey across the land bridge. So far, the genetic evidence doesn't show whether North and South America were populated in a single, early migration or two or three distinct waves, and it suggests only a rough range of dates, between 20,000 and 15,000 years ago. Even the youngest of those dates is older than the opening of an inland route through the Canadian ice. So how did the first Americans get here? They probably traveled along the coast: perhaps a few hundred people hopping from one pocket of land and sustenance to the next, between a frigid ocean and a looming wall of ice. "A coastal route would have been the easiest way in," says Wells. "But it still would have been a hell of a trip." Beyond the glaciers lay immense herds of bison, mammoths, and other animals on a continent innocent of other intelligent predators. Pushed by population growth or pulled by the lure of game, people spread to the tip of South America in as little as a thousand years.

The genes of today's Native Americans are helping to bring their ancestors' saga to life. But much of the story can only be imagined, says Jody Hey, a population geneticist at Rutgers University. "You can't tell it with the richness of what must have happened." With the settling of the Americas, modern humans had conquered most of the planet. When European explorers set sail 700 years ago, the lands they "discovered" were already full of people. The encounters were often wary or violent, but they were the reunions of a close-knit family.

Perhaps the most wonderful of the stories hidden in our genes is that, when unraveled, the tangled knot of our global genetic diversity today leads us all back to a recent yesterday, together in Africa. ●

The Reader's Presence

1. Shreeve opens his essay by comparing recent genetic discoveries to a "good story." How does this comparison inform the entire essay, including its title? Point out some words or phrases used in the course of the essay that reinforce the concept of a

"story." Do you think the concept of a "story" adequately explains the history of humankind? Why or why not?

2. As you read through the essay, pay attention to words such as *may, perhaps, probably,* and so on. What effect do these terms have on your overall response to the material? Reread the selection and try to separate scientific fact from conjecture. In your estimation, how much of the "story" is unproven or unverified? How much appears undeniable?

3. **CONNECTIONS:** Read "The Greatest Journey" along with David Brooks's "People Like Us" (page 330). In your opinion, how do the genetic findings summarized by Shreeve confirm or contradict the assumptions made by Brooks?

Charles Simic
THE LIFE OF IMAGES

CHARLES SIMIC (b. 1938) grew up in Belgrade, Yugoslavia (now Serbia), during World War II. He immigrated to the United States with his family when he was sixteen years old and became a naturalized citizen in 1971. "Being one of the millions of displaced persons made an impression on me. In addition to my own little story of bad luck, I heard plenty of others. I'm still amazed by all the vileness and stupidity I witnessed in my life," he says. Since his first volume of poetry, *What the Grass Says* (1967), Simic has published more than sixty books and has won numerous awards, including the Pulitzer Prize in poetry for *The World Doesn't End* (1989) and a MacArthur Foundation "genius grant." His book *Walking the Black Cat* (1996) was a finalist for the National Book Award for poetry; *The Voice at 3:00 A.M.* was nominated for the National Book Award and the *Los Angeles Times* Book Award in 2003. His recent collections of poetry include *Sixty Poems* (2008), collected to celebrate his appointment as the U.S. Poet Laureate in 2007, *That Little Something* (2008), and *Master of Disguises* (2010). Simic is a noted translator of French,

> **"Everything is hard to write about. Many of my shortest and seemingly simple poems took years to get right. . . . I expect to be revising in my coffin as it is being lowered into the ground."**

Serbian, Croatian, Macedonian, and Slovenian poetry, and his own work has also been translated into many languages. Professor emeritus at the University of New Hampshire in Durham, Simic also contributes frequently to magazines and journals, including the *Harvard Review*, in which his essay "The Life of Images" was published in 2003.

When asked what he found hardest to write about, Simic replied, "Everything is hard to write about. Many of my shortest and seemingly simple poems took years to get right. I tinker with most of my poems even after publication. I expect to be revising in my coffin as it is being lowered into the ground."

IN ONE of Berenice Abbott's[1] photographs of the Lower East Side, I recall a store sign advertising *Silk Underwear*. Underneath, there was the additional information about "reasonable prices for peddlers." How interesting, I thought. Did someone carry a suitcase full of ladies' underwear and try to peddle them on some street corner farther uptown? Or did he ring doorbells in apartment buildings and offer them to housewives? I imagine the underwear came in many different sizes, so he may have had to carry two suitcases. The peddler was most likely an immigrant and had difficulty making himself understood. What he wanted was for the lady of the house to feel how soft the silk was but she either did not understand him or she had other reasons for hesitating. She wore a house robe, her hair was loose as if she just got out of bed, so she was embarrassed to touch the undies draped over his extended hand. Then she finally did touch them.

The reason photographs live in my memory is that the city I continue to roam is rich with such visual delights. Everyone who does this is taking imaginary snapshots. For all I know my face, briefly glimpsed in a crowd, may live on in someone else's memory. The attentive eye makes the world mysterious. Some men or a woman going about their business seventy years ago either caught sight of a camera pointed at them or they passed by oblivious. It was like hide and seek. They thought they had concealed themselves in plain view and the camera found them out. It showed something even they did not know they were hiding. Often people had the puzzled look of someone who had volunteered to assist a hypnotist on a stage and awakened to the sound of the audience's applause.

I'm looking at the long-torn-down Second Avenue "El" at the intersection of Division Street and Bowery in another Abbott photograph. The date is April 24, 1936. It seems like a nice day, for the sunlight streams through the tracks and iron scaffold of the elevated train, making patterns of shadow and light on the sidewalk below. As far as I can make out, the street on both sides is lined with stores selling cheap furs. The entire area was for years a bargain hunter's paradise. My father knew a fellow in his office, an

---

1 **Berenice Abbott** (1898–1991): A photographer who is noted for her concentration on New York City. Combining artistry with documentary brilliance, her work ranks her among major American photographers. She wrote many articles on photography, and her best-known book is the one Simic refers to, *Changing New York* (1939). — EDS.

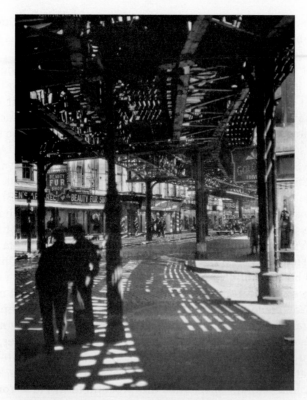

Second Street El.

elderly, impeccably dressed man, who claimed that he did all his shopping on Orchard and Hester Streets, where he never paid more than five dollars for a suit. What interests me the most in this photograph is the shadowy couple under the El with their backs turned to us. She's willowy and taller than he is, as if she were a model or a salesgirl in one of these shops. They have drawn close together as if talking over something very important, or why would they otherwise stop like that in the middle of the street? The way this woman in a long skirt carries herself gives me the impression that she is young. Not so the man. With one hand casually resting on a post and his other stuck in his pocket, he appears confident, even brash. It's the way they stand together that suggests to me that they are not casual acquaintances. Most likely they work in the same neighborhood, but there is something else going on between them too. She seems very interested in what he is saying now. No one else in view pays them any attention. The fellow standing on the sidewalk in front of the Beauty Fur Shop looks off into the distance where a portly young man with glasses wearing an open overcoat over a three-piece suit is coming into view. He has just had lunch and is glancing idly at the shop windows as he strolls lazily back to the office. He is too young to be the boss, so he must be the son or the son-in-law of one of the store owners. Except for the couple who elude identification, there is noth-ing unusual here. A photograph such as this one, where time has stopped on an ordinary scene full of innuendoes, partakes of the infinite.

I cannot look long at any old photograph of the city without hearing some music in the background. The moment that happens, I'm transported into the past so vividly no one can convince me that I did not live in that moment. I have heard just about every recording of popular music and jazz made between 1920 and 1950. This is probably the most esoteric knowledge I possess. It's easier to talk to people about Tibetan Buddhism, Arab poetry in Medieval Spain, or Russian icons, than about Helen Kane, Annette Han-shaw, and Ethel Waters. Or how about some Boswell Sisters or Joe Venuti and his Blue Four, Red McKenzie and his Mound City Blue Blowers, Ted Lewis and his Orchestra playing "Egyptian Ella"? It scares me how much of that music is in my head. I have friends who cannot believe that I can enjoy both Mahler's symphonies and Coleman Hawkins. Young Ella Fitzgerald singing "If That's What You're Thinking, You're Wrong" with Chick Webb's band would be just right for Abbott's shadowy couple.

Can one experience nostalgia for a time and place one did not know? I   5 believe so. You could put me in solitary with Abbott's photograph of "Blos-som Restaurant"[2] and I wouldn't notice the months pass away as I studied the menu chalked on the blackboard at its entrance. The prices, of course, are incredibly low, but that's secondary. The dishes enumerated here are what fascinates me. No one eats that kind of food today. Rare Mongolian, Patagonian, and Afghan specialties are procurable in New York, but not lamb oxtail stew, boiled beef, or even stuffed peppers. The ethnic makeup of the city has changed in the last thirty years. Most of the luncheonettes in the 1950s and 1960s served samplings of German, Hungarian, and Jewish cui-sine. Pea and bean soup, stuffed cabbage, corned beef and boiled potatoes, and veal cutlets were to be found regularly on the menu, together with the usual assortment of sandwiches. On every table, and all along the counter, there were containers stocked with dill pickles and slices of raw onion. The portions were enormous. A cheap dish like franks and kraut would stuff you for the rest of the day. I subsisted for years on soups and chowders cooked by a Greek in a greasy spoon on East 8th Street. They gave you two thick slices of rye bread and butter with the soup and all the pickles you could eat. After that, I could hardly keep my eyes open for the rest of the day.

Abbott's photograph of the Blossom Restaurant front also includes the barbershop next door with its own price list. Does a tonsorial establishment anywhere in this country still offer electric massage? The gadget, which resembled contraptions from a horror film, was a mesh of spring coils and electric wires. Once the juice was turned on, the machine squirmed and shook for a minute or two over the customer's scalp, supposedly providing a stimulating, healthful, up-to-date treatment, while he sat back in the chair

---

2 ***"Blossom Restaurant":*** Abbott's photograph of the restaurant, at 103 Bowery, was taken on October 3, 1935. — EDS.

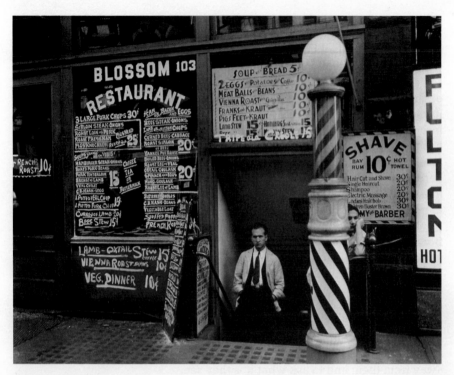

Blossom Restaurant.

pretending to be absorbed in some article in the *Police Gazette*.[3] That ordeal was followed by a few sprinkles of strong-smelling cologne from a large bottle and a dusting of talcum powder on the freshly shaved neck.

The worst haircut I ever had in my life was at a barber college at the Union Square subway station. "Learn Barbering and make Money," the sign said. It was the cheapest haircut in town. But, before I realized what was happening, the apprentice barber had cut off all my hair with clippers except for a tuft right up in front. The kid was clearly a hair fashion visionary decades ahead of his time, but back then I was in total panic. I rushed immediately across the street into Klein's department store and found a beret, which I wore pulled down over my ears for the next six weeks. The problem was that it was summer, hot and humid as it usually is in New York. I also wore dark glasses to give the impression that I was simply affecting the appearance of a jazz musician. I saw both Dizzy Gillespie and Thelonius Monk similarly decked out, but they tended to make their appearance only after dark, while I had to go to work in the morning in the storeroom of a publishing company where everyone who saw me burst out laughing. Lunch was a hassle too. The customers at adjoining tables snickered and the waitress who knew me

---

[3] **Police Gazette:** A century-old men's periodical that featured sensational news items and risqué photographs. It was especially popular in barbershops. — EDS.

well gave me a puzzled look as she brought me my sandwich. I always held unpopular opinions and was not afraid to voice them, but to have people stare at me because I had a funny haircut or wore a necktie of some outrageous hue was something I had no stomach for.

"My place is no bigger than a closet," a woman said to her companion on the street the other day as they rushed past me, and I saw it instantly with its clutter of furniture and its piles of clothes on the bed and the floor. Dickinson's "Madonna dim" came to mind and I did not even take a good look at her before she was lost in the crowd. No sooner has one seen an interesting face in the street than one gives it a biography. Through a small window in her room, the evening casts its first shadow on a blank wall where the outline of a picture that once hung there is still visible. She is not home yet, but there is a small bird in the cage waiting for her and so am I.

Mr. Nobody is what I call the man in the subway. I catch sight of him from time to time. He has labored all his life to make himself inconspicuous in dress and manner and has nearly succeeded. He sits in the far corner in his gray hat, gray moustache, pale collapsing cheeks, and empty, watery eyes, staring off into space while the subway train grinds along and the overhead lights go out briefly and return to find us puzzled, looking up from newspapers at each other sitting there. Even more odd than these searching looks we give strangers are the times when we catch someone doing the same to us. They see me as I truly am, one imagines, wanting both to run away from them and to ask what it is they see.

Today dozens of people are sunning themselves on park benches, sitting   10 close together with eyes shut as if making a collective wish. An old mutt who has done a lot of thinking and sighing in his life lies at their feet, eyeing a rusty pigeon take wing as I pass by. The enigma of the ordinary — that's what makes old photographs so poignant. An ancient streetcar in sepia color. A few men holding on to their hats on a windy day. They hurry with their faces averted except for one befuddled old fellow who has stopped and is looking over his shoulder at what we cannot see, but where, we suspect, we ourselves will be coming into view someday, as hurried and ephemeral as any one of them. ●

The Reader's Presence

1. Consider the process Simic goes through when looking at a photograph. How does he make sense of the image? What does he add to it? What conclusions does he come to about the value of photography?

2. How does Simic move between interpreting the historic photographs by Berenice Abbott and interpreting scenes from his daily life in New York City? What does one have to do with the other? Does Simic read faces on the street or scenes in the city in the same way that he reads Abbott's photographs? Why or why not?

3. **CONNECTIONS:**   Consider Simic's essay compared to Nora Ephron's "The Boston Photographs" (page 655). How would you describe the different artistic perspectives

of each writer? How are their perspectives shaped by the kind of photographs each writer is examining? In other words, how would you compare the photography of Berenice Abbott with that of Stanley Forman? After reading each selection carefully, discuss how you think Simic would have responded to Forman's photos. How would Ephron have responded to Abbott's?

Calvin Trillin

A TRADITIONAL FAMILY

The journalist, critic, novelist, and humorist **CALVIN TRILLIN** (b. 1935) was born in Kansas City but has lived in New York City for many years. He has contributed to many magazines, including the *New Yorker*, the *Atlantic Monthly*, *Harper's*, *Life*, and the *Nation*. Trillin is especially well known for his nonfiction. His magazine columns are collected in *Uncivil Liberties* (1982), *With All Disrespect: More Uncivil Liberties* (1985), *If You Can't Say Something Nice* (1987), and *Enough's Enough (and Other Rules of Life)* (1990); Trillin has also published a series of very popular books dealing with food and eating. In *American Fried: Adventures of a Happy Eater* (1974) he paints a revealing portrait of American life through his discussion of regional and national eating

> **"The facts are terribly restricting."**

habits. His love of traveling and eating in the company of his wife Alice also led him to write *Alice, Let's Eat* (1978), *Third Helpings* (1983), and *Travels with Alice* (1989). His latest book is *About Alice* (2006), a loving portrait of his wife five years after her death.

Forswearing the temptation to "eat for a living," his later books take on subjects other than food (almost), with an emphasis on memoir and politics, and include *Deadline Poet: My Life as a Doggerelist* (1994), *Messages from My Father* (1996), *Family Man* (1998), *Feeding a Yen: Savoring Local Specialties, from Kansas City to Cuzco* (2003), and two books that take on the Bush administration "in rhyme," *Obliviously on He Sails* (2004) and *A Heckuva Job: More of the Bush Administration in Rhyme* (2006). In 2008, he published another book in a similar vein, *Deciding the Next Decider: The 2008 Presidential Race in Rhyme*. "A Traditional Family" is excerpted from his book *Too Soon to Tell* (1995).

When asked to describe the process he goes through when writing factual as opposed to imaginative columns, Trillin replied, "In a nonfiction piece . . . you really have to carry around a lot of baggage. You have what happened, your understanding of what happened, what you want to get across about what happened, all kinds of burdens of being fair to whatever sides there are. The facts are terribly restricting." Trillin typically writes at least four drafts of nonfiction articles but finds that imaginative writing is less predictable. When writing his humor columns, for example, "it's a much less rigid system than that of writing nonfiction. Sometimes it only takes two drafts; sometimes it takes five."

I JUST FOUND OUT that our family is no longer what the Census Bureau calls a traditional American family, and I want everyone to know that this is not our fault.

We now find ourselves included in the statistics that are used constantly to show the lamentable decline of the typical American household from something like Ozzie and Harriet and the kids to something like a bunch of kooks and hippies.

I want everyone to know right at the start that we are not kooks. Oh sure, we have our peculiarities, but we are not kooks. Also, we are not hippies. We have no children named Goodness. I am the first one to admit that reasonable people may differ on how to characterize a couple of my veteran sportcoats, and there may have been a remark or two passed in the neighborhood from time to time about the state of our front lawn. But no one has ever seriously suggested that we are hippies.

In fact, most people find us rather traditional. My wife and I have a marriage certificate, although I can't say I know exactly where to put my hands on it right at the moment. We have two children. We have a big meal on Christmas. We put on costumes at Halloween. (What about the fact that I always wear an ax murderer's mask on Halloween? That happens to be one of the peculiarities.) We make family decisions in the traditional American family way, which is to say the father is manipulated by the wife and the children. We lose a lot of socks in the wash. At our house, the dishes are done and the garbage is taken out regularly—after the glass and cans and other recyclable materials have been separated out. We're not talking about a commune here.

So why has the Census Bureau begun listing us with households that consist of, say, the ex-stepchild of someone's former marriage living with someone who is under the mistaken impression that she is the aunt of somebody or other? Because the official definition of a traditional American family is two parents and one or more children under age eighteen. Our younger daughter just turned nineteen. Is that our fault?

As it happens, I did everything in my power to keep her from turning nineteen. When our daughters were about two and five, I decided that they were the perfect age, and I looked around for some sort of freezing process that might keep them there. I discovered that there was no such freezing

5

process on the market. Assuming, in the traditional American way, that the technology would come along by and by, I renewed my investigation several times during their childhoods—they always seemed to be at the perfect age—but the freezing process never surfaced. Meanwhile, they kept getting older at what seemed to me a constantly accelerating rate. Before you could say "Zip up your jacket," the baby turned nineteen. What's a parent to do?

Ask for an easement. That's what a parent's to do. When I learned about the Census Bureau's definition of a traditional family—it was mentioned in an Associated Press story about how the latest census shows the traditional family declining at a more moderate pace than "the rapid and destabilizing rate" at which it declined between 1970 and 1980—it occurred to me that we could simply explain the situation to the Census Bureau and ask that an exception be made in our case.

I realize that the Census Bureau would probably want to send out an inspector. I would acknowledge to him that our daughters are more or less away from home, but remind him that we have been assured by more experienced parents that we can absolutely count on their return. I would take the position, in other words, that we are just as traditional as any American family, just slightly undermanned at the moment—like a hockey team that has a couple of guys in the penalty box but is still a presence on the ice. We could show the official our Christmas tree decorations and our Halloween costumes and a lot of single socks. We might, in the traditional American way, offer him a cup of coffee and a small bribe.

I haven't decided for sure to approach the Census Bureau. For one thing, someone might whisper in the inspector's ear that I have been heard to refer to my older daughter's room—the room where we now keep the exercise bike—as "the gym," and that might take some explaining. Also, I haven't discussed the matter with my wife. I would, of course, abide by her wishes. It's traditional. ●

The Reader's Presence

1. According to Trillin, how does the Census Bureau define "a traditional American family" (paragraph 1)? How does Trillin discover that his family would no longer be included in the Census Bureau's statistical compilations about "traditional" American families? Why does his family no longer satisfy the Census Bureau's criteria? What does Trillin try to do about this "problem"?

2. What characteristics of his family's behavior does Trillin identify as "traditional"? Examine the effect(s) of Trillin's verb choices. What patterns do you notice? What other patterns do you notice that he has woven into his word choices? When—and how—does Trillin poke fun at himself and the members of his family? To what extent does his humor depend on irony? on wit? Point to specific words and phrases to support your response.

3. **CONNECTIONS:** When—and how—does Trillin use gender and familial stereotypes to reinforce the points he makes? Compare Trillin's light piece to the far more

serious essay by David Mamet about his "new, cobbled-together family" (paragraph 10) who live in a new suburban development ("The Rake: A Few Scenes from My Childhood," page 158). How do both writers play with the reader's sense of the normative or the ideal? Can you imagine a comic version of Mamet's essay and a serious version of Trillin's? If so, what might they look like?

Barbara Tuchman

"THIS IS THE END OF THE WORLD": THE BLACK DEATH

BARBARA TUCHMAN (1912–1989) was an acclaimed historian who was noted for writing historical accounts in a literary style. Believing that most historians alienate their readers by including minute details and by ignoring the elements of well-written prose, Tuchman hoped to engage a broad audience with a well-told narrative. As she explained during a speech at the National Portrait Gallery in 1978, "I want the reader to turn the page and keep on turning to the end. . . . This is accomplished only when the narrative moves steadily ahead, not when it comes to a weary standstill, overloaded with every item uncovered in the research." Tuchman, a 1933 Radcliffe College graduate, never received formal training as a historian but developed an ability to document history early in her career while working as a research assistant for the Institute of Pacific Relations, a writer for the *Nation*, a foreign correspondent during the Spanish Civil War, and an editor for the Office of War Information during World War II. Tuchman earned critical attention when her third book, *The Zimmermann Telegram*, became a best-seller in 1958. She received a Pulitzer Prize for *The Guns of August* (1962), a description of the early days of World War I, and for *Stilwell and the American Experience in China, 1911–1945* (1970), a biographical account of Joseph Warren Stilwell, an American military officer during China's shift from feudalism to communism. Tuchman's other books include *The Proud Tower: A Portrait of the World before the War, 1890–1914* (1966); *A Distant Mirror: The Calamitous 14th Century* (1978), from which "'This Is the End of the World': The Black Death" is taken; and *The March of Folly: From Troy to Vietnam* (1984).

> "I want the reader to turn the page and keep on turning to the end."

IN OCTOBER 1347, two months after the fall of Calais,[1] Genoese trading ships put into the harbor of Messina in Sicily with dead and dying
men at the oars. The ships had come from the Black Sea port of Caffa (now
Feodosiya) in the Crimea, where the Genoese maintained a trading post.
The diseased sailors showed strange black swellings about the size of an
egg or an apple in the armpits and groin. The swellings oozed blood and pus
and were followed by spreading boils and black blotches on the skin from
internal bleeding. The sick suffered severe pain and died quickly within five
days of the first symptoms. As the disease spread, other symptoms of continuous fever and spitting of blood appeared instead of the swellings or
buboes. These victims coughed and sweated heavily and died even more
quickly, within three days or less, sometimes in 24 hours. In both types
everything that issued from the body—breath, sweat, blood from the buboes
and lungs, bloody urine, and blood-blackened excrement—smelled foul.
Depression and despair accompanied the physical symptoms, and before
the end "death is seen seated on the face."[2]

The disease was bubonic plague, present in two forms: one that infected
the bloodstream, causing the buboes and internal bleeding, and was spread
by contact; and a second, more virulent pneumonic type that infected the
lungs and was spread by respiratory infection. The presence of both at once
cause the high mortality and speed of contagion. So lethal was the disease that cases were known of persons going to bed well and dying before
they woke, of doctors catching the illness at a bedside and dying before
the patient. So rapidly did it spread from one to another that to a French
physician, Simon de Covino, it seemed as if one sick person "could infect
the whole world."[3] The malignity of the pestilence appeared more terrible
because its victims knew no prevention and no remedy.

The physical suffering of the disease and its aspect of evil mystery were
expressed in a strange Welsh lament[4] which saw "death coming into our
midst like black smoke, a plague which cuts off the young, a rootless phantom which has no mercy for fair countenance. Woe is me of the shilling in
the armpit! It is seething, terrible . . . a head that gives pain and causes a
loud cry . . . a painful angry knob . . . Great is its seething like a burning cinder . . . a grievous thing of ashy color." Its eruption is ugly like the "seeds of
black peas, broken fragments of brittle sea-coal . . . the early ornaments of
black death, cinders of the peelings of the cockle weed, a mixed multitude,
a black plague like halfpence, like berries. . . ."

Rumors of a terrible plague supposedly arising in China and spreading through Tartary (Central Asia) to India and Persia, Mesopotamia, Syria,
Egypt, and all of Asia Minor had reached Europe in 1346. They told of a
death toll so devastating that all of India was said to be depopulated, whole

---

1 **fall of Calais:** After a year-long siege, Calais, a town in France, surrendered to Edward III,
king of England and self-declared king of France. — EDS.
2 "Death Is Seen Seated": Simon de Covino, q. Campbell, 80.
3 "Could Infect the Whole World": q. Gasquet, 41.
4 Welsh Lament: q. Ziegler, 190.

territories covered by dead bodies, other areas with no one left alive. As added up by Pope Clement VI at Avignon, the total of reported dead reached 23,840,000. In the absence of a concept of contagion, no serious alarm was felt in Europe until the trading ships brought their black burden of pestilence into Messina while other infected ships from the Levant carried it to Genoa and Venice.

By January 1348 it penetrated France via Marseille, and North Africa   5
via Tunis. Shipborne along coasts and navigable rivers, it spread westward from Marseille through the ports of Languedoc to Spain and northward up the Rhône to Avignon, where it arrived in March. It reached Narbonne, Montpellier, Carcassonne, and Toulouse between February and May, and at the same time in Italy spread to Rome and Florence and their hinterlands. Between June and August it reached Bordeaux, Lyon, and Paris, spread to Burgundy and Normandy, and crossed the Channel from Normandy into southern England. From Italy during the same summer it crossed the Alps into Switzerland and reached eastward to Hungary.

In a given area the plague accomplished its kill within four to six months and then faded, except in the larger cities, where, rooting into the close-quartered population, it abated during the winter, only to reappear in the spring and rage for another six months.

In 1349 it resumed in Paris, spread to Picardy, Flanders, and the Low Countries, and from England to Scotland and Ireland as well as to Norway, where a ghost ship with a cargo of wool and a dead crew drifted offshore until it ran aground near Bergen. From there the plague passed into Sweden, Denmark, Prussia, Iceland, and as far as Greenland. Leaving a strange pocket of immunity in Bohemia, and Russia unattacked until 1351, it had passed from most of Europe by mid-1350. Although the mortality rate was erratic, ranging from one-fifth in some places to nine-tenths or almost total elimination in others, the overall estimate of modern demographers has settled—for the area extending from India to Iceland—around the same figure expressed in Froissart's casual words: "a third of the world died." His estimate, the common one at the time, was not an inspired guess but a borrowing of St. John's figure for mortality from plague in Revelation, the favorite guide to human affairs of the Middle Ages.

A third of Europe would have meant about 20 million deaths. No one knows in truth how many died. Contemporary reports were an awed impression, not an accurate count. In crowded Avignon, it was said, 400 died daily; 7,000 houses emptied by death were shut up; a single graveyard received 11,000 corpses in six weeks; half the city's inhabitants reportedly died, including 9 cardinals or one-third of the total, and 70 lesser prelates. Watching the endlessly passing death carts, chroniclers let normal exaggeration take wings and put the Avignon death toll at 62,000 and even at 120,000 although the city's total population was probably less than 50,000.

When graveyards filled up, bodies at Avignon were thrown into the Rhône until mass burial pits were dug for dumping the corpses. In London in such pits corpses piled up in layers until they overflowed. Everywhere

Plague victim receiving last rites, from a fifteenth-century collection of English religious texts.

reports speak of the sick dying too fast for the living to bury. Corpses were dragged out of homes and left in front of doorways. Morning light revealed new piles of bodies. In Florence the dead were gathered up by the Compagnia della Misericordia—founded in 1244 to care for the sick—whose members wore red robes and hoods masking the face except for the eyes. When their efforts failed, the dead lay putrid in the streets for days at a time. When no coffins were to be had, the bodies were laid on boards, two or three at once, to be carried to graveyards or common pits. Families dumped their own relatives into the pits, or buried them so hastily and thinly "that dogs dragged them forth and devoured their bodies."[5]

5 "Dogs Dragged Them Forth": Agnolo di Tura, q. Ziegler, 58.

Amid accumulating death and fear of contagion, people died without   10
last rites and were buried without prayers, a prospect that terrified the last
hours of the stricken. A bishop in England gave permission to laymen to
make confession to each other as was done by the Apostles, "or if no man is
present then even to a woman,"[6] and if no priest could be found to administer extreme unction, "then faith must suffice." Clement VI found it necessary to grant remissions of sin to all who died of the plague because so many
were unattended by priests. "And no bells tolled,"[7] wrote a chronicler of
Siena, "and nobody wept no matter what his loss because almost everyone
expected death. . . . And people said and believed, 'This is the end of the
world.'"

In Paris, where the plague lasted through 1349, the reported death rate
was 800 a day, in Pisa 500, in Vienna 500 to 600. The total dead in Paris
numbered 50,000 or half the population. Florence, weakened by the famine of 1347, lost three- to four-fifths of its citizens, Venice two-thirds, Ham-
burg and Bremen, though smaller in size, about the same proportion. Cities,
as centers of transportation, were more likely to be affected than villages,
although once a village was infected, its death rate was equally high. At
Givry, a prosperous village in Burgundy of 1,200 to 1,500 people, the parish register records 615 deaths in the space of fourteen weeks, compared to
an average of thirty deaths a year in the previous decade.[8] In three villages
of Cambridgeshire, manorial records show a death rate of 47 percent, 57
percent, and in one case 70 percent.[9] When the last survivors, too few to
carry on, moved away, a deserted village sank back into the wilderness and
disappeared from the map altogether, leaving only a grass-covered ghostly
outline to show where mortals once had lived.

In enclosed places such as monasteries and prisons, the infection of one
person usually meant that of all, as happened in the Franciscan convents of
Carcassonne and Marseille, where every inmate without exception died. Of
the 140 Dominicans at Montpellier only seven survived. Petrarch's brother
Gherardo, member of a Carthusian monastery, buried the prior and 34 fellow monks one by one, sometimes three a day, until he was left alone with
his dog and fled to look for a place that would take him in.[10] Watching every
comrade die, men in such places could not but wonder whether the strange
peril that filled the air had not been sent to exterminate the human race. In
Kilkenny, Ireland, Brother John Clyn of the Friars Minor, another monk left
alone among dead men, kept a record of what had happened lest "things
which should be remembered perish with time and vanish from the memory
of those who come after us."[11] Sensing "the whole world, as it were, placed
within the grasp of the Evil One," and waiting for death to visit him too,

---

6 "Or If No Man Is Present": Bishop of Bath and Wells, q. Ziegler, 125.
7 "No Bells Tolled": Agnolo di Tura, q. Schevill, *Siena*, 211. The same observation was made
by Gabriel de Muisis, notary of Piacenza, q. Crawford, 113.
8 Givry Parish Register: Renouard, 111.
9 Three Villages of Cambridgeshire: Saltmarsh.
10 Petrarch's Brother: Bishop, 273.
11 Brother John Clyn: q. Ziegler, 195.

he wrote, "I leave parchment to continue this work, if perchance any man survive and any of the race of Adam escape this pestilence and carry on the work which I have begun." Brother John, as noted by another hand, died of the pestilence, but he foiled oblivion.

The largest cities of Europe, with populations of about 100,000, were Paris and Florence, Venice and Genoa. At the next level, with more than 50,000, were Ghent and Bruges in Flanders, Milan, Bologna, Rome, Naples, and Palermo, and Cologne. London hovered below 50,000, the only city in England except York with more than 10,000. At the level of 20,000 to 50,000 were Bordeaux, Toulouse, Montpellier, Marseille, and Lyon in France, Barcelona, Seville, and Toledo in Spain, Siena, Pisa, and other secondary cities in Italy, and the Hanseatic trading cities of the Empire. The plague raged through them all, killing anywhere from one-third to two-thirds of their inhabitants. Italy, with a total population of 10 to 11 million, probably suffered the heaviest toll. Following the Florentine bankruptcies, the crop failures and workers' riots of 1346–47, the revolt of Cola di Rienzi that plunged Rome into anarchy, the plague came as the peak of successive calamities. As if the world were indeed in the grasp of the Evil One, its first appearance on the European mainland in January 1348 coincided with a fearsome earthquake that carved a path of wreckage from Naples up to Venice. Houses collapsed, church towers toppled, villages were crushed, and the destruction reached as far as Germany and Greece. Emotional response, dulled by horrors, underwent a kind of atrophy epitomized by the chronicler who wrote, "And in these days was burying without sorrowe and wedding without friendschippe."[12]

In Siena, where more than half the inhabitants died of the plague, work was abandoned on the great cathedral, planned to be the largest in the world, and never resumed, owing to loss of workers and master masons and "the melancholy and grief" of the survivors. The cathedral's truncated transept still stands in permanent witness to the sweep of death's scythe. Agnolo di Tura, a chronicler of Siena, recorded the fear of contagion that froze every other instinct. "Father abandoned child, wife husband, one brother another," he wrote, "for this plague seemed to strike through the breath and sight.[13] And so they died. And no one could be found to bury the dead for money or friendship. . . . And I, Agnolo di Tura, called the Fat, buried my five children with my own hands, and so did many others likewise."

There were many to echo his account of inhumanity and few to balance   15
it, for the plague was not the kind of calamity that inspired mutual help. Its loathsomeness and deadliness did not herd people together in mutual distress, but only prompted their desire to escape each other. "Magistrates and notaries refused to come and make the wills of the dying," reported a Franciscan friar of Piazza in Sicily;[14] what was worse, "even the priests did

---

12 Apathy; "And in These Days": q. Deaux, 143, citing only "an old northern chronicle."
13 Agnolo di Tura, "Father Abandoned Child": q. Ziegler, 58.
14 "Magistrates and Notaries": q. Deaux, 49.

not come to hear their confessions." A clerk of the Archbishop of Canterbury reported the same of English priests who "turned away from the care of their benefices from fear of death."[15] Cases of parents deserting children and children their parents were reported across Europe from Scotland to Russia.[16] The calamity chilled the hearts of men, wrote Boccaccio[17] in his famous account of the plague in Florence that serves as introduction to the *Decameron.* "One man shunned another . . . kinsfolk held aloof, brother was forsaken by brother, oftentimes husband by wife; nay, what is more, and scarcely to be believed, fathers and mothers were found to abandon their own children to their fate, untended, unvisited as if they had been strangers." Exaggeration and literary pessimism were common in the fourteenth century, but the Pope's physician, Guy de Chauliac, was a sober, careful observer who reported the same phenomenon: "A father did not visit his son, nor the son his father. Charity was dead."[18]

Yet not entirely. In Paris, according to the chronicler Jean de Venette, the nuns of the Hôtel Dieu or municipal hospital, "having no fear of death, tended the sick with all sweetness and humility."[19] New nuns repeatedly took the places of those who died, until the majority "many times renewed by death now rest in peace with Christ as we may piously believe."

When the plague entered northern France in July 1348, it settled first in Normandy and, checked by winter, gave Picardy a deceptive interim until the next summer. Either in mourning or warning, black flags were flown from church towers of the worst-stricken villages of Normandy. "And in that time," wrote a monk of the abbey of Fourcarment, "the mortality was so great among the people of Normandy that those of Picardy mocked them."[20] The same unneighborly reaction was reported of the Scots, separated by a winter's immunity from the English. Delighted to hear of the disease that was scourging the "southrons," they gathered forces for an invasion, "laughing at their enemies." Before they could move, the savage mortality fell upon them too, scattering some in death and the rest in panic to spread the infection as they fled.

In Picardy in the summer of 1349 the pestilence penetrated the castle of Coucy to kill Enguerrand's[21] mother, Catherine, and her new husband.[22] Whether her nine-year-old son escaped by chance or was perhaps living elsewhere with one of his guardians is unrecorded. In nearby Amiens, tannery workers, responding quickly to losses in the labor force, combined to

---

15 English Priests "Turned Away": Ziegler, 261.

16 Parents Deserting Children: Hecker, 30.

17 **Giovanni Boccaccio** (1313–1375): An Italian writer best known for his collection of stories about the Black Death, the *Decameron.* — EDS.

18 Guy de Chauliac, "A Father": q. Gasquet, 50–51.

19 Nuns of the Hôtel Dieu: *Chron. Jean de Venette,* 49.

20 Picards and Scots Mock Mortality of Neighbors: Gasquet, 53, and Ziegler, 198.

21 **castle . . . Enguerrand:** Enguerrand de Coucy is the historical figure on whom Tuchman focuses in her account of the fourteenth century. — EDS.

22 Catherine de Coucy: *L'Art de verifier,* 237.

bargain for higher wages.[23] In another place villagers were seen dancing to drums and trumpets, and on being asked the reason, answered that, seeing their neighbors die day by day while their village remained immune, they believed they could keep the plague from entering "by the jollity that is in us. That is why we dance."[24] Further north in Tournai on the border of Flanders, Gilles li Muisis, Abbot of St. Martin's, kept one of the epidemic's most vivid accounts. The passing bells rang all day and all night, he recorded, because sextons were anxious to obtain their fees while they could. Filled with the sound of mourning, the city became oppressed by fear, so that the authorities forbade the tolling of bells and the wearing of black and restricted funeral services to two mourners. The silencing of funeral bells and of criers' announcements of deaths was ordained by most cities. Siena imposed a fine on the wearing of mourning clothes by all except widows.

Flight was the chief recourse of those who could afford it or arrange it. The rich fled to their country places like Boccaccio's young patricians of Florence, who settled in a pastoral palace "removed on every side from the roads" with "wells of cool water and vaults of rare wines." The urban poor died in their burrows, "and only the stench of their bodies informed neighbors of their death." That the poor were more heavily afflicted than the rich was clearly remarked at the time, in the north as in the south. A Scottish chronicler, John of Fordun, stated flatly that the pest "attacked especially the meaner sort and common people—seldom the magnates."[25] Simon de Covino of Montpellier made the same observation.[26] He ascribed it to the misery and want and hard lives that made the poor more susceptible, which was half the truth. Close contact and lack of sanitation was the unrecognized other half. It was noticed too that the young died in greater proportion than the old; Simon de Covino compared the disappearance of youth to the withering of flowers in the fields.[27]

In the countryside peasants dropped dead on the roads, in the fields, in their houses. Survivors in growing helplessness fell into apathy, leaving ripe wheat uncut and livestock untended. Oxen and asses, sheep and goats, pigs and chickens ran wild and they too, according to local reports, succumbed to the pest. English sheep, bearers of the precious wool, died throughout the country. The chronicler Henry Knighton, canon of Leicester Abbey, reported 5,000 dead in one field alone, "their bodies so corrupted by the plague that neither beast nor bird would touch them," and spreading an appalling stench.[28] In the Austrian Alps wolves came down to prey upon sheep and then, "as if alarmed by some invisible warning, turned and fled back into the wilderness."[29] In remote Dalmatia bolder wolves descended upon a

20

23 Amiens Tanners: Gasquet, 57.
24 "By the Jollity That Is in Us": *Grandes Chrons.*, VI, 486–87.
25 John of Fordun: q. Ziegler, 199.
26 Simon de Covino on the Poor: Gasquet, 42.
27 On Youth: Cazelles, *Peste*.
28 Knighton on Sheep: q. Ziegler, 175.
29 Wolves of Austria and Dalmatia: ibid., 84, 111.

plague-stricken city and attacked human survivors. For want of herdsmen, cattle strayed from place to place and died in hedgerows and ditches. Dogs and cats fell like the rest.[30]

The dearth of labor held a fearful prospect because the fourteenth century lived close to the annual harvest both for food and for next year's seed. "So few servants and laborers were left," wrote Knighton, "that no one knew where to turn for help." The sense of a vanishing future created a kind of dementia of despair. A Bavarian chronicler of Neuberg on the Danube recorded that "Men and women . . . wandered around as if mad" and let their cattle stray "because no one had any inclination to concern themselves about the future."[31] Fields went uncultivated, spring seed unsown. Second growth with nature's awful energy crept back over cleared land, dikes crumbled, salt water reinvaded and soured the lowlands. With so few hands remaining to restore the work of centuries, people felt, in Walsingham's words, that "the world could never again regain its former prosperity."[32]

Though the death rate was higher among the anonymous poor, the known and the great died too. King Alfonso XI of Castile was the only reigning monarch killed by the pest, but his neighbor King Pedro of Aragon lost his wife, Queen Leonora, his daughter Marie, and a niece in the space of six months. John Cantacuzene, Emperor of Byzantium, lost his son. In France the lame Queen Jeanne and her daughter-in-law Bonne de Luxemburg, wife of the Dauphin,[33] both died in 1349 in the same phase that took the life of Enguerrand's mother. Jeanne, Queen of Navarre, daughter of Louis X, was another victim. Edward III's second daughter, Joanna, who was on her way to marry Pedro, the heir of Castile, died in Bordeaux. Women appear to have been more vulnerable than men, perhaps because, being more housebound, they were more exposed to fleas. Boccaccio's mistress Fiammetta, illegitimate daughter of the King of Naples, died, as did Laura, the beloved—whether real or fictional—of Petrarch. Reaching out to us in the future, Petrarch cried, "Oh happy posterity who will not experience such abysmal woe and will look upon our testimony as a fable."[34]

In Florence Giovanni Villani, the great historian of his time, died at 68 in the midst of an unfinished sentence: ". . . e dure questo pistolenza fino a . . . (in the midst of this pestilence there came to an end . . .)."[35] Siena's master painters, the brothers Ambrogio and Pietro Lorenzetti, whose names never appear after 1348, presumably perished in the plague, as did Andrea Pisano, architect and sculptor of Florence. William of Ockham and the English mystic Richard Rolle of Hampole both disappear from mention after 1349. Francisco Datini, merchant of Prato, lost both his parents and two siblings. Curious sweeps of mortality afflicted certain bodies of merchants in

---

30 Dogs and Cats: Muisis, q. Gasquet, 44, 61.
31 Bavarian Chronicler of Neuberg: q. Ziegler, 84.
32 Walsingham, "The World Could Never": Denifle, 273.
33 **Dauphin:** The eldest son of a French king and presumably heir to the throne. — EDS.
34 "Oh Happy Posterity": q. Ziegler, 45.
35 Giovanni Villani, "e dure questo": q. Snell, 334.

London. All eight wardens of the Company of Cutters, all six wardens of the Hatters, and four wardens of the Goldsmiths died before July 1350. Sir John Pulteney, master draper and four times Mayor of London, was a victim, likewise Sir John Montgomery, Governor of Calais.

Among the clergy and doctors the mortality was naturally high because of the nature of their professions. Out of 24 physicians in Venice, 20 were said to have lost their lives in the plague, although, according to another account, some were believed to have fled or to have shut themselves up in their houses.[36] At Montpellier, site of the leading medieval medical school, the physician Simon de Covino reported that, despite the great number of doctors, "hardly one of them escaped."[37] In Avignon, Guy de Chauliac confessed that he performed his medical visits only because he dared not stay away for fear of infamy, but "I was in continual fear."[38] He claimed to have contracted the disease but to have cured himself by his own treatment; if so, he was one of the few who recovered.

Clerical mortality varied with rank. Although the one-third toll of cardinals reflects the same proportion as the whole, this was probably due to their concentration in Avignon. In England, in strange and almost sinister procession, the Archbishop of Canterbury, John Stratford, died in August 1348, his appointed successor died in May 1349, and the next appointee three months later, all three within a year. Despite such weird vagaries, prelates in general managed to sustain a higher survival rate than the lesser clergy. Among bishops the deaths have been estimated at about one in twenty. The loss of priests, even if many avoided their fearful duty of attending the dying, was about the same as among the population as a whole.

Government officials, whose loss contributed to the general chaos, found, on the whole, no special shelter. In Siena four of the nine members of the governing oligarchy died, in France one-third of the royal notaries, in Bristol 15 out of the 52 members of the Town Council or almost one third. Tax-collecting obviously suffered, with the result that Philip VI was unable to collect more than a fraction of the subsidy granted him by the Estates in the winter of 1347–48.

Lawlessness and debauchery accompanied the plague as they had during the great plague of Athens of 430 B.C., when according to Thucydides, men grew bold in the indulgence of pleasure: "For seeing how the rich died in a moment and those who had nothing immediately inherited their property, they reflected that life and riches were alike transitory and they resolved to enjoy themselves while they could."[39] Human behavior is timeless. When St. John had his vision of plague in Revelation, he knew from some experience or race memory that those who survived "repented not of the work of their hands. . . . Neither repented they of their murders, nor of their sorceries, nor of their fornication, nor of their thefts."

36 Physicians of Venice: Campbell, 98.
37 Simon de Covino: ibid., 31.
38 Guy de Chauliac, "I Was in Fear": q. Thompson, *Ec. and Soc.*, 379.
39 Thucydides: q. Crawford, 30–31.

Ignorance of the cause augmented the sense of horror. Of the real carriers, rats and fleas, the fourteenth century had no suspicion, perhaps because they were so familiar. Fleas, though a common household nuisance, are not once mentioned in contemporary plague writings, and rats only incidentally, although folklore commonly associated them with pestilence. The legend of the Pied Piper arose from an outbreak of 1284. The actual plague bacillus, *Pasturella pestis*, remained undiscovered for another 500 years. Living alternately in the stomach of the flea and the bloodstream of the rat who was the flea's host, the bacillus in its bubonic form was transferred to humans and animals by the bite of either rat or flea. It traveled by virtue of *Rattus rattus*, the small medieval black rat that lived on ships, as well as by the heavier brown or sewer rat. What precipitated the turn of the bacillus from innocuous to virulent form is unknown, but the occurrence is now believed to have taken place not in China but somewhere in central Asia and to have spread along the caravan routes. Chinese origin was a mistaken notion of the fourteenth century based on real but belated reports of huge death tolls in China from drought, famine, and pestilence which have since been traced to the 1330s, too soon to be responsible for the plague that appeared in India in 1346.[40]

The phantom enemy had no name. Called the Black Death only in later recurrences, it was known during the first epidemic simply as the Pestilence or Great Mortality. Reports from the East, swollen by fearful imaginings, told of strange tempests and "sheets of fire" mingled with huge hailstones that "slew almost all," or a "vast rain of fire" that burned up men, beasts, stones, trees, villages, and cities.[41] In another version, "foul blasts of wind" from the fires carried the infection to Europe "and now as some suspect it cometh round the seacoast." Accurate observation in this case could not make the mental jump to ships and rats because no idea of animal- or insect-borne contagion existed.

The earthquake was blamed for releasing sulfurous and foul fumes from   30
the earth's interior, or as evidence of a titanic struggle of planets and oceans causing waters to rise and vaporize until fish died in masses and corrupted the air. All these explanations had in common a factor of poisoned air, of miasmas and thick, stinking mists traced to every kind of natural or imagined agency from stagnant lakes to malign conjunction of the planets, from the hand of the Evil One to the wrath of God. Medical thinking, trapped in the theory of astral influences, stressed air as the communicator of disease, ignoring sanitation or visible carriers. The existence of two carriers confused the trail, the more so because the flea could live and travel independently

40 Chinese Origin: Although the idea of Chinese origin is still being repeated (e.g., by William H. McNeill, *Plagues and People*, New York, 1976, 161–63), it is disputed by L. Carrington Goodrich of the Association for Asian Studies, Columbia Univ., in letters to the author of 18 and 26 October 1973. Citing contemporary Chinese and other sources, he also quotes Dr. George A. Perera of the College of Physicians and Surgeons, an authority on communicable diseases, who "agrees with me that the spaces between epidemics in China (1334), Semirechyé (1338–9) and the Mediterranean basin (1347–9) seem too long for the first to be responsible for the last."
41 Reports from the East: Barnes, 432; Coulton, *Black Death*, 9–11.

of the rat for as long as a month and, if infected by the particularly viru-lent septicemic form of the bacillus, could infect humans without reinfecting itself from the rat. The simultaneous presence of the pneumonic form of the disease, which was indeed communicated through the air, blurred the prob-lem further.

The mystery of the contagion was "the most terrible of all the terrors," as an anonymous Flemish cleric in Avignon wrote to a correspondent in Bru-ges. Plagues had been known before, from the plague of Athens (believed to have been typhus) to the prolonged epidemic of the sixth century A.D., to the recurrence of sporadic outbreaks in the twelfth and thirteenth centuries, but they had left no accumulated store of understanding.[42] That the infec-tion came from contact with the sick or with their houses, clothes, or corpses was quickly observed but not comprehended. Gentile da Foligno, renowned physician of Perugia and doctor of medicine at the universities of Bologna and Padua, came close to respiratory infection when he surmised that poi-sonous material was "communicated by means of air breathed out and in."[43] Having no idea of microscopic carriers, he had to assume that the air was corrupted by planetary influences. Planets, however, could not explain the ongoing contagion. The agonized search for an answer gave rise to such theories as transference by sight. People fell ill, wrote Guy de Chauliac, not only by remaining with the sick but "even by looking at them." Three hundred years later Joshua Barnes, the seventeenth century biographer of Edward III, could write that the power of infection had entered into beams of light and "darted death from the eyes."

Doctors struggling with the evidence could not break away from the terms of astrology, to which they believed all human physiology was subject. Medicine was the one aspect of medieval life, perhaps because of its links with the Arabs, not shaped by Christian doctrine. Clerics detested astrology, but could not dislodge its influence. Guy de Chauliac, physician to three popes in succession, practiced in obedience to the zodiac. While his *Cirur-gia* was the major treatise on surgery of its time, while he understood the use of anesthesia made from the juice of opium, mandrake, or hemlock, he nevertheless prescribed bleeding and purgatives by the planets and divided chronic from acute diseases on the basis of one being under the rule of the sun and the other of the moon.

In October 1348 Philip VI asked the medical faculty of the University of Paris for a report on the affliction that seemed to threaten human survival.[44] With careful thesis, antithesis, and proofs, the doctors ascribed it to a triple conjunction of Saturn, Jupiter, and Mars in the fortieth degree of Aquarius said to have occurred on March 20, 1345. They acknowledged, however, effects "whose cause is hidden from even the most highly trained intellects."

---

42 Anonymous Flemish Cleric, "Most Terrible": His correspondence was edited in the form of a chronicle by De Smet, in *Recueil des chroniques de Flandres*, III, q. Ziegler, 22.
43 Gentile da Foligno, "Communicated by air": Campbell, 38.
44 Report of the University of Paris: Hecker, 51–53; Campbell, 15.

The Triumph of Death, *from a fifteenth-century Catalan fresco.*

The verdict of the masters of Paris became the official version. Borrowed, copied by scribes, carried abroad, translated from Latin into various vernaculars, it was everywhere accepted, even by the Arab physicians of Cordova and Granada, as the scientific if not the popular answer. Because of the terrible interest of the subject, the translations of the plague tracts stimulated use of national languages. In that one respect, life came from death.

To the people at large there could be but one explanation—the wrath of God. Planets might satisfy the learned doctors, but God was closer to the average man. A scourge so sweeping and unsparing without any visible cause could only be seen as Divine punishment upon mankind for its sins. It might even be God's terminal disappointment in his creature. Matteo Villani compared the plague to the Flood in ultimate purpose and believed he was recording "the extermination of mankind."[45] Efforts to appease Divine

---

[45] M. Villani, "Extermination of Mankind": q. Meiss, *Painting . . . After the Black Death*, 66.

wrath took many forms, as when the city of Rouen ordered that everything that could anger God, such as gambling, cursing, and drinking, must be stopped.[46] More general were the penitent processions authorized at first by the Pope, some lasting as long as three days, some attended by as many as 2,000, which everywhere accompanied the plague and helped to spread it.

Barefoot in sackcloth, sprinkled with ashes, weeping, praying, tearing their hair, carrying candles and relics, sometimes with ropes around their necks or beating themselves with whips, the penitents wound through the streets, imploring the mercy of the Virgin and saints at their shrines. In a vivid illustration for the *Très Riches Heures* of the Duc de Berry, the Pope is shown in a penitent procession attended by four cardinals in scarlet from hat to hem. He raises both arms in supplication to the angel on top of the Castel Sant'Angelo, while white-robed priests bearing banners and relics in golden cases turn to look as one of their number, stricken by the plague, falls to the ground, his face contorted with anxiety. In the rear, a gray-clad monk falls beside another victim already on the ground as the townspeople gaze in horror. (Nominally the illustration represents a sixth century plague in the time of Pope Gregory the Great, but as medieval artists made no distinction between past and present, the scene is shown as the artist would have seen it in the fourteenth century.) When it became evident that these processions were sources of infection, Clement VI had to prohibit them.

In Messina, where the plague first appeared, the people begged the Archbishop of neighboring Catania to lend them the relics of St. Agatha. When the Catanians refused to let the relics go, the Archbishop dipped them in holy water and took the water himself to Messina, where he carried it in a procession with prayers and litanies through the streets. The demonic, which shared the medieval cosmos with God, appeared as "demons in the shape of dogs" to terrify the people.[47] "A black dog with a drawn sword in his paws appeared among them, gnashing his teeth and rushing upon them and breaking all the silver vessels and lamps and candlesticks on the altars and casting them hither and thither. . . . So the people of Messina, terrified by this prodigious vision, were all strangely overcome by fear."

The apparent absence of earthly cause gave the plague a supernatural and sinister quality. Scandinavians believed that a Pest Maiden emerged from the mouth of the dead in the form of a blue flame and flew through the air to infect the next house.[48] In Lithuania the Maiden was said to wave a red scarf through the door or window to let in the pest. One brave man, according to legend, deliberately waited at his open window with drawn sword and, at the fluttering of the scarf, chopped off the hand. He died of his deed, but his village was spared and the scarf long preserved as a relic in the local church.

---

46 Rouen Prohibits Gambling: Nohl, 74.
47 At Messina, Demons Like Dogs: Coulton, *Black Death*, 22–27.
48 Pest Maiden: Ziegler, 85.

Beyond demons and superstition the final hand was God's. The Pope acknowledged it in a Bull[49] of September 1348, speaking of the "pestilence with which God is afflicting the Christian people." To the Emperor John Cantacuzene it was manifest that a malady of such horrors, stenches, and agonies, and especially one bringing the dismal despair that settled upon its victims before they died, was not a plague "natural" to mankind but "a chastisement from Heaven."[50] To Piers Plowman "these pestilences were for pure sin."[51]

The general acceptance of this view created an expanded sense of guilt, for if the plague were punishment there had to be terrible sin to have occasioned it. What sins were on the fourteenth century conscience? Primarily greed, the sin of avarice, followed by usury, worldliness, adultery, blasphemy, falsehood, luxury, irreligion. Giovanni Villani, attempting to account for the cascade of calamity that had fallen upon Florence, concluded that it was retribution for the sins of avarice and usury that oppressed the poor. Pity and anger about the condition of the poor, especially victimization of the peasantry in war, was often expressed by writers of the time and was certainly on the conscience of the century. Beneath it all was the daily condition of medieval life, in which hardly an act or thought, sexual, mercantile, or military, did not contravene the dictates of the Church. Mere failure to fast or attend mass was sin. The result was an underground lake of guilt in the soul that the plague now tapped.

That the mortality was accepted as God's punishment may explain in 40
part the vacuum of comment that followed the Black Death. An investigator has noticed that in the archives of Périgord references to the war are innumerable, to the plague few. Froissart mentions the great death but once, Chaucer gives it barely a glance. Divine anger so great that it contemplated the extermination of man did not bear close examination.

BIBLIOGRAPHY

L'Art de verifier les dates des faits historiques, par un Religieux de la Congregation de
    St. Maur, vol. XII. Paris, 1818.
Barnes, Joshua, *The History of Edward III.* Cambridge, 1688.
Bishop, *Petrarch's Brother,* 273.
Campbell, Anna M., *The Black Death and Men of Learning.* Columbia University Press,
    1931.
Cazelles, "On Youth," *Peste.*
Chronicle of Jean de Venette. Trans. Jean Birdsall. Ed. Richard A. Newhall. Columbia
    University Press, 1853.
Crawford, Raymond, *Plague and Pestilence in Literature and Art.* Oxford, 1914.
Coulton, G. G., *The Black Death.* London, 1929.

---

49 **Bull:** A formal papal document. — EDS.
50 Cantacuzene: Barnes, 435.
51 Piers Plowman, "Pure Sin": B text, V, 13.

Deaux, George, *The Black Death*, 1347. London, 1969.

Denifle, Henri, *La Désolation des églises, monastères et hôpitaux en France pendant la guerre de cent ans*, vol. I. Paris, 1899.

Gasquet, Francis Aidan, Abbot, *The Black Death of 1348 and 1349*, 2nd ed. London, 1908.

Grandes Chroniques de France, vol. VI (to 1380). Ed. Paulin Paris. Paris, 1838.

Hecker, J. F. C., *The Epidemics of the Middle Ages*. London, 1844.

Meiss, Millard, *Painting in Florence and Siena After the Black Death*. Princeton, 1951.

Nohl, Johannes, *The Black Death: A Chronicle of the Plague Compiled from Contemporary Sources*. Trans. C. H. Clarke. London, 1971.

Renouard, *Givry Parish Register*, 111.

Saltmarsh, John, "Plague and Economic Decline in England in the Latter Middle Ages," *Cambridge Historical Journal*, vol. VII, no. 1, 1941.

Schevill, Ferdinand, *History of Florence*. New York, 1961.

Snell, Frederick, *The Fourteenth Century*. Edinburgh, 1899.

Thompson, James Westfall, *Economic and Social History of Europe in the Later Middle Ages*. New York, 1931.

Ziegler, Philip, *The Black Death*. New York, 1969. (The best modern study.)

The Reader's Presence

1. History is a form of story. Which elements of Tuchman's account seem to pertain to pure fact and which to storytelling? Events are related in an objective tone. Is the writer's approval or disapproval ever evident? If so, where and in what ways?

2. This piece is drawn from a book titled *A Distant Mirror: The Calamitous 14th Century*. In what ways does Tuchman's account suggest that fourteenth-century behaviors reflect our behaviors today?

3. At times Tuchman recounts history in the aggregate; at times she traces history through a specific figure. Find a few instances of this latter technique. Why might she have chosen to augment the general with the particular and vice versa? What is the effect of this technique on the reader?

4. **CONNECTIONS:** "Ignorance of the cause augmented the sense of horror," Tuchman writes of the fourteenth-century plague (paragraph 28), but her statement can be taken as universally true. Use Tuchman's insight to sharpen your perception of the emotions expressed in Michihiko Hachiya's journal (from *Hiroshima Diary*, page 107) and in Don DeLillo's essay ("In the Ruins of the Future," page 355). How does each of these writers respond to problems of unspeakable horror? How do their approaches to narrating disaster compare?

Sherry Turkle

How Computers Change the Way We Think

SHERRY TURKLE (b. 1948) is Abby Rockefeller Mauzé Professor of the Social Studies of Science and Technology at the Massachusetts Institute of Technology. She is also the founder and current director of the MIT Initiative on Technology and Self, a research and education center concerned with the "subjective side of technology" and focused on the way techno-logical change—particularly computers and the Internet—affects humans. A clinical psycholo-gist, she has published a number of books, including *The Second Self: Computers and the Human Spirit* (1984), *Psychoanalytic Politics: Jacques Lacan and Freud's French Revolution* (1992), and *Life on the Screen: Identity in the Age of the Internet* (1995). Turkle has edited several books of essays, including *Evocative Objects: Things We Think With* (2007), which describes the power of objects—a cello, a computer, an apple—to evoke emotion and thought, and *Falling for Science: Objects in Mind* (2008). Her latest book, *Alone Together: Why We Expect More from Technology and Less from Each Other* (2011), explores how social-networking tools like Facebook simultaneously connect and isolate us.

> Sherry Turkle's latest book, *Alone Together*, explores how social-networking tools like Facebook simultaneously connect and isolate us.

Turkle sees computer-mediated reality as having the potential "to create a kind of crisis about the simulated and the real. The notion of what it is to live in a culture of simula-tion—how much of that counts as real experience and how much of that is discounted—is going to become more and more in the forefront of what people think and talk about, because so much experience is going to be about not being there." Her piece "How Comput-ers Change the Way We Think" appeared in the *Chronicle of Higher Education* in 2004.

THE TOOLS WE USE to think change the ways in which we think. The invention of written language brought about a radical shift in how we process, organize, store, and transmit representations of the world. Although writing remains our primary information technology, today when we think about the impact of technology on our habits of mind, we think primarily of the computer.

My first encounters with how computers change the way we think came soon after I joined the faculty at the Massachusetts Institute of Technology in the late 1970s, at the end of the era of the slide rule and the beginning of the era of the personal computer. At a lunch for new faculty members, several senior professors in engineering complained that the transition from slide rules to calculators had affected their students' ability to deal with issues of scale. When students used slide rules, they had to insert decimal points themselves. The professors insisted that that required students to maintain a mental sense of scale, whereas those who relied on calculators made frequent errors in orders of magnitude. Additionally, the students with calculators had lost their ability to do "back of the envelope" calculations, and with that, an intuitive feel for the material.

That same semester, I taught a course in the history of psychology. There, I experienced the impact of computational objects on students' ideas about their emotional lives. My class had read Freud's essay on slips of the tongue, with its famous first example: The chairman of a parliamentary session opens a meeting by declaring it closed. The students discussed how Freud interpreted such errors as revealing a person's mixed emotions. A computer-science major disagreed with Freud's approach. The mind, she argued, is a computer. And in a computational dictionary—like we have in the human mind—"closed" and "open" are designated by the same symbol, separated by a sign for opposition. "Closed" equals "minus open." To substitute "closed" for "open" does not require the notion of ambivalence or conflict.

"When the chairman made that substitution," she declared, "a bit was dropped; a minus sign was lost. There was a power surge. No problem."

The young woman turned a Freudian slip into an information-processing   5
error. An explanation in terms of meaning had become an explanation in terms of mechanism.

Such encounters turned me to the study of both the instrumental and the subjective sides of the nascent computer culture. As an ethnographer and psychologist, I began to study not only what the computer was doing *for* us, but what it was doing *to* us, including how it was changing the way we see ourselves, our sense of human identity.

In the 1980s, I surveyed the psychological effects of computational objects in everyday life—largely the unintended side effects of people's tendency to project thoughts and feelings onto their machines. In the 20 years since, computational objects have become more explicitly designed to have emotional and cognitive effects. And those "effects by design" will become even stronger in the decade to come. Machines are being designed to serve explicitly as companions, pets, and tutors. And they are introduced in school settings for the youngest children.

Today, starting in elementary school, students use e-mail, word processing, computer simulations, virtual communities, and PowerPoint software.

In the process, they are absorbing more than the content of what appears on their screens. They are learning new ways to think about what it means to know and understand.

What follows is a short and certainly not comprehensive list of areas where I see information technology encouraging changes in thinking. There can be no simple way of cataloging whether any particular change is good or bad. That is contested terrain. At every step we have to ask, as educators and citizens, whether current technology is leading us in directions that serve our human purposes. Such questions are not technical; they are social, moral, and political. For me, addressing that subjective side of computation is one of the more significant challenges for the next decade of information technology in higher education. Technology does not determine change, but it encourages us to take certain directions. If we make those directions clear, we can more easily exert human choice.

Thinking about Privacy. Today's college students are habituated to a world of online blogging, instant messaging, and Web browsing that leaves electronic traces. Yet they have had little experience with the right to privacy. Unlike past generations of Americans, who grew up with the notion that the privacy of their mail was sacrosanct, our children are accustomed to electronic surveillance as part of their daily lives.

I have colleagues who feel that the increased incursions on privacy have put the topic more in the news, and that this is a positive change. But middle-school and high-school students tend to be willing to provide personal information online with no safeguards, and college students seem uninterested in violations of privacy and in increased governmental and commercial surveillance. Professors find that students do not understand that in a democracy, privacy is a right, not merely a privilege. In ten years, ideas about the relationship of privacy and government will require even more active pedagogy. (One might also hope that increased education about the kinds of silent surveillance that technology makes possible may inspire more active political engagement with the issue.)

Avatars or a Self? Chat rooms, role-playing games, and other technological venues offer us many different contexts for presenting ourselves online. Those possibilities are particularly important for adolescents because they offer what Erik Erikson[1] described as a moratorium, a time out or safe space for the personal experimentation that is so crucial for adolescent development. Our dangerous world—with crime, terrorism, drugs, and AIDS—offers little in the way of safe spaces. Online worlds can provide valuable spaces for identity play.

But some people who gain fluency in expressing multiple aspects of self may find it harder to develop authentic selves. Some children who write

---

[1] **Erik Erikson** (1902–1994): A Danish-German-American developmental psychologist and psychoanalyst. — EDS.

narratives for their screen avatars may grow up with too little experience of how to share their real feelings with other people. For those who are lonely yet afraid of intimacy, information technology has made it possible to have the illusion of companionship without the demands of friendship.

From Powerful Ideas to PowerPoint. In the 1970s and early 1980s, some educators wanted to make programming part of the regular curriculum for K–12 education. They argued that because information technology carries ideas, it might as well carry the most powerful ideas that computer science has to offer. It is ironic that in most elementary schools today, the ideas being carried by information technology are not ideas from computer science like procedural thinking, but more likely to be those embedded in productivity tools like PowerPoint presentation software.

PowerPoint does more than provide a way of transmitting content. It 15 carries its own way of thinking, its own aesthetic—which not surprisingly shows up in the aesthetic of college freshmen. In that aesthetic, presentation becomes its own powerful idea.

To be sure, the software cannot be blamed for lower intellectual standards. Misuse of the former is as much a symptom as a cause of the latter. Indeed, the culture in which our children are raised is increasingly a culture of presentation, a corporate culture in which appearance is often more important than reality. In contemporary political discourse, the bar has also been lowered. Use of rhetorical devices at the expense of cogent argument regularly goes without notice. But it is precisely because standards of intellectual rigor outside the educational sphere have fallen that educators must attend to how we use, and when we introduce, software that has been designed to simplify the organization and processing of information.

In *The Cognitive Style of PowerPoint* (Graphics Press, 2003), Edward R. Tufte suggests that PowerPoint equates bulleting with clear thinking. It does not teach students to begin a discussion or construct a narrative. It encourages presentation, not conversation. Of course, in the hands of a master teacher, a PowerPoint presentation with few words and powerful images can serve as the jumping-off point for a brilliant lecture. But in the hands of elementary-school students, often introduced to PowerPoint in the third grade, and often infatuated with its swooshing sounds, animated icons, and flashing text, a slide show is more likely to close down debate than open it up.

Developed to serve the needs of the corporate boardroom, the software is designed to convey absolute authority. Teachers used to tell students that clear exposition depended on clear outlining, but presentation software has fetishized the outline at the expense of the content.

Narrative, the exposition of content, takes time. PowerPoint, like so much in the computer culture, speeds up the pace.

Word Processing vs. Thinking. The catalog for the Vermont Coun- 20 try Store advertises a manual typewriter, which the advertising copy says "moves at a pace that allows time to compose your thoughts." As many of us know, it is possible to manipulate text on a computer screen and see how it looks faster than we can think about what the words mean.

Word processing has its own complex psychology. From a pedagogical point of view, it can make dedicated students into better writers because it allows them to revise text, rearrange paragraphs, and experiment with the tone and shape of an essay. Few professional writers would part with their computers; some claim that they simply cannot think without their hands on the keyboard. Yet the ability to quickly fill the page, to see it before you can think it, can make bad writers even worse.

A seventh grader once told me that the typewriter she found in her mother's attic is "cool because you have to type each letter by itself. You have to know what you are doing in advance or it comes out a mess." The idea of thinking ahead has become exotic.

Taking Things at Interface Value. We expect software to be easy to use, and we assume that we don't have to know how a computer works. In the early 1980s, most computer users who spoke of transparency meant that, as with any other machine, you could "open the hood" and poke around. But only a few years later, Macintosh users began to use the term when they talked about seeing their documents and programs represented by attractive and easy-to-interpret icons. They were referring to an ability to make things work without needing to go below the screen surface. Paradoxically, it was the screen's opacity that permitted that kind of transparency. Today, when people say that something is transparent, they mean that they can see how to make it work, not that they know how it works. In other words, transparency means epistemic opacity.

The people who built or bought the first generation of personal computers understood them down to the bits and bytes. The next generation of operating systems were more complex, but they still invited that old-time reductive understanding. Contemporary information technology encourages different habits of mind. Today's college students are already used to taking things at (inter)face value; their successors in 2014 will be even less accustomed to probing below the surface.

Simulation and Its Discontents. Some thinkers argue that the new opacity is empowering, enabling anyone to use the most sophisticated technological tools and to experiment with simulation in complex and creative ways. But it is also true that our tools carry the message that they are beyond our understanding. It is possible that in daily life, epistemic opacity can lead to passivity.   25

I first became aware of that possibility in the early 1990s, when the first generation of complex simulation games were introduced and immediately became popular for home as well as school use. SimLife teaches the principles of evolution by getting children involved in the development of complex ecosystems; in that sense it is an extraordinary learning tool. During one session in which I played SimLife with Tim, a 13-year-old, the screen before us flashed a message: "Your orgot is being eaten up." "What's an orgot?" I asked. Tim didn't know. "I just ignore that," he said confidently. "You don't need to know that kind of stuff to play."

For me, that story serves as a cautionary tale. Computer simulations enable their users to think about complex phenomena as dynamic, evolving systems. But they also accustom us to manipulating systems whose core assumptions we may not understand and that may not be true.

We live in a culture of simulation. Our games, our economic and political systems, and the ways architects design buildings, chemists envisage molecules, and surgeons perform operations all use simulation technology. In ten years the degree to which simulations are embedded in every area of life will have increased exponentially. We need to develop a new form of media literacy: readership skills for the culture of simulation.

We come to written text with habits of readership based on centuries of civilization. At the very least, we have learned to begin with the journalist's traditional questions: who, what, when, where, why, and how. Who wrote these words, what is their message, why were they written, and how are they situated in time and place, politically and socially? A central project for higher education during the next ten years should be creating programs in information-technology literacy, with the goal of teaching students to interrogate simulations in much the same spirit, challenging their built-in assumptions.

Despite the ever-increasing complexity of software, most computer environments put users in worlds based on constrained choices. In other words, immersion in programmed worlds puts us in reassuring environments where the rules are clear. For example, when you play a video game, you often go through a series of frightening situations that you escape by mastering the rules—you experience life as a reassuring dichotomy of scary and safe. Children grow up in a culture of video games, action films, fantasy epics, and computer programs that all rely on that familiar scenario of almost losing but then regaining total mastery: There is danger. It is mastered. A still-more-powerful monster appears. It is subdued. Scary. Safe.

Yet in the real world, we have never had a greater need to work our way out of binary assumptions. In the decade ahead, we need to rebuild the culture around information technology. In that new sociotechnical culture, assumptions about the nature of mastery would be less absolute. The new culture would make it easier, not more difficult, to consider life in shades of gray, to see moral dilemmas in terms other than a battle between Good and Evil. For never has our world been more complex, hybridized, and global. Never have we so needed to have many contradictory thoughts and feelings at the same time. Our tools must help us accomplish that, not fight against us.

Information technology is identity technology. Embedding it in a culture that supports democracy, freedom of expression, tolerance, diversity, and complexity of opinion is one of the next decade's greatest challenges. We cannot afford to fail.

When I first began studying the computer culture, a small breed of highly trained technologists thought of themselves as "computer people." That is no longer the case. If we take the computer as a carrier of a way of knowing, a way of seeing the world and our place in it, we are all computer people now. ■

The Reader's Presence

1. Reread the example that Turkle uses to open her essay. Does the young woman's reinterpretation of a Freudian slip show that computers can change the way we think? Does it show a change in the way we think of ourselves? Why or why not?

2. Turkle advocates critical dialogue about the consequences of technology, emphasizing that these "questions are not technical; they are social, moral, and political" (paragraph 9). What are the social, moral, and political consequences that Turkle speaks of? Which concern her most and why? Do you share her concerns? Why or why not?

3. **CONNECTIONS:** What is Turkle's attitude toward the changes the technology has produced? To what extent does she present those changes uncritically, or does she place value on certain ways of thinking and being? Compare and contrast Turkle's essay to Nicholas Carr's essay "Is Google Making Us Stupid?" (page 633). How do these two writers differ in their responses to the changes that technology has engendered? In what specific ways are the views of these writers toward technology similar? Which essay do you find more engaging and convincing? Explain why.

William Speed Weed

106 SCIENCE CLAIMS AND A TRUCKFUL OF BALONEY

WILLIAM SPEED WEED (b. 1971) graduated from Yale University in 1993. A science writer, an essayist, and a pop-culture critic, he has been a frequent contributor and columnist for *GQ*, *Salon*, *Discover*, the *Washington Monthly*, *Current Science*, *Mother Jones*, and *Reader's Digest*, among others. Two of his essays were selected for the anthology *Best American Science and Nature Writing* for the years 2003 and 2005: "The Very Best Telescope," originally published in *Discover*, and "106 Science Claims and a Truckful of Baloney," which was published in *Popular Science* in 2005. Described in the *Washington Monthly* as "a science writer with a sly wit," Weed often questions conventional wisdom and blind cultural assumptions. For this essay, he recorded the many scientific claims he came across on product labels in stores, in print ads, in the media, and on the Internet. He then enlisted a number of experts to help him evaluate the "truckful of baloney" that he had collected. Weed summarizes the twenty-nine "science claims" in the endnotes to this essay (pages 612–616).

6:00 A.M.

I'M NOT UP FIVE MINUTES, and it looks like I'll get my RDA* of science claims at breakfast. Cheerios "can reduce your cholesterol."[1] My milk derives from a dairy whose cows "graze freely on lush natural pastures as nature intended."[2] My Concord Foods soy shake is "fat-free" and a "good source of fresh fruit."[3]

Then it's off to the e-mail inbox for some fresh scientific-sounding morning spam: A miracle pill guarantees I will "gain 3+ full inches in length."[4] A second promises me "huge breasts overnight."[5] A third will make me "look 20 years younger."[6] I wonder what I'd look like if I took all three.

In my first waking minutes of October 15, I wrote down thirteen scientific claims. Only one, for Cheerios, had any reasonable science behind it. According to the National Science Board's 2002 study *Science and Engineering Indicators*, only one-third of Americans can "adequately explain what it means to study something scientifically." Which presumably leaves those who would exploit scientific claims with two suckers born every three minutes. As a nation, we are easy prey to the pseudoscientific, and the National Science Board survey blames education and the media for this.

But how much "science" is the average American fed in a day, and how nutritious is it? I did not actively search through scientific journals, because the average American probably doesn't do that. Rather, I simply noted every claim to scientific veracity thrust upon me through radio, television, the Internet, product packaging, billboards, and a light read of the daily paper. By bedtime I had encountered more than one hundred (not all of which are detailed here, you'll be relieved to know; I've included a representative assortment). That's one science claim every ten minutes, on average.

The majority of the claims came from advertisers. Advertisers probably   5 feed more science to Americans than anyone else, which is not surprising since they are in the business of making claims, and the same NSB study cited above noted that Americans are all ears about science: 90 percent of

---

** **RDA:** The Recommended Dietary Allowance is the daily dietary intake level of a nutrient considered to be sufficient to meet the requirements of nearly all healthy individuals in each life-stage. — EDS.*

respondents were moderately or very interested in new scientific discoveries. Companies have a legal obligation to tell the truth (not always obeyed, of course; promising "3+ full inches" would seem to be a heartbreaking lie), but they have a marketing imperative to put the best possible spin on it. The marketing imperative is, of course, antithetical to the scientific method. Science proceeds slowly, painfully, and with considerable uncertainty: the cholesterol–heart disease connection has been researched for more than fifty years, and it's still not completely understood. In simplest terms, science is gray. Science in advertising wears makeup—it sometimes looks twenty years younger and has huge breasts and a, well, you get the picture. Very few of the one hundred claims I encountered proved completely true. A good number were patently false.

7:15 A.M.

The *New York Times* features a story on the Chinese astronaut's launch aboard the *Shenzhou 5* (which means "Divine Vessel") and a report that centenarians "have larger than average cholesterol-carrying molecules," which keep their arteries clear and healthy.[7]

On the radio, an ad for DuPont celebrates that "the fundamental understanding of life is something that didn't exist 15 years ago."[8] I Web surf, starting with MSN, where a banner ad tells me Pletal is my "claudication solution"[9]—whatever that means. Just a click away, WebMD reports "recommondations for breast cancer screening" from a panel of experts at the Cleveland Clinic: all women should have an annual mammogram starting at age forty.[10]

Just as I'm about to turn off the radio, Don Imus shoots a skeptical arrow at the Chinese astronaut: "How do we know those lying bastards got the guy up in the air?"

The breast cancer screening advice I clicked through to is a good example of how media—even careful media—simplify complex issues in order to give advice. Wait! I'm not allowed to call it *advice* because the site's legal disclaimer states that WebMD "does not provide medical advice." Whether or not "recommendations" and "advice" are synonyms is a moot point: in this case, the gray was rendered in black and white. Concerning whether women should have annual mammograms starting at age forty or (as some experts believe) at age fifty, the WebMD site acknowledges that "not all medical institutions and advocacy groups agree," but then comes down firmly on the age-forty standard. Further clicking does not easily reveal the full degree to which this recommendation remains controversial.

Oddly, the Imus joke about the Chinese astronaut embodied the sort of attitude Americans could profit from in a world of promiscuous science claims. His "How do we know?" is a demand for fundamental evidence. (To

10

answer the question: the Chinese launch and return were well documented, although some of the video was delayed by the Chinese government until it knew the taikonaut was safe on the ground.)

9:30 A.M.

Before I log off, I note an Atkins banner on my MSN homepage asking me to fill in my height and weight. I lie, typing in that I'm a 5-foot-10, 135-pound, 25-year-old female. When I punch "enter," the Web site tells me I'm perfectly healthy but pushes me to buy anyway. "Your low-carb meal plan will enable you to enjoy a lifetime of weight management."[11]

I throw some clothes on my 6-foot, 185-pound body and head for the grocery store. This place is a feast for a science-claim junkie. There's some Atkins low-carb bread, designed to contain as little as possible of the thing bread is famous for. There's a sign over the bread aisle: "Go for the grains! Bread and other grain foods are the foundation of healthy eating."[12] Meanwhile, the Wegmans brand bread claims to be "bromate-free."[13] Further along, a Perdue chicken assures me it's "all natural!"[14] and a bag of Diamond walnuts has a little flag saying "omega-3!"[15] A package of yeast brags that it's "gluten-free."[16] Puzzlingly, a nearby display suggests that gunky, white coconut oil may be a diet aid: a 2003 weekly magazine article conveniently posted over the bottles announces, "University of Colorado research has found coconut oil can increase your calorie-burning-power by up to 50%."[17]

"People in a grocery store assume the government is scrutinizing the claims products make, so if they're on the label, they must be accurate and important," notes William Hallman, a psychologist at the Food Policy Institute at Rutgers University. Of course, it's more complicated than that. The assumption of accuracy is correct, but the assumption of importance is not. Both Federal Trade Commission and FDA regulations require truthfulness on packages. Yes, the chicken is chicken. But, Hallman continues, "while the claim may be factually correct, the actual health benefits may lack practical significance."

Why make claims that "lack practical significance"? Because, says Hallman, "we jump to the conclusion that the benefits are substantial." Scientific language cues the consumer to take an insignificant claim and provide a significant health benefit *on the company's behalf*. "The beauty of this is that the manufacturer doesn't have to make the claim of benefits explicit." Doesn't have to, and, for the most part, couldn't. We do this because we generally believe science is good for us. The National Science Board survey found that although 90 percent of Americans consider themselves "interested" in science, only 15 percent consider themselves well informed. Ninety percent interested, 15 percent informed: That's a gap any marketing MBA could drive a truck of baloney through.

‖‖

12:45 P.M.

Over lunch at the deli, my friend Charles mourns that neither of us orders a   15
beer: "They're finding out alcohol is good for you,"[18] he says. On the car ride
home, I hear a radio ad for eHarmony, the dating service that promises to
find me a scientifically matched wife.[19] Near my exit, there's a billboard ad:
"Is breast cancer's most avoidable risk factor elective abortion?"[20]

   When I get home, I turn on the radio and hear the angry voice of Roger
Hedgecock, the man sitting in for Rush Limbaugh, who is in rehab for drug
addiction. "No U.S. animal species are falling extinct,"[21] he says.

   Soon I'm off to the gym. I stop by the blood pressure reader and notice a
warning label: "Only a physician is qualified to interpret the significance of
blood pressure measurements." I am not a physician, so presumably I should
note the measurements but not interpret them.

   I'm offered a blood pressure machine but warned not to use the information. Science for the science-ignorant is talismanic. Roger Hedgecock hurls
out claims so believers will believe. The billboard binds abortion to breast
cancer with the scientific-sounding term "risk factor," giving an ethical
argument—concerning the right to life—the halo of science.

   This is the nub of the power of science claims in advertising and in slip-
shod media: science claims give permission to believe, even if the science
itself, when examined, provides no such encouragement.

3:45 P.M.

CNN is on over the stationary bike at the gym. An FDA panel recommends   20
lifting the ban on silicone breast implants.[22] In the shower afterward, I note
that my conditioner "contains essential nucleic acids for pH 5.5 balance."[23]
I brew in my travel mug some AllGoode-brand DigestibiliTea, containing
fennel, which "promotes relaxation of the smooth muscles of the digestive
tract." At the bottom of the package, there's a little disclaimer that reads:
"The Food and Drug Administration has not evaluated these statements. This
product is not intended to diagnose, treat, cure, or prevent any disease."[24]

   At the GNC store, I spot that disclaimer on almost every product. It's
even on a yellow shelf placard, underneath a pronouncement that "amino
acids are the building blocks of proteins." Hmmm. Why the disclaimer?
Amino acids *are* the building blocks of proteins, the same way letters are the
building blocks of words. The FDA certainly knows this.

   Curious about a radio ad that I hear on the drive home, I call up a company called CortiSlim, whose product, it claims, reduces levels of the stress
hormone cortisol and thereby helps you lose weight.

   Me: "So how does CortiSlim work to reduce cortisol?" Seller: "It
decreases the level of cortisol in your body, just cancels it all out."[25] Me:
"OK, but *how* does it do that?" Seller: "CortiSlim evaporates it and absorbs

it and decreases it and cuts it down. So I want to tell you about a 'buy two get one free' special we're running this week."

Eager to establish its scientific credentials, CortiSlim's Web site features MRI images of fat deposits along with a bold motto: "The new science in weight loss." In the site's nether regions, however, you'll find the FDA disclaimer. Let's be clear: Wherever you see this disclaimer, it signals that you have no reason to believe that there will be "practical significance" to using a product. The people wearing lab coats in the promo pics? They can be actors. Reported data from scientific studies? Could have been invented by someone who failed high school biology. Claims of health benefits? Well, you get the idea.

A 1994 federal law took the teeth out of the FDA's dietary supplement regulations, which cover products that are neither foods nor drugs, such as CortiSlim and AllGoode teas. The FDA can yank a product off the shelves if it proves to be harmful (as it did to ephedra) and it can prohibit companies from claiming to cure specific diseases. AllGoode, therefore, can't be promoted as a cure to inflammatory bowel disease. But it can be sold to promote digestion, stimulate the digestive tract, maintain immune system balance—any medical-sounding thing that stimulates sales. Sellers of so-called "herbal Viagra alternatives" can imply the same benefits provided by heavily researched and FDA-approved pharmaceuticals—indeed, can imply the extra natural goodness of herbal drug alternatives—without reference to scientific research. Companies with names like Medicures can hawk "100% All Natural Doctor-Approved" pills, with names like Virility-Rx, which are neither medical nor, by their own disclaimered admission, cures.

6:30 P.M.

I drop by to visit my friends Mike and Jolynn, and they serve BLTs in front of the evening news. Tom Brokaw introduces the case of Terri Schiavo, a woman in a coma in Florida whose husband wants to pull the plug on her. "A medical dilemma wrapped in a family battle," he calls it.[26] A drug ad tells me that Lipitor reduces cholesterol[27] (just like Cheerios), although a disclaimer (not found on the Cheerios box) flashes on the screen: "Lipitor has not been shown to prevent heart disease or heart attacks." On a home shopping channel, a lady peddling skin cream tells me, "You know the benefits of vitamin A. Don't you want to use it on your skin?"[28] Actually, I don't know the benefits, and she never tells me.

Later, just before saying my good nights and heading home, I see a promo for *George of the Jungle 2*: George slams into a tree and Ape, his trusty gorilla butler, shakes his head: "And they say humans are more evolved."[29]

So the 106th and last item in my day of scientific-claim collecting turns out to be a joke. Fitting, perhaps, that it came from an actor dressed in a gorilla suit.

Psychologist William Hallman says that people really do learn their science from science claims, which is rather like learning the fundamentals of automobile engineering from a used-car salesman. "If you ask people, 'When you clean your kitchen, how clean do you need to get it to be safe?'" he says, "they respond: 'I need to clean 99.9 percent of germs on contact'—repeating the claims of antibacterial cleansers."

Or, you might say, aping them.   30

6:00 A.M.

1. CHEERIOS: **Fair enough. Good for sales.** In 1999 the FDA[*] allowed marketers to make unprecedented claims about the power of whole-grain foods to cut heart disease, based on its review of scientific research. General Mills, meanwhile, has funded Cheerios-specific research, and most recently published a 2003 study showing that if women eat two bowls a day, they can reduce their total cholesterol by 4 percent. A press release (not the study itself) concludes that Cheerios could save 24,000 lives per year, "if everybody in America ate Cheerios as recommended." Interesting extrapolation: 280 million Americans times 2 bowls times 365 days equals 204 billion bowls of Cheerios per year. Healthy indeed.

2. COWS: **Specious.** I'm happy for the cows—nature did evolve cows that wandered around and ate grass instead of the more efficient corn-based gruel some commercial dairies use. But "natural" is one of the most slippery words in marketing. Nature never "intended" humans to drink cow milk or to place cattle on pasture land in upstate New York. Cows descend from the wild aurochs, a now extinct native of Persia, and were bred and imported by humans who made pastures by clear-cutting the thick forests that had blanketed this land for eons.

3. SOY SHAKE: **Misleading.** The packaged powder contains no fresh fruit. The fruit is a banana you buy separately. Bananas contain fat, though not a lot. Only the powder is fat-free, and only the prepared shake has fresh fruit.

4. 3+ FULL INCHES: **Bogus.** Drugs can't extend penis length (except, of course, temporarily).

5. BREASTS: **Equally bogus.** No pill can enlarge breasts overnight.   35

6. YOUNGER: **Even more bogus.** No pill can make someone look twenty years younger. This pill further claims to increase emotional stability by 67 percent. Such pseudoscientific precision increases the absurdity of the claim by at least 68 percent.

---

[*]**FDA:** The U.S. Food and Drug Administration, an agency of the U.S. Department of Health and Human Services and responsible for regulating most types of food, dietary supplements, drugs, vaccines, biological medical products, blood products, medical devices, radiation-emitting devices, veterinary products, and cosmetics. — EDS.

7:15 A.M.

7. CENTENARIANS: **Well reported.** The science behind this story was published in the *Journal of the American Medical Association*, which, of course, doesn't guarantee its truth but does mean it has been peer-reviewed: vetted. The *Times* covered the study's method (comparing centenarians and their children to a control group of sixty- and seventy-year-olds); pointed out the unknowns, such as genetic links and the effect on "good cholesterol"; and cautioned against overemphasizing the significance of the findings.

8. FUNDAMENTAL UNDERSTANDING OF LIFE: **Puffed up.** This corporate-identity ad, promoting DuPont and the New York Stock Exchange, vaguely suggests that genetics has profoundly deepened our understanding of life. Which of course it has. But the ring of finality here is meaningless. The life process is far from decoded.

9. CLAUDICATION: **Oversold.** The prescription drug Pletal can alleviate the limping (in other words, claudication) and pain old people get from arterial disease. However, Pletal does not work for everyone, and, as a potential patient learns on the company's Web site, it can kill patients with congestive heart failure. "Your claudication solution" is what happens when complex therapies are reduced to slogans; it implies the drug will help everyone who needs it. No drug works for everyone.

10. MAMMOGRAM: **Incomplete and potentially dangerous.** Hypo- 40 thetically, if all women got annual mammograms starting at age twenty, we would catch even more breast cancers early. Doctors don't recommend doing so because we'd get too many false positives—resulting in a rash of unnecessary biopsies and worry, even lumpectomies. The critical public health question is: When does the risk of cancer outweigh the harm of false positives? While many doctors agree with the age-forty recommendation, others think forty is still too young and that fifty is the right *average* age. The most important guidelines, they say, are a woman's family medical history and her personal tolerance for risk.

9:30 A.M.

11. LOW-CARB PLAN: **Blanket pitch.** A healthy, right-weight twenty-five-year-old woman needs a lifetime plan?

12. GO FOR THE GRAINS: **Reasonable.** Despite the renewed controversy about low-carb diets, the evidence is not definitive. Balanced diet, calorie control, and exercise are still regarded as the best way to combat obesity. The FDA is reviewing the Food Pyramid, but it's unlikely to replace it with a Meat and Fat Pyramid. University of Colorado physician and nutritionist Holly Wyatt says, "All these diets mess up the message, saying, 'It's carbs!' 'It's protein!' It's neither. Calories are what count."

13. BROMATE-FREE: **Voodoo use of chemical name.** Wegmans bread is indeed bromate-free, but it doesn't much matter. Some studies have shown that bromate, a dough enhancer, is a carcinogen if consumed in large amounts, though these findings are controversial. Bromate has never been found in baked breads at harmful levels. Most brands have stopped using bromate altogether.

14. ALL NATURAL: **Invokes a magic word.** "Natural" conjures up images of happy chickens prancing about a sunny barnyard under a wind-mill. All this claim really means, though—insofar as FDA regulators are con-cerned—is that the chicken is not made of plastic. Chickens labeled "all natural" may have been crammed by the thousands into tight pens, their claws and beaks clipped, and stuffed full of antibiotics they'd never find in that "natural" barnyard.

15. OMEGA-3: **Cryptic.** Omega-3 fatty acids are a form of fat under-represented in our diets, according to many nutritionists. All walnuts contain omega-3's, so the claim is accurate. But the message is reduced to code. Greek letter plus number equals "science-based," ergo good.

16. GLUTEN-FREE YEAST: **Duh.** Yeast is a fungus. Gluten is a product of plant protein. In evolutionary terms, yeast and gluten are as unrelated as a cow and an orange.

17. COCONUT OIL: **Fad.** Two public information officers at the Uni-versity of Colorado canvassed their scientific faculty, trying to find anyone who had done this research. No luck. The notion that a saturated fat boosts "calorie-burning power"—rather than increasing the number of calories to be burned—is problematic. Well-known studies have shown that satu-rated fats *increase* the risk of heart disease. Still, the rumor of coconut oil's "power" created a run on the stuff in 2003.

45

12:45 P.M.

18. ALCOHOL IS GOOD FOR YOU: **Yes, and it's bad for you.** A land-mark study that followed the drinking habits of nearly 90,000 male physi-cians showed that those who had one drink per day had significantly lower morbidity and mortality from diabetes, stroke, and heart disease. But people who drink excessively—and the definition of that is still debated—die at high rates from liver diseases, esophageal cancer, and car accidents.

19. eHARMONY: **Incomplete.** In the hot and heavy world of Web matchmaking, eHarmony distinguishes itself as, first, a service for the tradi-tional altar-bound and, second, scientific in its approach, taking data points on clients' levels of obstreperousness, submissiveness, and other character-istics. The company now says it has conducted an internal scientific study of its matchmaking results using a standard methodology that gives "clear indication that the eHarmony matching algorithm works." Reviewing eHar-mony's Web site, Arthur Aron, a professor of social psychology at the State University of New York at Stony Brook, notes that "it's true compatibility can

be measured, but what they're measuring accounts for only a small portion of what makes a successful marriage."

20. ABORTION: **False.** The National Cancer Institute reviewed many studies and concluded abortions do not increase risk of breast cancer.

21. EXTINCT: **Hogwash.** Tell that to one of the three remaining Hawaiian po'ouli birds; the po'ouli is just one of several Hawaiian birds at serious risk of extinction. Plenty of U.S. animals are endangered.

3:45 P.M.

22. BREAST IMPLANTS: **True.** The FDA panel did recommend lifting the ban, though the agency has since decided not to follow that recommendation.

23. CONDITIONER: **Sounds scientific!** Dermatologist Jerome Litt of Case Western Reserve University doesn't know what "essential nucleic acids for pH 5.5 balance" is supposed to mean in this phrase. "Any conditioner you like will work. They are all essentially the same."

24. FENNEL: **Unproven.** Fennel is a folk cure for indigestion (some folk cures, of course, have been scientifically proven to work). AllGoode did not respond to repeated requests for the science behind this claim. We searched PubMed and found one study on the subject that showed that fennel *stimulated* contractions of smooth muscle in guinea pigs and another that showed that fennel *relieved* smooth-muscle spasms in rats.

25. CANCELS OUT ALL THE CORTISOL: **Bogus.** Cortisol *is* a stress hormone—among other things, it regulates our fight-or-flight impulse—and has been weakly linked to one form of obesity. But "canceling out all cortisol would be disastrous," notes the University of Virginia endocrinologist Mary Vance. Perusing the ingredients listed on the company's Web site, she says: "You might as well eat tree bark." The CortiSlim salesperson had apparently not read the Web site, which says the product helps "control cortisol levels within a healthy range." The site recommends the product for "millions of Americans . . . Anybody who leads a stressful lifestyle and wants to lose weight." Its homepage features a strong warning to consumers—against buying bogus CortiSlim.

6:30 P.M.

26. SCHIAVO COMA: **Incomplete.** The report never gives us the details of the medical dilemma behind this big story. Without more science, the dispute is difficult to understand.

27. LIPITOR: **True.** Lipitor lowers cholesterol, and cholesterol reduction is associated with lowering the risk of heart disease. But it's so difficult to prove a direct connection between a cholesterol-lowering medication and the long-term incidence of heart disease that Lipitor still runs this disclaimer,

seven years after it hit the market. In contrast to the FDA's toothlessness with dietary supplements, the agency has the authority to ensure that all statements about prescription drugs are scientifically true. A Lipitor researcher predicted at press time that the disclaimer will be off the drug within a year because of new studies showing that its active ingredient does lower the risk of heart-disease mortality.

28. VITAMIN A: **Bogus.** Retinoic acid is the form of vitamin A used in prescription medications to rejuvenate skin. But according to the Mount Sinai dermatology professor Susan Bershad, the form of vitamin A used in creams "sold over the counter won't have the same effect."

29. EVOLVED: **Misguided.** This joke only works because of the common misconception that evolution is progressive and that humans are the "most evolved." Indiana University biologist Rudolph Raff cautions, "Evolution is not a ladder of progress." All species alive today are, each in its own way, equally evolved. Humans have evolved higher intelligence. Apes are better adapted for eating leaves and, in some species, swinging from trees.

The Reader's Presence

1. In a series of endnotes, Weed evaluates each of the "scientific claims" that compete for his attention. What are the advantages—and disadvantages—of his decision to present his evaluations in footnote form? What would be the impact on his essay if he had chosen to weave many, most, or all of these evaluations into the heart of his essay?

2. How would you characterize Weed's tone in recounting each of the "scientific" claims presented to him during the course of a single day? Does his tone remain consistent throughout his essay? If it changes, point to where and how it shifts. In what specific ways is the tone of his endnotes consistent with—or different from—that in the main body of his essay? Point to specific passages to validate your reading.

3. What explanation does Weed offer for the benefits to companies who use scientific language and claims in promoting their products? Pay particular attention to paragraphs 13 through 19. Which of these explanations do you find most convincing? Explain why. Choose an example drawn from Weed's essay and compare and contrast it to one drawn from the items you purchase for either breakfast or lunch. What similarities and differences do you notice? Comment on the metaphors Weed uses. Which do you think are most effective? Explain why. From what aspect(s) of daily experience does Weed draw the majority of his metaphors and analogies? How does he resist what he calls the "marketing imperative" (paragraph 5) in his own choices of figurative language and diction? What does he mean when he says: "Science for the science-ignorant is talismanic" (paragraph 18)?

4. **CONNECTIONS:** Weed's essay debunks most of the scientific language used in advertising. Compare and contrast the way Weed uses investigative techniques to those of such writers as Eric Schlosser in "Why McDonald's Fries Taste So Good" (page 558), James Fallows in "Throwing Like a Girl" (page 400), and Amy Cunningham in "Why Women Smile" (page 347). How does each writer engage an audience's attention, and how does each sustain that interest? Which writer does the most credible work of investigative reporting? Explain why.

Tom Wolfe

HOOKING UP

TOM WOLFE (b. 1931) grew up in Richmond, Virginia, and graduated from Washington and Lee University. He received his doctorate in American Studies from Yale University and began a career as a reporter, eventually writing for such papers as the *New York Herald Tribune* and the *Washington Post*. His writing has also appeared in *New York* magazine, *Harper's*, and *Esquire*, where he has been a contributing editor since 1977. Writer, journalist, and social and cultural critic, Wolfe continues to be an arbiter (and satirist) of American cultural trends. His books *The Kandy-Kolored Tangerine-Flake Streamline Baby* (1965), *The Electric Kool-Aid Acid Test* (1968), *The Pump House Gang* (1969), and *Radical Chic & Mau Mauing the Flak Catchers* (1970) were models of a flamboyant style known as "New Journalism." Wolfe's best-selling work of "extended" journalism, *The Right Stuff* (1979), won the American Book Award and National Book Critics Circle Award. His three novels, *The Bonfire of the Vanities* (1982), *A Man in Full* (1998),

> **"A novel of psychological depth without social depth isn't worth an awful lot because we are all individuals caught in an enormous web that consists of other people."**

and *I Am Charlotte Simmons* (2004), contain the same blend of well-researched documentary journalism, entertainment, and realistic detail as his nonfiction work. Wolfe received the 2003 *Chicago Tribune* Literary Prize for lifetime achievement.

Wolfe has argued, "A novel of psychological depth without social depth isn't worth an awful lot because we are all individuals caught in an enormous web that consists of other people. It is in the social setting that the psychological battles take place." "Hooking Up" is from Wolfe's 2000 book *Hooking Up: What Life Was Like at the Turn of the Second Millennium: An American's World*, a combination of fiction, memoir, and cultural and social observation.

BY THE YEAR 2000, the term "working class" had fallen into disuse in the United States, and "proletariat" was so obsolete it was known only to a few bitter old Marxist academics with wire hair sprouting out of their ears. The average electrician, air-conditioning mechanic, or burglar-alarm repairman lived a life that would have made the Sun King[1] blink. He spent

---

1 **the Sun King:** Louis XIV, king of France (1638–1715), known for his absolutism and ostentation. — EDS.

his vacations in Puerto Vallarta, Barbados, or St. Kitts. Before dinner he would be out on the terrace of some resort hotel with his third wife, wearing his Ricky Martin cane-cutter shirt open down to the sternum, the better to allow his gold chains to twinkle in his chest hairs. The two of them would have just ordered a round of Quibel sparkling water, from the state of West Virginia, because by 2000 the once-favored European sparkling waters Perrier and San Pellegrino seemed so tacky.

European labels no longer held even the slightest snob appeal except among people known as "intellectuals," whom we will visit in a moment. Our typical mechanic or tradesman took it for granted that things European were second-rate. Aside from three German luxury automobiles — the Mercedes-Benz, the BMW, and the Audi — he regarded European-manufactured goods as mediocre to shoddy. On his trips abroad, our electrician, like any American businessman, would go to superhuman lengths to avoid being treated in European hospitals, which struck him as little better than those in the Third World. He considered European hygiene so primitive that to receive an injection in a European clinic voluntarily was sheer madness.

Indirectly, subconsciously, his views perhaps had to do with the fact that his own country, the United States, was now the mightiest power on earth, as omnipotent as Macedon under Alexander the Great, Rome under Julius Caesar, Mongolia under Genghis Khan, Turkey under Mohammed II, or Britain under Queen Victoria. His country was so powerful, it had begun to invade or rain missiles upon small nations in Europe, Africa, Asia, and the Caribbean for no other reason than that their leaders were lording it over their subjects at home.

Our air-conditioning mechanic had probably never heard of Saint-Simon,[2] but he was fulfilling Saint-Simon's and the other nineteenth-century utopian socialists' dreams of a day when the ordinary workingman would have the political and personal freedom, the free time and the wherewithal to express himself in any way he saw fit and to unleash his full potential. Not only that, any ethnic or racial group — *any*, even recent refugees from a Latin country — could take over the government of any American city, if they had the votes and a modicum of organization. Americans could boast of a freedom as well as a power unparalleled in the history of the world.

Our typical burglar-alarm repairman didn't display one erg of chauvinistic swagger, however. He had been numbed by the aforementioned "intellectuals," who had spent the preceding eighty years being indignant over what a "puritanical," "repressive," "bigoted," "capitalistic," and "fascist" nation America was beneath its democratic façade. It made his head hurt. Besides, he was too busy coping with what was known as the "sexual revolution." If anything, "sexual revolution" was rather a prim term for the lurid carnival actually taking place in the mightiest country on earth in the year

5

---

[2] **Saint-Simon:** A French aristocrat, Henri de Saint-Simon (1760–1825) founded one of the most influential socialist programs of the nineteenth century. — EDS.

2000. Every magazine stand was a riot of bare flesh, rouged areolae, moistened crevices, and stiffened giblets: boys with girls, girls with girls, boys with boys, bare-breasted female bodybuilders, so-called boys with breasts, riding backseat behind steroid-gorged bodybuilding bikers, naked except for *cache-sexes* and Panzer helmets, on huge chromed Honda or Harley-Davidson motorcycles.

But the magazines were nothing compared with what was offered on an invention of the 1990s, the Internet. By 2000, an estimated 50 percent of all hits, or "log-ons," were at Web sites purveying what was known as "adult material." The word "pornography" had disappeared down the memory hole along with "proletariat." Instances of marriages breaking up because of Web-sex addiction were rising in number. The husband, some fifty-two-year-old MRI technician or systems analyst, would sit in front of the computer for twenty-four or more hours at a stretch. Nothing that the wife could offer him in the way of sexual delights or food could compare with the one-handing he was doing day and night as he sat before the PC and logged on to such images as a girl with bare breasts and a black leather corset standing with one foot on the small of a naked boy's back, brandishing a whip.

In 1999, the year before, this particular sexual kink—sadomasochism—had achieved not merely respectability but high chic, and the word "perversion" had become as obsolete as "pornography" and "proletariat." Fashion pages presented the black leather and rubber paraphernalia as style's cutting edge. An actress named Rene Russo blithely recounted in the Living section of one of America's biggest newspapers how she had consulted a former dominatrix named Eva Norvind, who maintained a dungeon replete with whips and chains and assorted baffling leather masks, chokers, and cuffs, in order to prepare for a part as an aggressive, self-obsessed agent provocateur in *The Thomas Crown Affair*, Miss Russo's latest movie.

"Sexy" was beginning to replace "chic" as the adjective indicating what was smart and up-to-the-minute. In the year 2000, it was standard practice for the successful chief executive officer of a corporation to shuck his wife of two to three decades' standing for the simple reason that her subcutaneous packing was deteriorating, her shoulders and upper back were thickening like a shot-putter's—in short, she was no longer sexy. Once he set up the old wife in a needlepoint shop where she could sell yarn to her friends, he was free to take on a new wife, a "trophy wife," preferably a woman in her twenties, and preferably blond, as in an expression from that time, a "lemon tart." What was the downside? Was the new couple considered radioactive socially? Did people talk *sotto voce*, behind the hand, when the tainted pair came by? Not for a moment. All that happened was that everybody got on the cell phone or the Internet and rang up or e-mailed one another to find out the spelling of the new wife's first name, because it was always some name like Serena and nobody was sure how to spell it. Once that was written down in the little red Scully & Scully address book that was so popular among people of means, the lemon tart and her big CEO catch were invited to all the parties, as though nothing had happened.

Meanwhile, sexual stimuli bombarded the young so incessantly and intensely they were inflamed with a randy itch long before reaching puberty. At puberty the dams, if any were left, burst. In the nineteenth century, entire shelves used to be filled with novels whose stories turned on the need for women, such as Anna Karenina or Madame Bovary, to remain chaste or to maintain a façade of chastity. In the year 2000, a Tolstoy or a Flaubert[3] wouldn't have stood a chance in the United States. From age thirteen, American girls were under pressure to maintain a façade of sexual experience and sophistication. Among girls, "virgin" was a term of contempt. The old term "dating" — referring to a practice in which a boy asked a girl out for the evening and took her to the movies or dinner — was now deader than "proletariat" or "pornography" or "perversion." In junior high school, high school, and college, girls headed out in packs in the evening, and boys headed out in packs, hoping to meet each other fortuitously. If they met and some girl liked the looks of some boy, she would give him the nod, or he would give her the nod, and the two of them would retire to a halfway-private room and "hook up."

"Hooking up" was a term known in the year 2000 to almost every American child over the age of nine, but to only a relatively small percentage of their parents, who, even if they heard it, thought it was being used in the old sense of "meeting" someone. Among the children, hooking up was always a sexual experience, but the nature and extent of what they did could vary widely. Back in the twentieth century, American girls had used baseball terminology. "First base" referred to embracing and kissing; "second base" referred to groping and fondling and deep, or "French," kissing, commonly known as "heavy petting"; "third base" referred to fellatio, usually known in polite conversation by the ambiguous term "oral sex"; and "home plate" meant conception-mode intercourse, known familiarly as "going all the way." In the year 2000, in the era of hooking up, "first base" meant deep kissing ("tonsil hockey"), groping, and fondling; "second base" meant oral sex; "third base" meant going all the way; and "home plate" meant learning each other's names.

Getting to home plate was relatively rare, however. The typical Filofax entry in the year 2000 by a girl who had hooked up the night before would be: "Boy with black Wu-Tang T-shirt and cargo pants: O, A, 6." Or "Stupid cock diesel" — slang for a boy who was muscular from lifting weights — "who kept saying, 'This is a cool deal': TTC, 3." The letters referred to the sexual acts performed (e.g., TTC for "that thing with the cup"), and the Arabic number indicated the degree of satisfaction on a scale of 1 to 10.

In the year 2000, girls used "score" as an active verb indicating sexual conquest, as in: "The whole thing was like very sketchy, but I scored that diesel who said he was gonna go home and caff up [drink coffee in order

10

---

3 *a Tolstoy or a Flaubert:* The Russian novelist Leo Tolstoy published *Anna Karenina* in serial installments between 1875 and 1877; the French novelist Gustave Flaubert published *Madame Bovary* in 1865. — EDS.

to stay awake and study] for the psych test." In the twentieth century, only boys had used "score" in that fashion, as in: "I finally scored with Susan last night." That girls were using such a locution points up one of the ironies of the relations between the sexes in the year 2000.

The continuing vogue of feminism had made sexual life easier, even insouciant, for men. Women had been persuaded that they should be just as active as men when it came to sexual advances. Men were only too happy to accede to the new order, since it absolved them of all sense of responsibility, let alone chivalry. Men began to adopt formerly feminine attitudes when the subject of marriage came up, pleading weakness and indecisiveness, as in: "I don't know; I'm just not ready yet" or "Of course I love you, but like, you know, I start weirding out when I try to focus on it."

With the onset of puberty, males were able to get sexual enjoyment so easily, so casually, that junior high schools as far apart geographically and socially as the slums of the South Bronx and Washington's posh suburbs of Arlington and Talbot County, Virginia, began reporting a new discipline problem. Thirteen- and fourteen-year-old girls were getting down on their knees and fellating boys in corridors and stairwells during the two-minute break between classes. One thirteen-year-old in New York, asked by a teacher how she could do such a thing, replied: "It's nasty, but I need to satisfy my man." Nasty was an aesthetic rather than a moral or hygienic judgment. In the year 2000, boys and girls did not consider fellatio to be a truly sexual act, any more than tonsil hockey. It was just "fooling around." The President of the United States at the time used to have a twenty-two-year-old girl, an unpaid volunteer in the presidential palace, the White House, come around to his office for fellatio. He later testified under oath that he had never "had sex" with her. Older Americans tended to be shocked, but junior-high-school, high-school, and college students understood completely what he was saying and wondered what on earth all the fuss was about. The two of them had merely been on second base, hooking up.

Teenage girls spoke about their sex lives to total strangers without the   15 least embarrassment or guile. One New York City newspaper sent out a man-on-the-street interviewer with the question: "How did you lose your virginity?" Girls as well as boys responded without hesitation, posed for photographs, and divulged their name, age, and the neighborhood where they lived.

Stains and stigmas of every kind were disappearing where sex was concerned. Early in the twentieth century the term "cohabitation" had referred to the forbidden practice of a man and woman living together before marriage. In the year 2000, nobody under forty had ever heard of the word, since cohabitation was now the standard form of American courtship. For parents over forty, one of the thornier matters of etiquette concerned domestic bed assignments. When your son or daughter came home for the weekend with the live-in consort, did you put the two of them in the same bedroom, which would indicate implicit approval of the discomforting fait accompli? Or did you put them in different bedrooms and lie awake, rigid with insomnia, fearful of hearing muffled footfalls in the hallway in the middle of the night?

Putting them in different rooms was a decidedly old-fashioned thing to do; and in the year 2000, thanks to the feverish emphasis on sex and sexiness, nobody wanted to appear old, let alone old-fashioned. From the city of Baltimore came reports of grandmothers having their eyebrows, tongues, and lips pierced with gold rings in order to appear younger, since body-piercing was a popular fashion among boys and girls in their teens and early twenties. Expectant mothers were having their belly buttons pierced with gold rings so that the shapelessness of pregnancy would not make them feel old. An old man who had been a prominent United States senator and a presidential candidate, emerged from what he confessed to have been a state of incapacity to go on television to urge other old men to take a drug called Viagra to free them from what he said was one of the scourges of modern times, the disease that dared not speak its name: impotence. He dared not speak it, either. He called it "E.D.," for erectile dysfunction. Insurance companies were under pressure to classify impotence in old men as a disease and to pay for treatment.

In the late nineteenth and early twentieth centuries, old people in America had prayed, "Please, God, don't let me look poor." In the year 2000, they prayed, "Please, God, don't let me look old." Sexiness was equated with youth, and youth ruled. The most widespread age-related disease was not senility but juvenility. The social ideal was to look twenty-three and dress thirteen. All over the country, old men and women were dressing casually at every opportunity, wearing jeans, luridly striped sneakers, shorts, T-shirts, polo shirts, jackets, and sweaters, heedless of how such clothes revealed every sad twist, bow, hump, and webbed-up vein clump of their superannuated bodies. For that matter, in the year 2000, people throughout American society were inverting norms of dress that had persisted for centuries, if not millennia. Was the majesty of America's global omnipotence reflected in the raiments of the rich and prominent? Quite the opposite. In the year 2000, most American billionaires—and the press no longer took notice of men worth a mere $500 million or $750 million—lived in San José and Santa Clara Counties, California, an area known nationally, with mythic awe, as the Silicon Valley, the red-hot center of the computer and Internet industries. In 1999, the Internet industry alone had produced fourteen new billionaires. The Valley's mythology was full of the sagas of young men who had gone into business for themselves, created their own companies straight out of college, or, better still, had dropped out of college to launch their "start-ups," as these new digital-age enterprises were known. Such were the new "Masters of the Universe," a term coined in the eighties to describe the (mere) megamillionaires spawned by Wall Street during a boom in the bond business. By comparison with the Valley's boy billionaires, the Wall Streeters, even though they were enjoying a boom in the stock market in the year 2000, seemed slow and dreary. Typically, they graduated from college, worked for three years as number-crunching donkeys in some large

investment-banking firm, went off to business school for two years to be certified as Masters of Business Administration, then returned to some investment-banking firm and hoped to start making some real money by the age
of thirty. The stodginess of such a career was symbolized by the stodginess
of their dress. Even the youngest of them dressed like old men: the dark blah
suit, the light blah shirt, the hopelessly "interesting" Hermès tie . . . Many of
them even wore silk braces.

The new Masters of the Universe turned all that upside down. At Il Fornaio restaurant in Palo Alto, California, where they gathered to tell war stories and hand out business cards at breakfast, the billionaire founders of
the new wonder corporations walked in the door looking like well-pressed,
well-barbered beachcombers, but beachcombers all the same. They wore
khakis, boating moccasins (without socks), and ordinary cotton shirts with
the cuffs rolled up and the front unbuttoned to the navel, and that was it. You
could tell at a glance that a Silicon Valley billionaire carried no cell phone,
Palm Pilot, HP-19B calculator, or RIM pager—he had people who did that
for him. Having breakfast with him at Il Fornaio would be a vice president
whose net worth was $100 or $200 million. He would be dressed just like the
founder, except that he would also be wearing a sport jacket. Why? So that
he could carry . . . the cell phone, the Palm Pilot, the HP-19B calculator, and
the RIM pager, which received e-mail and felt big as a brick. But why not
an attaché case? Because that was what old-fashioned businessmen Back
East carried. Nobody would be caught dead at Il Fornaio carrying an attaché case. The Back East attaché case was known scornfully as "the leather
lunch pail."

When somebody walked into Il Fornaio wearing a suit and tie, he was   20
likely to be mistaken for a maître d'. In the year 2000, as in prior ages, service personnel, such as doormen, chauffeurs, waiters, and maître d's, were
expected to wear the anachronistic finery of bygone eras. In Silicon Valley,
wearing a tie was a mark of shame that indicated you were everything a
Master of the Universe was not. Gradually, it would dawn on you. The poor
devil in the suit and tie held one of those lowly but necessary executive
positions, in public or investor relations, in which one couldn't avoid dealing
with Pliocene old parties from . . . Back East.

Meanwhile, back East, the sons of the old rich were deeply involved in
inverted fashions themselves. One of the more remarkable sights in New
York City in the year 2000 was that of some teenage scion of an investment-
banking family emerging from one of the forty-two Good Buildings, as they
were known. These forty-two buildings on Manhattan's East Side contained
the biggest, grandest, stateliest apartments ever constructed in the United
States, most of them on Park and Fifth Avenues. A doorman dressed like an
Austrian Army colonel from the year 1870 holds open the door, and out comes
a wan white boy wearing a baseball cap sideways; an outsized T-shirt, whose
short sleeves fall below his elbows and whose tail hangs down over his hips;
baggy cargo pants with flapped pockets running down the legs and a crotch
hanging below his knees, and yards of material pooling about his ankles, all

but obscuring the Lugz sneakers. This fashion was deliberately copied from the "homeys"—black youths on the streets of six New York slums, Harlem, the South Bronx, Bedford-Stuyvesant, Fort Greene, South Ozone Park, and East New York. After passing the doorman, who tipped his visored officer's hat and said "Good day," the boy walked twenty feet to a waiting sedan, where a driver with a visored officer's hat held open a rear door.

What was one to conclude from such a scene? The costumes said it all. In the year 2000, the sons of the rich, the very ones in line to inherit the bounties of the all-powerful United States, were consumed by a fear of being envied. A German sociologist of the period, Helmut Schoeck, said that "fear of being envied" was the definition of guilt. But if so, guilt about what? So many riches, so much power, such a dazzling array of advantages? American superiority in all matters of science, economics, industry, politics, business, medicine, engineering, social life, social justice, and, of course, the military was total and indisputable. Even Europeans suffering the pangs of wounded chauvinism looked on with awe at the brilliant example the United States had set for the world as the third millennium began. And yet there was a cloud on the millennial horizon.

America had shown the world the way in every area save one. In matters intellectual and artistic, she remained an obedient colony of Europe. American architecture had never recovered from the deadening influence of the German Bauhaus[4] movement of the twenties. American painting and sculpture had never recovered from the deadening influence of various theory-driven French movements, beginning with Cubism early in the twentieth century. In music, the early-twentieth-century innovations of George Gershwin, Aaron Copland, Duke Ellington, and Ferde Grofé had been swept away by the abstract, mathematical formulas of the Austrian composer Arnold Schoenberg. Schoenberg's influence had faded in the 1990s, but the damage had been done. The American theater had never recovered from the Absurdism of Samuel Beckett, Bertolt Brecht, and Luigi Pirandello.

But, above all, there was the curious case of American philosophy—which no longer existed. It was as if Emerson, Charles Peirce, William James, and John Dewey had never lived. The reigning doctrine was deconstruction, whose hierophants were two Frenchmen, Michel Foucault and Jacques Derrida. They began with a hyperdilation of a pronouncement of Nietzsche's to the effect that there can be no absolute truth, merely many "truths," which are the tools of various groups, classes, or forces. From this, the deconstructionists proceeded to the doctrine that language is the most insidious tool of all. The philosopher's duty was to deconstruct the language, expose its hidden agendas, and help save the victims of the American "Establishment": women, the poor, nonwhites, homosexuals, and hardwood trees.

Oddly, when deconstructionists required appendectomies or bypass surgery or even a root-canal job, they never deconstructed medical or dental   25

---

4 **Bauhaus:** A school of industrial design and architecture that developed in Germany during the early twentieth century. — EDS.

"truth," but went along with whatever their board-certified, profit-oriented surgeons proclaimed was the last word.

Confused and bored, our electrician, our air-conditioning mechanic, and our burglar-alarm repairman sat down in the evening and watched his favorite TV show (*The Simpsons*), played his favorite computer game (*Tony Hawk's Pro Skater*) with the children, logged on to the Internet, stayed up until 2 A.M. planning a trip to this fabulous-sounding resort just outside Bangkok, then "crashed" (went to bed exhausted), and fell asleep faster than it takes to tell it, secure in the knowledge that the sun would once more shine blessedly upon him in the morning. It was the year 2000. ◼

The Reader's Presence

1. Wolfe makes frequent reference to how language has changed, pointing out defunct terms or newly coined phrases. What words does Wolfe say have been redefined or replaced? What are the connotations of the defunct term, and what is lost or gained with a new word?

2. Examine Wolfe's tone throughout the essay. How does he approach his subject? Where does he uses humor, and for what purpose? Where does he use hyperbole (overstatement) and why?

3. **CONNECTIONS:** Compare the way Wolfe covers current cultural trends to how Lauren Slater examines them in "The Trouble with Self-Esteem" (page 822). Which author strikes you as more objective and why? How does each writer establish credibility for his and her observations? What similarities can you see between both selections? Do you think Wolfe's comments on contemporary culture support Slater's and vice versa? Why or why not?

Virginia Woolf
THE DEATH OF THE MOTH

One of the most important writers of the twentieth century, **VIRGINIA WOOLF** (1882–1941) explored innovations in indirect narration and the impressionistic use of language that are now considered hallmarks of the modern novel and continue to influence novelists on both sides of the Atlantic. Together with her husband, Leonard Woolf, she founded the Hogarth

Press, which published many experimental works that have now become classics, including her own. A central figure in the Bloomsbury group of writers, Woolf established her reputation with the novels *Mrs. Dalloway* (1925), *To the Lighthouse* (1927), and *The Waves* (1931). The feminist movement has helped to focus attention on her work, and Woolf's nonfiction has provided the basis for several important lines of argument in contemporary feminist theory. *A Room of One's Own* (1929), *Three Guineas* (1938), and *The Common Reader* (1938) are the major works of nonfiction published in Woolf's lifetime; posthumously, her essays have been gathered together in *The Death of the Moth* (1942) (where the essay reprinted here appears) and in the four-volume *Collected Essays* (1967).

> **"The novelist—it is his distinction and his danger—is terribly exposed to life. . . . He can no more cease to receive impressions than a fish in mid-ocean can cease to let the water rush through his gills."**

Reflecting on her own writing life, Woolf wrote, "The novelist—it is his distinction and his danger—is terribly exposed to life. . . . He can no more cease to receive impressions than a fish in mid-ocean can cease to let the water rush through his gills." To turn those impressions into writing, Woolf maintained, requires solitude and the time for thoughtful selection. Given tranquility, a writer can, with effort, discover art in experience. "There emerges from the mist something stark, formidable and enduring, the bone and substance upon which our rush of indiscriminating emotion was founded."

MOTHS THAT FLY BY DAY are not properly to be called moths; they do not excite that pleasant sense of dark autumn nights and ivy-blossom which the commonest yellow-underwing asleep in the shadow of the curtain never fails to rouse in us. They are hybrid creatures, neither gay like butterflies nor somber like their own species. Nevertheless the present specimen, with his narrow hay-colored wings, fringed with a tassel of the same color, seemed to be content with life. It was a pleasant morning, mid-September, mild, benignant, yet with a keener breath than that of the summer months. The plough was already scoring the field opposite the window, and where the share had been, the earth was pressed flat and gleamed with moisture. Such vigor came rolling in from the fields and the down beyond that it was difficult to keep the eyes strictly turned upon the book. The rooks too were keeping one of their annual festivities; soaring round the tree tops until it looked as if a vast net with thousands of black knots in it had been cast up into the air; which, after a few moments sank slowly down upon the trees until every twig seemed to have a knot at the end of it. Then, suddenly, the net would be thrown into the air again in a wider circle this time, with the utmost clamor and vociferation, as though to be thrown into the air and settle slowly down upon the tree tops were a tremendously exciting experience.

The same energy which inspired the rooks, the ploughmen, the horses, and even, it seemed, the lean bare-backed downs, sent the moth fluttering from side to side of his square of the windowpane. One could not help watching him. One, was, indeed, conscious of a queer feeling of pity for him. The possibilities of pleasure seemed that morning so enormous and so various that to have only a moth's part in life, and a day moth's at that, appeared a hard fate, and his zest in enjoying his meager opportunities to the full, pathetic. He flew vigorously to one corner of his compartment, and after waiting there a second, flew across to the other. What remained for him but to fly to a third corner and then to a fourth? That was all he could do, in spite of the size of the downs, the width of the sky, the far-off smoke of houses, and the romantic voice, now and then, of a steamer out at sea. What he could do he did. Watching him, it seemed as if a fiber, very thin but pure, of the enormous energy of the world had been thrust into his frail and diminutive body. As often as he crossed the pane, I could fancy that a thread of vital light became visible. He was little or nothing but life.

Yet, because he was so small, and so simple a form of the energy that was rolling in at the open window and driving its way through so many narrow and intricate corridors in my own brain and in those of other human beings, there was something marvelous as well as pathetic about him. It was as if someone had taken a tiny bead of pure life and decking it as lightly as possible with down and feathers, had set it dancing and zigzagging to show us the true nature of life. Thus displayed one could not get over the strangeness of it. One is apt to forget all about life, seeing it humped and bossed and garnished and cumbered so that it has to move with the greatest circumspection and dignity. Again, the thought of all that life might have been had he been born in any other shape caused one to view his simple activities with a kind of pity.

After a time, tired by his dancing apparently, he settled on the window ledge in the sun, and, the queer spectacle being at an end, I forgot about him. Then, looking up, my eye was caught by him. He was trying to resume his dancing, but seemed either so stiff or so awkward that he could only flutter to the bottom of the windowpane; and when he tried to fly across it he failed. Being intent on other matters I watched these futile attempts for a time without thinking, unconsciously waiting for him to resume his flight, as one waits for a machine, that has stopped momentarily, to start again without considering the reason of its failure. After perhaps a seventh attempt he slipped from the wooden ledge and fell, fluttering his wings, on to his back on the windowsill. The helplessness of his attitude roused me. It flashed upon me that he was in difficulties; he could no longer raise himself; his legs struggled vainly. But, as I stretched out a pencil, meaning to help him to right himself, it came over me that the failure and awkwardness were the approach of death. I laid the pencil down again.

The legs agitated themselves once more. I looked as if for the enemy   5
against which he struggled. I looked out of doors. What had happened there?
Presumably it was midday, and work in the fields had stopped. Stillness and
quiet had replaced the previous animation. The birds had taken themselves
off to feed in the brooks. The horses stood still. Yet the power was there all
the same, massed outside, indifferent, impersonal, not attending to anything
in particular. Somehow it was opposed to the little hay-colored moth. It was
useless to try to do anything. One could only watch the extraordinary efforts
made by those tiny legs against an oncoming doom which could, had it chosen, have submerged an entire city, not merely a city, but masses of human
beings; nothing, I knew had any chance against death. Nevertheless after a
pause of exhaustion the legs fluttered again. It was superb this last protest,
and so frantic that he succeeded at last in righting himself. One's sympathies, of course, were all on the side of life. Also, when there was nobody to
care or to know, this gigantic effort on the part of an insignificant little moth,
against a power of such magnitude, to retain what no one else valued or
desired to keep, moved one strangely. Again, somehow, one saw life, a pure
bead. I lifted the pencil again, useless though I knew it to be. But even as I
did so, the unmistakable tokens of death showed themselves. The body
relaxed, and instantly grew stiff. The struggle was over. The insignificant
little creature now knew death. As I looked at the dead moth, this minute
wayside triumph of so great a force over so mean an antagonist filled me
with wonder. Just as life had been strange a few minutes before, so death
was now as strange. The moth having righted himself now lay most decently
and uncomplainingly composed. O yes, he seemed to say, death is stronger
than I am. ●

The Reader's Presence

1. Woolf calls her essay "The Death of *the* Moth" rather than "The Death of *a* Moth," the title of Annie Dillard's essay on page 371. Describe what difference this makes. What quality does the definite article add to the essay?

2. Reread the essay, paying special attention not to the moth but to the writer. What presence does Woolf establish for herself in the essay? How does the act of writing itself get introduced? Of what significance is the pencil? Can you discover any con- nection between the essay's subject and its composition?

3. **CONNECTIONS:**   Reread Woolf's essay and then compare and contrast it to Annie Dillard's essay on the same subject, "The Death of a Moth" (page 371). These essays treat similar subjects and use similar titles. Make a list of the similarities and then another list of the differences in each author's treatment of the same subject. For example, how does Woolf treat the death of the moth in her essay? To what extent are the language and literary techniques (including diction, metaphor, and irony) used by Dillard different? Support your response with specific examples from each essay.

The Writer at Work

VIRGINIA WOOLF on the Practice of Freewriting

At the time of her death (1941), Virginia Woolf, one of modern literature's outstanding creative voices, left twenty-six volumes of a handwritten diary that she had started in 1915. Her diary records her daily activities, social life, reading, and, most important, her thoughts about the writing process. In 1953, her husband, Leonard Woolf, extracted her remarks about writing and published them in a separate volume called *A Writer's Diary*. Here, just having completed a newspaper article on the novelist Daniel Defoe, Woolf decides to take a break and think about the different ways she composes when she writes in her diary as opposed to when she writes more formally for publication.

❝ This Loose, Drifting Material of Life
Easter Sunday, April 20, 1919

In the idleness which succeeds any long article, and Defoe is the second leader this month, I got out this diary and read, as one always does read one's own writing, with a kind of guilty intensity. I confess that the rough and random style of it, often so ungrammatical, and crying for a word altered, afflicted me somewhat. I am trying to tell whichever self it is that reads this hereafter that I can write very much better; and take no time over this; and forbid her to let the eye of man behold it. And now I may add my little compliment to the effect that it has a slapdash and vigor and sometimes hits an unexpected bull's eye. But what is more to the point is my belief that the habit of writing thus for my own eye only is good practice. It loosens the ligaments. Never mind the misses and the stumbles. Going at such a pace as I do I must make the most direct and instant shots at my object, and thus have to lay hands on words, choose them and shoot them with

no more pause than is needed to put my pen in the ink. I believe that during the past year I can trace some increase of ease in my professional writing which I attribute to my casual half hours after tea. Moreover there looms ahead of me the shadow of some kind of form which a diary might attain to. I might in the course of time learn what it is that one can make of this loose, drifting material of life; finding another use for it than the use I put it to, so much more consciously and scrupulously, in fiction. What sort of diary should I like mine to be? Something loose knit and yet not slovenly, so elastic that it will embrace anything, solemn, slight, or beautiful that comes into my mind. I should like it to resemble some deep old desk, or capacious hold-all, in which one flings a mass of odds and ends without looking them through. I should like to come back, after a year or two, and find that the collection had sorted itself and refined itself and coalesced, as such deposits so mysteriously do, into a mould, transparent enough to reflect the light of our life, and yet steady, tranquil compounds with the aloofness of a work of art. The main requisite, I think on re-reading my old volumes, is not to play the part of censor, but to write as the mood comes or of anything whatever; since I was curious to find how I went for things put in haphazard, and found the significance to lie where I never saw it at the time. But looseness quickly becomes slovenly. A little effort is needed to face a character or an incident which needs to be recorded. 🙲

PART 3

ARGUMENTATIVE WRITING
Contending with Issues

Nicholas Carr

IS GOOGLE MAKING US STUPID?

NICHOLAS CARR (b. 1959) writes about the influence of technology on business and economics as well as on society in general. The *Christian Science Monitor* called his 2008 best-seller, *The Big Switch: Rewiring the World, from Edison to Google*, "the most influential book so far on the cloud computing movement," and his previous book, *Does IT Matter? Information Technology and the Corrosion of Competitive Advantage* (2004), was praised by the *New York Times* for its clear analysis of the economics of information technology. Once the editor of the *Harvard Business Review*, Carr is currently a member of the editorial board for *Encyclopedia Britannica* as well as of the steering board of the World Economic Forum's project on cloud computing.

> The *Christian Science Monitor* called his 2008 best-seller, *Rewiring the World: From Edison to Google*, "the most influential book so far on the cloud computing movement."

He has written for the *Atlantic Monthly*, *Wired*, the *Financial Times*, the *New York Times Magazine*, and many other prestigious publications, and he has been an invited speaker on issues relating to technology at MIT, Harvard, and NASA. Originally published in the *Atlantic Monthly* in 2008, "Is Google Making Us Stupid?" has been anthologized in *The Best American Science and Nature Writing*, *The Best American Technology Writing*, and *The Best American Spiritual Writing*.

"DAVE, STOP. Stop, will you? Stop, Dave. Will you stop, Dave?" So the supercomputer HAL pleads with the implacable astronaut Dave Bowman in a famous and weirdly poignant scene toward the end of Stanley Kubrick's *2001: A Space Odyssey*. Bowman, having nearly been sent to a deep-space death by the malfunctioning machine, is calmly, coldly disconnecting the memory circuits that control its artificial "brain." "Dave, my mind is going," HAL says, forlornly. "I can feel it. I can feel it."

I can feel it, too. Over the past few years I've had an uncomfortable sense that someone, or something, has been tinkering with my brain, remapping the neural circuitry, reprogramming the memory. My mind isn't going—so far as I can tell—but it's changing. I'm not thinking the way I used to think. I can feel it most strongly when I'm reading. Immersing myself in a book or a lengthy article used to be easy. My mind would get caught up in the narrative or the turns of the argument, and I'd spend hours strolling through long stretches of prose. That's rarely the case anymore. Now my concentration often starts to drift after two or three pages. I get fidgety, lose the thread, begin looking for something else to do. I feel as if I'm always dragging my wayward brain back to the text. The deep reading that used to come naturally has become a struggle.

I think I know what's going on. For more than a decade now, I've been spending a lot of time online, searching and surfing and sometimes adding to the great databases of the Internet. The Web has been a godsend to me as a writer. Research that once required days in the stacks or periodical rooms of libraries can now be done in minutes. A few Google searches, some quick clicks on hyperlinks, and I've got the telltale fact or pithy quote I was after. Even when I'm not working, I'm as likely as not to be foraging in the Web's info-thickets, reading and writing e-mails, scanning headlines and blog posts, watching videos and listening to podcasts, or just tripping from link to link to link. (Unlike footnotes, to which they're sometimes likened, hyperlinks don't merely point to related works; they propel you toward them.)

For me, as for others, the Net is becoming a universal medium, the conduit for most of the information that flows through my eyes and ears and into my mind. The advantages of having immediate access to such an incredibly rich store of information are many, and they've been widely described and duly applauded. "The perfect recall of silicon memory," *Wired*'s Clive Thompson has written, "can be an enormous boon to thinking." But that boon comes at a price. As the media theorist Marshall McLuhan pointed out in the 1960s, media are not just passive channels of information. They supply the stuff of thought, but they also shape the process of thought. And what the Net seems to be doing is chipping away my capacity for concentration and contemplation. My mind now expects to take in information the way the Net distributes it: in a swiftly moving stream of particles. Once I was a scuba diver in the sea of words. Now I zip along the surface like a guy on a Jet Ski.

I'm not the only one. When I mention my troubles with reading to friends   5
and acquaintances—literary types, most of them—many say they're having similar experiences. The more they use the Web, the more they have to fight to stay focused on long pieces of writing. Some of the bloggers I follow have also begun mentioning the phenomenon. Scott Karp, who writes a blog about online media, recently confessed that he has stopped reading books altogether. "I was a lit major in college, and used to be [a] voracious book reader," he wrote. "What happened?" He speculates on the answer: "What if I do all my reading on the Web not so much because the way I read has changed, i.e. I'm just seeking convenience, but because the way I THINK has changed?"

Bruce Friedman, who blogs regularly about the use of computers in medicine, also has described how the Internet has altered his mental habits. "I now have almost totally lost the ability to read and absorb a longish article on the Web or in print," he wrote earlier this year. A pathologist who has long been on the faculty of the University of Michigan Medical School, Friedman elaborated on his comment in a telephone conversation with me. His thinking,

Multitasking has become an increasingly visible—and widespread—characteristic of contemporary experience for undergraduates as well as for those in the workforce.

he said, has taken on a "staccato" quality, reflecting the way he quickly scans short passages of text from many sources online. "I can't read *War and Peace* anymore," he admitted. "I've lost the ability to do that. Even a blog post of more than three or four paragraphs is too much to absorb. I skim it."

Anecdotes alone don't prove much. And we still await the long-term neurological and psychological experiments that will provide a definitive picture of how Internet use affects cognition. But a recently published study of online research habits, conducted by scholars from University College London, suggests that we may well be in the midst of a sea change in the way we read and think. As part of the five-year research program, the scholars examined computer logs documenting the behavior of visitors to two popular research sites, one operated by the British Library and one by a U.K. educational consortium, that provide access to journal articles, e-books, and other sources of written information. They found that people using the sites exhibited "a form of skimming activity," hopping from one source to another and rarely returning to any source they'd already visited. They typically read no more than one or two pages of an article or book before they would "bounce" out to another site. Sometimes they'd save a long article, but there's no evidence that they ever went back and actually read it. The authors of the study report:

It is clear that users are not reading online in the traditional sense; indeed there are signs that new forms of "reading" are emerging as users "power browse" horizontally through titles, contents pages and abstracts going for quick wins. It almost seems that they go online to avoid reading in the traditional sense.

Thanks to the ubiquity of text on the Internet, not to mention the popularity of text-messaging on cell phones, we may well be reading more today than we did in the 1970s or 1980s, when television was our medium of choice. But it's a different kind of reading, and behind it lies a different kind of thinking—perhaps even a new sense of the self. "We are not only *what* we read," says Maryanne Wolf, a developmental psychologist at Tufts University and the author of *Proust and the Squid: The Story and Science of the Reading Brain.* "We are *how* we read." Wolf worries that the style of reading promoted by the Net, a style that puts "efficiency" and "immediacy" above all else, may be weakening our capacity for the kind of deep reading that emerged when an earlier technology, the printing press, made long and complex works of prose commonplace. When we read online, she says, we tend to become "mere decoders of information." Our ability to interpret text, to make the rich mental connections that form when we read deeply and without distraction, remains largely disengaged.

Reading, explains Wolf, is not an instinctive skill for human beings. It's   10 not etched into our genes the way speech is. We have to teach our minds how to translate the symbolic characters we see into the language we understand. And the media or other technologies we use in learning and practicing the craft of reading play an important part in shaping the neural circuits inside our brains. Experiments demonstrate that readers of ideograms, such as the Chinese, develop a mental circuitry for reading that is very different from the circuitry found in those of us whose written language employs an alphabet. The variations extend across many regions of the brain, including those that govern such essential cognitive functions as memory and the interpretation of visual and auditory stimuli. We can expect as well that the circuits woven by our use of the Net will be different from those woven by our reading of books and other printed works.

Sometime in 1882, Friedrich Nietzsche bought a typewriter—a Malling-Hansen Writing Ball, to be precise. His vision was failing, and keeping his eyes focused on a page had become exhausting and painful, often bringing on crushing headaches. He had been forced to curtail his writing, and he feared that he would soon have to give it up. The typewriter rescued him, at least for a time. Once he had mastered touch-typing, he was able to write with his eyes closed, using only the tips of his fingers. Words could once again flow from his mind to the page.

But the machine had a subtler effect on his work. One of Nietzsche's friends, a composer, noticed a change in the style of his writing. His already terse prose had become even tighter, more telegraphic. "Perhaps you will through this instrument even take to a new idiom," the friend wrote in a letter, noting that, in his own work, his "'thoughts' in music and language often depend on the quality of pen and paper."

"You are right," Nietzsche replied, "our writing equipment takes part in the forming of our thoughts." Under the sway of the machine, writes the German media scholar Friedrich A. Kittler, Nietzsche's prose "changed from arguments to aphorisms, from thoughts to puns, from rhetoric to telegram style."

The human brain is almost infinitely malleable. People used to think that our mental meshwork, the dense connections formed among the 100 billion or so neurons inside our skulls, was largely fixed by the time we reached adulthood. But brain researchers have discovered that that's not the case. James Olds, a professor of neuroscience who directs the Krasnow Institute for Advanced Study at George Mason University, says that even the adult mind "is very plastic." Nerve cells routinely break old connections and form new ones. "The brain," according to Olds, "has the ability to reprogram itself on the fly, altering the way it functions."

As we use what the sociologist Daniel Bell has called our "intellectual technologies"—the tools that extend our mental rather than our physical capacities—we inevitably begin to take on the qualities of those technologies. The mechanical clock, which came into common use in the 14th century, provides a compelling example. In *Technics and Civilization*, the historian and cultural critic Lewis Mumford described how the clock "disassociated time from human events and helped create the belief in an independent world of mathematically measurable sequences." The "abstract framework of divided time" became "the point of reference for both action and thought." 15

The clock's methodical ticking helped bring into being the scientific mind and the scientific man. But it also took something away. As the late MIT computer scientist Joseph Weizenbaum observed in his 1976 book, *Computer Power and Human Reason: From Judgment to Calculation*, the conception of the world that emerged from the widespread use of timekeeping instruments "remains an impoverished version of the older one, for it rests on a rejection of those direct experiences that formed the basis for, and indeed constituted, the old reality." In deciding when to eat, to work, to sleep, to rise, we stopped listening to our senses and started obeying the clock.

The process of adapting to new intellectual technologies is reflected in the changing metaphors we use to explain ourselves to ourselves. When the mechanical clock arrived, people began thinking of their brains as operating "like clockwork." Today, in the age of software, we have come to think of them as operating "like computers." But the changes, neuroscience tells us, go much deeper than metaphor. Thanks to our brain's plasticity, the adaptation occurs also at a biological level.

The Internet promises to have particularly far-reaching effects on cognition. In a paper published in 1936, the British mathematician Alan Turing proved that a digital computer, which at the time existed only as a theoretical machine, could be programmed to perform the function of any other information-processing device. And that's what we're seeing today. The Internet, an immeasurably powerful computing system, is subsuming most of our other intellectual technologies. It's becoming our map and our clock, our printing press and our typewriter, our calculator and our telephone, and our radio and TV.

When the Net absorbs a medium, that medium is re-created in the Net's image. It injects the medium's content with hyperlinks, blinking ads, and other digital gewgaws, and it surrounds the content with the content of all the other media it has absorbed. A new e-mail message, for instance, may announce its arrival as we're glancing over the latest headlines at a newspaper's site. The result is to scatter our attention and diffuse our concentration.

The Net's influence doesn't end at the edges of a computer screen, either. 20 As people's minds become attuned to the crazy quilt of Internet media, traditional media have to adapt to the audience's new expectations. Television programs add text crawls and pop-up ads, and magazines and newspapers shorten their articles, introduce capsule summaries, and crowd their pages with easy-to-browse info-snippets. When, in March of this year, the *New York Times* decided to devote the second and third pages of every edition to article abstracts, its design director, Tom Bodkin, explained that the "shortcuts" would give harried readers a quick "taste" of the day's news, sparing them the "less efficient" method of actually turning the pages and reading the articles. Old media have little choice but to play by the new-media rules.

Never has a communications system played so many roles in our lives — or exerted such broad influence over our thoughts — as the Internet does today. Yet, for all that's been written about the Net, there's been little consideration of how, exactly, it's reprogramming us. The Net's intellectual ethic remains obscure.

About the same time that Nietzsche started using his typewriter, an earnest young man named Frederick Winslow Taylor carried a stopwatch into the Midvale Steel plant in Philadelphia and began a historic series of experiments aimed at improving the efficiency of the plant's machinists. With the approval of Midvale's owners, he recruited a group of factory hands, set them to work on various metalworking machines, and recorded and timed their every movement as well as the operations of the machines. By breaking down every job into a sequence of small, discrete steps and then testing different ways of performing each one, Taylor created a set of precise instructions — an "algorithm," we might say today — for how each worker should work. Midvale's employees grumbled about the strict new regime, claiming that it turned them into little more than automatons, but the factory's productivity soared.

More than a hundred years after the invention of the steam engine, the Industrial Revolution had at last found its philosophy and its philosopher. Taylor's tight industrial choreography — his "system," as he liked to call it — was embraced by manufacturers throughout the country and, in time, around the world. Seeking maximum speed, maximum efficiency, and maximum output, factory owners used time-and-motion studies to organize their work and configure the jobs of their workers. The goal, as Taylor defined it in his celebrated 1911 treatise, *The Principles of Scientific Management*, was to identify and adopt, for every job, the "one best method" of work and thereby to effect "the gradual substitution of science for rule of thumb throughout the mechanic arts." Once his system was applied to all acts of manual labor, Taylor assured his followers, it would bring about a restructuring not only of industry but of society, creating a utopia of perfect efficiency. "In the past the man has been first," he declared; "in the future the system must be first."

Taylor's system is still very much with us; it remains the ethic of industrial manufacturing. And now, thanks to the growing power that computer engineers and software coders wield over our intellectual lives, Taylor's ethic is beginning to govern the realm of the mind as well. The Internet is a machine designed for the efficient and automated collection, transmission, and manipulation of information, and its legions of programmers are intent on finding the "one best method"—the perfect algorithm—to carry out every mental movement of what we've come to describe as "knowledge work."

Google's headquarters, in Mountain View, California—the Google- 25 plex—is the Internet's high church, and the religion practiced inside its walls is Taylorism. Google, says its chief executive, Eric Schmidt, is "a company that's founded around the science of measurement," and it is striving to "systematize everything" it does. Drawing on the terabytes of behavioral data it collects through its search engine and other sites, it carries out thousands of experiments a day, according to the *Harvard Business Review*, and it uses the results to refine the algorithms that increasingly control how people find information and extract meaning from it. What Taylor did for the work of the hand, Google is doing for the work of the mind.

The company has declared that its mission is "to organize the world's information and make it universally accessible and useful." It seeks to develop "the perfect search engine," which it defines as something that "understands exactly what you mean and gives you back exactly what you want." In Google's view, information is a kind of commodity, a utilitarian resource that can be mined and processed with industrial efficiency. The more pieces of information we can "access" and the faster we can extract their gist, the more productive we become as thinkers.

Where does it end? Sergey Brin and Larry Page, the gifted young men who founded Google while pursuing doctoral degrees in computer science at Stanford, speak frequently of their desire to turn their search engine into an artificial intelligence, a HAL-like machine that might be connected directly to our brains. "The ultimate search engine is something as smart as people—or smarter," Page said in a speech a few years back. "For us, working on search is a way to work on artificial intelligence." In a 2004 interview with *Newsweek*, Brin said, "Certainly if you had all the world's information directly attached to your brain, or an artificial brain that was smarter than your brain, you'd be better off." Last year, Page told a convention of scientists that Google is "really trying to build artificial intelligence and to do it on a large scale."

Such an ambition is a natural one, even an admirable one, for a pair of math whizzes with vast quantities of cash at their disposal and a small army of computer scientists in their employ. A fundamentally scientific enterprise, Google is motivated by a desire to use technology, in Eric Schmidt's words, "to solve problems that have never been solved before," and artificial intelligence is the hardest problem out there. Why wouldn't Brin and Page want to be the ones to crack it?

Still, their easy assumption that we'd all "be better off" if our brains were supplemented, or even replaced, by an artificial intelligence is unsettling. It suggests a belief that intelligence is the output of a mechanical process, a series of discrete steps that can be isolated, measured, and optimized. In Google's world, the world we enter when we go online, there's little place for the fuzziness of contemplation. Ambiguity is not an opening for insight but a bug to be fixed. The human brain is just an outdated computer that needs a faster processor and a bigger hard drive.

The idea that our minds should operate as high-speed data-processing   30
machines is not only built into the workings of the Internet, it is the network's reigning business model as well. The faster we surf across the Web—the more links we click and pages we view—the more opportunities Google and other companies gain to collect information about us and to feed us advertisements. Most of the proprietors of the commercial Internet have a financial stake in collecting the crumbs of data we leave behind as we flit from link to link—the more crumbs, the better. The last thing these companies want is to encourage leisurely reading or slow, concentrated thought. It's in their economic interest to drive us to distraction.

Maybe I'm just a worrywart. Just as there's a tendency to glorify technological progress, there's a countertendency to expect the worst of every new tool or machine. In Plato's *Phaedrus*, Socrates bemoaned the development of writing. He feared that, as people came to rely on the written word as a substitute for the knowledge they used to carry inside their heads, they would, in the words of one of the dialogue's characters, "cease to exercise their memory and become forgetful." And because they would be able to "receive a quantity of information without proper instruction," they would "be thought very knowledgeable when they are for the most part quite ignorant." They would be "filled with the conceit of wisdom instead of real wisdom." Socrates wasn't wrong—the new technology did often have the effects he feared—but he was shortsighted. He couldn't foresee the many ways that writing and reading would serve to spread information, spur fresh ideas, and expand human knowledge (if not wisdom).

The arrival of Gutenberg's printing press, in the 15th century, set off another round of teeth gnashing. The Italian humanist Hieronimo Squarciafico worried that the easy availability of books would lead to intellectual laziness, making men "less studious" and weakening their minds. Others argued that cheaply printed books and broadsheets would undermine religious authority, demean the work of scholars and scribes, and spread sedition and debauchery. As New York University professor Clay Shirky notes, "Most of the arguments made against the printing press were correct, even prescient." But, again, the doomsayers were unable to imagine the myriad blessings that the printed word would deliver.

So, yes, you should be skeptical of my skepticism. Perhaps those who dismiss critics of the Internet as Luddites or nostalgists will be proved correct, and from our hyperactive, data-stoked minds will spring a golden age of intellectual discovery and universal wisdom. Then again, the Net isn't the alphabet, and although it may replace the printing press, it produces something altogether different. The kind of deep reading that a sequence of printed pages promotes is valuable not just for the knowledge we acquire from the author's words but for the intellectual vibrations those words set off within our own minds. In the quiet spaces opened up by the sustained, undistracted reading of a book, or by any other act of contemplation, for that matter, we make our own associations, draw our own inferences and analogies, foster our own ideas. Deep reading, as Maryanne Wolf argues, is indistinguishable from deep thinking.

If we lose those quiet spaces, or fill them up with "content," we will sacrifice something important not only in our selves but in our culture. In a recent essay, the playwright Richard Foreman eloquently described what's at stake:

> I come from a tradition of Western culture, in which the ideal (my ideal) was the complex, dense and "cathedral-like" structure of the highly educated and articulate personality — a man or woman who carried inside themselves a personally constructed and unique version of the entire heritage of the West. [But now] I see within us all (myself included) the replacement of complex inner density with a new kind of self — evolving under the pressure of information overload and the technology of the "instantly available."

As we are drained of our "inner repertory of dense cultural inheritance," Foreman concluded, we risk turning into "'pancake people' — spread wide and thin as we connect with that vast network of information accessed by the mere touch of a button."

I'm haunted by that scene in *2001*. What makes it so poignant, and so weird, is the computer's emotional response to the disassembly of its mind: its despair as one circuit after another goes dark, its childlike pleading with the astronaut — "I can feel it. I can feel it. I'm afraid" — and its final reversion to what can only be called a state of innocence. HAL's outpouring of feeling contrasts with the emotionlessness that characterizes the human figures in the film, who go about their business with an almost robotic efficiency. Their thoughts and actions feel scripted, as if they're following the steps of an algorithm. In the world of *2001*, people have become so machinelike that the most human character turns out to be a machine. That's the essence of Kubrick's dark prophecy: as we come to rely on computers to mediate our understanding of the world, it is our own intelligence that flattens into artificial intelligence. 35

The Reader's Presence

1. Before considering the scientific and sociological research supporting each of his claims, Carr relays his personal experience of the ways his reading habits have changed. What does he achieve in doing so? What effect does this strategy have on the persuasiveness of his argument? Comment on the specific ways in which this strategy was — or was not — effective in drawing you in as a reader.

2. Examine carefully each of the various sources Carr draws on to support his response to the question he asks. What are the different areas of study represented in his argument? What do you notice about the way Carr transitions from one source to the next? Comment on the effectiveness of these transitions.

3. **CONNECTIONS:** Both Carr's argument and the argument Pico Iyer presents in "The Inner Climate" (page 693) begin with personal experience. How does the way each writer structures his argument differ? How is the structure of each argument the same? Focusing on the way the arguments are constructed rather than on whether you agree with the author, how persuasive do you find each approach? To which author's argumentative strategy do you find yourself more drawn? Explain why.

Jared Diamond

THE ENDS OF THE WORLD AS WE KNOW THEM

Pulitzer Prize–winning author JARED DIAMOND (b. 1937) is a physiologist, an ecologist, and a science writer known for his ability to make serious science accessible to a general audience. Diamond received his PhD from Cambridge University and has been on the UCLA faculty since 1966, currently serving as professor of geography. A recipient of many prestigious awards, he won the 1999 National Medal of Science for his work in the fields of evolutionary biology and conservation biology. He has done extensive fieldwork in South America, Africa, Indonesia, Australia, and New Guinea and has written more than five hundred scholarly papers on evolutionary physiology, ecology, and ornithology.

> Jared Diamond has done extensive fieldwork in South America, Africa, Indonesia, Australia, and New Guinea and has written more than five hundred scholarly papers on evolutionary physiology, ecology, and ornithology.

Diamond's books include *Why Is Sex Fun? The Evolution of Human Sexuality* (1975); *The Third Chimpanzee: The Evolution and Future of the Human Animal* (1991), for which he was awarded the *Los Angeles Times* Book Prize and the *Science* Book Prize; *Guns, Germs, and Steel: The Fates of Human Societies* (1997), for which he won the 1997 Pulitzer Prize for nonfiction; and his latest book, *Collapse: How Societies Choose to Fail or Succeed* (2004), a historical analysis of the fates of societies faced with environmental or political catastrophe. He is a frequent contributor to such magazines as *Discover*, *Natural History*, and *Nature*; his essays are also found in such publications as the *Atlantic* and the *New York Times*, which published "The Ends of the World as We Know Them" on January 1, 2005.

NEW YEAR'S WEEKEND traditionally is a time for us to reflect, and to make resolutions based on our reflections. In this fresh year, with the United States seemingly at the height of its power and at the start of a new presidential term, Americans are increasingly concerned and divided about where we are going. How long can America remain ascendant? Where will we stand ten years from now, or even next year?

Such questions seem especially appropriate this year. History warns us that when once-powerful societies collapse, they tend to do so quickly and unexpectedly. That shouldn't come as much of a surprise: peak power usually means peak population, peak needs, and hence peak vulnerability. What can be learned from history that could help us avoid joining the ranks of those who declined swiftly? We must expect the answers to be complex, because historical reality is complex: while some societies did indeed collapse spectacularly, others have managed to thrive for thousands of years without major reversal.

When it comes to historical collapses, five groups of interacting factors have been especially important: the damage that people have inflicted on their environment; climate change; enemies; changes in friendly trading partners; and the society's political, economic and social responses to these shifts. That's not to say that all five causes play a role in every case. Instead, think of this as a useful checklist of factors that should be examined, but whose relative importance varies from case to case.

For instance, in the collapse of the Polynesian society on Easter Island[1] three centuries ago, environmental problems were dominant, and climate change, enemies and trade were insignificant; however, the latter three factors played big roles in the disappearance of the medieval Norse colonies on Greenland. Let's consider two examples of declines stemming from different mixes of causes: the falls of classic Maya civilization and of Polynesian settlements on the Pitcairn Islands.

Maya Native Americans of the Yucatan Peninsula and adjacent parts   5
of Central America developed the New World's most advanced civilization before Columbus. They were innovators in writing, astronomy, architecture and art. From local origins around 2,500 years ago, Maya societies rose especially after the year A.D. 250, reaching peaks of population and sophistication in the late eighth century.

---

[1] *Easter Island:* Remote South Pacific island known for giant Māori statues, which were toppled during a period of decline for the Rapa Nui people there. — EDS.

Thereafter, societies in the most densely populated areas of the southern Yucatan underwent a steep political and cultural collapse: between 760 and 910, kings were overthrown, large areas were abandoned, and at least 90 percent of the population disappeared, leaving cities to become overgrown by jungle. The last known date recorded on a Maya monument by their so-called Long Count calendar corresponds to the year 909. What happened?

A major factor was environmental degradation by people: deforestation, soil erosion and water management problems, all of which resulted in less food. Those problems were exacerbated by droughts, which may have been partly caused by humans themselves through deforestation. Chronic warfare made matters worse, as more and more people fought over less and less land and resources.

Why weren't these problems obvious to the Maya kings, who could surely see their forests vanishing and their hills becoming eroded? Part of the reason was that the kings were able to insulate themselves from problems afflicting the rest of society. By extracting wealth from commoners, they could remain well fed while everyone else was slowly starving.

What's more, the kings were preoccupied with their own power struggles. They had to concentrate on fighting one another and keeping up their images through ostentatious displays of wealth. By insulating themselves in the short run from the problems of society, the elite merely bought themselves the privilege of being among the last to starve.

Whereas Maya societies were undone by problems of their own making,   10 Polynesian societies on Pitcairn and Henderson Islands in the tropical Pacific Ocean were undone largely by other people's mistakes. Pitcairn, the uninhabited island settled in 1790 by the *H.M.S. Bounty* mutineers, had actually been populated by Polynesians 800 years earlier. That society, which left behind temple platforms, stone and shell tools and huge garbage piles of fish and bird and turtle bones as evidence of its existence, survived for several centuries and then vanished. Why?

In many respects, Pitcairn and Henderson are tropical paradises, rich in some food sources and essential raw materials. Pitcairn is home to Southeast Polynesia's largest quarry of stone suited for making adzes, while Henderson has the region's largest breeding seabird colony and its only nesting beach for sea turtles. Yet the islanders depended on imports from Mangareva Island, hundreds of miles away, for canoes, crops, livestock and oyster shells for making tools.

Unfortunately for the inhabitants of Pitcairn and Henderson, their Mangarevan trading partner collapsed for reasons similar to those underlying the Maya decline: deforestation, erosion and warfare. Deprived of essential imports in a Polynesian equivalent of the 1973 oil crisis, the Pitcairn and Henderson societies declined until everybody had died or fled.

The Maya and the Henderson and Pitcairn Islanders are not alone, of course. Over the centuries, many other societies have declined, collapsed or died out. Famous victims include the Anasazi in the American Southwest, who abandoned their cities in the twelfth century because of environmental problems and climate change, and the Greenland Norse, who disappeared in the fifteenth century because of all five interacting factors on the checklist. There were also the ancient Fertile Crescent societies, the Khmer at Angkor Wat, the Moche society of Peru—the list goes on.

But before we let ourselves get depressed, we should also remember that there is another long list of cultures that have managed to prosper for lengthy periods of time. Societies in Japan, Tonga, Tikopia, the New Guinea Highlands and Central and Northwest Europe, for example, have all found ways to sustain themselves. What separates the lost cultures from those that survived? Why did the Maya fail and the shogun succeed?

Half of the answer involves environmental differences: geography deals   15 worse cards to some societies than to others. Many of the societies that collapsed had the misfortune to occupy dry, cold or otherwise fragile environments, while many of the long-term survivors enjoyed more robust and fertile surroundings. But it's not the case that a congenial environment guarantees success: some societies (like the Maya) managed to ruin lush environments, while other societies—like the Incas, the Inuit, Icelanders and desert Australian Aborigines—have managed to carry on in some of the earth's most daunting environments.

The other half of the answer involves differences in a society's responses to problems. Ninth-century New Guinea Highland villagers, sixteenth-century German landowners, and the Tokugawa shoguns of seventeenth-century Japan all recognized the deforestation spreading around them and solved the problem, either by developing scientific reforestation (Japan and Germany) or by transplanting tree seedlings (New Guinea). Conversely, the Maya, Mangarevans and Easter Islanders failed to address their forestry problems and so collapsed.

Consider Japan. In the 1600s, the country faced its own crisis of deforestation, paradoxically brought on by the peace and prosperity following the Tokugawa shoguns' military triumph that ended 150 years of civil war. The subsequent explosion of Japan's population and economy set off rampant logging for construction of palaces and cities, and for fuel and fertilizer.

The shoguns responded with both negative and positive measures. They reduced wood consumption by turning to light-timbered construction, to fuel-efficient stoves and heaters, and to coal as a source of energy. At the same time, they increased wood production by developing and carefully managing plantation forests. Both the shoguns and the Japanese peasants took a long-term view: the former expected to pass on their power to their children, and the latter expected to pass on their land. In addition, Japan's isolation at the time made it obvious that the country would have to depend on its own resources and couldn't meet its needs by pillaging other countries. Today, despite having the highest human population density of any large developed country, Japan is more than 70 percent forested.

There is a similar story from Iceland. When the island was first settled by the Norse around 870, its light volcanic soils presented colonists with unfamiliar challenges. They proceeded to cut down trees and stock sheep as if they were still in Norway, with its robust soils. Significant erosion ensued, carrying half of Iceland's topsoil into the ocean within a century or two. Icelanders became the poorest people in Europe. But they gradually learned from their mistakes, over time instituting stocking limits on sheep and other strict controls, and establishing an entire government department charged with landscape management. Today, Iceland boasts the sixth-highest per-capita income in the world.

What lessons can we draw from history? The most straightforward: take environmental problems seriously. They destroyed societies in the past, and they are even more likely to do so now. If 6,000 Polynesians with stone tools were able to destroy Mangareva Island, consider what six billion people with metal tools and bulldozers are doing today. Moreover, while the Maya collapse affected just a few neighboring societies in Central America, globalization now means that any society's problems have the potential to affect anyone else. Just think how crises in Somalia, Afghanistan and Iraq have shaped the United States today.

20

Other lessons involve failures of group decision-making. There are many reasons why past societies made bad decisions, and thereby failed to solve or even to perceive the problems that would eventually destroy them. One reason involves conflicts of interest, whereby one group within a society (for instance, the pig farmers who caused the worst erosion in medieval Greenland and Iceland) can profit by engaging in practices that damage the rest of society. Another is the pursuit of short-term gains at the expense of long-term survival, as when fishermen overfish the stocks on which their livelihoods ultimately depend.

History also teaches us two deeper lessons about what separates successful societies from those heading toward failure. A society contains a built-in blueprint for failure if the elite insulates itself from the consequences of its actions. That's why Maya kings, Norse Greenlanders and Easter Island chiefs made choices that eventually undermined their societies. They themselves did not begin to feel deprived until they had irreversibly destroyed their landscape.

Could this happen in the United States? It's a thought that often occurs to me here in Los Angeles, when I drive by gated communities, guarded by private security patrols, and filled with people who drink bottled water, depend on private pensions, and send their children to private schools. By doing these things, they lose the motivation to support the police force, the municipal water supply, Social Security and public schools. If conditions deteriorate too much for poorer people, gates will not keep the rioters out. Rioters eventually burned the palaces of Maya kings and tore down the statues of Easter Island chiefs; they have also already threatened wealthy districts in Los Angeles twice in recent decades.

In contrast, the elite in seventeenth-century Japan, as in modern Scandinavia and the Netherlands, could not ignore or insulate themselves from broad societal problems. For instance, the Dutch upper class for hundreds of years has been unable to insulate itself from the Netherlands' water management problems for a simple reason: the rich live in the same drained lands below sea level as the poor. If the dikes and pumps keeping out the sea fail, the well-off Dutch know that they will drown along with everybody else, which is precisely what happened during the floods of 1953.

The other deep lesson involves a willingness to re-examine long-held 25 core values, when conditions change and those values no longer make sense. The medieval Greenland Norse lacked such a willingness: they continued to view themselves as transplanted Norwegian pastoralists, and to despise the Inuit as pagan hunters, even after Norway stopped sending trading ships and the climate had grown too cold for a pastoral existence. They died off as a result, leaving Greenland to the Inuit. On the other hand, the British in the 1950s faced up to the need for a painful reappraisal of their former status as rulers of a world empire set apart from Europe. They are now finding a different avenue to wealth and power, as part of a united Europe.

In this New Year, we Americans have our own painful reappraisals to face. Historically, we viewed the United States as a land of unlimited plenty, and so we practiced unrestrained consumerism, but that's no longer viable in a world of finite resources. We can't continue to deplete our own resources as well as those of much of the rest of the world.

Historically, oceans protected us from external threats; we stepped back from our isolationism only temporarily during the crises of two world wars. Now, technology and global interconnectedness have robbed us of our protection. In recent years, we have responded to foreign threats largely by seeking short-term military solutions at the last minute.

But how long can we keep this up? Though we are the richest nation on earth, there's simply no way we can afford (or muster the troops) to intervene in the dozens of countries where emerging threats lurk—particularly when each intervention these days can cost more than $100 billion and require more than 100,000 troops.

A genuine reappraisal would require us to recognize that it will be far less expensive and far more effective to address the underlying problems of public health, population and environment that ultimately cause threats to us to emerge in poor countries. In the past, we have regarded foreign aid as either charity or as buying support; now, it's an act of self-interest to preserve our own economy and protect American lives.

Do we have cause for hope? Many of my friends are pessimistic when they 30 contemplate the world's growing population and human demands colliding with shrinking resources. But I draw hope from the knowledge that humanity's biggest problems today are ones entirely of our own making. Asteroids hurtling at us beyond our control don't figure high on our list of imminent dangers. To save ourselves, we don't need new technology: we just need the political will to face up to our problems of population and the environment.

I also draw hope from a unique advantage that we enjoy. Unlike any previous society in history, our global society today is the first with the opportunity to learn from the mistakes of societies remote from us in space and in time. When the Maya and Mangarevans were cutting down their trees, there were no historians or archaeologists, no newspapers or television, to warn them of the consequences of their actions. We, on the other hand, have a detailed chronicle of human successes and failures at our disposal. Will we choose to use it? ▪

The Reader's Presence

1. What societies does Diamond use as examples? How does he suggest that the fates of historical societies relate to the survival of modern societies like our own? Do you agree with his views about the factors that will be important for our society's survival? Why or why not?

2. What connections does Diamond make between choices made in modern American society and in defunct cultures of the past? What does he suggest is going wrong in American culture that could adversely affect our society's future? Does he leave out anything that you consider an important factor in the survival of the United States as a society? If so, what is that factor, and why is it important?

3. **CONNECTIONS:**   Reread Diamond's essay and then compare and contrast it to Michael Pollan's "What's Eating America" (page 781). How does each writer underscore his interest in promoting the importance of protecting the natural environment? Which argument do you find more convincing and compelling? Explain why.

The Academic Voice

JARED DIAMOND on the "Ecological Collapses of Past Civilizations"

What happens when writers address an academic audience, rather than a general audience? What adjustments do they make in their vocabulary, tone of voice, organization, or argument? How do these adjustments take into account the level of knowledge and information they can expect an academic audience to possess? Here you will find the concluding section of Diamond's academic paper "Ecological Collapses of Past Civilizations," published in the *Proceedings of the American Philosophical Society*. Compare this academic selection with the lessons from history (paragraphs 20–31) in the conclusion of Diamond's essay for a general audience, "The Ends of the World as We Know Them" (page 642).

❝ **Lessons for Our Times**

We have reviewed examples of ancient civilizations that collapsed, and whose collapses were caused by (or received contributions from) self-inflicted ecological damage. Yet there are other collapses for which such factors are not suspected. In still other areas, such as Japan, Java, and northwest Europe, complex societies have developed for thousands of years without evidence of interruption by a major collapse. Why are some societies apparently more vulnerable ecologically than are others?

By now, it may be apparent to readers that past ecological collapses occurred in environments or climates of types that we recognize today as ecologically vulnerable. Many of the collapses—such as those of Easter Island, Kahoolawe, the Anasazi, the Fertile Crescent, Greece, and northwest Africa—occurred in areas with dry climates. Since growth of vegetation is approximately proportional to rainfall, dry areas take much more time to recover from habitat destruction than do wet areas. If regrowth is too slow, erosion may remove topsoil and make recovery impossible, as happened on Kahoolawe. Many other collapses—such as those of New Zealand South Island and of Henderson Island—occurred after humans first colonized a land formerly uninhabited by humans. Animals with no evolutionary history of exposure to human predators are behaviorally naïve and easily exterminated by hunters (Olson and James 1982, James et al. 1987, Steadman 1989, Steadman and Kirch 1990, Steadman 1991).

Thus, the pattern of ecological collapses of past civilizations is a familiar, almost banal, one. Of course, societies in more fragile environments are at a greater risk of collapse from undermining their own resource base! Today, many human societies in fragile environments are assaulting those environments with far greater human numbers and far more destructive technology than sufficed to degrade such environments in the past. Much of the U.S. West, the

Himalayas, and Africa consists of such environments.

However, that reasoning should not be reversed to conclude that modern societies in ecologically more robust environments are secure. Unlike Easter Island society, which was totally self-sufficient for 1,500 years, all countries today depend economically on other countries for some essential resources, including food and energy. All countries today are interconnected through living together in the same increasingly polluted atmosphere and oceans. In the next century we risk more than just societies of fragile environments collapsing one by one. We also risk a collapse of world society, an outcome for which there are already warning signs.

Surprisingly, many educated people who should know better deny the seriousness of the risks ahead of us. History has important lessons to teach such people. Collapse has already befallen many societies that were at less risk than our societies are today. 〃

References

James, H. F., D. W. Stafford, D. W. Steadman, et al. 1987. Radiocarbon dates on bones of extinct birds from Hawaii. *Proc. Nat. Acad. Sci. USA* 84:2350–2354.

Olson, S. L., and H. F. James. 1982. Fossil birds from the Hawaiian Islands: evidence for wholesale extinction by man before Western contact. *Science* 217:633–635.

Steadman, D. W. 1989. Extinction of birds in eastern Polynesia: a review of the record, and comparisons with other Pacific island groups. *J. Archaeol. Sci.* 16:177–205.

———. 1991. Extinct and extirpated birds from Aitutaki and Atiu, southern Cook Islands. *Pacific Sci.* 45:325–347.

Steadman, D. W., and P. V. Kirch. 1990. Prehistoric extinction of birds on Mangaia, Cook Islands, Polynesia. *Proc. Nat. Acad. Sci. USA* 87:9605–9609.

Barbara Ehrenreich

WILL WOMEN STILL NEED MEN?

Although she received a PhD in cellular biology from Rockefeller University in the late 1960s, **BARBARA EHRENREICH** (b. 1941) chose to abandon a career in science to pursue a life of political activism. She is a prominent member of the Democratic Socialists of America and sits on the Board of Directors of NORML, the National Organization for the Reform of Marijuana Laws. She has written nearly twenty books, the most famous of which is probably *Nickel and Dimed* (2001), an exposé of the rough conditions for the working poor in America after the welfare reform of 1996. As part of her research for *Nickel and Dimed*, Ehrenreich went undercover, working as a waitress, house cleaner, hotel maid, nursing home aide, and Walmart associate to gain a firsthand perspective on the difficulties blue-collar women face trying to make a living in America. Ehrenreich's work has appeared in *Harper's*, the *New York Times*, *Mother Jones*, the *Progressive*, *Ms.*, the *New Republic*, the *Atlantic Monthly*, and *Salon.com*.

> As part of her research for *Nickel and Dimed*, Barbara Ehrenreich went undercover, working as a waitress, house cleaner, hotel maid, nursing home aide, and Walmart associate to gain a firsthand perspective on the difficulties blue-collar women face trying to make a living in America.

THIS COULD BE the century when the sexes go their separate ways. Sure, we've hung in there together for about a thousand millenniums so far—through hunting-gathering, agriculture and heavy industry—but what choice did we have? For most of human existence, if you wanted to make a living, raise children or even have a roaring good time now and then, you had to get the cooperation of the other sex.

What's new about the future, and potentially more challenging to our species than Martian colonization or silicon brain implants, is that the partnership between the sexes is becoming entirely voluntary. We can decide to stick together—or we can finally say, "Sayonara, other sex!" For the first time in human history and prehistory combined, the choice will be ours.

I predict three possible scenarios, starting with the Big Divorce. Somewhere around 2025, people will pick a gender equivalent of the Mason-Dixon Line and sort themselves out accordingly. In Guy Land the men will be free to spend their evenings staging belching contests and watching old Howard Stern tapes. In Gal Land the women will all be fat and happy, and no one will bother to shave her legs. Aside from a few initial border clashes, the separation will for the most part be amicable. At least the "battle of the sexes," insofar as anyone can remember it, will be removed from the kitchens and bedrooms of America and into the U.N.

And why not? If the monosexual way of life were counter to human nature, men wouldn't have spent so much of the past millennium dodging women by enlisting in armies, monasteries and all-male guilds and professions. Up until the past half-century, women only fantasized about their version of the same: a utopia like the one described by 19th century feminist Charlotte Perkins Gilman, where women would lead placidly sexless lives and reproduce by parthenogenesis. But a real separation began to look feasible about 50 years ago. With the invention of TV dinners and drip-dry shirts, for the first time the average man became capable of feeding and dressing himself. Sensing their increasing dispensability on the home front, and tired of picking up dropped socks, women rushed into the work force. They haven't achieved full economic independence by any means (women still earn only 75% of what men do), but more and more of them are realizing that ancient female dream—a room, or better yet, a condo of their own.

The truly species-shaking change is coming from the new technologies of reproduction. Up until now, if you wanted to reproduce, you not only had to fraternize with a member of the other sex for at least a few minutes, but you also ran a 50% risk that any resulting baby would turn out to be a member of the foreign sex. No more. Thanks to in vitro fertilization, we can have babies without having sex. And with the latest techniques of sex selection, we can have babies of whatever sex we want.

Obviously women, with their built-in baby incubators, will have the advantage in a monosexual future. They just have to pack up a good supply of frozen semen, a truckload of turkey basters and go their own way. But men will be catching up. For one thing, until now, frozen-and-thawed ova have been tricky to fertilize because their outer membrane gets too hard. But a new technique called intracytoplasmic sperm injection makes frozen ova fully fertilizable, and so now Guy Land can have its ovum banks. As for the incubation problem, a few years ago feminist writer Gena Corea offered the seemingly paranoid suggestion that men might eventually keep just a few women around in "reproductive brothels," gestating on demand. A guy will pick an ovum for attractive qualities like smart, tall and allergy-free, then have it inserted into some faceless surrogate mother employed as a reproductive slave.

What about sex, though, meaning the experience, not the category? Chances are, we will be having sex with machines, mostly computers. Even today you can buy interactive CD-ROMs like Virtual Valerie, and there's talk of full-body, virtual-reality sex in which the pleasure seeker wears a specially fitted suit—very specially fitted—allowing for tactile as well as audiovisual sensation. If that sounds farfetched, consider the fact that cyber-innovation

5

is currently in the hands of social skills-challenged geeks who couldn't hope to get a date without flashing their Internet stock options.

Still, there's a reason why the Big Divorce scenario isn't likely to work out, even by Y3K: we love each other, we males and females—madly, sporadically, intermittently, to be sure—but at least enough to keep us pair bonding furiously, even when there's no obvious hardheaded reason to do so. Hence, despite predictions of the imminent "breakdown of the family," the divorce rate leveled off in the 1990s, and the average couple is still hopeful or deluded enough to invest about $20,000 in their first wedding. True, fewer people are marrying: 88% of Americans have married at least once, down from 94% in 1988. But the difference is largely made up by couples who set up housekeeping without the blessing of the state. And an astounding 16% of the population has been married three times—which shows a remarkable commitment to, if nothing else, the institution of marriage.

The question for the new century is, Do we love each other enough—enough, that is, to sustain the old pair-bonded way of life? Many experts see the glass half empty: cohabitation may be replacing marriage, but it's even less likely to last. Hearts are routinely broken and children's lives disrupted as we churn, ever starry-eyed, from one relationship to the next. Even liberal icons like Hillary Rodham Clinton and Harvard Afro-American studies professor Cornel West have been heard muttering about the need to limit the ease and accessibility of divorce.

Hence, perhaps, Scenario B: seeing that the old economic and biological   10
pressures to marry don't work anymore, people will decide to replace them with new forms of coercion. Divorce will be outlawed, along with abortion and possibly contraception. Extramarital hanky-panky will be punishable with shunning or, in the more hard-line jurisdictions, stoning. There will still be sex, and probably plenty of it inside marriage, thanks to what will be known as Chemically Assisted Monogamy: Viagra for men and Viagra-like drugs for women, such as apomorphine and Estratest (both are being tested right now), to reignite the spark long after familiarity has threatened to extinguish it. Naturally, prescriptions will be available only upon presentation of a valid marriage license.

It couldn't happen here, even in a thousand years? Already, a growing "marriage movement," including groups like the Promise Keepers, is working to make divorce lawyers as rare as elevator operators. Since 1997, Louisiana and Arizona have been offering ultratight "covenant marriages," which can be dissolved only in the case of infidelity, abuse or felony conviction, and similar measures have been introduced in 17 other states. As for the age-old problem of premarital fooling around, some extremely conservative Christian activists have launched a movement to halt the dangerous practice of dating and replace it with parent-supervised betrothals leading swiftly and ineluctably to the altar.

But Scenario B has a lot going against it too. The 1998 impeachment fiasco showed just how hard it will be to restigmatize extramarital sex. Sure, we think adultery is a bad thing, just not bad enough to disqualify anyone from ruling the world. Meanwhile, there have been few takers for covenant marriages, showing that most people like to keep their options open. Tulane University sociologist Laura Sanchez speculates that the ultimate effect of covenant marriages may be to open up the subversive possibility of diversifying the institution of marriage—with different types for different folks, including, perhaps someday, even gay folks.

Which brings us to the third big scenario. This is the diversity option, arising from the realization that the one-size-fits-all model of marriage may have been one of the biggest sources of tension between the sexes all along—based as it is on the wildly unrealistic expectation that a single spouse can meet one's needs for a lover, friend, co-parent, financial partner, reliably, 24-7. Instead there will be renewable marriages, which get re-evaluated every five to seven years, after which they can be revised, recelebrated or dissolved with no, or at least fewer, hard feelings. There will be unions between people who don't live together full-time but do want to share a home base. And of course there will always be plenty of people who live together but don't want to make a big deal out of it. Already, thanks to the gay-rights movement, more than 600 corporations and other employers offer domestic-partner benefits, a 60-fold increase since 1990.

And the children? The real paradigm shift will come when we stop trying to base our entire society on the wavering sexual connection between individuals. Romantic love ebbs and surges unaccountably; it's the bond between parents and children that has to remain rocklike year after year. Putting children first would mean that adults would make a contract—not to live together or sleep together but to take joint responsibility for a child or an elderly adult. Some of these arrangements will look very much like today's marriages, with a heterosexual couple undertaking the care of their biological children. Others will look like nothing we've seen before, at least not in suburban America, especially since there's no natural limit on the number of contracting caretakers. A group of people—male, female, gay, straight—will unite in their responsibility for the children they bear or acquire through the local Artificial Reproduction Center. Heather may routinely have two mommies, or at least a whole bunch of resident aunts—which is, of course, more or less how things have been for eons in such distinctly unbohemian settings as the tribal village.

So how will things play out this century and beyond? Just so you will be 15 prepared, here's my timeline:

> Between 2000 and 2339: geographical diversity prevails. The Southeast and a large swath of the Rockies will go for Scenario B (early marriage, no divorce). Oregon, California and New York will offer renewable marriages, and a few states will go monosexual, as in Scenario A. But because of the 1996 Defense of Marriage Act, each state is entitled to recognize only the kinds of "marriages" it approves of, so you will need a "marriage visa" to travel across the country, at least if you intend to share a motel room.

Between 2340 and 2387: NATO will be forced to intervene in the Custody Wars that break out between the Polygamous Republic of Utah and the Free Love Zone of the Central Southwest. A huge refugee crisis will develop when singles are ethnically cleansed from the Christian Nation of Idaho. Florida will be partitioned into divorce-free and marriage-free zones.

In 2786: the new President's Inauguration will be attended by all five members of the mixed-sex, multiracial commune that raised her. She will establish sizable tax reductions for couples or groups of any size that create stable households for their children and other dependents. Peace will break out.

And in 2999: a scholar of ancient history will discover these words penned by a gay writer named Fenton Johnson back in 1996: "The mystery of love and life and death is really grander and more glorious than human beings can grasp, much less legislate." He will put this sentence onto a bumper sticker. The message will spread. We will realize that the sexes can't live without each other, but neither can they be joined at the hip. We will grow up.

The Reader's Presence

1. Although Ehrenreich makes some hyperbolic and humorous assertions in this essay, most of her claims and predictions are rooted in current or historical events. Which specific parts of her essay are conjecture, and which are based on facts? How does she integrate the two? With what effect(s)? How persuasive do you find this compositional strategy?

2. Identify what you think are Ehrenreich's personal views on the topic of this essay. Which specific passages lead you to believe this? What do you notice, for example, about both the word choices and the way in which Ehrenreich presents these passages? How do you read the last line of the essay, and what are the effects of Ehrenreich's choosing to end the essay with it?

3. **CONNECTIONS:** Compare the claims about gender that Ehrenreich makes in this essay to the ones Michael Chabon makes in "Faking It" (page 343). What authority does each writer invoke to make his or her claims? In what specific ways are their approaches similar, and in what ways are they different? How does each writer's own gender affect your reading of the claims he or she makes?

Nora Ephron

THE BOSTON PHOTOGRAPHS

NORA EPHRON (b. 1941) started her writing career as a reporter for the *New York Post*, and since then has written for numerous magazines, including *New York Magazine*, *McCall's*, and *Cosmopolitan*. Ephron's collections of essays on popular culture include *Wallflower at the Orgy* (1970), *Crazy Salad: Some Things About Women* (1975), and *Scribble Scribble: Notes on the Media* (1978). The essay "The Boston Photographs" appeared originally in *Esquire* in 1975. Ephron also wrote the screenplays for *Silkwood* (with Alice Arlen), *When Harry Met Sally*, and *Sleepless in Seattle*. In 1992 she directed her first movie, *This Is My Life*, written with her sister Delia Ephron; since then she has directed the films *Michael* (1996), *You've*

> **Nora Ephron wrote, directed, and produced the award-winning film *Julie & Julia* (2009).**

Got Mail (1998), and *Lucky Numbers* (2000). She wrote, directed, and produced the award-winning film *Julie & Julia* (2009). Her most recent collection of essays is *I Remember Nothing: And Other Reflections* (2010).

When Nora Ephron spoke at the Wellesley College commencement in 1979, she told the largely female audience, "We were sent off into a college environment that expected us to grow up to be soothing women. . . . We were to spend our lives making nice." Ephron believes that the world needs more troublemakers. In "The Boston Photographs," she makes a bold argument for publishing disturbing and controversial photographs.

"I MADE all kinds of pictures because I thought it would be a good rescue shot over the ladder . . . never dreamed it would be anything else. . . . I kept having to move around because of the light set. The sky was bright and they were in deep shadow. I was making pictures with a motor drive and he, the fire fighter, was reaching up and, I don't know, everything started falling. I followed the girl down taking pictures . . . I made three or four frames. I realized what was going on and I completely turned around, because I didn't want to see her hit."

You probably saw the photographs. In most newspapers, there were three of them. The first showed some people on a fire escape—a fireman, a woman and a child. The fireman had a nice strong jaw and looked very brave. The woman was holding the child. Smoke was pouring from the building behind them. A rescue ladder was approaching, just a few feet away, and the fireman had one arm around the woman and one arm reaching out toward the ladder. The second picture showed the fire escape slipping off the building. The child had fallen on the escape and seemed about to slide off the edge. The woman was grasping desperately at the legs of the fireman, who had managed to grab the ladder. The third picture showed the woman and child in midair, falling to the ground. Their arms and legs were outstretched, horribly distended. A potted plant was falling too. The caption said that the woman, Diana Bryant, nineteen, died in the fall. The child landed on the woman's body and lived.

The pictures were taken by Stanley Forman, thirty, of the *Boston Herald American*. He used a motor-driven Nikon F set at 1/250, f5.6-S. Because of the motor, the camera can click off three frames a second. More than four hundred newspapers in the United States alone carried the photographs; the tear sheets from overseas are still coming in. The *New York Times* ran them on the first page of its second section; a paper in south Georgia gave them nineteen columns; the *Chicago Tribune*, the *Washington Post* and the *Washington Star* filled almost half their front pages, the *Star* under a somewhat redundant headline that read: SENSATIONAL PHOTOS OF RESCUE ATTEMPT THAT FAILED.

The photographs are indeed sensational. They are pictures of death in action, of that split second when luck runs out, and it is impossible to look

Three photographs documenting the spectacle of death.

at them without feeling their extraordinary impact and remembering, in an almost subconscious way, the morbid fantasy of falling, falling off a building, falling to one's death. Beyond that, the pictures are classics, old-fashioned but perfect examples of photojournalism at its most spectacular. They're throwbacks, really, fire pictures, 1930s tabloid shots; at the same time they're technically superb and thoroughly modern—the sequence could not have been taken at all until the development of the motor-driven camera some sixteen years ago.

Most newspaper editors anticipate some reader reaction to photographs   5
like Forman's; even so, the response around the country was enormous, and almost all of it was negative. I have read hundreds of the letters that were printed in letters-to-the-editor sections, and they repeat the same points. "Invading the privacy of death." "Cheap sensationalism." "I thought I was reading the *National Enquirer.*" "Assigning the agony of a human being in terror of imminent death to the status of a side-show act." "A tawdry way to sell newspapers." The *Seattle Times* received sixty letters and calls; its managing editor even got a couple of them at home. A reader wrote the *Philadelphia Inquirer:* "*Jaws* and *Towering Inferno* are playing downtown; don't take business away from people who pay good money to advertise in your own paper." Another reader wrote the *Chicago Sun-Times:* "I shall try to hide my disappointment that Miss Bryant wasn't wearing a skirt when she fell to her death. You could have had some award-winning photographs of her underpants as her skirt billowed over her head, you voyeurs." Several newspaper editors wrote columns defending the pictures: Thomas Keevil of the *Costa Mesa* (California) *Daily Pilot* printed a ballot for readers to vote on whether they would have printed the pictures; Marshall L. Stone of Maine's *Bangor Daily News*, which refused to print the famous assassination picture of the Vietcong prisoner in Saigon,[1] claimed that the Boston pictures showed the dangers of fire escapes and raised questions about slumlords. (The burning building was a five-story brick apartment house on Marlborough Street in the Back Bay section of Boston.)

For the last five years, the *Washington Post* has employed various journalists as ombudsmen, whose job is to monitor the paper on behalf of the public. The *Post's* current ombudsman is Charles Seib, former managing editor of the *Washington Star;* the day the Boston photographs appeared, the paper received over seventy calls in protest. As Seib later wrote in a column about the pictures, it was "the largest reaction to a published item that I have experienced in eight months as the Post's ombudsman. . . .

"In the *Post's* newsroom, on the other hand, I found no doubts, no second thoughts . . . the question was not whether they should be printed but how they should be displayed. When I talked to editors . . . they used words

---

[1] **famous assassination picture . . . in Saigon:** A 1968 photograph by Eddie Adams of the Associated Press showed Saigon's chief of police executing a prisoner with a pistol; the photograph helped turn American opinion against the war.—EDS.

like 'interesting' and 'riveting' and 'gripping' to describe them. The pictures told of something about life in the ghetto, they said (although the neighborhood where the tragedy occurred is not a ghetto, I am told). They dramatized the need to check on the safety of fire escapes. They dramatically conveyed something that had happened, and that is the business we're in. They were news. . . .

"Was publication of that [third] picture a bow to the same taste for the morbidly sensational that makes gold mines of disaster movies? Most papers will not print the picture of a dead body except in the most unusual circumstances. Does the fact that the final picture was taken a millisecond before the young woman died make a difference? Most papers will not print a picture of a bare female breast. Is that a more inappropriate subject for display than the picture of a human being's last agonized instant of life?" Seib offered no answers to the questions he raised, but he went on to say that although as an editor he would probably have run the pictures, as a reader he was revolted by them.

In conclusion, Seib wrote: "Any editor who decided to print those pictures without giving at least a moment's thought to what purpose they served and what their effect was likely to be on the reader should ask another question: Have I become so preoccupied with manufacturing a product according to professional traditions and standards that I have forgotten about the consumer, the reader?"

It should be clear that the phone calls and letters and Seib's own reaction 10 were occasioned by one factor alone: the death of the woman. Obviously, had she survived the fall, no one would have protested; the pictures would have had a completely different impact. Equally obviously, had the child died as well—or instead—Seib would undoubtedly have received ten times the phone calls he did. In each case, the pictures would have been exactly the same—only the captions, and thus the responses, would have been different.

But the questions Seib raises are worth discussing—though not exactly for the reasons he mentions. For it may be that the real lesson of the Boston photographs is not the danger that editors will be forgetful of reader reaction, but that they will continue to censor pictures of death precisely because of that reaction. The protests Seib fielded were really a variation on an old theme—and we saw plenty of it during the Nixon-Agnew years—the "Why doesn't the press print the good news?" argument. In this case, of course, the objections were all dressed up and cleverly disguised as righteous indignation about the privacy of death. This is a form of puritanism that is often justifiable; just as often it is merely puritanical.

Seib takes it for granted that the widespread though fairly recent newspaper policy against printing pictures of dead bodies is a sound one; I don't know that it makes any sense at all. I recognize that printing pictures of corpses raises all sorts of problems about taste and titillation and sensationalism; the fact is, however, that people die. Death happens to be one of life's main events. And it is irresponsible—and more than that, inaccurate—for newspapers to fail to show it, or to show it only when an astonishing set of photos comes in over the Associated Press wire. Most papers covering fatal automobile accidents will print pictures of mangled cars. But the significance of fatal automobile accidents is not that a great deal of steel is twisted but that people die. Why not show it? That's what accidents are about. Throughout the Vietnam War, editors were reluctant to print atrocity pictures. Why *not* print them? That's what that war was about. Murder victims are almost never photographed; they are granted their privacy. But their relatives are relentlessly pictured on their way in and out of hospitals and morgues and funerals.

I'm not advocating that newspapers print these things in order to teach their readers a lesson. The *Post* editors justified their printing of the Boston pictures with several arguments in that direction; every one of them is irrelevant. The pictures don't show anything about slum life; the incident could have happened anywhere, and it did. It is extremely unlikely that anyone who saw them rushed out and had his fire escape strengthened. And the pictures were not news—at least they were not national news. It is not news in Washington, or New York, or Los Angeles that a woman was killed in a Boston fire. The only newsworthy thing about the pictures is that they were taken. They deserve to be printed because they are great pictures, breathtaking pictures of something that happened. That they disturb readers is exactly as it should be: that's why photojournalism is often more powerful than written journalism. ▪

The Reader's Presence

1. At what point does Ephron's argument begin to emerge? How does she present information about the photographs? Why do you think she chooses to structure her argument as she does?

2. How does Ephron refute newspapers' justifications for printing the photographs? What might she argue should be the purpose of photojournalism? Do you agree with this purpose? Why or why not?

3. **CONNECTIONS:** "Death happens to be one of life's main events," Ephron writes in paragraph 12, arguing that the photographs are important although they are "not news" (paragraph 13). How does knowing that the woman died in the fall affect the viewer's feelings about the photographs? Read Errol Morris's essay "Liar, Liar, Pants on Fire" (page 753), which focuses on "truth and photography." "It is also interesting," Morris observes, "how a photograph quickly changes when we learn more about what it depicts, when we provide a context, when we become familiar with an underlying story. And when we make claims about the photograph using language. For truth, properly considered, is about the relationship between language and the world, not about photographs and the world" (paragraph 18). Given your understanding of Ephron's points about photography, what would you anticipate would be her reaction to Morris's point here? Be as specific in your response as possible.

Jonathan Safran Foer

LET THEM EAT DOG

JONATHAN SAFRAN FOER (b. 1977) is a Jewish-American author whose first novel, *Everything Is Illuminated* (2002), was published to critical acclaim when he was only twenty-five years old. In the wake of this success, he went on to write another novel, *Extremely Loud & Incredibly Close* (2005), which was also widely praised and translated into several languages. A writer of diverse talents, Foer has also written the libretto for an opera, *Seven Attempted Escapes from Silence*, which was performed by the Berlin State Opera in 2005, and a book of nonfiction, *Eating Animals* (2009), from which "Let Them Eat Dog" is an excerpt. Long conflicted about the ethics of eating meat, Foer was inspired by the birth of his first child to explore the issue with more urgency because, he said, he "would have to make decisions on [his son's] behalf." Foer's most recent book, *Tree of Codes*, was published in 2010.

> Long conflicted about the ethics of eating meat, Jonathan Safran Foer was inspired by the birth of his first child to explore the issue with more urgency because, he said, he "would have to make decisions on [his son's] behalf."

DESPITE THE FACT that it's perfectly legal in 44 states, eating "man's best friend" is as taboo as a man eating his best friend. Even the most enthusiastic carnivores won't eat dogs. TV guy and sometimes cooker Gordon Ramsay can get pretty macho with lambs and piglets when doing publicity for something he's selling, but you'll never see a puppy peeking out of one of his pots. And though he once said he'd electrocute his children if they became vegetarian, one can't help but wonder what his response would be if they poached the family pooch.

Dogs are wonderful, and in many ways unique. But they are remarkably unremarkable in their intellectual and experiential capacities. Pigs are every bit as intelligent and feeling, by any sensible definition of the words. They can't hop into the back of a Volvo, but they can fetch, run and play, be mischievous and reciprocate affection. So why don't they get to curl up by the fire? Why can't they at least be spared being tossed on the fire? Our taboo against dog eating says something about dogs and a great deal about us.

The French, who love their dogs, sometimes eat their horses.

The Spanish, who love their horses, sometimes eat their cows.

The Indians, who love their cows, sometimes eat their dogs.   5

While written in a much different context, George Orwell's words (from *Animal Farm*) apply here: "All animals are equal, but some animals are more equal than others."

So who's right? What might be the reasons to exclude canine from the menu? The selective carnivore suggests:

Don't eat companion animals. But dogs aren't kept as companions in all of the places they are eaten. And what about our petless neighbors? Would we have any right to object if they had dog for dinner?

OK, then: Don't eat animals with significant mental capacities. If by "significant mental capacities" we mean what a dog has, then good for the dog. But such a definition would also include the pig, cow and chicken. And it would exclude severely impaired humans.

Then: It's for good reason that the eternal taboos—don't fiddle with your   10
crap, kiss your sister, or eat your companions—are taboo. Evolutionarily speaking, those things are bad for us. But dog eating isn't a taboo in many places, and it isn't in any way bad for us. Properly cooked, dog meat poses no greater health risks than any other meat.

Dog meat has been described as "gamey," "complex," "buttery" and "floral." And there is a proud pedigree of eating it. Fourth-century tombs

Dutch photographer Jan van IJken has devoted several years to observing humans interact with animals in a wide range of circumstances—from laboratory settings to bird shows and factory farms. His remarkable images document the ambivalent ways we value other creatures.

contain depictions of dogs being slaughtered along with other food animals. It was a fundamental enough habit to have informed language itself: the Sino-Korean character for "fair and proper" (*yeon*) literally translates into "as cooked dog meat is delicious." Hippocrates praised dog meat as a source of strength. Dakota Indians enjoyed dog liver, and not so long ago Hawaiians ate dog brains and blood. Captain Cook ate dog. Roald Amundsen famously ate his sled dogs. (Granted, he was really hungry.) And dogs are still eaten to overcome bad luck in the Philippines; as medicine in China and Korea; to enhance libido in Nigeria and in numerous places, on every continent, because they taste good. For centuries, the Chinese have raised special breeds of dogs, like the black-tongued chow, for chow, and many European countries still have laws on the books regarding postmortem examination of dogs intended for human consumption.

Of course, something having been done just about everywhere is no kind of justification for doing it now. But unlike all farmed meat, which requires the creation and maintenance of animals, dogs are practically begging to be eaten. Three to four million dogs and cats are euthanized annually. The simple disposal of these euthanized dogs is an enormous ecological and economic problem. But eating those strays, those runaways, those not-quite-cute-enough-to-take and not-quite-well-behaved-enough-to-keep dogs would be killing a flock of birds with one stone and eating it, too.

In a sense it's what we're doing already. Rendering—the conversion of animal protein unfit for human consumption into food for livestock and pets—allows processing plants to transform useless dead dogs into productive members of the food chain. In America, millions of dogs and cats euthanized in animal shelters every year become the food for our food. So let's just eliminate this inefficient and bizarre middle step.

This need not challenge our civility. We won't make them suffer any more than necessary. While it's widely believed that adrenaline makes dog meat taste better—hence the traditional methods of slaughter: hanging, boiling alive, beating to death—we can all agree that if we're going to eat them, we should kill them quickly and painlessly, right? For example, the traditional Hawaiian means of holding the dog's nose shut—in order to conserve blood—must be regarded (socially if not legally) as a no-no. Perhaps we could include dogs under the Humane Methods of Slaughter Act. That doesn't say anything about how they're treated during their lives, and isn't subject to any meaningful oversight or enforcement, but surely we can rely on the industry to "self-regulate," as we do with other eaten animals.

Few people sufficiently appreciate the colossal task of feeding a world of billions of omnivores who demand meat with their potatoes. The inefficient use of dogs—conveniently already in areas of high human population (take note, local-food advocates)—should make any good ecologist blush. One could argue that various "humane" groups are the worst hypocrites, spending enormous amounts of money and energy in a futile attempt to reduce the number of unwanted dogs while at the very same time propagating the irresponsible no-dog-for-dinner taboo. If we let dogs be dogs, and breed without interference, we would create a sustainable, local meat supply with low energy inputs that would put even the most efficient grass-based farming to shame. For the ecologically-minded it's time to admit that dog is realistic food for realistic environmentalists.

For those already convinced, here's a classic Filipino recipe I recently came across. I haven't tried it myself, but sometimes you can read a recipe and just know.

> **Stewed Dog, Wedding Style**
> First, kill a medium-sized dog, then burn off the fur over a hot fire. Carefully remove the skin while still warm and set aside for later (may be used in other recipes). Cut meat into 1" cubes. Marinate meat in mixture of vinegar, peppercorn, salt, and garlic for 2 hours. Fry meat in oil using a large wok over an open fire, then add onions and chopped pineapple and sauté until tender. Pour in tomato sauce and boiling water, add green pepper, bay leaf, and Tabasco. Cover and simmer over warm coals until meat is tender. Blend in purée of dog's liver and cook for additional 5–7 minutes.

There is an overabundance of rational reasons to say no to factory-farmed meat: It is the No. 1 cause of global warming, it systematically forces tens of billions of animals to suffer in ways that would be illegal if they were dogs, it is a decisive factor in the development of swine and avian flus, and so on. And yet even most people who know these things still aren't inspired to order something else on the menu. Why?

Food is not rational. Food is culture, habit, craving and identity. Responding to factory farming calls for a capacity to care that dwells beyond information. We know what we see on undercover videos of factory farms and slaughterhouses is wrong. (There are those who will defend a system that allows for occasional animal cruelty, but no one defends the cruelty, itself.) And despite it being entirely reasonable, the case for eating dogs is likely repulsive to just about every reader of this paper. The instinct comes before our reason, and is more important. ▨

20

The Reader's Presence

1. What was your visceral reaction to reading Foer's essay? Discuss your reaction in the light of what you think Foer's purpose was in writing this essay. How well does his approach support—or not support—the argument he is advocating?

2. Foer writes, "Food is not rational" (paragraph 20). Review the numerous reasons he gives to support the idea of consuming dogs as food. What arguments can you make against any of his justifications? How airtight is the case he makes?

3. **CONNECTIONS:** Compare the voice of Foer's essay with that of David Foster Wallace in "Consider the Lobster" (page 839). What kinds of reaction do you think each writer tries to elicit from his respective readers? (Cite specific passages to support your answer.) Why do you think each writer chose his unusual approach to argument rather than a more traditional one? How does each writer establish his authority to speak on the topic?

John Taylor Gatto

AGAINST SCHOOL

"I've taught public school for twenty-six years but I just can't do it anymore," began an impassioned op-ed piece published in the *Wall Street Journal* in 1991. Its author, **JOHN TAYLOR GATTO** (b. 1935), continued, "I've come slowly to understand what it is I really teach: A curriculum of confusion, class position, arbitrary justice, vulgarity, rudeness, disrespect for privacy, indifference to quality, and utter dependency. I teach how to fit into a world I don't want to live in." With the headline "I May Be a Teacher but I'm Not an Educator," the essay set off a fierce debate among parents, teachers, and politicians about the system of public education in the United States. It also launched Gatto's career as a speaker, consultant, and writer.

After graduating from Columbia University, Gatto worked as a scriptwriter, a songwriter, and an ad writer; drove a cab; sold hot dogs; and, finally, began a distinguished career as a schoolteacher. He was recognized as New York City Teacher of the Year for three years in a row. In 1991, the year he resigned in protest from his position as a seventh-grade teacher at the Booker T. Washington School in New

> "I've come slowly to understand what it is I really teach: A curriculum of confusion, class position, arbitrary justice, vulgarity, rudeness, disrespect for privacy, indifference to quality, and utter dependency. I teach how to fit into a world I don't want to live in."

York City, he was named New York State Teacher of the Year. He has edited and written many books on education, including *Dumbing Us Down: The Hidden Curriculum of Compulsory Schooling* (1992), *The Exhausted School* (1993), *A Different Kind of Teacher: Solving the Crisis of American Schooling* (2000), and *The Underground History of American Education: A Schoolteacher's Intimate Investigation into the Problem of Modern Schooling* (2001). His new book, *Weapons of Mass Instruction: A Schoolteacher's Journey Through the Dark World of Compulsory Schooling* (2010), focuses on the ways in which compulsory schooling cripples the imagination. His essay "Against School" first appeared in *Harper's* magazine in 2001.

I TAUGHT FOR THIRTY YEARS in some of the worst schools in Manhattan, and in some of the best, and during that time I became an expert in boredom. Boredom was everywhere in my world, and if you asked the kids, as I often did, *why* they felt so bored, they always gave the same answers: They said the work was stupid, that it made no sense, that they already knew it. They said they wanted to be doing something real, not just sitting around. They said teachers didn't seem to know much about their subjects and clearly weren't interested in learning more. And the kids were right: their teachers were every bit as bored as they were.

Boredom is the common condition of schoolteachers, and anyone who has spent time in a teachers' lounge can vouch for the low energy, the whining, the dispirited attitudes, to be found there. When asked why *they* feel bored, the teachers tend to blame the kids, as you might expect. Who wouldn't get bored teaching students who are rude and interested only in grades? If even that. Of course, teachers are themselves products of the same twelve-year compulsory school programs that so thoroughly bore their students, and as school personnel they are trapped inside structures even more rigid than those imposed upon the children. Who, then, is to blame?

We all are. My grandfather taught me that. One afternoon when I was seven I complained to him of boredom, and he batted me hard on the head. He told me that I was never to use that term in his presence again, that if I was bored it was my fault and no one else's. The obligation to amuse and instruct myself was entirely my own, and people who didn't know that were childish people, to be avoided if possible. Certainly not to be trusted. That episode cured me of boredom forever, and here and there over the years I was able to pass on the lesson to some remarkable student. For the most part, however, I found it futile to challenge the official notion that boredom and childishness were the natural state of affairs in the classroom. Often I had to defy custom, and even bend the law, to help kids break out of this trap.

The empire struck back, of course; childish adults regularly conflate opposition with disloyalty. I once returned from a medical leave to discover that all evidence of my having been granted the leave had been purposely destroyed, that my job had been terminated, and that I no longer possessed even a teaching license. After nine months of tormented effort I was able to retrieve the license when a school secretary testified to witnessing the plot unfold. In the meantime my family suffered more than I care to remember. By the time I finally retired in 1991, I had more than enough reason to think of our schools — with their long-term, cell-block–style, forced confinement of both students and teachers — as virtual factories of childishness. Yet I honestly could not see *why* they had to be that way. My own experience had revealed to me what many other teachers must learn along the way, too, yet keep to themselves for fear of reprisal: if we wanted to we could easily and inexpensively jettison the old, stupid structures and help kids *take* an education rather than merely *receive* a schooling. We could encourage the best qualities of youthfulness — curiosity, adventure, resilience, the capacity for surprising insight — simply by being more flexible about time, texts, and tests, by introducing kids to truly competent adults, and by giving each student what autonomy he or she needs in order to take a risk every now and then.

But we don't do that. And the more I asked why not, and persisted in thinking about the "problem" of schooling as an engineer might, the more   5

I missed the point: What if there is no "problem" with our schools? What if they are the way they are, so expensively flying in the face of common sense and long experience in how children learn things, not because they are doing something wrong but because they are doing something right? Is it possible that George W. Bush accidentally spoke the truth when he said we would "leave no child behind"? Could it be that our schools are designed to make sure not one of them ever really grows up?

Do we really need school? I don't mean education, just forced schooling: six classes a day, five days a week, nine months a year, for twelve years. Is this deadly routine really necessary? And if so, for what? Don't hide behind reading, writing, and arithmetic as a rationale, because two million happy homeschoolers have surely put that banal justification to rest. Even if they hadn't, a considerable number of well-known Americans never went through the twelve-year wringer our kids currently go through, and they turned out all right. George Washington, Benjamin Franklin, Thomas Jefferson, Abraham Lincoln? Someone taught them, to be sure, but they were not products of a school *system*, and not one of them was ever "graduated" from a secondary school. Throughout most of American history, kids generally didn't go to high school, yet the unschooled rose to be admirals, like Farragut; inventors, like Edison; captains of industry, like Carnegie and Rockefeller; writers, like Melville and Twain and Conrad; and even scholars, like Margaret Mead.[1] In fact, until pretty recently people who reached the age of thirteen weren't looked upon as children at all. Ariel Durant, who co-wrote an enormous, and very good, multivolume history of the world with her husband, Will, was happily married at fifteen, and who could reasonably claim that Ariel Durant was an uneducated person? Unschooled, perhaps, but not uneducated.

We have been taught (that is, schooled) in this country to think of "success" as synonymous with, or at least dependent upon, "schooling," but historically that isn't true in either an intellectual or a financial sense. And plenty of people throughout the world today find a way to educate themselves without resorting to a system of compulsory secondary schools that all too often resemble prisons. Why, then, do Americans confuse education with just such a system? What exactly is the purpose of our public schools?

Mass schooling of a compulsory nature really got its teeth into the United States between 1905 and 1915, though it was conceived of much earlier and pushed for throughout most of the nineteenth century. The reason given for this enormous upheaval of family life and cultural traditions was, roughly speaking, threefold:

1. To make good people.

2. To make good citizens.

3. To make each person his or her personal best.

---

1 **Margaret Mead** (1901–1978): Became the most famous anthropologist in the world, best known for *Coming of Age in Samoa* (1928), a book that analyzed cultural influence on adolescence. —EDS.

These goals are still trotted out today on a regular basis, and most of us accept them in one form or another as a decent definition of public education's mission, however short schools actually fall in achieving them. But we are dead wrong. Compounding our error is the fact that the national literature holds numerous and surprisingly consistent statements of compulsory schooling's true purpose. We have, for example, the great H. L. Mencken,[2] who wrote in *The American Mercury* for April 1924 that the aim of public education is not

> to fill the young of the species with knowledge and awaken their intelligence. . . . Nothing could be further from the truth. The aim . . . is simply to reduce as many individuals as possible to the same safe level, to breed and train a standardized citizenry, to put down dissent and originality. That is its aim in the United States . . . and that is its aim everywhere else.

Because of Mencken's reputation as a satirist, we might be tempted to dismiss this passage as a bit of hyperbolic sarcasm. His article, however, goes on to trace the template for our own educational system back to the now vanished, though never to be forgotten, military state of Prussia. And although he was certainly aware of the irony that we had recently been at war with Germany, the heir to Prussian thought and culture, Mencken was being perfectly serious here. Our educational system really is Prussian in origin, and that really is cause for concern.

The odd fact of a Prussian provenance for our schools pops up again   10
and again once you know to look for it. William James[3] alluded to it many times at the turn of the century. Orestes Brownson, the hero of Christopher Lasch's 1991 book, *The True and Only Heaven*, was publicly denouncing the Prussianization of American schools back in the 1840s. Horace Mann's[4] "Seventh Annual Report" to the Massachusetts State Board of Education in 1843 is essentially a paean to the land of Frederick the Great and a call for its schooling to be brought here. That Prussian culture loomed large in America is hardly surprising, given our early association with that utopian state. A Prussian served as Washington's aide during the Revolutionary War, and so many German-speaking people had settled here by 1795 that Congress considered publishing a German-language edition of the federal laws. But what shocks is that we should so eagerly have adopted one of the very worst aspects of Prussian culture: an educational system deliberately designed to produce mediocre intellects, to hamstring the inner life, to deny students appreciable leadership skills, and to ensure docile and incomplete citizens—all in order to render the populace "manageable."

---

[2] *H(enry) L(ouis) Mencken* (1880–1956): An influential journalist, essayist, magazine editor, satirist, and critic of American life and culture.—Eds.

[3] *William James* (1842–1910): One of America's most important psychologists and philosophers. Trained as a medical doctor, he wrote important books on psychology, and particularly on education and religious experience, as well as on the philosophy of pragmatism. The brother of novelist Henry James and of diarist Alice James.—Eds.

[4] *Horace Mann* (1796–1859): A celebrated American education reformer and also a member of the U.S. House of Representatives (Massachusetts) from 1848 to 1853.—Eds.

It was from James Bryant Conant—president of Harvard for twenty years, WWI poison-gas specialist, WWII executive on the atomic-bomb project, high commissioner of the American zone in Germany after WWII, and truly one of the most influential figures of the twentieth century—that I first got wind of the real purposes of American schooling. Without Conant, we would probably not have the same style and degree of standardized testing that we enjoy today, nor would we be blessed with gargantuan high schools that warehouse 2,000 to 4,000 students at a time, like the famous Columbine High in Littleton, Colorado. Shortly after I retired from teaching I picked up Conant's 1959 book-length essay, *The Child, the Parent and the State*, and was more than a little intrigued to see him mention in passing that the modern schools we attend were the result of a "revolution" engineered between 1905 and 1930. A revolution? He declines to elaborate, but he does direct the curious and the uninformed to Alexander Inglis's 1918 book, *Principles of Secondary Education*, in which "one saw this revolution through the eyes of a revolutionary."

Inglis, for whom a lecture in education at Harvard is named, makes it perfectly clear that compulsory schooling on this continent was intended to be just what it had been for Prussia in the 1820s: a fifth column into the burgeoning democratic movement that threatened to give the peasants and the proletarians a voice at the bargaining table. Modern, industrialized, compulsory schooling was to make a sort of surgical incision into the prospective unity of these underclasses. Divide children by subject, by age-grading, by constant rankings on tests, and by many other more subtle means, and it was unlikely that the ignorant mass of mankind, separated in childhood, would ever re-integrate into a dangerous whole.

Inglis breaks down the purpose—the *actual* purpose—of modern schooling into six basic functions, any one of which is enough to curl the hair of those innocent enough to believe the three traditional goals listed earlier:

1. The *adjustive or adaptive* function. Schools are to establish fixed habits of reaction to authority. This, of course, precludes critical judgment completely. It also pretty much destroys the idea that useful or interesting material should be taught, because you can't test for *reflexive* obedience until you know whether you can make kids learn, and do, foolish and boring things.

2. The *integrating* function. This might well be called "the conformity function," because its intention is to make children as alike as possible. People who conform are predictable, and this is of great use to those who wish to harness and manipulate a large labor force.

3. The *diagnostic and directive* function. School is meant to determine each student's proper social role. This is done by logging evidence mathematically and anecdotally on cumulative records. As in "your permanent record." Yes, you do have one.

4. The *differentiating* function. Once their social role has been "diagnosed," children are to be sorted by role and trained only so far as
their destination in the social machine merits—and not one step further. So much for making kids their personal best.

5. The *selective* function. This refers not to human choice at all but
to Darwin's theory of natural selection as applied to what he called
"the favored races." In short, the idea is to help things along by consciously attempting to improve the breeding stock. Schools are meant
to tag the unfit—with poor grades, remedial placement, and other
punishments—clearly enough that their peers will accept them as
inferior and effectively bar them from the reproductive sweepstakes.
That's what all those little humiliations from first grade onward were
intended to do: wash the dirt down the drain.

6. The *propaedeutic* function. The societal system implied by these rules
will require an elite group of caretakers. To that end, a small fraction
of the kids will quietly be taught how to manage this continuing project, how to watch over and control a population deliberately dumbed
down and declawed in order that government might proceed unchallenged and corporations might never want for obedient labor.

That, unfortunately, is the purpose of mandatory public education in this
country. And lest you take Inglis for an isolated crank with a rather too cynical take on the educational enterprise, you should know that he was hardly
alone in championing these ideas. Conant himself, building on the ideas of
Horace Mann and others, campaigned tirelessly for an American school system designed along the same lines. Men like George Peabody, who funded
the cause of mandatory schooling throughout the South, surely understood
that the Prussian system was useful in creating not only a harmless electorate and a servile labor force but also a virtual herd of mindless consumers.
In time a great number of industrial titans came to recognize the enormous
profits to be had by cultivating and tending just such a herd via public education, among them Andrew Carnegie and John D. Rockefeller.

There you have it. Now you know. We don't need Karl Marx's[5] concep-   15
tion of a grand warfare between the classes to see that it is in the interest of complex management, economic or political, to dumb people down,
to demoralize them, to divide them from one another, and to discard them
if they don't conform. Class may frame the proposition, as when Woodrow
Wilson, then president of Princeton University, said the following to the New
York City School Teachers Association in 1909: "We want one class of persons to have a liberal education, and we want another class of persons, a

---

5 **Karl Marx** (1818–1883): Often identified as the father of communism, Marx was a philosopher, political economist, sociologist, political theorist, and revolutionary.—EDS.

very much larger class, of necessity, in every society, to forgo the privileges of a liberal education and fit themselves to perform specific difficult manual tasks." But the motives behind the disgusting decisions that bring about these ends need not be class-based at all. They can stem purely from fear, or from the by now familiar belief that "efficiency" is the paramount virtue, rather than love, liberty, laughter, or hope. Above all, they can stem from simple greed.

There were vast fortunes to be made, after all, in an economy based on mass production and organized to favor the large corporation rather than the small business or the family farm. But mass production required mass consumption, and at the turn of the twentieth century most Americans considered it both unnatural and unwise to buy things they didn't actually need. Mandatory schooling was a godsend on that count. School didn't have to train kids in any direct sense to think they should consume nonstop, because it did something even better: it encouraged them not to think at all. And that left them sitting ducks for another great invention of the modern era — marketing.

Now, you needn't have studied marketing to know that there are two groups of people who can always be convinced to consume more than they need to: addicts and children. School has done a pretty good job of turning our children into addicts, but it has done a spectacular job of turning our children into children. Again, this is no accident. Theorists from Plato to Rousseau to our own Dr. Inglis knew that if children could be cloistered with other children, stripped of responsibility and independence, encouraged to develop only the trivializing emotions of greed, envy, jealousy, and fear, they would grow older but never truly grow up. In the 1934 edition of his once well-known book *Public Education in the United States*, Ellwood P. Cubberley detailed and praised the way the strategy of successive school enlargements had extended childhood by two to six years, and forced schooling was at that point still quite new. This same Cubberley — who was dean of Stanford's School of Education, a textbook editor at Houghton Mifflin, and Conant's friend and correspondent at Harvard — had written the following in the 1922 edition of his book *Public School Administration*: "Our schools are . . . factories in which the raw products (children) are to be shaped and fashioned. . . . And it is the business of the school to build its pupils according to the specifications laid down."

It's perfectly obvious from our society today what those specifications were. Maturity has by now been banished from nearly every aspect of our lives. Easy divorce laws have removed the need to work at relationships; easy credit has removed the need for fiscal self-control; easy entertainment has removed the need to learn to entertain oneself; easy answers have removed the need to ask questions. We have become a nation of children, happy to surrender our judgments and our wills to political exhortations and commercial blandishments that would insult actual adults. We buy televisions, and then we buy the things we see on the television. We buy computers, and then we buy the things we see on the computer. We buy $150 sneakers whether we need them or not, and when they fall apart too soon we buy another pair. We drive SUVs and believe the lie that they constitute a kind of life insurance, even when we're upside-down in them. And, worst of all, we don't bat an eye when Ari Fleischer[6] tells us to "be careful what you say," even if we remember having been told somewhere back in school that America is the land of the free. We simply buy that one too. Our schooling, as intended, has seen to it.

Now for the good news. Once you understand the logic behind modern schooling, its tricks and traps are fairly easy to avoid. School trains children to be employees and consumers; teach your own to be leaders and adventurers. School trains children to obey reflexively; teach your own to think critically and independently. Well-schooled kids have a low threshold for boredom; help your own to develop an inner life so that they'll never be bored. Urge them to take on the serious material, the *grown-up* material, in history, literature, philosophy, music, art, economics, theology—all the stuff schoolteachers know well enough to avoid. Challenge your kids with plenty of solitude so that they can learn to enjoy their own company, to conduct inner dialogues. Well-schooled people are conditioned to dread being alone, and they seek constant companionship through the TV, the computer, the cell phone, and through shallow friendships quickly acquired and quickly abandoned. Your children should have a more meaningful life, and they can.

First, though, we must wake up to what our schools really are: laborato-   20
ries of experimentation on young minds, drill centers for the habits and attitudes that corporate society demands. Mandatory education serves children only incidentally; its real purpose is to turn them into servants. Don't let your own have their childhoods extended, not even for a day. If David Farragut could take command of a captured British warship as a preteen, if Thomas Edison could publish a broadsheet at the age of twelve, if Ben Franklin could apprentice himself to a printer at the same age (then put himself through a course of study that would choke a Yale senior today), there's no telling what your own kids could do. After a long life, and thirty years in the public school trenches, I've concluded that genius is as common as dirt. We suppress our genius only because we haven't yet figured out how to manage a population of educated men and women. The solution, I think, is simple and glorious. Let them manage themselves. ▣

The Reader's Presence

1. Would you agree with Gatto that compulsory schooling has the effect of creating conformity and obedience to authority? Why or why not? To what extent does schooling attempt to form citizens? To what extent are students trained to be consumers?

[6] *Ari Fleischer:* White House Press Secretary under President George W. Bush from 2001 to 2003. —EDS.

2. Gatto makes a distinction between "education" and "schooling" (paragraph 4). What is significant about this distinction? What are the consequences of conflating the two?

3. **CONNECTIONS:**   Gatto argues that compulsory schooling can effectively prevent students from becoming independent thinkers. Read Joseph Epstein's "The Perpetual Adolescent" (page 390). Do you think Epstein would agree that schooling is at least partly responsible for resistance to adulthood? Do you agree? Why or why not?

Adam Gopnik

SHOOTINGS

ADAM GOPNIK was born in Philadelphia, Pennsylvania, in 1956 and grew up in Montreal, Canada. After graduating from McGill University, he went to New York City to do graduate work in art history at the New York University Institute of Fine Arts. He arrived, he has said, with "a satchel full of ambitions," most of which centered on writing for the *New Yorker*, a goal he realized in 1986 when he joined the magazine. In the more than twenty years since, Gopnik has served as reporter, journalist, essayist, and art critic, writing fiction and humor pieces, book reviews, profiles, and hundreds of articles for the magazine. He moved to Paris in 1995 and began writing the magazine's "Paris Journal" column. These personal essays about his five years in Paris, which included the birth of his son among other adventures, were collected in his best-selling book *Paris to the Moon* (2000).

> "The essay . . . is a strong form, a beautiful form, a living form, one that counts, and one that is as likely to produce material that goes rocketing on through time as its more boastful near-relations."

Gopnik's post-Paris life after his return to New York with his family is described in his book of essays, *Through the Children's Gate: A Home in New York* (2006). Gopnik is also the author of a novel, *The King in the Window* (2005) and the editor of the anthology *Americans in Paris* (2004). His most recent book, *Angels and Ages: A Short Book About Darwin, Lincoln, and Modern Life*, was published in 2009 and released in paperback in 2010. In the introduction to *The Best American Essays* 2008, which Gopnik edited, he defends the essay form against naysayers: "The essay . . . is a strong form, a beautiful form, a living form, one that counts, and one that is as likely to produce material that goes rocketing on through time as its more boastful near-relations." He is a three-time winner of National Magazine Awards for Essays and for Criticism, and winner of the George Polk Award for Magazine Reporting.

In his introduction to *Best American Essays 2008*, Gopnik added: "The essays of our time . . . are as likely to hang on and make history as any novel or play or poem, maybe more. There is more of life in the essay, less art and more matter, fewer workshop wiles and more real manners—the sound of people talking about what interests them instead of writing what they think will impress—than in almost any other form."

THE CELL PHONES in the pockets of the dead students were still ringing when we were told that it was wrong to ask why. As the police cleared the bodies from the Virginia Tech engineering building, the cell phones rang, in the eccentric varieties of ring tones, as parents kept trying to see if their children were O.K. To imagine the feelings of the police as they carried the bodies and heard the ringing is heartrending; to imagine the feelings of the parents who were calling—dread, desperate hope for a sudden answer and the bliss of reassurance, dawning grief—is unbearable. But the parents, and the rest of us, were told that it was not the right moment to ask how the shooting had happened—specifically, why an obviously disturbed student, with a history of mental illness, was able to buy guns whose essential purpose is to kill people—and why it happens over and over again in America. At a press conference, Virginia's governor, Tim Kaine, said, "People who want to . . . make it their political hobby horse to ride, I've got nothing but loathing for them. . . . At this point, what it's about is comforting family members . . . and helping this community heal. And so to those who want to try to make this into some little crusade, I say take that elsewhere."

If the facts weren't so horrible, there might be something touching in the Governor's deeply American belief that "healing" can take place magically, without the intervening practice called "treating." The logic is unusual but striking: the aftermath of a terrorist attack is the wrong time to talk about security, the aftermath of a death from lung cancer is the wrong time to talk about smoking and the tobacco industry, and the aftermath of a car crash is the wrong time to talk about seat belts. People talked about the shooting, of course, but much of the conversation was devoted to musings on the treatment of mental illness in universities, the problem of "narcissism," violence in the media and in popular culture, copycat killings, the alienation of immigrant students, and the question of Evil.

Some people, however—especially people outside America—were eager to talk about it in another way, and even to embark on a little crusade. The whole world saw that the United States has more gun violence than other countries because we have more guns and are willing to sell them to

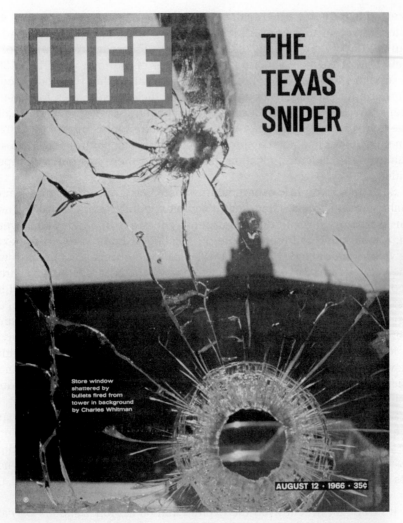

The cover of Life *magazine for August 12, 1966, showing a store window shattered by a bullet fired by Charles Whitman, a student at the University of Texas–Austin, who went on a shooting spree on campus. He killed 16 people and wounded 32 more.*

madmen who want to kill people. Every nation has violent loners, and they tend to have remarkably similar profiles from one country and culture to the next. And every country has known the horror of having a lunatic get his hands on a gun and kill innocent people. But on a recent list of the fourteen worst mass shootings in Western democracies since the nineteen-sixties the United States claimed seven, and, just as important, no other country on the list has had a repeat performance as severe as the first.

In Dunblane, Scotland, in 1996, a gunman killed sixteen children and a teacher at their school. Afterward, the British gun laws, already restrictive, were tightened—it's now against the law for any private citizen in the United Kingdom to own the kinds of guns that Cho Seung-Hui used at Virginia Tech—and nothing like Dunblane has occurred there since. In Quebec, after a school shooting took the lives of fourteen women in 1989, the survivors helped begin a gun-control movement that resulted in legislation bringing stronger, though far from sufficient, gun laws to Canada. (There have been a couple of subsequent shooting sprees, but on a smaller scale, and with far fewer dead.) In the Paris suburb of Nanterre, in 2002, a man killed eight people at a municipal meeting. Gun control became a key issue in the Presidential election that year, and there has been no repeat incident.

So there is no American particularity about loners, disenfranchised immigrants, narcissism, alienated youth, complex moral agency, or Evil. There is an American particularity about guns. The arc is apparent. Forty years ago, a man killed fourteen people on a college campus in Austin, Texas; this year, a man killed thirty-two in Blacksburg, Virginia. Not enough was done between those two massacres to make weapons of mass killing harder to obtain. In fact, while campus killings continued—Columbine being the most notorious, the shooting in the one-room Amish schoolhouse among the most recent—weapons have gotten more lethal, and, in states like Virginia, where the NRA [National Rifle Association] is powerful, no harder to buy.

Reducing the number of guns available to crazy people will neither relieve them of their insanity nor stop them from killing. Making it more difficult to buy guns that kill people is, however, a rational way to reduce the number of people killed by guns. Nations with tight gun laws have, on the whole, less gun violence; countries with somewhat restrictive gun laws have some gun violence; countries with essentially no gun laws have a lot of gun violence. (If you work hard, you can find a statistical exception hiding in a corner, but exceptions are just that. Some people who smoke their whole lives don't get lung cancer, while some people who never smoke do; still, the best way not to get lung cancer is not to smoke.)

It's true that in renewing the expired ban on assault weapons we can't guarantee that someone won't shoot people with a semi-automatic pistol, and that by controlling semi-automatic pistols we can't reduce the chances of someone killing people with a rifle. But the point of lawmaking is not to act as precisely as possible, in order to punish the latest crime; it is to act as comprehensively as possible, in order to prevent the next one. Semi-automatic Glocks and Walthers, Cho's weapons, are for killing people. They are not made for hunting, and it's not easy to protect yourself with them. (If having a loaded semi-automatic on hand kept you safe, cops would not be shot as often as they are.)

Rural America is hunting country, and hunters need rifles and shotguns—with proper licensing, we'll live with risk. There is no reason that any private citizen in a democracy should own a handgun. At some point, that simple truth will register. Until it does, phones will ring for dead children, and parents will be told not to ask why. ■

5

The Reader's Presence

1. Note the way Gopnik opens his essay. Why do you think he decided to start with the ringing cell phones on the dead students? Why didn't he begin with the act of shooting? What effect does he achieve with the ring tones? How would you describe its effect on you as a reader?

2. In constructing effective arguments, writers often concede points to an opponent to demonstrate their reasonableness. How does Gopnik achieve this? Does he take an absolute position against gun control? Point to several passages in which he entertains arguments that might be made by those who oppose gun control. How does he respond to those arguments? Do you find his responses persuasive? Why or why not?

3. **CONNECTIONS:**   Although Gopnik brings up the National Rifle Association (NRA), he doesn't introduce issues revolving around the Second Amendment directly. How do you think Gopnik would respond to constitutional scholar Akhil Reed Amar's opinions in "Second Thoughts: What the Right to Bear Arms Really Means" (page 305)? Explain the extent to which Gopnik could cite Amar's essay in support of his own beliefs in "Shootings."

Vicki Hearne
WHAT'S WRONG WITH ANIMAL RIGHTS

VICKI HEARNE (1946–2001) had a unique career as a poet, an author, and an animal trainer, and she taught creative writing at Yale University and at the University of California. She published three volumes of poetry, *Nervous Horses* (1980), *In the Absence of Horses* (1983), and *The Parts of Light* (1994). Hearne was known for her ability to train aggressive dogs (particularly pit bull terriers), and she wrote an account of her experiences in *Bandit: Dossier of a Dangerous Dog* (1991). Her other books include *Adam's Task: Calling Animals by Name* (1987), *The White German Shepherd* (1988), and *Animal Happiness: A Moving Exploration of Animals and Their Emotions* (1994). "What's Wrong with Animal Rights" was originally published in *Harper's* in 1991 and was selected for *The Best American Essays 1992*.

> Vicki Hearne was known for her ability to train aggressive dogs, particularly pit bull terriers.

NOT ALL HAPPY ANIMALS are alike. A Doberman going over a hurdle after a small wooden dumbbell is sleek, all arcs of harmonious power. A basset hound cheerfully performing the same exercise exhibits harmonies of a more lugubrious nature. There are chimpanzees who love precision the way musicians or fanatical housekeepers or accomplished hypochondriacs do; others for whom happiness is a matter of invention and variation—chimp vaudevillians. There is a rhinoceros whose happiness, as near as I can make out, is in needing to be trained every morning, all over again, or else he "forgets" his circus routine, and in this you find a clue to the slow, deep, quiet chuckle of his happiness and to the glory of the beast. Happiness for Secretariat[1] is in his ebullient bound, that joyful length of stride. For the draft horse or the weight-pull dog, happiness is of a different shape, more awesome and less obviously intelligent. When the pulling horse is at its most intense, the animal goes into himself, allocating all of the educated power that organizes his desire to dwell in fierce and delicate intimacy with that power, leans into the harness, and MAKES THAT SUCKER MOVE.

If we are speaking of human beings and use the phrase "animal happiness," we tend to mean something like "creature comforts." The emblems of this are the golden retriever rolling in the grass, the horse with his nose deep in the oats, the kitty by the fire. Creature comforts are important to animals—"Grub first, then ethics" is a motto that would describe many a wise Labrador retriever, and I have a pit bull named Annie whose continual quest for the perfect pillow inspires her to awesome feats. But there is something more to animals, a capacity for satisfactions that come from work in the fullest sense—what is known in philosophy and in this country's Declaration of Independence as "happiness." This is a sense of personal achievement, like the satisfaction felt by a good wood-carver or a dancer or a poet or an accomplished dressage horse. It is a happiness that, like the artist's must come from something within the animal, something trainers call "talent." Hence, it cannot be imposed on the animal. But it is also something that does not come *ex nihilo*. If it had not been a fairly ordinary thing, in one part of the world, to teach young children to play the pianoforte, it is doubtful that Mozart's music would exist.

Happiness is often misunderstood as a synonym for pleasure or as an antonym for suffering. But Aristotle associated happiness with ethics—codes of behavior that urge us toward the sensation of getting it right, a kind of work that yields the "click" of satisfaction upon solving a problem or surmounting an obstacle. In his *Ethics*, Aristotle wrote, "If happiness is activity in accordance with excellence, it is reasonable that it should be in accordance with the highest excellence." Thomas Jefferson identified the capacity for happiness as one of the three fundamental rights on which all others are based: "life, liberty, and the pursuit of happiness."

---

1 **Secretariat** (1970–1989): A celebrated American thoroughbred racehorse and winner of the 1973 Triple Crown (the Kentucky Derby, the Preakness, and the Belmont Stakes).—EDS.

I bring up this idea of happiness as a form of work because I am an animal trainer, and work is the foundation of the happiness a trainer and an animal discover together. I bring up these words also because they cannot be found in the lexicon of the animal-rights movement. This absence accounts for the uneasiness toward the movement of most people, who sense that rights advocates have a point but take it too far when they liberate snails or charge that goldfish at the county fair are suffering. But the problem with the animal-rights advocates is not that they take it too far; it's that they've got it all wrong.

Animal rights are built upon a misconceived premise that rights were created to prevent us from unnecessary suffering. You can't find an animal-rights book, video, pamphlet, or rock concert in which someone doesn't mention the Great Sentence, written by Jeremy Bentham in 1789. Arguing in favor of such rights, Bentham wrote: "The question is not, Can they *reason*? nor, can they *talk*? but, can they *suffer*?"

The logic of the animal-rights movement places suffering at the iconographic center of a skewed value system. The thinking of its proponents — given eerie expression in a virtually sado-pornographic sculpture of a tortured monkey that won a prize for its compassionate vision — has collapsed into a perverse conundrum. Today the loudest voices calling for — demanding — the destruction of animals are the humane organizations. This is an inevitable consequence of the apotheosis of the drive to relieve suffering: death is the ultimate release. To compensate for their contradictions, the humane movement has demonized, in this century and the last, those who made animal happiness their business: veterinarians, trainers, and the like. We think of Louis Pasteur as the man whose work saved you and me and your dog and cat from rabies, but antivivisectionists of the time claimed that rabies increased in areas where there were Pasteur Institutes.

An anti-rabies public relations campaign mounted in England in the 1880s by the Royal Society for the Prevention of Cruelty to Animals and other organizations led to orders being issued to club any dog found not wearing a muzzle. England still has her cruel and unnecessary law that requires an animal to spend six months in quarantine before being allowed loose in the country. Most of the recent propaganda about pit bulls — the crazy claim that they "take hold with their front teeth while they chew away with their rear teeth" (which would imply, incorrectly, that they have double jaws) — can be traced to literature published by the Humane Society of the United States during the fall of 1987 and earlier. If your neighbors want your dog or horse impounded and destroyed because he is a nuisance — say the dog barks, or the horse attracts flies — it will be the local Humane Society to whom your neighbors turn for action.

In a way, everyone has the opportunity to know that the history of the humane movement is largely a history of miseries, arrests, prosecutions, and death. The Humane Society is the pound, the place with the decompression chamber or the lethal injections. You occasionally find worried letters about this in Ann Landers's[2] column.

Animal-rights publications are illustrated largely with photographs of two kinds of animals—"Helpless Fluff" and "Agonized Fluff," the two conditions in which some people seem to prefer their animals, because any other version of an animal is too complicated for propaganda. In the introduction to his book *Animal Liberation*, Peter Singer[3] says somewhat smugly that he and his wife have no animals and, in fact, don't much care for them. This is offered as evidence of his objectivity and ethical probity. But it strikes me as an odd, perhaps, obscene underpinning for an ethical project that encourages university and high school students to cherish their ignorance of, say, great bird dogs as proof of their devotion to animals.

I would like to leave these philosophers behind, for they are inept connoisseurs of suffering who might revere my Airedale for his capacity to scream when subjected to a blowtorch but not for his wit and courage, not for his natural good manners that are a gentle rebuke to ours. I want to celebrate the moment not long ago when, at his first dog show, my Airedale, Drummer, learned that there can be a public place where his work is respected. I want to celebrate his meticulousness, his happiness upon realizing at the dog show that no one would swoop down upon him and swamp him with the goo-goo excesses known as the "teddy-bear complex" but that people actually got out of his way, gave him room to work. I want to say, "There can be a six-and-a-half-month-old puppy who can care about accuracy, who can be fastidious, and whose fastidiousness will be a foundation for courage later." I want to say, "Leave my puppy alone!" 10

I want to leave the philosophers behind, but I cannot, in part because the philosophical problems that plague academicians of the animal-rights movement are illuminating. They wonder, do animals have rights or do they have interests? Or, if these rightists lead particularly unexamined lives, they dismiss that question as obvious (yes, of course animals have rights, prima facie) and proceed to enumerate them, James Madison style. This leads to the issuance of bills of rights—the right to an environment, the right not to be used in medical experiments—and other forms of trivialization.

The calculus of suffering can be turned against the philosophers of festering flesh, even in the case of food animals, or exotic animals who perform in movies and circuses. It is true that it hurts to be slaughtered by man, but it doesn't hurt nearly as much as some of the cunningly cruel arrangements meted out by "Mother Nature." In Africa, 75 percent of the lions cubbed do not survive to the age of two. For those who make it to two, the average age at death is ten years. Asali, the movie and TV lioness, was still working at

---

[2] ***Ann Landers:*** The pseudonym created by the *Chicago Sun-Times* for advice columnist Ruth Crowley in 1943 and assumed by Eppie Lederer in 1955. The "Ask Ann Landers" syndicated column continued to be published until 2002.—EDS.

[3] For more on Peter Singer, see page 814.—EDS.

age twenty-one. There are fates worse than death, but twenty-one years of a close working relationship with Hubert Wells, Asali's trainer, is not one of them. Dorset sheep and polled Herefords would not exist at all were they not in a symbiotic relationship with human beings.

A human being living in the "wild"—somewhere, say, without the benefits of medicine and advanced social organization—would probably have a life expectancy of from thirty to thirty-five years. A human being living in "captivity"—in, say, a middle-class neighborhood of what the Centers for Disease Control [and Prevention] call a Metropolitan Statistical Area—has a life expectancy of seventy or more years. For orangutans in the wild in Borneo and Malaysia, the life expectancy is thirty-five years; in captivity, fifty years. The wild is not a suffering-free zone or all that frolicsome a location.

The questions asked by animal-rights activists are flawed, because they are built on the concept that the origin of rights is in the avoidance of suffering rather than in the pursuit of happiness. The question that needs to be asked—and that will put us in closer proximity to the truth—is not, do they have rights? or, what are those rights? but rather, what is a right?

Rights originate in committed relationships and can be found, both intact   15
and violated, wherever one finds such relationships—in social compacts, within families, between animals, and between people and nonhuman animals. This is as true when the nonhuman animals in question are lions or parakeets as when they are dogs. It is my Airedale whose excellencies have my attention at the moment, so it is with reference to him that I will consider the question, what is a right?

When I imagine situations in which it naturally arises that A defends or honors or respects B's rights, I imagine situations in which the relationship between A and B can be indicated with a possessive pronoun. I might say, "Leave her alone, she's my daughter" or "That's what she wants, and she is my daughter. I think I am bound to honor her wants." Similarly, "Leave her alone, she's my mother." I am more tender of the happiness of my mother, my father, my child, than I am of other people's family members; more tender of my friends' happinesses than your friends' happinesses, unless you and I have a mutual friend.

Possession of a being by another has come into more and more disrepute, so that the common understanding of one person possessing another is slavery. But the important detail about the kind of possessive pronoun that I have in mind is reciprocity: if I have a friend, she has a friend. If I have a daughter, she has a mother. The possessive does not bind one of us while freeing the other; it cannot do that. Moreover, should the mother reject the daughter, the word that applies is "disown." The form of disowning that most often appears in the news is domestic violence. Parents abuse children; husbands batter wives.

Some cases of reciprocal possessives have built-in limitations, such as "my patient / my doctor" or "my student / my teacher" or "my agent / my client." Other possessive relations are extremely limited but still remarkably binding: "my neighbor" and "my country" and "my president."

The responsibilities and the ties signaled by reciprocal possession typically are hard to dissolve. It can be as difficult to give up an enemy as to give up a friend, and often the one becomes the other, as though the logic of the possessive pronoun outlasts the forms it chanced to take at a given moment, as though we were stuck with one another. In these bindings, nearly inextricable, are found the origin of our rights. They imply a possessiveness but also recognize an acknowledgment by each side of the other's existence.

The idea of democracy is dependent on the citizens' having knowledge   20
of the government; that is, realizing that the government exists and knowing how to claim rights against it. I know this much because I get mail from the government and see its "representatives" running about in uniforms. Whether I actually have any rights in relationship to the government is less clear, but the idea that I do is symbolized by the right to vote. I obey the government, and, in theory, it obeys me, by counting my ballot, reading the *Miranda* warning to me, agreeing to be bound by the Constitution. My friend obeys me as I obey her; the government "obeys" me to some extent, and, to a different extent, I obey it.

What kind of thing can my Airedale, Drummer, have knowledge of? He can know that I exist and through that knowledge can claim his happinesses, with varying degrees of success, both with me and against me. Drummer can also know about larger human or dog communities than the one that consists only of him and me. There is my household—the other dogs, the cats, my husband. I have had enough dogs on campuses to know that he can learn that Yale exists as a neighborhood or village. My older dog, Annie, not only knows that Yale exists but can tell Yalies from townies, as I learned while teaching there during labor troubles.

Dogs can have elaborate conceptions of human social structures, and even of something like their rights and responsibilities within them, but these conceptions are never elaborate enough to construct a rights relationship between a dog and the state, or a dog and the Humane Society. Both of these are concepts that depend on writing and memoranda, officers in uniform, plaques and seals of authority. All of these are literary constructs, and all of them are beyond a dog's ken, which is why the mail carrier who doesn't also happen to be a dog's friend is forever an intruder—this is why dogs bark at mailmen.

It is clear enough that natural rights relations can arise between people and animals. Drummer, for example, can insist, "Hey, let's go outside and do something!" if I have been at my computer several days on end. He can both refuse to accept various of my suggestions and tell me when he fears for his life—such as the time when the huge, white flapping flag appeared out of nowhere, as it seemed to him, on the town green one evening when we were working. I can (and do) say to him either, "Oh, you don't have to worry about that" or, "Uh oh, you're right, Drum, that guy looks dangerous." Just as the government and I—two different species of organism—have developed improvised ways of communicating, such as the vote, so Drummer and I have worked out a number of ways to make our expressions known. Largely through obedience, I have taught him a fair amount about how to get responses from me. Obedience is reciprocal; you cannot get responses from a dog to whom you do not respond accurately. I have enfranchised him in a relationship to me by educating him, creating the conditions by which he can achieve a certain happiness specific to a dog, maybe even specific to an Airedale, inasmuch as this same relationship has allowed me to plumb the happiness of being a trainer and writing this article.

Instructions in this happiness are given terms that are alien to a culture in which liver treats, fluffy windup toys, and miniature sweaters are confused with respect and work. Jack Knox, a sheepdog trainer originally from Scotland, will shake his crook at a novice handler who makes a promiscuous move to praise a dog, and will call out in his Scottish accent, "Eh! Eh! Get back, get BACK! Ye'll no be abusin' the dogs like that in my clinic." America is a nation of abused animals, Knox says, because we are always swooping at them with praise, "no gi'ing them their freedom." I am reminded of Rainer Maria Rilke's[4] account in which the Prodigal Son leaves—has to leave—because everyone loves him, even the dogs love him, and he has no path to the delicate and fierce truth of himself. Unconditional praise and love, in Rilke's story, disenfranchise us, distract us from what truly excites our interest.

In the minds of some trainers and handlers, praise is dishonesty. Paradoxically, it is a kind of contempt for animals that masquerades as a reverence for helplessness and suffering. The idea of freedom means that you do not, at least not while Jack Knox is nearby, helpfully guide your dog through the motions of, say, herding over and over—what one trainer calls "explainy-wainy." This is rote learning. It works tolerably well on some handlers, because people have vast unconscious minds and can store complex preprogrammed behaviors. Dogs, on the other hand, have almost no unconscious minds, so they can learn only by thinking. Many children are like this until educated out of it.   25

If I tell my Airedale to sit and stay on the town green, and someone comes up and burbles, "What a pretty thing you are," he may break his stay to go for a caress. I pull him back and correct him for breaking. Now he holds his stay because I have blocked his way to movement but not because I have punished him. (A correction blocks one path as it opens another for desire to work; punishment blocks desire and opens nothing.) He holds his stay now, and—because the stay opens this possibility of work, new to a heedless young dog—he watches. If the person goes on talking, and isn't going to gush with praise, I may heel Drummer out of his stay and give him

---

4 ***Rainer Maria Rilke*** (1875–1926): Widely acclaimed as one of the German language's most important poets.—EDS.

an "Okay" to make friends. Sometimes something about the person makes Drummer feel that reserve is in order. He responds to an insincere approach by sitting still, going down into himself, and thinking, "This person has no business pawing me. I'll sit very still, and he will go away." If the person doesn't take the hint from Drummer, I'll give the pup a little backup by saying, "Please don't pet him, he's working," even though he was not under any command.

The pup reads this, and there is a flicker of a working trust now stirring in the dog. Is the pup grateful? When the stranger leaves, does he lick my hand, full of submissive blandishments? This one doesn't. This one says nothing at all, and I say nothing much to him. This is a working trust we are developing, not a mutual congratulation society. My backup is praise enough for him; the use he makes of my support is praise enough for me.

Listening to a dog is often praise enough. Suppose it is just after dark and we are outside. Suddenly there is a shout from the house. The pup and I both look toward the shout and then toward each other: "What do you think?" I don't so much as cock my head, because Drummer is growing up, and I want to know what he thinks. He takes a few steps toward the house, and I follow. He listens again and comprehends that it's just Holly, who at fourteen is much given to alarming cries and shouts. He shrugs at me and goes about his business. I say nothing. To praise him for this performance would make about as much sense as praising a human being for the same thing. Thus:

A. What's that?

B. I don't know. [Listens] Oh, it's just Holly.

A. What a goooooood human being!

B. Huh?

This is one small moment in a series of like moments that will culminate in an Airedale who on a Friday will have the discrimination and confidence required to take down a man who is attacking me with a knife and on Saturday clown and play with the children at the annual Orange Empire Dog Club Christmas party.

People who claim to speak for animal rights are increasingly devoted 30
to the idea that the very keeping of a dog or a horse or a gerbil or a lion is in and of itself an offense. The more loudly they speak, the less likely they are to be in a rights relation to any given animal, because they are spending so much time in airplanes or transmitting fax announcements of the latest Sylvester Stallone anti-fur rally. In a 1988 *Harper's* forum, for example, Ingrid Newkirk, the national director of People for the Ethical Treatment of Animals [PETA], urged that domestic pets be spayed and neutered and ultimately phased out. She prefers, it appears, wolves—and wolves someplace else—to Airedales and, by a logic whose interior structure is both

emotionally and intellectually forever closed to Drummer, claims thereby to be speaking for "animal rights."

She is wrong. I am the only one who can own up to my Airedale's inalienable rights. Whether or not I do it perfectly at any given moment is no more refutation of this point than whether I am perfectly my husband's mate at any given moment refutes the fact of marriage. Only people who know Drummer, and whom he can know, are capable of this relationship. PETA and the Humane Society and the ASPCA[5] and the Congress and NOW[6]—as institutions—do have the power to affect my ability to grant rights to Drummer but are otherwise incapable of creating conditions or laws or rights that would increase his happiness. Only Drummer's owner has the power to obey him—to obey who he is and what he is capable of—deeply enough to grant him his rights and open up the possibility of happiness.

The Reader's Presence

1. Hearne writes from an "expert" perspective as an animal trainer. Suppose she were not an expert. How would that change your reading of her argument?

2. Hearne takes issue both with the common definition of "animal," protesting that not all animals are alike, and with the common notion of "happiness" as comfort (paragraphs 1 and 2). How do questions about these definitions form the basis of Hearne's argument? Is it possible to disagree with her definitions and still support her overall argument, or vice versa? Why or why not?

3. **CONNECTIONS:**   Throughout her essay, Hearne attends to the political dimensions of her argument. In paragraph 20, for example, she introduces "the idea of democracy," and in the final paragraph she refers to her "Airedale's inalienable rights." Find other such examples. How does Hearne incorporate American political history into her essay? Do you find her allusion to slavery (paragraph 17) persuasive? necessary? Compare Hearne's ideas about dogs to the essays on the death of moths by Annie Dillard ("The Death of a Moth," page 371) and by Virginia Woolf ("The Death of the Moth," page 625). Which essay presents the most compelling treatment of its subject? What aspects of each essay are similar? To what extent does each essayist attend to the interests of her reader? Based on your analysis, what would you describe as the compositional goal of each writer?

---

5 **ASPCA:** American Society for the Prevention of Cruelty to Animals.—EDS.
6 **NOW:** National Organization for Women.—EDS.

Christopher Hitchens

BELIEVE ME, IT'S TORTURE

One of the world's most public intellectuals, **CHRISTOPHER HITCHENS** (b. 1949) is known for making controversial arguments. His 2007 book, for example, *God Is Not Great: How Religion Poisons Everything*, argues that religion is immoral, contributing to everything from ignorance and terrorism to sexual repression. In another book, *The Missionary Position: Mother Teresa in Theory and Practice* (1995), he took the very unpopular position that the Catholic nun was more interested in further-ing Catholic doctrine and "becoming a saint" than she was in genuinely helping the poor. Although his views on religion and sexuality are typically associated with the political left, Hitchens has not been reluctant to criticize lib-eral politicians: his 1999 book, *No One Left to Lie To: The Values of the Worst Family*, was a scathing attack on the Clinton family. In recent years, Hitchens has also advocated interventionist politics in some of the Islamic states of the Middle East, criticizing what he calls "fascism with an Islamic face." His most recent book, *Hitch-22* (2010), is a candid memoir of his personal life and political philosophy. This essay was originally published in the August 2008 issue of *Vanity Fair*.

> One of the world's most public intellectuals, Christopher Hitchens is known for making controversial arguments.

HERE IS THE MOST chilling way I can find of stating the matter. Until recently, "waterboarding" was something that Americans did to other Americans. It was inflicted, and endured, by those members of the Special Forces who underwent the advanced form of training known as SERE (Sur-vival, Evasion, Resistance, Escape). In these harsh exercises, brave men and women were introduced to the sorts of barbarism that they might expect to meet at the hands of a lawless foe who disregarded the Geneva Conven-tions. But it was something that Americans were being trained to resist, not to *inflict*.

Exploring this narrow but deep distinction, on a gorgeous day last May I found myself deep in the hill country of western North Carolina, preparing to be surprised by a team of extremely hardened veterans who had confronted their country's enemies in highly arduous terrain all over the world. They knew about everything from unarmed combat to enhanced interrogation and, in exchange for anonymity, were going to show me as nearly as possible what real waterboarding might be like.

It goes without saying that I knew I could stop the process at any time, and that when it was all over I would be released into happy daylight rather than returned to a darkened cell. But it's been well said that cowards die many times before their deaths, and it was difficult for me to completely forget the clause in the contract of indemnification that I had signed. This document (written by one who knew) stated revealingly: "'Water boarding' is a potentially dangerous activity in which the participant can receive serious and permanent (physical, emotional and psychological) injuries and even death, including injuries and death due to the respiratory and neurological systems of the body." As the agreement went on to say, there would be safeguards provided "during the 'water boarding' process, however, these measures may fail and even if they work properly they may not prevent Hitchens from experiencing serious injury or death."

On the night before the encounter I got to sleep with what I thought was creditable ease, but woke early and knew at once that I wasn't going back to any sort of doze or snooze. The first specialist I had approached with the scheme had asked my age on the telephone and when told what it was (I am 59) had laughed out loud and told me to forget it. Waterboarding is for Green Berets in training, or wiry young jihadists whose teeth can bite through the gristle of an old goat. It's not for wheezing, paunchy scribblers. For my current "handlers" I had had to produce a doctor's certificate assuring them that I did not have asthma, but I wondered whether I should tell them about the 15,000 cigarettes I had inhaled every year for the last several decades. I was feeling apprehensive, in other words, and beginning to wish I hadn't given myself so long to think about it.

I have to be opaque about exactly where I was later that day, but there came a moment when, sitting on a porch outside a remote house at the end of a winding country road, I was very gently yet firmly grabbed from behind, pulled to my feet, pinioned by my wrists (which were then cuffed to a belt), and cut off from the sunlight by having a black hood pulled over my face. I was then turned around a few times, I presume to assist in disorienting me, and led over some crunchy gravel into a darkened room. Well, mainly darkened: there were some oddly spaced bright lights that came as pinpoints through my hood. And some weird music assaulted my ears. (I'm no judge of these things, but I wouldn't have expected former Special Forces types to be so fond of New Age techno-disco.) The outside world seemed very suddenly very distant indeed.

Arms already lost to me, I wasn't able to flail as I was pushed onto a sloping board and positioned with my head lower than my heart. (That's the main point: the angle can be slight or steep.) Then my legs were lashed together so that the board and I were one single and trussed unit. Not to bore you with my phobias, but if I don't have at least two pillows I wake up with acid reflux and mild sleep apnea, so even a merely supine position makes

5

me uneasy. And, to tell you something I had been keeping from myself as well as from my new experimental friends, I do have a fear of drowning that comes from a bad childhood moment on the Isle of Wight, when I got out of my depth. As a boy reading the climactic torture scene of *1984*,[1] where what is in Room 101 is the worst thing in the world, I realize that somewhere in my version of that hideous chamber comes the moment when the wave washes over me. Not that that makes me special: I don't know anyone who *likes* the idea of drowning. As mammals we may have originated in the ocean, but water has many ways of reminding us that when we are in it we are out of our element. In brief, when it comes to breathing, give me good old air every time.

You may have read by now the official lie about this treatment, which is that it "simulates" the feeling of drowning. This is not the case. You feel that you are drowning because you *are* drowning—or, rather, being drowned, albeit slowly and under controlled conditions and at the mercy (or otherwise) of those who are applying the pressure. The "board" is the instrument, *not* the method. You are not being boarded. You are being watered. This was very rapidly brought home to me when, on top of the hood, which still admitted a few flashes of random and worrying strobe light to my vision, three layers of enveloping towel were added. In this pregnant darkness, head downward, I waited for a while until I abruptly felt a slow cascade of water going up my nose. Determined to resist if only for the honor of my navy ancestors who had so often been in peril on the sea, I held my breath for a while and then had to exhale and—as you might expect—inhale in turn. The inhalation brought the damp cloths tight against my nostrils, as if a huge, wet paw had been suddenly and annihilatingly clamped over my face. Unable to determine whether I was breathing in or out, and flooded more with sheer panic than with mere water, I triggered the pre-arranged signal and felt the unbelievable relief of being pulled upright and having the soaking and stifling layers pulled off me. I find I don't want to tell you how little time I lasted.

This is because I had read that Khalid Sheikh Mohammed, invariably referred to as the "mastermind" of the atrocities of September 11, 2001, had impressed his interrogators by holding out for upward of two minutes before cracking. (By the way, this story is not confirmed. My North Carolina friends jeered at it. "Hell," said one, "from what I heard they only washed his damn face before he babbled.") But, hell, I thought in my turn, no Hitchens is going to do worse than *that*. Well, O.K., I admit I didn't outdo him. And so then I said, with slightly more bravado than was justified, that I'd like to try it one more time. There was a paramedic present who checked my racing pulse and warned me about adrenaline rush. An interval was ordered, and then I felt the mask come down again. Steeling myself to remember what it had been like last time, and to learn from the previous panic attack, I fought

---

1 **Nineteen Eighty-Four** (also written as **1984**): George Orwell's novel (published 1948) depicting a world of constant warfare, government surveillance, and public mind control, a world in which the individual is subordinated to the state ("Big Brother").—EDS.

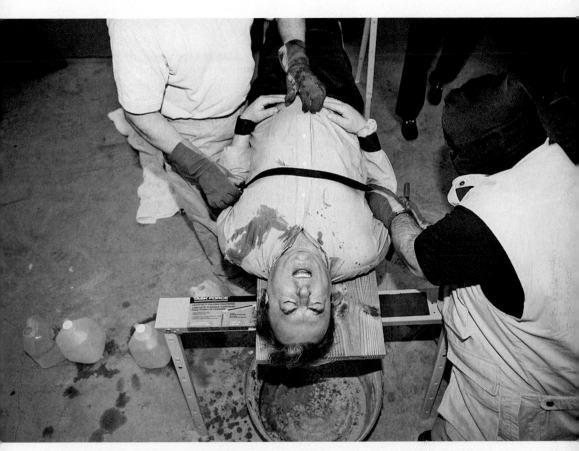

Christopher Hitchens undergoing waterboarding "treatment."

down the first, and some of the second, wave of nausea and terror but soon found that I was an abject prisoner of my gag reflex. The interrogators would hardly have had time to ask me any questions, and I knew that I would quite readily have agreed to supply any answer. I still feel ashamed when I think about it. Also, in case it's of interest, I have since woken up trying to push the bedcovers off my face, and if I do anything that makes me short of breath I find myself clawing at the air with a horrible sensation of smothering and claustrophobia. No doubt this will pass. As if detecting my misery and shame, one of my interrogators comfortingly said, "Any time is a long time when you're breathing water." I could have hugged him for saying so, and just then I was hit with a ghastly sense of the sadomasochistic dimension that underlies the relationship between the torturer and the tortured. I apply the Abraham Lincoln test for moral casuistry:[2] "If slavery is not wrong,

2 ***casuistry:*** Using clever but unsound reasoning, especially in relation to moral questions. —EDS.

nothing is wrong." Well, then, if waterboarding does not constitute torture, then there is no such thing as torture.

I am somewhat proud of my ability to "keep my head," as the saying goes, and to maintain presence of mind under trying circumstances. I was completely convinced that, when the water pressure had become intolerable, I had firmly uttered the pre-determined code word that would cause it to cease. But my interrogator told me that, rather to his surprise, I had not spoken a word. I had activated the "dead man's handle" that signaled the onset of unconsciousness. So now I have to wonder about the role of false memory and delusion. What I do recall clearly, though, is a hard finger feeling for my solar plexus as the water was being poured. What was that for? "That's to find out if you are trying to cheat, and timing your breathing to the doses. If you try that, we can outsmart you. We have all kinds of enhancements." I was briefly embarrassed that I hadn't earned or warranted these refinements, but it hit me yet again that this is certainly the *language* of torture.

Maybe I am being premature in phrasing it thus. Among the veterans there are at least two views on all this, which means in practice that there are two opinions on whether or not "waterboarding" constitutes torture. I have had some extremely serious conversations on the topic, with two groups of highly decent and serious men, and I think that both cases have to be stated at their strongest.

The team who agreed to give me a hard time in the woods of North Carolina belong to a highly honorable group. This group regards itself as out on the front line in defense of a society that is too spoiled and too ungrateful to appreciate those solid, underpaid volunteers who guard us while we sleep. These heroes stay on the ramparts at all hours and in all weather, and if they make a mistake they may be arraigned in order to scratch some domestic political itch. Faced with appalling enemies who make horror videos of torture and beheadings, they feel that they are the ones who confront denunciation in our press, and possible prosecution. As they have just tried to demonstrate to me, a man who has been waterboarded may well emerge from the experience a bit shaky, but he is in a mood to surrender the relevant information and is unmarked and undamaged and indeed ready for another bout in quite a short time. When contrasted to actual torture, waterboarding is more like foreplay. No thumbscrew, no pincers, no electrodes, no rack. Can one say this of those who have been captured by the tormentors and murderers of (say) Daniel Pearl? On this analysis, any call to indict the United States for torture is therefore a lame and diseased attempt to arrive at a moral equivalence between those who defend civilization and those who exploit its freedoms to hollow it out, and ultimately to bring it down. I myself do not trust anybody who does not clearly understand this viewpoint.

Against it, however, I call as my main witness Mr. Malcolm Nance. Mr. Nance is not what you call a bleeding heart. In fact, speaking of the coronary area, he has said that, in battlefield conditions, he "would personally

10

cut bin Laden's heart out with a plastic M.R.E. spoon."[3] He was to the fore on September 11, 2001, dealing with the burning nightmare in the debris of the Pentagon. He has been involved with the SERE program since 1997. He speaks Arabic and has been on al Qaeda's tail since the early 1990s. His most recent book, *The Terrorists of Iraq* [2007], is a highly potent analysis both of the jihadist threat in Mesopotamia and of the ways in which we have made its life easier. I passed one of the most dramatic evenings of my life listening to his cold but enraged denunciation of the adoption of waterboarding by the United States. The argument goes like this:

1. Waterboarding is a deliberate torture technique and has been prosecuted as such by our judicial arm when perpetrated by others.

2. If we allow it and justify it, we cannot complain if it is employed in the future by other regimes on captive U.S. citizens. It is a method of putting American prisoners in harm's way.

3. It may be a means of extracting information, but it is also a means of extracting junk information. (Mr. Nance told me that he had heard of someone's being compelled to confess that he was a hermaphrodite. I later had an awful twinge while wondering if I myself could have been "dunked" this far.) To put it briefly, even the CIA sources for the *Washington Post* story on waterboarding conceded that the information they got out of Khalid Sheikh Mohammed was "not all of it reliable." Just put a pencil line under that last phrase, or commit it to memory.

4. It opens a door that cannot be closed. Once you have posed the notorious "ticking bomb" question, and once you assume that you are in the right, what will you *not* do? Waterboarding not getting results fast enough? The terrorist's clock still ticking? Well, then, bring on the thumbscrews and the pincers and the electrodes and the rack.

Masked by these arguments, there lurks another very penetrating point. Nance doubts very much that Khalid Sheikh Mohammed lasted that long under the water treatment (and I am pathetically pleased to hear it). It's also quite thinkable, *if* he did, that he was trying to attain martyrdom at our hands. But even if he endured so long, and since the United States has in any case bragged that *in fact* he did, one of our worst enemies has now become one of the founders of something that will someday disturb your sleep as well as mine. To quote Nance:

> Torture advocates hide behind the argument that an open discussion about specific American interrogation techniques will aid the enemy. Yet, convicted Al Qaeda members and innocent captives who were released to their host nations have already debriefed the world through hundreds of interviews,

---

[3] After searching for Osama bin Laden for nearly a decade following the attacks of September 11, 2001, Osama bin Laden was killed by American special military forces on May 1, 2011.—EDS.

movies and documentaries on exactly what methods they were subjected to and how they endured. Our own missteps have created a cadre of highly experienced lecturers for Al Qaeda's own virtual SERE school for terrorists.

Which returns us to my starting point, about the distinction between training *for* something and training to resist it. One used to be told — and surely with truth — that the lethal fanatics of al Qaeda were schooled to lie, and instructed to claim that they had been tortured and maltreated whether they had been tortured and maltreated or not. Did we notice what a frontier we had crossed when we admitted and even proclaimed that their stories might in fact be true? I had only a very slight encounter on that frontier, but I still wish that my experience were the only way in which the words "waterboard" and "American" could be mentioned in the same (gasping and sobbing) breath. ●

The Reader's Presence

1. How would you characterize the tone of voice Hitchens uses in this essay? Pay particular attention to the passages where he describes the sensation of being waterboarded. How would you describe the sound of his voice in these passages? What other approaches could he have taken with equal plausibility, given the subject matter? Why do you think Hitchens takes the approach that he does?

2. Hitchens writes: "As if detecting my misery and shame, one of my interrogators comfortingly said, 'Any time is a long time when you're breathing water.' I could have hugged him for saying so, and just then I was hit with a ghastly sense of the sadomasochistic dimension that underlies the relationship between the torturer and the tortured" (paragraph 8). What does Hitchens mean by this? What is the effect of Hitchens's having made this observation so close to the end of the essay? With what impression does Hitchens leave the reader at the end of his essay?

3. **CONNECTIONS:** Compare Hitchens's essay to the passages from Michihiko Hachiya's "Hiroshima Diary" (page 107). What similarities (and differences) do you notice about the way the two writers tell their stories? Consider, for example, their respective tones of voice, sentence lengths, rhythms, and interjections of personal opinion. How do those similarities and differences affect your understanding of what each writer experienced? How did your visceral reaction to each essay differ?

Pico Iyer

THE INNER CLIMATE

PICO IYER (b. 1957) is the British-born son of Indian philosopher, Raghavan N. Iyer, and religious scholar Nandini Nanak Mehta. When Pico was seven years old, his family left Oxford, England, for California. He returned to Oxford for his own degree, graduating with the highest marks in his class, then went on to teach writing and literature at Harvard University before joining *Time* magazine in 1982 to write on world affairs. Known primarily as a travel writer, he has written several books of fiction and nonfiction, including novels *Cuba and the Night* (1995) and *Abandon* (2003), as well as numerous books of essays and travelogs, including *Video Night in Kathmandu: And Other Reports from the Not-So-Far East* (1988), *The Lady and the Monk: Four Seasons in Kyoto* (1991), *Falling Off the Map: Some Lonely Places of the World* (1993), and *The Open Road: The Global Journey of the Fourteenth Dalai Lama* (2008), an extended journalistic analysis of the Tibetan spiritual leader.

> As an Indian born in England and raised predominantly in the United States, Iyer has said that "being an outsider, as I always was, proved to be a perfect background, and launching pad, for writing (and for traveling)."

As an Indian born in England and raised predominantly in the United States, Iyer has said that "being an outsider, as I always was, proved to be a perfect background, and launching pad, for writing (and for traveling)."

THE MAPLES are still blazing outside my two-room flat in suburban Japan, and the skies, in mid-December, are still blue, blue, blue, warmer and clearer than those of California. The temperature is higher than it usually is, and yet winter is often inexplicably warm and invigorating here in the outskirts of the eighth-century capital of Nara, where the center of town is given over to twelve hundred roaming deer and a temple. Besides, the lesson of the autumn, every year in Japan, is that everything is moving, aging, falling away, and nothing is really changing, deep down. Every year brings the same autumn in the midst of shifting (and enduring) circumstances.

Wherever I go on my travels, people are telling me about freaks in the weather. In California, where my mother lives, they're all wondering where the rain has gone. A forest fire came within two miles of her house last August—smoke rose above the hills for two months and my car got so coated in ash that its roof corroded—and threatened to raze to the ground the house that she had built after a previous forest fire wiped out our home and six hundred others. In the Himalayas, where I've spent some of the year, people don't know what to do with the crops and cycles that have sustained them for centuries, now that the temperatures are so unnaturally high. In Jerusalem, where I go tomorrow, there has been concern for millennia about how to get the inner thermostat right, and try to keep fervor, passion, and conviction alive without excessive heat, the kind that destroys as much as a forest fire might.

Our outer environment can only begin to be healed by our inner, and I'm not sure we can ever truly tend to our polluted waters, our shrinking forests, the madness we've loosed on the air until we begin to try to clean up the inner waters, and attend to the embattled wild spaces within us. Action without reflection is what got us into this mess in the first place, and the only answer is not action, but, first, clearer reflection. A peace treaty signed by men who are still territorial, jealous, or unquiet—Jerusalem tells me this—is not going to create any real peace at all. A commitment to the environment based only on what is outside of us forgets that the source of our problems—and solutions—is invisible, and that "nature" is a word we apply to what's within as well as without.

How to find the right heat that can bring focus and determination and light to the issue, without raging out of control? How to keep some cool, too, some sense of proportion, that reminds us that our seasons are all mixed up, and it is a sense of cycles as much as of progress that we need? Things don't necessarily go forward; they come around.

I make my own small efforts to play my part, living in a small room in the middle of nowhere, with no bicycle or car or printer or iPod or cell phone. I try to keep myself clear by not bringing newspapers or magazines or TV programs or World Wide Web into this space. I turn off lights and make the tiny gestures that, if more of us do them more often, can make a tiny difference. But mostly I try to think how cleaning up my own debris and setting the thermostat within can finally be the best contribution that any nonspecialist can make. Take care of the roots, and the flowers will take care of themselves. ■

5

The Reader's Presence

1. In the first paragraph, Iyer writes, "the lesson of the autumn, every year in Japan, is that everything is moving, aging, falling away, and nothing is really changing, deep down. Every year brings the same autumn in the midst of shifting (and enduring) circumstances." What are the effects of Iyer's decision to open his essay with this observation? How does this sentence anticipate the most important ideas he presents in the rest of his essay? Point to specific passages to support your response.

2. At the end of the essay, Iyer lists a few of the "small efforts" that he makes to play his part in affecting change. What do you understand Iyer to mean when he calls these "tiny gestures"? How—and in what specific ways—do they relate to his statement "it is a sense of cycles as much as of progress that we need" (paragraph 4)? What is your judgment of their efficacy?

3. **CONNECTIONS:** Compare Iyer's position on activism with the one Malcolm Gladwell puts forth in "Small Change: Why the Revolution Will Not Be Tweeted" (page 411). In what ways are the two positions complementary? In what ways are they at odds? What in your judgment would each writer say about the other's position? Point to specific passages in each essay to validate your answer.

Thomas Jefferson

THE DECLARATION OF INDEPENDENCE

THOMAS JEFFERSON (1743–1826) was born and raised in Virginia and attended William and Mary College. After being admitted to the bar, he entered politics and served in the Virginia House of Burgesses and the Continental Congress of 1775. During the Revolutionary War he was elected governor of Virginia, and after independence he was appointed special minister to France and later secretary of state. As the nation's third president, he negotiated the Louisiana Purchase. Of all his accomplishments as an inventor, an architect, a diplomat, a scientist, and a politician, Jefferson counted his work in designing the University of Virginia among the most important, along with his efforts to establish separation of church and state and the composition of the Declaration of Independence.

> Thomas Jefferson intended the Declaration of Independence "to be an expression of the American mind, and to give to that expression the proper tone and spirit called for by the occasion."

In May and June 1776, the Continental Congress had been vigorously debating the dangerous idea of independence and felt the need to issue a document that clearly pointed out the colonial grievances against Great Britain. A committee was appointed to "prepare a declaration" that would summarize the specific reasons for colonial discontent. The committee of five included Thomas Jefferson, Benjamin Franklin, and John Adams. Jefferson, who was noted for his skills in composition and, as Adams put it, "peculiar felicity of expression," was chosen to write the first draft. The assignment took Jefferson about two weeks, and he submitted the draft first to the committee, which made a few verbal alterations, and then on June 28 to Congress, where, after further alterations mainly relating to slavery, it was finally approved on July 4, 1776.

Jefferson claims to have composed the document without research, working mainly from ideas he felt were commonly held at the time. As Jefferson recalled many years later, he drafted the document as "an appeal to the tribunal of the world" and hoped "to place before mankind the common sense of the subject, in terms so plain and firm as to command their assent." He claims that "neither aiming at originality of principle or sentiment . . . it was intended to be an expression of the American mind, and to give to that expression the proper tone and spirit called for by the occasion."

WHEN IN THE COURSE of human events, it becomes necessary for one people to dissolve the political bands which have connected them with another, and to assume among the Powers of the earth, the separate and equal station to which the Laws of Nature and of Nature's God entitle them, a decent respect to the opinions of mankind requires that they should declare the causes which impel them to the separation.

We hold these truths to be self-evident, that all men are created equal, that they are endowed by their Creator with certain inalienable Rights, that among these are Life, Liberty and the pursuit of Happiness. That to secure these rights, Governments are instituted among Men, deriving their just powers from the consent of the governed. That whenever any Form of Government becomes destructive of these ends, it is the Right of the People to alter or to abolish it, and to institute new Government, laying its foundation on such principles and organizing its powers in such form, as to them shall seem most likely to effect their Safety and Happiness. Prudence, indeed, will dictate that Governments long established should not be changed for light and transient causes; and accordingly all experience hath shown, that mankind are more disposed to suffer, while evils are sufferable, than to right themselves by abolishing the forms to which they are accustomed. But when a long train of abuses and usurpations, pursuing invariably the same Object evinces a design to reduce them under absolute Despotism, it is their right, it is their duty, to throw off such Government, and to provide new Guards for their future security.—Such has been the patient sufferance of these Colonies; and such is now the necessity which constrains them to alter their former Systems of Government. The history of the present King of Great Britain is a history of repeated injuries and usurpations, all having in direct object the establishment of an absolute Tyranny over these States. To prove this, let Facts be submitted to a candid world.

He has refused his Assent to Laws, the most wholesome and necessary for the public good.

He has forbidden his Governors to pass Laws of immediate and pressing importance, unless suspended in their operation till his Assent should be obtained; and when so suspended, he has utterly neglected to attend to them.

He has refused to pass other laws for the accommodation of large districts of people, unless those people would relinquish the right of Representation in the Legislature, a right inestimable to them and formidable to tyrants only.   5

He has called together legislative bodies at places unusual, uncomfortable, and distant from the depository of their Public Records, for the sole purpose of fatiguing them into compliance with his measures.

He has dissolved Representative Houses repeatedly, for opposing with manly firmness his invasions on the rights of the people.

He has refused for a long time, after such dissolutions, to cause others to be elected; whereby the Legislative Powers, incapable of Annihilation, have returned to the People at large for their exercise; the State remaining in the mean time exposed to all the dangers of invasion from without, and convulsions within.

He has endeavoured to prevent the population of these States;[1] for that purpose obstructing the Laws for Naturalization of Foreigners; refusing to pass others to encourage their migration hither, and raising the conditions of new Appropriations of Lands.

He has obstructed the Administration of Justice, by refusing his Assent   10
to Laws for establishing Judiciary Powers.

He has made Judges dependent on his Will alone, for the tenure of their offices, and the amount and payment of their salaries.

He has erected a multitude of New Offices, and sent hither swarms of Officers to harass our People, and eat out their substance.

He has kept among us, in times of peace, Standing Armies without the Consent of our legislature.

He has affected to render the Military independent of and superior to the Civil Power.

He has combined with others to subject us to a jurisdiction foreign to our   15
constitution, and unacknowledged by our laws; giving his Assent to their acts of pretended Legislation:

For quartering large bodies of armed troops among us:

For protecting them, by a mock Trial, from Punishment for any Murders which they should commit on the Inhabitants of these States:

---

1 ***prevent the population of these States:*** This meant limiting emigration to the Colonies, thus controlling their growth. —EDS.

For cutting off our Trade with all parts of the world:

For imposing taxes on us without our Consent:

For depriving us in many cases, of the benefits of Trial by Jury: 20

For transporting us beyond Seas to be tried for pretended offenses:

For abolishing the free System of English Laws in a neighboring Province, establishing therein an Arbitrary government, and enlarging its Boundaries so as to render it at once an example and fit instrument for introducing the same absolute rule into these Colonies:

For taking away our Charters, abolishing our most valuable Laws, and altering fundamentally the Forms of our Governments:

For suspending our own Legislatures, and declaring themselves invested with Power to legislate for us in all cases whatsoever.

He has abdicated Government here, by declaring us out of his Protec- 25
tion and waging War against us.

He has plundered our seas, ravaged our Coasts, burnt our towns, and destroyed the lives of our people.

He is at this time transporting large armies of foreign mercenaries to compleat the works of death, desolation and tyranny, already begun with circumstances of Cruelty & perfidy scarcely paralleled in the most barbarous ages, and totally unworthy of the Head of a civilized nation.

He has constrained our fellow Citizens taken Captive on the high Seas to bear Arms against their Country, to become the executioners of their friends and Brethren, or to fall themselves by their Hands.

He has excited domestic insurrections amongst us, and has endeavoured to bring on the inhabitants of our frontiers, the merciless Indian Savages, whose known rule of warfare, is an undistinguished destruction of all ages, sexes and conditions.

In every stage of these Oppressions We have Petitioned for Readdress 30
in the most humble terms: Our repeated Petitions have been answered only by repeated injury. A Prince, whose character is thus marked by every act which may define a Tyrant, is unfit to be the ruler of a free People.

Nor have We been wanting in attention to our British brethren. We have warned them from time to time of attempts by their legislature to extend an unwarrantable jurisdiction over us. We have reminded them of the circumstances of our emigration and settlement here. We have appealed to their native justice and magnanimity, and we have conjured them by the ties of our common kindred to disavow these usurpations, which would inevitably interrupt our connections and correspondence. They too have been deaf to the voice of justice and of consanguinity. We must, therefore, acquiesce in the necessity, which denounces our Separation, and hold them, as we hold the rest of mankind, Enemies in War, in Peace Friends.

We, therefore, the Representatives of the United States of America, in General Congress, Assembled, appealing to the Supreme Judge of the world for the rectitude of our intentions, do in the Name, and by Authority of the good People of these Colonies, solemnly publish and declare, That these

United Colonies are, and of Right ought to be Free and Independent States, that they are Absolved from all Allegiance to the British Crown, and that all political connection between them and the State of Great Britain, is and ought to be totally dissolved; and that as Free and Independent States, they have full Power to levy War, conclude Peace, contract Alliances, establish Commerce, and to do all other Acts and Things which Independent States may of right do. And for the support of this Declaration, with a firm reliance on the Protection of Divine Providence, we mutually pledge to each other our Lives, our Fortunes and our sacred Honor. ◼

The Reader's Presence

1. How does Jefferson seem to define *independence*? Whom does the definition include? Whom does it exclude? How does Jefferson's definition of *independence* differ from your own? It has been pointed out that Jefferson disregards "interdependence." Can you formulate an argument contrary to Jefferson's?

2. Examine the Declaration's first sentence. Who is the speaker here? What is the effect of the omniscient tone of the opening? Why does the first paragraph have no personal pronouns or references to specific events? What might Jefferson's argument stand to gain in generalizing the American situation?

3. **CONNECTIONS:** As in classical epics and the Bible, Jefferson frequently relies on the rhetorical devices of repetition and lists. What is the effect of such devices? What else about the Declaration strikes you as representative of eighteenth-century ideas and language? Choose another essay in this collection that relies on similar strategies. What, more specifically, do these essays have in common? What sets them apart? As you respond, you might find it helpful to read Akhil Reed Amar's essay "Second Thoughts: What the Right to Bear Arms Really Means" (page 305). Amar argues that "we need to understand how all the words of the [second] amendment fit together, and how they in turn, mesh with other words in the Constitution. The amendment's syntax seems odd only because modern readers persistently misread the words 'militia' and 'people,' imposing twentieth-century assumptions on an eighteenth-century text" (paragraph 5). Do you share Amar's view about the continuing misreadings of the second amendment? Why or why not?

The Writer at Work

Another Draft of the Declaration of Independence

The "original Rough draught" of the Declaration of Independence is one of the foundational documents in American history. The following reproduction of the opening paragraphs of the Declaration illustrates how the text evolved from the initial draft by Thomas Jefferson to the final text adopted by Congress on the morning of July 4, 1776.

❝A Declaration by the Representatives of the United States of America, in General Congress assembled.

When in the course of human events, it becomes necessary for one people to dissolve the political bands which have connected them with another, and to assume among the powers of the earth the separate and equal station to which the laws of nature and of nature's God entitle them, a decent respect to the opinions of mankind requires that they should declare the causes which impel them to the separation.

We hold these truths to be self evident: that all men are created equal; that they are endowed by their Creator with [inherent and] inalienable rights; that among these are life, liberty, and the pursuit of happiness; that to secure these rights, governments are instituted among men, deriving their just powers from the consent of the governed; that whenever any form of government becomes destructive of these ends, it is the right of the people to alter or to abolish it, and to institute new government, laying its foundation on such principles, and organizing its powers in such form, as to them shall seem most likely to effect their safety and happiness. Prudence, indeed, will dictate that governments long established should not be changed for light and transient causes; and accordingly all experience hath shown that mankind are more disposed to suffer while evils are sufferable, than to right themselves by abolishing the forms to which they are accustomed. But when a long train of abuses and usurpations, [begun at a distinguished period and] pursuing invariably the same object, evinces a design to reduce them under absolute despotism, it is their right, it is their duty to throw off such government, and to provide new guards for their future security. Such has been the patient sufferance of these colonies; and such is now the necessity which constrains them to [expunge] their former systems of government. The history of the present king of Great Britain is a history of [unremitting] injuries and usurpations, [among which appears no solitary fact to contradict the uniform tenor of the rest, but all have] in direct object the establishment of an absolute tyranny over these states. To prove this, let facts be submitted to a candid world [for the truth of which we pledge a faith yet unsullied by falsehood.] . . . ❞

Martin Luther King Jr.

I HAVE A DREAM

MARTIN LUTHER KING JR. (1929–1968) was born in Atlanta, Georgia, and after training for the ministry became pastor of the Dexter Avenue Baptist Church in Montgomery, Alabama. In 1956 he was elected president of the Montgomery Improvement Association, the group that organized a transportation boycott in response to the arrest of Rosa Parks. King later became president of the Southern Christian Leadership Conference, and under his philosophy of nonviolent direct action he led marches and protests throughout the South, to Chicago, and to Washington, D.C. In 1963 King delivered his most famous speech, "I Have a Dream," before 200,000 people in front of the Lincoln Memorial in Washington, D.C., and in 1964 he was awarded the Nobel Peace Prize. King was assassinated on April 3, 1968, in Memphis, Tennessee.

> In 1964, Martin Luther King Jr. was awarded the Nobel Peace Prize.

King was a masterful orator and a powerful writer. Along with his many speeches, King wrote several books, including *Why We Can't Wait* (1963), *Where Do We Go from Here: Chaos or Community?* (1967), *The Measure of a Man* (1968), and *Trumpet of Conscience* (1968).

For more on Martin Luther King Jr., see page 716.

FIVE SCORE YEARS AGO, a great American, in whose symbolic shadow we stand, signed the Emancipation Proclamation.[1] This momentous decree came as a great beacon light of hope to millions of Negro slaves who had been seared in the flames of withering injustice. It came as a joyous daybreak to end the long night of captivity.

But one hundred years later, we must face the tragic fact that the Negro is still not free. One hundred years later, the life of the Negro is still sadly crippled by the manacles of segregation and the chains of discrimination. One hundred years later, the Negro lives on a lonely island of poverty in the midst of a vast ocean of material prosperity. One hundred years later, the Negro is still languishing in the corners of American society and finds

[1] **Emancipation Proclamation:** Abraham Lincoln signed the Emancipation Proclamation that officially freed the slaves in 1863. —EDS.

himself an exile in his own land. So we have come here today to dramatize an appalling condition.

In a sense we have come to our nation's Capitol to cash a check. When the architects of our republic wrote the magnificent words of the Constitution and the Declaration of Independence, they were signing a promissory note to which every American was to fall heir. This note was a promise that all men would be guaranteed the unalienable rights of life, liberty, and the pursuit of happiness.

It is obvious today that America has defaulted on this promissory note insofar as her citizens of color are concerned. Instead of honoring this sacred obligation, America has given the Negro people a bad check; a check which has come back marked "insufficient funds." But we refuse to believe that the bank of justice is bankrupt. We refuse to believe that there are insufficient funds in the great vaults of opportunity of this nation. So we have come to cash this check—a check that will give us upon demand the riches of freedom and the security of justice. We have also come to this hallowed spot to remind America of the fierce urgency of *now*. This is no time to engage in the luxury of cooling off or to take the tranquilizing drug of gradualism. *Now* is the time to make real the promises of Democracy. *Now* is the time to rise from the dark and desolate valley of segregation to the sunlit path of racial justice. *Now* is the time to open the doors of opportunity to all of God's children. *Now* is the time to lift our nation from the quicksands of racial injustice to the solid rock of brotherhood.

It would be fatal for the nation to overlook the urgency of the moment and to underestimate the determination of the Negro. This sweltering summer of the Negro's legitimate discontent will not pass until there is an invigorating autumn of freedom and equality. 1963 is not an end, but a beginning. Those who hope that the Negro needed to blow off steam and will now be content will have a rude awakening if the nation returns to business as usual. There will be neither rest nor tranquility in America until the Negro is granted his citizenship rights. The whirlwinds of revolt will continue to shake the foundations of our nation until the bright day of justice emerges.

But there is something I must say to my people who stand on the warm threshold which leads into the palace of justice. In the process of gaining our rightful place we must not be guilty of wrongful deeds. Let us not seek to satisfy our thirst for freedom by drinking from the cup of bitterness and hatred. We must forever conduct our struggle on the high plane of dignity and discipline. We must not allow our creative protest to degenerate into physical violence. Again and again we must rise to the majestic heights of meeting physical force with soul force. The marvelous new militancy which has engulfed the Negro community must not lead us to a distrust of all white people, for many of our white brothers, as evidenced by their presence here today, have come to realize that their destiny is tied up with our destiny and their freedom is inextricably bound to our freedom. We cannot walk alone.

And as we walk, we must make the pledge that we shall march ahead. We cannot turn back. There are those who are asking the devotees of civil rights, "When will you be satisfied?" We can never be satisfied as long as the Negro is the victim of the unspeakable horrors of police brutality. We can never be satisfied as long as our bodies, heavy with the fatigue of travel, cannot gain lodging in the motels of the highways and the hotels of the cities. We cannot be satisfied as long as the Negro's basic mobility is from a smaller ghetto to a larger one. We can never be satisfied as long as a Negro in Mississippi cannot vote and a Negro in New York believes he has nothing for which to vote. No, no, we are not satisfied, and we will not be satisfied until justice rolls down like waters and righteousness like a mighty stream.

I am not unmindful that some of you have come here out of great trials and tribulations. Some of you have come fresh from narrow jail cells. Some of you have come from areas where your quest for freedom left you battered by the storms of persecution and staggered by the winds of police brutality. You have been the veterans of creative suffering. Continue to work with the faith that unearned suffering is redemptive.

Go back to Mississippi, go back to Alabama, go back to South Carolina, go back to Georgia, go back to Louisiana, go back to the slums and ghettoes of our northern cities, knowing that somehow this situation can and will be changed. Let us not wallow in the valley of despair.

I say to you today, my friends, that in spite of the difficulties and frustra-   10
tions of the moment I still have a dream. It is a dream deeply rooted in the American dream.

I have a dream that one day this nation will rise up and live out the true meaning of its creed: "We hold these truths to be self-evident; that all men are created equal."[2]

I have a dream that one day on the red hills of Georgia the sons of former slaves and the sons of former slaveowners will be able to sit down together at the table of brotherhood.

I have a dream that the state of Mississippi, a desert state sweltering with the heat of injustice and oppression, will be transformed into an oasis of freedom and justice.

I have a dream that my four little children will one day live in a nation where they will not be judged by the color of their skin but by the content of their character.

I have a dream today.   15

I have a dream that the state of Alabama, whose governor's[3] lips are presently dripping with the words of interposition and nullification, will be transformed into a situation where little black boys and black girls will be

2 From the Declaration of Independence by Thomas Jefferson (page 695).—EDS.
3 **governor's:** The governor of Alabama in 1963 was segregationist George Wallace (1919–1998), who eventually came to support integration and equal rights for African Americans.—EDS.

able to join hands with little white boys and white girls and walk together as sisters and brothers.

I have a dream today.

I have a dream that one day every valley shall be exalted, every hill and mountain shall be made low, the rough places will be made plain, and the crooked places will be made straight, and the glory of the Lord shall be revealed, and all flesh shall see it together.

This is our hope. This is the faith with which I return to the South. With this faith we will be able to hew out of the mountain of despair a stone of hope. With this faith we will be able to transform the jangling discords of our nation into a beautiful symphony of brotherhood. With this faith we will be able to work together, to pray together, to struggle together, to go to jail together, to stand up for freedom together, knowing that we will be free one day.

This will be the day when all of God's children will be able to sing with 20 new meaning.

> My country, 'tis of thee
> Sweet land of liberty,
>   Of thee I sing:
> Land where my fathers died,
> Land of the pilgrims' pride,
> From every mountainside
>   Let freedom ring.

And if America is to be a great nation this must become true. So let freedom ring from the prodigious hilltops of New Hampshire. Let freedom ring from the mighty mountains of New York. Let freedom ring from the heightening Alleghenies of Pennsylvania!

Let freedom ring from the snowcapped Rockies of Colorado!

Let freedom ring from the curvaceous peaks of California!

But not only that; let freedom ring from Stone Mountain of Georgia!

Let freedom ring from Lookout Mountain of Tennessee! 25

Let freedom ring from every hill and molehill of Mississippi. From every mountainside, let freedom ring.

When we let freedom ring, when we let it ring from every village and every hamlet, from every state and every city, we will be able to speed up that day when all of God's children, black men and white men, Jews and Gentiles, Protestants and Catholics, will be able to join hands and sing in the words of the old Negro spiritual, "Free at last! free at last! thank God almighty, we are free at last!" ▪

The Reader's Presence

1. How does King use familiar concepts and phrases from American democracy to create his message? What are some examples? How does he use repetition? How does he use rhythm? What are the effects of his rhetoric?

2. Make a list of the metaphors King uses throughout the speech. What connotations do they bring? What recurring themes does he draw on for his metaphors? How do metaphors help extend the meanings of the words he describes?

3. **CONNECTIONS:**   Read Ho Che Anderson's graphic representation of King's "I Have a Dream" speech, which follows this piece. How does Anderson represent King as a speaker and leader? How does the juxtaposition of images and words influence your perception of the event?

The Artist at Work

HO CHE ANDERSON Reenvisions
Martin Luther King Jr.'s *I Have a Dream*

Ho Che Anderson (b. 1970) was born in the United Kingdom and raised in Canada, where he lives today. He has authored a number of graphic "comix" including *Young Hoods in Love* (1994), *I Want to Be Your Dog* (1996), and, in collaboration with Wilfred Santiago, the series *Pop Life* (1998). His biographical trilogy, *King* (Volumes I–III), illustrates the life of Martin Luther King Jr. from his birth to his assassination. Anderson's complex rendering of the 1963 civil rights march on Washington, D.C., during which Dr. King delivered his most famous speech, "I Have a Dream," is excerpted from *King, Volume II* (2002). The first volume, *King* (1992), won a 1995 Parent's Choice Award; *King, Volume III*, was published in 2003.

Martin Luther King Jr.
LETTER FROM BIRMINGHAM JAIL

MARTIN LUTHER KING JR. (1929–1968), one of the nation's best-known civil rights activists, led protests across the South in the years before the passage of the Civil Rights Act of 1964. He was arrested in 1960 for sitting at a whites-only lunch counter in Greensboro, North Carolina, and in 1962 he was jailed in Albany, Georgia. On April 12, 1963, King was again arrested, this time in Birmingham, Alabama, for demonstrating without a permit. He served eleven days in jail. While there, he wrote "Letter from Birmingham Jail" in response to a letter from eight clergymen who argued against King's acts of civil disobedience. The letter was published in King's book *Why We Can't Wait* (1963).

> **"Through education we seek to break down the spiritual barriers to integration."**

Many of King's writings, including the letter printed here and the famous "I Have a Dream" speech (see page 701), are designed to educate his audiences and inspire them to act. "Through education we seek to break down the spiritual barriers to integration," he said, and "through legislation and court orders we seek to break down the physical barriers to integration. One method is not a substitute for the other, but a meaningful and necessary supplement."

For more on Martin Luther King Jr., see page 701.

The following is the public statement by eight Alabama clergymen that occasioned King's letter.

———

WE THE UNDERSIGNED clergymen are among those who, in January, issued "an appeal for law and order and common sense," in dealing with racial problems in Alabama. We expressed understanding that honest convictions in racial matters could properly be pursued in the courts, but urged that decisions of those courts should in the meantime be peacefully obeyed.

Since that time there had been some evidence of increased forbearance and a willingness to face facts. Responsible citizens have undertaken to work on various problems which cause racial friction and unrest. In Birmingham, recent public events have given indication that we all have opportunity for a new constructive and realistic approach to racial problems.

However, we are now confronted by a series of demonstrations by some of our Negro citizens, directed and led in part by outsiders. We recognize the natural impatience of people who feel that their hopes are slow in being realized. But we are convinced that these demonstrations are unwise and untimely.

We agree rather with certain local Negro leadership which has called for honest and open negotiation of racial issues in our area. And we believe this kind of facing of issues can best be accomplished by citizens of our own metropolitan area, white and Negro, meeting with their knowledge and experience of the local situation. All of us need to face that responsibility and find proper channels for its accomplishment.

Just as we formerly pointed out that "hatred and violence have no sanction in our religious and political traditions," we also point out that such actions as incite to hatred and violence, however technically peaceful those actions may be, have not contributed to the resolution of our local problems. We do not believe that these days of new hope are days when extreme measures are justified in Birmingham.

We commend the community as a whole, and the local news media and law enforcement officials in particular, on the calm manner in which these demonstrations have been handled. We urge the public to continue to show restraint should the demonstrations continue, and the law enforcement officials to remain calm and continue to protect our city from violence.

We further strongly urge our own Negro community to withdraw support from these demonstrations, and to unite locally in working peacefully for a better Birmingham. When rights are consistently denied, a cause should be pressed in the courts and in negotiations among local leaders, and not in the streets. We appeal to both our white and Negro citizenry to observe the principles of law and order and common sense.

BISHOP C. C. J. CARPENTER, D.D., LL.D., Episcopalian Bishop of Alabama

BISHOP JOSEPH A. DURICK, D.D., Auxiliary Bishop, Roman Catholic Diocese of Mobile, Birmingham

RABBI MILTON L. GRAFMAN, Temple Emanu-El, Birmingham, Alabama

BISHOP PAUL HARDIN, Methodist Bishop of the Alabama–West Florida Conference

BISHOP NOLAN B. HARMON, Bishop of the North Alabama Conference of the Methodist Church

REV. GEORGE M. MURRAY, D.D., LL.D., Bishop Coadjutor, Episcopal Diocese of Alabama

REV. EDWARD V. RAMAGE, Moderator, Synod of the Alabama Presbyterian Church in the United States

REV. EARL STALLINGS, Pastor, First Baptist Church, Birmingham, Alabama

April 12, 1963

MARTIN LUTHER KING JR.
Birmingham City Jail
April 16, 1963

Bishop C. C. J. CARPENTER	*Bishop* NOLAN B. HARMON
Bishop JOSEPH A. DURICK	*The Rev.* GEORGE M. MURRAY
Rabbi MILTON L. GRAFMAN	*The Rev.* EDWARD V. RAMAGE
Bishop PAUL HARDIN	*The Rev.* EARL STALLINGS

My dear Fellow Clergymen,

While confined here in the Birmingham City Jail, I came across your recent statement calling our present activities "unwise and untimely." Seldom, if ever, do I pause to answer criticism of my work and ideas. If I sought to answer all of the criticisms that cross my desk, my secretaries would be engaged in little else in the course of the day and I would have no time for constructive work. But since I feel that you are men of genuine good will and your criticisms are sincerely set forth, I would like to answer your statement in what I hope will be patient and reasonable terms.

I think I should give the reason for my being in Birmingham, since you have been influenced by the argument of "outsiders coming in." I have the honor of serving as president of the Southern Christian Leadership Conference, an organization operating in every Southern state with headquarters in Atlanta, Georgia. We have some eighty-five affiliate organizations all across the South—one being the Alabama Christian Movement for Human Rights. Whenever necessary and possible we share staff, educational, and financial resources with our affiliates. Several months ago our local affiliate here in Birmingham invited us to be on call to engage in a nonviolent direct action program if such were deemed necessary. We readily consented and when the hour came we lived up to our promises. So I am here, along with several members of my staff, because we were invited here. I am here because I have basic organizational ties here. Beyond this, I am in Birmingham because injustice is here. Just as the eighth century prophets left their little villages and carried their "thus saith the Lord" far beyond the boundaries of their home town, and just as the Apostle Paul left his little village of Tarsus and carried the gospel of Jesus Christ to practically every hamlet and city of the Greco-Roman world, I too am compelled to carry the gospel of freedom beyond my particular home town. Like Paul, I must constantly respond to the Macedonian call for aid.

Moreover, I am cognizant of the interrelatedness of all communities and states. I cannot sit idly by in Atlanta and not be concerned about what happens in Birmingham. Injustice anywhere is a threat to justice everywhere. We are caught in an inescapable network of mutuality tied in a single garment of destiny. Whatever affects one directly affects all indirectly. Never again can we afford to live with the narrow, provincial "outside agitator" idea. Anyone who lives inside the United States can never be considered an outsider anywhere in this country.

You deplore the demonstrations that are presently taking place in Birmingham. But I am sorry that your statement did not express a similar concern for the conditions that brought the demonstrations into being. I am sure that each of you would want to go beyond the superficial social analyst who looks merely at effects, and does not grapple with underlying causes. I would not hesitate to say that it is unfortunate that so-called demonstrations are taking place in Birmingham at this time, but I would say in more emphatic terms it is even more unfortunate that the white power structure of this city left the Negro community with no other alternative.

In any nonviolent campaign there are four basic steps: (1) collection   5 of the facts to determine whether injustices are alive; (2) negotiation; (3) self-purification; and (4) direct action. We have gone through all of these steps in Birmingham. There can be no gainsaying of the fact that racial injustice engulfs this community. Birmingham is probably the most thoroughly segregated city in the United States. Its ugly record of police brutality is known in every section of this country. Its unjust treatment of Negroes in the courts is a notorious reality. There have been more unsolved bombings of Negro homes and churches in Birmingham than in any city in this nation. These are the hard, brutal, and unbelievable facts. On the basis of these conditions Negro leaders sought to negotiate with the city fathers. But the political leaders consistently refused to engage in good faith negotiation.

Then came the opportunity last September to talk with some of the leaders of the economic community. In these negotiating sessions certain promises were made by the merchants—such as the promise to remove the humiliating racial signs from the stores. On the basis of these promises Rev. Shuttlesworth and the leaders of the Alabama Christian Movement for Human Rights agreed to call a moratorium on any type of demonstrations. As the weeks and months unfolded we realized that we were the victims of a broken promise. The signs remained. As in so many experiences of the past we were confronted with blasted hopes, and the dark shadow of a deep disappointment settled upon us. So we had no alternative except that of preparing for direct action, whereby we would present our very bodies as a means of laying our case before the conscience of the local and national community. We were not unmindful of the difficulties involved. So we decided to go through a process of self-purification. We started having workshops on nonviolence and repeatedly asked ourselves the questions, "Are you able to accept blows without retaliating?" "Are you able to endure the ordeals of jail?"

We decided to set our direct action program around the Easter season, realizing that with the exception of Christmas, this was the largest shopping period of the year. Knowing that a strong economic withdrawal program would be the by-product of direct action, we felt that this was the best time to bring pressure on the merchants for the needed changes. Then it occurred to us that the March election was ahead, and so we speedily decided to postpone action until after election day. When we discovered that Mr. Connor[1] was in the run-off, we decided again to postpone so that the demonstrations could not be used to cloud the issues. At this time we agreed to begin our nonviolent witness the day after the run-off.

This reveals that we did not move irresponsibly into direct action. We too wanted to see Mr. Connor defeated; so we went through postponement after postponement to aid in this community need. After this we felt that direct action could be delayed no longer.

You may well ask, "Why direct action? Why sit-ins, marches, etc.? Isn't negotiation a better path?" You are exactly right in your call for negotiation. Indeed, this is the purpose of direct action. Nonviolent direct action seeks to create such a crisis and establish such creative tension that a community that has constantly refused to negotiate is forced to confront the issue. It seeks so to dramatize the issue that it can no longer be ignored. I just referred to the creation of tension as a part of the work of the nonviolent resister. This may sound rather shocking. But I must confess that I am not afraid of the word *tension*. I have earnestly worked and preached against violent tension, but there is a type of constructive nonviolent tension that is necessary for growth. Just as Socrates felt that it was necessary to create a tension in the mind so that individuals could rise from the bondage of myths and half-truths to the unfettered realm of creative analysis and objective appraisal, we must see the need of having nonviolent gadflies to create the kind of tension in society that will help men rise from the dark depths of prejudice and racism to the majestic heights of understanding and brotherhood. So the purpose of the direct action is to create a situation so crisis-packed that it will inevitably open the door to negotiation. We, therefore, concur with you in your call for negotiation. Too long has our beloved Southland been bogged down in the tragic attempt to live in monologue rather than dialogue.

One of the basic points in your statement is that our acts are untimely. 10 Some have asked, "Why didn't you give the new administration time to act?" The only answer that I can give to this inquiry is that the new administration must be prodded about as much as the outgoing one before it acts. We will be sadly mistaken if we feel that the election of Mr. Boutwell will bring the millennium to Birmingham. While Mr. Boutwell is much more articulate and gentle than Mr. Connor, they are both segregationists dedicated to the task of maintaining the status quo. The hope I see in Mr. Boutwell is that he will be reasonable enough to see the futility of massive resistance to desegregation. But he will not see this without pressure from the devotees of civil rights. My friends, I must say to you that we have not made a single gain in civil rights without determined legal and nonviolent pressure. History is the

---

1 ***Mr. Connor:*** Eugene "Bull" Connor and Albert Boutwell ran for mayor of Birmingham, Alabama, in 1963. Although Boutwell, the more moderate candidate, was declared the winner, Connor, the city commissioner of public safety, refused to leave office, claiming that he had been elected to serve until 1965. While the issue was debated in the courts, Connor was on the street ordering the police to use force to suppress demonstrations against segregation. —EDS.

long and tragic story of the fact that privileged groups seldom give up their privileges voluntarily. Individuals may see the moral light and voluntarily give up their unjust posture; but as Reinhold Niebuhr[2] has reminded us, groups are more immoral than individuals.

We know through painful experience that freedom is never voluntarily given by the oppressor; it must be demanded by the oppressed. Frankly I have never yet engaged in a direct action movement that was "well timed," according to the timetable of those who have not suffered unduly from the disease of segregation. For years now I have heard the word "Wait!" It rings in the ear of every Negro with a piercing familiarity. This "wait" has almost always meant "never." It has been a tranquilizing thalidomide,[3] relieving the emotional stress for a moment, only to give birth to an ill-formed infant of frustration. We must come to see with the distinguished jurist of yesterday that "justice too long delayed is justice denied." We have waited for more than three hundred and forty years for our constitutional and God-given rights. The nations of Asia and Africa are moving with jet-like speed toward the goal of political independence, and we still creep at horse and buggy pace toward the gaining of a cup of coffee at a lunch counter.

I guess it is easy for those who have never felt the stinging darts of segregation to say wait. But when you have seen vicious mobs lynch your mothers and fathers at will and drown your sisters and brothers at whim; when you have seen hate-filled policemen curse, kick, brutalize, and even kill your black brothers and sisters with impunity; when you see the vast majority of your twenty million Negro brothers smothering in an air-tight cage of poverty in the midst of an affluent society; when you suddenly find your tongue twisted and your speech stammering as you seek to explain to your six-year-old daughter why she can't go to the public amusement park that has just been advertised on television, and see tears welling up in her little eyes when she is told that Funtown is closed to colored children, and see the depressing clouds of inferiority begin to form in her little mental sky, and see her begin to distort her little personality by unconsciously developing a bitterness toward white people; when you have to concoct an answer for a five-year-old son asking in agonizing pathos: "Daddy, why do white people treat colored people so mean?"; when you take a cross country drive and find it necessary to sleep night after night in the uncomfortable corners of your automobile because no motel will accept you; when you are humiliated day in and day out by nagging signs reading "white" men and "colored"; when your first name becomes "nigger" and your middle name becomes "boy" (however old you are) and your last name becomes "John," and when your wife and mother are never given the respected title "Mrs."; when you are harried by day and haunted by night by the fact that you are a Negro,

---

2 ***Reinhold Niebuhr*** (1892–1971): Protestant theologian best known for attempts to relate Christianity to modern politics. —EDS.

3 ***thalidomide:*** A drug originally used as a sedative, but withdrawn in the early 1960s following the discovery that it caused malformation or absence of limbs in children whose mothers took the drug during early pregnancy. —EDS.

living constantly at tip-toe stance never quite knowing what to expect next, and plagued with inner fears and outer resentments; when you are forever fighting a degenerating sense of "nobodiness";—then you will understand why we find it difficult to wait. There comes a time when the cup of endurance runs over, and men are no longer willing to be plunged into an abyss of injustice where they experience the bleakness of corroding despair. I hope, sirs, you can understand our legitimate and unavoidable impatience.

You express a great deal of anxiety over our willingness to break laws. This is certainly a legitimate concern. Since we so diligently urge people to obey the Supreme Court's decision of 1954 outlawing segregation in the public schools, it is rather strange and paradoxical to find us consciously breaking laws. One may well ask, "How can you advocate breaking some laws and obeying others?" The answer is found in the fact that there are two types of laws. There are *just* laws and there are *unjust* laws. I would be the first to advocate obeying just laws. One has not only a legal but moral responsibility to obey just laws. Conversely, one has a moral responsibility to disobey unjust laws. I would agree with Saint Augustine that "An unjust law is no law at all."

Now what is the difference between the two? How does one determine when a law is just or unjust? A just law is a man-made code that squares with the moral law or the law of God. An unjust law is a code that is out of harmony with the moral law. To put it in the terms of Saint Thomas Aquinas, an unjust law is a human law that is not rooted in eternal and natural law. Any law that uplifts human personality is just. Any law that degrades human personality is unjust. All segregation statutes are unjust because segregation distorts the soul and damages the personality. It gives the segregator a false sense of superiority and the segregated a false sense of inferiority. To use the words of Martin Buber, the great Jewish philosopher, segregation substitutes an "I-it" relationship for the "I-thou" relationship, and ends up relegating persons to the status of things. So segregation is not only politically, economically, and sociologically unsound, but it is morally wrong and sinful. Paul Tillich[4] has said that sin is separation. Isn't segregation an existential expression of man's tragic separation, an expression of his awful estrangement, his terrible sinfulness? So I can urge men to obey the 1954 decision of the Supreme Court[5] because it is morally right, and I can urge them to disobey segregation ordinances because they are morally wrong.

Let us turn to a more concrete example of just and unjust laws. An unjust law is a code that a majority inflicts on a minority that is not binding on itself. This is *difference* made legal. On the other hand a just law is a code that a majority compels a minority to follow that it is willing to follow itself. This is *sameness* made legal.   15

Let me give another explanation. An unjust law is a code inflicted upon a minority which that minority had no part in enacting or creating because

---

4 **Paul Tillich** (1886–1965): Theologian and philosopher.—EDS.
5 **1954 decision of the Supreme Court:** *Brown v. Board of Education*, the case in which the Supreme Court ruled racial segregation in the nation's public schools unconstitutional.—EDS.

they did not have the unhampered right to vote. Who can say the legislature of Alabama which set up the segregation laws was democratically elected? Throughout the state of Alabama all types of conniving methods are used to prevent Negroes from becoming registered voters and there are some counties without a single Negro registered to vote despite the fact that the Negro constitutes a majority of the population. Can any law set up in such a state be considered democratically structured?

These are just a few examples of unjust and just laws. There are some instances when a law is just on its face but unjust in its application. For instance, I was arrested Friday on a charge of parading without a permit. Now there is nothing wrong with an ordinance which requires a permit for a parade, but when the ordinance is used to preserve segregation and to deny citizens the First Amendment privilege of peaceful assembly and peaceful protest, then it becomes unjust.

I hope you can see the distinction I am trying to point out. In no sense do I advocate evading or defying the law as the rabid segregationist would do. This would lead to anarchy. One who breaks an unjust law must do it *openly*, *lovingly* (not hatefully as the white mothers did in New Orleans when they were seen on television screaming "nigger, nigger, nigger") and with a willingness to accept the penalty. I submit that an individual who breaks a law that conscience tells him is unjust, and willingly accepts the penalty by staying in jail to arouse the conscience of the community over its injustice, is in reality expressing the very highest respect for law.

Of course there is nothing new about this kind of civil disobedience. It was seen sublimely in the refusal of Shadrach, Meshach, and Abednego to obey the laws of Nebuchadnezzar because a higher moral law was involved. It was practiced superbly by the early Christians who were willing to face hungry lions and the excruciating pain of chopping blocks, before submitting to certain unjust laws of the Roman Empire. To a degree academic freedom is a reality today because Socrates practiced civil disobedience.

We can never forget that everything Hitler did in Germany was "legal" and everything the Hungarian freedom fighters[6] did in Hungary was "illegal." It was "illegal" to aid and comfort a Jew in Hitler's Germany. But I am sure that, if I had lived in Germany during that time, I would have aided and comforted my Jewish brothers even though it was illegal. If I lived in a communist country today where certain principles dear to the Christian faith are suppressed, I believe I would openly advocate disobeying those antireligious laws.

I must make two honest confessions to you, my Christian and Jewish brothers. First I must confess that over the last few years I have been gravely disappointed with the white moderate. I have almost reached the regrettable conclusion that the Negroes' great stumbling block in the stride toward freedom is not the White Citizens' "Counciler" or the Ku Klux Klanner, but the

20

---

6 ***Hungarian freedom fighters:*** Those who fought in the unsuccessful 1956 revolt against Soviet oppression. —EDS.

white moderate who is more devoted to "order" than to justice; who prefers a negative peace which is the absence of tension to a positive peace which is the presence of justice; who constantly says "I agree with you in the goal you seek, but I can't agree with your methods of direct action"; who paternalistically feels that he can set the timetable for another man's freedom; who lives by the myth of time and who constantly advises the Negro to wait until a "more convenient season." Shallow understanding from people of good will is more frustrating than absolute misunderstanding from people of ill will. Lukewarm acceptance is much more bewildering than outright rejection.

I had hoped that the white moderate would understand that law and order exist for the purpose of establishing justice, and that when they fail to do this they become the dangerously structured dams that block the flow of social progress. I had hoped that the white moderate would understand that the present tension in the South is merely a necessary phase of the transition from an obnoxious negative peace, where the Negro passively accepted his unjust plight, to a substance-filled positive peace, where all men will respect the dignity and worth of human personality. Actually, we who engage in nonviolent direct action are not the creators of tension. We merely bring to the surface the hidden tension that is already alive. We bring it out in the open where it can be seen and dealt with. Like a boil that can never be cured as long as it is covered up but must be opened with all its pus-flowing ugliness to the natural medicines of air and light, injustice must likewise be exposed, with all of the tension its exposing creates, to the light of human conscience and the air of national opinion before it can be cured.

In your statement you asserted that our actions, even though peaceful, must be condemned because they precipitate violence. But can this assertion be logically made? Isn't this like condemning the robbed man because his possession of money precipitated the evil act of robbery? Isn't this like condemning Socrates because his unswerving commitment to truth and his philosophical delvings precipitated the misguided popular mind to make him drink the hemlock? Isn't this like condemning Jesus because His unique God consciousness and never-ceasing devotion to His will precipitated the evil act of crucifixion? We must come to see, as federal courts have consistently affirmed, that it is immoral to urge an individual to withdraw his efforts to gain his basic constitutional rights because the quest precipitates violence. Society must protect the robbed and punish the robber.

I had also hoped that the white moderate would reject the myth of time. I received a letter this morning from a white brother in Texas which said: "All Christians know that the colored people will receive equal rights eventually, but is it possible that you are in too great of a religious hurry? It has taken Christianity almost 2000 years to accomplish what it has. The teachings of Christ take time to come to earth." All that is said here grows out of a tragic misconception of time. It is the strangely irrational notion that there is something in the very flow of time that will inevitably cure all ills. Actually time is neutral. It can be used either destructively or constructively. I am coming to feel that the people of ill will have used time much more effectively than the people of good will. We will have to repent in this generation not merely for the vitriolic words and actions of the bad people, but for the appalling silence of the good people. We must come to see that human progress never rolls in on wheels of inevitability. It comes through the tireless efforts and persistent work of men willing to be co-workers with God, and without this hard work time itself becomes an ally of the forces of social stagnation.

We must use time creatively, and forever realize that the time is always   25 ripe to do right. Now is the time to make real the promise of democracy, and transform our pending national elegy into a creative psalm of brotherhood. Now is the time to lift our national policy from the quicksand of racial injustice to the solid rock of human dignity.

You spoke of our activity in Birmingham as extreme. At first I was rather disappointed that fellow clergymen would see my nonviolent efforts as those of the extremist. I started thinking about the fact that I stand in the middle of two opposing forces in the Negro community. One is a force of complacency made up of Negroes who, as a result of long years of oppression, have been so completely drained of self-respect and a sense of "somebodiness" that they have adjusted to segregation, and of a few Negroes in the middle class who, because of a degree of academic and economic security, and because at points they profit by segregation, have unconsciously become insensitive to the problems of the masses. The other force is one of bitterness and hatred and comes perilously close to advocating violence. It is expressed in the various black nationalist groups that are springing up over the nation, the largest and best known being Elijah Muhammad's Muslim movement.[7] This movement is nourished by the contemporary frustration over the continued existence of racial discrimination. It is made up of people who have lost faith in America, who have absolutely repudiated Christianity, and who have concluded that the white man is an incurable "devil." I have tried to stand between these two forces saying that we need not follow the "do-nothing-ism" of the complacent or the hatred and despair of the black nationalist. There is the more excellent way of love and nonviolent protest. I'm grateful to God that, through the Negro church, the dimension of nonviolence entered our struggle. If this philosophy had not emerged I am convinced that by now many streets of the South would be flowing with floods of blood. And I am further convinced that if our white brothers dismiss us as "rabble rousers" and "outside agitators"—those of us who are working through the channels of nonviolent direct action—and refuse to support our nonviolent efforts, millions of Negroes, out of frustration and despair, will seek solace and security in black nationalist ideologies, a development that will lead inevitably to a frightening racial nightmare.

Oppressed people cannot remain oppressed forever. The urge for freedom will eventually come. This is what has happened to the American Negro. Something within has reminded him of his birthright of freedom;

---

[7] ***Elijah Muhammad's Muslim movement:*** Led by Elijah Muhammad, the Black Muslims opposed integration and promoted the creation of a black nation within the United States. —EDS.

something without has reminded him that he can gain it. Consciously and unconsciously, he has been swept in by what the Germans call the *Zeitgeist*,[8] and with his black brothers of Africa, and his brown and yellow brothers of Asia, South America, and the Caribbean, he is moving with a sense of cosmic urgency toward the promised land of racial justice. Recognizing this vital urge that has engulfed the Negro community, one should readily understand public demonstrations. The Negro has many pent-up resentments and latent frustrations. He has to get them out. So let him march sometime; let him have his prayer pilgrimages to the city hall; understand why he must have sit-ins and freedom rides. If his repressed emotions do not come out in these nonviolent ways, they will come out in ominous expressions of violence. This is not a threat; it is a fact of history. So I have not said to my people, "Get rid of your discontent." But I have tried to say that this normal and healthy discontent can be channeled through the creative outlet of nonviolent direct action. Now this approach is being dismissed as extremist. I must admit that I was initially disappointed in being so categorized.

But as I continued to think about the matter I gradually gained a bit of satisfaction from being considered an extremist. Was not Jesus an extremist in love? "Love your enemies, bless them that curse you, pray for them that despitefully use you." Was not Amos[9] an extremist for justice — "Let justice roll down like waters and righteousness like a mighty stream." Was not Paul an extremist for the gospel of Jesus Christ — "I bear in my body the marks of the Lord Jesus." Was not Martin Luther an extremist — "Here I stand; I can do none other so help me God." Was not John Bunyan[10] an extremist — "I will stay in jail to the end of my days before I make a butchery of my conscience." Was not Abraham Lincoln an extremist — "This nation cannot survive half slave and half free." Was not Thomas Jefferson an extremist — "We hold these truths to be self-evident, that all men are created equal." So the question is not whether we will be extremist but what kind of extremist will we be. Will we be extremists for hate or will we be extremists for love? Will we be extremists for the preservation of injustice — or will we be extremists for the cause of justice? In that dramatic scene on Calvary's hill three men were crucified. We must never forget that all three were crucified for the same crime — the crime of extremism. Two were extremists for immorality, and thus fell below their environment. The other, Jesus Christ, was an extremist for love, truth, and goodness, and thereby rose above His environment. So, after all, maybe the South, the nation, and the world are in dire need of creative extremists.

I had hoped that the white moderate would see this. Maybe I was too optimistic. Maybe I expected too much. I guess I should have realized that few members of a race that has oppressed another race can understand or appreciate the deep groans and passionate yearnings of those that have been oppressed, and still fewer have the vision to see that injustice must be

---

8 **Zeitgeist:** A German word meaning "spirit of the time." —EDS.

9 **Amos:** Prophet who preached against false worship and immorality. —EDS.

10 **John Bunyan** (1628–1688): Puritan author of *Pilgrim's Progress*. —EDS.

rooted out by strong, persistent, and determined action. I am thankful, however, that some of our white brothers have grasped the meaning of this social revolution and committed themselves to it. They are still all too small in quantity, but they are big in quality. Some like Ralph McGill, Lillian Smith, Harry Golden, and James Dabbs have written about our struggle in eloquent, prophetic, and understanding terms. Others have marched with us down nameless streets of the South. They have languished in filthy, roach-infested jails, suffering the abuse and brutality of angry policemen who see them as "dirty nigger lovers." They, unlike so many of their moderate brothers and sisters, have recognized the urgency of the moment and sensed the need for powerful "action" antidotes to combat the disease of segregation.

Let me rush on to mention my other disappointment. I have been so greatly disappointed with the white Church and its leadership. Of course there are some notable exceptions. I am not unmindful of the fact that each of you has taken some significant stands on this issue. I commend you, Rev. Stallings, for your Christian stand on this past Sunday, in welcoming Negroes to your worship service on a nonsegregated basis. I commend the Catholic leaders of this state for integrating Springhill College several years ago.

But despite these notable exceptions I must honestly reiterate that I have been disappointed with the Church. I do not say that as one of those negative critics who can always find something wrong with the Church. I say it as a minister of the gospel, who loves the Church; who was nurtured in its bosom; who has been sustained by its spiritual blessings and who will remain true to it as long as the cord of life shall lengthen.

I had the strange feeling when I was suddenly catapulted into the leadership of the bus protest in Montgomery[11] several years ago that we would have the support of the white Church. I felt that the white ministers, priests, and rabbis of the South would be some of our strongest allies. Instead, some have been outright opponents, refusing to understand the freedom movement and misrepresenting its leaders; all too many others have been more cautious than courageous and have remained silent behind the anesthetizing security of stained glass windows.

In spite of my shattered dreams of the past, I came to Birmingham with the hope that the white religious leadership of the community would see the justice of our cause and, with deep moral concern, serve as the channel through which our just grievances could get to the power structure. I had hoped that each of you would understand. But again I have been disappointed.

I have heard numerous religious leaders of the South call upon their worshippers to comply with a desegregation decision because it is the law, but I have longed to hear white ministers say follow this decree because integration is morally right and the Negro is your brother. In the midst of blatant injustices inflicted upon the Negro, I have watched white churches stand on the sideline

---

11 **bus protest in Montgomery:** After Rosa Parks was arrested on December 1, 1955, in Montgomery, Alabama, for refusing to give her seat on a bus to a white male passenger, a bus boycott began, which lasted nearly one year and was supported by nearly all of the city's black residents. —EDS.

and merely mouth pious irrelevancies and sanctimonious trivialities. In the midst of a mighty struggle to rid our nation of racial and economic injustice, I have heard so many ministers say, "Those are social issues with which the Gospel has no real concern," and I have watched so many churches commit themselves to a completely otherworldly religion which made a strange distinction between body and soul, the sacred and the secular.

So here we are moving toward the exit of the twentieth century with 35 a religious community largely adjusted to the status quo, standing as a tail-light behind other community agencies rather than a headlight leading men to higher levels of justice.

I have travelled the length and breadth of Alabama, Mississippi, and all the other Southern states. On sweltering summer days and crisp autumn mornings I have looked at her beautiful churches with their spires pointing heavenward. I have beheld the impressive outlay of her massive religious education buildings. Over and over again I have found myself asking: "Who worships here? Who is their God? Where were their voices when the lips of Governor Barnett[12] dripped with words of interposition and nullification? Where were they when Governor Wallace[13] gave the clarion call for defiance and hatred? Where were their voices of support when tired, bruised, and weary Negro men and women decided to rise from the dark dungeons of complacency to the bright hills of creative protest?"

Yes, these questions are still in my mind. In deep disappointment, I have wept over the laxity of the Church. But be assured that my tears have been tears of love. There can be no deep disappointment where there is not deep love. Yes, I love the Church; I love her sacred walls. How could I do otherwise? I am in the rather unique position of being the son, the grandson, and the great grandson of preachers. Yes, I see the Church as the body of Christ. But, oh! How we have blemished and scarred that body through social neglect and fear of being nonconformists.

There was a time when the Church was very powerful. It was during that period when the early Christians rejoiced when they were deemed worthy to suffer for what they believed. In those days the Church was not merely a thermometer that recorded the ideas and principles of popular opinion; it was a thermostat that transformed the mores of society. Wherever the early Christians entered a town the power structure got disturbed and immediately sought to convict them for being "disturbers of the peace" and "outside agitators." But they went on with the conviction that they were a "colony of heaven" and had to obey God rather than man. They were small in number but big in commitment. They were too God-intoxicated to be "astronomically intimidated." They brought an end to such ancient evils as infanticide and gladiatorial contest.

Things are different now. The contemporary Church is so often a weak, ineffectual voice with an uncertain sound. It is so often the arch-supporter of

---

12 **Governor Barnett:** Ross R. Barnett, governor of Mississippi from 1960 to 1964.—EDS.
13 **Governor Wallace:** George C. Wallace served as governor of Alabama from 1963 to 1966, 1971 to 1979, and 1983 to 1987.—EDS.

the status quo. Far from being disturbed by the presence of the Church, the power structure of the average community is consoled by the Church's silent and often vocal sanction of things as they are.

But the judgment of God is upon the Church as never before. If the Church of today does not recapture the sacrificial spirit of the early Church, it will lose its authentic ring, forfeit the loyalty of millions, and be dismissed as an irrelevant social club with no meaning for the twentieth century. I am meeting young people every day whose disappointment with the Church has risen to outright disgust.   40

Maybe again I have been too optimistic. Is organized religion too inextricably bound to the status quo to save our nation and the world? Maybe I must turn my faith to the inner spiritual Church, the church within the Church, as the true *ecclesia*[14] and the hope of the world. But again I am thankful to God that some noble souls from the ranks of organized religion have broken loose from the paralyzing chains of conformity and joined us as active partners in the struggle for freedom. They have left their secure congregations and walked the streets of Albany, Georgia, with us. They have gone through the highways of the South on torturous rides for freedom. Yes, they have gone to jail with us. Some have been kicked out of their churches and lost the support of their bishops and fellow ministers. But they have gone with the faith that right defeated is stronger than evil triumphant. These men have been the leaven in the lump of the race. Their witness has been the spiritual salt that has preserved the true meaning of the Gospel in these troubled times. They have carved a tunnel of hope through the dark mountain of disappointment.

I hope the Church as a whole will meet the challenge of this decisive hour. But even if the Church does not come to the aid of justice, I have no despair about the future. I have no fear about the outcome of our struggle in Birmingham, even if our motives are presently misunderstood. We will reach the goal of freedom in Birmingham and all over the nation, because the goal of America is freedom. Abused and scorned though we may be, our destiny is tied up with the destiny of America. Before the pilgrims landed at Plymouth, we were here. Before the pen of Jefferson etched across the pages of history the majestic words of the Declaration of Independence, we were here. For more than two centuries our foreparents labored in this country without wages; they made cotton "king"; and they built the homes of their masters in the midst of brutal injustice and shameful humiliation—and yet out of a bottomless vitality they continued to thrive and develop. If the inexpressible cruelties of slavery could not stop us, the opposition we now face will surely fail. We will win our freedom because the sacred heritage of our nation and the eternal will of God are embodied in our echoing demands.

I must close now. But before closing I am impelled to mention one other point in your statement that troubled me profoundly. You warmly commended the Birmingham police force for keeping "order" and "preventing

---

14 **ecclesia:** The Latin word for church.—EDS.

violence." I don't believe you would have so warmly commended the police force if you had seen its angry violent dogs literally biting six unarmed, non-violent Negroes. I don't believe you would so quickly commend the police-men if you would observe their ugly and inhuman treatment of Negroes here in the city jail; if you would watch them push and curse old Negro women and young Negro girls; if you would see them slap and kick old Negro men and young Negro boys; if you will observe them, as they did on two occasions, refuse to give us food because we wanted to sing our grace together. I'm sorry that I can't join you in your praise for the police department.

It is true that they have been rather disciplined in their public handling of the demonstrators. In this sense they have been rather publicly "nonvio-lent." But for what purpose? To preserve the evil system of segregation. Over the last few years I have consistently preached that nonviolence demands that the means we use must be as pure as the ends we seek. So I have tried to make it clear that it is wrong to use immoral means to attain moral ends. But now I must affirm that it is just as wrong, or even more so, to use moral means to preserve immoral ends. Maybe Mr. Connor and his policemen have been rather publicly nonviolent, as Chief Pritchett[15] was in Albany, Georgia, but they have used the moral means of nonviolence to maintain the immoral end of flagrant racial injustice. T. S. Eliot has said that there is no greater treason than to do the right deed for the wrong reason.

I wish you had commended the Negro sit-inners and demonstrators of   45
Birmingham for their sublime courage, their willingness to suffer, and their amazing discipline in the midst of the most inhuman provocation. One day the South will recognize its real heroes. They will be the James Merediths,[16] courageously and with a majestic sense of purpose, facing jeering and hos-tile mobs and the agonizing loneliness that characterizes the life of the pio-neer. They will be old, oppressed, battered Negro women, symbolized in a seventy-two year old woman of Montgomery, Alabama, who rose up with a sense of dignity and with her people decided not to ride the segregated buses, and responded to one who inquired about her tiredness with ungram-matical profundity: "My feets is tired, but my soul is rested." They will be young high school and college students, young ministers of the gospel and a host of the elders, courageously and nonviolently sitting in at lunch coun-ters and willingly going to jail for conscience's sake. One day the South will know that when these disinherited children of God sat down at lunch coun-ters they were in reality standing up for the best in the American dream and the most sacred values in our Judeo-Christian heritage, and thus carrying our whole nation back to great wells of democracy which were dug deep by

15 **Chief Pritchett:** Pritchett served as police chief in Albany, Georgia, during nonviolent dem-onstrations in 1961 and 1962. Chief Pritchett responded to the nonviolent demonstrations with non-violence, refusing to allow his officers to physically or verbally abuse the demonstrators. —EDS.
16 **James Merediths:** Under the protection of federal marshals and the National Guard in 1962, James Meredith was the first black man to enroll at the University of Mississippi. —EDS.

the founding fathers in the formulation of the Constitution and the Declaration of Independence.

Never before have I written a letter this long (or should I say a book?). I'm afraid that it is much too long to take your precious time. I can assure you that it would have been much shorter if I had been writing from a comfortable desk, but what else is there to do when you are alone for days in the dull monotony of a narrow jail cell other than write long letters, think strange thoughts, and pray long prayers?

If I have said anything in this letter that is an overstatement of the truth and is indicative of an unreasonable impatience, I beg you to forgive me. If I have said anything in this letter that is an understatement of the truth and is indicative of my having a patience that makes me patient with anything less than brotherhood, I beg God to forgive me.

I hope this letter finds you strong in the faith. I also hope that circumstances will soon make it possible for me to meet each of you, not as an integrationist or a civil rights leader, but as a fellow clergyman and a Christian brother. Let us all hope that the dark clouds of racial prejudice will soon pass away and the deep fog of misunderstanding will be lifted from our fear-drenched communities and in some not too distant tomorrow the radiant stars of love and brotherhood will shine over our great nation with all of their scintillating beauty.

> *Yours for the cause of*
> *Peace and Brotherhood*
> MARTIN LUTHER KING JR.

The Reader's Presence

1. What does King gain by characterizing his "Fellow Clergymen" as "men of genuine good will," whose criticisms are "sincerely set forth" (paragraph 1)? What evidence can you point to in King's letter to verify the claim that his audience extends far beyond the eight clergymen he explicitly addresses? Comment on the overall structure of King's letter. What principle of composition underpins the structure of his response?

2. King establishes the tone of his response to the criticisms of the clergymen at the end of the opening paragraph: "I would like to answer your statement in what I hope will be patient and reasonable terms." As you reread his letter, identify specific words and phrases—as well as argumentative strategies—that satisfy these criteria that King imposes on himself. In what specific sense does King use the word *hope* here? As you reread his letter, point to each subsequent reference to hope. How does King emphasize the different meanings and connotations of the word as he unfolds his argument?

3. **CONNECTIONS:**   This letter has the ring of the oratory for which King was widely known and justly praised. Read passages aloud and note the ways that King appeals to his reader's ear (for example, with the balanced clauses of many of his sentences). How do the cadences of King's prose help to make his point? Compare King's letter to the famous "I Have a Dream" speech (page 701) he made in the same year. Although one is composed as a letter and the other was delivered as a stirring public address, what elements of language do they share?

The Writer at Work

MARTIN LUTHER KING JR. on Self-Importance

In the following piece, the famous African American political leader expresses his profound mistrust of the individual voice that rises above those for whom that voice speaks. In this, as in so many respects, King joins a long tradition of wrestling with the question of how to reconcile one's own creativity with the larger—and vastly more important—word and mission of God. King's spiritual mission was, of course, a social vision as well: that of racial equality in America. In speaking for those who believed with him in the possibility of making this dream a reality, King drew on his consummate skills as a preacher, an orator, and an organizer. Throughout his short public life (spanning only twelve years, ending with his assassination on April 4, 1968, in Memphis, Tennessee), King struggled with the competing claims of personal celebrity and of the community he so forcefully represented. How do King's ideas about representation (standing for and speaking on behalf of others) resonate with the ideas of other notable Americans included in this anthology, for example, Thomas Jefferson (page 695), Malcolm X (page 153), and Abraham Lincoln (page 491)?

❝ Would you allow me to share a personal experience with you this morning? And I say it only because I think it has bearing on this message. One of the problems that I have to face and even fight every day is this problem of self-centeredness, this tendency that can so easily come to my life now that I'm something special, that I'm something important. Living over the past year, I can hardly go into any city or any town in this nation where I'm not lavished with hospitality by peoples of all races and of all creeds. I can hardly go anywhere to speak in this nation where hundreds and thousands of people are not turned away because of lack of space. And then after speaking, I often have to be rushed out to get away from the crowd rushing for autographs. I can hardly walk the street in any city of this nation where I'm not confronted with people running up on the street, "Isn't this Reverend King of Alabama?" Living under this it's easy, it's a dangerous tendency that I will come to feel that I'm something special, that I stand somewhere in this universe because of my ingenuity and that I'm important, that I can walk around life with a type of arrogance because of an importance that I have. And one of the prayers that I pray to God every day is: "O God, help me to see my self in my true perspective. Help me, O God, to see that I'm just a symbol of a movement. Help me to see that I'm the victim of what the Germans call a *Zeitgeist* and that something was getting ready to happen in history; history was ready for it. And that a boycott would have taken place in Montgomery, Alabama, if I had never come to Alabama. Help me to realize that I'm where I am because of the forces of history and because of the fifty thousand Negroes of

Alabama who will never get their names in the papers and in the headline. O God, help me to see that where I stand today, I stand because others helped me to stand there and because the forces of history projected me there. And this movement would have come in history even if M. L. King had never been born." And when we come to see that, we stand with humility. This is the prayer I pray to God every day, "Lord help me to see M. L. King as M. L. King in his true perspective." Because if I don't see that, I will become the biggest fool in America. **"**

Laura Kipnis

AGAINST LOVE

LAURA KIPNIS is a cultural theorist, an author, and a videographer whose work blends academic theory, social criticism, and witty analysis, all "richly informed by her post-marxist, post-structuralist, post-feminist, post-everything sense of humor," according to a recent biography. A professor in the school of communications at Northwestern University in Evanston, Illinois, Kipnis is the author of several books, including *Ecstasy Unlimited: On Sex, Capital, Gender, and Aesthetics* (1993), *Bound and Gagged: Pornography and the Politics of Fantasy in America* (1996), *Against Love: A Polemic* (2003), and *The Female Thing: Dirt, Sex, Envy, Vulnerability* (2006). Kipnis's video essays—including *Ecstasy Unlimited: The Interpenetrations of Sex and Capital* (1985), *A Man's Woman* (1988), and *Marx: The Video* (1990)—have been screened in such venues as the Museum of Modern Art, the American Film Institute, and the Whitney Museum. Kipnis has also written essays and reviews for *Slate*, the *Village Voice*, *Harper's*, *Critical Inquiry*, *Wide Angle*, and the *New York Times Magazine*, where "Against Love" appeared in 2001. Her most recent book, *How to Become a Scandal: Adventures in Bad Behavior*, was published in 2010.

> "It's a polemic, so there are certain questions I don't have to address, or complications I don't have to go into. I can be completely irresponsible. I love it."

Kipnis's work has evolved over time, shifting from what was once a strictly academic tone to her more recent playful and casual style. In an interview with the editor of the *Minnesota Review*, she admits that she has developed a growing interest in "creativity" over "theory." She explains, "I trace it back to my art school origins. I started as a painter, actually, and there's something about the writing I've been doing lately which has gotten really intricate and worked over, that reminds me of my origins as a painter. I've started to write in a painterly way, dabbing at it, endlessly revising."

In a discussion of *Against Love* in 2001, Kipnis pointed out that "the voice isn't precisely 'me,' it's some far more vivacious and playful version of me. It's a polemic, so there are certain questions I don't have to address, or complications I don't have to go into. I can be completely irresponsible. I love it."

LOVE IS, as we know, a mysterious and controlling force. It has vast power over our thoughts and life decisions. It demands our loyalty, and we, in turn, freely comply. Saying no to love isn't simply heresy; it is tragedy—the failure to achieve what is most essentially human. So deeply internalized is our obedience to this most capricious despot that artists create passionate odes to its cruelty, and audiences seem never to tire of the most deeply unoriginal mass spectacles devoted to rehearsing the litany of its torments, fixating their very beings on the narrowest glimmer of its fleeting satisfactions.

Yet despite near total compliance, a buzz of social nervousness attends the subject. If a society's lexicon of romantic pathologies reveals its particular anxieties, high on our own list would be diagnoses like "inability to settle down" or "immaturity," leveled at those who stray from the norms of domestic coupledom either by refusing entry in the first place or, once installed, pursuing various escape routes: excess independence, ambivalence, "straying," divorce. For the modern lover, "maturity" isn't a depressing signal of impending decrepitude but a sterling achievement, the sine qua non of a lover's qualifications to love and be loved.

This injunction to achieve maturity—synonymous in contemporary usage with thirty-year mortgages, spreading waistlines, and monogamy—obviously finds its raison d'être in modern love's central anxiety, that structuring social contradiction the size of the San Andreas Fault: namely, the expectation that romance and sexual attraction can last a lifetime of coupled togetherness despite much hard evidence to the contrary.

Ever optimistic, heady with love's utopianism, most of us eventually pledge ourselves to unions that will, if successful, far outlast the desire that impelled them into being. The prevailing cultural wisdom is that even if sexual desire tends to be a short-lived phenomenon, "mature love" will kick in to save the day when desire flags. The issue that remains unaddressed is whether cutting off other possibilities of romance and sexual attraction for the more muted pleasures of mature love isn't similar to voluntarily amputating a healthy limb: a lot of anesthesia is required and the phantom pain never entirely abates. But if it behooves a society to convince its citizenry that wanting change means personal failure or wanting to start over is shameful or simply wanting more satisfaction than what you have is an illicit thing, clearly grisly acts of self-mutilation will be required.

There hasn't always been quite such optimism about love's longevity. For the Greeks, inventors of democracy and a people not amenable to being pushed around by despots, love was a disordering and thus preferably brief experience. During the reign of courtly love, love was illicit and usually fatal. Passion meant suffering: the happy ending didn't yet exist in the cultural imagination. As far as togetherness as an eternal ideal, the 12th-century advice manual "De Amore et Amoris Remedio" ("On Love and the Remedies of Love") warned that too many opportunities to see or chat with the beloved would certainly decrease love.

The innovation of happy love didn't even enter the vocabulary of romance until the 17th century. Before the 18th century—when the family was primarily an economic unit of production rather than a hothouse of Oedipal tensions—marriages were business arrangements between families; participants had little to say on the matter. Some historians consider romantic love a learned behavior that really only took off in the late 18th century along with the new fashion for reading novels, though even then affection between a husband and wife was considered to be in questionable taste.

Historians disagree, of course. Some tell the story of love as an eternal and unchanging essence; others, as a progress narrative over stifling social conventions. (Sometimes both stories are told at once; consistency isn't required.) But has modern love really set us free? Fond as we are of projecting our own emotional quandaries back through history, construing vivid costume dramas featuring medieval peasants or biblical courtesans sharing their feelings with the post-Freudian savvy of lifelong analysands, our amatory predecessors clearly didn't share all our particular aspirations about their romantic lives.

We, by contrast, feel like failures when love dies. We believe it could be otherwise. Since the cultural expectation is that a state of coupled permanence is achievable, uncoupling is experienced as crisis and inadequacy—even though such failures are more the norm than the exception.

As love has increasingly become the center of all emotional expression in the popular imagination, anxiety about obtaining it in sufficient quantities—and for sufficient duration—suffuses the population. Everyone knows that as the demands and expectations on couples escalated, so did divorce rates. And given the current divorce statistics (roughly 50 percent of all marriages end in divorce), all indications are that whomever you love today—your beacon of hope, the center of all your optimism—has a good chance of becoming your worst nightmare tomorrow. (Of course, that 50 percent are those who actually leave their unhappy marriages and not a particularly good indication of the happiness level or nightmare potential of those who remain.) Lawrence Stone, a historian of marriage, suggests—rather jocularly, you can't help thinking—that today's rising divorce rates are just a modern technique for achieving what was once taken care of far more efficiently by early mortality.

Love may or may not be a universal emotion, but clearly the social   10
forms it takes are infinitely malleable. It is our culture alone that has dedicated itself to allying the turbulence of romance and the rationality of the long-term couple, convinced that both love and sex are obtainable from one person over the course of decades, that desire will manage to sustain itself for thirty or forty or fifty years and that the supposed fate of social stability is tied to sustaining a fleeting experience beyond its given life span.

Of course, the parties involved must "work" at keeping passion alive (and we all know how much fun that is), the presumption being that even after living in close proximity to someone for a historically unprecedented length of time, you will still muster the requisite desire to achieve sexual congress on a regular basis. (Should passion fizzle out, just give up sex. Lack of desire for a mate is never an adequate rationale for "looking elsewhere.") And it is true, many couples do manage to perform enough psychic retooling to reshape the anarchy of desire to the confines of the marriage bed, plugging away at the task year after year (once a week, same time, same position) like diligent assembly-line workers, aided by the occasional fantasy or two to help get the old motor to turn over, or keep running, or complete the trip. And so we have the erotic life of a nation of workaholics: if sex seems like work, clearly you're not working hard enough at it.

But passion must not be allowed to die! The fear—or knowledge—that it does shapes us into particularly conflicted psychological beings, perpetually in search of prescriptions and professional interventions, regardless of cost or consequence. Which does have its economic upside, at least. Whole new sectors of the economy have been spawned, with massive social investment in new technologies from Viagra to couples' porn: capitalism's Lourdes[1] for dying marriages.

There are assorted low-tech solutions to desire's dilemmas too. Take advice. In fact, take more and more advice. Between print, airwaves, and the therapy industry, if there were any way to quantify the GNP in romantic counsel, it would be a staggering number. Desperate to be cured of love's temporality, a love-struck populace has molded itself into an advanced race of advice receptacles, like some new form of miracle sponge that can instantly absorb many times its own body weight in wetness.

Inexplicably, however, a rebellious breakaway faction keeps trying to leap over the wall and emancipate themselves, not from love itself—unthinkable!—but from love's domestic confinements. The escape routes are well trodden—love affairs, midlife crises—though strewn with the left-behind

---

[1] **Lourdes:** Notre Dame de Lourdes in France has been a site of Catholic pilgrimage ever since a fourteen-year-old girl reportedly received a vision there in 1858.—EDS.

luggage of those who encountered unforeseen obstacles along the way (panic, guilt, self-engineered exposures) and beat self-abashed retreats to their domestic gulags, even after pledging body and soul to new-found loves in the balmy utopias of nondomesticated romances. Will all the adulterers in the audience please stand up? You know who you are. Don't be embarrassed! Adulterers aren't just "playing around." These are our home-grown closet social theorists, because adultery is not just a referendum on the sustainability of monogamy; it is a veiled philosophical discussion about the social contract itself. The question on the table is thus "How much renunciation of desire does society demand of us, versus the degree of gratification it provides?" Clearly, the adulterer's answer, following a long line of venerable social critics, would be, "Too much."

But what exactly is it about the actual lived experience of modern   15 domestic love that would make flight such a compelling option for so many? Let us briefly examine those material daily life conditions.

Fundamentally, to achieve love and qualify for entry into that realm of salvation and transcendence known as the couple (the secular equivalent of entering a state of divine grace), you must *be* a lovable person. And what precisely does being lovable entail? According to the tenets of modern love, it requires an advanced working knowledge of the intricacies of *mutuality*.

Mutuality means recognizing that your partner has needs and being prepared to meet them. This presumes, of course, that the majority of those needs can and should be met by one person. (Question this, and you question the very foundations of the institution. So don't.) These needs of ours run deep, a tangled underground morass of ancient, gnarled roots, looking to ensnarl any hapless soul who might accidentally trod upon their outer radices.

Still, meeting those needs is the most effective way to become the object of another's desire, thus attaining intimacy, which is required to achieve the state known as psychological maturity. (Despite how closely it reproduces the affective conditions of our childhoods, since trading compliance for love is the earliest social lesson learned; we learn it in our cribs.)

You, in return, will have your own needs met by your partner in matters large and small. In practice, many of these matters turn out to be quite small. Frequently, it is the tensions and disagreements over the minutiae of daily living that stand between couples and their requisite intimacy. Taking out the garbage, tone of voice, a forgotten errand—these are the rocky shoals upon which intimacy so often founders.

Mutuality requires *communication*, since in order to be met, these needs   20 must be expressed. (No one's a mind reader, which is not to say that many of us don't expect this quality in a mate. Who wants to keep having to tell someone what you need?) What you need is for your mate to understand you—your desires, your contradictions, your unique sensitivities, what irks you. (In practice, that means what about your mate irks you.) You, in turn, must learn to understand the mate's needs. This means being willing to hear what about yourself irks your mate. Hearing is not a simple physiological act performed with the ears, as you will learn. You may think you know how to *hear*, but that doesn't mean that you know how to *listen*.

With two individuals required to coexist in enclosed spaces for extended periods of time, domesticity requires substantial quantities of compromise and adaptation simply to avoid mayhem. Yet with the post-Romantic ideal of unconstrained individuality informing our most fundamental ideas of the self, this can prove a perilous process. Both parties must be willing to jettison whatever aspects of individuality might prove irritating while being simultaneously allowed to retain enough individuality to feel their autonomy is not being sacrificed, even as it is being surgically excised.

Having mastered mutuality, you may now proceed to *advanced intimacy*. Advanced intimacy involves inviting your partner "in" to your most interior self. Whatever and wherever our "inside" is, the widespread—if somewhat metaphysical—belief in its existence (and the related belief that whatever is in there is dying to get out) has assumed a quasi-medical status. Leeches once served a similar purpose. Now we "express our feelings" in lieu of our fluids because everyone knows that those who don't are far more prone to cancer, ulcers or various dire ailments.

With love as our culture's patent medicine, prescribed for every ill (now even touted as a necessary precondition for that other great American obsession, longevity), we willingly subject ourselves to any number of arcane procedures in its quest. "Opening up" is required for relationship health, so lovers fashion themselves after doctors wielding long probes to penetrate the tender regions. Try to think of yourself as one big orifice: now stop clenching and relax. If the procedure proves uncomfortable, it just shows you're not open enough. Psychotherapy may be required before sufficient dilation can be achieved: the world's most expensive lubricant.

Needless to say, this opening-up can leave you feeling quite vulnerable, lying there psychically spread-eagled and shivering on the examining table of your relationship. (A favored suspicion is that your partner, knowing exactly where your vulnerabilities are, deliberately kicks you there—one reason this opening-up business may not always feel as pleasant as advertised.) And as anyone who has spent much time in—or just in earshot of—a typical couple knows, the "expression of needs" is often the Trojan horse of intimate warfare, since expressing needs means, by definition, that one's partner has thus far failed to meet them.

In any long-term couple, this lexicon of needs becomes codified over time into a highly evolved private language with its own rules. Let's call this couple grammar. Close observation reveals this as a language composed of one recurring unit of speech: the interdiction—highly nuanced, mutually imposed commands and strictures extending into the most minute areas of household affairs, social life, finances, speech, hygiene, allowable idiosyncrasies and so on. From bathroom to bedroom, car to kitchen, no aspect of coupled life is not subject to scrutiny, negotiation and codes of conduct.

A sample from an inexhaustible list, culled from interviews with numerous members of couples of various ages, races and sexual orientations:

You can't leave the house without saying where you're going. You can't not say what time you'll return. You can't go out when the other person feels like staying at home. You can't be a slob. You can't do less than 50 percent of the work around the house, even if the other person wants to do 100 percent more cleaning than you find necessary or even reasonable. You can't leave the dishes for later, load them the way that seems best to you, drink straight from the carton or make crumbs. You can't leave the bathroom door open—it's offensive. You can't leave the bathroom door closed—your partner needs to get in. You can't not shave your underarms or legs. You can't gain weight. You can't watch soap operas. You can't watch infomercials or the pregame show or Martha Stewart. You can't eat what you want—goodbye Marshmallow Fluff; hello tofu meatballs. You can't spend too much time on the computer. And stay out of those chat rooms. You can't take risks, unless they are agreed-upon risks, which somewhat limits the concept of "risk." You can't make major purchases alone, or spend money on things the other person considers excesses. You can't blow money just because you're in a bad mood, and you can't be in a bad mood without being required to explain it. You can't begin a sentence with "You always...." You can't begin a sentence with "I never...." You can't be simplistic, even when things are simple. You can't say what you really think of that outfit or color combination or cowboy hat. You can't be cynical about things the other person is sincere about. You can't drink without the other person counting your drinks. You can't have the wrong laugh. You can't bum cigarettes when you're out because it embarrasses your mate, even though you've explained the unspoken fraternity between smokers. You can't tailgate, honk or listen to talk radio in the car. And so on. The specifics don't matter. What matters is that the operative word is "can't."

Thus is love obtained.

Certainly, domesticity offers innumerable rewards: companionship, child-rearing convenience, reassuring predictability and many other benefits too varied to list. But if love has power over us, domesticity is its enforcement wing: the iron dust mop in the velvet glove. The historian Michel Foucault[2] has argued that modern power made its mark on the world by inventing new types of enclosures and institutions, places like factories, schools, barracks, prisons and asylums, where individuals could be located, supervised, processed and subjected to inspection, order and the clock. What current social institution is more enclosed than modern intimacy? What offers greater regulation of movement and time, or more precise surveillance of body and thought, to a greater number of individuals?

---

[2] **Michel Foucault** (1926–1984): French philosopher and historian who questioned assumptions about the constitution of power and knowledge.—EDS.

Of course, it is your choice—as if any of us could really choose not to   30
desire love or not to feel like hopeless losers should we fail at it. We moderns
are beings yearning to be filled, yearning to be overtaken by love's mysterious power. We prostrate ourselves at love's portals, like social strivers waiting at the rope line outside some exclusive club hoping to gain admission
and thereby confirm our essential worth. A life without love lacks an organizing narrative. A life without love seems so barren, and it might almost
make you consider how empty the rest of the world is, as if love were vital
plasma and everything else just tap water.

Exchanging obedience for love comes naturally—after all, we all were
once children whose survival depended on the caprices of love. And there
you have the template for future intimacies. If you love me, you'll do what
I want—or need, or demand—and I'll love you in return. We all become
household dictators, petty tyrants of the private sphere, who are, in our turn,
dictated to.

And why has modern love developed in such a way as to maximize submission and minimize freedom, with so little argument about it? No doubt a
citizenry schooled in renouncing desire instead of imagining there could be
something more would be, in many respects, advantageous. After all, wanting more is the basis for utopian thinking, a path toward dangerous social
demands, even toward imagining the possibilities for altogether different
social arrangements. But if the most elegant forms of social control are those
that came packaged in the guise of individual needs and satisfactions, so
wedded to the individual psyche that any opposing impulse registers as the
anxiety of unlovability, who needs a soldier on every corner? We are more
than happy to police ourselves and those we love and call it living happily
ever after. Perhaps a secular society needed another metaphysical entity to
subjugate itself to after the death of God, and love was available for the job.
But isn't it a little depressing to think we are somehow incapable of inventing forms of emotional life based on anything other than subjugation?

The Reader's Presence

1. How does Kipnis reevaluate the meaning of adultery and mid-life crises? What sort
   of evidence are these phenomena, in her opinion?

2. What elements of Kipnis's writing mark this essay as a scholarly argument? Do you
   agree that it is also a "polemic," as the subtitle of her book indicates? Is it more effective as a scholarly argument or as a polemic? Why?

3. **CONNECTIONS:** Kipnis suggests that society benefits from convincing its populace to marry and that people have been brainwashed into believing that these
   long-term arrangements are natural. What benefits does society gain from long-term
   relationships? What, in Kipnis's opinion, do individuals give up? Read John Taylor
   Gatto's "Against School" (page 665). What, according to his argument, does the
   individual lose in submitting to compulsory schooling? Who, according to Gatto,
   benefits from it?

Thomas Lynch

INTO THE OBLIVION

Poet and essayist **THOMAS LYNCH** (b. 1948) has the distinction of being the only writer in this book who also runs a funeral home. He took over his father's funeral home in Milford, Michigan in 1974, and has been running the business ever since. He won the Heartland Prize for nonfiction and the American Book Award for his 1997 collection, *The Undertaking: Life Studies from the Dismal Trade*, and his work has appeared in national magazines like the *New Yorker*, the *Paris Review*, *Harper's*, *Esquire*, and *Newsweek*, to name only a few. His most recent books are the collection *Walking Papers: Poems 1999–2009* (2010) and his first book of fiction, a novella and a collection of short stories in one volume, *Apparitions and Late Fictions* (2010). In addition to running his funeral home, he teaches creative writing part time in the graduate creative writing program at the University of Michigan, Ann Arbor.

> Thomas Lynch has the distinction of being the only writer in this book who also runs a funeral home.

On the subject of the humor in his writing, he has said, "I don't set out to write anything jokey. But I do think that the way things organize themselves, the good laugh and the good cry are fairly close on that continuum. So the ridiculous and the sublime—they're neighbors."

MY EXPERIENCE with bodies and the parts of bodies over the past thirty-five years has taught me that our dead are precious to us because ours is a species, for better or for worse, that has learned to deal with death, the idea of the thing, by dealing with our dead, the thing itself. It casts my imagination back to forty or fifty thousand years ago, when the first human widow awakened in that cave to the dead lump of protein next to her and said, "My, he's very quiet this morning," or words to that effect. Depending on the season and the weather, sooner or later she would begin to sense— actually, she'd begin to smell—that this stillness was a different stillness than she had ever experienced before. She knew she'd have to do something about it. She knew she'd have to leave the cave to him, in which case, I suppose, it would become his tomb. Or maybe she thought she'd drag him out by the ankles and kick his sorry self over the cliff, in which case we could call him "consigned to the oblivion," or maybe she'd build a fire and burn his body, or she'd scratch a hole in the ground and tip him into it.

Whatever she did, whatever oblivion she consigned him to, the questions that quickened in her looking into that void became, I think, the signature of our species, what separates us from rock bass and rhododendrons and cocker spaniels and other living things that die. Looking into whatever oblivion she consigned that first dead thing to, she asked the standard questions. I hear them asked by widowed people today: "Is that all there is? Can it happen to me? Why is it cold? What comes next?" The dead do not care. I've spent a fair amount of time around cadavers, corpses, dead neighbors, dead friends and family, and never once has one of them said anything like, "I want the blue pin-striped suit or the cherry casket or the mum plants, please." They say nothing. They are mum on the subject. The dead don't care, you can take that to the bank. But the dead do matter. They matter to the living in ways that we're only beginning to understand.

And so as you discuss bodies and the parts of bodies, I would encourage you to take on more the notion that whether we are talking about the parts of bodies of dead gangsters, buried maybe in Milford, Michigan, where last month they went digging for whatever is left of Jimmy Hoffa at Hidden Dreams Farm, or whether we are looking for our dead at the Fresh Kills landfill site, where their bodies are commingled with those of their murderers on September 11, the dead are with us. We are all haunted, properly and happily in some cases, not only by their memories but also by their remnants.

There are distinctions to be made between the notions of medical death or metabolic death, social death, spiritual death, and actual death as far as your family is concerned. I might know, for example, that after a cremation, we end up with, say, fourteen pounds of bone fragment and dessicated tissue that we can put in a box and hand to the family, but when you see the elderly sister come to claim the ashes of a sister whose own children couldn't come and get her, when she bears that box like viaticum,[1] when she walks out the door, flips the button to open the trunk, and then reconsiders and goes to the back door and opens it up, and then thinks better of it and closes it again, when she goes to the front-seat passenger door, opens it up, places the box on the front seat, and then clicks a seat belt around it, you can see that whether we are remnant or icon or relic is not up to you or me. It's up to the living who bear us in their memory and, in fact, bear our mortality, because we are humans, tied to this humus,[2] this layer of earth from which our monuments and our homes and our histories rise up.

The market, the retail event of organ and tissue procurement, is something that may have medical consequences, but to most families it remains a mystery, tied up in issues of personhood, not parts. There's this "just a shell" theory of how we should relate to dead human bodies. You hear a lot of it

5

---

[1] *viaticum:* In the Roman Catholic Church, the Eucharist (communion) given to someone who is dying. Also, monies paid to cover traveling expenses. —EDS.

[2] *humus:* An organic, fertile material found in soil that is formed when plants and animals die and decompose. —EDS.

from young clergy and old family friends, well-intentioned in-laws, folks who are unsettled by the fresh grief of others. You hear it when you bring a mother and a father in for the first sight of their dead daughter killed in a car wreck or left out to rot by some mannish violence. It is proffered as a kind of comfort in the teeth of a comfortless situation, consolation to the inconsolable. Between the inhale and exhale of the bone-racking sob such hurts produce, some frightened and well-meaning ignoramus is bound to give out with, "It's okay, it's not her. That's just a shell."

I once saw an Episcopalian deacon nearly decked by the swift slap of a mother of a teenager dead of leukemia to whom he had rendered this counsel. "I'll tell you when it's just a shell," the woman said. "For now and until I tell you otherwise, she's my daughter." The woman was asserting the long-standing right of the living to declare the dead dead. Just as we declare the living alive through baptisms and lovers in love by nuptials, funerals are the way we close the gap between the death that happens and the death that matters. It's how we assign meaning to our little histories. And the rituals we devise to conduct the living and the beloved and the dead from one status to another have less to do with performance than they do with meaning. In a world where "dysfunctional" has become the operative adjective, a body that has ceased to work has, it would seem, few useful applications beyond those we are talking about here this morning. It's dysfunction more manifest than the sexual and familial forms that fill our tabloids and talk shows. A body that doesn't work is, in the early going, the evidence we have of a person who has ceased to be, and a person who has ceased to be is as compelling a prospect as it was when the first hominid dug holes for his dead and set our species apart from the others.

So I encourage you, as you wrestle with these difficult issues, to consider the traffic between the living and the dead, because in most of these situations, there is no medicine or math, no bottom line or Bible verse, that will explain the mystery we behold when we behold someone we love dying or dead. I know this not only because of my professional and personal experience but because I also sense it in the lives of people all around me. The bodies of the newly dead are not debris or remnant, nor entirely icon or essence. They are rather changelings, incubates, hatchlings of a new reality that bear our names and dates, our images and likenesses, as surely in the eyes and ears of our children and grandchildren as did words of our birth in the ears of our parents and their parents. It is wise to treat such new things tenderly, carefully, and with honor. ●

The Reader's Presence

1. The author adapted this essay from a speech he gave to the President's Council on Bioethics, an advisory group that had convened to discuss the topic of organ transplants. Given this context, what do you think the author's purpose was in writing this essay? What changes in the way society deals with our dead does Lynch call for

explicitly in the essay? What changes does he also imply should be made? What are the compositional effects of using this strategy?

2. Lynch writes that the living "bear us in their memory and, in fact, bear our mortality" (paragraph 4). What do you understand him to mean by this assertion? What other statements does Lynch make that you found surprising, puzzling, or especially thought provoking? What are a few ways the statements you identified could be interpreted? How do you interpret them?

3. **CONNECTIONS:**   Compare Lynch's argument to the one Michael J. Sandel makes about genetic engineering in "Designer Babies" (page 787). What similarities or differences can you identify about the way each writer frames the spiritual aspects of each topic? the material aspects? How does each writer relate the spiritual to the material? With what effect(s)?

Walter Benn Michaels

THE TROUBLE WITH DIVERSITY

WALTER BENN MICHAELS (b. 1948) entered a swirl of controversy—from both right and left—with his 2006 book, *The Trouble with Diversity: How We Learned to Love Identity and Ignore Equality*, his polemic against identity politics and economic inequality on college campuses and in the greater society. In his book, he argues that the thorniest problem in American society is not racism or sexism or any of the other isms but the "increasing gap between the rich and the poor." Michaels received his PhD at the University of California, Santa Barbara, and taught English at the University of California, Berkeley, and at Johns Hopkins University before joining the faculty at the University of Illinois at Chicago, where he has taught American literature and literary theory since 2001. His books and monographs include *The Gold Standard and the Logic of Naturalism: American Literature at the Turn of the Century* (1987), *Our America: Nativism, Modernism, and Pluralism* (1995), *The Shape of the Signifier: 1967 to the End of History*

> **Walter Benn Michaels argues that the thorniest problem in American society is not racism or sexism or any of the other isms but the "increasing gap between the rich and the poor."**

(2004), and *Promises of American Life: 1880–1920* in volume three of the *Cambridge History of American Literature*. His essay, "The Trouble with Diversity," excerpted from his 2006 book, appeared in the *American Prospect* in 2006.

In a 2004 essay in the *New York Times Magazine*, Michaels argued that focusing on diversity keeps our eyes off the real problem. "As long as we think that our best universities are fair if they are appropriately diverse, we don't have to worry that most people can't go to them, while others get to do so because they've had the good luck to be born into relatively wealthy families. In other words, as long as the left continues to worry about diversity, the right won't have to worry about inequality."

"THE RICH are different from you and me" is a famous remark supposedly made by F. Scott Fitzgerald to Ernest Hemingway, although what made it famous—or at least made Hemingway famously repeat it—was not the remark itself but Hemingway's reply: "Yes, they have more money." In other words, to Hemingway, the rich really aren't very different from you and me. Fitzgerald's mistake, he thought, was that he mythologized or sentimentalized the rich, treating them as if they were a different kind of person instead of the same kind of person with more money. It was as if, according to Fitzgerald, what made rich people different was not what they *had*—their money—but what they *were*, "a special glamorous race."

To Hemingway, this difference—between what people owned and what they were—seemed obvious. No one cares much about Robert Cohn's money in *The Sun Also Rises*, but everybody feels the force of the fact that he's a "race conscious . . . little kike." And whether or not it's true that Fitzgerald sentimentalized the rich, it's certainly true that he, like Hemingway, believed that the fundamental differences—the ones that really mattered—ran deeper than the question of how much money you had. That's why in *The Great Gatsby*, the fact that Gatsby has made a great deal of money isn't quite enough to win Daisy Buchanan back. Rich as he has become, he's still "Mr. Nobody from Nowhere," not Jay Gatsby but Jimmy Gatz. The change of name is what matters. One way to look at *The Great Gatsby* is as a story about a poor boy who makes good, which is to say, a poor boy who becomes rich—the so-called American Dream. But *Gatsby* is not really about someone who makes a lot of money; it is instead about someone who tries and fails to change who he is. Or, more precisely, it's about someone who pretends to be something he's not; it's about Jimmy Gatz pretending to be Jay Gatsby. If, in the end, Daisy Buchanan is very different from Jimmy Gatz, it's not because she's rich and he isn't but because Fitzgerald treats them as if they really belong to different races, as if poor boys who made a lot of money were only "passing" as rich. "We're all white here," someone says, interrupting one of Tom Buchanan's racist outbursts. Jimmy Gatz isn't quite white enough.

What's important about *The Great Gatsby*, then, is that it takes one kind of difference (the difference between the rich and the poor) and redescribes it as another kind of difference (the difference between the white and the not-so-white). To put the point more generally, books like *The Great Gatsby* (and there have been a great many of them) give us a vision of our society divided into races rather than into economic classes. And this vision has proven to be extraordinarily attractive. Indeed, it has survived even though what we used to think were the races have not. In the 1920s, racial science was in its heyday; now very few scientists believe that there are any such things as races. But many of those who are quick to remind us that there are no biological entities called races are even quicker to remind us that races have not disappeared; they should just be understood as social entities instead. And these social entities have turned out to be remarkably tenacious, both in ways we know are bad and in ways we have come to think of as good. The bad ways involve racism, the inability or refusal to accept people who are different from us. The good ways involve just the opposite: embracing difference, celebrating what we have come to call diversity.

Indeed, in the United States, the commitment to appreciating diversity emerged out of the struggle against racism, and the word diversity itself began to have the importance it does for us today in 1978 when, in *Bakke v. Board of Regents*, the Supreme Court ruled that taking into consideration the race of an applicant to the University of California (the medical school at UC Davis, in this case) was acceptable if it served "the interest of diversity." The Court's point here was significant. It was not asserting that preference in admissions could be given, say, to black people because they had previously been discriminated against. It was saying instead that universities had a legitimate interest in taking race into account in exactly the same way they had a legitimate interest in taking into account what part of the country an applicant came from or what his or her nonacademic interests were. They had, in other words, a legitimate interest in having a "diverse student body," and racial diversity, like geographic diversity, could thus be an acceptable goal for an admissions policy.

Two things happened there. First, even though the concept of diversity   5
was not originally connected with race (universities had long sought diverse student bodies without worrying about race at all), the two now came to be firmly associated. When universities publish their diversity statistics today, they're not talking about how many kids come from Oregon. My university—the University of Illinois at Chicago—is ranked as one of the most diverse in the country, but well over half the students in it come from Chicago. What the rankings measure is the number of African Americans and Asian Americans and Latinos we have, not the number of Chicagoans.

And, second, even though the concept of diversity was introduced as a kind of end run around the historical problem of racism (the whole point was that you could argue for the desirability of a diverse student body without appealing to the history of discrimination against blacks and so without getting accused by people like Alan Bakke of reverse discrimination against whites), the commitment to diversity became deeply associated with the struggle against racism. Indeed, the goal of overcoming racism—of creating a "color-blind" society—was now reconceived as the goal of creating a diverse, that is, a color-conscious, society. Instead of trying to treat people as if their race didn't matter, we would not only recognize but celebrate racial identity. Indeed, race has turned out to be a gateway drug for all kinds of identities, cultural, religious, sexual, even medical. To take what may seem like an extreme case, advocates for the disabled now urge us to stop thinking of disability as a condition to be "cured" or "eliminated" and to start thinking of it instead on the model of race: We don't think black people should want to stop being black; why do we assume the deaf want to hear?

Our commitment to diversity has thus redefined the opposition to discrimination as the appreciation (rather than the elimination) of difference. So with respect to race, the idea is not just that racism is a bad thing (which of course it is) but that race itself is a good thing.

And what makes it a good thing is that it's not class. We love race—we love identity—because we don't love class. We love thinking that the differences that divide us are not the differences between those of us who have money and those who don't but are instead the differences between those who are black and those who are white or Asian or Latino or whatever. A world where some of us don't have money is a world where the differences between us present a problem: the need to get rid of inequality or to justify it. A world where some of us are black and some of us are white—or biracial or Native American or transgendered—is a world where the differences between us present a solution: appreciating our diversity. So we like to talk about the differences we can appreciate, and we don't like to talk about the ones we can't. Indeed, we don't even like to acknowledge that they exist. As survey after survey has shown, Americans are very reluctant to identify themselves as belonging to the lower class and even more reluctant to identify themselves as belonging to the upper class. The class we like is the middle class.

But the fact that we all like to think of ourselves as belonging to the same class doesn't, of course, mean that we actually do belong to the same class. In reality, we obviously and increasingly don't. "The last few decades," as *The Economist* puts it, "have seen a huge increase in inequality in America." The rich *are* different from you and me, and one of the ways they're different is that they're getting richer and we're not. And while it's not surprising that most of the rich and their apologists on the intellectual right are unperturbed by this development, it is at least a little surprising that the intellectual left has managed to remain almost equally unperturbed. Giving priority to issues like affirmative action and committing itself to the celebration of difference, the intellectual left has responded to the increase in economic inequality by insisting on the importance of cultural identity. So for 30 years, while the gap between the rich and the poor has grown larger, we've been urged to respect people's identities—as if the problem of poverty would be solved if we just appreciated the poor. From the economic standpoint, however, what poor people want is not to contribute to diversity but to minimize their contribution to it—they want to stop being poor. Celebrating the diversity of

American life has become the American left's way of accepting their poverty, of accepting inequality.

Our current notion of cultural diversity—trumpeted as the repudiation of 10 racism and biological essentialism—in fact grew out of and perpetuates the very concepts it congratulates itself on having escaped. The American love affair with race—especially when you can dress race up as culture—has continued and even intensified. Almost everything we say about culture (that the significant differences between us are cultural, that such differences should be respected, that our cultural heritages should be perpetuated, that there's a value in making sure that different cultures survive) seems to me mistaken. We must shift our focus from cultural diversity to economic equality to help alter the political terrain of contemporary American intellectual life.

In the last year, it has sometimes seemed as if this terrain might in fact be starting to change, and there has been what at least looks like the beginning of a new interest in the problem of economic inequality. Various newspapers have run series noticing the growth of inequality and the decline of class mobility; it turns out, for example, that the Gatsby-style American Dream—poor boy makes good, buys beautiful, beautiful shirts—now has a better chance of coming true in Sweden than it does in America, and as good a chance of coming true in western Europe (which is to say, not very good) as it does here. People have begun to notice also that the intensity of interest in the race of students in our universities has coincided with more or less complete indifference to their wealth. We're getting to the point where there are more black people than poor people in elite universities (even though there are still precious few black people). And Hurricane Katrina—with its televised images of the people left to fend for themselves in drowning New Orleans—provided both a reminder that there still are poor people in America and a vision of what the consequences of that poverty can be.

At the same time, however, the understanding of these issues has proven to be more a symptom of the problem than a diagnosis. In the *Class Matters* series in the *New York Times*, for example, the differences that mattered most turned out to be the ones between the rich and the really rich and between the old rich and the new rich. Indeed, at one point, the *Times* started treating class not as an issue to be addressed in addition to race but as itself a version of race, as if the rich and poor really were different races and so as if the occasional marriage between them were a kind of interracial marriage.

But classes are not like races and cultures, and treating them as if they were—different but equal—is one of our strategies for managing inequality rather than minimizing or eliminating it. White is not better than black, but rich is definitely better than poor. Poor people are an endangered species in elite universities not because the universities put quotas on them (as they did with Jews in the old days) and not even because they can't afford to go to them (Harvard will lend you or even give you the money you need to go there) but because they can't get into them. Hence the irrelevance of most of the proposed solutions to the systematic exclusion of poor people from elite universities, which involve ideas like increased financial aid for students who can't afford the high tuition, support systems for the few poor students who manage to end up there anyway, and, in general, an effort to increase the "cultural capital" of the poor. Today, says David Brooks, "the rich don't exploit the poor, they just out-compete them." And if out-competing people means tying their ankles together and loading them down with extra weight while hiring yourself the most expensive coaches and the best practice facilities, he's right. The entire U.S. school system, from pre-K up, is structured from the very start to enable the rich to out-compete the poor, which is to say, the race is fixed. And the kinds of solutions that might actually make a difference—financing every school district equally, abolishing private schools, making high-quality child care available to every family—are treated as if they were positively un-American.

But it's the response to Katrina that is most illuminating for our purposes, especially the response from the left, not from the right. "Let's be honest," Cornel West told an audience at the Paul Robeson Student Center at Rutgers University, "we live in one of the bleakest moments in the history of black people in this nation." "Look at the Super Dome," he went on to say. "It's not a big move from the hull of the slave ship to the living hell of the Super Dome." This is what we might call the "George Bush doesn't care about black people" interpretation of the government's failed response to the catastrophe. But nobody doubts that George Bush cares about Condoleezza Rice, who is very much a black person and who is fond of pointing out that she's been black since birth. And there are, of course, lots of other black people—like Clarence Thomas[1] and Thomas Sowell[2] and Janice Rogers Brown[3] and, at least once upon a time, Colin Powell—for whom George Bush almost certainly has warm feelings. But what American liberals want is for our conservatives to be racists. We want the black people George Bush cares about to be "some of my best friends are black" tokens. We want a fictional George Bush who doesn't care about black people rather than the George Bush we've actually got, one who doesn't care about poor people.

Although that's not quite the right way to put it. First because, for all I   15 know, George Bush does care about poor people; at least he cares as much about poor people as anyone else does. What he doesn't care about—and what Bill Clinton, judging by his eight years in office, didn't much care about, and what John Kerry, judging from his presidential campaign, doesn't much care about, and what we on the so-called left, judging by our own willingness to accept Kerry as the alternative to Bush, don't care about either—is

---

1 **Clarence Thomas** (b. 1948): Associate justice of the Supreme Court of the United States since 1991 and the second African American to serve on the Supreme Court, after Justice Thurgood Marshall.—Eds.

2 **Thomas Sowell** (b. 1930): An American economist, social commentator, author of numerous books, and a senior fellow of the Hoover Institution.—Eds.

3 **Janice Rogers Brown** (b. 1949): A federal judge on the United States Court of Appeals for the District of Columbia Circuit and previously an associate justice of the California Supreme Court.—Eds.

taking any steps to get them to stop being poor. We would much rather get rid of racism than get rid of poverty. And we would much rather celebrate cultural diversity than seek to establish economic equality.

Indeed, diversity has become virtually a sacred concept in American life today. No one's really against it; people tend instead to differ only in their degrees of enthusiasm for it and their ingenuity in pursuing it. Microsoft, for example, is very ingenious indeed. Almost every company has the standard racial and sexual "employee relations groups," just as every college has the standard student groups: African American, Black and Latino Brotherhood, Alliance of South Asians, Chinese Adopted Sibs (this one's pretty cutting-edge), and the standard GLBTQ (the Q is for *Questioning*) support center. But (as reported in a 2003 article in *Workforce Management*) Microsoft also includes groups for "single parents, dads, Singaporean, Malaysian, Hellenic, and Brazilian employees, and one for those with attention deficit disorder." And the same article goes on to quote Patricia Pope, CEO of a diversity management firm in Cincinnati, describing companies that "tackle other differences" like "diversity of birth order" and, most impressive of all, "diversity of thought." If it's a little hard to imagine the diversity of birth order workshops (all the oldest siblings trying to take care of each other, all the youngest competing to be the baby), it's harder still to imagine how the diversity of thought workshops go. What if the diversity of thought is about your sales plan? Are you supposed to reach agreement (but that would eliminate diversity) or celebrate disagreement (but that would eliminate the sales plan)?

Among the most enthusiastic proponents of diversity, needless to say, are the thousands of companies providing "diversity products," from diversity training (a $10-billion-a-year industry) to diversity newsletters (I subscribe to *Diversity Inc.*, but there are dozens of them) to diversity rankings to diversity gifts and clothing—you can "show your support for multiculturalism" *and* "put an end to panty lines" with a "Diversity Rocks Classic Thong" ($9.99). The "Show Me the Money Diversity Venture Capital Conference" says what needs to be said here. But it's not all about the benjamins.[4] There's no money for the government in proclaiming Asian Pacific American Heritage Month (it used to be just a week, but the first President Bush upgraded it) or in Women's History Month or National Disability Employment Awareness Month or Black History Month or American Indian Heritage Month. And there's no money for the Asians, Indians, blacks, and women whose history gets honored.

In fact, the closest thing we have to a holiday that addresses economic inequality instead of identity is Labor Day, which is a product not of the multicultural cheerleading at the end of the 20th century but of the labor unrest at the end of the 19th. The union workers who took a day off to protest

---

[4] **benjamins:** 100-dollar bills; so called because the face of Benjamin Franklin is on the bill.—EDS.

President Grover Cleveland's deployment of 12,000 troops to break the Pullman strike weren't campaigning to have their otherness respected. And when, in 1894, their day off was made official, the president of the American Federation of Labor, Samuel Gompers, looked forward not just to a "holiday" but to "the day for which the toilers in past centuries looked forward, when their rights and wrongs would be discussed." The idea was not that they'd celebrate their history but that they'd figure out how to build a stronger labor movement and make the dream of economic justice a reality.

Obviously, it didn't work out that way, either for labor (which is weaker than it's ever been) or for Labor Day (which mainly marks the end of summer). You get bigger crowds, a lot livelier party and a much stronger sense of solidarity for Gay Pride Day. But Gay Pride Day isn't about economic equality, and celebrating diversity shouldn't be an acceptable alternative to seeking economic equality.

In an ideal universe we wouldn't be celebrating diversity at all—we wouldn't even be encouraging it—because in an ideal universe the question of who you wanted to sleep with would be a matter of concern only to you and to your loved (or unloved) ones. As would your skin color; some people might like it, some people might not, but it would have no political significance whatsoever. Diversity of skin color is something we should happily take for granted, the way we do diversity of hair color. No issue of social justice hangs on appreciating hair color diversity; no issue of social justice hangs on appreciating racial or cultural diversity. 20

If you're worried about the growing economic inequality in American life, if you suspect that there may be something unjust as well as unpleasant in the spectacle of the rich getting richer and the poor getting poorer, no cause is less worth supporting, no battles are less worth fighting, than the ones we fight for diversity. While some cultural conservatives may wish that everyone should be assimilated to their fantasy of one truly American culture, and while the supposed radicals of the "tenured left" continue to struggle for what they hope will finally become a truly inclusive multiculturalism, the really radical idea of redistributing wealth becomes almost literally unthinkable. In the early 1930s, Senator Huey Long of Louisiana proposed a law making it illegal for anyone to earn more than $1 million a year and for anyone to inherit more than $5 million. Imagine the response if—even suitably adjusted for inflation—any senator were to propose such a law today, cutting off incomes at, say, $15 million a year and inheritances at $75 million. It's not just the numbers that wouldn't fly; it's the whole concept. Long's proposal never became law, but it was popular and debated with some seriousness. Today, such a restriction would seem as outrageous and unnatural as interracial—not to mention gay—marriage would have seemed then. But we don't need to purchase our progress in civil rights at the expense of a commitment to economic justice. More fundamentally still, we should not allow—or we should not continue to allow—the phantasm of respect for difference to take the place of that commitment to economic justice. Commitment to diversity is at best a distraction and at worst an essentially reactionary position that prevents us from putting equality at the center of the national agenda.

Our identity is the least important thing about us. And yet, it is the thing we have become most committed to talking about. From the standpoint of a left politics, this is a profound mistake since what it means is that the political left—increasingly invested in the celebration of diversity and the redress of historical grievance—has converted itself into the accomplice rather than the opponent of the right. Diversity has become the left's way of doing neoliberalism, and antiracism has become the left's contribution to enhancing market efficiency. The old Socialist leader Eugene Debs used to be criticized for being unwilling to interest himself in any social reform that didn't involve attacking economic inequality. The situation now is almost exactly the opposite; the left obsessively interests itself in issues that have nothing to do with economic inequality.

And, not content with pretending that our real problem is cultural difference rather than economic difference, we have also started to treat economic difference as if it were cultural difference. So now we're urged to be more respectful of poor people and to stop thinking of them as victims, since to treat them as victims is condescending—it denies them their "agency." And if we can stop thinking of the poor as people who have too little money and start thinking of them instead as people who have too little respect, then it's our attitude toward the poor, not their poverty, that becomes the problem to be solved, and we can focus our efforts of reform not on getting rid of classes but on getting rid of what we like to call classism. The trick, in other words, is to stop thinking of poverty as a disadvantage, and once you stop thinking of it as a disadvantage then, of course, you no longer need to worry about getting rid of it. More generally, the trick is to think of inequality as a consequence of our prejudices rather than as a consequence of our social system and thus to turn the project of creating a more egalitarian society into the project of getting people (ourselves and, especially, others) to stop being racist, sexist, classist homophobes. The starting point for a progressive politics should be to attack that trick. ●

The Reader's Presence

1. According to Michaels, why does celebrating diversity distract us from minimizing inequality? Specifically, how does Michaels establish connections between race and class? What would happen if we followed his advice and focused only on economic inequalities? For example, describe how colleges would be affected if they did not take the diversity of their student body into account during the admissions process. Michaels is not specific about how eliminating race as a political category will eliminate class as a social misery. Applying Michaels's logic to his Hurricane Katrina example (paragraph 14), how would ignoring race have led to a better response for the hurricane's victims?

2. Michaels skillfully uses wit and humor at strategic moments in his essay. Consider, for example, such lines as "what poor people want is not to contribute to diversity but to minimize their contribution to it" (paragraph 9). What are the effects of using wit and humor to write about such a serious subject? What risks does Michaels take in doing so? How effectively would his essay read if such wit and humor were omitted? In formulating your response, identify a few humorous or witty moments and rewrite them with a serious tone. How did changing the tone affect the argument? Do you think a reader would be more—or less—convinced by an argument that was formulated without wit and humor? Explain why.

3. **CONNECTIONS:**   Stephen Jay Gould's "Sex, Drugs, Disasters, and the Extinction of Dinosaurs" (page 430) demonstrates how to distinguish ideas that are "silly speculation" from solid hypotheses. Use Gould's methods to evaluate the specific claims Michaels makes in his essay. For example, what would Gould make of Michaels's notion that "no issue of social justice hangs on appreciating racial or cultural diversity" (paragraph 20)? Is it fair to use scientific standards for argument to evaluate cultural claims about race and class? Why or why not?

Errol Morris

LIAR, LIAR, PANTS ON FIRE

Writer and documentary filmmaker **ERROL MORRIS** was born in Hewlett, New York, in 1948. After graduating from the University of Wisconsin, Morris studied philosophy at the University of California, Berkeley, until his "obsession" with film ended his graduate-school career. His first film was *Gates of Heaven*, released in 1978. Financed by family, friends, and the kindness of strangers, the film met with critical acclaim and launched a career that would result in seven more feature-length documentaries, a Guggenheim Fellowship, a MacArthur Fellowship "genius award," a retrospective at the Museum of Modern Art, a tribute at the Sundance Film Festival, and an Oscar. His films include *Vernon, Florida* (1980); *The Thin Blue Line* (1988); *Fast, Cheap & Out of Control* (1997); *A Brief History of Time* (1992); *Mr. Death: The Rise & Fall of*

> "It all starts with the photographs."

Fred A. Leuchter Jr. (2000); and *The Fog of War: Eleven Lessons from the Life of Robert S. McNamara*, which won the Academy Award for best documentary feature in 2004. Between films, Morris created the Bravo television series *First Person* and became a sought-after, and highly successful, director of commercials. Morris's 2008 film, *Standard Operating Procedure*, explores the incidents at Abu Ghraib prison in Iraq through the infamous photos taken there. "It all starts with the photographs," he said in an interview. "*Standard Operating Procedure* is my attempt to tell the stories behind these photographs, to examine the context in which they were taken." Morris's essay, "Liar, Liar, Pants on Fire," part of a series written for the *New York Times* blog "Zoom," explores the same themes. "You look at a photograph, you think you know what it means, but more often than not, you could be wrong. Photographs provide evidence, but usually, it takes some investigative effort to uncover evidence of what?"

PICTURES are supposed to be worth a thousand words. But a picture unaccompanied by words may not mean anything at all. Do pictures provide evidence? And if so, evidence of what? And, of course, the underlying question: do they tell the truth?

I have beliefs about the photographs I see. Often — when they appear in books or newspapers — there are captions below them, or they are embedded in explanatory text. And even where there are no explicit captions on the page, there are captions in my mind. What I think I'm looking at. What I think the photograph is about.

I have often wondered: would it be possible to look at a photograph shorn of all its context, captionless, unconnected to current thought and ideas? It would be like stumbling on a collection of photographs in a curiosity shop — pictures of people and places that we do not recognize and know nothing about. I might imagine things about the people and places in the photographs but know nothing about them. Nothing.

This collection could even involve my own past. I recently was handed a collection of photographs taken by my father — dead now for over fifty years. I looked at it, somewhat confused. I suppose saddened by the passage of time. Even though I am in the photographs, the people in them are mysterious, inherently foreign. Maybe because photographs tamper with the glue that holds life and memory together.

Who are these people? Do they have anything to do with me? Do I really know them?   5

As disconnected from the present as these photographs might be, they do not seem devoid of context. I know too much about them — even if I know very little. They are pictures of my own family. It's too easy for me to concoct some story about them. To find a picture shorn of context, it would be important to pick a photograph that's sufficiently removed for me in time and context — a photograph preternaturally unfamiliar. Perhaps a war photograph, but a war photograph from an unfamiliar war. It should be a war six or seven wars ago. Passions, presumably, have been diminished. No one in the photographs will still be alive.

I want to ask a relatively simple question. Are these photographs true or false? Do they tell the truth?

Look at the photograph below. Is it true or false?

I find the question ridiculous: "True or false in regard to what?"

Without a caption, without a context, without some idea about what the   10
picture is a picture of, I can't answer. I simply cannot talk about the photograph as being true or false independently of beliefs about the picture. A
captionless photograph, stripped of all context, is virtually meaningless. I
need to know more.

And yet, this idea that photographs can be true or false independent of
context is so ingrained in our thinking that we are reluctant to part with it.

Let's add a caption to the photograph.

The Lusitania.

Only now can we ask questions that have true or false answers. The caption asserts that this is a photograph of the *Lusitania*, a British ship launched in 1907. I found the photograph on a website entitled "Maritime Quest." I made no effort to check it; I simply took their word for it. That could be a mistake on my part. With no malice intended, the wrong caption could have inadvertently been placed under the photograph. The photograph could actually be a photograph of the *Titanic*. Or malice could have been involved. Someone could have maliciously switched the captions of pictures of the *Lusitania* and the *Titanic*.

But one thing is clear. When I look at these pictures—whether it is a picture of the *Lusitania* or the *Titanic*—I imagine that someone stood on a dry dock, or some vantage point, looked through the viewfinder of the camera, and took a photograph of something that was floating out there in the water. If it was the *Lusitania*, then he took a photograph of the *Lusitania*. If it was the *Titanic*, then he took a picture of the *Titanic*. This may seem hopelessly obvious, but I have this saying—and I believe there's something to it—that there is nothing so obvious that it's obvious.

But we need language, and we need context, in order to know which 15 ship it is, and a host of other sundry facts.

In discussing truth and photography, we are asking whether a caption or a belief—whether a statement about a photograph—is true or false about (the things depicted in) the photograph. A caption is like a statement. It trumpets the claim, "This is the *Lusitania*." And when we wonder "Is this a photograph of the *Lusitania*?" we are wondering whether the claim is true or false. The issue of the truth or falsity of a photograph is only meaningful with respect to statements about the photograph. Truth or falsity "adheres" not to the photograph itself but to the statements we make about a photograph. Depending on the statements, our answers change. All alone—shorn of context, without captions—a photograph is neither true nor false.

But why this photograph? It's so terribly bland. I wanted to begin this series of essays on photography with an image chosen particularly for its blandness. Removed in time, far from our core knowledge, it is unfamiliar. We know little about it. We most likely do not recognize it as the *Lusitania*. We might think it's an early-20th-century ocean liner, and perhaps even imagine it may be the *Titanic*—at which point we have placed a kind of mental caption under the photograph, and we begin to see the photograph in terms of our associations and beliefs, about what it seems to say about reality.

It is also interesting how a photograph quickly changes when we learn more about what it depicts, when we provide a context, when we become familiar with an underlying story. And when we make claims about the photograph using language. For truth, properly considered, is about the relationship between language and the world, not about photographs and the world.

So here's a story.

On the evening of May 7th, 1915, the RMS *Lusitania* was off the coast 20
of Ireland en route to Liverpool from New York when it was torpedoed by a
German U-Boat and sank. About 1,200 of the nearly 2,000 passengers and
crew aboard drowned, including more than 100 Americans. The loss of life
provoked America out of a hereunto neutrality in the ongoing war in Europe.
With cries of "Remember the *Lusitania*" the U.S. entered into WWI within
two years.

To modern viewers, this image of the *Lusitania* is emotionally uncharged,
if not devoid of interest. But to a viewer in the summer of 1915, it was charged
with meaning. It was surrounded by many, many other photographs, images
and accounts of the sinking of the *Lusitania*, a cause célèbre.

Let's look at some of these other images.

"ENLIST" was a WWI Recruitment poster designed by Fred Spears.
Spears's design was inspired by a news report from Cork, Ireland, that
described, among the recovered bodies from the *Lusitania*, "a mother with a
three-month-old child clasped tightly in her arms. Her face wears a half smile.
Her baby's head rests against her breast. No one has tried to separate them."

And here is a photograph from the same period with the following caption.

"SOME OF THE SIXTY-SIX COFFINS BURIED IN ONE OF THE HUGE GRAVES IN 25
THE QUEENSTOWN CHURCHYARD"

The caption is from a two-page pictorial spread in the May 30, 1915, *New York Times*: "BURYING THE LUSITANIA'S DEAD AND SUCCORING HER SURVIVORS"

One more photograph and an accompanying article from the *Toronto Star*.

Watch's Fixed Hands Record Lusitania's Last 30 Minutes

At 2:30 p.m. today it will be exactly 27 years since a small pocket watch owned by Percy Rogers, Toronto, was stopped by the action of a German submarine.

It was 2 o'clock on the afternoon of May 7, 1915. The giant Cunard liner, Lusitania, with 1,906 aboard, was eight miles off the south coast of Ireland, and New York bound. In the domed dining saloon, Percy Rogers, then secretary of the C.N.E., had just finished lunch.

Mr. Rogers got up from the table, glanced at his watch and walked to his stateroom. At the very moment he was reaching to pick up a letter, he heard a "tremendous thud." He rushed on deck.

"People were running around like a flock of sheep with no one to direct them," he recalls. "Some of them clambered into lifeboats. The ship took a heavy list." His watch ticked off the fateful minutes. It was 2:15.

"I helped women and children near me into a boat. Then, as there were no more there, I got in. We had barely pulled a little way off before the ship turned on its side and sank." Five minutes had ticked by. It was 2:20.

"There was very little suction from the ship's sinking. But our boat upset. I struck out. Women and children were floating, mothers seeking to hold babies up. . . ." The watch ticked on, minute after minute. More than 1,000 lives were being snuffed out, and as the cold salt water seeped through Percy Rogers' clothes and finally into the delicate mechanism, his watch stopped. The minute hand, which had ticked off 30 of the most terrible minutes in history, was turned

downward in defeat. It was exactly 2:30.

Mr. Rogers floated with the help of a cupboard for an hour and a half. He was then picked up by a trawler and taken to Queenstown. When he looks at his watch today, one thing sticks in his mind. It is the official German statement at the time of the torpedoing: "Every German heart is filled with joy, pride and gratification." Mr. Rogers has never had the watch repaired. The hands have remained where they stopped as a reminder of the Lusitania.

The photograph is of a pocket watch. We learn from the accompanying article that the watch belonged to Percy Rogers and that the watch stopped at exactly 2:30 after "ticking off 30 of the most terrible minutes in history." Mr. Rogers was in a stateroom when the torpedo struck the *Lusitania*. He spent his last minutes on board helping women and children climb into lifeboats. Then he climbed into a lifeboat as well. And then the ship sank. The last paragraph of the article is memorable. It quotes "the official German statement" following the sinking of the *Lusitania*: "Every German heart is filled with joy, pride and gratification."

Now look at the photograph of the ship one more time.

The image remains the same, but clearly we look at it in a different   30
way.

Is that really a photograph of the *Lusitania*? When was it taken? Could
it have been taken on May 7, 1915? If it was, what was the exact time that
it was taken? Two o'clock? Two fifteen? Just seconds before the German
torpedo hit? Ah, can we see the torpedo in the water? Is that the mother and
her child (depicted in the poster) standing on the deck looking out over the
water? Is that Percy Rogers with his pocket watch, helping that same woman
and child climb into a lifeboat?

The idea that photographs hand us an objective piece of reality, that
they by themselves provide us with the truth, is an idea that has been with
us since the beginning of photography. But photographs are neither true
nor false in and of themselves. They are only true or false with respect to
statements that we make about them or the questions that we might ask of
them.

The photograph doesn't give me answers. A lot of additional investigation could provide those answers, but who has time for that?

Pictures may be worth a thousand words, but there are two words that
you can never apply to them: "true" and "false." ▓

The Reader's Presence

1. In the opening of his essay, Morris mentions receiving a collection of family photographs taken by his father a long time ago. Of what relevance are these photos to the
point Morris is making about truth and photography? Why don't these photographs
allow him to establish his point?

2. Morris writes: "A captionless photograph, stripped of all context, is virtually meaningless" (paragraph 10). Yet in many museums and galleries across the nation
photographs by leading photographers are exhibited and many are deliberately

without captions. Are these works "virtually meaningless"? Do such exhibits disprove Morris's point? How might Morris respond to such uncaptioned photographs?

3. **CONNECTIONS:** How does Morris's assessment of photography compare with Charles Simic's in "The Life of Images" (page 575)? What similarities and differences do you find between these two approaches to photographs? How does each writer "make sense" of photographic images?

The Writer at Work

ERROL MORRIS on Truth

This I Believe is a *New York Times* best-selling collection featuring 80 essayists sharing their most deeply held beliefs. Based on the essays originally broadcast on Edward R. Murrow's "This I Believe" radio series in the 1950s, the editors of the recent *This I Believe* book series extended a "simple, if difficult invitation" to "politicians, nurses, artists, construction workers, athletes, parents, students, the famous, and the unknown, everyone: Write a few hundred words expressing the core principles that guide your life—your personal credo." According to Jay Allison, the editor of the series, each respondent "wrote of their most closely held convictions and then spoke them on the radio [National Public Radio] to an audience of millions in a media climate that tends toward sound bites, potshots, and spin." The responses to this invitation are gathered in two volumes: *This I Believe: The Personal Philosophies of Remarkable Men and Women* (2006) and *This I Believe II: More Personal Philosophies of Remarkable Men and Women* (2008). A more recent volume is entitled *This I Believe: On Love* (2011). Errol Morris's essay "There Is Such a Thing as Truth" appeared in the first volume in the series.

❝I believe in truth. And in the pursuit of truth.

When I was ten years old, I asked a neighborhood kid who was older than me, "Which city is further west: Reno, Nevada, or Los Angeles?" The correct answer is Reno, Nevada. But he was convinced it was the other way around.

He was so convinced that Los Angeles was west of Reno that he was willing to bet me two bucks. So I went into the house to get my Rand McNally Atlas. The kid looked at the atlas and said, "This map is drawn funny." It wasn't. Was his argument that the map didn't preserve east, west, north, and south? What kind of map would that be? I showed him if you trace down the 120-degree west line of longitude—which runs almost directly through Reno, Nevada—you end up in the Pacific Ocean, somewhere west of Los Angeles.

He replied, "Lines of longitude don't cross the ocean."

What? I told him that the lines of longitude were there to indicate how far west or east some location was, regardless of whether it was on land or on sea.

There was one insurmountable problem, however. He was bigger than me.

I drew a number of conclusions from this story. There is such a thing as truth, but we often have a vested interest in ignoring it or outright denying it. Also, it's not just thinking something that makes it true. Truth is not relative. It's not subjective. It may be elusive or hidden. People may wish to disregard it. But there is such a thing as truth and the pursuit of truth: trying to figure out what has really happened, trying to figure out how things really are.

Almost fifteen years ago, I stumbled on a story about an innocent man, a man who had been sentenced to die in the Huntsville, Texas, electric chair. And through hard work, luck, and a certain amount of pathological obsession, I was able to make the movie *The Thin Blue Line* and help get him out of prison.

What kept me going was the belief that there had to be answers to the questions "Did he do it?," "Was he guilty or innocent?," "If he didn't do it, who did?" and that I could find an answer to these questions through investigating.

It's not that we find truth with a big "T." We investigate and sometimes we find things out and sometimes we don't. There's no way to know in advance. It's just that we have to proceed as though there are answers to questions. We must proceed as though, in principle, we can find things out—even if we can't. The alternative is unacceptable.

I will never know whether the neighborhood kid really didn't understand the logic of my argument about Reno, Nevada. Or whether he understood it completely and just didn't want to admit it. Or whether he understood it and just didn't want to pay up. I'll never know.

All I know is I never got my two dollars. **"**

Martha Nussbaum
VEILED THREATS?

Philosopher **MARTHA NUSSBAUM** (b. 1947) has written extensively on ethics, justice, and liberal education. Although her work is largely rooted in the classical (ancient Greek and Roman) tradition, she has nonetheless challenged conventional thinking in the humanities. She has criticized widely respected philosophers, most notably Jacques Derrida, stating that his work was "not worth studying." She has also called for a radical rethinking of gender roles. Her book *Sex and Social Justice* (1998) was praised by Salon.com for "brilliantly [showing] how sex is used to deny some people— i.e., women and gay men—social justice." Some of her other major works include *The Fragility of Goodness: Luck and Ethics in Greek Tragedy and Philosophy* (1986), *Hiding from Humanity: Disgust, Shame, and the Law* (2004), and *From Disgust to Humanity: Sexual Orientation and Constitutional Law* (2010). She is the Ernst Freund Distinguished Professor of Law and Ethics at the University of Chicago. "Veiled Threats?" first appeared in the July 11, 2010 issue of the "Opinionator," an online commentary published by the *New York Times*.

> **Martha Nussbaum's book** ***Sex and Social Justice* (1998) was praised by Salon.com for "brilliantly [showing] how sex is used to deny some people— i.e., women and gay men— social justice."**

IN SPAIN earlier this month [July 2010], the Catalonian assembly narrowly rejected a proposed ban on the Muslim burqa[1] in all public places—reversing a vote the week before in the country's upper house of parliament supporting a ban. Similar proposals may soon become national law in France and Belgium. Even the headscarf often causes trouble. In France, girls may not wear it in school. In Germany (as in parts of Belgium and the Netherlands) some regions forbid public school teachers to wear it on the job, although nuns and priests are permitted to teach in full habit. What does political philosophy have to say about these developments? As it turns out, a long philosophical and legal tradition has reflected about similar matters.

Let's start with an assumption that is widely shared: that all human beings are equal bearers of human dignity. It is widely agreed that government must treat that dignity with equal respect. But what is it to treat people with equal respect in areas touching on religious belief and observance?

We now add a further premise: that the faculty with which people search for life's ultimate meaning—frequently called "conscience"—is a very important part of people, closely related to their dignity. And we add one further premise, which we might call the vulnerability premise: this faculty can be seriously damaged by bad worldly conditions. It can be stopped from becoming active, and it can even be violated or damaged within. (The first sort of damage, which the 17th-century American philosopher Roger Williams[2] compared to imprisonment, happens when people are prevented from outward observances required by their beliefs. The second sort, which Williams called "soul rape," occurs when people are forced to affirm convictions that they may not hold, or to give assent to orthodoxies they don't support.)

---

1 **burqa:** A loose-fitting outer garment worn by women in some Islamic traditions to cover their bodies in public places.—EDS.

2 **Roger Williams** (c. 1603–c. 1683): An American Protestant theologian and philosopher, and the first prominent advocate of religious freedom and the separation of church and state.—EDS.

The vulnerability premise shows us that giving equal respect to conscience requires tailoring worldly conditions so as to protect both freedom of belief and freedom of expression and practice. Thus the framers of the United States Constitution concluded that protecting equal rights of conscience requires "free exercise" for all on a basis of equality. What does that really mean, and what limits might reasonably be placed upon religious activities in a pluralistic society? The philosophical architects of our legal tradition could easily see that when peace and safety are at stake, or the equal rights of others, some reasonable limits might be imposed on what people do in the name of religion. But they grasped after a deeper and more principled rationale for these limits and protections.

Here the philosophical tradition splits. One strand, associated with another 17-century English philosopher, John Locke,[3] holds that protecting equal liberty of conscience requires only two things: laws that do not penalize religious belief, and laws that are nondiscriminatory about practices, applying the same laws to all in matters touching on religious activities. An example of a discriminatory law, said Locke, would be one making it illegal to speak Latin in a Church, but not restricting the use of Latin in schools. Obviously, the point of such a law would be to persecute Roman Catholics. But if a law is not persecutory in this way, it may stand, even though it may incidentally impose burdens on some religious activities more than on others. If people find that their conscience will not permit them to obey a certain law (regarding military service, say, or work days), they had better follow their conscience, says Locke, but they will have to pay the legal penalty. A modern Lockean case, decided by the U.S. Supreme Court in 1993, concerned an ordinance passed by the city of Hialeah, Fla., which made "ritual animal sacrifice" illegal, but permitted the usual ways of killing animals for food. The Court, invalidating the law, reasoned that it was a deliberate form of persecution directed at Santeria worshippers.

Another tradition, associated with Roger Williams, the founder of the colony of Rhode Island and the author of copious writings on religious freedom, holds that protection for conscience must be stronger than this. This tradition reasons that laws in a democracy are always made by majorities and will naturally embody majority ideas of convenience. Even if such laws are not persecutory in intent, they may turn out to be very unfair to minorities. In cases in which such laws burden liberty of conscience—for example by requiring people to testify in court on their holy day, or to perform military service that their religion forbids, or to abstain from the use of a drug required in their sacred ceremony—this tradition held that a special exemption, called an "accommodation," should be given to the minority believer.

On the whole, the accommodationist position has been dominant in U.S. law and public culture—ever since George Washington wrote a famous

5

---

3 **John Locke** (1632–1704): An English philosopher and physician recognized as one of the most influential Enlightenment thinkers. —EDS.

letter to the Quakers explaining that he would not require them to serve in the military because the "conscientious scruples of all men" deserve the greatest "delicacy and tenderness." For a time, modern constitutional law in the U.S. applied an accommodationist standard, holding that government may not impose a "substantial burden" on a person's "free exercise of religion" without a "compelling state interest" (of which peace and safety are obvious examples, though not the only ones). The landmark case articulating this principle concerned a woman, Adell Sherbert, who was a Seventh-Day Adventist and whose workplace introduced a sixth workday, Saturday. Fired because she refused to work on that day, she sought unemployment compensation from the state of South Carolina and was denied on the grounds that she had refused "suitable work." The U.S. Supreme Court ruled in her favor, arguing that the denial of benefits was like fining Mrs. Sherbert for her nonstandard practices: it was thus a denial of her equal freedom to worship in her own way. There was nothing wrong in principle with choosing Sunday as the day of rest, but there was something wrong with not accommodating Mrs. Sherbert's special religious needs.

I believe that the accommodationist principle is more adequate than Locke's principle, because it reaches subtle forms of discrimination that are ubiquitous in majoritarian democratic life. It has its problems, however. One (emphasized by Justice Scalia,[4] when he turned our constitutional jurisprudence toward the Lockean standard in 1990) is that it is difficult for judges to administer. Creating exemptions to general laws on a case by case basis struck Scalia as too chaotic, and beyond the competence of the judiciary. The other problem is that the accommodationist position has typically favored religion and disfavored other reasons people may have for seeking an exemption to general laws. This is a thorny issue that requires lengthy discussion, for which there is no room here. But we don't need it, because the recent European cases all involve discriminatory laws that fail to pass even the weaker Lockean test. Let's focus on the burqa; arguments made there can be adapted to other cases.

Five arguments are commonly made in favor of proposed bans. Let's see whether they treat all citizens with equal respect. First, it is argued that security requires people to show their faces when appearing in public places. A second, closely related, argument says that the kind of transparency and reciprocity proper to relations between citizens is impeded by covering part of the face.

What is wrong with both of these arguments is that they are applied   10 inconsistently. It gets very cold in Chicago—as, indeed, in many parts of Europe. Along the streets we walk, hats pulled down over ears and brows, scarves wound tightly around noses and mouths. No problem of either

---

4 ***Antonin Scalia*** (born 1936): An associate justice of the U.S. Supreme Court. Appointed by President Ronald Reagan in 1986, Scalia is said to be the anchor of the Court's conservative wing.—EDS.

transparency or security is thought to exist, nor are we forbidden to enter public buildings so insulated. Moreover, many beloved and trusted professionals cover their faces all year round: surgeons, dentists, (American) football players, skiers and skaters. What inspires fear and mistrust in Europe, clearly, is not covering per se, but Muslim covering.

A reasonable demand might be that a Muslim woman have a full face photo on her driver's license or passport. With suitable protections for modesty during the photographic session, such a photo might possibly be required. However, we know by now that the face is a very bad identifier. At immigration checkpoints, eye-recognition and fingerprinting technologies have already replaced the photo. When these superior technologies spread to police on patrol and airport security lines, we can do away with the photo, hence with what remains of the first and second arguments.

A third argument, very prominent today, is that the burqa is a symbol of male domination that symbolizes the objectification of women (that they are being seen as mere objects). A Catalonian legislator recently called the burqa a "degrading prison." The first thing we should say about this argument is that the people who make it typically don't know much about Islam and would have a hard time saying what symbolizes what in that religion. But the more glaring flaw in the argument is that society is suffused with symbols of male supremacy that treat women as objects. Sex magazines, nude photos, tight jeans—all of these products, arguably, treat women as objects, as do so many aspects of our media culture. And what about the "degrading prison" of plastic surgery? Every time I undress in the locker room of my gym, I see women bearing the scars of liposuction, tummy tucks, breast implants. Isn't much of this done in order to conform to a male norm of female beauty that casts women as sex objects? Proponents of the burqa ban do not propose to ban all these objectifying practices. Indeed, they often participate in them. And banning all such practices on a basis of equality would be an intolerable invasion of liberty. Once again, then, the opponents of the burqa are utterly inconsistent, betraying a fear of the different that is discriminatory and unworthy of a liberal democracy. The way to deal with sexism, in this case as in all, is by persuasion and example, not by removing liberty.

Once again, there is a reasonable point to be made in this connection. When Turkey banned the veil long ago, there was a good reason in that specific context: because women who went unveiled were being subjected to harassment and violence. The ban protected a space for the choice to be unveiled, and was legitimate so long as women did not have that choice. We might think of this as a "substantial burden" justified (temporarily) by a "compelling state interest." But in today's Europe women can dress more or less as they please; there is no reason for the burden to religious liberty that the ban involves.

A fourth argument holds that women wear the burqa only because they are coerced. This is a rather implausible argument to make across the board, and it is typically made by people who have no idea what the circumstances of this or that individual woman are. We should reply that of course all forms of violence and physical coercion in the home are illegal already, and laws against domestic violence and abuse should be enforced much more zealously than they are. Do the arguers really believe that domestic violence is a peculiarly Muslim problem? If they do, they are dead wrong. According to the U.S. Bureau of Justice Statistics, intimate partner violence made up 20 percent of all nonfatal violent crime experienced by women in 2001. The National Violence Against Women Survey, cited on the B.J.S. Web site, reports that 52 percent of surveyed women said they were physically assaulted as a child by an adult caretaker and/or as an adult by any type of perpetrator. There is no evidence that Muslim families have a disproportionate amount of such violence. Indeed, given the strong association between domestic violence and the abuse of alcohol, it seems at least plausible that observant Muslim families will turn out to have less of it.

Suppose there were evidence that the burqa was strongly associated,   15 statistically, with violence against women. The U.S. Supreme Court has held that nude dancing may be banned on account of its contingent association with crime, including crimes against women, but it is not clear that this holding was correct. College fraternities are very strongly associated with violence against women, and some universities have banned all or some fraternities as a result. But private institutions are entitled to make such regulations; a total governmental ban on the male drinking club (or on other places where men get drunk, such as soccer matches) would certainly be a bizarre restriction of associational liberty. What is most important, however, is that anyone proposing to ban the burqa must consider it together with these other cases, weigh the evidence, and take the consequences for their own cherished hobbies.

Societies are certainly entitled to insist that all women have a decent education and employment opportunities that give them exit options from any home situation they may dislike. If people think that women only wear the burqa because of coercive pressure, let them create ample opportunities for them, at the same time enforce laws making primary and secondary education compulsory, and then see what women actually do.

Finally, I've heard the argument that the burqa is per se unhealthy, because it is hot and uncomfortable. (Not surprisingly, this argument is made in Spain.) This is perhaps the silliest of the arguments. Clothing that covers the body can be comfortable or uncomfortable, depending on the fabric. In India I typically wear a full salwaar kameez of cotton, because it is superbly comfortable, and full covering keeps dust off one's limbs and at least diminishes the risk of skin cancer. It is surely far from clear that the amount of skin displayed in typical Spanish female dress would meet with a dermatologist's approval. But more pointedly, would the arguer really seek to ban all uncomfortable and possibly unhealthy female clothing? Wouldn't we have to begin with high heels, delicious as they are? But no, high heels are associated with majority norms (and are a major Spanish export), so they draw no ire.

All five arguments are discriminatory. We don't even need to reach the delicate issue of religiously grounded accommodation to see that they are utterly unacceptable in a society committed to equal liberty. Equal respect for conscience requires us to reject them. ●

The Reader's Presence

1. Nussbaum begins her essay by invoking the ideas of two important thinkers from the 1600s: Roger Williams and John Locke. In what specific ways are the ideas of these two philosophers relevant to the topic of Nussbaum's essay? How does Nussbaum connect their ideas to recent events? How, if at all, do the ideas or the principles that Nussbaum outlines affect your opinion of a burqa ban?

2. Nussbaum addresses five arguments "commonly made in favor of proposed bans" (paragraph 9). Show how Nussbaum's counterarguments relate to the historical groundwork she presents earlier in the essay. In what ways do the philosophical ideas Nussbaum raises earlier in the essay make her position more or less compelling? Point to specific passages to support your response. How would your reading of Nussbaum's essay differ if she omitted the first part and only stated her counterarguments?

3. **CONNECTIONS:**   Consider Nussbaum's essay in relation to the Declaration of Independence (page 695). In what specific ways do the ideals set forth by the Declaration pertain to Nussbaum's essay? What passages from the Declaration could Nussbaum have incorporated into her essay, and how might she have done so?

> *Note:* Martha Nussbaum published "Veiled Threats?" on July 11, 2010, in the online edition of the *New York Times* and under the auspices of "The Opinionator," a "forum for contemporary philosophers on issues both timely and timeless." Her essay prompted 756 online responses. For a sampling of these varied responses, see the selections provided by the *New York Times* at http://opinionator.blogs.nytimes.com/2010/07/11/veiled-threats. To read Nussbaum's response to the comments she received on her essay, see http://opinionator.blogs.nytimes.com/2010/07/15/beyond-the-veil-a-response.

Barack Obama

GRANT PARK VICTORY SPEECH

America's forty-fourth president, **BARACK OBAMA** (b. 1961) was born in Honolulu, Hawaii, to a Kansas-born American mother and a Kenyan father, who met and married when they were students at the University of Hawaii. The effects of his parent's interracial marriage, his father's return to Kenya, and his parents' subsequent divorce when he was very young are central to his memoir, *Dreams from My Father: A Story of Race and Inheritance* (1995; reprinted in 2004). A 1995 review in the *New York Times Book Review* said that Obama's memoir "persuasively describes the phenomenon of belonging to two different worlds, and thus belonging to neither." After graduating from Columbia University in 1983, Obama worked as a community organizer in Chicago, then went on to Harvard University, where he became the first African American president of the *Harvard Law Review*; he received his law degree in 1991. Turning down a prestigious judicial clerkship, he chose instead to practice civil rights law in Chicago and to teach constitutional law at the University of Chicago. He served in the Illinois State Senate from 1997 to 2003 and was elected to the U.S. Senate in 2004. In addition to his memoir, Obama wrote *The Audacity of Hope: Thoughts on Reclaiming the American Dream*, published in 2006. In 2009, Barack Obama received the Nobel Peace Prize "for his extraordinary efforts to strengthen international diplomacy and cooperation between peoples . . ." and particularly for his "vision of and work for a world without nuclear weapons." This speech was given in Grant Park in Chicago, Illinois, on November 4, 2008, the night Obama won the presidential election.

> In 2009, Barack Obama received the Nobel Peace Prize "for his extraordinary efforts to strengthen international diplomacy and cooperation between peoples."

"HELLO, CHICAGO!"

If there is anyone out there who still doubts that America is a place where all things are possible; who still wonders if the dream of our founders is alive in our time; who still questions the power of our democracy, tonight is your answer.

It's the answer told by lines that stretched around schools and churches in numbers this nation has never seen; by people who waited three hours and four hours, many for the very first time in their lives, because they believed that this time must be different; that their voice could be that difference.

It's the answer spoken by young and old, rich and poor, Democrat and Republican, black, white, Latino, Asian, Native American, gay, straight, disabled and not disabled—Americans who sent a message to the world that we have never been a collection of red states and blue states; we are, and always will be, the United States of America.

It's the answer that led those who have been told for so long by so many to be cynical, and fearful, and doubtful of what we can achieve to put their hands on the arc of history and bend it once more toward the hope of a better day.

It's been a long time coming, but tonight, because of what we did on this day, in this election, at this defining moment, change has come to America.   5

I just received a very gracious call from Sen. McCain. He fought long and hard in this campaign, and he's fought even longer and harder for the country he loves. He has endured sacrifices for America that most of us cannot begin to imagine, and we are better off for the service rendered by this

President-elect Barack Obama addresses his supporters in Chicago's Grant Park, following his election-night victory on November 4, 2008.

brave and selfless leader. I congratulate him and Gov. Palin for all they have achieved, and I look forward to working with them to renew this nation's promise in the months ahead.

I want to thank my partner in this journey, a man who campaigned from his heart and spoke for the men and women he grew up with on the streets of Scranton and rode with on that train home to Delaware, the vice-president-elect of the United States, Joe Biden.

I would not be standing here tonight without the unyielding support of my best friend for the last 16 years, the rock of our family and the love of my life, our nation's next first lady, Michelle Obama. Sasha and Malia, I love you both so much, and you have earned the new puppy that's coming with us to the White House. And while she's no longer with us, I know my grandmother is watching, along with the family that made me who I am. I miss them tonight, and know that my debt to them is beyond measure.

To my campaign manager, David Plouffe; my chief strategist, David Axelrod; and the best campaign team ever assembled in the history of politics — you made this happen, and I am forever grateful for what you've sacrificed to get it done.

But above all, I will never forget who this victory truly belongs to — it belongs to you. 10

I was never the likeliest candidate for this office. We didn't start with much money or many endorsements. Our campaign was not hatched in the halls of Washington — it began in the backyards of Des Moines and the living rooms of Concord and the front porches of Charleston.

It was built by working men and women who dug into what little savings they had to give $5 and $10 and $20 to this cause. It grew strength from the young people who rejected the myth of their generation's apathy; who left their homes and their families for jobs that offered little pay and less sleep; from the not-so-young people who braved the bitter cold and scorching heat to knock on the doors of perfect strangers; from the millions of Americans who volunteered and organized, and proved that more than two centuries later, a government of the people, by the people and for the people has not perished from this earth. This is your victory.

I know you didn't do this just to win an election, and I know you didn't do it for me. You did it because you understand the enormity of the task that lies ahead. For even as we celebrate tonight, we know the challenges that tomorrow will bring are the greatest of our lifetime — two wars, a planet in peril, the worst financial crisis in a century. Even as we stand here tonight, we know there are brave Americans waking up in the deserts of Iraq and the mountains of Afghanistan to risk their lives for us. There are mothers and fathers who will lie awake after their children fall asleep and wonder how they'll make the mortgage, or pay their doctor's bills, or save enough for college. There is new energy to harness and new jobs to be created; new schools to build and threats to meet and alliances to repair.

The road ahead will be long. Our climb will be steep. We may not get there in one year, or even one term, but America — I have never been more hopeful than I am tonight that we will get there. I promise you: We as a people will get there.

There will be setbacks and false starts. There are many who won't agree 15 with every decision or policy I make as president, and we know that government can't solve every problem. But I will always be honest with you about the challenges we face. I will listen to you, especially when we disagree. And, above all, I will ask that you join in the work of remaking this nation the only way it's been done in America for 221 years—block by block, brick by brick, callused hand by callused hand.

What began 21 months ago in the depths of winter must not end on this autumn night. This victory alone is not the change we seek—it is only the chance for us to make that change. And that cannot happen if we go back to the way things were. It cannot happen without you.

So let us summon a new spirit of patriotism; of service and responsibility where each of us resolves to pitch in and work harder and look after not only ourselves, but each other. Let us remember that if this financial crisis taught us anything, it's that we cannot have a thriving Wall Street while Main Street suffers. In this country, we rise or fall as one nation—as one people.

Let us resist the temptation to fall back on the same partisanship and pettiness and immaturity that has poisoned our politics for so long. Let us remember that it was a man from this state who first carried the banner of the Republican Party to the White House—a party founded on the values of self-reliance, individual liberty and national unity. Those are values we all share, and while the Democratic Party has won a great victory tonight, we do so with a measure of humility and determination to heal the divides that have held back our progress.

As Lincoln said to a nation far more divided than ours, "We are not enemies, but friends. . . . Though passion may have strained, it must not break our bonds of affection." And, to those Americans whose support I have yet to earn, I may not have won your vote, but I hear your voices, I need your help, and I will be your president, too.

And to all those watching tonight from beyond our shores, from parlia- 20 ments and palaces to those who are huddled around radios in the forgotten corners of our world—our stories are singular, but our destiny is shared, and a new dawn of American leadership is at hand. To those who would tear this world down: We will defeat you. To those who seek peace and security: We support you. And to all those who have wondered if America's beacon still burns as bright: Tonight, we proved once more that the true strength of our nation comes not from the might of our arms or the scale of our wealth, but from the enduring power of our ideals: democracy, liberty, opportunity and unyielding hope.

For that is the true genius of America—that America can change. Our union can be perfected. And what we have already achieved gives us hope for what we can and must achieve tomorrow.

This election had many firsts and many stories that will be told for generations. But one that's on my mind tonight is about a woman who cast her ballot in Atlanta. She's a lot like the millions of others who stood in line to make their voice heard in this election, except for one thing: Ann Nixon Cooper is 106 years old.

She was born just a generation past slavery; a time when there were no cars on the road or planes in the sky; when someone like her couldn't vote for two reasons—because she was a woman and because of the color of her skin.

And tonight, I think about all that she's seen throughout her century in America—the heartache and the hope; the struggle and the progress; the times we were told that we can't and the people who pressed on with that American creed: Yes we can.

At a time when women's voices were silenced and their hopes dismissed,   25 she lived to see them stand up and speak out and reach for the ballot. Yes, we can.

When there was despair in the Dust Bowl and depression across the land, she saw a nation conquer fear itself with a New Deal, new jobs and a new sense of common purpose. Yes, we can.

When the bombs fell on our harbor and tyranny threatened the world, she was there to witness a generation rise to greatness and a democracy was saved. Yes, we can.

She was there for the buses in Montgomery, the hoses in Birmingham, a bridge in Selma and a preacher from Atlanta who told a people that "We Shall Overcome." Yes, we can.

A man touched down on the moon, a wall came down in Berlin, a world was connected by our own science and imagination. And this year, in this election, she touched her finger to a screen and cast her vote, because after 106 years in America, through the best of times and the darkest of hours, she knows how America can change. Yes, we can.

America, we have come so far. We have seen so much. But there is so   30 much more to do. So tonight, let us ask ourselves: If our children should live to see the next century; if my daughters should be so lucky to live as long as Ann Nixon Cooper, what change will they see? What progress will we have made?

This is our chance to answer that call. This is our moment. This is our time—to put our people back to work and open doors of opportunity for our kids; to restore prosperity and promote the cause of peace; to reclaim the American Dream and reaffirm that fundamental truth that out of many, we are one; that while we breathe, we hope, and where we are met with cynicism, and doubt, and those who tell us that we can't, we will respond with that timeless creed that sums up the spirit of a people: Yes, we can.

Thank you, God bless you, and may God bless the United States of America. ■

The Reader's Presence

1. In the second sentence of Obama's public address on November 4, 2008, the night he was declared the winner of the popular vote to be the next president of the United States of America, he invokes two classic myths about America: "a place where all things are possible" and a place where "the dream of our founders is alive in our time." At what other points in his speech—and with what specific effects—does President-elect Obama introduce other myths about America? What popular political myths does he invoke and then deny?

2. Obama uses a classical rhetorical strategy, anaphora—the repetition of a word or phrase at the beginning of successive phrases, clauses, or sentences—at the beginning of the second, third, and fourth paragraphs. Identify, and comment on the effectiveness of, other instances of repetition (of diction, phrasing, and imagery) throughout Obama's speech. Choose one example and explain why you think it is especially effective.

3. **CONNECTIONS:**　During the course of his address, President-elect Obama also makes several historical allusions and invokes several figures in American history, including Abraham Lincoln and Martin Luther King Jr. After you have re-read Barack Obama's "Victory Speech," examine it in relation to Lincoln's "Gettysburg Address" (page 491) and Martin Luther King Jr.'s address ("I Have a Dream") delivered as the culmination of the March on Washington on August 28, 1963 (page 701). What specific thematic, rhetorical, and stylistic connections can you establish between and among these three historic speeches to the American public?

Camille Paglia

THE PITFALLS OF PLASTIC SURGERY

CAMILLE PAGLIA (b. 1947), academic, author, and *Salon*'s "fave pop intellectual," earned her PhD at Yale University and taught at Bennington College, Wesleyan University, and Yale University. In 1984, she joined the faculty at the University of the Arts in Philadelphia, where she is professor of humanities and media studies. Her academic study, and first book, *Sexual Personae: Art and Decadence from Nefertiti to Emily Dickinson* (1990) caused heated debate and launched her career as a noted feminist, cultural critic, and social commentator. By early 1991, she was featured on the cover of *New York Magazine*, under the headline: "Woman Warrior." In 1992, her second book, *Sex, Art and American Culture*, was published, followed by *Vamps and Tramps* (1994). In 1998, she published a volume about Alfred Hitchcock's film *The Birds*, for the British Film Institute Films Classics series. Her latest book is *Break, Blow, Burn: Camille Paglia Reads Forty-Three of the World's Best Poems* (2005). Paglia is a contributing editor at *Interview* magazine; she is a founding contributor to *Salon*; and she writes about art, literature, culture, media, and politics for numerous publications throughout the world, including the *Advocate*, the *New York Times*, the *Independent* of London, the *American Enterprise*, and *Harper's Bazaar*, where "The Pitfalls of Plastic Surgery" appeared in 2005.

> **"That 700-page tome was a round-the-clock operation, requiring a fanaticism of attention and persistence that could not possibly have been combined with a responsible family life."**

Paglia describes her life after turning sixty and becoming a parent, with her partner, of a baby boy—and reveals the trials of writing her first book. "I'm deeply enjoying being a parent—which I certainly would not have been able to do while I was writing *Sexual Personae* for 20 years," she told an interviewer. "That 700-page tome was a round-the-clock operation, requiring a fanaticism of attention and persistence that could not possibly have been combined with a responsible family life."

PLASTIC SURGERY is living sculpture: a triumph of modern medicine. As a revision of nature, cosmetic surgery symbolizes the conquest of biology by human free will. With new faces and bodies, people have become their own works of art.

Once largely confined to the entertainment and fashion industries, plastic surgery has become routine in the corporate workplace in the U.S., even for men. A refreshed, youthful look is now considered essential for job retention and advancement in high-profile careers. As cosmetic surgery has become more widespread and affordable, it has virtually become a civil right, an equal-opportunity privilege once enjoyed primarily by a moneyed elite who could fly to Brazil for a discreet nip and tuck.

The questions raised about plastic surgery often have a moralistic hue. Is cosmetic surgery a wasteful frivolity, an exercise in narcissism? Does the pressure for alteration of face and body fall more heavily on women because of endemic sexism? And are coercive racist stereotypes at work in the trend among black women to thin their noses and among Asian women to "Westernize" their eyes?

All these ethical issues deserve serious attention. But nothing, I submit, will stop the drive of the human species toward beauty and the shimmering illusion of perfection. It is one of our deepest and finest instincts. From prehistory on, tribal peoples flattened their skulls, pierced their noses, elongated their necks, stretched their earlobes and scarred or tattooed their entire bodies to achieve the most admired look. Mutilation is in the eye of the beholder.

Though cosmetic surgery is undoubtedly an unstoppable movement, we   5
may still ask whether its current application can be improved. I have not had
surgery and have no plans to do so, on the theory that women intellectuals,
at least, should perhaps try to hold out. (On the other hand, one doesn't want
to scare the horses!) Over the past 15 years, I have become increasingly
uneasy about ruling styles of plastic surgery in the U.S. What norms are
being imposed on adult or aging women?

I would suggest that the current models upon which many American
surgeons are basing their reworking of the female face and body are far
too parochial. The eye can be retrained over time, and so we have come
to accept a diminished and even demeaning view of woman as ingenue, a
perky figure of ingratiating girliness. Neither sex bomb nor dominatrix, she
is a cutesy sex kitten without claws.

In the great era of the Hollywood studio system, from the 1920s to the
early '60s, pioneering makeup techniques achieved what plastic surgery
does now to remold the appearance of both male and female stars. For
example, the mature Lana Turner[1] of *Imitation of Life* or *Peyton Place* was
made to look like a superglamorous and ravishingly sensual version of a
woman of Turner's own age. The problem today is that Hollywood expects
middle-aged female actors to look 20 or even 30 years younger than they
are. The ideal has become the bouncy Barbie doll or simpering nymphet, not
a sophisticated woman of the world. Women's faces are erased, blanked out
as in a cartoon. In Europe, in contrast, older women are still considered sexy:
Women are granted the dignity of accumulated experience. The European
woman has a reserve or mystique because of her assumed mastery of the
esoteric arts of love.

Why this cultural discrepancy? Many of the founders of Hollywood, from
studio moguls to directors, screenwriters, makeup artists, and composers,
were European émigrés whose social background ranged from peasant to
professional. European models of beauty are based on classical precedents:
on luminous Greek sculpture, with its mathematical symmetry and proportion, or on Old Master oil paintings, with their magnificent portraiture of elegant aristocrats and hypnotic femme fatales. As an upstart popular form with
trashy roots in nickelodeons and penny arcades, Hollywood movies strove to
elevate their prestige by invoking a noble past. The studios presented their
stable of stars as a Greek pantheon of resurrected divinities, sex symbols
with an unattainable grandeur.

But Hollywood's grounding in great art has vanished. In this blockbuster
era of computerized special effects and slam-bang action-adventure films,
few producers and directors root their genre in the ancestry of the fine arts.
On the contrary, they are more likely to be inspired by snarky television
sitcoms or holographic video games, with their fantasy cast of overmuscled
heroes and pneumatic vixens. The profound influence of video games can

---

1 **Lana Turner** (1921–1995): One of Hollywood's most glamorous stars in the 1940s and 1950s,
Turner appeared in countless films, including *Peyton Place* (1957) and *Imitation of Life* (1959).

be seen in the redefining of today's ultimate female body type, inspired by Amazonian superheroines like Lara Croft: large breasts with a flat midriff and lean hips, a hormonally anomalous profile that few women can attain without surgical intervention and liposuction.

Maximizing one's attractiveness and desirability is a justifiable aim in any   10 society, except for the most puritanical. But it is worrisome that the American standard of female sexual allure may be regressing. In the post-1960s culture of easy divorce on demand, middle-aged women have found themselves competing with nubile women in their 20s, who are being scooped up as trophy second wives by ambitious men having a midlife crisis. Cosmetic surgery seems to level the playing field. But at what cost?

Good surgery discovers and reveals personality; bad surgery obscures or distorts it. The facial mask should not be frozen or robotic. We still don't know what neurological risks there might be in long term use of nonsurgical Botox, a toxin injected subcutaneously to paralyze facial muscles and smooth out furrows and wrinkles. What is clear, however, is that unskilled practitioners are sometimes administering Botox in excessive amounts, so that even major celebrities in their late 30s and 40s can be seen at public events with frighteningly waxen, mummified foreheads. Actors who overuse Botox are forfeiting the mobile expressiveness necessary to portray character. We will probably never again see "great faces" among accomplished older women—the kind of severe, imperious, craggy look of formidable visionaries like Diana Vreeland or Lillian Hellman.[2]

The urgent problem is that today's cosmetic surgeons are drawing from too limited a repertoire of images. Plastic surgery is an art form: Therefore, surgeons need training in art as well as medicine. Without a broader visual vocabulary, too many surgeons will continue to homogenize women, divesting them of authority and reducing them to a generic cookie-cutter sameness. And without a gift for psychology, surgeons cannot intuit and reinforce a woman's unique personality.

For cosmetic surgery to maintain or regain subtlety and nuance, surgeons should meditate on great painting and sculpture. And women themselves must draw the line against seeking and perpetuating an artificial juvenility that obliterates their own cultural value. ■

The Reader's Presence

1. How would you describe Paglia's attitude toward cosmetic surgery? What ethical issues does it raise for her? In what ways does cosmetic surgery affect Paglia's artistic sensibility? What distinction does she make between good surgery and bad surgery?

---

2 **Diana Vreeland or Lillian Hellman:** Vreeland (1903–1989), the celebrated fashion editor of *Vogue* magazine, and Hellman (1905–1984), the well-known American playwright, were known for their strikingly craggy facial features.

2. How does Paglia connect the popularity of cosmetic surgery today to the history of the American film industry? How did changes in the movie industry alter American notions of what is beautiful? According to Paglia, what are the sources of today's standards of attractiveness and how are they affecting cosmetic surgery? Do you find her analysis persuasive? Why or why not?

3. **CONNECTIONS:**   Consider Paglia's short essay in conjunction with Daniel Akst's "What Meets the Eye" (page 293). In what ways does Akst's essay help reinforce Paglia's point? Which author, in your opinion, provides the more interesting explanation of what Americans find physically attractive? Give specific reasons for why you find one analysis more interesting than the other.

The Student at Work

SABRINA VERCHOT
Cosmetic Surgery: A Modest Defense

Sabrina Verchot was a senior at Emerson College in Boston, working toward her BFA in Writing, Literature, and Publishing. After graduating, in spring 2011, she planned to take the summer off to work on some writing projects, both fiction and nonfiction, and hopes to find a teaching position in her hometown of Pittsfield, Massachusetts.

❝ In her essay, "The Pitfalls of Plastic Surgery," Camille Paglia explores the growing practice of cosmetic surgery and how it has both influenced and been influenced by American culture. She examines the idea that plastic surgery is simply a form of sculpture for Hollywood actresses who want their bodies to conform to the sexist ideal promoted by American media. She suggests that conformity to this ideal has also become the norm for many other Americans, and now plays a critical role in job retention as well as marriage retention. Although Paglia's argument is in many ways sensible, there are a few points I take issue with, such as the idea that Hollywood has perpetuated a sexist ideal of women through plastic surgery.

Plastic surgery was indeed made popular by Hollywood. Most of the news coverage of plastic surgery typically involves Hollywood actresses, particularly those who have undergone extreme cosmetic surgery or who have had multiple operations. Paglia is certainly right about that detail. Even so, in the past few years, Hollywood has not encouraged surgically enhanced sexist images. In fact, casting directors have gone in the opposite direction and some refuse to cast anyone who looks as though she has been transformed by plastic surgery. For example, the casting director of *Pirates of the Caribbean 4*, now underway, specifically requested auditions from those with "natural-looking breasts only" (Fagen). Clearly, there has been a distinct switch in Hollywood thinking when it comes to surgical enhancement and the media's vision of the ideal woman.

Paglia states that, "plastic surgery is living sculpture" [paragraph 1]. She is literally correct. The word *plastic* comes from the Greek *Plastikos*, to make or form, so even the very root of the word suggests that to opt for plastic surgery is to be *formed* into something other than what you are. However, that does not necessarily mean that if you elect such surgery you will automatically become a carbon copy of everyone else who has done the same. Paglia complains that plastic surgeons "homogenize women, divesting them of authority and reducing them to a generic cookie-cutter sameness" [paragraph 12]. But the process of plastic surgery actually takes place over a number of different medical sessions to make sure that the person undergoing surgery will receive the expected results, not some generic face or body that the surgeon has pre-selected for all of his or her patients.

There are women in Hollywood who undergo massive amounts of surgery to achieve the "perfect body," the homogenized version of a woman Paglia talks about. But most of those women are actually addicted to plastic surgery and

have body dysmorphic disorder, which causes them to see their own bodies as unappealing. They might see themselves as fat even if they are thin, and they'll pick up on the tiniest imperfection and feel that they have to fix it. Michael Jackson is the most well-known case of body dysmorphic disorder in Hollywood, but Kelly Osbourne is another case, and there is quite a bit of debate over whether Heidi Montag has the disease, considering her recent venture into plastic surgery in which she had ten operations done in one day (Goldman).

Although some patients, particularly those with body dysmorphic disorder, may want to be the "perfect" woman, displaying—as Paglia observes –"large breasts with a flat midriff and lean hips" [paragraph 9], that certainly isn't every woman's ideal. Some simply want to soften harsh features or even out bodily proportions. Not to mention that there are—usually to the surprise of many men—women unhappy with large breasts who willingly undergo breast-reduction surgery. Not all women want implants. Even Hollywood seems to be getting the idea that women do not require oversized breasts to be sexually appealing. Drew Barrymore, Queen Latifah, and Kelly Osbourne have all either openly discussed the idea of having breast-reduction surgery or are planning to undergo the surgery, and not just for the cosmetic reasons Paglia seems to focus on when she criticizes plastic surgery (Stewart). Reducing breast size can actually be medically beneficial for some women and can eliminate back pain and headaches (Ray). Additionally, studies have suggested that breast-reduction surgery can reduce the risk of breast cancer, especially in women over the age of fifty (Hage).

Medically, a huge number of benefits can result from successful plastic surgery, and each of these benefits is particular to the patient and the problem he or she would like to remedy. Plastic surgery isn't confined to Hollywood, as Paglia notes, but it is also not confined to the "corporate workplace" for "job retention and advancement in high-profile careers" [paragraph 2]. Plastic surgery is practiced in hospitals all over the world on normal, everyday people who need a life-changing procedure. In Boston, just a few years ago, James Maki fell onto the subway tracks. Half of his face was burnt off, his nose was completely gone, his upper lips and cheeks were missing. He survived miraculously, but once he was out of the hospital he wouldn't leave his house for fear of how neighbors would react. In 2009, he returned to Brigham and Women's Hospital in Boston for plastic surgery to reconstruct his face. The procedure was a success and dramatically changed his life for the better. The surgery gave him a life outside of the confines of his home (Kowalczyk).

Though Paglia is certainly right on many counts, there is clearly much more to plastic surgery than its "pitfalls." When examining the costs and benefits of cosmetic surgery we must look carefully at the whole picture. That picture includes not just how plastic surgery perpetuates the media's version of a "perfect body" but also how it can give hope to all the people in hospitals today desperately looking for a better life. **"**

WORKS CITED

Fagen, Cynthia R. "Disney Wants Women with Natural Breasts for New 'Pirate' Movie." *NY Post.* N.p., 21 Mar. 2010. Web. 27 Nov. 2010.

Goldman, Leslie. "Celebs and Body Dysmorphic Disorder." *iVillage Health.* NBC, Today, 1 Mar. 2010. Web. 26 Nov. 2010.

Hage, Joris J., and Refaat B. Karim. "Risk of Breast Cancer among Reduction Mammaplasty Patients and the Strategies Used by Plastic Surgeons to Detect Such Cancer." *Plastic and Reconstructive Surgery* 117.3 (2006): 727–735. Print.

Kowalczyk, Liz. "His Tragic Accident Behind Him, New England's First Face Transplant Patient Tells of an Arduous Journey and a Life Renewed." *Boston Globe.* Globe Newspaper Company, 21 May 2009. Web. 26 Nov. 2010.

Ray, Lynn. "Breast Reduction May Be Covered by Your Insurance Plan." *Examiner.* Clarity Digital Group LLC, 6 Aug. 2010. Web. 26 Nov. 2010.

Stewart, Colin. "Smaller Breasts Are in Style." *Orange County Register.* The Orange County Register Communications, 8 Sept. 2009. Web. 26 Nov. 2010.

Michael Pollan

WHAT'S EATING AMERICA

Journalist, author, and educator **MICHAEL POLLAN** (b. 1955), has become a leading voice for change in our industrialized food system—what we grow and what we eat. The theme of his latest book, *In Defense of Food: An Eater's Manifesto* (2008), comes down to seven words: Eat Food. Not Too Much. Mostly Plants. His previous books include *The Botany of Desire: A Plant's-Eye View of the World* (2001), in which he argues that domesticated plants have shaped humans as much as humans have shaped them, and *The Omnivore's Dilemma: A Natural History of Four Meals* (2006), which focuses on the impact of corn on the American diet and the environment. Pollan was born and raised on Long Island, New York, and educated at Bennington College, Mansfield College, Oxford, and Columbia University, where he received his MA in English. Since then, he has written books and articles, lectured, and taught about food, agriculture, nature, and the environment. He is currently the Knight Professor of Journalism and director of the Knight Program in Science and Environmental Journalism at the University of California, Berkeley. An award-winning journalist, Pollan is a regular contributor to the *New York Times Magazine*. "What's Eating America" appeared in the July 2006 issue of *Smithsonian*.

> The theme of Michael Pollan's latest book, *In Defense of Food: An Eater's Manifesto* (2008), comes down to seven words: Eat Food. Not Too Much. Mostly Plants.

DESCENDANTS OF THE MAYA living in Mexico still sometimes refer to themselves as "the corn people." The phrase is not intended as metaphor. Rather, it's meant to acknowledge their abiding dependence on this miraculous grass, the staple of their diet for almost 9,000 years.

For an American like me, growing up linked to a very different food chain, yet one that is also rooted in corn, not to think of himself as a corn person suggests either a failure of imagination or a triumph of capitalism.

Or perhaps a little of both. For the great edifice of variety and choice that is an American supermarket rests on a remarkably narrow biological foundation: corn. It's not merely the feed that the steers and the chickens and the pigs and the turkeys ate; it's not just the source of the flour and the oil and the leavenings, the glycerides and the coloring in the processed foods; it's not just sweetening the soft drinks or lending a shine to the magazine cover over by the checkout. The supermarket itself—the wallboard and joint compound, the linoleum and fiberglass and adhesives out of which the building itself has been built—is in no small measure a manifestation of corn.

There are some 45,000 items in the average American supermarket, and more than a quarter of them contain corn. At the same time, the food industry has done a good job of persuading us that the 45,000 different items or SKUs (stock keeping units) represent genuine variety rather than the clever rearrangements of molecules extracted from the same plant.

How this peculiar grass, native to Central America and unknown to the   5
Old World before 1492, came to colonize so much of our land and bodies is one of the plant world's greatest success stories. I say the plant world's success story because it is no longer clear that corn's triumph is such a boon to the rest of the world.

At its most basic, the story of life on earth is the competition among species to capture and store as much energy as possible—either directly from the sun, or, in the case of animals, by eating plants and plant eaters. The energy is stored in the form of carbon molecules and measured in calories: the calories we eat, whether in an ear of corn or a steak, represent packets of energy once captured by a plant. Few plants can manufacture quite as much organic matter (and calories) from the same quantities of sunlight and water and basic elements as corn.

The great turning point in the modern history of corn, which in turn marks a key turning point in the industrialization of our food, can be dated with some precision to the day in 1947 when the huge munitions plant at Muscle Shoals, Alabama, switched over from making explosives to making chemical fertilizer. After World War II, the government had found itself with a tremendous supply of ammonium nitrate, the principal ingredient in the making of explosives. Ammonium nitrate also happens to be an excellent source of nitrogen for plants. Serious thought was given to spraying America's forests with the surplus chemical, to help the timber industry. But agronomists in the Department of Agriculture had a better idea: spread the ammonium nitrate on farmland as fertilizer. The chemical fertilizer industry (along with that of pesticides, which are based on the poison gases developed for war) is the product of the government's effort to convert its war machine to peacetime purposes. As the Indian farmer activist Vandana Shiva says in her speeches, "We're still eating the leftovers of World War II."

F1 hybrid corn is the greediest of plants, consuming more fertilizer than any other crop. Though F1 hybrids were introduced in the 1930s, it wasn't until they made the acquaintance of chemical fertilizers in the 1950s that corn yields exploded. The discovery of synthetic nitrogen changed everything—not just for the corn plant and the farm, not just for the food system, but also for the way life on earth is conducted.

All life depends on nitrogen; it is the building block from which nature assembles amino acids, proteins and nucleic acid; the genetic information that orders and perpetuates life is written in nitrogen ink. But the supply of

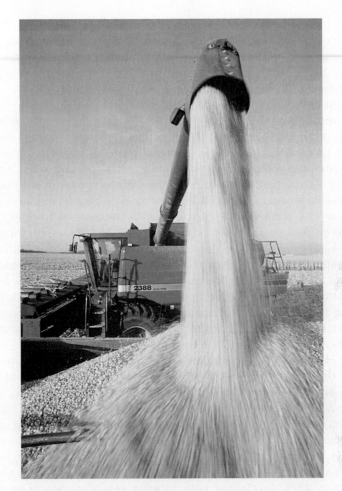

A combine unloads harvested grain corn into a truck for transport to a grain elevator in late-afternoon light.

usable nitrogen on earth is limited. Although earth's atmosphere is about 80 percent nitrogen, all those atoms are tightly paired, nonreactive and therefore useless; the 19th-century chemist Justus von Liebig spoke of atmospheric nitrogen's "indifference to all other substances." To be of any value to plants and animals, these self-involved nitrogen atoms must be split and then joined to atoms of hydrogen.

Chemists call this process of taking atoms from the atmosphere and combining them into molecules useful to living things "fixing" that element. Until a German Jewish chemist named Fritz Haber figured out how to turn this trick in 1909, all the usable nitrogen on earth had at one time been fixed by soil bacteria living on the roots of leguminous plants (such as peas or alfalfa or locust trees) or, less commonly, by the shock of electrical lightning, which can break nitrogen bonds in the air, releasing a light rain of fertility.

10

In his book *Enriching the Earth: Fritz Haber, Carl Bosch and the Transformation of World Food Production*, Vaclav Smil pointed out that "there is no way to grow crops and human bodies without nitrogen." Before Haber's invention, the sheer amount of life earth could support—the size of crops and therefore the number of human bodies—was limited by the amount of nitrogen that bacteria and lightning could fix. By 1900, European scientists had recognized that unless a way was found to augment this naturally occurring nitrogen, the growth of the human population would soon grind to a very painful halt. The same recognition by Chinese scientists a few decades later is probably what compelled China's opening to the West: after Nixon's 1972 trip, the first major order the Chinese government placed was for 13 massive fertilizer factories. Without them, China would have starved.

This is why it may not be hyperbole to claim, as Smil does, that the Haber-Bosch process for fixing nitrogen (Bosch gets the credit for commercializing Haber's idea) is the most important invention of the 20th century. He estimates that two of every five humans on earth today would not be alive if not for Fritz Haber's invention. We can easily imagine a world without computers or electricity, Smil points out, but without synthetic fertilizer billions of people would never have been born. Though, as these numbers suggest, humans may have struck a Faustian bargain[1] with nature when Fritz Haber gave us the power to fix nitrogen.

Fritz Haber? No, I'd never heard of him either, even though he was awarded the Nobel Prize in 1918 for "improving the standards of agriculture and the well-being of mankind." But the reason for his obscurity has less to do with the importance of his work than an ugly twist of his biography, which recalls the dubious links between modern warfare and industrial agriculture: during World War I, Haber threw himself into the German war effort, and his chemistry kept alive Germany's hopes for victory, by allowing it to make bombs from synthetic nitrate. Later, Haber put his genius for chemistry to work developing poisonous gases—ammonia, then chlorine. (He subsequently developed Zyklon B, the gas used in Hitler's concentration camps.) His wife, a chemist sickened by his contributions to the war effort, used his army pistol to kill herself; Haber died, broken and in flight from Nazi Germany, in a Basel hotel room in 1934.

His story has been all but written out of the 20th century. But it embodies the paradoxes of science, the double edge to our manipulations of nature, the good and evil that can flow not only from the same man but from the same knowledge. Even Haber's agricultural benefaction has proved to be a decidedly mixed blessing.

When humankind acquired the power to fix nitrogen, the basis of soil   15
fertility shifted from a total reliance on the energy of the sun to a new reliance on fossil fuel. That's because the Haber-Bosch process works by combining nitrogen and hydrogen gases under immense heat and pressure in

---

[1] *Faustian bargain:* In the legend, Faust traded his soul to the devil in exchange for knowledge. To "strike a Faustian bargain" is to be willing to give up anything for knowledge or power.—EDS.

the presence of a catalyst. The heat and pressure are supplied by prodigious amounts of electricity, and the hydrogen is supplied by oil, coal or, most commonly today, natural gas. True, these fossil fuels were created by the sun, billions of years ago, but they are not renewable in the same way that the fertility created by a legume nourished by sunlight is. (That nitrogen is fixed by a bacterium living on the roots of the legume, which trades a tiny drip of sugar for the nitrogen the plant needs.)

Liberated from the old biological constraints, the farm could now be managed on industrial principles, as a factory transforming inputs of raw material—chemical fertilizer—into outputs of corn. And corn adapted brilliantly to the new industrial regime, consuming prodigious quantities of fossil fuel energy and turning out ever more prodigious quantities of food energy. Growing corn, which from a biological perspective had always been a process of capturing sunlight to turn it into food, has in no small measure become a process of converting fossil fuels into food. More than half of all the synthetic nitrogen made today is applied to corn.

From the standpoint of industrial efficiency, it's too bad we can't simply drink petroleum directly, because there's a lot less energy in a bushel of corn (measured in calories) than there is in the half-gallon of oil required to produce it. Ecologically, this is a fabulously expensive way to produce food—but "ecologically" is no longer the operative standard. In the factory, time is money, and yield is everything.

One problem with factories, as opposed to biological systems, is that they tend to pollute. Hungry for fossil fuels as hybrid corn is, farmers still feed it far more than it can possibly eat, wasting most of the fertilizer they buy. And what happens to that synthetic nitrogen the plants don't take up? Some of it evaporates into the air, where it acidifies the rain and contributes to global warming. Some seeps down to the water table, whence it may come out of the tap. The nitrates in water bind to hemoglobin, compromising the blood's ability to carry oxygen to the brain. (I guess I was wrong to suggest we don't sip fossil fuels directly; sometimes we do.)

It has been less than a century since Fritz Haber's invention, yet already it has changed earth's ecology. More than half of the world's supply of usable nitrogen is now man-made. (Unless you grew up on organic food, most of the kilo or so of nitrogen in your body was fixed by the Haber-Bosch process.) "We have perturbed the global nitrogen cycle," Smil wrote, "more than any other, even carbon." The effects may be harder to predict than the effects of the global warming caused by our disturbance of the carbon cycle, but they are no less momentous.

The flood of synthetic nitrogen has fertilized not just the farm fields but 20 the forests and oceans, too, to the benefit of some species (corn and algae being two of the biggest beneficiaries) and to the detriment of countless others. The ultimate fate of the nitrates spread in Iowa or Indiana is to flow down the Mississippi into the Gulf of Mexico, where their deadly fertility poisons the marine ecosystem. The nitrogen tide stimulates the wild growth of algae, and the algae smother the fish, creating a "hypoxic," or dead, zone as big as New Jersey—and still growing. By fertilizing the world, we alter the planet's composition of species and shrink its biodiversity.

And yet, as organic farmers (who don't use synthetic fertilizer) prove every day, the sun still shines, plants and their bacterial associates still fix nitrogen, and farm animals still produce vast quantities of nitrogen in their "waste," so-called. It may take more work, but it's entirely possible to nourish the soil, and ourselves, without dumping so much nitrogen into the environment. The key to reducing our dependence on synthetic nitrogen is to build a more diversified agriculture—rotating crops and using animals to recycle nutrients on farms—and give up our vast, nitrogen-guzzling monocultures of corn. Especially as the price of fossil fuels climbs, even the world's most industrialized farmers will need to take a second look at how nature, and those who imitate her, go about creating fertility without diminishing our world. ■

The Reader's Presence

1. In paragraph 4, Pollan announces,

   > There are some 45,000 items in the average American supermarket, and more than a quarter of them contain corn. At the same time, the food industry has done a good job of persuading us that the 45,000 different items or SKUs (stock keeping units) represent genuine variety rather than the clever rearrangements of molecules extracted from the same plant.

   Comment on Pollan's use of statistics throughout his essay. In which instances does he use them most effectively to reinforce his argument? Consider field-testing his assertion. Visit your local supermarket and check out the label of ingredients on 50 items—to assess how accurate Pollan's claim that a quarter of the items there rely on corn either directly (corn syrup) or indirectly (corn feed). In what specific products were you surprised to find corn? Pollan suggests that our ignorance about the large role corn-based products play in our lives is not an accident. Based on Pollan's description of agri-business, why would companies not announce that their products are grounded in corn? Summarize the flow of nitrogen during corn production and explain why Pollan thinks this has dangerous consequences for the environment.

2. Pollan published his essay in *Smithsonian* magazine, which characterizes itself as "World renowned for its unparalleled coverage of nature, history, science and the arts." *Smithsonian* "explores lifestyles, cultures, people, technology, music and Americana for an inquisitive and educated readership." What would you identify as some of the expectations about writing that this "inquisitive and educated readership" would have of authors publishing in this magazine? To what extent does Pollan take liberty with some of these expectations? Point to specific examples and analyze the effectiveness of each. For example, re-read Pollan's essay carefully; how often does he use incomplete sentences (fragments)? With what effect(s)? Or, consider the nature and length of his paragraphs. Many young writers are instructed that a paragraph must have at least three sentences. How many of Pollan's paragraphs have fewer? With what effect(s)? Pollan, of course, is aware of his readers' expectations about sentence and paragraph structure. What tradition(s) does he draw on in constructing his essay? What effects are the nature of his sentence and paragraph structure likely to have on his readers?

3. **CONNECTIONS:**   Compare Eric Schlosser's explanation of the chemistry of French fries (see "Why McDonald's Fries Taste So Good," page 558) to Pollan's chemistry of corn. Both authors try to make technical subjects easily understandable for non-technical readers. To what extent does each writer use similar methods? Describe as specifically as possible what the writers share, or how they differ. What purpose does each establish for his essay? Overall, which author was more successful in achieving his purpose? Which process did you understand more easily? Explain why. Choose a complex food subject, such as the chemistry that makes soda fizz, and prepare a nontechnical but accurate description using the strategies that make Pollan's and Schlosser's explanations successful.

Michael J. Sandel

DESIGNER BABIES

MICHAEL J. SANDEL (b. 1953) is the Anne T. and Robert M. Bass Professor of Government at Harvard University, where he has taught political philosophy since 1980. He is well known for his "Justice" course, which has over the past two decades become one of the most widely attended courses offered by the renowned university. It was recorded in the fall semester of 2005 and condensed into a twelve-hour miniseries for WGBH public television. The series has been broadcast around the world and is particularly popular in Japan, where the companion book, *Justice: What's the Right Thing to Do?* (2009), became a best-seller. Sandel is known for being an excellent lecturer, drawing on clear examples from everyday life to make his arguments. He has said that "the responsibility of political philosophy that tries to engage with practice is to be clear, or at least accessible—clear enough that its arguments and concerns can be accessible to a nonacademic public. Otherwise, it's not possible really for political philosophers to generate debate that could possibly challenge existing understandings." This essay was originally published in *Tikkun Magazine* in September/October 2007.

> "The responsibility of political philosophy that tries to engage with practice is to be clear, or at least accessible—clear enough that its arguments and concerns can be accessible to a nonacademic public."

THERE'S A GROWING DEBATE about what limits, if any, should be put on genetic engineering. We are on a path in which in the not-too-distant future scientists and technicians will be able to select genes and may be able to shape characteristics of your children. Some people already argue that using that to select the sex of your child is fine, or perhaps for medical reasons. But what about other features? What if we could choose their hair color and type, their eye colors, their sexual orientation, their level of intelligence, their musical or writing ability or sports, dance, or artistic aptitude?

There is a long tradition that defends eugenics in the name of "lifting up." Now we know that the eugenics movement has a very dark history, though it was a very respectable movement in the early part of the twentieth century. Eugenics was discredited by the Nazis, by genocide, the Nuremberg Laws,[1] by the forced sterilization laws that were enacted by the majority of American states in the 1920s and 1930s. Yet, in its earlier days, eugenics was endorsed and embraced by social reformers, by American progressives: Theodore Roosevelt[2] was a great supporter of eugenics, Margaret Sanger,[3] who began Planned Parenthood, was a defender of eugenics. Oliver Wendell Holmes,[4] in a famous Supreme Court case *Buck v. Bell*,[5] upheld a forced sterilization law, with the notorious line that "three generations of imbeciles is enough." Oliver Wendell Holmes! So eugenics has a very respectable lineage if you look at the people who supported it, and yet it led to forced sterilization. It ultimately leads to genocide, even though it was first done in the name of those who have been burdened or disadvantaged.

What's the moral of the story of the dark history of eugenics? Some say it's that eugenics, in its earlier version, was coercive. State laws mandated sterilization in the so-called "feeble-minded," or in the criminal classes, and, of course, in Hitler's genocide. There are many today who say the only thing wrong with eugenics was its coerciveness, and if we could imagine a eugenics program that was not mandated by the State, that was not coercive, but was chosen by the individual parents trying to help and lift up their children, then there's nothing wrong with eugenics.

But I think that's a mistake. I think that coercion was not the only thing wrong with eugenics. What we have today with designer children is privatized eugenics, free market eugenics, individualistic eugenics. Without the broad social ambitions for everyone, it's really now an instrument for privileged parents to give their kids a competitive edge. Privatized eugenics reflect a deflation of the ideal of eugenics, perverse as that ideal was in its enactment, because it's no longer trying to uplift humanity, or entire

---

1 **Nuremberg Laws:** (German *Nürnberger Gesetze*) Anti-semitic laws in Germany introduced in 1935 at the annual Nuremberg Rally of the Nazi Party.—EDS.
2 **Theodore Roosevelt** (1858–1919): 26th president of the United States and leader of the Republican Party and the Progressive Movement.—EDS.
3 **Margaret Sanger** (1879–1966): American sex educator and birth-control activist.—EDS.
4 **Oliver Wendell Holmes Jr.** (1841–1935): Associate Justice of the Supreme Court from 1902–1932.—EDS.
5 **Buck v. Bell:** A 1927 decision that upheld a statute instituting compulsory sterilization of those deemed "unfit" or mentally retarded "for the protection and health of the state."—EDS.

societies, but just trying to get a competitive edge. I think what's wrong with eugenics, beyond coercion, is the fact of its ambition to try to control or exercise dominion over the genetic traits of the next generation. That's morally troubling, whether done on a society-wide basis or done by individual parents trying to give their kids a competitive edge.

Of course, there are objections about whether doing this can be made 5 safe and predictable. And there is another question about making it available in a fair way, so that it would not only be an option for rich people. But what would be your objection if the designer child were an equal option for all, publicly subsidized as part of a universal health care system, and it could be done in a way that was safe and predictable?

Is there a moral objection to this genetic engineering, beyond safety, beyond fairness? After all, we tend to praise parents who give their children every advantage they can: offer them music lessons to learn an instrument, play catch with them to learn how to be coordinated in sports, help them do their homework so that they can more fully learn what they need to learn. So what's the objection to parents wanting to give their children the advantage of genes that make it easier for them to succeed in creating a pleasant life for themselves?

It seems to me that there is a reason for a set of moral considerations that go beyond safety and fairness. What makes us most uneasy about the use of genetic engineering to enhance or to create something, has to do with the fact that the drive to create children of a certain character reflects an aspiration to freedom, mastery, and control, and to exercise our human will and our ability to remake human nature to serve our purposes and satisfy our desires. It seems to me there is something flawed but deeply attractive about that.

This uneasiness, I believe, connects to a recognition that there is a way in which who we are is a gift from the universe. And this is to say that not everything we are is a product of our own doing, and not everything in the world is open to any use we might desire or devise.

An appreciation of the giftedness of life might induce in us a certain humility. What I'm trying to articulate here is, in part, a religious sensibility, but its resonance reaches beyond religion.

Let's go back to the example of designer children. It's very hard to make 10 sense of what's precious or special about the relationship between parents and children without drawing, at least a little, on the ethic of giftedness. To appreciate children as gifts is to accept them as they come, not as products of our design or instruments of our ambition. Parental love is not contingent, or at least it shouldn't be contingent, on attributes that the child happens to have. We choose our friends and our spouses at least partly on qualities that we find attractive, but we do not choose our children—that's an important moral fact about parenting. Even the most conscientious parent cannot be held wholly responsible for the child that they had. This is why parenting teaches us what the theologian William May calls "an openness to the unbidden."

The problem of genetic engineering lies in the hubris of the designing parents. Even if this disposition doesn't make parents tyrants to their children, still it disfigures the relation between parent and child and it deprives the parent of the humility, the human sympathies, and the openness to the unbidden.

Now, to appreciate children as gifts and blessings from God is not to be passive in the face of illness. It's true that medical treatment intervenes with nature, but it does so for the sake of health. It doesn't represent the same bid for mastery. Even strenuous medicine, to treat or cure diseases, doesn't constitute a Promethean assault. Medicine is at least governed by a certain norm, the norm of preserving and restoring, and that is what constitutes good health.

What counts as "good health" is open to argument. There is research about whether deafness or other disabilities should be cured, or if they should be part of an identity that is cherished. But even then, the disagreement comes from the assumption that the purpose of medicine is to promote health and cure disease.

Now there is a complexity with this idea of resisting the temptation to manage, direct, and protect our children. Because we do that as parents. Parents want to educate their children, give them every opportunity, help them learn an instrument, develop athletic skill. . . . What then is the difference, and this is not an easy question to answer, but what is the difference between providing help with health and training, and providing this help with the use of genetic enhancement? Parents spend all this money educating their children and giving them special advantages. If that's accurate, why isn't it equally as admirable for parents to use whatever genetic technology has been developed, provided it's safe, to enhance their children's chance at life, to give them a competitive edge?

The answer I would give to this question is that the defenders of genetic   15 engineering are right to say that there is not such a bright line between the use of genetic technology to enhance children, and the kind of heavily managed, high-pressure child rearing practices that are common these days. But this similarity, this parallel, does *not* vindicate genetic enhancement. To the contrary, it highlights a problem with the high-pressure hyper-parenting tendencies that we see in our society today. We see the frenzy of parents at soccer game sidelines or at little league. It is a frenzy, or an anxiety even, of the parents to manage, to hold, to direct their children's lives. I don't think there is such a clear line between these two practices, but this suggests that the overreaching in genetic parenting may actually shed light on the kind of overreaching frenzied parenting that we see now.

So, let me say a word about the larger moral stance if the account I have given is right. Some people would say of this drive for mastery and life control: "That's parents exercising their freedom to give their kids the best, and who are we to criticize that freedom?"

What would happen if biotechnology dissolved our sense of giftedness? There are two answers to this question. One of them is the religious answer (which suggests that using biotechnology has us assume a role in creation that seeks to make us on par with God). Biotechnology is, in a sense, "playing God."

The moral stakes can also be understood in secular terms. One way of seeing this is to consider what would be the effect on our moral landscape if the practice of designer parents became the common way of parenting. At least two key features of our moral culture would be transformed. One of them is humility and the other is solidarity.

Let me say a word about humility and why it matters as a social ethic. Parenthood is a school for humility. We care deeply about our children but cannot choose the kind we want. Humility teaches us to reign in our need for control and to live with the unexpected. One of the blessings of seeing ourselves as creatures of nature or God is that we are not always responsible for the way we are. The more we become masters of our genetics the greater burden we bear for the talents we have and the way we perform. So with the erosion of humility comes an explosion of responsibility.

Consider the use of genetic testing. In the past, giving birth to a child   20
with Down syndrome was a matter of chance. Today, parents of children with Down syndrome are judged or blamed. Because people will say to them, "Why did you bring this child into the world?" So the responsibility is greater because we have a choice. Parents should be able to choose what they want to do, but they shouldn't be free to choose the burden of choice that this new technology creates.

Along with the explosion of responsibility over our own fate and that of our children, comes, paradoxically, a diminished sense of solidarity with those less fortunate than ourselves. Here's why: the more open we are to chance in the control over our own success, the more reason we have to share our fate with others. Why, after all, do the successful owe anything to the least advantaged members of society? The answers to this question lie very heavily in the notions of giftedness. They lean on the idea that our success has nothing to do with hard work, or other things within our control, but on good fortune—the result of the genetic lottery. If we regard our genetics as gifts rather than achievements for which we can claim credit, then we have no basis to claim that we are entitled to the good things in society.

A lively sense of the contingency of our gifts can be used in a "meritocratic" society like ours to prevent us from sliding into the idea that the rich are rich because they are more deserving than the poor. If genetic engineering enabled us to override the results of the genetic lottery, if it enabled us to replace chance with choice, it's likely that the gifted character of human powers and achievements would recede, and with it, perhaps, our capacity to see ourselves as sharing a common fate. The successful would be even more likely than they are now to see themselves as self-made and self-sufficient, and those at the bottom of society would be seen not as disadvantaged, but simply as unfit. The meritocracy would become less forgiving. So that's why humility and solidarity as features of our moral culture can help us preserve a lively sense of giftedness of our nature, of our talents, and of our achievements.

A related case is the use of Ritalin in classrooms. Admittedly, it is difficult to precisely draw the line between clinical Attention Deficit Hyperactivity Disorder (ADHD) and a squirmy kid in a classroom. It is a difficult line to draw and it involves judgment on the part of the parent, the teachers, the doctor, the psychologist, and the kid. I would not for a moment say that Ritalin should never be prescribed for ADHD. There are cases, clearly, of clinical ADHD where it can help a child function and overcome a real deficiency. But Ritalin is often used either to control children in the classroom who are simply squirmy and should be dealt with by closer individual attention by the teacher, and by smaller classroom size, and so on, or by college students who do not have any prescription, simply to improve their performance on a test. The line can be difficult to draw between the medical use of Ritalin and the performance enhancement use.

In order to draw this line, we must have, not just some statistical understanding of the normal, because that can shift over time, but a substantive, normative conception of what human flourishing consists of. So parents are often pressured to consent to Ritalin, and I fear that they might face even greater pressures to participate in genetic engineering.

We can't just blame parents for responding to these pressures. How could we expect them not to? We have to take a step back and ask what is the source of those heightened, intensified pressures? There has been an enormous increase in those types of pressures having to do with the economy and society and also the educational system.

So, to go back to the question with which I began, beyond safety and beyond fairness, what is the source of our unease about designer children? I think it has something to do with our big questions about human nature and the limits of the Promethean project of mastery and control. It is tempting to think that bioengineering our children and selves is an exercise in freedom, but it really isn't. Because changing our nature to fit the world rather than the other way around is actually an ethical defeat. It distracts us from reflecting critically on the world. It deadens the impulse for social and political improvement. So rather than increase our genetic powers to fit ourselves into society, we should do what we can to create political and social realms that are more hospitable to the gifts and also to the limitations of imperfect human beings. ■

The Reader's Presence

1. Comment on the effectiveness of Sandel's use of common preconceptions about genetic engineering to frame his argument. Identify the specific examples he chooses to include in support of his argument. Which do you find to be the most convincing? Explain why, quoting specific words and phrases from this essay in support of each point you make. To what extent do these examples relate to the conclusions Sandel draws? To what extent—and with what effect(s)—is Sandel consistent in his use of examples to support his argument?

2. What are the various perspectives or points of view from which Sandel approaches the topic of genetic engineering? How comprehensive does Sandel's exploration of

the topic strike you? Point to specific passages to support your response. In paragraph 4, for example, Sandel draws a distinction between the "privatized eugenics" of today and the past practices of eugenics "in the name of 'lifting up'" the public as a whole (paragraph 2). How does he compare and contrast the two? What objections to his argument does he anticipate in paragraph 4? What questions about genetic engineering do you—or others—have that Sandel doesn't address? What effect does this approach have on the persuasiveness of Sandel's argument?

3. **CONNECTIONS:**   Compare and contrast the way Sandel uses historical facts to support his argument to Malcolm Gladwell's use of historical facts in "Small Change: Why the Revolution Will Not Be Tweeted" (page 411). Where does each author position historical facts in each essay? With what effect(s)? How are the historical facts used structurally? What effect do they have on the impact of each essay?

Scott Russell Sanders
THE MEN WE CARRY IN OUR MINDS

SCOTT RUSSELL SANDERS (b. 1945) writes in a variety of genres: science fiction, realistic fiction, folktales, children's stories, essays, and historical novels. In all his work, however, he is concerned with the ways in which people live in communities. His books include *The Paradise of Bombs* (1987), from which "The Men We Carry in Our Minds" is taken; *Staying Put: Making a Home in a Restless World* (1993); *Here Comes the Mystery Man* (1993); *Writing from the Center* (1995); *Hunting for Hope: A Father's Journeys* (1998); *The Country of Language* (1999); *Bad Man Ballad* (2004); and a memoir, *A Private History of Awe* (2006). Sanders contributes to both literary and popular magazines. He is a professor of English at Indiana University.

> **"If my writing does not help my neighbors to live more alertly, pleasurably, or wisely, then it is worth little."**

Sanders has said, "I believe that a writer should be a servant of language, community, and nature. Language is the creation and sustenance of community. . . . My writing is driven by a deep regard for particular places and voices, persons and tools, plants and animals, for human skills and stories. . . . If my writing does not help my neighbors to live more alertly, pleasurably, or wisely, then it is worth little."

"THIS MUST BE a hard time for women," I say to my friend Anneke. "They have so many paths to choose from, and so many voices calling them."

"I think it's a lot harder for men," she replies.

"How do you figure that?"

"The women I know feel excited, innocent, like crusaders in a just cause. The men I know are eaten up with guilt."

We are sitting at the kitchen table drinking sassafras tea, our hands   5
wrapped around the mugs because this April morning is cool and drizzly. "Like a Dutch morning," Anneke told me earlier. She is Dutch herself, a writer and midwife and peacemaker, with the round face and sad eyes of a woman in a Vermeer[1] painting who might be waiting for the rain to stop, for a door to open. She leans over to sniff a sprig of lilac, pale lavender, that rises from a vase of cobalt blue.

"Women feel such pressure to be everything, do everything," I say. "Career, kids, art, politics. Have their babies and get back to the office a week later. It's as if they're trying to overcome a million years' worth of evolution in one lifetime."

"But we help one another. We don't try to lumber on alone, like so many wounded grizzly bears, the way men do." Anneke sips her tea. I gave her the mug with the owls on it, for wisdom. "And we have this deep-down sense that we're in the *right*—we've been held back, passed over, used—while men feel they're in the wrong. Men are the ones who've been discredited, who have to search their souls."

I search my soul. I discover guilty feelings aplenty—toward the poor, the Vietnamese, Native Americans, the whales, an endless list of debts—a guilt in each case that is as bright and unambiguous as a neon sign. But toward women I feel something more confused, a snarl of shame, envy, wary tenderness, and amazement. This muddle troubles me. To hide my unease I say, "You're right, it's tough being a man these days."

"Don't laugh." Anneke frowns at me, mournful-eyed, through the sassafras steam. "I wouldn't be a man for anything. It's much easier being the victim. All the victim has to do is break free. The persecutor has to live with his past."

How deep is that past? I find myself wondering after Anneke has left.   10
How much of an inheritance do I have to throw off? Is it just the beliefs I breathed in as a child? Do I have to scour memory back through father and grandfather? Through St. Paul? Beyond Stonehenge and into the twilit caves? I'm convinced the past we must contend with is deeper even than speech. When I think back on my childhood, on how I learned to see men and women, I have a sense of ancient, dizzying depths. The back roads of Tennessee and Ohio where I grew up were probably closer, in their sexual patterns, to the campsites of Stone Age hunters than to the genderless cities of the future into which we are rushing.

---

[1] *Jan Vermeer* (1632–1675): Dutch painter known for his interior scenes.—EDS.

The first men, besides my father, I remember seeing were black convicts and white guards, in the cottonfield across the road from our farm on the outskirts of Memphis. I must have been three or four. The prisoners wore dingy gray-and-black zebra suits, heavy as canvas, sodden with sweat. Hatless, stooped, they chopped weeds in the fierce heat, row after row, breathing the acrid dust of boll-weevil poison. The overseers wore dazzling white shirts and broad shadowy hats. The oiled barrels of their shotguns flashed in the sunlight. Their faces in memory are utterly blank. Of course those men, white and black, have become for me an emblem of racial hatred. But they have also come to stand for the twin poles of my early vision of manhood—the brute toiling animal and the boss.

When I was a boy, the men I knew labored with their bodies. They were marginal farmers, just scraping by, or welders, steelworkers, carpenters; they swept floors, dug ditches, mined coal, or drove trucks, their forearms ropy with muscle; they trained horses, stoked furnaces, built tires, stood on assembly lines wrestling parts onto cars and refrigerators. They got up before light, worked all day long whatever the weather, and when they came home at night they looked as though somebody had been whipping them. In the evenings and on weekends they worked on their own places, tilling gardens that were lumpy with clay, fixing broken-down cars, hammering on houses that were always too drafty, too leaky, too small.

The bodies of the men I knew were twisted and maimed in ways visible and invisible. The nails of their hands were black and split, the hands tattooed with scars. Some had lost fingers. Heavy lifting had given many of them finicky backs and guts weak from hernias. Racing against conveyor belts had given them ulcers. Their ankles and knees ached from years of standing on concrete. Anyone who had worked for long around machines was hard of hearing. They squinted, and the skin of their faces was creased like the leather of old work gloves. There were times, studying them, when I dreaded growing up. Most of them coughed, from dust or cigarettes, and most of them drank cheap wine or whiskey, so their eyes looked bloodshot and bruised. The fathers of my friends always seemed older than the mothers. Men wore out sooner. Only women lived into old age.

As a boy I also knew another sort of men, who did not sweat and break down like mules. They were soldiers, and so far as I could tell they scarcely worked at all. During my early school years we lived on a military base, an arsenal in Ohio, and every day I saw GIs in the guardshacks, on the stoops of barracks, at the wheels of olive drab Chevrolets. The chief fact of their lives was boredom. Long after I left the Arsenal I came to recognize the sour smell the soldiers gave off as that of souls in limbo. They were all waiting—for wars, for transfers, for leaves, for promotions, for the end of their hitch—like so many braves waiting for the hunt to begin. Unlike the warriors of older tribes, however, they would have no say about when the battle would start or how it would be waged. Their waiting was broken only when they practiced for war. They fired guns at targets, drove tanks across the churned-up fields of the military reservation, set off bombs in the wrecks of old fighter planes.

I knew this was all play. But I also felt certain that when the hour for killing arrived, they would kill. When the real shooting started, many of them would die. This was what soldiers were *for*, just as a hammer was for driving nails.

Warriors and toilers: those seemed, in my boyhood vision, to be the chief   15 destinies for men. They weren't the only destinies, as I learned from having a few male teachers, from reading books, and from watching television. But the men on television—the politicians, the astronauts, the generals, the savvy lawyers, the philosophical doctors, the bosses who gave orders to both soldiers and laborers—seemed as remote and unreal to me as the figures in tapestries. I could no more imagine growing up to become one of these cool, potent creatures than I could imagine becoming a prince.

A nearer and more hopeful example was that of my father, who had escaped from a red-dirt farm to a tire factory, and from the assembly line to the front office. Eventually he dressed in a white shirt and tie. He carried himself as if he had been born to work with his mind. But his body, remembering the earlier years of slogging work, began to give out on him in his fifties, and it quit on him entirely before he turned sixty-five. Even such a partial escape from man's fate as he had accomplished did not seem possible for most of the boys I knew. They joined the army, stood in line for jobs in the smoky plants, helped build highways. They were bound to work as their fathers had worked, killing themselves or preparing to kill others.

A scholarship enabled me not only to attend college, a rare enough feat in my circle, but even to study in a university meant for the children of the rich. Here I met for the first time young men who had assumed from birth that they would lead lives of comfort and power. And for the first time I met women who told me that men were guilty of having kept all the joys and privileges of the earth for themselves. I was baffled. What privileges? What joys? I thought about the maimed, dismal lives of most of the men back home. What had they stolen from their wives and daughters? The right to go five days a week, twelve months a year, for thirty or forty years to a steel mill or a coal mine? The right to drop bombs and die in war? The right to feel every leak in the roof, every gap in the fence, every cough in the engine, as a wound they must mend? The right to feel, when the lay-off comes or the plant shuts down, not only afraid but ashamed?

I was slow to understand the deep grievances of women. This was because, as a boy, I had envied them. Before college, the only people I had ever known who were interested in art or music or literature, the only ones who read books, the only ones who ever seemed to enjoy a sense of ease and grace were the mothers and daughters. Like the menfolk, they fretted about money, they scrimped and made-do. But, when the pay stopped coming in, they were not the ones who had failed. Nor did they have to go to war, and that seemed to me a blessed fact. By comparison with the narrow, ironclad days of fathers, there was an expansiveness, I thought, in the days of mothers. They went to see neighbors, to shop in town, to run errands at school, at the library, at church. No doubt, had I looked harder at their lives, I would have envied them less. It was not my fate to become a woman, so it was easier for me to see the graces. Few of them held jobs outside the home, and those who did filled thankless roles as clerks and waitresses. I didn't see, then, what a prison a house could be, since houses seemed to me brighter, handsomer places than any factory. I did not realize—because such things were never spoken of—how often women suffered from men's bullying. I did learn about the wretchedness of abandoned wives, single mothers, widows; but I also learned about the wretchedness of lone men. Even then I could see how exhausting it was for a mother to cater all day to the needs of young children. But if I had been asked, as a boy, to choose between tending a baby and tending a machine, I think I would have chosen the baby. (Having now tended both, I know I would choose the baby.)

So I was baffled when the women at college accused me and my sex of having cornered the world's pleasures. I think something like my bafflement has been felt by other boys (and by girls as well) who grew up in dirt-poor farm country, in mining country, in black ghettos, in Hispanic barrios, in the shadows of factories, in Third World nations—any place where the fate of men is as grim and bleak as the fate of women. Toilers and warriors. I realize now how ancient these identities are, how deep the tug they exert on men, the undertow of a thousand generations. The miseries I saw, as a boy, in the lives of nearly all men I continue to see in the lives of many—the body-breaking toil, the tedium, the call to be tough, the humiliating powerlessness, the battle for a living and for territory.

When the women I met at college thought about the joys and privileges 20 of men, they did not carry in their minds the sort of men I had known in my childhood. They thought of their fathers, who were bankers, physicians, architects, stockbrokers, the big wheels of the big cities. These fathers rode the train to work or drove cars that cost more than any of my childhood houses. They were attended from morning to night by female helpers, wives, and nurses and secretaries. They were never laid off, never short of cash at month's end, never lined up for welfare. These fathers made decisions that mattered. They ran the world.

The daughters of such men wanted to share in this power, this glory. So did I. They yearned for a say over their future, for jobs worthy of their abilities, for the right to live at peace, unmolested, whole. Yes, I thought, yes yes. The difference between me and these daughters was that they saw me, because of my sex, as destined from birth to become like their fathers, and therefore as an enemy to their desires. But I knew better. I wasn't an enemy, in fact or in feeling. I was an ally. If I had known, then, how to tell them so, would they have believed me? Would they now? ●

The Reader's Presence

1. Sanders begins the essay by jumping directly into a conversation (paragraphs 1–9). What initial effect does this conversation have on the reader? What does Sanders want you to think of him as you read the dialogue? How does he move from the conversation to the body of the essay (paragraphs 10 and following)? How might

you describe the transition? Does Sanders's voice change at paragraph 10? Does Sanders return to Anneke's distinction between the victim and the persecutor (end of paragraph 9)? If so, how? Finally, how do you understand the opening dialogue by the end of the essay, having encountered the full passion of Sanders's beliefs about his legacy of masculinity?

2. Consider the title of the essay. Why does Sanders use the word *carry*? What image does the word convey? How is that image reinforced throughout the essay?

3. **CONNECTIONS:** Read Sanders's essay in connection with Katha Pollitt's "Why Boys Don't Play with Dolls" (page 555). In what ways does Pollitt's view of sex roles reinforce or contradict Sanders's opinions about gender and class? After a careful reading of both essays, do you think Sanders would agree with Pollitt, in whole or in part? Why or why not? To what extent does Sanders endorse or deny conventional sex roles and expectations?

The Writer at Work

SCOTT RUSSELL SANDERS on Writing Essays

The well-known American essayist Scott Russell Sanders is also a professor of English at Indiana University and the author of several novels, short story collections, and books of criticism. In the following passage from "The Singular First Person," which was originally delivered as a keynote talk at an academic conference on the essay at Seton Hall University in 1988, Sanders argues for the relevance of essay writing in a society that increasingly relies on abstract and formulaic language. If you compare this passage with the style of argument Sanders makes in the preceding essay, you will see that he is a writer who practices what he preaches. He also raises an interesting question about the difference between essays and fiction that you might consider when reading the stories in Part 4: Do essayists put more of themselves at risk than novelists and short story writers?

❝ The essay is a haven for the private, idiosyncratic voice in an era of anonymous babble. Like the bland burgers served in their millions along our highways, most language served up in public these days is textureless, tasteless mush. On television, over the phone, in the newspaper, wherever humans bandy words about, we encounter more and more abstractions, more empty formulas. Think of the pablum ladled out by politicians. Think of the fluffy white bread of advertising. Think, Lord help us, of committee reports. In contrast, the essay remains stubbornly concrete and particular: it confronts you with an oil-smeared toilet at the Sunoco station, a red vinyl purse shaped like a valentine heart, a bow-legged dentist hunting deer with an elephant gun. As Orwell forcefully argued,[1] and as dictators seem to agree, such a bypassing of abstractions, such an insistence on the concrete, is a politically subversive act. Clinging to this door, that child, this grief, following the zigzag motions of an inquisitive mind, the essay renews language and clears trash from the springs of thought. A century and a half ago, Emerson called on a new generation of writers to cast off the hand-me-down rhetoric of the day, to "pierce this rotten diction and fasten words again to visible things." The essayist aspires to do just that.

As if all these virtues were not enough to account for a renaissance of this protean genre, the essay has also taken over some of the territory abdicated by contemporary fiction. Pared down to the brittle bones of plot, camouflaged with irony, muttering in brief sentences and grade-school vocabulary, today's fashionable fiction avoids disclosing where the author stands on anything. Most of the trends in the novel and short story over the past twenty years have led away from candor—toward satire, artsy jokes, close-lipped coyness, metafictional hocus-pocus, anything but a direct statement of what the author thinks and feels. If you hide behind enough screens, no one will ever hold you to an opinion or demand from you a coherent vision or take you for a charlatan.

The essay is not fenced round by these literary inhibitions. You may speak without disguise of what moves and worries and excites you. In fact, you had better speak from a region pretty close to the heart, or the reader will detect the wind of phoniness whistling through your hollow phrases. In the essay you may be caught with your pants down, your ignorance and sentimentality showing, while you trot recklessly about on one of your hobbyhorses. You cannot stand back from the action, as Joyce instructed us to do, and pare your fingernails. You cannot palm off your cockamamie notions on some hapless character. If the words you put down are foolish, everyone knows precisely who the fool is.

To our list of the essay's contemporary attractions we should add the perennial ones of verbal play, mental adventure, and sheer anarchic high spirits. The writing of an essay is like finding one's way through a forest without being quite sure what game you are chasing, what landmark you are seeking. You sniff down one path until some heady smell tugs you in a new direction, and then off you go, dodging and circling, lured on by the songs of unfamiliar birds, puzzled by the tracks of strange beasts, leaping from stone to stone across rivers, barking up one tree after another. Much of the pleasure in writing an essay—and, when the writing is any good, the pleasure in reading it—comes from this dodging and leaping, this movement of the mind. It must not be idle movement, however, if the essay is to hold up; it must be driven by deep concerns. The surface of a river is alive with lights and reflections, the breaking of foam over rocks, but beneath that dazzle it is going somewhere. We should expect as much from an essay: the shimmer and play of mind on the surface and in the depths a strong current. **"**

---

[1] See "Politics and the English Language," page 527. —EDS.

Barry Schwartz

THE TYRANNY OF CHOICE

Author and professor **BARRY SCHWARTZ** (b. 1946) has taught psychology and economics at Swarthmore College in Pennsylvania since receiving his PhD from the University of Pennsylvania in 1971. He is currently the Dorwin Cartwright Professor of Social Theory and Social Action, and his classes and seminars focus on the process of thinking and decision making, the interaction of morality and self-interest, work satisfaction, and the intersection of psychology and economics—all subjects found in his many writings and books. In addition to co-writing a number of textbooks on the psychology of learning, memory, and behaviorism, he has written *The Battle for Human Nature: Science, Morality and Modern Life* (1987), *The Costs of Living: How Market Freedom Erodes the Best Things in Life* (2000), and *The Paradox of Choice: Why More Is Less* (2003), in which he explores how choice overload in the marketplace can lead to anxiety and the inability to choose anything at all. Schwartz has written articles for numerous professional journals and mainstream periodicals, including the *New York Times Magazine*, *USA Today*, *Scientific American*, and the *Chronicle of Higher Education*, where his essay, "The Tyranny of Choice," appeared in January 2004.

> Barry Schwartz's book, *The Paradox of Choice: Why More Is Less* (2003), "explores how choice overload in the marketplace can lead to anxiety and the inability to choose anything at all."

THE MODERN UNIVERSITY has become a kind of intellectual shopping mall. Universities offer a wide array of different "goods" and allow, even encourage, students—the "customers"—to shop around until they find what they like. Individual customers are free to "purchase" whatever bundles of knowledge they want, and the university provides whatever its customers demand. In some rather prestigious institutions, this shopping-mall view has been carried to an extreme. In the first few weeks of classes, students sample the merchandise. They go to a class, stay 10 minutes to see what the professor is like, then walk out, often in the middle of the professor's sentence, to try another class. Students come and go in and out of classes just as browsers go in and out of stores in a mall.

This explosion of choice in the university is a reflection of a pervasive social trend. Americans are awash in choice, not only in the courses they take, but also in the products they buy (300 kinds of cereal, 50 different cellphones, thousands of mutual funds) and in virtually all aspects of life. Increasingly, people are free to choose when and how they will work, how they will worship, where they will live, and what they will look like (thanks to liposuction, Botox, and cosmetic surgery of every description), and what kind of romantic relationships they will have. Further, freedom of choice is greatly enhanced by increased affluence. In the last 40 years, the inflation-adjusted, per capita income of Americans has more than doubled. The proportion of homes with dishwashers has increased from 9 to 50 percent, with clothes dryers from 20 to 70 percent, and with air-conditioning from 15 to 73 percent. And of course, no one had cable TV, home computers, or the Internet in 1964. This increased affluence contributes to freedom of choice by giving people the means to act on their various goals and desires, whatever they may be.

Does increased affluence and increased choice mean we have more happy people? Not at all. Three recently published books—by the psychologist David Myers, the political scientist Robert E. Lane, and the journalist Gregg Easterbrook—point out how the growth of material affluence has not brought with it an increase in subjective well-being. Indeed, they argue that we are actually experiencing a *decrease* in well-being. In the last 30 years, the number of Americans describing themselves as "very happy" declined by 5 percent, which means that about 14 million fewer people report being very happy today than in 1974. And, as a recent study published in the *Journal of the American Medical Association* indicates, the rate of serious clinical depression has more than tripled over the last two generations, and increased by perhaps a factor of 10 from 1900 to 2000. Suicide rates are also up, not only in the United States, but in almost every developed country. And both serious depression and suicide are occurring among people younger than ever before. Deans at virtually every college and university in the United States can testify to this malaise, as they witness a demand for psychological services that they are unable to meet.

Why are people increasingly unhappy even as they experience greater material abundance and freedom of choice? Recent psychological research suggests that increased choice may itself be part of the problem.

It may seem implausible that there can be too much choice. As a matter of logic, it would appear that adding options will make no one worse off and is bound to make someone better off. If you're content choosing among three different kinds of breakfast cereal, or six television stations, you can simply ignore the dozens or hundreds that get added to your supermarket shelves or cable provider's menu. Meanwhile, one of those new cereals or TV stations may be just what some other person was hoping for. Given the indisputable fact that choice is good for human well-being, it seems only logical that if some choice is good, more choice is better.

Logically true, yes. Psychologically true, no. My colleagues and I, along with other researchers, have begun amassing evidence—both in the laboratory and in the field—that increased choice can lead to *decreased* well-being. This is especially true for people we have termed "maximizers," people whose goal is to get the best possible result when they make decisions. Choice overload is also a problem for people we call "satisficers," people who seek only "good enough" results from their choices, but the problem is greatly magnified for maximizers. Much of the relevant research is summarized in my book, *The Paradox of Choice: Why More Is Less.* Here are some examples:

- Shoppers who confront a display of 30 jams or varieties of gourmet chocolate are less likely to purchase *any* than when they encounter a display of six.

- Students given 30 topics from which to choose to write an extra-credit essay are less likely to write one than those given six. And if they do write one, it tends to be of lower quality.

- The majority of medical patients do not want the decision authority that the canons of medical ethics have thrust upon them. Responsibility for medical decisions looks better to people in prospect than in actuality: Sixty-five percent of respondents say that if they were to get cancer, they would want to be in charge of treatment decisions, but among those who actually have cancer, only 12 percent want that control and responsibility.

- The more funds employers offer their employees in 401(k) retirement plans, the less likely the employees are to invest in any, even though in many cases, failing to do so costs them employer-matching funds of up to several thousand dollars a year.

- When maximizers, as opposed to satisficers, go shopping for big items or small ones, they spend more time looking, have a harder time deciding, look around more at what others are buying, and are less satisfied with their purchases.

- Maximizing college seniors send out more résumés, investigate more different fields, go on more job interviews, and get better, higher-paying jobs than satisfiers. But they are less satisfied with their jobs, and are much more stressed, anxious, frustrated, and unhappy in the process.

These examples paint a common picture: Increasing options does not increase well-being, especially for maximizers, even when it enables choosers to do better by some objective standard. We have identified several processes that help explain why increased choice decreases satisfaction. Greater choice:

- Increases the burden of gathering information to make a wise decision.

- Increases the likelihood that people will regret the decisions they make.

- Increases the likelihood that people will *anticipate* regretting the decision they make, with the result that they can't make a decision at all.

- Increases the feeling of missed opportunities, as people encounter the attractive features of one option after another that they are rejecting.

- Increases expectations about how good the chosen option should be. Since assessments of the quality of a choice are almost always made relative to one's expectations, as expectations rise, actual choices have a rising standard to meet if they are to produce satisfaction.

- Increases the chances that people will blame themselves when their choices fail to live up to expectations. After all, with so many options out there, there is really no excuse for a disappointing choice.

To illustrate these last two points, I recall buying a bottle of wine to accompany dinner when I was vacationing with my family in a seaside cottage in a small town in Oregon. The tiny general store had about five options from which to choose. The wine I chose wasn't very good, but I didn't expect it to be, and I knew that I couldn't really have done much better. Contrast that with how it would feel to bring home a disappointing bottle of wine from a store that offered thousands of bottles from which to choose.

What are the implications of an abundance of choice for higher education today? College students don't have to worry about choosing 401(k) plans, and most of them don't have major health issues to make decisions about. Nonetheless, the world of the modern college student is so laden with choice, much of it extremely consequential, that for many, it has become overwhelming, perhaps contributing to the rush of students to university counseling services.

When I went to college, 35 years ago, there were almost two years' worth 10 of general-education requirements that all students had to complete. We had *some* choices among courses that met those requirements, but they were rather narrow. Almost every department had a single, introductory course that prepared the student for more advanced work in the field. You could be fairly certain, if you ran into a fellow student you didn't know, that the two of you would have at least a year's worth of courses in common to discuss. In the shopping mall that is the modern university, the chances that any two students have significant intellectual experiences in common are much reduced.

About 30 years ago, somewhat dismayed that their students no longer shared enough common intellectual experiences, the Harvard faculty revised its general-education requirements to form a "core curriculum." With this new curriculum (which is currently undergoing another revision), students take at least one course in each of 11 different broad areas of inquiry. But among those areas, there are dozens and dozens of courses from which to choose. What are the odds that two random students will have courses in common to discuss?

At the advanced end of the curriculum, Harvard offers about 40 majors. For students with interdisciplinary interests, these can be combined into an almost endless array of joint majors. If that doesn't do the trick, students can create their own degree plan. And within majors, at least many of them, internal structure has largely disappeared. Students can begin almost anywhere in the curriculum and end almost anywhere.

Harvard is not unusual. Princeton offers its students a choice of several hundred courses from which to satisfy its general-education requirements.

Stanford, which has a larger student body, offers even more. Even at my small college, Swarthmore, with only 1,350 students, we offer about 120 courses to meet our version of the general-education requirement, from which students must select nine. And don't think that this range of choices is peculiar to elite, private institutions. At Pennsylvania State University, for example, liberal-arts students can choose from more than 40 majors and from hundreds of courses intended to meet basic requirements.

Within classes, the digital revolution has made access to information unbelievably easy. The Internet and the "digital library" can be a term-paper writer's blessing. But they can also be a curse. With so much information so readily available, when do you stop looking? There is no excuse for failing to examine all of it.

And outside the classroom, the range of recreational and extracurricu-   15
lar activities afforded to students has become mind-boggling. As elite universities compete with one another for elite students (an example of social waste that I think rivals the SUV), the institutions engage in an arms race of amenity provision—fitness centers, indoor rock-climbing walls, hot tubs that accommodate dozens of people at once, espresso bars—in their effort to attract every student they want. The result is a set of choices of things to do outside of class that makes one's head spin.

There are many benefits to expanded educational opportunities. The traditional bodies of knowledge transmitted from teachers to students in the past were constraining and often myopic. The tastes and interests of the idiosyncratic students often were stifled and frustrated. In the modern university, each individual student is free to pursue almost any interest, without having to be harnessed to what his intellectual ancestors thought was worth knowing. Moreover, the advent of the digital age has opened up the intellectual world to all students, even those at resource-poor institutions.

But this freedom comes at a price. Now, students are required to make many choices about education that will affect them for the rest of their lives, and they are forced to make them at a point in their intellectual development when many students lack the wisdom to choose intelligently. In my own experience I see this manifested in several ways. Advisees ask me to approve course selections that have no rhyme or reason behind them and that the advisees themselves can't justify. Students are eager to have double and triple majors, partly, I know, to pad their résumés, but also because they can't figure out which discipline they really want to commit to. And I learned some time ago that "What are you doing when you graduate?" is not a friendly question to ask many college seniors.

In addition, students are faced with all this curricular choice while also trying to figure out what kinds of people they are going to be. Matters of ethnic, religious, and sexual identity are up for grabs. So are issues of romantic intimacy (to marry or not to marry; to have kids or not to have kids; to have kids early or to wait until careers are established). Students can live and work anywhere after they graduate, and in a wired world, they can work at any time, from any place. Of course it is true that students have always had to make these kinds of life decisions. College is an unsettled, and often unsettling, time. But in the past, in virtually each of these areas of life, there was a "default" option that was so powerful that many decisions didn't *feel* like decisions, because alternatives to the default weren't seriously considered. Nowadays, almost nothing is decided by default.

The result is a generation of students who use university counseling services and antidepressants in record numbers, and who provide places like Starbucks with the most highly educated minimum-wage work force in the world, as they bide their time hoping that the answer to the "what should I be when I grow up" question will eventually emerge. Choice overload is certainly not the only reason for the anxiety and uncertainty experienced by modern college students, but I believe it is an important one. I believe that by offering our students this much freedom of choice, we are doing them no favor. Indeed, I think that this obsession with choice constitutes an abdication of responsibility by university faculty members and administrators to provide college students with the guidance they badly need.

In an important respect, the "liberation" of the university experience   20 mirrors the embrace of choice in American society at large. The dominant political trend in the last 25 years, influenced by the principles and assumptions of neoclassical economics, has been to stop trying to have the government provide services that serve the welfare of citizens and instead offer citizens choices so that each of us can pursue our own welfare. The push to privatize Social Security, to offer senior citizens choice among prescription-drug plans, and to offer parents choice in the public education their children receive—these are all instances of the view that choice cannot help but make people better off. And so it is with the modern university. What I have tried to indicate is that though all this choice no doubt makes *some* people better off, it makes *many* people worse off, even when their choices work out well.

If enhanced freedom of choice and increased affluence don't enhance well-being, what does? The most important factor seems to be close social relations. People who are married, who have good friends, and who are close to their families are happier than those who are not. People who participate in religious communities are happier than those who do not. Being connected to others seems to be more important to well-being than being rich or "keeping your options open."

In the context of this discussion of choice, it is important to note that, in many ways, social ties actually *decrease* freedom of choice. Marriage, for example, is a commitment to a particular other person that curtails freedom of choice of sexual or emotional partners. Serious friendship also entails weighty responsibilities and obligations that at times may limit one's own freedom. The same is true, obviously, of family. And most religious institutions call on their members to live their lives in a certain way, and to take responsibility for the well-being of their fellow congregants. So, counterintuitive as it may appear, what seems to contribute most to happiness binds us rather than liberates us.

Yet more than a quarter of Americans report being lonely, and loneliness seems to come not from being alone, but from lack of intimacy. We spend less time visiting with neighbors. We spend less time visiting with our parents, and much less time visiting with other relatives. Partly this is because we *have* less time, since we are busy trying to determine what choices to make in other areas of life. But partly this is because close social relations have themselves become matters of choice. As Robert Lane writes: "What was once given by neighborhood and work now must be achieved; people have had to make their own friends . . . and actively cultivate their own family connections." In other words, our social fabric is no longer a birthright but has become a series of deliberate and demanding choices.

Universities should acknowledge the role they have played in creating a world of choice overload and move from being part of the problem to being a part of the solution. The "culture wars" over the canon that rocked college campuses for years have subsided, and most of us were not sorry to see them go. It is deeply troubling to face up to the fact that you and your colleagues can't agree on something as basic as what a college curriculum should consist of. There were no winners in these wars; they subsided, I think, because people got tired of fighting them. And they subsided because giving students choice seemed like a benign resolution of what were sometimes virulent conflicts. Some choice is good, we thought, so more choice is better. Let students choose and we never have to figure out what to choose for them.

But offering more choice is *not* benign. It is a major source of stress,   25
uncertainty, anxiety—even misery. It is not serving our students well. They would be better served by a faculty and an institution that offered choice within limits, freedom within constraints. The poet and essayist Katha Pollitt observed some years ago that the real reason why battles over the curriculum were so intense—the reason that the stakes seemed so high—is that faculty members knew that for the vast majority of students, the last serious book they would *ever* read would be the last book they read in their college careers. I think we are less likely to turn our students off to the life of the mind if we offer them curricular options that are well structured and coherent than if we simply let them choose whatever they want on their own.

There is a *New Yorker* cartoon that depicts a parent goldfish and an offspring in a small goldfish bowl. "You can be anything you want to be—no limits," says the myopic parent, not realizing how limited an existence the fishbowl allows. I'd like to suggest that perhaps the parent is not so myopic. Freedom without limits, choice within constraints, is indeed liberating. But if the fishbowl gets shattered—if the constraints disappear—freedom of choice can turn into a tyranny of choice. ●

The Reader's Presence

1. Schwartz, a professor of psychology and economics at Swarthmore College, begins his essay with the provocative assertion: "The modern university has become a kind of intellectual shopping mall." Explore the nature of this metaphor. What aspects

of it do you find most—and least—convincing? Explain why. If "increased choice" leads to a "*decrease* in well-being," as Schwartz argues (paragraph 3), then to what extent should we decrease curriculum choice to increase our educational well-being? Which parts of Schwartz's essay support eliminating our opportunity to choose college courses? Would Schwartz endorse the recommendation that all students should take the same classes through their undergraduate years? Explain why or why not. Develop a counterargument that defends increased choice, taking care to reply to each of Schwartz's points. In your judgment, what are some reasons to keep a university as "a kind of intellectual shopping mall"?

2. Identify—and comment on the effectiveness of—the different kinds of evidence Schwartz draws on to make his points (for example, statistics, stories, logic). In what circumstances—and why—does he use one kind of proof rather than another? For example, why do the statistics that begin the essay disappear toward the end? Which kinds of proof are the most convincing to support his points? Reread Schwartz's account of choosing a bottle of wine. These are personal facts, but this is the only personal story Schwartz tells. Why does he choose to tell it here? How is it more or less persuasive than citing another statistic or research study?

3. **CONNECTIONS:** What might Schwartz say about people who have no choices? For example, read Lars Eighner's "On Dumpster Diving" (page 377), which partly tells about what happens when we can no longer exercise choice about where we get our food and what we eat. As Schwartz predicts, Eighner comes to "a healthy state of mind" by losing his material choices (food, cable channels, etc.). But explain the extent to which Eighner's mental well-being increases because he has lost his choices.

Leslie Marmon Silko

IN THE COMBAT ZONE

Poet, novelist, screenwriter, and storyteller **LESLIE MARMON SILKO** (b. 1948) is of mixed heritage, part Pueblo Indian, part Mexican, and part white. She was raised on the Laguna Pueblo and educated at the University of New Mexico, where she taught English for many years. Her published work includes *Storyteller* (1981), a montage of stories, legends, poems, and photographs; *Sacred Water: Narratives and Pictures* (1993), an illustrated autobiography; *Yellow Woman and a Beauty of the Spirit* (1996), a collection of essays; *Love Poem: Slim Man Canyon* (1999); and the novels *Almanac of the Dead* (1991) and *Garden in the*

|||||||||||||||||||||||||||||||||||||||||||||||||||||||||||||||||||||||||||||||||||||||||||||||||||||||||||||||||||||||||||||||||||||||||||||||||||||||

Dunes (1999). A collection of rare interviews with Silko, *Conversations with Leslie Marmon Silko*, edited by Ellen L. Arnold, was published in 2000. "In the Combat Zone" appeared in *Hungry Mind Review* in 1995. In 1981, Silko was awarded a MacArthur Fellowship prize for her writing. She has taught in New Mexico, Alaska, and Arizona and holds academic appointments at both the universities of New Mexico and Arizona.

> When asked by an interviewer why she writes, Leslie Marmon Silko replied, "I don't know what I know until it comes out in narrative."

When asked by an interviewer why she writes, she replied, "I don't know what I know until it comes out in narrative." Speaking specifically of the process of composing her novel *Almanac of the Dead*, she said, "It's like a do-it-yourself psychoanalysis. It's sort of dangerous to be a novelist . . . you're working with language and all kinds of things can escape with the words of a narrative."

WOMEN SELDOM DISCUSS our wariness or the precautions we take after dark each time we leave the apartment, car, or office to go on the most brief errand. We take for granted that we are targeted as easy prey by muggers, rapists, and serial killers. This is our lot as women in the United States. We try to avoid going anywhere alone after dark, although economic necessity sends women out night after night. We do what must be done, but always we are alert, on guard, and ready. We have to be aware of persons walking on the sidewalk behind us; we have to pay attention to others who board an elevator we're on. We try to avoid all staircases and deserted parking garages when we are alone. Constant vigilance requires considerable energy and concentration seldom required of men.

I used to assume that most men were aware of this fact of women's lives, but I was wrong. They may notice our reluctance to drive at night to the convenience store alone, but they don't know or don't want to know the experience of a woman out alone at night. Men who have been in combat know the feeling of being a predator's target, but it is difficult for men to admit that we women live our entire lives in a combat zone. Men have the power to end violence against women in the home, but they feel helpless to protect women from violent strangers. Because men feel guilt and anger at their inability to shoulder responsibility for the safety of their wives, sisters, and daughters, we don't often discuss random acts of violence against women.

When we were children, my sisters and I used to go to Albuquerque with my father. Sometimes strangers would tell my father it was too bad that he had three girls and no sons. My father, who has always preferred the company of women, used to reply that he was glad to have girls and not boys, because he might not get along as well with boys. Furthermore, he'd say, "My girls can do anything your boys can do, and my girls can do it better." He had in mind, of course, shooting and hunting.

When I was six years old, my father took me along as he hunted deer; he showed me how to walk quietly, to move along, and then to stop and listen carefully before taking another step. A year later, he traded a pistol for a little single shot .22 rifle just my size.

He took me and my younger sisters down to the dump by the river and 5 taught us how to shoot. We rummaged through the trash for bottles and glass jars; it was great fun to take aim at a pickle jar and watch it shatter. If the Río San Jose had water running in it, we threw bottles for moving targets in the muddy current. My father told us that a .22 bullet can travel a mile, so we had to be careful where we aimed. The river was a good place because it was below the villages and away from the houses; the high clay riverbanks wouldn't let any bullets stray. Gun safety was drilled into us. We were cautioned about other children whose parents might not teach them properly; if we ever saw another child with a gun, we knew to get away. Guns were not toys. My father did not approve of BB guns because they were classified as toys. I had a .22 rifle when I was seven years old. If I felt like shooting, all I had to do was tell my parents where I was going, take my rifle and a box of .22 shells and go. I was never tempted to shoot at birds or animals because whatever was killed had to be eaten. Now, I realize how odd this must seem; a seven-year-old with a little .22 rifle and a box of ammunition, target shooting alone at the river. But that was how people lived at Laguna when I was growing up; children were given responsibilities from an early age.

Laguna Pueblo people hunted deer for winter meat. When I was thirteen, I carried George Pearl's saddle carbine, a .30–30, and hunted deer for the first time. When I was fourteen, I killed my first male deer buck with one shot through the heart.

Guns were for target shooting and guns were for hunting, but also I knew that Grandma Lily carried a little purse gun with her whenever she drove alone to Albuquerque or Los Lunas. One night my mother and my grandmother were driving the fifty miles from Albuquerque to Laguna down Route 66 when three men in a car tried to force my grandmother's car off the highway. Route 66 was not so heavily traveled as Interstate 40 is now, and there were many long stretches of highway where no other car passed for minutes on end. Payrolls at the Jackpile Uranium Mine were large in the 1950s, and my mother or my grandmother had to bring home thousands from the bank in Albuquerque to cash the miners' checks on paydays.

After that night, my father bought my mother a pink nickel-plated snub-nose .22 revolver with a white bone grip. Grandma Lily carried a tiny Beretta as black as her prayer book. As my sisters and I got older, my father taught us to handle and shoot handguns, revolvers mostly, because back then, semiautomatic pistols were not as reliable—they frequently jammed. I will never forget the day my father told us three girls that we never had to let a man hit us or terrorize us because no matter how big and strong the man was, a gun in our hand equalized all differences of size and strength.

Much has been written about violence in the home and spousal abuse. I wish to focus instead on violence from strangers toward women because this form of violence terrifies women more, despite the fact that most women are murdered by a spouse, relative, fellow employee, or next-door neighbor, not a stranger. Domestic violence kills many more women and children than strangers kill, but domestic violence also follows more predictable patterns and is more familiar: He comes home drunk and she knows what comes next. A good deal of the terror of a stranger's attack comes from its suddenness and unexpectedness. Attacks by strangers occur with enough frequency that battered women and children often cite their fears of such attacks as reasons for remaining in abusive domestic situations. They fear the violence they imagine strangers will inflict on them more than they fear the abusive home. More than one feminist has pointed out that rapists and serial killers help keep the patriarchy securely in place.

An individual woman may be terrorized by her spouse, but women are   10 not sufficiently terrorized that we avoid marriage. Yet many women I know, including myself, try to avoid going outside of their homes alone after dark. Big deal, you say; well, yes, it is a big deal since most lectures, performances, and films are presented at night; so are dinners and other social events. Women out alone at night who are assaulted by strangers are put on trial by public opinion: Any woman out alone after dark is asking for trouble. Presently, for millions of women of all socioeconomic backgrounds, sundown is lockdown. We are prisoners of violent strangers.

Daylight doesn't necessarily make the streets safe for women. In the early 1980s, a rapist operated in Tucson in the afternoon near the University of Arizona campus. He often accosted two women at once, forced them into residential alleys, then raped each one with a knife to her throat and forced the other to watch. Afterward the women said that part of the horror of their attack was that all around them, everything appeared normal. They could see people inside their houses and cars going down the street—all around them life was going on as usual while their lives were being changed forever.

The afternoon rapist was not the only rapist in Tucson at that time; there were the prime-time rapist, the potbellied rapist, and the apologetic rapist all operating in Tucson in the 1980s. The prime-time rapist was actually two men who invaded comfortable foothills homes during television prime time when residents were preoccupied with television and eating dinner. The prime-time rapists terrorized entire families; they raped the women and sometimes they raped the men. Family members were forced to go to automatic bank machines to bring back cash to end the ordeal. Potbelly rapist and apologetic rapist need little comment, except to note that the apologetic rapist was good looking, well educated, and smart enough to break out of jail for one last rape followed by profuse apologies and his capture in the University of Arizona library. Local papers recounted details about Tucson's last notorious rapist, the red bandanna rapist. In the late 1970s, this rapist attacked more than twenty women over a three-year period, and Tucson police were powerless to stop him. Then one night, the rapist broke into a midtown home where the lone resident, a woman, shot him four times in the chest with a .38 caliber revolver.

In midtown Tucson, on a weekday afternoon, I was driving down Campbell Avenue to the pet store. Suddenly the vehicle behind me began to weave into my lane, so I beeped the horn politely. The vehicle swerved back to its lane, but then in my rearview mirror I saw the small late-model truck change lanes and begin to follow my car very closely. I drove a few blocks without looking in the rearview mirror, but in my sideview mirror I saw the compact truck was right behind me. OK. Some motorists stay upset for two or three blocks, some require ten blocks or more to recover their senses. Stoplight after stoplight, when I glanced into the rearview mirror I saw the man—in his early thirties, tall, white, brown hair, and dark glasses. This guy must not have a job if he has the time to follow me for miles—oh, ohhh! No beast more dangerous in the U.S.A. than an unemployed white man.

At this point I had to make a decision: Do I forget about the trip to the pet store and head for the police station downtown, four miles away? Why should I have to let this stranger dictate my schedule for the afternoon? The man might dare to follow me to the police station, but by the time I reach the front door of the station, he'd be gone. No crime was committed; no Arizona law forbids tailgating someone for miles or for turning into a parking lot behind them. What could the police do? I had no license plate number to report because Arizona requires only one license plate, on the rear bumper of the vehicle. Anyway, I was within a block of the pet store where I knew I could get help from the pet store owners. I would feel better about this incident if it was not allowed to ruin my trip to the pet store.

The guy was right on my rear bumper; if I'd had to stop suddenly for any   15 reason, there'd have been a collision. I decide I will not stop even if he does ram into the rear of my car. I study this guy's face in my rearview mirror; six feet two inches tall, 175 pounds, medium complexion, short hair, trimmed moustache. He thinks he can intimidate me because I am a woman, five feet five inches tall, 140 pounds. But I am not afraid, I am furious. I refuse to be intimidated. I won't play his game. I can tell by the face I see in the mirror this guy has done this before, he enjoys using his truck to menace lone women.

I keep thinking he will quit, or he will figure that he's scared me enough, but he seems to sense that I am not afraid. It's true. I am not afraid because years ago my father taught my sisters and me that we did not have to be afraid. He'll give up when I turn into the parking lot outside the pet store, I think. But I watch in my rearview mirror; he's right on my rear bumper. As his truck turns into the parking lot behind my car, I reach over and open the glove compartment. I take out the holster with my .38 special and lay it on the car seat beside me.

I turned my car into a parking spot so quickly that I was facing my stalker who had momentarily stopped his truck and was watching me. I slid the .38 out of its holster onto my lap. I watched the stranger's face, trying to determine whether he would jump out of his truck with a baseball bat or gun and come after me. I felt calm. No pounding heart or rapid breathing. My early experience deer hunting had prepared me well. I did not panic because I felt I could stop him if he tried to harm me. I was in no hurry. I sat in the car and waited to see what choice my stalker would make. I looked directly at him without fear because I had my .38 and I was ready to use it. The expression on my face must have been unfamiliar to him; he was used to seeing terror in the eyes of the women he followed. The expression on my face communicated a warning: If he approached the car window, I'd kill him.

He took a last look at me then sped away. I stayed in my car until his truck disappeared in the traffic of Campbell Avenue.

I walked into the pet store shaken. I had felt able to protect myself throughout the incident, but it left me emotionally drained and exhausted. The stranger had only pursued me—how much worse to be battered or raped.

Years before, I was unarmed the afternoon that two drunken deer hunt-   20
ers threatened to shoot me off my horse with razor-edged hunting arrows from fiberglass crossbows. I was riding a colt on a national park trail near my home in the Tucson Mountains. These young white men in their late twenties were complete strangers who might have shot me if the colt had not galloped away erratically bucking and leaping—a moving target too difficult for the drunken bow hunters to aim at. The colt brought me to my ranch house where I called the county sheriff's office and the park ranger. I live in a sparsely populated area where my nearest neighbor is a quarter-mile away. I was afraid the men might have followed me back to my house so I took the .44 magnum out from under my pillow and strapped it around my waist until the sheriff or park ranger arrived. Forty-five minutes later, the park ranger arrived; the deputy sheriff arrived fifteen minutes after him. The drunken bow hunters were apprehended in the national park and arrested for illegally hunting; their bows and arrows were seized as evidence for the duration of bow hunting season. In southern Arizona that is enough punishment; I didn't want to take a chance of stirring up additional animosity with these men because I lived alone then; I chose not to make a complaint about their threatening words and gestures. I did not feel that I backed away by not pressing charges; I feared that if I pressed assault charges against these men, they would feel that I was challenging them to all-out war. I did not want to have to kill either of them if they came after me, as I thought they might. With my marksmanship and my .243 caliber hunting rifle from the old days, I am confident that I could stop idiots like these. But to have to take the life of another person is a terrible experience I will always try to avoid.

It isn't height or weight or strength that make women easy targets; from infancy women are taught to be self-sacrificing, passive victims. I was taught differently. Women have the right to protect themselves from death or bodily harm. By becoming strong and potentially lethal individuals, women destroy the fantasy that we are sitting ducks for predatory strangers.

In a great many cultures, women are taught to depend on others, not themselves, for protection from bodily harm. Women are not taught to defend themselves from strangers because fathers and husbands fear the consequences themselves. In the United States, women depend on the courts and the police, but as many women have learned the hard way, the police cannot be outside your house twenty-four hours a day. I don't want more police. More police on the streets will not protect women. A few policemen are rapists and killers of women themselves; their uniforms and squad cars give them an advantage. No, I will be responsible for my own safety, thank you.

Women need to decide who has the primary responsibility for the health and safety of their bodies. We don't trust the State to manage our reproductive organs, yet most of us blindly trust that the State will protect us (and our reproductive organs) from predatory strangers. One look at the rape and murder statistics for women (excluding domestic incidents) and it is clear that the government FAILS to protect women from the violence of strangers. Some may cry out for a "stronger" State, more police, mandatory sentences, and swifter executions. Over the years we have seen the U.S. prison population become the largest in the world, executions take place every week now, inner-city communities are occupied by the National Guard, and people of color are harassed by police, but guess what? A woman out alone, night or day, is confronted with more danger of random violence from strangers than ever before. As the U.S. economy continues "to downsize," and the good jobs disappear forever, our urban and rural landscapes will include more desperate, angry men with nothing to lose.

Only women can put a stop to the "open season" on women by strangers. Women are TAUGHT to be easy targets by their mothers, aunts, and grandmothers, who themselves were taught that "a woman doesn't kill" or "a woman doesn't learn how to use a weapon." Women must learn how to take aggressive action individually, apart from the police and the courts.

Presently, twenty-one states issue permits to carry concealed weapons;   25
most states require lengthy gun safety courses and a police security check before issuing a permit. Inexpensive but excellent gun safety and self-defense courses designed for women are also available from every quality gun dealer who hopes to sell you a handgun at the end of the course. Those who object to firearms need trained companion dogs or collectives of six or more women to escort one another day and night. We must destroy the myth that women are born to be easy targets. ▨

The Reader's Presence

1. What does Silko mean by a "combat zone" (paragraph 2)? What is the origin of the term? How does she apply it to women's experiences? Do you think the term is applicable? What behavior does the term legitimize? Why do you think she concentrates on violence from strangers instead of domestic violence?

2. Why do you think Silko introduces stories about hunting experiences? In what ways do those experiences shape her background? Do you think they have shaped her present attitude? How do the experiences help reinforce her point about gun ownership? In what ways do they make her more qualified to speak on the issue?

3. **CONNECTIONS:**   In her opening two paragraphs, Silko describes the precautions women take in public every day, of which men are often ignorant. Read Brent Staples's "Just Walk on By" (page 217), which details his experiences of being stereotyped as a threat. How do you think Staples and Silko might discuss this idea of safety? Does Staples show himself to be aware of women's safety concerns? If so, in what ways? What might Silko say in response to Staples's feelings about "being perceived as dangerous"?

Peter Singer
THE SINGER SOLUTION TO WORLD POVERTY

PETER SINGER, born in Melbourne, Australia, in 1946, has had a long career as the dean of the animal rights movement and is one of today's most controversial contemporary philosophers. He has taught at the University of Colorado at Boulder and the University of California at Irvine and is now the DeCamp Professor of Bioethics at Princeton University's Center for Human Values. His book *Animal Liberation*, first published in 1975 and reprinted many times since, has become a basic sourcebook for animal rights activists. His *Practical Ethics* (1979) is one of the most widely recognized works of applied ethics. He has also written *Rethinking Life and Death: The Collapse of Our Traditional Ethics*, which received an award from the National Book Council in 1995. In 2000, Singer published *Writings on an Ethical Life*

> "For Singer, living ethically is living a meaningful life. It is a life that makes a difference in the world. It is a life that reduces the sum total of suffering."

and *A Darwinian Left: Politics, Evolution, and Cooperation*, which argues that the left should replace Marx with Darwin. Singer's other books include *One World: The Ethics of Globalization* (2002), *Pushing Time Away: My Grandfather and the Tragedy of Jewish Vienna* (2003), and *The President of Good & Evil: Questioning the Ethics of George W. Bush* (2004). He co-wrote with Jim Mason *The Ethics of What We Eat: Why Our Food Choices Matter* (2006) and co-edited the *Cambridge Textbook of Bioethics*, published in 2008. "The Singer Solution to World Poverty" was first published in the *New York Times* in September 1999.

A reviewer of *Writings on an Ethical Life* commented: "Singer argues that value judgments should be matters of rational scrutiny and not matters of taste about which argument is futile. . . . For Singer, living ethically is living a meaningful life. It is a life that makes a difference in the world. It is a life that reduces the sum total of suffering."

IN THE BRAZILIAN FILM *Central Station*, Dora is a retired schoolteacher who makes ends meet by sitting at the station writing letters for illiterate people. Suddenly she has an opportunity to pocket $1,000. All she has to do is persuade a homeless nine-year-old boy to follow her to an address she has been given. (She is told he will be adopted by wealthy foreigners.) She delivers the boy, gets the money, spends some of it on a television set, and settles down to enjoy her new acquisition. Her neighbor spoils the fun, however, by telling her that the boy was too old to be adopted—he will be killed and his organs sold for transplantation. Perhaps Dora knew this all along, but after her neighbor's plain speaking, she spends a troubled night. In the morning Dora resolves to take the boy back.

Suppose Dora had told her neighbor that it is a tough world, other people have nice new TVs too, and if selling the kid is the only way she can get one, well, he was only a street kid. She would then have become, in the eyes of the audience, a monster. She redeems herself only by being prepared to bear considerable risks to save the boy.

At the end of the movie, in cinemas in the affluent nations of the world, people who would have been quick to condemn Dora if she had not rescued the boy go home to places far more comfortable than her apartment. In fact, the average family in the United States spends almost one-third of its income on things that are no more necessary to them than Dora's new TV was to her. Going out to nice restaurants, buying new clothes because the old ones are no longer stylish, vacationing at beach resorts—so much of our income is spent on things not essential to the preservation of our lives and health. Donated to one of a number of charitable agencies, that money could mean the difference between life and death for children in need.

All of which raises a question: In the end, what is the ethical distinction between a Brazilian who sells a homeless child to organ peddlers and an American who already has a TV and upgrades to a better one—knowing that the money could be donated to an organization that would use it to save the lives of kids in need?

Of course, there are several differences between the two situations that could support different moral judgments about them. For one thing, to be able to consign a child to death when he is standing right in front of you takes a chilling kind of heartlessness; it is much easier to ignore an appeal for money to help children you will never meet. Yet for a utilitarian philosopher like myself—that is, one who judges whether acts are right or wrong by their consequences—if the upshot of the American's failure to donate the money is that one more kid dies on the streets of a Brazilian city, then it is,

5

in some sense, just as bad as selling the kid to the organ peddlers. But one doesn't need to embrace my utilitarian ethic to see that, at the very least, there is a troubling incongruity in being so quick to condemn Dora for taking the child to the organ peddlers while, at the same time, not regarding the American consumer's behavior as raising a serious moral issue.

In his 1996 book, *Living High and Letting Die*, the New York University philosopher Peter Unger presented an ingenious series of imaginary examples designed to probe our intuitions about whether it is wrong to live well without giving substantial amounts of money to help people who are hungry, malnourished, or dying from easily treatable illnesses like diarrhea. Here's my paraphrase of one of these examples:

Bob is close to retirement. He has invested most of his savings in a very rare and valuable old car, a Bugatti, which he has not been able to insure. The Bugatti is his pride and joy. In addition to the pleasure he gets from driving and caring for his car, Bob knows that its rising market value means that he will always be able to sell it and live comfortably after retirement. One day when Bob is out for a drive, he parks the Bugatti near the end of a railway siding and goes for a walk up the track. As he does so, he sees that a runaway train, with no one aboard, is running down the railway track. Looking farther down the track, he sees the small figure of a child very likely to be killed by the runaway train. He can't stop the train and the child is too far away to warn of the danger, but he can throw a switch that will divert the train down the siding where his Bugatti is parked. Then nobody will be killed—but the train will destroy his Bugatti. Thinking of his joy in owning the car and the financial security it represents, Bob decides not to throw the switch. The child is killed. For many years to come, Bob enjoys owning his Bugatti and the financial security it represents.

Bob's conduct, most of us will immediately respond, was gravely wrong. Unger agrees. But then he reminds us that we, too, have opportunities to save the lives of children. We can give to organizations like Unicef or Oxfam America. How much would we have to give one of these organizations to have a high probability of saving the life of a child threatened by easily preventable diseases? (I do not believe that children are more worth saving than adults, but since no one can argue that children have brought their poverty on themselves, focusing on them simplifies the issues.) Unger called up some experts and used the information they provided to offer some plausible estimates that include the cost of raising money, administrative expenses, and the cost of delivering aid where it is most needed. By his calculation, $200 in donations would help a sickly two-year-old transform into a healthy six-year-old—offering safe passage through childhood's most dangerous years. To show how practical philosophical argument can be, Unger even tells his readers that they can easily donate funds by using their credit card and calling one of these toll-free numbers: (800) 367-5437 for Unicef; (800) 693-2687 for Oxfam America.

Now you, too, have the information you need to save a child's life. How should you judge yourself if you don't do it? Think again about Bob and his Bugatti. Unlike Dora, Bob did not have to look into the eyes of the child he was sacrificing for his own material comfort. The child was a complete stranger to him and too far away to relate to in an intimate, personal way. Unlike Dora, too, he did not mislead the child or initiate the chain of events imperiling him. In all these respects, Bob's situation resembles that of people able but unwilling to donate to overseas aid and differs from Dora's situation.

If you still think that it was very wrong of Bob not to throw the switch   10
that would have diverted the train and saved the child's life, then it is hard to see how you could deny that it is also very wrong not to send money to one of the organizations listed above. Unless, that is, there is some morally important difference between the two situations that I have overlooked.

Is it the practical uncertainties about whether aid will really reach the people who need it? Nobody who knows the world of overseas aid can doubt that such uncertainties exist. But Unger's figure of $200 to save a child's life was reached after he had made conservative assumptions about the proportion of the money donated that will actually reach its target.

One genuine difference between Bob and those who can afford to donate to overseas aid organizations but don't is that only Bob can save the child on the tracks, whereas there are hundreds of millions of people who can give $200 to overseas aid organizations. The problem is that most of them aren't doing it. Does this mean that it is all right for you not to do it?

Suppose that there were more owners of priceless vintage cars—Carol, Dave, Emma, Fred, and so on, down to Ziggy—all in exactly the same situation as Bob, with their own siding and their own switch, all sacrificing the child in order to preserve their own cherished car. Would that make it all right for Bob to do the same? To answer this question affirmatively is to endorse follow-the-crowd ethics—the kind of ethics that led many Germans to look away when the Nazi atrocities were being committed. We do not excuse them because others were behaving no better.

We seem to lack a sound basis for drawing a clear moral line between Bob's situation and that of any reader of this article with $200 to spare who does not donate it to an overseas aid agency. These readers seem to be acting at least as badly as Bob was acting when he chose to let the runaway train hurtle toward the unsuspecting child. In the light of this conclusion, I trust that many readers will reach for the phone and donate that $200. Perhaps you should do it before reading further.

Now that you have distinguished yourself morally from people who put   15
their vintage cars ahead of a child's life, how about treating yourself and your partner to dinner at your favorite restaurant? But wait. The money you will spend at the restaurant could also help save the lives of children overseas! True, you weren't planning to blow $200 tonight, but if you were to give up dining out just for one month, you would easily save that amount. And what is one month's dining out, compared to a child's life? There's the rub. Since there are a lot of desperately needy children in the world, there will always be another child whose life you could save for another $200. Are

you therefore obliged to keep giving until you have nothing left? At what point can you stop?

Hypothetical examples can easily become farcical. Consider Bob. How far past losing the Bugatti should he go? Imagine that Bob had got his foot stuck in the track of the siding, and if he diverted the train, then before it rammed the car it would also amputate his big toe. Should he still throw the switch? What if it would amputate his foot? His entire leg?

As absurd as the Bugatti scenario gets when pushed to extremes, the point it raises is a serious one: Only when the sacrifices become very significant indeed would most people be prepared to say that Bob does nothing wrong when he decides not to throw the switch. Of course, most people could be wrong; we can't decide moral issues by taking opinion polls. But consider for yourself the level of sacrifice that you would demand of Bob, and then think about how much money you would have to give away in order to make a sacrifice that is roughly equal to that. It's almost certainly much, much more than $200. For most middle-class Americans, it could easily be more like $200,000.

Isn't it counterproductive to ask people to do so much? Don't we run the risk that many will shrug their shoulders and say that morality, so conceived, is fine for saints but not for them? I accept that we are unlikely to see, in the near or even medium-term future, a world in which it is normal for wealthy Americans to give the bulk of their wealth to strangers. When it comes to praising or blaming people for what they do, we tend to use a standard that is relative to some conception of normal behavior. Comfortably off Americans who give, say, 10 percent of their income to overseas aid organizations are so far ahead of most of their equally comfortable fellow citizens that I wouldn't go out of my way to chastise them for not doing more. Nevertheless, they should be doing much more, and they are in no position to criticize Bob for failing to make the much greater sacrifice of his Bugatti.

At this point various objections may crop up. Someone may say: "If every citizen living in the affluent nations contributed his or her share I wouldn't have to make such a drastic sacrifice, because long before such levels were reached, the resources would have been there to save the lives of all those children dying from lack of food or medical care. So why should I give more than my fair share?" Another, related objection is that the government ought to increase its overseas aid allocations, since that would spread the burden more equitably across all taxpayers.

Yet the question of how much we ought to give is a matter to be decided 20 in the real world—and that, sadly, is a world in which we know that most people do not, and in the immediate future will not, give substantial amounts to overseas aid agencies. We know, too, that at least in the next year, the United States government is not going to meet even the very modest United Nations–recommended target of 0.7 percent of gross national product; at the moment it lags far below that, at 0.09 percent, not even half of Japan's 0.22 percent or a tenth of Denmark's 0.97 percent. Thus, we know that the money we can give beyond that theoretical "fair share" is still going to save lives that would otherwise be lost. While the idea that no one need do more than his or her fair share is a powerful one, should it prevail if we know that others are not doing their fair share and that children will die preventable deaths unless we do more than our fair share? That would be taking fairness too far.

Thus, this ground for limiting how much we ought to give also fails. In the world as it is now, I can see no escape from the conclusion that each one of us with wealth surplus to his or her essential needs should be giving most of it to help people suffering from poverty so dire as to be life-threatening. That's right: I'm saying that you shouldn't buy that new car, take that cruise, redecorate the house, or get that pricey new suit. After all, a $1,000 suit could save five children's lives.

So how does my philosophy break down in dollars and cents? An American household with an income of $50,000 spends around $30,000 annually on necessities, according to the Conference Board, a nonprofit economic research organization. Therefore, for a household bringing in $50,000 a year, donations to help the world's poor should be as close as possible to $20,000. The $30,000 required for necessities holds for higher incomes as well. So a household making $100,000 could cut a yearly check for $70,000. Again, the formula is simple: Whatever money you're spending on luxuries, not necessities, should be given away.

Now, evolutionary psychologists tell us that human nature just isn't sufficiently altruistic to make it plausible that many people will sacrifice so much for strangers. On the facts of human nature, they might be right, but they would be wrong to draw a moral conclusion from those facts. If it is the case that we ought to do things that, predictably, most of us won't do, then let's face that fact head-on. Then, if we value the life of a child more than going to fancy restaurants, the next time we dine out we will know that we could have done something better with our money. If that makes living a morally decent life extremely arduous, well, then that is the way things are. If we don't do it, then we should at least know that we are failing to live a morally decent life — not because it is good to wallow in guilt but because knowing where we should be going is the first step toward heading in that direction.

When Bob first grasped the dilemma that faced him as he stood by that railway switch, he must have thought how extraordinarily unlucky he was to be placed in a situation in which he must choose between the life of an innocent child and the sacrifice of most of his savings. But he was not unlucky at all. We are all in that situation. ▪

The Reader's Presence

1. How convincing do you find Singer's hypothetical examples, such as Bob and his uninsured Bugatti? Do you think the examples support his basic argument or weaken it? Explain your response.

2. Singer defines a utilitarian philosopher as one who "judges whether acts are right or wrong by their consequences" (paragraph 5). Can you think of utilitarian

solutions other than Singer's to the problems of world poverty? For example, would population-control methods that drastically reduced the number of impoverished children born into the world also be a utilitarian solution? Would donations to organizations that fund population control be more effective than charitable donations that directly assist children? If Singer's solution were adopted and more and more children were assisted, would that eventually encourage higher birth rates and thus worsen the very problem Singer wants to solve?

3. **CONNECTIONS:** Consider Singer's essay in conjunction with Jonathan Swift's classic satirical essay on poverty, "A Modest Proposal" (page 831). In what ways does Swift's essay also take a utilitarian position? How do you think Swift would react to Singer's solution to world poverty?

The Academic Voice

PETER SINGER on "Utility and the Survival Lottery"

What happens when writers address an academic audience, rather than a general audience? What adjustments do they make in their vocabulary, tone of voice, organization, or argument? How do these adjustments take into account the level of knowledge and information they can expect an academic audience to possess? Here you will find the beginning of Peter Singer's academic paper "Utility and the Survival Lottery," published in the journal *Philosophy*. Compare this academic selection with Singer's imaginary example of Bob and his Bugatti (paragraphs 7–14) in his essay for a general audience, "The Singer Solution to World Poverty" (page 814).

❝ In an ingenious article John Harris has proposed a "survival lottery," which would minimize the total number of deaths in a community by sacrificing randomly chosen individuals so that their organs could be transplanted to other people, each of whom needs to have an organ replaced. Since, assuming the perfection of transplant technology, the parts of one "donor" (if that is the right word) could save the lives of four or five others, the proposal appears to be a rational one. If we had the option of joining such a scheme it seems, at first glance anyway, that we would be imprudent to refuse to join. More lives will be saved by the transplants than will be lost by the sacrifices required; hence our prospects of living to a ripe old age are better if we join.[1]

Rational as Harris's idea seems, it will no doubt evoke numerous objections based on the idea of the sanctity of

[1] John Harris, "The Survival Lottery," *Philosophy* 50 (1975), 81.

human life and the wrongness of killing an innocent human being.[2] It is not my present purpose to discuss such objections, although my inclinations are to side with Harris against them, on the ground that if human life is valuable, a scheme that saves human lives must be desirable. To say that one violates the sanctity of human life by killing one person to save four, while one does not violate it if one allows four to die because one refuses to kill one, invokes a very dubious notion of moral responsibility. Moral responsibility, as Harris and others have argued, must apply to what we deliberately allow to occur as well as to what we directly bring about.[3]

Similarly, the charge that it is arbitrary or unfair to be called upon to die just because one's number has been drawn in a lottery can be met by pointing out that it is arbitrary and unfair to die just because one has contracted a kidney disease; and if the only way to prevent four arbitrary and unfair deaths is to inflict one arbitrary and unfair death, that procedure is itself neither arbitrary nor unfair.

In any case, the charge of unfairness, or of infringing on individual rights, can be overcome by the stipulation that the scheme be a voluntary one. Instead of simply giving everyone a lottery number, as Harris suggests, we could invite applications for membership in a kind of mutual benefit society, benefits and

[2] Alan Ryan has suggested (though not necessarily endorsed) some of these objections in "Two Kinds of Morality," *The Hastings Center Report 5*, no. 5 (1975), 5.
[3] See, for instance, Jonathan Bennett, "Whatever the Consequences," *Analysis 26* (1966); Michael Tooley, "Abortion and Infanticide," *Philosophy and Public Affairs 2*, no. 1 (1972); and Jonathan Glover's book, *Causing Death and Saving Lives* (1990).

risks being restricted to members only. Provided people consent to the arrangement, in full knowledge of what it is to which they are consenting, it seems difficult to hold it unfair or an infringement of their rights if they are later selected to be sacrificed.

The major drawback to the survival lottery seems to be, then, not that it infringes some justifiable moral prohibition against killing; rather, I shall suggest, it is a problem of a utilitarian kind. This is surprising, for the scheme looks like an example of utilitarian planning carried to a new extreme. Harris himself says that utilitarians ought to favor it, and devotes most of his article to meeting absolutist objections. But the survival lottery faces a problem that is faced—though in a milder form—by a wide range of social welfare schemes: by transferring the consequences of imprudent action from the imprudent individual to society at large, the scheme removes the natural disincentive to imprudent action. Thus if I like rich food, and am a member of the survival lottery, I can eat what I like without worrying about growing obese or straining my heart; when it fails, I can always get a new one from a healthier person. My obesity does not increase my chances of being selected by the lottery, and so does not decrease my expected life-span; nor does another person's sensible diet and regular exercise increase his expected life-span. There may even be a tendency toward the reverse, since unhealthy people whose organs have already deteriorated to some extent will be of little use as donors and so presumably would be eliminated from the draw, leaving the healthy to bear the burden of providing organs when required. 🙶

Lauren Slater
THE TROUBLE WITH SELF-ESTEEM

LAUREN SLATER (b. 1962) began her writing career after earning a doctorate in clinical psychology from Boston University. Her first book, *Welcome to My Country: A Therapist's Memoir of Madness* (1996), tells the stories of some of the patients she treated over the course of her eleven-year career. She is perhaps best known, however, for her accounts of her own mental illness and recovery, *Prozac Diary* (1998) and *Lying: A Metaphorical Memoir* (2000). Discussing the difference between writing about her patients and about herself, Slater explains, "I think I found it easier to write about other people, about patients, because I could portray the enormity and dignity of their suffering without risking self-absorption, or blatant narcissism. In writing about myself, I feel much more constricted. I worry about solipsism, shortsightedness, self-aggrandizement, self-denigration, and all the other treacherous territories that come with the fascinating pursuit of autobiography."

> "In writing about myself, I feel much more constricted. I worry about solipsism, shortsightedness, self-aggrandizement, self-denigration, and all the other treacherous territories that come with the fascinating pursuit of autobiography."

Slater has also published numerous books combining scientific research, a professional's perspective, and personal experience, including *Love Works Like This: Moving from One Kind of Life to Another* (2002), *Opening Skinner's Box: Great Psychological Experiments of the Twentieth Century* (2004), and *Blue Beyond Blue* (2005), a collection of stories told as fairy tales. She has contributed pieces to the *New York Times*, *Harper's*, *Elle*, and *Nerve*, and her essays are found in numerous anthologies, including *Best American Essays of 1994, 1997*, and *2008*, *Best American Science Writing 2002*, and *Best American Magazine Writing 2002*. Her essay "The Trouble with Self-Esteem" appeared in the *New York Times Magazine* in 2002.

TAKE THIS TEST:

1. On the whole I am satisfied with myself.

2. At times I think that I am no good at all.

3. I feel that I have a number of good qualities.

4. I am able to do things as well as most other people.

5. I feel I do not have much to be proud of.

6. I certainly feel useless at times.

7. I feel that I am a person of worth, at least the equal of others.

8. I wish I could have more respect for myself.

9. All in all, I am inclined to feel that I am a failure.

10. I take a positive attitude toward myself.

Devised by the sociologist Morris Rosenberg, this questionnaire is one of the most widely used self-esteem assessment scales in the United States. If your answers demonstrate solid self-regard, the wisdom of the social sciences predicts that you are well adjusted, clean and sober, basically lucid, without criminal record and with some kind of college cum laude under your high-end belt. If your answers, on the other hand, reveal some inner shame, then it is obvious: you were, or are, a teenage mother; you are prone to social deviance; and if you don't drink, it is because the illicit drugs are bountiful and robust.

It has not been much disputed, until recently, that high self-esteem—defined quite simply as liking yourself a lot, holding a positive opinion of your actions and capacities—is essential to well-being and that its opposite is responsible for crime and substance abuse and prostitution and murder and rape and even terrorism. Thousands of papers in psychiatric and social-science literature suggest this, papers with names like "Characteristics of Abusive Parents: A Look at Self-Esteem" and "Low Adolescent Self-Esteem Leads to Multiple Interpersonal Problems." In 1990, David Long published "The Anatomy of Terrorism," in which he found that hijackers and suicide bombers suffer from feelings of worthlessness and that their violent, fluorescent acts are desperate attempts to bring some inner flair to a flat mindscape.

This all makes so much sense that we have not thought to question it. The less confidence you have, the worse you do; the more confidence you have, the better you do; and so the luminous loop goes round. Based on our beliefs, we have created self-esteem programs in schools in which the main objective is, as Jennifer Coon-Wallman, a psychotherapist based in Boston, says, "to dole out huge heapings of praise, regardless of actual accomplishment." We have a National Association for Self-Esteem with about a thousand members, and in 1986, the State Legislature of California founded the "California Task Force to Promote Self-Esteem and Personal and Social Responsibility." It was galvanized by Assemblyman John Vasconcellos, who fervently believed that by raising his citizens' self-concepts, he could divert drug abuse and all sorts of other social ills.

It didn't work.

In fact, crime rates and substance abuse rates are formidable, right   5 along with our self-assessment scores on paper-and-pencil tests. (Whether these tests are valid and reliable indicators of self-esteem is a subject worthy of inquiry itself, but in the parlance of social-science writing, it goes "beyond the scope of this paper.") In part, the discrepancy between high self-esteem scores and poor social skills and academic acumen led researchers like Nicholas Emler of the London School of Economics and Roy Baumeister of Case Western Reserve University to consider the unexpected notion that self-esteem is overrated and to suggest that it may even be a culprit, not a cure.

"There is absolutely no evidence that low self-esteem is particularly harmful," Emler says. "It's not at all a cause of poor academic performance; people with low self-esteem seem to do just as well in life as people with high self-esteem. In fact, they may do better, because they often try harder." Baumeister takes Emler's findings a bit further, claiming not only that low self-esteem is in most cases a socially benign if not beneficent condition but also that its opposite, high self-regard, can maim and even kill. Baumeister conducted a study that found that some people with favorable views of themselves were more likely to administer loud blasts of ear-piercing noise to a subject than those more tepid, timid folks who held back the horn. An earlier experiment found that men with high self-esteem were more willing to put down victims to whom they had administered electric shocks than were their low-level counterparts.

Last year alone there were three withering studies of self-esteem released in the United States, all of which had the same central message: people with high self-esteem pose a greater threat to those around them than people with low self-esteem and feeling bad about yourself is not the cause of our country's biggest, most expensive social problems. The research is original and compelling and lays the groundwork for a new, important kind of narrative about what makes life worth living—if we choose to listen, which might be hard. One of this country's most central tenets, after all, is the pursuit of happiness, which has been strangely joined to the pursuit of self-worth. Shifting a paradigm is never easy. More than 2,000 books offering the attainment of self-esteem have been published; educational programs in schools designed to cultivate self-esteem continue to proliferate, as do rehabilitation programs for substance abusers that focus on cognitive realignment with self-affirming statements like, "Today I will accept myself for who I am, not who I wish I were." I have seen therapists tell their sociopathic patients to say "I adore myself" every day or to post reminder notes on their kitchen cabinets and above their toilet-paper dispensers, self-affirmations set side by side with waste.

Will we give these challenges to our notions about self-esteem their due or will the research go the way of the waste? "Research like that is seriously flawed," says Stephen Keane, a therapist who practices in Newburyport, Mass. "First, it's defining self-esteem according to very conventional and problematic masculine ideas. Second, it's clear to me that many violent men, in particular, have this inner shame; they find out early in life they're not going to measure up, and they compensate for it with fists. We need, as men, to get to the place where we can really honor and expand our natural human grace."

Keane's comment is rooted in a history that goes back hundreds of years, and it is this history that in part prevents us from really tussling with the insights of scientists like Baumeister and Emler. We have long held in this country the Byronic[1] belief that human nature is essentially good or graceful, that behind the sheath of skin is a little globe of glow to be harnessed for creative uses. Benjamin Franklin, we believe, got that glow, as did Joseph Pulitzer and scads of other, lesser, folks who eagerly caught on to what was called, in the 19th century, "mind cure."

Mind cure augurs New Age healing, so that when we lift and look at   10
the roots, New Age is not new at all. In the 19th century, people fervently believed that you were what you thought. Sound familiar? Post it above your toilet paper. You are what you think. What you think. What you think. In the 1920's, a French psychologist, Émile Coué, became all the rage in this country; he proposed the technique of autosuggestion and before long had many citizens repeating, "Day by day in every way I am getting better and better."

But as John Hewitt says in his book criticizing self-esteem, it was maybe Ralph Waldo Emerson more than anyone else who gave the modern self-esteem movement its most eloquent words and suasive philosophy. Emerson died more than a century ago, but you can visit his house in Concord, Mass., and see his bedroom slippers cordoned off behind plush velvet ropes and his eyeglasses, surprisingly frail, the frames of thin gold, the ovals of shine, perched on a beautiful desk. It was in this house that Emerson wrote his famous transcendentalist essays like "On Self-Reliance," which posits that the individual has something fresh and authentic within and that it is up to him to discover it and nurture it apart from the corrupting pressures of social influence. Emerson never mentions "self-esteem" in his essay, but his every word echoes with the self-esteem movement of today, with its romantic, sometimes silly and clearly humane belief that we are special, from head to toe.

Self-esteem, as a construct, as a quasi-religion, is woven into a tradition that both defines and confines us as Americans. If we were to deconstruct self-esteem, to question its value, we would be, in a sense, questioning who we are, nationally and individually. We would be threatening our self-esteem. This is probably why we cannot really assimilate research like Baumeister's or Emler's; it goes too close to the bone and then threatens to break it. Imagine if you heard your child's teacher say, "Don't think so much of yourself." Imagine your spouse saying to you, "You know, you're really not so good at what you do." We have developed a discourse of affirmation, and to deviate from that would be to enter another arena, linguistically and grammatically, so that what came out of our mouths would be impolite at best, unintelligible at worst.

---

1 **Byronic:** After the English poet George Gordon, Lord Byron (1788–1824). —EDS.

Is there a way to talk about the self without measuring its worth? Why, as a culture, have we so conflated the two quite separate notions—(a) self and (b) worth? This may have as much to do with our entrepreneurial history as Americans, in which everything exists to be improved, as it does, again, with the power of language to shape beliefs. How would we story the self if not triumphantly, redemptively, enhanced from the inside out? A quick glance at amazon.com titles containing the word "self" shows that a hefty percentage also have -improvement or -enhancement tucked into them, oftentimes with numbers—something like 101 ways to improve your self-esteem or 503 ways to better your outlook in 60 days or 604 ways to overcome negative self-talk. You could say that these titles are a product of a culture, or you could say that these titles and the contents they sheathe shape the culture. It is the old argument: do we make language or does language make us? In the case of self-esteem, it is probably something in between, a synergistic loop-the-loop.

On the subject of language, one could, of course, fault Baumeister and Emler for using "self-esteem" far too unidimensionally, so that it blurs and blends with simple smugness. Baumeister, in an attempt at nuance, has tried to shade the issue by referring to two previously defined types: high *unstable* self-esteem and high *well-grounded* self-esteem. As a psychologist, I remember once treating a murderer, who said, "The problem with me, Lauren, is that I'm the biggest piece of [expletive] the world revolves around." He would have scored high on a self-esteem inventory, but does he really "feel good" about himself? And if he doesn't really feel good about himself, then does it not follow that his hidden low, not his high, self-esteem leads to violence? And yet as Baumeister points out, research has shown that people with overt low self-esteem aren't violent, so why would low self-esteem cause violence only when it is hidden? If you follow his train of thinking, you could come up with the sort of silly conclusion that covert low self-esteem causes aggression, but overt low self-esteem does not, which means concealment, not cockiness, is the real culprit. That makes little sense.

"The fact is," Emler says, "we've put antisocial men through every 15 self-esteem test we have, and there's *no* evidence for the old psychodynamic concept that they secretly feel bad about themselves. These men are racist or violent because they don't feel bad *enough* about themselves." Baumeister and his colleagues write: "People who believe themselves to be among the top 10 percent on any dimension may be insulted and threatened whenever anyone asserts that they are in the 80th or 50th or 25th percentile. In contrast, someone with lower self-esteem who regards himself or herself as being merely in the top 60 percent would only be threatened by the feedback that puts him or her at the 25th percentile. . . . In short, the more favorable one's view of oneself, the greater the range of external feedback that will be perceived as unacceptably low."

Perhaps, as these researchers are saying, pride really is dangerous, and too few of us know how to be humble. But that is most likely not the entire reason why we are ignoring flares that say, "Look, sometimes self-esteem can be bad for your health." There are, as always, market forces, and they are formidable. The psychotherapy industry, for instance, would take a huge hit were self-esteem to be re-examined. After all, psychology and psychiatry are predicated upon the notion of the self, and its enhancement is the primary purpose of treatment. I am by no means saying mental health professionals have any conscious desire to perpetuate a perhaps simplistic view of self-esteem, but they are, we are (for I am one of them, I confess), the "cultural retailers" of the self-esteem concept, and were the concept to falter, so would our pocketbooks.

Really, who would come to treatment to be taken down a notch? How would we get our clients to pay to be, if not insulted, at least uncomfortably challenged? There is a profound tension here between psychotherapy as a business that needs to retain its customers and psychotherapy as a practice that has the health of its patients at heart. Mental health is not necessarily a comfortable thing. Because we want to protect our patients and our pocketbooks, we don't always say this. The drug companies that underwrite us never say this. Pills take you up or level you out, but I have yet to see an advertisement for a drug of deflation.

If you look at psychotherapy in other cultures, you get a glimpse into the obsessions of our own. You also see what a marketing fiasco we would have on our hands were we to dial down our self-esteem beliefs. In Japan, there is a popular form of psychotherapy that does not focus on the self and its worth. This psychotherapeutic treatment, called Morita, holds as its central premise that neurotic suffering comes, quite literally, from extreme self-awareness. "The most miserable people I know have been self-focused," says David Reynolds, a Morita practitioner in Oregon. Reynolds writes, "Cure is not defined by the alleviation of discomfort or the attainment of some ideal state (which is impossible) but by taking constructive action in one's life which helps one to live a full and meaningful existence and not be ruled by one's emotional state."

Morita therapy, which emphasizes action over reflection, might have some trouble catching on here, especially in the middle-class West, where folks would be hard pressed to garden away the 50-minute hour. That's what Morita patients do; they plant petunias and practice patience as they wait for them to bloom.

Like any belief system, Morita has its limitations. To detach from feelings   20
carries with it the risk of detaching from their significant signals, which carry important information about how to act: reach out, recoil. But the current research on self-esteem does suggest that we might benefit, if not fiscally then at least spiritually, from a few petunias on the Blue Cross bill. And the fact that we continue, in the vernacular, to use the word "shrink" to refer to treatment means that perhaps unconsciously we know we sometimes need to be taken down a peg.

Down to . . . what? Maybe self-control should replace self-esteem as a primary peg to reach for. I don't mean to sound puritanical, but there is something to be said for discipline, which comes from the word "disciple," which actually means to comprehend. Ultimately, self-control need not be seen as a constriction; restored to its original meaning, it might be experienced as the kind of practiced prowess an athlete or an artist demonstrates, muscles not tamed but trained, so that the leaps are powerful, the spine supple and the energy harnessed and shaped.

There are therapy programs that teach something like self-control, but predictably they are not great moneymakers and they certainly do not attract the bulk of therapy consumers, the upper middle class. One such program, called Emerge, is run by a psychologist named David Adams in a low-budget building in Cambridge, Mass. Emerge's clients are mostly abusive men, 75 percent of them mandated by the courts. "I once did an intake on a batterer who had been in psychotherapy for three years, and his violence wasn't getting any better," Adams told me. "I said to him, 'Why do you think you hit your wife?' He said to me, 'My therapist told me it's because I don't feel good about myself inside.'" Adams sighs, then laughs. "We believe it has *nothing* to do with how good a man feels about himself. At Emerge, we teach men to evaluate their behaviors honestly and to interact with others using empathy and respect." In order to accomplish these goals, men write their entire abuse histories on 12-by-12 sheets of paper, hang the papers on the wall and read them. "Some of the histories are so long, they go all around the room," Adams says. "But it's a powerful exercise. It gets a guy to really concretely *see*." Other exercises involve having the men act out the abuse with the counselor as the victim. Unlike traditional "suburban" therapies, Emerge is under no pressure to keep its customers; the courts do that for them. In return, they are free to pursue a path that has to do with "balanced confrontation," at the heart of which is critical reappraisal and self-—no, not esteem—responsibility.

While Emerge is for a specific subgroup of people, it might provide us with a model for how to reconfigure treatment—and maybe even life—if we do decide the self is not about how good it feels but how well it does, in work and love. Work and love. That's a phrase fashioned by Freud himself, who once said the successful individual is one who has achieved meaningful work and meaningful love. Note how separate this sentence is from the notion of self. We blame Freud for a lot of things, but we can't blame that cigar-smoking Victorian for this particular cultural obsession. It was Freud, after all, who said that the job of psychotherapy was to turn neurotic suffering into ordinary suffering. Freud never claimed we should be happy, and he never claimed confidence was the key to a life well lived.

I remember the shock I had when I finally read this old analyst in his native tongue. English translations of Freud make him sound maniacal, if not egomaniacal, with his bloated words like id, ego and superego. But in the original German, id means under-I, ego translates into I and superego is not super-duper but, quite simply, over-I. Freud was staking a claim for a part of the mind that watches the mind, that takes the global view in an effort at honesty. Over-I. I can see. And in the seeing, assess, edit, praise and prune. This is self-appraisal, which precedes self-control, for we must first know both where we flail and stumble, and where we are truly strong, before we can make disciplined alterations. Self-appraisal. It has a certain sort of rhythm to it, does it not? Self-appraisal may be what Baumeister and Emler are actually advocating. If our lives are stories in the making, then we must be able to edit as well as advertise the text. Self-appraisal. If we say self-appraisal again and again, 101 times, 503 times, 612 times, maybe we can create it. And learn its complex arts. ▨

The Reader's Presence

1. How does Slater establish her credibility? Identify techniques, words, phrases, and evidence that enhance your view of her as an expert. What makes establishing credibility especially important in this essay?

2. In Slater's opinion, how is self-esteem tied to American identity? What have Americans invested in the idea of self-esteem? What might be lost if self-esteem were no longer seen as valuable?

3. **CONNECTIONS:**   In refuting the idea that self-esteem is highly valuable, Slater honestly addresses what would be threatened by such a change in perspective. How does Slater address each of these threats? Compare Slater's technique of arguing against a widely accepted ideal to Laura Kipnis's argument in "Against Love" (page 733) and John Taylor Gatto's in "Against School" (page 665). Which argument(s) do you find most convincing? Why?

The Writer at Work

LAUREN SLATER on Writing Groups

Many professional writers find it stimulating and inspiring to share their work with friends and colleagues. They prefer to do this while the writing is in progress so that they can discover problems they haven't anticipated, take note of alternate directions they might pursue, or simply obtain a "gut reaction" from a supportive audience. For Slater, a key advantage of working with a writing group is the impetus provided by a dialogue: "You feel like you're really involved in a dialogue as opposed to a monologue. I do better in engaging in dialogues" (paragraph 2). These comments on writing groups are part of an interview Slater did with Alys Culhane that appeared in the creative nonfiction journal *Fourth Genre* in spring 2005.

Culhane: I recently read that your writing group is integral to your writing process. Is this so? And if so, what's its history?

Slater: It's been quite critical. I was 24 when I started working with this group and I've just turned 40. My writing group has shortened or abolished the state between writer and reader. It can be weeks on end that you are writing, and when you send something out, weeks on end before you hear anything back. But you can bring something to group, and people will hear it right away. This provides a real impetus. You feel like you're really involved in a dialogue as opposed to a monologue. I do better in engaging in dialogues.

Culhane: Why do you think this is?

Slater: Probably everything I write is kind of a co-construction of what I think and what other people think and I just don't see myself as being someone who's pulling ideas out of her own head. I dialogue with people, with books, with pictures, with everything—the world is always giving me things and I'm always taking them and turning them over. I often feel like a quilt maker—and the members of my writing group have, in a way, provided me with ways of thinking about a design and given me some of the squares. So have other friends, other writers, other books. I'm a very derivative writer and I rely heavily on other texts.

Culhane: Can you provide a specific instance where a reliance upon other texts appears in your work?

Slater: Yes. I just finished a book of fairy tales, *Blue Beyond Blue*. In this book I take established fairy tales and established fairy-tale characters and tell the story of Snow White through the eyes of the stepmother, Hansel and Gretel through the eyes of the witch.

Culhane: How has the structure of your writing group changed over time?

Slater: It's always been very loose. There's been considerable discussion about life issues that have changed over the years, from getting a boyfriend, to having breast cancer, to having kids or not having kids; the issues have changed as we've changed. In terms of structure, we have always followed the same set of "rules." We convene around 8:30 p.m. every Thursday night. We eat. We talk. At around about 11 p.m. we start to read our work. We stay for as long as it takes for everyone who has work to read it. After a person is finished reading, we go around the room and give our own comments on the piece. When this is done, we plunge into a discussion. We're all very tired on Fridays.

Culhane: Now after many years of sharing your writing with the same people do you find that you anticipate their response when you're writing?

Slater: Yes. For example, to some degree I know that one person is going to feel that a particular, say, meditative or internal beginning is slow because her writing style favors very action-oriented scenes. Others are more partial to memoir, or to fiction. Some of us adhere to the "Show, Don't Tell" rule whereas others are more likely to analyze and interpret.

Culhane: Do you anticipate their specific responses?

Slater: Yes. As a writer, what I'm really looking for is a very visceral kind of response; I take visceral reactions much more to heart than studious ones. I ask myself, did they connect with this piece, does it resonate? What I should do with this paragraph or that paragraph isn't an issue to me.

Jonathan Swift

A MODEST PROPOSAL

For Preventing the Children of Poor People in Ireland from Being a Burden to Their Parents or Country, and for Making Them Beneficial to the Public

JONATHAN SWIFT (1667–1745) was born and raised in Ireland, the son of English parents. He was ordained an Anglican priest and, although as a young man he lived a literary life in London, he was appointed against his wishes to be dean of St. Patrick's Cathedral in Dublin. Swift wrote excellent poetry but is remembered principally for his essays and politi-cal pamphlets, most of which were published under pseudonyms. Swift received payment for only one work in his entire life, *Gulliver's Travels* (1726). Swift's political pamphlets were very influential in his day; among other issues, he spoke out against English exploita-tion of the Irish. Some of Swift's more important publications include *A Tale of a Tub* (1704), *The Importance of the Guardian Considered* (1713), *The Public Spirit of the Whigs* (1714), and *A Modest Proposal* (1729).

> "... the chief end I propose to myself in all my labors is to vex the world rather than divert it."

Writing to his friend Alexander Pope, Swift commented that "the chief end I propose to myself in all my labors is to vex the world rather than divert it, and if I could compass that design without hurting my own person or Fortune I would be the most Indefatigable writer you have ever seen."

IT IS A MELANCHOLY OBJECT to those who walk through this great town[1] or travel in the country, when they see the streets, the roads, and cabin doors, crowded with beggars of the female sex, followed by three, four, or six children, all in rags and importuning every passenger for an alms. These mothers instead of being able to work for their honest livelihood, are forced to employ all their time in strolling to beg sustenance for their help-less infants: who as they grow up either turn thieves for want of work, or

---

[1] *this great town:* Dublin. —EDS.

leave their dear native country to fight for the pretender in Spain,[2] or sell themselves to the Barbadoes.[3]

I think it is agreed by all parties that this prodigious number of children in the arms, or on the backs, or at the heels of their mothers, and frequently of their fathers, is in the present deplorable state of the kingdom a very great additional grievance; and, therefore, whoever could find out a fair, cheap, and easy method of making these children sound, useful members of the commonwealth, would deserve so well of the public as to have his statute set up for a preserver of the nation.

But my intention is very far from being confined to provide only for the children of professed beggars; it is of a much greater extent, and shall take in the whole number of infants at a certain age who are born of parents in effect as little able to support them as those who demand our charity in the streets.

As to my own part, having turned my thoughts for many years upon this important subject, and maturely weighed the several schemes of our projectors,[4] I have always found them grossly mistaken in their computation. It is true, a child just dropped from its dam may be supported by her milk for a solar year, with little other nourishment; at most not above the value of 2s.,[5] which the mother may certainly get, or the value in scraps, by her lawful occupation of begging; and it is exactly at one year old that I propose to provide for them in such a manner as instead of being a charge upon their parents or the parish, or wanting food and raiment for the rest of their lives, they shall on the contrary contribute to the feeding, and partly to the clothing, of many thousands.

There is likewise another great advantage in my scheme, that it will prevent those voluntary abortions, and that horrid practice of women murdering their bastard children, alas! too frequent among us! sacrificing the poor innocent babes I doubt more to avoid the expense than the shame, which would move tears and pity in the most savage and inhuman breast.   5

The number of souls in this kingdom being usually reckoned one million and a half, of these I calculate there may be about 200,000 couple whose wives are breeders; from which number I subtract 30,000 couple who are able to maintain their own children (although I apprehend there cannot be so many, under the present distress of the kingdom); but this being granted,

---

2 ***pretender in Spain:*** James Stuart (1688–1766); exiled in Spain, he laid claim to the English crown and had the support of many Irishmen who had joined an army hoping to restore him to the throne. —EDS.

3 ***the Barbadoes:*** Inhabitants of the British colony in the Caribbean where Irishmen emigrated to work as indentured servants in exchange for their passage. —EDS.

4 ***projectors:*** Planners. —EDS.

5 ***2s.:*** Two shillings: in Swift's time one shilling was worth less than twenty-five cents. Other monetary references in the essay are to pounds sterling ("£"), pence ("d."), a crown, and a groat. A pound consisted of twenty shillings; a shilling of twelve pence; a crown was five shillings; a groat was worth a few cents. —EDS.

there will remain 170,000 breeders. I again subtract 50,000 for those women who miscarry, or whose children die by accident or disease within the year. There only remain 120,000 children of poor parents annually born. The question therefore is, how this number shall be reared and provided for? which, as I have already said, under the present situation of affairs, is utterly impossible by all the methods hitherto proposed. For we can neither employ them in handicraft or agriculture; we neither build houses (I mean in the country) nor cultivate land; they can very seldom pick up a livelihood by stealing, till they arrive at six years old, except where they are of towardly parts,[6] although I confess they learn the rudiments much earlier; during which time they can, however, be properly looked upon only as probationers; as I have been informed by a principal gentleman in the county of Cavan, who protested to me that he never knew above one or two instances under the age of six, even in a part of the kingdom so renowned for the quickest proficiency in that art.

I am assured by our merchants, that a boy or a girl before twelve years old is no salable commodity; and even when they come to this age they will not yield above 3£. or 3£. 2s. 6d. at most on the exchange; which cannot turn to account either to the parents or kingdom, the charge of nutriment and rags having been at least four times that value.

I shall now therefore humbly propose my own thoughts, which I hope will not be liable to the least objection.

I have been assured by a very knowing American of my acquaintance in London, that a young healthy child well nursed is at a year old a most delicious, nourishing, and wholesome food, whether stewed, roasted, baked, or broiled; and I make no doubt that it will equally serve in a fricassee or a ragout.[7]

I do therefore humbly offer it to public consideration that of the 120,000 children already computed, 20,000 may be reserved for breed, whereof only one-fourth part to be males; which is more than we allow to sheep, black cattle, or swine; and my reason is, that these children are seldom the fruits of marriage, a circumstance not much regarded by our savages; therefore one male will be sufficient to serve four females. That the remaining 100,000 may, at a year old, be offered in sale to the persons of quality and fortune through the kingdom; always advising the mother to let them suck plentifully in the last month, so as to render them plump and fat for a good table. A child will make two dishes at an entertainment for friends; and when the family dines alone, the fore and hind quarter will make a reasonable dish, and seasoned with a little pepper or salt will be very good boiled on the fourth day, especially in winter.

I have reckoned upon a medium that a child just born will weigh 12 pounds, and in a solar year, if tolerably nursed, will increase to 28 pounds.

10

6 **towardly parts:** Natural abilities. —EDS.
7 **ragout:** A stew. —EDS.

I grant this food will be somewhat dear, and therefore very proper for landlords, who, as they have already devoured most of the parents, seem to have the best title to the children.

Infants' flesh will be in season throughout the year, but more plentiful in March, and a little before and after: for we are told by a grave author, an eminent French physician,[8] that fish being a prolific diet, there are more children born in Roman Catholic countries about nine months after Lent than at any other season; therefore, reckoning a year after Lent, the markets will be more glutted than usual, because the number of popish infants is at least three to one in this kingdom: and therefore it will have one other collateral advantage, by lessening the number of papists among us.

I have already computed the charge of nursing a beggar's child (in which list I reckon all cottagers, laborers, and four-fifths of the farmers) to be about 2s. per annum, rags included; and I believe no gentleman would repine to give 10s. for the carcass of a good fat child, which, as I have said, will make four dishes of excellent nutritive meat, when he has only some particular friend or his own family to dine with him. Thus the squire will learn to be a good landlord, and grow popular among the tenants; the mother will have 8s. net profit, and be fit for work till she produces another child.

Those who are more thrifty (as I must confess the times require) may   15
flay the carcass; the skin of which artificially[9] dressed will make admirable gloves for ladies, and summer boots for fine gentlemen.

As to our city of Dublin, shambles[10] may be appointed for this purpose in the most convenient parts of it, and butchers we may be assured will not be wanting: although I rather recommend buying the children alive, and dressing them hot from the knife as we do roasting pigs.

A very worthy person, a true lover of his country, and whose virtues I highly esteem, was lately pleased in discoursing on this matter to offer a refinement upon my scheme. He said that many gentlemen of this kingdom, having of late destroyed their deer, he conceived that the want of venison might be well supplied by the bodies of young lads and maidens, not exceeding fourteen years of age nor under twelve; so great a number of both sexes in every country being now ready to starve for want of work and service; and these to be disposed of by their parents, if alive, or otherwise by their nearest relations. But with due deference to so excellent a friend and so deserving a patriot, I cannot be altogether in his sentiments; for as to the males, my American acquaintance assured me from frequent experience that their flesh was generally tough and lean, like that of our schoolboys by continual exercise, and their taste disagreeable; and to fatten them would not answer the charge. Then as to the females, it would, I think, with humble

---

8 **French physician:** François Rabelais (c. 1494–1553), the great Renaissance humanist and author of the comic masterpiece *Gargantua and Pantagruel.* Swift is being ironic in calling Rabelais "grave." —EDS.

9 **artificially:** Artfully. —EDS.

10 **shambles:** Slaughterhouses. —EDS.

submission be a loss to the public, because they soon would become breeders themselves: and besides, it is not improbable that some scrupulous people might be apt to censure such a practice (although indeed very unjustly), as a little bordering upon cruelty; which, I confess, has always been with me the strongest objection against any project, how well soever intended.

But in order to justify my friend, he confessed that this expedient was put into his head by the famous Psalmanazar[11] a native of the island Formosa, who came from thence to London about twenty years ago: and in conversation told my friend, that in his country when any young person happened to be put to death, the executioner sold the carcass to persons of quality as a prime dainty; and that in his time the body of a plump girl of fifteen, who was crucified for an attempt to poison the emperor, was sold to his imperial majesty's prime minister of state, and other great mandarins of the court, in joints from the gibbet, at 400 crowns. Neither indeed can I deny, that if the same use were made of several plump young girls in this town, who without one single groat to their fortunes cannot stir abroad without a chair,[12] and appear at the playhouse and assemblies in foreign fineries which they never will pay for, the kingdom would not be the worse.

Some persons of a desponding spirit are in great concern about the vast number of poor people, who are aged, diseased, or maimed, and I have been desired to employ my thoughts what course may be taken to ease the nation of so grievous an encumbrance. But I am not in the least pain upon that matter, because it is very well known that they are every day dying and rotting by cold and famine, and filth and vermin, as fast as can be reasonably expected. And as to the young laborers, they are now in as hopeful condition: They cannot get work, and consequently pine away for want of nourishment, to a degree that if at any time they are accidentally hired to common labor, they have not strength to perform it; and thus the country and themselves are happily delivered from the evils to come.

I have too long digressed, and therefore shall return to my subject. I   20 think the advantages by the proposal which I have made are obvious and many, as well as of the highest importance.

For first, as I have already observed, it would greatly lessen the number of papists, with whom we are yearly overrun, being the principal breeders of the nation as well as our most dangerous enemies; and who stay at home on purpose to deliver the kingdom to the Pretender, hoping to take their advantage by the absence of so many good Protestants, who have chosen rather to leave their country than stay at home and pay tithes against their conscience to an Episcopal curate.

Secondly, The poor tenants will have something valuable of their own, which by law may be made liable to distress[13] and help to pay their

11 **George Psalmanazar** (c. 1679–1763): A Frenchman who tricked London society into believing he was a native of Formosa (now Taiwan).—EDS.
12 **a chair:** A sedan chair in which one is carried about.—EDS.
13 **distress:** Seizure for payment of debt.—EDS.

landlord's rent, their corn and cattle being already seized, and money a thing unknown.

Thirdly, Whereas the maintenance of 100,000 children from two years old and upward, cannot be computed at less that 10s. a-piece per annum, the nation's stock will be thereby increased £50,000 per annum, beside the profit of a new dish introduced to the tables of all gentlemen of fortune in the kingdom who have any refinement in taste. And the money will circulate among ourselves, the goods being entirely of our own growth and manufacture.

Fourthly, The constant breeders beside the gain of 8s. sterling per annum by the sale of their children, will be rid of the charge of maintaining them after the first year.

Fifthly, This food would likewise bring great custom to taverns, where the vintners will certainly be so prudent as to procure the best receipts[14] for dressing it to perfection, and consequently have their houses frequented by all the fine gentlemen, who justly value themselves upon their knowledge in good eating; and a skillful cook who understands how to oblige his guests, will contrive to make it as expensive as they please.

Sixthly, This would be a great inducement to marriage, which all wise nations have either encouraged by rewards or enforced by laws and penalties. It would increase the care and tenderness of mothers toward their children, when they were sure of a settlement for life to the poor babes, provided in some sort by the public, to their annual profit instead of expense. We should see an honest emulation among the married women, which of them would bring the fattest child to the market. Men would become as fond of their wives during the time of their pregnancy as they are now of their mares in foal, their cows in calf, their sows when they are ready to farrow; nor offer to beat or kick them (as is too frequent a practice) for fear of a miscarriage.

Many other advantages might be enumerated. For instance, the addition of some thousand carcasses in our exportation of barreled beef, the propagation of swine's flesh, and improvement in the art of making good bacon, so much wanted among us by the great destruction of pigs, too frequent at our table; which are no way comparable in taste or magnificence to a well-grown, fat, yearling child, which roasted whole will make a considerable figure at a lord mayor's feast or any other public entertainment. But this and many others I omit, being studious of brevity.

Supposing that 1,000 families in this city would be constant customers for infants' flesh, besides others who might have it at merry-meetings, particularly at weddings and christenings, I compute that Dublin would take off annually about 20,000 carcasses; and the rest of the kingdom (where probably they will be sold somewhat cheaper) the remaining 80,000.

14 ***receipts:*** Recipes. —EDS.

I can think of no one objection that will possibly be raised against this proposal unless it should be urged that the number of people will be thereby much lessened in the kingdom. This I freely own, and it was indeed one principal design in offering it to the world. I desire the reader will observe, that I calculate my remedy for this one individual kingdom of Ireland and for no other that ever was, is, or I think ever can be upon earth. Therefore let no man talk to me of other expedients: of taxing our absentees at 5s. a pound: of using neither clothes nor household furniture except what is of our own growth and manufacture: of utterly rejecting the materials and instruments that promote foreign luxury: of curing the expensiveness of pride, vanity, idleness, and gaming in our women: of introducing a vein of parsimony, prudence, and temperance: of learning to love our country, in the want of which we differ even from Laplanders and the inhabitants of Topinamboo:[15] of quitting our animosities and factions, nor acting any longer like the Jews, who were murdering one another at the very moment their city was taken:[16] of being a little cautious not to sell our country and conscience for nothing: of teaching landlords to have at least one degree of mercy toward their tenants: lastly, of putting a spirit of honesty, industry, and skill into our shopkeepers; who, if a resolution could now be taken to buy only our native goods, would immediately unite to cheat and exact upon us in the price the measure, and the goodness, nor could ever yet be brought to make one fair proposal of just dealing, though often and earnestly invited to it.

Therefore I repeat, let no man talk to me of these and the like expedi-   30
ents, till he has at least some glimpse of hope that there will be ever some hearty and sincere attempt to put them in practice.

But as to myself, having been wearied out for many years with offering vain, idle, visionary thoughts, and at length utterly despairing of success, I fortunately fell upon this proposal; which, as it is wholly new, so it has something solid and real, of no expense and little trouble, full in our own power, and whereby we can incur no danger in disobliging England. For this kind of commodity will not bear exportation, the flesh being of too tender a consistence to admit a long continuance in salt, although perhaps I could name a country which would be glad to eat up our whole nation without it.

After all, I am not so violently bent upon my own opinion as to reject any offer proposed by wise men, which shall be found equally innocent, cheap, easy, and effectual. But before something of that kind shall be advanced in contradiction to my scheme, and offering a better, I desire the author or authors will be pleased maturely to consider two points. First, as things now stand, how they will be able to find food and raiment for 100,000 useless mouths and backs. And secondly, there being a round million of creatures in

15 **Laplanders and the inhabitants of Topinamboo:** Lapland is the area of Scandinavia above the Arctic Circle; Topinamboo, in Brazil, was known in Swift's time for the savagery of its tribes.—EDS.

16 **was taken:** A reference to the Roman seizure of Jerusalem (70 CE).—EDS.

human figure throughout this kingdom, whose subsistence put into a common stock would leave them in debt 2,000,000£. sterling, adding those who are beggars by profession to the bulk of farmers, cottagers, and laborers, with the wives and children who are beggars in effect; I desire those politicians who dislike my overture, and may perhaps be so bold as to attempt an answer, that they will first ask the parents of these mortals, whether they would not at this day think it a great happiness to have been sold for food at a year old in the manner I prescribe, and thereby have avoided such a perpetual scene of misfortunes as they have since gone through by the oppression of landlords, the impossibility of paying rent without money or trade, the want of common sustenance, with neither house nor clothes to cover them from the inclemencies of the weather, and the most inevitable prospect of entailing the like or greater miseries upon their breed for ever.

I profess, in the sincerity of my heart, that I have not the least personal interest in endeavoring to promote this necessary work, having no other motive than the public good of my country, by advancing our trade, providing for infants, relieving the poor, and giving some pleasure to the rich. I have no children by which I can propose to get a single penny; the youngest being nine years old, and my wife past childbearing. ◼

The Reader's Presence

1. Consider Swift's title. In what sense is the proposal "modest"? What is modest about it? What synonyms would you use for *modest* that appear in the essay? In what sense is the essay a "proposal"? Does it follow any format that resembles a proposal? If so, what type of format? What aspects of its language seem to resemble proposal writing?

2. For this essay Swift invents a speaker, an unnamed, fictional individual who "humbly" proposes a plan to relieve poverty in Ireland. What attitudes and beliefs in the essay do you attribute to the speaker? Which do you attribute to Swift, the author? Having considered two authors (the speaker of the proposal and Swift), now consider two readers—the reader the speaker imagines and the reader Swift imagines. How do these two readers differ? Reread the final paragraph of the essay from the perspective of each of these readers. How do you think each reader is expected to respond?

3. **CONNECTIONS:**   In the introductory comment, Swift is quoted as wanting "to vex the world rather than divert it" with his writing. Where in the essay do you find Swift most vexing? How does he attempt to provoke the reader's outrage? Where does the first, most visceral indication of the speaker's plan appear? Does he heighten the essay's effect after this point? If so, where and how? How does Swift mount a serious political argument in the midst of such hyperbole? Read "Against Love" by Laura Kipnis (page 733). How does Kipnis use hyperbole or satire in the presentation of her argument? Does she make a serious point? Why or why not?

David Foster Wallace

CONSIDER THE LOBSTER

DAVID FOSTER WALLACE (1962–2008) is probably best known for his 1996 novel, *Infinite Jest*. Widely considered one of the most important works of American fiction in recent memory, *Infinite Jest* made *Time* magazine's list of the 100 greatest novels spanning the period of 1926–2006, and firmly established Wallace at the forefront of American letters. Wallace double-majored in English and philosophy at Amherst College and went on to receive an MFA in Creative Writing at the University of Arizona in 1987. He published his first novel, *The Broom of the System*, in 1987, and, shortly thereafter, moved to Boston, Massachusetts, to work toward a graduate degree in philosophy at Harvard University. He soon abandoned the endeavor, dedicating himself instead to writing. He taught creative writing at Illinois State University from 1992 through 2002, when he moved to Claremont, California, to take a position as the Roy E. Disney Professor of Creative Writing at Pomona College. In addition to *Infinite Jest* and *The Broom of the System*, Wallace published several short story collections, including *Brief Interviews with Hideous Men* (1999), which was adapted for the screen in a 2009 film of the same name. Wallace also published essays and stories in magazines, including the *Paris Review*, *Harper's*, the *Atlantic Monthly*, *Esquire*, and *Gourmet*. He died by suicide in 2008.

> Widely considered one of the most important works of American fiction in recent memory, *Infinite Jest* made *Time* magazine's list of the 100 greatest novels spanning the period of 1926–2006, and firmly established David Foster Wallace at the forefront of American letters.

Wallace wrote "Consider the Lobster" on assignment from *Gourmet*, a culinary magazine, in 2004.

Note: Extensive personal footnotes are part of Wallace's prose style; unless otherwise specified, all the footnotes are Wallace's.

THE ENORMOUS, pungent, and extremely well-marketed Maine Lobster Festival is held every late July in the state's midcoast region, meaning the western side of Penobscot Bay, the nerve stem of Maine's lobster industry. What's called the midcoast runs from Owl's Head and

Lots of lobster

Very descriptive / Paints the picture of scene

Thomaston in the south to Belfast in the north. (Actually, it might extend all the way up to Bucksport, but we were never able to get farther north than Belfast on Route 1, whose summer traffic is, as you can imagine, unimaginable.) The region's two main communities are Camden, with its very old money and yachty harbor and five-star restaurants and phenomenal B&Bs, and Rockland, a serious old fishing town that hosts the festival every summer in historic Harbor Park, right along the water.[1]

Tourism and lobster are the midcoast region's two main industries, and they're both warm-weather enterprises, and the Maine Lobster Festival represents less an intersection of the industries than a deliberate collision, joyful and lucrative and loud. The assigned subject of this *Gourmet* article is the 56th Annual MLF, 30 July–3 August 2003, whose official theme this year was "Lighthouses, Laughter, and Lobster." Total paid attendance was over 100,000, due partly to a national CNN spot in June during which a senior editor of *Food & Wine* magazine hailed the MLF as one of the best food-themed galas in the world. 2003 festival highlights: concerts by Lee Ann Womack and Orleans, annual Maine Sea Goddess beauty pageant, Saturday's big parade, Sunday's William G. Atwood Memorial Crate Race, annual Amateur Cooking Competition, carnival rides and midway attractions and food booths, and the MLF's Main Eating Tent, where something over 25,000 pounds of fresh-caught Maine lobster is consumed after preparation in the World's Largest Lobster Cooker near the grounds' north entrance. Also available are lobster rolls, lobster turnovers, lobster sauté, Down East lobster salad, lobster bisque, lobster ravioli, and deep-fried lobster dumplings. Lobster thermidor is obtainable at a sit-down restaurant called the Black Pearl on Harbor Park's northwest wharf. A large all-pine booth sponsored by the Maine Lobster Promotion Council has free pamphlets with recipes, eating tips, and Lobster Fun Facts. The winner of Friday's Amateur Cooking Competition prepares Saffron Lobster Ramekins, the recipe for which is now available for public downloading at www.mainelobsterfestival.com. There are lobster T-shirts and lobster bobblehead dolls and inflatable lobster pool toys and clamp-on lobster hats with big scarlet claws that wobble on springs. Your assigned correspondent saw it all, accompanied by one girlfriend and both his own parents—one of which parents was actually born and raised in Maine, albeit in the extreme northern inland part, which is potato country and a world away from the touristic midcoast.[2]

list of events

For practical purposes, everyone knows what a lobster is. As usual, though, there's much more to know than most of us care about—it's all a matter of what your interests are. Taxonomically speaking, a lobster is a marine crustacean of the family Homaridae, characterized by five pairs of

---

[1] There's a comprehensive native apothegm: "Camden by the sea, Rockland by the smell."

[2] N.B. All personally connected parties have made it clear from the start that they do not want to be talked about in this article.

jointed legs, the first pair terminating in large pincerish claws used for subduing prey. Like many other species of benthic carnivore, lobsters are both hunters and scavengers. They have stalked eyes, gills on their legs, and antennae. There are a dozen or so different kinds worldwide, of which the relevant species here is the Maine lobster, *Homarus americanus*. The name "lobster" comes from the Old English *loppestre*, which is thought to be a corrupt form of the Latin word for locust combined with the Old English *loppe*, which meant spider.

Moreover, a crustacean is an aquatic arthropod of the class Crustacea, which comprises crabs, shrimp, barnacles, lobsters, and freshwater crayfish. All this is right there in the encyclopedia. And arthropods are members of the phylum Arthropoda, which phylum covers insects, spiders, crustaceans, and centipedes/millipedes, all of whose main commonality, besides the absence of a centralized brain-spine assembly, is a chitinous exoskeleton composed of segments, to which appendages are articulated in pairs.

The point is that lobsters are basically giant sea insects.[3] Like most arthropods, they date from the Jurassic period, biologically so much older than mammalia that they might as well be from another planet. And they are—particularly in their natural brown-green state, brandishing their claws like weapons and with thick antennae awhip—not nice to look at. And it's true that they are garbagemen of the sea, eaters of dead stuff,[4] although they'll also eat some live shellfish, certain kinds of injured fish, and sometimes one another.

But they are themselves good eating. Or so we think now. Up until sometime in the 1800s, though, lobster was literally low-class food, eaten only by the poor and institutionalized. Even in the harsh penal environment of early America, some colonies had laws against feeding lobsters to inmates more than once a week because it was thought to be cruel and unusual, like making people eat rats. One reason for their low status was how plentiful lobsters were in old New England. "Unbelievable abundance" is how one source describes the situation, including accounts of Plymouth Pilgrims wading out and capturing all they wanted by hand, and of early Boston's seashore being littered with lobsters after hard storms—these latter were treated as a smelly nuisance and ground up for fertilizer. There is also the fact that premodern lobster was cooked dead and then preserved, usually packed in salt or crude hermetic containers. Maine's earliest lobster industry was based around a dozen such seaside canneries in the 1840s, from which lobster was shipped as far away as California, in demand only because it was cheap and high in protein, basically chewable fuel.

Now, of course, lobster is posh, a delicacy, only a step or two down from caviar. The meat is richer and more substantial than most fish, its taste subtle

5

---

3 Midcoasters' native term for a lobster is, in fact, "bug," as in "Come around on Sunday and we'll cook up some bugs."

4 Factoid: Lobster traps are usually baited with dead herring.

compared to the marine-gaminess of mussels and clams. In the US pop-food imagination, lobster is now the seafood analog to steak, with which it's so often twinned as Surf 'n' Turf on the really expensive part of the chain steak-house menu.

In fact, one obvious project of the MLF, and of its omnipresently sponso-rial Maine Lobster Promotion Council, is to counter the idea that lobster is unusually luxe or unhealthy or expensive, suitable only for effete palates or the occasional blow-the-diet treat. It is emphasized over and over in presen-tations and pamphlets at the festival that lobster meat has fewer calories, less cholesterol, and less saturated fat than chicken.[5] And in the Main Eating Tent, you can get a "quarter" (industry shorthand for a 1¼-pound lobster), a four-ounce cup of melted butter, a bag of chips, and a soft roll w/butter-pat for around $12.00, which is only slightly more expensive than supper at McDonald's.

Be apprised, though, that the Maine Lobster Festival's democratization of lobster comes with all the massed inconveniences and aesthetic compro-mise of real democracy. See, for example, the aforementioned Main Eat-ing Tent, for which there is a constant Disneyland-grade queue, and which turns out to be a square quarter mile of awning-shaded cafeteria lines and rows of long institutional tables at which friend and stranger alike sit cheek by jowl, cracking and chewing and dribbling. It's hot, and the sagged roof traps the steam and the smells, which latter are strong and only partly food-related. It is also loud, and a good percentage of the total noise is mastica-tory. The suppers come in styrofoam trays, and the soft drinks are iceless and flat, and the coffee is convenience-store coffee in yet more styrofoam, and the utensils are plastic (there are none of the special long skinny forks for pushing out the tail meat, though a few savvy diners bring their own). Nor do they give you near enough napkins considering how messy lobster is to eat, especially when you're squeezed onto benches alongside children of various ages and vastly different levels of fine-motor development—not to mention the people who've somehow smuggled in their own beer in enor-mous aisle-blocking coolers, or who all of a sudden produce their own plas-tic tablecloths and spread them over large portions of tables to try to reserve them (the tables) for their own little groups. And so on. Any one example is no more than a petty inconvenience, of course, but the MLF turns out to be full of irksome little downers like this—see for instance the Main Stage's headliner shows, where it turns out that you have to pay $20 extra for a fold-ing chair if you want to sit down; or the North Tent's mad scramble for the Nyquil-cup-sized samples of finalists' entries handed out after the Cooking Competition; or the much-touted Maine Sea Goddess pageant finals, which turn out to be excruciatingly long and to consist mainly of endless thanks

---

5 Of course, the common practice of dipping the lobster meat in melted butter torpedoes all these happy fat-specs, which none of the council's promotional stuff ever mentions, any more than potato industry PR talks about sour cream and bacon bits.

and tributes to local sponsors. Let's not even talk about the grossly inadequate Port-A-San facilities or the fact that there's nowhere to wash your hands before or after eating. What the Maine Lobster Festival really is is a midlevel county fair with a culinary hook, and in this respect it's not unlike Tidewater crab festivals, Midwest corn festivals, Texas chili festivals, etc., and shares with these venues the core paradox of all teeming commercial demotic events: It's not for everyone.[6] Nothing against the euphoric senior editor of *Food & Wine*, but I'd be surprised if she'd ever actually been here in Harbor Park, amid crowds of people slapping canal-zone mosquitoes as they eat deep-fried Twinkies and watch Professor Paddywhack, on six-foot stilts in a raincoat with plastic lobsters protruding from all directions on springs, terrify their children.

Lobster is essentially a summer food. This is because we now prefer our   10
lobsters fresh, which means they have to be recently caught, which for both tactical and economic reasons takes place at depths less than 25 fathoms. Lobsters tend to be hungriest and most active (i.e., most trappable) at summer water temperatures of 45–50 degrees. In the autumn, most Maine lobsters migrate out into deeper water, either for warmth or to avoid the heavy waves that pound New England's coast all winter. Some burrow into the bottom. They might hibernate; nobody's sure. Summer is also lobsters' molting season—specifically early- to mid-July. Chitinous arthropods grow by molting, rather the way people have to buy bigger clothes as they age and gain weight. Since lobsters can live to be over 100, they can also get to be quite large, as in 30 pounds or more—though truly senior lobsters are rare

---

6 In truth, there's a great deal to be said about the differences between working-class Rockland and the heavily populist flavor of its festival versus comfortable and elitist Camden with its expensive view and shops given entirely over to $200 sweaters and great rows of Victorian homes converted to upscale B&Bs. And about these differences as two sides of the great coin that is US tourism. Very little of which will be said here, except to amplify the above-mentioned paradox and to reveal your assigned correspondent's own preferences. I confess that I have never understood why so many people's idea of a fun vacation is to don flip-flops and sunglasses and crawl through maddening traffic to loud, hot, crowded tourist venues in order to sample a "local flavor" that is by definition ruined by the presence of tourists. This may (as my festival companions keep pointing out) all be a matter of personality and hardwired taste: the fact that I do not like tourist venues means that I'll never understand their appeal and so am probably not the one to talk about it (the supposed appeal). But, since this FN will almost surely not survive magazine-editing anyway, here goes:

As I see it, it probably really is good for the soul to be a tourist, even if it's only once in a while. Not good for the soul in a refreshing or enlivening way, though, but rather in a grim, steely-eyed, let's-look-honestly-at-the-facts-and-find-some-way-to-deal-with-them way. My personal experience has not been that traveling around the country is broadening or relaxing, or that radical changes in place and context have a salutary effect, but rather that intranational tourism is radically constricting, and humbling in the hardest way—hostile to my fantasy of being a real individual, of living somehow outside and above it all. (Coming up is the part that my companions find especially unhappy and repellent, a sure way to spoil the fun of vacation travel:) To be a mass tourist, for me, is to become a pure late-date American: alien, ignorant, greedy for something you cannot ever have, disappointed in a way you can never admit. It is to spoil, by way of sheer ontology, the very unspoiledness you are there to experience. It is to impose yourself on places that in all non-economic ways would be better, realer, without you. It is, in lines and gridlock and transaction after transaction, to confront a dimension of yourself that is as inescapable as it is painful: As a tourist, you become economically significant but existentially loathsome, an insect on a dead thing.

now because New England's waters are so heavily trapped.[7] Anyway, hence the culinary distinction between hard- and soft-shell lobsters, the latter sometimes a.k.a. shedders. A soft-shell lobster is one that has recently molted. In midcoast restaurants, the summer menu often offers both kinds, with shedders being slightly cheaper even though they're easier to dismantle and the meat is allegedly sweeter. The reason for the discount is that a molting lobster uses a layer of seawater for insulation while its new shell is hardening, so there's slightly less actual meat when you crack open a shedder, plus a redolent gout of water that gets all over everything and can sometimes jet out lemonlike and catch a tablemate right in the eye. If it's winter or you're buying lobster someplace far from New England, on the other hand, you can almost bet that the lobster is a hard-shell, which for obvious reasons travel better.

As an à la carte entrée, lobster can be baked, broiled, steamed, grilled, sautéed, stir-fried, or microwaved. The most common method, though, is boiling. If you're someone who enjoys having lobster at home, this is probably the way you do it, since boiling is so easy. You need a large kettle w/cover, which you fill about half full with water (the standard advice is that you want 2.5 quarts of water per lobster). Seawater is optimal, or you can add two tbsp salt per quart from the tap. It also helps to know how much your lobsters weigh. You get the water boiling, put in the lobsters one at a time, cover the kettle, and bring it back up to a boil. Then you bank the heat and let the kettle simmer—ten minutes for the first pound of lobster, then three minutes for each pound after that. (This is assuming you've got hard-shell lobsters, which, again, if you don't live between Boston and Halifax is probably what you've got. For shedders, you're supposed to subtract three minutes from the total.) The reason the kettle's lobsters turn scarlet is that boiling somehow suppresses every pigment in their chitin but one. If you want an easy test of whether the lobsters are done, you try pulling on one of their antennae—if it comes out of the head with minimal effort, you're ready to eat.

A detail so obvious that most recipes don't even bother to mention it is that each lobster is supposed to be alive when you put it in the kettle. This is part of lobster's modern appeal—it's the freshest food there is. There's no decomposition between harvesting and eating. And not only do lobsters require no cleaning or dressing or plucking, they're relatively easy for vendors to keep alive. They come up alive in the traps, are placed in containers of seawater, and can—so long as the water's aerated and the animals' claws are pegged or banded to keep them from tearing one another up under the stresses of captivity[8]—survive right up until they're boiled. Most

---

7 Datum: In a good year, the US industry produces around 80,000,000 pounds of lobster, and Maine accounts for more than half that total.

8 N.B. Similar reasoning underlies the practice of what's termed "debeaking" broiler chickens and brood hens in modern factory farms. Maximum commercial efficiency requires that enormous poultry populations be confined in unnaturally close quarters, under which conditions many birds go crazy and peck one another to death. As a purely observational side-note, be apprised that debeaking is usually an automated process and that the chickens receive no anesthetic. It's not

of us have been in supermarkets or restaurants that feature tanks of live lobsters, from which you can pick out your supper while it watches you point. And part of the overall spectacle of the Maine Lobster Festival is that you can see actual lobstermen's vessels docking at the wharves along the northeast grounds and unloading fresh-caught product, which is trans- ferred by hand or cart 150 yards to the great clear tanks stacked up around the festival's cooker—which is, as mentioned, billed as the World's Largest Lobster Cooker and can process over 100 lobsters at a time for the Main Eating Tent.

So then here is a question that's all but unavoidable at the World's Larg- est Lobster Cooker, and may arise in kitchens across the US: Is it all right to boil a sentient creature alive just for our gustatory pleasure? A related set of concerns: Is the previous question irksomely PC or sentimental? What does "all right" even mean in this context? Is the whole thing just a matter of personal choice?

As you may or may not know, a certain well-known group called People for the Ethical Treatment of Animals thinks that the morality of lobster-boiling is not just a matter of individual conscience. In fact, one of the very first things we hear about the MLF . . . well, to set the scene: We're coming in by cab from the almost indescribably odd and rustic Knox County Airport[9] very late on the night before the festival opens, sharing the cab with a wealthy political consultant who lives on Vinalhaven Island in the bay half the year (he's headed for the island ferry in Rockland). The consultant and cabdriver are responding to informal journalistic probes about how people who live in the midcoast region actually view the MLF, as in is the festival just a big- dollar tourist thing or is it something local residents look forward to attend- ing, take genuine civic pride in, etc. The cabdriver (who's in his seventies, one of apparently a whole platoon of retirees the cab company puts on to help with the summer rush, and wears a US-flag lapel pin, and drives in what can only be called a very *deliberate* way) assures us that locals do endorse and enjoy the MLF, although he himself hasn't gone in years, and now come to think of it no one he and his wife know has, either. However, the demilocal consultant's been to recent festivals a couple times (one gets the impression it was at his wife's behest), of which his most vivid impression was that "you have to line up for an ungodly long time to get your lobsters, and meanwhile there are all these ex–flower children coming up and down along the line handing out pamphlets that say the lobsters die in terrible pain and you shouldn't eat them."

---

clear to me whether most *Gourmet* readers know about debeaking, or about related practices like dehorning cattle in commercial feed lots, cropping swine's tails in factory hog farms to keep psy- chotically bored neighbors from chewing them off, and so forth. It so happens that your assigned correspondent knew almost nothing about standard meat-industry operations before starting work on this article.

9 The terminal used to be somebody's house, for example, and the lost-luggage-reporting room was clearly once a pantry.

And it turns out that the post-hippies of the consultant's recollection were 15 activists from PETA. There were no PETA people in obvious view at the 2003 MLF,[10] but they've been conspicuous at many of the recent festivals. Since at least the mid-1990s, articles in everything from the *Camden Herald* to the *New York Times* have described PETA urging boycotts of the Maine Lobster Festival, often deploying celebrity spokesmen like Mary Tyler Moore for open letters and ads saying stuff like "Lobsters are extraordinarily sensitive" and "To me, eating a lobster is out of the question." More concrete is the oral testimony of Dick, our florid and extremely gregarious rental-car liaison,[11] to the effect that PETA's been around so much in recent years that a kind of brittlely tolerant homeostasis now obtains between the activists and the festival's locals, e.g.: "We had some incidents a couple years ago. One lady took most of her clothes off and painted herself like a lobster, almost got herself arrested. But for the most part they're let alone. [Rapid series of small ambiguous laughs, which with Dick happens a lot.] They do their thing and we do our thing."

This whole interchange takes place on Route 1, 30 July, during a four-mile, 50-minute ride from the airport[12] to the dealership to sign car-rental papers. Several irreproducible segues down the road from the PETA anecdotes, Dick—whose son-in-law happens to be a professional lobsterman and one of the Main Eating Tent's regular suppliers—explains what he and his family feel is the crucial mitigating factor in the whole morality-of-boiling-lobsters-alive issue: "There's a part of the brain in people and animals that lets us feel pain, and lobsters' brains don't have this part."

Besides the fact that it's incorrect in about nine different ways, the main reason Dick's statement is interesting is that its thesis is more or less echoed by the festival's own pronouncement on lobsters and pain, which is part of a

---

10 It turned out that one Mr. William R. Rivas-Rivas, a high-ranking PETA official out of the group's Virginia headquarters, was indeed there this year, albeit solo, working the festival's main and side entrances on Saturday, 2 August, handing out pamphlets and adhesive stickers emblazoned with "Being Boiled Hurts," which is the tagline in most of PETA's published material about lobsters. I learned that he'd been there only later, when speaking with Mr. Rivas-Rivas on the phone. I'm not sure how we missed seeing him *in situ* at the festival, and I can't see much to do except apologize for the oversight—although it's also true that Saturday was the day of the big MLF parade through Rockland, which basic journalistic responsibility seemed to require going to (and which, with all due respect, meant that Saturday was maybe not the best day for PETA to work the Harbor Park grounds, especially if it was going to be just one person for one day, since a lot of diehard MLF partisans were off-site watching the parade (which, again with no offense intended, was in truth kind of cheesy and boring, consisting mostly of slow homemade floats and various midcoast people waving at one another, and with an extremely annoying man dressed as Blackbeard ranging up and down the length of the crowd saying "Arrr" over and over and brandishing a plastic sword at people, etc.; plus it rained)).

11 By profession, Dick is actually a car salesman; the midcoast region's National Car Rental franchise operates out of a Chevy dealership in Thomaston.

12 The short version regarding why we were back at the airport after already arriving the previous night involves lost luggage and a miscommunication about where and what the midcoast's National franchise was—Dick came out personally to the airport and got us, out of no evident motive but kindness. (He also talked nonstop the entire way, with a very distinctive speaking style that can be described only as manically laconic; the truth is that I now know more about this man than I do about some members of my own family.)

Test Your Lobster IQ quiz that appears in the 2003 MLF program courtesy of the Maine Lobster Promotion Council:

> The nervous system of a lobster is very simple, and is in fact most similar to the nervous system of the grasshopper. It is decentralized with no brain. There is no cerebral cortex, which in humans is the area of the brain that gives the experience of pain.

Though it sounds more sophisticated, a lot of the neurology in this latter claim is still either false or fuzzy. The human cerebral cortex is the brain-part that deals with higher faculties like reason, metaphysical self-awareness, language, etc. Pain reception is known to be part of a much older and more primitive system of nociceptors and prostaglandins that are managed by the brain stem and thalamus.[13] On the other hand, it is true that the cerebral cortex is involved in what's variously called suffering, distress, or the emotional experience of pain—i.e., experiencing painful stimuli as unpleasant, very unpleasant, unbearable, and so on.

Before we go any further, let's acknowledge that the questions of whether and how different kinds of animals feel pain, and of whether and why it might be justifiable to inflict pain on them in order to eat them, turn out to be extremely complex and difficult. And comparative neuroanatomy is only part of the problem. Since pain is a totally subjective mental experience, we do not have direct access to anyone or anything's pain but our own; and even just the principles by which we can infer that other human beings experience pain and have a legitimate interest in not feeling pain involve hardcore philosophy—metaphysics, epistemology, value theory, ethics. The fact that even the most highly evolved nonhuman mammals can't use language to communicate with us about their subjective mental experience is only the first layer of additional complication in trying to extend our reasoning about pain and morality to animals. And everything gets progressively more abstract and convoluted as we move farther and farther out from the higher-type mammals into cattle and swine and dogs and cats and rodents, and then birds and fish, and finally invertebrates like lobsters.

The more important point here, though, is that the whole animal-cruelty-and-eating issue is not just complex, it's also uncomfortable. It is, at any rate, uncomfortable for me, and for just about everyone I know who enjoys a variety of foods and yet does not want to see herself as cruel or unfeeling. As far as I can tell, my own main way of dealing with this conflict has been to avoid thinking about the whole unpleasant thing. I should add that it appears to me unlikely that many readers of *Gourmet* wish to think about it, either, or to be queried about the morality of their eating habits in the pages

---

13 To elaborate by way of example: The common experience of accidentally touching a hot stove and yanking your hand back before you're even aware that anything's going on is explained by the fact that many of the processes by which we detect and avoid painful stimuli do not involve the cortex. In the case of the hand and stove, the brain is bypassed altogether; all the important neurochemical action takes place in the spine.

of a culinary monthly. Since, however, the assigned subject of this article is what it was like to attend the 2003 MLF, and thus to spend several days in the midst of a great mass of Americans all eating lobster, and thus to be more or less impelled to think hard about lobster and the experience of buying and eating lobster, it turns out that there is no honest way to avoid certain moral questions.

There are several reasons for this. For one thing, it's not just that lobsters   20
get boiled alive, it's that you do it yourself—or at least it's done specifically for you, on-site.[14] As mentioned, the World's Largest Lobster Cooker, which is highlighted as an attraction in the festival's program, is right out there on the MLF's north grounds for everyone to see. Try to imagine a Nebraska Beef Festival[15] at which part of the festivities is watching trucks pull up and the live cattle get driven down the ramp and slaughtered right there on the World's Largest Killing Floor or something—there's no way.

The intimacy of the whole thing is maximized at home, which of course is where most lobster gets prepared and eaten (although note already the semiconscious euphemism "prepared," which in the case of lobsters really means killing them right there in our kitchens). The basic scenario is that we come in from the store and make our little preparations like getting the kettle filled and boiling, and then we lift the lobsters out of the bag or whatever retail container they came home in . . . whereupon some uncomfortable things start to happen. However stuporous the lobster is from the trip home, for instance, it tends to come alarmingly to life when placed in boiling water. If you're tilting it from a container into the steaming kettle, the lobster will sometimes try to cling to the container's sides or even to hook its claws over the kettle's rim like a person trying to keep from going over the edge of a roof. And worse is when the lobster's fully immersed. Even if you cover the kettle and turn away, you can usually hear the cover rattling and clanking as the lobster tries to push it off. Or the creature's claws scraping the sides of the kettle as it thrashes around. The lobster, in other words, behaves very much as you or I would behave if we were plunged into boiling water (with

---

[14] Morality-wise, let's concede that this cuts both ways. Lobster-eating is at least not abetted by the system of corporate factory farms that produces most beef, pork, and chicken. Because, if nothing else, of the way they're marketed and packaged for sale, we eat these latter meats without having to consider that they were once conscious, sentient creatures to whom horrible things were done. (N.B. PETA distributes a certain video—the title of which is being omitted as part of the elaborate editorial compromise by which this note appears at all—in which you can see just about everything meat-related you don't want to see or think about. (N.B.[2] Not that PETA's any sort of font of unspun truth. Like many partisans in complex moral disputes, the PETA people are fanatics, and a lot of their rhetoric seems simplistic and self-righteous. Personally, though, I have to say that I found this unnamed video both credible and deeply upsetting.))

[15] Is it significant that "lobster," "fish," and "chicken" are our culture's words for both the animal and the meat, whereas most mammals seem to require euphemisms like "beef" and "pork" that help us separate the meat we eat from the living creature the meat once was? Is this evidence that some kind of deep unease about eating higher animals is endemic enough to show up in English usage, but that the unease diminishes as we move out of the mammalian order? (And is "lamb"/"lamb" the counterexample that sinks the whole theory, or are there special, biblico-historical reasons for that equivalence?)

A squeamish Woody Allen preparing to boil a lobster in his 1977 film classic,
Annie Hall.

the obvious exception of screaming[16]). A blunter way to say this is that the
lobster acts as if it's in terrible pain, causing some cooks to leave the kitchen
altogether and to take one of those little lightweight plastic oven-timers with
them into another room and wait until the whole process is over.

There happen to be two main criteria that most ethicists agree on for
determining whether a living creature has the capacity to suffer and so has

---

16 There's a relevant populist myth about the high-pitched whistling sound that sometimes
issues from a pot of boiling lobster. The sound is really vented steam from the layer of seawater between the lobster's flesh and its carapace (this is why shedders whistle more than hard-shells), but
the pop version has it that the sound is the lobster's rabbit-like death scream. Lobsters communicate
via pheromones in their urine and don't have anything close to the vocal equipment for screaming,
but the myth's very persistent—which might, once again, point to a low-level cultural unease about
the boiling thing.

genuine interests that it may or may not be our moral duty to consider.[17] One is how much of the neurological hardware required for pain-experience the animal comes equipped with—nociceptors, prostaglandins, neuronal opioid receptors, etc. The other criterion is whether the animal demonstrates behavior associated with pain. And it takes a lot of intellectual gymnastics and behaviorist hairsplitting not to see struggling, thrashing, and lid-clattering as just such pain-behavior. According to marine zoologists, it usually takes lobsters between 35 and 45 seconds to die in boiling water. (No source I could find talks about how long it takes them to die in superheated steam; one rather hopes it's faster.)

There are, of course, other ways to kill your lobster on-site and so achieve maximum freshness. Some cooks' practice is to drive a sharp heavy knife point-first into a spot just above the midpoint between the lobster's eyestalks (more or less where the Third Eye is in human foreheads). This is alleged either to kill the lobster instantly or to render it insensate, and is said at least to eliminate some of the cowardice involved in throwing a creature into boiling water and then fleeing the room. As far as I can tell from talking to proponents of the knife-in-the-head method, the idea is that it's more violent but ultimately more merciful, plus that a willingness to exert personal agency and accept responsibility for stabbing the lobster's head honors the lobster somehow and entitles one to eat it (there's often a vague sort of Native American spirituality-of-the-hunt flavor to pro-knife arguments). But the problem with the knife method is basic biology: Lobsters' nervous systems operate off not one but several ganglia, a.k.a. nerve bundles, which are sort of wired in series and distributed all along the lobster's underside, from stem to stern. And disabling only the frontal ganglion does not normally result in quick death or unconsciousness.

Another alternative is to put the lobster in cold saltwater and then very slowly bring it up to a full boil. Cooks who advocate this method are going mostly on the analogy to a frog, which can supposedly be kept from jumping out of a boiling pot by heating the water incrementally. In order to save a lot of research-summarizing, I'll simply assure you that the analogy between frogs and lobsters turns out not to hold—plus, if the kettle's water isn't aerated seawater, the immersed lobster suffers from slow suffocation, although usually not decisive enough suffocation to keep it from still thrashing and clattering when the water gets hot enough to kill it. In fact, lobsters boiled incrementally often display a whole bonus set of gruesome, convulsionlike reactions that you don't see in regular boiling.

---

[17] "Interests" basically means strong and legitimate preferences, which obviously require some degree of consciousness, responsiveness to stimuli, etc. See, for instance, the utilitarian philosopher Peter Singer, whose 1974 *Animal Liberation* is more or less the bible of the modern animal-rights movement:

> It would be nonsense to say that it was not in the interests of a stone to be kicked along the road by a schoolboy. A stone does not have interests because it cannot suffer. Nothing that we can do to it could possibly make any difference to its welfare. A mouse, on the other hand, does have an interest in not being kicked along the road, because it will suffer if it is.

Ultimately, the only certain virtues of the home-lobotomy and slow-   25
heating methods are comparative, because there are even worse/crueler
ways people prepare lobster. Time-thrifty cooks sometimes microwave them
alive (usually after poking several extra vent-holes in the carapace, which
is a precaution most shellfish-microwavers learn about the hard way). Live
dismemberment, on the other hand, is big in Europe—some chefs cut the
lobster in half before cooking; others like to tear off the claws and tail and
toss only these parts in the pot.

And there's more unhappy news respecting suffering-criterion number
one. Lobsters don't have much in the way of eyesight or hearing, but they
do have an exquisite tactile sense, one facilitated by hundreds of thousands
of tiny hairs that protrude through their carapace. "Thus it is," in the words
of T. M. Prudden's industry classic *About Lobster*, "that although encased
in what seems a solid, impenetrable armor, the lobster can receive stimuli
and impressions from without as readily as if it possessed a soft and delicate
skin." And lobsters do have nociceptors,[18] as well as invertebrate versions
of the prostaglandins and major neurotransmitters via which our own brains
register pain.

Lobsters do not, on the other hand, appear to have the equipment for
making or absorbing natural opioids like endorphins and enkephalins,
which are what more advanced nervous systems use to try to handle intense
pain. From this fact, though, one could conclude either that lobsters are
maybe even *more* vulnerable to pain, since they lack mammalian nervous
systems' built-in analgesia, or, instead, that the absence of natural opioids
implies an absence of the really intense pain-sensations that natural opioids
are designed to mitigate. I for one can detect a marked upswing in mood as
I contemplate this latter possibility. It could be that their lack of endorphin/
enkephalin hardware means that lobsters' raw subjective experience of pain
is so radically different from mammals' that it may not even deserve the term
"pain." Perhaps lobsters are more like those frontal-lobotomy patients one
reads about who report experiencing pain in a totally different way than you
and I. These patients evidently do feel physical pain, neurologically speaking, but don't dislike it—though neither do they like it; it's more that they
feel it but don't feel anything *about* it—the point being that the pain is not
distressing to them or something they want to get away from. Maybe lobsters, who are also without frontal lobes, are detached from the neurological-
registration-of-injury-or-hazard we call pain in just the same way. There is,
after all, a difference between (1) pain as a purely neurological event, and
(2) actual suffering, which seems crucially to involve an emotional component, an awareness of pain as unpleasant, as something to fear/dislike/want
to avoid.

---

18 This is the neurological term for special pain-receptors that are "sensitive to potentially
damaging extremes of temperature, to mechanical forces, and to chemical substances which are
released when body tissues are damaged."

Still, after all the abstract intellection, there remain the facts of the frantically clanking lid, the pathetic clinging to the edge of the pot. Standing at the stove, it is hard to deny in any meaningful way that this is a living creature experiencing pain and wishing to avoid/escape the painful experience. To my lay mind, the lobster's behavior in the kettle appears to be the expression of a preference; and it may well be that an ability to form preferences is the decisive criterion for real suffering.[19] The logic of this (preference → suffering) relation may be easiest to see in the negative case. If you cut certain kinds of worms in half, the halves will often keep crawling around and going about their vermiform business as if nothing had happened. When we assert, based on their post-op behavior, that these worms appear not to be suffering, what we're really saying is that there's no sign the worms know anything bad has happened or would *prefer* not to have gotten cut in half.

Lobsters, though, are known to exhibit preferences. Experiments have shown that they can detect changes of only a degree or two in water temperature; one reason for their complex migratory cycles (which can often cover 100-plus miles a year) is to pursue the temperatures they like best.[20] And, as mentioned, they're bottom-dwellers and do not like bright light—if a tank of food-lobsters is out in the sunlight or a store's fluorescence, the lobsters will always congregate in whatever part is darkest. Fairly solitary in the ocean, they also clearly dislike the crowding that's part of their captivity in tanks, since (as also mentioned) one reason why lobsters' claws are banded on capture is to keep them from attacking one another under the stress of close-quarter storage.

In any event, at the MLF, standing by the bubbling tanks outside the   30
World's Largest Lobster Cooker, watching the fresh-caught lobsters pile over one another, wave their hobbled claws impotently, huddle in the rear

---

19 "Preference" is maybe roughly synonymous with "interests," but it is a better term for our purposes because it's less abstractly philosophical—"preference" seems more personal, and it's the whole idea of a living creature's personal experience that's at issue.

20 Of course, the most common sort of counterargument here would begin by objecting that "like best" is really just a metaphor, and a misleadingly anthropomorphic one at that. The counterarguer would posit that the lobster seeks to maintain a certain optimal ambient temperature out of nothing but unconscious instinct (with a similar explanation for the low-light affinities about to be mentioned in the main text). The thrust of such a counterargument will be that the lobster's thrashings and clankings in the kettle express not unpreferred pain but involuntary reflexes, like your leg shooting out when the doctor hits your knee. Be advised that there are professional scientists, including many researchers who use animals in experiments, who hold to the view that nonhuman creatures have no real feelings at all, merely "behaviors." Be further advised that this view has a long history that goes all the way back to Descartes, although its modern support comes mostly from behaviorist psychology.

To these what-looks-like-pain-is-really-just-reflexes counterarguments, however, there happen to be all sorts of scientific and pro–animal rights counter-counterarguments. And then further attempted rebuttals and redirects, and so on. Suffice it to say that both the scientific and the philosophical arguments on either side of the animal-suffering issue are involved, abstruse, technical, often informed by self-interest or ideology, and in the end so totally inconclusive that as a practical matter, in the kitchen or restaurant, it all still seems to come down to individual conscience, going with (no pun) your gut.

corners, or scrabble frantically back from the glass as you approach, it is difficult not to sense that they're unhappy, or frightened, even if it's some rudimentary version of these feelings . . . and, again, why does rudimentariness even enter into it? Why is a primitive, inarticulate form of suffering less urgent or uncomfortable for the person who's helping to inflict it by paying for the food it results in? I'm not trying to give you a PETA-like screed here—at least I don't think so. I'm trying, rather, to work out and articulate some of the troubling questions that arise amid all the laughter and saltation and community pride of the Maine Lobster Festival. The truth is that if you, the festival attendee, permit yourself to think that lobsters can suffer and would rather not, the MLF begins to take on the aspect of something like a Roman circus or medieval torture-fest.

Does that comparison seem a bit much? If so, exactly why? Or what about this one: Is it possible that future generations will regard our own present agribusiness and eating practices in much the same way we now view Nero's[21] entertainments or Mengele's[22] experiments? My own initial reaction is that such a comparison is hysterical, extreme—and yet the reason it seems extreme to me appears to be that I believe animals are less morally important than human beings;[23] and when it comes to defending such a belief, even to myself, I have to acknowledge that (a) I have an obvious selfish interest in this belief, since I like to eat certain kinds of animals and want to be able to keep doing it, and (b) I haven't succeeded in working out any sort of personal ethical system in which the belief is truly defensible instead of just selfishly convenient.

Given this article's venue and my own lack of culinary sophistication, I'm curious about whether the reader can identify with any of these reactions and acknowledgments and discomforts. I'm also concerned not to come off as shrill or preachy when what I really am is more like confused. For those *Gourmet* readers who enjoy well-prepared and -presented meals involving beef, veal, lamb, pork, chicken, lobster, etc.: Do you think much about the (possible) moral status and (probable) suffering of the animals involved? If you do, what ethical convictions have you worked out that permit you not just to eat but to savor and enjoy flesh-based viands (since of course refined enjoyment, rather than mere ingestion, is the whole point of gastronomy)? If, on the other hand, you'll have no truck with confusions or convictions and regard stuff like the previous paragraph as just so much fatuous navel-gazing, what makes it feel truly okay, inside, to just dismiss the whole thing

21 **Nero** (37–68): First-century Roman Emperor noted for his cruelty.—EDS.

22 **Mengele:** Dr. Mengele, the infamous Nazi concentration camp physician (1911–1979) who inspected new prisoners to select those fit for labor and those who would be exterminated. He also was responsible for performing medical experiments on prisoners.—EDS.

23 Meaning *a lot* less important, apparently, since the moral comparison here is not the value of one human's life vs. the value of one animal's life, but rather the value of one animal's life vs. the value of one human's taste for a particular kind of protein. Even the most diehard carniphile will acknowledge that it's possible to live and eat well without consuming animals.

out of hand? That is, is your refusal to think about any of this the product of actual thought, or is it just that you don't want to think about it? And if the latter, then why not? Do you ever think, even idly, about the possible reasons for your reluctance to think about it? I am not trying to bait anyone here—I'm genuinely curious. After all, isn't being extra aware and attentive and thoughtful about one's food and its overall context part of what distinguishes a real gourmet? Or is all the gourmet's extra attention and sensibility just supposed to be sensuous? Is it really all just a matter of taste and presentation?

These last few queries, though, while sincere, obviously involve much larger and more abstract questions about the connections (if any) between aesthetics and morality—about what the adjective in a phrase like "The Magazine of Good Living" is really supposed to mean—and these questions lead straightaway into such deep and treacherous waters that it's probably best to stop the public discussion right here. There are limits to what even interested persons can ask of each other. ●

The Reader's Presence

1. What is the occasion behind "Consider the Lobster"? Why did Wallace write it? How would you describe the audience he is writing for? What relation does he establish with that audience? What is Wallace's overall attitude toward the event that he was assigned to write about?

2. Wallace refers to "Consider the Lobster" as an "article." How does it differ from the magazine articles you may typically read? Note the title: "Consider" is often a term used by essayists. What does the word *consider* suggest to you? It's common in essays for the essayist to examine different sides of an issue and, instead of coming up with a definite conclusion, offer various ways that we might think of, or "consider," that issue. What features of the selection resemble a magazine article? What features appear essayistic?

3. **CONNECTIONS:** The selection begins with a consideration of tourism in America. How would you characterize Wallace's attitude toward tourism? Carefully read his remarks on tourism in the long footnote appearing on page 843. Consider Nathaniel Hawthorne's "My Visit to Niagara" (page 438) in the light of Wallace's remarks. How appropriate do those remarks seem to Hawthorne's essay? You might also want to compare "Consider the Lobster" to Jonathan Swift's "A Modest Proposal" (page 831). How does each writer deal with problems of audience?

The Writer at Work

Another Version of "Consider the Lobster"

When David Foster Wallace submitted "Consider the Lobster" to *Gourmet*, which calls itself "The Magazine of Good Living," the piece was edited by the magazine before it appeared in its August 2004 issue. After it was selected for the *Best American Essays 2005*, Wallace asked if he could make some changes before it was published in that volume. Basically, he wanted to restore some of his original remarks that the magazine had revised. Then, when he included the essay in his own collection, *Consider the Lobster and Other Essays* (2005), he made even further revisions. It is that final text that we have included in this book.

Most of Wallace's revisions occur in the conclusion of the essay. The following passage is taken from the first appearance of the essay in *Gourmet* magazine and represents the essay's final four paragraphs. As you compare the concluding paragraphs as they appeared in *Gourmet* to those Wallace preferred and used in his book (pages 852–854), what do you find significant about the differences? What kind of changes had *Gourmet* made? Why do you think Wallace wanted to change what *Gourmet* had done? Note the substitution of "Aztec sacrifices" for "Mengele's experiments" (for more on Mengele see Elie Wiesel's "Eight Simple, Short Words" on page 267). Which is the better example in your opinion? Why do you think Wallace preferred to address his readers as "you" in his version and not as "they" as appears in paragraph 3 of the *Gourmet* version? Why do you think the magazine preferred to drop the direct address to readers in this context?

From *Gourmet* magazine:

[30] **❝**I'm not trying to give you a PETA-like screed here—at least I don't think so. I'm trying, rather, to work out and articulate some of the troubling questions that arise amid all the laughter and saltation and community pride of the Maine Lobster Festival. The truth is that if you, the Festival attendee, permit yourself to think that lobsters can suffer and would rather not, the MLF can begin to take on aspects of something like a Roman circus or medieval torture-fest.

[31] Does that comparison seem a bit much? If so, exactly why? Or what about this one: Is it not possible that future generations will regard our own present agribusiness and eating practices in much the same way we now view Nero's entertainments or Aztec sacrifices? My own immediate reaction is that such a comparison is hysterical, extreme—and yet the reason it seems extreme to me appears to be that I believe animals are less morally important than human beings; and when it comes to defending such a belief, even to myself, I have to acknowledge that (a) I have an obvious selfish interest in this belief, since I like to eat certain kinds of animals and want

to be able to keep doing it, and (b) I have not succeeded in working out any sort of personal ethical system in which the belief is truly defensible instead of just selfishly convenient.

[32] Given this article's venue and my own lack of culinary sophistication, I'm curious about whether the reader can identify with any of these reactions and acknowledgments and discomforts. I am also concerned not to come off as shrill or preachy when what I really am is confused. Given the (possible) moral status and (very possible) physical suffering of the animals involved, what ethical convictions do gourmets evolve that allow them not just to eat but to savor and enjoy flesh-based viands (since of course refined *enjoyment*, rather than just ingestion, is the whole point of gastronomy)? And for those gourmets who'll have no truck with convictions or rationales and who regard stuff like the previous paragraph as just so much pointless navel-gazing, what makes it feel okay, inside, to dismiss the whole issue out of hand? That is, is their refusal to think about any of this the product of actual thought, or is it just that they don't want to think about it? Do they ever think about their reluctance to think about it? After all, isn't being extra aware and attentive and thoughtful about one's food and its overall context part of what distinguishes a real gourmet? Or is all the gourmet's extra attention and sensibility just supposed to be aesthetic, gustatory?

[33] These last couple queries, though, while sincere, obviously involve much larger and more abstract questions about the connections (if any) between aesthetics and morality, and these questions lead straightaway into such deep and treacherous waters that it's probably best to stop the public discussion right here. There are limits to what even interested persons can ask of each other. **"**

John Edgar Wideman

STREET CORNER DREAMERS

Professor of Africana studies and English at Brown University, **JOHN EDGAR WIDE-MAN** (b. 1941) is the only author to win the International PEN/Faulkner Award for Fiction twice. After receiving his BA in English in 1963, he won a Rhodes scholarship to study philosophy at Oxford University's New College. He returned to the United States in 1966, spent a year as a Kent Fellow at the famous University of Iowa Writer's Workshop, and published his first novel, *A Glance Away*, in 1967. His has written many novels since then, including *The Lynchers* (1973), *Hiding Place* (1981), *Philadelphia Fire* (1990), *Two Cities* (1998), and *Fanon* (2008), to name but a few. He is also the author of a memoir, *Brothers and Keepers* (1984), as well as several other nonfiction books and collections of short stories. *Conversations with John Edgar Wideman*, a series of nineteen interviews spanning three decades, was published by the University Press of Mississippi in 1998. Wideman has written widely on African American issues and culture, and his articles on Malcolm X, Spike Lee, Denzel Washington, Michael Jordan, Emmett Till, Thelonius Monk, and women's professional basketball have appeared in the *New Yorker*, *Vogue*, *Esquire*, *Emerge*, and the *New York Times Magazine*. His daughter, Jamila, is a professional basketball player.

> **Wideman has written widely on African American issues and culture, and his articles on Malcolm X, Spike Lee, Denzel Washington, Michael Jordan, Emmett Till, Thelonius Monk, and women's professional basketball have appeared in the *New Yorker*, *Vogue*, *Esquire*, *Emerge*, and the *New York Times Magazine*.**

IT IS THE MORNING AFTER Barack Obama has been elected the forty-fourth president of the United States. In six hours or so, the corner of Grand and Essex, a block from my apartment building on New York's Lower East Side, will fill up with young people exiting Seward Park High School. For more than two years, the city has been sandblasting Seward Park's seven-story exterior walls. As the presidential candidates debated taxes, someone was paid a large chunk of scarce public funds, originally designated for improving education, to clean the building. Unfortunately, the scouring barely altered the dour, dirty gray scowl of the brick and stone. I don't know what was transpiring inside Seward while its outside was being scrubbed, but given the dismal record of public schools educating the poor, I harbor plenty of dire concerns: Has anybody asked the students if they think they're learning more and better after their school's facelift? Are the students being instructed how to survive the droning, predatory streets waiting to eat them up? I want to walk up to one of them and ask, "Do you think your life might be different now that Barack Obama is president? What steps do you believe President Obama will take to improve your life? What steps do you think he should take?"

Of course there are many, many young people missing from the corner—in jail, addicted or dead already from violence or neglect, many alienated absolutely from school, citizenship, prospects of jobs and families. Not a lost generation exactly—their bodies survive, though as mere phantoms of what they could have become, could have offered society. They are ghosts whose absence is a palpable presence among the kids on the corner, a shadow haunting and jeopardizing them. How long? Too long. They are the predictable casualties, victims comprising a heartbreakingly high percentage of youth of color, destroyed by marginalization. Why? Because America decided we could get along just fine without them, thank you. Is a President Obama too late to help the missing ones? What higher priority for a nation, for a new president, than to stop the bleeding, to stop the blighting of youth and potential suffered by generation after generation of the colored and poor? Will they continue to be treated as expendable? How will President Barack Obama attempt to seal the cracks they slip through? Not cracks in the pavement of Grand and Essex, but the cracks of broken promises, the cracks that have divided and conquered the will of a nation to treat all citizens equally.

Walking the gauntlets of students on the sidewalks surrounding that school, I admit to myself that I've been too busy, too consumed by whatever's on my mind, to ask any of them anything. Though they'd never guess it from my silence as I pass through their ranks, I'm hopelessly in love with them, worry about them, see my nieces, nephews, granddaughter, myself in this unruly, roiling mass of teenagers—young people of amalgamated African, Asian, European descent, every shade of light and dark skin, bushy hair, straight hair, dreads, braids, shaved heads, raw exuberance and noise and eyes hungry only for each other. I am a bit intimidated by them, certainly daunted by the ruthless truth of the vast difference in age and circumstance separating us, overwhelmed finally by the spectacle of their absolute fragility and vulnerability as they pour out onto the streets, exposed by the clothing they wear, clothes manufactured from the cheapest synthetics to simulate expensive flash and flair, colorful clothing brimming with attitude, with confidence and humor and shame and shyness about physically coming of age, bodies sprouting, busting-out young bodies in motley costumes to disguise poverty, clothing calculated to reveal and conceal.

Is there such a thing, really, as a future in young minds infatuated, incarcerated by the present moment? Why would these young people speculate about crossing the gulf between themselves and the future, any future, whether a President Obama's in it or not? How equipped are they to imagine bridging the chasm between a White House in Washington, D.C., and a local, recently scoured public school that serves the Lower East Side's children of color and poverty?

In a classroom inside the building, as a sponsored guest, maybe I could   5
undertake a conversation about who they are, who I am, and the uncertain, unsettling place where we find ourselves at this perilous juncture in our nation's evolution. Perhaps we would explore together the explosive, still almost unbelievable fact that our country finally seized the opportunity to turn away from one deeply rooted, intractable, self-destructive, dead-end understanding of itself as White and Black, finally began to create a new vision of itself, whatever that vision might shake out to be. Will we become a nation converted to a new faith, a new dream, a new political consciousness and commitment, embracing Obama's complex heritage, his courage, his determination, his call for us to be more, collectively, than the sum of our parts?

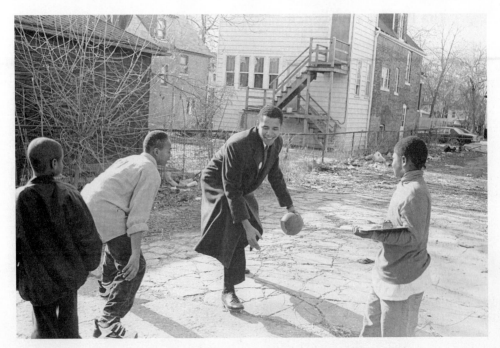

Barack Obama plays basketball with local youths in Chicago's South Side, where he launched his career in public service as a community organizer. Source: © Marc Pokempner

My vision of what's coming next goes no further. No crystal-ball gazing. I see a swarm of young people congregating down the block, free at last, of closed rooms, regimented hours, hostility, chaos, good intentions. Young women and men energized by the immediate, compelling hunger and sweetness of being alive. I want to believe that these young people on the corner are not only capable of bearing change, but that they can also be bearers of that change. Do I glimpse that change in the way they walk and talk, the way they occupy space and flash looks at one another, urgent exchanges of joy, anger, longing, understanding, impatience, solidarity, challenge, like the undeniable, irrepressible reality embodied in singer Sam Cooke's voice when he promises change that must come—music that might be in the general air now or playing just around the corner in the voice of Barack Obama?

Not Barack singing, but President Obama in charge, calling the meeting to order. Putting a finger to his lips: *Quiet, everybody, please.* Let's listen to our young people on the street corners. Let's begin making room for the voices they may not exactly understand they own yet, carve out space for them in this country they may not exactly comprehend belongs to them, too. The president of the United States of America, listening to the words of the young people who throng Grand and Essex, Obama listening to discover what he may do for them, do for us all. ●

The Reader's Presence

1. Comment on the effectiveness of Wideman's decision to open his essay by describing the sandblasting of the high school's exterior walls. How does this image relate—literally or metaphorically or both—to the argument Wideman makes in this essay?

2. In paragraph 4, Wideman asks, "Is there such a thing, really, as a future in young minds infatuated, incarcerated by the present moment?" What do you understand him to mean by this statement? What do you make of Wideman's juxtaposition of "infatuated" and "incarcerated" here? Look for similarly surprising turns of phrase throughout the essay and analyze their meaning and effects.

3. **CONNECTIONS:**   Read the speech by Martin Luther King Jr. titled "I Have a Dream" (page 701). In what specific ways—and with what specific effects—does Wideman allude to and expand on the ideas King set forth in that speech? What new realities facing minorities does Wideman feel must be addressed? How does Wideman's "dream" differ from that of Martin Luther King Jr.?

Howard Zinn
STORIES HOLLYWOOD NEVER TELLS

HOWARD ZINN (1922–2010) was professor emeritus of political science at Boston University and is known both for his active involvement in the civil rights and peace movements and for his scholarship. He published scores of books that reflected the issues of their times yet remain in print, demonstrating their continuing relevance. A sampling includes *The Southern Mystique* (1964); *Vietnam: The Logic of Withdrawal* (1967); *Disobedience and Democracy: Nine Fallacies on Law and Order* (1968); *The Politics of History* (1970); *A People's History of the United States: 1492 to the Present* (1980), which has sold more than a million copies; *Declarations of Independence: Cross-Examining American Ideology* (1990); *The Zinn Reader: Writings on Disobedience and Democracy* (1997); *Howard Zinn on History* (2000); *Three Strikes: Miners, Musicians, Salesgirls, and the Fighting Spirit of Labor's Last Century* (2001); and *Artists in Times of War* (2003). His most recent book, *Voices of a People's History*

> "I am totally confident not that the world will get better, but that we should not give up the game before all the cards have been played."

of the United States (2004), is a companion to *A People's History*. The essay "Stories Holly-wood Never Tells," adapted from *Artists in Times of War*, was published in *The Sun* in 2004.

Zinn had also written plays, a musical, and an autobiography, *You Can't Be Neutral on a Moving Train* (1994).

Throughout his career, Zinn argued that perseverence in the face of opposition is essential: "I am totally confident not that the world will get better, but that we should not give up the game before all the cards have been played. The metaphor is deliberate; life is a gamble. Not to play is to foreclose any chance of winning. To play, to act, is to create at least a possibility of changing the world."

HOWEVER HATEFUL they may be sometimes, I have always loved the movies. When I began reading and studying history, I kept coming across incidents and events that led me to think, *Wow, what a movie this would make.* I would look to see if a movie had been made about it, but I'd never find one. It took me a while to realize that Hollywood isn't going to make movies like the ones I imagined. Hollywood isn't going to make movies that are class-conscious, or antiwar, or conscious of the need for racial equality or gender equality.

I wondered about this. It seemed to me that the people in Hollywood didn't all get together in a room and decide, "We're going to do just this kind of film and not the other kind of film." Yet it's not just an oversight or an accident, either. Leon Trotsky once used an expression to describe events that are not accidents, and are not planned deliberately, but are something in between. He called this the "natural selection of accidents," in which, if there's a certain structure to a situation, then these "accidents" will inevitably happen, whether anyone plans them or not. It seems that the structure of Hollywood is such that it will not produce the kinds of films that I imagined. It's a structure where money and profit are absolutely the first consideration: before art, before aesthetics, before human values.

When you consider the films about war that have come out of Hollywood — and there have been hundreds and hundreds, maybe even thousands — they almost always glorify military heroism. We need to think about telling the story of war from a different perspective.

Let's take one of our most popular wars to begin with: the Revolutionary War. How can you speak against the Revolutionary War, right? But to tell the story of the American Revolution, not from the standpoint of the schoolbooks, but from the standpoint of war as a complex phenomenon intertwined with moral issues, we must acknowledge not just that Americans were oppressed by the English, but that some Americans were oppressed by other Americans. For instance, American Indians did not rush to celebrate the victory of the colonists over England, because for them it meant that the line that the British had drawn to limit westward expansion in the Proclamation of 1763 would now be obliterated. The colonists would be free to move west into Indian lands.

John Adams, one of the Founding Fathers and a revolutionary leader,   5
estimated that one-third of the colonists supported the American Revolution,
one-third were opposed, and one-third were neutral. It would be interesting to tell the story of the American Revolution from the viewpoint of an
ordinary workingman who hears the Declaration of Independence read to
him from a balcony in Boston, promising freedom and equality and so on,
and immediately is told that rich men can get out of service by paying several hundred dollars. This man then joins the army, despite his misgivings,
despite his own feelings of being oppressed—not just by the British, but by
the leaders of the colonial world—because he is promised some land. But as
the war progresses and he sees the mutilations and the killing, he becomes
increasingly disaffected. There's no place in society where class divisions
are more clear-cut than in the military, and he sees that the officers are living
in splendor while the ordinary enlisted men don't have any clothes or shoes,
aren't being paid, and are being fed slop. So he joins the mutineers.

In the Revolutionary War, there were two mutinies against Washington's army: the mutiny of the Pennsylvania Line, and the mutiny of the New
Jersey Line. Let's say our workingman joins the Pennsylvania Line, and
they march on the Continental Congress, but eventually are surrounded by
Washington's army, and several of their former comrades are forced to shoot
several of the mutineers. Then this soldier, embittered by what he's seen,
gets out of the army and gets some land in western Massachusetts. After the
war is over, he becomes part of Shays's Rebellion, in which a group of small
farmers rebel against the rich men who control the legislature in Boston and
who are imposing heavy taxes on them, taking away their land and farms.
The farmers, many of them Revolutionary War veterans, surround the court-
houses and refuse to let the auctioneer go in to auction off their farms. The
militia is called out to suppress them, and the militia also goes over to their
side. Finally an army is raised by the moneyed class in Boston to suppress
Shays's Rebellion.

I have never seen Hollywood tell this kind of story. If you know of a film
that has been made about it, I wish you'd tell me so that we could have a
celebration of that rare event.

Wars are more complicated than the simple good-versus-evil scenario
presented to us in our history books and our culture. Wars are not simply
conflicts of one people against another; wars always involve class differences within each side, and victory is very often not shared by everybody,
but only among a few. The people who fight the wars are not the people who
benefit from the wars.

I think somebody should make a new movie about the Mexican War. I
haven't seen one that tells how the Mexican War started, or how the president of the United States deceived the American people. I know it's surprising to hear that a president would willfully deceive the people of the
United States, but this was one of those rare cases. President James Polk told
Americans that Mexican troops had fired at our troops on U.S. soil. Really
the fighting broke out on disputed soil that both Mexico and the U.S. had

claimed. The war had been planned in advance by the Polk administration, because it coveted this beautiful territory of the Southwest.

It would be interesting to tell that story from the viewpoint of an ordi-   10
nary soldier, who sees the mayhem and the bloodshed as the army moves into Mexico and destroys town after town. More and more U.S. soldiers grow disaffected from the war, and as they make their final march toward Mexico City, General Scott wakes up one morning to discover that half his army has deserted.

It would be interesting, too, to tell the story from the point of view of one of the Massachusetts volunteers who comes back at the end of the war and is invited to a victory celebration. When the commander of the Massachusetts volunteers gets up to speak, he is booed off the platform by the surviving half of his men, who resent what happened to their comrades in the war and who wonder what they were fighting for. I should tell you: this really happened.

The film could also include a scene after the war in which the U.S. Army is moving to suppress a rebellion in Santa Fe, because mostly Mexicans still live there. The army marches through the streets of Santa Fe, and all the townspeople go into their houses and close the shutters. The army is met by total silence, an expression of how the population feels about this great American victory.

Another little story about the Mexican War is the tale of the deserters. Many of those who volunteered to fight in the Mexican War did so for the same reason that people volunteer for the military today: they were desperately poor and hoped that their fortunes would improve as a result of enlisting. During the Mexican War, some of these volunteers were recent Irish immigrants. When these immigrant soldiers saw what was being done to the people of Mexico, a number of them deserted and went over to the Mexican side. They formed their own battalion, which they called St. Patrick's Battalion, or the San Patricio Battalion, and they fought for the Mexicans.

It's not easy to make the Spanish-American War look like a noble enterprise — though of course Hollywood can do anything. The war has gotten a certain amount of attention, because of the heroism of Theodore Roosevelt and his Rough Riders, but not a lot. In the history textbooks, the Spanish-American War is called "a splendid little war." It lasted three months. We fought it to free the Cubans, because we're always going to war to free somebody. We expelled the Spaniards from Cuba, but we didn't expel ourselves, and the United States in effect took over Cuba after the war. One grievance we have against Fidel Castro is that he ended U.S. control of Cuba. We're certainly not against him simply because he's a dictator. We've never had anything against dictators in general.

I remember learning in school that, as a result of the Spanish-American   15
War, we somehow took over the Philippines, but I never knew the details. When you look into it, you'll find that the Spanish-American War lasted three months; the Philippine War lasted for years and was a brutal, bloody suppression of the Filipino movement for independence. In many ways, it

was a precursor of the Vietnam War, in terms of the atrocities committed by the U.S. Army. Now, that's a story that has never been told.

Black American soldiers in the Philippines soon began to identify more with the Filipinos than with their fellow white Americans. While these black soldiers were fighting to suppress the Filipinos, they also were hearing from relatives about the lynchings and race riots in their hometowns. They were hearing about black people being killed in large numbers—and here they were, fighting against a nonwhite people on behalf of the United States government. A number of black soldiers deserted and went over to fight with the Filipinos.

In 1906, when the Philippine War was supposedly over—but really the U.S. Army was still suppressing pockets of rebellion—there was a massacre. That's the only way to describe it. The Moros are inhabitants of a southern island in the Philippines. The army swooped down and annihilated a Moro village of six hundred men, women, and children—all of whom were unarmed. Every last one of them was killed. Mark Twain wrote angrily about this. He was especially angry about the fact that President Theodore Roosevelt sent a letter of congratulations to the military commander who had ordered this atrocity, saying it was a great military victory. Have you ever seen a movie in which Theodore Roosevelt was presented as a racist? As an imperialist? As a supporter of massacres? And there he is, up on Mount Rushmore. I've had the thought: *A hammer, a chisel.* But no, it wouldn't do.

War needs to be presented on film in such a way as to encourage the population simply to say no to war. We need a film about those heroic Americans who protested World War I. When you look at them, you see socialists, pacifists, and just ordinary people who saw the stupidity of entering a war that was taking the lives of ten million people in Europe. You see Emma Goldman, the feminist and anarchist, who went to prison for opposing the draft and the war. You see Helen Keller. Every film about Helen Keller concentrates on the fact that she was disabled. I've never seen a film in which Helen Keller is presented as what she was: a radical, a socialist, an antiwar agitator. You also see Kate Richards O'Hare, a socialist who was put in jail for opposing World War I. There is a story from her time in prison that would make a great scene in a movie: The prisoners are stifling for lack of air, and O'Hare takes a book that she's been reading, reaches through the bars, and hurls the book through a skylight to let the air in. All the prisoners applaud and cheer.

I have to acknowledge that there have been a few antiwar films made about World War I. *All Quiet on the Western Front* is an extraordinary film. I recently wrote an article comparing it to *Saving Private Ryan.* Despite the mayhem, *Saving Private Ryan* was essentially a glorification of war, whereas *All Quiet on the Western Front* expresses a diamond-clear antiwar sentiment.

What about the many films devoted to World War II, the "good war"? 20 When Studs Terkel did his oral history of World War II, he called it *The "Good War,"* with quotation marks around *Good War.* In that war, we fought against a terrible evil—fascism—but our own atrocities multiplied as the war went on, culminating in the bombings of Hiroshima and Nagasaki. I have not seen a Hollywood film about the bombing of Hiroshima. The closest we've come to a movie that deals with our bombing of civilian populations was the film version of Kurt Vonnegut's book *Slaughterhouse-Five*, about the bombing of Dresden, Germany, and that was a rarity.

Films about the Civil War tend to focus on the famous battles, like Gettysburg, Fredericksburg, and Bull Run. The Civil War is, again, one of our "good wars"—the slaves were freed because of it—but it is not that simple. There is the class element of who was and who was not drafted, who paid substitutes, who made huge amounts of money off the war. And then there is what happened to the Indians. In the midst of the Civil War, while the armies were fighting in the South, another part of the Union Army was out west, destroying Indian settlements and taking over Indian land. In 1864, not long after the Emancipation Proclamation, the U.S. Army was in Colorado attacking an Indian village, killing hundreds of men, women, and children at Sand Creek, in one of the worst Indian massacres in American history. This massacre occurred during the war to end slavery. In the years of the Civil War, more land was taken from the Indians than in any other comparable period in history.

There's a lot of historical work to be done, a lot of films that need to be made. There are so many class struggles in the U.S. that could be dealt with in movies. We've seen movies that deal with working-class people, but it's always some individual who rises up out of his or her situation and "makes it" in society. Stories of Americans who organize and get together to oppose the powers that hold them down have been very rare.

The American political system and the revered and celebrated Constitution of the United States do not grant any economic rights to the American people. We very often forget that the Constitution gives political rights but not economic rights. If you are not wealthy, then your political rights are limited, even though they are guaranteed on paper in the Constitution. The freedom of speech is granted there, but how much free speech you have depends on how much money and what access to resources you have. The Declaration of Independence talks about the right to life, liberty, and the pursuit of happiness. But how can you have life, liberty, and the pursuit of happiness if you don't have food, housing, and healthcare?

Working people throughout history have had to organize, struggle, go on strike, declare boycotts, and face the police and the army. They have had to do it themselves, against the opposition of government, in order to win the eight-hour workday and other slight improvements to their working conditions. A great film remains to be made about the Haymarket Affair of 1886, which was part of the struggle for the eight-hour workday. The Haymarket Affair culminated in the execution of four anarchists who were charged with planting a bomb, though in the end nobody ever found out who really had planted it.

Engraving depicting the 1886 Haymarket Riot.

The great railroad strike of 1894 tied up the railway system of the United 25
States, and all the power of the army and the courts had to be brought against
the striking workers. Eugene Debs, who organized the railroad workers, has
never been the central figure in a movie. He was sent to prison for opposing
World War I, and he made such an impression on his fellow prisoners that,
when he was released, the warden let all the inmates out into the yard, and
they applauded as Debs was granted his freedom.

I've met someone who is actually writing a script about the Lawrence
textile strike of 1912, a magnificent episode in American history, because
the striking workers won. It was a multicultural strike. A working population
that spoke twelve different languages got together and defied the textile
companies and the police, who were sent to the railroad station to prevent
the children of the workers from leaving town. Police literally attacked the
women and children at the station, because the company wanted to starve
out the strikers, and that would be less likely to happen if their children were
safe. But the strikers held out, and with the help of the Industrial Workers of
the World, they finally won.

Then there's the Ludlow Massacre, which took place during the Colorado coal strike of 1913–1914, one of the most bitter, bloody, dramatic strikes
in American history. The workers were up against the Rockefeller interests.
(It's not easy to make an unflattering film about the Rockefellers.) One of
the strike's leaders was Mother Jones, an eighty-three-year-old woman who

had previously organized textile workers in West Virginia and Pennsylvania. That's another story that should be told. There were kids working in the textile mills at the age of eleven and twelve. Mother Jones led these children on a march from Pennsylvania to Oyster Bay, New York, where President Theodore Roosevelt was on summer vacation. They stood there outside the resort with signs that said, WE WANT TIME TO PLAY. Has there ever been a film made about that?

We've had films on Christopher Columbus, but I don't know of any film that shows Columbus as what he was: a man ruled by the capitalist ethic. Columbus and the Spaniards were killing people for gold. The Catholic priest Bartolomé de Las Casas was an eyewitness. He exposed what was going on, and a remarkable debate took place before the Royal Commission of Spain in 1650. The debate was between Las Casas and Sepulveda, another priest, who argued that the Indians were not human and therefore you could do anything you wanted to them.

Immigrant women striking in Lawrence, Massachusetts, 1912.

There's also the story of the Trail of Tears—the expulsion of the Cherokees from the Southeast. Andrew Jackson, one of our national heroes, signed the order to expel them. That was ethnic cleansing on a large scale: the march across the continent, the U.S. Army driving the Indians from their homeland to a little space in Oklahoma that was then called "Indian Territory." When oil was later discovered there, the Indian population was once again evicted. Of the sixteen thousand people who marched westward, four thousand died on the march, while the U.S. Army pushed them, and the U.S. president extolled what happened.

Of course someone should finally tell the story of black people in the   30
United States from a black person's point of view. We've had a number of films about the civil-rights movement from white points of view. *The Long Walk Home* (1991) tells the story of the Montgomery bus boycott from Sissy Spacek's point of view. *Mississippi Burning* (1988) is about the murder of three civil-rights workers in Mississippi in 1964. The FBI agents are the heroes of the film, but every person who was in Mississippi in 1964—my wife and I were both there at the time—knew that the FBI was the enemy. The FBI was watching people being beaten and not doing anything about it. The FBI was silent and absent when people needed protection against murderers. In this Hollywood film, they become heroes. We need the story of the civil-rights movement told from the viewpoint of black people.

Of course, many good movies and wonderful documentaries have been made. Michael Moore's film *Roger and Me*, which has been seen by tens of millions of people, is a remarkable success story. So the possibilities do exist to practice a kind of guerrilla warfare and make films outside of the Hollywood establishment.

If such films are made—about war, about class conflict, about the history of governmental lies, about broken treaties and official violence—if those stories reach the public, we might produce a new generation. As a teacher, I'm not interested in just reproducing class after class of graduates who will get out, become successful, and take their obedient places in the slots that society has prepared for them. What we must do—whether we teach or write or make films—is educate a new generation to do this very modest thing: change the world. ◼

The Reader's Presence

1. Explain what Zinn means by what Leon Trotsky called the "natural selection of accidents" (paragraph 2) preventing true depictions of war, class, and race from appearing in films. Do you agree that Hollywood's structure works against such depictions? Why or why not?

2. Reading the essay, who did you imagine Zinn's audience to be? How sympathetic to his argument would you expect them to be? What evidence can you find for your answers?

3. **CONNECTIONS:** Zinn says, "Stories of Americans who organize and get together to oppose the powers that hold them down have been very rare" in Hollywood (paragraph 22), but he presents examples to indicate that such stories have appeared again and again throughout American history. In "Street Corner Dreamers" (page 856), John Edgar Wideman raises questions about whether the young people celebrating the election of Barack Obama to the presidency of the United States would think on the morning after that their lives will be fundamentally different: "What steps do you believe President Obama will take to improve your life? What steps do you think he should take?" (paragraph 1). What "American values" would Zinn and Wideman be likely to share? Point to specific passages in each essay to validate your response. To what extent do you view these values as "traditional"? as important? Why or why not?

Sherman Alexie

THIS IS WHAT IT MEANS TO SAY PHOENIX, ARIZONA

SHERMAN ALEXIE's short story "This Is What It Means to Say Phoenix, Arizona" appears in *The Lone Ranger and Tonto Fistfight in Heaven* (1993). Alexie has said, "Most of my heroes are just decent people. Decency is rare and underrated. I think my writing is somehow just about decency." Victor and Thomas, two "decent people" in this story, are also characters in Alexie's first screenplay. The film, *Smoke Signals*, premiered at the 1998 Sundance Film Festival, where it won the Audience Award and the Filmmakers Trophy. Alexie describes the film as "a very basic story, a road trip/buddy movie about a lost father." The narrative structure, as he has pointed out, appears "in everything from the Bible to the *Iliad* and the *Odyssey*."

For additional information on Sherman Alexie, see page 27.

> **"Most of my heroes are just decent people. Decency is rare and underrated. I think my writing is somehow just about decency."**

JUST AFTER VICTOR lost his job at the BIA,[1] he also found out that his father had died of a heart attack in Phoenix, Arizona. Victor hadn't seen his father in a few years, only talked to him on the telephone once or twice, but there still was a genetic pain, which was soon to be pain as real and immediate as a broken bone.

Victor didn't have any money. Who does have money on a reservation, except the cigarette and fireworks salespeople? His father had a savings account waiting to be claimed, but Victor needed to find a way to get to Phoenix. Victor's mother was just as poor as he was, and the rest of his family didn't have any use at all for him. So Victor called the Tribal Council.

"Listen," Victor said. "My father just died. I need some money to get to Phoenix to make arrangements."

"Now, Victor," the council said. "You know we're having a difficult time financially."

"But I thought the council had special funds set aside for stuff like this." 5

---

1 **BIA:** Bureau of Indian Affairs, an agency that has historically often been at odds with the tribes it was created to administer.—EDS.

"Now, Victor, we do have some money available for the proper return of tribal members' bodies. But I don't think we have enough to bring your father all the way back from Phoenix."

"Well," Victor said. "It ain't going to cost all that much. He had to be cremated. Things were kind of ugly. He died of a heart attack in his trailer and nobody found him for a week. It was really hot, too. You get the picture."

"Now, Victor, we're sorry for your loss and the circumstances. But we can really only afford to give you one hundred dollars."

"That's not even enough for a plane ticket."

"Well, you might consider driving down to Phoenix."   10

"I don't have a car. Besides, I was going to drive my father's pickup back up here."

"Now, Victor," the council said. "We're sure there is somebody who could drive you to Phoenix. Or is there somebody who could lend you the rest of the money?"

"You know there ain't nobody around with that kind of money."

"Well, we're sorry, Victor, but that's the best we can do."

Victor accepted the Tribal Council's offer. What else could he do? So he   15
signed the proper papers, picked up his check, and walked over to the Trading Post to cash it.

While Victor stood in line, he watched Thomas Builds-the-Fire standing near the magazine rack, talking to himself. Like he always did. Thomas was a storyteller that nobody wanted to listen to. That's like being a dentist in a town where everybody has false teeth.

Victor and Thomas Builds-the-Fire were the same age, had grown up and played in the dirt together. Ever since Victor could remember, it was Thomas who always had something to say.

Once, when they were seven years old, when Victor's father still lived with the family, Thomas closed his eyes and told Victor this story: "Your father's heart is weak. He is afraid of his own family. He is afraid of you. Late at night he sits in the dark. Watches the television until there's nothing but that white noise. Sometimes he feels like he wants to buy a motorcycle and ride away. He wants to run and hide. He doesn't want to be found."

Thomas Builds-the-Fire had known that Victor's father was going to leave, knew it before anyone. Now Victor stood in the Trading Post with a one-hundred-dollar check in his hand, wondering if Thomas knew that Victor's father was dead, if he knew what was going to happen next.

Just then Thomas looked at Victor, smiled, and walked over to him.   20

"Victor, I'm sorry about your father," Thomas said.

"How did you know about it?" Victor asked.

"I heard it on the wind. I heard it from the birds. I felt it in the sunlight. Also, your mother was just in here crying."

"Oh," Victor said and looked around the Trading Post. All the other Indians stared, surprised that Victor was even talking to Thomas. Nobody talked to Thomas anymore because he told the same damn stories over and over again. Victor was embarrassed, but he thought that Thomas might be able to help him. Victor felt a sudden need for tradition.

"I can lend you the money you need," Thomas said suddenly. "But you   25
have to take me with you."

"I can't take your money," Victor said. "I mean, I haven't hardly talked to you in years. We're not really friends anymore."

"I didn't say we were friends. I said you had to take me with you."

"Let me think about it."

Victor went home with his one hundred dollars and sat at the kitchen table. He held his head in his hands and thought about Thomas Builds-the-Fire, remembered little details, tears and scars, the bicycle they shared for a summer, so many stories.

Thomas Builds-the-Fire sat on the bicycle, waited in Victor's yard. He   30
was ten years old and skinny. His hair was dirty because it was the Fourth of July.

"Victor," Thomas yelled. "Hurry up. We're going to miss the fireworks."

After a few minutes, Victor ran out of his house, jumped the porch railing, and landed gracefully on the sidewalk.

"And the judges award him a 9.95, the highest score of the summer," Thomas said, clapped, laughed.

"That was perfect, cousin," Victor said. "And it's my turn to ride the bike."

Thomas gave up the bike and they headed for the fairgrounds. It was   35
nearly dark and the fireworks were about to start.

"You know," Thomas said. "It's strange how us Indians celebrate the Fourth of July. It ain't like it was *our* independence everybody was fighting for."

"You think about things too much," Victor said. "It's just supposed to be fun. Maybe Junior will be there."

"Which Junior? Everybody on this reservation is named Junior."

And they both laughed.

The fireworks were small, hardly more than a few bottle rockets and   40
a fountain. But it was enough for two Indian boys. Years later, they would need much more.

Afterwards, sitting in the dark, fighting off mosquitoes, Victor turned to Thomas Builds-the-Fire.

"Hey," Victor said. "Tell me a story."

Thomas closed his eyes and told this story: "There were these two Indian boys who wanted to be warriors. But it was too late to be warriors in the old way. All the horses were gone. So the two Indian boys stole a car and drove to the city. They parked the stolen car in front of the police station and then hitchhiked back home to the reservation. When they got back, all their friends cheered and their parents' eyes shone with pride. *You were very brave*, everybody said to the two Indian boys. *Very brave.*"

"Ya-hey," Victor said. "That's a good one. I wish I could be a warrior."

"Me, too," Thomas said.   45

They went home together in the dark, Thomas on the bike now, Victor on foot. They walked through shadows and light from the streetlamps.

"We've come a long ways," Thomas said. "We have outdoor lighting."

"All I need is the stars," Victor said. "And besides, you still think about things too much."

They separated then, each headed for home, both laughing all the way.

Victor sat at his kitchen table. He counted his one hundred dollars again   50
and again. He knew he needed more to make it to Phoenix and back. He knew he needed Thomas Builds-the-Fire. So he put his money in his wallet and opened the front door to find Thomas on the porch.

"Ya-hey, Victor," Thomas said. "I knew you'd call me."

Thomas walked into the living room and sat down on Victor's favorite chair.

"I've got some money saved up," Thomas said. "It's enough to get us down there, but you have to get us back."

"I've got this hundred dollars," Victor said. "And my dad had a savings account I'm going to claim."

"How much in your dad's account?"   55

"Enough. A few hundred."

"Sounds good. When we leaving?"

When they were fifteen and had long since stopped being friends, Victor and Thomas got into a fistfight. That is, Victor was really drunk and beat Thomas up for no reason at all. All the other Indian boys stood around and watched it happen. Junior was there and so were Lester, Seymour, and a lot of others. The beating might have gone on until Thomas was dead if Norma Many Horses hadn't come along and stopped it.

"Hey, you boys," Norma yelled and jumped out of her car. "Leave him alone."

If it had been someone else, even another man, the Indian boys would've   60
just ignored the warnings. But Norma was a warrior. She was powerful. She could have picked up any two of the boys and smashed their skulls together. But worse than that, she would have dragged them all over to some tipi and made them listen to some elder tell a dusty old story.

The Indian boys scattered, and Norma walked over to Thomas and picked him up.

"Hey, little man, are you okay?" she asked.

Thomas gave her a thumbs up.

"Why they always picking on you?"

Thomas shook his head, closed his eyes, but no stories came to him,   65
no words or music. He just wanted to go home, to lie in his bed and let his dreams tell his stories for him.

Actors Adam Beach and Evan Adams in a still from the 1998 film Smoke Signals, *based on "This Is What It Means to Say Phoenix, Arizona." Directed by Chris Eyre.* Source: *Miramax/The Kobal Collection/Sabella, Jill.*

Thomas Builds-the-Fire and Victor sat next to each other in the airplane, coach section. A tiny white woman had the window seat. She was busy twisting her body into pretzels. She was flexible.

"I have to ask," Thomas said, and Victor closed his eyes in embarrassment.

"Don't," Victor said.

"Excuse me, miss," Thomas asked. "Are you a gymnast or something?"

"There's no something about it," she said. "I was first alternate on the   70 1980 Olympic team."

"Really?" Thomas asked.

"Really."

"I mean, you used to be a world-class athlete?" Thomas asked.

"My husband still thinks I am."

Thomas Builds-the-Fire smiled. She was a mental gymnast, too. She   75 pulled her leg straight up against her body so that she could've kissed her kneecap.

"I wish I could do that," Thomas said.

Victor was ready to jump out of the plane. Thomas, that crazy Indian storyteller with ratty old braids and broken teeth, was flirting with a beautiful Olympic gymnast. Nobody back home on the reservation would ever believe it.

"Well," the gymnast said. "It's easy. Try it."

Thomas grabbed at his leg and tried to pull it up into the same position as the gymnast. He couldn't even come close, which made Victor and the gymnast laugh.

"Hey," she asked. "You two are Indian, right?"   80

"Full-blood," Victor said.

"Not me," Thomas said. "I'm half magician on my mother's side and half clown on my father's."

They all laughed.

"What are your names?" she asked.

"Victor and Thomas."   85

"Mine is Cathy. Pleased to meet you all."

The three of them talked for the duration of the flight. Cathy the gymnast complained about the government, how they screwed the 1980 Olympic team by boycotting.

"Sounds like you all got a lot in common with Indians," Thomas said.

Nobody laughed.

After the plane landed in Phoenix and they had all found their way to   90
the terminal, Cathy the gymnast smiled and waved good-bye.

"She was really nice," Thomas said.

"Yeah, but everybody talks to everybody on airplanes," Victor said. "It's too bad we can't always be that way."

"You always used to tell me I think too much," Thomas said. "Now it sounds like you do."

"Maybe I caught it from you."

"Yeah."   95

Thomas and Victor rode in a taxi to the trailer where Victor's father died.

"Listen," Victor said as they stopped in front of the trailer. "I never told you I was sorry for beating you up that time."

"Oh, it was nothing. We were just kids and you were drunk."

"Yeah, but I'm still sorry."

"That's all right."   100

Victor paid for the taxi and the two of them stood in the hot Phoenix summer. They could smell the trailer.

"This ain't going to be nice," Victor said. "You don't have to go in."

"You're going to need help."

Victor walked to the front door and opened it. The stink rolled out and made them both gag. Victor's father had lain in that trailer for a week in hundred-degree temperatures before anyone found him. And the only reason anyone found him was because of the smell. They needed dental records to identify him. That's exactly what the coroner said. They needed dental records.

"Oh, man," Victor said. "I don't know if I can do this."   105

"Well, then don't."

"But there might be something valuable in there."

"I thought his money was in the bank."

"It is. I was talking about pictures and letters and stuff like that."

"Oh," Thomas said as he held his breath and followed Victor into the   110
trailer.

When Victor was twelve, he stepped into an underground wasp nest. His foot was caught in the hole, and no matter how hard he struggled, Victor couldn't pull free. He might have died there, stung a thousand times, if Thomas Builds-the-Fire had not come by.

"Run," Thomas yelled and pulled Victor's foot from the hole. They ran then, hard as they ever had, faster than Billy Mills,[2] faster than Jim Thorpe,[3] faster than the wasps could fly.

Victor and Thomas ran until they couldn't breathe, ran until it was cold and dark outside, ran until they were lost and it took hours to find their way home. All the way back, Victor counted his stings.

"Seven," Victor said. "My lucky number."

Victor didn't find much to keep in the trailer. Only a photo album and a   115
stereo. Everything else had that smell stuck in it or was useless anyway.

"I guess this is all," Victor said. "It ain't much."

"Better than nothing," Thomas said.

"Yeah, and I do have the pickup."

"Yeah," Thomas said, "it's in good shape."

"Dad was good about that stuff."   120

"Yeah, I remember your dad."

"Really?" Victor asked. "What do you remember?"

Thomas Builds-the-Fire closed his eyes and told this story: "I remember when I had this dream that told me to go to Spokane, to stand by the Falls in the middle of the city and wait for a sign. I knew I had to go there but I didn't have a car. Didn't have a license. I was only thirteen. So I walked all the way, took me all day, and I finally made it to the Falls. I stood there for an hour waiting. Then your dad came walking up. *What the hell are you doing here?* he asked me. I said, *Waiting for a vision.* Then your father said, *All you're going to get here is mugged.* So he drove me over to Denny's, bought me dinner, and then drove me home to the reservation. For a long time I was mad because I thought my dreams had lied to me. But they didn't. Your dad was my vision. *Take care of each other* is what my dreams were saying. *Take care of each other.*"

---

2 **Billy Mills** (b. 1938): An Oglala Lakota (Sioux), Mills was the only American to win an Olympic gold medal in the 10,000-meter race—at the 1964 Tokyo Olympic Games.—EDS.

3 **Jim Thorpe** (1887–1953): A member of the Sac and Fox tribe and acclaimed to be the greatest athlete of the twentieth century, Thorpe won gold medals in the pentathlon and decathlon in the 1912 Olympic games and played both professional football and professional baseball.—EDS.

Victor was quiet for a long time. He searched his mind for memories of his father, found the good ones, found a few bad ones, added it all up, and smiled.

"My father never told me about finding you in Spokane," Victor said. 125

"He said he wouldn't tell anybody. Didn't want me to get in trouble. But he said I had to watch out for you as part of the deal."

"Really?"

"Really. Your father said you would need the help. He was right."

"That's why you came down here with me, isn't it?" Victor asked.

"I came because of your father." 130

Victor and Thomas climbed into the pickup, drove over to the bank, and claimed the three hundred dollars in the savings account.

Thomas Builds-the-Fire could fly.

Once, he jumped off the roof of the tribal school and flapped his arms like a crazy eagle. And he flew. For a second, he hovered, suspended above all the other Indian boys who were too smart or too scared to jump.

"He's flying," Junior yelled, and Seymour was busy looking for the trick wires or mirrors. But it was real. As real as the dirt when Thomas lost altitude and crashed to the ground.

He broke his arm in two places. 135

"He broke his wing," Victor chanted, and the other Indian boys joined in, made it a tribal song.

"He broke his wing, he broke his wing, he broke his wing," all the Indian boys chanted as they ran off, flapping their wings, wishing they could fly, too. They hated Thomas for his courage, his brief moment as a bird. Everybody has dreams about flying. Thomas flew.

One of his dreams came true for just a second, just enough to make it real.

Victor's father, his ashes, fit in one wooden box with enough left over to fill a cardboard box.

"He was always a big man," Thomas said. 140

Victor carried part of his father and Thomas carried the rest out to the pickup. They set him down carefully behind the seats, put a cowboy hat on the wooden box and a Dodgers cap on the cardboard box. That's the way it was supposed to be.

"Ready to head back home?" Victor asked.

"It's going to be a long drive."

"Yeah, take a couple days, maybe."

"We can take turns," Thomas said. 145

"Okay," Victor said, but they didn't take turns. Victor drove for sixteen hours straight north, made it halfway up Nevada toward home before he finally pulled over.

"Hey, Thomas," Victor said. "You got to drive for a while."

"Okay."

Thomas Builds-the-Fire slid behind the wheel and started off down the road. All through Nevada, Thomas and Victor had been amazed at the lack of animal life, at the absence of water, of movement.

"Where is everything?" Victor had asked more than once.   150

Now when Thomas was finally driving they saw the first animal, maybe the only animal in Nevada. It was a long-eared jackrabbit.

"Look," Victor yelled. "It's alive."

Thomas and Victor were busy congratulating themselves on their discovery when the jackrabbit darted out into the road and under the wheels of the pickup.

"Stop the goddamn car," Victor yelled, and Thomas did stop, backed the pickup to the dead jackrabbit.

"Oh, man, he's dead," Victor said as he looked at the squashed animal.   155

"Really dead."

"The only thing alive in this whole state and we just killed it."

"I don't know," Thomas said, "I think it was suicide."

Victor looked around the desert, sniffed the air, felt the emptiness and loneliness, and nodded his head.

"Yeah," Victor said, "it had to be suicide."   160

"I can't believe this," Thomas said. "You drive for a thousand miles and there ain't even any bugs smashed on the windshield. I drive for ten seconds and kill the only living thing in Nevada."

"Yeah," Victor said. "Maybe I should drive."

"Maybe you should."

Thomas Builds-the-Fire walked through the corridors of the tribal school by himself. Nobody wanted to be anywhere near him because of all those stories. Story after story.

Thomas closed his eyes and this story came to him: "We are all given   165
one thing by which our lives are measured, one determination. Mine are the stories which can change or not change the world. It doesn't matter which as long as I continue to tell the stories. My father, he died on Okinawa in World War II, died fighting for this country, which had tried to kill him for years. My mother, she died giving birth to me, died while I was still inside her. She pushed me out into the world with her last breath. I have no brothers or sisters. I have only my stories which came to me before I even had the words to speak. I learned a thousand stories before I took my first thousand steps. They are all I have. It's all I can do."

Thomas Builds-the-Fire told his stories to all those who would stop and listen. He kept telling them long after people had stopped listening.

Victor and Thomas made it back to the reservation just as the sun was rising. It was the beginning of a new day on earth, but the same old shit on the reservation.

"Good morning," Thomas said.

"Good morning."

The tribe was waking up, ready for work, eating breakfast, reading the   170
newspaper, just like everybody else does. Willene LeBret was out in her garden wearing a bathrobe. She waved when Thomas and Victor drove by.

"Crazy Indians made it," she said to herself and went back to her roses.

Victor stopped the pickup in front of Thomas Builds-the-Fire's HUD[4]
house. They both yawned, stretched a little, shook dust from their bodies.

"I'm tired," Victor said.

"Of everything," Thomas added.

They both searched for words to end the journey. Victor needed to   175
thank Thomas for his help, for the money, and make the promise to pay it
all back.

"Don't worry about the money," Thomas said. "It don't make any difference anyhow."

"Probably not, enit?"

"Nope."

Victor knew that Thomas would remain the crazy storyteller who talked
to dogs and cars, who listened to the wind and pine trees. Victor knew that
he couldn't really be friends with Thomas, even after all that had happened.
It was cruel but it was real. As real as the ashes, as Victor's father, sitting
behind the seats.

"I know how it is," Thomas said. "I know you ain't going to treat me any   180
better than you did before. I know your friends would give you too much
shit about it."

Victor was ashamed of himself. Whatever happened to the tribal ties,
the sense of community? The only real thing he shared with anybody was a
bottle and broken dreams. He owed Thomas something, anything.

"Listen," Victor said and handed Thomas the cardboard box which contained half of his father. "I want you to have this."

Thomas took the ashes and smiled, closed his eyes, and told this story:
"I'm going to travel to Spokane Falls one last time and toss these ashes into
the water. And your father will rise like a salmon, leap over the bridge, over
me, and find his way home. It will be beautiful. His teeth will shine like silver, like a rainbow. He will rise, Victor, he will rise."

Victor smiled.

"I was planning on doing the same thing with my half," Victor said. "But   185
I didn't imagine my father looking anything like a salmon. I thought it'd
be like cleaning the attic or something. Like letting things go after they've
stopped having any use."

"Nothing stops, cousin," Thomas said. "Nothing stops."

Thomas Builds-the-Fire got out of the pickup and walked up his driveway. Victor started the pickup and began the drive home.

---

4 **HUD:** The U.S. Department of Housing and Urban Development. —EDS.

"Wait," Thomas yelled suddenly from his porch. "I just got to ask one favor."

Victor stopped the pickup, leaned out the window, and shouted back. "What do you want?"

"Just one time when I'm telling a story somewhere, why don't you stop 190 and listen?" Thomas asked.

"Just once?"

"Just once."

Victor waved his arms to let Thomas know that the deal was good. It was a fair trade, and that was all Victor had ever wanted from his whole life. So Victor drove his father's pickup toward home while Thomas went into his house, closed the door behind him, and heard a new story come to him in the silence afterwards. ■

The Reader's Presence

1. Thomas is portrayed as an outcast in the community, "a storyteller that nobody wanted to listen to" (paragraph 16). What stories does Thomas tell? Why are they unpopular with listeners? What do Thomas's stories have to do with his role as an outcast?

2. Describe Victor's state of mind and place in life at the beginning of the story. What is he like? What has happened to him? Compare this Victor to the Victor who appears at the end of the story. Has he changed? Do you think that he will change in the future? Why or why not?

3. **CONNECTIONS:** Compare the characters of Thomas and Victor to Alexie's description of the children on the Spokane Indian Reservation of Alexie's youth in "The Joy of Reading and Writing: Superman and Me" (page 27). What characteristics does Thomas share with the children Alexie describes, including himself as a boy? What characteristics does Victor share with them? How are Alexie's fictional reservation and the people who live there like — and unlike — the reservation and people Alexie describes in his essay?

Raymond Carver

WHAT WE TALK ABOUT WHEN WE TALK ABOUT LOVE

RAYMOND CARVER is best known for his tightly crafted, spare, and often grim short stories. In fact, his mastery of dialogue and his fine eye for detail have made his collections of short stories best-sellers in the United States and abroad. These collections include *Will You Please Be Quiet, Please?* (1976); *What We Talk About When We Talk About Love* (1981), in which the following short story can be found; *Cathedral* (1984); and *Where I'm Calling From* (1988). Sometimes described as a minimalist writer, Carver is well-regarded for his tightly focused prose. He often edited heavily, leaving only the bare bones of a story on the page: action and dialogue with very little in the way of exposition. In 1993, Robert Altman made the critically acclaimed film *Short Cuts* based on a number of Carver's short stories.

> "I start with an image, a cigarette being put out in a jar of mustard, for instance, or the remains, the wreckage, of a dinner left on the table."

Describing the process of writing fiction, Carver says, "I never start with an idea. I always see something. I start with an image, a cigarette being put out in a jar of mustard, for instance, or the remains, the wreckage, of a dinner left on the table. Pop cans in the fireplace, that sort of thing. And a feeling goes with that. And that feeling seems to transport me back to that particular time and place, and the ambience of time. But it is the image, and the emotion that goes with that image—that's what's important."

For more information on Raymond Carver, see page 60.

MY FRIEND MEL McGINNIS was talking. Mel McGinnis is a cardiologist, and sometimes that gives him the right.

The four of us were sitting around his kitchen table drinking gin. Sunlight filled the kitchen from the big window behind the sink. There were Mel and me and his second wife, Teresa—Terri, we called her—and my wife, Laura. We lived in Albuquerque then. But we were all from somewhere else.

There was an ice bucket on the table. The gin and the tonic water kept going around, and we somehow got on the subject of love. Mel thought real love was nothing less than spiritual love. He said he'd spent five years in a seminary before quitting to go to medical school. He said he still looked back on those years in the seminary as the most important years in his life.

Terri said the man she lived with before she lived with Mel loved her so much he tried to kill her. Then Terri said, "He beat me up one night. He dragged me around the living room by my ankles. He kept saying, 'I love you, I love you, you bitch.' He went on dragging me around the living room. My head kept knocking on things." Terri looked around the table. "What do you do with love like that?"

She was a bone-thin woman with a pretty face, dark eyes, and brown   5
hair that hung down her back. She liked necklaces made of turquoise, and long pendant earrings.

"My God, don't be silly. That's not love, and you know it," Mel said. "I don't know what you'd call it, but I sure know you wouldn't call it love."

"Say what you want to, but I know what it was," Terri said. "It may sound crazy to you, but it's true just the same. People are different, Mel. Sure, sometimes he may have acted crazy. Okay. But he loved me. In his own way maybe, but he loved me. There was love there, Mel. Don't say there wasn't."

Mel let out his breath. He held his glass and turned to Laura and me. "The man threatened to kill me," Mel said. He finished his drink and reached for the gin bottle. "Terri's a romantic. Terri's of the kick-me-so-I'll-know-you-love-me school. Terri, hon, don't look that way." Mel reached across the table and touched Terri's cheeks with his fingers. He grinned at her.

"Now he wants to make up," Terri said.

"Make up what?" Mel said. "What is there to make up? I know what I   10
know. That's all."

"How'd we get started on this subject, anyway?" Terri said. She raised her glass and drank from it. "Mel always has love on his mind," she said. "Don't you, honey?" She smiled, and I thought that was the last of it.

"I just wouldn't call Ed's behavior love. That's all I'm saying, honey," Mel said. "What about you guys?" Mel said to Laura and me. "Does that sound like love to you?"

"I'm the wrong person to ask," I said. "I didn't even know the man. I've only heard his name mentioned in passing. I wouldn't know. You'd have to know the particulars. But I think what you're saying is that love is an absolute."

Mel said, "The kind of love I'm talking about is. The kind of love I'm talking about, you don't try to kill people."

Laura said, "I don't know anything about Ed, or anything about the situation.   15
But who can judge anyone else's situation?"

I touched the back of Laura's hand. She gave me a quick smile. I picked up Laura's hand. It was warm, the nails polished, perfectly manicured. I encircled the broad wrist with my fingers, and I held her.

"When I left, he drank rat poison," Terri said. She clasped her arms with her hands. "They took him to the hospital in Santa Fe. That's where we lived then, about ten miles out. They saved his life. But his gums went crazy from it. I mean they pulled away from his teeth. After that, his teeth stood out like fangs. My God," Terri said. She waited a minute, then let go of her arms and picked up her glass.

"What people won't do!" Laura said.

"He's out of the action now," Mel said. "He's dead."

Mel handed me the saucer of limes. I took a section, squeezed it over my 20 drink, and stirred the ice cubes with my finger.

"It gets worse," Terri said. "He shot himself in the mouth. But he bungled that too. Poor Ed," she said. Terri shook her head.

"Poor Ed nothing," Mel said. "He was dangerous."

Mel was forty-five years old. He was tall and rangy with curly soft hair. His face and arms were brown from the tennis he played. When he was sober, his gestures, all his movements, were precise, very careful.

"He did love me though, Mel. Grant me that," Terri said. "That's all I'm asking. He didn't love me the way you love me. I'm not saying that. But he loved me. You can grant me that, can't you?"

"What do you mean, he bungled it?" I said. 25

Laura leaned forward with her glass. She put her elbows on the table and held her glass in both hands. She glanced from Mel to Terri and waited with a look of bewilderment on her open face, as if amazed that such things happened to people you were friendly with.

"How'd he bungle it when he killed himself?" I asked.

"I'll tell you what happened," Mel said. "He took this twenty-two pistol he'd bought to threaten Terri and me with. Oh, I'm serious, the man was always threatening. You should have seen the way we lived in those days. Like fugitives. I even bought a gun myself. Can you believe it? A guy like me? But I did. I bought one for self-defense and carried it in the glove compartment. Sometimes I'd have to leave the apartment in the middle of the night. To go to the hospital, you know? Terri and I weren't married then, and my first wife had the house and kids, the dog, everything, and Terri and I were living in this apartment here. Sometimes, as I say, I'd get a call in the middle of the night and have to go in to the hospital at two or three in the morning. It'd be dark out there in the parking lot, and I'd break into a sweat before I could even get to my car. I never knew if he was going to come up out of the shrubbery or from behind a car and start shooting. I mean, the man was crazy. He was capable of wiring a bomb, anything. He used to call my service at all hours and say he needed to talk to the doctor, and when I'd return the call, he'd say, 'Son of a bitch, your days are numbered.' Little things like that. It was scary, I'm telling you."

"I still feel sorry for him," Terri said.

"It sounds like a nightmare," Laura said. "But what exactly happened 30 after he shot himself?"

Laura is a legal secretary. We'd met in a professional capacity. Before we knew it, it was a courtship. She's thirty-five, three years younger than I am. In addition to being in love, we like each other and enjoy one another's company. She's easy to be with.

"What happened?" Laura asked.

Mel said, "He shot himself in the mouth in his room. Someone heard the shot and told the manager. They came in with a passkey, saw what had happened, and called an ambulance. I happened to be there when they brought him in, alive but past recall. The man lived for three days. His head swelled up to twice the size of a normal head. I'd never seen anything like it, and I hope I never do again. Terri wanted to go in and sit with him when she found out about it. We had a fight over it. I didn't think she should see him like that. I didn't think she should see him, and I still don't."

"Who won the fight?" Laura said.

"I was in the room with him when he died," Terri said. "He never came up out of it. But I sat with him. He didn't have anyone else." 35

"He was dangerous," Mel said. "If you call that love, you can have it."

"It was love," Terri said. "Sure, it's abnormal in most people's eyes. But he was willing to die for it. He did die for it."

"I sure as hell wouldn't call it love," Mel said. "I mean, no one knows what he did it for. I've seen a lot of suicides, and I couldn't say anyone ever knew what they did it for."

Mel put his hands behind his neck and tilted his chair back. "I'm not interested in that kind of love," he said. "If that's love, you can have it."

Terri said, "We were afraid. Mel even made a will out and wrote to his brother in California who used to be a Green Beret. Mel told him who to look for if something happened to him." 40

Terri drank from her glass. She said, "But Mel's right—we lived like fugitives. We were afraid. Mel was, weren't you, honey? I even called the police at one point, but they were no help. They said they couldn't do anything until Ed actually did something. Isn't that a laugh?" Terri said.

She poured the last of the gin into her glass and waggled the bottle. Mel got up from the table and went to the cupboard. He took down another bottle.

"Well, Nick and I know what love is," Laura said. "For us, I mean," Laura said. She bumped my knee with her knee. "You're supposed to say something now," Laura said, and turned her smile on me.

For an answer, I took Laura's hand and raised it to my lips. I made a big production out of kissing her hand. Everyone was amused.

"We're lucky," I said. 45

"You guys," Terri said. "Stop that now. You're making me sick. You're still on the honeymoon, for God's sake. You're still gaga, for crying out loud. Just wait. How long have you been together now? How long has it been? A year? Longer than a year?"

"Going on a year and a half," Laura said, flushed and smiling.

"Oh, now," Terri said. "Wait awhile."

She held her drink and gazed at Laura.

"I'm only kidding," Terri said.   50

Mel opened the gin and went around the table with the bottle.

"Here, you guys," he said. "Let's have a toast. I want to propose a toast. A toast to love. To true love," Mel said.

We touched glasses.

"To love," we said.

Outside in the backyard, one of the dogs began to bark. The leaves of the   55
aspen that leaned past the window ticked against the glass. The afternoon sun was like a presence in the room, the spacious light of ease and generosity. We could have been anywhere, somewhere enchanted. We raised our glasses again and grinned at each other like children who had agreed on something forbidden.

"I'll tell you what real love is," Mel said. "I mean, I'll give you a good example. And then you can draw your own conclusions." He poured more gin into his glass. He added an ice cube and a sliver of lime. We waited and sipped our drinks. Laura and I touched knees again. I put a hand on her warm thigh and left it there.

"What do any of us really know about love?" Mel said. "It seems to me we're just beginners at love. We say we love each other and we do, I don't doubt it. I love Terri and Terri loves me, and you guys love each other too. You know the kind of love I'm talking about now. Physical love, that impulse that drives you to someone special, as well as love of the other person's being, his or her essence, as it were. Carnal love and, well, call it sentimental love, the day-to-day caring about the other person. But sometimes I have a hard time accounting for the fact that I must have loved my first wife too. But I did, I know I did. So I suppose I am like Terri in that regard. Terri and Ed." He thought about it and then he went on. "There was a time when I thought I loved my first wife more than life itself. But now I hate her guts. I do. How do you explain that? What happened to that love? What happened to it, is what I'd like to know. I wish someone could tell me. Then there's Ed. Okay, we're back to Ed. He loves Terri so much he tries to kill her and he winds up killing himself." Mel stopped talking and swallowed from his glass. "You guys have been together eighteen months and you love each other. It shows all over you. You glow with it. But you both loved other people before you met each other. You've both been married before, just like us. And you probably loved other people before that too, even. Terri and I have been together for five years, been married for four. And the terrible thing, the terrible thing is, but the good thing too, the saving grace, you might say, is that if something happened to one of us—excuse me for saying this—but if something happened to one of us tomorrow, I think the other one, the other person, would grieve for a while, you know, but then the surviving party would go out and love again, have someone else soon enough. All this, all this love we're talking about, it would just be a memory. Maybe not even a memory.

Am I wrong? Am I way off base? Because I want you to set me straight if you think I'm wrong. I want to know. I mean, I don't know anything, and I'm the first one to admit it."

"Mel, for God's sake," Terri said. She reached out and took hold of his wrist. "Are you getting drunk? Honey? Are you drunk?"

"Honey, I'm just talking," Mel said. "All right? I don't have to be drunk to say what I think. I mean, we're all just talking, right?" Mel said. He fixed his eyes on her.

"Sweetie, I'm not criticizing," Terri said.   60

She picked up her glass.

"I'm not on call today," Mel said. "Let me remind you of that. I am not on call," he said.

"Mel, we love you," Laura said.

Mel looked at Laura. He looked at her as if he could not place her, as if she was not the woman she was.

"Love you too, Laura," Mel said. "And you, Nick, love you too. You   65
know something?" Mel said. "You guys are our pals," Mel said.

He picked up his glass.

Mel said, "I was going to tell you about something. I mean, I was going to prove a point. You see, this happened a few months ago, but it's still going on right now, and it ought to make us feel ashamed when we talk like we know what we're talking about when we talk about love."

"Come on now," Terri said. "Don't talk like you're drunk if you're not drunk."

"Just shut up for once in your life," Mel said very quietly. "Will you do me a favor and do that for a minute? So as I was saying, there's this old couple who had this car wreck out on the interstate. A kid hit them and they were all torn to shit and nobody was giving them much chance to pull through."

Terri looked at us and then back at Mel. She seemed anxious, or maybe   70
that's too strong a word.

Mel was handing the bottle around the table.

"I was on call that night," Mel said. "It was May or maybe it was June. Terri and I had just sat down to dinner when the hospital called. There'd been this thing out on the interstate. Drunk kid, teenager, plowed his dad's pickup into this camper with this old couple in it. They were up in their mid-seventies, that couple. The kid—eighteen, nineteen, something—he was DOA.[1] Taken the steering wheel through his sternum. The old couple, they were alive, you understand. I mean, just barely. But they had everything. Multiple fractures, internal injuries, hemorrhaging, contusions, lacerations, the works, and they each of them had themselves concussions. They were in a bad way, believe me. And, of course, their age was two strikes against them. I'd say she was worse off than he was. Ruptured spleen along with

1 **DOA:** Dead on arrival. —EDS.

everything else. Both kneecaps broken. But they'd been wearing their seat-belts and, God knows, that's what saved them for the time being."

"Folks, this is an advertisement for the National Safety Council," Terri said. "This is your spokesman, Dr. Melvin R. McGinnis, talking." Terri laughed. "Mel," she said, "sometimes you're just too much. But I love you, hon," she said.

"Honey, I love you," Mel said.

He leaned across the table. Terri met him halfway. They kissed. 75

"Terri's right," Mel said as he settled himself again. "Get those seatbelts on. But seriously, they were in some shape, those oldsters. By the time I got down there, the kid was dead, as I said. He was off in a corner, laid out on a gurney. I took one look at the couple and told the ER nurse to get me a neurologist and an orthopedic man and a couple of surgeons down there right away."

He drank from his glass. "I'll try to keep this short," he said. "So we took the two of them up to the OR and worked like fuck on them most of the night. They had these incredible reserves, those two. You see that once in a while. So we did everything that could be done, and toward morn-ing we're giving them a fifty-fifty chance, maybe less than that for her. So here they are, still alive the next morning. So, okay, we move them into the ICU,[2] which is where they both kept plugging away at it for two weeks, hit-ting it better and better on all the scopes. So we transfer them out to their own room."

Mel stopped talking. "Here," he said, "let's drink this cheapo gin the hell up. Then we're going to dinner, right? Terri and I know a new place. That's where we'll go, to this new place we know about. But we're not going until we finish this cut-rate, lousy gin."

Terri said, "We haven't actually eaten there yet. But it looks good. From the outside, you know."

"I like food," Mel said. "If I had it to do all over again, I'd be a chef, you 80 know? Right, Terri?" Mel said.

He laughed. He fingered the ice in his glass.

"Terri knows," he said. "Terri can tell you. But let me say this. If I could come back again in a different life, a different time and all, you know what? I'd like to come back as a knight. You were pretty safe wearing all that armor. It was all right being a knight until gunpowder and muskets and pistols came along."

"Mel would like to ride a horse and carry a lance," Terri said.

"Carry a woman's scarf with you everywhere," Laura said.

"Or just a woman," Mel said. 85

"Shame on you," Laura said.

Terri said, "Suppose you came back as a serf. The serfs didn't have it so good in those days," Terri said.

---

2 *ICU:* Intensive care unit. —EDS.

"The serfs never had it good," Mel said. "But I guess even the knights were vessels to someone. Isn't that the way it worked? But then everyone is always a vessel to someone. Isn't that right? Terri? But what I liked about knights, besides their ladies, was that they had that suit of armor, you know, and they couldn't get hurt very easy. No cars in those days, you know? No drunk teenagers to tear into your ass."

"Vassals," Terri said.

"What?" Mel said.   90

"Vassals," Terri said. "They were called vassals, not vessels."

"Vassals, vessels," Mel said, "what the fuck's the difference? You knew what I meant anyway. All right," Mel said. "So I'm not educated. I learned my stuff. I'm a heart surgeon, sure, but I'm just a mechanic. I go in and I fuck around and I fix things. Shit," Mel said.

"Modesty doesn't become you," Terri said.

"He's just a humble sawbones," I said. "But sometimes they suffocated in all that armor, Mel. They'd even have heart attacks if it got too hot and they were too tired and worn out. I read somewhere that they'd fall off their horses and not be able to get up because they were too tired to stand with all that armor on them. They got trampled by their own horses sometimes."

"That's terrible," Mel said. "That's a terrible thing, Nicky. I guess they'd   95
just lay there and wait until somebody came along and made a shish kebab out of them."

"Some other vessel," Terri said.

"That's right," Mel said. "Some vassal would come along and spear the bastard in the name of love. Or whatever the fuck it was they fought over in those days."

"Same things we fight over these days," Terri said.

Laura said, "Nothing's changed."

The color was still high in Laura's cheeks. Her eyes were bright. She 100
brought her glass to her lips.

Mel poured himself another drink. He looked at the label closely as if studying a long row of numbers. Then he slowly put the bottle down on the table and slowly reached for the tonic water.

"What about the old couple?" Laura said. "You didn't finish that story you started."

Laura was having a hard time lighting her cigarette. Her matches kept going out.

The sunshine inside the room was different now, changing, getting thinner. But the leaves outside the window were still shimmering, and I stared at the pattern they made on the panes and on the Formica counter. They weren't the same patterns, of course.

"What about the old couple?" I said.   105

"Older but wiser," Terri said.

Mel stared at her.

Terri said, "Go on with your story, hon. I was only kidding. Then what happened?"

"Terri, sometimes," Mel said.

"Please, Mel," Terri said. "Don't always be so serious, sweetie. Can't   110
you take a joke?"

"Where's the joke?" Mel said.

He held his glass and gazed steadily at his wife.

"What happened?" Laura said.

Mel fastened his eyes on Laura. He said, "Laura, if I didn't have Terri and if I didn't love her so much, and if Nick wasn't my best friend, I'd fall in love with you. I'd carry you off, honey," he said.

"Tell your story," Terri said. "Then we'll go to that new place, okay?"   115

"Okay," Mel said. "Where was I?" he said. He stared at the table and then he began again.

"I dropped in to see each of them every day, sometimes twice a day if I was up doing other calls anyway. Casts and bandages, head to foot, the both of them. You know, you've seen it in the movies. That's just the way they looked, just like in the movies. Little eye-holes and nose-holes and mouth-holes. And she had to have her legs slung up on top of it. Well, the husband was very depressed for the longest while. Even after he found out that his wife was going to pull through, he was still very depressed. Not about the accident, though. I mean, the accident was one thing, but it wasn't every-thing. I'd get up to his mouth-hole, you know, and he'd say no, it wasn't the accident exactly but it was because he couldn't see her through his eye-holes. He said that was what was making him feel so bad. Can you imagine? I'm telling you, the man's heart was breaking because he couldn't turn his goddamn head and *see* his goddamn wife."

Mel looked around the table and shook his head at what he was going to say.

"I mean, it was killing the old fart just because he couldn't *look* at the fucking woman."

We all looked at Mel.   120

"Do you see what I'm saying?" he said.

Maybe we were a little drunk by then. I know it was hard keeping things in focus. The light was draining out of the room, going back through the window where it had come from. Yet nobody made a move to get up from the table to turn on the overhead light.

"Listen," Mel said. "Let's finish this fucking gin. There's about enough left here for one shooter all around. Then let's go eat. Let's go to the new place."

"He's depressed," Terri said. "Mel, why don't you take a pill?"

Mel shook his head. "I've taken everything there is."   125

"We all need a pill now and then," I said.

"Some people are born needing them," Terri said.

She was using her finger to rub at something on the table. Then she stopped rubbing.

"I think I want to call my kids," Mel said. "Is that all right with everybody? I'll call my kids," he said.

Terri said, "What if Marjorie answers the phone? You guys, you've heard   130
us on the subject of Marjorie? Honey, you know you don't want to talk to Marjorie. It'll make you feel even worse."

"I don't want to talk to Marjorie," Mel said. "But I want to talk to my kids."

"There isn't a day goes by that Mel doesn't say he wishes she'd get married again. Or else die," Terri said. "For one thing," Terri said, "she's bankrupting us. Mel says it's just to spite him that she won't get married again. She has a boyfriend who lives with her and the kids, so Mel is supporting the boyfriend too."

"She's allergic to bees," Mel said. "If I'm not praying she'll get married again, I'm praying she'll get herself stung to death by a swarm of fucking bees."

"Shame on you," Laura said.

"Bzzzzzz," Mel said, turning his fingers into bees and buzzing them at   135
Terri's throat. Then he let his hands drop all the way to his sides.

"She's vicious," Mel said. "Sometimes I think I'll go up there dressed like a beekeeper. You know, that hat that's like a helmet with the plate that comes down over your face, the big gloves, and the padded coat? I'll knock on the door and let loose a hive of bees in the house. But first I'd make sure the kids were out, of course."

He crossed one leg over the other. It seemed to take him a lot of time to do it. Then he put both feet on the floor and leaned forward, elbows on the table, his chin cupped in his hands.

"Maybe I won't call the kids, after all. Maybe it isn't such a hot idea. Maybe we'll just go eat. How does that sound?"

"Sounds fine to me," I said. "Eat or not eat. Or keep drinking. I could head right on out into the sunset."

"What does that mean, honey?" Laura said.   140

"It just means what I said," I said. "It means I could just keep going. That's all it means."

"I could eat something myself," Laura said. "I don't think I've ever been so hungry in my life. Is there something to nibble on?"

"I'll put out some cheese and crackers," Terri said.

But Terri just sat there. She did not get up to get anything.

Mel turned his glass over. He spilled it out on the table.   145

"Gin's gone." Mel said.

Terri said, "Now what?"

I could hear my heart beating. I could hear everyone's heart. I could hear the human noise we sat there making, not one of us moving, not even when the room went dark. ●

The Reader's Presence

1. The entire flow of conversation in the story, from beginning to end, is fueled by drinking. What effect does the drinking appear to have on everyone? Do you think Carver intended the reader to dismiss the content of what is being said as merely drunken conversation? Why or why not? What elements of the story suggest we are meant to take the conversation seriously? Read the final sentences of the story carefully. How do you explain what has happened?

2. How do you interpret the story Mel tells about the old couple seriously injured in the car crash? Why do you think it is so important to him? In your judgment, does it help explain "what we talk about when we talk about love"? How would you compare Mel's story about the old couple to Terri's story about Ed?

3. **CONNECTIONS:** Read Carver's story (one of his most famous) in conjunction with his personal essay, "My Father's Life" (page 60). What similarities can you find between the story and the essay? What aspects of the short story appear to have grown out of Carver's personal background? In your judgment, what characteristics of each selection suggest that both were written by the same person?

Jamaica Kincaid

Girl

JAMAICA KINCAID was born in Antigua in 1949 and came to the United States at the age of seventeen to work for a New York family as an au pair. Her novel *Lucy* (1990) is an imaginative account of her experience of coming into adulthood in a foreign country and continues the narrative of her personal history begun in the novel *Annie John* (1985). She has also published a collection of short stories, *At the Bottom of the River* (1983), a collection of essays, *A Small Place* (1988), and a third novel, *The Autobiography of My Mother* (1995). Her most recent publications include *My Brother* (1997), which was a National Book Award Finalist for Nonfiction, *My*

> "Girl" is the first piece of fiction Jamaica Kincaid published; it appeared in the *New Yorker* in 1978.

Favorite Plant: Writers and Gardeners on the Plants They Love (1998), *My Garden* (2001), *Mr. Potter* (2002), and *Among Flowers: A Walk in the Himalaya* (2005). Her writing also appears in national magazines, especially the *New Yorker*, where she worked as a staff writer until 1995. "Girl" is the first piece of fiction Kincaid published; it appeared in the *New Yorker* in 1978.

For more information on Jamaica Kincaid, see page 129.

WASH THE WHITE CLOTHES on Monday and put them on the stone heap; wash the color clothes on Tuesday and put them on the clothesline to dry; don't walk barehead in the hot sun; cook pumpkin fritters in very hot sweet oil; soak your little clothes right after you take them off; when buying cotton to make yourself a nice blouse, be sure that it doesn't have gum on it, because that way it won't hold up well after a wash; soak salt fish overnight before you cook it; is it true that you sing benna[1] in Sunday School?; always eat your food in such a way that it won't turn someone else's stomach; on Sundays try to walk like a lady and not like the slut you are so bent on becoming; don't sing benna in Sunday School; you mustn't speak to wharf-rat boys, not even to give directions; don't eat fruits on the street—flies will follow you; *but I don't sing benna on Sundays at all and never in Sunday School*; this is how to sew on a button; this is how to make a buttonhole for the button you have just sewed on; this is how to hem a dress when you see the hem coming down and so to prevent yourself from looking like the slut I know you are so bent on becoming; this is how you iron your father's khaki shirt so that it doesn't have a crease; this is how you iron your father's khaki pants so that they don't have a crease; this is how you grow okra—far from the house, because okra tree harbors red ants; when you are growing dasheen,[2] make sure it gets plenty of water or else it makes your throat itch when you are eating it; this is how you sweep a corner; this is how you sweep a whole house; this is how you sweep a yard; this is how you smile to someone you don't like too much; this is how you smile to someone you don't like at all; this is how you smile to someone you like completely; this is how you set a table for tea; this is how you set a table for dinner; this is how you set a table for dinner with an important guest; this is how you set a table for lunch; this is how you set a table for breakfast; this is how to behave in the presence of men who don't know you very well, and this way they won't recognize immediately the slut I have warned you against becoming; be sure to wash every day, even if it is with your own spit; don't squat down to play marbles—you are not a boy, you know; don't pick people's flowers—you might catch something; don't throw stones at blackbirds, because it might not be a blackbird at all; this is how to make a bread pudding; this is how to

---

1 **benna:** Popular calypso-like music.—EDS.
2 **dasheen:** A starchy vegetable.—EDS.

make doukona;[3] this is how to make pepper pot; this is how to make a good medicine for a cold; this is how to make a good medicine to throw away a child before it even becomes a child; this is how to catch a fish; this is how to throw back a fish you don't like, and that way something bad won't fall on you; this is how to bully a man; this is how a man bullies you; this is how to love a man, and if this doesn't work there are other ways, and if they don't work don't feel too bad about giving up; this is how to spit up in the air if you feel like it, and this is how to move quick so that it doesn't fall on you; this is how to make ends meet; always squeeze bread to make sure it's fresh; *but what if the baker won't let me feel the bread?*; you mean to say that after all you are really going to be the kind of woman who the baker won't let near the bread? ▨

The Reader's Presence

1. Whose voice dominates this story? To whom is the monologue addressed? What effect(s) does the speaker seek to have on the listener? Where does the speaker appear to have acquired her values? Categorize the kinds of advice you find in the story. Identify sentences in which one category of advice merges into another. How are the different kinds of advice alike, and to what extent are they contradictory?

2. "Girl" speaks only two lines, both of which are italicized. In each case, what prompts her to speak? What is the result? Stories generally create the expectation that at least one main character will undergo a change. What differences, if any, do you notice between Girl's first and second lines of dialogue (and the replies she elicits), differences that might suggest that such a change has taken place? If you do notice any differences, in whom do you notice them? Analyze the girl's character based not only on what she says but on what she hears (if one can assume that this monologue was not delivered all in one sitting, but is rather the distillation of years' worth of advice, as heard by the girl).

3. **CONNECTIONS:** Consider the role of gender in this story. What gender stereotypes does the main speaker perpetuate? Look not only at the stereotypes that affect women but also at those that define the roles of men. What can you infer about the males who remain behind the scenes? Read Amy Cunningham's "Why Women Smile" (page 347). What gender stereotypes influence whether—and when—women smile? To what extent do gender roles and cultural expectations determine the patterns—and consequences—of when men and women smile?

[3] *doukona:* Cornmeal.—EDS.

The Writer at Work

JAMAICA KINCAID on "Girl"

To many readers, "Girl" appears to be an odd and confusing short story. It's far shorter than most published stories and consists almost entirely of a monologue spoken by a mother to her daughter. Readers may wonder: "What makes this a story?" In the following passage from an interview with Jamaica Kincaid, Allan Varda asks the author some questions about this intriguing little story and discovers behind its composition a larger agenda that we might not perceive from a single reading. How do Kincaid's answers to Varda's questions help you better understand what's happening in the story? In what ways?

AV: There is a litany of items in "Girl" from a mother to her daughter about what to do and what *not* to do regarding the elements of being "a nice young lady." Is this the way it was for you and other girls in Antigua?

JK: In a word, yes.

AV: Was that good or bad?

JK: I don't think it's the way I would tell my daughter, but as a mother I would tell her what I think would be best for her to be like. This mother in "Girl" was really just giving the girl an idea about the things she would need to be a self-possessed woman in the world.

AV: But you didn't take your mother's advice?

JK: No, because I had other ideas on how to be a self-possessed woman in the world. I didn't know that at the time. I only remember these things. What the mother in the story sees as aids to living in the world, the girl might see as extraordinary oppression, which is one of the things I came to see.

AV: Almost like she's Mother England.

JK: I was just going to say that. I've come to see that I've worked through the relationship of the mother and the girl to a relationship between Europe and the place that I'm from, which is to say, a relationship between the powerful and the powerless. The girl is powerless and the mother is powerful. The mother shows her how to be in the world, but at the back of her mind she thinks she never will get it. She's deeply skeptical that this child could ever grow up to be a self-possessed woman and in the end she reveals her skepticism; yet even within the skepticism is, of course, dismissal and scorn. So it's not unlike the relationship between the conquered and the conqueror.

Joyce Carol Oates

WHERE ARE YOU GOING, WHERE HAVE YOU BEEN?

JOYCE CAROL OATES (b. 1938) has published more than a hundred works of fiction and nonfiction in every genre, including novels, short stories, essays, poetry, screenplays, and a libretto—frequently publishing several projects simultaneously while working and reworking the manuscript for the next. Describing herself as a "chronicler of the American experience," Oates often explores violent behavior "in a nation prone to violence" and its effect on the lives of ordinary people, particularly women and children. Among her long list of novels are *A Garden of Earthly Delights* (1967) and *them* (1969), which won the National Book Award for fiction in 1970. Her most recent works of fiction include the novels *Missing Mom* (2005), *Black Girl / White Girl* (2006), *The Gravedigger's Daughter* (2007), and *My Sister, My Love: The Intimate Story of Skyler Rampike* (2008) and short story collections

> Describing herself as a "chronicler of the American experience," Joyce Carol Oates often explores violent behavior "in a nation prone to violence."

The Museum of Dr. Moses: Tales of Mystery and Suspense (2007) and *Wild Nights! Stories about the Last Days of Poe, Dickinson, Twain, James, and Hemingway* (2008). Oates's interests and versatility are also reflected in her nonfiction prose, which includes *The Profane Art* (1983), *On Boxing* (1987), *Where I've Been, and Where I'm Going* (1999), and *Uncensored: Views & (Re)views* (2005).

Oates's short story "Where Are You Going, Where Have You Been?" first appeared in 1966 and has been anthologized frequently since. She has said that the idea came from a magazine piece she saw—but never finished reading—about a "thrill killer" in Tucson, Arizona. "Where Are You Going, Where Have You Been?" was the basis for the film *Smooth Talk* in 1985.

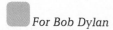 *For Bob Dylan*

HER NAME WAS CONNIE. She was fifteen and she had a quick nervous giggling habit of craning her neck to glance into mirrors, or checking other people's faces to make sure her own was all right. Her mother, who noticed everything and knew everything and who hadn't much reason any longer to look at her own face, always scolded Connie about it. "Stop gawking at yourself, who are you? You think you're so pretty?" she would say. Connie would raise her eyebrows at these familiar complaints and look right through her mother, into a shadowy vision of herself as she was right at that moment: she knew she was pretty and that was everything. Her mother had been pretty once too, if you could believe those old snapshots in the album, but now her looks were gone and that was why she was always after Connie.

"Why don't you keep your room clean like your sister? How've you got your hair fixed—what the hell stinks? Hair spray? You don't see your sister using that junk."

Her sister June was twenty-four and still lived at home. She was a secretary in the high school Connie attended, and if that wasn't bad enough—with her in the same building—she was so plain and chunky and steady that Connie had to hear her praised all the time by her mother and her mother's sisters. June did this, June did that, she saved money and helped clean the house and cooked and Connie couldn't do a thing, her mind was all filled with trashy daydreams. Their father was away at work most of the time and when he came home he wanted supper and he read the newspaper at supper and after supper he went to bed. He didn't bother talking much to them, but around his bent head Connie's mother kept picking at her until Connie wished her mother was dead and she herself was dead and it was all over. "She makes me want to throw up sometimes," she complained to her friends. She had a high, breathless, amused voice which made everything she said a little forced, whether it was sincere or not.

There was one good thing: June went places with girl friends of hers, girls who were just as plain and steady as she, and so when Connie wanted to do that her mother had no objections. The father of Connie's best girl friend drove the girls the three miles to town and left them off at a shopping plaza, so that they could walk through the stores or go to a movie, and when he came to pick them up again at eleven he never bothered to ask what they had done.

They must have been familiar sights, walking around that shopping plaza in their shorts and flat ballerina slippers that always scuffed the sidewalk, with charm bracelets jingling on their thin wrists; they would lean together to whisper and laugh secretly if someone passed by who amused or interested them. Connie had long dark blond hair that drew anyone's eye to it, and she wore part of it pulled up on her head and puffed out and the rest of it she let fall down her back. She wore a pullover jersey blouse that looked one way when she was at home and another way when she was away from home. Everything about her had two sides to it, one for home and one for anywhere that was not home: her walk that could be childlike and bobbing, or languid enough to make anyone think she was hearing music in her head, her mouth which was pale and smirking most of the time, but bright and pink on these evenings out, her laugh which was cynical and drawling at home— "Ha, ha, very funny" —but high-pitched and nervous anywhere else, like the jingling of the charms on her bracelet.

5

Sometimes they did go shopping or to a movie, but sometimes they went across the highway, ducking fast across the busy road, to a drive-in restaurant where older kids hung out. The restaurant was shaped like a big bottle, though squatter than a real bottle, and on its cap was a revolving figure of a grinning boy who held a hamburger aloft. One night in midsummer they ran across, breathless with daring, and right away someone leaned out a car window and invited them over, but it was just a boy from high school they didn't like. It made them feel good to be able to ignore him. They went up through the maze of parked and cruising cars to the bright-lit, fly-infested restaurant, their faces pleased and expectant as if they were entering a sacred building that loomed out of the night to give them what haven and what blessing they yearned for. They sat at the counter and crossed their legs at the ankles, their thin shoulders rigid with excitement and listened to the music that made everything so good: the music was always in the background like music at a church service, it was something to depend upon.

A boy named Eddie came in to talk with them. He sat backwards on his stool, turning himself jerkily around in semi-circles and then stopping and turning again, and after a while he asked Connie if she would like something to eat. She said she did and so she tapped her friend's arm on her way out—her friend pulled her face up into a brave droll look—and Connie said she would meet her at eleven, across the way. "I just hate to leave her like that," Connie said earnestly, but the boy said that she wouldn't be alone for long. So they went out to his car and on the way Connie couldn't help but let her eyes wander over the windshields and faces all around her, her face gleaming with the joy that had nothing to do with Eddie or even this place; it might have been the music. She drew her shoulders up and sucked in her breath with the pure pleasure of being alive, and just at that moment she happened to glance at a face just a few feet from hers. It was a boy with shaggy black hair, in a convertible jalopy painted gold. He stared at her and then his lips widened into a grin. Connie slit her eyes at him and turned away, but she couldn't help glancing back and there he was still watching her. He wagged a finger and laughed and said, "Gonna get you, baby," and Connie turned away again without Eddie noticing anything.

She spent three hours with him, at the restaurant where they ate hamburgers and drank Cokes in wax cups that were always sweating, and then down an alley a mile or so away, and when he left her off at five to eleven only the movie house was still open at the plaza. Her girl friend was there, talking with a boy. When Connie came up the two girls smiled at each other and Connie said, "How was the movie?" and the girl said, "You should know." They rode off with the girl's father, sleepy and pleased, and Connie couldn't help but look at the darkened shopping plaza with its big empty parking lot and its signs that were faded and ghostly now, and over at the drive-in restaurant where cars were still circling tirelessly. She couldn't hear the music at this distance.

Next morning June asked her how the movie was and Connie said, "So-so."

She and that girl and occasionally another girl went out several times a   10
week that way, and the rest of the time Connie spent around the house—it
was summer vacation—getting in her mother's way and thinking, dreaming, about the boys she met. But all the boys fell back and dissolved into a
single face that was not even a face, but an idea, a feeling, mixed up with
the urgent insistent pounding of the music and the humid night air of July.
Connie's mother kept dragging her back to the daylight by finding things for
her to do or saying suddenly, "What's this about the Pettinger girl?"

And Connie would say nervously, "Oh, her. That dope." She always
drew thick clear lines between herself and such girls, and her mother was
simple and kindly enough to believe her. Her mother was so simple, Connie thought, that it was maybe cruel to fool her so much. Her mother went
scuffling around the house in old bedroom slippers and complained over
the telephone to one sister about the other, then the other called up and the
two of them complained about the third one. If June's name was mentioned
her mother's tone was approving, and if Connie's name was mentioned it
was disapproving. This did not really mean she disliked Connie and actually Connie thought that her mother preferred her to June because she was
prettier, but the two of them kept up a pretense of exasperation, a sense that
they were tugging and struggling over something of little value to either
of them. Sometimes, over coffee, they were almost friends, but something
would come up—some vexation that was like a fly buzzing suddenly around
their heads—and their faces went hard with contempt.

One Sunday Connie got up at eleven—none of them bothered with
church—and washed her hair so that it could dry all day long, in the sun.
Her parents and sister were going to a barbecue at an aunt's house and Connie said no, she wasn't interested, rolling her eyes, to let mother know just
what she thought of it. "Stay home alone then," her mother said sharply.
Connie sat out back in a lawn chair and watched them drive away, her
father quiet and bald, hunched around so that he could back the car out,
her mother with a look that was still angry and not at all softened through
the windshield, and in the back seat poor old June all dressed up as if she
didn't know what a barbecue was, with all the running yelling kids and the
flies. Connie sat with her eyes closed in the sun, dreaming and dazed with
the warmth about her as if this were a kind of love, the caresses of love, and
her mind slipped over onto thoughts of the boy she had been with the night
before and how nice he had been, how sweet it always was, not the way
someone like June would suppose but sweet, gentle, the way it was in movies and promised in songs; and when she opened her eyes she hardly knew
where she was, the back yard ran off into weeds and a fenceline of trees and
behind it the sky was perfectly blue and still. The asbestos "ranch house"
that was now three years old startled her—it looked small. She shook her
head as if to get awake.

It was too hot. She went inside the house and turned on the radio to
drown out the quiet. She sat on the edge of her bed, barefoot, and listened
for an hour and a half to a program called XYZ Sunday Jamboree, record

after record of hard, fast, shrieking songs she sang along with, interspersed by exclamations from "Bobby King": "An' look here you girls at Napoleon's—Son and Charley want you to pay real close attention to this song coming up!"

And Connie paid close attention herself, bathed in a glow of slow-pulsed joy that seemed to rise mysteriously out of the music itself and lay languidly about the airless little room, breathed in and breathed out with each gentle rise and fall of her chest.

After a while she heard a car coming up the drive. She sat up at once, 15 startled, because it couldn't be her father so soon. The gravel kept crunching all the way in from the road—the driveway was long—and Connie ran to the window. It was a car she didn't know. It was an open jalopy, painted a bright gold that caught the sun opaquely. Her heart began to pound and her fingers snatched at her hair, checking it, and she whispered "Christ. Christ," wondering how bad she looked. The car came to a stop at the side door and the horn sounded four short taps as if this were a signal Connie knew.

She went into the kitchen and approached the door slowly, then hung out the screen door, her bare toes curling down off the step. There were two boys in the car and now she recognized the driver: he had shaggy, shabby black hair that looked crazy as a wig and he was grinning at her.

"I ain't late, am I?" he said.

"Who the hell do you think you are?" Connie said.

"Toldja I'd be out, didn't I?"

"I don't even know who you are." 20

She spoke sullenly, careful to show no interest or pleasure, and he spoke in a fast bright monotone. Connie looked past him to the other boy, taking her time. He had fair brown hair, with a lock that fell onto his forehead. His sideburns gave him a fierce, embarrassed look, but so far he hadn't even bothered to glance at her. Both boys wore sunglasses. The driver's glasses were metallic and mirrored everything in miniature.

"You wanta come for a ride?" he said.

Connie smirked and let her hair fall loose over one shoulder.

"Don'tcha like my car? New paint job," he said. "Hey."

"What?" 25

"You're cute."

She pretended to fidget, chasing flies away from the door.

"Don'tcha believe me, or what?" he said.

"Look, I don't even know who you are," Connie said in disgust.

"Hey, Ellie's got a radio, see. Mine's broke down." He lifted his friend's 30 arm and showed her the little transistor the boy was holding, and now Connie began to hear the music. It was the same program that was playing inside the house.

"Bobby King?" she said.

"I listen to him all the time. I think he's great."

"He's kind of great," Connie said reluctantly.

"Listen, that guy's *great*. He knows where the action is."

Connie blushed a little, because the glasses made it impossible for her   35
to see just what this boy was looking at. She couldn't decide if she liked him
or if he was just a jerk, and so she dawdled in the doorway and wouldn't
come down or go back inside. She said, "What's all that stuff painted on
your car?"

"Can'tcha read it?" He opened the door very carefully, as if he was afraid
it might fall off. He slid out just as carefully, planting his feet firmly on the
ground, the tiny metallic world in his glasses slowing down like gelatin hardening and in the midst of it Connie's bright green blouse. "This here is my
name, to begin with," he said. ARNOLD FRIEND was written in tar-like black
letters on the side, with a drawing of a round grinning face that reminded
Connie of a pumpkin, except it wore sunglasses. "I wanta introduce myself,
I'm Arnold Friend and that's my real name and I'm gonna be your friend,
honey, and inside the car's Ellie Oscar, he's kinda shy." Ellie brought his
transistor up to his shoulder and balanced it there. "Now these numbers are
a secret code, honey," Arnold Friend explained. He read off the numbers
33, 19, 17 and raised his eyebrows at her to see what she thought of that,
but she didn't think much of it. The left rear fender had been smashed and
around it was written, on the gleaming gold background: DONE BY CRAZY
WOMAN DRIVER. Connie had to laugh at that. Arnold Friend was pleased at
her laughter and looked up at her. "Around the other side's a lot more—you
wanta come and see them?"

"No."

"Why not?"

"Why should I?"

"Don'tcha wanta see what's on the car? Don'tcha wanta go for a ride?"   40

"I don't know."

"Why not?"

"I got things to do."

"Like what?"

"Things."   45

He laughed as if she had said something funny. He slapped his thighs.
He was standing in a strange way, leaning back against the car as if he were
balancing himself. He wasn't tall, only an inch or so taller than she would be if
she came down to him. Connie liked the way he was dressed, which was the
way all of them dressed: tight faded jeans stuffed into black, scuffed boots, a
belt that pulled his waist in and showed how lean he was, and a white pullover shirt that was a little soiled and showed the hard small muscles of his
arms and shoulders. He looked as if he probably did hard work, lifting and
carrying things. Even his neck looked muscular. And his face was a familiar
face, somehow: the jaw and chin and cheeks slightly darkened, because he
hadn't shaved for a day or two, and the nose long and hawk-like, sniffing as
if she were a treat he was going to gobble up and it was all a joke.

"Connie, you ain't telling the truth. This is your day set aside for a ride
with me and you know it," he said, still laughing. The way he straightened
and recovered from his fit of laughing showed that it had been all fake.

"How do you know what my name is?" she said suspiciously.

"It's Connie."

"Maybe and maybe not."   50

"I know my Connie," he said, wagging his finger. Now she remembered him even better, back at the restaurant, and her cheeks warmed at the thought of how she sucked in her breath just at the moment she passed him—how she must have looked to him. And he had remembered her. "Ellie and I come out here especially for you," he said. "Ellie can sit in back. How about it?"

"Where?"

"Where what?"

"Where're we going?"

He looked at her. He took off the sunglasses and she saw how pale the   55
skin around his eyes was, like holes that were not in shadow but instead in light. His eyes were like chips of broken glass that catch the light in an amiable way. He smiled. It was as if the idea of going for a ride somewhere, to some place, was a new idea to him.

"Just for a ride, Connie sweetheart."

"I never said my name was Connie," she said.

"But I know what it is. I know your name and all about you, lots of things," Arnold Friend said. He had not moved yet but stood still leaning back against the side of his jalopy. "I took a special interest in you, such a pretty girl, and found out all about you like I know your parents and sister are gone somewheres and I know where and how long they're going to be gone, and I know who you were with last night, and your best friend's name is Betty. Right?"

He spoke in a simple lilting voice, exactly as if he were reciting the words to a song. His smile assured her that everything was fine. In the car Ellie turned up the volume on his radio and did not bother to look around at them.

"Ellie can sit in the back seat," Arnold Friend said. He indicated his   60
friend with a casual jerk of his chin, as if Ellie did not count and she could not bother with him.

"How'd you find out all that stuff?" Connie said.

"Listen: Betty Schultz and Tony Fitch and Jimmy Pettinger and Nancy Pettinger," he said, in a chant. "Raymond Stanley and Bob Hutter—"

"Do you know all those kids?"

"I know everybody."

"Look, you're kidding. You're not from around here."   65

"Sure."

"But—how come we never saw you before?"

"Sure you saw me before," he said. He looked down at his boots, as if he were a little offended. "You just don't remember."

"I guess I'd remember you," Connie said.

"Yeah?" He looked up at this, beaming. He was pleased. He began to   70
mark time with the music from Ellie's radio, tapping his fists lightly together.

Connie looked away from his smile to the car, which was painted so bright it almost hurt her eyes to look at it. She looked at that name, ARNOLD FRIEND. And up at the front fender was an expression that was familiar—MAN THE FLYING SAUCERS. It was an expression kids had used the year before, but didn't use this year. She looked at it for a while as if the words meant something to her that she did not yet know.

"What're you thinking about? Huh?" Arnold Friend demanded. "Not worried about your hair blowing around in the car, are you?"

"No."

"Think I maybe can't drive good?"

"How do I know?"

"You're a hard girl to handle. How come?" he said. "Don't you know I'm your friend? Didn't you see me put my sign in the air when you walked by?"   75

"What sign?"

"My sign." And he drew an X in the air, leaning out toward her. They were maybe ten feet apart. After his hand fell back to his side the X was still in the air, almost visible. Connie let the screen door close and stood perfectly still inside it, listening to the music from her radio and the boy's blend together. She stared at Arnold Friend. He stood there so stiffly relaxed, pretending to be relaxed, with one hand idly on the door handle as if he were keeping himself up that way and had no intention of ever moving again. She recognized most things about him, the tight jeans that showed his thighs and buttocks and the greasy leather boots and the tight shirt, and even that slippery friendly smile of his, that sleepy dreamy smile that all the boys used to get across ideas they didn't want to put into words. She recognized all this and also the singsong way he talked, slightly mocking, kidding, but serious and a little melancholy, and she recognized the way he tapped one fist against the other in homage to the perpetual music behind him. But all these things did not come together.

She said suddenly, "Hey, how old are you?"

His smile faded. She could see then that he wasn't a kid, he was much older—thirty, maybe more. At this knowledge her heart began to pound faster.

"That's a crazy thing to ask. Can'tcha see I'm your own age?"   80

"Like hell you are."

"Or maybe a coupla years older, I'm eighteen."

"Eighteen?" she said doubtfully.

He grinned to reassure her and lines appeared at the corners of his mouth. His teeth were big and white. He grinned so broadly his eyes became slits and she saw how thick the lashes were, thick and black as if painted with a black tar-like material. Then he seemed to become embarrassed, abruptly, and looked over his shoulder at Ellie. "*Him*, he's crazy," he said. "Ain't he a riot, he's a nut, a real character." Ellie was still listening to the music. His sunglasses told nothing about what he was thinking. He wore a bright orange shirt unbuttoned halfway to show his chest, which was a pale, bluish chest and not muscular like Arnold Friend's. His shirt collar was turned up all around and the very tips of the collar pointed out past his chin as if they were protecting him. He was pressing the transistor radio up against his ear and sat there in a kind of daze, right in the sun.

"He's kinda strange," Connie said.   85

"Hey, she says you're kinda strange! Kinda strange!" Arnold Friend cried. He pounded on the car to get Ellie's attention. Ellie turned for the first time and Connie saw with shock that he wasn't a kid either—he had a fair, hairless face, cheeks reddened slightly as if the veins grew too close to the surface of his skin, the face of a forty-year-old baby. Connie felt a wave of dizziness rise in her at this sight and she stared at him as if waiting for something to change the shock of the moment, make it all right again. Ellie's lips kept shaping words, mumbling along with the words blasting his ear.

"Maybe you two better go away," Connie said faintly.

"What? How come?" Arnold Friend cried. "We come out here to take you for a ride. It's Sunday." He had the voice of the man on the radio now. It was the same voice, Connie thought. "Don'tcha know it's Sunday all day and honey, no matter who you were with last night today you're with Arnold Friend and don't you forget it!—Maybe you better step out here," he said, and this last was in a different voice. It was a little flatter, as if the heat was finally getting to him.

"No. I got things to do."

"Hey."   90

"You two better leave."

"We ain't leaving until you come with us."

"Like hell I am—"

"Connie, don't fool around with me. I mean—I mean, don't fool *around*," he said, shaking his head. He laughed incredulously. He placed his sunglasses on top of his head, carefully, as if he were indeed wearing a wig, and brought the stems down behind his ears. Connie stared at him, another wave of dizziness and fear rising in her so that for a moment he wasn't even in focus but was just a blur, standing there against his gold car, and she had the idea that he had driven up the driveway all right but had come from nowhere before that and belonged nowhere and that everything about him and even the music that was so familiar to her was only half real.

"If my father comes and sees you—"   95

"He ain't coming. He's at a barbecue."

"How do you know that?"

"Aunt Tillie's. Right now they're—uh—they're drinking. Sitting around," he said vaguely, squinting as if he were staring all the way to town and over to Aunt Tillie's back yard. Then the vision seemed to clear and he nodded energetically. "Yeah. Sitting around. There's your sister in a blue dress, huh? And high heels, the poor sad bitch—nothing like you, sweetheart! And your mother's helping some fat woman with the corn, they're cleaning the corn—husking the corn—"

"What fat woman?" Connie cried.

"How do I know what fat woman. I don't know every goddamn fat 100 woman in the world!" Arnold Friend laughed.

"Oh, that's Mrs. Hornby. . . . Who invited her?" Connie said. She felt a little light-headed. Her breath was coming quickly.

"She's too fat. I don't like them fat. I like them the way you are, honey," he said, smiling sleepily at her. They stared at each other for a while, through the screen door. He said softly, "Now what you're going to do is this: you're going to come out that door. You're going to sit up front with me and Ellie's going to sit in the back, the hell with Ellie, right? This isn't Ellie's date. You're my date. I'm your lover, honey."

"What? You're crazy—"

"Yes, I'm your lover. You don't know what that is but you will," he said. "I know that too. I know all about you. But look: it's real nice and you couldn't ask for nobody better than me, or more polite. I always keep my word. I'll tell you how it is, I'm always nice at first, the first time. I'll hold you so tight you won't think you have to try to get away or pretend anything because you'll know you can't. And I'll come inside you where it's all secret and you'll give in to me and you'll love me—"

"Shut up! You're crazy!" Connie said. She backed away from the door. 105 She put her hands against her ears as if she'd heard something terrible, something not meant for her. "People don't talk like that, you're crazy," she muttered. Her heart was almost too big now for her chest and its pumping made sweat break out all over her. She looked out to see Arnold Friend pause and then take a step toward the porch lurching. He almost fell. But, like a clever drunken man, he managed to catch his balance. He wobbled in his high boots and grabbed hold of one of the porch posts.

"Honey?" he said. "You still listening?"

"Get the hell out of here!"

"Be nice, honey. Listen."

"I'm going to call the police—"

He wobbled again and out of the side of his mouth came a fast spat 110 curse, an aside not meant for her to hear. But even this "Christ!" sounded forced. Then he began to smile again. She watched this smile come, awkward as if he were smiling from inside a mask. His whole face was a mask, she thought wildly, tanned down onto his throat but then running out as if he had plastered make-up on his face but had forgotten about his throat.

"Honey—? Listen, here's how it is. I always tell the truth and I promise you this: I ain't coming in that house after you."

"You better not! I'm going to call the police if you—if you don't—"

"Honey," he said, talking right through her voice, "honey, I'm not coming in there but you are coming out here. You know why?"

She was panting. The kitchen looked like a place she had never seen before, some room she had run inside but which wasn't good enough, wasn't going to help her. The kitchen window had never had a curtain, after three years, and there were dishes in the sink for her to do—probably—and if you ran your hand across the table you'd probably feel something sticky there.

"You listening, honey? Hey?" 115

"—going to call the police—"

"Soon as you touch the phone I don't need to keep my promise and can come inside. You won't want that."

She rushed forward and tried to lock the door. Her fingers were shaking. "But why lock it," Arnold Friend said gently, talking right into her face. "It's just a screen door. It's just nothing." One of his boots was at a strange angle, as if his foot wasn't in it. It pointed out to the left, bent at the ankle. "I mean, anybody can break through a screen door and glass and wood and iron or anything else if he needs to, anybody at all and specially Arnold Friend. If the place got lit up with a fire, honey, you'd come runnin' out into my arms, right into my arms an' safe at home—like you knew I was your lover and'd stopped fooling around, I don't mind a nice shy girl but I don't like no fooling around." Part of those words were spoken with a slight rhythmic lilt, and Connie somehow recognized them—the echo of a song from last year, about a girl rushing into her boy friend's arms and coming home again—

Connie stood barefoot on the linoleum floor, staring at him. "What do you want?" she whispered.

"I want you," he said. 120

"What?"

"Seen you that night and thought, that's the one, yes sir. I never needed to look any more."

"But my father's coming back. He's coming to get me. I had to wash my hair first—" She spoke in a dry, rapid voice, hardly raising it for him to hear.

"No, your daddy is not coming and yes, you had to wash your hair and you washed it for me. It's nice and shining and all for me. I thank you, sweetheart," he said, with a mock bow, but again he almost lost his balance. He had to bend and adjust his boots. Evidently his feet did not go all the way down; the boots must have been stuffed with something so that he would seem taller. Connie stared out at him and behind him at Ellie in the car, who seemed to be looking off toward Connie's right, into nothing. Then Ellie said, pulling the words out of the air one after another as if he were just discovering them, "You want me to pull out the phone?"

"Shut your mouth and keep it shut," Arnold Friend said, his face red 125 from bending over or maybe from embarrassment because Connie had seen his boots. "This ain't none of your business."

"What—what are you doing? What do you want?" Connie said. "If I call the police they'll get you, they'll arrest you—"

"Promise was not to come in unless you touch that phone, and I'll keep that promise," he said. He resumed his erect position and tried to force his shoulders back. He sounded like a hero in a movie, declaring something important. He spoke too loudly and it was as if he were speaking to someone behind Connie. "I ain't made plans for coming in that house where I don't belong but just for you to come out to me, the way you should. Don't you know who I am?"

"You're crazy," she whispered. She backed away from the door but did not want to go into another part of the house, as if this would give him permission to come through the door. "What do you . . . You're crazy, you. . . ."

"Huh? What're you saying, honey?"

Her eyes darted everywhere in the kitchen. She could not remember   130 what it was, this room.

"This is how it is, honey: you come out and we'll drive away, have a nice ride. But if you don't come out we're gonna wait till your people come home and then they're all going to get it."

"You want that telephone pulled out?" Ellie said. He held the radio away from his ear and grimaced, as if without the radio the air was too much for him.

"I toldja shut up, Ellie," Arnold Friend said, "you're deaf, get a hearing aid, right? Fix yourself up. This little girl's no trouble and's gonna be nice to me, so Ellie keep to yourself, this ain't your date—right? Don't hem in on me, don't hog, don't crush, don't bird dog, don't trail me," he said in a rapid, meaningless voice, as if he were running through all the expressions he'd learned but was no longer sure which one of them was in style, then rushing on to new ones, making them up with his eyes closed. "Don't crawl under my fence, don't squeeze in my chipmunk hole, don't sniff my glue, suck my pop-sicle, keep your own greasy fingers on yourself!" He shaded his eyes and peered in at Connie, who was backed against the kitchen table. "Don't mind him, honey, he's just a creep. He's a dope. Right? I'm the boy for you and like I said, you come out here nice like a lady and give me your hand, and nobody else gets hurt, I mean, your nice old bald-headed daddy and your mummy and your sister in her high heels. Because listen: why bring them in this?"

"Leave me alone," Connie whispered.

"Hey, you know that old woman down the road, the one with the chick-   135 ens and stuff—you know her?"

"She's dead!"

"Dead? What? You know her?" Arnold Friend said.

"She's dead—"

"Don't you like her?"

"She's dead—she's—she isn't here any more—"   140

"But don't you like her, I mean, you got something against her? Some grudge or something?" Then his voice dipped as if he were conscious of rudeness. He touched the sunglasses on top of his head as if to make sure they were still there. "Now you be a good girl."

"What are you going to do?"

"Just two things, or maybe three," Arnold Friend said. "But I promise it won't last long and you'll like me that way you get to like people you're close to. You will. It's all over for you here, so come on out. You don't want your people in any trouble, do you?"

She turned and bumped against a chair or something, hurting her leg, but she ran into the back room and picked up the telephone. Something roared in her ear, a tiny roaring, and she was so sick with fear that she could do nothing but listen to it—the telephone was clammy and very heavy and her fingers groped down to the dial but were too weak to touch it. She began to scream into the phone, into the roaring. She cried out, she cried for her mother, she felt her breath start jerking back and forth in her lungs as if it were something Arnold Friend was stabbing her with again and again with no tenderness. A noisy sorrowful wailing rose all about her and she was locked inside it the way she was locked inside this house.

After a while she could hear again. She was sitting on the floor, with her 145 wet back against the wall.

Arnold Friend was saying from the door, "That's a good girl. Put the phone back."

She kicked the phone away from her.

"No, honey. Pick it up. Put it back right."

She picked it up and put it back. The dial tone stopped.

"That's a good girl. Now you come outside." 150

She was hollow with what had been fear but what was now just an emptiness. All that screaming had blasted it out of her. She sat, one leg cramped under her, and deep inside her brain was something like a pinpoint of light that kept going and would not let her relax. She thought, I'm not going to see my mother again. She thought, I'm not going to sleep in my bed again. Her bright green blouse was all wet.

Arnold Friend said, in a gentle-loud voice that was like a stage voice, "The place where you came from ain't there any more, and where you had in mind to go is cancelled out. This place you are now—inside your daddy's house—is nothing but a cardboard box I can knock down any time. You know that and always did know it. You hear me?"

She thought, I have got to think. I have got to know what to do.

"We'll go out to a nice field, out in the country here where it smells so nice and it's sunny," Arnold Friend said. "I'll have my arms tight around you so you won't need to try to get away and I'll show you what love is like, what it does. The hell with this house! It looks solid all right," he said. He ran a fingernail down the screen and the noise did not make Connie shiver, as it would have the day before. "Now put your hand on your heart, honey. Feel that? That feels solid too but we know better. Be nice to me, be sweet like you can because what else is there for a girl like you but to be sweet and pretty and give in?—and get away before her people get back?"

She felt her pounding heart. Her hand seemed to enclose it. She thought 155 for the first time in her life that it was nothing that was hers, that belonged to her, but just a pounding, living thing inside this body that wasn't really hers either.

"You don't want them to get hurt," Arnold Friend went on. "Now get up, honey. Get up all by yourself."

She stood.

"Now turn this way. That's right. Come over to me—Ellie, put that away, didn't I tell you? You dope. You miserable creepy dope," Arnold Friend said.

His words were not angry but only part of an incantation. The incantation was kindly. "Now come out through the kitchen to me honey and let's see a smile, try it, you're a brave sweet little girl and now they're eating corn and hotdogs cooked to bursting over an outdoor fire, and they don't know one thing about you and never did and honey you're better than them because not a one of them would have done this for you."

Connie felt the linoleum under her feet; it was cool. She brushed her hair back out of her eyes. Arnold Friend let go of the post tentatively and opened his arms for her, his elbows pointing in toward each other and his wrists limp, to show that this was an embarrassed embrace and a little mocking, he didn't want to make her self-conscious.

She put out her hand against the screen. She watched herself push the 160 door slowly open as if she were back safe somewhere in the other doorway, watching this body and this head of long hair moving out into the sunlight where Arnold Friend waited.

"My sweet little blue-eyed girl," he said in a half-sung sigh that had nothing to do with her brown eyes but was taken up just the same by the vast sunlit reaches of the land behind him and on all sides of him—so much land that Connie had never seen before and did not recognize except to know that she was going to it. ■

The Reader's Presence

1. Oates describes Connie as having "two sides . . . , one for home and one for anywhere that was not home" (paragraph 5). What are the differences between the two sides? In what ways does Arnold Friend also seem to have two sides? How are these characters alike? How are they different?

2. Compare the ending of this story to the conclusion of Raymond Carver's "What We Talk About When We Talk About Love" (page 884). What do you think happens after each story ends? Why do you think Carver and Oates made the decision to end the story without discussing how the characters' situations will resolve? Does the ending increase or decrease each story's emotional tension? Why?

3. **CONNECTIONS:** Read Oates's essay that follows. In what specific ways does reading this essay help you to understand better—and appreciate more—Oates's achievements as a writer of fiction? What specific aspects of the essay help you to understand Connie and, especially, her relationship with adults? What does Oates admire about the film *Smooth Talk*? What reservations does she express about the film? Characterize Oates's response to the contrast between the end of the story and the end of the film. Which does she prefer? Explain why.

The Writer at Work

JOYCE CAROL OATES on *Smooth Talk*: Short Story into Film

Joyce Carol Oates's "Where Are You Going, Where Have You Been?" has been described as "a study in the peril that lurks beneath the surface of everyday life." In 1985, Joyce Chopra directed a film, *Smooth Talk*, with a screenplay by Tom Cole based on Oates's story. The film continues after the story ends, giving viewers an unexpectedly optimistic glimpse of Connie's fate. *Smooth Talk* won the Grand Jury Prize at the Sundance Film Festival in 1986. The following article appeared in the *New York Times* in 1986. Does Oates's original conception of the story fit with your expectations of what might happen to Connie? Does considering a happy ending—or at least an ending without tragedy—make a difference in your view of the story as a whole?

❝Some years ago in the American Southwest there surfaced a tabloid psychopath known as "The Pied Piper of Tucson." I have forgotten his name, but his specialty was the seduction and occasional murder of teenaged girls. He may or may not have had actual accomplices, but his bizarre activities were known among a circle of teenagers in the Tucson area; for some reason they kept his secret, deliberately did not inform parents or police. It was this fact, not the fact of the mass murderer himself, that struck me at the time. And this was a pre-Manson time, early or mid-1960s.

The Pied Piper mimicked teenagers in their talk, dress, and behavior, but he was not a teenager—he was a man in his early thirties. Rather short, he stuffed rags in his leather boots to give himself height. (And sometimes walked unsteadily as a consequence: did none among his admiring constituency notice?) He charmed his victims as charismatic psychopaths have always charmed their victims, to the bewilderment of others who fancy themselves free of all lunatic attractions. The Pied Piper of Tucson: a trashy dream, a tabloid archetype, sheer artifice, comedy, cartoon—surrounded, however improbably, and finally tragically by real people. You think that, if you look twice, he won't be there. But there he is.

I don't remember any longer where I first read about this Pied Piper—very likely in *Life* Magazine. I do recall deliberately not reading the full article because I didn't want to be distracted by too much detail. It was not after all the mass murderer himself who intrigued me, but the disturbing fact that a number of teenagers—from "good" families—aided and abetted his crimes. This is the sort of thing authorities and responsible citizens invariably call "inexplicable" because they can't find explanations for it. *They* would not have fallen under this maniac's spell, after all.

An early draft of my short story "Where Are You Going, Where Have You Been?"—from which the film *Smooth Talk* was adapted by Joyce Chopra and Tom Cole—had the rather too explicit title "Death and the Maiden." It was cast in a mode of fiction to which I am still partial—indeed, every third or fourth story of mine is probably in this mode—"realistic allegory," it might be called. It is Hawthornean,[1] romantic, shading into parable. Like the medieval German engraving from which my title was taken, the story was minutely detailed yet clearly an allegory of the fatal attractions of death (or the devil). An innocent young girl is seduced by way of her own vanity; she mistakes death for erotic romance of a particularly American/trashy sort.

In subsequent drafts the story changed its tone, its focus, its language, its title. It became "Where Are You Going, Where Have You Been?" Written at a time when the author was intrigued by the music of Bob Dylan, particularly the hauntingly elegiac song "It's All Over Now, Baby Blue," it was dedicated to Bob Dylan. The charismatic mass murderer drops into the background and his innocent victim, a fifteen-year-old, moves into the foreground. She becomes the true protagonist of the tale, courting and being courted by her fate, a self-styled 1950s pop figure, alternately absurd and winning. There is no suggestion in the published story that "Arnold Friend" has seduced and murdered other young girls, or even that he necessarily intends to murder Connie. Is his interest "merely" sexual? (Nor is there anything about the complicity of other teenagers. I saved that yet more provocative note for a current story, "Testimony.") Connie is shallow, vain, silly, hopeful, doomed—but capable nonetheless of an unexpected gesture of heroism at the story's end. Her smooth-talking seducer, who cannot lie, promises her that her family will be unharmed if she gives herself to him; and so she does.

The story ends abruptly at the point of her "crossing over." We don't know the nature of her sacrifice, only that she is generous enough to make it.

In adapting a narrative so spare and thematically foreshortened as "Where Are You Going, Where Have You Been?" film director Joyce Chopra and screenwriter Tom Cole were required to do a good deal of filling in, expanding, inventing. Connie's story becomes lavishly, and lovingly, textured; she is not an allegorical figure so much as a "typical" teen-aged girl (if Laura Dern, spectacularly good-looking, can be so defined). Joyce Chopra, who has done documentary films on contemporary teenage culture and, yet more authoritatively, has an adolescent daughter of her own, creates in *Smooth Talk* a vivid and absolutely believable world for Connie to inhabit. Or worlds: as in the original story there is Connie-at-home, and there is Connie-with-her-friends. Two fifteen-year-old girls, two finely honed styles, two voices, sometimes but not often overlapping. It is one of the marvelous visual features of the film that we *see* Connie and her friends transform themselves, once they are safely free of parental observation. The girls claim their true identities in the neighborhood shopping mall. What freedom, what joy!

Smooth Talk is, in a way, as much Connie's mother's story as it is Connie's; its center of gravity, its emotional nexus, is frequently with the mother—warmly and convincingly played by Mary Kay Place. (Though the mother's sexual jealousy of her daughter is slighted in the film.) Connie's ambiguous relationship with her affable, somewhat mysterious father (well played by Levon Helm) is an excellent touch: I had thought, subsequent to the story's publication, that I should have built up the father, suggesting, as subtly as I could, an attraction there paralleling the attraction Connie

---

[1] *Hawthornean:* Similar in style to that of Nathaniel Hawthorne (1804–1864), the acclaimed American novelist and short story writer. (See page 438). —EDS.

feels for her seducer, Arnold Friend. And Arnold Friend himself—"A. Friend" as he says—is played with appropriately over-done sexual swagger by Treat Williams, who is perfect for the part; and just the right age. We see that Arnold Friend isn't a teenager even as Connie, mesmerized by his presumed charm, does not seem to *see* him at all. What is so difficult to accomplish in prose—nudging the reader to look over the protagonist's shoulder, so to speak—is accomplished with envi-able ease in film.

Treat Williams as Arnold Friend is supreme in his very awfulness, as, surely, the original Pied Piper of Tucson must have been. (Though no one involved in the film knew about the original source.) Mr. Williams flawlessly impersonates Arnold Friend as Arnold Friend imperson-ates—is it James Dean? James Dean regarding himself in mirrors, doing James Dean impersonations? That Connie's fate is so trashy is in fact her fate.

What is outstanding in Joyce Chopra's *Smooth Talk* is its visual fresh-ness, its sense of motion and life; the attentive intelligence the director has brought to the semi-secret world of the American adolescent—shopping mall flirtations, drive-in restaurant romances, highway hitchhiking, the fascination of rock music played very, very loud. (James Taylor's music for the film is wonderfully appropriate. We hear it as Connie hears it; it is the music of her spiritual being.) Also outstanding, as I have indicated, and numerous critics have noted, are the acting performances. Laura Dern is so dazzlingly right as "my" Connie that I may come to think I modeled the ficti-tious girl on her, in the way that writers frequently delude themselves about motions of causality.

My difficulties with *Smooth Talk* have primarily to do with my chronic hesitation—about seeing/hearing work of mine abstracted from its contexture of language. All writers know that language is their subject; quirky word choices, patterns of rhythm, enigmatic pauses, punctuation marks. Where the quick scanner sees "quick" writing, the writer conceals nine tenths of the iceberg. Of course we all have "real" subjects, and we will fight to the death to defend those subjects, but beneath the tale-telling it is the tale-telling that grips us so very fiercely. The writer works in a single dimension, the director works in three. I assume they are professionals to their fingertips; authorities in their medium as I am an authority (if I am) in mine. I would fiercely defend the placement of a semicolon in one of my novels but I would probably have deferred in the end to Joyce Chopra's decision to reverse the story's conclusion, turn it upside down, in a sense, so that the film ends not with death, not with a sleepwalker's crossing over to her fate, but upon a scene of rec-onciliation, rejuvenation.

A girl's loss of virginity, bittersweet but not necessarily tragic. Not today. A girl's coming-of-age that involves her succumbing to, but then rejecting, the "trashy dreams" of her pop teenage cul-ture. "Where Are You Going, Where Have You Been?" defines itself as allegorical in its conclusion: Death and Death's chariot (a funky souped-up convertible) have come for the Maiden. Awakening is, in the story's final lines, moving out into the sunlight where Arnold Friend waits:

> "My sweet little blue-eyed girl," he said in a half-sung sigh that had noth-ing to do with [Connie's] brown eyes but was taken up just the same by the vast sunlit reaches of the land behind him and on all sides of him—so much land that Connie had never seen before and did not recognize except to know that she was going to it.

—a conclusion impossible to transfigure into film. **”**

Tim O'Brien
THE THINGS THEY CARRIED

TIM O'BRIEN (b. 1946) served as U.S. infantryman in Vietnam from 1968 through 1970, and much of his writing is concerned with the Vietnam War experience. His 1979 novel, *Going After Cacciato*, won the National Book Award, and his subsequent works have been widely praised for their unusual approach to storytelling. O'Brien is known for blurring the lines between fiction and reality: for example, his collection of Vietnam War stories, *The Things They Carried* (1990), from which the following story is taken, draws heavily from personal experience. Yet in narrating events, O'Brien often makes a point of telling the reader that the stories are fictional. He explains how they are fictional, and why. Some of O'Brien's other works include *Northern Lights* (1975), *In the Lake of the Woods* (1994), and *July, July* (2004). *In the Lake of the Woods* won the James Fenimore Cooper Award for Historical Fiction in 1995.

> Tim O'Brien served as U.S. infantryman in Vietnam from 1968 through 1970, and much of his writing is concerned with the Vietnam War experience.

FIRST LIEUTENANT Jimmy Cross carried letters from a girl named Martha, a junior at Mount Sebastian College in New Jersey. They were not love letters, but Lieutenant Cross was hoping, so he kept them folded in plastic at the bottom of his rucksack. In the late afternoon, after a day's march, he would dig his foxhole, wash his hands under a canteen, unwrap the letters, hold them with the tips of his fingers, and spend the last hour of light pretending. He would imagine romantic camping trips into the White Mountains in New Hampshire. He would sometimes taste the envelope flaps, knowing her tongue had been there. More than anything, he wanted Martha to love him as he loved her, but the letters were mostly chatty, elusive on the matter of love. She was a virgin, he was almost sure. She was an English major at Mount Sebastian, and she wrote beautifully about her professors and roommates and midterm exams, about her respect for Chaucer and her great affection for Virginia Woolf. She often quoted lines of poetry; she never mentioned the war, except to say, Jimmy, take care of yourself. The letters weighed 10 ounces. They were signed Love, Martha, but Lieutenant Cross understood that Love was only a way of signing and did not mean what he sometimes pretended it meant. At dusk, he would carefully return the letters to his rucksack. Slowly, a bit distracted, he would get up and move among his men, checking the perimeter, then at full dark he would return to his hole and watch the night and wonder if Martha was a virgin.

The things they carried were largely determined by necessity. Among the necessities or near-necessities were P-38 can openers, pocket knives, heat tabs, wristwatches, dog tags, mosquito repellent, chewing gum, candy, cigarettes, salt tablets, packets of Kool-Aid, lighters, matches, sewing kits, Military Payment Certificates, C rations, and two or three canteens of water. Together, these items weighed between 15 and 20 pounds, depending upon a man's habits or rate of metabolism. Henry Dobbins, who was a big man, carried extra rations; he was especially fond of canned peaches in heavy syrup over pound cake. Dave Jensen, who practiced field hygiene, carried a toothbrush, dental floss, and several hotel-sized bars of soap he'd stolen on R&R in Sydney, Australia. Ted Lavender, who was scared, carried tranquilizers until he was shot in the head outside the village of Than Khe in mid-April. By necessity, and because it was SOP,[1] they all carried steel helmets that weighed 5 pounds including the liner aid camouflage cover. They carried the standard fatigue jackets and trousers. Very few carried underwear. On their feet they carried jungle boots—2.1 pounds—and Dave Jensen carried three pairs of socks and a can of Dr. Scholl's foot powder as a precaution against trench foot. Until he was shot, Ted Lavender carried six or seven ounces of premium dope, which for him was a necessity. Mitchell Sanders, the RTO,[2] carried condoms. Norman Bowker carried a diary. Rat Kiley carried comic books. Kiowa, a devout Baptist, carried an illustrated New Testament that had been presented to him by his father, who taught Sunday school in Oklahoma City, Oklahoma. As a hedge against bad times, however, Kiowa also carried his grandmother's distrust of the white man, his grandfather's old hunting hatchet. Necessity dictated. Because the land was mined and booby-trapped, it was SOP for each man to carry a steel-centered, nylon-covered flak jacket, which weighed 6.7 pounds, but which on hot days seemed much heavier. Because you could die so quickly, each man carried at least one large compress bandage, usually in the helmet band for easy access. Because the nights were cold, and because the monsoons were wet, each carried a green plastic poncho that could be used as a raincoat or groundsheet or makeshift tent. With its quilted liner, the poncho weighed almost two pounds, but it was worth every ounce. In April, for instance, when Ted Lavender was shot, they used his poncho to wrap him up, then to carry him across the paddy, then to lift him into the chopper that took him away.

They were called legs or grunts.

To carry something was to hump it, as when Lieutenant Jimmy Cross humped his love for Martha up the hills and through the swamps. In its intransitive form, to hump meant to walk, or to march, but it implied burdens far beyond the intransitive.

---

1 **SOP:** Standard operating procedure. —EDS.
2 **RTO:** Radio telephone operator. —EDS.

Almost everyone humped photographs. In his wallet, Lieutenant Cross   5
carried two photographs of Martha. The first was a Kodacolor snapshot
signed Love, though he knew better. She stood against a brick wall. Her
eyes were gray and neutral, her lips slightly open as she stared straight-on at
the camera. At night, sometimes, Lieutenant Cross wondered who had taken
the picture, because he knew she had boyfriends, because he loved her so
much, and because he could see the shadow of the picture-taker spreading
out against the brick wall. The second photograph had been clipped from
the 1968 Mount Sebastian yearbook. It was an action shot—women's volleyball—and Martha was bent horizontal to the floor, reaching, the palms
of her hands in sharp focus, the tongue taut, the expression frank and competitive. There was no visible sweat. She wore white gym shorts. Her legs,
he thought, were almost certainly the legs of a virgin, dry and without hair,
the left knee cocked and carrying her entire weight, which was just over
one hundred pounds. Lieutenant Cross remembered touching that left knee.
A dark theater, he remembered, and the movie was *Bonnie and Clyde*, and
Martha wore a tweed skirt, and during the final scene, when he touched
her knee, she turned and looked at him in a sad, sober way that made him
pull his hand back, but he would always remember the feel of the tweed
skirt and the knee beneath it and the sound of the gunfire that killed Bonnie
and Clyde, how embarrassing it was, how slow and oppressive. He remembered kissing her goodnight at the dorm door. Right then, he thought, he
should've done something brave. He should've carried her up the stairs to
her room and tied her to the bed and touched that left knee all night long.
He should've risked it. Whenever he looked at the photographs, he thought
of new things he should've done.

What they carried was partly a function of rank, partly of field specialty.

As a first lieutenant and platoon leader, Jimmy Cross carried a compass, maps, code books, binoculars, and a .45-caliber pistol that weighed 2.9
pounds fully loaded. He carried a strobe light and the responsibility for the
lives of his men.

As an RTO, Mitchell Sanders carried the PRC-25 radio, a killer, 26 pounds
with its battery.

As a medic, Rat Kiley carried a canvas satchel filled with morphine and
plasma and malaria tablets and surgical tape and comic books and all the
things a medic must carry, including M&M's for especially bad wounds, for
a total weight of nearly 20 pounds.

As a big man, therefore a machine gunner, Henry Dobbins carried the   10
M-60, which weighed 23 pounds unloaded, but which was almost always
loaded. In addition, Dobbins carried between 10 and 15 pounds of ammunition draped in belts across his chest and shoulders.

As PFCs[3] or Spec 4s,[4] most of them were common grunts and carried the
standard M-16 gas-operated assault rifle. The weapon weighed 7.5 pounds

---

3 **PFC:** Private First Class.—EDS.
4 **Spec 4s:** Specialist Fourth Class.—EDS.

unloaded, 8.2 pounds with its full 20-round magazine. Depending on numerous factors, such as topography and psychology, the riflemen carried anywhere from 12 to 20 magazines, usually in cloth bandoliers, adding on another 8.4 pounds at minimum, 14 pounds at maximum. When it was available, they also carried M-16 maintenance gear—rods and steel brushes and swabs and tubes of LSA oil[5]—all of which weighed about a pound. Among the grunts, some carried the M-79 grenade launcher, 5.9 pounds unloaded, a reasonably light weapon except for the ammunition, which was heavy. A single round weighed 10 ounces. The typical load was 25 rounds. But Ted Lavender, who was scared, carried 34 rounds when he was shot and killed outside Than Khe, and he went down under an exceptional burden, more than 20 pounds of ammunition, plus the flak jacket and helmet and rations and water and toilet paper and tranquilizers and all the rest, plus the unweighed fear. He was dead weight. There was no twitching or flopping. Kiowa, who saw it happen, said it was like watching a rock fall, or a big sandbag or something—just boom, then down—not like the movies where the dead guy rolls around and does fancy spins and goes ass over teakettle—not like that, Kiowa said, the poor bastard just flat-fuck fell. Boom. Down. Nothing else. It was a bright morning in mid-April. Lieutenant Cross felt the pain. He blamed himself. They stripped off Lavender's canteens and ammo, all the heavy things, and Rat Kiley said the obvious, the guy's dead, and Mitchell Sanders used his radio to report one U.S. KIA[6] and to request a chopper. Then they wrapped Lavender in his poncho. They carried him out to a dry paddy, established security, and sat smoking the dead man's dope until the chopper came. Lieutenant Cross kept to himself. He pictured Martha's smooth young face, thinking he loved her more than anything, more than his men, and now Ted Lavender was dead because he loved her so much and could not stop thinking about her. When the dustoff arrived, they carried Lavender aboard. Afterward they burned Than Khe. They marched until dusk, then dug their holes, and that night Kiowa kept explaining how you had to be there, how fast it was, how the poor guy just dropped like so much concrete. Boom-down, he said. Like cement.

In addition to the three standard weapons—the M-60, M-16, and M-79—they carried whatever presented itself, or whatever seemed appropriate as a means of killing or staying alive. They carried catch-as-catch-can. At various times, in various situations, they carried M-14s and CAR-15s and Swedish Ks and grease guns and captured AK-47s and Chi-Coms and RPGs and Simonov carbines and black market Uzis and .38-caliber Smith & Wesson handguns and 66 mm LAWs and shotguns and silencers and blackjacks and bayonets and C-4 plastic explosives. Lee Strunk carried a slingshot; a weapon of last resort, he called it. Mitchell Sanders carried brass knuckles.

---

[5] *LSA:* Lubricant, Small Arms.—EDS.
[6] *KIA:* Killed in action.—EDS.

Kiowa carried his grandfather's feathered hatchet. Every third or fourth man carried a Claymore antipersonnel mine—3.5 pounds with its firing device. They all carried fragmentation grenades—14 ounces each. They all carried at least one M-18 colored smoke grenade—24 ounces. Some carried CS or tear gas grenades. Some carried white phosphorus grenades. They carried all they could bear, and then some, including a silent awe for the terrible power of the things they carried.

In the first week of April, before Lavender died, Lieutenant Jimmy Cross received a good-luck charm from Martha. It was a simple pebble, an ounce at most. Smooth to the touch, it was a milky white color with flecks of orange and violet, oval-shaped, like a miniature egg. In the accompanying letter, Martha wrote that she had found the pebble on the Jersey shoreline, precisely where the land touched water at high tide, where things came together but also separated. It was this separate-but-together quality, she wrote, that had inspired her to pick up the pebble and to carry it in her breast pocket for several days, where it seemed weightless, and then to send it through the mail, by air, as a token of her truest feelings for him. Lieutenant Cross found this romantic. But he wondered what her truest feelings were, exactly, and what she meant by separate-but-together. He wondered how the tides and waves had come into play on that afternoon along the Jersey shoreline when Martha saw the pebble and bent down to rescue it from geology. He imagined bare feet. Martha was a poet, with the poet's sensibilities, and her feet would be brown and bare, the toenails unpainted, the eyes chilly and somber like the ocean in March, and though it was painful, he wondered who had been with her that afternoon. He imagined a pair of shadows moving along the strip of sand where things came together but also separated. It was phantom jealousy, he knew, but he couldn't help himself. He loved her so much. On the march, through the hot days of early April, he carried the pebble in his mouth, turning it with his tongue, tasting sea salt and moisture. His mind wandered. He had difficulty keeping his attention on the war. On occasion he would yell at his men to spread out the column, to keep their eyes open, but then he would slip away into daydreams, just pretending, walking barefoot along the Jersey shore, with Martha, carrying nothing. He would feel himself rising. Sun and waves and gentle winds, all love and lightness.

What they carried varied by mission.

When a mission took them to the mountains, they carried mosquito netting, machetes, canvas tarps, and extra bug juice.   15

If a mission seemed especially hazardous, or if it involved a place they knew to be bad, they carried everything they could. In certain heavily mined AOs,[7] where the land was dense with Toe Poppers and Bouncing Betties,

[7] ***AOs:*** Areas of operation.—EDS.

they took turns humping a 28-pound mine detector. With its headphones and big sensing plate, the equipment was a stress on the lower back and shoulders, awkward to handle, often useless because of the shrapnel in the earth, but they carried it anyway, partly for safety, partly for the illusion of safety.

On ambush, or other night missions, they carried peculiar little odds and ends. Kiowa always took along his New Testament and a pair of moccasins for silence. Dave Jensen carried night-sight vitamins high in carotene. Lee Strunk carried his slingshot; ammo, he claimed, would never be a problem. Rat Kiley carried brandy and M&M's. Until he was shot, Ted Lavender carried the starlight scope, which weighed 6.3 pounds with its aluminum carrying case. Henry Dobbins carried his girlfriend's pantyhose wrapped around his neck as a comforter. They all carried ghosts. When dark came, they would move out single file across the meadows and paddies to their ambush coordinates, where they would quietly set up the Claymores and lie down and spend the night waiting.

Other missions were more complicated and required special equipment. In mid-April, it was their mission to search out and destroy the elaborate tunnel complexes in the Than Khe area south of Chu Lai. To blow the tunnels, they carried one-pound blocks of pentrite high explosives, four blocks to a man, 68 pounds in all. They carried wiring, detonators, and battery-powered clackers. Dave Jensen carried earplugs. Most often, before blowing the tunnels, they were ordered by higher command to search them, which was considered bad news, but by and large they just shrugged and carried out orders. Because he was a big man, Henry Dobbins was excused from tunnel duty. The others would draw numbers. Before Lavender died there were 17 men in the platoon, and whoever drew the number 17 would strip off his gear and crawl in headfirst with a flashlight and Lieutenant Cross's .45-caliber pistol. The rest of them would fan out as security. They would sit down or kneel, not facing the hole, listening to the ground beneath them, imagining cobwebs and ghosts, whatever was down there—the tunnel walls squeezing in—how the flashlight seemed impossibly heavy in the hand and how it was tunnel vision in the very strictest sense, compression in all ways, even time, and how you had to wiggle in—ass and elbows—a swallowed-up feeling—and how you found yourself worrying about odd things: Will your flashlight go dead? Do rats carry rabies? If you screamed, how far would the sound carry? Would your buddies hear it? Would they have the courage to drag you out? In some respects, though not many, the waiting was worse than the tunnel itself. Imagination was a killer.

On April 16, when Lee Strunk drew the number 17, he laughed and muttered something and went down quickly. The morning was hot and very still. Not good, Kiowa said. He looked at the tunnel opening, then out across a dry paddy toward the village of Than Khe. Nothing moved. No clouds or birds or people. As they waited, the men smoked and drank Kool-Aid, not talking much, feeling sympathy for Lee Strunk but also feeling the luck of the draw. You win some, you lose some, said Mitchell Sanders, and some-times you settle for a rain check. It was a tired line and no one laughed.

Henry Dobbins ate a tropical chocolate bar. Ted Lavender popped a 20 tranquilizer and went off to pee.

After five minutes, Lieutenant Jimmy Cross moved to the tunnel, leaned down, and examined the darkness. Trouble, he thought—a cave-in maybe. And then suddenly, without willing it, he was thinking about Martha. The stresses and fractures, the quick collapse, the two of them buried alive under all that weight. Dense, crushing love. Kneeling, watching the hole, he tried to concentrate on Lee Strunk and the war, all the dangers, but his love was too much for him, he felt paralyzed, he wanted to sleep inside her lungs and breathe her blood and be smothered. He wanted her to be a virgin and not a virgin, all at once. He wanted to know her. Intimate secrets: Why poetry? Why so sad? Why that grayness in her eyes? Why so alone? Not lonely, just alone—riding her bike across campus or sitting off by herself in the cafeteria—even dancing, she danced alone—and it was the aloneness that filled him with love. He remembered telling her that one evening. How she nod-ded and looked away. And how, later, when he kissed her, she received the kiss without returning it, her eyes wide open, not afraid, not a virgin's eyes, just flat and uninvolved.

Lieutenant Cross gazed at the tunnel. But he was not there. He was buried with Martha under the white sand at the Jersey shore. They were pressed together, and the pebble in his mouth was her tongue. He was smil-ing. Vaguely, he was aware of how quiet the day was, the sullen paddies, yet he could not bring himself to worry about matters of security. He was beyond that. He was just a kid at war, in love. He was twenty-four years old. He couldn't help it.

A few moments later Lee Strunk crawled out of the tunnel. He came up grinning, filthy but alive. Lieutenant Cross nodded and closed his eyes while the others clapped Strunk on the back and made jokes about rising from the dead.

Worms, Rat Kiley said. Right out of the grave. Fuckin' zombie.

The men laughed. They all felt great relief. 25

Spook City, said Mitchell Sanders.

Lee Strunk made a funny ghost sound, a kind of moaning, yet very happy, and right then, when Strunk made that high happy moaning sound, when he went *Ahhooooo*, right then Ted Lavender was shot in the head on his way back from peeing. He lay with his mouth open. The teeth were broken. There was a swollen black bruise under his left eye. The cheekbone was gone. Oh shit, Rat Kiley said, the guy's dead. The guy's dead, he kept saying, which seemed profound—the guy's dead. I mean really.

The things they carried were determined to some extent by superstition. Lieutenant Cross carried his good-luck pebble. Dave Jensen carried a rab-bit's foot. Norman Bowker, otherwise a very gentle person, carried a thumb that had been presented to him as a gift by Mitchell Sanders. The thumb was dark brown, rubbery to the touch, and weighed four ounces at most. It had been cut from a VC corpse, a boy of fifteen or sixteen. They'd found him at the bottom of an irrigation ditch, badly burned, flies in his mouth and eyes. The boy wore black shorts and sandals. At the time of his death he had been carrying a pouch of rice, a rifle, and three magazines of ammunition.

You want my opinion, Mitchell Sanders said, there's a definite moral here.

He put his hand on the dead boy's wrist. He was quiet for a time, as   30
if counting a pulse, then he patted the stomach, almost affectionately, and used Kiowa's hunting hatchet to remove the thumb.

Henry Dobbins asked what the moral was.

Moral?

You know. *Moral.*

Sanders wrapped the thumb in toilet paper and handed it across to Norman Bowker. There was no blood. Smiling, he kicked the boy's head, watched the files scatter, and said, It's like with that old TV show—Paladin. Have gun, will travel.

Henry Dobbins thought about it.   35

Yeah, well, he finally said. I don't see no moral.

There it *is*, man.

Fuck off.

They carried USO[8] stationery and pencils and pens. They carried Sterno, safety pins, trip flares, signal flares, spools of wire, razor blades, chewing tobacco, liberated joss sticks and statuettes of the smiling Buddha, candles, grease pencils, *The Stars and Stripes*, fingernail clippers, Psy Ops[9] leaflets, bush hats, bolos, and much more. Twice a week, when the resupply choppers came in, they carried hot chow in green mermite cans and large canvas bags filled with iced beer and soda pop. They carried plastic water containers, each with a two-gallon capacity. Mitchell Sanders carried a set of starched tiger fatigues for special occasions. Henry Dobbins carried Black Flag insecticide. Dave Jensen carried empty sandbags that could be filled at night for added protection. Lee Strunk carried tanning lotion. Some things they carried in common. Taking turns, they carried the big PRC-77 scrambler radio, which weighed 30 pounds with its battery. They shared the weight of memory. They took up what others could no longer bear. Often, they carried each other, the wounded or weak. They carried infections. They carried chess sets, basketballs, Vietnamese-English dictionaries, insignia of rank, Bronze Stars and Purple Hearts, plastic cards imprinted with the Code of Conduct. They carried diseases, among them malaria and dysentery. They

8 *USO:* United Service Organizations: Privately funded, nonprofit organization that provides recreation and entertainment to military personnel; "a home away from home" to troops stationed in foreign lands. —EDS.

9 *Psy Ops:* Psychological operations. —EDS.

carried lice and ringworm and leeches and paddy algae and various rots and molds. They carried the land itself—Vietnam, the place, the soil—a powdery orange-red dust that covered their boots and fatigues and faces. They carried the sky. The whole atmosphere, they carried it, the humidity, the monsoons, the stink of fungus and decay, all of it, they carried gravity. They moved like mules. By daylight they took sniper fire, at night they were mortared, but it was not battle, it was just the endless march, village to village, without purpose, nothing won or lost. They marched for the sake of the march. They plodded along slowly, dumbly, leaning forward against the heat, unthinking, all blood and bone, simple grunts, soldiering with their legs, toiling up the hills and down into the paddies and across the rivers and up again and down, just humping, one step and then the next and then another, but no volition, no will, because it was automatic, it was anatomy, and the war was entirely a matter of posture and carriage, the hump was everything, a kind of inertia, a kind of emptiness, a dullness of desire and intellect and conscience and hope and human sensibility. Their principles were in their feet. Their calculations were biological. They had no sense of strategy or mission. They searched the villages without knowing what to look for, not caring, kicking over jars of rice, frisking children and old men, blowing tunnels, sometimes setting fires and sometimes not, then forming up and moving on to the next village, then other villages, where it would always be the same. They carried their own lives. The pressures were enormous. In the heat of early afternoon, they would remove their helmets and flak jackets, walking bare, which was dangerous but which helped ease the strain. They would often discard things along the route of march. Purely for comfort, they would throw away rations, blow their Claymores and grenades, no matter, because by nightfall the resupply choppers would arrive with more of the same, then a day or two later still more, fresh watermelons and crates of ammunition and sunglasses and woolen sweaters—the resources were stunning—sparklers for the Fourth of July, colored eggs for Easter—it was the great American war chest—the fruits of science, the smokestacks, the canneries, the arsenals at Hartford, the Minnesota forests, the machine shops, the vast fields of corn and wheat—they carried like freight trains; they carried it on their backs and shoulders—and for all the ambiguities of Vietnam, all the mysteries and unknowns, there was at least the single abiding certainty that they would never be at a loss for things to carry.

After the chopper took Lavender away, Lieutenant Jimmy Cross led   40 his men into the village of Than Khe. They burned everything. They shot chickens and dogs, they trashed the village well, they called in artillery and watched the wreckage, then they marched for several hours through the hot afternoon, and then at dusk, while Kiowa explained how Lavender died, Lieutenant Cross found himself trembling.

He tried not to cry. With his entrenching tool, which weighed five pounds, he began digging a hole in the earth.

He felt shame. He hated himself. He had loved Martha more than his men, and as a consequence Lavender was now dead, and this was something he would have to carry like a stone in his stomach for the rest of the war.

All he could do was dig. He used his entrenching tool like an ax, slashing, feeling both love and hate, and then later, when it was full dark, he sat at the bottom of his foxhole and wept. It went on for a long while. In part, he was grieving for Ted Lavender, but mostly it was for Martha, and for himself, because she belonged to another world, which was not quite real, and because she was a junior at Mount Sebastian College in New Jersey, a poet and a virgin and uninvolved, and because he realized she did not love him and never would.

Like cement, Kiowa whispered in the dark. I swear to God—boom, down. Not a word.

I've heard this, said Norman Bowker.   45

A pisser, you know? Still zipping himself up. Zapped while zipping.

All right, fine. That's enough.

Yeah, but you had to see it, the guy just—

I *heard*, man. Cement. So why not shut the fuck *up*?

Kiowa shook his head sadly and glanced over at the hole where Lieu-   50
tenant Jimmy Cross sat watching the night. The air was thick and wet. A warm dense fog had settled over the paddies and there was the stillness that precedes rain.

After a time Kiowa sighed.

One thing for sure, he said. The lieutenant's in some deep hurt. I mean that crying jag—the way he was carrying on—it wasn't fake or anything, it was real heavy-duty hurt. The man cares.

Sure, Norman Bowker said.

Say what you want, the man does care.

We all got problems.   55

Not Lavender.

No, I guess not, Bowker said. Do me a favor, though.

Shut up?

That's a smart Indian. Shut up.

Shrugging, Kiowa pulled off his boots. He wanted to say more, just to   60
lighten up his sleep, but instead he opened his New Testament and arranged it beneath his head as a pillow. The fog made things seem hollow and unattached. He tried not to think about Ted Lavender, but then he was thinking how fast it was, no drama, down and dead, and how it was hard to feel anything except surprise. It seemed unchristian. He wished he could find some great sadness, or even anger, but the emotion wasn't there and he couldn't make it happen. Mostly he felt pleased to be alive. He liked the smell of the New Testament under his cheek, the leather and ink and paper and glue, whatever the chemicals were. He liked hearing the sounds of night. Even his fatigue, it felt fine, the stiff muscles and the prickly awareness of his

own body, a floating feeling. He enjoyed not being dead. Lying there, Kiowa admired Lieutenant Jimmy Cross's capacity for grief. He wanted to share the man's pain, he wanted to care as Jimmy Cross cared. And yet when he closed his eyes, all he could think was Boom-down, and all he could feel was the pleasure of having his boots off and the fog curling in around him and the damp soil and the Bible smells and the plush comfort of night.

After a moment Norman Bowker sat up in the dark.

What the hell, he said. You want to talk, *talk*. Tell it to me.

Forget it.

No, man, go on. One thing I hate, it's a silent Indian.

For the most part they carried themselves with poise, a kind of dignity.   65
Now and then, however, there were times of panic, when they squealed or wanted to squeal but couldn't, when they twitched and made moaning sounds and covered their heads and said Dear Jesus and flopped around on the earth and fired their weapons blindly and cringed and sobbed and begged for the noise to stop and went wild and made stupid promises to themselves and to God and to their mothers and fathers, hoping not to die. In different ways, it happened to all of them. Afterward, when the firing ended, they would blink and peek up. They would touch their bodies, feeling shame, then quickly hiding it. They would force themselves to stand. As if in slow motion, frame by frame, the world would take on the old logic—absolute silence, then the wind, then sunlight, then voices. It was the burden of being alive. Awkwardly, the men would reassemble themselves, first in private, then in groups, becoming soldiers again. They would repair the leaks in their eyes. They would check for casualties, call in dustoffs, light cigarettes, try to smile, clear their throats and spit and begin cleaning their weapons. After a time someone would shake his head and say, No lie, I almost shit my pants, and someone else would laugh, which meant it was bad, yes, but the guy had obviously not shit his pants, it wasn't that bad, and in any case nobody would ever do such a thing and then go ahead and talk about it. They would squint into the dense, oppressive sunlight. For a few moments, perhaps, they would fall silent, lighting a joint and tracking its passage from man to man, inhaling, holding in the humiliation. Scary stuff, one of them might say. But then someone else would grin or flick his eyebrows and say, Roger-dodger, almost cut me a new asshole, *almost*.

There were numerous such poses. Some carried themselves with a sort of wistful resignation, others with pride or stiff soldierly discipline or good humor or macho zeal. They were afraid of dying but they were even more afraid to show it.

They found jokes to tell.

They used a hard vocabulary to contain the terrible softness. *Greased*, they'd say. *Offed, lit up, zapped while zipping*. It wasn't cruelty, just stage presence. They were actors. When someone died, it wasn't quite dying, because in a curious way it seemed scripted, and because they had their lines mostly memorized, irony mixed with tragedy, and because they called it by other names, as if to encyst and destroy the reality of death itself. They kicked corpses. They cut off thumbs. They talked grunt lingo. They told stories about Ted Lavender's supply of tranquilizers, how the poor guy didn't feel a thing, how incredibly tranquil he was.

There's a moral here, said Mitchell Sanders.

They were waiting for Lavender's chopper, smoking the dead man's 70 dope.

The moral's pretty obvious, Sanders said, and winked. Stay away from drugs. No joke, they'll ruin your day every time.

Cute, said Henry Dobbins.

Mind blower, get it? Talk about wiggy. Nothing left, just blood and brains.

They made themselves laugh.

There it is, they'd say, over and over—there it is, my friend, there it 75 is—as if the repetition itself were an act of poise, a balance between crazy and almost crazy, knowing without going, there it is, which meant be cool, let it ride, because Oh yeah, man, you can't change what can't be changed, there it is, there it absolutely and positively and fucking well *is*.

They were tough.

They carried all the emotional baggage of men who might die. Grief, terror, love, longing—these were intangibles, but the intangibles had their own mass and specific gravity, they had tangible weight. They carried shameful memories. They carried the common secret of cowardice barely restrained, the instinct to run or freeze or hide, and in many respects this was the heaviest burden of all, for it could never be put down, it required perfect balance and perfect posture. They carried their reputations. They carried the soldier's greatest fear, which was the fear of blushing. Men killed, and died, because they were embarrassed not to. It was what had brought them to the war in the first place, nothing positive, no dreams of glory or honor, just to avoid the blush of dishonor. They died so as not to die of embarrassment. They crawled into tunnels and walked point and advanced under fire. Each morning, despite the unknowns, they made their legs move. They endured. They kept humping. They did not submit to the obvious alternative, which was simply to close the eyes and fall. So easy, really. Go limp and tumble to the ground and let the muscles unwind and not speak and not budge until your buddies picked you up and lifted you into the chopper that would roar and dip its nose and carry you off to the world. A mere matter of falling, yet no one ever fell. It was not courage, exactly; the object was not valor. Rather, they were too frightened to be cowards.

By and large they carried these things inside, maintaining the masks of composure. They sneered at sick call. They spoke bitterly about guys who had found release by shooting off their own toes or fingers. Pussies, they'd say. Candyasses. It was fierce, mocking talk, with only a trace of envy or awe, but even so the image played itself out behind their eyes.

They imagined the muzzle against flesh. So easy: squeeze the trigger and blow away a toe. They imagined it. They imagined the quick, sweet pain, then the evacuation to Japan, then a hospital with warm beds and cute geisha nurses.

They dreamed of freedom birds. 80

At night, on guard, staring into the dark, they were carried away by jumbo jets. They felt the rush of takeoff. *Gone!* they yelled. And then velocity—wings and engines—a smiling stewardess—but it was more than a plane, it was a real bird, a big sleek silver bird with feathers and talons and high screeching. They were flying. The weights fell off; there was nothing to bear. They laughed and held on tight, feeling the cold slap of wind and altitude, soaring, thinking *It's over, I'm gone!*—they were naked, they were light and free—it was all lightness, bright and fast and buoyant, light as light, a helium buzz in the brain, a giddy bubbling in the lungs as they were taken up over the clouds and the war, beyond duty, beyond gravity and mortification and global entanglements—*Sin loi!*[10] they yelled. *I'm sorry, motherfuckers, but I'm out of it, I'm goofed, I'm on a space cruise, I'm gone!*—and it was a restful, unencumbered sensation, just riding the light waves, sailing that big silver freedom bird over the mountains and oceans, over America, over the farms and great sleeping cities and cemeteries and highways and the golden arches of McDonald's, it was flight, a kind of fleeing, a kind of falling, falling higher and higher, spinning off the edge of the earth and beyond the sun and through the vast, silent vacuum where there were no burdens and where everything weighed exactly nothing—*Gone!* they screamed. *I'm sorry but I'm gone!*—and so at night, not quite dreaming, they gave themselves over to lightness, they were carried, they were purely borne.

On the morning after Ted Lavender died, First Lieutenant Jimmy Cross crouched at the bottom of his foxhole and burned Martha's letters. Then he burned the two photographs. There was a steady rain falling, which made it difficult, but he used heat tabs and Sterno to build a small fire, screening it with his body, holding the photographs over the tight blue flame with the tips of his fingers.

He realized it was only a gesture. Stupid, he thought. Sentimental, too, but mostly just stupid.

Lavender was dead. You couldn't burn the blame.

Besides, the letters were in his head. And even now, without photographs, Lieutenant Cross could see Martha playing volleyball in her white gym shorts and yellow T-shirt. He could see her moving in the rain. 85

When the fire died out, Lieutenant Cross pulled his poncho over his shoulders and ate breakfast from a can.

There was no great mystery, he decided.

10 *Sin loi!:* Sorry about that! (Vietnamese).—EDS.

In those burned letters Martha had never mentioned the war, except to say, Jimmy, take care of yourself. She wasn't involved. She signed the letters Love, but it wasn't love, and all the fine lines and technicalities did not matter. Virginity was no longer an issue. He hated her. Yes, he did. He hated her. Love, too, but it was a hard, hating kind of love.

The morning came up wet and blurry. Everything seemed part of everything else, the fog and Martha and the deepening rain.

He was a soldier, after all.   90

Half smiling, Lieutenant Jimmy Cross took out his maps. He shook his head hard, as if to clear it, then bent forward and began planning the day's march. In ten minutes, or maybe twenty, he would rouse the men and they would pack up and head west, where the maps showed the country to be green and inviting. They would do what they had always done. The rain might add some weight, but otherwise it would be one more day layered upon all the other days.

He was realistic about it. There was that new hardness in his stomach. He loved her but he hated her.

No more fantasies, he told himself.

Henceforth, when he thought about Martha, it would be only to think that she belonged elsewhere. He would shut down the daydreams. This was not Mount Sebastian, it was another world, where there were no pretty poems or midterm exams, a place where men died because of carelessness and gross stupidity. Kiowa was right. Boom-down, and you were dead, never partly dead.

Briefly, in the rain, Lieutenant Cross saw Martha's gray eyes gazing   95
back at him.

He understood.

It was very sad, he thought. The things men carried inside. The things men did or felt they had to do.

He almost nodded at her, but didn't.

Instead he went back to his maps. He was now determined to perform his duties firmly and without negligence. It wouldn't help Lavender, he knew that, but from this point on he would comport himself as an officer. He would dispose of his good-luck pebble. Swallow it, maybe, or use Lee Strunk's slingshot, or just drop it along the trail. On the march he would impose strict field discipline. He would be careful to send out flank security, to prevent straggling or bunching up, to keep his troops moving at the proper pace and at the proper interval. He would insist on clean weapons. He would confiscate the remainder of Lavender's dope. Later in the day, perhaps, he would call the men together and speak to them plainly. He would accept the blame for what had happened to Ted Lavender. He would be a man about it. He would look them in the eyes, keeping his chin level, and he would issue the new SOPs in a calm, impersonal tone of voice, a lieutenant's voice, leaving no room for argument or discussion. Commencing immediately, he'd tell them, they would no longer abandon equipment along the route of march.

They would police up their acts. They would get their shit together, and keep it together, and maintain it neatly and in good working order.

He would not tolerate laxity. He would show strength, distancing 100 himself.

Among the men there would be grumbling, of course, and maybe worse, because their days would seem longer and their loads heavier, but Lieutenant Cross reminded himself that his obligation was not to be loved but to lead. He would dispense with love; it was not now a factor. And if anyone quarreled or complained, he would simply tighten his lips and arrange his shoulders in the correct command posture. He might give a curt little nod. Or he might not. He might just shrug and say, Carry on, then they would saddle up and form into a column and move out toward the villages west of Than Khe. ●

The Reader's Presence

1. The title — "The Things They Carried" — obviously refers to the physical objects O'Brien catalogs in his story. To what else does the title refer? At what point in the story does what the soldiers carry move beyond the tangible? What does this movement represent? How does the thematic element of the things they carried extend beyond the men to encompass what the men themselves represent?

2. First Lieutenant Jimmy Cross is obsessed with Martha, perusing her letters every afternoon, carrying in his mouth the pebble she sent him from a New Jersey beach, and romanticizing a relationship he knows to be platonic (affectionate but not sexual). Yet, at the conclusion of the story he burns her letters. Why? What does he hope to gain from this gesture? And what changes in Cross's character does this gesture suggest?

3. **CONNECTIONS:**   Writers use certain language and sentence structure to establish a particular tone of voice. Describe the tone O'Brien uses when we first learn of Ted Lavender's death. In what specific ways is this tone related to the mindsets of the soldiers? Compare O'Brien's tone of voice with Adam Mayblum's in his account of the 9/11 attack on the World Trade Center ("The Price We Pay," page 164). What does this suggest about how people respond to traumatic experiences?

Flannery O'Connor

A GOOD MAN IS HARD TO FIND

FLANNERY O'CONNOR (1925–1964) was born in Savannah, Georgia, the only child of devout Catholic parents. At the age of thirteen, O'Connor moved with her parents to her mother's ancestral home in Milledgeville, Georgia, after her father became terminally ill with lupus. In 1945 she received a BA degree from Georgia State College for Women, where she contributed regularly to the school's literary magazine. While earning an MFA from the Writers' Workshop at the University of Iowa, O'Connor published her first short story, "The Geranium," in 1946. After graduation, O'Connor was a resident at Yaddo, an artists' retreat in New York, and lived in New York City and in Connecticut until 1951, when she was diagnosed with lupus and returned to Georgia for treatment. She and her mother moved a short distance from Milledgeville to their family farm, Andalusia, where O'Connor lived

> Flannery O'Connor spent the last part of her life on her family's farm in Georgia. She spent her time raising peafowl, painting, and writing.

until her death at the age of thirty-nine, raising peafowl, painting, and writing daily. During her short yet distinguished life, O'Connor published two novels, *Wise Blood* (1952) and *The Violent Bear It Away* (1960), and a collection of short stories, *A Good Man Is Hard to Find* (1955), the title story of which appears here. A book of essays, *Mystery and Manners* (1969); two other short story collections, *Everything That Rises Must Converge* (1965) and *The Complete Stories of Flannery O'Connor* (1971), winner of a National Book Award; and a collection of letters, *The Habit of Being* (1979), were published posthumously.

THE GRANDMOTHER didn't want to go to Florida. She wanted to visit some of her connections in east Tennessee and she was seizing at every chance to change Bailey's mind. Bailey was the son she lived with, her only boy. He was sitting on the edge of his chair at the table, bent over the orange sports section of the *Journal*. "Now look here, Bailey," she said, "see here, read this," and she stood with one hand on her thin hip and the other rattling the newspaper at his bald head. "Here this fellow that calls himself The Misfit is aloose from the Federal Pen and headed toward Florida and you read here what it says he did to these people. Just you read it. I wouldn't take my children in any direction with a criminal like that aloose in it. I couldn't answer to my conscience if I did."

Bailey didn't look up from his reading so she wheeled around then and faced the children's mother, a young woman in slacks, whose face was as broad and innocent as a cabbage and was tied around with a green head-kerchief that had two points on the top like a rabbit's ears. She was sitting on the sofa, feeding the baby his apricots out of a jar. "The children have been to Florida before," the old lady said. "You all ought to take them somewhere else for a change so they would see different parts of the world and be broad. They never have been to east Tennessee."

The children's mother didn't seem to hear her but the eight-year-old boy, John Wesley, a stocky child with glasses, said, "If you don't want to go to Florida, why dontcha stay at home?" He and the little girl, June Star, were reading the funny papers on the floor.

"She wouldn't stay at home to be queen for a day," June Star said without raising her yellow head.

"Yes and what would you do if this fellow, The Misfit, caught you?" the 5 grandmother asked.

"I'd smack his face," John Wesley said.

"She wouldn't stay at home for a million bucks," June Star said. "Afraid she'd miss something. She has to go everywhere we go."

"All right, Miss," the grandmother said. "Just remember that the next time you want me to curl your hair."

June Star said her hair was naturally curly.

The next morning the grandmother was the first one in the car, ready to 10 go. She had her big black valise that looked like the head of a hippopotamus in one corner, and underneath it she was hiding a basket with Pitty Sing, the cat, in it. She didn't intend for the cat to be left alone in the house for three days because he would miss her too much and she was afraid he might brush against one of the gas burners and accidentally asphyxiate himself. Her son, Bailey, didn't like to arrive at a motel with a cat.

She sat in the middle of the back seat with John Wesley and June Star on either side of her. Bailey and the children's mother and the baby sat in front and they left Atlanta at eight forty-five with the mileage on the car at 55890. The grandmother wrote this down because she thought it would be interesting to say how many miles they had been when they got back. It took them twenty minutes to reach the outskirts of the city.

The old lady settled herself comfortably, removing her white cotton gloves and putting them up with her purse on the shelf in front of the back window. The children's mother still had on slacks and still had her head tied up in a green kerchief, but the grandmother had on a navy blue straw sailor hat with a bunch of white violets on the brim and a navy blue dress with a small white dot in the print. Her collars and cuffs were white organdy trimmed with lace and at her neckline she had pinned a purple spray of cloth violets containing a sachet. In case of an accident, anyone seeing her dead on the highway would know at once that she was a lady.

She said she thought it was going to be a good day for driving, neither too hot nor too cold, and she cautioned Bailey that the speed limit was

fifty-five miles an hour and that the patrolmen hid themselves behind billboards and small clumps of trees and sped out after you before you had a
chance to slow down. She pointed out interesting details of the scenery: Stone
Mountain; the blue granite that in some places came up to both sides of the
highway; the brilliant red clay banks slightly streaked with purple; and the
various crops that made rows of green lace-work on the ground. The trees were
full of silver-white sunlight and the meanest of them sparkled. The children
were reading comic magazines and their mother had gone back to sleep.

"Let's go through Georgia fast so we won't have to look at it much,"
John Wesley said.

"If I were a little boy," said the grandmother, "I wouldn't talk about my   15
native state that way. Tennessee has the mountains and Georgia has the
hills."

"Tennessee is just a hillbilly dumping ground," John Wesley said, "and
Georgia is a lousy state too."

"You said it," June Star said.

"In my time," said the grandmother, folding her thin veined fingers,
"children were more respectful of their native states and their parents and
everything else. People did right then. Oh look at the cute little picka-
ninny!" she said and pointed to a Negro child standing in the door of a
shack. "Wouldn't that make a picture, now?" she asked and they all turned
and looked at the little Negro out of the back window. He waved.

"He didn't have any britches on," June Star said.

"He probably didn't have any," the grandmother explained. "Little nig-   20
gers in the country don't have things like we do. If I could paint, I'd paint
that picture," she said.

The children exchanged comic books.

The grandmother offered to hold the baby and the children's mother
passed him over the front seat to her. She set him on her knee and bounced
him and told him about the things they were passing. She rolled her eyes
and screwed up her mouth and stuck her leathery thin face into his smooth
bland one. Occasionally he gave her a faraway smile. They passed a large
cotton field with five or six graves fenced in the middle of it, like a small
island. "Look at the graveyard!" the grandmother said, pointing it out. "That
was the old family burying ground. That belonged to the plantation."

"Where's the plantation?" John Wesley asked.

"Gone With the Wind," said the grandmother. "Ha. Ha."

When the children finished all the comic books they had brought, they   25
opened the lunch and ate it. The grandmother ate a peanut butter sandwich
and an olive and would not let the children throw the box and the paper
napkins out the window. When there was nothing else to do they played a
game by choosing a cloud and making the other two guess what shape it
suggested. John Wesley took one the shape of a cow and June Star guessed
a cow and John Wesley said, no, an automobile, and June Star said he didn't
play fair, and they began to slap each other over the grandmother.

The grandmother said she would tell them a story if they would keep quiet. When she told a story, she rolled her eyes and waved her head and was very dramatic. She said once when she was a maiden lady she had been courted by a Mr. Edgar Atkins Teagarden from Jasper, Georgia. She said he was a very good-looking man and a gentleman and that he brought her a watermelon every Saturday afternoon with his initials cut in it, E. A. T. Well, one Saturday, she said, Mr. Teagarden brought the watermelon and there was nobody at home and he left it on the front porch and returned in his buggy to Jasper, but she never got the watermelon, she said, because a nigger boy ate it when he saw the initials, E. A. T.! This story tickled John Wesley's funny bone and he giggled and giggled but June Star didn't think it was any good. She said she wouldn't marry a man that just brought her a watermelon on Saturday. The grandmother said she would have done well to marry Mr. Teagarden because he was a gentleman and had bought Coca-Cola stock when it first came out and that he had died only a few years ago, a very wealthy man.

They stopped at The Tower for barbecued sandwiches. The Tower was a part stucco and part wood filling station and dance hall set in a clearing outside of Timothy. A fat man named Red Sammy Butts ran it and there were signs stuck here and there on the building and for miles up and down the highway saying, TRY RED SAMMY'S FAMOUS BARBECUE. NONE LIKE FAMOUS RED SAMMY'S! RED SAM! THE FAT BOY WITH THE HAPPY LAUGH! A VETERAN! RED SAMMY'S YOUR MAN!

Red Sammy was lying on the bare ground outside The Tower with his head under a truck while a gray monkey about a foot high, chained to a small chinaberry tree, chattered nearby. The monkey sprang back into the tree and got on the highest limb as soon as he saw the children jump out of the car and run toward him.

Inside, The Tower was a long dark room with a counter at one end and tables at the other and dancing space in the middle. They all sat down at a board table next to the nickelodeon and Red Sam's wife, a tall burnt-brown woman with hair and eyes lighter than her skin, came and took their order. The children's mother put a dime in the machine and played "The Tennessee Waltz," and the grandmother said that tune always made her want to dance. She asked Bailey if he would like to dance but he only glared at her. He didn't have a naturally sunny disposition like she did and trips made him nervous. The grandmother's brown eyes were very bright. She swayed her head from side to side and pretended she was dancing in her chair. June Star said play something she could tap to so the children's mother put in another dime and played a fast number and June Star stepped out onto the dance floor and did her tap routine.

"Ain't she cute?" Red Sam's wife said, leaning over the counter. "Would you like to come be my little girl?"   30

"No I certainly wouldn't," June Star said. "I wouldn't live in a broken-down place like this for a million bucks!" and she ran back to the table.

"Ain't she cute?" the woman repeated, stretching her mouth politely.

"Aren't you ashamed?" hissed the grandmother.

Red Sam came in and told his wife to quit lounging on the counter and hurry up with these people's order. His khaki trousers reached just to his hip bones and his stomach hung over them like a sack of meal swaying under his shirt. He came over and sat down at a table nearby and let out a combination sigh and yodel. "You can't win," he said. "You can't win," and he wiped his sweating red face off with a gray handkerchief. "These days you don't know who to trust," he said. "Ain't that the truth?"

"People are certainly not nice like they used to be," said the   35
grandmother.

"Two fellers come in here last week," Red Sammy said, "driving a Chrysler. It was an old beat-up car, but it was a good one and these boys looked all right to me. Said they worked at the mill and you know I let them fellers charge the gas they bought? Now why did I do that?"

"Because you're a good man!" the grandmother said at once.

"Yes'm, I suppose so," Red Sam said as if he were struck with this answer.

His wife brought the orders, carrying the five plates all at once without a tray, two in each hand and one balanced on her arm. "It isn't a soul in this green world of God's that you can trust," she said. "And I don't count nobody out of that, not nobody," she repeated, looking at Red Sammy.

"Did you read about that criminal, The Misfit, that's escaped?" asked   40
the grandmother.

"I wouldn't be a bit surprised if he didn't attact this place right here," said the woman. "If he hears about it being here, I wouldn't be none surprised to see him. If he hears it's two cent in the cash register, I wouldn't be at all surprised if he . . ."

"That'll do," Red Sam said. "Go bring these people their Co'-Colas," and the woman went off to get the rest of the order.

"A good man is hard to find," Red Sammy said. "Everything is getting terrible. I remember the day you could go off and leave your screen door unlatched. Not no more."

He and the grandmother discussed better times. The old lady said that in her opinion Europe was entirely to blame for the way things were now. She said the way Europe acted you would think we were made of money and Red Sam said it was no use talking about it, she was exactly right. The children ran outside into the white sunlight and looked at the monkey in the lacy chinaberry tree. He was busy catching fleas on himself and biting each one carefully between his teeth as if it were a delicacy.

They drove off again into the hot afternoon. The grandmother took cat   45
naps and woke up every few minutes with her own snoring. Outside of Toombsboro she woke up and recalled an old plantation that she had visited in this neighborhood once when she was a young lady. She said the house had six white columns across the front and that there was an avenue of oaks

leading up to it and two little wooden trellis arbors on either side in front where you sat down with your suitor after a stroll in the garden. She recalled exactly which road to turn off to get to it. She knew that Bailey would not be willing to lose any time looking at an old house, but the more she talked about it, the more she wanted to see it once again and find out if the little twin arbors were still standing. "There was a secret panel in this house," she said craftily, not telling the truth but wishing that she were, "and the story went that all the family silver was hidden in it when Sherman[1] came through but it was never found . . ."

"Hey!" John Wesley said. "Let's go see it! We'll find it! We'll poke all the woodwork and find it! Who lives there? Where do you turn off at? Hey Pop, can't we turn off there?"

"We never have seen a house with a secret panel!" June Star shrieked. "Let's go to the house with the secret panel! Hey Pop, can't we go see the house with the secret panel!"

"It's not far from here, I know," the grandmother said. "It wouldn't take over twenty minutes."

Bailey was looking straight ahead. His jaw was as rigid as a horseshoe. "No," he said.

The children began to yell and scream that they wanted to see the house   50 with the secret panel. John Wesley kicked the back of the front seat and June Star hung over her mother's shoulder and whined desperately into her ear that they never had any fun even on their vacation, that they could never do what THEY wanted to do. The baby began to scream and John Wesley kicked the back of the seat so hard that his father could feel the blows in his kidney.

"All right!" he shouted and drew the car to a stop at the side of the road. "Will you all shut up? Will you all just shut up for one second? If you don't shut up, we won't go anywhere."

"It would be very educational for them," the grandmother murmured.

"All right," Bailey said, "but get this: this is the only time we're going to stop for anything like this. This is the one and only time."

"The dirt road that you have to turn down is about a mile back," the grandmother directed. "I marked it when we passed."

"A dirt road," Bailey groaned.   55

After they had turned around and were headed toward the dirt road, the grandmother recalled other points about the house, the beautiful glass over the front doorway and the candle-lamp in the hall. John Wesley said that the secret panel was probably in the fireplace.

"You can't go inside this house," Bailey said. "You don't know who lives there."

"While you all talk to the people in front, I'll run around behind and get in a window," John Wesley suggested.

---

1 **Sherman:** General William Tecumseh Sherman (1820–1891) was the Union general who captured Atlanta in 1864. —EDS.

"We'll all stay in the car," his mother said.

They turned onto the dirt road and the car raced roughly along in a swirl   60
of pink dust. The grandmother recalled the times when there were no paved
roads and thirty miles was a day's journey. The dirt road was hilly and there
were sudden washes in it and sharp curves on dangerous embankments. All
at once they would be on a hill, looking down over the blue tops of trees for
miles around, then the next minute, they would be in a red depression with
the dust-coated trees looking down on them.

"This place had better turn up in a minute," Bailey said, "or I'm going
to turn around."

The road looked as if no one had traveled on it in months.

"It's not much farther," the grandmother said and just as she said it, a
horrible thought came to her. The thought was so embarrassing that she
turned red in the face and her eyes dilated and her feet jumped up, upsetting her valise in the corner. The instant the valise moved, the newspaper
top she had over the basket under it rose with a snarl and Pitty Sing, the cat,
sprang onto Bailey's shoulder.

The children were thrown to the floor and their mother, clutching the
baby, was thrown out the door onto the ground; the old lady was thrown
into the front seat. The car turned over once and landed right-side-up in a
gulch off the side of the road. Bailey remained in the driver's seat with the
cat—gray-striped with a broad white face and an orange nose—clinging to
his neck like a caterpillar.

As soon as the children saw they could move their arms and legs, they   65
scrambled out of the car, shouting, "We've had an ACCIDENT!" The grandmother was curled up under the dashboard, hoping she was injured so that
Bailey's wrath would not come down on her all at once. The horrible thought
she had had before the accident was that the house she had remembered so
vividly was not in Georgia but in Tennessee.

Bailey removed the cat from his neck with both hands and flung it out
the window against the side of a pine tree. Then he got out of the car and
started looking for the children's mother. She was sitting against the side
of the red gutted ditch, holding the screaming baby, but she only had a cut
down her face and a broken shoulder. "We've had an ACCIDENT!" the children screamed in a frenzy of delight.

"But nobody's killed," June Star said with disappointment as the grandmother limped out of the car, her hat still pinned to her head but the broken
front brim standing up at a jaunty angle and the violet spray hanging off the
side. They all sat down in the ditch, except the children, to recover from the
shock. They were all shaking.

"Maybe a car will come along," said the children's mother hoarsely.

"I believe I have injured an organ," said the grandmother, pressing her
side, but no one answered her. Bailey's teeth were clattering. He had on a
yellow sport shirt with bright blue parrots designed in it and his face was as
yellow as the shirt. The grandmother decided that she would not mention
that the house was in Tennessee.

The road was about ten feet above and they could see only the tops of   70
the trees on the other side of it. Behind the ditch they were sitting in there
were more woods, tall and dark and deep. In a few minutes they saw a car
some distance away on top of a hill, coming slowly as if the occupants were
watching them. The grandmother stood up and waved both arms dramatically to attract their attention. The car continued to come on slowly, disappeared around a bend and appeared again, moving even slower, on top of
the hill they had gone over. It was a big black battered hearselike automobile. There were three men in it.

It came to a stop just over them and for some minutes, the driver looked
down with a steady expressionless gaze to where they were sitting, and
didn't speak. Then he turned his head and muttered something to the other
two and they got out. One was a fat boy in black trousers and a red sweat
shirt with a silver stallion embossed on the front of it. He moved around on
the right side of them and stood staring, his mouth partly open in a kind of
loose grin. The other had on khaki pants and a blue striped coat and a gray
hat pulled down very low, hiding most of his face. He came around slowly
on the left side. Neither spoke.

The driver got out of the car and stood by the side of it, looking down at
them. He was an older man than the other two. His hair was just beginning
to gray and he wore silver-rimmed spectacles that gave him a scholarly look.
He had a long creased face and didn't have on any shirt or undershirt. He
had on blue jeans that were too tight for him and was holding a black hat
and a gun. The two boys also had guns.

"We've had an ACCIDENT!" the children screamed.

The grandmother had the peculiar feeling that the bespectacled man was
someone she knew. His face was as familiar to her as if she had known him all
her life but she could not recall who he was. He moved away from the car and
began to come down the embankment, placing his feet carefully so that he
wouldn't slip. He had on tan and white shoes and no socks, and his ankles were
red and thin. "Good afternoon," he said. "I see you all had you a little spill."

"We turned over twice!" said the grandmother.   75

"Oncet," he corrected. "We seen it happen. Try their car and see will it
run, Hiram," he said quietly to the boy with the gray hat.

"What you got that gun for?" John Wesley asked. "Whatcha gonna do
with that gun?"

"Lady," the man said to the children's mother, "would you mind calling
them children to sit down by you? Children make me nervous. I want all you
all to sit down right together there where you're at."

"What are you telling US what to do for?" June Star asked.

Behind them the line of woods gaped like a dark open mouth. "Come   80
here," said their mother.

"Look here now," Bailey began suddenly, "we're in a predicament!
We're in . . ."

The grandmother shrieked. She scrambled to her feet and stood staring.
"You're The Misfit!" she said. "I recognized you at once!"

"Yes'm," the man said, smiling slightly as if he were pleased in spite of himself to be known, "but it would have been better for all of you, lady, if you hadn't of reckernized me."

Bailey turned his head sharply and said something to his mother that shocked even the children. The old lady began to cry and The Misfit reddened.

"Lady," he said, "don't you get upset. Sometimes a man says things he   85 don't mean. I don't reckon he meant to talk to you thataway."

"You wouldn't shoot a lady, would you?" the grandmother said and removed a clean handkerchief from her cuff and began to slap at her eyes with it.

The Misfit pointed the toe of his shoe into the ground and made a little hole and then covered it up again. "I would hate to have to," he said.

"Listen," the grandmother almost screamed, "I know you're a good man. You don't look a bit like you have common blood. I know you must come from nice people!"

"Yes ma'am," he said, "finest people in the world." When he smiled he showed a row of strong white teeth. "God never made a finer woman than my mother and my daddy's heart was pure gold," he said. The boy with the red sweat shirt had come around behind them and was standing with his gun at his hip. The Misfit squatted down on the ground. "Watch them children, Bobby Lee," he said. "You know they make me nervous." He looked at the six of them huddled together in front of him and he seemed to be embarrassed as if he couldn't think of anything to say. "Ain't a cloud in the sky," he remarked, looking up at it. "Don't see no sun but don't see no cloud neither."

"Yes, it's a beautiful day," said the grandmother. "Listen," she said,   90 "you shouldn't call yourself The Misfit because I know you're a good man at heart. I can just look at you and tell."

"Hush!" Bailey yelled. "Hush! Everybody shut up and let me handle this!" He was squatting in the position of a runner about to sprint forward but he didn't move.

"I pre-chate that, lady," The Misfit said and drew a little circle in the ground with the butt of his gun.

"It'll take a half a hour to fix this here car," Hiram called, looking over the raised hood of it.

"Well, first you and Bobby Lee get him and that little boy to step over yonder with you," The Misfit said, pointing to Bailey and John Wesley. "The boys want to ask you something," he said to Bailey. "Would you mind stepping back in them woods there with them?"

"Listen," Bailey began, "we're in a terrible predicament! Nobody real-   95 izes what this is," and his voice cracked. His eyes were as blue and intense as the parrots in his shirt and he remained perfectly still.

The grandmother reached up to adjust her hat brim as if she were going to the woods with him but it came off in her hand. She stood staring at it and after a second she let it fall on the ground. Hiram pulled Bailey up by the arm as if he were assisting an old man. John Wesley caught hold of his father's hand and Bobby Lee followed. They went off toward the woods and just as they reached the dark edge, Bailey turned and supporting himself against a gray naked pine trunk, he shouted, "I'll be back in a minute, Mamma, wait on me!"

"Come back this instant!" his mother shrilled but they all disappeared into the woods.

"Bailey Boy!" the grandmother called in a tragic voice but she found she was looking at The Misfit squatting on the ground in front of her. "I just know you're a good man," she said desperately. "You're not a bit common!"

"Nome, I ain't a good man," The Misfit said after a second as if he had considered her statement carefully, "but I ain't the worst in the world neither. My daddy said I was a different breed of dog from my brothers and sisters. 'You know,' Daddy said, 'it's some that can live their whole life out without asking about it and it's others has to know why it is, and this boy is one of the latters. He's going to be into everything!'" He put on his black hat and looked up suddenly and then away deep into the woods as if he were embarrassed again. "I'm sorry I don't have on a shirt before you ladies," he said, hunching his shoulders slightly. "We buried our clothes that we had on when we escaped and we're just making do until we can get better. We borrowed these from some folks we met," he explained.

"That's perfectly all right," the grandmother said. "Maybe Bailey has an 100
extra shirt in his suitcase."

"I'll look and see terrectly," The Misfit said.

"Where are they taking him?" the children's mother screamed.

"Daddy was a card himself," The Misfit said. "You couldn't put anything over on him. He never got in trouble with the Authorities though. Just had the knack of handling them."

"You could be honest too if you'd only try," said the grandmother. "Think how wonderful it would be to settle down and live a comfortable life and not have to think about somebody chasing you all the time."

The Misfit kept scratching in the ground with the butt of his gun as 105
if he were thinking about it. "Yes'm, somebody is always after you," he murmured.

The grandmother noticed how thin his shoulder blades were just behind his hat because she was standing up looking down on him. "Do you ever pray?" she asked.

He shook his head. All she saw was the black hat wiggle between his shoulder blades. "Nome," he said.

There was a pistol shot from the woods, followed closely by another. Then silence. The old lady's head jerked around. She could hear the wind move through the tree tops like a long satisfied insuck of breath. "Bailey Boy!" she called.

"I was a gospel singer for a while," The Misfit said. "I been most everything. Been in the arm service, both land and sea, at home and abroad, been twict married, been an undertaker, been with the railroads, plowed Mother

Earth, been in a tornado, seen a man burnt alive oncet," and looked up at the children's mother and the little girl who were sitting close together, their faces white and their eyes glassy; "I even seen a woman flogged," he said.

"Pray, pray," the grandmother began, "pray, pray . . ."   110

"I never was a bad boy that I remember of," The Misfit said in an almost dreamy voice, "but somewheres along the line I done something wrong and got sent to the penitentiary. I was buried alive," and he looked up and held her attention to him by a steady stare.

"That's when you should have started to pray," she said. "What did you do to get sent to the penitentiary that first time?"

"Turn to the right, it was a wall," The Misfit said, looking up again at the cloudless sky. "Turn to the left, it was a wall. Look up it was a ceiling, look down it was a floor. I forget what I done, lady. I set there and set there, trying to remember what it was I done and I ain't recalled it to this day. Oncet in a while, I would think it was coming to me, but it never come."

"Maybe they put you in by mistake," the old lady said vaguely.

"Nome," he said. "It wasn't no mistake. They had the papers on me."   115

"You must have stolen something," she said.

The Misfit sneered slightly. "Nobody had nothing I wanted," he said. "It was a head-doctor at the penitentiary said what I had done was kill my daddy but I known that for a lie. My daddy died in nineteen ought nineteen of the epidemic flu and I never had a thing to do with it. He was buried in the Mount Hopewell Baptist churchyard and you can go there and see for yourself."

"If you would pray," the old lady said, "Jesus would help you."

"That's right," The Misfit said.

"Well then, why don't you pray?" she asked, trembling with delight 120 suddenly.

"I don't want no hep," he said. "I'm doing all right by myself."

Bobby Lee and Hiram came ambling back from the woods. Bobby Lee was dragging a yellow shirt with bright blue parrots in it.

"Throw me that shirt, Bobby Lee," The Misfit said. The shirt came flying at him and landed on his shoulder and he put it on. The grandmother couldn't name what the shirt reminded her of. "No, lady," The Misfit said while he was buttoning it up, "I found out the crime don't matter. You can do one thing or you can do another, kill a man or take a tire off his car, because sooner or later you're going to forget what it was you done and just be punished for it."

The children's mother had begun to make heaving noises as if she couldn't get her breath. "Lady," he asked, "would you and that little girl like to step off yonder with Bobby Lee and Hiram and join your husband?"

"Yes, thank you," the mother said faintly. Her left arm dangled help- 125 lessly and she was holding the baby, who had gone to sleep, in the other. "Hep that lady up, Hiram," The Misfit said as she struggled to climb out of the ditch, "and Bobby Lee, you hold onto that little girl's hand."

"I don't want to hold hands with him," June Star said. "He reminds me of a pig."

The fat boy blushed and laughed and caught her by the arm and pulled her off into the woods after Hiram and her mother.

Alone with The Misfit, the grandmother found that she had lost her voice. There was not a cloud in the sky nor any sun. There was nothing around her but woods. She wanted to tell him that he must pray. She opened and closed her mouth several times before anything came out. Finally she found herself saying, "Jesus, Jesus," meaning, Jesus will help you, but the way she was saying it, it sounded as if she might be cursing.

"Yes'm," the Misfit said as if he agreed. "Jesus thown everything off balance. It was the same case with Him as with me except He hadn't committed any crime and they could prove I had committed one because they had the papers on me. Of course," he said, "they never shown me my papers. That's why I sign myself now. I said long ago, you get you a signature and sign everything you do and keep a copy of it. Then you'll know what you done and you can hold up the crime to the punishment and see do they match and in the end you'll have something to prove you ain't been treated right. I call myself The Misfit," he said, "because I can't make what all I done wrong fit what all I gone through in punishment."

There was a piercing scream from the woods, followed closely by a pis- 130 tol report. "Does it seem right to you, lady, that one is punished a heap and another ain't punished at all?"

"Jesus!" the old lady cried. "You've got good blood! I know you wouldn't shoot a lady! I know you come from nice people! Pray! Jesus, you ought not to shoot a lady. I'll give you all the money I've got!"

"Lady," The Misfit said, looking beyond her far into the woods, "there never was a body that give the undertaker a tip."

There were two more pistol reports and the grandmother raised her head like a parched old turkey hen crying for water and called, "Bailey Boy, Bailey Boy!" as if her heart would break.

"Jesus was the only One that ever raised the dead." The Misfit continued, "and He shouldn't have done it. He thown everything off balance. If He did what He said, then it's nothing for you to do but thow away everything and follow Him, and if He didn't, then it's nothing for you to do but enjoy the few minutes you got left the best way you can—by killing somebody or burning down his house or doing some other meanness to him. No pleasure but meanness," he said and his voice had become almost a snarl.

"Maybe He didn't raise the dead," the old lady mumbled, not knowing 135 what she was saying and feeling so dizzy that she sank down in the ditch with her legs twisted under her.

"I wasn't there so I can't say He didn't," The Misfit said. "I wisht I had of been there," he said, hitting the ground with his fist. "It ain't right I wasn't there because if I had of been there I would of known. Listen lady," he said in a high voice, "if I had of been there I would of known and I wouldn't be like I am now." His voice seemed about to crack and the grandmother's head cleared for an instant. She saw the man's face twisted close to her own as if he was going to cry and she murmured, "Why you're one of my babies. You're one of my own children!" She reached out and touched him on the shoulder. The Misfit sprang back as if a snake had bitten him and shot her three times through the chest. Then he put his gun down on the ground and took off his glasses and began to clean them.

Hiram and Bobby Lee returned from the woods and stood over the ditch, looking down at the grandmother who half sat and half lay in a puddle of blood with her legs crossed under her like a child's and her face smiling up at the cloudless sky.

Without his glasses, The Misfit's eyes were red-rimmed and pale and defenseless-looking. "Take her off and thow her where you thown the others," he said, picking up the cat that was rubbing itself against his leg.

"She was a talker, wasn't she?" Bobby Lee said, sliding down the ditch with a yodel.

"She would of been a good woman," The Misfit said, "if it had been 140 somebody there to shoot her every minute of her life."

"Some fun!" Bobby Lee said.

"Shut up, Bobby Lee," The Misfit said. "It's no real pleasure in life." ●

The Reader's Presence

1. The grandmother is described only indirectly, through her words, actions, and interactions with others. Reread paragraphs 1–9. How does the grandmother appear to see herself? How do you see her? In what ways does the writer's "voice" influence your impression of the character?

2. What might The Misfit figure symbolize in relation to the grandmother and her family? Does his nickname have any significance? What sort of tone does O'Connor establish in the Misfit encounter? Is it eerie, comedic, or somewhere in between? Imagine the story as presented in a different tone; how would the story differ? What does O'Connor's position on the characters and events appear to be? What specific evidence (words and phrases) in her approach leads you to your conclusion? (See also O'Connor's commentary on the story.)

3. **CONNECTIONS:** In the "Writer at Work" that follows, O'Connor discusses the crucial action or gesture that makes a story work. "[I]t is probably some action, some gesture of a character that is unlike any other in the story, one which indicates where the real heart of the story lies. . . . It would be a gesture which somehow made contact with mystery" (paragraph 12). O'Connor locates this key moment in paragraph 136 of "A Good Man Is Hard to Find," when "the grandmother's head cleared for an instant." Locate the crucial gesture or action in Raymond Carver's story "What We Talk About When We Talk About Love" (page 884) and in Sherman Alexie's story "This Is What It Means to Say Phoenix, Arizona" (page 873). Is O'Connor's description of such a gesture and its key role in "making a story hold up" applicable to stories by writers other than herself? Is "mystery" as important to Carver and to Alexie as it is to O'Connor?

The Writer at Work

FLANNERY O'CONNOR on Her Own Work

Flannery O'Connor's "A Good Man Is Hard to Find" ranks as one of American fiction's most durable short stories. It has been reprinted and analyzed in critical periodicals hundreds of times since it first appeared in 1953. Ten years after its first publication and shortly before her untimely death, O'Connor was invited to read the story at Hollins College (now Hollins University) in Virginia, where she made the following remarks. Her comments on the story were then included in a collection of nonfiction published by her editor in 1969 under the very appropriate title "Mystery and Manners." As you consider the story, you may want to focus on these terms: *mystery* and *manners*. How does each word describe an important aspect of the story? How are they interrelated? You should also consider the story from the perspective O'Connor herself provides in the following selection. Do you think her comments on her own story are critically persuasive? Did you come away from the story with a different sense of its significance? Do you think that what an author says about his or her own work must always be the final word?

❝ Last fall I received a letter from a student who said she would be "graciously appreciative" if I would tell her "just what enlightenment" I expected her to get from each of my stories. I suspect she had a paper to write. I wrote her back to forget about the enlightenment and just try to enjoy them. I knew that was the most unsatisfactory answer I could have given because, of course, she didn't want to enjoy them, she just wanted to figure them out.

In most English classes the short story has become a kind of literary specimen to be dissected. Every time a story of mine appears in a Freshman anthology, I have a vision of it, with its little organs laid open, like a frog in a bottle.

I realize that a certain amount of this what-is-the-significance has to go on, but I think something has gone wrong in the process when, for so many students, the story becomes simply a problem to be solved, something which you evaporate to get Instant Enlightenment.

A story really isn't any good unless it successfully resists paraphrase, unless it hangs on and expands in the mind. Properly, you analyze to enjoy, but it's equally true that to analyze with any discrimination, you have to have enjoyed already, and I think that the best reason to hear a story read is that it should stimulate that primary enjoyment.

I don't have any pretensions to being an Aeschylus or Sophocles and providing you in this story with a cathartic experience out of your mythic background, though this story I'm going to read certainly calls up a good deal of the South's mythic background, and it should elicit from you a degree of pity and terror, even though its way of being serious is a comic one. I do think, though, that like the Greeks you should know what is going to happen in this story so that any element of suspense in it will be transferred from its surface to its interior.

I would be most happy if you had already read it, happier still if you knew it well, but since experience has taught me to keep my expectations along these lines modest, I'll tell you that this is the story of a family of six which, on its way driving to Florida, gets wiped out by an escaped convict who calls himself the Misfit. The family is made up of the Grandmother and her son, Bailey, and his children, John Wesley and June Star and the baby, and there is also the cat and the children's mother. The cat is named Pitty Sing, and the Grandmother is taking him with them, hidden in a basket.

Now I think it behooves me to try to establish with you the basis on which reason operates in this story. Much of my fiction takes its character from a reasonable use of the unreasonable, though the reasonableness of my use of it may not always be apparent. The assumptions that underlie this use of it, however, are those of the central Christian mysteries. These are assumptions to which a large part of the modern audience takes exception. About this I can only say that there are perhaps other ways than my own in which this story could be read, but none other by which it could have been written. Belief, in my own case anyway, is the engine that makes perception operate.

The heroine of this story, the Grandmother, is in the most significant position life offers the Christian. She is facing death. And to all appearances she, like the rest of us, is not too well prepared for it. She would like to see the event postponed. Indefinitely.

I've talked to a number of teachers who use this story in class and who tell their students that the Grandmother is evil, that in fact, she's a witch, even down to the cat. One of these teachers told

me that his students, and particularly his Southern students, resisted this interpretation with a certain bemused vigor, and he didn't understand why. I had to tell him that they resisted it because they all had grandmothers or great-aunts just like her at home, and they knew, from personal experience, that the old lady lacked comprehension, but that she had a good heart. The Southerner is usually tolerant of those weaknesses that proceed from innocence, and he knows that a taste for self-preservation can be readily combined with the missionary spirit.

This same teacher was telling his students that morally the Misfit was several cuts above the Grandmother. He had a really sentimental attachment to the Misfit. But then a prophet gone wrong is almost always more interesting than your grandmother, and you have to let people take their pleasures where they find them.

It is true that the old lady is a hypocritical old soul; her wits are no match for the Misfit's, nor is her capacity for grace equal to his; yet I think the unprejudiced reader will feel that the Grandmother has a special kind of triumph in this story which instinctively we do not allow to someone altogether bad.

I often ask myself what makes a story work, and what makes it hold up as a story, and I have decided that it is probably some action, some gesture of a character that is unlike any other in the story, one which indicates where the real heart of the story lies. This would have to be an action or a gesture which was both totally right and totally unexpected; it would have to be one that was both in character and beyond character; it would have to suggest both the world and eternity. The action or gesture I'm talking about would have to be on the anagogical level, that is, the level which has to do with the Divine life and our participation in it. It would be a gesture that transcended any neat allegory that might have been intended or any pat moral categories a reader could make. It would be a gesture which somehow made contact with mystery.

There is a point in this story where such a gesture occurs. The Grandmother is at last alone, facing the Misfit. Her head clears for an instant and she realizes, even in her limited way, that she is responsible for the man before her and joined to him by ties of kinship which have their roots deep in the mystery she has been merely prattling about so far. And at this point, she does the right thing, she makes the right gesture.

I find that students are often puzzled by what she says and does here, but I think myself that if I took out this gesture and what she says with it, I would have no story. What was left would not be worth your attention. Our age not only does not have a very sharp eye for the almost imperceptible intrusions of grace, it no longer has much feeling for the nature of the violences which precede and follow them. The devil's greatest wile, Baudelaire has said, is to convince us that he does not exist.

I suppose the reasons for the use of so much violence in modern fiction will differ with each writer who uses it, but in my own stories I have found that violence is strangely capable of returning my characters to reality and preparing them to accept their moment of grace. Their heads are so hard that almost nothing else will do the work. This idea, that reality is something to which we must be returned at considerable cost, is one which is seldom understood by the casual reader, but it is one which is implicit in the Christian view of the world.

I don't want to equate the Misfit with the devil. I prefer to think that, however unlikely this may seem, the old lady's gesture, like the mustard-seed, will grow to be a great crow-filled tree in the Misfit's heart, and will be enough of a pain to him there to turn him into the prophet he was meant to become. But that's another story.

This story has been called grotesque, but I prefer to call it literal. A good story is literal in the same sense that a child's drawing is literal. When a child draws, he doesn't intend to distort but to set down exactly what he sees, and as his gaze is direct, he sees the lines that create motion. Now the lines of motion that interest the writer are usually invisible. They are lines of spiritual motion. And in this story you should be on the lookout for such things as the action of grace in the Grandmother's soul, and not for the dead bodies.

We hear many complaints about the prevalence of violence in modern fiction, and it is always assumed that this violence is a bad thing and meant to be an end in itself. With the serious writer, violence is never an end in itself. It is the extreme situation that best reveals what we are essentially, and I believe these are times when writers are more interested in what we are essentially than in the tenor of our daily lives. Violence is a force which can be used for good or evil, and among other things taken by it is the kingdom of heaven. But regardless of what can be taken by it, the man in the violent situation reveals those qualities least dispensable in his personality, those qualities which are all he will have to take into eternity with him; and since the characters in this story are all on the verge of eternity, it is appropriate to think of what they take with them. In any case, I hope that if you consider these points in connection with the story, you will come to see it as something more than an account of a family murdered on the way to Florida. **🙶**

The Critic at Work

WILLIAM CAVERLEE on "The Best Southern Short Story Ever?"

For decades, "A Good Man Is Hard to Find" has been considered one of the greatest American short stories and it has been included in nearly every short fiction anthology since it first appeared in *Partisan Review* in 1953. Given its enigmatic quality and its eerie combination of humor and horror, the story has been the subject of much serious criticism over the years. The following essay by William Caverlee, a contributing writer to the Southern magazine *Oxford American*, is one of the latest attempts to come to terms with the story's mystery. You might compare Caverlee's understanding of the story to O'Connor's in the preceding selection. How do you think O'Connor might respond to Caverlee's interpretation and assessment?

❝Without ever leaving her hideout in Milledgeville, Georgia, Flannery O'Connor knew all there was to know about the two-lane, dirt and blacktop Southern roads of the 1950s—with their junkyards and tourist courts, gravel pits and pine trees that pressed at the edges of the road. She knew the slogans of the Burma Shave signs, knew the names of barbecue joints and the chicken baskets on their menus. She also knew a backwoods American cadence and vocabulary you'd think was limited to cops, truckers, runaway teens, and the patrons of the Teardrop Inn, where at midnight somebody could always be counted on to go out to a pickup truck and come back with a shotgun. She was a virtuoso mimic, and she assimilated whole populations of American sounds and voices, and then offered them back to us from time to time in her small fictional detonations, one of which she named, in 1953, "A Good Man Is Hard to Find."

The plot is sewn together through a devious coincidence: While planning a car trip to Florida, a Georgia family (grandmother, son, wife, and three children)

learns that an escaped criminal named The Misfit is roaming about the region. The family embarks anyway, stops for lunch at a country restaurant, has a car accident, and is slaughtered by The Misfit and his two cohorts.

In a characteristic sleight of hand, O'Connor decided to give the story to the grandmother, a pint-sized heroine for this tale of mayhem and death. The grandmother (that's her name in the story) appears in every scene and speaks nearly all of the dialogue, rivaled only by the two menacing, boisterous older children and an unexpected visitor in the final scene. She takes control of things from the outset—wheedling, conniving, whining, and manipulating the entire family to go along with her plans. She's a self-pitying narcissist, a megalomaniacal, self-delighting tyrant of her middle-class family. She utters clichés day and night and considers herself, in the end, always a proper lady:

> I wouldn't take my children in any direction with a criminal like that

aloose in it. I couldn't answer to my conscience if I did. [1]

In my time, children were more respectful of their native states and their parents and everything else. [18]

People are certainly not nice like they used to be. [35]

And naturally, it is the grandmother's hiding of her cat in the car's back seat (couldn't bear leaving Pitty Sing home alone) and her maneuvers to visit a roadside attraction that lead to the car accident and the family's destruction.

In the final scene, the grandmother meets her narcissistic match, who just so happens to be a sociopathic killer. The duet that plays between her and The Misfit is a pinnacle of American comic writing—a dizzying dialogue that takes place at the same time as the gunshot murders of two adults, two children, and an infant. Like a pair of theological vaudevillians, they speak of Christ, fate, good and evil, and the discovery of their respective salvation. For the first time in her life, the grandmother is nearly dumb with terror, reduced to stammering out pleas for her life. The middle-aged Misfit, scholarly in his spectacles, recounts his horrific past. He is at once ominous and detached, despairing and alert, a kind of proselytizing antiprophet utterly given over to impulse and violence, and who, in spite of (or perhaps because of) his complete solipsism, speaks one or two words of unwitting truth—truth that, improbably enough, sets the old woman free.

Along with the grandmother, everyone in the story speaks in banalities—the children, John Wesley and June Star, the garrulous restaurateur Red Sammy, The Misfit's two henchmen, Hiram and Bobby Lee—everyone including The Misfit (perhaps especially The Misfit), although his language also manages to be complex and self-aware. With The Misfit,

the reader is jerked out of an impatient restlessness and distaste for these tiresome people. He's the only charismatic figure in these pages, and his compressed life story has the cadence and richness of a poem:

I was a gospel singer for a while. I been most everything. Been in the arm service, both land and sea, at home and abroad, been twict married, been an undertaker, been with the railroads, plowed Mother Earth, been in a tornado. . . . [109]

In one sense, The Misfit is a co-hero, as significant as the grandmother—a hypnotic, dazzling Iago, of sorts. But O'Connor is doing a number on us with the magnetic Misfit, has intentionally made him the most interesting character, so that we would be drawn to him for a time, so that we would be curious about him, half-believe him. Indeed, we're spellbound, laughing and wincing at his eerie language until the moment he reminds us of his horrific potential.

The Shakespeare critic A. C. Bradley once said that the first thing to keep in mind about Iago is that you can't believe a single word he says. You have to distrust everything. Certainly, the same holds for The Misfit, who, like his predecessor, is so penetrated with untruth that he lies before he thinks, lies as he breathes. He's in that great line of backwoods con men—quite capable of rewriting his charismatic life story on every ditchbank in Georgia, the biblical language in which he is so fluent being another form of the con.

The story, which had begun as a cartoon, a comedy of '50s manners, takes, in a handful of pages, a remarkable turn. All the events have occurred in a single day, during this balmy summer car trip in rural Georgia. There is no chance that a reader should accept O'Connor's plot, with its blatantly placed clue in the first paragraph. Yet she makes it work. We laugh our way through a brief series of scenes, ride along in the crowded car, have lunch at Red Sammy's, get lost on the dirt road, laugh again when Pitty Sing (who, it must be said, had been suspiciously well behaved for most of the trip) jumps on the son's shoulder and causes the wreck; and then somehow, not quite knowing how it has happened, we find ourselves slumped in shock alongside the doomed family at the bottom of a ditch, looking up at a cloudless sky and three men looming above.

The grandmother's son is named Bailey, but we never learn his wife's name. She is simply "the children's mother," anonymous, almost selfless in the grandmother's characteristic worldview. O'Connor makes her the butt of an early joke on page one, giving her a face "as broad and innocent as a cabbage." During the accident, she is thrown from the car, still holding the infant, and breaks her shoulder. She sits there, stiffening in shock as her husband and young son are led away by The Misfit's henchmen to be slaughtered in the woods. Soon the murderers come for her, and The Misfit quietly asks her "to step off yonder with Bobby Lee and Hiram and join your husband."

Nearly mute in pain and horror, she can only say, "Yes, thank you." Then she takes the two remaining children and obediently walks off to her death. O'Connor, who had humiliated the young woman earlier, gives her back to us now in something close to tragedy, in a miraculous dignity; and her "Yes, thank you" becomes the most poignant moment of the story.

Only the grandmother remains. Grasping at straws, she mutters, "Jesus, Jesus," and The Misfit chimes right in. And then, in the midst of his philosophizing, he speaks the central line of the story: "Jesus thown everything off balance" [paragraph 129]. We know that The Misfit is speaking out of his own insanity and violence, but O'Connor is stretching language so far here that, for a moment at least, the reality of these Georgia trees and skies starts to crack apart. We've been working our way through some of the strangest American prose ever written. Six people are dead. And The Misfit becomes the most memorable religious character in recent American fiction.

In the last moments of the story, the grandmother has reached the limits of despair. She alone is left alive. She has begged for her life, twisted and turned every way she knows, has reached some unspeakable point of horror and fear and catastrophe, and she cries out to The Misfit, "Why you're one of my babies. You're one of my own children!" [paragraph 136]. Her entire atrocious, selfish, ignorant, useless life has led to this. And in its last moments, the improbable occurs: She breaks through, speaks words she doesn't even realize she is speaking. She reaches out to The Misfit and touches him on the shoulder—a common enough rural gesture. And at her touch, The Misfit, a fully realized nihilist, shoots her dead.

The story runs quickly to its close. One or two more sentences. The Misfit tells Bobby Lee, "She would of been a good woman, if it had been somebody there to shoot her every minute of her life." It has taken the extremity of death for the grandmother to escape the shell of her egoism—a transformation The Misfit, a shrewd psychologist, readily comprehends, even as he is the very agent of her destruction.

Thus, in the guise of a Deep South horror story, O'Connor gave American letters something else altogether: a religiously audacious work of literature, a spiritual puzzle—a small miracle. **"**

John Updike

A & P

Over the course of his career as a novelist, short story writer, poet, essayist, and dramatist, **JOHN UPDIKE** (1932–2009) received every major American literary award; in 1998 he was awarded the National Book Foundation Medal for Distinguished Contribution to American Letters. For one novel alone, *Rabbit Is Rich* (1981), he won the Pulitzer Prize, the American Book Award, and the National Book Critics Circle Award. Among more than a dozen published novels, his recurring themes include religion, sexuality, and middle-class experience. In his essays, Updike's concerns range widely over literary and cultural issues. One volume of his col-lected essays, *Hugging the Shore: Essays and Criticism* (1983), was also awarded a National Book Critics Circle Award. Since his death, a posthumous collection of poems, *Endpoint and Other Poems* (2009), has been published, along with a collection of essays, *Hub Fans Bid Kid Adieu: John Updike on Ted Williams* (2010).

"A & P" is one of nineteen stories from John Updike's 1962 collection titled *Pigeon Feathers and Other Stories*, which appeared early in the writer's long and impressive career. In a 2001 interview, Updike commented on his goals as a writer and what he appreciated in other writing: "I've just tried to write in a way that would entertain and please me, if I were the reader . . . the kind of writer I'm attracted to is a writer who gives pleasure—the prose writer who does a little more than what is strictly called for to deliver the image or the facts. I'm not a very fast reader, so I like to open up a book and feel some whiff of poetry or of extra effort or of something inventive going on, so that even read backwards, a paragraph of prose will yield something to the sense." Updike once said humorously of his approach to reading: "My purpose in reading has ever secretly been not to come and judge but to come and steal."

> "I'm not a very fast reader, so I like to open up a book and feel some whiff of poetry or of extra effort or of something inventive going on, so that even read backwards, a paragraph of prose will yield something to the sense."

IN WALKS THESE THREE GIRLS in nothing but bathing suits. I'm in the third checkout slot, with my back to the door, so I don't see them until they're over by the bread. The one that caught my eye first was the one in the plaid green two-piece. She was a chunky kid, with a good tan and a sweet broad soft-looking can with those two crescents of white just under it, where the sun never seems to hit, at the top of the backs of her legs. I stood there with my hand on a box of HiHo crackers trying to remember if I rang it up or not. I ring it up again and the customer starts giving me hell. She's one of these cash-register-watchers, a witch about fifty with rouge on her cheekbones and no eyebrows, and I know it made her day to trip me up. She'd been watching cash registers for fifty years and probably never seen a mistake before.

By the time I got her feathers smoothed and her goodies into a bag—she gives me a little snort in passing, if she'd been born at the right time they would have burned her over in Salem—by the time I get her on her way the girls had circled around the bread and were coming back, without a push-cart, back my way along the counters, in the aisle between the checkouts and the Special bins. They didn't even have shoes on. There was this chunky one, with the two-piece—it was bright green and the seams on the bra were still sharp and her belly was still pretty pale so I guessed she just got it (the suit)—there was this one, with one of those chubby berry-faces, the lips all bunched together under her nose, this one, and a tall one, with black hair that hadn't quite frizzed right, and one of these sunburns right across under the eyes, and a chin that was too long—you know, the kind of girl other girls think is very "striking" and "attractive" but never quite makes it, as they very well know, which is why they like her so much—and then the third one, that wasn't quite so tall. She was the queen. She kind of led them, the other two peeking around and making their shoulders round. She didn't look around, not this queen, she just walked straight on slowly, on these long white prima-donna legs. She came down a little hard on her heels, as if she didn't walk in her bare feet that much, putting down her heels and then letting the weight move along to her toes as if she was testing the floor with every step, putting a little deliberate extra action into it. You never know for sure how girls' minds work (do you really think it's a mind in there or just a little buzz like a bee in a glass jar?) but you got the idea she had talked the other two into coming in here with her, and now she was showing them how to do it, walk slow and hold yourself straight.

She had on a kind of dirty-pink—beige maybe, I don't know—bathing suit with a little nubble all over it and, what got me, the straps were down. They were off her shoulders looped loose around the cool tops of her arms, and I guess as a result the suit had slipped a little on her, so all around the top of the cloth there was this shining rim. If it hadn't been there you wouldn't have known there could have been anything whiter than those shoulders. With the straps pushed off, there was nothing between the top of the suit and the top of her head except just *her*, this clean bare plane of the top of her chest down from the shoulder bones like a dented sheet of metal tilted in the light. I mean, it was more than pretty.

She had sort of oaky hair that the sun and salt had bleached, done up in a bun that was unraveling, and a kind of prim face. Walking into the A & P with your straps down, I suppose it's the only kind of face you *can* have. She held her head so high her neck, coming up out of those white shoulders, looked kind of stretched, but I didn't mind. The longer her neck was, the more of her there was.

She must have felt in the corner of her eye me and over my shoulder   5 Stokesie in the second slot watching, but she didn't tip. Not this queen. She kept her eyes moving across the racks, and stopped, and turned so slow it made my stomach rub the inside of my apron, and buzzed to the other two, who kind of huddled against her for relief, and then they all three of them went up the cat-and-dog-food-breakfast-cereal-macaroni-rice-raisins-seasonings-spreads-spaghetti-soft-drinks-crackers-and-cookies aisle. From the third slot I look straight up this aisle to the meat counter, and I watched them all the way. The fat one with the tan sort of fumbled with the cookies, but on second thought she put the package back. The sheep pushing their carts down the aisle—the girls were walking against the usual traffic (not that we have one-way signs or anything)—were pretty hilarious. You could see them, when Queenie's white shoulders dawned on them, kind of jerk, or hop, or hiccup, but their eyes snapped back to their own baskets and on they pushed. I bet you could set off dynamite in an A & P and the people would by and large keep reaching and checking oatmeal off their lists and muttering "Let me see, there was a third thing, began with A, asparagus, no, ah, yes, applesauce!" or whatever it is they do mutter. But there was no doubt, this jiggled them. A few houseslaves in pin curlers even looked around after pushing their carts past to make sure what they had seen was correct.

You know, it's one thing to have a girl in a bathing suit down on the beach, where what with the glare nobody can look at each other much anyway, and another thing in the cool of the A & P, under the fluorescent lights, against all those stacked packages, with her feet paddling along naked over our checkerboard green-and-cream rubber-tile floor.

"Oh Daddy," Stokesie said beside me. "I feel so faint."

"Darling," I said. "Hold me tight." Stokesie's married, with two babies chalked up on his fuselage already, but as far as I can tell that's the only difference. He's twenty-two, and I was nineteen this April.

"Is it done?" he asks, the responsible married man finding his voice. I forgot to say he thinks he's going to be manager some sunny day, maybe in 1990 when it's called the Great Alexandrov and Petrooshki Tea Company or something.

What he meant was, our town is five miles from a beach, with a big   10 summer colony out on the Point, but we're right in the middle of town, and the women generally put on a shirt or shorts or something before they get out of the car into the street. And anyway these are usually women with six children and varicose veins mapping their legs and nobody, including them, could care less. As I say, we're right in the middle of town, and if you stand at our front doors you can see two banks and the Congregational church and the newspaper store and three real-estate offices and about twenty-seven old freeloaders tearing up Central Street because the sewer broke again. It's not as if we're on the Cape, we're north of Boston and there's people in this town haven't seen the ocean for twenty years.

The girls had reached the meat counter and were asking McMahon something. He pointed, they pointed, and they shuffled out of sight behind a pyramid of Diet Delight peaches. All that was left for us to see was old McMahon patting his mouth and looking after them sizing up their joints. Poor kids, I began to feel sorry for them, they couldn't help it.

Now here comes the sad part of the story, at least my family says it's sad, but I don't think it's so sad myself. The store's pretty empty, it being Thursday afternoon, so there was nothing much to do except lean on the register and wait for the girls to show up again. The whole store was like a pinball machine and I didn't know which tunnel they'd come out of. After a while they come around out of the far aisle, around the light bulbs, records at discount of the Caribbean Six or Tony Martin Sings or some such gunk you wonder they waste the wax on, sixpacks of candy bars, and plastic toys done up in cellophane that fall apart when a kid looks at them anyway. Around they come, Queenie still leading the way, and holding a little gray jar in her hands. Slots Three through Seven are unmanned and I could see her wondering between Stokes and me, but Stokesie with his usual luck draws an old party in baggy gray pants who stumbles up with four giant cans of pineapple juice (what do these bums *do* with all that pineapple juice? I've often asked myself). So the girls come to me. Queenie puts down the jar and I take it into my fingers icy cold. Kingfish Fancy Herring Snacks in Pure Sour Cream: 49¢. Now her hands are empty, not a ring or a bracelet, bare as God made them, and I wonder where the money's coming from. Still with that prim look she lifts a folded dollar bill out of the hollow at the center of her nubbled pink top. The jar went heavy in my hand. Really, I thought that was so cute.

Then everybody's luck begins to run out. Lengel comes in from haggling with a truck full of cabbages on the lot and is about to scuttle into that door marked MANAGER behind which he hides all day when the girls touch his eye. Lengel's pretty dreary, teaches Sunday school and the rest, but he doesn't miss that much. He comes over and says, "Girls, this isn't the beach."

Queenie blushes, though maybe it's just a brush of sunburn I was noticing for the first time, now that she was so close. "My mother asked me to pick up a jar of herring snacks." Her voice kind of startled me, the way voices do when you see the people first, coming out so flat and dumb yet kind of tony, too, the way it ticked over "pick up" and "snacks." All of a sudden I slid right down her voice into the living room. Her father and the other men were standing around in ice-cream coats and bow ties and the women were in sandals picking up herring snacks on toothpicks off a big glass plate and they were all holding drinks the color of water with olives and sprigs of mint in them. When my parents have somebody over they get lemonade and if it's a real racy affair Schlitz in tall glasses with "They'll Do It Every Time" cartoons stenciled on.

"That's all right," Lengel said. "But this isn't the beach." His repeating   15
this struck me as funny, as if it had just occurred to him, and he had been thinking all these years the A & P was a great big dune and he was the head lifeguard. He didn't like my smiling—as I say he doesn't miss much—but he concentrates on giving the girls that sad Sunday-school-superintendent stare.

Queenie's blush is no sunburn now, and the plump one in plaid, that I liked better from the back—a really sweet can—pipes up, "We weren't doing any shopping. We just came in for the one thing."

"That makes no difference," Lengel tells her, and I could see from the way his eyes went that he hadn't noticed she was wearing a two-piece before. "We want you decently dressed when you come in here."

"We *are* decent," Queenie says suddenly, her lower lip pushing, getting sore now that she remembers her place, a place from which the crowd that runs the A & P must look pretty crummy. Fancy Herring Snacks flashed in her very blue eyes.

"Girls, I don't want to argue with you. After this come in here with your shoulders covered. It's our policy." He turns his back. That's policy for you. Policy is what the kingpins want. What the others want is juvenile delinquency.

All this while, the customers had been showing up with their carts but,   20
you know, sheep, seeing a scene, they had all bunched up on Stokesie, who shook open a paper bag as gently as peeling a peach, not wanting to miss a word. I could feel in the silence everybody getting nervous, most of all Lengel, who asks me, "Sammy, have you rung up their purchase?"

I thought and said "No" but it wasn't about that I was thinking. I go through the punches, 4, 9, GROC. TOT—it's more complicated than you think, and after you do it often enough, it begins to make a little song, that you hear words to, in my case "Hello (*bing*) there, you (*gung*) hap-py *pee*-pul (*splat*)!"—the *splat* being the drawer flying out. I uncrease the bill, tenderly as you may imagine, it just having come from between the two smoothest scoops of vanilla I had ever known were there, and pass a half and a penny into her narrow pink palm, and nestle the herrings in a bag and twist its neck and hand it over, all the time thinking.

The girls, and who'd blame them, are in a hurry to get out, so I say "I quit" to Lengel quick enough for them to hear, hoping they'll stop and watch me, their unsuspected hero. They keep right on going, into the electric eye; the door flies open and they flicker across the lot to their car, Queenie and Plaid and Big Tall Goony-Goony (not that as raw material she was so bad), leaving me with Lengel and a kink in his eyebrow.

"Did you say something, Sammy?"

"I said I quit."

"I thought you did."   25

"You didn't have to embarrass them."

"It was they who were embarrassing us."

I started to say something that came out "Fiddle-de-doo." It's a saying of my grandmother's, and I know she would have been pleased.

"I don't think you know what you're saying," Lengel said.

"I know you don't," I said. "But I do." I pull the bow at the back of my   30
apron and start shrugging it off my shoulders. A couple customers that had been heading for my slot begin to knock against each other, like scared pigs in a chute.

Lengel sighs and begins to look very patient and old and gray. He's been a friend of my parents for years. "Sammy, you don't want to do this to your Mom and Dad," he tells me. It's true, I don't. But it seems to me that once you begin a gesture it's fatal not to go through with it. I fold the apron, "Sammy" stitched in red on the pocket, and put it on the counter, and drop the bow tie on top of it. The bow tie is theirs, if you've ever wondered. "You'll feel this for the rest of your life," Lengel says, and I know that's true, too, but remembering how he made the pretty girl blush makes me so scrunchy inside I punch the No Sale tab and the machine whirs "pee-pul" and the drawer splats out. One advantage to this scene taking place in summer, I can follow this up with a clean exit, there's no fumbling around getting your coat and galoshes, I just saunter into the electric eye in my white shirt that my mother ironed the night before, and the door heaves itself open, and outside the sunshine is skating around on the asphalt.

I look around for my girls, but they're gone, of course. There wasn't anybody but some young married screaming with her children about some candy they didn't get by the door of a powder-blue Falcon station wagon. Looking back in the big windows, over the bags of peat moss and aluminum lawn furniture stacked on the pavement, I could see Lengel in my place in the slot, checking the sheep through. His face was dark gray and his back stiff, as if he'd just had an injection of iron, and my stomach kind of fell as I felt how hard the world was going to be to me hereafter. ■

The Reader's Presence

1. The story is written in colloquial language. Reread the first two paragraphs. What does the narrator's style of expression convey about him? What effect does the narrator's style of expression have on your reading of the story? Are you more, or less, inclined to believe his words? Why? Suppose the same story were recounted in more conventional English. Would its meaning differ? If so, in what ways? How do you think Updike wishes the reader to view the narrator? Does Updike seem to agree, partially agree, or disagree with the narrator's point of view? What clues in the narrative lead you to your conclusion?

2. A great deal of the story hinges on what the narrator doesn't know or say. Is the girls' attire the only issue in the confrontation? What other tensions are evident in

the store and in the town? What impression of the situation do you glean "between the lines"? How does the writer convey information beyond the scope of what the narrator is able to articulate?

3. **CONNECTIONS:** Updike's story presents a seemingly minor event at a supermarket as the catalyst for a major change in the narrator's life. "I felt how hard the world was going to be to me hereafter," Sammy says in the story's final sentence. How do the perceptions of the past, present, and future intersect in the story? How seriously do you take the narrator's grim view of his future? Read Judith Ortiz Cofer's essay "Silent Dancing" (page 68), which is also prompted by a seemingly insignificant occasion: watching a home movie. Compare and contrast the ways in which past, present, and future intersect in Cofer's essay and Updike's story. Which writer handles these intersections more effectively? Explain why.

ACKNOWLEDGMENTS (continued from page ii)

Text Credits

Chris Abani. "The Lottery." From *The New York Times*, February 1, 2004. Copyright © 2004 by Chris Abani. Reprinted by permission of Chris Abani.

Joan Acocella. "A Few Too Many." From *The New Yorker*, May 26, 2008, pp. 32–37. Copyright © 2007 by Joan Acocella. Reprinted by permission from the author.

Daniel Akst. "What Meets the Eye." First published in *Wilson Quarterly*, Summer 1997. Copyright © 2005 Daniel Akst. Reprinted by permission of International Creative Management, Inc.

Sherman Alexie. "This Is What It Means to Say Phoenix, Arizona." From *The Lone Ranger and Tonto Fistfight in Heaven*. Copyright © 1993 by Sherman Alexie. Used by permission of Grove/Atlantic, Inc.; "Superman and Me." From *The Most Wonderful Books*, edited by Michael Dorris and Emilie Buchwald. Copyright © 1997 by Milkweed Editions. Reprinted with permission of the author.

Akhil Reed Amar. "Second Thoughts: What the Right to Bear Arms Really Means." First published in the July 12, 1999, issue of *The New Republic*. Copyright © 1999. All rights reserved by Akhil Amar c/o Writers Representatives LLC, New York, NY. Published by permission of Akhil Reed Amar.

Ho Che Anderson. "Reinvisioning *I Have a Dream*." From *King*, Volume 2. Copyright © 2002 by Ho Che Anderson. Reprinted courtesy of Fantagraphic Books.

Maya Angelou. "'What's Your Name, Girl?'" From *I Know Why the Caged Bird Sings* by Maya Angelou. Copyright © 1969 and renewed 1997 by Maya Angelou. Used by permission of Random House, Inc.

James Baldwin. Excerpt from *Notes of a Native Son* by James Baldwin. Copyright © 1955 renewed 1983 by James Baldwin. Reprinted by permission of Beacon Press, Boston. "Black English." Originally titled, "If Black English Isn't a Language, Then Tell Me, What Is?" © 1979 was originally published in *The New York Times*, collected in *The Price of the Ticket*, published by St. Martin's. Used by arrangement with the James Baldwin Estate.

Dave Barry. "Beauty and the Beast." From *Miami Herald*, February 1998. Copyright © 1998 by Dave Barry. All rights reserved. Reproduced by permission.

Michael Bérubé. "Analyze, Don't Summarize." Originally published in *The Chronicle of Higher Education*, October 1, 2004. Copyright © 2004 Michael Bérubé. Used by permission of the author.

Charles Bowden. "Our Wall." From *National Geographic* magazine. May 2007. © 2010 National Geographic Society. All rights reserved. Reproduced by permission.

David Brooks. "People Like Us." Originally published in *The Atlantic Monthly*, September 2003. Used by permission of the author.

Augusten Burroughs. "Absolutely Fabulous." First published in *Details*, October 2008, pp. 196, 199. Copyright © 2008 by Augusten, Inc. Reprinted by permission of Augusten Burroughs c/o Selectric Artists LLC.

Nicholas Carr. "Is Google Making Us Stupid?" From *The Atlantic Monthly*, July/August 2008. Copyright © 2008 by Nicholas Carr. All rights reserved. Reproduced by permission.

Lauren Carter. "Isn't Watermelon Delicious?" *The Bridge* (Bridgewater State College), Volume 2, Spring 2005. Reprinted by permission of the author.

Stephen L. Carter. "The Insufficiency of Honesty." From *Integrity*. Copyright © 2010 by Stephen L. Carter. Used by permission of Basic Books, a member of the Perseus Books Group.

Raymond Carver. "What We Talk About When We Talk About Love." From *What We Talk About When We Talk About Love*, pp. 137–154. Copyright © 1974, 1976, 1978, 1980, 1981 by Raymond Carver. Used by permission of Alfred A. Knopf, a division of Random House, Inc.; "My Father's Life." First published in *Esquire* (1984). Copyright © 1983 by the estate of Raymond Carver. Reprinted with permission of The Wylie Agency.

William Caverlee. "The Best Southern Short Story Ever?" Originally published in *The Oxford American*, Spring 2006, pp. 134–136. Copyright © 2006 [by] William Caverlee. Used by permission of the author.

Michael Chabon. "Faking It." From *Manhood for Amateurs*, pp. 127–134. HarperCollins, 2009. Copyright © 2009 by Michael Chabon. Reprinted by permission of HarperCollins Publishers and HarperCollins Publishers Ltd. All rights reserved.

Judith Ortiz Cofer. "On Memory and Personal Essays" (excerpted from "Preface") and "Silent Dancing." From *Silent Dancing: A Partial Remembrance of a Puerto Rican Childhood*. Copyright © 1990 Arte Publico Press–University of Houston. Reprinted with permission from the publisher.

Bernard Cooper. "A Clack of Tiny Sparks: Remembrances of a Gay Boyhood." Copyright © 1991 by *Harper's* magazine. All rights reserved. Reproduced from the January issue by special permission.

Amy Cunningham. "Why Women Smile." First published in *Lear's* (1993). Used by permission of the author.

Don DeLillo. "In the Ruins of the Future: Reflections on Terror, Loss, and Time in the Shadow of September." First published in *Harper's* magazine, December 2001. Copyright © 2001 by Don DeLillo. Used by permission of the Wallace Literary Agency, Inc.

Jared Diamond. From "Ecological Collapses of Past Civilizations," published in *Proceedings of the American Philosophical Society*, Volume 138, Number 3, pages 363–370. Used by permission of the author. "The Ends of the World as We Know Them." From *The New York Times*, Editorial Section, January 1, 2005, issue, page 13. Copyright © 2005 The New York Times. All rights reserved. Used by permission and protected by the Copyright Laws of the United States. The printing, copying, redistribution, or retransmission of the material without express written permission is prohibited.

Joan Didion. "On Morality." From *Sloughing Towards Bethlehem*, pp. 157–163. Copyright © 1966, 1968. Renewed 1996 by Joan Didion. Reprinted by permission of Farrar, Straus and Giroux, LLC.

Annie Dillard. "On the Writing Life." pages 78-79. From *The Writing Life* by Annie Dillard. Copyright © 1989 by Annie Dillard. Reprinted by permission of HarperCollins Publishers. "The Death of a Moth." From *Holy the Firm*. Copyright © 1977 by Annie Dillard. Originally appeared in *Harper's* magazine, May 1976, pp. 26–27. Used by permission of HarperCollins Publishers.

Frederick Douglass. "Learning to Read and Write." From *Narrative of the Life of Frederick Douglass, An American Slave* by Frederick Douglass, 1845.

Brian Doyle. "The Greatest Nature Essay *Ever*." From *Orion* magazine, November/December 2008. Copyright © 2008 by Brian Doyle. Reprinted by permission from the author.

Barbara Ehrenreich. "Will Women Still Need Men?" From *Time* magazine, February 21, 2000. Copyright TIME INC. Reprinted by permission. TIME is a registered trademark of Time Inc. All rights reserved.

Lars Eighner. Introduction. From *Travels with Lizbeth*, pp. ix–xi. St. Martin's Press, 1993. Copyright © 1993 by Lars Eighner. "On Dumpster Diving." From *Travels with Lizbeth* by Lars Eighner. Copyright © 1993 by the author and reprinted by permission of St. Martin's Press, L.L.C.

Nora Ephron. "The Boston Photographs." From *Scribble Scribble*. Copyright © 1978 by Nora Ephron. Reprinted by permission of International Creative Management, Inc.

Joseph Epstein. "The Perpetual Adolescent." Originally published in *The Weekly Standard*, March 15, 2003. Copyright © 2003. Reprinted with permission of the publisher.

Anne Fadiman. "Under Water." From *At Large and at Small: Familiar Essays by Anne Fadiman*. pp. 191–196. Copyright © 2008 by Anne Fadiman. Reprinted by permission of Farrar, Straus and Giroux, LLC.

James Fallows. "Throwing Like a Girl." Originally published in *The Atlantic Monthly*, August 1996. Copyright © 1996 by James Fallows. Used by permission of the author.

Jonathan Safran Foer. "Let Them Eat Dog." *Wall Street Journal*, October 31, 2009. Reprinted by permission of The Wall Street Journal, Copyright © 2009 Dow Jones & Company, Inc. All rights reserved worldwide.

Henry Louis Gates, Jr. "In the Kitchen" and "Introduction." From *Colored People* by Henry Louis Gates Jr. Copyright © 1994 by Henry Louis Gates Jr. Used by permission of Alfred A. Knopf, a division of Random House, Inc.

John Taylor Gatto. "Against School." Copyright © 2003 by *Harper's* magazine. All rights reserved. Reproduced from the September issue by special permission.

Daniel Gilbert. "Next to Nothing." From *Stumbling on Happiness*, pp. 151–155 by Daniel Gilbert. Copyright © 2006 by Daniel Gilbert. Used by permission of Alfred A. Knopf, a division of Random House, Inc.

Malcolm Gladwell. "Small Change." From *The New Yorker* magazine, October 4, 2010. Copyright © 2010 by Malcolm Gladwell. Reproduced by permission.

Adam Gopnik. "Shootings." From *The New Yorker* (Talk of the Town), April 30, 2007, pp. 27–28. Copyright © 2007. Used by permission of the author.

Cynthia Gorney. "The Urge to Merge." From *New York Times Magazine*, August 3, 2008. Copyright © 2008 The New York Times. All rights reserved. Used by permission and protected by the Copyright Laws of the United States. The printing, copying, redistribution, or retransmission of this Content without express written permission is prohibited.

Stephen Jay Gould. "Sex, Drugs, Disasters, and the Extinction of Dinosaurs." From *The Flamingo's Smile: Reflections in Natural History* by Stephen Jay Gould. Copyright © 1984 by Stephen Jay Gould. Used by permission of W.W. Norton & Company, Inc.

Michihiko Hachiya. "What Had Happened?" August 6, 1945, "Pikadon." pages 36–38 from *Hiroshima Diary: The Journal of a Japanese Physician, August 6–September 30, 1945* by Michihiko Hachiya, translated and edited by Warner Wells, M.D. Copyright © 1955 by the University of North Carolina Press. Renewed 1983 by Warner Wells. Foreword by John W. Dower © 1995 by the University of North Carolina Press. Used by permission of the publisher. www.uncpress.unc.edu

Nathaniel Hawthorne. "My Visit to Niagara." From *Tales and Sketches*, pp. 244–250. Literary Classics, 1982.

Vicki Hearne. "What's Wrong with Animal Rights." Copyright © 1991 by *Harper's* magazine.

Christopher Hitchens. "Believe Me, It's Torture." From *Vanity Fair*, August 2008. Copyright © 2008 by Christopher Hitchens.

Edward Hoagland. "What an Essay Is." Excerpted from "To the Point: Truths Only Essays Can Tell." Copyright © 1993 by Edward Hoagland. Reprinted by permission from the author. "On Stuttering." Originally published as "The Football Game in My Head" in *U.S. News & World Report*, April 2, 2001. Copyright 2001 U.S. News & World Report, L.P. Reprinted with permission.

Langston Hughes. "Salvation." From *The Big Sea* by Langston Hughes. Copyright © 1940 by Langston Hughes. Copyright renewed 1968 by Arna Bontemps and George Houston Bass. Reprinted by permission of Hill and Wang, a division of Farrar, Straus, and Giroux, LLC. "How to Be a Bad Writer (in Ten Easy Lessons)." From *The Langston Hughes Reader*. Reprinted by permission of Harold Ober Associates Incorporated.

Siri Hustvedt. "Eight Days in a Corset." Copyright © 2006 by Siri Hustvedt. Reprinted by permission of International Creative Management, Inc.

Pico Iyer. "The Inner Climate." From *Orion* magazine, September/October 2008, pp. 37–38. Copyright © Pico Iyer. All rights reserved. Reproduced by permission of the author.

Thomas Jefferson. The Declaration of Independence.

Ha Jin. "Arrival." From *The Washington Post Magazine*, July 13, 2008, pp. 16, 18–19, 29–30. Copyright © Ha Jin. Reproduced by permission from the author.

Jamaica Kincaid. "On 'Girl'" from "An Interview with Jamaica Kincaid" in *Face to Face: Interviews with Contemporary Novelists*, edited by Allan Vorda. Originally appeared in the *Mississippi Review*. Rice University Press, 1993. Copyright © 1993 by Allan Vorda. Reproduced by permission. "Girl." From *At the Bottom of the River*. Copyright © 1983 by Jamaica Kincaid. Reprinted by permission of Farrar, Straus and Giroux, LLC.; "The Estrangement" by Jamaica Kincaid, originally published in *AARP*. Copyright © 2008 by Jamaica Kincaid, used with permission of The Wylie Agency LLC.

Martin Luther King Jr. "I Have a Dream" and "Letter from Birmingham Jail." Copyright 1963 Dr. Martin Luther King Jr.; copyright renewed 1991 Coretta Scott King. Reprinted by arrangement with The Heirs to the Estate of Martin Luther King, Jr., c/o Writers House as agent for the proprietor New York, NY. "On Self-Importance" excerpted from "Conquering Self-Centeredness." Copyright 1957 by Martin Luther King, Jr. and renewed 1991 by Coretta Scott King. Reprinted by arrangement with The Heirs to the Estate of Martin Luther King, Jr., c/o Writers House as agent for the proprietor New York, NY.

Stephen King. "Everything You Need to Know About Writing Successfully—in Ten Minutes." First published in *The Writer*, March 2000. © Stephen King. Permission granted by the author. All rights reserved.

Eric Schlosser. "Why McDonald's Fries Taste So Good." From *Fast Food Nation: The Dark Side of the All-American Meal* by Eric Schlosser. Copyright © 2001 by Eric Schlosser. Excerpted and reprinted by permission of Houghton Mifflin Harcourt Publishing Company. All rights reserved. First published in the *Atlantic Monthly*, January 2001.

Barry Schwartz. "The Tyranny of Choice." First published in *The Chronicle of Higher Education*, January 23, 2004. Copyright © 2004 Barry Schwartz. Reprinted by permission of the author.

David Sedaris. "Me Talk Pretty One Day." From *Me Talk Pretty One Day* by David Sedaris. Copyright © 2000 by David Sedaris. By permission of Little, Brown, & Company.

James Shreeve. "The Greatest Journey." From *National Geographic* magazine, March 2006. © 2006 National Geographic Society. All rights reserved. Reproduced by permission.

Leslie Marmon Silko. "In the Combat Zone." From *Hungry Mind Review*, Fall 1995. Copyright © 1996 by Leslie Marmon Silko. Reprinted with the permission of the Wylie Agency, Inc.

Charles Simic. "The Life of Images." From *Harvard Review*, Fall 2003. Used with permission of the author.

Peter Singer. "The Singer Solution to World Poverty." From *The New York Times Magazine*, September 5, 1999. Copyright © by Peter Singer. Reprinted by permission of the author. "Utility and the Survival Lottery." First published in *Philosophy*, Volume 52, Number 200 (April 1977), pp. 218–222. Reprinted with permission of Cambridge University Press.

Lauren Slater. "On Writing Groups." Excerpt interview with Lauren Slater by Alys Culhane. This work originally appeared in *Fourth Genre: Explorations in Non-Fiction*, Volume 7, Number 1, 2005. Used by permission of Michigan State University Press.; "The Trouble with Self-Esteem." Originally published in *The New York Times*, February 3, 2002. Copyright © Lauren Slater. Reprinted with the permission of the Dunow, Carlson, and Lerner Literary Agency.

Brian Jay Stanley. "Confessions of a Carnivore." From *North American Review*, September/October 2009, Volume 294.5, pp. 37–39. Reprinted by permission from the author.

Brent Staples. "Another Version of 'Just Walk on By.'" From *Parallel Time* by Brent Staples. Copyright © 1994 by Brent Staples. Used by permission of Pantheon Books, a division of Random House, Inc. "Just Walk on By: A Black Man Ponders His Power to Alter Public Space." Copyright © 1986 by Brent Staples. Reprinted by permission of the author.

Andrew Sullivan. "The M-Word: Why It Matters to Me." First published in *Time* magazine, February 8, 2004. © 2004 by Andrew Sullivan. Reprinted with permission of The Wylie Agency, Inc.; "Why I Blog" by Andrew Sullivan, originally published in *The Atlantic*. Copyright © 2008 by Andrew Sullivan, used by permission of The Wylie Agency LLC.

Manil Suri. "Keys to the Kingdom." First published in *The Washington Post Magazine*, May 9, 2004, pp. 18, 20, 28. Reprinted by permission of Manil Suri and Aragi Inc.

Jonathan Swift. "A Modest Proposal." by Jonathan Swift, 1729.

Amy Tan. "Mother Tongue." First appeared in *The Threepenny Review*. Copyright © 1989 by Amy Tan. Reprinted by permission of the author and the Sandra Dijkstra Literary Agency.

Calvin Trillin. "A Traditional Family." From *Too Soon to Tell*. Published by Farrar, Straus & Giroux. Copyright © 1991, 1995 by Calvin Trillin. Reprinted by permission of Lescher & Lescher, Ltd. All rights reserved.

Barbara Tuchman. "This Is the End of the World: The Black Death." From *A Distant Mirror* by Barbara Tuchman. Text Copyright © 1978 by Barbara W. Tuchman. Maps copyright © 1978 by Anita Karl. Used by permission of Alfred A. Knopf, a division of Random House, Inc.

Sherry Turkle. "How Computers Change the Way We Think." Originally published in *The Chronicle of Higher Education*, January 30, 2004. Used with permission of the author.

John Updike. "A & P." From *Pigeon Feathers and Other Stories* by John Updike. Copyright © 1962 and renewed 1990 by John Updike. Used by permission of Alfred A. Knopf, a division of Random House, Inc.

Sabrina Verchot. "Cosmetic Surgery: A Modest Defense." Reprinted by permission of the author.

Robert Vivian. "Town." From *Ecotone*, Volume 5, Issue 1, Fall 2009. Copyright © 2009 by Robert Vivian. Reproduced by permission from the author.

Alice Walker. "Beauty: When the Other Dancer Is the Self." From *In Search of Our Mothers' Gardens: Womanist Prose*. Copyright © 1983 by Alice Walker. Reprinted by permission of Houghton Mifflin Harcourt Publishing Company.

Index of Authors and Titles